Introducing Corporate Finance

Second edition

Diana Beal
Michelle Goyen
Abul Shamsuddin

WILEY
John Wiley & Sons Australia, Ltd

Second edition published 2008 by
John Wiley & Sons Australia, Ltd
42 McDougall Street, Milton Qld 4064

Typeset in 10.5/12pt Times

First edition published 2005

National Library of Australia
Cataloguing-in-Publication data

Beal, Diana.
Introducing corporate finance.

2nd ed.
Bibliography.
Includes index.
ISBN 978 0 470 81376 8 (pbk.).

1. Corporations — Finance — Textbooks. I. Goyen,
Michelle, 1962–. II. Shamsuddin, Abul F.M. III. Title.

658.15

Cover and internal design images: John Wiley & Sons Australia/Photo by Kari-Ann Tapp

Edited by Sharon Nevile

Typeset in India by Aptara

Printed in China by
Printplus Limited

10 9 8 7 6 5 4 3 2 1

Introducing Corporate Finance

Second edition

About the authors

Diana Beal is an Associate Professor in Finance at the University of Southern Queensland (USQ), where she has taught courses in business finance, personal finance, applied microeconomics, macroeconomics, financial markets and financial institutions management. Her initial training was as an economist and she worked for the government, both federal and state, for eight years. Since joining USQ in 1988 Diana has completed a Masters degree and a PhD in economics. She also has a commerce degree, and can therefore read between the lines of a balance sheet. Diana has always had an interest in both business and personal finance and has traded property, shares, collectibles, forex and options. In addition, she ran her own business for 15 years before joining USQ.

Michelle Goyen is a lecturer at the University of Southern Queensland, where she has enjoyed teaching corporate finance for over a decade. Michelle has an Honours degree in Accounting and Financial Management from the University of New England and a Masters of Commerce from the University of Southern Queensland. Prior to becoming an academic, she worked in a variety of industries, the most relevant of which was benchmarking the performance of small firms. Michelle is especially interested in the application of theory to real world settings and in considering how people's behaviour modifies predicted outcomes. Her main research interests are investor behaviour and the valuation of initial public offers in Australia.

Abul Shamsuddin is Associate Professor of Finance at the University of Newcastle, where he has taught corporate finance, investments, derivatives and risk management and financial institutions management. Prior to taking up this position in 2003, Abul taught at the University of New England and Simon Fraser University for over 15 years. He received his PhD in 1994 from Simon Fraser University, Canada. Abul is a co-author of *Introducing Corporate Finance* (1st edn) and *Investments: Analysis and Management*. His current research interests include asset pricing, market volatility and capital market integration. He has published articles in *The Journal of Empirical Finance*, *International Journal of Forecasting*, *Pacific-Basin Finance Journal*, *The Review of Income and Wealth* and *Journal of International Financial Markets, Institutions & Money*, among others. He has held visiting appointments at the Australian National University, La Trobe University and Simon Fraser University. Abul is a Senior Associate of the Financial Services Institute of Australasia and has previously served as Assistant Dean and Discipline Head at the University of Newcastle.

Brief contents

Contents

PART 4
SPECIAL TOPICS IN CORPORATE FINANCE 557

Chapter 15
Risk management 558

Chapter 16
Capital restructuring — takeovers and divestments 600

Chapter 17
International corporate finance 642

Preface

Introducing Corporate Finance, second edition, has been designed to meet the needs of students in their first course in finance. The authors have drawn on their extensive teaching experience to ensure that this book provides the answers to those questions most frequently asked by students of corporate finance. The language used is also targeted to a student's first exposure to finance (either undergraduate or postgraduate) rather than at the level that would appear in the academic journals, and discipline-specific jargon is introduced with plain English explanations.

In addition to accessible language and sound pedagogy, three further features of *Introducing Corporate Finance* will be of interest to students. The first of these is the inclusion of real world examples at the start of each chapter and within chapters when appropriate. The second, the 'behavioural perspective' features, aims to inspire students to consider how the chapter material relates to the decisions people make. Behavioural perspectives are an innovation in a corporate finance textbook. Discussions of behavioural finance have also been introduced to weave a richer tapestry in the area of corporate finance. Third, corporate governance issues are highlighted where relevant throughout the text. This feature will assist students to further relate the material they are studying to current events in the corporate world.

Features of the text

Sound pedagogy

Learning objectives are presented at the start of each chapter. They also become signposts throughout the chapter, with chapter content firmly linked to the objectives. The material in the chapter summaries is organised around each of the learning objectives to further reinforce the relationships.

Definitions for key terms are included in the text, the margins and the glossary. This approach gives students an efficient way to navigate when searching for a particular concept. The glossary contains all key terms and the corresponding page references to the place where the term appears in the text.

Clarity of method for calculations is achieved by presenting equations and examples throughout the chapters. The equations are numbered and presented in a manner that makes them easy to find when reviewing chapter material; they are also listed in a glossary of equations. A clearly identifiable example is presented for each type of calculation relevant to the text. All steps are shown so that those students who lack a strong background in mathematics will understand how to perform any calculations without having to look beyond this textbook.

Section breaks for review are included in the 'finance workshop' features for each chapter. The finance workshops provide students with an opportunity to test their comprehension of material in a section of the chapter before moving on to new material. They are presented wherever there are calculations, so students have ready reference to the examples in the section when trying these for the first time.

Self-test problems are presented at the end of the chapters. These problems are relatively easy and the answers are provided. They will allow students to review their understanding prior to attempting work set for them by their instructor.

Questions are presented at the end of each chapter. These questions deal primarily with the key concepts included in the chapter material and are of varying difficulty. The questions require written answers.

Financial problems are also included at the end of each chapter. They give students the opportunity to attempt calculations at a higher level than those presented in the self-test problems. Again, the degree of difficulty varies to give instructors latitude in deciding how far their students need to go.

Case studies are presented at the end of the textbook. These allow students to demonstrate their abilities in identifying the practical issues they could face in the workplace. The case studies are designed to simulate real business problems and require students to use what they have learnt from a number of chapters. The 'case matrix' identifies which chapters must be completed prior to attempting a case study. The cases are of varying degrees of difficulty.

Content linked to current corporate events

The opening scenario for each chapter, taken predominantly from recent articles appearing in the financial press, highlights the relevance of the chapter material to the business world. Students are alerted to the relationship of the chapter material to the real world scenario where the content appears in the chapter. The 'finance world' features within chapters contain further references to current corporate situations.

Content linked to research in behavioural finance

The discipline of corporate finance is about making decisions. It is also about developing techniques that will help managers to make the best possible decisions at the time (in a wealth maximising sense, of course). The proportion of working students has increased dramatically over the last decade and students are now less willing to accept those theoretical concepts that are inconsistent with the behaviour they observe in their working lives. The 'behavioural perspective' features help students to understand how abstraction from reality has been used to develop our more simplified models of people's behaviour. They also alert students to situations where the models discussed in the text may not hold when people behave differently from the way finance theory assumes they do.

Content linked to corporate governance issues

Corporate governance issues are discussed, using recent articles appearing in the financial press, where they relate to the text content. This feature allows students to assess the role of corporate governance in the business world and links decision making to issues of corporate governance.

How to use this book

Introducing Corporate Finance, second edition, has been designed with you — the student — in mind. Our aim is to provide you with a book that both communicates the subject matter and facilitates learning. We have incorporated the following elements to achieve this.

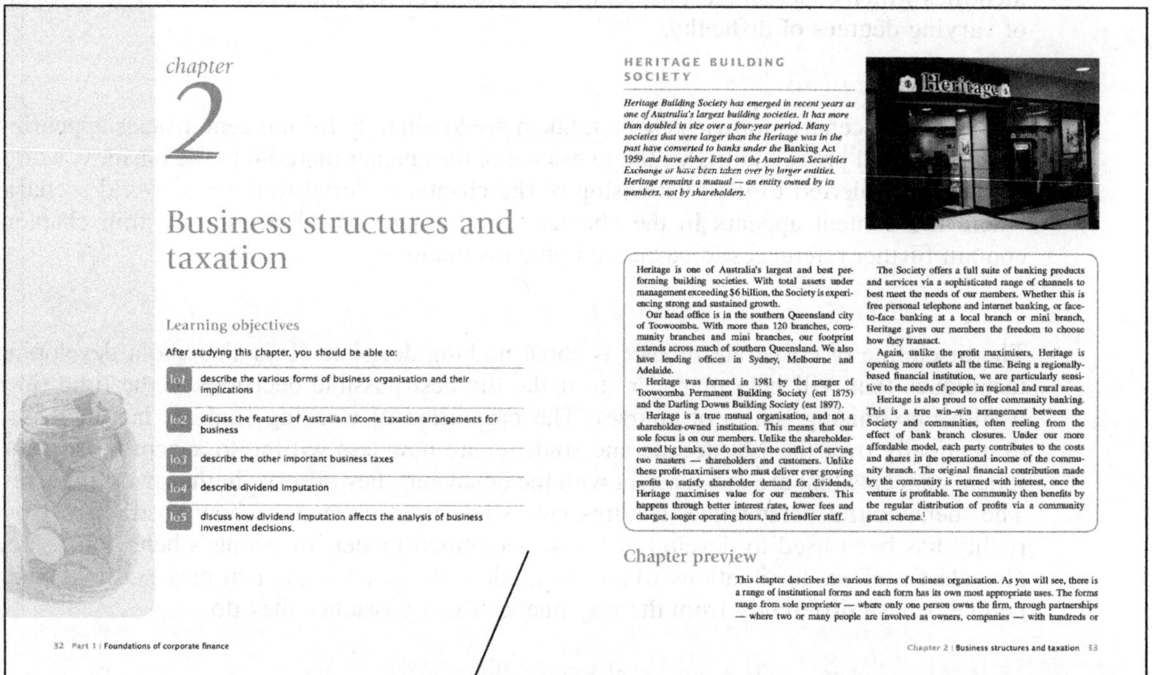

chapter
2

Business structures and taxation

Learning objectives

After studying this chapter, you should be able to:

lo1 describe the various forms of business organisation and their implications

lo2 discuss the features of Australian income taxation arrangements for business

lo3 describe the other important business taxes

lo4 describe dividend imputation

lo5 discuss how dividend imputation affects the analysis of business investment decisions.

32 Part 1 | Foundations of corporate finance

HERITAGE BUILDING SOCIETY

Heritage Building Society has emerged in recent years as one of Australia's largest building societies. It has more than doubled in size over a four-year period. Many societies that were larger than the Heritage was in the past have converted to banks under the Banking Act 1959 *and have either listed on the Australian Securities Exchange or have been taken over by larger entities. Heritage remains a mutual — an entity owned by its members, not by shareholders.*

Heritage is one of Australia's largest and best performing building societies. With total assets under management exceeding $6 billion, the Society is experiencing strong and sustained growth.

Our head office is in the southern Queensland city of Toowoomba. With more than 120 branches, community branches and mini branches, our footprint extends across much of southern Queensland. We also have lending offices in Sydney, Melbourne and Adelaide.

Heritage was formed in 1981 by the merger of Toowoomba Permanent Building Society (est 1875) and the Darling Downs Building Society (est 1897).

Heritage is a true mutual organisation, and not a shareholder-owned institution. This means that our sole focus is on our members. Unlike the shareholder-owned big banks, we do not have the conflict of serving two masters — shareholders and customers. Unlike these profit-maximisers who must deliver ever growing profits to satisfy shareholder demand for dividends, Heritage maximises value for our members. This happens through better interest rates, lower fees and charges, longer operating hours, and friendlier staff.

The Society offers a full suite of banking products and services via a sophisticated range of channels to best meet the needs of our members. Whether this is free personal telephone and internet banking, or face-to-face banking at a local branch or mini branch, Heritage gives our members the freedom to choose how they transact.

Again, unlike the profit maximisers, Heritage is opening more outlets all the time. Being a regionally-based financial institution, we are particularly sensitive to the needs of people in regional and rural areas.

Heritage is also proud to offer community banking. This is a true win–win arrangement between the Society and communities, often reeling from the effect of bank branch closures. Under our more affordable model, each party contributes to the costs and shares in the operational income of the community branch. The original financial contribution made by the community is returned with interest, once the venture is profitable. The community then benefits by the regular distribution of profits via a community grant scheme.[1]

Chapter preview

This chapter describes the various forms of business organisation. As you will see, there is a range of institutional forms and each form has its own most appropriate uses. The forms range from sole proprietor — where only one person owns the firm, through partnerships — where two or many people are involved as owners, companies — with hundreds or

Chapter 2 | Business structures and taxation 33

Chapter opening double-page spread The double-page chapter opener displays, at a glance, the learning objectives for the chapter content and a chapter opening article or scenario that introduces the topic and aligns it to a relevant contemporary business environment.

HERITAGE BUILDING SOCIETY

Heritage Building Society has emerged in recent years as one of Australia's largest building societies. It has more than doubled in size over a four-year period. Many societies that were larger than the Heritage was in the past have converted to banks under the Banking Act 1959 *and have either listed on the Australian Securities Exchange or have been taken over by larger entities. Heritage remains a mutual — an entity owned by its members, not by shareholders.*

Heritage is one of Australia's largest and best performing building societies. With total assets under management exceeding $6 billion, the Society is experiencing strong and sustained growth.

Our head office is in the southern Queensland city of Toowoomba. With more than 120 branches, community branches and mini branches, our footprint extends across much of southern Queensland. We also have lending offices in Sydney, Melbourne and Adelaide.

Heritage was formed in 1981 by the merger of Toowoomba Permanent Building Society (est 1875) and the Darling Downs Building Society (est 1897).

Heritage is a true mutual organisation, and not a shareholder-owned institution. This means that our sole focus is on our members. Unlike the shareholder-owned big banks, we do not have the conflict of serving two masters — shareholders and customers. Unlike these profit-maximisers who must deliver ever growing profits to satisfy shareholder demand for dividends, Heritage maximises value for our members. This happens through better interest rates, lower fees and charges, longer operating hours, and friendlier staff.

The Society offers a full suite of banking products and services via a sophisticated range of channels to best meet the needs of our members. Whether this is free personal telephone and internet banking, or face-to-face banking at a local branch or mini branch, Heritage gives our members the freedom to choose how they transact.

Again, unlike the profit maximisers, Heritage is opening more outlets all the time. Being a regionally-based financial institution, we are particularly sensitive to the needs of people in regional and rural areas.

Heritage is also proud to offer community banking. This is a true win–win arrangement between the Society and communities, often reeling from the effect of bank branch closures. Under our more affordable model, each party contributes to the costs and shares in the operational income of the community branch. The original financial contribution made by the community is returned with interest, once the venture is profitable. The community then benefits by the regular distribution of profits via a community grant scheme.[1]

Chapter preview

This chapter describes the various forms of business organisation. As you will see, there is a range of institutional forms and each form has its own most appropriate uses. The forms range from sole proprietor — where only one person owns the firm, through partnerships — where two or many people are involved as owners, companies — with hundreds or

Chapter 2 | Business structures and taxation 33

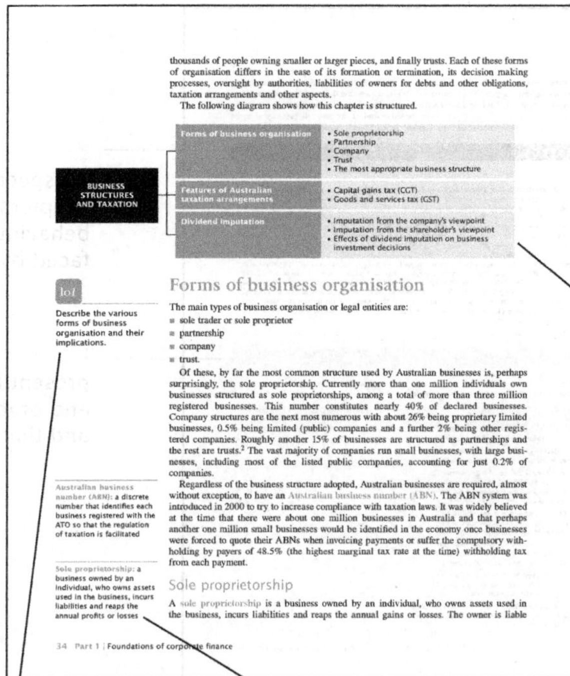

thousands of people owning smaller or larger pieces, and finally trusts. Each of these forms of organisation differs in the ease of its formation or termination, its decision making processes, oversight by authorities, liabilities of owners for debts and other obligations, taxation arrangements and other aspects.

The following diagram shows how this chapter is structured.

BUSINESS STRUCTURES AND TAXATION

- Forms of business organisation
  - Sole proprietorship
  - Partnership
  - Company
  - Trust
  - The most appropriate business structure
- Features of Australian taxation arrangements
  - Capital gains tax (CGT)
  - Goods and services tax (GST)
- Dividend imputation
  - Imputation from the company's viewpoint
  - Imputation from the shareholder's viewpoint
  - Effects of dividend imputation on business investment decisions

Forms of business organisation

lo1 Describe the various forms of business organisation and their implications.

The main types of business organisation or legal entities are:

- sole trader or sole proprietor
- partnership
- company
- trust.

Of these, by far the most common structure used by Australian businesses is, perhaps surprisingly, the sole proprietorship. Currently more than one million individuals own businesses structured as sole proprietorships, among a total of more than three million registered businesses. This number constitutes nearly 40% of declared businesses. Company structures are the next most numerous with about 26% being proprietary limited businesses, 0.5% being limited (public) companies and a further 2% being other registered companies. Roughly another 15% of businesses are structured as partnerships and the rest are trusts.[2] The vast majority of companies run small businesses, with large businesses, including most of the listed public companies, accounting for just 0.2% of companies.

Australian business number (ABN): a discrete number that identifies each business registered with the ATO so that the regulation of taxation is facilitated

Regardless of the business structure adopted, Australian businesses are required, almost without exception, to have an **Australian business number (ABN)**. The ABN system was introduced in 2000 to try to increase compliance with taxation laws. It was widely believed at the time that there were about one million businesses in Australia and that perhaps another one million small businesses would be identified in the economy once businesses were forced to quote their ABNs when invoicing payments or suffer the compulsory withholding by payers of 48.5% (the highest marginal tax rate at the time) withholding tax from each payment.

Sole proprietorship

Sole proprietorship: a business owned by an individual, who owns assets used in the business, incurs liabilities and reaps the annual profits or losses

A **sole proprietorship** is a business owned by an individual, who owns assets used in the business, incurs liabilities and reaps the annual gains or losses. The owner is liable

34 Part 1 | Foundations of corporate finance

Illustrative chapter road map This diagram presents the main sections of the chapter structure.

Learning objectives Learning objectives are clearly stated beside the relevant discussion in the chapter.

Chapter preview The chapter preview provides a brief summary of the topics, processes and procedures developed within the chapter.

Key terms Key terms are bolded and defined in the text at first mention in the chapter. A glossary is also included at the end of the book.

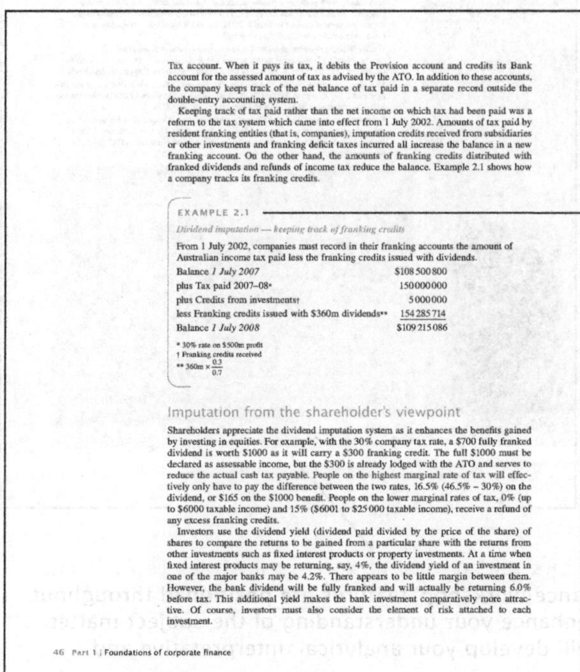

Tax account. When it pays its tax, it debits the Provision account and credits its Bank account for the assessed amount of tax as advised by the ATO. In addition to these accounts, the company keeps track of the net balance of tax paid in a separate record outside the double-entry accounting system.

Keeping track of tax paid rather than the net income on which tax had been paid was a reform to the tax system which came into effect from 1 July 2002. Amounts of tax paid by resident franking entities (that is, companies), imputation credits received from subsidiaries or other investments and franking deficit taxes incurred all increase the balance in a new franking account. On the other hand, the amounts of franking credits distributed with franked dividends and refunds of income tax reduce the balance. Example 2.1 shows how a company tracks its franking credits.

EXAMPLE 2.1

Dividend imputation — keeping track of franking credits

From 1 July 2002, companies must record in their franking accounts the amount of Australian income tax paid less the franking credits issued with dividends.

Balance *1 July 2007*	$108 500 800
plus Tax paid 2007–08*	150 000 000
plus Credits from investments†	5 000 000
less Franking credits issued with $360m dividends**	154 285 714
Balance *1 July 2008*	$109 215 086

* 30% rate on $500m profit
† Franking credits received
** $360\text{m} \times \frac{0.3}{0.7}$

Imputation from the shareholder's viewpoint

Shareholders appreciate the dividend imputation system as it enhances the benefits gained by investing in equities. For example, with the 30% company tax rate, a $700 fully franked dividend is worth $1000 as it will carry a $300 franking credit. The full $1000 must be declared as assessable income, but the $300 is already lodged with the ATO and serves to reduce the actual cash tax payable. People on the highest marginal rate of tax will effectively only have to pay the difference between the two rates, 16.5% (46.5% – 30%) on the dividend, or $165 on the $1000 benefit. People on the lower marginal rates of tax, 0% (up to $6000 taxable income) and 15% ($6001 to $25 000 taxable income), receive a refund of any excess franking credits.

Investors use the dividend yield (dividend paid divided by the price of the share) of shares to compare the returns to be gained from a particular share with the returns from other investments such as fixed interest products or property investments. At a time when fixed interest products may be returning, say, 4%, the dividend yield of an investment in one of the major banks may be 4.2%. There appears to be little margin between them. However, the bank dividend will be fully franked and will actually be returning 6.0% before tax. This additional yield makes the bank investment comparatively more attractive. Of course, investors must also consider the element of risk attached to each investment.

46 Part 1 | Foundations of corporate finance

Worked examples The worked examples are positioned strategically throughout the chapters to provide a step-by-step illustration of calculations using financial equations.

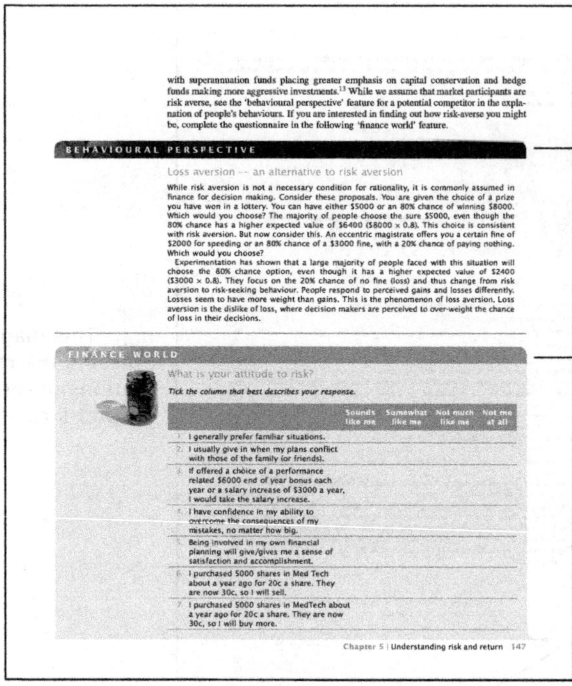

with superannuation funds placing greater emphasis on capital conservation and hedge funds making more aggressive investments.[13] While we assume that market participants are risk averse, see the 'behavioural perspective' feature for a potential competitor in the explanation of people's behaviours. If you are interested in finding out how risk-averse you might be, complete the questionnaire in the following 'finance world' feature.

BEHAVIOURAL PERSPECTIVE

Loss aversion -- an alternative to risk aversion

While risk aversion is not a necessary condition for rationality, it is commonly assumed in finance for decision making. Consider these proposals. You are given the choice of a prize you have won in a lottery. You can have either $5000 or an 80% chance of winning $8000. Which would you choose? The majority of people choose the sure $5000, even though the 80% chance has a higher expected value of $6400 ($8000 × 0.8). This choice is consistent with risk aversion. But now consider this. An eccentric magistrate offers you a certain fine of $2000 for speeding or an 80% chance of a $3000 fine, with a 20% chance of paying nothing. Which would you choose?

Experimentation has shown that a large majority of people faced with this situation will choose the 80% chance option, even though it has a higher expected value of $2400 ($3000 × 0.8). They focus on the 20% chance of no fine (loss) and thus change from risk aversion to risk-seeking behaviour. People respond to perceived gains and losses differently. Losses seem to have more weight than gains. This is the phenomenon of loss aversion. Loss aversion is the dislike of loss, where decision makers are perceived to over-weight the chance of loss in their decisions.

FINANCE WORLD

What is your attitude to risk?

Tick the column that best describes your response.

	Sounds like me	Somewhat like me	Not much like me	Not me at all
1. I generally prefer familiar situations.				
2. I usually give in when my plans conflict with those of the family (or friends).				
3. If offered a choice of a performance related $6000 end of year bonus each year or a salary increase of $3000 a year, I would take the salary increase.				
4. I have confidence in my ability to overcome the consequences of my mistakes, no matter how big.				
5. Being involved in my own financial planning will give/gives me a sense of satisfaction and accomplishment.				
6. I purchased 5000 shares in Med Tech about a year ago for 20c a share. They are now 30c, so I will sell.				
7. I purchased 5000 shares in MedTech about a year ago for 20c a share. They are now 30c, so I will buy more.				

Chapter 5 | Understanding risk and return 147

Behavioural perspective 'Behavioural perspective' features appear in most chapters to provide insights from behavioural finance into various issues faced by financial managers.

Finance world 'Finance world' features present a range of finance industry insights and practices relevant to the chapter topic and that reinforce the key issues raised.

Table 2.1 Appropriate business structures for given objectives

Objective	Best structures
Ease of establishment	Sole proprietorship; partnership
Low cost of establishment	Sole proprietorship; partnership
Limited legal liability	Company
Ease of management and control	Sole proprietorship; partnership
Low regulatory oversight, compliance costs	Sole proprietorship; partnership
Ease of raising capital	Company
Managing income taxation	Company; trust
Ability to manage capital gains tax (CGT)*	Sole proprietorship; partnership; trust
Likelihood of business continuity	Company
Ease of transfer of ownership	Listed company

* Companies pay the same rate of tax on capital gains as on ordinary income.

FINANCE WORKSHOP 2.1

1. Close this textbook and then see if you can list from your understanding of each business structure five objectives best achieved by:
   (a) a sole proprietorship or partnership
   (b) a company structure.
2. Greg Gringovitch is a fitter and turner by trade. He saw a gap in the medical appliances market when his son developed a muscular degeneration problem. Greg developed a gadget called 'The Thing' which helped his son stay mobile. After Greg and his wife joined a support group that helped families cope with this disease, Greg made a number of 'Things'. As it became apparent that 'The Thing' could help many people, it was suggested to Greg that he develop both Australian and export markets. Suggest a business structure that you believe would serve Greg well for the first stage of the development of his business. Would this recommendation change if Greg's turnover increased to $1 million per annum?

lo2

Discuss the features of Australian income taxation arrangements for business.

Features of Australian income taxation arrangements

Taxation impacts to a greater or lesser extent on many decisions taken in business. As you read through the later chapters of this book, you will find taxation arrangements affect to a greater or lesser extent many issues of concern to financial managers — not least the planning of investments, sourcing finance and capital structures. The most important taxes from the points of view of financial managers are income tax, capital gains tax (CGT) and the goods and services tax (GST). This section deals with income tax.

Chapter 2 | Business structures and taxation 41

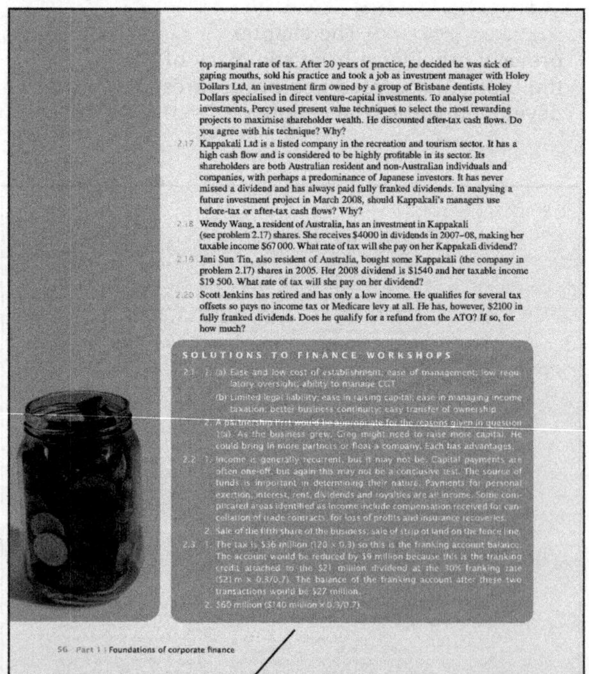

top marginal rate of tax. After 20 years of practice, he decided he was sick of gaping mouths, sold his practice and took a job as investment manager with Holey Dollars Ltd, an investment firm owned by a group of Brisbane dentists. Holey Dollars specialised in direct venture-capital investments. To analyse potential investments, Percy used present value techniques to select the most rewarding projects to maximise shareholder wealth. He discounted after-tax cash flows. Do you agree with his technique? Why?

2.17 Kappakali Ltd is a listed company in the recreation and tourism sector. It has a high cash flow and is considered to be highly profitable in its sector. Its shareholders are both Australian resident and non-Australian individuals and companies, with perhaps a predominance of Japanese investors. It has never missed a dividend and has always paid fully franked dividends. In analysing a future investment project in March 2008, should Kappakali's managers use before-tax or after-tax cash flows? Why?

2.18 Wendy Wang, a resident of Australia, has an investment in Kappakali (see problem 2.17) shares. She receives $4000 in dividends in 2007–08, making her taxable income $67 000. What rate of tax will she pay on her Kappakali dividend?

2.19 Jani Sun Tin, also resident of Australia, bought some Kappakali (the company in problem 2.17) shares in 2005. Her 2008 dividend is $1540 and her taxable income $19 500. What rate of tax will she pay on her dividend?

2.20 Scott Jenkins has retired and has only a low income. He qualifies for several tax offsets so pays no income tax or Medicare levy at all. He has, however, $2100 in fully franked dividends. Does he qualify for a refund from the ATO? If so, for how much?

SOLUTIONS TO FINANCE WORKSHOPS

2.1 1. (a) Ease and low cost of establishment; ease of management; low regulatory oversight; ability to manage CGT
(b) Limited legal liability; ease in raising capital; ease in managing income taxation; better business continuity; easy transfer of ownership
2. A partnership first would be appropriate for the reasons given in question 1(a). As the business grew, Greg might need to raise more capital. He could bring in more partners or float a company. Each has advantages.

2.2 1. Income is generally recurrent, but it may not be. Capital payments are often one-off, but again this may not be a conclusive test. The source of funds is important in determining their nature. Payments for personal exertion, interest, rent, dividends and royalties are all income. Some complicated areas identified as income include compensation received for cancellation of trade contracts, for loss of profits and insurance recoveries.
2. Sale of the fifth share of the business; sale of strip of land on the fence line.

2.3 1. The tax is $36 million (120 × 0.3) so this is the franking account balance. The account would be reduced by $9 million because this is the franking credit attached to the $21 million dividend at the 30% franking rate ($21 m × 0.3/0.7). The balance of the franking account after these two transactions would be $27 million.
2. $60 million ($140 million × 0.3/0.7)

56 Part 1 | Foundations of corporate finance

Finance workshops and end-of-chapter solutions to finance workshops 'Finance workshop' features are positioned throughout the chapters to enhance your understanding of the subject matter. These features will develop your analytical, interpretative and calculation skills.

This well-established winding-up process is under legal review in Australia in 2007. On 15 September 2005, Justice Emmett in the Federal Court of Australia handed down a decision favouring the plaintiff in the case of *Sons of Gwalia (Administrator Appointed) vs Margaretic* [2005] FCA 1305. Margaretic maintained that he had been misled by the company about its future prospects when he bought the shares and thus he should be ranked with other creditors, instead of after them, in the determination of final payments. In early February 2007, the High Court of Australia upheld this decision. The following 'corporate financial governance' feature offers one newspaper's comment on this decision.

CORPORATE FINANCIAL GOVERNANCE

Gwalia redefines shareholder rights

ALAN KOHLER

Now that High Court has ruled that misled shareholders rank with creditors in a wind-up, surely the next step is for fraud on the market theory to be applied in Australia.

That would complete the revolution in shareholder rights that began with this week's Sons of Gwalia judgement in favour of the plaintiff, Luka Margaretic.

...

Luka Margaretic bought 20 000 shares in Sons of Gwalia 11 days before it went broke and in doing so he claims to have relied on misleading information to the effect that the company was a going concern, when it wasn't.

...

This week's Sons of Gwalia judgement elevates [shareholder] claimants to the status of creditors.

In my experience, virtually every company collapse is accompanied by some jiggery-pokery, or at least a failure by directors to tell the market the company is in trouble.

This is one of the most difficult decisions a director ever has to make in his or her life: at what point do you raise the flag, knowing that to do so would effectively represent voluntary corporate euthanasia? The Sons of Gwalia decision makes this even sharper.

The decision might also render insolvencies impossibly unwieldy, as receivers and liquidators have to deal with the claims of the shareholders as well as the creditors, and have to wait until the courts determine whether the shareholders were misled before making any payments — at least that's what a lot of practitioners and lawyers are now saying.

As a result, there is now a clamour for the law to be amended urgently to keep shareholders in their place; that is behind employees and creditors in the queue for money in the event of insolvency.

Interestingly, Justice Michael Kirby seemed to invite that in his judgement with the (six to one) majority, and actually spelt out how the law could be amended. He wrote: One way would have been simply to delete from section 563A of the Act the words 'a debt owed by a company to a person in the person's capacity as a member of the company, whether by way of dividends, profits or otherwise' and substitute 'a debt owed by a company to a person who is a member of the company.'

But then he goes on: 'It should not be assumed that the inclusion of shareholder claims, such as those of the respondent, with the debts of general creditors is contrary to the will of the Parliament or the result of a slip or oversight requiring a measure of judicial inventiveness and surgery. By sticking to a variation of a time-honoured statutory phrase, it can be assumed that the Act was intended to effect only a limited subordination of claims brought by people who happen to be shareholders.'

Anyway, the Government will now be asked to do what Kirby suggests, which could be an uncomfortable decision, especially this year. Does John Howard really want to reduce consumer protections during an election year? And in any case, will it be supported by the Senate? That is far from clear.[3]

Chapter 2 | Business structures and taxation 39

'Corporate financial governance' features These features apply the chapter content and profile current, topical industry issues and developments in Australia and internationally.

Executive summary The executive summary lists the expected learning outcomes for the chapter, reiterating the core issues explored in the chapter and reinforcing key points.

executive summary

lo1 describe the various forms of business organisation and their implications

- Australian businesses are required, almost without exception, to have an Australian business number (ABN).
- The ABN system was introduced in 2000 to try to increase compliance with taxation laws.
- A sole proprietorship is a business owned by an individual who owns assets used in the business, incurs liabilities and reaps the annual profits or losses.
- Sole proprietors have freedom to run their businesses any way they wish, so long as their activities remain within the law.
- Sole proprietorships are easy and cheap to establish.
- Sole proprietors often use their own names as trading names.
- Sole proprietors may register trading names with state authorities under the relevant state business names Act.
- In terms of legal liability for debts and costs of their actions, sole proprietors carry unlimited liability.
- Sole proprietors may expand their businesses by arranging debt finance but, by definition, they cannot raise funds by selling equity.
- Sole proprietors may sell or transfer ownership of their businesses by transferring the trading names and the assets.
- At the death of a sole proprietor, the sole proprietor structure is dissolved, even though the business as such may be sold as a going concern and may indeed keep its old trading name.
- The advantages of the sole proprietorship structure are:
  - the speed and ease of establishment
  - lack of formalities (such as reports to stakeholders)
  - freedom in decision making enjoyed by the owner.
- Disadvantages include:
  - the potential limited life of the firm — if the owner dies, the firm may also die
  - financing limited by definition to debt finance
  - unlimited liability for debts
  - no formal sharing of management responsibilities (but expertise may still be purchased by means of skilled employees, consultants or advisers).
- A partnership is an association of two or more people carrying on a business in common with a view to profit.
- Partnerships are easy to set up with a minimum of formalities and many partnerships use their own names as their trading names.
- Taxation law takes the view that the existence of a partnership is a matter of fact which may be deduced from the evidence available. Such evidence includes:
  - the existence of a formal partnership agreement
  - contributions of capital and labour by the partners
  - any forms of evidence signifying the partners' intentions to collaborate
  - jointly entered relevant contracts
  - jointly held and operated bank accounts
  - notifications to stakeholders that a partnership exists.

48 Part 1 | Foundations of corporate finance

- A franked dividend is a dividend carrying an attached franking or tax credit.
- A fully franked dividend carries a tax credit equal to the full 30% company tax paid on the underlying profit.
- A partly franked dividend carries a tax credit less than the full 30% company tax paid on the underlying profit.
- An unfranked dividend carries no tax credit.

lo5 discuss how dividend imputation affects the analysis of business investment decisions

- Where a company believes the majority of its shareholders can take advantage of the dividend imputation, it should undertake investments and manage the firm's operations to maximise its before-tax cash flows.
- Where a company believes the majority of its shareholders can take advantage of the dividend imputation, it should analyse potential projects using pre-tax cash flows.
- Where shareholders cannot claim the full benefits of the tax credits, the full integration of the two tax regimes cannot be realised and the tax paid by the firm on its income becomes relevant to business finance decisions.

Key terms

allowable deductions, p. 42
assessable income, p. 42
Australian business number (ABN), p. 34
company, p. 37
corporate governance, p. 38
dividend imputation, p. 45
franked dividends, p. 45
fully franked dividends, p. 45
joint venture, p. 37
marginal tax rate, p. 40
partly franked dividends, p. 45
partnership, p. 35
sole proprietorship, p. 34
taxable income, p. 42
trust, p. 40
unfranked dividend, p. 45

Learning chart

Learning objective	Questions	Self-test problems	Financial problems
lo1 describe the various forms of business organisation and their implications	2.1, 2.2, 2.3, 2.4, 2.5, 2.6, 2.7, 2.8		2.1, 2.2, 2.3, 2.4
lo2 discuss the features of Australian income taxation arrangements for business	2.9, 2.10, 2.11	2.1, 2.2, 2.3	2.5, 2.6, 2.7, 2.8, 2.13, 2.14, 2.15, 2.18, 2.19
lo3 describe the other important business taxes	2.12, 2.13, 2.14		2.9, 2.10, 2.11, 2.12

continued

Chapter 2 | Business structures and taxation 51

Learning chart The learning chart aligns the end-of-chapter questions and problems to the chapter learning objectives, making it an easy-to-reference chart for assignment activities.

Questions Questions test your understanding of the material presented in the chapter, and encourage considered responses.

Learning objective	Questions	Self-test problems	Financial problems
lo4 describe dividend imputation	2.15, 2.16, 2.17, 2.18	2.4, 2.5	2.13, 2.14, 2.15, 2.18, 2.19, 2.20
lo5 discuss how dividend imputation affects the analysis of business investment decisions	2.19, 2.20		2.16, 2.17

Questions

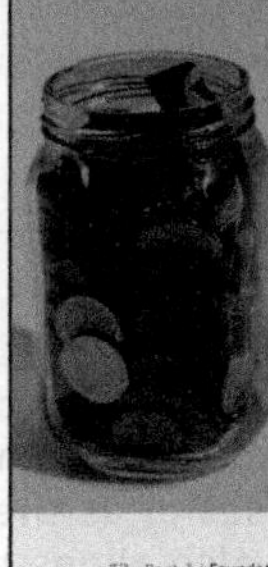

2.1 What is an ABN?
2.2 Why should suppliers of goods and services be sure to quote an ABN on their invoices?
2.3 Why is sole proprietorship so commonly used as the structure of Australian businesses?
2.4 David Black Plumbing ceases trading with $20000 owed to EZ Plumbing Supplies. David Black, the sole owner of the defunct business, owns his house and several flats. Who is legally liable for the $20 000 — David Black or EZ Plumbing?
2.5 Filcher Partners are lawyers who want to bring in a new full partner. Explain how the finances might be arranged to achieve this.
2.6 Dana Stevens is an orthodontist in a suburban dental practice run as a partnership. There are no professional employees, the only employees being the two receptionists and the three dental assistants. Dana draws a wage fortnightly and always says she is the lowest paid employee in the firm. Can this claim be correct? Why?
2.7 'A company cannot be sued; it is the board who are sued in the case of negligence.' Is this statement correct? Why?
2.8 Traders use trusts to minimise their income tax. Explain this statement with an example.
2.9 Most income received by resident individuals in Australia is assessable income including legacies, lottery prizes and gambling wins. Is this true? Explain.
2.10 Prime Paints suffered a fire and lost $180 000 worth of stock. $150 000 was claimed and received from its insurer. Is this assessable income?
2.11 The claiming of interest expenses as tax deductions has been a highly litigated area. Explain the factors underlying this.
2.12 Explain the basis of CGT.
2.13 What rate of tax is currently levied as CGT?
2.14 GST is an unfair tax that disadvantages business. Do you agree? Why?
2.15 Explain the theoretical basis for dividend imputation.
2.16 If a taxpayer receives a $700 fully franked dividend, she will pay tax on $700. Is this correct?
2.17 A taxpayer receives $2100 in fully franked dividends and has a 30% marginal tax rate. What extra tax liability will the taxpayer have on the dividends?
2.18 John is happy to be told by his accountant that he has $4500 in franking credits. Explain to John what this means.

52 Part 1 | Foundations of corporate finance

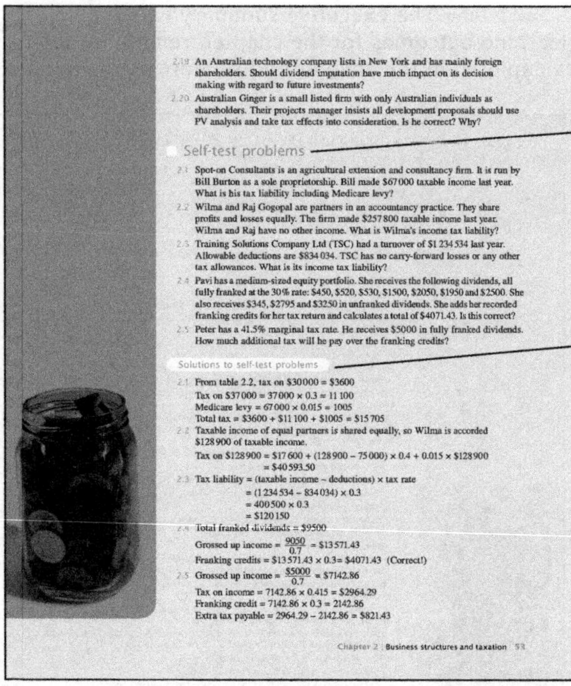

Self-test problems and solutions These present a range of corporate finance scenarios that will guide your learning and foster confidence with the subject matter before you proceed to the next category of activity.

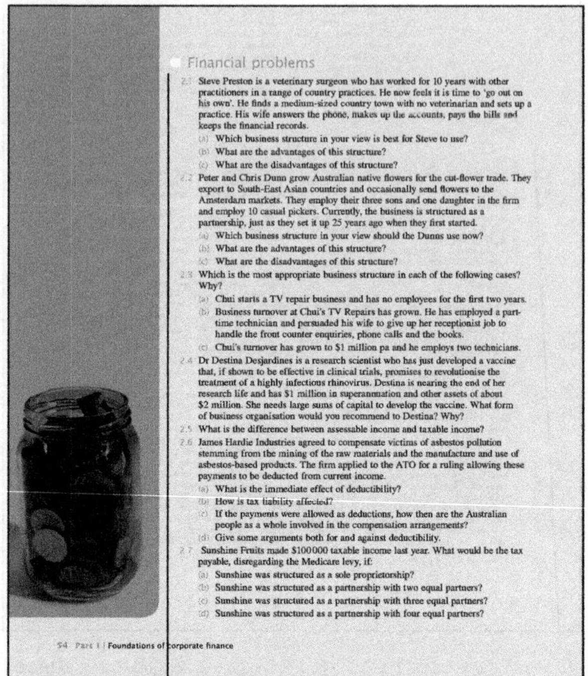

Financial problems These problems are designed to develop your skills in analysing, interpreting, evaluating, communicating and calculating a range of finance related activities.

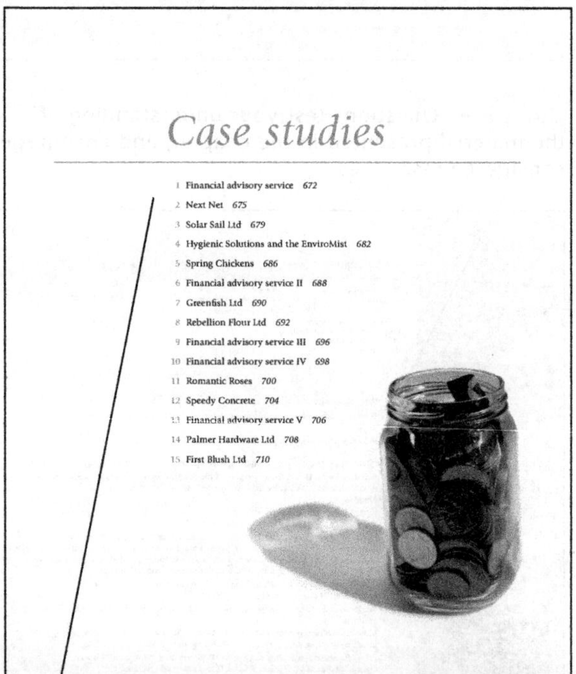

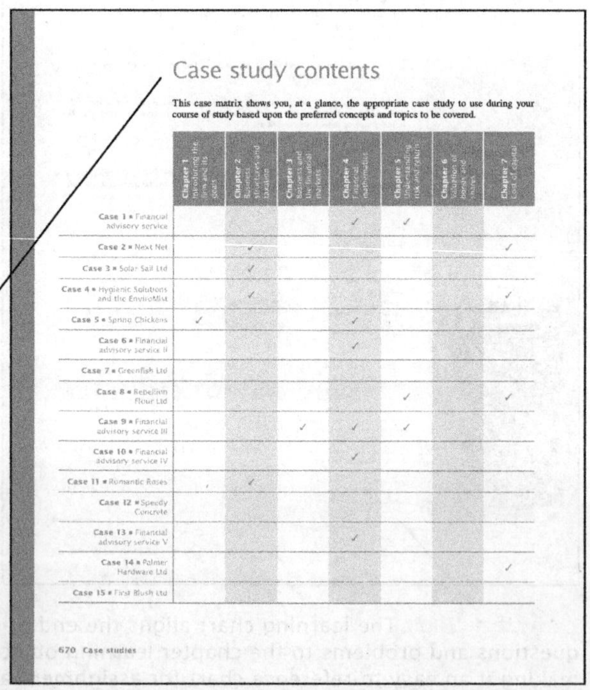

End-of-book case studies This collection of case studies, aligned to various topics throughout the text, encourages a detailed assessment of typical corporate finance scenarios. The case studies can be used as individual learning exercises or as the basis for group work activity. A case study matrix also aligns the topics presented in each case study to the relevant chapter.

Resources

All supplementary materials for both lecturer and student will be available in Blackboard or WebCT for ease of course preparation and administration. Please contact your Wiley sales representative for more information on accessing the following resources.

For the lecturer

Solutions manual

Prepared by the authors, this resource provides solutions to all the end-of-chapter activities and end-of-book case studies.

PowerPoint presentation

Prepared by James Williams, University of Newcastle. This PowerPoint presentation summarises the key learning outcomes of each chapter and offers an integrated resource for teaching.

Test bank

Prepared by Chris Deeley, Charles Sturt University, for the first edition and revised by James Williams, University of Newcastle. The test bank presents an extensive selection of assessment questions plus a selection of examination style questions and accompanying solutions. The test bank also includes exam papers, providing lecturers with a range of activities that can be used for mid-term and end-of-semester examinations.

For the student

Student practice test

The student practice test is a unique self-testing resource that is freely available to students using the text. Each chapter is supported with over 30 interactive multiple choice and true/false questions that will develop your understanding of the topics and enhance your learning outcomes during the course. You can randomise the questions, select the number of questions in the test, select a time limit in which to complete the test, email the results and store the results of past tests.

Study skills in finance

As each student learns differently, this website offers a set of study skills to help you maximise your learning during the course. In addition, web links to relevant media, financial analysis and regulatory agencies will be included.

Acknowledgements

The authors and publisher would like to thank the following copyright holders, organisations and individuals for permission to reproduce copyright material in this book.

Images

• © Newspix/Alan Pryke: **p. 3** • © John Wiley & Sons Australia/Taken by Kari-Ann Tapp: **pp. 33, 211** • © Banana Stock: **p. 59** • © Australian Stock Exchange Limited ABN 98 008 624 691 (ASX) 2003. All rights reserved. This material is reproduced with the permission of ASX. This material should not be reproduced, stored in a retrieval system or transmitted in any form whether in whole or in part without the prior written permission of ASX: **pp. 79, 134** • © Corbis Corporation: **p. 93** • Purestock Superstock: **p. 129** • © Photodisc: **p. 177** (top right); **p. 267**/Getty Images/Don Farall; **p. 421, p. 643** • Screenshots reprinted by permission from Microsoft Corporation: **p. 223** • Copyright Digital Vision: **p. 307** • Digital Stock/Corbis Corporation: **pp. 357, 385, 509** • © Australian Bankers' Association, Submission to the Financial System Inquiry, Sept. 1996. p.61**:** **p. 394** • Corbis Digital Stock: **pp. 467, 601** • 'Is your dividend policy liquidating your business?', 2002, © Australia and New Zealand Banking Group Limited: **p. 474** (top) • Commonwealth Copyright Administration: **p. 480** (top)/Top overall statutory tax rates on domestic source dividend income, *International Comparison of Australia's Taxes*, by Warburton and Hendy, (2006), p. 206, Copyright Commonwealth of Australia, reproduced by permission; **p. 483**/*International Comparison of Australia's Taxes*, by Warburton and Hendy, (2006) p. 207. Copyright Commonwealth of Australia, reproduced by permission; **pp. 612, 614**/*Corporations Act 2001*© Commonwealth of Australia • © Corbis Royalty Free: **p. 559** • Reserve Bank of Australia: **p. 616**/Sources: Australian Venture Capital Journal; RBA; Thomson Financial. Reproduced with permission of Reserve Bank of Australia www.rba.gov.au; **p. 625**/Sources: RBA; Thomson Financial. Reproduced with permission of Reserve Bank of Australia www.rba.gov.au.

Text

• © David Brearley, *The Australian*, 10 August 2002: **p. 3** • © Group of 100. www.group100.com.au: **pp. 11–12** • © Westpac: **pp. 14–15, 646–7** • © ANZ: **pp. 17–18, 423** • Journalists Copyright: **pp. 20–1**/Adele Ferguson, *BRW*, 29 June 2006; **pp. 559–60**/© Ken Boag • Heritage Building Society Limited: **p. 33** • 'Gwalie redefines shareholder rights', by Alan Kohler, *The Age*, 3 February 2007: **p. 39** • ABC Learning Centres: **pp. 59–60, 87–8** • © GE: **pp. 65, 373** • ABS *Year Book Australia 2006*, 1301.0/ABS data is used with permission from the Australian Bureau of Statistics/www.abs.gov.au: **p. 73** • ASX, **pp. 78–80**/© Australian Stock Exchange Limited ABN 98 008 624 691 (ASX) 2003. All rights reserved. This material is reproduced with the permission of ASX. This material should not be reproduced, stored in a retrieval system or transmitted in any form whether in whole or in part without the prior written permission of ASX • 'The Lex Column', 12 August 2006, © Financial Times Ltd: **pp. 153–4** • © Aspect Huntley: **pp. 177, 178** • 'Sydney Airport rejigs debt in expansion plan', by Steve Creedy, *The Australian*, 20 July 2006: **pp. 224–5** • 'The cost-of-capital furphies', by Paul Kerin, *BRW*, 20 July 2006: **pp. 238–9** • 'Centennial falls out of favour', by Stephen Wisenthal, *Australian Financial Review*, 23 November 2006: **p. 267** • 'Brambles Industries Ltd — BIL', *The Bulletin*, 22 November

2006, vol. 124, no. 48: **pp. 284–5** • © AAP: **p. 287**/10 August 2006; **p. 372** • 'Analysts scrutinise Twiggy's scheme', by Matthew Stevens, *The Australian*, 17 November 2006: **pp. 307–8** • 'More than 'social welfare' in disguise' by Hugh Alexander Grossman, *The Age*, 16 February 2006: **pp. 332–3** • Commonwealth Copyright Administration: **p. 357/** © Australian Government Export Finance and Insurance Corporation; **p. 362**/Australian Government Insolvency and Trustee Service Australia. Copyright Commonwealth of Australia, reproduced by permission • © Commonwealth Bank: **pp. 369–70** • Centre for Australian Financial Institutions: **p. 385**/from 'Economic and Social Impacts of the Closure of the Only Bank Branch in Rural Communities' by Dr. Diana Beal & Deborah Ralston, Centre for Australian Financial Institutions, CAFI, Report produced for CreditCare • © CSL Limited: **p. 400** • © Veda Advantage. www.vedaadvantage.com: **p. 402** • © National Australia Bank Limited: **pp. 427–8, 472–3** • 'Perfect year to offer public a piece of the action', by Michael Evans, *SMH*, 31 December 2005: **pp. 447–9** • 'Investors overwhelm BHP $3.5b buyback', by Jamie Freed, *SMH*, 31 December 2005: **p. 491** • Reproduced with the kind permission of the University of New South Wales, publishers of the *Australian Journal of Management*, where the paper first appeared in vol. 29, no. 2, pp. 225–42, 2004: **pp. 563–4** • © SFE Corporation Limited: **pp. 575–6** • *Business Times*, Singapore, 26 May, 2005 © Singapore Press Holdings: **pp. 585–6** • Simon Evans, *Australian Financial Review*, 14 February 2007: **p. 601** • 'Application to APRA for a non-bank spin-off' by Scott Murdoch, *The Australian*, 13 March 2007, p. 23: **p. 628** • © The Economist Newspaper Ltd, London: **pp. 650–1**.

Every effort has been made to trace ownership of copyright material. Information that will help to rectify any error or omission in subsequent editions will be welcome. In such cases, please contact the Permissions Section of John Wiley & Sons Australia, Ltd who will arrange for the payment of the usual fee.

part 1

Foundations of corporate finance

chapter

1

Introducing the firm and its goals

Learning objectives

After studying this chapter, you should be able to:

- **lo1** describe the range of goals of firms, including the significant wealth-maximisation objective
- **lo2** discuss the roles of financial managers
- **lo3** grasp the importance of the principal–agent problem
- **lo4** discuss the role of ethics
- **lo5** discuss some of the challenges facing modern firms
- **lo6** describe the nature of rationality in decision making.

HIH INSURANCE COLLAPSES WITH $5.5 BILLION OWING

HIH, a major insurance company in Australia, collapsed early this decade. Its latest set of audited accounts at the time showed net assets of almost $1 billion, but it later transpired that, rather than having net assets, the company had net liabilities of about $5.5 billion. Ray Williams was managing director for most of the company's history. The following article refers to hearings of the HIH Royal Commission, which inquired into the failure.

The profligate philanthropist

DAVID BREARLEY

Wayne Martin, the [HIH] commission's tenacious counsel, hit hard when Williams finally appeared on Tuesday, day 129 of the hearing.

Dr Raymond Reginald Williams AM, he suggested, was a vain man who loved his honorifics and donated no end of HIH cash to secure them. Monash University, to which he channelled a good share of the HIH millions, bestowed the honorary doctorate. The Order of Australia came with a citation acknowledging his boundless generosity, but not HIH's role in underwriting it.

Anyone in Williams's sights — client, servant or otherwise — was liable for summary reward. Swiss watches worth $10 000 apiece were the standard thank-you for 15 years' service at HIH. An invoice for 38 of them arrived on January 9, 2000, the same day staff were told to stop processing claims because of cashflow problems.

There were baubles and trinkets for all — including high-end jelly beans — but those in Williams's inner orbit prospered in special ways. Stuart Korchinski received a Saab convertible from the boss and $20 000 worth of home airconditioning, apparently while occupying the position of audit general manager. There was also a $250 000 loan, which appears to have been written off.

Executive expense accounts for calendar 2000 show Korchinski's claims topping $100 000, although he was never, strictly speaking, an executive. He was, however, the ultimate Williams insider — his jogging partner. In May 2000, Williams authorised $17 000 for three Korchinskis to attend a family funeral in Canada; seven months later he signed off on a $910 000 termination payout for Korchinski, whose contract suggests he was entitled to considerably less than that.

...

On Williams's own evidence, his directors never once blinked at his loose ways with shareholders' money (Williams's personal shareholding in HIH was insubstantial), even as the company careered towards oblivion. But why would they, when executive bonuses were soaring, from $340 000 in 1998–99 to $7.2 million in 2001. The last days of Pompeii seem tame by comparison.

...

The donations, he [Williams] insists, are the legitimate acts of a good corporate citizen. The other gifts reflect a sense of common decency and a commitment to staff motivation. And the authority for it all resides in the office of chief executive, which invests its occupant with prudence and honour. This is an article of faith with Williams, who regards supreme executive status as Catholics regard the papacy.

...

Bad call.[1]

In 2001, HIH consisted of more than 240 companies, of which eight were licensed insurers. Liquidators were appointed in 2001 and in the period since have identified the assets and liabilities of the companies, held creditors' meetings and established schemes of arrangement. In mid-2006, both the Australian and UK administrators paid a 5% distribution to some eligible creditors. The final outcome for individual creditors, expected perhaps by 2010, depends on the company with which they had dealings. Total payments to some creditors may be as high as 40%, but others are expected to be less than 5%.

Chapter preview

The HIH report gives you a real-life example of what part of this chapter is about. The collapse of HIH was a major event in Australian business history. Not only did employees and shareholders lose considerable sums of money, but the market for many types of insurance products virtually collapsed overnight. This was because HIH had undercut reasonable market prices and thus put an artificial cap on pricing while at the same time capturing large market shares. The loss of insurance cover meant that, for a considerable period, builders could not work, some professionals could not risk working and many community events had to be cancelled. Government, several years later, is still dealing with the effects on the public liability insurance industry. Additionally, the courts are dealing with the legal issues that arose from the conduct of various individuals during the HIH collapse, and are likely to continue to do so for many years.

Many of the issues raised by the HIH collapse are covered in this chapter: the goals of firms, the goals of finance managers, the roles of finance managers, the principal–agent problem and the need for ethical behaviour. We also consider some of the challenges facing modern business. Finally, we introduce some concepts from behavioural finance that help us understand the way people make decisions.

The following diagram shows how this chapter is structured.

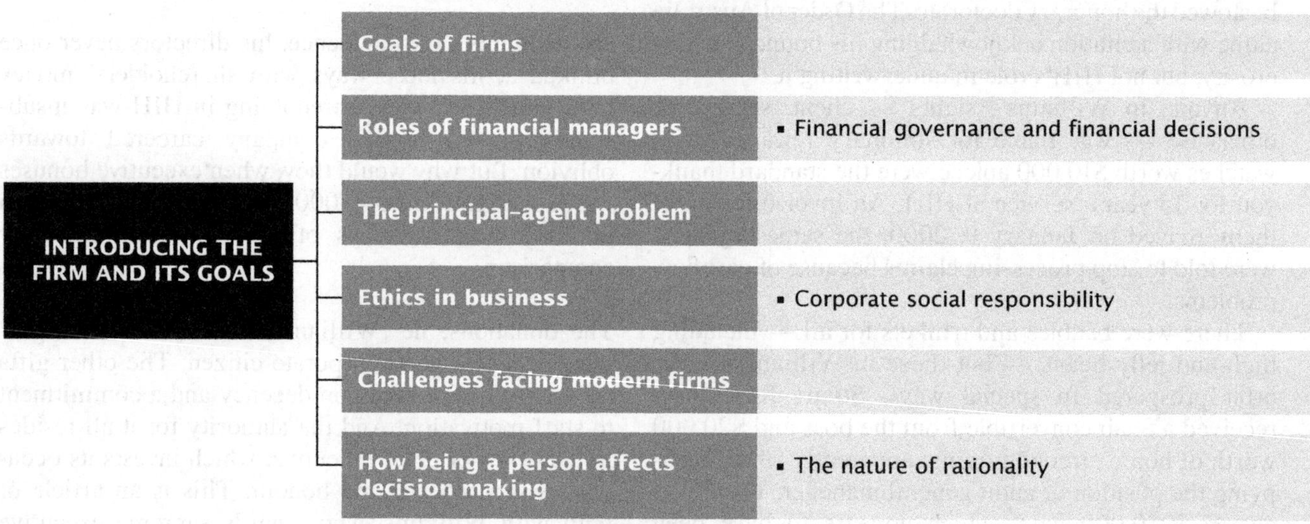

lo1

Describe the range of goals of firms, including the significant wealth-maximisation objective.

Goals of firms

Firms come in all sizes — small, medium and large. Firms are owned by sole operators, partnerships of two to 20 people or perhaps some hundreds, or by thousands of individual shareholders and large investment institutions in the case of listed public corporations. This book has been written to cover the financial decisions faced by all these firms, no matter how small or large and no matter how they are owned. However, in practice it is likely that small firms will take a less rigorous approach to decision making and financial analyses than is advocated here because these firms tend not to employ people trained in finance. Additionally, the management of many small firms judge that the benefits of employing a financial manager or a financial consultant do not exceed the costs. This judgement may in fact be an error, as time inevitably will reveal.

Every business has a reason or reasons for being. Because of different sizes and ownership structures, it is to be expected that there would be a range of goals among firms. For example, the Grey family partnership, which owns a small auto electrical business, might want to earn enough to live comfortably, put away some funds to educate their children, not work on Saturday or Sunday, earn a reputation for doing good work on time and at a reasonable cost, and have a good relationship with all their customers so that old ones return and new ones are attracted by word of mouth rather than expensive advertising campaigns. Eventually, the family might want to sell the business to fund a comfortable retirement.

In contrast, the ownership of a large corporation is much more removed from the operations of the company. The owners are you and me — through our direct shareholdings and indirectly through our superannuation funds and managed funds. What are our goals? Are they the same as the Greys? This is unlikely. Because the owners are not closely connected with the everyday operations of the firm, it is likely that the goals are simplified. Some owners will want only to make good returns; others will be concerned with returns, but would also want their firm to have good employment policies and labour relations or to make all possible attempts not to harm the natural environment in the course of business operations.

So the range of primary business goals includes:

- maximal wealth for owners
- maximal profits
- adequate profits — termed 'satisficing' where owners are happy with reasonable profits and company growth
- high revenue growth — especially for corporations where managers are rewarded for achieving such growth goals
- large market share
- limited working hours
- high reputation for product quality and service
- good employee relations and employment policies — a good place to work
- minimal or no harm to the natural environment — no pollution or land degradation
- ethical treatment of all parties associated with the business — a good corporate citizen.

Some of these goals will not be pursued by all businesses, some are difficult to achieve, some are difficult to measure and some need good returns in order to be able to fund their pursuit. Others are interdependent, and sometimes one goal must be sacrificed to some extent to achieve another. Take wealth maximisation, for example. Wealth maximisation by owners is a simple concept and must stem from at least good, if not maximal, returns in the form of either annual net cash inflows or capital appreciation. In turn, net cash in flows maximisation as a concept sounds simple enough, but can be difficult to achieve in practice. For example, are we thinking of short-run maximum profits or of long-run profits? Is there a difference? Yes, there is.

Consider the case of Jonno, a travelling house painter, who does paint jobs for people and then moves on. He is in business, and he buys paint and completes jobs by adding his labour. He has no plans to return to a particular area again and moves from state to state according to whim. He plans to stay in business only as long as it takes to save for a small fishing boat. He may well maximise his short-run profits by charging as much as he thinks the market will bear so he just gets each job. He could buy cheap paint. After all, the customers can not tell the difference, and he will be well away by the time the green paint fades and the white paint blisters and cracks. Why should he decrease his profits by buying expensive, high-quality paint? He will try to maximise his short-run profits, because the long term is not relevant to him. Jonno is pursuing **profit maximisation.**

Profit maximisation: implies a business is managed to maximise the difference between revenues and expenses in any period

By contrast, consider the case of Len, a lawnmowing and landscaping contractor, who works in the same region he lives in. He wants his customers to be pleased with the way he tends their gardens, and he wants them to get him back every two or three weeks. When he does landscaping jobs, he puts in durable timbers because he knows he will lose future business if the timbers rot or are eaten by termites within a few years. Thus, this businessman will tend to charge reasonable prices (not the maximum the market will bear) and will buy good-quality, more expensive materials. He is much more likely to try to maximise his long-run profits, and his pricing behaviour will be very different from the businessman in the first case. Thus, the element of time is important in our considerations. Len is pursuing **wealth maximisation**. He is managing his business to maximise the 'present value' of its present and future cash flows. We will learn more about this concept on the following pages.

Wealth maximisation: implies that the business is managed so that the present and future cash flows discounted at an appropriate rate will give a present value (PV) that is maximised

Both Jonno and Len in these two very different business scenarios try to run their business at a profit, probably as high a profit as they can achieve. But Len is putting in place the foundations for future cash flows and future wealth while Jonno is 'burning his bridges' and practically guaranteeing that he will not be invited back for future business.

Did you notice that we distinguished between profit maximisation and wealth maximisation in the range of business goals? Len and Jonno are operating their businesses with different time horizons. If we compare the profit figures for the two businesses, Jonno's will look to be the better performing business, but which business would you prefer to buy into?

The maximisation of owners' or shareholders' wealth is taken to be the optimal objective for the firm. This concept takes into account future earnings (and from this basis stems Len's concern to keep his current customers happy so that they provide the foundation for his future earnings). Earnings means profits and profits are a good thing for a firm to have. However, be aware it is possible for a firm to have large profits but not be able to pass these on to the owners because there is no spare cash. The profits are 'soaked up' by increased stock, debtors and necessary purchases of fixed assets.

Further, maximising profits ignores how much risk the firm had to take to generate the profits. As we see in chapter 5, if owners of firms are exposed to increased risk, they will want a higher return than they would for safer investments. Risk can be incorporated into managers' decisions when the objective of the firm is maximising wealth.

Another drawback of profit maximisation where owners and managers are different people is that managers have been known to manipulate profit figures. They can do this by changing the way some items are accounted for, reporting revenues early or costs late, or by failing to report some items at all. The collapses of companies like Harris Scarfe and HIH in Australia and Enron in the United States have shown that the profit figures in financial statements are sometimes not representative of the real situation.

The objective of maximising owners' wealth factors in the **time value of money**. The time value of money concept merely proposes, and I'm sure you will all agree, that $10 in the hand now is worth more to you than the same $10 if you were to receive it later; say, in one year's time. Regardless of the effects of inflation on your purchasing power, you could invest the $10 at, say, 5% with your local financial institution and have $10.50 at the end of

Time value of money: the concept that a dollar is worth more the sooner it is received

12 months. Put another way, we could say that the present value (PV) of $10.50 to be received in 12 months' time, when discounted back to the present at 5% pa, is $10. **Discounting** is the process of calculating the present value (PV) of a future amount. It incorporates the required return for the funds. Thus, as we saw with Len's lawnmowing and landscaping business, wealth maximisation implies that the business is managed so that the present and future cash flows discounted at an appropriate rate will give a present value that is maximised. For public corporations, the present value is the **market capitalisation** (share price multiplied by the number of issued shares) and, for other businesses, the **market value** of the firm.

Discounting: the process of calculating the present value (PV) of a future amount. The discount factor incorporates the required return for the funds.

Market capitalisation: the total value of a corporation as measured by the price of each issued share multiplied by the number of issued shares

Market value: the price willing buyers are prepared to pay and willing sellers are prepared to accept

The present value of the firm is thus the sum of all expected future cash flows discounted at an appropriate rate. Mathematically, this can be represented by equation 1.1.

$$PV = \frac{CF_1}{(1+k)} + \frac{CF_2}{(1+k)^2} + \frac{CF_3}{(1+k)^3} + \ldots + \frac{CF_n}{(1+k)^n} \quad [1.1]$$

where CF = cash flow for the period

n = number of periods

k = an appropriate discount rate

We learn how to calculate present values in chapter 4. We investigate the matter of an appropriate discount rate in chapter 7 and learn to calculate it. For the time being, we can interpret equation 1.1 as the value of the firm. Equation 1.1 tells us that a firm is worth the total of its future cash flows when they are discounted to their present values. In the special situation of corporations that pay dividends, equation 1.1 can be restated in terms of dividends received by the shareholders. Thus, the present value of the company is the perceived current value of future dividends. We examine this idea further when we calculate the value of securities.

The total market capitalisation of a company is the price per share multiplied by the number of issued shares. For example, a company with one million issued shares, which are currently selling for $1 each, has a market capitalisation of $1 million, which is the investing public's perception of the present value of future dividends. The market's perception of firm value tends to change, sometimes quite rapidly, even when the underlying 'true' present value has not changed at all. This can happen because the market price can change rapidly; for example, under the influence of excessive supply or demand.

To sum up, maximising owners' wealth has the following advantages over maximising profit as the objective of the firm. Wealth maximisation:

- uses a long-run perspective of the business
- takes future cash flows into account
- takes risk into consideration
- does not rely on accounting numbers
- considers the time value of money.

Thus wealth maximisation is taken to be the chief financial goal of the firm within the context of other non-exclusive goals such as ethical operations. Assuming wealth maximisation as the goal of the firm has the further benefit of giving us a quantifiable objective. A quantifiable objective allows us to model the impact of decisions on firm value. Without this assumption, it becomes much more difficult to predict how owners will assess managers' decisions and invalidates many of the techniques covered in this book.

FINANCE WORKSHOP 1.1

Aquila Investments Ltd is a small firm specialising in project investments that have clearly defined starting and ending points. The firm always invests in projects that use well-tested technology so that the risk of cost escalations is small.

Aquila has two projects under review in January 2008. Both require an initial investment of $10 million and in both cases the funds will need to be spent almost immediately the project is agreed to and signed off. Each project will terminate in five years. Aquila has only $10 million to invest, so must select either one of these projects or neither. The projects have the following anticipated cash flows (in $ million).

	Year 1	Year 2	Year 3	Year 4	Year 5
Project A	0	1	3	16	0
Project B	3	4	5	6	2

Aquila has wealth maximisation for its shareholders as its principal goal. Consider the implications of equation 1.1 for the analysis of the projects. Which project *in principle* should yield the greater increase in wealth? Why?

lo2

Roles of financial managers

Discuss the roles of financial managers.

If we accept wealth maximisation for owners to be the chief financial goal of the firm, what then are the goals and the roles of the financial manager? The goals should be the same as the owners' goals, as achieving the owners' goals is the task for which the financial manager is employed. In smaller firms, the owners and employed executives are much more likely to meet often, either formally or informally, and owners' goals are more easily transmitted. In large firms, this does not happen and we will discuss that issue in the next major section.

How do financial managers in large firms with many shareholders know what the owners (the shareholders) want? The transmission mechanism is the annual general meeting and the right of shareholders to request special general meetings. Shareholders at annual general meetings elect directors to represent them. Shareholders also on occasion are asked to vote on important issues or projects. If shareholders become strongly dissatisfied about the way their company is being run or about a particular project, they may request a special general meeting to have the issue discussed.

The financial manager has many roles to play in the essential task of managing the flow of funds through the firm. While some firms split the various functions between many individuals and other smaller firms may have one person doing the whole job, the roles or tasks of the financial manager may include overseeing or undertaking the following:

- the accounting and reporting functions
- managing cash and other short-term assets (discussed in chapters 10 and 11), raising funds (discussed in chapters 12 and 13) and managing excess funds
- taxation management, including compliance, forecasts and planning (discussed in chapter 2)
- risk management (discussed in chapter 15), on both the revenue and expenses sides of the business

- developmental financial analyses of projected investments and projects (discussed in chapters 7, 8 and 9) and capital restructures (discussed in chapter 16)
- forecasting the impact of financial decisions (discussed in chapter 14)
- audit management, both internal and external
- investor relations, including share registers and advice to shareholders, dividend policy (discussed in chapter 13), and (for listed companies) managing discussions with investment analysts, disclosures to the relevant securities exchanges, such as the ASX, and compliance with exchange rules.

The accounting and reporting functions include the daily keeping of the accounts, invoicing, receipting payments and paying bills, the keeping of asset registers and depreciation schedules, and the annual or biannual compilation and summary accounts. In addition, the accounting function includes the presentation and reporting of the annual financial statements to all interested parties. These parties include shareholders, regulators, creditors and the general public.

The cash management function includes planning and implementing the cash needs of the business (which is a complex task, particularly in a retail business), banking and maintenance of security systems for the cash. Raising funds involves planning and organising loans from banks and other financial institutions, perhaps arranging lease finance and, for corporations, perhaps issuing equities.

Taxation management includes compliance with all the taxation legislation and submitting the appropriate returns, forecasting taxation liabilities and planning and organising business activities, where possible, to manage the taxation effects. A simple example of such taxation management is the case of a farmer who buys in more stock feed in late June. This purchase increases his costs and business tax deductions, thus reducing his tax liability, but is essentially 'money in the bank' until drought comes and he has to feed it out.

Risk management is undertaken on both the revenue and expenses sides of business operations. Depending on the nature of the business, price variations may be managed with futures and forward supply contracts that allow a firm to lock in future selling prices now; cost variations may be managed with similar **financial derivatives** contracts and forward supply contracts. Financial derivatives are contracts that are derived from the value of some underlying assets and are used to manage risk. Derivatives include futures, swaps and forward rate agreements (FRAs), which are all discussed in chapter 15.

Financial derivatives: contracts that are derived from the value of some underlying assets and are used to manage risk

Financial managers employ a number of analytical techniques including net present value (NPV) and internal rate of return (IRR) to examine the viability of proposed investments, projects or products. In addition, they may undertake financial analyses of mergers, takeovers and other capital restructuring proposals. Financial managers should want to make decisions that increase the value of the firm. They can use the forecasting techniques outlined in chapter 14 to help them assess the likely impact of their decisions.

Another function of financial management is the audit of the firm's accounting and corporate governance systems. Internal audits are completed to ensure systems and processes are working well and to keep management informed. Qualified independent auditors conduct audits to ensure processes and transactions are properly managed and financial reports reflect a true and fair view of the financial position and performance of the entity. External auditors report their findings to the shareholders of companies and the owners of other types of business structures.

Investor relations are very important to public corporations. Public corporations can have thousands of shareholders and these stakeholders must be kept informed. They are advised of all the important news within the company. Additionally, firms with shareholders must keep an up-to-date share register. Most medium to large public corporations employ specialist firms to manage their share registration function. Dedicated share registries such as Computershare have developed the software and expertise to complete the transfer and registration tasks for share sales efficiently. The task can thus be completed at lower cost externally than a firm could achieve itself. Furthermore, listed public companies (not all public companies are listed on a stock exchange) must keep the listing exchange informed of any developments that might be price-sensitive. Any developments that might cause the share price to move up or down must be communicated to the exchange as soon as possible. Large listed public companies also meet investment analysts reasonably frequently to brief them of current and future events within the business because such analysts can have a significant influence on institutional sale or purchase of the company's shares.

Financial governance and financial decisions

As you can see, the primary duty of a firm's financial manager (sometimes called the chief financial officer or CFO) is to assist the chief executive officer (CEO) and the other executives to carry out board policy to optimise the financial and economic benefits that stem from all investments. All of the systems and processes that are put in place to achieve this aim are called the financial governance in the firm. **Financial governance** therefore comprises all the financial and management accounting systems and processes including the accounting for both capital and external liabilities, financial reporting, internal controls and internal audit, external audit, forecasting, strategic planning, operational planning and budgeting, purchasing, payments and communication. Financial governance is one part of the corporate governance of a firm. **Corporate governance** is the management of firms so that the actions of managers are in accord with the stated objectives of the operations.

Financial governance: the financial and management accounting systems and other financial processes that are put in place to achieve the objectives of the firm

Corporate governance: the management of the firm so that the actions of managers are in accord with the stated objectives

To illustrate the financial governance process for you, let's consider briefly what decisions are made in a going concern (an operating business) that is contemplating a new project and therefore new investment. Suppose the firm is structured as a company and it grows sweet corn under irrigation in northern New South Wales and north Queensland. It is geographically diversified to take advantage of the ability to extend the growing season so that it can supply corn to its major retail customers for as long a period as possible. The firm is thinking about investing in farmland in the Ord in Western Australia to increase its production dramatically, reduce its production risk from pests and diseases and further increase its supply period. The firm is also thinking about putting in a snap-freezing works so excess production in the Ord can be frozen and sold throughout the year as frozen corn on the cob.

What decisions must be made in regard to this investment? First, assuming the firm has collected all the production and financial information necessary to make the decision, the firm (its financial managers) must decide whether the investment will return adequate and acceptable benefits, given the goals of the firm. You will find information on this decision in chapter 2 (on taxation) and in chapters 4 (financial mathematics), 5 (required rates of return), 7 (cost of capital), and 8 and 9 (investment analysis).

Assuming the firm decides to go ahead with the investment, it must then make further financial decisions. How will the investment be funded? Will it use debt or equity? You will find answers to these questions after studying chapters 3 (overview of the financial markets), 7 (capital structure), 12 (long-term external finance), 13 (internal finance), 14 (financial evaluation) and 15 (risk management).

While this major task of planning a substantial new investment is taking place, the other responsibilities of the financial manager continue. Suppose the firm had funds which were in excess of current requirements; it would want to invest these funds at the best possible return for its desired level of risk. You will find information on this decision in chapters 3 (financial markets), 6 (valuation of bonds and shares), 10 (short-term finance) and 12 (long-term finance). Moreover, the firm must continue to manage its working capital and current assets effectively (see chapters 10 and 11). It must remember the needs of its owners (shareholders) and manage the returns to them (chapter 13).

To summarise, the most important classes of financial decisions comprise:

- new investment decisions
- investment funding decisions
- management of short-term funding and working capital
- management of long-term funding and capital structure
- dividend policy
- risk management.

lo3

Grasp the importance of the principal–agent problem.

The principal–agent problem

Principal–agent problem: the scope for conflict or division between principals (owners) and agents (managers) over the goals of the firm that are being pursued by its policy and management decisions

Agency costs: the losses borne by the owners of the firm that can be attributed to the agent having different objectives from the owners (or principals)

Even though this phrase sounds like a difficulty with the chief agent, the **principal–agent problem** really has nothing to do with first agents or second agents. Instead, it concerns an owner as principal and a manager as agent. Managers work for the owners as their agents. As we have seen, the owners expect their agents to carry out their wishes and to run businesses with the goals of the owners as their primary objectives. However, managers may not do so. They may have other objectives and agendas.

Remember the report about HIH at the start of this chapter? The CEO of HIH donated millions of the company's funds to Monash University and was subsequently rewarded with a personal honour for his generosity with other people's (the shareholders') funds. The CEO could argue that this was good advertising for the firm but, if HIH was not acknowledged as the donor, then it did not constitute advertising expenditure and did not generate any benefits for the owners of HIH. This type of expenditure is an agency cost. **Agency costs** are the losses borne by the owners of the firm that can be attributed to the agent having different objectives from the owners (or principals). In addition to direct costs, as in the HIH donation, agency costs include the cost of monitoring the agent's behaviour (by requiring regular reporting) and bonding costs (or the cost of trying to align the manager's objectives to those of the owners).

FINANCE WORLD

CFO code — where the CFO fits in

A code of conduct for CFOs has been developed in Australia by a group representative of Australia's largest companies — companies that recognise that accurate financial information is imperative if capital markets are to function properly.

The code and additional commentary may be found at the website of the Group of 100.

The Code of Conduct

This code provides that CFOs and senior finance officers influencing financial performance will:

1. Discharge their duties at the highest level of honesty and integrity having regard to their position and their organisation. Integrity is the quality from which public trust is derived and a benchmark against which the CFO must measure all decision making.
2. Observe the rule and spirit of the law and comply with the ethical and technical requirements of any relevant regulatory or professional body.

3. Respect all the confidentiality of all confidential information acquired in the course of business and not make improper use or disclose such confidential information to third parties without specific authorisation or legal requirement.
4. Observe the principles of independence, accuracy and integrity in dealings with the Board, audit committees, board committees, internal and external auditors and other senior managers within the organisation and other relevant bodies external to the organisation.
5. Disclose to the Board any actual or perceived conflicts of interest of a direct or indirect nature of which the CFO becomes aware and which the CFO believes could compromise in any way the reputation or performance of the organisation.
6. Maintain the principle of transparency in the preparation and delivery of financial information to both internal and external users.
7. Exercise diligence and good faith in the preparation of financial information and ensure that such information is accurate, timely and represents a true and fair view of the financial performance and condition of the organisation and complies with all applicable legislative requirements.
8. Ensure the maintenance of a sound system of internal controls to safeguard the organisation's assets and to manage risk exposure through appropriate forms of control.
9. Set a standard for honesty, fairness, integrity, diligence and competency in respect of the position of CFO that will encourage emulation by others within the organisation.
10. Remain committed, at all times, to observing, developing and implementing the principles embodied in this Code in a conscientious, consistent and rigorous manner.[2]

One of the problems encountered with corporate governance is perverse incentives. In other words, incentive schemes are set up in order to achieve one thing but in fact they are structured in such a way that they achieve something else. For example, a board of directors might offer a CEO a large parcel of share options if certain revenue levels are reached, on the basis that if revenue increases, profit increases and owners' wealth increases. This is an example of a bonding cost. However, the CEO may just focus on increasing revenue, so the objectives of principal and agent remain divergent. This is what happened with HIH. HIH consistently underpriced risk in its insurance businesses and gained large market shares. This meant that revenue was large and kept on increasing, but profitability was low or negative, and the company ultimately failed as claims and costs exceeded the ability of the company to pay. The HIH collapse was so large that it precipitated crises in the professional indemnity, construction insurance and several other insurance markets.

FINANCE WORKSHOP 1.2

1. Briefly state the nature of the principal–agent problem.
2. Consider some of the other gifts reported in the HIH story as being given away by the CEO. Which gifts do you think were legitimate business expenses and which revealed different objectives on the part of the CEO from those we expect the shareholders would be interested in?

lo4

Ethics in business

Discuss the role of ethics.

Ethics: moral principles or rules of conduct that indicate the acceptability of behaviour within a community

What actions are right or wrong? Such judgements are in the province of ethics. **Ethics** are moral principles or rules of conduct that indicate the acceptability of behaviour within a community. The answer to any specific question of ethical acceptability may be found in the social framework of the community concerned. In turn, the generally accepted codes of behaviour or social norms that make up the social fabric stem from religious, legal and traditional foundations. For a newcomer to any community, the last-named source of behavioural constraint may be the hardest to master, because tradition may be oral rather than written and based on tacit assumptions that native inhabitants inherently understand.

Ethical codes differ between cultures and communities. However, there are many common principles. If it is accepted that ethical laws are based on the desire of humankind to live without conflict with neighbours and without fear for life and property, then prohibitions on homicide, violence and injury to person and property, and attacks on honour and reputation will be universal prescriptions. In addition, duties such as protection, support and furthering the wellbeing of others, and being truthful and keeping promises are generally respected.

Ethical codes and standards have not always been applied universally to all parts of society. Things have improved in some areas, but not in others. People in lower social classes for a long time were considered fair game for oppression in the workplace; inhabitants of other communities or continents were prime candidates for slavery; draught animals were starved in the name of economy and flogged to death when weakness prevented them from exerting the required force; and other animals were killed slowly and painfully for sport. While the ethical pool has widened over time and additional classes of people and other species have had their rights recognised or have been given rights for the first time, still more needs to be done. Even in our society, for example, there are still people who condone and profit from blood sports that the majority find unacceptable. Moreover, the need for thought about ethical problems has grown enormously as life has become more complicated and developing technology has expanded our views on what is possible.

Regard for objectives and values other than the pursuit of profits, revenues, market share and so on, and respect for the laws of the communities in which business operates generally speaking have been forced upon business by concerned and aware investors. This movement is called the ethical or social investment paradigm. Kinder and Domini[3] traced the movement back to the Quakers who, in the seventeenth century, could not reconcile the idea of investing for profit in slavery, yet holding the belief that all humankind was equal before God.

The ethical investment movement holds the view that investors cannot completely divorce their social concerns from their investment behaviour. Thus, concerned investors apply screens to their investments. They do not want to support some activities and they do want to positively encourage others. The types of activities that social investors have not wanted to support include:

- the arms and munitions industries
- the tobacco industry
- the nuclear industry
- the gambling industry
- unsafe products
- unsustainable use of natural resources
- poor employee conditions
- bullying tactics with suppliers.

Activities and industries that have been viewed as socially good and ethically acceptable include:

- recycling of resources
- nature conservation
- reduction of pollution
- good employee management/benefits/involvement
- concern for diversity/minorities/those with disabilities.

For many years, social investors were themselves seen as a minority group — not to be taken seriously by the mainstream. The ethical investment movement could see that, even though a few funds managers perceived opportunities for profits in constructing ethical investment unit trusts, a transmission mechanism was necessary to make investment managers and company boards aware of the issues and to convince them that the movement had strength and had become part of the modern business environment.

That transmission mechanism was found — shareholder activism at the annual general meetings (AGMs) of listed and other companies. Even the largest companies were not immune to shareholder resolutions demanding more sensitive behaviour. The 2002 AGM of the Commonwealth Bank, for example, was presented with a resolution that the bank should not support financially activities which resulted in the destruction of high-conservation-value forests. The ANZ Bank, as shown in finance workshop 1.3, has taken note of ethical behaviour issues and the Westpac Bank has joined with other large international banking institutions to adopt a comprehensive set of principles for managing social and environmental issues (see the following 'corporate financial governance' feature).

CORPORATE FINANCIAL GOVERNANCE

Westpac adopts the Equator Principles

In June 2003, Westpac joined nine leading banks from seven countries in announcing their adoption of the Equator Principles, a voluntary set of guidelines which have been developed for managing social and environmental issues relating to the financing of projects. Today, there are approximately 40 signatories to the Equator Principles, which cover more than 80% of the global project-financing market.

In adopting the Equator Principles, we agree to provide loans only to those projects whose sponsors can demonstrate their ability and willingness to comply with processes that ensure that projects are developed in a socially responsible manner, according to sound environmental management practices.

In 2006, Westpac joined a number of leading financial institutions from around the world to announce the launch of the revised Equator Principles. The revised Principles now apply to all project financings with capital costs above USD10 million.

The full text of the principles, as well as frequently asked questions, can be found on the Equator Principles website.

Embedding the Equator Principles

We have drafted our Equator Principles policy and engaged an external environmental consulting firm to assist with its implementation. Specific procedures have been embedded within the Project and Structured Debt procedural manual and the Equator Principles are being applied to all project finance transactions being considered by the bank.

Training has been conducted on the Equator Principles with 13 representatives from Project and Structured Debt, Syndications, Relationship Management, Portfolio Management, Credit Policy and Credit Approvals.

Reporting on performance

A full case study on our progress in implementing the Equator Principles was published in our 2004 Stakeholder Impact Report.

In 2006, we closed 14 project finance transactions. The assets financed were all located in Australia, six were greenfield developments, one an expansion of an existing asset and seven the refinancing of an existing asset. The asset classes involved were tollroads, electricity generation, oil and gas production and pipelines, mining and social infrastructure. Our role in these transactions was as Joint Lead Arranger and Underwriter, Sole Underwriter, Sole Lender and Club Participant.

The Equator Principles were applied to all transactions notwithstanding that one was below the revised Equator Principles threshold of US$10m. A number of transactions were declined during the past year, several for reasons including environmental concerns.[4]

(12 months to September 2006)	Number	Loan value – Westpac share	Equator Principles category		
			A	B	C
Transactions closed	14	A$933m	0	13	1
Transactions pending (credit approved – not closed)	8	n/a	0	6	2

Merchants and consumers who enter markets face not only possible contravention of basic social principles such as the integrity of property ownership (for example, fraud, misrepresentation, credit card theft and theft of information and intellectual property), but also the possibility of enhanced ethical violations due to the advance of technology. There are possibly hundreds of different types of cases; the following are just a few.

- *Exploitation of resources overseas by Australian firms using cheap technology that would not be acceptable legally or ethically here.* An example is the Australian mining company BHP at the Ok Tedi mine in Papua. It dumped enormous quantities of overburden (soil and rock) into the Ok Tedi and Fly rivers every day and this pollution has destroyed the ecology of the river. Apart from any ethical considerations for other species, the river used to provide the livelihood of local people.
- *Importation of goods which do not comply with Australian health and safety standards.* We have in place comprehensive standards for the quality of foodstuffs produced in Australia. For example, the maximum allowable limit for the heavy metal, cadmium, in peanuts is 0.5 mg/kg. On numerous occasions when the Australian peanut crop has produced less than the required output, importers have brought in peanuts from China to be used in manufactured peanut foods, such as peanut paste and chocolate products. Only the vigilance of the Quarantine Service has stopped peanuts with much higher levels of cadmium from entering the Australian food market.
- *Paying bribes to secure sales contracts.* In some countries, the paying of bribes or commissions in order to secure contracts is a normal part of doing business. Australian exporters are often put into difficult positions when trying to sell into these countries (for example, selling grain into Iraq). Hence the firms involved in these markets should have written governance policies to guide staff.
- *Shifting of manufacturing offshore.* Closing down old plants in Australia and sourcing production from other countries, where labour costs are low, may improve profitability but there is an ethical question if costs are low in the new supply country because safety standards are compromised or hours of work are exploitive.

- *Industrial espionage.* An employee of a rival supplier bidding for a large contract offers to come to work for your firm — provided he is given a large 'golden hello' which is outside the normal remuneration in the industry — and he promises to bring his intimate knowledge of the rival's costings with him. Can the firm ethically employ this person?
- *Conspiracy with other firms to cheat consumers.* During the 1990s, the property market on the Gold Coast in Queensland boomed. House and unit construction increased dramatically. Unscrupulous developers devised a system whereby they could 'gouge' additional profits from the market by setting up a two-tier price system, called 'marketeering'. They charged the locals one price, but negotiated much higher prices with other people who did not know the market. They offered free trips to the Gold Coast to people living in other states and then subjected them to high-pressure sales techniques. Many people signed up only to find in a few months that their 'dream' investment property had been significantly over-priced and the year-round demand for accommodation by tenants had failed to materialise. Banks, solicitors and real estate agents were all implicated in this fraud. The Queensland Government strengthened the *Property Agents and Motor Dealers Act 2000* to deal with the issue and also introduced a compulsory five-day 'cooling off' period for all property deals.
- *Invasion of privacy through insecure system controls on databanks.* The *Privacy Act 1988* prohibits data collected for one purpose being used for another purpose without the consent of the affected people. Thus, for example, customer lists may not be sold to other firms so that those firms can direct advertising to people known to be interested in a particular issue. Merchants may build comprehensive databanks on their customers. There are many aspects to the ethical management of these databanks. Not least, there is an arguable case that it is ethically incumbent upon managers to ensure data are as accurate as possible, up-to-date, and accessible only on a need-to-know basis. Such data, once recorded — accurately or inaccurately — may be shared with other computers. If security systems are not comprehensive, the potential to invade privacy is created in a way never before possible.

What do ethics have to do with making financial decisions? BHP was subjected to international condemnation for the decision not to construct a tailings dam to contain the Ok Tedi mine's waste. As we see in chapter 8, large capital investment projects like the construction of a mine are difficult to reverse. BHP had to take substantial losses to get out of its Ok Tedi investment and has invested significant amounts trying to restore its environmental image. Similarly, moving production offshore may not increase the value of the firm if the firm's customers have strong feelings about purchasing domestically produced goods. The 'Buy Australian' campaigns specifically encourage consumers to purchase Australian made products when they can. Being ethical is not necessarily inconsistent with wealth maximisation, especially if we look beyond the short term.

Whistleblowing: informing (usually by employees of the perpetrators) the relevant authorities of malpractice or dangers to the public or the environment

Whistleblowing presents a further threat to firms that behave either illegally or unethically. 'Whistleblowing' is a reasonably new term in the language and it means 'informing (usually by employees of the perpetrators) the relevant authorities of malpractice or dangers to the public or the environment'. Usually the actions that are the subject of whistleblowing are illegal as well as unethical. A person contemplating whistleblowing has to think very carefully about the consequences. Assuming there has been illegal activity, whistleblowers run several risks:

- sacking by disgruntled management if their identity is revealed
- personal vilification
- loss of future employment benefits
- no punishment for the miscreants because regulators or investigators are lax
- ingrained culture of corruption wins the power struggle and no changes are made.

Even with knowledge of the risks that are being run, there are fortunately still people in our society who feel so strongly when they observe consistent and organised malpractice being effected for profit that they are willing to risk their personal financial health in making the wrongs publicly known. Legislation has been passed to try to protect whistle-blowers, but it does not always achieve that aim.

Corporate social responsibility

Corporate social responsibility: the firm has wider responsibilities in relation to objectives and people apart from the owners or shareholders

Corporate social responsibility (CSR) is a concept that has gained some prominence in the last decade or so. CSR means that the firm has responsibilities in relation to objectives and people apart from the owners or shareholders. Objectives often associated with CSR include a responsibility to manage natural assets sustainably and not to pollute by chemical discharge, smell, noise, dust or other irritants; fair treatment of employees and an ethical attitude towards clients. The other people or stakeholders include employees, customers, suppliers, regulators and the public at large.

Contemporary academic literature contains many references to corporations 'doing well by doing good'. The motivation behind these corporate actions can be explained within the conventional economic framework of wealth maximisation, as well as through ethical motivation. The involvement of public relations is the reason that CSR can be fitted within conventional theory, as a favourable corporate image will tend to enhance the ability to continue in business and to maximise long-run wealth.

People who are aware of the need to conserve what little high-conservation-value eco-systems we have left understand that the financial services sector funds the activities that are destroying those ecosystems. If those funds were withdrawn or denied, then there would be less uncaring destruction. The banks are starting to consider these issues, as well as issues of equity and social justice, as the following article indicates.

FINANCE WORLD

ANZ: new small loans program for people on low incomes

Accessing low-cost, fair and safe financial poducts and services can be difficult and distressing for some Australians, Our research shows that around six per cent of adults have minimal access to financial services. This includes people who are on low incomes or unemployed, people with disabilities and those from Indigenous communities. These people may feel too intimidated to enter a bank branch, let alone apply for a loan to cover unexpected costs. In some cases, they borrow from 'loan sharks' or payday lenders at interest rates of up to 1000%, simply because they believe they have no other options.

Our products and services help many Australians to build their assets and create a secure future. But the policies and practices of our industry have also — in part — contributed to financial exclusion. We know there are some basic things we can and should do to make a difference for people struggling to understand their finances or facing financial hardship.

To help address some of these problems, ANZ and the Brotherhood of St Laurence have teamed up to launch our 'Progress Loans' pilot, a small loans program providing low-income earners with access to mainstream credit. Progress Loans offers eligible customers loans of between \$500 and \$3000, at an interest rate of

12.7%, to pay for essential household items like fridges and washing machines, education and medical expenses.

Progress Loans is the culmination of more than 18 months of consultation and development work. It brings together ANZ's resources and expertise in financial services with the Brotherhood's knowledge and experience in providing personal loans to meet the needs of people on low incomes.

Progress Loans recognises the role we can play in enhancing the lives of Australians, particularly some of the most vulnerable groups in our community by improving access to mainstream financial services.[5]

FINANCE WORKSHOP 1.3

The ANZ Bank has taken the concept of CSR to heart with the development of many corporate programs dealing with CSR issues. These include:

- screening for environmental and social impacts of transactions/portfolios/ industries supported
- adoption of a sustainability policy for suppliers — all new suppliers are required to self-assess their social and environmental performance
- ANZ Volunteers — a program whereby staff are allowed one paid leave day per year to perform voluntary work in the community
- community giving by staff — ANZ matches donations up to $1 million each year
- community giving by customers — ANZ provides facilities through which customers can make donations
- community giving by shareholders.

The donations by shareholders scheme is called the ANZ Dividend Charity Program, announced in July 2006. Under this scheme, shareholders are able to instruct the ANZ share registry to pay all or part of their dividends to selected charities. All the charities involved have 'deductible gift recipient' status; thus, all donations made to these charities are allowable income-tax deductions. ANZ will match these donations on a dollar-for-dollar basis up to $250 000 in the first 12 months.

1. What positive arguments would you present to a friend who asks you if she should register to donate her ANZ dividends?
2. What issues would you expect your cynical friend, Joe, to raise and cite against the whole concept of CSR and its many practical manifestations?

lo5

Challenges facing modern firms

Discuss some of the challenges facing modern firms.

Perhaps the most significant challenge of all those facing modern firms can be encapsulated in one word — change — or more correctly in two words — rapid change. Firms face rapid change in all facets of their business dealings. Successful firms will rise to the challenge and turn threats into opportunities. Less proactive (or slowly reactive) firms will become overwhelmed by change, will become less profitable and will eventually die or be taken over.

We can construct a framework to help us consider the most important aspects of change. Change affects businesses by means of:

- the external environment
- advancing technology
- social advances and the expectations of customers and the community.

In Australia, the external environment for businesses has changed predominantly through globalisation and all its implications and the deregulation of the financial markets. Globalisation has led to an increasingly interconnected world where national economies are becoming more and more dependent on each other. It could be argued that globalisation started when the first people moved north out of Africa, but the movement to interconnectedness has accelerated rapidly in the last few decades. For business, globalisation may be viewed as either a threat or an opportunity; as firms increasingly specialise, they source materials and labour from the optimal locations globally, not just nationally, and in turn market their goods and services worldwide.

Deregulation of the financial markets in Australia has taken place in the last two decades in an environment of deregulation globally. Deregulation has seen an increase in market efficiency and competition, the introduction of many new financial products and the pricing of financial products much more in line with the 'true' market prices. This trend towards more accurate pricing has seen the consequent decrease in cross-subsidisation between products, where excess profits on one set of products made up for under-charging on another set. This is the reason that financial institutions seem to charge more in fees these days than in the past. Previously, they made higher returns from interest charges and absorbed some of the costs of providing other services; now they earn lower interest margins, have cut cross-subsidisation and charge higher fees for services rendered.

A further consequence of deregulation is the rapid introduction and adoption of improved technology in the financial markets. Electronic banking, including Internet banking services and EFTPOS (electronic funds transfer at point of sale), has brought significant benefits to businesses which have welcomed this technology and adopted it quickly. The same is true for many of the other changes brought about by deregulation in the financial markets. Businesses which have decided to welcome and deal with change have benefited, while businesses which have been forced belatedly to adopt new measures have generally not shared in the benefits to the same degree.

Advancing technology allows businesses to do things better and cheaper. For manufacturers, new technology allows them to produce more efficiently. For example, car manufacturers have installed hundreds, if not thousands, of robots in their plants to produce cars both more cheaply and of higher quality than car workers were able to do previously. Plants using the new technology gain the advantages. Plants not quickly adopting the same new technology put themselves at a disadvantage, as their competitors are able to offer high-quality cars more cheaply.

New technology is continually being developed for all sorts of processes in all sorts of businesses. It is by no means limited to manufacturers. Retailers, for example, may benefit from advances in payment systems (EFTPOS, credit and debit cards, smart cards); stock control and re-order systems using bar coding; and Internet commerce. As in the case of production technology, some firms will adopt new technology quickly and reap the benefits. Others will be slow and lose competitiveness. The slowest and most reactionary will normally lose the race altogether and in time go out of business.

The final facet of change that is important to business is social change. Views of what is right and acceptable within a society or community are continually changing. Possibly the most important aspects for businesses to be aware of relate to employees and employment conditions, safety of products and the treatment of the natural environment. Not so long ago, employers were able to treat employees harshly. They were able to sell unsafe products and dump their waste products into the natural environment, virtually without penalty. Over the last few decades, the situation with regard to all these matters has changed dramatically. For example, excess employees now are routinely offered redundancy packages and retraining rather than being sacked with little warning and no compensation. Products found to be unsafe are routinely recalled for modification or destruction and purchasers are compensated. Pollution of the air or waterways is controlled or prohibited in many cases.

While the situation with many of these issues is much better now than it was even a few decades ago, change has not stopped. People's views will continue to evolve and modify, and successful businesses will alter their behaviour to accommodate the changing social environment in which they operate. Honouring the social contract between businesses and the societies in which they operate will mean that businesses have to continue to be ready to meet new obligations socially, legally and economically. The most successful businesses will meet the challenges by employing new people with tertiary education and well-developed skills as well as by developing skills and insights among current employees through mind-expanding staff development programs.

The following 'corporate financial governance' feature highlights one of the effects of social change — the issue of CSR. Accountability and transparency in relation to corporate donations and corporate governance are now very important.

CORPORATE FINANCIAL GOVERNANCE

Corporates see the light

ADELE FERGUSON

More companies are realising they can lift their share price through corporate responsibility.

...

The real problem with CSR is a lack of transparency and accountability. There are no rules covering disclosure of non-political donations, and that means many companies do not disclose information about philanthropic ventures they support, and even fewer put a dollar figure on how much they give away.

Transparency is improving, but it still has a long way to go. Not enough public companies put a note in their annual reports outlining who they give money to, and even fewer put a dollar figure on how much they spend on their CSR programs. Fewer still measure the success of the programs. Given that shareholders, not the directors or executives, own the company, it is incumbent on all companies to let shareholders know exactly how their money is being spent.

Companies such as BHP Billiton go to great lengths to outline how much they spend on CSR and sustainable development. Others, such as Foster's Group, have seen the light more recently. From this year, Foster's will detail its CSR program and put a dollar figure on how much it spends, and it will start quantifying the success of its various projects.

...

Foster's and 11 other companies, including ANZ Banking Group, Pacific Brands and Australian Gas Light, have started to measure and benchmark their corporate community contributions using the London Benchmarking Group methodology. There are many such organisations, with different models. For instance, there is the Global Reporting Initiative, which is another framework for reporting CSR or sustainable development, and BHP Billiton belongs to the One Percent Club, which asks members to give 1% or more of their pre-tax profit. BHP Billiton's chairman, Don Argus, is passionate about the importance of CSR, and he has formed a subcommittee of the board to emphasise its strong strategic focus.

The point is CSR has nothing to do with pure philanthropy. It is about enhancing the appeal of the company, for all concerned. The best corporate philanthropy is also beneficial for the company. Companies embracing CSR believe it will play a bigger role in the future, particularly if it can outgrow its image as being 'nice to have' and come to be regarded as a mainstream activity to manage risk and capture opportunities.

…

CSR is becoming mainstream. For example, stockbrokers such as Deutsche Bank and Citigroup are starting to count CSR as part of the risk profile of a company. In March, Citigroup released a 112-page report enititled *Riding With the Cowboys or Hanging With the Sheriff*, which measures the effect on mining companies of good corporate practice versus bad corporate practice. It argues that in the past, mining companies kept costs low by clamping down on unionism, cutting corners with health and safety and taking risks with waste disposal. Now, many of them take into account social costs when they do business.[6]

lo6

Describe the nature of rationality in decision making.

How being a person affects decision making

Throughout this book, we will discuss methods and tools that financial managers can use to analyse problems and to assist them to make decisions. Underlying all decisions are either specifically enunciated or assumed goals. In this chapter, we have discussed the goal of maximising wealth. But even as we accept this objective as a reasonable goal for business, we may observe in everyday events that not all decisions are taken to maximise wealth. In reality, many other factors come into consideration and many decision makers have an attitude that 'near enough is good enough' or 'she'll be right'.

We noted earlier that an advantage of assuming wealth maximisation as the goal of the firm was that it provides a quantifiable objective that allows us to predict how the owners of the firm will respond to management's decisions. There is no generally accepted alternative goal that can challenge and supplant wealth maximisation as a driving force for our decisions. This does not, however, mean that wealth maximisation is a universal description of the way people really behave in all circumstances. Included throughout this book you will find special 'behavioural perspective' features. In these, we deal with some observed phenomena that reveal non-maximisation anomalies in order to share with you some common behaviour in the real business world.

Given that we have the technology to allow carefully programmed computers to make logical decisions based solely on the wealth maximisation criterion, why do we still leave the financial decisions of firms to people? People are not computationally equipped to make perfect decisions — we make mistakes. Some mistakes can be attributed to random error and others occur because we have biases in our decision making processes. Understanding the way we make decisions helps us to overcome biases that are negative and allows us to capitalise on the short cuts that the human mind uses effectively that can't yet be replicated by computers! The 'behavioural perspective' features will help you to detect the flaws in your own decisions and to understand why other people make the choices they do. We begin our discussion of the impact that people have on decisions by considering the role and nature of rationality.

Rational behaviour: implies decisions are made after an amount of reasoning so that ultimate decisions are not foolish or absurd, and are based on the desire to satisfy objectives and maximise or at least optimise outcomes

The nature of rationality

Finance theory stems from the theories of economics, a discipline that prides itself among all the branches of the social sciences on its strong framework of rigorously developed theory. A fundamental principle of the traditional finance and economics disciplines is that decision makers behave rationally. **Rational behaviour** implies decisions are made after an amount of reasoning so that ultimate decisions are not foolish or absurd, and are based on the desire to satisfy objectives and maximise or at least optimise outcomes. Normally, optimised outcomes are taken to relate to material wellbeing and would include owner's objectives such as limited working hours.

The traditional finance and economics literature is resplendent with the assumption that people are 'rational wealth maximisers'. These people always have the objective of increasing their wealth as much as possible because they, rationally, prefer to have more dollars than less. Rational wealth maximisers do systematic and comprehensive analysis before they make decisions, and the choices they make are always in favour of the option that is most likely to increase their wealth by the largest amount possible.

However, economics is not the only strongly theory-based social science that studies human behaviour. Psychology is strictly the study of the human soul and mind and, as such, has much to contribute to the study of decision making. Unlike economists, psychologists perceive rationality 'in terms of the process employed to make a decision, whether or not it happens to lead to the best results'.[7] In recent years economists — not satisfied to accept the versions of rationality which have been handed down by their predecessors, and aware of the many observed anomalies among decision makers — have adopted the psychologists' view of rationality and have incorporated process rationality into their thinking.

Thus, new branches of both economics and finance have developed — behavioural economics and behavioural finance. Both sub-disciplines are endeavouring to develop new theory to better explain human decision making. Especially, the new theory should be able to explain the systematic errors and inconsistencies that are commonly observed in both consumer and business decisions.

Some of these issues will be highlighted in the 'behavioural perspectives' features throughout this book. For example, the following feature tells you about the behaviour of the board of Home Depot, the largest home-improvement retailer in the world, when it came to rewarding the CEO for his services.

BEHAVIOURAL PERSPECTIVE

$210 million for quitting

The board of a firm, as we know, represents the owners and is appointed to formulate policies to achieve the firm's objectives. One of these objectives normally is to maximise owners' wealth. It is interesting then that the board of Home Depot changed the benchmark for chairman and chief executive Robert Nardelli's performance pay. It had been linked to returns to shareholders, but the linkage was changed to earnings per share. At the time the company was performing rather poorly on the first measure, but quite well on the second. The result was that Nardelli's performance pay increased to a seemingly outrageous amount, even though the shares lost 8.2% in value (and the owners therefore lost wealth) during his six-year tenure. Why would the board do this?

Shareholders had been unhappy with the company's corporate governance in relation to share options and with the size of Nardelli's pay packet, particularly as the company had been suffering a lacklustre share price. Just before the company's 2006 annual meeting, several shareholders asked why the benchmark for Nardelli's performance pay had been altered. Discussion of the issue was avoided at the meeting — indeed, Nardelli told the company's directors not to attend.

In 2007, Home Depot announced Nardelli would resign after six years in the job. Under his employment contract, Nardelli was entitled to a $210 million severance package. The head of the US Financial Services Committee, Barney Frank, suggested that 'Mr. Nardelli's contribution to raising Home Depot's stock value consists of quitting and receiving hundreds of millions of dollars to do so'. You can judge what the market thought of his departure by the 4% increase in the share price in one day's trading after the news was released to the market.[8]

executive summary

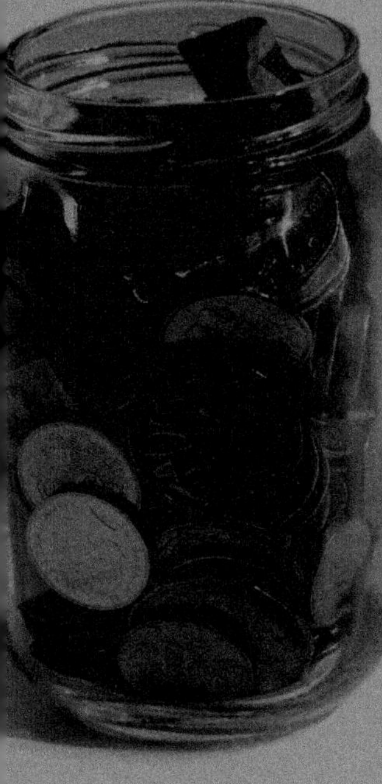

lo1 describe the range of goals of firms, including the significant wealth-maximisation objective

- Firms have a wide range of goals, which stem from the goals of the owners and, to some extent, the managers.
- Firms' goals include:
  - maximal wealth for owners
  - maximal profits
  - adequate profits — termed 'satisficing', where owners are happy with reasonable profits and company growth
  - high revenue growth — especially for corporations where managers are rewarded for achieving such growth goals
  - large market share
  - limited working hours
  - high reputation for product quality and service
  - good employee relations and employment policies — a good place to work
  - minimal or no harm to the natural environment — no pollution or land degradation
  - ethical treatment of all parties associated with the business — a good corporate citizen.
- Goals are often interdependent and not all may be achievable simultaneously.
- Maximisation of owners' wealth is taken to be the premier objective.
- Maximisation of owners' wealth takes into account a long-term view, future cash flows and the time value of money, and includes risk.

lo2 discuss the roles of financial managers

- The financial manager plays many roles:
  - the accounting and reporting functions
  - cash management, raising funds and managing excess funds
  - taxation management, including compliance, forecasts and planning
  - risk management, on both the revenue and expenses sides of the business
  - developmental financial analyses of projected investments, projects, capital restructures
  - forecasting the impact of financial decisions
  - audit management, both internal and external
  - investor relations, including share registers and advice to shareholders, and (for listed companies) managing discussions with investment analysts, disclosures to the relevant stock exchanges and compliance with exchange rules.
- Financial management is part of corporate governance, which is the whole management of the firm so that the actions of the managers are guided by and in accordance with the stated objectives of the firm.

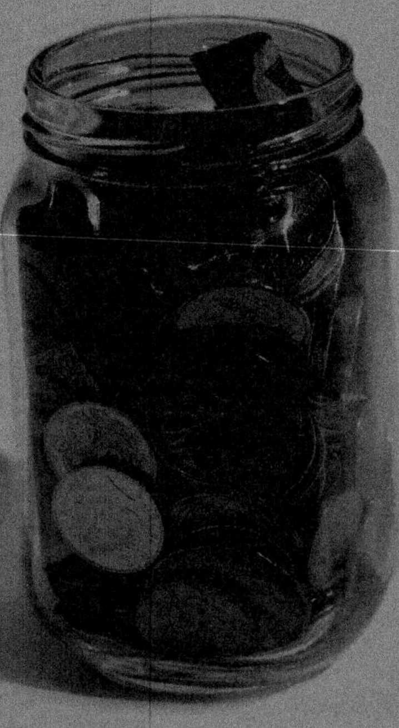

lo3 grasp the importance of the principal–agent problem

- The principal–agent problem is the scope for conflict between owners and managers over the goals which are being pursued through policy and management decisions.
- This difficulty can cause transfers of wealth from owners to others as in the HIH case.
- Agency costs are the losses borne by the owners of the firm that can be attributed to the agent having different objectives to the owners.
- One of the issues encountered with the principal–agent problem is the existence of perverse incentives.
- Perverse incentives are incentives that are set up to achieve an outcome (such as increased profit) but in fact are structured in such a way that they are used to achieve another outcome (such as a bonus payment for a manager)

lo4 discuss the role of ethics

- Ethical behaviour is conduct that is acceptable within a given community.
- Ethical codes differ among communities, but there are many common principles which facilitate people living together in reasonable harmony.
- Acceptable behaviours change over time.
- Business faces continual demands to act with greater responsibility toward those entities with recognised rights.
- Corporate social responsibility, meaning that business has responsibilities toward others apart from owners, is gaining greater acceptance as a management issue.
- The ethical investment movement holds the view that investors cannot completely divorce their social concerns from their investment behaviour and thus apply screens to their investments.
- Social investors have not wanted to support:
  - the arms and munitions industries
  - the tobacco industry
  - the nuclear industry
  - the gambling industry
  - unsafe products
  - unsustainable use of natural resources
  - poor employee conditions
  - bullying tactics with suppliers.
- Activities which have been viewed as ethically acceptable include:
  - recycling of resources
  - nature conservation
  - reduction of pollution
  - good employee management/benefits/involvement
  - concern for diversity/minorities/those with disabilities.

lo5 discuss some of the challenges facing modern firms

- Firms face rapid change in all facets of their business dealings.
- Successful firms will rise to the challenge posed by change and turn threats into opportunities.
- Less proactive (or slowly reactive) firms will become overwhelmed by change and will become less profitable.
- Change affects businesses by means of:
  - the external environment
  - advancing technology
  - social advances and the expectations of customers and the community.
- Globalisation and the deregulation of the financial markets have been the chief forces of change in the external environment.
- Advancing technology allows businesses to do things better and cheaper. Firms using new technology gain advantages and firms not quickly adopting the same new technology put themselves at a disadvantage.
- Social change continues, with views continually altering of what constitutes acceptable behaviour.
- Possibly the most important aspects for businesses relate to employment conditions, product safety and the treatment of the natural environment, and standards for all these are continually being raised.

lo6 describe the nature of rationality in decision making

- Rational behaviour implies decisions are made after an amount of reasoning so that ultimate decisions are not foolish or absurd, and are based on the desire to satisfy objectives.
- Traditionally in the disciplines of finance and economics it is assumed that decision makers behave rationally; that is, that they make their decisions to maximise results or at least optimise outcomes.
- Psychology is strictly the study of the human soul and mind and has much to contribute to the study of decision making. Unlike economists, psychologists perceive rationality in terms of the process employed to make a decision, whether or not it happens to lead to the best results.
- In recent years economists have adopted the psychologists' view of rationality and have incorporated process rationality into their thinking.

Key terms

agency costs, p. 11
corporate governance, p. 10
corporate social responsibility, p. 17
discounting, p. 7
ethics, p. 13
financial derivatives, p. 9
financial governance, p. 10
market capitalisation, p. 7
market value, p. 7
principal–agent problem, p. 11
profit maximisation, p. 6
rational behaviour, p. 21
time value of money, p. 6
wealth maximisation, p. 6
whistleblowing, p. 16

Learning chart

Learning objective	Questions	Financial problems
lo1 describe the range of goals of firms including the significant wealth-maximisation objective	1.1, 1.2, 1.3, 1.4	1.1, 1.2, 1.3, 1.4
lo2 discuss the roles of financial managers	1.5, 1.6, 1.7, 1.8, 1.9	1.5, 1.6, 1.7, 1.8
lo3 grasp the importance of the principal–agent problem	1.10, 1.11, 1.12	1.9, 1.10, 1.11
lo4 discuss the role of ethics	1.13, 1.14, 1.15	1.3, 1.12, 1.13
lo5 discuss some of the challenges facing modern business	1.16, 1.17, 1.18	1.14, 1.15, 1.16, 1.17, 1.18
lo6 describe the nature of rationality in decision making	1.19	1.19

Questions

1.1 Now that you have studied this chapter, what do you consider to be the key issues with regard to the firm's goals raised by the HIH news report reproduced at the start of the chapter?

1.2 The growth of consumer power through consumer protection groups and state offices of fair trading, and the development of product safety laws have all made the cost of product manufacture and selling higher. Are these forces detrimental to profit maximisation?

1.3 Argue the case that the growth of consumer power has strengthened the chance of firms to maximise the wealth of their shareholders.

1.4 Would a manager, confronted with a given set of circumstances, necessarily make the same decision when pursuing either profit- or wealth-maximising objectives? Explain with an example.

1.5 Based on your experience in buying a car or a mobile phone, what is one way a CFO could manage price risk on inputs which form a large part of the firm's operating costs? What difficulties do you foresee in trying to implement this strategy?

1.6 Why do most listed companies outsource the management of their share registers?

1.7 Internal auditors normally report to the chief financial officer.

(a) What do you think are the roles of the internal auditor?

(b) Is there likely to be an adversarial or collegial relationship between the internal auditor and the chief financial officer?

(c) Which type of relationship is likely to be most beneficial to the firm?

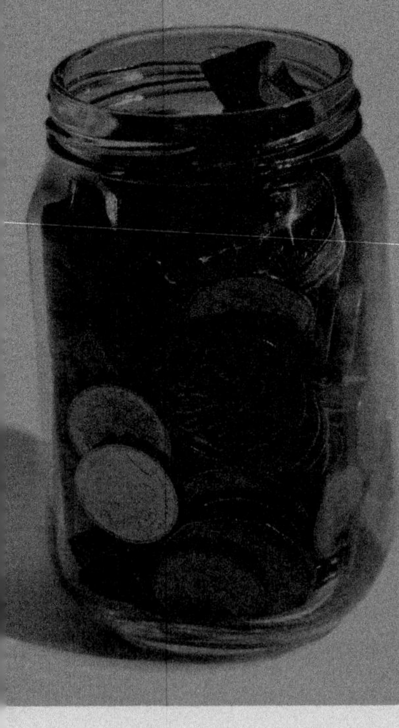

1.8 Why would a firm not want to keep more working capital than necessary in a cheque account?

1.9 Would a listed company want to maximise or minimise dividends? Argue both cases.

1.10 What are some of the reasons that might motivate a corporate chief executive officer (CEO) *not* to try to maximise shareholders' wealth in relation to the firm's activities?

1.11 Explain agency cost and, from the HIH story that opens this chapter, give some sources of agency cost.

1.12 The marketing manager of a listed company wants to maximise sales, the finance manager wants to maximise revenue, the CEO wants to maximise profit. Why might these various officers of the firm have different goals?

1.13 Genuine Used Cars is a second-hand car dealer with a landscaped yard on a busy highway serving Sydney. The plants used to 'decorate' the yard are all high water users. Drought is setting in and the local council has asked businesses to conserve as much water as possible. Town water is still available, bore water may be accessed in fairly shallow bores and the council is encouraging businesses to install underground tanks to conserve rain water. Which source of water should the firm use to gain the most 'brownie points' ethically? Should the firm change the plants for more efficient water users?

1.14 An Australian publishing company has purchased rights to a US textbook and contracted Australian academics to re-work it for the Australian environment. The US publisher supplies pdf files only, so the Australian firm needs to have these files converted into Word so that the authors can work electronically. This sort of conversion work is now routinely sent to several Asian countries where the pay rates are lower than in Australia. Firms in two countries quote for the job — one at half the price of the other. The country with the cheaper quote is well known for its poor labour conditions; employees in both countries enjoy lower standards of living than employees in Australia. What do you believe are the issues for the product-development manager in deciding to award the contract?

1.15 An investment firm supports the coal-mining industry with infrastructure funds and also invests in tree plantations for paper pulp production. Are the environmental 'goods' attached to the plantations cancelled out by the environmental 'bads' of the coal mining?

1.16 In view of the information given in the chapter opening article on page 3, could Ray Williams's largesse have been distributed in a way more acceptable to shareholders?

1.17 Given the circumstances in question 1.14, discuss how the export of Australian jobs may be good for Australians.

1.18 One of the most striking effects of globalisation in recent decades has been the export of both manufacturing and service jobs from the advanced nations to newly developing nations such as China and India. From your experiences as a consumer of goods and services, discuss examples from both manufacturing and service industries where jobs have been exported from Australia.

1.19 How is the concept of rationality different in the disciplines of finance and psychology?

Financial problems

1.1 Read the following excerpt from *Business Review Weekly*[9] and then answer the questions.

> Almost every local biotechnology company aims to follow the same basic plan: license interesting-sounding research or technology from a university or research institute, further develop the drug or treatment and run early-stage clinical trials. Then, if the results are promising, license the product to one of the big pharmaceutical companies with the resources to conduct expensive later-stage trials. If the drug or device makes it to market, royalties follow.
>
> In the case of the Gardasil, the original discoveries were made in the 1980s and 1990s at the University of Queensland by researchers led by Professor Ian Frazer. The drug was licensed to CSL in 1995 and on-licensed a couple of years later to Merck, which conducted the phase two and three trials. CSL and the University of Queensland will receive royalty payments on Gardasil sales: CSL will receive 7% and it is believed the university will receive 1%. After a further licensing deal signed in 2005, both will receive further royalty payments from a similar vaccine now in the final stages of development by a rival pharmaceutical company, GlaxoSmithKline.

(a) In purchasing a licence over an experimental drug in 1995, was CSL trying to maximise profits or shareholder wealth?

(b) For what financial reasons would CSL have sold a right to Merck, a global pharmaceutical company, a couple of years later?

(c) Why would CSL also have sold rights to GlaxoSmithKline?

1.2 Beth Glasgow runs a roadhouse in an isolated part of the Northern Territory. The various motor fuels (ULP, diesel, etc.) sell at a mark-up of 20% (while competition in the cities and coastal towns in Australia keeps mark-ups down to 4–5%). Groceries sell at 50% more than landed cost. Beth has a restricted liquor licence and sells beer at a 100% mark-up.

(a) Is Beth maximising profits or wealth?

(b) How can she stay in business when charging high prices?

(c) If 'normal' roadhouses have average margins of 15% and sell for seven times net profit, Beth reckons her business is worth at least 10 times net profits. Do you agree?

1.3 Toowoomba Computer Works (TCW) has employed a programmer to write business programs for their clients. She writes a program which will be ideal to teach first-year accounting students the rudiments of electronic financial record-keeping. It sells for $200 per copy. TCW decides to give 100 copies free to the local university to be distributed to students in whatever way the course lecturer decides. The firm also gives the university a free site licence.

(a) Would this action tend to work against TCW's avowed objective of wealth maximisation?

(b) Is there an ethical problem here for any of the parties?

1.4 Dan Levy is in partnership with three others in their business, Outdoor Camping World. (Outdoor World had been Dan's business and Camping World had been run by the other three until they merged the businesses last year. They merged the names, too, so they might keep all their old customers, even though it doesn't make much sense.) Dan argues that the firm should maximise gross profit margins [(selling price – buying price)/selling price] on each item of stock.

(a) Do you think this is a valid financial objective?

(b) Is this objective consistent with maximisation of partners' wealth?

(c) What problems do you see in operationalising this objective?

1.5 It has been reported that Ray Williams, CEO of HIH, gave away at least $20 million of HIH shareholders' funds inappropriately as gifts. In what areas of his duties do you think the chief financial officer of HIH was derelict?

1.6 Brian Brickston is an accountant at a medium-sized manufacturing firm. He is nearing retirement and has specialised during his working life in cost accounting — that is, working out in minute detail how much each type of widget costs to manufacture with the firm's current equipment. Sandy Sharp, his supervisor, has arranged to go on long service leave and Brian is to head the accounts department while Sandy is away. The firm is approached to quote on the cost of a completely new line. Brian wants to use his normal costing techniques, but the new young product-development manager insists the present value of money must be considered in analysing the 10-year project. Who is correct? Why?

1.7 The CFO of a firm must decide whether to replace a fully-depreciated six-year-old machine that currently costs twice the price of the machine in place.

(a) What issues would you advise her to consider?

(b) What method would be your recommended analytical technique to back the decision?

1.8 The CFO of a building society wants to take the transport of its spare cash and cash requirements away from its own security force and award a contract to a transport firm. Why would he do this?

1.9 On what bases could you argue the collapse of HIH was an example of the principal–agent problem?

1.10 How could a board of a company ensure that the managers of the firm all have the same objective as the board?

1.11 The incorporation of ethics into business practices has been characterised as 'doing well by doing good'.

(a) Why would firms want to 'do good'?

(b) Give some examples of a firm 'doing good' by employees, the general community and the natural environment.

1.12 Some commentators argue that business has no role in 'doing good'. Do you think this argument is more congruent with the profit or wealth maximisation objective? Why?

1.13 Tinsel Tin Company, an Australian company, mines tin using cheap resource-wasteful techniques in a tropical country. The effects of the mining include pollution of freshwater streams almost from their sources to the sea. The local people used to fish, hunt near, get drinking water from and swim in these streams, but now none of these things are possible. Local people now buy canned meat for protein. It is relatively cheap but tends to be poor quality with a very high fat content. As a result, the local people are now much fatter than they used to be and they suffer poorer health. Tinsel has supplied a fully equipped medical clinic but expects the local people to supply the staff. Discuss each of the questions on the following page.

(a) Has Tinsel contravened, in your view, its ethical responsibilities?

(b) Is it possible to trade off an ethical 'bad' with an ethical 'good'?

(c) Has Tinsel done enough to compensate for the change they have brought about in the local people's lives?

1.14 What are the advantages to business of deregulation?

1.15 What makes new technology acceptable to business?

1.16 What important changes in technology have retailers adopted in the last few decades? Give examples from your experience as a consumer with regard to, say, a 2-litre container of milk.

1.17 How has the social contract between manufacturers and the community changed in the last few years with regard to the safety of products? How do you see this as a consumer?

1.18 How has the social contract between business and the community changed in the last few years with regard to the natural environment? Give examples from both secondary and tertiary (service) industries.

1.19 Recently the price of a mining share listed on the ASX ran from the 20–30 cent range to more than $7 in three days on the news of a large copper discovery. Do you think this rise in price was rational? What information would you need for it to be rational to buy the shares at many dollars per share instead of many shares per dollar?

SOLUTIONS TO FINANCE WORKSHOPS

1.1 Project B in principle will yield the greater benefits. This is because the cash flows start sooner and are greater earlier than those of Project A. To prove this to yourself, assume a discount rate of 10%. By the end of year 2, project B has gained over $6 million in PV terms, while project A has only $0.82 million.

1.2 The aims of the agent are different from those of the principal. None of the gifts could be justified as legitimate. For example, the $10 000 watches for some employees may represent 20–25% of annual salary. These were given for length of service, whether the service was good, bad or indifferent, when normally such a gift may be worth less than $100. The $10 000 gifts could not be seen to be in the shareholders' interests.

1.3 An easy way to make donations to a chosen charity; ANZ matches the donations. Arguments against: firms are in business to maximise the wealth of the shareholders — these donations and extra employee costs may not be in shareholders' best interests; it is not ANZ's business to act as a society police officer.

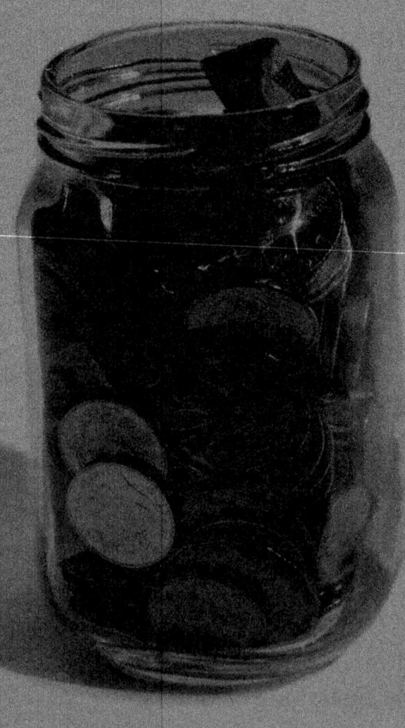

End notes

1 Excerpts from Brearley, David 2002, 'The profligate philanthropist', *The Australian*, 10 August, p. 21.

2 Group of 100, 'The Code of Conduct', www.group100.com.au.

3 Kinder, PD & Domini, AL 1990, 'Social screening: paradigms old and new', in BR Bruce (ed.), *The investment research guide to socially responsible investing*, Colloquium on Socially Responsible Investing, Alamo, Texas.

4 Westpac 2007, ‘Equator principles’, www.westpac.com.au.

5 ANZ 2007, ‘Building financial literacy and inclusion’ (Community), *Contact 06 — Shareholder Update*, p. 11.

6 Excerpts from Ferguson, Adele 2006, ‘Corporates see the light’, *Business Review Weekly*, 29 June – 5 July, pp. 10–11.

7 Schwarz, H 1998, *Rationality gone awry: decision-making inconsistent with economic and financial theory*, Praeger, Westport, Connecticut, p. 13.

8 Information from Zimmerman, A, Lloyd, ME & Lublin, J 2007, ‘Nardelli leaves Home Depot, will get $210M’, Dow Jones News Service, 4 January.

9 Excerpt from Quinlivan, B 2006, ‘From research to revenue’, *Business Review Weekly*, 29 June – 5 July, p. 64.

chapter

2

Business structures and taxation

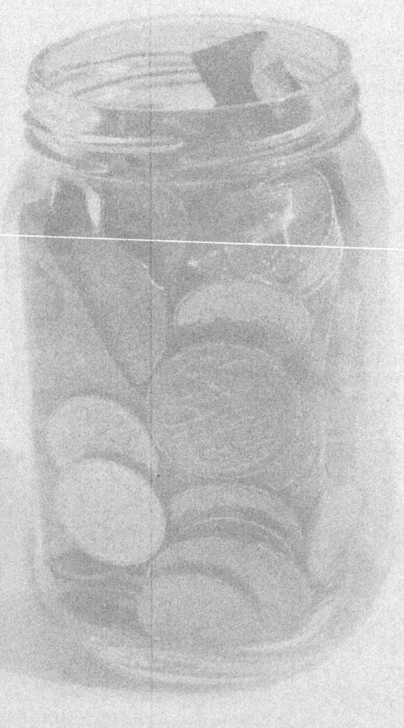

Learning objectives

After studying this chapter, you should be able to:

- **lo1** describe the various forms of business organisation and their implications
- **lo2** discuss the features of Australian income taxation arrangements for business
- **lo3** describe the other important business taxes
- **lo4** describe dividend imputation
- **lo5** discuss how dividend imputation affects the analysis of business investment decisions.

HERITAGE BUILDING SOCIETY

Heritage Building Society has emerged in recent years as one of Australia's largest building societies. It has more than doubled in size over a four-year period. Many societies that were larger than the Heritage was in the past have converted to banks under the Banking Act 1959 *and have either listed on the Australian Securities Exchange or have been taken over by larger entities. Heritage remains a mutual — an entity owned by its members, not by shareholders.*

Heritage is one of Australia's largest and best performing building societies. With total assets under management exceeding $6 billion, the Society is experiencing strong and sustained growth.

Our head office is in the southern Queensland city of Toowoomba. With more than 120 branches, community branches and mini branches, our footprint extends across much of southern Queensland. We also have lending offices in Sydney, Melbourne and Adelaide.

Heritage was formed in 1981 by the merger of Toowoomba Permanent Building Society (est 1875) and the Darling Downs Building Society (est 1897).

Heritage is a true mutual organisation, and not a shareholder-owned institution. This means that our sole focus is on our members. Unlike the shareholder-owned big banks, we do not have the conflict of serving two masters — shareholders and customers. Unlike these profit-maximisers who must deliver ever growing profits to satisfy shareholder demand for dividends, Heritage maximises value for our members. This happens through better interest rates, lower fees and charges, longer operating hours, and friendlier staff.

The Society offers a full suite of banking products and services via a sophisticated range of channels to best meet the needs of our members. Whether this is free personal telephone and internet banking, or face-to-face banking at a local branch or mini branch, Heritage gives our members the freedom to choose how they transact.

Again, unlike the profit maximisers, Heritage is opening more outlets all the time. Being a regionally-based financial institution, we are particularly sensitive to the needs of people in regional and rural areas.

Heritage is also proud to offer community banking. This is a true win–win arrangement between the Society and communities, often reeling from the effect of bank branch closures. Under our more affordable model, each party contributes to the costs and shares in the operational income of the community branch. The original financial contribution made by the community is returned with interest, once the venture is profitable. The community then benefits by the regular distribution of profits via a community grant scheme.[1]

Chapter preview

This chapter describes the various forms of business organisation. As you will see, there is a range of institutional forms and each form has its own most appropriate uses. The forms range from sole proprietor — where only one person owns the firm, through partnerships — where two or many people are involved as owners, companies — with hundreds or thousands of people owning smaller or larger pieces, and finally trusts. Each of these forms of organisation differs in the ease of its formation or termination, its decision making processes, oversight by authorities, liabilities of owners for debts and other obligations, taxation arrangements and other aspects.

The following diagram shows how this chapter is structured.

BUSINESS STRUCTURES AND TAXATION		
	Forms of business organisation	▪ Sole proprietorship ▪ Partnership ▪ Company ▪ Trust ▪ The most appropriate business structure
	Features of Australian taxation arrangements	▪ Capital gains tax (CGT) ▪ Goods and services tax (GST)
	Dividend imputation	▪ Imputation from the company's viewpoint ▪ Imputation from the shareholder's viewpoint ▪ Effects of dividend imputation on business investment decisions

lo1

Describe the various forms of business organisation and their implications.

Forms of business organisation

The main types of business organisation or legal entities are:

- sole trader or sole proprietor
- partnership
- company
- trust.

Of these, by far the most common structure used by Australian businesses is, perhaps surprisingly, the sole proprietorship. Currently more than one million individuals own businesses structured as sole proprietorships, among a total of more than three million registered businesses. This number constitutes nearly 40% of declared businesses. Company structures are the next most numerous with about 26% being proprietary limited businesses, 0.5% being limited (public) companies and a further 2% being other registered companies. Roughly another 15% of businesses are structured as partnerships and the rest are trusts.[2] The vast majority of companies run small businesses, with large businesses, including most of the listed public companies, accounting for just 0.2% of companies.

Australian business number (ABN): a discrete number that identifies each business registered with the ATO so that the regulation of taxation is facilitated

Regardless of the business structure adopted, Australian businesses are required, almost without exception, to have an **Australian business number (ABN)**. The ABN system was introduced in 2000 to try to increase compliance with taxation laws. It was widely believed at the time that there were about one million businesses in Australia and that perhaps another one million small businesses would be identified in the economy once businesses were forced to quote their ABNs when invoicing payments or suffer the compulsory withholding by payers of 48.5% (the highest marginal tax rate at the time) withholding tax from each payment.

Sole proprietorship: a business owned by an individual, who owns assets used in the business, incurs liabilities and reaps the annual profits or losses

Sole proprietorship

A **sole proprietorship** is a business owned by an individual, who owns assets used in the business, incurs liabilities and reaps the annual gains or losses. The owner is liable for debts and other potential liabilities and must fund any losses. Owners do not pay themselves wages; instead, they make periodic drawings against potential profits. The whole of the calculated profits are taxed as income in the hands of the proprietor, regardless of whether the cash is paid out. (In many cases, proprietors continue to invest profits in their businesses as either higher inventories or increases in fixed assets.)

A sole proprietorship is the easiest business structure to set up. Typically people with urges to start businesses just put together the assets necessary and open their doors for business under their own names. If they want to use trading names, such as *Seafresh Seafoods* or *Nifty Gadgets*, instead of their own names they must register the name with state authorities under the relevant state Business Names Act.

Sole proprietors have freedom to run their businesses any way they wish, so long as their activities remain within the law. In terms of legal liability for debts and costs of their actions (for example, legally proved negligence) they carry unlimited liability. Sole proprietors may expand their businesses by arranging debt finance but, by definition, they cannot raise funds by selling equity. Although legally they can do so, they would no longer be sole proprietors if they did.

Sole proprietors may sell or transfer ownership of their businesses by transferring the trading names and the assets. Normally, any debts are settled at the time of transfer, so that the new proprietors may bring in their own new liabilities and the debts of the old owners do not continue. However, liabilities such as the accrued long-service leave of employees, if properly accounted for in the books, would probably carry over to the new owner rather than being paid out to the employees at the time of transfer. At the death of a sole proprietor, the sole proprietor structure in itself is dissolved, even though the business as such may be sold as a going concern and may indeed keep its old trading name.

The advantages of the sole proprietorship structure are:

- speed and ease of establishment
- lack of formalities (for example, reports to stakeholders)
- freedom in decision making enjoyed by the owner.

Disadvantages include:

- the potential limited life of the firm — if the owner dies, the firm may also die
- financing is limited by definition to debt finance
- unlimited liability for debts
- no formal sharing of management responsibilities (but expertise may still be purchased by means of skilled employees, consultants or advisers).

Sole proprietor structures are common among small businesses just starting up; for example, tradespeople serving the public (although many of these soon evolve into partnerships with spouses), small retail establishments and farms.

Partnership

Partnership: an association of two or more people carrying on a business in common with a view to profit

A **partnership** is an association of two or more people carrying on a business in common with a view to profit. This is the gist of the definitions included in the various state partnership Acts. Commonwealth taxation law takes a wider view and includes those associations where people earn income jointly, such as from property held as tenants in common. Partners may agree on their relationship and duties with either an informal oral or a formal written agreement. An agreement written specifically to cover exactly each situation is the most prudent way to operate a partnership.

Partnership agreements, at a minimum, should include full details of:

- contributions of capital by partners
- contributions of labour by partners
- how profits or losses are to be shared
- duration of the partnership
- procedures for admitting a new partner or withdrawal (including death) of a partner
- powers of partners to write cheques, raise funds and operate the bank accounts.

Taxation law takes the view that the existence of a partnership is a matter of fact that may be deduced from the evidence available. Such evidence includes:

- the existence of a formal partnership agreement
- contributions of capital and labour by the partners
- any forms of evidence signifying the partners' intentions to collaborate
- jointly entered relevant contracts
- jointly held and operated bank accounts
- notifications to stakeholders that a partnership exists.

The courts have held that no one of these factors will be conclusive evidence of a partnership's existence. However, a combination of the factors will be considered strong evidence. In addition, the Australian Taxation Office (ATO) has issued a ruling defining the factors that it will consider when determining if a partnership exists.

Like the sole proprietorship, partnerships are easy to set up with a minimum of formalities. Many partnerships use their own names as their trading names; for example, *AS and JB Cato*, but can use a registered trading name such as *Cato Plumbing*. In terms of legal liability for debts and costs of their actions, the partners carry unlimited liability. Partnerships may expand their businesses by arranging debt finance. In addition, they can raise extra funds by selling equity through admission of more partners who would bring in additional cash or other assets.

Partnerships may sell or transfer ownership of their businesses by transferring the trading names and the assets. More commonly, with the consent of all partners, one or more partners withdraw or new partners are admitted with the financial consideration being calculated in accordance with the partnership agreement. In these cases the assets of the partnership, including intangibles such as goodwill, which may not have appeared up to that time in the books, are valued and liabilities are subtracted to estimate the value of each partner's share.

A partnership cannot legally employ any of the partners. However, typically partners have to have funds on which to live during the year until annual profits are calculated at the end of the accounting period. Thus, it is common for a partner to be paid a 'salary'. This salary is merely an early distribution of the partner's agreed share of the profits. Some partners may be paid salaries and some not, depending on their relative contributions of effort and capital, and as defined in the partnership agreement.

The payment of interest to a partner for funds lent to the partnership creates an interesting partnership issue. Any interest paid to partners, generally on their capital contributions, is not allowable as a tax deduction. It is considered merely another way of distributing partnership profits. However, the situation is different if a partner lends the partnership funds on a commercial basis in order to increase the partnership's capacity to earn assessable income. The partner in question makes the loan as an individual not as a partner. Hence, the interest is deductible by the partners but is assessable income for the maker of the loan. (Naturally, interest on loans received from non-related parties is generally deductible if used to earn assessable income.)

All profits are considered to be distributed. If cash is not actually paid out for the full distribution, the unpaid balance is added to the partners' capital accounts and thus constitutes an increase in each partner's capital contribution. Profits from partnerships are taxed in full in the hands of the individual partners. Partnerships submit a tax return that shows the taxable income of the partnership and how that income was distributed among the partners. The partners then show those amounts on their individual returns.

Joint venture: an association of individuals or corporations who agree under a contract to pursue a common goal or engage in a common undertaking with the aim of making a profit by combining their resources without forming a legal partnership

Another form of business association which is similar to a partnership but is not a true partnership is a **joint venture**. Joint venture agreements are used for mining and property syndicates, sharefarming agreements, publishing and entertainment arrangements and some research and development agreements for new industrial products and infrastructure. Often among joint venturers one group has the ideas, skills or intellectual property and the other group has the capital. Distinctions between joint ventures and partnerships stem from the inability of joint venturers to bind their co-venturers in various contractual areas and from the ways interests in the ventures may be divested.

Company

Company: an association of entities with a common objective formed under the *Corporations Act 2001* that is legally separate from its owners

A **company** is an association of entities (individuals or corporations) with a common objective. It constitutes a separate legal entity from its owners. As such, the company structure has been a significant force in the development of business in the past 300 years. Because the company is separate from its owners, legal liability of the owners is limited, and that limit is normally the amount of each owner's investment in the company. The limitation of legal liability has made the company structure popular where the underlying business carries high risk.

Companies in effect make a trade-off with the society in which they operate. In return for the limitation of legal liability, they are subjected to greater regulation and compliance costs than either partnerships or sole proprietors. Mostly companies in Australia are formed under the system of regulation provided for in the *Corporations Act 2001*. Prospective companies apply to the Australian Securities and Investments Commission (ASIC), the companies' regulator. If all legal requirements have been complied with, ASIC issues a certificate of incorporation; the company assumes a legal identity of its own from the moment of issue.

Companies raise funds by issuing shares or by contracting for debt finance. Debt may be secured by a charge over assets or over uncalled capital. The relevant part of the Corporations Act, section 124, provides that:

> A company has the legal capacity and powers of an individual both in and outside this jurisdiction. A company also has all the powers of a body corporate, including the power to:
> (a) issue and cancel shares in the company;
> (b) issue debentures;
> (c) grant options over unissued shares in the company;
> (d) distribute any of the company's property among the members, in kind or otherwise;
> (e) give security by charging uncalled capital;
> (f) grant a floating charge over the company's property.

The owners of companies are the shareholders who meet at least annually. At the annual general meeting (AGM), shareholders vote on significant decisions for the company and/or suggested changes in its constitution, as well as elect the board of directors. The board is responsible for the policy direction and day-to-day running of the company, and normally the day-to-day management is undertaken by a group of employed management executives.

While this situation theoretically should work well, globally there have been many instances recently where the system has broken down to a spectacular degree. 'Corporate governance has broken down!' shout the tabloid headlines. **Corporate governance** as a term sounds complicated, but it is not. It merely means the management of corporations so that decisions and actions are made and taken in accord with acknowledged corporate objectives. In Australia, there have been the recent collapses of One.Tel, Pasminco, HIH Insurance, Sons of Gwalia (gold miners) and ION Ltd (a major supplier of parts and components to the motor vehicle industry), while the United States has suffered the demise of WorldCom and Enron. Another failure of a global company was that of the Italian dairy company Parmalat. Fortunately, the Australian Parmalat subsidiaries were not dragged into the failure. In all cases, evidence has come to light of directors failing in their oversight duties (through personal incompetence and having too many directorships), auditors not being sufficiently removed from the firms and managers being allowed to get away with extravagant behaviour. Legislators and regulators have vowed to put stronger controls in place.

Corporate governance: the management of the firm so that the actions of managers are in accord with the stated objectives

Moreover, as we see in chapter 1 with the discussion of the principal–agent problem, the company structure runs the risk of a division developing between the objectives of the owners and the motives of the managers. Nowhere is this more apparent than in the matter of executive salary packages, an issue has deepened the divide between shareholders and executives. The 'behavioural perspectives' feature at the end of chapter 1 also illustrates that linking executive benefits to the share price through options and other share deals, while theoretically aligning the executives' objectives to those of shareholders, does not always result in the desired outcomes.

Ownership is easily transferred through the sale of shares. Companies are formed in either of two categories — private or public. Private companies are designated 'Pty Ltd' or 'Proprietary Limited'. Public companies merely carry the designation 'Ltd'. Many public companies are listed on the securities exchange, the ASX, although not all public companies are so listed. Listing brings its own regulation and compliance issues, together with benefits. One benefit for shareholders of a listed firm is that they always know the value of their shares because the market provides up-to-date share prices. Thus, the owners of shares in a listed company may check the current share price, sell if it is acceptable and have the funds in hand in three days. Owners of shares in unlisted public companies or of private companies have to find a potential buyer first, negotiate a price, sell if that is acceptable and wait until payment is made.

Because of the separate entity structure, companies continue to operate if one part-owner dies or indeed if all shareholders die at the same time. The shares would be transferred eventually to beneficiaries and the company would continue, essentially without noticing the change in ownership, at least in the short term.

In the event of company failure, a process laid down in the *Corporations Act 2001* is followed. Either the company passes a resolution or a court orders 'winding up'. A liquidator is appointed and management of the firm's assets and liabilities passes to that person. The liquidator ascertains the financial position of the firm as accurately as possible. That is, the assets are realised to raise cash and all debts and obligations are identified. The Corporations Act stipulates the order in which obligations are to be paid in the event that the cash raised does not cover all the debts (which is normally the case). Traditionally, shareholders are last in line to receive a payout and frequently their payment is zero. In other words, all of the firm's formal capital will have been dissipated by its operations or by losses sustained in the winding-up process.

This well-established winding-up process is under legal review in Australia in 2007. On 15 September 2005, Justice Emmett in the Federal Court of Australia handed down a decision favouring the plaintiff in the case of *Sons of Gwalia (Administrator Appointed) vs Margaretic* [2005] FCA 1305. Margaretic maintained that he had been misled by the company about its future prospects when he bought the shares and thus he should be ranked with other creditors, instead of after them, in the determination of final payments. In early February 2007, the High Court of Australia upheld this decision. The following 'corporate financial governance' feature offers one newspaper's comment on this decision.

CORPORATE FINANCIAL GOVERNANCE

Gwalia redefines shareholder rights

ALAN KOHLER

Now that High Court has ruled that misled shareholders rank with creditors in a wind-up, surely the next step is for fraud on the market theory to be applied in Australia.

That would complete the revolution in shareholder rights that began with this week's Sons of Gwalia judgement in favour of the plaintiff, Luka Margaretic.

...

Luka Margaretic bought 20 000 shares in Sons of Gwalia 11 days before it went broke and in doing so he claims to have relied on misleading information to the effect that the company was a going concern, when it wasn't.

...

This week's Sons of Gwalia judgement elevates [shareholder] claimants to the status of creditors.

In my experience, virtually every company collapse is accompanied by some jiggery-pokery, or at least a failure by directors to tell the market the company is in trouble.

This is one of the most difficult decisions a director ever has to make in his or her life: at what point do you raise the flag, knowing that to do so would effectively represent voluntary corporate euthanasia? The Sons of Gwalia decision makes this even sharper.

The decision might also render insolvencies impossibly unwieldy, as receivers and liquidators have to deal with the claims of the shareholders as well as the creditors, and have to wait until the courts determine whether the shareholders were misled before making any payments — at least that's what a lot of practitioners and lawyers are now saying.

As a result, there is now a clamour for the law to be amended urgently to keep shareholders in their place; that is behind employees and creditors in the queue for money in the event of insolvency.

Interestingly, Justice Michael Kirby seemed to invite that in his judgement with the (six to one) majority, and actually spelt out how the law could be amended. He wrote: One way would have been simply to delete from section 563A of the Act the words 'a debt owed by a company to a person in the person's capacity as a member of the company, whether by way of dividends, profits or otherwise' and substitute 'a debt owed by a company to a person who is a member of the company.'

But then he goes on: 'It should not be assumed that the inclusion of shareholder claims, such as those of the respondent, with the debts of general creditors is contrary to the will of the Parliament or the result of a slip or oversight requiring a measure of judicial inventiveness and surgery. By sticking to a variation of a time-honoured statutory phrase, it can be assumed that the Act was intended to effect only a limited subordination of claims brought by people who happen to be shareholders.'

Anyway, the Government will now be asked to do what Kirby suggests, which could be an uncomfortable decision, especially this year. Does John Howard really want to reduce consumer protections during an election year? And in any case, will it be supported by the Senate? That is far from clear.[3]

Companies are taxed as separate entities at company-tax rate. (Remember the opening article in this chapter where Heritage Building Society proudly claimed it is a mutual, working for the benefit of its members and not for shareholders. Note that mutuals are taxed as if they were companies.) Each company submits an income tax return and pays the assessed amount of tax. In Australia today, the dividend imputation system allows tax credits to shareholders for the dividends received, so that the tax which has already been paid by the company on taxable income is recognised. Dividend imputation is discussed in more detail later in this chapter.

Trust

Trust: a legal structure where property is nominally owned by one party, the trustee, on behalf of others, who are the beneficiaries

The **trust** is a creation of common law which has developed from medieval times. The popularity of trusts as business structures waxes and wanes depending on current taxation legislation. During the 1980s and 1990s, for example, the number of trusts used as business vehicles in Australia increased dramatically because they provided taxation advantages, especially for family businesses. Trusts are not separate legal entities.

Trusts comprise five essential elements:

- the trustee, who is the legal owner of the trust property
- the trust property
- the beneficiary or beneficiaries, who have rights to receive financial benefits
- the personal obligation on the part of the trustee to deal with the property
- the trust deed, which contains the arrangements for the management of the trust.

Among the types of trusts available, the most commonly used business structure is the discretionary trust. Other trust structures, such as unit trusts, superannuation trusts, family trusts and charitable trusts — all of which are classed as 'express' trusts — are available and may be used to advantage depending on the situation and type of business. Discretionary trusts give the trustee unlimited discretion to allocate both capital and income among the beneficiaries, and even to select beneficiaries from among a designated group.

Trustees may be natural persons or bodies corporate (that is, companies). Hence, many trustees are proprietary limited companies to limit legal liability and to provide for long-term continuity and succession. Trusts submit income tax returns, but may or may not pay tax directly on taxable income. Trustees provide the details of distributions of income on the tax return and the individual beneficiaries pay the assessed taxation on their total taxable incomes. Some income is taxed with the trusts.

Marginal tax rate: the tax rate applied to the next dollar of taxable income

The chief advantage of the trust structure is the ability of the trustee to direct income where it will be least tax-disadvantaged. In other words, income may be directed to beneficiaries who otherwise have low incomes and enjoy low **marginal rates of tax**, rather than to beneficiaries with high marginal rates of tax. For example, the annual income of $100 000 from running a hardware store set up as a trust, if directed to one beneficiary who had other income of more than $60 000 and thus was levied tax at the top marginal rate, might attract income tax of $46 500 but, if directed to and split evenly among five family-member beneficiaries who otherwise had low incomes, might attract only the lower marginal rates, and thus result in an aggregate tax payment that is much lower.

The most appropriate business structure

Students and people new to business often ask which is the best (most beneficial) business structure. The best depends on individual circumstances and individual motivations. Table 2.1 provides a guide to the most appropriate structures for achieving given objectives.

Table 2.1 Appropriate business structures for given objectives

Objective	Best structures
Ease of establishment	Sole proprietorship; partnership
Low cost of establishment	Sole proprietorship; partnership
Limited legal liability	Company
Ease of management and control	Sole proprietorship; partnership
Low regulatory oversight, compliance costs	Sole proprietorship; partnership
Ease of raising capital	Company
Managing income taxation	Company; trust
Ability to manage capital gains tax (CGT)*	Sole proprietorship; partnership; trust
Likelihood of business continuity	Company
Ease of transfer of ownership	Listed company

* Companies pay the same rate of tax on capital gains as on ordinary income.

FINANCE WORKSHOP 2.1

1. Close this textbook and then see if you can list from your understanding of each business structure five objectives best achieved by:
   (a) a sole proprietorship or partnership
   (b) a company structure.
2. Greg Gringovitch is a fitter and turner by trade. He saw a gap in the medical appliances market when his son developed a muscular degeneration problem. Greg developed a gadget called 'The Thing' which helped his son stay mobile. After Greg and his wife joined a support group that helped families cope with this disease, Greg made a number of 'Things'. As it became apparent that 'The Thing' could help many people, it was suggested to Greg that he develop both Australian and export markets. Suggest a business structure that you believe would serve Greg well for the first stage of the development of his business. Would this recommendation change if Greg's turnover increased to $1 million per annum?

lo2

Discuss the features of Australian income taxation arrangements for business.

Features of Australian income taxation arrangements

Taxation impacts to a greater or lesser extent on many decisions taken in business. As you read through the later chapters of this book, you will find taxation arrangements affect to a greater or lesser extent many issues of concern to financial managers — not least the planning of investments, sourcing finance and capital structures. The most important taxes from the points of view of financial managers are income tax, capital gains tax (CGT) and the goods and services tax (GST). This section deals with income tax.

Taxable income: assessable income less legitimate deductions

Assessable income: includes most forms of income earned by resident taxpayers, both in Australia and overseas

Income tax is levied in Australia on individuals' and companies' **taxable income**. Taxable income is assessable income less allowable deductions. **Assessable income** includes most forms of income earned by resident taxpayers, both in Australia and overseas. Because there is a long history of people trying to avoid paying tax, the taxation legislation, regulations, cases, rulings and determinations form a complex and comprehensive web that serves to catch almost all forms of monetary benefits. The most notable exemptions for individuals are some war service pensions, legacies, scholarships, gifts, lottery prizes and gambling wins (unless the gambler is running a gambling business). For businesses and companies, almost all monies received are assessable. The only exceptions are receipts that are not revenue, such as loans and capital injections.

Distinguishing between income and capital can sometimes be difficult. Income is often periodically or frequently received, whereas capital may be received infrequently. However, this is not a fail-safe test. There is a large body of case law which builds the pattern of what is assessable income and what constitutes capital. (Some parts of capital receipts may still be taxable under the capital gains tax legislation.) Some of the classes of transactions that the courts have identified as income include:

- compensation received for cancellation of trade contracts
- compensation, such as insurance recovery, for the loss of trading stock
- compensation for the loss of profits.

Allowable deductions: generally, for the computation of income tax liability, expenses incurred to earn assessable income

Assessable income may be reduced by **allowable deductions**. For individuals, allowable deductions are few. For businesses, allowable deductions include many classes of expenses and the general rule is that expenditure incurred to earn assessable income is an allowable deduction.

Income tax is collected under the authority of two Income Tax Assessment Acts, 1936 and 1997. The later Act introduced some new material, clarified some of the old and left some of the old so that the 1936 Act still applies in part. Allowable deductions were covered in the 1936 Act under section 51(1) and this is considered to be the most litigated section of the Act as taxpayers battled to reduce their tax liability and the Commissioner fought to increase the public revenue. The comparable section under the new Act is s. 8-1.

Section 8-1 can be divided into two parts, the so-called positive and negative limbs. There are two positive and four negative limbs. Taxpayers should test first against the positive to see if a deduction is possible, then test against the negative to ensure that the deduction is not denied. Section 8-1(1) provides:

> You can deduct from your assessable income any loss or outgoing to the extent that:
> (a) it is incurred in gaining or producing your assessable income; or
> (b) it is necessarily incurred in carrying on a business for the purposes of gaining or producing your assessable income.

Section 8-1(2) provides:

> However, you cannot deduct a loss or outgoing under this section to the extent that:
> (a) it is loss or outgoing of capital, or of a capital nature; or
> (b) it is loss or outgoing of a private or domestic nature; or
> (c) it is incurred in relation to gaining or producing your exempt income; or
> (d) a provision of this Act prevents you from deducting it.

Even though the term 'necessarily' in s. 8-1(1)(b) appears to be strict in meaning, the courts have interpreted this section liberally to mean that the outgoing must have an appropriate relationship to carrying on a business. The negative limbs are comparatively straightforward. An example of a specific denial of deductibility in another part of the Act is superannuation contributions for employees who are supported by their employers with superannuation contributions.

Examples of business deductions are advertising, borrowing expenses, cost of sales, depreciation, electricity, freight, insurance, legal and motor vehicle expenses, rent, repairs and salaries. Some classes of expenses have been the subject of more legal battles than others, and these difficult areas may include interest expenses, repairs, bad debts, legal expenses, gifts and car expenses.

Taxation rates for individuals (including their partnership and trust income) are progressive, meaning that higher income brackets attract increased rates of tax. The taxation rates for resident individuals are given in table 2.2. The taxation on exactly $75 000 of taxable income is $17 100, made up of the marginal rates of each of the lower steps in the tax scale. No tax is paid on the first $6000, 15% is paid of the next $24 000, 30% is paid of the next $45 000 and so on. Thus, the average rate of tax on $75 000 is 22.8%, but the marginal rate for any income in excess of that figure is 40%. In addition, most individuals pay a 1.5% Medicare levy, the exceptions being some low-income earners and people who are otherwise supported for their medical needs, such as some Veterans' Affairs pensioners.

Table 2.2: Taxation rates for Australian resident individuals, 2007–08 (announced in the 2007–08 Budget)

Taxable income ($)	Tax on income up to the threshold ($)*	Marginal rate of tax (%)
0–6 000	nil	nil
6 001–30 000	nil	15
30 001–75 000	3 600	30
75 001–150 000	17 100	40
>150 000	47 100	45

* The tax on the threshold of each income range is the sum of the tax on each of the lower ranges. For example, the tax on $30 000 is the sum of 0 plus $24 000 × 0.15, which equals $3600.

Marginal rates of tax are important because we often analyse alternative income-producing activities in terms of how they affect marginal income. For example, an investor with a salary of $75 000 may invest in a property to gain a $5000 net return each year or invest in shares to gain a $10 000 gross return. Any analysis of the after-tax effects uses the marginal rate of tax, because of the assumption that the base income of $75 000 will continue no matter what decision is made about this investment. This technique allows us to do the analysis more efficiently because we don't have to calculate the full taxable income and taxation liability for each scenario. We just consider the incremental income of the $5000 net return and the $10 000 gross return less the allowable deductions for expenses.

The taxation rate for companies is currently a flat 30%. Companies generally pay their tax in quarterly instalments, 21 days after the end of each quarter. The ATO advises each quarterly payer of its instalment rate, which is the tax rate that is applied to the taxable income earned each quarter.

The most important of the other business taxes are capital gains tax and the goods and services tax.

lo3

Describe the other important business taxes.

Capital gains tax (CGT)

Capital gains tax (CGT) is paid on gains made on the disposal of certain assets purchased after 19 September 1985. No CGT is payable until a CGT event occurs. The *Income Tax Assessment Act 1997* exhaustively lists events that have CGT consequences and labels them from A1 to L7, thus grouping transactions into classes of CGT events. The most common such event is the sale of a non-depreciable asset. For example, the sale of land is CGT event A1. Other CGT events are loss or destruction of an applicable asset (label C1), transfer to a trust, grant of a lease and owners' cessation of Australian residency. However, a most important exemption from the tax is any gain made on the sale of an individual taxpayer's main residence.

The CGT system has been simplified since September 1999 so that individuals pay CGT at their marginal rates on half of any gains made. Thus, for an investor on the top marginal rate, the CGT rate is 23.25% including the 1.5% Medicare levy. Companies are not granted this 50% discount on realised capital gains.

Capital losses cannot be claimed against ordinary income to reduce income tax, but must be written off against current capital gains or quarantined and carried forward until sufficient capital gains are made so that they may be written off. In a future year when capital gains are made, the carried-forward capital loss is first deducted from the total gain, then the net gain, if any, is subjected to the 50% discount rule before the tax rate is applied. Gains and losses on non-depreciable assets owned for less than 12 months are included in taxable income and are not subject to CGT rules.

Goods and services tax (GST)

While the GST regime has imposed a good deal of paperwork on business and has prompted many business managers to improve their record-keeping and accounting systems, it is not a tax on business. Businesses collect the tax on most sales and pay the tax on most purchases. The tax collected from consumers is remitted to the ATO and the tax paid on purchases is refunded by the ATO. In practice, only the net tax is paid to the ATO and any excess tax that businesses have paid above their collections in any period is reimbursed by the ATO.

Some supplies (sales) made by business are GST-free. These include food, health supplies, education, child care, religious services, water and sewage, precious metals and farmland. However, as with most things associated with taxation, nothing is simple. Not all foods are tax-free. Live animals (such as beef cattle consigned to an abattoir are not food — yet!), unprocessed grains, hot takeaway food and restaurant meals are all subject to GST. The current rate of GST is 10% levied on the selling price, so that the asking price becomes the final price including GST. In other words, by law marked prices must include the GST amount.

Businesses conducting an enterprise have to register for GST administration if their annual turnover exceeds $75 000 (from 1 July 2007). Additionally, smaller businesses may register voluntarily. Once registered, entities are liable to account for GST collected on their sales and taxable supplies and they may claim the tax paid on their purchased inputs, so long as they keep the tax invoices setting out the amounts of tax paid on each purchase.

FINANCE WORKSHOP 2.2

1. Explain to a friend the differences in the nature of income and capital. What are some of the areas where the courts have identified complicated cash flows as income?
2. Su Chee Zong runs a 'retail trading warehouse'. His 2007–08 receipts include cash sales; credit-card sales; insurance recoveries for stock lost in a fire; funds from the sale of a one-fifth share in the business to his cousin; compensation for the loss of an exclusive agency for a kitchen mixer; compensation for the sale of a strip of land along the fence line with his neighbouring business; and compensation from the manufacturer of rubber goods for the loss and disposal of some hose stock which perished. Which of these categories do you think are not ordinary assessable income?

lo4

Describe dividend imputation.

Dividend imputation: the system where dividends carry an additional benefit in the form of an attached tax credit for the relevant amount of tax paid by the company on its profits

Franked dividend: a dividend carrying an attached franking or tax credit

Fully franked dividend: a dividend that carries a tax credit equal to the full 30% company tax paid on the underlying profit

Partly franked dividend: a dividend that carries a tax credit less than the full 30% company tax paid on the underlying profit

Unfranked dividend: a dividend that carries no tax credit

Dividend imputation

Dividend imputation was introduced into the Australian financial scene in 1987. This change in the tax system was made to encourage and expand investment in equities and to quell complaints of double taxation of dividends. Dividends had been taxed once through the tax on company profits and again as personal income in the hands of shareholders. Dividend imputation is the system where **franked dividends** carry additional benefits in the form of attached tax credits for the relevant amount of tax paid by the company on its profits.

Where a company pays full tax on profits, it may distribute **fully franked dividends** that carry with them an amount of franking credits or tax credited against the shareholder's account at the ATO. A fully franked dividend carries a tax credit equal to the full 30% company tax paid on the underlying profit. A **partly franked dividend** carries a tax credit less than the full 30% company tax paid on the underlying profit. An **unfranked dividend** carries no tax credit. Partly franked and unfranked dividends are paid by companies that have not paid sufficient Australian tax in the past to have enough franking credits in their accounts to pay fully franked dividends. For example, NAB is a profitable bank that normally pays a great deal of tax and usually pays fully franked dividends. In 2002 it could only attach 90% franking to its 75-cent final dividend because it had insufficient franking credits available to pay a fully franked dividend after sustaining losses on its overseas operations the previous year. In 2005–06, it could only distribute 80% franked dividends.

You may wonder how a company may not pay 30% taxation on the full amount of its current year's income. One explanation is the case where a company has past-year losses that it writes off against current income. Thus, for example, a biotechnology company makes $100 million in profits this year, but has $60 million in past losses that it writes off against the profits. Its taxable income is then $40 million and it may pay $12 million in tax. However, it may decide for various reasons to distribute $50 million in dividends. In this case, if it has no previous excess franking credits to distribute, the dividend to its shareholders cannot be fully franked. That is, there is only $12 million in the franking account and a fully franked dividend would require about $21.4 million.

Imputation from the company's viewpoint

The dividend imputation system works like this. A company calculates its net profit and estimates its tax liability. It debits Income Tax Expense and credits a Provision for Income

Tax account. When it pays its tax, it debits the Provision account and credits its Bank account for the assessed amount of tax as advised by the ATO. In addition to these accounts, the company keeps track of the net balance of tax paid in a separate record outside the double-entry accounting system.

Keeping track of tax paid rather than the net income on which tax had been paid was a reform to the tax system which came into effect from 1 July 2002. Amounts of tax paid by resident franking entities (that is, companies), imputation credits received from subsidiaries or other investments and franking deficit taxes incurred all increase the balance in a new franking account. On the other hand, the amounts of franking credits distributed with franked dividends and refunds of income tax reduce the balance. Example 2.1 shows how a company tracks its franking credits.

EXAMPLE 2.1

Dividend imputation — keeping track of franking credits

From 1 July 2002, companies must record in their franking accounts the amount of Australian income tax paid less the franking credits issued with dividends.

Balance *1 July 2007*	$108 500 800
plus Tax paid 2007–08*	150 000 000
plus Credits from investments†	5 000 000
less Franking credits issued with $360m dividends**	154 285 714
Balance *1 July 2008*	$109 215 086

* 30% rate on $500m profit

† Franking credits received

** $360m \times \frac{0.3}{0.7}$

Imputation from the shareholder's viewpoint

Shareholders appreciate the dividend imputation system as it enhances the benefits gained by investing in equities. For example, with the 30% company tax rate, a $700 fully franked dividend is worth $1000 as it will carry a $300 franking credit. The full $1000 must be declared as assessable income, but the $300 is already lodged with the ATO and serves to reduce the actual cash tax payable. People on the highest marginal rate of tax will effectively only have to pay the difference between the two rates, 16.5% (46.5% – 30%) on the dividend, or $165 on the $1000 benefit. People on the lower marginal rates of tax, 0% (up to $6000 taxable income) and 15% ($6001 to $25 000 taxable income), receive a refund of any excess franking credits.

Investors use the dividend yield (dividend paid divided by the price of the share) of shares to compare the returns to be gained from a particular share with the returns from other investments such as fixed interest products or property investments. At a time when fixed interest products may be returning, say, 4%, the dividend yield of an investment in one of the major banks may be 4.2%. There appears to be little margin between them. However, the bank dividend will be fully franked and will actually be returning 6.0% before tax. This additional yield makes the bank investment comparatively more attractive. Of course, investors must also consider the element of risk attached to each investment.

lo5

Discuss how dividend imputation affects the analysis of business investment decisions.

Effects of dividend imputation on business investment decisions

Dividend imputation credits are available to most resident taxpayers (the few exceptions will be discussed later). Where a company believes the majority of its shareholders can take advantage of the system, it should undertake investments and manage the firm's operations to maximise its before-tax cash flows. Maximising the company's before-tax cash flows will maximise shareholders' wealth. Shareholders measure their wealth by using their after-tax cash flow and this measure for each shareholder when aggregated will not necessarily be the same as company after-tax cash flow. *Tax paid by the company on its earnings is irrelevant.*

Effectively, where a company believes itself to be in this situation, the company is no longer paying tax in its own right. It pays tax on behalf of its shareholders who are treated as if they were sole traders or partners in their own businesses. The final reckoning for each year's tax payments comes only with the submission of each individual shareholder's tax return and the tax assessment that is issued soon afterwards. Thus, shareholders should not be concerned about, and should not support managers who are concerned about, minimising their company's income taxation. Shareholders' after-tax cash flow is dependent purely on:

- their share of the company's pre-tax cash flow, which is paid as dividends
- their own individual marginal rate of tax.

There are some exceptions to these conclusions. In any case where shareholders cannot claim the full benefits of the tax credits, *the full integration of the two tax regimes cannot be realised and the tax paid by the firm on its income becomes relevant to business finance decisions*. Cases where shareholders cannot claim full benefits include non-resident shareholders, tax-exempt shareholders and shareholders who do not qualify under certain share holding period requirements that were introduced to reduce tax minimisation. In addition, the dividend imputation scheme is only available to companies paying dividends. The owners of firms run under all the other business structures pay tax on their business profits at their own individual marginal rates. *Taxation effects are relevant to business decisions for owners who cannot take full benefit of tax credits.* These issues are discussed further in chapters 7 and 14.

FINANCE WORKSHOP 2.3

1. A company makes an initial \$120 million profit and pays the full 30% tax. It then pays out a fully franked dividend of \$21 million. What is the balance in its franking account after these transactions?
2. Smart Electronics, a resident Australian company, has \$235 million in its franking account and wants to pay a fully franked \$140 million dividend. By how much will the franking credit reduce its franking account?

executive summary

lo1 describe the various forms of business organisation and their implications

- Australian businesses are required, almost without exception, to have an Australian business number (ABN).
- The ABN system was introduced in 2000 to try to increase compliance with taxation laws.
- A sole proprietorship is a business owned by an individual who owns assets used in the business, incurs liabilities and reaps the annual profits or losses.
- Sole proprietors have freedom to run their businesses any way they wish, so long as their activities remain within the law.
- Sole proprietorships are easy and cheap to establish.
- Sole proprietors often use their own names as trading names.
- Sole proprietors may register trading names with state authorities under the relevant state business names Act.
- In terms of legal liability for debts and costs of their actions, sole proprietors carry unlimited liability.
- Sole proprietors may expand their businesses by arranging debt finance but, by definition, they cannot raise funds by selling equity.
- Sole proprietors may sell or transfer ownership of their businesses by transferring the trading names and the assets.
- At the death of a sole proprietor, the sole proprietor structure is dissolved, even though the business as such may be sold as a going concern and may indeed keep its old trading name.
- The advantages of the sole proprietorship structure are:
  - the speed and ease of establishment
  - lack of formalities (such as reports to stakeholders)
  - freedom in decision making enjoyed by the owner.
- Disadvantages include:
  - the potential limited life of the firm — if the owner dies, the firm may also die
  - financing limited by definition to debt finance
  - unlimited liability for debts
  - no formal sharing of management responsibilities (but expertise may still be purchased by means of skilled employees, consultants or advisers).
- A partnership is an association of two or more people carrying on a business in common with a view to profit.
- Partnerships are easy to set up with a minimum of formalities and many partnerships use their own names as their trading names.
- Taxation law takes the view that the existence of a partnership is a matter of fact which may be deduced from the evidence available. Such evidence includes:
  - the existence of a formal partnership agreement
  - contributions of capital and labour by the partners
  - any forms of evidence signifying the partners' intentions to collaborate
  - jointly entered relevant contracts
  - jointly held and operated bank accounts
  - notifications to stakeholders that a partnership exists.

- Partnership agreements, at a minimum, should include full details of:
  - contributions of capital by partners
  - contributions of labour by partners
  - how profits or losses are to be shared
  - duration of the partnership
  - procedures for admitting a new partner or withdrawal (including death) of a partner
  - powers of partners to write cheques, raise funds and operate the bank accounts.
- Partnerships carry unlimited liability for debts and costs of their actions.
- Partnerships may expand their businesses by arranging debt finance and they can raise extra funds by selling equity through admission of more partners who would bring in additional cash or other assets.
- Partnerships may sell or transfer ownership of their businesses by transferring the trading names and the assets.
- More commonly, with the consent of all partners, one or more partners withdraw or new partners are admitted with the financial consideration being calculated in accordance with the partnership agreement.
- A partnership cannot legally employ any of the partners but it is common for a partner to be paid a 'salary', which is merely an early distribution of the partner's agreed share of the profits.
- All profits are considered to be distributed. If cash is not actually paid out for the full distribution, the unpaid balance is added to the partners' capital accounts and thus constitutes an increase in each partner's capital contribution.
- Profits from partnerships are taxed in full in the hands of the individual partners. Partnerships submit a tax return showing the taxable income of the partnership and how that income was distributed among the partners.
- A company, which is legally separate from its owners, is an entity formed under the *Corporations Act 2001*.
- A company is an association of people with a common objective.
- Companies make a trade-off with the society in which they operate: in return for the limitation of legal liability, they are subjected to greater regulation and compliance costs than either partnerships or sole proprietors.
- Prospective companies apply to the Australian Securities and Investments Commission (ASIC), the companies' regulator, for incorporation.
- If all legal requirements have been complied with, ASIC issues a certificate of incorporation; the company assumes a legal identity of its own from the moment of issue.
- Companies raise funds by issuing shares or by contracting for debt finance.
- Debt may be secured by a charge over assets or over uncalled capital.
- The owners of companies are the shareholders who meet at least annually at the annual general meeting (AGM).
- At the AGM, shareholders vote on significant decisions for the company and/or suggested changes in its constitution, as well as elect the board of directors.
- The board is responsible for the policy direction and day-to-day running of the company, and normally the day-to-day management is undertaken by a group of employed management executives.
- Corporate governance means the management of corporations so that decisions and actions are made and taken in accord with acknowledged corporate objectives.

- A trust is a legal structure where property is nominally owned by one party, the trustee, on behalf of others who are the beneficiaries.
- Income of trusts may be taxed within the trust or in the hands of the beneficiaries.
- Among the types of trusts available, the most commonly used business structure is the discretionary trust.
- The chief advantage of the trust structure is the ability of the trustee to direct income where it will be least tax-disadvantaged.

lo2 discuss the features of Australian income taxation arrangements for business

- Income tax is levied in Australia on individuals' and companies' taxable income.
- Taxable income is assessable income less legitimate deductions.
- Assessable income includes most forms of income earned by resident taxpayers both in Australia and overseas.
- Distinguishing between income and capital receipts can sometimes be difficult, but income is often periodically or frequently received whereas capital may be received infrequently.
- For businesses, allowable deductions include many classes of expenses and the general rule is that expenditure incurred to earn assessable income is an allowable deduction.
- Allowable deductions do not include an expense that is:
  - a loss or outgoing of capital, or of a capital nature
  - a loss or outgoing of a private or domestic nature
  - incurred in relation to gaining or producing exempt income.
- Individuals are taxed at stepped progressive rates.
- Companies are taxed at a flat rate.
- Marginal rates of tax are important because we often analyse alternative income-producing activities in terms of how they affect marginal income.

lo3 describe the other important business taxes

- Capital gains tax (CGT) is paid on gains made on the disposal of certain assets purchased after 19 September 1985.
- No CGT is payable until a CGT event occurs and the most common such event is the sale of the asset.
- GST is added to selling prices of goods and services.
- GST is not a tax on business because GST outgoings are claimed back from the ATO (and GST charged is remitted to the ATO).
- The GST regime has imposed a good deal of paperwork on business.

lo4 describe dividend imputation

- Dividend imputation is the system where dividends carry an additional benefit in the form of an attached tax credit for the relevant amount of tax paid by the company on its profits.

- A franked dividend is a dividend carrying an attached franking or tax credit.
- A fully franked dividend carries a tax credit equal to the full 30% company tax paid on the underlying profit.
- A partly franked dividend carries a tax credit less than the full 30% company tax paid on the underlying profit.
- An unfranked dividend carries no tax credit.

lo5 discuss how dividend imputation affects the analysis of business investment decisions

- Where a company believes the majority of its shareholders can take advantage of the dividend imputation, it should undertake investments and manage the firm's operations to maximise its before-tax cash flows.
- Where a company believes the majority of its shareholders can take advantage of the dividend imputation, it should analyse potential projects using pre-tax cash flows.
- Where shareholders cannot claim the full benefits of the tax credits, the full integration of the two tax regimes cannot be realised and the tax paid by the firm on its income becomes relevant to business finance decisions.

Key terms

allowable deductions, p. 42
assessable income, p. 42
Australian business number (ABN), p. 34
company, p. 37
corporate governance, p. 38
dividend imputation, p. 45
franked dividends, p. 45
fully franked dividends, p. 45
joint venture, p. 37
marginal tax rate, p. 40
partly franked dividends, p. 45
partnership, p. 35
sole proprietorship, p. 34
taxable income, p. 42
trust, p. 40
unfranked dividend, p. 45

Learning chart

Learning objective	Questions	Self-test problems	Financial problems
lo1 describe the various forms of business organisation and their implications	2.1, 2.2, 2.3, 2.4, 2.5, 2.6, 2.7, 2.8		2.1, 2.2, 2.3, 2.4
lo2 discuss the features of Australian income taxation arrangements for business	2.9, 2.10, 2.11	2.1, 2.2, 2.3	2.5, 2.6, 2.7, 2.8, 2.13, 2.14, 2.15, 2.18, 2.19
lo3 describe the other important business taxes	2.12, 2.13, 2.14		2.9, 2.10, 2.11, 2.12

continued

Learning objective	Questions	Self-test problems	Financial problems
lo4 describe dividend imputation	2.15, 2.16, 2.17, 2.18	2.4, 2.5	2.13, 2.14, 2.15, 2.18, 2.19, 2.20
lo5 discuss how dividend imputation affects the analysis of business investment decisions	2.19, 2.20		2.16, 2.17

Questions

2.1 What is an ABN?

2.2 Why should suppliers of goods and services be sure to quote an ABN on their invoices?

2.3 Why is sole proprietorship so commonly used as the structure of Australian businesses?

2.4 David Black Plumbing ceases trading with $20 000 owed to EZ Plumbing Supplies. David Black, the sole owner of the defunct business, owns his house and several flats. Who is legally liable for the $20 000 — David Black or EZ Plumbing?

2.5 Filcher Partners are lawyers who want to bring in a new full partner. Explain how the finances might be arranged to achieve this.

2.6 Dana Stevens is an orthodontist in a suburban dental practice run as a partnership. There are no professional employees, the only employees being the two receptionists and the three dental assistants. Dana draws a wage fortnightly and always says she is the lowest paid employee in the firm. Can this claim be correct? Why?

2.7 'A company cannot be sued; it is the board who are sued in the case of negligence.' Is this statement correct? Why?

2.8 Traders use trusts to minimise their income tax. Explain this statement with an example.

2.9 Most income received by resident individuals in Australia is assessable income including legacies, lottery prizes and gambling wins. Is this true? Explain.

2.10 Prime Paints suffered a fire and lost $180 000 worth of stock. $150 000 was claimed and received from its insurer. Is this assessable income?

2.11 The claiming of interest expenses as tax deductions has been a highly litigated area. Explain the factors underlying this.

2.12 Explain the basis of CGT.

2.13 What rate of tax is currently levied as CGT?

2.14 GST is an unfair tax that disadvantages business. Do you agree? Why?

2.15 Explain the theoretical basis for dividend imputation.

2.16 If a taxpayer receives a $700 fully franked dividend, she will pay tax on $700. Is this correct?

2.17 A taxpayer receives $2100 in fully franked dividends and has a 30% marginal tax rate. What extra tax liability will the taxpayer have on the dividends?

2.18 John is happy to be told by his accountant that he has $4500 in franking credits. Explain to John what this means.

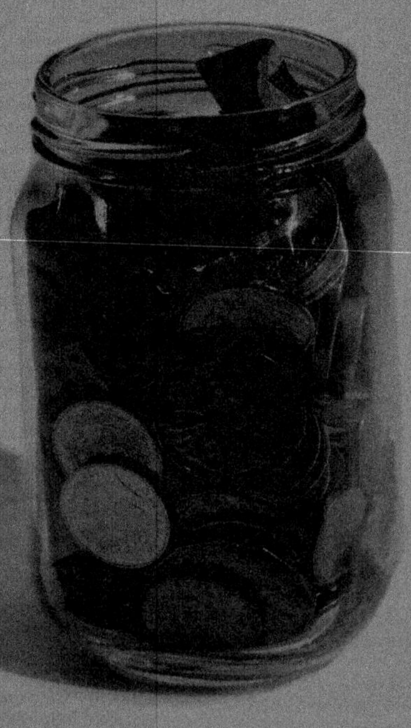

2.19 An Australian technology company lists in New York and has mainly foreign shareholders. Should dividend imputation have much impact on its decision making with regard to future investments?

2.20 Australian Ginger is a small listed firm with only Australian individuals as shareholders. Their projects manager insists all development proposals should use PV analysis and take tax effects into consideration. Is he correct? Why?

Self-test problems

2.1 Spot-on Consultants is an agricultural extension and consultancy firm. It is run by Bill Burton as a sole proprietorship. Bill made \$67 000 taxable income last year. What is his tax liability including Medicare levy?

2.2 Wilma and Raj Gogopal are partners in an accountancy practice. They share profits and losses equally. The firm made \$257 800 taxable income last year. Wilma and Raj have no other income. What is Wilma's income tax liability?

2.3 Training Solutions Company Ltd (TSC) had a turnover of \$1 234 534 last year. Allowable deductions are \$834 034. TSC has no carry-forward losses or any other tax allowances. What is its income tax liability?

2.4 Pavi has a medium-sized equity portfolio. She receives the following dividends, all fully franked at the 30% rate: \$450, \$520, \$530, \$1500, \$2050, \$1950 and \$2500. She also receives \$345, \$2795 and \$3250 in unfranked dividends. She adds her recorded franking credits for her tax return and calculates a total of \$4071.43. Is this correct?

2.5 Peter has a 41.5% marginal tax rate. He receives \$5000 in fully franked dividends. How much additional tax will he pay over the franking credits?

Solutions to self-test problems

2.1 From table 2.2, tax on \$30 000 = \$3600

Tax on \$37 000 = 37 000 × 0.3 = 11 100

Medicare levy = 67 000 × 0.015 = 1005

Total tax = \$3600 + \$11 100 + \$1005 = \$15 705

2.2 Taxable income of equal partners is shared equally, so Wilma is accorded \$128 900 of taxable income.

Tax on \$128 900 = \$17 600 + (128 900 – 75 000) × 0.4 + 0.015 × \$128 900

= \$40 593.50

2.3 Tax liability = (taxable income – deductions) × tax rate

= (1 234 534 – 834 034) × 0.3

= 400 500 × 0.3

= \$120 150

2.4 Total franked dividends = \$9500

$$\text{Grossed up income} = \frac{9050}{0.7} = \$13\,571.43$$

Franking credits = \$13 571.43 × 0.3= \$4071.43 (Correct!)

2.5 $$\text{Grossed up income} = \frac{\$5000}{0.7} = \$7142.86$$

Tax on income = 7142.86 × 0.415 = \$2964.29

Franking credit = 7142.86 × 0.3 = 2142.86

Extra tax payable = 2964.29 – 2142.86 = \$821.43

Financial problems

2.1 Steve Preston is a veterinary surgeon who has worked for 10 years with other practitioners in a range of country practices. He now feels it is time to 'go out on his own'. He finds a medium-sized country town with no veterinarian and sets up a practice. His wife answers the phone, makes up the accounts, pays the bills and keeps the financial records.

(a) Which business structure in your view is best for Steve to use?

(b) What are the advantages of this structure?

(c) What are the disadvantages of this structure?

2.2 Peter and Chris Dunn grow Australian native flowers for the cut-flower trade. They export to South-East Asian countries and occasionally send flowers to the Amsterdam markets. They employ their three sons and one daughter in the firm and employ 10 casual pickers. Currently, the business is structured as a partnership, just as they set it up 25 years ago when they first started.

(a) Which business structure in your view should the Dunns use now?

(b) What are the advantages of this structure?

(c) What are the disadvantages of this structure?

2.3 Which is the most appropriate business structure in each of the following cases? Why?

(a) Chui starts a TV repair business and has no employees for the first two years.

(b) Business turnover at Chui's TV Repairs has grown. He has employed a part-time technician and persuaded his wife to give up her receptionist job to handle the front counter enquiries, phone calls and the books.

(c) Chui's turnover has grown to $1 million pa and he employs two technicians.

2.4 Dr Destina Desjardines is a research scientist who has just developed a vaccine that, if shown to be effective in clinical trials, promises to revolutionise the treatment of a highly infectious rhinovirus. Destina is nearing the end of her research life and has $1 million in superannuation and other assets of about $2 million. She needs large sums of capital to develop the vaccine. What form of business organisation would you recommend to Destina? Why?

2.5 What is the difference between assessable income and taxable income?

2.6 James Hardie Industries agreed to compensate victims of asbestos pollution stemming from the mining of the raw materials and the manufacture and use of asbestos-based products. The firm applied to the ATO for a ruling allowing these payments to be deducted from current income.

(a) What is the immediate effect of deductibility?

(b) How is tax liability affected?

(c) If the payments were allowed as deductions, how then are the Australian people as a whole involved in the compensation arrangements?

(d) Give some arguments both for and against deductibility.

2.7 Sunshine Fruits made $100 000 taxable income last year. What would be the tax payable, disregarding the Medicare levy, if:

(a) Sunshine was structured as a sole proprietorship?

(b) Sunshine was structured as a partnership with two equal partners?

(c) Sunshine was structured as a partnership with three equal partners?

(d) Sunshine was structured as a partnership with four equal partners?

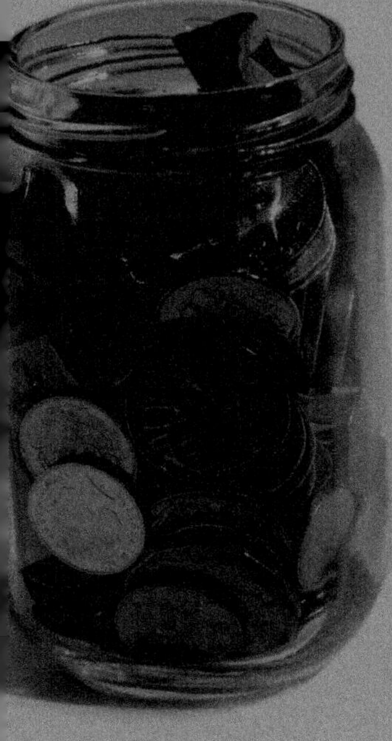

(e) Sunshine was structured as a partnership with five equal partners?

(f) Sunshine was structured as a company (company tax only)?

2.8 Jane Winter lent $100 000 to her accountancy partnership at 5% interest, the cash rate at the time.

(a) Can the partnership claim the interest as a tax deduction?

(b) Explain where the deduction and the interest income will appear in the tax returns.

2.9 Since the calculation of a CGT liability was simplified in September 1999, a taxpayer making an assessable capital gain and paying the top marginal tax rate of 45% plus 1.5% Medicare levy effectively pays only 23.25% on the gain. Explain why the rate is not (0.5 × 45%) + 1.5%, making 24%.

2.10 A gain on the sale of an individual's main residence is CGT exempt. Explain why you think Parliament enacted this provision.

2.11 Tom bought an investment property in 2000 for $150 000 and sold it again in April 2007 for $280 000. He had no other capital gains or losses in the year and had $75 000 other taxable income. How much tax will he pay on his gain?

2.12 Alpha Agents and Traders buys timber fence posts from a small-time timber cutter (not registered for GST) at $10 each. Freight is another $2 per post. Alpha adds 40% mark-up and the 10% GST. What is the selling price per post?

2.13 Jim earns a salary of $60 000 and has legitimate deductions, mainly donations, of $1000. He has investments and receives $5600 in fully franked dividends.

(a) What would be his tax liability (including the 1.5% Medicare levy) if the dividends had been unfranked?

(b) By how much does his taxable income increase through receipt of the franking credits?

(c) What is his net tax (including 1.5% Medicare levy) if the dividends are fully franked?

2.14 Frenelli South Entertainments Ltd (FSE) is a company which provides after-dinner speakers. Its total fee income last year was $9.8 million and its disbursements to the speakers were $8.2 million. In addition, there were $600 000 in tax-deductible expenses.

(a) What are FSE's taxable income and tax liability for the year?

(b) FSE has a policy of paying out 80% of taxable income as dividends and has 1 million issued shares. What is the dividend per share and what amount will be the franking credit per share?

(c) What will be the balance in the franking credit account at FSE after the dividend payment, if the balance at the start of the year was $200 000?

2.15 IXL Ltd is a manufacturer that carried forward past losses of $5 million from 2005–06. It made a profit in 2006–07 and wrote off all the past losses. Its taxable income was thus reduced and it paid only $1.5 million in income tax. It had a nil balance in its franking credit account at the start of 2006–07.

(a) What was its taxable income in 2006–07?

(b) The directors decide to distribute $7 million in dividends of $1 per share. Can these dividends be fully franked?

(c) How much is the franking credit per share?

2.16 Percy Porcelain graduated from university with a degree in dentistry. Within a few years he started his own practice, saved diligently and invested well in shares and property. Percy always looked for tax-effective investments as he hated paying the top marginal rate of tax. After 20 years of practice, he decided he was sick of gaping mouths, sold his practice and took a job as investment manager with Holey Dollars Ltd, an investment firm owned by a group of Brisbane dentists. Holey Dollars specialised in direct venture-capital investments. To analyse potential investments, Percy used present value techniques to select the most rewarding projects to maximise shareholder wealth. He discounted after-tax cash flows. Do you agree with his technique? Why?

2.17 Kappakali Ltd is a listed company in the recreation and tourism sector. It has a high cash flow and is considered to be highly profitable in its sector. Its shareholders are both Australian resident and non-Australian individuals and companies, with perhaps a predominance of Japanese investors. It has never missed a dividend and has always paid fully franked dividends. In analysing a future investment project in March 2008, should Kappakali's managers use before-tax or after-tax cash flows? Why?

2.18 Wendy Wang, a resident of Australia, has an investment in Kappakali (see problem 2.17) shares. She receives $4000 in dividends in 2007–08, making her taxable income $67 000. What rate of tax will she pay on her Kappakali dividend?

2.19 Jani Sun Tin, also resident of Australia, bought some Kappakali (the company in problem 2.17) shares in 2005. Her 2008 dividend is $1540 and her taxable income $19 500. What rate of tax will she pay on her dividend?

2.20 Scott Jenkins has retired and has only a low income. He qualifies for several tax offsets so pays no income tax or Medicare levy at all. He has, however, $2100 in fully franked dividends. Does he qualify for a refund from the ATO? If so, for how much?

SOLUTIONS TO FINANCE WORKSHOPS

2.1 1. (a) Ease and low cost of establishment; ease of management; low regulatory oversight; ability to manage CGT

(b) Limited legal liability; ease in raising capital; ease in managing income taxation; better business continuity; easy transfer of ownership

2. A partnership first would be appropriate for the reasons given in question 1(a). As the business grew, Greg might need to raise more capital. He could bring in more partners or float a company. Each has advantages.

2.2 1. Income is generally recurrent, but it may not be. Capital payments are often one-off, but again this may not be a conclusive test. The source of funds is important in determining their nature. Payments for personal exertion, interest, rent, dividends and royalties are all income. Some complicated areas identified as income include compensation received for cancellation of trade contracts, for loss of profits and insurance recoveries.

2. Sale of the fifth share of the business; sale of strip of land on the fence line.

2.3 1. The tax is $36 million (120 × 0.3) so this is the franking account balance. The account would be reduced by $9 million because this is the franking credit attached to the $21 million dividend at the 30% franking rate ($21 m × 0.3/0.7). The balance of the franking account after these two transactions would be $27 million.

2. $60 million ($140 million × 0.3/0.7).

End notes

1 Source: Heritage Building Society 2007, 'Corporate information', http://secure.heritageonline.com.au.

2 Australian Bureau of Statistics 2005, *ABS business register: counts of businesses, June 2004*, cat. no. 8161.0.55.001.

3 Excerpts from Kohler, Alan 2007, 'Gwalia redefines shareholder rights', *The Age*, 3 February.

chapter

3

Business and the financial markets

Learning objectives

After studying this chapter, you should be able to:

- lo1 describe the roles of the financial markets
- lo2 discuss how business operations are financed
- lo3 describe the financial service institutions in the financial markets
- lo4 differentiate between different sectors of the financial markets
- lo5 discuss the main forms of debt offered in the financial markets
- lo6 understand equity and its raising
- lo7 discuss the role of regulators and the ASX.

ABC LEARNING CENTRES

ABC Learning Centres Ltd (ASX code: ABS) is a childcare services company that started operations in Brisbane and is still based there. The directors have pursued a strong growth strategy and the following information highlights that growth.

	2006	2001	Change (%)
Number of childcare centres at 30 June	1547	43	3500
Revenue ($ millions)	631	13	4750
Operating profit after tax ($ millions)	81	3.25	2400
Earnings per share — basic (cents)	27.7	29.9	–7
Full-year fully franked dividend (cents)	15	14	7

Source: ABC Learning Centres Ltd.[1]

Here are some extracts from ABC's 2006 annual report (pp. 4–5, 23–4).

CEO's report

ABC is now an international childcare provider with an increasingly strong financial and shareholder focus. During the year, we have repaid debt and funded acquisitions and further growth opportunities.

Consolidation and international expansion

In the last 12 months, ABC has evolved into a substantially different company. We are a significantly larger company and now also an international organisation.

During the year, we commenced our expansion into the US, gaining a substantial part of the largest childcare market in the world.

We cemented our position as the leading childcare provider in the Australian market through our acquisitions of Kids Campus and Hutchison's Child Care Services and are now Australia's leading provider of childcare services.

Our financial position has been strengthened with an additional capital raising underpinning our acquisitions and funding our future growth opportunities.

These initiatives have positioned ABC at the forefront of the childcare industry, enabling us to continue to provide the highest quality of care for children and families in our centres and strategically positioning us to capitalise on these investments over the longer term.

Directors' report

Capital management

During the year, ABC has raised sufficient capital to repay debt and fund acquisitions and further growth opportunities. Our net debt position at the end of June was $29.3 million. We can now feel comfortable in increasing the debt position of the Company as we continue to grow.

The breadth and scale of our operations now means that we have also moved into the ASX Top 100 list of companies. The Company and its operations are now attracting the attention of a new set of institutional shareholders and one of our priorities is to engage with this market to build understanding of our development strategy.

Significant changes in state of affairs

The following significant changes in the state of affairs of the Group occurred during the year:

(i) On 13 September 2005, the Company issued 10 000 000 ordinary shares at $6.00 per share to raise capital to reduce debt and to fund the Company's ongoing acquisition program;

(ii) On 15 December 2005, the Company issued 37 200 000 ordinary shares at $7.00 to raise funds for the acquisition of the Learning Care Group, Inc. and to fund the Company's ongoing acquisition program;

(iii) On 11 January 2006, the Company acquired the Learning Care Group, Inc. for US$159 100 000;

(iv) On 9 May 2006, the Company issued 44 104 239 ordinary shares at an issue price of $7.30 each to a range of institutional and professional investors to refinance the Company balance sheet to place the Company in a strong position to take advantage of global acquisition opportunities;

(v) In May 2006, the Company acquired Kids Campus Limited for $127 897 000; and

(vi) On 14 June 2006, the Company issued 38 087 542 ordinary shares at an issue price of $7.30 each to a range of institutional and professional investors to refinance ABC's balance sheet to place the Company in a strong position to take advantage of global acquisition opportunities.

Significant events after balance date

On 7 July 2006 the company announced an off-market takeover bid of Hutchison's Child Care Services Ltd for $1.50 per ordinary share. On 25 September 2006 the Company declared the takeover bid unconditional and commenced compulsory acquisition of the remaining shares.

On 6 September 2006 the company acquired 100% of The Children's Courtyard LLP, the ninth largest childcare provider in the US for US$66 million.

Chapter preview

The information given on this and the previous page was released by ABC Learning Centres Ltd in its annual reports. It is apparent that the company is growing strongly — from managing 43 centres at 30 June 2001 to 187 centres in 2003, 660 in 2005 and more than 1500 in 2006. The centres include about 500 located in the United States.

How does a company fund such rapid expansion? There are only two ways — through increases in debt or equity. You will see from the statement in the 2006 annual report that ABC has raised a great deal of additional capital — more than 130 million shares in 2006 alone, thus taking issued capital to 393 million shares (or $1.6 billion) at 30 June 2006.

You will also observe that the CEO notes in his report that the firm has repaid debt during the year and 'can now feel comfortable in increasing the debt position' again. Can you explain this apparent paradox? The company has just repaid debt but now is happy to increase it again?

Our focus in this chapter is on funding sources in general. After reading this chapter, you will understand more of the business financing environment, what this statement means and why the company is taking this path.

The following diagram shows how this chapter is structured.

BUSINESS AND THE FINANCIAL MARKETS

- **The roles of the financial markets**
- **Financing business operations**
  - Direct finance
  - Intermediate finance
- **Types of financial institutions**
  - Authorised deposit-taking institutions (ADIs)
  - Registered financial corporations (RFCs)
- **Classifying the markets**
  - Primary and secondary markets
  - Public and private markets
  - Money and capital markets
- **Debt and equity**
  - The effect of debt on risk
  - The effect of debt on control
  - The effect of varying taxation treatments of payments to debt and equity
- **Forms of debt**
- **Equity instruments**
- **Regulators and regulation**
  - Reserve Bank of Australia
  - Australian Prudential Regulation Authority
  - Australian Securities and Investments Commission
  - Australian Securities Exchange

The roles of the financial markets

lo1

Describe the roles of the financial markets.

The financial markets in Australia, and indeed in any country, fulfil many roles, not least of which are:

- provision of platforms where the supply of funds by surplus units (potential lenders) and the demand for funds by deficit units (potential borrowers) may be reconciled and priced through trading (this allows businesses to raise the funds they need to operate and the pricing mechanism allows funds to be allocated among competing users)
- facilitation of business and trade, thus making the production and exchange of goods and services easier and more efficient
- facilitation of saving by individuals to allow for future consumption
- provision of financial services which allow participants to balance their risk tolerance with their requirements for both returns and cash.

The ABC Learning Centres fund raising is a good example of the financial markets in operation. There is no doubt that the existence of the financial markets makes the raising of funds easier for ABC. This means that management can get on with the task of providing child care so that parents can more easily do the tasks necessary to earn a living and raise their families. The incentive of returns from firms such as ABC encourages individuals to save, thereby putting off consumption in the near term so that it can be enjoyed at a later time. Saving eventually transforms into investment.

In Australia, savers are typically individuals and foreign entities. In other words, individuals and foreign entities normally supply the finance necessary in the system, although businesses and governments sometimes supply funds. The borrowers are usually businesses and governments but, notwithstanding this situation, most individuals have borrowed funds at some time in their lives. Australians rely heavily on the savings of foreign entities to fund our investment and, sometimes, government spending and consumption. This is seen by many economists to be a fundamental weakness in our economic situation. Many see it as stemming from over-indulgence in consumption ('enjoy now, pay later'), which contributes to our chronically weak currency. The Australian dollar (AUD), they assert, will always sell at a discount to what we see as its correct price, if we need to sell more and more AUD to fund our lifestyle and investment needs.

Apart from the savers and borrowers, there are other entities in the markets that provide financial services and, additionally, who oversee the markets. The first group is composed of the financial institutions and the second of the regulators. Financial institutions are banks, building societies and credit unions — collectively called 'authorised deposit-taking institutions' (ADIs) — and many other types of financial services institutions — collectively called 'registered financial corporations' (RFCs). RFCs include money market corporations, pastoral finance companies, finance companies, general financiers and intragroup financiers. The regulators are the Reserve Bank of Australia (RBA), the Australian Prudential Regulation Authority (APRA) and the Australian Securities and Investments Commission (ASIC).

FINANCE WORKSHOP 3.1

From your recall of the previous section, what is the role of the financial markets for both savers and investors? Give an example to illustrate each role and explain fully how each example is an apt case.

lo2

Discuss how business operations are financed.

Financing business operations

Financing business operations takes place either directly or indirectly. In the next two sections, we will examine these operations in turn.

Direct finance

Direct finance takes place when the saver who is the supplier of funds makes a deal directly with the business that needs the funds. Such a supply could take place from an individual or company to a sole proprietor, a partnership, a trust or a company. Thus, funds might be supplied by a relative to a sole proprietor or a partnership. Alternatively, the funds might be supplied by a solicitor or other professional, such as an accountant or auditor, who has funds to invest. Other common situations are the supply of funds by individuals in a family to a trust, or the supply of funds by one company to a related company. Apart from these 'related party' transactions, there is of course the very common direct supply of funds to companies by investors through public offerings of equity (and, to a lesser extent, debt).

What do all these situations have in common? The link is information. With direct funding, the supplier must know the entity that needs the funds. If the supplier does not know of an entity needing funds, then no supply can be made. Think of the situation where there were no financial services companies. Would all suppliers of funds find entities that

Transaction costs: the costs, in terms of both time and explicit cash costs, of effecting a transaction or deal

Hoarding: savings held outside the financial system and thus not available for financial investment

needed money? The answer is probably not, so savers would tend not to bother trying to find investments. Without companies supplying financial services, the **transaction costs** (the time and cost of finding appropriate borrowers) would be too high. The result would be that some savings would be put under the mattress, in the biscuit tin or the flowerpot, or wherever such spare cash is kept. This is called **hoarding**. Hoarding results in decreased economic growth as not all money that could fund investment is available, so the rate of economic expansion is reduced.

Intermediated finance

Intermediated finance, which takes place through an intermediary or financial institution, is much more common than direct finance. As we have already seen, and will examine in more detail shortly, there are many different types of financial institutions in Australia today. The key to their existence is that they provide much needed services and, even though people complain over the levels of their fees, they provide those services at costs which are less than the transaction costs savers and borrowers would have to bear if there were no financial institutions.

lo3

Describe the financial service institutions in the financial markets.

Types of financial institutions

There are several types of financial institutions in Australia, the various types being the product of history, past and present market niches, and past and present regulatory regimes.

Authorised deposit-taking institutions (ADIs)

Financial institutions in Australia may be divided into two major classes — ADIs and RFCs. The ADIs, which are registered under the *Banking Act 1959*, comprise the banks, building societies and credit unions. At February 2007, there were 14 Australian-owned banks:

- the big four (ANZ, Commonwealth, NAB and Westpac)
- the regionals (for example, Adelaide Bank, Suncorp-Metway)
- the new entrants who diversified into banking (for example, AMP from insurance and funds management and Elders Rural Bank from its stock and station agency business).

In addition, there were 10 foreign-subsidiary banks such as Bank of China, ING Bank and BankWest. Moreover, there are another 30 banks here represented by branches. These include some of the biggest banks in the world: ABN AMRO, Barclays, Citibank, Deutsche Bank, JPMorgan Chase, Rabobank Nederland and Standard Chartered.[2]

Building societies are now fewer in number, at 14, than perhaps they have been in the last 100 years. This is because, in the quest for efficiency and the ability to compete in the highly-competitive financial services markets, many former building societies have transformed themselves into banks (such as Suncorp-Metway and St George Bank) and others have merged to gain critical mass. Credit unions stem from a similar background to building societies, in that both tended to develop from the desire of individuals or communities to provide financial services for themselves. Both use the mutual or cooperative society as their business structures. The difference between the two classes of institutions now is that credit unions have remained predominantly small and numerous (about 140 entities) and focused on serving individuals' financial needs. On the other hand, building societies have tended to join the bigger world of global finance and are attempting to compete with the banks in most forms of finance.

In terms of size, the banks dominate the ADI markets. At September 2006, the banks controlled $1650 billion in assets, while the building societies held $19 billion and the credit unions managed $37 billion. Of the banks' assets, some $77 billion was held as bills receivable (almost always business finance) and $420 billion was commercial loans. In contrast, building societies' commercial lending amounted to only $900 million and credit unions' commercial lending totalled $1200 million.[3]

The ADIs, as their name implies, take deposits from savers and lend that money out to borrowers, both individuals and businesses, who need funds. In addition, ADIs themselves arrange for loans of funds so they can expand their businesses faster than the rate of received deposits will allow. Hence, ADIs currently manage their assets (the loans they make plus their fixed assets, such as premises and equipment); their liabilities (deposits plus any loans they contract to expand their funds available); and their equity or capital (their ownership or proprietorship funds) to ensure that these funds are returning optimal amounts.

Registered financial corporations (RFCs)

RFCs include money market corporations, pastoral finance companies, finance companies, general financiers and intra-group financiers. These companies are registered under the *Financial Sector (Collection of Data) Act 2001.*

The quest for efficiency in the financial service sector has encouraged specialisation in the past. Thus, pastoral finance companies such as Dalgety Ltd and Primac Elders Ltd developed expertise in valuing both rural properties and stock and were able to build profitable finance businesses by using that expertise in making loans. On the other hand, finance companies such as AGC and Esanda developed their expertise in lending for the purchase of consumer goods and in efficient debt-collection methods. Money market corporations specialised in short-term finance. Specialisation was encouraged by registrations of financial institutions in separate categories under the *Financial Corporations Act 1974*.

Deregulation in the financial markets, changing competitive pressures and changes to governing legislation such as the *Corporations Act 2001* and the credit Acts of the various states have wrought great changes in the financial service sector. In some cases, specialisation has remained and in others the divisions between categories of financial providers have tended to blur. Businesses looking for finance can approach money market corporations, pastoral finance companies, finance companies and general financiers. Pastoral finance companies still tend to specialise in rural lending. Finance companies have a competitive edge in lease financing, wholesale or 'floor plan' financing and factoring — the financing of accounts receivable. General financiers such as GE Money (see the next 'finance world' feature) offer a wide range of finance, such as loans for and leasing of vehicles, credit card finance and commercial loans.

There are other financial institutions, such as superannuation funds and insurance companies, that operate in the financial markets but provide business finance only in a roundabout way. Managers of funds within these firms invest in cash (very short-term debt), fixed interest, property and equities, and thereby supply funds in the financial markets.

FINANCE WORKSHOP 3.2

ADIs and RFCs play different roles in the financial system. Explain what differences currently exist and how they came about. Assume you are the finance manager in several types of businesses and explain which institutions you would approach for finance.

FINANCE WORLD

About GE Money Australia and New Zealand

In August 1995, we acquired the credit card operations of the Coles Myer Group in Australia. This formed the basis of GE Money Australia and New Zealand, which has grown rapidly over the past 10 years through acquisitions, new product introduction and organic growth. Acquisitions have included Nissan Financial Services in 1998, Avco Financial Services in 1999, AGC Australia and New Zealand in 2002 and, in 2004, the Australian Financial Investments Group whose brands include Wizard Home Loans.

Today we are one of Australia's leading consumer finance companies, offering a vast range of consumer lending products, including personal loans, auto loans, credit cards, mortgages, insurance and promotional retail finance. We have assets in excess of A$30 billion and over 3 million customers across Australia and New Zealand.

Our financial services are distributed through numerous sales channels, including over 12 000 retailers, 700 auto dealers, 5 500 brokers, 400 branches and the internet. By providing accessible credit at the right time and place, our clients are better able to acquire new customers, generate incremental sales and strengthen their customer relationships. GE Money in Australia and New Zealand is a full service provider of financing solutions, managing credit applications, credit authorisation, billing, remittance and customer service processing utilising six-sigma quality methodology to minimise defects and ensure operational excellence.

GE Money is part of the global GE network, a company with a AAA rating and global lending experience.[4]

lo4

Differentiate between different sectors of the financial markets.

Classifying the markets

The financial markets are extremely broad-ranging and can be confusing for a novice market watcher. The market classifications that are discussed here are:

- primary and secondary
- public and private
- money and capital.

A further division is debt and equity, but this distinction is so important to business that we examine these sources of capital in more detail in the next section.

None of these markets has a single physical presence like the cattle market at the local saleyards or the hobby, plant and craft market held every second Sunday down at the police youth club. The financial markets are either electronic, with buyers and sellers participating from hundreds of locations with a centralised electronic server, or physically decentralised, with millions of transactions taking place each year but with price discovery and transmission in the market taking place through highly effective information systems. Physically decentralised markets could not operate well without efficient information systems, because potential traders would have to spend a great deal of their working time just trying to find out what are reasonable price ranges. Such inefficiencies would hinder the efficient allocation of resources and the funding of the best and most productive investments.

Price discovery: the process of finding and settling on a price that is acceptable to both parties to a transaction

An important function of markets is that they allow **price discovery**. Price discovery is the process of finding and settling on a price that is acceptable to both parties to a transaction. Just imagine you were trying to buy a new car, but had no idea of a reasonable price for such a vehicle and nor did the seller. Where would you start to negotiate the price? At \$5000, \$10 000, \$20 000, \$50 000? How would you know if you had no yardstick for value? It would be even more difficult when, as with securities, there is often no easily valued physical presence to examine. Price information systems are critical.

Primary and secondary markets

Primary market: the market in which securities are offered for the first time

Securities: tradeable instruments that represent an ownership interest or the right to receive payment on a debt

As the name implies, the **primary market** is the market in which securities are offered for the first time. **Securities** are documents that provide evidence of a loan or the ownership of shares, a bond or a commercial bill. You could think of a security merely as a receipt for the transfer of funds, but it is a receipt that normally is worth money and can be resold in the market, unlike the receipt you get from Woolworths when you buy the week's groceries. Thus, when ABC Learning Centres issues new shares, these shares form part of the primary market. They are new and are being issued for the first time. They have increased the stock of shares in the market. Similarly, businesses raising funds through the issue of units, notes or debentures are increasing the stock of these securities in the market and hence are operating in the primary market.

Secondary markets: deal with sales of securities that have been issued by their respective firms in the past and do not increase the stock of securities

The **secondary markets** deal with securities that have been issued by their respective firms in the past. If you like, these are second-hand securities but, unlike most second-hand cars, they do not necessarily decrease in value. Indeed, many securities increase dramatically in value over time, and it does not matter how many owners an individual parcel of shares or an individual bond has had. Thus, transactions in the secondary markets do not increase the stock of securities; they merely change the distribution of ownership. The Australian Securities Exchange (ASX) is a prime example of a secondary market principally for the trading of equities, but also for trading selected debt instruments.

The existence of active secondary markets for securities supports the primary markets by supplying liquidity, confidence and the ability to manage risk. Investors thinking of buying particular securities may buy with confidence when they know they can sell at any time and regain their liquidity within a few days. In contrast, investors contemplating the purchase of securities that lack active secondary markets must be reasonably sure that they will not need the funds at any time before maturity. If they do need the funds, they may face difficulty in finding buyers, high transaction costs or price discounts.

The secondary markets also act as a price-discovery mechanism for the primary markets when new issues are contemplated. In addition, the secondary markets allow investors to restructure their portfolios in line with their changing preferences for risk and return. The relationship between risk and return is discussed in detail in chapter 5.

Public and private markets

Public issues: issues of securities to the public; they require the release of a prospectus or product disclosure statement

Prospectus: a document that provides details of a new issue of securities to the public

When firms want to raise extra funds, they can do so publicly or privately. In **public issues**, the firm is asking people or entities that do not have a close relationship with it to provide funding. In order to entice them to hand over their funds, the firm must provide full details of its business, its past financial performance and its future prospects. This is achieved by means of a **prospectus** (or product disclosure statements for public trusts). A prospectus is a document that provides details of a new issue of securities to the public. It normally contains details of past financial performance and projected future performance. It also may contain taxation implications for investors. Compiling a prospectus is time-consuming and expensive. The various reports from professionals such as accountants, auditors and taxation experts that are included in the prospectus are costly. Prospectuses must be approved by ASIC. Therefore, public issues are issues of securities to the public and require the release of a prospectus.

Private placements: issues of securities made by negotiation directly with purchasers

Private placements, on the other hand, are issues of securities made by negotiation directly with purchasers. Normally public issues are larger than private placements, but this is not necessarily so. There are several reasons for this, but basically it comes down to cost.

The mechanics of using a public issue for fund-raising are costly — applications to process, cheques to be banked, reconciliations to be made and ultimately securities to be issued. Moreover, to ensure the issue is a success, some firms buy a guarantee of success by paying an underwriter. An underwriter agrees to fund any shortfall in the monies raised in return for an underwriting fee. Hence, to spread these costs and thus reduce the transaction costs per dollar raised, public offerings tend to be relatively large. These issues are discussed more thoroughly in chapter 12.

In contrast, a private placement takes place by negotiation between the firm or its agent and selected private individuals or financial institutions. The details of the issue are worked out between the two to their mutual satisfaction. No prospectus or special reports are necessary, as the supplier of funds normally has had a relationship with the firm previously and has been following its financial performance. Even though this process may be facilitated by a **merchant bank** or other financial institution, its cost normally is quite low in comparison with costs associated with a public offering. A merchant bank is a financial institution that is not registered or regulated under the *Banking Act 1959* but which carries out many of the functions of a bank, especially in the wholesale or commercial banking areas.

Merchant bank: a financial institution that is not registered or regulated under the *Banking Act 1959* but which carries out many of the functions of a bank, especially in the wholesale or commercial banking areas

Another advantage of private placements is that funds may be raised very quickly. In Australia, currently the merchant banks tend not to be household names, but are often subsidiaries of either domestic or foreign financial institutions. For example, Macquarie Bank, which is a licensed bank, has several merchant bank subsidiaries such as Macquarie Leasing.

In recent years, many firms have raised funds by both methods. Often a public offering has followed several private placements, as existing shareholders apply pressure to be included in raising additional funds. Their argument is that their holdings are diluted each time a private placement of shares is made to other parties. For example, suppose a firm has one million issued shares and you hold 50 000 shares or 5%. The firm issues privately a further 200 000 shares to XYZ Nominees, thus making 1 200 000 shares on issue. You still hold 50 000 shares, but now your holding has shrunk to 4.16%. If this process went on for further issues, your holding would shrink progressively to 4%, 3%, 2% and so on, and you would have progressively less voting power in your firm.

Money and capital markets

Money markets: deal in short-term debt; that is, debt that has less than one year to maturity

Money markets deal in short-term debt; that is, debt that has less than one year to maturity. For businesses looking for funds, the major instruments traded are commercial bills and promissory notes. Entities with funds to invest could buy these instruments or certificates of deposit, which are all offered by the private sector. Treasury notes used to be offered by the Commonwealth Government, but have not been made available since late 2003. Commercial bills and promissory notes are discussed further in chapter 10 and we calculate prices for them in chapter 4.

Re-purchase agreements or **repos:** securities that are bought or sold with an agreement to reverse the original transaction at a later date

Treasury notes ('T-notes') were loans issued by the Commonwealth Government to raise short-term finance to fund its day-to-day expenditures. They were issued by a tender process and thus the market in its collective wisdom set the eventual price and yield (interest rate), which was normally fairly close to the cash rate. Amounts offered in each tender usually ranged from $200 million to $500 million. The Reserve Bank of Australia (RBA), for the Commonwealth, now uses **re-purchase agreements** or **'repos'** over longer-term securities to achieve short-term funding. Re-purchase agreements are securities that are bought or sold with an agreement to reverse the original transaction at a later date.

Certificates of deposit (CDs) are issued by banks. They are normally issued for periods ranging from a few days up to 180 days. They are essentially loans issued by banks and are payable to the bearer (current holder). Their credit risk is low. Businesses may buy these certificates (thus, effectively making a deposit with the respective bank) but retain the flexibility of selling them and regaining cash at any time. CDs are discount securities, meaning that they are sold at less than their face value, but pay their face value on maturity.

Capital markets: deal in long-term instruments; that is, instruments with maturities greater than one year

In contrast, the **capital markets** deal in long-term instruments; that is, instruments with maturities greater than one year. Long-term corporate debt — such as that involved with the issue of debentures, secured or unsecured notes, leases and loans with terms greater than one year — as well as the equity instruments such as shares and convertible notes are all issued and traded in this market.

Debt and equity

Business needs funds to operate. Funds are needed to have change in the cash registers, to purchase stock, to pay all cash expenses such as wages, rent, freight, phone bills and taxes, and to pay for capital goods such as delivery trucks, machinery, land and buildings. There are three sources of those funds: equity (funds supplied by the owners), debt (funds supplied by lenders) and revenue (funds supplied by customers). Most firms cannot rely on customers to supply all the funds needed all the time. Typically, firms start with an injection of capital by the owners. However, as firms grow, owners cannot always supply all the funds needed and funds from external sources, such as debt, are sought. Sometimes, owners invite others to share in the ownership by selling part of the equity.

Financial structure: the mix of all sources of debt and equity that fund the assets owned by the business

How does a business owner decide which source of funds — debt or equity — or which combination of funding is best? This decision encompasses what is called the financial structure of the business. The **financial structure** is the mix of debt and equity or all the items that appear in the liability section of the balance sheet and that fund the assets owned by the business. The balance sheet shows values relating to the business at a point in time. It consists basically of two classes of values — assets and liabilities. Assets (A) are funded by liabilities (L) and equity (E), and total assets equal the total of liabilities and equity. Put another way, equity equals assets minus liabilities: $E = A - L$.

Chapter 14 includes a discussion of the balance sheet. If you have not worked with financial statements before, or are a little rusty with the concepts, the first two sections of chapter 14 are recommended reading at this point.

In accordance with the assumption that business managers desire to maximise owners'/shareholders' wealth, the aim in planning and designing the financial structure is to minimise the cost of raising and using the desired level of funding. How managers achieve that aim is a major issue that encompasses much of the discussion in the remainder of this book.

Maturity or **term to maturity:** the contracted time that may elapse before the borrowed funds are to be repaid

With the goal of minimising the cost of funding, managers are obviously interested in the cost of each potential source of funds. We explore the cost of funds in chapters 7 and 10. However, cost can not be the only issue. Suitability of funding is important. What does 'suitability' mean? After all, a dollar is a dollar. Suitability really relates to maturity of the funds. The **maturity** or **term to maturity** of funds is the time that the contract stipulates may elapse before the funds are to be repaid. Firms need both short-term funds and long-term funds. It would be inappropriate, for example, for a firm to arrange a seven-day loan to purchase a factory site in an industrial estate. A seven-year loan would be much more apt. Similarly, a financial institution such as a building society, running its own business of funding 25-year housing loans, is far more comfortable taking in large long-term fixed deposits than many small, at-call savings deposits.

Apart from the need for funds to have appropriate maturity to suit the financing task at hand, there are other issues that a financial manager must consider. The most important of these are:

- the effect of debt on risk
- the effect of debt on control
- the varying taxation treatments of servicing payments to debt and equity.

The effect of debt on risk

Risk: defined in finance as the chance that the actual outcome from an investment will be different from the expected outcome

While lenders mostly prefer more to less and thus would like interest rates to be as high as possible, interest rates in the debt markets are set effectively by the supply and demand for funds and the perceived individual **risk** of each lending proposal. Risk may be perceived by some to mean only the possibility of loss, but in finance risk is defined as the chance that the actual outcome from an investment will be different from the expected outcome. Thus, it is a measure of volatility, so includes gains as well as losses. We consider risk further in chapter 5.

Financial risk: the risk involved in using debt as a source of finance

Financial distress: occurs when a firm's financial obligations can not be met or can be met only with major difficulty

Funds raised in the market as debt will often be cheaper than equity funds. Rational financial managers will thus go to the debt markets every time funds are needed, won't they? No, they will not. Why not? The answer to this question concerns the effect of debt in increasing **financial risk**. Financial risk is the risk involved in using debt as a source of finance. Debt must be serviced. That is, the providers of debt finance want to be paid for the use of their money and, of course, that is the nature of interest charged and interest payments made. So a firm with debt has fixed commitments to pay interest out of usually scarce cash balances. At any interest rate, the higher the debt, the higher the commitments to pay interest and normally to repay the debt within or at a given time. If at any time revenue falls below expected or planned levels, or cash costs are higher than expected, a firm with high debt faces the possibility of **financial distress**. Financial distress occurs when a firm's financial obligations can not be met or can be met only with major difficulty. Similarly, financial distress can occur where a firm has variable rate loans, interest rates rise and interest payments increase above planned levels. Firms with no debt are shielded from interest rate risk and do not face the possibility of financial distress from this source (although they are not immune to distress from other causes).

Financial distress can become so acute that the firm fails. Such was the case with many high-profile firms in the period 2000–2003 when, for example, HIH and One.Tel failed in Australia, Enron and World.Com failed in the United States and Parmalat failed in Italy. These firms simply ran out of cash and were unable to meet their financial obligations. In such cases, liquidators are appointed.

Liquidators are specialist professionals who identify the assets and liabilities of each failed business, liquidate the assets at the best prices available, identify the order in which creditors will be repaid and eventually pay creditors to the extent to which funds are available. Creditors with recognised first charges (security of first ranking) over assets are normally paid first and often are paid in full. Creditors with security of lower ranking may be paid a proportion of the value owed to them or indeed receive nothing. In cases of major failure, owners or shareholders are likely to receive nothing. Liquidators incur costs and charge their own fees. These costs and fees are effectively paid by the creditors, who receive less from the fixed pool of remaining funds because the liquidators are paid first. However, the alternative to this system of orderly cleaning-up of the financial mess left by a failed firm is possibly no payment at all for creditors.

The effect of debt on control

Normally, providers of debt funding have little or no control over the operations of a business. It is tempting to say that, provided a firm meets its contractual obligations regarding the debt, funds providers have no control over the operations of businesses. However, anecdotal evidence tends to suggest that this has not always been so in the case of small businesses. There have been cases reported in the press of banks trying to influence operational decisions of businesses even when they were not in loan default.

Notwithstanding these cases, lenders, unlike shareholders or partners, have no voting rights at firm meetings. However, once a firm defaults, lenders are able to exert considerable influence to try to protect their interests. This influence may be brought to bear through the appointment of administrators, receivers or liquidators. Administrators and receivers often run the firm for a period to try to trade their way out of the difficulty, or to maximise the value of the assets by ensuring they are part of a going concern. This was the case with the collapse of Ansett Airlines in 2001. The administrators ran the airline in a curtailed form for a period while trying to find a buyer, because airline assets are worth more when part of a going concern than as individual pieces of property or plant.

The effect of varying taxation treatments of payments to debt and equity

The payment to service debt is of course interest and the payments to service equity are dividends. Interest is a deductible expense for firms where that interest expense is incurred for the purposes of gaining assessable income. Difficulties have arisen and litigation ensued where the times of incurring the interest expense and earning the assessable income have tended to move apart. In *Steele's* case[5] in 1999, interest expense was incurred well before the asset yielded assessable income and, in *Brown's* case[6] in the same year, a loan used to finance a business was still being serviced with interest payments after the business had ceased yielding assessable income. In each case, the High Court and the Full Federal Court respectively found against the ATO and held that interest is deductible so long as that connection to assessable income remains.

Dividends, on the other hand, are not tax-deductible. However, as discussed in chapter 2, the difference in tax treatment for interest and dividends is not relevant to a financial manager's funding decisions where the tax payments of the company are fully integrated with the tax ation of its shareholders through dividend imputation. In these cases, a company effectively is no longer paying tax in its own right. It pays tax on behalf of its shareholders who are treated, in regard to their shareholding, as if they were sole traders or partners in their own businesses. The exceptions to this conclusion are discussed in chapter 2 and also apply here.

lo5

Discuss the main forms of debt offered in the financial markets.

Forms of debt

The principal sources of debt for businesses are other businesses, financial institutions and the financial markets. The principal forms are:

- trade credit
- overdrafts
- inventory or floor-plan finance
- promissory notes and commercial bills
- long-term bank loans

- debentures and unsecured notes
- corporate bonds.

These types of debt comprise four with shorter maturities listed first followed by three longer-maturity instruments. These are all discussed in greater detail in chapters 10 and 12. There are many other less significant forms of debt finance, some of which are discussed later in this book.

Trade credit: allows a purchase to be made without the immediate payment of cash

Trade credit is granted by one firm to another to facilitate trade. The granting of trade credit allows a purchase to be made without the immediate payment of cash or the use of a credit card. At one extreme, granting trade credit may be the only way sales can be made. However, normally trade credit is granted to reduce the paperwork that would be necessary to deal with many small billings and payments, or to obviate the need to entrust cash or pre-signed cheques to employees sent out to make purchases or collect ordered stock. Trade credit is usually granted for 30 days, although seven-day accounts are becoming more common, especially for purchases that are not likely to be repeated within a short period. Trade credit is usually free (to the receiver, not the provider). Exceptions and variations are discussed in the later chapters. The volume of trade credit granted is enormous, as nearly all business entities grant credit to other entities at some time or other.

Overdraft: a permitted over-drawing of funds beyond the credit balance in the account

Overdrafts are provided by financial institutions on current or cheque accounts. An overdraft is a permitted over-drawing of funds beyond the credit balance in the account. Thus, a firm with a \$50 000 overdraft limit on a current account with a \$10 000 credit balance can write a cheque for \$30 000 on the account and have it successfully cleared. The bank will use the \$10 000 of the business's own funds and \$20 000 of the overdraft limit to clear the cheque. Thus, this business can spend another \$30 000 before the money runs out. Successful applicants for overdrafts are normally charged establishment fees and account keeping fees, as well as an interest rate on outstanding funds based on the indicator or benchmark rate plus a margin for perceived risk. Recently, the average margin has been about 3.5%, so that the average overdraft rate has been about 3.5% above the cash rate. Overdrafts are a major source of business finance.

Inventory finance or **floor-plan finance:** provided to car and whitegoods dealers to buy stock to place on showroom floors; secured by the stock itself

In Australia, **inventory finance** or **floor-plan finance** is normally provided by finance companies. Finance companies were established by the major banks to lend to the riskier end of the retail (consumer) market during the period when banks' activities were constrained by heavy regulation. Nowadays, that constraint has decreased considerably. Nevertheless, floor-plan finance is a major part of finance companies' business.

Finance is provided to car and whitegoods dealers to buy stock to place on showroom floors. The loans are secured by the stock. Apart from providing finance to the retailer, a profitable business relationship often develops between the financier and the retailer. Retailers may use the financier as a preferred supplier of finance for their customers when they make purchases. Floor-plan finance is a significant source of finance for retailers with high-value inventories. A dealer, for example, with 30 new vehicles on a showroom floor or in nearby storage would have about \$1 million of stock in these new units alone. In addition, there would be second-hand vehicles plus parts stock that must be financed.

Promissory notes: 'P-notes' are promises by the borrowers to repay the face value of the instrument at a stated future date

Commercial bills: promises by the borrowers to repay at a stated future date the face value of the instrument, which is normally guaranteed by a third party such as a bank

Face value: the amount that will be repaid upon maturity of the debt security. It is specified at the time the security is issued.

Promissory notes and **commercial bills** are forms of short-term finance that, unlike trade credit, overdrafts and inventory finance, are marketable. That is, the debt may be sold from lender to lender. Promissory notes ('P-notes') and commercial bills are promises to repay the **face value** of the instrument at a stated future date. Both are discount securities — the price of the security will be less than the face value until the maturity date. Maturities range normally from 30 days to 180 days. The chief difference between the two securities is that commercial bills are usually guaranteed ('accepted') by a bank, so that the risk of default is small, whereas P-notes carry the risk associated with the borrower.

In early 2007 when the cash rate was 6.25%, the commercial bill rate remained in the range 6.35–6.5%. Thus, it is obvious that bill finance is considerably cheaper than overdraft finance. Even so, smaller firms tend to stay with overdraft finance due to its simplicity and ease of establishment.

Long-term bank loans come in many forms with many variations in conditions. The full array are explored in chapter 12. However, some of the most popular are fully drawn advances, instalment loans and interest-only loans. Fully drawn advances are loans where the full contracted sum is drawn initially and the principal is repaid according to a set schedule. The interest rate is normally variable and the timing of interest payments may be left open to negotiation during the term of the loan. Instalment loans are also fully drawn at the outset, but are subject to a schedule of fixed repayments, comprising both principal and interest, over the course of the loan. Interest-only loans are repaid at the maturity of the contract, but interest is paid on the loan amount during the interim.

In Australia, at November 2006 bank loans to non-financial corporations amounted to more than $330 billion.[7] Total bank loans amounted to about double the bill finance.

Debentures: fixed-term debt securities issued under a prospectus. They are secured by assets.

Unsecured notes: fixed-term debt securities issued under a prospectus. Unlike debentures, they are not secured by assets.

Corporate bonds: debt instruments where the issuer receives the face value of the bonds at the outset and pays a coupon, usually six-monthly. The face value is repaid when the bonds mature.

Coupon: the stated rate of interest paid on a bond

Debentures and **unsecured notes** are sources of finance limited to companies and, in Australia, normally limited to finance companies and general financiers. They are debt securities issued under a prospectus; debentures are secured by assets, unsecured notes are not. They have fixed maturities and pay interest periodically. As an unsecured loan, unsecured notes carry a higher interest rate than debentures to compensate investors for considerably higher risk. Debentures and unsecured notes may be traded.

In November 2006, finance companies and general financiers had about $67 billion in borrowings outstanding from Australian residents, including P-notes, bills, debentures and unsecured notes.[8] In the environment of the time, the interest rates on debentures were about 6.15% depending on maturity.

Corporate bonds have really only started to develop rapidly as a source of business funding since 1999. A company issuing bonds receives the face value (or close to it) of the bonds at the outset and pays a stated rate of interest ('the **coupon**'), usually six-monthly until the bonds mature. At maturity, investors are paid back the face value. Corporate bonds are normally unsecured. Because of the lack of a formal security mechanism, credit rankings carried out by ratings firms such as Moody's and Standard & Poor's are extremely important. Corporate bonds in Australia are ranked AAA, AA, A and BBB, with AAA being the highest ranking (that is, the bond with the lowest perceived credit risk). In December 2006, the yields for bonds of the first three rankings with 1–5 years to maturity were, respectively, 6.6%, 6.63% and 6.76%.[9] Bonds with BBB ranking, issued by firms considered to present high credit risk, are the so-called 'junk' bonds. They are perceived not to have a risk profile suitable for investment by fund managers managing funds on behalf of others. Table 3.1 provides a summary of the forms of debt described so far.

Table 3.1 Debt classified by term to maturity

Short-term debt (< 1 year)	Long-term debt (> 1 year)
Trade credit	Debentures
Overdraft	Unsecured notes
Floor-plan finance	Corporate bonds
Promissory notes	
Commercial bills	

The corporate bond market is in its infancy in Australia, but has been growing strongly. This has been because large companies have seen the opportunity to move from intermediated finance to direct finance through the capital markets. From the funds supply side, funds managers have welcomed the opportunity to invest in relatively low-risk fixed-interest products at a time when the supply of Commonwealth bonds is falling due to the repayment and contraction of Commonwealth Government debt. In November 2006, the corporate bond market comprised $45 billion outstanding, about nine times its size in 1997.[10] Another similar instrument growing strongly in popularity is the kangaroo bond, a long-term debt security issued in the Australian market by non-residents of Australia. The following 'finance world' feature provides more information on this security.

We learn how to calculate the value of a bond in chapter 6 and calculate the return on a bond in chapter 7.

FINANCE WORLD

Kangaroo bonds

Kangaroo bonds are long-term debt securities issued by non-residents in the Australian domestic market. They are denominated in Australian dollars, documented to Australian legal requirements, settled through Austraclear, a central depository providing clearing and settlement facilities to the Australian financial markets, and listed on the Australian Securities Exchange.

The rapid growth in Kangaroo bond issues in the Australian market has given rise to an interest in the nature, trend and impact of this type of bond on Australia's international investment statistics. While Kangaroo bonds have been issued for a number of years, this article focuses on the period from 2000–01, when they became significant in terms of Australia's international investment position.

The growth of non-government bonds, such as Kangaroo bonds, is due in part to the reduction of Australian government bond issues. Non-resident financial institutions are the dominant issuers and most are resident in the United States of America (USA).

...

One of the notable contributors to the growth in the non-government bond market has been the increase in non-resident bond issuers (Kangaroo bonds). Kangaroo bonds issued increased to $15.2b in 2003–04 from a level of $1.8b in 2002–03. In 2004–05, non-resident borrowers entered the bond market with $8.4b in issues, of which approximately $5.8b (70%) were taken up by residents.

For Australian investors, Kangaroo bonds became attractive during this period, as did all highly rated corporate bond issues. The credit spread (the price difference between AA bonds from corporate issuers when compared with similarly denominated government issues) decreased in the first half of 2003 then picked up again in 2004. With the decreasing availability of government bonds, AA corporate bonds were being favoured as the best alternative in fixed income securities. This lowered the cost of borrowing for corporate borrowers and helped to increase the attractiveness of Australian denominated debt for non-resident issuers.

...

Anecdotally, it is suggested that two main drivers explained trends in Kangaroo bond transactions. From the issuer's point of view, the first commonly quoted reason for the growth in Kangaroo bonds was a desire to diversify funding. Diversifying currency exposures for issuers lowers the risks associated with foreign borrowings. The second is the widening interest rate basis swap. This widening effectively made it cheaper for borrowers to hedge against interest rate movements.[11]

FINANCE WORKSHOP 3.3

Suppose you were starting up your own business. Your firm develops innovative software for niche business uses, such as keeping track of breeding and genetic records at laboratories that breed predator insects for use in agriculture. Assuming the business grows successfully, what debt instruments for which purposes would you expect to use in:

(a) the first year of business

(b) the next 5 years of business

(c) the long term?

lo6

Understand equity and its raising.

Equity instruments

Equity instruments by their very nature relate to corporations. The other forms of business structures do not have equity instruments, even though they have owners and the owners have equity in their businesses.

Although there are many variations in the way shares are issued (for example, by way of initial public offers, employee share plans and rights issues), there are three main types of shares or equity instruments. They are:

- ordinary shares (fully paid)
- contributing shares or partly paid ordinary shares
- preference shares.

Ordinary share: evidence of part-ownership of a company

Ordinary shares are the most common form of equity instrument. All corporations have ordinary shares on issue and a share is proof of part-ownership of a company. If a corporation has 1 000 000 shares issued, then a person holding 10 000 shares owns 1% of the business. That person will be entitled to dividends and will be paid on the basis of so many cents per share, possibly twice a year. When two dividend payments are made, the first payment of the financial year is called an interim dividend and the latter is the final dividend. If the business is a listed company and its shares are quoted on a stock exchange, then the price of the shares will be set by the forces of supply and demand on the day. Theoretically, the price of the share will be the present value (PV) of expected future dividends. We learn how to calculate the price of an ordinary share in chapter 6 and calculate the return in chapter 7.

Shares rank behind the claims of all other interested parties. Thus, in the matter of dividends, shareholders may experience many periods when no payments are received because the firm has not made sufficient profits. Similarly, in the case of the winding-up of the company, shareholders often receive nothing as there are not sufficient assets to realise to pay out the shareholders as well as the higher priority claimants, such as secured debt holders.

Contributing shares or **partly paid shares:** ordinary shares where the full subscription amount has not yet been paid to the issuing company

Contributing shares or **partly paid shares** historically have not been a particularly important instrument in the general industrial market; rather, they have been favoured by mining and exploration companies. Government privatisations, including the sale of part of Telstra by the Commonwealth Government and the sale of its holding of Suncorp-Metway by the Queensland Government were managed in this fashion.

The rationale for offering partly paid shares stems mainly from marketing concerns, but also from a belief that there may not be sufficient funds available to take up the offer of investment. In the case of both Telstra and Suncorp-Metway, the government vendors were concerned that as many people as possible, especially among their political constituents, could take up the shares and thus assume ownership of important formerly public assets. If the price of a fully paid share were to be set at a bit under $6, for example, some people might say they could not afford a reasonably-sized parcel of, say, 500 shares, but they could find $1500. You might quite reasonably suggest that they could buy 250 shares at about $6 instead but human nature is a funny thing (see the following 'behavioural perspective' discussion). Some potential investors would then say it was not worth the bother, so would not invest at all. By setting the price at $3, with a further $3 to be paid in, say 18 months, more people are attracted to the offer as they don't see the initial price as a barrier and they are able to save the final instalment money in the intervening time. Partly paid shares have recently been called instalment receipts.

Preference shares: hybrid equity instruments with some characteristics of equity and some of debt. They normally have a fixed dividend that has preference over the payment of ordinary dividends.

Preference shares are a hybrid equity instrument with some characteristics of equity and some of debt. Preference shares normally have a fixed dividend that has preference over the payment of ordinary dividends. Thus, a company may issue 10% preference shares which have rights to a fixed 10% dividend attached. This is a characteristic of debt. Additionally, preference shares may have a stipulated repayment time when the company effectively repurchases the shares or they may instead convert to ordinary shares. In the event of a company's liquidation, preference shares rank for repayment after debt but before ordinary shares. We learn how to price preference shares in chapter 6 and to calculate the return in chapter 7.

lo7

Discuss the role of regulators and the ASX.

Regulators and regulation

The discussion so far has introduced you to many different markets. Just as in our daily lives, there are people operating in the financial markets who desire to profit personally at the expense of others to a degree which goes beyond normal legal and ethical standards. In our daily lives we have the police and the legal system to protect our interests. In the financial markets, we have regulators and a comprehensive body of legislation to ensure a standard of behaviour is maintained.

The Australian financial markets are regulated by three government bodies working closely together plus another, the Australian Competition and Consumer Commission (ACCC), which keeps a watching brief with regard to competition and consumer welfare. The chief government regulators are the:

- Reserve Bank of Australia (RBA)
- Australian Prudential Regulation Authority (APRA)
- Australian Securities and Investments Commission (ASIC).

In addition, the Australian Securities Exchange (ASX) is charged with a regulatory role in relation to listed corporations.

BEHAVIOURAL PERSPECTIVE

Framing choices

People have preferences that are innate (part of their character make-up) or that have been instilled in them through their upbringing, education and socio-cultural environments. These personal preferences will affect the decisions they make. If the choice theory which underlies both consumer and business decisions is to be considered acceptably robust, then decision makers should have a fixed order of preferences in any given situation and the fixed order should be independent of the methods used to discover the preferences.

However, it has been shown that preference decisions are affected by the context of the data supporting them, the framing. In experimentation, subjects were asked to choose between two bets, essentially one with a high probability of winning a small amount (for example, a 90% chance of winning $101) and the other with a low probability of winning a large amount (for example, a 9% chance of winning $1000). The expected values were about the same, so the subjects were expected to show indifference. They were also asked to value each bet in terms of the minimum amounts they would accept to sell the rights to each bet or the maximum amounts they would pay to buy each bet. People who preferred the small amount assigned larger values to the large-amount bet, even though it had a smaller probability. The converse was also found. This phenomenon is called preference reversal and it contravenes the principle that decision makers have fixed orders of preferences.

Dominance refers to consistency in appreciation of better attributes. It implies that the most outstanding attribute or benefit will consistently maintain its premier position, no matter how it is presented. If outcome A is better than outcome B in all respects, then A will be preferred to B. This principle is based on the idea, with which most of us will readily agree, that more is preferred to less. Experimentation testing this principle incorporated the following choices and found the principle does not always hold.

(i) A. a sure $240; or B. a 25% chance to gain $1000 and a 75% chance to gain $0;

(ii) C. a sure loss of $750; or D. a 75% chance to lose $1000 and a 25% chance to lose $0.[12]

The expected values are: A $240; B $250 (0.25 × 1000); C –$750; and D –$750 (0.75 × –1000).

The responses from experimentation were: A was chosen by 84% of players; B by 16%; C by 13%; and D by 87%.

A total of 73% of subjects selected both A and D, while 3% chose B and C. However, the sum of B and C (equal to a loss of $500 in aggregate) is clearly a more favourable outcome than the sum of A and D (equal to a loss of $510), yet only 3% preferred this better outcome. We discuss expected values further in chapter 5.

A rational investor would be indifferent to the choice of either 500 partly paid shares that required a payment of $3 today, or 250 fully paid shares at $6 paid today (assuming a further 250 shares could be purchased for $6 at the time the second $3 instalment was to be made on the partially paid shares). The 'frame' in this example is the investor's view of what constitutes a 'reasonably-sized parcel' of shares. Neither of the alternatives dominates the other.

Reserve Bank of Australia

The RBA was set up under the *Reserve Bank Act 1959* as Australia's central bank. It has an important role in ensuring the stability of the financial system as a whole. Without the services of the RBA in managing the financial system, business would not enjoy the financial stability that it currently does and would not be able to operate so easily within the financial system.

The RBA, under its Act, is obliged to manage the economy to facilitate the stability of prices and the full employment of the economy's resources. To achieve these ends, it controls monetary policy independently of the government in power. Monetary policy in Australia is essentially managed through the control of the price of money. The RBA board sets the cash rate — the interest rate at which funds are lent overnight between banks. Once that rate is announced, officers of the RBA conduct open market operations to ensure that the desired rate is maintained.

Open market operations are the buying and selling of Commonwealth Government securities — Commonwealth bonds — by the RBA in the money and capital markets. The RBA also enters re-purchase agreements or 'repos' with holders of securities, whereby securities are bought or sold with an attached agreement to sell or buy back the same securities at a later date. In addition, the RBA may buy or sell foreign exchange ('forex') or make forex swaps in order to change the supply of funds in the Australian financial system. We look at swaps in detail in chapter 15.

Note that, contrary to general belief, the RBA does not have a formal 'lender of the last resort' role when a financial institution gets into financial difficulties. However, that does not rule out government taking a role and 'bailing out' depositors/investors when a financial institution fails. Such actions are usually taken for political reasons rather than for the protection of financial stability in the system, although it could be argued that the action is taken to prevent contagion or the spread of financial instability. In effect, such rescue missions use taxes paid by most of the people to redistribute funds to those people who have suffered financial loss. The RBA, however, may increase liquidity in the whole system through open-market operations in a time of crisis to try to prevent the spread of instability.

Australian Prudential Regulation Authority

APRA is the prudential regulator of ADIs. APRA was set up in July 1998, after the Wallis Financial Systems Inquiry recommended in 1997 that prudential regulation of the three types of authorised deposit-taking institutions — banks, building societies and credit unions — reside with the one body. Previously the RBA had regulated banks.

APRA generally takes the view that the management of these ADIs must remain responsible for sound operations and prudent processes. However, to give that management guidance as to what constitutes prudent management, Australian authorities adopted the Bank of International Settlements' (BIS) capital adequacy guidelines. The capital contributed by shareholders is essentially the last line of defence for any banking institution, should it encounter liquidity problems. Therefore, APRA specifies a minimum level of capital to be held by ADIs. The minimum capital to be held is determined by the types of assets the ADI holds. The loans made by ADIs are the major part of their assets, and the deposits they receive are part of their liabilities.

Australian Securities and Investments Commission

ASIC was formed at the same time as APRA in 1998 to continue and expand the role undertaken by the previous Australian Securities Commission. ASIC administers the *Corporations Act 2001*, which provides for federal regulation of companies.

ASIC is concerned with the management and maintenance of financial market integrity, consumer protection and maintenance of confidence by all stakeholders in the financial system. A feature of regulation in this area in recent times is harmonisation of rules and requirements for most types of financial products including investments, insurance and superannuation. The *Financial Services Reform Act 2001* was passed by Parliament, after an extensive consultation period, to introduce a large suite of reforms, all aimed at lifting the standard of services across the financial service industry, improving confidence and ensuring that most products are regulated in a similar manner.

Australian Securities Exchange

The ASX through its subsidiary ASX Markets Supervision regulates the behaviour of companies that are listed with it and traded on it with respect to the handling and release of information about operations, and results that might be expected to be market-sensitive. Market-sensitive information is information that could be expected to have an impact on the share price. Thus, news of a major new contract might lift a firm's share price, as potential buyers perceive that the company may make higher profits and dividends in future. They will be willing to pay more now. If many people have the same view, the price of the share will be bid up. In contrast, news that a company had suffered another major loss overseas will be highly likely to depress the share price.

Issues with the dissemination of price-sensitive information include timing and scope of distribution. The ASX demands that such information be available to all stakeholders as quickly as possible. Thus, news should not be bottled up within the company for weeks or even more days than necessary. The reason for this is that the longer news is withheld, the more likely that insider trading can occur. Insider trading occurs when one or two investors gain information in advance of the general investing public and use that information to buy or sell shares in order to make personal profits before a general buying or selling movement builds up. Insider trading destroys confidence in the system.

The other issue with regard to information concerns the briefing of analysts. Financial service providers often employ analysts to undertake research on firms listed on the ASX. In order to do their jobs, the analysts often visit firms and receive briefings on future prospects. Firms are happy to do this, because when analysts recommend to their clients to buy the firm's shares it helps to keep share prices buoyant and helps in future capital raisings. When does this sort of briefing move from a legitimate exercise to the first step in insider trading? The ASX has wrestled with this issue and has declared that the gist of the information given in such briefings should also be released to the general public.

Firms that do not comply with ASX listing requirements may have trading in their shares suspended. Similarly, firms that do not respond appropriately to an ASX query may have trading suspended. In addition to these requirements, the ASX operates two electronic screening systems that aim to detect transactions that fall outside given parameters. These transactions are then investigated to determine that no illegal activity has occurred.

The following 'corporate financial governance' feature highlights the operations of ASX Markets Supervision. For further information about any aspects of these operations, go to the Australian Securities Exchange website.

CORPORATE FINANCIAL GOVERNANCE

ASX Markets Supervision — the ASX markets supervisor

On 1 July 2006 ASX placed its operational supervisory functions in a separate subsidiary called ASX Markets Supervision. ASX Markets Supervision is a subsidiary of ASX Limited. The subsidiary was created to provide greater transparency and accountability of ASX's supervisory operations, strengthen market integrity and address the perception of conflict between ASX's regulatory and commercial functions. ASX Markets Supervision comprises the three core elements of supervision, Issuers, Participants and Enforcement, along with the Disciplinary Tribunal.

The head of ASX Markets Supervision is the Chief Supervisory Officer (CSO) (currently Eric Mayne) who makes all operational supervisory decisions. The CSO does not report to the CEO of ASX but reports to the Board of ASX Markets Supervision.

ASX Markets Supervision organisation chart

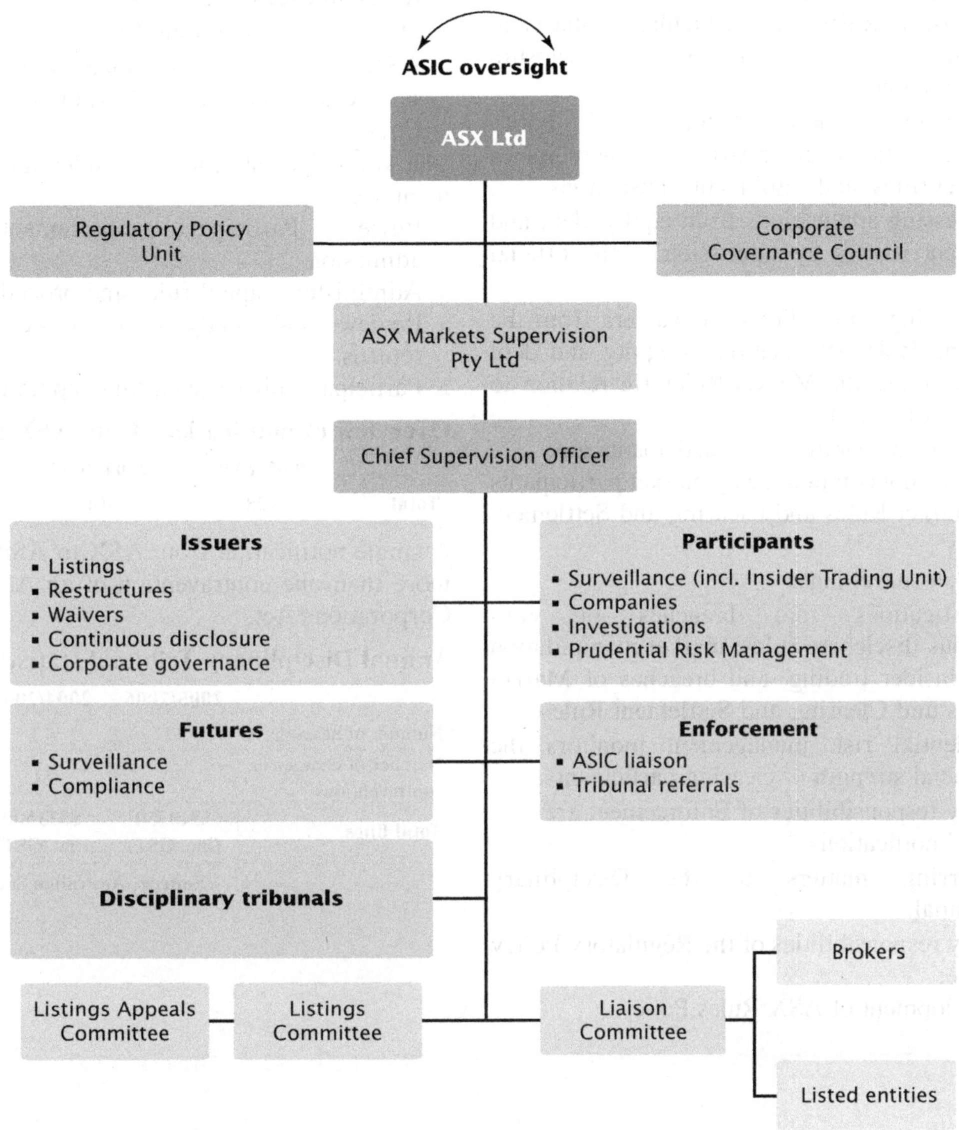

How ASX supervises the market

ASX Markets Supervision oversees compliance with ASX's Operating Rules (Listing Rules, Market Rules, Clearing Rules and Settlement Rules). This involves:

- Supervising listed entities
- Supervising trading activity in the market
- Supervising market participants such as stockbrokers, and clearing and settlement operators
- Meeting the regulatory obligations of ASX under the Corporations Act and
- Cooperating with other regulatory bodies like ASIC and ACCC.

The key responsibilities of Issuers are:

- Monitoring compliance by listed entities with the Listing Rules, with particular emphasis on continuous and periodic disclosure requirements
- Reviewing proposals for listed entity reorganisations and restructures, new issues of securities, and significant transactions
- Processing applications from equity, debt and warrant issuers for admission to the official list
- Processing applications for waivers from the Listing Rules (in relation to equity and debt issuers) and the Market Rules (in relation to warrant issuers).

The key responsibilities of Participants are:

- Monitoring compliance by market participants of Market Rules and Clearing and Settlement Rules
- Market surveillance
- Investigations into breaches of continuous disclosure rules, market manipulation and insider trading, and breaches of Market Rules and Clearing and Settlement Rules
- Prudential risk management monitors the financial strength of clearing participants.

The key responsibilities of Enforcement are:

- ASIC notifications
- Referring matters to the Disciplinary Tribunal.

The key responsibilities of the Regulatory Policy Unit are:

- Development of ASX Rules Policy
- Responding to government papers
- Rules amendments policy
- Streamlining Operating Rules
- ASX corporate governance policy, including secretariat for ASX Corporate Governance Council.

The key responsibilities of Prudential Risk Management are:

- Review Participant requirements prior to admission
- Administers capital rules and procedures
- Review and analysis of participant capital returns
- Participant advice regarding capital requirements.

Overview of notifications from ASX to ASIC

	2005/2006	2004/2005
Total	128	101

A single notification from ASX to ASIC may include more than one contravention of an ASX Rule or the Corporations Act.

Annual Disciplinary Tribunal statistics

	2005/2006	2004/2005	2003/2004
Number of hearings	17	13	17
Number of charges or contraventions	30	51	68
Total fines	$310 750 (inc. GST)	$533 500 (inc. GST)	$915 200 (inc. GST)

Source: Australian Securities Exchange.[13]

executive summary

lo1 describe the roles of the financial markets

- The financial markets in Australia fulfil many roles, not least of which are:
  - facilitating business and trade, making the production and exchange of goods and services easier and more efficient
  - facilitating saving by individuals to allow for future consumption
  - providing financial services which allow participants to balance their risk tolerance with their requirements for both returns and cash.

lo2 discuss how business operations are financed

- Business operations are financed directly or indirectly through intermediation.
- Direct finance takes place when the saver, who is the supplier of funds, makes a deal directly with the business that needs the funds.
- Direct financiers may be related parties or unrelated members of the public who contribute funds in public offers.
- Intermediated finance is supplied by ADIs and RFCs.

lo3 describe the financial service institutions in the financial markets

- The institutions that supply financial services are the ADIs and the RFCs.
- ADIs are the banks, building societies and credit unions, of which the banks are by far the largest institutions with about 97% of the market.
- The RFCs include the money market corporations, pastoral finance companies, finance companies, general financiers and intra-group financiers.

lo4 differentiate between different sectors of the financial markets

- The whole structure of the financial markets can be divided in many ways, such as into primary and secondary, public and private, money and capital, and debt and equity.
- The primary market is the market in which securities are offered for the first time, while the secondary markets deal with sales of securities which have been issued by their respective firms in the past.
- Public issues are issues of securities to the public, normally by means of a prospectus. A prospectus is a document that provides details of a new issue of securities to the public. It normally contains details of past financial performance and projected future performance. Private placements are issues of securities made by negotiation directly with purchasers. Many private placements are facilitated by merchant banks that bring together suppliers and users of funds in return for fees.
- Money markets deal in short-term debt; that is, debt that has less than one year to maturity. The capital markets deal in long-term instruments; that is, instruments with maturities greater than one year.
- Debt provides funds that must be repaid to lenders; equity finance provides funds which owners supply and for which there is no right of repayment. Managers must decide on the debt and equity mix in financing.

- The mix of debt and equity is called the 'financial structure' of the business. The aim of structuring finances is to minimise the cost of finance for the business.
- Debt increases financial risk in a business. Debt must be serviced with the payment of interest. Eventually debt must be repaid. The call on cash may lead to financial distress.

lo5 discuss the main forms of debt offered in the financial markets

The principal forms of debt are:
- trade credit — allowing the easy purchase of goods and services
- overdrafts — a common business loan facility attached to a cheque account
- inventory or floor-plan finance — to finance the purchase of stock
- promissory notes and commercial bills — very common short-term finance provided at favourable interest rates
- long-term bank loans
- debentures and unsecured notes — finance provided in the debt markets
- corporate bonds — a strongly growing area of debt finance for corporations.

lo6 understand equity and its raising

- There are three main types of shares or equity instruments. They are ordinary shares (fully paid), contributing shares or partly paid ordinary shares, and preference shares.
- Ordinary shares are the most common equity instrument.
- Ordinary shares are proof of part-ownership in a corporation.
- Ordinary shares rank behind the claims of all other interested parties in the event of the firm's being wound up.
- Contributing or partly paid shares are normally ordinary shares where only part of the subscription price has been paid.
- Partly paid shares are attractive to firms wanting to expand their shareholder base and allow those shareholders to contract for larger eventual stakes in the company.
- Preference shares are hybrid shares with aspects of debt as well as equity.
- Preference shares normally have a fixed dividend with preference over ordinary shares with regard to payment.

lo7 discuss the role of regulators and the ASX

- The chief government regulators are the Reserve Bank of Australia (RBA), the Australian Prudential Regulation Authority (APRA), and the Australian Securities and Investments Commission (ASIC). The RBA has an important role in ensuring the stability of the financial system as a whole.
- The RBA under its Act is obliged to manage the economy to facilitate the stability of prices and the full employment of the economy's resources.
- To achieve these ends, the RBA controls monetary policy independently of the government in power.
- Monetary policy in Australia is essentially managed through the control of the price of money.

- The RBA board sets the cash rate, the interest rate at which funds are lent overnight between banks. Once that rate is announced, officers of the bank buy or sell cash to ensure that the desired rate is maintained in the market.
- Contrary to general belief, the RBA does not have a formal 'lender of the last resort' role when a financial institution gets into financial difficulties.
- APRA is the prudential regulator of authorised deposit-taking institutions — banks, building societies and credit unions.
- APRA generally takes the view that that the management of ADIs must remain responsible for sound operations and prudent processes.
- APRA has adopted the Bank of International Settlements' (BIS) capital adequacy guidelines.
- The capital contributed by shareholders is essentially the last line of defence for any banking institution, should it encounter liquidity problems. Therefore, APRA specifies a minimum level of capital be held by ADIs.
- The minimum capital is determined by the types of assets the ADI holds.
- ASIC administers the *Corporation Act 2001*, which provides for federal regulation of companies.
- ASIC is concerned with the management and maintenance of financial market integrity, consumer protection and maintenance of confidence by all stakeholders in the financial system.
- A feature of regulation in this area in recent times is harmonisation of rules and requirements for most types of financial products including investments, insurance and superannuation.
- The ASX regulates the behaviour of companies that are listed with it and traded on it with respect to the handling and release of information about operations and results that might be expected to be market-sensitive.
- Issues with the dissemination of price-sensitive information include timing and scope of distribution.
- The ASX demands that such information be available to all stakeholders as quickly as possible.
- Firms that do not comply with ASX listing requirements may have trading in their shares suspended.
- ASX uses a fully owned subsidiary, ASX Markets Supervision, to manage supervision and compliance.

Key terms

secondary markets, p. 66
securities, p. 66
term to maturity, p. 68
trade credit, p. 71
transaction costs, p. 63
unsecured notes, p. 72

Learning chart

Learning objective	Questions	Self-test problems	Financial problems
lo1 describe the roles of the financial markets	3.1, 3.2	3.1	
lo2 discuss how business operations are financed	3.3, 3.4	3.1, 3.2	3.1, 3.2, 3.3, 3.4
lo3 describe the financial service institutions in the financial markets	3.5, 3.6		
lo4 differentiate between different sectors of the financial markets	3.7, 3.8, 3.9, 3.10, 3.11, 3.12		
lo5 discuss the main forms of debt offered in the financial markets	3.13, 3.14, 3.15, 3.16		3.1, 3.2, 3.3, 3.4
lo6 understand equity and its raising	3.17		3.1, 3.2, 3.3, 3.4
lo7 discuss the role of regulators and the ASX	3.18, 3.18, 3.20		

Questions

3.1 'Savers overseas fund our lavish Australian lifestyle', says Rob Steele, a self-promoting financial expert. What is the evidence for this remark?

3.2 We regularly see the most recent balance of trade reported on the evening TV news and normally imports exceed exports. Why is that? What effect would you expect this imbalance to have on the value of our dollar?

3.3 Define direct finance. Is it necessary to know the borrower of funds personally to be able to lend surplus funds? Give an example where:
(a) it is necessary to know the borrower
(b) it is not necessary to know the borrower.

3.4 Explain the role of intermediation. Who are the intermediaries in the Australian financial system?

3.5 What are ADIs? Which class of institutions controls the majority of ADI assets?

3.6 'Loans from banks are a good source of funding for my business. If my business fails, I don't have to apologise to anyone personally; it's just a book entry and it doesn't hurt anybody.' Is this true? Explain your reasoning.

3.7 What are the primary financial markets? Why is it critically important for the effective operation of the primary markets to have well-developed secondary markets where investors can trade with confidence?

3.8 Explain why a firm looking for $1 million probably would not try to raise it by public issue.

3.9 The ASX provides a secondary market in equities. Who provides a secondary market in debt instruments in Australia?

3.10 What is a prospectus? Why do firms prepare these documents?

3.11 Differentiate money and capital markets. Who operates in each market in Australia?

3.12 Define financial structure. Why are managers interested in this issue?

3.13 'Debt can be risky. You can lose your business through having it.' Is this true? Explain your reasoning.

3.14 Explain the circumstances when a firm should not take into account taxation requirements when deciding on a funding mix.

3.15 What is the role of floor-plan finance? Which firms are large providers of this type of finance?

3.16 Why are commercial bills popular with firms wanting finance? How could a firm use commercial bills to fund long-term financing needs?

3.17 Why did the government use partly paid shares as the instruments of choice for the first and second tranches of the sale of Telstra?

3.18 What is the current role of the RBA in relation to small business?

3.19 What are the chief concerns of ASIC?

3.20 In what aspects of a listed firm's behaviour is the ASX most interested? Why?

Self-test problems

3.1 Kate and Anna Shutak own a profitable nature-tours business, Shutak Tours. Kate leads many of the tours and Anna mostly looks after the bookings and administration. They own the building from which the firm operates, which was recently valued at $400 000. It cost them $200 000 six years ago. They also have about $55 000 of fixtures, fittings and office equipment. They own two station wagons that they use for personal travel when these vehicles are not needed to transport tourists. They have a 4-wheel drive bus for desert travel. The cars are worth about $15 000 each and the bus, worth $110 000, is leased under an arrangement whereby they do not actually own the vehicle but pay a monthly leasing fee. Their financing arrangements are as follows: $50 000 overdraft drawn to $22 000, trade creditors $15 500, fully drawn advance of $200 000 repaid to $85 600.

(a) What is the gross value of Shutak Tours' assets?

(b) What is the net value of Shutak Tours' assets?

(c) If you owned Shutak Tours, would you sell the business (including the listed assets) for either of the values you worked out in (a) and (b)? Explain.

(d) What percentage of total assets were funded by debt?

(e) What is the ratio of debt to equity? Do you think this is a conservative or risky ratio?

3.2 (a) From the data given in the opening scene to this chapter, calculate approximately how many shares were on issue by ABC Learning Centres in both 2001 and 2006. (Your answer may not exactly correspond with numbers in the annual reports because of averaging or issues made throughout the year.)

(b) From the data given in the opening scene to this chapter, calculate the payout ratios for each year. Payout ratio is the ratio of dividend payments to earnings. Why would a firm not pay almost 100% of its earnings as dividends?

Solutions to self-test problems

3.1 (a) Gross assets are:

Building	$400 000	Current market price is most relevant
Fittings	55 000	
Cars	30 000	Assume valued as business assets
Bus	nil	Leased, not owned
Total	$485 000	

(b) Liabilities are:

Overdraft	$22 000	The agreed limit is irrelevant
Trade creditors	15 000	
FDA	85 000	Current amount outstanding
Total	$122 000	
Net assets	$363 000	$485 000 − $122 000

(c) I would not sell the business for either $485 000 or $363 000. There are two issues here. First, there is the matter of the debts. If the business is structured as a partnership, then the debts 'belong' to the owners (if a company, the debts would be the responsibility of the company and may be transferred with the assets on sale). Thus the owners on sale of the business would have to pay back the $122 000 in debts. So they would not accept $363 000 for their business.

However, if they accepted the gross value of the listed assets alone, they are not putting any value on the operations of the business. We know it is a profitable business. Hence it has something more to sell apart from the physical assets. This is called goodwill. The owners could calculate a value for the goodwill of the business by multiplying the average annual profit by a factor that appears reasonable. Then, to arrive at a sale price for the business, they would add this value to the value of the gross assets.

(d) $\frac{\text{Debt}}{\text{total assets}} = \frac{122\,000}{485\,000} = 25$

(e) $\frac{\text{Debt}}{\text{equity}} = \frac{122\,000}{363\,000} = 33.6\%$. This would normally be viewed as conservative.

3.2 (a) The data give us profits after tax and earnings per share. Therefore $\frac{\text{profits}}{\text{earnings per share}}$ should give us an indication of the number of shares.

In 2001, $\frac{\$3.25\text{m}}{0.299} = 10.87$ million shares.

In 2006, $\frac{\$81\text{m}}{0.277} = 292.4$ million shares.

(b) Payout (2001) $= \frac{0.14}{0.299} = 46.8\%$

Payout (2006) $= \frac{0.15}{0.277} = 54.2\%$

Firms use internally generated funds to finance expansion. Hence, it is to be expected that a strongly growing firm such as ABC would have a relatively low payout ratio. (The major banks, in contrast, pay out 60–65% of earnings.)

Financial problems

3.1 Alison Toogood owns and runs a toy store. Sales amounted to about $400 000 last year and the cost of goods sold was about 70% of sales. Alison spent another $80 000 on wages, rent, rates, phone, power, insurance and other cash costs. She runs the business as a sole trader and drew $500 per week for living expenses. The business has been valued as a going concern at $360 000 (she refused an offer of this amount yesterday) plus the value of the stock, which is about $90 000. She has a cheque account with a $50 000 overdraft limit. The current balance in this account is $10 000 in the red (negative). She also has a fully drawn advance of $70 000 on which she paid last year about $6000 interest.

(a) What was the profit made by the toy shop last year?

(b) What is the value of Alison's equity in the business?

(c) What percentage of assets is funded by equity and what percentage by debt?

(d) What is the debt-to-equity ratio (that is, debt/equity)?

(e) If Alison negotiated another loan of $50 000 for a major increase in stock levels, what would the new debt-to-equity ratio be? Would Alison be exposed to more or less risk? Explain.

(f) Alison expects to be able to sell the first batch of the new lines of stock within 2–3 months, so she decides to raise the funds by way of a 180-day commercial bill. The bank quotes her 3% as the cost for the full 180-day period. As commercial bills are issued at a discount (that is, interest due plus the principal equal the face value), about how much will Alison get in cash for a bill with a $50 000 face value?

(g) Alison's overdraft costs her about 8% pa. Which source of funding would you advise? Why?

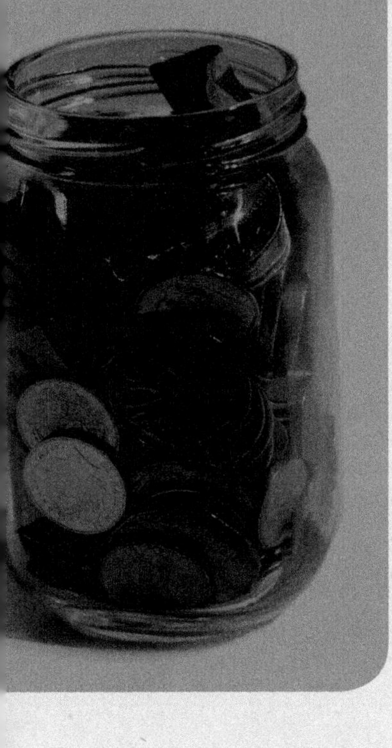

3.2 ABC Learning Centres has grown strongly in the last few years, as we have seen. At June 2004, the firm owned 327 childcare centres; a year later, the number had doubled to 660 centres. Here is the liabilities portion of the 2005 balance sheet.

	2005 $000	2004 $000
Current liabilities		
Payables	52 214	4 605
Interest bearing liabilities	4 456	19 671
Current tax liabilities	3 061	1 954
Provisions	6 079	246
Total current liabilities	**65 810**	**26 476**
Non-current liabilities		
Interest bearing liabilities	195 665	83 353
Non-current tax liabilities	57 539	1 664
Provisions	911	1

Total non-current liabilities	**254 115**	**85 018**
Total liabilities	**319 925**	**111 494**
Net assets	**845 534**	**202 559**
Equity		
Contributed equity	676 935	174 009
Reserves	114 033	3 871
Retained profits	54 566	24 679
Total equity	**845 534**	**202 559**

(a) Ignoring both the current and non-current provisions, what proportion of total assets was funded by debt in each year, 2004 and 2005? What do these percentages tell us?

(b) Explain which segments of debt have increased and which decreased in the 2004–05 year. How would each of these changes impact upon the profits of the firm?

(c) What changes are reflected in the equity section of the balance sheet? Why (do you think) did the directors make the decisions that produced these results?

(d) What is the 2005 debt-to-equity ratio? Is this conservative or risky?

3.3 Woolworths Ltd is another firm which has grown strongly in the 2004–05 year, with expansion into new non-traditional trading areas. Here is the liabilities portion of the 2005 balance sheet.

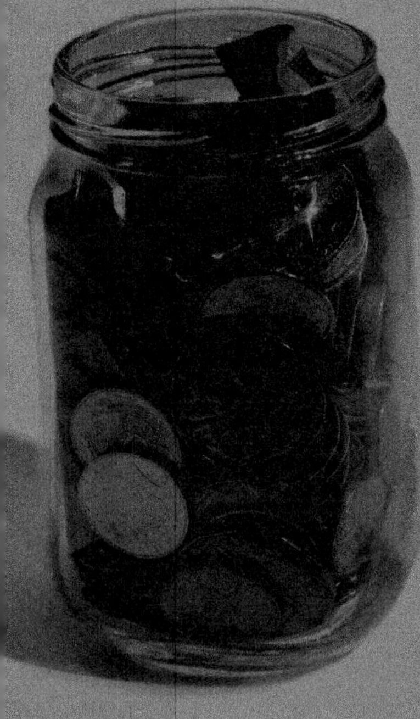

	As at 26 June 2005	**As at 27 June 2004**
	$m	**$m**
Accounts payable	2 335.6	2 176.3
Accruals	651.9	554.5
Interest bearing liabilities	235.5	18.0
Current tax liabilities	105.5	132.2
Provisions	393.5	348.0
Total current liabilities	**3 722.0**	**3 229.0**
Interest beaing liabilities	2 614.0	494.8
Deferred tax liabilities	12.4	4.5
Provisions	412.4	364.6
Total non-current liabilities	**3 038.8**	**863.9**
Total liabilities	**6 760.8**	**4 092.9**
Net assets	**2 197.1**	**2 052.5**
Contributed equity	977.9	575.4
Reserves	207.9	184.6
Retained profits	978.0	704.3
Equity attributable to the members of Woolworths Limited	**2 163.8**	**1 464.3**
Woolworths Income Notes	–	583.0

Outside equity interest in controlled entities:		
Reserves	0.9	0.9
Retained profits	32.4	4.3
Total outside equity interest	**33.3**	**5.2**
Total equity	**2 197.1**	**2 052.5**

(a) Ignoring both the current and non-current provisions, what proportion of total assets was funded by debt in each year, 2004 and 2005. What do these percentages tell us?

(b) Explain which segments of debt have increased and which decreased in the 2004–05 year. How would each of these changes impact upon the profits of the firm?

(c) What changes are reflected in the equity section of the balance sheet? Why (do you think) did the directors make the decisions that produced these results?

(d) What is the 2005 debt-to-equity ratio? Is this conservative or risky?

3.4 CSL Ltd, another well-known Australian firm, is highly profitable but has not expanded as fast in the 2004–05 year as ABC and Woolworths. Here is the liabilities portion of the 2005 balance sheet.

	2005	**2004**
	$000	**$000**
Current liabilities		
Payables	398 555	458 502
Interest-bearing liabilities	21 861	13 297
Current tax liabilities	37 130	26 903
Provisions	75 171	199 406
Total current liabilities	**532 717**	**698 108**
Non-current liabilities		
Payables	–	3 314
Interest-bearing liabilities	1 003 035	851 033
Deferred tax liabilities	106 814	80 577
Provisions	157 218	168 309
Total non-current liabilities	**1 267 067**	**1 103 233**
Total liabilities	**1 799 784**	**1 801 341**
Net assets	**2 074 512**	**2 074 042**
Equity		
Contributed equity	1 223 034	1 502 417
Reserves	(62 091)	77 373
Retained profits	913 569	494 252
Total equity	**2 074 512**	**2 074 042**

(a) How can we tell CSL has not expanded greatly in the 2004–05 year?

(b) Ignoring both the current and non-current provisions, what proportion of total assets was funded by debt in each year, 2004 and 2005. What do these percentages tell us?

(c) Explain which segments of debt have increased and which decreased in the 2004–05 year. How would each of these changes impact upon the profits of the firm?

(d) What changes are reflected in the equity section of the balance sheet? Why (do you think) did the directors make the decisions that produced these results?

(e) What is the 2005 debt-to-equity ratio? Is this conservative or risky?

(f) Of the three firms — ABC, Woolworths and CSL — CSL at the end of 2004–05 had the highest price in the share market relative to earnings (at least double the ratios of the other two firms). Do you think it rational of investors to bid the price of CSL up to such high levels? Why would they do so?

SOLUTIONS TO FINANCE WORKSHOPS

3.1 Role of the financial markets is to:

- provide a platform where the supply of funds by surplus units (potential lenders) and the demand for funds by deficit units (potential borrowers) may be reconciled and priced through trading (which allows businesses to raise the funds they need to operate and the pricing mechanism allows funds to be allocated among competing users)
- facilitate business and trade, thus making the production and exchange of goods and services easier and more efficient
- facilitate the saving of individuals for future consumption
- provide financial services which allow participants to balance their risk tolerance with their requirements for both returns and cash.

Examples (in order of these points):

- share market offers of IPOs allow savers to invest and users to be funded; also provide a price mechanism
- listing on the stock exchange or funding by intermediaries are both funding mechanism which facilitate trade
- deposit accounts at ADIs assist savers to save
- the multitude of unit trusts offered by funds managers allow investors to select the risk structure they prefer.

3.2 ADIs are the institutions registered under the *Banking Act 1959*. They are mostly the 'banks'; they dominate the retail end of the markets, taking deposits small and large, and lending in most forms available. RFCs are the 'others' — non-bank financial institutions (NBFIs). They are generally artifacts of past regulation where such regulation encouraged institutions to specialise. Thus, money market corporations and merchant banks operated in the large-dollar wholesale markets; finance companies served consumers and producers in higher-risk areas; pastoral houses specialised in rural finance; general financiers found niche high-risk areas to service.

Small to medium business generally — major banks, equity market
Large business generally — major banks, equity market, direct debt markets

Consumer finance for retailers — general financiers such as GE Money
Floor plan finance for car retailers — general financiers, finance companies, major banks
Large pastoral holdings — major banks, pastoral houses
Land and housing developer — major banks; general financiers

3.3 (a) First year, general financing of the business: trade credit; overdraft; FDA if no prospect of paying down the overdraft balance periodically so that it fluctuates from positive to negative.

(b) Next 5 years, general financing of the business: overdraft, FDA, commercial bills (if short-term periods of finance required for defined projects).

(c) Long term, general financing of the business: FDA, commercial bills (if short-term periods of finance required for defined projects).

End notes

1 Data derived from ABC Learning Centres Ltd annual reports, various years.

2 You may access the APRA website, www.apra.gov.au, for a full and up-to-date list of ADIs.

3 *Reserve Bank of Australia Bulletin*, January 2007, tables B1, B2, B7, B8.

4 GE Money 2006, 'Introducing GE Money', www.gemoney.com.au.

5 99 ATC 4242 *Steele vs the Federal Commissioner of Taxation*. Steele borrowed funds to acquire an asset to be developed for income-producing purposes in the future. Steele won the right for tax deductibility in these circumstances.

6 99 ATC 4600 *Brown vs the Federal Commissioner of Taxation*. Brown won the right to claim interest as a tax deduction long after the business for which the loan was received had ceased yielding income.

7 *Reserve Bank of Australia Bulletin*, January 2007, table D5.

8 *Reserve Bank of Australia Bulletin*, January 2007, table B10.

9 *Reserve Bank of Australia Bulletin*, January 2007, table F3.

10 *Reserve Bank of Australia Bulletin*, January 2007, table D4.

11 ABS, *Year book Australia, 2006*, cat. no. 1301.0, www.abs.gov.au.

12 Schwarz, H 1998, *Rationality gone awry: decision-making inconsistent with economic and financial theory,* Praeger, Westport, Connecticut, p. 88.

13 ASX 2007, 'Supervision subsidiary — ASX Markets Supervision' and 'Statistics', www.asx.com.au.

chapter

4

Financial mathematics

Learning objectives

After studying this chapter, you should be able to:

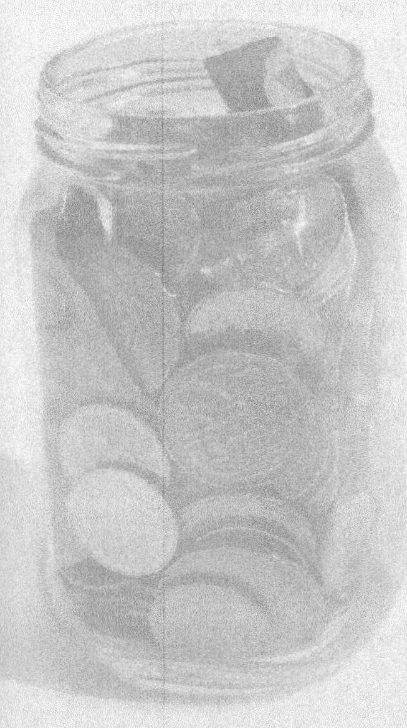

lo1	discuss cash flows, interest and the time value of money
lo2	solve simple interest problems
lo3	compute the prices of discount securities
lo4	understand the compound interest formula so that you can calculate both future and present values
lo5	calculate both present and future values of annuities
lo6	calculate both present and future values of unequal amounts.

A PHONE CALL TO YOUR ADVANTAGE

Ring, ring ... ring, ring.

'Hello?'

'Is that Sue Tait?'

'Yes, it is.'

'Sue, this is Mark Mitchell here from the Translotto Company. I have some good news for you. You have just won a prize ... that is, we think you have won a prize. Do you hold ticket number 452 867 584?'

'Yes, I have a ticket. Just a sec, I'll go and get it ... Hello, Mark, my number is 452 967 584.'

'Sue, did you say "967"?'

'Yes, I did. No, it's not. My hand is shaking so much I misread the number. It's "867". Is that the number you wanted?'

'Yes, 452 867 584. Is that the number on your ticket?'

'Yes, it is. What did I win?'

'Sue, you have a choice. You can take $1 million now or you can elect to take 21 annual payments of $60 000 starting now with the first $60 000. Which would you rather do?'

'Oh, I don't know. Can I have some time to think about it?'

'Yes, Sue, you can. How about if I call you again early Monday morning? My advice would be to take the 21 annual payments because that's $1 260 000 but, of course, we are not supposed to give you advice, just give you the good news.'

'Thanks, Mark, I'll look forward to your call and, in the meantime, I'll seek advice. Good-bye and thanks again.'

What would your advice be?

Chapter preview

This chapter is about financial mathematics, and when you have completed studying it you will have all the necessary tools to advise Sue on the best course of action. In addition, you will understand how both simple and compound interest problems are solved, how financial institutions work out loan repayment schedules, how commercial bills are priced, how bonds are priced and much more.

The chapter starts with a discussion of simple interest and shows how the simple interest equation may be manipulated to solve problems. The discussion then moves on to compound interest, which is by far the more common type of interest charged within the Australian financial system. Compound interest is examined in relation to both single sums and streams of equal payments, which are called annuities. Several interesting applications of the compound interest concepts are discussed. We make extensive use of the principles and techniques presented in this chapter throughout the remainder of this book.

The diagram on the following page shows how this chapter is structured.

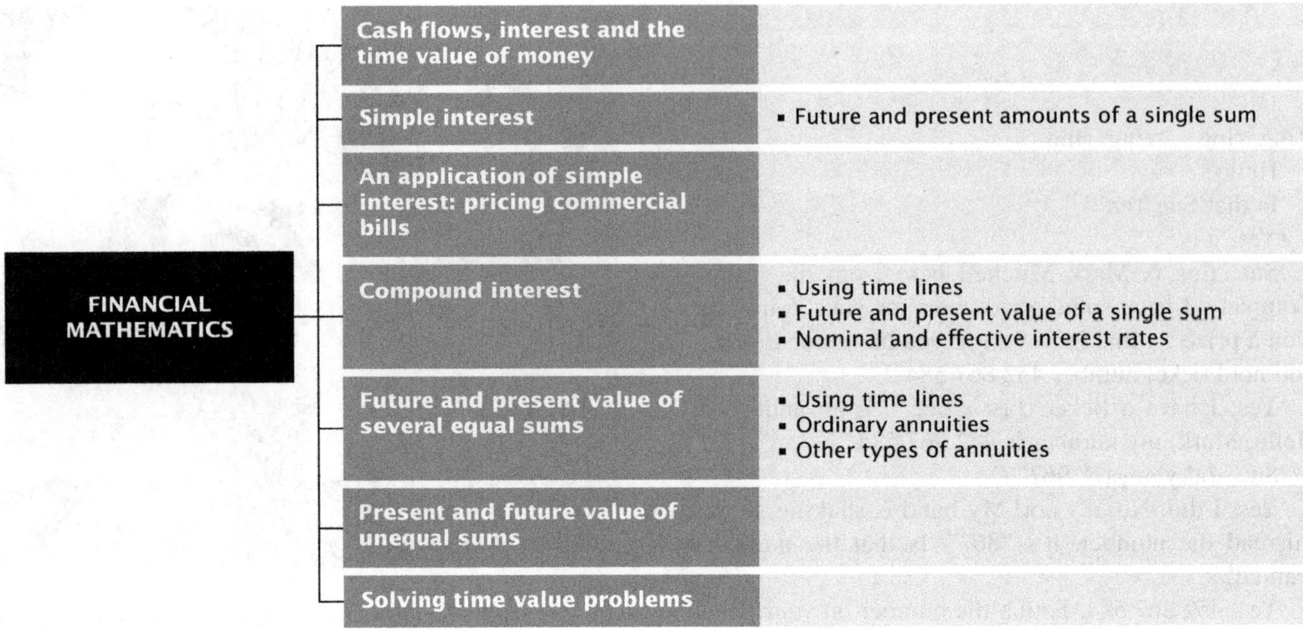

Cash flows, interest and the time value of money

lo1

Discuss cash flows, interest and the time value of money.

Cash flow: funds flowing either into or out of a business; that is, cash receipts or cash expenses

Before we discuss simple interest, compound interest and all the other interesting concepts and applications in this chapter, there are three fundamental issues of which you must be aware. These are cash flows, interest rates and the time value of money.

In this chapter, we are concerned with cash flows, not profits, losses, capital gains or capital losses. We are interested only in the payments of cash that are made between one party and another. The reasons we deal with cash are that we want to be able to compare values at different points in time, we want to be able to reduce multiple flows to single values and we want to be able to make rational decisions. We want to be able to make decisions based on values that are not obscured by accounting rules or accounting choices.

When a business owner contracts to buy some new premises, for example, and arranges for a mortgage at a financial institution, what cash flows ensue from this contract? The buyer lodges a deposit with the real estate agent handling the purchase at the time of signing the contract. At settlement, normally a representative of the financial institution will attend and hand over a bank cheque in return for the deed. The deed is then kept by the financial institution as security for the loan. The bank has exchanged cash for another asset, which is the loan. Subsequently, when the real estate agent is advised that settlement has taken place, the agent deducts fees from the deposit that has been held in trust and remits the balance to the seller. Thus, the seller normally receives two payments — the larger payment directly from the mortgagee and the balance of the deposit from the real estate agent. The buyer makes one payment immediately in the form of the deposit, and then spends the next several years making a multitude of payments to pay off the mortgage loan. The real estate agent receives one cash flow that is kept in trust until settlement, when fees are earned and deducted and the balance is remitted to the seller.

Even though the buyer has not seen one dollar of the cash flow that is the loan, effectively the cash has flowed from the bank to the buyer and then on to the seller. In time, the buyer pays that cash back and the flow of cash is reversed. In addition, there will be the cash flow comprising interest expense that also must be paid to compensate the lenders for the use of their money. This chapter investigates how that interest expense is calculated.

What is interest? Before the concept of money was developed, people lent goods to each other. When returning the same goods or other goods in compensation for the original loans, the borrowers sometimes added a bit extra in recognition of the service which had been rendered by the lender. This bit extra is called 'rent' by economists. Once 'money' (in forms such as printed paper, printed plastics, metals, leaves, seeds, shells) has been developed by communities to facilitate the exchange of goods and services, it too is often loaned or rented by one person or entity to another, so that the borrower can take advantage of the purchasing power the money represents. The rent or price charged for the temporary use of money is called **interest**.

Interest: the price charged for the temporary use of money

Interest performs an allocative role in economies. If people are willing and able to pay the prices asked for particular goods or services, then they are able to purchase those items and enjoy the benefits of consumption. Thus, prices are the mechanism by which allocation of scarce goods and services is made to users. Similarly with money; people willing to pay the interest charges, at whatever levels they are set, enjoy the benefits of the purchasing power the lenders are offering. For borrowers, interest can be thought of as a penalty for wanting to consume before income is earned. For lenders, on the other hand, interest is compensation for putting off consumption until a later period.

Interest rates are set by the interaction of supply and demand. Put more explicitly, the level of interest rates stems from individuals' time preference for consumption (delayed consumption produces savings which underlie the supply of loanable funds) and production opportunities facing entrepreneurs and investors. Production opportunities translate into demand for funds.

At low interest rates, there will be many investment projects that are expected to be able to generate sufficient cash surpluses above their costs and, combined, these projects will result in a strong demand for funds. At the same time, when interest rates are low, consumers will have little incentive not to consume and to save for future consumption. It is thought that most people have a positive time preference for consumption — that is, they would rather spend and consume now than in the future. In order to encourage savings, interest rates may have to rise. However, as rates rise, fewer projects will prove to be worthy of funding.

In addition to our concern with cash flows and the nature of interest, we are interested in this chapter with the **time value of money**. The time value of money is the notion that a dollar is worth more the sooner it is received. This is because the dollar represents purchasing power which may be rented out to others and earn a return, if the owner does not need it immediately for consumption. Suppose you see an advertisement for a well-used vehicle at El Cheapo Car Dealers. The price is $5000, payable either now or in three months' time. Which is the better deal, or is there no difference? Intuitively, we probably all know that paying in three months' time is to be preferred, even when we have the money on hand now. Why? Because, if we don't pay over the cash now, we can keep it in our bank account and earn 4% pa interest ourselves for the three months. This interest payment amounts to 1% for three months or $50. With $50 we can fill the fuel tank at least once as well as buy the car with the $5000.

Time value of money: the concept that a dollar is worth more the sooner it is received

Thus, the principle with the time value of money is that money received now is worth more than the same amount received in the future because of the return that could be earned on the money between now and the future date. When cash sums are received at different times, we need to express them all in terms of a common date — either today or a future date — so that they may be validly added or otherwise manipulated. A common example of this phenomenon in business relates to investments in productive capacity. Money is spent now to purchase machinery, for example, but the returns are received over many years to come. As we see in chapters 8 and 9, to analyse this investment correctly, all the returns should be brought to a common date.

lo2

Solve simple interest problems.

Simple interest: interest calculated on the original sum borrowed

Simple interest

Simple interest is interest calculated on the original or principal sum borrowed, *P*. The money we borrow today is stated in terms of today's dollars, so it is the present value (PV) of the loan. Many financial contracts specify the rate of interest to be paid, and that rate is applied to the original sum borrowed. Almost intuitively, we know that, if we borrow \$100 from a friend for one year and she says she needs to charge 5% interest, we will owe her \$105 at the end of the year. Similarly, if we borrowed the sum for two years at the same rate of interest, we can quickly deduce that we will owe her \$110 at the end of two years.

The equation for the calculation of simple interest is equation 4.1.

$$\textbf{Interest} = \boldsymbol{Pin} \qquad [4.1]$$

where P = principal sum borrowed
i = simple interest rate
n = number of periods

EXAMPLE 4.1

The calculation of simple interest

Jim's Welding Works borrows \$20 000 from Jim's brother for a period of 1 year at a simple interest rate of 6% pa.

(a) What interest is owed at the end of the year?

Interest = Pin

Interest = \$20 000 × 0.06 × 1
= \$1200

Converting interest rate and period of loan to the same units

If Jim had borrowed the money for a period longer than 1 year, say 2 years, then the interest would be

\$20 000 × 0.06 × 2 = \$2400.

Sometimes the interest rate and the period of the loan are not quoted in the same units (for example, the interest rate may be quoted per annum but the period of the loan may be 5 months). There are two approaches to solve this problem — either convert the interest rate per period to the period of the loan or express the period of the loan in the units in which the interest rate is quoted.

(b) What would be the interest charge if Jim had needed the \$20 000 for only 7 months? Clearly, the interest payable would be proportionately reduced from that payable on a 1-year loan.

One approach to calculate the interest payable is to express the interest rate in the same units as the period of the loan (that is, months). To convert a simple annual interest rate to a monthly rate, we simply divide by 12 (because there are 12 months in a year). Therefore 6% (0.06) per annum equates to $\frac{6\%}{12}\left(\frac{0.06}{12}\right)$ per month, which is 0.5% (0.005) per month. Now we have the interest rate and the period of the loan in the same units and we can substitute the figures into equation 4.1.

$$\text{Interest} = Pin$$

$$\begin{aligned}\text{Interest} &= \$20\,000 \times 0.005 \times 7\\ &= \$700\end{aligned}$$

The alternative approach is to express the period of the loan in the same units as the interest rate, which is in years. In this case, we simply divide the period by 12, making $\frac{7}{12}$ years.

$$\text{Interest} = Pin$$

$$\begin{aligned}\text{Interest} &= \$20\,000 \times 0.06 \times \tfrac{7}{12}\\ &= \$700\end{aligned}$$

Simple interest is applied to many sorts of bank deposits, such as savings accounts and term deposits, as well as many types of loans. Loans between relatives and business partners, for example, are often based on simple interest. Debenture loans and commercial loans made by financial institutions on an interest-only basis also operate on a simple interest basis. Simple interest is used because it is appropriate to calculate the interest on the original sum involved and it is also easy to calculate.

Future and present amounts of a single sum

When Jim borrowed the $20000 in example 4.1, he would have been interested at the outset in how much he would have to repay at the end of the borrowing period, so he could think about how he could manage his finances in order to repay the debt on time. The sum that must be repaid, *FS*, at the end of a loan period consists of the original sum borrowed (the principal) plus the interest. We can build an equation for this calculation by simply adding the principal, *P*, on to the interest that we calculated using equation 4.1, *Pin*, so:

$$\begin{aligned}\text{Principal} + \text{interest} &= FS\\ &= P + Pin\\ &= P(1 + in)\end{aligned}$$

$$\boldsymbol{FS = P(1 + in)} \qquad [4.2]$$

where FS = sum that must be repaid

P = principal sum borrowed

i = simple interest rate

n = number of periods

Equation 4.2 enables us to calculate how much Jim would owe his brother at the end of one year if he borrowed $20000 for one year at 6% per annum.

$$FS = P(1 + in)$$
$$= \$20000(1 + 0.06 \times 1)$$
$$= \$21\,200$$

Another situation that often arises is that firms advertise goods for sale, with payment required only in one year's time. You might want to compare this offer with the price for cash paid immediately. What is the equivalent price now? We can build an equation to solve this problem. The future sum is made up of the principal sum plus interest. We can calculate the principal for the known future value if we know the rate of interest that our funds could attract.

$$P = \frac{FS}{(1 + in)} \quad [4.3]$$

where P = principal sum borrowed

FS = sum that must be repaid

i = simple interest rate

n = number of periods

EXAMPLE 4.2

The present amount of a future sum

The price of a road bike is advertised as $30000 for immediate delivery, with payment required in exactly 1 year's time. The same model is available now at another dealer for $29000 cash. Which is the better price, if money can earn 6% pa?

$$P = \frac{FS}{(1 + in)}$$

$$P = \frac{\$30000}{(1 + 0.06 \times 1)}$$
$$= \$28\,301.89$$

(You can check this calculation by applying a 6% pa interest rate to $28 301.89 for one year. The answer is exactly $30000.)

Which is the better price? The deferred payment deal is better, because the bike is really costing only $28 302. (One thing that complicates this sort of calculation is the effect of tax. In Australia, income tax reduces the actual interest rate on the funds if they were invested to something less than 6%.) Try a new calculation for yourself. What would the decision be, if funds could earn 3.5% after tax?

An application of simple interest: pricing commercial bills

lo3

Compute the prices of discount securities.

We will now examine some corporate finance examples that use simple interest. Remember example 4.1(b), where the simple annual interest rate was 6% but Jim's loan was for only seven months instead of the full year. The rate was calculated as 0.035 (or 0.005 × 7) for that single seven-month period. This is a useful way to think of applying interest rates, because many financial securities are issued and priced for periods of less than one year.

You may remember from when we examine promissory notes and commercial bills briefly in chapter 3 that such securities are normally issued for periods of 30 to 180 days, but the interest rates are quoted on an annual basis. This is the normal situation or convention in Australia. For example, the interest rate to be charged on a loan of funds by way of a 180-day commercial bill may be quoted as 6% pa. You will notice this quoted rate does not match the term of the bill because it is a rate of interest for one year and the bill is a loan for 180 days.

To find out how much interest must be paid on the bill, we first convert the annual rate by pro-rating (reducing the value to correspond with the period required), as we did on page 97 in part (b) of example 4.1. This is then the rate charged for the specific period, or the periodic rate. For our 180-day commercial bill, the periodic rate is $0.06 \times \frac{180}{365}$ or 0.0296.

Another way to consider this problem is to work out how many of the required periods (in the case of this example, of 180 days) there are in each year. There are 2.0277 180-day periods in a 365-day year ($\frac{180}{365} = 2.0277$). Then the rate per period is the annual rate divided by the number of periods per year. Continuing the example, the rate for the period of 180 days is $\frac{0.06}{2.0277}$ or 0.0296.

One issue that immediately springs to mind when considering pro-rating interest rates to periods of less than one year is: how many days are there in a year? We all know 365 days is the usual answer, but how do financial institutions cope with leap years? The answer is that, if a loan period spans 29 February, interest is charged for that day. However, in making calculations involving leap years, the year is assumed to have only the standard 365 days.

To summarise, some of the most important rules for solving commercial bill pricing problems are:

1. Interest rates are quoted on a simple annual basis (as if for one year) and pro-rated for the actual period of the loan.
2. Pro-rating takes place on the basis of the exact number of days divided by 365.
3. In a leap year, 29 February is charged for if the loan is outstanding over this day, but the year is assumed still to have 365 days.

With these rules to hand, some commercial bill problems may be illustrated.

EXAMPLE 4.3

Calculating the proceeds from a commercial bill

Pholin's Fish Foods arranges finance through a $40000 commercial bill for 90 days at 5.6%. How much will Pholin receive, disregarding any fees? (Remember, commercial bills are a discount security and the initial sum Pholin receives will be the face value of the bill less the interest Pholin will owe at the end of the period.)

Using equation 4.3:

$$P = \frac{FS}{(1 + in)}$$

$$P = \frac{\$400000}{\left(1 + 0.056 \times \frac{90}{365}\right)}$$

$$= \frac{\$400000}{(1 + 0.0138)}$$

$$= \$39455.51$$

(In this textbook, we will adhere to the convention of rounding at four decimal places. Thus, 0.013 808 2 becomes 0.0138.)

Effectively, what has happened here is that the simple annual interest rate (5.6%) has been reduced to match the time for which the funds have been borrowed (that is, reduced to $\frac{90}{365}$ of 5.6%, to 1.38% for the 90-day period). Then the principal, *P*, has been found. The principal sum represents the present amount. The principal sum, *P*, plus the interest owing at the end of the period ($544.49) together equal the face value (or future sum) of the bill, $40000.

EXAMPLE 4.4

Calculating the interest rate of a commercial bill

Ace Baking Co. arranges to issue a 180-day $100000 commercial bill through its bank. The bank advises that $97600 will be available from the loan. What is the annual rate of interest being charged?

$$P = \frac{FS}{(1 + in)}$$

$$P = 97600 = \frac{100000}{(1 + in)}$$

$$1 + in = \frac{100000}{97600}$$

$$= 1.0246$$

$$in = 0.0246$$

As the bill is for 180 days, $n = \frac{180}{365}$

$$i = 0.0246 \times \frac{180}{365}$$

$$= 0.0498$$

Yield: the amount produced or the return based on the initial investment

In example 4.4, the commercial bill with a face value of $100000 gives the borrower $97600. The bill is said to yield $2400 or 4.98% pa. The **yield** is the amount produced or the return based on the initial investment; yields are normally expressed as percentages. Yield can also be thought of as the effective cost to the borrower.

While yields describe the returns made in relation to the initial investments, commercial bills or promissory notes may be sold from one investor to another. When a bill is offered

Discount rate: (in relation to pricing a security) the percentage difference between the face value and the purchase price of the security

for resale, it may be described as being sold at a given yield or a given **discount rate**. As we already know, a yield relates to P or the actual amount borrowed, but a discount relates to the face value or future sum, FS, of the bill. In Australia, we normally trade commercial bills in terms of yield. However, in some other economies, for example in the United States, short-term securities are traded on a discount basis.

In the case of the Ace bill in example 4.4, suppose the holder sold the bill for \$98 000 when it had 120 days to maturity. In terms of the face value, the bill has been discounted by what percentage? The equation may be worked out as follows:

$$\text{Selling price } (SP) = \text{face value } (FS) - \text{discount}$$

The amount of discount is calculated like any interest amount. Remember Simple interest = Pin, so the discount = $FSin$.

$$SP = FS - FSin$$

This yields equation 4.4.

$$\mathbf{SP = FS(1 - in)} \qquad [4.4]$$

where SP = selling price (or present value)
FS = sum that must be repaid (or face value)
i = simple interest rate
n = number of periods (expressed in years)

EXAMPLE 4.5

Calculating the discount rate of a commercial bill sold before maturity

Suppose the holder sold the bill for \$98 000 when it had 120 days to maturity. In terms of its \$100 000 face value, by what percentage has the bill been discounted?

$$98\,000 = 100\,000(1 - in)$$
$$0.98 = 1 - in$$
$$in = 1 - 0.98$$
$$= 0.02$$
$$\text{As } n = \frac{120}{365}$$
$$i = 0.02 \times \frac{365}{210}$$
$$= 0.0608$$

Thus, the bill has been discounted in relation to its face value at an annual rate of 6.08%. For the same sale, the yield on this bill in relation to the funds owed may be calculated and is 6.21%. Try that calculation yourself. These two interest rates demonstrate for you an immutable relationship between yields and discount rates for the same bill transaction. The yield percentage will always be a higher number than the discount rate. This is because the interest amount denominated in dollars is a proportion of a lower value with yield than it is with a discount. Thus, the same value as a proportion of a lower value will give a higher percentage than the same value expressed as a proportion of a higher amount.

FINANCE WORKSHOP 4.1

Here are some commercial bill problems. Remember, the equation to use is:

$$P = \frac{FS}{(1 + in)}$$

1. August Road Diamonds arranges finance through a $100 000 commercial bill for 180 days at 7%. How much money, disregarding any fees, will August Road receive?
2. The August Road bill is sold when there are 60 days to run to yield 8%. What is the price?

lo4

Understand the compound interest formula so that you can calculate both future and present values.

Compound interest: interest calculated on the actual amount outstanding each period

Time line: a diagrammatic representation of cash flows, either received or paid or both

Present value: the value (in today's dollars) of a future amount calculated for a given discount rate

Future value: the value of an amount of today's dollars at a specific time in the future; future value is calculated by compounding at a given rate

Compound interest

Compound interest is based on the idea that, while interest charged on an outstanding principal amount or debt remains unpaid, interest should be charged on that new part of the debt as well as the original principal. Thus, if a loan has interest charged on a daily basis but repayments are made on a monthly basis, the balance will increase every day by an increasing amount until a payment is made. In effect, increasing amounts of interest are added at the end of each day to the total amount owed. Then the balance will drop by the amount of the repayment. Following that payment, the cycle will start again. The daily balance will increase, then drop, and so on.

Using time lines

Time lines are very handy tools for analysing cash flow problems. A time line is a diagrammatic representation of cash flows, either received or paid or both. Thus, a time line might look like this, where *PV* equals **present value** or value now (time = zero) and *FV* is a **future value** at the end of denominated time period.

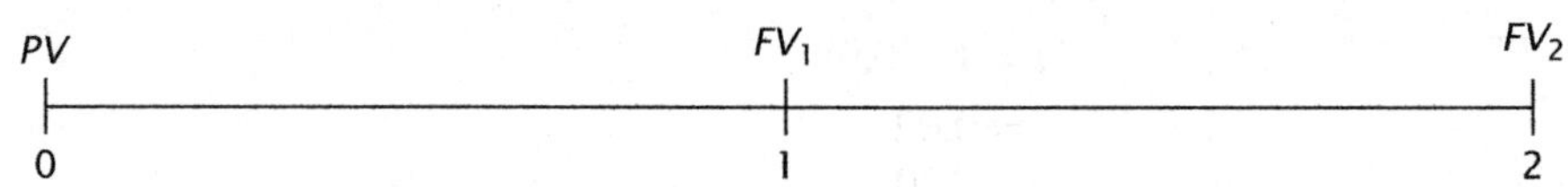

Time 0 is now or the time relating to a PV. The future value (FV) relates to a time in the future and may, in the diagram, be either at the end of period 1 or at the end of period 2.

Future and present value of a single sum

To deal with compound interest problems, we need to develop equations as we did with simple interest. The sum of the principal amount, *P*, plus interest, gives the balance at the end of the first period, or future value, FV_1. The principal amount can also be thought of as the present value. Given a compounding rate of *k* that is charged for a period, the amount of interest charged will be equal to *Pk*. Then the balance at the end of the first period will be: $FV_1 = P + Pk = P(1 + k)$. The amount of interest charged at the end of the first period is exactly the same as would be charged as simple interest. If no repayments have been made, more interest will be charged in the second period and that interest will be charged on FV_1, not on *P*, as FV_1 is the total amount outstanding. So the total amount outstanding at the end of the second period, FV_2, will be FV_1 plus the interest on FV_1.

$$
\begin{aligned}
FV_2 &= FV_1 + kFV_1 \\
&= (1 + k)FV_1 \\
&= (1 + k)[P(1 + k)] \\
&= P(1 + k)^2
\end{aligned}
$$

Shown on a time line, this would look like the following.

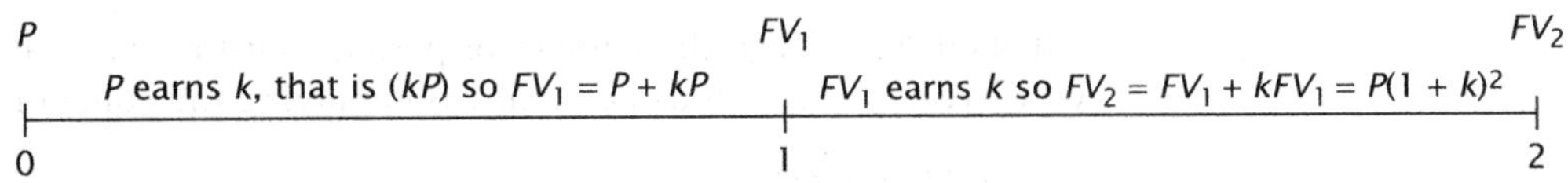

The total interest charged is more than the amounts that would have been charged as simple interest. Interest in the second period is charged on both principal and interest, and thus interest is charged on unpaid interest. This process will continue for as many periods as are relevant until a repayment is made. Thus the general rule for the future value of a sum, given compounding interest, is equation 4.5. So far we have used the symbol P to represent principal of a simple interest loan. For the compound interest equations, we refer to PV rather than P because the discounting and compounding processes have more applications than simply calculating loans.

$$\boldsymbol{FV_n = PV(1 + k)^n} \qquad [4.5]$$

where FV_n = future value at the end of the nth period
PV = present value
k = compounding rate
n = number of periods

EXAMPLE 4.6

Calculating compound interest

Dog-eared Paperbacks is a second-hand book business. The partnership which owns the store is saving to buy new shelving so the business can display its 10 000 titles more effectively. Dog-eared has saved \$20 000 this year and can invest the funds at 7% pa. What amount will they have at the end of 5 years?

$$
\begin{aligned}
FV_n &= PV(1 + k)^n \\
FV_5 &= 20\,000(1.07)^5 \\
&= 20\,000(1.4025) = \$28\,051
\end{aligned}
$$

What would be the effect if the partners in Dog-eared Paperbacks were able to invest the funds with a compounding period of less than one year? Suppose they were able to invest at the same nominal annual rate of 7%, but interest was compounded at monthly intervals. Your understanding of the concept of compounding will tell you that the value of the future balance with monthly compounding will be greater than it was with annual compounding, because interest will be earned on interest which is recognised sooner as earned and added to the balance. Let's see what happens to the balance.

EXAMPLE 4.7

Calculating interest compounding monthly

Dog-eared Paperbacks saved \$20000 this year and invests the funds at 7% pa, compounding monthly. What amount will they have at the end of 5 years? The compounding rate must first be calculated for the monthly period. This is, $\frac{0.07}{12}$, which equals 0.0058. Then the number of periods must be calculated. This number is 60 (5 years × 12 months per year). By applying the equation:

$$FV_n = PV(1 + k)^n$$

$$FV_n = 20000(1 + 0.0058)^{60}$$

$$= 20000 \times 1.4148$$

$$= \$28296$$

As expected, the sum at the end of 5 years has increased by more than \$200 (\$28296 − 28051 = \$245), because interest has been earned on interest sooner in each period. This example shows you that it is a good idea to think of n always as 'number of periods' during which compounding takes place, rather than 'number of years'.

Discount rate: the interest factor that is used to calculate a present value (PV) from a future value (FV)

The FV equation may be manipulated so that it will give the present value (PV) of a future sum. We introduce the concept of discounting in chapter 1. Discounting calculates the present value of a future sum by taking the time value of money into consideration. The future value is discounted back to the present value using the **discount rate**.

The PV or discount equation (equation 4.6) is derived from the FV equation:

$$FV_n = PV\,(1 + k)^n$$

$$\mathbf{PV = \frac{FV_n}{(1 + k)^n}} \qquad [4.6]$$

where PV = present value
FV_n = future value at the end of the nth period
k = discount rate
n = number of periods

Suppose a business expects to receive \$500000 in 10 years' time. The manager might want to know what that amount is worth today. To calculate this value, we need to know how much could be earned by the money if it were received today. Assume money could earn 8% pa.

$$PV = \frac{FV_n}{(1 + k)^n}$$

$$= \frac{500000}{(1.08)^{10}}$$

$$= \frac{500\,000}{2.1589}$$

$$= \$231\,599$$

This shows you that \$231 599 in the hand is worth almost twice that in the future, if that future is far enough away!

EXAMPLE 4.8

Calculating the present value of a future sum

Dog-eared Paperbacks gets a quote for the sort of shelving it wants and decides to build an extension as well. The partners think they can afford to do the work, now estimated to cost \$60 000, in 3 years' time. How much do they need to have now to fund this expense if they can earn 6% pa, compounded monthly, or 0.5% per month?

$$PV = \frac{FV_n}{(1 + k)^n}$$

$$PV = \frac{60\,000}{(1.005)^{36}}$$

$$= \frac{60\,000}{1.1967}$$

$$= \$50\,139$$

In addition to solving these sorts of problems by use of the equations, it is possible to look up FV and PV tables. Table 1 in the appendix gives you the future value of \$1 at the end of many different periods at many different rates of return. Table 2 gives you the present value of \$1 due at the end of different time periods at many different rates of return.

To read these tables, select the time period and the desired interest rate, then read off the compounding or discount factor. For example, if you want to find the value of \$1 invested for 10 years at 10% pa, use table 1 to look up n = 10 in the left-hand column and 10% across the top. Read off the compounding factor of 2.5937. The final step is to multiply the dollar amount in question by the factor to get the FV. The value of \$1 invested is \$2.59. The value of \$1000 invested is \$2593.70.

To discount a future value to calculate a PV, look up the discount factor in table 2 in the same fashion. The discount factor for a future value to be received in 10 years with a 10% interest (discount) rate is 0.3855 and is the value for the divisor part $[(1 + k)^n]$ of the PV equation. Because the discount factor is the value for $\frac{1}{(1+k)^n}$, the cash flow need only be multiplied by the discount factor, not divided. Thus, if a future sum is \$2593.70, the PV is approximately \$1000, after allowing for rounding (2593.70 × 0.3855). You can always check your logic and numeracy by remembering that the PV will always be smaller in size than the cash flow number you started with. If the time period or discount rate you are dealing with is not given in the tables, you will have to use the appropriate equations, 4.5 and 4.6.

Nominal rate: the advertised or quoted annual rate that does not reflect the impact of multiple compounding periods during the year

Nominal and effective interest rates

The **nominal rate** is a rate of interest that does not reflect the impact of compounding. A 6% pa rate quoted for a 180-day bill is a nominal rate, because it is based on simple interest and does not consider reinvesting the face value of a 180-day bill again to get a return for the whole year. The interest rates you see advertised by banks for their products are also nominal rates. You may see a rate of 7.5% per annum quoted for a home loan, but this won't tell you how much interest you will actually pay in a year — the interest you pay on your mortgage depends on how often interest is compounded during the year.

Effective rate: reflects the impact of multiple compounding during the year

The rate that reflects the number of times interest is compounded each year is called the **effective rate**. The nominal rate equals the effective rate only when interest is compounded annually (that is, once per year). The effective rate allows financial managers to compare interest rates or returns on the same bases. For example, the rates charged for a series of short-term commercial bills could be compared with the cost of longer-term finance to find which is the better deal. The returns earned by investing a series of four 90-day bills can be compared to an alternative investment in two 180-day bills, or to a one-year term deposit. The effective rate is the most appropriate rate to use when comparing loans or investments that have different terms.

The equation for annual effective rate is:

$$k_{eff} = \left(1 + \frac{j}{m}\right)^m - 1 \qquad [4.7]$$

where k_{eff} = annual effective rate

j = nominal annual rate

m = number of compounding periods each year

EXAMPLE 4.9

Calculating the annual effective rate

An interest rate is quoted as 12%, compounded monthly. What is the annual effective rate?

$$k_{eff} = \left(1 + \frac{j}{m}\right)^m - 1$$

$$k_{eff} = \left(1 + \frac{0.12}{12}\right)^{12} - 1$$

$$= (1.01)^{12} - 1$$

$$= 1.1268 - 1$$

$$= 0.1268 \text{ or } 12.68\%$$

When do you apply the effective annual rate rather than the nominal rate? The general rule is that the timing of the cash flows and the compounding period need to be equal. When you are quoted a nominal annual rate, and compounding and cash flows occur monthly, divide the annual nominal rate by the number of compounding periods as in example 4.7. This results in a higher annual effective rate than the nominal rate (calculate the effective annual rate for example 4.7 and see). However, when you have a compounding period shorter than the cash flow period (for example, compounding occurs monthly but payments are made annually) you will need to calculate and apply the effective annual rate to discount or compound your cash flows. What if several cash flows occur during the compounding period? If you make daily deposits in your bank account and interest accrues weekly, for example, your interest is calculated as if you made all deposits on the day interest accrues. We do not use the effective rate to calculate the week's interest in this case.

FINANCE WORKSHOP 4.2

The equations you may find useful in these questions are as follows:

$FV_n = PV(1 + k)^n$

$FS = P(1 + in)$

$$k_{eff} = \left(1 + \frac{j}{m}\right)^m - 1$$

1. Don's Boots supplies protective clothing and footwear to mining companies. He is owed \$50 000 for a large order. The customer is having temporary cash flow problems and comes to an arrangement with Don that the debt will be paid in 6 months' time. They agree on 6.0% pa compounding monthly as an appropriate interest rate. How much will Don be owed at the end of the 6 months?
2. How much would be owed if Don and the miner had agreed on 6.0% pa compounding 6-monthly?
3. How much would be owed if Don and the miner had agreed on 6% pa simple interest?
4. What are the annual effective rates in each case (1–3) above?

Future and present value of several equal sums

lo5

Calculate both present and future values of annuities.

Annuity: a series of equal cash flows that are evenly spaced over time

Ordinary annuity: a series of equal cash flows that are evenly spaced over time and are received at the end of each period

Annuity due: the first payment is made at the inception of the annuity

Deferred annuity: the first payment is made after several periods have elapsed

Perpetuity: an ordinary annuity that has cash flows that continue forever

One of the most useful techniques that can be learned in the area of financial mathematics concerns the manipulation of annuities. An **annuity** is a series of equal cash flows that are evenly spaced over time. Even though the word 'annuity' stems from the Latin *annus*, a year, the equal-length periods need not be years. They can be any period; for example, 3 months, 60 days, 5 days, and so on.

There are four sorts of annuities:

- **ordinary annuity** (where the payments flow at the end of each even-length period)
- **annuity due** (where the first payment is received on the day of the valuation)
- **deferred annuity** (where the first payment is deferred for a period greater than the subsequent even-length periods)
- **perpetuity** (where the cash flows continue regularly forever).

Using time lines

As already noted, time lines are very useful tools for analysing cash flow problems. They are especially useful where numerous cash flows are involved. Take this case, for example.

\$'000

−100	10	5	12	5	15	8	35	45
0	1	2	3	4	5	6	7	8

This time line tells us that someone will pay \$100000 now, but will receive cash flows at the end of each of the next eight years. The obvious question: Is this project or proposal worth undertaking? As you will be aware now, it all depends on the value that is put on money or the discount rate. Discount rates are based on the opportunity return that might otherwise be earned and the effects of inflation. There is no one correct discount rate for all time periods and all situations. Discount rates are selected to fit the analysis appropriately given the current and expected market conditions, current and expected inflation rates and the desired return on the part of the investor. We learn how to calculate a discount rate that is consistent with maximising the value of the firm in chapter 7.

Ordinary annuities

Ordinary annuities occur very frequently in business finance, and thus understanding them and being able to calculate PVs, FVs and the periodic instalments or cash flows (C) is an important skill. The repayment of instalment loans and mortgage loans offered by financial institutions constitute annuities. The initial loan amount is the PV and the regular repayment amount is the C. Similarly, analysts pricing bonds in the financial markets use annuity calculations as well as the PV of single sums to arrive at theoretically correct prices as bases for trading.

Equations 4.8 and 4.9 are used to calculate the PV and the FV of ordinary annuities.

$$PVA = C\left\{\frac{1-(1+k)^{-n}}{k}\right\} \qquad [4.8]$$

$$FVA_n = C\left\{\frac{(1+k)^{-n}-1}{k}\right\} \qquad [4.9]$$

where PVA = present value of an ordinary annuity at the end of the nth period
FVA_n = future value of an annuity at the end of the nth period
C = periodic cash flow
k = compounding or discount rate
n = number of periods

EXAMPLE 4.10

Calculating the present value of an ordinary annuity

Thompson's Foundry casts speciality bronze plaques for community groups who want to honour local citizens. The manager wants to buy a new piece of equipment that she thinks will net \$10000 each year for 5 years. After 5 years, the equipment will be worn out. The demand for these plaques is seasonal, with most orders coming in the three months before Christmas. What is the PV of these future cash flows? (The manager wants to know this so that she can compare this figure and the current cost of the machine.) Assume the cash is all received by Christmas Day. (This assumption is to approximate the condition of an annuity that the funds are received at the end of each period.)

The firm's funds can earn 6% pa in the next best alternative use, so the manager will want to earn at least this rate of return. By using this best alternative rate in the calculation, the manager is ensuring th`at this alternative opportunity is allowed for in the calculations. Then, if the PV of the cash flows exceeds the cost now of the machine, the manager is ensuring that the wealth of the firm is increased as much as possible in the circumstances.

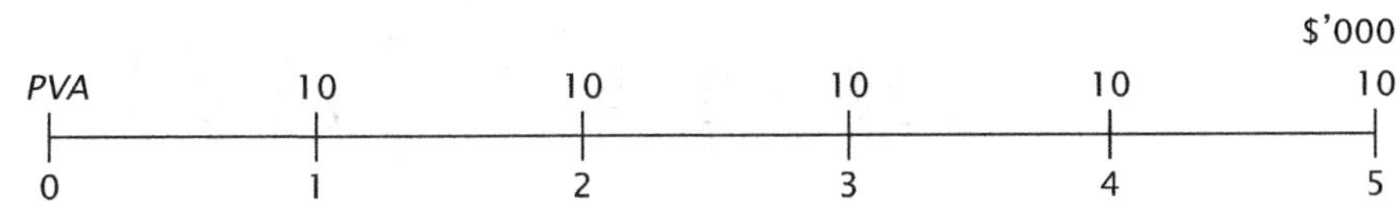

$$PVA = C\left\{\frac{[1-(1+k)^{-n}]}{k}\right\}$$

$$PVA = 10\,000\frac{[1-1.06^{-5}]}{0.06}$$

$$= 10\,000 \times 4.2123$$

$$= \$42\,123$$

Suppose the current cost of the equipment is \$30 000. Should the manager go ahead with buying the equipment? Based on these figure and assuming the data are correct, she should because there is more than \$12 000 gain in present-value terms. Generally speaking, projects should be undertaken where the PV of future cash inflows is greater than the initial outlay.

These equations may look complicated, but they really are not. It's just a matter of practice. If you are calculating a PVA using a scientific calculator and your maths is a bit rusty, start with the $(1 + k)^{-n}$ part. The discount rate, k, is 6% and the n is 5 years. Input 1.06 and hit the y^x button, then input 5 and hit the = button. Next press the $1/x$ button (to give you the *negative n*) and you will have solved this first bit of the equation. The answer is 0.7473. Now, press the +/– key to make the displayed value negative. Press + and 1, then = to get 0.2527 (you have subtracted 0.7473 from 1) then divide by 0.06 to get 4.2123. Then as your C is \$10 000, multiply the 10 000 by 4.2123 to get 42 123. The PVA of \$10 000 for 5 years at 6% discount rate is \$42 123. After you have tried a number of problems, your finger will dance over the calculator and find its own way onto the right buttons.

PV annuity problems are extremely common in finance. Think of a fully drawn business loan or a mortgage loan financing a house or a factory site and building (see the discussion in the following 'finance world' feature). The lender advances a sum at the present time, and the borrower normally repays the loan with periodic repayments, all of the same amount. For example, a 15-year business loan of \$100 000 at 6% pa nominal may be repaid with 180 monthly payments of \$843.86. Similarly, a \$10 000 loan at 6% for two years, compounded monthly, may be repaid with 24 payments of \$443.21. Table 4.1 shows you the amortisation or repayment schedule for such a loan, taken out on 1 January 2008, and the repayments made on the first day of each month for 24 months.

There are many websites available that will show you how long various loans will take to repay at various interest rates. Just use your search engine and type in 'loan calculator'. FV annuity problems are less common, but still have applicability in finance as investors think of accumulating future amounts.

Table 4.1 Amortisation of a $10 000 loan borrowed on 1 January 2008

Loan amortisation data												
Month Year	**Feb 2008**	**March 2008**	**April 2008**	**May 2008**	**June 2008**	**July 2008**	**Aug 2008**	**Sept 2008**	**Oct 2008**	**Nov 2008**	**Dec 2008**	**Jan 2009**
Payment ($)	443.21	443.21	443.21	443.21	443.21	443.21	443.21	443.21	443.21	443.21	443.21	443.21
Principal paid ($)	393.21	395.17	397.15	399.13	401.13	403.14	405.15	407.18	409.21	411.26	413.31	415.38
Interest paid ($)	50.00	48.03	46.06	44.07	42.08	40.07	38.06	36.03	33.99	31.95	29.89	27.82
Total interest ($)	50.00	98.03	144.09	188.16	230.24	270.31	308.37	344.40	378.39	410.34	440.23	468.05
Balance ($)	9606.79	9211.62	8814.47	8415.34	8014.21	7611.08	7205.92	6798.75	6389.54	5978.28	5564.96	5149.58
Month Year	**Feb 2009**	**March 2009**	**April 2009**	**May 2009**	**June 2009**	**July 2009**	**Aug 2009**	**Sept 2009**	**Oct 2009**	**Nov 2009**	**Dec 2009**	**Jan 2010**
Payment ($)	443.21	443.21	443.21	443.21	443.21	443.21	443.21	443.21	443.21	443.21	443.21	443.21
Principal paid ($)	417.46	419.55	421.64	423.75	425.87	428.00	430.14	432.29	434.45	436.62	438.81	441.00
Interest paid ($)	25.75	23.66	21.56	19.45	17.34	15.21	13.07	10.92	8.75	6.58	4.40	2.21
Total interest ($)	493.80	517.46	539.03	558.48	575.82	591.02	604.09	615.01	623.76	630.34	634.74	636.95
Balance ($)	4732.12	4312.58	3890.93	3467.18	3041.31	2613.31	2183.17	1750.88	1316.43	879.81	441.00	0.00

EXAMPLE 4.11

Calculating the future value of an ordinary annuity

Carson's Camping Supplies decides to set aside funds to build up a retirement nest egg for the couple who run the business as partners. They think they can put away \$20 000 pa starting in 1 year's time and they have 18 years to go before they want to retire. Using a conservative estimate, they think their funds can gain 8% pa after tax. How much will they have at the end of 18 years?

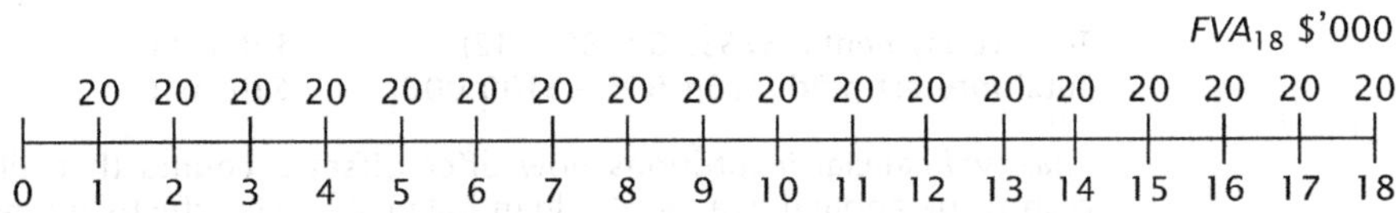

$$FVA_n = C\left\{\frac{[(1 + k)^{-n} - 1]}{k}\right\}$$

$$FVA_{18} = 20\,000\frac{[1.08^{18} - 1]}{0.08}$$

$$= 20\,000 \times 37.4502$$

$$= \$749\,005$$

With this example the value of compound interest becomes really apparent. The Carsons invest \$360 000 (\$20 000 × 18) of their own funds over the period, but their nest egg is worth \$749 005 at the end of the period due to the earning of interest (returns) and interest on interest.

Just as with the FV and PV of a single sum, tables are available in the appendix at the end of this book to provide the compounding and discount factors for the calculation of FVs and PVs of ordinary annuities. Table 3 gives the factor for the FVA of \$1 per period for many periods and table 4 gives the discount factors for the PVA of \$1 per period for many periods. In addition, there are many times in business that monthly, quarterly or annual periods are inappropriate. It is more appropriate to use daily discount rates in situations where cash flows are received many times during the year. For example, a manufacturer analysing a potential investment in new production machinery from which the output would be sold every weekday would find it more appropriate to use daily rates than to assume all cash flows were received on 31 December. Daily discounting always results in higher PVs than end-of-period discounting, because the funds are received earlier in every case. Table 5 in the appendix gives the factors for calculating PVAs, given equal daily cash flows.

As exercises in using these tables, look up the compounding factor for the Carsons case (example 4.11) using table 3: $n = 18$, the rate is 8% and the factor is 37.4502. Multiplying the \$20 000 annual payment by the factor gives an FVA of \$749 004. Similarly, look up the Thompson's discount factor (example 4.10) in table 4: $n = 5$ and the rate is 6%. This gives a factor of 4.2124. Again, multiplying the annual payment of \$10 000 by the factor, 4.2124, gives a PVA of \$42 124.

FINANCE WORLD

Annuity mathematics and interest

Calculating the repayment of a fully drawn business loan or a traditional home loan is an application of annuity mathematics. Consider the following loan proposal:

Loan amount	$100 000	
Term (years)	30	
Interest rate	8.02%	(compounded monthly)
Scheduled monthly repayment	$735.16	
Total repayments ($735.16 × 30 × 12)	$264 656	
Total interest paid ($264 656 − $100 000)	$164 656	

Many financial institutions now offer offset accounts that allow all of a borrower's spare cash to be applied against the loan balance.[1] This effectively means that for the purposes of calculating interest the outstanding loan balance is reduced by the amount of spare cash in the borrower's offset account. If the amount of cash is substantial, it can dramatically reduce both the interest paid and the time it takes to pay off the loan. Consider the following scenario based on the loan proposal above.

Income after tax (monthly)	$5000
Expenses (monthly)	$3775
Scheduled monthly repayment	$735.16
Savings (monthly after expenses and scheduled repayment)	$489.84

Assume that the borrower leaves all their savings in the offset account. The balance will eventually reach the amount still owing on the loan and they can pay off the loan in full. Because the savings are offset against the loan balance each month, the borrower is effectively making a repayment each month of $1225 (that is, $735.16 + $489.84). This would see the loan repaid in 119 payments (just less than 10 years), and the last payment (about $500) would not need to be as much as the $1220.99 necessary if 119 equal payments were made. The total amount repaid would be $145 299 and the total interest paid would be $45 299 (based on the 119 equal payments) or about $145 050 and $45 050 based on payments of $1225. This amounts to a saving of $119 357 or $119 606 over the original loan proposal.

Is it worth paying off your loan early? The PV of the loan does not change if you make larger payments over a shorter period. The opportunity cost concept comes in here — if you cannot find an investment that generates an after-tax return greater than the rate you pay on your mortgage, then you should utilise an offset account. Alternatively, if you have credit card debt (where interest charges are higher than the mortgage rate) you should pay off that debt first.

FINANCE WORKSHOP 4.3

1. Prove to yourself that the $735.16 monthly repayment in the original loan proposal is correct.
2. Prove the reduced time of the offset arrangement is correct. *Note:* this is a trial and error problem. Select a time period and try to get the computed factor as close as possible to $\frac{PVA}{C}$, which is 81.6326 [loan of $100 000, divided by the monthly repayment plus the monthly savings: $\frac{\$100\,000}{\$735.16 + \$489.84}$].

Other types of annuities

We will now examine the annuity due, deferred annuity and perpetuity.

Annuity due

An annuity due is only an ordinary annuity with an extra payment added on to the front end of the series of cash flows. A common example in finance of annuities due is leasing finance. With lease finance, the first payment is due immediately the lease is signed and then payments are made at regular intervals thereafter. (Payments made or received on the first day of each period are assumed to have the same value as a payment made on the last day of the period before.)

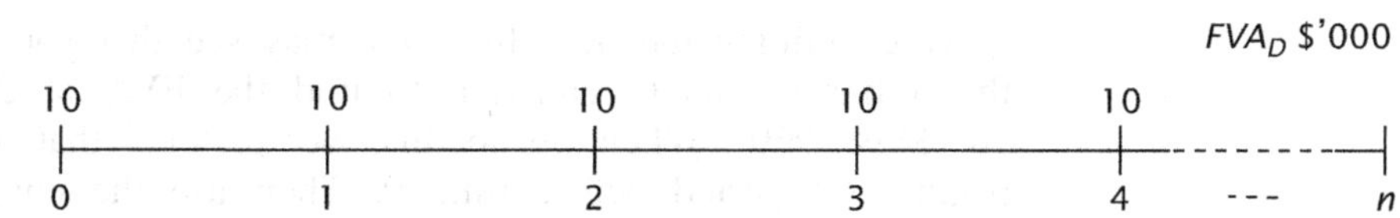

The equation for the FV of an ordinary annuity may be converted for use as the equation for the FV of an annuity due by adding '1' to n and subtracting '1' from the calculated compounding factor. Thus the equation is:

$$FVA_D = C\left\{\frac{[(1+k)^{n+1}-1]}{k}-1\right\} \qquad [4.10]$$

where FVA_D = future value of an annuity due
C = periodic cash flow
k = compounding rate
n = number of periods

The number of time periods, n, is increased by '1' because the extra payment at time zero can be thought of as being received at the end of an additional period that ends at exactly time zero. Look at the time line. However, the whole compounding factor must be decreased by '1' because there is no payment on the final day of the nth period such as would be received with an ordinary annuity. (The final payment is received at the beginning of the last period.)

EXAMPLE 4.12

Calculating the future value of an annuity due

Brown's Castings wants to replace a large grinding machine in 21 years' time. The manager has been advised that the machine will cost in the order of \$2.25 million at that time and that he should budget to reserve about \$60000 per year, starting now, to pay for the machine. With one instalment invested now and a further 20 annual instalments, there will be 21 instalments of \$60000 altogether. Is this advice correct? Will there be \$2.25 million available at the end of year 21, given that the funds can earn 5%?

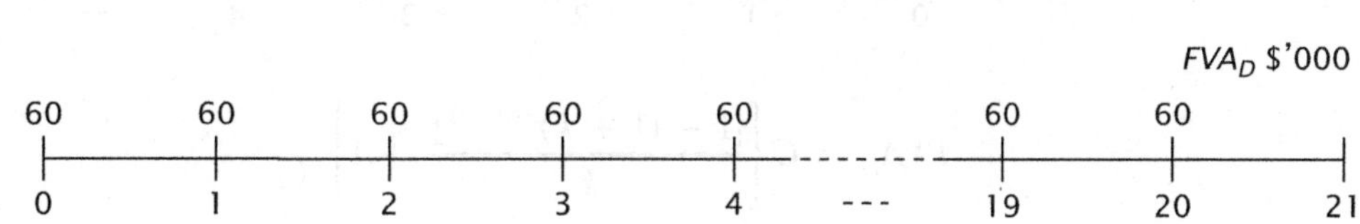

$$FVA_D = C\left\{\frac{[(1 + k)^{n+1} - 1]}{k} - 1\right\}$$

$$FVA_D = 60\,000\left(\left\{\frac{[(1.05)^{22} - 1]}{0.05}\right\} - 1\right)$$

$$= \$2\,250\,313$$

By examining the time line, you may see that you can solve this problem by using the ordinary annuity equation to find the FVA of 20 payments at the end of year 20 ($1 983 960). When we do this, we 'pretend' that we have an ordinary annuity that begins one period before time 0. Then use the equation for compounding a single sum to increase that sum by the 5% return to find the value at the end of year 21 ($2 083 158). To this amount, you will have to add the compounded value in 21 years of one payment of $60 000 received now [$60\,000(1.05)^{21}$ = $167 157]. The total amount is $2 250 315, which is close enough to the value previously calculated after allowing for rounding.

Similarly, the equation for the PV of an annuity due may be built. The number of time periods is reduced by '1', because there is one less period for the funds to earn interest, and the discount factor is increased by '1' as the payment made at time zero carries its full value as its PV. Hence, the equation for the PVA_D is:

$$\boldsymbol{PVA_D = C\left\{\frac{[1 - (1 + k)^{-(n-1)}]}{k} + 1\right\}} \qquad [4.11]$$

where PVA_D = present value of an annuity due
C = periodic cash flow
k = discount rate
n = number of periods

EXAMPLE 4.13

Calculating the present value of an annuity due

What is the PVA_D of Sue's prize option (in the opening page of this chapter) of 21 payments of $60 000, given a discount rate of 5% (which is a reasonable assumption of the interest rate she could earn on funds)?

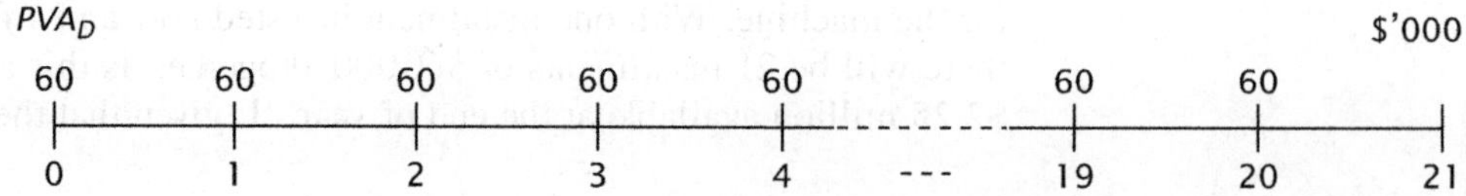

$$PVA_D = C\left\{\frac{[1 - (1 + k)^{-(n-1)}]}{k} + 1\right\}$$

$$PVA_{120} = 60\,000\left(\left\{\frac{[1 - 1.05^{-20}]}{0.05}\right\} + 1\right)$$

$$= \$807\,732$$

If Sue were studying this course, she would now have the skills to decide which prize to accept from Translotto. She has the option of $1 million now or a series of payments for which the PV is $807 732, given a discount rate of 5%. While the difference between the amounts is substantial, Sue would have to be sure in her mind that 5% was the appropriate discount rate. If, for example, she could be sure to earn 8% pa after tax on her funds, the PV of the series of $60 000 payments would be less than the $807 732. On the other hand, if she felt reasonably certain that she could earn only 3% pa after tax, then the PV of the cash flow would rise to more than $950 000. Once she had decided on the most appropriate rate, she could then make her selection of the prize with confidence.

Deferred annuity

A deferred annuity has its first payment made after several periods have elapsed. Thus, solving a deferred annuity PV problem is undertaken in two parts. First, solve the annuity part as an ordinary annuity. Thus, for the following time line, find the PVA at time * of the six payments of $60 000, then deal with the deferred part by discounting the single-sum PVA* back to the present to find PV**.

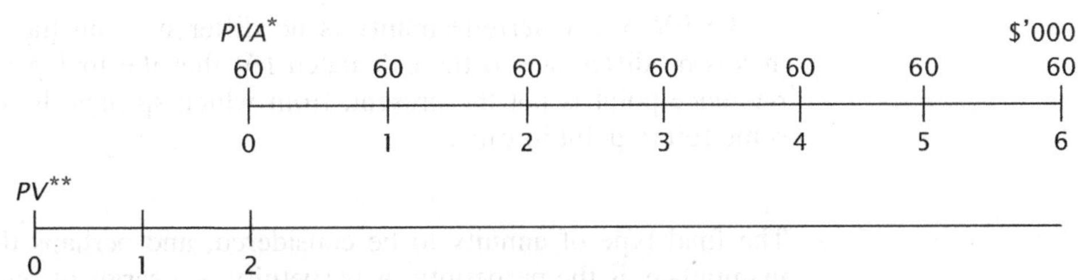

Equation 4.12 is used to calculate the PV of a deferred annuity, PVA_B.

$$PVA_B = C\left\{\frac{[1 - (1 + k)^{-n}]}{k}\right\}(1 + k)^{-b} \quad [4.12]$$

where PVA_B = present value of a deferred annuity
C = periodic cash flow
k = discount rate
n = number of annuity periods
b = number of periods before the annuity begins

For example, suppose Sue's prize of 21 annual payments were to start in early January 2010. What is its PV at 1 January 2007? We can solve this problem by thinking of the stream of payments as an ordinary annuity starting in two years' time at 1 January 2009 with the first payment actually received in the first week of January 2010. For simplicity, we will show the calculation for the ordinary annuity deferred two years.

EXAMPLE 4.14

Calculating the present value of a deferred annuity

Sue's prize of 21 annual payments is deferred 2 years and she receives her first payment at the end of year 3. What is the PV, given a 5% discount rate?

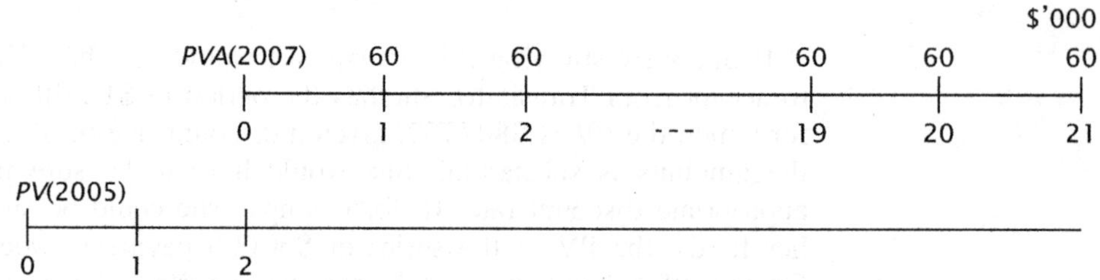

$$PVA_B = C\left\{\frac{[1-(1+k)^{-n}]}{k}\right\}(1+k)^{-b}$$

$$PV = 60\,000\left[\frac{1-(1.05)^{-21}}{0.05}\right](1.05)^{-2}$$

$$= 769\,269\ (0.9070)$$
$$= \$697\,750$$

So we can see by this calculation that Sue would lose the equivalent of about $110 000 if the first payment of the prize were delayed 3 years.

The FV of a deferred annuity is no different from the FV of an ordinary annuity. It makes no difference to the calculated FV that the first payment is deferred, because the reference point is not the present, from which springs the concept of being deferred, but some future point in time.

Perpetuity

The final type of annuity to be considered, and perhaps the simplest to understand and manipulate, is the perpetuity. A perpetuity is a series of regular equal payments that continue forever. While forever is a long time, and you might argue that nothing lasts forever, which is true, the concept of perpetuity is still a useful one. Some cash flows have no determined limit. An example is a 10% preference share. With this security, the 10% payment will continue to be made while ever the company issuing the shares is solvent. There is no determined limit to the stream of payments. The equation for the PV of a perpetuity is:

$$PVP = \frac{C}{k} \qquad [4.13]$$

where PVP = present value of a perpetuity
C = periodic cash flow
k = discount rate

EXAMPLE 4.15

Calculating the present value of a perpetuity

Boon's Best Bakery Co. issues 10% $2 preference shares that pay a 20c dividend per share for as far into the future as anyone cares to analyse. What should be the current price of each share, given a discount rate of 5%?

$$PVP = \frac{C}{k}$$

$$PVP = \frac{0.2}{0.05} = \$4$$

The following 'behavioural perspective' feature opens with a report on a situation where consumers should do some PV calculations, but typically do not. Most people took the expensive option.

BEHAVIOURAL PERSPECTIVE

Retailer understands customers' foibles

Dateline: *Pottsville Marketing World*, Monday 23 The Pottsville branch of the major home furnishings retailer Narvey Hormann (NH) reported a very successful sales result from its promotion last month. In the current environment of ever-expanding housing developments around Pottsville and the influx of young families, the sales manager of NH had conceived a plan for a monster weekend sale on the last weekend of the month.

The specials offered that weekend were for purchases of any household goods of the customers' choice valued at $20 000. Customers could choose:

- $1000 immediate cash back, 48 monthly payments of $553 starting in 30 days, 1% interest per month
- 48 monthly payments of $500
- $18 000 cash within three business days.

Million-Dollar Malcolm Marshall reported to our PMW sleuth that 53 young couples had signed up to the deals and happily taken home the smaller items of their purchases. Malcolm confided that the first option had been the most popular, with 35 couples taking this option and only five taking the second option. Thirteen canny purchasers had agreed to the cash deal.

Why do you think this rather tongue-in-cheek report refers to the cash buyers as 'canny' or shrewd in their decision making? One additional piece of information you might like to consider when thinking about this report is this. Housing equity loans are currently available at most banks in Pottsville at 8% and special personal loans for householders are available at 9%.

Present and future value of unequal amounts

lo6

Calculate both present and future values of unequal amounts.

As we have already learned, an annuity involves a cash flow of equal amounts. A stream of unequal amounts is therefore not an annuity and cannot be manipulated by use of the annuity equations. Thus, any problem with different amounts must be solved using the single-sum equations for either the FV or PV, as required. Let's look at a time line example for a PV. To find the PV of the cash flows here, we need to take each flow in turn and discount it back to the present. Once all values are in present-day terms, we can add like to like and thus calculate the total PV.

EXAMPLE 4.16

Calculating the PV of unequal amounts

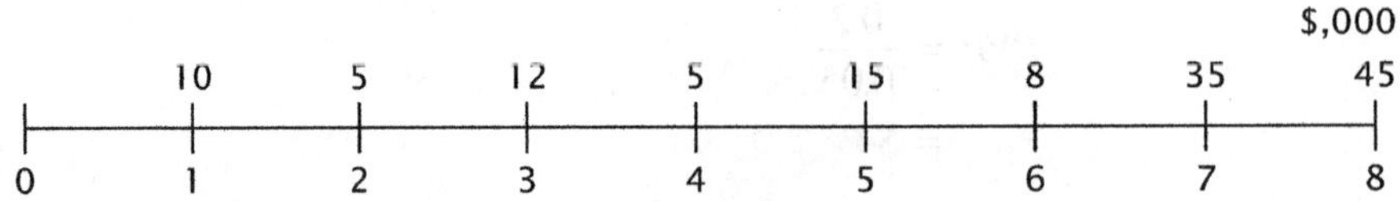

The PV of the positive cash flows, at a 5% discount rate, is:

$$PV = \frac{10000}{1.05} + \frac{5000}{(1.05)^2} + \frac{12000}{(1.05)^3} + \frac{5000}{(1.05)^4} + \frac{15000}{(1.05)^5} + \frac{8000}{(1.05)^6} + \frac{35000}{(1.05)^7} + \frac{45000}{(1.05)^8}$$

$$= 9524 + 4535 + 10366 + 4113 + 11752 + 5970 + 24874 + 30458$$

$$= \$101592$$

So, having done this calculation, what can we say about this project? Is it worth doing? We can't make this judgement until we know how much the project will cost. If it were to cost $100000 to start the project, then we might go ahead as our costs are covered in PV terms. Whether a business would actually commit to this project depends on:

- how good the data are (are these values likely to be accurate?)
- how the project fits with the business objectives
- whether the excess of $1592 is considered good enough, given the risk
- whether a 5% return on the funds is adequate.

Don't worry about these decisions at this stage; we learn more about them in chapter 8.

Solving time value problems

On first delving into the area, some students find financial mathematics rather daunting. There is no need for it to be. As we have shown, the use of a time line can be of immeasurable help in defining what information is available, what information is missing and what type of problem it is. Thus, we could develop a few steps in solving these problems.

These are:

1. Draw a time line and insert the cash flows, both in and out, at the appropriate places.
2. Identify what component of the required information is unknown.
3. Decide the class of problem (for example, FV or PV) so that the correct equations may be chosen.
4. Write down the equation(s), manipulate them so that the unknown value is on the left-hand side, insert the values as given and solve.

executive summary

lo1 discuss cash flows, interest and the time value of money

- Cash flows are relevant to project evaluation, not profits, losses, capital gains or capital losses.
- Interest is the price charged for the temporary use of money.
- Interest performs an allocative role in economies, by sharing out scarce funds to users.
- For borrowers, interest can be thought of as a penalty for wanting to consume before income is earned.
- For lenders, on the other hand, interest is compensation for putting off consumption until a later time.
- The time value of money is the concept that a dollar is worth more the sooner it is received. Money now is worth more than the same amount received in the future.
- When cash sums are received at different times, their values need to be brought to a common date, either today or a future date, so that they may be validly added or otherwise manipulated.

lo2 solve simple interest problems

- Simple interest is interest calculated on the original sum borrowed.
- Simple interest is applied to many sorts of bank deposits, such as savings accounts and term deposits, as well as many types of loans.
- The calculation of values relating to commercial bills provides an example of simple interest problems.

lo3 compute the prices of discount securities

- The yield is the amount produced or the return based on the initial investment.
- In Australia, we normally trade commercial bills in terms of yield.
- When a bill is offered for re-sale, it may be described as being sold at a given yield or a given discount.
- A discount rate in relation to pricing a security relates to the face value, not the funds borrowed (PV).
- Some of the most important conventions or rules for solving commercial bill problems are:
  - Interest rates are quoted on a nominal annual basis (as if for one year) and pro-rated for the actual period of the loan.
  - Pro-rating takes place on the basis of the exact number of days divided by 365.
  - In a leap year, 29 February is charged for if the loan is outstanding over this day, but the year is assumed still to have 365 days.

lo4 understand the compound interest formula so that you can calculate both future and present values

- Compound interest is interest calculated on the actual outstanding amount each period and this amount may comprise the whole or part of the initial principal plus unpaid interest.

- The total interest charged under a compound-interest arrangement is more than that which would have been charged with simple interest.
- Compound interest is applied to many different types of loans such as personal and credit-card finance, mortgages and overdrafts.
- The FV formula may be manipulated so that it will give the PV of a future sum.
- The discount rate is the rate of interest that is used to calculate the PV from an FV.
- The nominal interest rate is the advertised or quoted annual rate that does not reflect the impact of multiple compounding periods during the year.
- The effective interest rate reflects the impact of multiple compounding during the year.
- One basis point is one-hundredth of 1% — 0.01%; there are 100 basis points in 1%.

lo5 calculate both present and future values of annuities

- An annuity is a series of equal cash flows which are evenly spaced over time.
- There are four sorts of annuities:
  - ordinary (where the payments flow at the end of each even-length period)
  - annuity due (where the first payment is received on the day of the valuation)
  - deferred (where the first payment is deferred for a period greater than the subsequent even-length periods)
  - perpetuity (where the cash flows continue regularly for ever).
- It is easiest to use a time line to show yourself pictorially when cash flows occur when solving PV or FV problems.

lo6 calculate both present and future values of unequal amounts

- A stream of unequal amounts is not an annuity and cannot be manipulated by use of the annuity formulae.
- Any problem with different amounts must be solved using the single-sum formulae for either the FV or PV as required.
- Once all cash flows are in FV or PV terms, we can add like to like and thus calculate the total FV or PV.
- The use of a time line helps to define what information is available, what information is missing and what type of problem it is. A few steps to help solve these problems are:
  - Draw a timeline and insert the cash flows, both in and out, at the appropriate places.
  - Identify what component of the required information is unknown.
  - Decide in your own mind the class of problem so that the correct formulae may be chosen.
- Write down the formula(e), manipulate so that the unknown value is on the left-hand side, insert the values as given and solve.

Key terms

annuity, p. 107
annuity due, p. 107
cash flows, p. 94
compound interest, p. 102
deferred annuity, p. 107
discount rate (in relation to pricing a security), p. 101
discount rate, p. 104

effective rate, p. 106
future value, p. 102
interest, p. 95
nominal rate, p. 105
ordinary annuity, p. 107
perpetuity, p. 107
present value, p. 102
simple interest, p. 96
time line, p. 102
time value of money, p. 95
yield, p. 100

Learning chart

Learning objective	Questions	Self-test problems	Financial problems
lo*1* discuss cash flows, interest and the time value of money	4.1, 4.2, 4.3		
lo2 solve simple interest problems	4.4, 4.5	4.1	
lo3 compute the prices of discount securities	4.6, 4.7, 4.8, 4.9	4.2	4.1, 4.2, 4.3, 4.4, 4.5, 4.6, 4.7, 4.8, 4.9, 4.10, 4.11, 4.12
lo4 understand the compound interest formula so that you can calculate both future and present values	4.10, 4.11, 4.12	4.3	4.13, 4.14, 4.15
lo5 calculate both present and future values of annuities	4.13, 4.14, 4.15, 4.16, 4.17, 4.18 4.19	4.4, 4.5	4.16, 4.17, 4.18, 4.19, 4.20, 4.21, 4.22, 4.23, 4.24, 4.25
lo6 calculate both present and future values of unequal amounts	4.20		4.24

Questions

4.1. Explain in your own words why an expected $100 Christmas present is worth less to you in January of the same calendar year than an expected $100 April birthday present.

4.2 Georgi buys a new utility with which to make deliveries in his business. The ute costs $22 000. Georgi's bookkeeper charges $4500 depreciation for the use of the ute for the year, so that its written down value at the end of the year is $17 500. Which of these figures is/are cash flow(s)?

4.3 Rigo sells some land which is no longer integral to his business's expansion plans. The sale price is $220 000; the transaction costs are $6000; the land cost $100 000 and Rigo's capital gain is $114 000. Which of these values are cash flows?

4.4 A2Z Banking Co. advertises that it pays 0.5% higher than cash rate on all savings accounts with the interest paid 3-monthly on lowest balance. Does this specification describe simple interest? How could a bank pay more than cash rate and still make a profit?

4.5 Sunni borrows $2000 from her friend Greta for one year at 5% pa simple interest. Is the interest payable more or less (or the same) as 5% compounding annually?

4.6 Yield in relation to a commercial bill is a percentage of what dollar amount?

4.7 A discount in relation to a commercial bill is a percentage of what dollar amount?

4.8 How many days are assumed to be in a year for the calculation values of commercial bills?

4.9 How many days are assumed to be in leap years for the calculation of values of commercial bills?

4.10 Jill has $1000 saved and can invest it at 5% pa simple interest or compounding monthly. Which deal will give her more funds at the end of 12 months?

4.11 The present value (PV) of $20 000 received in two years' time is always more than the PV of the same sum received in four years' time, assuming each will be received with 100% certainty. Is this true? Why?

4.12 Explain the difference between nominal and effective rates of interest.

4.13 An annuity is a series of ________ payments received at the ________ of several ________ length periods. Fill in the blanks.

4.14 The payments in an annuity due occur when in each of the equal-length periods?

4.15 Fung is thinking of buying either an annuity or an annuity due for a retirement income stream. How could she structure her finances so that an annuity becomes effectively an annuity due?

4.16 Assume you have been given a monthly annuity due, which is deferred for six months. How many months must elapse before you receive the first payment?

4.17 Give an example of a perpetuity.

4.18 Are coupons and bond yields the same thing?

4.19 As the stock market falls, bonds normally become more attractive and investors rush to buy bonds. What happens to bond prices and to bond yields?

4.20 Explain to your friend the value of using time lines to help solve cash flow problems.

Self-test problems

4.1 Bill gets a loan from his mum to buy a cheap second-hand car. His mum lets him have $5000 for 4 years at 5% simple interest. Bill contracts to pay the interest to his mum annually and to pay back the debt at the end of four years. How much is the annual interest and how much is paid at the end of year 4?

4.2 Bankeast supplies 91-day commercial bill finance to a customer. The face value of the bill is $100 000 and the nominal annual interest rate is 6.2%. How much does the customer receive?

4.3 Steve has $200 000 in his superannuation fund which is earning an average 10% compounded monthly. How much will this portion of his savings be worth in 10 years? How much more than growth of 10% annually will this amount be?

4.4 Singer's Sinking Fund receives $200 per month for 8 years and earns on average 6% pa. What is the future value of the fund?

4.5 Ace Charities has $1 000 000 in a fund earning 5.04% pa. How much can the charity spend each month for 10 years?

Solutions to self-test problems

4.1 Using the formula, Interest = Pin

Annual interest = $5000 \times 0.05 \times 1$ = \$250

Final repayment = \$5000 + 250 = \$5250

4.2 Using the formula, $PV = \dfrac{FV}{(1 + in)}$

$$PV = \frac{\$100000}{(1 + 0.062 \times \frac{91}{365})}$$

$$= \frac{100000}{(1 + 0.01546)}$$

$$= \$98\,477.78$$

4.3 Using the formula, $FV = PV\,(1 + k)^n$

$$FV = 200000\left(1 + \frac{0.1}{12}\right)^{120}$$

$$= 200000\,(1.0083)^{120}$$

$$= \$539\,265$$

$FV = 200000(1.1)^{10}$ = \$518 748 (for 10% annual growth)

Difference = \$539 265 − 518 748 = \$20 517

4.4 $$FV = C\frac{[(1+i)^n - 1]}{i}$$

$$= 200\frac{[1.005^{96} - 1]}{0.005}$$

$$= \$24\,565.71$$

4.5 $$PV = C\frac{[1 - (1+i)^{-n}]}{i}$$

$$= 1000000\,\frac{[1 - 1.0042^{-120}]}{0.0042}$$

$$= \$10\,626.11$$

Financial problems

4.1 Sue Chee's Fruit and Veges arranges for finance using a 6.5% pa \$50 000 commercial bill for 90 days. How much does she receive?

4.2 If Sue Chee's bill was for 180 days, how much would she receive?

4.3 Frank's Fishing Co. contracts with a bank to sell a \$100 000 180-day commercial bill with a 10% yield. How much will Frank receive?

4.4 Dim Sum Ltd buys a 90-day \$100 000 bill at 6% yield. How much will Dim Sum pay?

4.5 Jane's adviser offers her a chance to fund a commercial bill. The bill is for \$50 000 and 183 days at 8%. How much must Jane invest?

4.6 David's Hardware is offered 180-day \$100 000 bill finance yielding \$93 000. What is the yield?

4.7 Judy's Consulting Services looks for high-yield investments. She is offered this deal: \$100 000 commercial bill, 90 days, \$96 500 to pay. What is the yield?

4.8 Aquila Investments offers a borrower a \$50 000 180-day bill for \$48 000. What is the yield?

4.9 Don Ltd bought a $100 000 commercial bill in the secondary market with 100 days to maturity. It was discounted at 8%. How much did the company pay?

4.10 A 180-day $100 000 bill was sold for $93 000. What was the discount rate?

4.11 Joe bought a $100 000 90-day bill for $96 500. What was the discount rate?

4.12 A $50 000 180-day bill was discounted at 8% and sold to Ngai. How much did she pay?

4.13 Jean invested her lottery prize of $80 000 in a fund which pays 6% pa. How much will she have at the end of 8 years?

4.14 Joan invested her lottery prize of $80 000 in a fund which pays 6% pa, compounded monthly. How much will she have at the end of 8 years?

4.15 Agricola Ltd extends 'interest-free' terms to customers. It has made sales that will bring in $100 000 at the end of 2 years. How much is the $100 000 worth now if money can earn 6% pa compounded monthly?

4.16 Agrico has contracted an interest-only loan. It must repay the principal of $500 000 in six years' time. How much must it invest at the end of each year to have exactly $500 000 put aside if funds earn 6%?

4.17 If Sootico borrowed $500 000 now at 6% compounding monthly, how much must it repay monthly to pay off the loan in six years?

4.18 A 7% coupon $10 000 bond with semi-annual payments has seven payments to maturity. (The latest payment was received yesterday.) What is its price if it yields 5.2%?

4.19 Sam Lee is saving for his retirement. He invests a regular $1000 per month for 20 years and earns 8% pa compounded monthly on his investment. How much does he have on his retirement?

4.20 Sam says he will live for 18 years after he retires. He intends to spend all of his nest-egg of $590 000 through monthly payments from his pension fund. He budgets on the fund earning 5% pa compounded monthly. How much can he draw each month?

4.21 Here are some details of $100 000 high-risk bonds. Calculate the current price in each case.

Coupon (%)	Required yield (%)	Interest payable	Time to maturity
12	10	6-monthly	4.5 years
12	15	6-monthly	5 years
12	15	6-monthly	5 years + 1 day*
10	12	3-monthly	3 years
12	8	3-monthly	4 years
8	6	6-monthly	4 years

* An interest payment is due on this day.

4.22 A $100 000 8% bond with 6 years to maturity is sold for $93 970. What is its yield, if interest is paid 6-monthly?

4.23 A $50 000 9% (6-monthly interest) bond is purchased by a dealer for $51 880. If it has 3 years to maturity, what is its yield?

4.24 Sam is negotiating to purchase an annuity of $50 000 pa for 10 years. Funds currently earn 6% pa. To sweeten the deal, the supplier offers either to:

(a) make it an annuity due (with 10 payments in total) or

(b) add an extra payment of $10 000 to be paid immediately.

Which is the better deal for Sam, if the price remains the same?

4.25 Jo is offered a $3000 monthly pension for 15 years with the first payment deferred 24 months. What is the correct price of the pension now if funds earn 8% pa?

SOLUTIONS TO FINANCE WORKSHOPS

4.1 1. $$\frac{100000}{\left(1 + 0.07 \times \frac{180}{365}\right)} = \$96\,663.13$$

2. $$\frac{100000}{\left(1 + 0.08 \times \frac{60}{365}\right)} = \$98\,702$$

4.2 1. $$FV = 50000\left(1 + \frac{0.06}{12}\right)^{6} = \$51\,518.87$$

2. $$FV = 50000\left(1 + \frac{0.06}{2}\right) = \$51\,500$$

3. $$FV = 50000\left(1 + \frac{0.06}{2}\right) = \$51\,500$$

4. $$k_{eff1} = \left(1 + \frac{0.06}{12}\right)^{12} - 1 = 0.0617$$

$$k_{eff2} = \left(1 + \frac{0.06}{2}\right)^{2} - 1 = 0.0609$$

k_{eff3} — no compounding involved

4.3 1. $$PV = C\left\{\frac{[1 - (1 + k)^{-n}]}{k}\right\}$$

$$C = \frac{PV}{\left\{\frac{[1 - (1 + k)^{-n}]}{k}\right\}}$$

$$= \frac{100\,000}{\left\{\frac{[1 - (1 + 0.006\,683\,3)^{-360}]}{0.006\,683\,3}\right\}}$$

$$= \frac{100\,000}{\frac{[1 - 0.090\,90]}{0.006\,683\,3}}$$

$$= \frac{100000}{136.0255}$$

$$= \$735.16$$

2. At say 10 years $\frac{[1 - (1 + k)^{-n}]}{k} = \frac{[1 - (1 + 0.006\,683\,3)^{-120}]}{0.006\,683\,3} = 82.797$

At 9 years, $\frac{[1 - (1 + 0.006\,683\,3)^{-108}]}{0.006\,683\,3} = 76.751$

At 9 years 10 months, $\frac{[1 - (1 + 0.006\,683\,3)^{-118}]}{0.006\,683\,3} = 81.448$

At 10 years 2 months, $\frac{[1 - (1 + 0.006\,683\,3)^{-119}]}{0.006\,683\,3} = 81.900$

(The difference between this answer and the computed value is in the rounding of the decimal places.)

End notes

1 Examples of such offset arrangements include Heritage Building Society's 'Mortgage Crusher' and St George Bank's 'Mortgage Equaliser'.

chapter 5

chapter

5

Understanding risk and return

Learning objectives

After studying this chapter, you should be able to:

lo1 explain the term 'return'

lo2 explain the difference between ex post and ex ante returns and calculate each of these for a share

lo3 explain how risk is defined in the discipline of finance

lo4 calculate ex post and ex ante levels of risk using the standard deviation

lo5 explain how a person's risk profile influences their investment decisions

lo6 describe the relationship between risk and expected return

lo7 explain how risk is reduced by diversification

lo8 explain how risk is measured in the Capital Asset Pricing Model (CAPM) and apply the model.

INVESTMENT OPTIONS FOR THE UNISUPER SUPERANNUATION FUND

Product	Description	Financial year return % 2001–02	Financial year return % 2005–06
Cash	Includes short-term money market investments such as bank bills and promissory notes, and short-term fixed interest securities.	4.3	5.50
Capital stable	Over half of the assets held are fixed interest bonds. The remaining assets are held in roughly equal proportions. These assets are: ▪ cash ▪ property (commercial, industrial and residential real estate, owned directly or held indirectly through listed property trusts) ▪ overseas listed shares ▪ Australian listed shares.	*	7.78
Conservative balanced	About 45% of the assets are held as fixed interest bonds. About 20% of the assets are held as Australian listed shares. The remainder is divided between: ▪ cash ▪ property (as described above) ▪ overseas listed shares.	–1.3	11.24
Balanced	About 25% in each of: ▪ Australian listed shares ▪ overseas listed shares About 30% in: ▪ fixed interest bonds. The remainder is divided between: ▪ property ▪ alternative investments (infrastructure — for example, roads and airports; and private equity investments — unlisted Australian shares and other investments).	–2.8	14.48
Growth	About 30% of the assets are held as Australian listed shares. About 30% of the assets are held as overseas listed shares. The remainder is divided between: ▪ fixed interest bonds ▪ alternative investments (as already described) ▪ property.	–6.1	17.39

continued

continued

Product	Description	Financial year return %	
		2001–02	2005–06
Socially responsible shares	Sustainable investment criteria are used to select: ▪ Australian listed shares (around 55%) ▪ overseas listed shares.	*	21.2
Shares	▪ Australian listed shares (around 55%) ▪ overseas listed shares.	–11.0	21.14

* These investment options were newly created, so no historical return was available.

Source: UniSuper.[1]

Chapter preview

The variety of investment options available to members of the UniSuper superannuation fund is shown on the opening page of this chapter. Have a look at the investment alternatives, the types of assets that are used to generate income for the alternatives and how much return was earned by each of the alternatives in the 2001–02 and the 2005–06 financial years. Did you wonder why one superannuation fund would offer so many alternatives? Did you wonder why some alternatives gave positive returns and some made losses? Did you wonder why the superannuation fund would bother continuing with the shares alternative when it made an 11% loss the first year?

Members of the superannuation fund elect which alternative their contributions are held in. Why do the members of UniSuper make different choices? Why do some people choose to make all of their investments in property? Why do other people choose not to own a place to live, choosing to own shares or their own businesses instead? The answers to these questions require an understanding of the concepts of risk and return. Applying the theory in this chapter will help you to provide informed answers about why people don't make identical investment choices.

The following diagram shows how this chapter is structured.

UNDERSTANDING RISK AND RETURN

- **What is return?**
- **Calculating returns**
  - Ex post returns
  - Ex ante returns
- **What is risk?**
- **Measuring risk?**
  - Ex ante standard deviation
  - Ex post standard deviation
  - Attitudes to risk
- **The relationship between risk and return**
  - Required rates of return
- **Reducing risk**
- **The Capital Asset Pricing Model**
  - Using CAPM to identify over- and under-priced shares
  - Is CAPM the best model of risk and return?

lo1

Explain the term 'return'.

Return: the gain or loss achieved by making an investment

What is return?

People invest their surplus funds in the expectation of making a positive **return**. A return is the gain or loss achieved by making an investment. If you buy a corporate bond, you get a flow of returns from the interest you receive. The issuing company uses the funds raised by issuing the bond to invest in projects that generate a flow of returns for the company. These returns are used to pay the interest on the bonds. The company can also raise funds by issuing shares. Shareholders get their stream of returns from the dividends they receive. They also get a return from any gain or loss they make when they sell their shares in the secondary market. Returns are positive when you make a gain and negative when you make a loss.

Figure 5.1 shows the historical annual returns on Australian shares and Commonwealth Treasury bonds with a 10-year maturity. It shows how much return shareholders and bondholders received over the period from January 1986 to January 2007. In the next section of this chapter we will see how returns are calculated. The remainder of the chapter is devoted to explaining why different assets — shares and bonds, for example — can have such very different returns over the same time period.

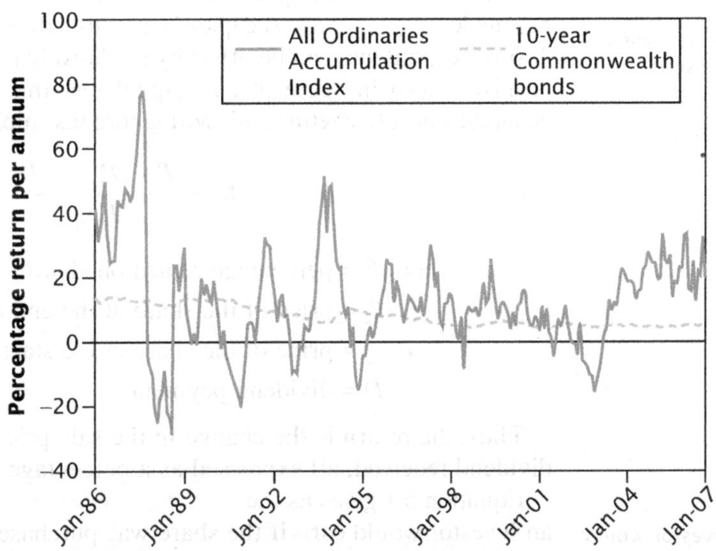

Figure 5.1 Annual returns on shares and Commonwealth bonds

Source: Index values were obtained from the SIRCA core research data,[2] and the *Australian Financial Review*, and Commonwealth bond returns were obtained from the Reserve Bank of Australia.[3]

lo2

Explain the difference between ex post and ex ante returns and calculate each of these for a share.

Calculating returns

There are two types of returns we can calculate. The first is measured after the return has occurred (ex post returns). The second involves estimating returns that are expected to occur in a future period (ex ante returns). The choice as to which type of return will be calculated depends on the nature of the decision you are to make. If you are using historical data, you will calculate the ex post return as you are looking at events that have already happened. If you are using expectations about the future, you will calculate the ex ante return because these events have not yet happened.

Investors are interested in after-tax returns. We discuss dividend imputation and capital gains tax in chapter 2. The level of franking credits, the investor's ability to utilise them and the capital gains tax implications of selling a share are all relevant to the investment decision. To keep the calculations in this chapter simple, we will calculate only before-tax returns. The impact of imputation on returns are covered in chapter 7 and the principles of capital gains discussed in the context of investment appraisal in chapter 9 can also be applied to security returns.

Ex post returns

Ex post or **realised returns:** those returns that relate to past periods

The returns in figure 5.1 are **ex post** or **realised returns**. This means that these returns can be readily observed from collecting data relating to past periods. The following discussion relates to calculating the returns on shares. We could apply the same principles to obtaining returns on any assets by substituting other relevant cash flows for dividends in equation 5.1. We use equation 5.1 to calculate the percentage return on a share for a single period. The equation tells us that the return on a share for a given period depends on the capital gain or loss plus any dividends we received over the period, D. A **capital gain** is made when the price of the share is higher at the end of the period, P_t, than it was at the start of the period, P_{t-1}. When the ending share price is lower than the price at the start of the period, the shareholder has made a **capital loss**. A capital gain plus a dividend payment will result in a positive return. A small capital loss can be offset by a relatively large dividend payment, giving the investor a positive return in aggregate. A capital loss that is larger than any dividend payment will generate a negative return. We will ignore tax implications to keep our discussion simple.

Capital gain: arises when the price of an asset increases

Capital loss: arises when the price of an asset decreases

$$R = \frac{P_t - P_{t-1} + D}{P_{t-1}} \times 100 \qquad [5.1]$$

where R = percentage return on share

P_t = price of the share at the end of the period

P_{t-1} = price of the share at the start of the period

D = dividend payment

Thus, the return is the change in the sale price compared to the purchase price plus any dividend received, all expressed as a percentage of the purchase price of the share.

Holding period return: the return an investor would earn if the share was purchased at the start of the period and sold at the end of the period

Equation 5.1 gives us the **holding period return**. The holding period return is the return an investor would earn if the share was purchased at the start of the period, $t - 1$, and sold at the end of the period, t. This means that the holding period return we calculate could relate to any period from a day to a number of years because it depends on the length of period we specify. You could, for example, calculate the holding period return for a share in A Ltd as 50% over a five-year period of ownership. You could also calculate the holding period return of a share in B Ltd to be 5% over a six-month period of ownership. Even if we ignore any potential impact from differences in risk for the moment, we cannot use these two holding period returns to unequivocally say both investments are as good as each other or that one is better than the other. To be able to compare the returns of two investments in any meaningful way, we need to have equal-length holding periods. By convention, returns are expressed on an annual percentage basis. We calculate the annual return on a share using the price at the start of the year, P_{t-1}, the price at the end of the year, P_t, and the dividends received through the year. Not only should holding period returns be expressed in the same length of time for comparison, they should also occur at about the same point in time. It would not be sensible to compare the annual return for a share in A Ltd that was calculated for 1997 to a share in B Ltd for the 2008 calendar year.

EXAMPLE 5.1

Realised (ex post) return on a share

An investor paid $35.06 each for Cochlear Ltd shares at the start of November 2002. During the year, she received an interim dividend of 33c and a final dividend of 44c. She sold the shares at the end of October 2003 for $28.91 each. What was the holding period return for the share?

$$R = \frac{P_t - P_{t-1} + D}{P_{t-1}} \times 100$$

$$R = \frac{28.91 - 35.06 + 0.33 + 0.44}{35.06} \times 100$$

$$= \frac{-5.38}{35.06} \times 100$$

$$= -15.3\%$$

The holding period (in this case annual) percentage return from Cochlear shares was a loss of 15.3%.

With the benefit of perfect hindsight, we can say that purchasing Cochlear shares and selling them when our investor in example 5.1 did was not a good investment. She decreased her net wealth over the year because the capital loss was greater than the dividends paid. This does not mean that the purchase of Cochlear shares today would give a poor return (the annual return was 42% for the year ending 30 June 2006). One reason we would not judge Cochlear harshly for the return in example 5.1 is that the share market overall experienced losses during 2002 and early 2003. This explains why the share investment alternative for the UniSuper superannuation fund at the start of the chapter made losses in the same periods. The **All Ordinaries Accumulation Index** is frequently used as a measure of the overall performance of the Australian share market. The index is constructed by taking the share prices of a group of companies listed on the ASX and weighting them according to their relative size in the market. It is assumed that dividends paid by the companies are reinvested, so they increase the index. Reinvestment of dividends occurs when any dividend paid by a company is used by the investor to purchase more shares in that company.

All Ordinaries Accumulation Index: constructed by taking the share prices of a group of companies listed on the ASX and weighting them according to their relative size in the market. It is assumed that dividends paid by the companies are reinvested, so they increase the index.

Using the All Ordinaries Accumulation Index as a measure of share market performance over the period from 1900 to 2006, figure 5.2 shows that there were negative annual returns in 22 of the 107 years. In three of these years, losses were in the range of 20–30%.[5]

FINANCE WORKSHOP 5.1

1. You paid $6.05 each for shares in Aluma Ltd a year ago. The company paid a dividend of 30c per share during the year. You sold the shares for $6.30 this morning. What was your annual return?
2. Check Cochlear's current share price and most recent dividends to calculate the holding period return from 1 July 2006 to now. The data are available at www.asx.com.au. Cochlear's share price code is COH.

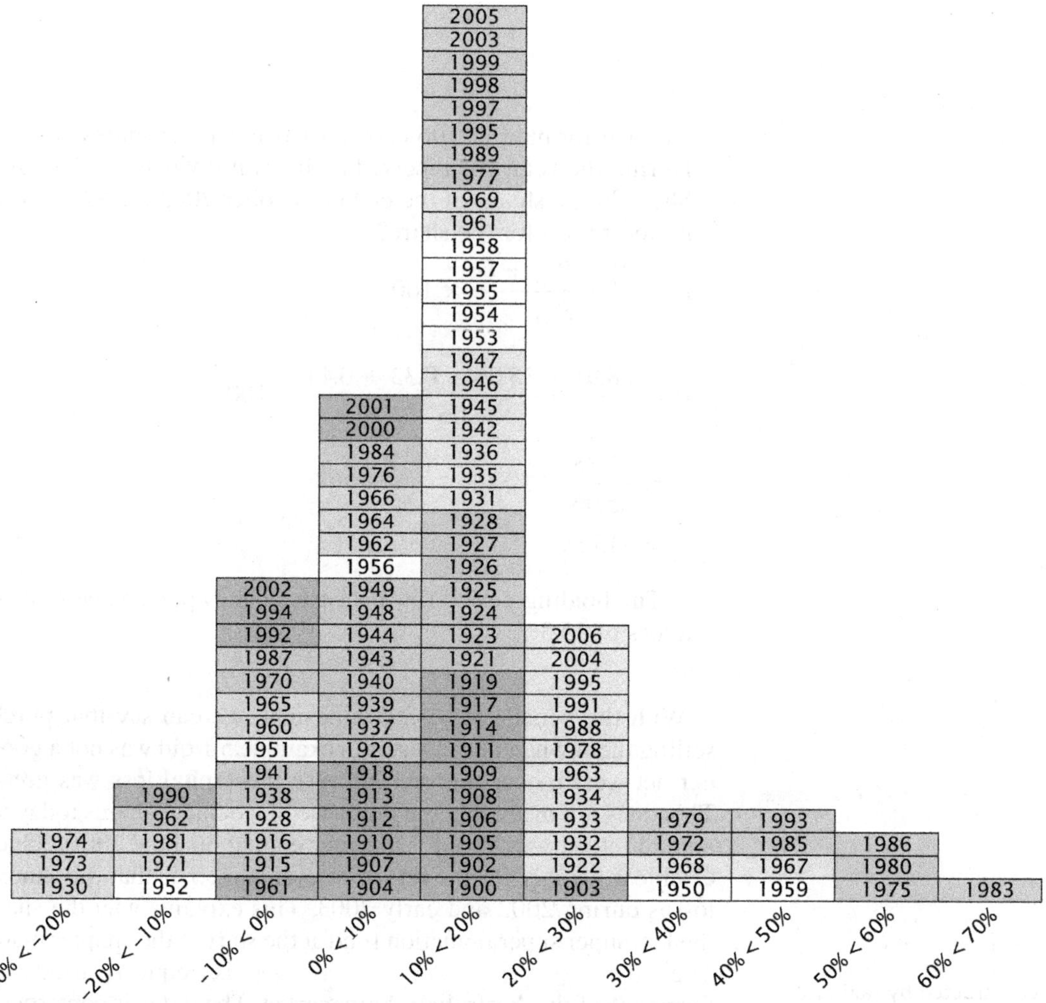

Figure 5.2 Annual performance of Australian shares 1900–2006

Source: Australian Securities Exchange.[4] Index values post-2002 were obtained from the *Australian Financial Review*.

Ex ante returns

Ex ante returns: those that investors expect to receive in the future

Investors make investments in the expectation of making positive returns and the future is always uncertain. It is the investor's estimation of **ex ante returns** that drives the decision to make an investment. Past returns are relevant only if they can be used to help understand how the company's future cash flows will be generated. Look again at the negative return we calculated for Cochlear in example 5.1. We have already discussed how the market as a whole performed poorly over the holding period, but are there any other factors that can help us to understand the loss? If we look closely at the activities of the company we find that it generates a large proportion of its income from sales in the United States. The Australian dollar appreciated against the US dollar over this period, so if Cochlear continued to charge the same US dollar price for its products, the strong exchange rate would result in less Australian dollar profits for the company. If we expect the Australian dollar to be worth relatively less compared to the US dollar in the future, we would also expect the Australian dollar cash flows to increase. At the point of making an investment decision, the future returns, rather than the historical returns, are relevant to that investment decision.

Expected return: the probability-weighted average of possible outcomes associated with the investments

While ex post returns are observable from past data, ex ante returns have not happened yet so they cannot be observed. Calculating the **expected return** on an investment is more difficult because it is subjective. It involves forecasting all the possible values the return could take and assigning probabilities to each of these possible outcomes. The possible outcomes are weighted (that is, multiplied) by their respective probabilities and then summed to obtain the expected return. This process is captured in the application of equation 5.2. Equation 5.2 can be used for shares as well as for other types of investments.

$$E(R) = \sum_{i=1}^{n} O_i p_i \qquad [5.2]$$

where $E(R)$ = expected return on the investment

n = number of possible outcomes for the investment

O_i = ith possible outcome

p_i = probability of the ith possible outcome occurring

Equation 5.2 tells us that the investor's expected return depends on the assessment of possible return outcomes and the probabilities associated with each of these outcomes.

The first step in calculating an expected return is to identify the possible outcomes for the return on the shares. Theoretically, your potential loss could be up to 100% of the purchase price, while your potential gain could be infinite. Neither of these extremes is probable, but there is still a wide range of possible return. In example 5.2 for simplicity's sake we will assume there are only four possible outcomes — you can apply the method used to any number of possible outcomes you would care to assign probabilities for. The probabilities in this example have been assigned in a subjective manner. This means that individual investors would assess the probabilities differently as they are based on a fairly vague notion of likelihood. When assigning probabilities to possible outcomes, it is critical that your total probability does not exceed 100%, because one of the possible outcomes must eventuate and, notwithstanding current vernacular, you can never be more than 100% certain that something will happen.

The following 'behavioural perspective' feature discusses how some people can take an irrational view of the use of probabilities.

BEHAVIOURAL PERSPECTIVE

Decision weights and probabilities

Consider the case of Rick Miller, the chief financial officer for BG Investments (BGI), a large national investment firm. Rick is used to making decisions that involve the expenditure of millions of dollars. The BGI board of directors is considering buying several stores — either in a chain of cheap fast-food outlets or in a chain of restaurants with a reputation for high-quality food and service. Rick has been asked to make a recommendation to the board. The revenue, cost and income analyses have been completed.

Rick thinks the two proposals are approximately equal in value but is leaning towards the higher-quality chain when a point of conflict arises over the franchise fees BGI would have to pay. The higher quality chain determines the non-adjustable franchise fees charged to owners *after* calculating the expected value of the cash flows for the restaurant. In contrast, the cheaper-food outlets have a flat fee. Upon thorough analysis of the most likely outcomes, the flat fee should prove to be about 30% higher per $1000 of sales than the probability-based fee and this difference will tip the balance so that the cheaper-food outlets will be less profitable in both the short and long runs. Rick, however, is adamant that he will not recommend that his firm should commit to a contract where there are probability-based outcomes. He changes his decision and recommends the cheaper-food outlets with the potentially lower returns. Why does he make this decision? (It is especially strange when we remember that most financial analyses of any reasonable complexity contain numerous estimates and assumptions based on probability distributions.)

The principle involved here relates to decision weighting. Decision weighting involves the weights decision makers put on possible outcomes and which influence final decisions. Certainty is often preferred by decision makers and over-weighted in relation to other options with probability-weighted outcomes of higher monetary value. This is known as the Allais Paradox, first reported by Frenchman Maurice Allais in the 1950s. Allais conducted a series of experiments that showed that, in choosing between two options, we cancel out what is the same for the two outcomes and focus on the differences in order to make a choice. Once we make a selection, that preference should hold if an identical amount is added to or subtracted from both options (that is, change both options so they are both worth proportionately more or less than the original option and their relative attractiveness has not changed).

In practice, the equivalent addition to or subtraction from an option may change preferences. Further, there should be no preference between equivalent outcomes. Experimentation has shown that subjects have indeed exhibited preference where there was no basis in terms of higher probabilities. The results are pretty much the same for student subjects and executive subjects,[6] suggesting that this is a phenomenon that does not decrease with experience in making decisions.

Is it rational to select a certain alternative with a lower expected value over a risky alternative that has a higher expected value? People do seem to give certainty a premium in decision making,[7] which results in certain outcomes with lower expected values than the alternatives being selected. Decision theorists have mixed opinions about the rationality of taking the sure thing when it comes to gains, but being prepare to risk all when faced with realising losses. We will explore this aspect further in the next 'behavioural perspective' feature.

EXAMPLE 5.2

Expected (ex ante) return on a share

Your analysis of Cochlear has resulted in the following four possible outcomes for next year's return. You have assigned the following probabilities.

Possible return (%)	Likelihood	Probability (%)
12	not very likely	20
8	most likely	60
2	unlikely	15
–5	remote	5

$$E(R) = \sum_{i=1}^{n} O_i p_i$$

$$\begin{aligned} E(R) &= (0.12 \times 0.20) + (0.08 \times 0.60) + (0.02 \times 0.15) + (-0.05 \times 0.05) \\ &= 0.024 + 0.048 + 0.003 - 0.0025 \\ &= 0.0725 \text{ or } 7.25\% \end{aligned}$$

Given your forecasts, the expected return on a Cochlear share is 7.25%.

You will notice in example 5.2 that the expected return is not equal to any of the possible returns. This is due to the role the weightings play in the calculation of expected return. The most likely outcome is heavily weighted and contributes 4.8% to the expected return while the least likely outcome (the chance of a loss) decreases the expected return by 0.25%. We have to wait until the end of the holding period to determine what the actual return will be. If our assumption that there are only four possible outcomes is true (and we know it is not!) the return on Cochlear shares could be as low as –5% or as high as 12%.

FINANCE WORKSHOP 5.2

You have identified the following possible annual returns and their probabilities for Aluma Ltd shares.

Possible return (%)	Probability (%)
15	25
10	30
5	30
0	13
–10	2

What is your expected annual return?

lo3

Explain how risk is defined in the discipline of finance.

What is risk?

We tend to think about risk in everyday situations as the chance that something will go wrong. To fully appreciate what risk means in the world of finance, we need to expand our pessimistic view of risk (the chance that something will go wrong) to a more balanced concept that includes the potential for something to go really well. In chapter 3 we define **risk** as the chance that the actual outcome from an investment will be different from the expected outcome. The everyday usage of the word 'risky' tends to have the negative connotation of being dangerous and again is a pessimistic view. When we describe something as 'risky' in finance, we are saying that the returns are variable or that the actual outcome can be different from the expected outcome. The terms 'risk' and 'risky' are value neutral when used in finance.

The definition of risk tells us that the realised (or ex post) returns over the life of a risky investment can be different from the expected (or ex ante) returns that were forecast at the outset of the investment. Ex post returns on a risky asset could end up as large gains or losses, and very different from the expected return. How different the ex post return can be depends on the probability distribution of possible returns. In finance, risk is synonymous with uncertainty.[8]

Consider a research company (Rescon) that has developed a new and highly efficient air-conditioning system. The airconditioners are manufactured by a number of different companies under licence. The manufacturers currently pay the licence fee to Rescon based on the number of units they make. As production levels vary, so does the amount of money received by Rescon. The possible outcomes for Rescon's licence revenue are shown in panel A of figure 5.3. Revenues for the next year could range from zero (if the manufacturers all decide they won't produce any airconditioners) to $4 million (if they all decide to produce nothing but Rescon's systems). Based on the probabilities of the possible outcomes, Rescon expects $2 million in revenue for the coming year.

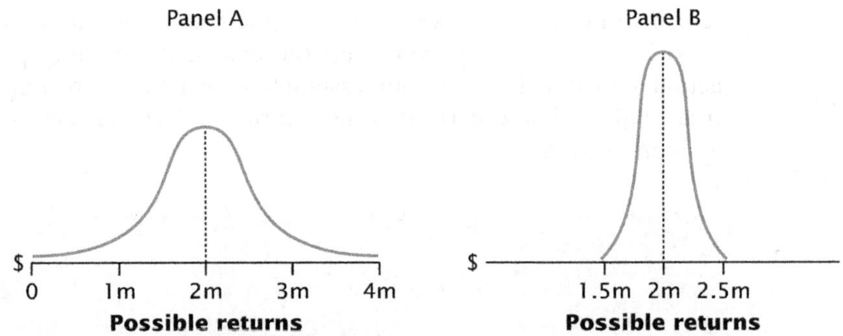

Figure 5.3 Distribution of possible outcomes

What if Rescon were to change the way they structure their licence fees? Rescon could charge each manufacturer a set amount each year for the right to produce the airconditioners. As shown in panel B of figure 5.3, this policy would reduce the number of possible outcomes for the licence revenue that Rescon would collect. The company would set the fee so its expected revenue was still \$2 million. Revenues would vary from the expected amount only if the number of companies holding the licences changed. The new policy would reduce the risk associated with Rescon's revenues because the number of possible outcomes has been restricted. The panel B revenues are less risky because there is no chance that revenues will be zero and there is no chance that revenues will be \$4 million. Rescon can feel more confident that the actual and expected outcomes will be close together. Generally speaking, the wider the dispersion of the possible future returns, the greater the chance that the ex post return will be different from the expected return. Distributions and dispersion are discussed in greater detail in the next section.

lo4

Calculate ex post and ex ante levels of risk using the standard deviation.

Measuring risk

Risk is defined as the chance that an actual outcome would be different from the expected outcome. Before the measures of risk are introduced in the following sections, there are a few statistical concepts that you need to be familiar with. In this section, we will discuss random variables, probability distributions and the concept of a standard distribution.

When the outcome of a future event cannot be known with certainty, as is the case with investment returns, the measurement of the outcome of an event (the actual return, that is) is called a random variable. Random variables can take on any value within a possible range of values. Investment returns, for example, can take on any value from –100% (you have lost your entire investment) to infinity (the gain you make is limited only by the performance of the underlying company) and all possible measures between these extremes (for example, –7.56% and 39.487%) are possible investment outcomes. Combining all possible outcomes for a random variable with their associated probabilities gives us the probability distribution of the random variable. The probability distribution of a random variable like investment returns will be a curve with an area equal to 1. Figure 5.4 shows a probability distribution.

Normal distribution: a symmetric and bell-shaped curve centred on the expected value of a variable

The probability distribution in figure 5.4 is called the **normal distribution**. The normal distribution is a symmetric and bell-shaped curve centred on the expected value of a variable. The mean (or average of possible values for the variable) and the mode (the most frequently occurring value of a variable) are both equal to the expected value of the variable. The mean is shown as $\bar{R}$ at the centre of the distribution. The symmetry of the normal curve tells us that some actual outcome, say five above the expected value, is just as probable as an actual outcome of five below the expected value. The difference between the expected value and an actual outcome is called a deviation — the observed value 'deviates' from what was expected. The shape of the normal distribution tells us that small deviations are much more likely than large deviations from the expected value. This is the same as saying that the realised outcomes will be clustered around the expected outcome.

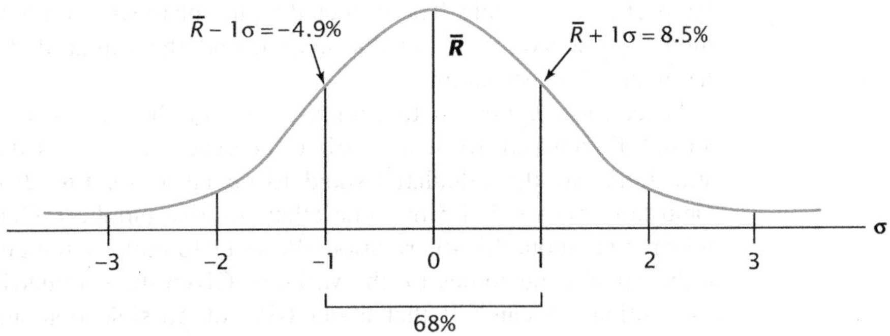

Figure 5.4 The standard deviation and normal distributions

Consistent with the definition of risk, the measurement of risk is about determining how probable it is that a realised outcome will deviate from the expected one. The width of a distribution shows us the dispersion of possible values for the variable and by how much a realised outcome is likely to deviate from the expected. The **variance** of a distribution measures this dispersion and is denoted by the symbol σ^2. The variance is the squared deviation of the variable from its expected value. If we try to calculate a measure of risk using the deviations from the expected value (or mean) for historical data the answer will always be zero. Consider a distribution with an expected value of 10%. We observe one outcome in each of the next two periods and find that the outcome for the first period is 5% and is 15% for the second period. This gives us a deviation of –5% (5 – 10) for the first period and a deviation of +5% (15 – 10) for the second period. When we add the deviations we will get zero (–5 + 5 = 0). A negative deviation of some particular size is exactly as likely as a positive deviation of the same size when we are using a symmetric distribution. By squaring the deviation, the impact of the sign of the realised outcome is eliminated and we are left with only the impact of the size of the deviation. Continuing with our two observations, but this time squaring the deviations, we get a dispersion measure of fifty ($-5^2 + 5^2 = 50$).

Variance: the squared deviation of the variable from its expected value

By squaring the deviations, we have changed the initial unit of measure so our answer of 50 does not indicate a dispersion of 50%, but is in fact a dispersion of 50 'square per cents'. If you are having trouble with this concept, think back to your school maths when you were required to calculate how much paint you would need to paint a room by working out the area to be painted. The answer should be some amount of square metres. Did you ever accidentally get an answer that was some amount of cubic metres? If you did, you worked out the volume rather than the area (and filled the room with paint!). Just as square metres measure something different from cubic metres, a 'square per cent' is not the same as the type of percentage we use to measure returns. The variance gives us a measure of dispersion, but that number measure is not on the same measurement basis as the variable of interest. To convert the variance to the same measure of the variable, we take the square root of the variance. This measure is the **standard deviation** (σ) and is the one we use to measure risk.

Standard deviation: the square root of the variance

Have another look at figure 5.4, paying particular attention to the numbers at the bottom of the curve. The expected value $E(R)$ is equal to zero and three standard deviations are shown on the left and the right of the expected value. No matter what the variable or its expected value, a normal distribution always has the majority of its possible outcomes within the range of the expected value minus three standard deviations and the expected value plus three standard deviations ($E(R) \pm 3\sigma$). This feature of the normal distribution allows us to say that the distribution is fully described by its expected value and the standard deviation. Another way of saying this is that knowing the expected value and the standard deviation is enough for us to be able to construct the normal distribution for that particular variable. The expected value (or mean) of a historical data set identifies the middle (or location) of the distribution and the standard deviation tells us a lot about the range of observations.

We can use figure 5.4 to demonstrate how the standard deviation is interpreted for a normal distribution. As stated earlier, the expected value of the distribution in figure 5.4 is zero. Let's say the calculated standard deviation for this distribution is one (although it could have been 0.5, 1.5 or some other positive number). Combining these two pieces of information about this distribution allows us to make some powerful conclusions about all of the possible outcomes for the variable. Given the symmetrical bell shape of the normal distribution we can tell that about 68% of possible outcomes fall in the range of the expected value plus or minus one standard deviation. Another way to say this is that the probability of observing a realised outcome that has a value between –1 and 1 is 68%. And 95% of the possible outcomes (the expected return plus or minus two standard deviations) will be in the range of –2 and 2. Given a mean of zero and a standard deviation of 1, the probability of observing an outcome that lies between –2 and 2 is 95%. The area under the normal curve covered by the range of the expected value plus or minus three standard deviations (–3 to 3) is 99.7%. The final conclusion we can draw is that only 0.3% of possible outcomes fall outside the range of the expected value plus or minus three standard deviations.

The bigger the standard deviation, the greater the likelihood of later observing an actual outcome that is different from the expected outcome. The smaller the standard deviation, the less likely it is that the actual outcome will be too different from the expected value.

Ex post and ex ante standard deviations are calculated using different equations, as we see in the next two sections. The ex ante standard deviation takes the probability of each possible outcome into consideration because the event has not yet happened. The ex post standard deviation does not use probabilities because all of the observations come from events that have already happened. We can be certain about the outcome of something that has already happened, so do not need to use probabilities to take uncertainty into account.

Ex ante standard deviation

Go back to the expected licensing revenues of Rescon as shown in figure 5.3. Panel A shows the wide distribution of possible outcomes under the variable charge plan. With possible outcomes ranging from zero to $4 million, the dispersion of potential outcomes is large and so is the chance that the actual outcome will be very different from the expected outcome. Panel B, with the same expected outcome of $2 million, shows that a very large proportion of the possible outcomes lies in the range $1.5–2.5 million. Therefore, the actual revenues in panel B have a lower chance of being different from the expected outcome. For symmetric distributions (like the ones in panels A and B) the appropriate measure of risk is the **ex ante standard deviation**. As we discussed in the previous section, the standard deviation is the square root of the variance. The **ex ante variance** is the probability weighted average of the deviations of possible returns from the expected return. Equation 5.3 is used to calculate the ex ante variance.

ex ante standard deviation: the square root of the ex ante variance

ex ante variance: the probability-weighted average of squared deviations of possible returns from the expected return

$$\sigma^2 = \sum_{i=1}^{n} (O_i - E(R))^2 p_i \qquad [5.3]$$

where σ^2 = variance

O_i = ith possible outcome

$E(R)$ = expected return on the investment

n = number of possible outcomes

p_i = probability of the ith possible outcome occurring

The term in the brackets of equation 5.3 tells us to subtract the expected return, $E(R)$, from each possible outcome to measure the possible deviation. The deviation is then squared to remove the effect of negative deviations and include only the impact of the size of the deviation. The squared deviation is then weighted (multiplied) by the probability that the particular outcome, O_i, will occur. This process is repeated for each possible outcome and then we total the calculations. This process is demonstrated in example 5.3.

EXAMPLE 5.3

Ex ante variance

We calculated the expected return for Cochlear in example 5.2 to be 7.25%. Using this and the following probabilities, calculate the variance of Cochlear's possible returns.

Possible return (%)	Probability (%)
12	20
8	60
2	15
–5	5

$$\sigma^2 = \sum_{i=1}^{n} (O_i - E(R))^2 p_i$$

$$\begin{aligned}\sigma^2 &= [(0.12 - 0.0725)^2 0.2] + [(0.08 - 0.0725)^2 0.6] + [(0.02 - 0.0725)^2 0.15] \\ &\quad + [(-0.05 - 0.0725)^2 0.05] \\ &= (0.002\,256 \times 0.2) + (0.000\,056\,3 \times 0.6) + (0.002\,756 \times 0.15) + (0.015\,006 \times 0.05) \\ &= 0.000\,451 + 0.000\,033\,8 + 0.000\,413 + 0.000\,75 \\ &= 0.001\,649 \text{ or } 0.1649 \text{ square per cent}\end{aligned}$$

Equation 5.4 calculates the ex ante standard deviation and is simply the square root of the variance given in equation 5.3.

$$\sigma = \sqrt{\sum_{i=1}^{n} (O_i - E(R))^2 p_i} \qquad [5.4]$$

where σ = standard deviation

O_i = ith possible outcome

$E(R)$ = expected return on the investment
n = number of possible outcomes
p_i = probability of the ith possible outcome occurring

EXAMPLE 5.4
Ex ante standard deviation

Using the information about Cochlear given in example 5.3, calculate the standard deviation of Cochlear's possible returns.

$$\sigma = \sqrt{\sum_{i=1}^{n}(O_i - E(R))^2 p_i}$$

$$\sigma = \sqrt{[(0.12 - 0.0725)^2 0.2] + [(0.08 - 0.0725)^2 0.6][(0.02 - 0.0725)^2 0.15] + [(-0.05 - 0.0725)^2 0.05]}$$
$$= \sqrt{(0.002\,256 \times 0.2)(0.000\,0563 \times 0.6) + (0.002\,756 \times 0.15) + (0.015\,006 \times 0.05)}$$
$$= \sqrt{0.000\,451 + 0.000\,0338 + 0.000\,413 + 0.000\,75}$$
$$= \sqrt{0.001649}$$
$$= 0.040\,61 \text{ or } 4.06\%$$

If the distribution of Cochlear's expected returns is normal, an expected return of 7.25% and a standard deviation of 4.06% tell us that about 68% of possible outcomes fall in the range of 3.19% to 11.31%. And 95% of the possible outcomes (the expected return plus or minus two standard deviations) will be in the range of −0.87% to 15.37%.

Ex post standard deviation

Ex post standard deviation: the square root of the ex post variance

Ex post variance: the weighted average of the squared deviations of observed returns from the mean return

Although the past is not generally a good predictor of the future, you will often see historical standard deviations presented as a measure of risk. The ex post standard deviation is the square root of the ex post variance. The ex post variance is the average of the deviations of actual returns from the mean return. Equation 5.5 is used to calculate the ex post (or historical) variance.

$$\sigma^2 = \frac{\sum_{t=1}^{T}(R_t - \bar{R})^2}{T-1} \quad [5.5]$$

where σ^2 = variance
R_t = observed outcome for time period t
$\bar{R}$ = mean return of the observed outcomes
T = number of observations

Deviations from the expected return (E(R)) were used to calculate the ex ante variance and standard deviation. The ex post variance and standard deviation use the mean return ($\bar{R}$) as the centre of the distribution. Before we can use equation 5.5, we need to calculate the mean (or average) return for our observations. Equation 5.6 is used to do this.

$$\bar{R} = \frac{\sum_{t=1}^{T} R_t}{T} \qquad [5.6]$$

where $\bar{R}$ = mean return of the observed outcomes

R_t = observed outcome for time period t

T = number of observations

Equation 5.7 is used to calculate the ex post standard deviation.

$$\sigma = \sqrt{\frac{\sum_{t=1}^{T} (R_t - \bar{R})^2}{T - 1}} \qquad [5.7]$$

where σ = standard deviation

R_t = observed outcome for time period t

$\bar{R}$ = mean return of the observed outcomes

T = number of observations

Example 5.5 demonstrates how the mean and historical standard deviations are calculated. The example uses the returns on an ordinary share, but you can use equations 5.6 and 5.7 for calculating standard deviations and means in general.

EXAMPLE 5.5

Mean, ex post variance and standard deviation

The following table contains the monthly returns for Cochlear Ltd for a 4-month period. Calculate the ex post standard deviation for Cochlear's returns.

Month	Return (%)
July	−4.96
August	6.14
September	−3.12
October	9.15

We first use equation 5.6 to calculate the mean return ($\bar{R}$):

$$\bar{R} = \frac{\sum_{t=1}^{T} R_t}{T}$$

$$\bar{R} = \frac{-0.0496 + 0.0614 - 0.0312 + 0.0915}{4}$$

$$= \frac{0.0721}{4}$$

$$= 0.018 \text{ or } 1.8\%$$

Having calculated the mean monthly return for Cochlear, we use 1.8% in equation 5.5 to calculate the ex post variance.

$$\sigma^2 = \frac{\sum_{t=1}^{T}(R_t - \bar{R})^2}{T - 1}$$

$$\sigma^2 = \frac{(-0.0496 - 0.018)^2 + (0.0614 - 0.018)^2 + (-0.0312 - 0.018)^2 + (0.0915 - 0.018)^2}{4 - 1}$$

$$= \frac{(-0.0676)^2 + (0.0434)^2 + (-0.0492)^2 + (0.0735)^2}{3}$$

$$= \frac{0.00457 + 0.001884 + 0.002421 + 0.005402}{3}$$

$$= 0.00476 \text{ or } 4.8 \text{ square per cent}$$

The ex post standard deviation is then the square root of the variance.

$$\sigma = \sqrt{\frac{\sum_{t=1}^{T}(R_t - \bar{R})^2}{T - 1}}$$

$$\sigma = \sqrt{\frac{(-0.0496 - 0.018)^2 + (0.0614 - 0.018)^2 + (-0.0312 - 0.018)^2 + (0.0915 - 0.018)^2}{4 - 1}}$$

$$= \sqrt{\frac{(-0.0676)^2 + (0.0434)^2 + (-0.0492)^2 + (0.0735)^2}{3}}$$

$$= \sqrt{\frac{0.00457 + 0.001884 + 0.002421 + 0.005402}{3}}$$

$$= \sqrt{0.00476}$$

$$= 0.06898 \text{ or } 6.9\%$$

If the monthly returns on the Cochlear shares in example 5.5 come from a normal distribution, the mean return, $\bar{R}$, of 1.8% locates the centre of the symmetric distribution. With a standard deviation of 6.9%, adding one standard deviation to the mean (8.7%) and subtracting one standard deviation from the mean (–5.1%) gives us the range in which about 68% of all observed returns for Cochlear fall. We can find the range for around 95% of all observed returns by adding and subtracting two standard deviations (2 × 6.9% = 13.8%) from the mean. This means that 95% of historical returns information we used for Cochlear will lie between the values of –12.0 and 15.6%. Similarly, 99.7% of all observed returns lie within three standard deviations from the mean of a normal distribution. The chance that an observed return will fall outside the range of –18.9% and 22.5% is only 0.3%. If we assume that Cochlear's past distribution of returns is similar to the distribution of future returns, knowing the range of returns allows us to be fairly confident that the company will not make a 100% gain or loss in a month. However, it is important to note that a 100% gain or loss in a month is possible, but there is a less than 0.3% chance that it would occur.

A large standard deviation indicates that many of the observations were very different from the mean outcome. If you want to use the ex post standard deviation as a proxy for future risk, and the standard deviation is large, you won't have much confidence that the future outcome will equal the historic mean. Therefore, a large standard deviation indicates high risk. Conversely, a small standard deviation indicates that returns fall within a relatively narrow range and indicates lower risk.

The standard deviation provides us with a useful measure of risk when possible outcomes follow a normal distribution. If the distribution of possible outcomes is asymmetric (or lopsided) or if it is too tall or too flat to be consistent with a normal distribution, we cannot draw conclusions about the probability that an observed outcome will fall within a specific range centred on the mean. In these cases, the standard deviation is not a reliable measure of risk.

FINANCE WORKSHOP 5.3

1. You should have calculated the expected return of Aluma Ltd as 8.05% in finance workshop 5.2. Use this and the following possible returns and probabilities to calculate the ex ante standard deviation for Aluma.

Possible return (%)	Probability (%)
15	25
10	30
5	30
0	13
−10	2

2. Use the following annual returns for Aluma Ltd to calculate the ex post standard deviation.

Year	Return (%)
2003	9.5
2004	7
2005	-8
2006	-3
2007	5

lo5

Explain how a person's risk profile influences their investment decisions.

Attitudes to risk

Individuals respond differently to uncertainty. Some people dislike taking risks and avoid doing so unless it is absolutely essential. Other people enjoy the thrill of not knowing how a situation will turn out and actively seek out risky situations. A person's attitude to risk (or **risk preference**) is part of his or her personality and researchers are still unsure if attitudes to risk are the result of life experiences or determined at birth by genetics[9] or a combination of both factors. Observed differences in the amount of risk people are willing to take have been linked to gender, income level, wealth, level of education and occupation. Civil servants, for example, tend to avoid risk while self-employed people are less likely to do so.[10]

Risk preference: represents a person's attitude to risk

We can categorise risk preferences according to the level of risk a person can comfortably tolerate. The three groups used in finance are risk averse, risk neutral and risk seeking.

Risk-averse: a person who will not participate in a fair game

Would you be willing to bet $100 on the toss of an unbiased coin? If your answer is 'no', then you are displaying behaviour that is consistent with risk aversion. A **risk-averse**

Fair game: one where the expected value of participating is zero

person will not participate in a fair game. The coin toss offered to you is an example of a fair game. A fair game is one where the expected value (or return) of participating is zero. We can use equation 5.2 to calculate the expected value of the coin toss as:

$$E(R) = \sum_{i=1}^{n} O_i p_i$$
$$= (100 \times 0.5) + (-100 \times 0.5)$$
$$= 50 - 50$$
$$= \$0$$

The expected value of the coin toss, as for all fair games, is zero. A gain of $100 or a loss of $100 are the only two possible outcomes for this game, so if you play it once you will not get an actual outcome of $0. Given the equal probabilities of gain and loss, if you played the game a number of times you could expect that your total gains minus your losses would amount to zero in the long run.

A risk-averse person will not choose to play this fair game. They will prefer the certain outcome of keeping the $100 that would be used for the game to the chance of either increasing or reducing their wealth by $100. This is the attitude most people have to risk.

Risk-neutral: a person who is indifferent to participating in a fair game

Were you unsure if you would play our fair coin toss game? Did you have to carefully consider before you decided? These considerations are likely to be made by a person who has a neutral attitude to risk. A risk-neutral person is indifferent to participating in a fair game. From this person's perspective, there is no expected gain so they would not take steps to avoid playing the game, as would a risk-averse investor, nor will they actively seek such games to play.

Did you jump at the chance to bet on the toss of a coin? Would you be willing to play another game where you bet $100 on the toss of a coin that you know to be biased and gives you only a 40% chance of winning? People who would agree to play this game are classified as risk seeking.

Risk-seeking: a person who will reject a certain outcome in favour of a riskier game that has an equal or lower expected return

A risk-seeking person will reject a certain outcome in favour of a game with an equal or lower expected value.[11] The expected value of the second game is negative.

$$E(R) = \sum_{i=1}^{n} O_i p_i$$
$$= (100 \times 0.4) + (-100 \times 0.6)$$
$$= 40 - 60$$
$$= -\$20$$

It will be a bit of a mystery to the risk-averse among you as to why anyone would accept this second game. Risk seekers will participate in the game because they get enjoyment from taking the risk. The enjoyment they get from taking risk will offset the decrease in the expected monetary value of the game. They like the uncertainty that comes with playing the game, possibly more than they like the gain that may come from winning.[12]

Market participants have different risk tolerances and these influence their investment choices. Traditional finance theory is based on the assumption that market participants are risk averse. This assumption implies that market participants will not choose to invest when the probabilities for losing or gaining a dollar amount generate an expected value of zero. Risk-averse investors will invest only when they think the expected value of the investment is positive (that is, the investment is not a fair game, but one biased in the investor's favour). Institutional traders display the impact of their risk tolerances in their selected portfolios, with superannuation funds placing greater emphasis on capital conservation and hedge funds making more aggressive investments.[13] While we assume that market participants are risk averse, see the 'behavioural perspective' feature for a potential competitor in the explanation of people's behaviours. If you are interested in finding out how risk-averse you might be, complete the questionnaire in the following 'finance world' feature.

BEHAVIOURAL PERSPECTIVE

Loss aversion — an alternative to risk aversion

While risk aversion is not a necessary condition for rationality, it is commonly assumed in finance for decision making. Consider these proposals. You are given the choice of a prize you have won in a lottery. You can have either $5000 or an 80% chance of winning $8000. Which would you choose? The majority of people choose the sure $5000, even though the 80% chance has a higher expected value of $6400 ($8000 × 0.8). This choice is consistent with risk aversion. But now consider this. An eccentric magistrate offers you a certain fine of $2000 for speeding or an 80% chance of a $3000 fine, with a 20% chance of paying nothing. Which would you choose?

Experimentation has shown that a large majority of people faced with this situation will choose the 80% chance option, even though it has a higher expected value of $2400 ($3000 × 0.8). They focus on the 20% chance of no fine (loss) and thus change from risk aversion to risk-seeking behaviour. People respond to perceived gains and losses differently. Losses seem to have more weight than gains. This is the phenomenon of loss aversion. Loss aversion is the dislike of loss, where decision makers are perceived to over-weight the chance of loss in their decisions.

FINANCE WORLD

What is your attitude to risk?

Tick the column that best describes your response.

	Sounds like me	Somewhat like me	Not much like me	Not me at all
1. I generally prefer familiar situations.				
2. I usually give in when my plans conflict with those of the family (or friends).				
3. If offered a choice of a performance related $6000 end of year bonus each year or a salary increase of $3000 a year, I would take the salary increase.				
4. I have confidence in my ability to overcome the consequences of my mistakes, no matter how big.				
5. Being involved in my own financial planning will give/gives me a sense of satisfaction and accomplishment.				
6. I purchased 5000 shares in Med Tech about a year ago for 20c a share. They are now 30c, so I will sell.				
7. I purchased 5000 shares in MedTech about a year ago for 20c a share. They are now 30c, so I will buy more.				

8. I often put off making financial decisions because I am afraid of making a mistake.	
9. I think you must have a lot of spare money to bother thinking about investments.	
10. I believe that opportunity usually knocks only once.	
11. Reports of the ups and downs of the stock market are boring.	
12. If I were offered a cash benefit now or twice the sum in 12 months' time, I would take the cash now.	
13. If I received a $60 000 inheritance and decided to invest it, I would invest in shares.	
14. If I received a $60 000 inheritance and decided to invest it, I would invest in fixed interest deposits.	
15. I can handle big losses and disappointments with little difficulty.	
16. I would keep a share investment even if it lost 50% of the purchase price in the first year, so long as I thought it would make big gains in a few years' time.	
17. If I had to choose a comfortable life or an exciting one, I would choose the comfortable one.	

How to score your reponses

For questions 1, 2, 3, 6, 8, 9, 10, 11, 12, 14 and 17 score as:

Sounds like me	Somewhat like me	Not much like me	Not me at all
1	2	3	4

For questions 4, 5, 7, 13, 15 and 16 score as:

Sounds like me	Somewhat like me	Not much like me	Not me at all
4	3	2	1

Your score

Please note that this evaluation does not include questions that allow the identification of risk-seeking personalities.

15–35 Youare very risk averse. As a cautious and conservative person, you prefer to avoid most risks if possible. You are unlikely to take on additional risks, even if the expected return for the opportunity is large.

36–52 Youprefer a middle course. You will take risks, but only if the expected return of the decision is positive and quite large.

53–68 Ascore in this range indicates that you are less risk averse than most people and may even have the profile of a risk-neutral person. You will take more risk than the previous two groups. You will take risks that result in positive expected returns, and these expected returns would not have to be as high as they would be for the previous group. You are confident in your decisions. You take a longer term approach and are not so concerned about short-term hiccups in your plans.

FINANCE WORKSHOP 5.4

Calculate the standard deviation of returns for the following two shares.

Year	Grace Corp. (%)	Blunding Ltd (%)
2001	–4	–1.5
2002	–2	–3.5
2003	0.5	1.6
2004	6.3	8.9

1. Which of the assets has had the highest level of risk?
2. Given what you have learnt about your level of risk tolerance in the previous 'finance world' questionnaire, would you prefer to own shares in Grace Corp. or Blunding Ltd?

lo6

Describe the relationship between risk and expected return.

The relationship between risk and return

If most people are risk averse and want to avoid risk, why would anyone make risky investments when they could earn a return by depositing their money in the bank? Risk aversion means you dislike risk in much the same way that a lot of people dislike going to work every day. The incentive to go to work is the income given in return for labour. The incentive for risk-averse investors to take on risk is the additional expected return.

Have another look at figure 5.1. Although it shows ex post returns rather than ex ante, we can still draw some conclusions about the relationship between risk and expected return. The most obvious difference between the two time series of returns is that the return on shares is much more volatile. A volatile time series will have a relatively large standard deviation and will be classified as risky. The range of returns on the All Ordinaries Accumulation Index (AOAI) over the period included nominal annual gains of over 75% to annual losses exceeding 25%. The nominal annual returns on the 10-year Commonwealth bonds didn't do much better than 14%, but did not make a loss either. The standard deviation of the AOAI (the risky asset) for the period 1986–2006 was 12.74%, while the standard deviation for 10-year Commonwealth bonds (that have a much lower level of risk) was 5.49%.

Looking at the data in figure 5.1, we can conclude that risk is positively related to average annual return. This positive relationship means that risk and return increase (or decrease) together. Ex post, the riskier investment as represented by the AOAI generated higher returns, a larger standard deviation and larger losses than the less risky investment in Commonwealth bonds. While this relationship is not surprising when we use 21 years of data, a negative relationship is sometimes observed when shorter time horizons are used. The UniSuper information at the start of this chapter provides us with evidence that a negative relationship between risk and return can be observed during the 2002 financial year.

The risk–return relationship that is of real interest in finance is the positive relationship between risk and expected (or ex ante) return. The higher the risk, the greater the expected return. The ex ante relationship should hold because risk-averse investors will take on risk only if the expected return is high enough to compensate them for the discomfort of holding higher risk investments. This does not mean the positive relationship will always be observed from historical data — expectations are formed about an uncertain future event and they are not always correct!

Required rates of return

Required rate of return: (on an investment) the minimum level of return that is acceptable to an investor, given the level of risk associated with that investment

Risk-averse people require a higher return for taking on a higher level of risk. A **required rate of return** is the minimum level of return that is acceptable to an investor for assuming the level of risk associated with an investment. Investors have a required rate of return in mind when considering making an investment. Theory tells us they will then calculate the expected return on the investment and compare this to the required return. If the expected returns are greater than the required returns, investors will make those investments because they expect to be fully compensated for the risk of the investments. If the expected returns are lower than the required returns, investors will not receive sufficient compensation for assuming the level of risk of the investments.

Even if they make identical assessments of risk and expected outcomes, not all risk-averse people will accept and reject the same investments. While many people can be categorised as risk averse, not all of these will have an identical risk tolerance. Some will require relatively less compensation for taking on an additional amount of risk; some will require relatively more. Traditional finance theory relies heavily on the assumption of risk-averse investors. However, the range of risk tolerances within this category does not present difficulties for theory, if the broad concept of risk aversion applies to the way market participants behave in aggregate.

Reducing risk

lo7

Explain how risk is reduced by diversification.

Portfolio: a collection of different assets

Diversification: the spread of different assets held in a portfolio

We have discussed the positive relationship between risk and required return, but how much additional return can an investor expect for taking on additional risk? Before we can attempt to quantify the relationship, we need to consider the implications of holding more than one investment at a time. A **portfolio** is a collection of different assets. If you own shares in a number of companies, you have formed a portfolio. Another example of a typical portfolio for an individual consists of some shares, some bonds or term deposits and ownership of the house that the investor lives in. **Diversification** refers to the spread of different asset types you hold in your portfolio. A portfolio of shares in two different companies is not well diversified because the range of assets is very small. A portfolio of shares and bonds from numerous companies and some real estate is more diversified.

The main objective of holding a diversified portfolio is to reduce the risk of investment. The return on one coalmining company might be much the same as the return on another coalmining company. Both will be affected by the world price for coal, the exchange rates for the Australian dollar and the currencies of coal-importing countries, and by how seriously the world is taking the Kyoto Protocol at a particular time. We would expect the changes in the returns on these two coalmining shares would take place at around the same time and would be for about the same proportional amount.

Correlation: a measure of the way two variables move relative to each other

Correlation is a measure of the way two variables move relative to each other. The returns on our two coalmining companies would be positively correlated. Positive correlation means that both variables increase together and fall together. Perfect positive correlation means that the variables increase and decrease by the same amount. Negative correlation describes the situation where two variables move in opposite directions. A coalmining company and a manufacturer of solar panels might have negatively correlated returns. Both companies are involved in producing energy but the coalminer relies on non-renewable resources while the solar panel manufacturer focuses on a renewable source of energy. Regulations that require a reduction in greenhouse gas emissions would be expected to generate increased returns for the solar panel maker. The same regulations would likely cause a reduction in the return for the coalmining company. Perfect negative correlation means that the variables move in the opposite direction to each other and they move by the same amount as each other.

If you construct a portfolio of assets that are perfectly positively correlated — shares in all of the Australian coalmining companies, for example — you will not achieve any risk reduction. If your portfolio contains assets with less than perfect positive correlation — shares in a variety of companies, for example — there will be some reduction in risk. A portfolio that contains assets that are negatively correlated will have the least risk of the three portfolios discussed so far. Not many shares are negatively correlated with others, so portfolio diversification usually relies on shares that are not perfectly positively correlated to reduce risk. When risk is reduced in a portfolio, the actual outcome from investing will be closer to the expected outcome because the distribution of outcomes is smaller.

To see how a very basic example of diversification works, consider a wheat farming operation in Australia. The return for the wheat farmer depends on the size and quality of the crop. These, in turn, depend on the weather. If the crop receives enough (but not too much) rain, the return will be high. Not enough rain means lower crop yields and lower financial return, while drought conditions usually mean negative returns as the cost of planting the crop cannot be recovered. An El Nino weather pattern is usually associated with insufficient rain in Australia when there is plenty of rain on the other side of the Pacific, and vice versa. The Australian wheat farming operation could reduce its risk by planting crops on both sides of the Pacific, if this were a feasible strategy given national boundaries. This geographic diversification would mean that losses from one region would be offset by gains in the other growing region. The cash flows from the two wheat growing operations would be negatively correlated. However, the potential gains will not be as great as a strategy of planting twice the wheat in Australia in a good year, but the potential losses won't be as large either. In effect, the distribution of expected returns (and therefore risk) has become smaller.

Systematic risk: the risk that is common to all business

Unsystematic risk: comes from the way a particular business conducts its activities

A major implication of the risk reduction that comes from diversification is that investors will gain higher returns only from taking more systematic risk. **Systematic risk** is the risk that is common to all businesses (or the market). Some examples of systematic risk include the level of economic activity, interest rates, consumer spending and other such factors that influence the market as a whole. While all firms have some level of systematic risk, different firms can have different levels of systematic risk. We will consider this further when we look at the Capital Asset Pricing Model. **Unsystematic risk** (or firm-specific risk) comes from the way a particular business conducts its activities. Some examples of unsystematic risk include the type of business the firm does (mining, manufacturing, retailing or service, for example), the financial structure of the business and the location of the business.

Total risk: includes both systematic and unsystematic risk

Combining assets that have less than perfect positive correlations in a portfolio will reduce unsystematic risk. A given set of market conditions can mean that one type of firm will thrive while another type of firm will struggle under those conditions, as was the case with our wheat farming business. Figure 5.5 shows how increasing the number of assets in a portfolio reduces the total level of risk. The diagram shows the portfolio risk of two different portfolios, *a* and *b*. **Total risk** includes both systematic and unsystematic risk. It is measured by σ (on the *y*-axis) and is represented by the curve on the diagram. Portfolio *a* has a level of total risk (σ_a) and consists of a relatively small number of assets (a_n) as shown on the *x*-axis. Portfolio *b* has total risk of σ_b and includes a larger number of assets (b_n). Assume both portfolios have the same level of systematic risk as shown by the line that runs parallel to the *x*-axis.

Portfolio *a* has the higher level of total risk because the relatively low level of diversification means that a significant amount of unsystematic risk remains. Portfolio *b* has a lower level of portfolio risk $\sigma_a > \sigma_b$ because the variations attributable to unsystematic risk factors on one asset are offset by the variations in unsystematic risk on other assets in the portfolio. In fact, the number of assets in portfolio *b* means that the total risk is similar to the level of systematic risk. Investors can not expect to get higher returns by taking on unsystematic risk. The owner of portfolio *a* should not expect higher returns than the owner of portfolio *b* as both portfolios have the same level of systematic risk. Investors should expect to receive the same level of return on two portfolios with the same level of systematic risk. Theoretically, an investor will not gain by taking on more unsystematic risk; investors can expect higher returns only if they take on higher levels of systematic risk.

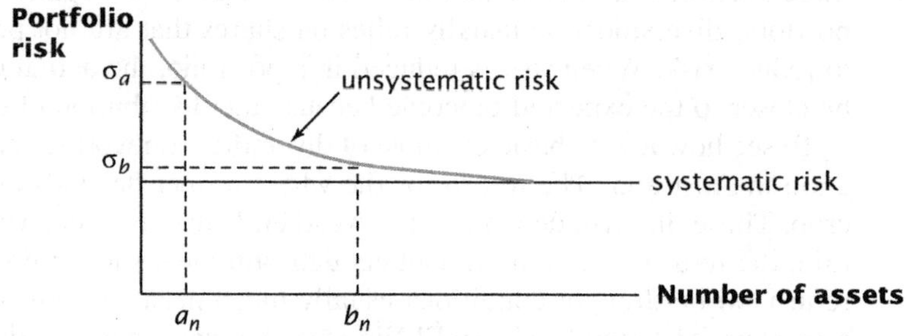

Figure 5.5 Diversification and the reduction of unsystematic risk

lo8

Explain how risk is measured in the Capital Asset Pricing Model (CAPM) and apply the model.

Capital Asset Pricing Model (CAPM): generates an expected return for a risky asset based on the asset's level of systematic risk, the expected return on the market portfolio and a risk-free asset

The Capital Asset Pricing Model

Ex ante and ex post standard deviations were introduced as measures of risk earlier in the chapter. The standard deviation is a measure of total risk and includes both systematic and unsystematic risk. Theory tells us that increased expected returns are associated only with systematic risk and the **Capital Asset Pricing Model (CAPM)** provides a quantifiable relationship between expected return and systematic risk. The CAPM generates an expected return for a risky asset based on the asset's level of systematic risk, the return on the market portfolio and a risk-free asset. Equation 5.8 shows the CAPM.

$$E(R) = R_f + \beta\,(E(R_m) - R_f) \quad [5.8]$$

where $E(R)$ = expected return on the investment
R_f = return on the risk-free asset
$E(R_m)$ = expected return on the market portfolio
β = systematic risk of the asset

The CAPM is derived from portfolio theory, which states that the optimal portfolio to hold consists of an investment in the market portfolio of all risky assets and an investment in the risk-free asset. Theoretically, the market portfolio should be consistent with holding all types of risky assets from around the world. This would include shares in companies from all nations, corporate debt issued by many companies in many countries, real estate in different locations around the world, precious metals, jewellery, works of art, classic cars and any other valuable and risky asset that you can think of. As it is not possible to identify all of these assets, let alone track the changes in their value, the return on the market is usually approximated by a domestic share price index in the application of the CAPM. Therefore, the optimal portfolio will include a diversified portfolio of shares. The return on the market is the **benchmark** for the performance of risky assets in the CAPM because it represents the level of return expected for assets with the same level of systematic risk as the market. The AIOI shown in figure 5.1 is an example of a market return benchmark.

Benchmark: sets the standard for assessing the level of risk and the expected return

Equity risk premium: indicates how much additional return can be expected by moving from the risk-free asset to the market portfolio of risky assets

The risk-free rate represents the return an investor could gain without taking on any risk. The optimal portfolio will include some level of the risk-free asset in addition to the portfolio of shares mentioned earlier. The risk-free rate is usually measured as the return on government-issued debt (the 10-year Commonwealth bonds shown in figure 5.1, for example). Subtracting the risk-free rate from the market portfolio ($E(R_m) - R_f$) gives the **equity risk premium** (ERP). The usual explanation for the risk premium required to hold shares is based on investor risk aversion.[14] The ERP shows how much additional return can be expected by moving from the risk-free asset to the portfolio of risky assets. Our basic relationship between risk and return for risk-averse investors indicates that the ex ante ERP should be positive. If investors are going to take on more risk, they will expect higher returns. Looking at figure 5.1 again, you can see that the ex post ERP (shown as the gap between the return on the 10-year Commonwealth bonds and the AIOI) was positive in most years. It was, however, negative in a number of years (1988, 1990 and 1995, for example). This does not mean that investors didn't expect a premium for taking risk in these years. Investors in risky assets expected a risk premium, but ex post the market for shares did not generate returns above the risk-free rate.

The risk-free rate is observable in the market via the returns on government-issued debt with different maturities. The expected return on the market, however, is much more difficult to assess. Historical average ERP is sometimes used rather than estimating the return on the market.[15] However, this method relies on the assumptions that the ex ante ERP will be in line with the ex post average, and that past returns on the market are a good indicator of future returns. The size of the ex post ERP does vary between time periods (as we can see in figure 5.1) and the ex ante ERP also varies with market sentiment.[16] Additionally, the size of the ex post ERP over time appears much larger than would be predicted by theory. This disparity is called the 'equity premium puzzle'.[17] The following 'finance world' feature discusses the relationship between risk and the level of the ERP.

FINANCE WORLD

The risk and return trade-off

The following article discusses the impact of terrorist attacks on financial markets. The article was published in the UK in the week following the bombings on the London transport system.

Disaster response — The LEX Column

Markets are the last bastions of optimism; in an era of nuclear proliferation and environmental threats, the standard valuation tool for companies assumes that earnings grow in perpetuity. History suggests that war and 'clashes of civilisations' are bad for financial assets. What does the market today suggest about the probability of such events?

Anecdotally, investors discount a more dangerous world since September 11. As with other actual or attempted terrorist attacks, most asset classes shrugged off the news from London on Thursday. Similarly, analysts generally think that oil prices contain a Dollars 20 or so premium to reflect geopolitical risk. Gold, an armageddon as well as inflation hedge, is near its nominal highs.

Finding hard evidence that capital markets are ready for trouble is tougher. Some believe the equity risk premium (the return investors require to hold equities over government bonds) had a one-off rise after 9/11. Yet measuring the current ERP requires subjective assumptions about earnings growth. Many think the ERP is actually near its all-time low.

An alternative is the Vix index — the expected volatility of the S&P 500 implied by option prices. This has risen in the past six months, perhaps reflecting fears of a nuclear Iran and war in the Middle East. But the Vix has its flaws. Behavioural quirks mean more investors buy puts than calls. The index soared during the second Clinton administration, an era that was unambiguously less geopolitically risky than today.

In any case, equities do not really isolate the relevant type of risk. Their volatility might reflect fears of a slowdown, overkill by the Federal Reserve or of US imbalances finally coming home to roost. An alternative measure is real bond yields. In the US these have usually fallen during wars, reflecting safe-haven status and economic insensitivity. During discrete events too, for example the Cuban missile crisis, equities fell while bonds held firm.

The six months after September 11 followed this pattern; long-term real bond yields fell sharply. So what should be made of the sharp reversal in yields during 2006? Prices might be distorted by, for example, the activity of Asian central banks or by changing views of central bank competence. Still, the basic message is that the price of safe assets has fallen. Since geopolitical risks have probably risen, this suggests complacency.

Yet there is an opposite and gloomier conclusion. America's 20th century experience was exceptional. In most countries, war risks include the collapse of governments and property rights, not just recession. In such circumstances the price of 'risk free' assets plummets along with everything else. This outcome is hard to imagine for the US. Still, for professional doom-mongers, the rise in real yields from post-9/11 lows suggests that what was once viewed as a manageable catastrophe is now thought to herald a new era of existential threats.[18]

Beta: a relative measure that describes how the return on the asset is related to the return on the market portfolio

Beta (β) is the measure of the risky asset's level of systematic risk. Beta is a relative measure that describes how the return on the asset moves with the return on the market portfolio. Beta is estimated by regressing the return on the asset on the return on the market. The asset specific beta is used to weight the ERP, so the expected return reflects the level of systematic risk for the asset.

The market portfolio has a beta of 1 because beta, in this case, measures the movement of the market against itself and it is not possible for the market to move in a different manner from itself. A risky asset with a beta of 1 will move with the market. This means that a 1% increase in expected return for the market will result in a 1% increase in expected return for the asset. Similarly, an expected market decrease of 1% will cause a 1% decrease in expected return for the asset. An asset with a beta of 1 has the same amount of systematic risk as the market portfolio. A risky asset with a beta of 2 will move twice as much as the market. For this asset, the 1% increase in expected return for the market will result in a 2% increase in expected return for the asset. Assets with betas greater than one have higher levels of systematic risk than the market portfolio. An asset with a negative beta moves in the opposite direction from the market. If the risky asset has a beta of –1, a 1% increase in the market will result in a 1% decrease in the expected return of the risky asset. While assets with negative betas would be valuable for designing portfolios, they are very rare. Assets with betas less than one have less systematic risk than the market portfolio does. A beta of zero indicates that the expected return on the risky asset is not related to changes in the expected return on the market. Figure 5.6 shows how expected return (as a percentage) on the risky asset relates to the expected return on the market (as a percentage) for some different levels of beta. The asset with a beta of zero is not shown as there is no linear relationship between the expected return on this asset and the expected return on the market.

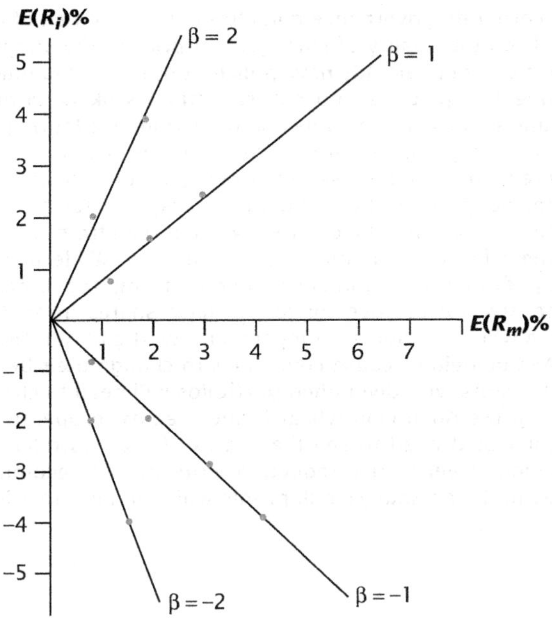

Figure 5.6 Beta and expected returns

EXAMPLE 5.6

Applying the CAPM

You expect a return on the market of 8% and the risk-free rate to be 4%. If the beta for Cochlear Ltd is 0.522, what is the expected return for a Cochlear share?

$$E(R) = R_f + \beta\,(E(R_m) - R_f)$$
$$E(R) = 0.04 + 0.522\,(0.08 - 0.04)$$
$$= 0.04 + 0.522\,(0.04)$$
$$= 0.04 + 0.020\,88$$
$$= 0.060\,88 \text{ or } 6.09\%$$

Therefore, given these expectations of the market return and the risk-free rate, the expected return on a Cochlear share is 6.09%.

CORPORATE FINANCIAL GOVERNANCE

Governance and risk

In chapter 1 we define corporate governance as the management of corporations. Principle 7 of the ASX's *Principles of good corporate governance and best practice recommendations*[19] is that the board and management should 'recognise and manage risk'. To achieve this, there should be a 'sound system of risk oversight and management and internal control'. The principle also recommends that 'material changes to the company's risk profile' be disclosed to investors.

How will the corporate governance guidelines affect the risk of the firm? The answer to this question depends on the quality of management prior to the adoption of the guidelines. Well-managed companies would already have policies on risk management and would have systems of risk management in place, so no risk reduction is likely to occur in these firms. Poorly managed companies may achieve some risk reduction by adopting better systems and internal controls. However, the guidelines are not legal requirements.

How will any reductions in the risk of a firm impact on investors? The type of risk that could be reduced by the adoption of the ASX guidelines is unsystematic (or firm specific) risk. Investors holding a diversified portfolio of assets will not gain from reductions of unsystematic risk. Think of our wheat farmer example of diversification. While it would be very costly for an Australian wheat farmer to commence operations on the other side of the Pacific, it is relatively inexpensive for an investor to purchase shares in an Australian wheat producing company and in a wheat producing company in, say, the USA. If the risk disclosure recommendations in the ASX guidelines cause companies to change their behaviours so they can report reduced risks, investors with diversified portfolios will need to change their positions to avoid increased risk — if the Australian wheat farmer begins to operate on the Pacific coast of the USA, the investor would need to sell the shares of the Australian or the US company to get back to the previous level of risk reduction. Principle 7's recommendation for disclosure of material changes to the company's risk profile will help investors in their portfolio decisions.

Using CAPM to identify over- and under-priced shares

Figure 5.6 shows the relationship of expected return to the return on the market portfolio for some different levels of beta. Figure 5.7 shows the relationship of expected return to different levels of beta, given the return on the market and the risk-free rate. The upward sloping line is the graphical representation of the CAPM given the risk-free rate of 4% and the return on the market of 8% used in example 5.6. This line is called the security market line and it shows the expected returns for a given level of beta. As we discussed in the previous section, the market portfolio has a beta of 1. We can see the market portfolio on the security market line with a beta of 1 and an expected return of 8% (that is, the expected return on the market). If you chose not to invest in risky assets (beta equals 0), figure 5.7 shows that you could expect to receive the risk-free rate of 4%. The expected return calculated for Cochlear in example 5.6 is also shown on the security market line.

We say that assets are fairly priced if they generate an expected return that lies on the security market line. What about Share A and Share B in figure 5.7? The market price of Share A suggests that its forecast future cash flows are expected to generate a return of 9%. With a beta of 0.75, the CAPM expected return for Share A is 7%. You could purchase Share A at its current market price and earn more return than could be expected for the level of systematic risk you are taking by making the investment. If this is the case, we say that the market has underpriced Share A. You would be willing to pay more for Share A given its level of systematic risk. As enough investors recognise the underpricing of Share A, the demand for the share will increase and so will the price. How far will the price increase? We would expect the price to increase to the point where the present value of the forecast future cash flows represented a return of 7%. At this point, Share A will sit on the security market line. If you can identify under-priced shares you should purchase them. The price of these assets should increase in the future.

With a beta of 1.25 and a forecast return of 7%, we say that Share B is overpriced. Share B lies below the security market line because the expected return from CAPM for a share with a beta of 1.25 is 9%. You would be paying too much to purchase an asset that sits below the security market line because its forecast future cash flows will not generate sufficient return for the level of risk you are taking. If you own any overpriced shares you should sell them. The price of these assets should fall in the future.

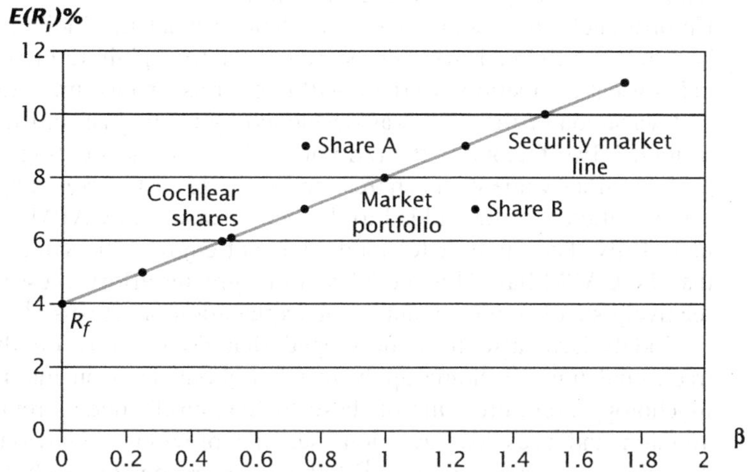

Figure 5.7 Identifying overpriced and underpriced shares

EXAMPLE 5.7

Identifying overpriced and underpriced shares

You expect a return on the market of 8% and the risk-free rate to be 4%. The beta for Share C is 1.1 and it is priced to return 8.1%. Is Share C fairly priced? Would you buy or sell Share C?

$$E(R) = R_f + \beta\,(E(R_m) - R_f)$$
$$E(R) = 0.04 + 1.1\,(0.08 - 0.04)$$
$$= 0.084 \text{ or } 8.4\%$$

Given the risk-free rate, the expected market return and the systematic risk of Share C, the expected return is 8.4%. Share C is priced to return 8.1% which is less than you could get for other assets with the same level of systematic risk. Share C will lie below the security market line and it is overpriced. You would not purchase Share C at its current price as the price can be expected to fall in the future.

FINANCE WORKSHOP 5.5

You expect a return on the market of 8% and the risk-free rate to be 4%. If the beta for Aluma Ltd is –0.03, what is the expected return for Aluma shares?

Is CAPM the best model of risk and return?

There has been much criticism of the CAPM on theoretical grounds[20] and the empirical tests of the model provide mixed evidence on how useful the CAPM is for explaining returns on shares.[21] The CAPM is a single factor model — it rests on the assumption that market risk fully describes the relevant risk when pricing risky assets. Much of the theoretical model development since the CAPM was published has been the result of the search for additional risk factors that more fully explain the relationship between risk and return. These multi-factor models are often variants of Arbitrage Pricing Theory (APT).[22] Unfortunately, the theory does not identify what the individual risk factors are, or even how many individual risk factors are needed to explain returns. Thus, the APT has not provided great competition to the CAPM as far as finance practitioners are concerned.

Arbitrage Pricing Theory: systematic risk comes from a number of factors

A variation of the APT was developed by using past returns to search for common risk factors.[23] Two factors — the ratio of the book (or accounting) value of a company's equity to the market value of its shares, and the size of the company as measured by its market capitalisation — when added to the beta measure in CAPM were found to explain returns more fully. The three factor model has not enjoyed the same popularity with practitioners that the CAPM has. This model requires greater effort in estimation while offering only a relatively small improvement in the explanation of returns.[24]

Models have also been developed that do not rely on the standard assumptions of traditional finance. Some apply insights about decision making and risk taken from the psychology literature. One of these 'behavioural' models replaces the assumption of risk aversion and uses loss aversion (see the previous 'behavioural perspective' feature) to describe people's preferences.[25] Other more recent research has suggested that unsystematic risk does have a role to play in asset pricing.[26]

Although the flaws in the CAPM demonstrate that the model is imperfect, it is the model most widely embraced by practitioners. More complicated models will need to outperform the CAPM by a large margin to justify their costs of application. Research into the role of risk and return on asset pricing continues and may one day provide a significantly better model that can be readily used in practice. Until that time, the CAPM provides us with a fundamental way to structure thought about risk and return.

FINANCE WORKSHOP 5.6

1. Why does the UniSuper fund offer so many alternatives?
2. Why do members make different choices about their investment options?
3. Why did some options give positive returns while some made losses?
4. Why would UniSuper continue to offer the shares option when it made a loss of 11%?

executive summary

lo1 explain the term 'return'

- A return is the gain or loss achieved by making an investment.
- Companies issue debt and equity and use the funds raised to increase the earnings of the firm.
- The cash flows from the investments a company makes are used to pay debtholders their return in the form of interest and equity holders in the form of dividends and increased value per share.

lo2 explain the difference between ex post and ex ante returns and calculate each of these for a share

- There are two types of return we calculate: ex post and ex ante.
- Ex post returns are those that relate to past periods. These returns are observable and easily measured.
- Past dividends and any price change are used to measure ex post returns on a share.
- A capital gain arises when the price of an asset increases. A capital loss arises when the price of an asset decreases.
- The return calculated for the period an investment is owned is called the holding period return.
- Returns should be measured over the same time period to make any meaningful comparisons. Return is normally compared on an annual basis.
- Ex ante returns are those that investors expect to receive in the future. These are not observable and measurement is more subjective than for ex post returns.
- The expected return is the average of the probability-weighted possible outcomes associated with the investment.
- Possible outcomes each have a probability assigned to them. The total probability of all possible outcomes must not exceed 100%.
- The calculated expected return can be a different number to any of the identified possible outcomes.

lo3 explain how risk is defined in the discipline of finance

- Risk is the chance that the actual outcome from an investment will be different from the expected outcome.
- How risky an asset is depends on the dispersion of its expected returns. A wide distribution of returns indicates high risk. A narrow distribution of returns indicates lower risk.

lo4 calculate ex post and ex ante levels of risk using the standard deviation

- A random variable is a possible outcome that is drawn from the distribution of possible outcomes for that variable.
- The normal distribution is symmetric and bell-shaped and is fully described by the expected value (or mean) and the standard deviation.

- If returns are normally distributed, the mean plus or minus one standard deviation will cover approximately 68% of returns. The mean plus or minus two standard deviations cover about 95% of observations. And 99.7% of all observations in a normal distribution fall within three standard deviations of the mean.
- We measure risk to determine how probable it is that the realised outcome will vary from an expected one.
- The ex ante variance is the probability-weighted average of deviations of possible returns from the expected return.
- The ex ante standard deviation is the square root of the ex ante variance. It is used to measure the risk of expected returns when the distribution is symmetric.
- The ex post variance is the weighted average of the deviations of observed returns from the mean return. The ex post standard deviation is the square root of the variance.
- The larger the standard deviation of expected returns, the greater the chance that the ex post outcome will be different to the expected outcome.
- Due to the subjectivity of the calculation of the ex ante standard deviation, the standard deviation of ex post outcomes is sometimes used as a substitute risk measure.

lo5 explain how a person's risk profile influences their investment decisions

- Different people have different views on how much risk they feel comfortable in taking.
- A risk preference represents a person's attitude to risk.
- In finance, people are categorised into three groups on the basis of their risk preferences. The groups are risk averse, risk neutral and risk seeking.
- A risk-averse person will not participate in a fair game (that is, a game where the expected value of participation is zero).
- A risk-neutral person is indifferent to participating in a fair game. That is, this person will sometimes participate in a fair game and sometimes not. A risk-neutral person doesn't have a firm rule about playing fair games.
- A risk-seeking person will reject a certain outcome in favour of a game with an equal or lower expected value. A risk-seeking person might play a game where it is a reasonable expectation that they will lose their money. A risk-seeking person thinks it is fun to take risks.
- Traditional finance theory is based on the assumption that market participants are risk averse. Differing degrees within the category of risk aversion are used to explain differing preferences for assets with varying levels of risk.

lo6 describe the relationship between risk and expected return

- Risk-averse investors are willing to take on more risk if the expected return is high enough to compensate them for the risk.
- This feature of risk aversion leads us to the conclusion that there is a positive relationship between risk and expected return.
- Historically, the return on equities is more volatile (riskier) than the return on bonds. On average, equities provide higher returns than bonds.
- The required rate of return on an investment is the minimum level of return that is acceptable to an investor given the level of risk associated with that investment.

- People making investment decisions compare the expected return to the required return. If the expected return is higher, they will invest. If the required return is higher, they will not invest as the expected return is insufficient to compensate them for that level of risk.

lo7 explain how risk is reduced by diversification

- A portfolio is a collection of different assets.
- Diversification is the spread of different assets held in a portfolio.
- The objective of holding a diversified portfolio is to reduce risk.
- Correlation is a measure of the way two variables move relative to each other.
- Positive correlation indicates that the two variables move in the same direction.
- Negative correlation indicates that the two variables move in opposite directions.
- A portfolio of assets that have perfectly positively correlated returns is not diversified because no risk reduction has been achieved.
- The most risk reduction would occur if the assets in the portfolio were negatively correlated with each other — but negatively correlated assets are difficult to find.
- A portfolio of assets that have less than perfect positive correlation will achieve some risk reduction.
- Systematic risk is the risk that is common to all businesses. It cannot be reduced by diversification because it is the risk of investing per se.
- Unsystematic risk comes from the way a particular business conducts its activities. Unsystematic risk can be reduced by combining different assets.
- A well-diversified portfolio contains only systematic risk. The unsystematic risk associated with each individual asset is offset by the unsystematic risks of the other assets in the portfolio.
- Total risk, as measured by the standard deviation, includes both systematic and unsystematic risk.
- Theoretically, investors cannot expect to gain higher returns by increasing unsystematic risk. Higher expected returns can be expected only from increasing the level of systematic risk.

lo8 explain how risk is measured in the Capital Asset Pricing Model (CAPM) and apply the model

- Portfolio theory states that the optimal portfolio consists of an investment in the market portfolio of all risky assets and an investment in the risk-free asset.
- The CAPM generates an expected return for a risky asset based on the asset's level of systematic risk, the return on the market portfolio and a risk-free asset.
- The return on the market portfolio is measured using a benchmark share price index.
- The risk-free rate is measured as the return on government-issued bonds.
- The equity risk premium indicates how much additional return can be expected by moving from the risk-free asset to the market portfolio of risky assets.
- The asset's beta is used to measure the level of systematic risk.
- Beta is a relative measure that describes how the return on the asset is related to the return on the market portfolio. It is estimated by regressing the return on the asset on the return on the market.

- An asset with a beta of one will move in the same direction as the market and by the same amount as the market movement.
- An asset with a beta of two will move in the same direction as the market and by twice the amount as the market movement.
- An asset with a beta of negative one will move in the opposite direction to the market and by the same amount as the market movement.
- The security market line shows the expected returns for a given level of beta.
- Assets that sit on the security market line are fairly priced.
- Assets that sit above the security market line are underpriced. These assets should be purchased as their prices will be expected to rise in the future.
- Assets that sit below the security market line are overpriced. These assets should be sold (or not purchased) as their prices will be expected to fall in the future.
- CAPM has been challenged on theoretical grounds and has not received unanimous support when tested for its predictive ability.
- No model has yet been developed that is capable of replacing the CAPM in a practical sense.

Key terms

All Ordinaries Accumulation Index, p. 133
Arbitrage Pricing Theory, p. 158
benchmark, p. 152
beta, p. 154
Capital Asset Pricing Model (CAPM), p. 152
capital gain, p. 132
capital loss, p. 132
correlation, p. 150
diversification, p. 150
equity risk premium, p. 153
ex ante returns, p. 134
ex ante standard deviation, p. 140
ex ante variance, p. 140
ex post returns, p. 132
ex post standard deviation, p. 142
ex post variance, p. 142
expected return, p. 135
fair game, p. 146
holding period return, p. 132
normal distribution, p. 138
portfolio, p. 150
realised returns, p. 132
required rate of return, p. 150
return, p. 131
risk, p. 137
risk-averse, p. 145
risk-neutral, p. 146
risk preference, p. 145
risk-seeking, p. 146
standard deviation, p. 139
systematic risk, p. 151
total risk, p. 151
unsystematic risk, p. 151
variance, p. 139

Learning chart

Learning objective	Question	Self-test problems	Financial problems
lo*1* explain the term 'return'	5.1, 5.4, 5.7,		
lo*2* explain the difference between ex post and ex ante returns and calculate each of these for a share	5.2, 5.3, 5.5, 5.6	5.1, 5.3	5.1, 5.2, 5.3, 5.5, 5.14, 5.15, 5.17, 5.18, 5.19
lo*3* explain how risk is defined in the discipline of finance	5.8, 5.9		

lo4 calculate ex post and ex ante levels of risk using the standard deviation		5.2, 5.4	5.4, 5.6, 5.7, 5.8, 5.9, 5.14, 5.16, 5.17, 5.18
lo5 explain how a person's risk profile influences their investment decisions	5.10, 5.11, 5.13		5.20
lo6 describe the relationship between risk and expected return	5.12, 5.15		5.10, 5.20
lo7 explain how risk is reduced by diversification	5.14, 5.16, 5.17, 5.18, 5.19		
lo8 explain how risk is measured in the Capital Asset Pricing Model (CAPM) and apply the model	5.20, 5.21, 5.22	5.5	5.11, 5.12, 5.13, 5.19, 5.21

Questions

5.1 What is a 'return'? Demonstrate your understanding by explaining how to calculate the return on a bond and the return on a share.

5.2 What are ex post and ex ante returns and why do we differentiate between them?

5.3 Explain the nature of capital gains and losses and explain how they affect the calculation of returns.

5.4 What is a 'holding period return'? What is the conventional time period used when discussing returns?

5.5 Look at figure 5.1. What does the graph tell you about risk and ex post returns?

5.6 Your friend has calculated an expected return of 4.7% for CSL Ltd. He is confused, as 4.7% was not identified as a possible outcome. Explain to your friend how this result can occur.

5.7 What is the maximum possible percentage loss you can make on the purchase of an ordinary share? What is the maximum possible percentage gain you can make on the purchase of an ordinary share? Explain your answers.

5.8 How is the definition of risk in finance different from the way people ordinarily think of risk? Why is the distinction important?

5.9 What is a 'standard deviation'? What does it tell us when a distribution is normal? Use figure 5.4 to help your explanation.

5.10 You have been offered the choice of two games. The first game gives you the chance of doubling your money or losing it all. The second game gives you the chance of winning 50% of your bet or losing 50% of it. Which game would be preferred by:

(a) a risk-averse person

(b) a risk-neutral person

(c) a risk-seeking person?

5.11 Explain what is meant by the term 'risk aversion' and provide a rationale for risk-averse investors participating in the market.

5.12 Define 'expected return' and 'required return'. What is the relationship between these two concepts?

5.13 Do all risk-averse investors make the same investment decisions? Why?

5.14 What is 'correlation'? Demonstrate your understanding by examining the situation of perfect positive correlation of two assets and by explaining what will happen with perfect negative correlation.

5.15 What is diversification and how does it work? Which would be the riskier of the following portfolios?
(a) Five residential properties that are leased out
(b) Two residential properties for leasing and shares in five listed companies
(c) Bonds issued by the Australian government

5.16 Can you achieve risk reduction by combining positively correlated assets? Explain your answer.

5.17 What is 'systematic risk'? What is 'unsystematic risk'? Give some examples of sources of both types of risk to demonstrate your understanding.

5.18 Which type of risk does diversification reduce? Explain why only one type of risk can be reduced by diversification.

5.19 Are higher expected returns associated with increased total risk or increased systematic risk? Why?

5.20 The CAPM uses the expected return on the market portfolio to calculate the expected return on a risky asset. What is the market portfolio? Describe one of the indices that is used to approximate the market portfolio.

5.21 (a) Explain how the following asset's returns would respond to a 1% increase in the market return:
i) $\beta = 1$
ii) $\beta = 2$
iii) $\beta = -1$
(b) Explain how much systematic risk the following assets have compared to the market:
i) $\beta = 1$
ii) $\beta = 2$
iii) $\beta = -1$

5.22 You identify several shares with forecast returns that lie above the security market line. Should you buy or sell these shares? Why?

Self-test problems

5.1 Share prices and annual dividends for Magnolia Ltd are as follows:

Year	Share price ($)	Dividend ($)
0	4.35	
1	4.60	0.40
2	4.20	0.42
3	4.37	0.40

What is the annual return for each of the 3 years?

5.2 Using the data in problem 1, calculate the standard deviation of the Magnolia Ltd returns.

5.3 The possible cash flows and their associated probabilities for an investment are as follows.

Cash flow ($)	Probability
100 000	30
200 000	40
500 000	30

What is the expected outcome for the investment?

5.4 Using the data in problem 3, calculate the standard deviation of the investment's cash flows.

5.5 If the expected market return and risk-free rate are 11% and 5.5%, respectively, what is the expected return on an asset with a beta of 1.5?

Solutions to self-test problems

5.1 $$R = \frac{P_t - P_{t-1} + D}{P_{t-1}} \times 100$$

$$R_{Year1} = \frac{4.60 - 4.35 + 0.40}{4.35} \times 100$$

$$R_{Year1} = \frac{0.65}{4.35} \times 100 = 14.94\%$$

$$R_{Year2} = \frac{4.20 - 4.60 + 0.42}{4.60} \times 100$$

$$R_{Year2} = \frac{0.02}{4.60} \times 100 = 0.44\%$$

$$R_{Year3} = \frac{4.37 - 4.20 + 0.40}{4.20} \times 100$$

$$R_{Year3} = \frac{0.57}{4.20} \times 100 = 13.57\%$$

5.2 $$\bar{R} = \frac{\sum_{t=1}^{T} R_t}{T}$$

$$\bar{R} = \frac{0.1494 + 0.0044 + 0.1357}{3}$$

$$\bar{R} = \frac{0.2895}{3}$$

$$\bar{R} = 0.0965 = 9.65\%$$

$$\sigma^2 = \frac{\sum_{t=1}^{T}(R_t - \bar{R})^2}{T-1}$$

$$\sigma^2 = \frac{(0.1494-0.0965)^2 + (0.0044-0.0965)^2 + (0.1357-0.0965)^2}{2}$$

$$\sigma^2 = 0.006415$$

$$\sigma = \sqrt{\sigma^2}$$

$$\sigma = \sqrt{0.006415} = 0.0801 \text{ or } 8.01\%$$

5.3 $$E(R) = \sum_{i=1}^{n} O_i p_i$$

$$\begin{aligned} E(R) &= (100000 \times 0.3) + (200000 \times 0.4) + (500000 \times 0.3) \\ &= 30000 + 80000 + 150000 \\ &= \$260000 \end{aligned}$$

5.4 $$\sigma = \sqrt{\sum_{t=1}^{n}(O_i - E(R))^2 P_i}$$

$$\sigma = \sqrt{[(100000-260000)^2 0.3] + [(200000-260000)^2 0.4] + [(500000-260000)^2 0.3]}$$

$$= \sqrt{7680000000 + 1440000000 + 17280000000}$$

$$= \sqrt{26400000000}$$

$$= \$162480.77$$

5.5 $$\begin{aligned} E(R) &= R_f + \beta\,(E(R_m) - R_f) \\ E(R) &= 0.055 + 1.5(0.11 - 0.055) \\ &= 13.75\% \end{aligned}$$

Financial problems

5.1 You paid \$5.60 for a share and received dividends of \$0.23 during the year you owned the share. You sold the share for \$5.95 at the end of the year. What was your holding period return?

5.2 Calculate the annual return on the following shares.

	ABC Ltd	DEF Ltd	HIJ Ltd
Purchase price (\$)	5.00	7.00	8.00
Annual dividend (\$)	0.50	0	1.50
Selling price (\$)	5.07	7.80	6.50

5.3 You have forecast the following possible returns and associate probabilities for shares of Green Ltd:

Possible return (%)	Probability (%)
25	0.05
15	0.4
5	0.4
−5	0.1
−8	0.05

Calculate the expected return.

5.4 Calculate the variance and standard deviation of returns for the Green Ltd shares in problem 5.3.

5.5 Calculate the return on the following shares:

		Possible outcome (% return)		
Economic condition	**Probability (%)**	**KLM Ltd**	**NOP Ltd**	**QRS Ltd**
Boom	5	30	25	20
Good	10	25	20	16
Average	50	10	12	8
Poor	20	4	2	0
Bust	15	−25	−15	−10

5.6 Calculate the standard deviations of KLM Ltd, NOP Ltd and QRS Ltd from the information given in problem 5.5. Which asset has the highest level of risk?

5.7 The returns on Blue Ltd shares for the last 5 years are as follows:

Year	Return (%)
1	12
2	8
3	3.6
4	−4.7
5	0.6

Calculate the variance and standard deviation for Blue Ltd.

5.8 Calculate the standard deviation of returns for the following three assets.

	ABC Ltd (%)	DEF Ltd (%)	HIJ Ltd (%)
2000	6	12	10
2001	2	4	5
2002	−5	−3	0
2003	1	−3	2

Which asset has the highest level of risk?

5.9 Use the standard deviations you calculated in problem 5.8 and assume the returns are drawn from a normal distribution. In what range of returns will 68% of all observations fall?

5.10 The standard deviation and expected returns for two portfolios are as follows.

	Portfolio 1	Portfolio 2
Expected return	6%	10%
Ex ante standard deviation	10%	10%

(a) Which portfolio would you prefer to hold? Why?

(b) Why can two portfolios with the same standard deviation have different expected returns?

5.11 Look at the beta for each of the following companies. Using just this information, make some predictions about the return for each company.

Company	Beta
Red Ltd	1.7
Blue Ltd	1
Green Ltd	0
Purple Ltd	−0.1

5.12 You have forecast the return on the All Ordinaries Accumulation Index to be 6% in the coming year. The rate on 10-year Treasury bonds is 4.5%. Calculate the expected return for the companies identified in problem 5.11.

5.13 What is the expected return for a share with a beta of 1.5 when the return on the market is expected to be 15% and the risk-free rate is 3%?

5.14 Microsplat is a highly successful manufacturer and vendor of computer software. The company has been growing rapidly and has never paid a dividend. Share prices for the last 10 years are as follows:

Year	Price ($)	Year	Price ($)
1996	1.20	2001	27.39
1997	4.60	2002	30.02
1998	5.90	2003	35.78
1999	10.36	2004	40.69
2000	23.79	2005	42.50

(a) Calculate the annual return for each year.

(b) Calculate the variance and standard deviation of the annual returns.

5.15 Two assets have the same level of risk. You have collected the following information about the last year of operation for each of the assets:

	Asset 1	Asset 2
Purchase price	100 000	80 000
Net operating cash inflow	7 000	4 000
Selling price (today)	110 000	84 000

(a) Calculate the return on each of the assets.

(b) Assume you are a risk-averse investor. Which of these assets would you prefer to have owned?

5.16 You have calculated the following historical annual returns data for three companies:

	Annual returns		
Year	Company 1	Company 2	Company 3
1	0.046	0.013	−0.003
2	0.053	0.066	0.051
3	0.017	0.042	0.082
4	0.13	−0.008	−0.069
5	0.016	0.057	0.067

(a) Calculate the standard deviation for shares in each of the companies.
(b) Which share has the highest level of risk? Which has the lowest?

5.17 You have collected the following monthly closing prices for shares in three companies (CAT, CBA and CSL):

	CAT	CBA	CSL
July	5.10	32.11	31.14
August	4.80	31.10	28.25
September	4.79	31.42	22.37
October	3.62	30.20	21.61
November	3.62	28.86	17.30
December	3.65	27.18	23.13
January	3.55	27.34	21.47

(a) Assuming the companies paid no dividends over the period, calculate the monthly return for each of the shares.
(b) Which of the shares had the highest standard deviation and what does this tell you about the associated risk?

5.18 You have forecast the returns and associated probabilities for the following three companies:

ABC		DEF		XYZ	
Return (%)	Probability (%)	Return (%)	Probability (%)	Return (%)	Probability (%)
5.01	25	17.05	5	15.51	10
3.7	25	9.55	25	7.7	30
3	25	6.69	40	3.14	50
2.17	25	3.2	30	-11.95	10

(a) Calculate the expected return on each share.
(b) Calculate the variance for each share.
(c) Calculate the standard deviation for each share.

5.19 You have forecast an equity risk premium of 7%. The risk-free rate is 5%. Beta for the following three companies is shown in the table that follows.

Company	Beta
Sims Ltd	1.26
Simpsons Ltd	0.80
Knight-Day Ltd	−0.64

(a) What is the expected return for shares in each company?

(b) Which company has the highest level of risk? How can you tell?

(c) Which company's shares would you like to be holding when the market takes a downturn? Why?

5.20 Complete the risk preference survey in the 'finance world' feature on page 147. Use this knowledge of your risk preferences to identify your preferred investment from those identified in problem 5.19.

5.21 You expect a return on the market of 15% and the risk-free rate to be 3%. The beta for Zed Ltd is 0.89 and it is priced to return 14%. Is Zed Ltd fairly priced? Would you buy or sell Zed Ltd?

SOLUTIONS TO FINANCE WORKSHOPS

5.1 Using equation 5.1 $R = \frac{P_t - P_{t-1} + D}{P_{t-1}} \times 100$

$$R = \frac{6.30 - 6.05 + 0.30}{6.05} \times 100$$

$= 0.0909$ or 9.09%

5.2 Using equation 5.2 $E(R) = \sum_{i=1}^{n} O_i p_i$

$$E(R) = (0.15 \times 0.25) + (0.10 \times 0.30) + (0.05 \times 0.30) + (0 \times 0.13) + (-0.10 \times 0.02)$$

$= 0.0375 + 0.03 + 0.015 + 0 - 0.002$

$= 0.0805$ or 8.05%

5.3 1. Using equation 5.4 $\sigma = \sqrt{\sum_{t=1}^{n} (R_i - E(R))^2 p_i}$

$$\sigma = \sqrt{(0.15 - 0.0805)^2 0.25 + (0.10 - 0805)^2 0.30 + (0.05 - 0.0805)^2 0.30 + (0 - 0.0805)^2 0.13 + (-0.1 - 0.0805)^2 0.02}$$

$= \sqrt{0.001208 + 0.000114 + 0.000279 + 0.000842 + 0.000652}$

$= \sqrt{0.003095}$

$= 0.05563$ or 5.56%

2. Using equations 5.6 $\bar{R} = \frac{\sum_{t=1}^{T} R_t}{T}$ and 5.7 $\sigma = \sqrt{\frac{\sum_{t=1}^{T} (R_t - R)^2}{T-1}}$

$$\bar{R} = \frac{0.095 + 0.07 - 0.08 - 0.03 + 0.05}{5} = 2.1\%$$

$$\sigma = \sqrt{\frac{(0.095-0.021)^2+(0.07-0.021)^2+(-0.08-0.021)^2+(-0.03-0.021)^2+(0.05-0.021)^2}{5-1}}$$

$$= \sqrt{\frac{0.02152}{4}}$$

$$= 0.073\,35 \text{ or } 7.34\%$$

5.4 Using equations 5.6 $\bar{R} = \frac{\sum_{t=1}^{T} R_t}{T}$ and 5.7 $\sigma = \sqrt{\frac{\sum_{t=1}^{T}(R_t - \bar{R})^2}{T-1}}$

$$\bar{R} = \frac{-0.04 - 0.02 + 0.005 + 0.063}{4} = 0.002$$

$$\sigma_G = \sqrt{\frac{(-0.04 - 0.002)^2 + (-0.02 - 0.002)^2 + (0.005 - 0.002)^2 + (0.063 - 0.002)^2}{4-1}}$$

$$= \sqrt{\frac{0.001764 + 0.000\,484 + 0.000\,009 + 0.003721}{3}}$$

$$= 0.044\,639 \text{ or } 4.464\%$$

$$\bar{R}_B = \frac{-0.015 - 0.035 + 0.016 + 0.089}{4} = 0.013\,75$$

$$\sigma_B = \sqrt{\frac{(-0.015 - 0.01375)^2 + (-0.035 - 0.01375)^2 + (0.016 - 0.01375)^2 + (0.089 - 0.01375)^2}{4-1}}$$

$$= \sqrt{\frac{0.000\,827 + 0.002\,377 + 0.000\,005\,06 + 0.005\,663}{3}}$$

$$= 0.054\,378 \text{ or } 5.44\%$$

1. Blunding Ltd has the higher level of risk (5.44 > 4.46).
2. The answer to this question depends upon your personal risk preferences.

5.5 Using equation 5.8 $E(R) = R_f + \beta\,(E(R_m) - R_f)$

$$E(R) = 0.04 + -0.03(0.08 - 0.04)$$
$$= 0.0388 \text{ or } 3.88\%$$

5.6
1. The UniSuper fund offers a range of investment alternatives to suit the range of risk preferences of the fund members.
2. We would expect that different members choose different investment options because they have different risk preferences.
3. Ex post, some options have positive returns because the assets held in these did well over the previous year. The cash product is an example of an option with positive returns. Shares, on the other hand, had large negative returns because the share market as a whole did poorly in the first years reported in the chapter opening scenario. The 'balanced' and 'growth' options did not do as poorly as the shares option because they contained assets other than shares and the performance of these assets was not as bad.

4. Ex ante, we would expect the 'shares' option to have much higher returns than the cash option because the former has much higher risk than the latter. The realised returns, however, may not meet our expectations — that is what risk is all about. The shares option would not be expected to continue generating negative returns in the longer term.

End notes

1 Data derived from UniSuper 2006, *Investing for the future*, and the series of historical returns available at www.unisuper.com.au.

2 SIRCA, *ASX daily data*, www.sirca.usyd.edu.au. Data available only by subscription. The All Ordinaries Accumulation Index was used to measure the return on shares. This index is constructed by taking the share prices of a group of companies listed on the ASX and weighting them according to their relative size in the market. The index value increases when dividends are paid by the companies because it is assumed that all dividends are reinvested in the paying company. This means that any dividends that you receive would be used to purchase more shares in the company that paid the dividend. Annual returns were calculated at the end of each month by summing the monthly returns for the previous 12 months on a rolling basis.

3 Reserve Bank of Australia 2006, *FO2 Capital market yields — government bonds*, www.rba.gov.au.

4 Australian Securities Exchange, *Annual performance of Australian shares, including dividends, 1900–2006*, www.asx.com.au.

5 ASX, *Annual performance of Australian shares, including dividends, 1900–2002*, www.asx.com.au.

6 Webber, M 1998, 'The resilience of the Allais paradox', *Ethics*, vol. 109, no. 1, pp. 94–118.

7 Kahneman, D & Tversky, A 1979, 'Prospect theory: an analysis of decision under risk', *Econometrica*, vol. 47, no. 2, pp. 263–81.

8 Economists tend to differentiate between risk and uncertainty on the ability of the decision maker to assign a probability to an event. This distinction may be important from a theoretical perspective, but means little in practical application.

9 Roberts, P 1994, ' Risk (popular leisure activities)', *Psychology Today*, viewed 18 June 2003, http://global.factiva.com.

10 Hartog, J, Ferrer-i-Carbonella, A & Smith, N 2002, 'Linking measured risk aversion to individual characteristics', *Kyklos*, vol. 55, no. 1, pp. 3–26.

11 Kahneman, D & Tversky, A 1982, 'The psychology of preferences', *Scientific American*, vol. 246, pp. 160–73.

12 This discussion is based on the assumption that people are making rational decisions about participating in the games. If there is low cost information available that allows prospective participants to assess the probabilities of winning or losing, rational players will use this information and incorporate it into their decision making process. Assessing the probabilities of a coin toss game that uses a fair coin would have to be one of the lowest cost pieces of reliable information a participant would ever have access to! If the potential participant does not include this information in the decision, he or she would not be considered rational.

13 Tarashev, N, Tsatsoronis, K & Karampatos, D 2003, 'Investors' attitude toward risk: what can we learn from options?', *BIS Quarterly Review*, June, pp. 57–66, www.bis.org.

14 Scheicher, M 2003, 'What drives investor risk aversion? Daily evidence from the German equity market', *BIS Quarterly Review*, June, pp. 67–74, www.bis.org.

15 The ex ante form of the CAPM is shown in equation 5.8. When the CAPM is applied to historical data, the observed return on the market is used in place of the expected return on the market. In this situation, the CAPM generates a required return for investors rather than an expected return.

16 For research on the changes in the ERP over time see, for example, Banasal, R & Lundblad, C 2002, 'Market efficiency, asset returns and the size of the risk premium in global equity markets', *Journal of Econometrics*, vol. 109, no. 2, pp. 195–237.

17 See, for example, Benartzi, S & Thaler, R 1995,'Myopic loss aversion and the equity premium puzzle', *Quarterly Journal of Economics*, vol. 110, no. 1, pp. 73–91.

18 'Disaster response — The LEX column', *Financial Times*, 12 August 2006, p. 12.

19 ASX Corporate Governance Council 2003, *Principles of good corporate governance and best practice recommendations*, www.asx.com.au.

20 Most notably the critique of Roll, R 1977, 'A critique of the asset pricing theory's tests, part 1: on the past and potential testability of the theory', *Journal of Financial Economics*, March, pp. 129–76. One of Roll's main arguments is that the market portfolio should include all risky assets (not just the market index for one country) and thus, the market portfolio cannot be observed. This makes the CAPM untestable. A hypothesis that cannot be tested cannot be rejected (if tests show CAPM does not predict, then lack of predictive ability can be attributed to measurement issues and the hypothesis is not rejected). A theory that cannot generate testable hypothesis is not generally considered to be sound.

21 Bartholdy and Peare found, using a variety of specifications, it explained 3% of the differences in share returns at best. See Bartholdy, J & Peare, P 2005, 'Estimation of expected return: CAPM vs Fama and French', *International Review of Financial Analysis*, vol. 14, no. 4, pp. 407–27.

22 Ross, S 1976, 'The arbitrage theory of capital asset pricing', *Journal of Economic Theory*, December, pp. 343–62.

23 Fama, E & French, K 1992, 'The cross-section of expected returns', *Journal of Finance*, vol. 47, no. 2, pp. 427–65.

24 Bartholdy and Peare (see note 21) found that the Fama and French three factor model explained 5% of the difference in share returns. They suggest that this incremental explanatory power was insufficient to justify the additional costs of estimation.

25 Barberis, N, Huang, M & Santos, T 2001, 'Prospect theory and asset prices', *Quarterly Journal of Economics*, vol. 116, no. 1, pp. 1–53.

26 See Malkiel, B & Xu, Y 1997, 'Risk and return revisited', *Journal of Portfolio Management*, vol. 27, no. 4, pp. 9–14; Goyal, A & Santa-Clara, P 2003, 'Idiosyncratic Risk Matters', *Journal of Finance*, vol. 58, no. 3, pp. 975–1007.

part 2

Investment choices

chapter

6

Valuation of bonds and shares

Learning objectives

After studying this chapter, you should be able to:

- lo1 explain the difference between price and value
- lo2 discuss how prices are set in securities markets
- lo3 define the concept of intrinsic value
- lo4 calculate the intrinsic value of a bond
- lo5 calculate the intrinsic value of a preference share
- lo6 calculate the intrinsic value of an ordinary share
- lo7 discuss and apply the price–earnings ratio approach.

SHOULD YOU PURCHASE THESE SHARES? INVESTMENT ANALYSTS' RECOMMENDATIONS

Billabong International Limited (BBG)

Previously Reviewed: 13/7/06(YMW26)

Price: $14.69

Recommendation: Buy

BUY	ACCUM	HOLD	REDUCE	SELL
	$14.80	$16.80	$19.80	$21.50

Note: Marker indicates price of $14.69 at publication date.

Sector
Speciality Retailing
Market Cap
$3 040.8m
52 Week High/Low
$16.49 – $12.37

Risk

Business Risk: Medium   Pricing Risk: Medium

Year	06/04(a)	06/05(a)	06/06(a)	06/07(e)	06/08(e)
NPAT ($m)	89.9	125.3	145.9	172.7	209.4
EPS (c)	44.4	61.0	70.8	83.3	100.9
% Change	13.0	37.3	16.1	17.6	21.1
DPS (c)	26.5	38.0	44.0	52.0	63.0
Franking (%)	100.0	100.0	100.0	100.0	100.0
Dividend Yield (%)	1.80	2.59	3.00	3.54	4.29
PER	33.09	24.08	20.75	17.64	14.56

Source: *Aspect Huntley analyst estimates*

Avge Annual Growth Rates	10yr	5yr	1yr
Earnings per Share	–	27.3%	15.5%
Dividends per Share	–	27.6%	15.8%

MYOB Limited (MYO)

Previously Reviewed: 8/3/06(SCG9)

Price: $0.95

Recommendation: Accumulate

BUY	ACCUM	HOLD	REDUCE	SELL

$0.85 $1.00 $1.20 $1.50

Note: Marker indicates price of $0.95 at publication date.

Sector

Accounting software provider

Market Cap

386.7m

52 Week High/Low

$1.24 – $0.80

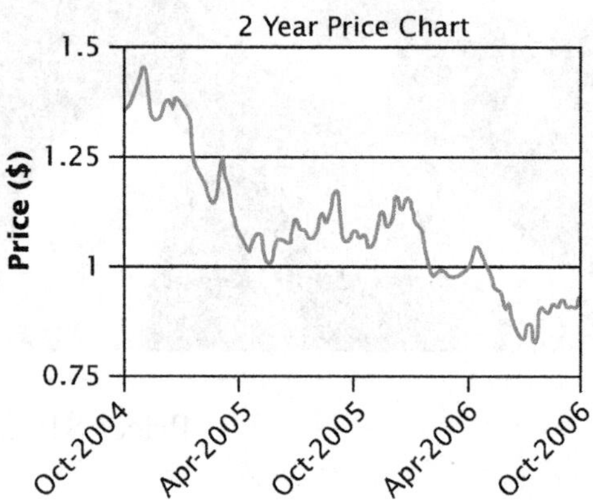

Risk

Business Risk: Medium Pricing Risk: Medium

Year	12/04(a)	12/05(a)	12/06(e)	12/07(e)
NPAT ($m)	14.1	17.7	18.1	21.2
EPS (c)	4.6	4.4	4.6	5.5
% Change	22.9	–4.6	4.5	20.2
DPS (c)	2.3	2.8	3.0	3.5
Franking (%)	100.0	100.0	100.0	100.0
Dividend Yield (%)	2.40	2.90	3.20	3.70
PER	20.70	21.60	20.70	17.30

***Source:** Aspect Huntley analyst estimates*

Avge Annual Growth Rates	10yr	5yr	1yr
Earnings per Share	9.7%	–9.3%	51.2%
Dividends per Share	–	6.2%	200.0%

Source: Aspect Huntley.[1]

The first recommendation — for Billabong International Limited (BBG) — was released by Huntley Investment Information Ltd on 31 August 2006. The 'previously reviewed' date 13/07/06 refers to the last time Huntleys gave investment advice about the purchase or sale of Billabong shares. The 'price' of $14.69 is the quoted price on the ASX at the time the recommendation was published. The price range over the last year '52 week high/low' is shown on the left-hand side, above the price chart that shows how the price has changed over the previous two years.

The recommendation also includes a price bar that recommends an action for investors in five different price ranges. The bar shows that Huntleys recommend the purchase of Billabong shares as long as the price is below $14.80 (which it was at the time the advice was given). Huntleys consider that a share price of $21.50 is too high for Billabong and recommend that shares be sold if the market reaches that price. An assessment of the business and price (the share price volatility) risk is shown under the price bar. The remaining information in the recommendation includes three years of historic data for variables of interest to investors and two years of the analysts' forecasts of these variables.

The second recommendation — for MYOB Limited (MYO) — was released on 30 August 2006. The recommendation for this firm is to 'accumulate'. The price bar shows the current price of $0.95 is higher than the recommended buy price of $0.85. 'Accumulate' means that the firm is 'undervalued, but there is time to purchase'. So how is a 'buy' recommendation different to an 'accumulate'? You could say that purchasing MYOB at an amount below the price of $0.85 is a 'bargain' and that purchasing at a price below $1.00 is still good buying. The 'hold' price range of $1.00 to $1.20 is the range that the analysts think is about right for MYOB. The 'reduce' price range of $1.20 to $1.50 is considered too high by the analysts, while any price over $1.50 would indicate the seller was getting much more than the analysts think the company is worth.

Chapter preview

The investment recommendation about Billabong International Ltd on page 177 of this chapter is an example of some summary advice given by investment analysts. The advice, given the share price at the time of the report, is to buy the shares. This means that the analyst considers that Billabong shares are worth more than their current purchase price. You would not necessarily get the same advice from a different broker.

We start this chapter by looking at the difference between price and value (or price and what an asset is worth), and which measure of value is most relevant to finance. The main part of the chapter is devoted to measuring the intrinsic value of bonds and ordinary and preference shares. Understanding how 'value' is measured gives the financial manager an understanding of how much return is required by security holders. This required return is important for determining the cost of capital, which we explore in detail in chapter 7.

The following diagram shows how this chapter is structured.

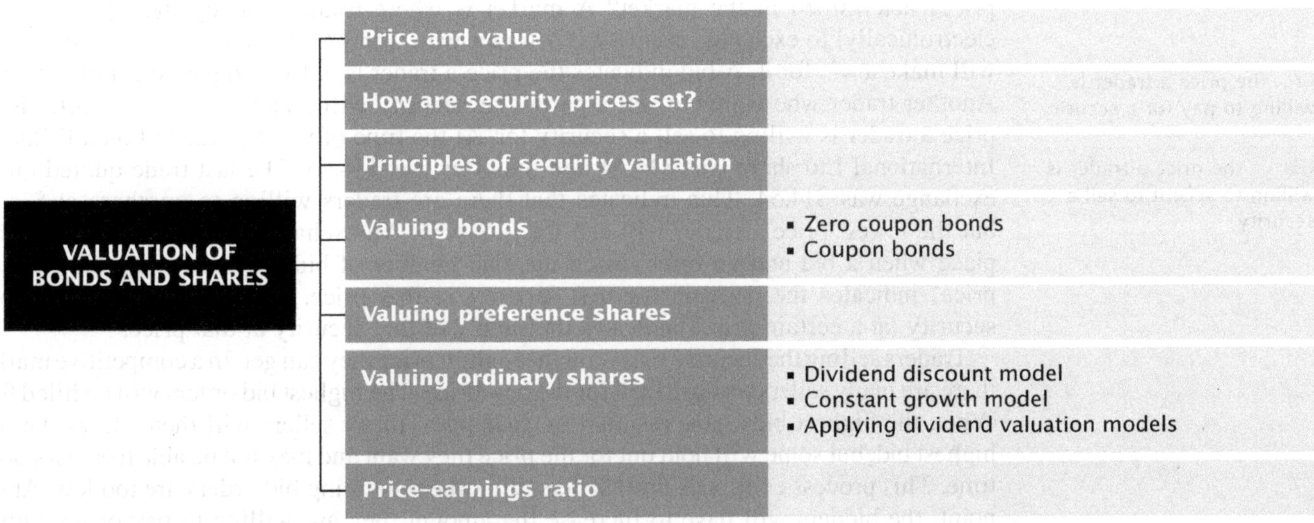

lo1

Explain the difference between price and value.

Price: the amount of money needed to acquire an asset

Value: the worth of an asset to an individual

Price and value

Oscar Wilde once said that 'people know the price of everything, and the value of nothing'. How can price and value be different? The **price** is the amount of money that is paid to purchase something — prices are set by the market forces of supply and demand. The **value** of an asset is what that asset is worth to a person.

Consider the price of $30 for a ticket to see the rock band Wolfmother live in concert. If you really like the band, you might be willing to pay twice that to see them — you would value the ticket at $60. If wild horses couldn't drag you to see the band, you won't be willing to pay $30 for a ticket — you would place a much lower value on the ticket (or even want to be paid to attend!). Price and value can be quite different amounts.

Based on Huntleys' investment advice on pages 177 and 178, the price of Billabong shares ($14.69) was below their value ($16.80 to $19.80), while the price ($0.95) and value ($1.00 to $1.20) for MYOB Ltd shares are closer together.

lo2

How are security prices set?

Discuss how prices are set in securities markets.

Securities: tradable instruments that represent an ownership interest or the right to receive payment on a debt

In chapter 3 we define **securities** as tradable instruments that represent an ownership interest or the right to receive payment on a debt. As we discuss in chapter 3, securities include ordinary and preference shares, debentures, notes, bills, government and semi-government bonds. An important characteristic normally found in securities is that they are easily interchangeable — an investor who wants to purchase an ordinary share of Billabong Ltd, for example, will not have a preference for a particular ordinary share issued by the company because all of the shares will carry the same entitlements. The only preference an investor would have is in regard to the price paid for the share.

The price of a security is easy to observe when it is traded in an active market. As we see in chapter 3, Australian listed securities are traded on the Australian Securities Exchange (ASX). Brokers have access to electronic systems that show the price for the last trade of a particular share. People who trade for themselves online using a discount broker like E-Trade can also access the most recent information. The ASX website provides prices free to the public for all but the most recent trades of listed securities.[2] How are these prices determined in the market? A market is where traders get together (physically or electronically) to exchange securities. A trader who wants to purchase a particular security will make a **bid** for it. A bid indicates the price a trader is willing to pay to get the security. Another trader who wants to sell a particular security will make an **offer**. An offer is the price a trader is willing to sell a security for. At the time of writing, the bid on a Billabong International Ltd share was $14.54 and the offer was $14.55. The last trade quoted on the exchange was $14.54. This indicates that there are traders willing to purchase at $14.54, but the lowest price a trader will sell for is $14.55. An exchange of the security will take place when a bid and an offer match up. The number of bids for a security (at a certain price) indicates the demand for that security at that price. The number of offers for a security (at a certain price) indicates the supply of that security at that price.

Bid: the price a trader is willing to pay for a security

Offer: the price a trader is willing to accept to sell a security

Traders selling the security will want the highest price they can get. In a competitive market, there are many sellers trying to sell for the best price. The highest bid orders will be filled first. When the highest bids have resulted in exchanges, many sellers will then accept the next highest bid, but some will hold out for the price they want and may not be able to sell for some time. This process continues until sellers think the remaining bid orders are too low. At this point, the bidders will have to increase the amount they are willing to pay or go without purchasing the security. Purchasers who still wish to buy at a higher price increase their bids. Sellers still wishing to sell at the lower price decrease their offers. The next exchange takes place when there is a bid and an offer at the same price and the process begins again.

How high a trader is willing to bid depends on the value she has given the security. How low another trader is willing to offer depends on his valuation of the security. The market price represents the most widely held view of the value of the security at that point in time. Price approximates the aggregate values of individual traders.

FINANCE WORLD

Consensus forecasts

What does it really mean to say that price approximates the aggregate values of individual traders? If people are trading shares when they think that the value of the company has changed, or if they think that the market price is different from the value, we can say that the price in the most recent trades reflects the average of the traders' own beliefs about the actual value of the share. In this case, a falling share price would indicate that, on average, traders think that the value of the share is lower than it was when the market opened. Some traders will think that the market price is incorrect and the value is higher than the current price. These traders will be purchasing more as the share price falls, but a falling price indicates that these traders are in the minority. We devote the rest of the chapter to calculating intrinsic values, but let's consider some of the variables that affect value first. Table 6.1 contains information about BHP Billiton Ltd.

Table 6.1 Variables affecting the value of the shares of BHP Billiton Ltd

		Consensus forecasts		
	Last result	1 year ahead	2 years ahead	3 years ahead
Earnings per share	$2.30	$2.86	$2.72	$2.31
Price–earnings ratio	12.17	9.78	10.28	12.14
Growth rate	79.1%	24.31%	−4.92%	−15.28%
Number of analysts		14	12	9

Source: Datastream International.[3]

The first column shows us that analysts forecast earnings per share, the price–earnings ratio and earnings growth for BHP Billiton. These variables can be used when calculating the value of an ordinary share and they will be explained later in the chapter. The second column shows the historic rate for each variable. The 2006 earnings per share, for example, was $2.30. Fourteen analysts have generated forecasts for the next financial year and 12 have forecast for the following financial year as well. The third and fourth columns show an average of these analyst forecasts.

Not all analysts will be using forecast earnings of $2.86 for the coming year and $2.72 for two years ahead. They can all have different expectations, but these differences will tend to offset each other because some will be higher and some lower. Therefore, we can say that the majority view of the value of BHP Billiton Ltd is consistent with using the consensus forecast earnings, and this should have a strong influence on the price of BHP shares. We learn more about forecasting in chapter 14.

lo3

Define the concept of intrinsic value.

Principles of security valuation

Book value: the accounting measure of an asset's worth

There are many ways we can measure the broad concept of 'value'. One that you may already be familiar with is **book value**. Book value is the accounting measure of an asset's worth. The book value of a machine, for example, is measured as the cost of purchasing the machine minus the accumulated depreciation that has been charged against the machine over the period of ownership. We look at book values further in chapter 14.

The book value of a share is measured by the accounting amounts for total assets minus total liabilities (this equals total equity), all divided by the number of ordinary shares issued (equation 6.1).

Coupon payments: the regular interest payments received by the holder of a bond

$$\textbf{Book value of a share} = \frac{\textbf{total assets} - \textbf{total liabilities}}{\textbf{number of ordinary shares issued}} \quad [6.1]$$

Intrinsic value: (of a security) the present value of expected future cash flows discounted at the investor's required rate of return

Securities represent the rights to future cash flows. Book value does not provide us with a good representation of future cash flows. The cash flows of a security can come from dividends, **coupon payments**, redemption by the issuer or from the sale of the security on the secondary market. We can use the forecast pattern of cash flows and the investor's required rate of return (see chapter 5) to calculate a value for a security. The **intrinsic value** of a security is the present value of the expected future cash flows of the security discounted at the investor's required rate of return. We will devote the rest of this chapter to measuring the intrinsic value of bonds, ordinary shares and preference shares.

If investors were all forecasting cash flows and discounting them at their required rates of return to calculate intrinsic value, why would some think Billabong shares are a good buy at $15 while others consider the shares too expensive? Intrinsic value, like beauty, is in the eye of the beholder. One source of variation in the calculation of intrinsic values comes from the individual investor's view of risk. Even if all market players forecast the same cash flows for the share, they can still have different intrinsic values for that asset. As we discuss in chapter 5, people who have a lower tolerance to risk will have a higher required return and the required return is the discount rate that should be applied to future cash flows. Given that systematic risk, rather than total risk, drives the returns earned on a security, a difference in investors' perceptions of the level of systematic risk associated with the security will result in individuals applying different discount rates to the same forecast cash flows. A higher discount rate will lead to a lower intrinsic value calculation. A person that has calculated a low intrinsic value for a share will not be willing to pay as much for it as a person who has calculated a higher intrinsic value for the same share. Further, the assumption that all investors are risk averse does not mean they will all use the same discount rate. Some risk-averse investors are relatively more risk averse than others.

Another source of variation arises from the uncertainty associated with the future cash flows. The amount of uncertainty about cash flows varies between securities. We can fore-cast the coupons and be pretty certain of the amount and timing of the cash flows for a debt instrument. As we discuss in chapter 3, the size and timing of the coupons and the amount paid by the issuer at maturity are normally specified in the contract. Like coupon payments, the future dividends from preference shares are not usually difficult to forecast. The difficulty in forecasting cash flows from equities stems from their infinite lives — they don't have a maturity value. In addition to having an infinite life, the size of dividends on ordinary shares can vary because dividends are declared by the company's board. Dividends are not always paid at regular intervals. We investigate the size and timing of dividend payments in chapter 13. When forecasting involves some judgement, be it about the level of risk or the expected cash flows, individuals will form different opinions. Consequently, intrinsic values will vary.

An investor's required return, the amount and timing of the security's cash flows and the level of risk associated with these cash flows are the key elements in determining a security's value. The basic security valuation model is equation 6.2.

$$V = \sum_{t=1}^{n} \frac{CF_t}{(1+r)^t} \qquad [6.2]$$

where V = intrinsic (or present) value of a security producing expected future cash flows, CF_t, in periods 1 to n

CF_t = cash flow to be received in period t

r = investor's required rate of return

Equation 6.2 shows us that intrinsic value is determined by the present value of future cash flows. The symbol Σ is the Greek letter 'sigma'. It tells us to take the sum of the calculations that follow this symbol. The $t = 1$ that appears below the sigma tells us to start at time period 1. The n above the symbol tells us to keep going until we get to time period n. As we discuss in chapter 4, interest rates are quoted in annual nominal terms by convention. The same convention is observed for required rates of return and the rates we use in this text are all expressed on an annual basis unless specifically stated otherwise.

EXAMPLE 6.1

Intrinsic value

You have been offered an investment that will pay \$15 a year from today, \$20 in 2 years' time and \$125 in 3 years when the investment matures. Your required rate of return is 10% pa. What is your intrinsic value for this investment?

$$V = \sum_{t=1}^{n} \frac{CF_t}{(1+r)^t}$$

Where C_1 = \$15 cash flow to be received in period 1

C_2 = \$20 cash flow to be received in period 2

C_3 = \$125 cash flow to be received in period 3

r = 10% pa, the required rate of return.

$$V = \frac{15}{(1+0.1)^1} + \frac{20}{(1+0.1)^2} + \frac{125}{(1+0.1)^3}$$

$$= \frac{15}{1.1} + \frac{20}{1.21} + \frac{125}{1.331}$$

$$= 13.64 + 16.53 + 93.91$$

$$= \$124.08$$

The value of the investment in example 6.1 is \$124.08, given a required return of 10%. If you could purchase this investment for \$100 (or at any price below \$124.08), would you? Given your intrinsic value of \$124.08, the opportunity to acquire it for \$100 would mean you were earning more than your required return, so the investment would be very attractive. If you could purchase the investment for \$124.08 you would still purchase it because it will earn your required return and you will be appropriately compensated for the level of risk you are taking with the investment. If the investment was offered to you for \$130 (or at any price above \$124.08) you would not purchase it because it would be returning less than your required return. Another person with a required return of 12% would give this investment a lower intrinsic value. Another with a required return of 8% would calculate a higher intrinsic value. To test your understanding, work out each of these values to ascertain the maximum each investor would be willing to pay for the investment.

Valuing bonds

lo4

Calculate the intrinsic value of a bond.

In this section we will adapt our basic security valuation model and apply it to valuing longer term debt securities. As we discuss in chapter 3, these debt securities include debentures, unsecured notes and corporate bonds. We can also apply this same valuation technique to government and semi-government bonds. The term 'bond' will be used to refer to all of these securities for the remainder of this chapter.

Coupon: the stated rate of interest paid on a bond

A bond normally pays a regular income stream (the **coupon**) and has a face value that is repaid to the holder at maturity. The term 'coupon' (French for 'piece cut off') stems from the days when bonds were paper instruments and the coupons, which were effectively receipts, were printed on the bottom of the bond. Each time interest was paid, a coupon was physically cut off the bond and given back to the borrower as a receipt. Anybody could tell how many coupon payments were outstanding by counting the remaining coupons.

Zero coupon bonds

A zero coupon bond, as the name suggests, does not make regular coupon payments over the security's life. Even though zero coupon bonds are not the most common form of bond, we deal with them first because the calculation of their value is relatively simple. We then move on to more complex valuations.

The cash flow pattern on a zero coupon bond is similar to that of the discount securities we discuss in chapter 4. The purchase price at the time of issue will be at a **deep discount** to the face value of the bond. Interest accrues (but is not paid to the holder) at regular intervals over the life of the bond and the face value is repaid at maturity. Equation 6.3 shows us that the intrinsic value of a zero coupon bond is equal to present value of the maturity cash flow.

Deep discount: a purchase price (at the time of issue) for a security that is well below its face value

$$V_b = \frac{F}{(1+r_b)^n} \qquad [6.3]$$

where V_b = intrinsic value of the bond

F = bond's face (or maturity) value

r_b = bondholder's required return

n = number of periods

To use equation 6.3, we need to adjust the required annual return so that the period the return refers to is equal to the length of the compounding period. As we discuss in chapter 4, rates of return are expressed in annual terms by convention. However, we have specified semi-annual compounding in example 6.2. To use the nominal interest rate when compounding is more frequent than annual, we must divide the annual required return, r_b, by the number of compounding periods, m. In example 6.2, $m = 2$ because we have semi-annual compounding (that is, the compounding period is six months). Additionally, we must multiply the number of years to maturity, n, by the number of compounding times each year, m, to make sure the total number of time periods equals the total number of compounding periods.

EXAMPLE 6.2

Valuing a zero coupon bond

A zero coupon bond has a face value of \$100 000 and 3 years to maturity. Interest accrues on the bond twice a year (semi-annually). The investor's required return is 5% pa. What is the value of the bond?

$$V_b = \frac{F}{(1+r_b)^n}$$

$$V_b = \frac{100\,000}{\left(1+\frac{0.05}{2}\right)^{3\times 2}}$$

$$= \frac{100\,000}{(1.025)^6}$$

$$= \frac{100\,000}{(1.1597)}$$

$$= \$86\,229.20$$

For an investor with a required rate of return of 5%, this bond has an intrinsic value of $86 229.20. The intrinsic value of $86 229.20 indicates the maximum that this investor would be willing to pay for the bond. A purchase price higher than the intrinsic value means that the investor will not earn his or her required return.

FINANCE WORKSHOP 6.1

Everycar Ltd is issuing zero coupon bonds that mature in 5 years and have a face value of $1000. If your required rate of return is 5% pa, what is the value of the bond to you?

Coupon bonds

Rather than accrue interest for payment at maturity (as was the case for zero coupon bonds), it is more common for bonds to have coupon payments made over the life of the security. An 8% July 2010 $1000 corporate bond, for example, matures in July 2010 and is said to have an 8% or $80 coupon. The dollar coupon amount is calculated as a percentage of the face value (0.08 × $1000). The face value in our example is $1000 and this is the amount that will be paid to the holder at maturity in July 2010. With semi-annual coupon payments, $40 would be paid every six months over the life of the bond $\left(\frac{0.08}{2} \times \$1000\right)$.

Fixed interest: the coupon received on the bond stays the same over the bond's life

The cash flows of a **fixed interest** coupon bond form an annuity plus a single sum when the face value is repaid. This cash flow pattern is used in equation 6.4 to calculate intrinsic value.

$$V_b = \sum_{t=1}^{n} \frac{C_t}{(1+r_b)^t} + \frac{F}{(1+r_b)^n} \qquad [6.4]$$

where V_b = intrinsic value of the bond
C_t = coupon payment in period t
F = bond's face (or maturity) value
r_b = bondholder's required return
n = number of periods

This equation shows us that the value of a bond to an investor is the present value of the future cash flows from the bond, discounted at the bondholder's required rate of return.

EXAMPLE 6.3

Valuing a fixed interest coupon bond

A bond with 2 years to maturity has a coupon of 5% and a face value of $100 000. Coupons are paid semi-annually. The investor's required return is 6% pa. What is the investor's intrinsic value for this bond?

$$V_b = \sum_{t=1}^{n} \frac{C_t}{\left(1+\frac{r_b}{m}\right)^t} + \frac{F}{\left(1+\frac{r_b}{m}\right)^{nm}}$$

$$V_b = \sum_{t=1}^{n} \frac{2500}{\left(1+\frac{0.06}{2}\right)^t} + \frac{100000}{\left(1+\frac{0.06}{2}\right)^{2\times 2}}$$

$$= \frac{2500}{(1+0.03)^1} + \frac{2500}{(1+0.03)^2} + \frac{2500}{(1+0.03)^3} + \frac{2500}{(1+0.03)^4} + \frac{100000}{(1+0.03)^4}$$

$$= \frac{2500}{1.03} + \frac{2500}{1.0609} + \frac{2500}{1.0927} + \frac{2500}{1.1255} + \frac{100000}{1.1255}$$

$$= 2427.18 + 2356.49 + 2287.91 + 2221.24 + 88\,849.40$$

$$= \$98\,142.22$$

The maximum that the investor would be willing to pay for this bond is $98 142.22.

The first part of equation 6.4 calculates the present value of the annuity that is made up of the coupon payments. We could use the present value of an annuity equation given in chapter 4 to calculate this part of the equation more efficiently, as follows:

$$V_b = C\left[\frac{1-(1+r_b)^{-n}}{r_b}\right] + \frac{F}{(1+r_b)^n}$$

The last half calculates the present value of the face value of the bond. Again, it is essential to have the required return match the number of compounding periods. If we calculate the value this way, the PV of the coupons is $9292.75. Together with the PV of the face value, the intrinsic value of the bond is the same as we calculated in the example.

Not all Australian corporate issues of bonds follow the basic cash flow patterns of the bond in example 6.3. Rather than repay the face value at maturity, the bonds issued by Mariner Credit Corporation Ltd, for example, make monthly payments of principal and interest. The interest on these bonds is calculated on the amount of face value yet to be repaid (the same way interest is calculated on a mortgage). We use equation 6.4 to value these bonds but do not show any payment of face value at maturity.

Some issuers offer a fixed coupon rate for a specified period then move to a variable rate until maturity. In 2005, the Australian Central Credit Union issued July 2015 bonds with a face value of $100 that pay quarterly coupons at 9% pa for the first five years. Interest payments for the last five years depend on the level of a benchmark (the bank bill swap rate in this case). We cannot use equation 6.4 to value these bonds for two reasons; firstly, the cash flows for the variable interest period cannot be reliably predicted and secondly, the cash flows in the latter period will not form an annuity.

The Australian Central Credit Union bonds are also redeemable on 31 July each year. In this case, the issuer can choose to repay the face value of the bond plus any accrued interest prior to the maturity date of 2015. So, even if we could forecast the interest payments for the 2010–15 period with perfect accuracy, we would have to assume that no redemption would occur before we could use equation 6.4 to value these bonds.

A further complication arises when the bond can be converted to the ordinary shares of the issuer before or at maturity (see chapter 12 for more details). We can not use equation 6.4 to value convertible debt unless we are able to generate a reliable forecast of the maturity value of the security and these forecasts can be very difficult.

FINANCE WORKSHOP 6.2

A bond with 6 years to maturity has a coupon of 3% pa and a face value of $100 000. Your required rate of return is 4% pa. Coupons are paid semi-annually. What is your intrinsic value for this bond?

lo5

Calculate the intrinsic value of a preference share.

Valuing preference shares

Preference shares, as discussed in chapter 3, are hybrid securities that have features of both debt and equity. The similarity to debt is that they normally have a fixed coupon based on a face value. The similarity to equity is that they don't usually have a maturity date — dividend payments will continue to be made while the company issuing the shares is solvent. We can value the cash flows associated with a typical preference share as a perpetuity. Equation 6.5 is equivalent to the calculation of the present value of a perpetuity in equation 4.12.

$$V_p = \frac{D}{r_p} \qquad [6.5]$$

where V_p = intrinsic value of the preference share
D = dividend payment
r_p = preference shareholder's required return

EXAMPLE 6.4

Valuing a preference share

Weblink Ltd issues $5 preference shares which pay a 50c dividend per share annually. The company is financially stable and dividends are expected to continue indefinitely. What is the intrinsic value of a share if the investor has a required return of 8%?

$$V_p = \frac{D}{r_p}$$

$$V_p = \frac{0.50}{0.08}$$

$$= \$6.25$$

If dividend payments are made more than once a year, we need to make the required rate of return and the number of compounding periods equivalent. If Weblink Ltd made semi-annual dividend payments, we would divide the annual dividend and the required rate of return by two. The dividend would be 25 cents and the required rate of return 4%. Is the intrinsic value still the same? Do the calculation and see.

Example 6.4 values a 'typical' preference share. A range of preference share securities with different characteristics is available in the market. Some preference shares are redeemable; that is, the company buys them back at a future date. In October 2003, Grain Corp Ltd issued redeemable preference shares where redemption could occur after 30 September 2006. Such preference shares are much more akin to debt than equity and are valued using the bond valuation equation 6.4 with the redemption amount in the place of the face value. Some preference shares can be converted to the ordinary shares of the issuer (see chapter 12 for more detail). These shares are rather more difficult to value because the value at conversion is not known until close to that time.

It is also possible for preference shares to have varying dividends. The dividend on participating preference shares depends, to some extent, on the level of profit generated by the firm. Participating preference shares usually receive a minimum dividend amount but can participate in additional dividends (as ordinary shareholders do) when company profits reach some pre-specified level. Reset preference shares have their dividends adjusted if and when some future event happens. We discuss variable dividend preference shares further in chapter 12. Participating and reset preference shares can not be valued using equation 6.5 because their dividend cash flows are not perpetuities.

FINANCE WORKSHOP 6.3

An investor wishes to work out the value of a 10% preference share. The face value of the share is $100 and the dividends are paid semi-annually. If the investor's required rate of return is 12%, what is the intrinsic value of the share?

lo6

Calculate the intrinsic value of an ordinary share.

Valuing ordinary shares

This section of the chapter is devoted to valuing ordinary shares. Three models are examined. Two of these — the dividend discount model and the constant growth model — use the shares' cash flows as a variable. These models are not applicable in certain circumstances, especially for valuing a company that does not pay dividends. The third model we use to value ordinary shares is the price–earnings multiple.

Dividend discount model

As for bonds and preference shares, the intrinsic value of an ordinary share is the present value of the future cash flows using the investor's required rate of return. If we expect to own a share for a finite period, we calculate intrinsic value by forecasting the dividends we will receive and the price we expect to get for the share when we sell it. If we can do that, we can adapt the basic security valuation shown in equation 6.2 to give us the value for the period we intend to hold the share. This equation is called the dividend discount model.

$$V_e = \sum_{t=1}^{n} \frac{D_t}{(1 + r_e)^t} + \frac{P_n}{(1 + r_e)^n} \qquad [6.6]$$

where V_e = intrinsic value of the ordinary share
r_e = shareholder's required return
D_t = dividend payment in period t
P_n = market price of the share at time n
n = number of periods

The first part of the equation is the sum of the discounted forecast dividend cash flows and is analogous to the present value of the coupons received on a bond. The final part of the equation is the present value of the price we will receive when we sell the share and is analogous to the discounted face value on a bond. As with all of our valuation models, we need to ensure that the required rate of return matches the timing of the expected cash flows.

EXAMPLE 6.5

Valuing an ordinary share with a finite holding period

You are considering the purchase of a parcel of Cochlear shares. The shares pay dividends semi-annually and you have forecast the next four dividends to be 35c, 37c, 42c and 45c. You have a contract to sell the shares in 2 years' time (just after the last dividend is received) for \$65 each. If your required return is 11%, what is the intrinsic value of a Cochlear share to you?

$$V_e = \sum_{t=1}^{n} \frac{D_t}{(1+r_e)^t} + \frac{P_n}{(1+r_e)^n}$$

$$V_e = \frac{0.35}{(1+0.055)^1} + \frac{0.37}{(1+0.055)^2} + \frac{0.42}{(1+0.055)^3} + \frac{0.45}{(1+0.055)^4} + \frac{65.00}{(1+0.055)^4}$$

$$= 0.33 + 0.33 + 0.36 + 0.36 + 52.47$$

$$= \$53.85$$

Therefore, the intrinsic value of the share to you is \$53.85 and this is the maximum price you would be prepared to pay for a share.

FINANCE WORKSHOP 6.4

You expect Sansanqua Ltd to pay the following dividends at the end of each of the next 4 years:

Year	Dividend
1	0.50
2	0.75
3	0.80
4	0.85

You have a contract that requires you to sell your shares in the company for \$6.50 immediately after you receive the fourth yearly dividend. If your required return is 10%, what is the intrinsic value of a Sansanqua share?

Example 6.5 depicts a very simplistic situation. While the bond valuation equation 6.4 and the finite holding period share valuation equation 6.6 appear very similar, two factors make the intrinsic value of a share much more difficult to determine than is the case for coupon bonds. The first arises when forecasting dividends and the second involves estimating the price we will get when we sell the share in a future period. Without a contract to sell the shares, how can you estimate the future price of the share? These issues are discussed in the following sections.

Coupon bonds have regular payments of the same amount that are specified in the debt contract. The cash flows for ordinary shares are much less certain. The dividends paid on ordinary shares are largely determined by the company's profitability and can be difficult to predict. We may be able to make reasonable forecasts for a couple of years, but uncertainty increases with time. If we could somehow know all the future dividends, we could use equation 6.6 to obtain the value of all future cash flows (which should be close to the price) at the end of year two. One way to tackle the uncertainty of dividends is to make a simplifying assumption that dividends grow as the firm matures and becomes more profitable. We can use this method to forecast the future cash flows of the share when we think dividends will increase over time and that the increase is best represented by a percentage of the last dividend. Example 6.6 is a simple example of calculating future dividends based on the assumption that dividends will increase proportionally over time. In reality, dividends vary with company performance and companies can follow different policies with respect to dividend payments. We discuss these dividend policy alternatives in chapter 13.

EXAMPLE 6.6

Forecasting dividends with proportional growth

The last semi-annual dividend paid by ABC Ltd was 32 cents. You forecast the dividend growth rate as 10% pa. What are your dividend forecasts for the next 2 years?

Dividend forecasts are shown below. If the growth rate is 10% pa and dividends are semi-annual, the semi-annual growth rate is 5%. Starting with the last dividend of 32c, we forecast the next dividend by multiplying that by one plus the growth rate (and remember that we need a semi-annual growth rate for a semi-annual dividend). We take the same approach with all subsequent dividends, using the dividend for the last period as our starting point. An alternative way to make these calculations is shown in the last column.

$$\text{first dividend} = 0.32 \times 1.05 = 0.336 = 0.32\,(1.05)^1$$
$$\text{second dividend} = 0.336 \times 1.05 = 0.3528 = 0.32\,(1.05)^2$$
$$\text{third dividend} = 0.3528 \times 1.05 = 0.3704 = 0.32\,(1.05)^3$$
$$\text{fourth dividend} = 0.3704 \times 1.05 = 0.3890 = 0.32\,(1.05)^4$$

Constant growth model

The second major difficulty in valuing a share is the infinite life of the security. Ordinary shares have no maturity date and we need to incorporate this feature into our valuation. If the value of a security is the present value of its future cash flows, then the value of that security in, say, a year's time will be the present value of the future cash flows occurring after one year's time. Purchasing a share gives you the right to receive its future cash flows. Consider the timing of your share purchase. If you purchase one year from today, you would be willing to pay the present value of the future cash flows from the purchase date to infinity. Alternatively, you could purchase the share today. If you purchase today, you would be willing to pay the same amount you would pay in one year's time (discounted to today's dollars) plus the present value of the cash flows that would occur between today and the end of one year. Therefore, it doesn't matter if we forecast the dividends to infinity or if we forecast the dividends for one period, then forecast the value at the end of that period. If we make a consistent assumption about the growth rate, the results of both calculations should be the same and we do not need to calculate the price for the end of the holding period. This means we can not get around the problem of forecasting dividends forever by forecasting an ending value for our investment as we did with the basic dividend discount model.

We all know that the future is uncertain. Around the turn of the century analysts' forecasts for BHP would have been consistent with the stable growth that is normally associated with the company. Have another look at the growth forecasts for BHP in the 'finance world' feature on page 181. The realised earnings growth for the 2005–06 year was an astounding 79%. Such a high growth rate is unusual even in the context of the commodities boom driven by demand from China (the historic average annual growth rate during 2001–06 was about 32%). Analysts don't normally forecast such unusually high (or low) growth rates. In fact, the forecast growth for BHP shown in the 'finance world' feature shows that analysts expected earnings to increase again in 2007, but to fall in 2008 and 2009. Will BHP achieve the forecast growth rate in 2007? We couldn't answer this question at the time of writing this book, but you will be able to answer it now. BHP's performance all depends on the price for commodities in the world market. No matter how well a company is managed, external factors can cause cash flows to decrease (or increase).

The point is that we make the best estimates of the future that we can, given that we don't have crystal balls or infinite resources to use on research. In many cases, we can use a constant growth rate that we expect to approximate actual growth for at least the medium term. The further into the future the cash flows occur, the greater the uncertainty about the size of the cash flows. Fortunately, the discounting process reflects this uncertainty by heavily penalising cash flows that occur later in the future stream. This means that the further into the future a cash flow occurs, the less it adds to the present value — so distant cash flows are relatively unimportant. To reinforce this idea, look back to finance workshop 6.4. Notice the PVs of 50c and 80c were less than 15c different? This happens because the cash flows occur two years apart and a dollar today is worth more than a dollar in two years' time.

If we do make the assumption of constant growth we can use equation 6.7 to calculate the value of a share.

$$V_e = \frac{D_1}{r_e - g} \qquad [6.7]$$

where V_e = intrinsic value of the ordinary share
D_1 = dividend to be paid in the next period
r_e = shareholder's required return
g = expected growth in dividends

Equation 6.7 is used when we forecast a constant level of growth in dividends forever. It can also be used for shares that pay a constant fixed dividend (that is, $g = 0$) forever. A growth rate of zero reduces equation 6.7 to the same equation we used to value preference shares (equation 6.5).

EXAMPLE 6.7

Valuing an ordinary share with constant growth

CSR Ltd is a mature company that has experienced a growth rate of 2% pa for the last 5 years. You expect that this growth rate will continue indefinitely. Dividends are paid semi-annually. The most recent dividend was 15c and was paid last week. What is the intrinsic value of a CSR ordinary share if your required rate of return is 6% pa?

$$V_e = \frac{D_1}{r_e - g}$$

$$V_e = \frac{0.15(1 + 0.01)}{0.03 - 0.01}$$

$$= \frac{0.1515}{0.02}$$

$$= \$7.58$$

The intrinsic value of the CSR share is $7.58.

Notice that we took the current dividend ($D_0 = 0.15$) and increased that by one plus the growth rate to calculate D_1. What if you are valuing the shares of a relatively new company that is enjoying a high growth rate at the moment, but you think this growth will not be continued to infinity? Example 6.8 shows how we can incorporate changing growth rates into our calculations.

EXAMPLE 6.8

Valuing an ordinary share with changing growth

The Technobrat company started operating 3 years ago. The company was originally based on one product — a virtual reality machine that was easy to use and moderately priced. During the last 3 years, the company has ploughed all of its resources into research and development and has come up with a range of very marketable products. The first ever dividend was paid this month. From now on, the company expects to be able to pay annual dividends and continue to have sufficient funds for further research and development. The recently paid dividend was 20c per share. Your analysis of Technobrat has led you to expect a growth rate of 15% pa for the next three years. As new competitors move into the market and the research and development team doesn't have as many brilliant ideas, you expect the growth rate to stabilise at 3% pa. As Technobrat's operations have a fairly high level of systematic risk your required rate of return is 18%. What valuation will you give the shares of Technobrat?

$$V_e = \frac{D_1}{(1 + r_e)^1} + \frac{D_2}{(1 + r_e)^2} + \frac{D_3}{(1 + r_e)^3} + \frac{D_4}{r_e - g}\left(\frac{1}{(1 + r_e)^3}\right)$$

$$V_e = \frac{0.20(1+0.15)}{(1+0.18)} + \frac{0.20(1+0.15)^2}{(1+0.18)^2} + \frac{0.20(1+0.15)^3}{(1+0.18)^3} + \frac{0.20(1+0.15)^3(1.03)}{0.18-0.03}\left(\frac{1}{(1+0.18)^3}\right)$$

$$= \frac{0.23}{1.18} + \frac{0.2645}{1.3924} + \frac{0.3042}{1.643} + \frac{0.3133}{0.15}(0.6086)$$
$$= 0.1949 + 0.19 + 0.1851 + 1.2712$$
$$= \$1.84$$

The first thing to note in example 6.8 is that the 15% growth rate is sustained for only three years. We can apply the constant growth model only when growth will not change again. Therefore, to value Technobrat's shares, we needed to forecast the dividends for periods one to three and discount these at the required return as we would to value a share with a finite holding period. In the second part of the calculation, we apply the constant growth model for dividends received after year three. We can apply the constant growth model here because the new 3% growth rate is expected to continue to infinity. The constant growth model gives us the intrinsic value of a share one time period before the first constant growth dividend is received. This is, of course, just the price of the share at the end of time period three. This price has to be discounted back to today's dollars. In this example, we apply the constant growth model after three years of dividends have been received. We therefore need to discount the value from the constant growth model by three years to get it to today's dollars. Given the assumptions we made about growth and timing, the intrinsic value of a Technobrat share is $1.84.

A major constraint of the constant growth model is that it can not be applied to securities when the investor's required rate of return is lower than the growth rate. Required rates of return will fall in periods of low interest rates. If economic circumstances dictate low required returns, and the company you are trying to value is expected to maintain a relatively good growth rate and you apply the constant growth model, you will end up with a negative share price. Clearly, this would not then reflect the intrinsic value of a security enjoying good growth forecasts. While the growth rate may be higher than the required return in the short term, the situation would not be expected to continue in the long term.

FINANCE WORKSHOP 6.5

Palmco Ltd is an established firm with a solid history of paying semi-annual dividends. You expect the current annual growth rate of 3% to continue indefinitely. The last dividend paid was recently and was 15c per share. If your required rate of return is 10% pa, what is the intrinsic value of a Palmco share?

Applying dividend valuation models

Blue chip: companies that are well established and have a good track record for financial stability

The dividend discount and constant growth valuation models can not be applied to all companies. These models do not fit well with any unpredictable variability in future dividends. The models should work better when valuing **blue chip** companies. Blue chip companies are those that are well established and have a good track record for being financially stable. They have a solid dividend history, paying dividends in good times and bad, so they tend to have a fairly predictable pattern of dividend payments. Blue chip companies got their name because the blue chips in a poker game are the most expensive (or valuable).[4] Some examples of Australian blue chips are BHP Billiton, the Commonwealth Bank and Coles Ltd.

Smaller companies might want to pay a stable dividend but may not have enough cash to maintain the dividend level. The *Corporations Act 2001* specifies that dividends can be paid only out of current profits or past period profits kept as retained earnings. Younger companies may not have enough retained profits to keep the dividend stable in years of low profits. New companies that are experiencing rapid growth may not pay a dividend at all — they keep the money to fund their growth options. We take an in-depth look at different dividend policies in chapter 13.

While many investors like to receive regular dividend payments, others don't want to receive dividends at the current time. They might prefer cash flows some years down the track; they might have a preference for receiving extra shares in the company instead of getting a cash dividend; or they might prefer a large capital gain when they sell the shares at a later date. (A preference for a capital gain rather than dividends is usually influenced by the investor's current marginal tax rate and their expected marginal tax rate in the future.) In some cases, investors might prefer to have the company retain the cash to achieve some objective that is not wealth related (see the next 'behavioural perspective' feature).

The standard valuation models that have been presented in this chapter can not accommodate this type of preference for not receiving dividends. Some companies don't pay dividends (the most famous of these is the US corporation, Microsoft, which started paying dividends only in 2002) and investors that do not need income from shares over their investment horizon will purchase shares in companies that don't pay dividends. We discuss these different investor needs further in chapter 13. For the time being, it is important to note that we can not value shares that do not pay dividends by using the dividend discount or constant growth models.

BEHAVIOURAL PERSPECTIVE

A non-wealth motive for investing

Traditional finance theory is based on the assumption that investors are homogeneous with respect to the objective of maximising wealth or monetary return. The growth of ethical investment funds in Australia could be interpreted as an indication that some investors want to go beyond wealth maximisation and hold investments that reflect personal values.

Australian ethical investors tend to avoid companies producing tobacco or armaments, those involved in uranium mining or gambling or dealing with repressive regimes. Positive energy and resource usage practices, recycling, sustainable land use, fair labour practices and reafforestation are considered desirable characteristics for ethical investments. Thus, the notion of 'ethical investment' covers a range of social issues.[5]

Why would ethical investors consider social issues when evaluating investments? From a theoretical perspective, you would expect ethical investors to earn lower returns because their investment universe has been constrained (this results from fewer diversification opportunities — see chapter 5). Research suggests that ethical funds generate the same size returns as other funds, so investors could rationally expect to maximise wealth by adding a social dimension to their investment decisions.

'Green' investors are a subset of ethical investors who choose to purchase the shares of a company because the company engages in activities that are environmentally positive. Earth Sanctuaries Ltd (ESL) was an Australian company specialising in conserving native plants and animals. A survey of the shareholders of this company found that the main reason for purchasing shares in this company was to protect endangered Australian flora and fauna. These investors did not place nearly as much emphasis on financial returns as would be suggested by traditional finance theory — they were not wealth maximisers, at least with respect to their investment in ESL.[6]

Utility is a measure of satisfaction. Utility is synonymous with the terms 'satisfaction', 'welfare', 'happiness' and 'wellbeing'.[7] Utility is difficult to measure because it cannot be directly observed. The finance discipline overcame this problem by using the assumption that wealth measures utility. If green investors are evaluating the environmental performance of a company in order to maximise their wealth, we would expect to see financial considerations as the primary motivation for purchasing the shares of a green company. If green investors are maximising their utility, we would expect to see environmental considerations as a driving force in the green individual's selection of an investment. This does not imply that green investors will disregard financial performance, but does indicate the importance of environmental criteria. If green investors have social as well as financial goals, wealth maximisation will be an insufficient explanation of ethical investor behaviour.

FINANCE WORLD

The uncertainty of dividends

Forecasting dividends is not an easy task. Forecasts based on the most thorough analysis can still turn out to be incorrect. The following are examples of unexpected changes in dividends.

- Gold producer Dominion Mining declared a dividend for the first time in 13 years. High gold prices combined with a change in the way the gold was extracted at one mine increased production by 150% and reduced costs by 45%.[8] After years of losses, it would have been difficult to forecast that any dividend would be paid.
- SDI, manufacturer of products used by dentists, reported an earnings decline of 79% for the 2004–05 financial year. The fall in earnings was attributed to a fault in one of the company's products, problems with distributors and high silver prices. After seven years of solid performance, the company halved its dividend.[9]
- While the dividends on preference shares are easier to forecast than those on ordinary shares, they are still not certain. Village Roadshow Ltd suspended dividends on its preference shares so the company would have more cash to use in its film production unit. Investors complained to ASIC. ASIC's response was that the company was legally permitted to suspend the dividends.[10]

lo7

Discuss and apply the price–earnings ratio approach.

Market capitalisation: the total dollar value of all issued shares. Market value is used to determine the dollar value per share.

Earnings per share: the total forecast earnings of the firm divided by the number of ordinary shares on issue

Price–earnings ratio: compares the price per share to the forecast EPS

Price–earnings ratio

The analyst's report for Billabong International on the opening page of this chapter indicates that the company was trading at about 21 times its 2006 earnings at the end of the 2005–06 financial year (see the PER figure for 06/06). This means that current market capitalisation divided by total earnings is equal to about 21. We can work out the current market capitalisation by multiplying the number of shares issued by the current market price. Using total capitalisation and total earnings is rather cumbersome and it makes more sense to relate the price of one share to the earnings per share (EPS). This per share calculation is the price–earnings ratio (PE). The analyst's report tells us that the current price per Billabong share is 21 times the forecast EPS.

The price–earnings multiple is defined in equation 6.8.

$$PE = \frac{P_O}{EPS} \qquad [6.8]$$

where PE = price–earnings ratio

P_O = current price of an ordinary share

EPS = forecast earnings per share

Analysts pay a lot of attention to earnings results and devote considerable resources to developing earnings forecasts. The decisions that financial managers make are reflected in earnings and we discuss this further in chapters 13 and 14.

Earnings indicate profitability, but before we can compare the profitability of two firms we need to take the size of each of the operations into consideration. If UVW Ltd can generate $1 million profit with 100 000 shares on issue, it will have a higher EPS than XYZ Ltd generating $1 million with one million shares on issue. Calculating the EPS standardises the total earnings for companies and puts them on a more comparable per share footing.

$$\text{EPS} = \frac{\text{net profit (loss)}}{\text{number of shares on issue}}$$

EXAMPLE 6.9

Calculating EPS

Calculate the EPS for UVW Ltd and XYZ Ltd. The forecast earnings for both companies are $1 million for the coming financial year. UVW has issued 100 000 ordinary shares and XYZ has issued 1 million ordinary shares.

$$EPS_{UVW} = \frac{1\,000\,000}{100\,000}$$
$$= \$10$$

$$EPS_{XYZ} = \frac{1\,000\,000}{1\,000\,000}$$
$$= \$1$$

Once we have a forecast EPS we get the value of the share by using the relationship in equation 6.8 as follows:

$$P_0 = PE \times EPS$$

We multiply the EPS by the PE ratio to value the share.

EXAMPLE 6.10

Valuing an ordinary share with the PE multiple

You have forecast the earnings per share of Sandilines Ltd at $3. Your research indicates that an appropriate PE is 7. What is the value of a Sandilines ordinary share?

$$PE = \frac{P_0}{EPS}$$
$$P_0 = PE \times EPS$$
$$= 7 \times 3$$
$$= \$21$$

The PE ratio for Billabong for 2006 and the PE ratios you see quoted daily in the financial press are historical and are not useful for determining value. A change in the historical PE of a company can be due solely to a change in the general level of prices in the share market rather than with changes in the value of the company. Analysts use a PE multiple based on the PEs of comparable firms and make adjustments for differences attributable to risk and gearing and any other factors they consider relevant.

Earnings tend to be more volatile than dividends, so using the PE method of valuation is not 'easier' when we take this into account. Determining the appropriate PE to apply to an earnings forecast requires much skill and experience. The PE ratios given earlier, in the 'finance world' feature on consensus forecasts, are forecasts of the multiple one and two years ahead. Theoretically, if you use the same assumptions in your forecasts of dividends and earnings, valuations using PE or the constant growth model should give the same dollar value.

FINANCE WORKSHOP 6.6

Your profit forecast for Calla Ltd for the next financial year is $2.4 million. Calla has 1 million shares on issue and is currently trading at $5 per share. What is Calla's PE ratio?

CORPORATE FINANCIAL GOVERNANCE

Corporate governance and share valuation

An interesting question that is currently being debated in the finance literature is the impact of corporate governance on share valuation.

Tippett surveyed Australian investors who own shares in BHP Billiton for their views on the importance of a number of corporate governance and ethical issues.[11] The top ranked 'ethical' issue was professional and good business practice by management. The five most important governance issues for these investors were:

1. excessively high directors' remuneration
2. related-party transactions
3. insufficient share of profits paid out as dividends
4. lack of independence of auditors
5. late payment of dividends.

It is not hard to see how the first four of these governance issues relate to firm performance. If directors are paying themselves too much, they are reducing the amount of firm funds available for investment and for return to shareholders. If directors and managers use their position in the company to give favourable treatment to other businesses (from which they or their family members gain returns), shareholders lose because the wealth maximising contract for the firm has not been taken. Directors have an obligation to maximise shareholder wealth. When they make decisions to maximise their own wealth instead (via contracts that are not 'at arm's length') they have a conflict of interest. We expect directors who are maximising shareholder wealth to retain cash in the company for investment in projects that increase shareholder wealth. If the company does not have any projects that will achieve this, the cash should be returned to shareholders so they can invest it elsewhere. If cash is being retained in a company that does not have worthwhile projects to undertake, there is a good chance that the directors and managers plan to use the cash to build themselves an empire rather than maximise shareholder wealth. Likewise, auditors can not maintain independence when the accounting firm that provides the audit service also provides other services to the company. In this situation, there is potential for the auditors to provide a biased audit report because the accounting firm does not want to lose the revenue from the other services provided. A potential conflict of interest occurs where the accounting firm has the objective of maximising its profits rather than adhering to its duty to shareholders to provide certification that the financial statements are fairly presented.

How important are these governance issues to share valuation? While shareholders have indicated which governance issues they consider to be most important, they were not asked to rank governance issues relative to the traditional investor decision criteria of dividends, future expectations and financial stability.[12] We expect that these traditional investor concerns make the largest contribution to establishing share value.

executive summary

lo1 explain the difference between price and value

- Price is the amount of money needed to acquire an asset.
- Value represents the worth of an asset to an individual.
- Price is determined by the interaction of sellers and purchasers while value is determined independently of price.

lo2 discuss how prices are set in securities markets

- Securities are tradable instruments that represent an ownership interest or the right to receive payment on a debt.
- Securities include ordinary and preference shares, debentures, notes, bills, government and semi-government bonds.
- Traders selling a security will want to get the highest price they can for it. Traders wanting to purchase the security will want to pay as little as they can for it.
- The price of a listed security is determined by the last bid and offer that resulted in a trade.
  - A bid indicates the price a trader is willing to pay for a security.
  - An offer is the price a trader is willing to accept to sell a security.
- How much a trader is willing to pay for a security is determined by its intrinsic value to the trader. The maximum a trader will pay is equal to the trader's intrinsic value for the investment.
- Price approximates the average intrinsic values of individual traders.

lo3 define the concept of intrinsic value

- Value can be measured in a variety of ways.
- Book value is the accounting measure of a security's worth.
- Because securities represent the right to future cash flows, a more appropriate measure of value for finance is the present value of the security's cash flows.
- Depending on the type of security, cash flows come from dividends, coupon payments, redemption by the issuer or from the sale of the security on the market.
- The intrinsic value of a security is the present value of expected future cash flows.
- The intrinsic value of a security can vary between investors. Sources of variation include different risk tolerances and differing perceptions of the risk of the security. These two factors influence the investor's required rate of return. Another important source of variation comes from the estimation of future cash flows associated with the security.
- The dividend payments on ordinary shares are difficult to forecast over the life of the security because there is no maturity date on an ordinary share. Dividends are determined by the company board and there is no legal requirement to pay dividends at regular intervals.
- The higher an investor's required return for a security, the lower the intrinsic value of the security to that investor.
- Investors compare intrinsic value to the market price to determine if they should purchase the security.

- If the intrinsic value is higher than the market price, the investor will purchase the security because she is expecting the security to generate more than her required rate of return.
- If the intrinsic value is lower than the market price, the investor will not purchase the security (or will sell the security if he currently owns it) because he is expecting the security to generate less than his required rate of return.

lo4 calculate the intrinsic value of a bond

- A bond normally pays a regular income stream and has a face value that is repaid to the holder at maturity.
- Coupon payments are the regular interest payments received by the holder of a bond.
- Zero coupon bonds do not make regular coupon payments and are issued at a deep discount to face value.
- The valuation of a zero coupon bond is similar to the valuation of a short-term discount security.
- By convention, rates of return are expressed in annual terms. If compounding on a security occurs more frequently than annually, the required annual return must be adjusted so that the period the return refers to is equal to the length of the compounding period.
- Bonds can have fixed or variable interest rates.
- Fixed interest means that the coupon received on the bond stays the same over the bond's life.
- For fixed interest bonds, the dollar coupon amount is calculated as a percentage of face value. The present value of the coupon stream forms an annuity.
- The intrinsic value of the bond is the present value of the coupon stream plus the present value of the face (or maturity) value.
- The required rate of return must match the time period between the receipts of the regular coupon payments.
- Rather than paying the face value at maturity, convertible notes may be 'repaid' with ordinary shares at or before maturity.
- We cannot use equation 6.4 to value variable rate bonds or convertible notes.

lo5 calculate the intrinsic value of a preference share

- An infinite stream of dividends (and thus, no maturity date) forms the cash flow pattern for a typical preference share.
- Typical preference shares are 'hybrid' securities. The dividends are for a fixed amount (like a fixed interest coupon) but they have infinite lives (like ordinary shares).
- The typical preference share is valued as a perpetuity.
- The required return must match the time period between the receipts of the dividend payments.
- Redeemable preference shares might be repurchased by the issuer prior to the maturity date.
- Convertible preference shares might be changed to ordinary shares.
- Participating preference shares receive a fixed minimum amount of dividend each period, but may receive higher dividends if the company achieves some pre-specified level of profit for the period.

- Reset preference shares enjoy a change in the level of dividend if some pre-specified event occurs in the future.
- We can't use equation 6.5 to value redeemable, convertible or reset preference shares.

lo6 calculate the intrinsic value of an ordinary share

- The dividend discount model calculates intrinsic value by finding the present value of the share's future dividends and the estimated amount that will be received when the share is sold.
- The further into the future a dividend occurs, the less certain we can be about the forecast. If the circumstances are right, we can make the simplifying assumption that dividends grow by some percentage for some specific period of time.
- The constant growth model can be used to value ordinary shares when the growth rate in dividends is expected to remain the same for the foreseeable future.
- We do not forecast a selling price when applying the constant growth model to value an ordinary share because the price at any given time should be equal to the present value of all the future dividends to infinity.
- The constant growth model will produce the same valuation as the dividend discount model if the same assumptions are made about dividends and the selling price used in the dividend discount model is based on the present value of the share's future cash flows.
- The constant growth model can be applied only when the growth rate is not expected to change.
- The required rate of return used to discount the share's cash flows must match the period between dividends.
- The discounting process gives more weight to cash flows that occur early in the life of the security. This means that the later (and more uncertain) cash flows do not 'drive' the calculation of value. Therefore, a lower degree of accuracy is needed for cash flows that occur later in the life of the security.
- The dividend discount and constant growth models should work best on blue chip companies where a track record has been established for dividend payments.
- Discount each dividend separately until the company reaches a stage of constant growth. At that point, the constant growth model can be applied. The constant growth model gives the present value of the future dividends on the first day of the period when the model is applied. This means that the value from the constant growth model needs to be discounted by the number of periods when dividends did not grow at a constant rate.
- Dividends for smaller and newer companies tend to be less predictable than they are for blue chips.
- Some investors prefer not to receive dividends at the current time. Some profitable companies do not pay dividends.
- The constant growth model cannot be applied when the forecast growth rate is larger than the investor's required rate of return.

lo7 discuss and apply the price–earnings ratio approach

- The price–earnings (PE) ratio compares the price per share to the forecast EPS.
- Earnings per share (EPS) are the total forecast earnings of the firm divided by the number of ordinary shares on issue.

- Analysts forecast earnings and regularly use the PE ratio to value ordinary shares.
- While forecasting earnings is a difficult task, determining the appropriate PE ratio to apply to a particular company requires a great deal of knowledge and skill.

Key terms

bid, p. 180
blue chip, p. 193
book value, p. 181
coupon, p. 183
coupon payments, p. 181
deep discount, p. 184
earnings per share, p. 195
fixed interest, p. 185
intrinsic value, p. 181
market capitalisation, p. 195
offer, p. 180
price, p. 179
price–earnings ratio, p. 195
securities, p. 180
value, p. 179

Learning chart

Learning objective	Questions	Self-test problems	Financial problems
lo1 explain the difference between price and value	6.1		
lo2 discuss how prices are set in securities markets	6.2, 6.3		
lo3 define the concept of intrinsic value	6.4, 6.5, 6.6, 6.7		6.1
lo4 calculate the intrinsic value of a bond	6.8, 6.9, 6.10	6.1	6.3, 6.4, 6.5, 6.6, 6.7, 6.8, 6.9, 6.24, 6.25
lo5 calculate the intrinsic value of a preference share	6.11, 6.12, 6.13, 6.14	6.2	6.10, 6.12, 6.13, 6.26
lo6 calculate the intrinsic value of an ordinary share	6.15, 6.16, 6.17, 6.18	6.3, 6.4, 6.5	6.2, 6.11, 6.14, 6.15, 6.16, 6.17, 6.18, 6.19, 6.20, 6.27
lo7 discuss and apply the price–earnings ratio approach	6.19, 6.20		6.21, 6.22, 6.23

Questions

6.1 What is the difference between price and value?
6.2 What is meant by the terms ‘bid’ and ‘offer’?
6.3 Describe how prices are set for listed securities.
6.4 What is book value and how does it relate to the cash flows of a security?
6.5 What is the intrinsic value of a security and why do we focus on intrinsic values in finance?

6.6 Describe the variables that are used to determine a security's intrinsic value and explain the role of each variable.

6.7 Do analysts and traders all have the same intrinsic value for a security? Why?

6.8 Explain what is meant by the term 'coupon' and describe how the coupon payment is calculated for a fixed interest bond.

6.9 What are the three main types of long-term debt securities? What cash flows does an investor receive from a coupon bond?

6.10 What is a zero coupon bond? Is the calculation of the intrinsic value of a zero coupon bond different from that for a coupon bond? Explain.

6.11 What do preference shares have in common with bonds and ordinary shares? How is the valuation of a typical preference share different from the valuation of a coupon bond or an ordinary share?

6.12 If dividends are paid semi-annually on a preference share and we adjust the required return to reflect this, is the intrinsic value any different to a share with the same total dividend paid annually and an annual required return? Use an annual dividend of $1 and a required return of 9% to demonstrate your understanding.

6.13 How are redeemable preference shares and convertible preference shares different to 'normal' preference shares? Can redeemable or convertible preference shares be valued with equation 6.5?

6.14 How are participating preference shares and reset preference shares different to 'normal' preference shares? Can participating or reset preference shares be valued with equation 6.5?

6.15 Are people likely to be able to forecast a constant growth rate to infinity with any degree of accuracy? Is this important in the discounting process over long periods of time? Why?

6.16 Not all companies pay stable or growing dividends and not all investors want to purchase shares in companies that pay dividends. Explain why these behaviours are observed.

6.17 Explain the difference between the dividend discount model and the constant growth model. Why do we have two models?

6.18 What is the most difficult aspect of valuing ordinary shares?

6.19 Explain why you should not use a PE multiple from the financial press to value a share.

6.20 Is there a theoretical relationship between the constant growth model and the PE method of valuation? What does the relationship depend on?

Self-test problems

6.1 Repco Ltd has issued unsecured notes with 4 more years to maturity. The notes have a face value of $100 and a coupon of 10% pa. Coupons are paid semi-annually with the next one due in 6 months' time. If your required rate of return is 8% pa, what is the intrinsic value of a Repco note?

6.2 What is the intrinsic value of a preference share that pays an annual dividend of $1 if your required return is 7% per annum?

6.3 You have saved up some money for a trip to Europe and plan to travel in 4 years' time. Rather than keep your money in the bank, you are considering the purchase of shares in Banksia Ltd. You have forecast the following dividends for the next 4 years.

Year	Dividend
1	1
2	1.20
3	1.25
4	1.30

You predict that you will be able to sell your shares for $10 each on the day after you receive the year 4 dividend. After analysis, you decide that the appropriate discount rate is 12%. What is the intrinsic value of a Banksia share?

6.4 XYZ Ltd's next dividend will be $0.20. Dividends are paid semi-annually. You expect a dividend growth rate of 7% pa. Forecast XYZ's dividends for the next three years.

6.5 If you expect the growth rate for XYZ (see question 6.4) to continue indefinitely and your required return is 15% pa, what is the intrinsic value of the share?

Solutions to self-test problems

6.1 $$V_b = \sum_{t=1}^{n} C\left[\frac{1-(1+r_b)^{-n}}{r_b}\right] + \frac{F}{(1+r_b)^n}$$

$$V_b = \frac{0.10 \times 100}{2}\left[\frac{1-\left(1+\frac{0.08}{2}\right)^{-4\times 2}}{\frac{0.08}{2}}\right] + \frac{100}{\left(1+\frac{0.08}{2}\right)^{4\times 2}}$$

$$= 5[6.7327] + \frac{100}{1.3686}$$

$$= \$106.73$$

6.2 $$V_p = \frac{D}{r_p}$$

$$V_p = \frac{1.00}{0.07}$$

$$= \$14.29$$

6.3 $$V_e = \frac{D_1}{(1+0.12)} + \frac{D_2}{(1+0.12)^2} + \frac{D_3}{(1+0.12)^3} + \frac{D_4}{(1+0.12)^4} + \frac{P_4}{(1+0.12)^4}$$

$$V_e = \frac{1.00}{1.12} + \frac{1.20}{1.2544} + \frac{1.25}{1.4049} + \frac{1.30}{1.5735} + \frac{10}{1.5735}$$

$$= 0.8929 + 0.9566 + 0.8897 + 7.1814$$

$$= \$9.92$$

6.4 The question gives the next dividend, so the dividend for the first period does not need to be calculated.

First dividend = \$0.20

Second dividend = $0.20 \times (1 + 0.07/2)$	\$0.207
Third dividend = $0.20 \times (1 + 0.07/2)^2$	\$0.2142
Fourth dividend = $0.20 \times (1 + 0.07/2)^3$	\$0.2217
Fifth dividend = $0.20 \times (1 + 0.07/2)^4$	\$0.2295
Sixth dividend = $0.20 \times (1 + 0.07/2)^5$	\$0.2375

6.5 $$V_e = \frac{D_1}{r_e - g}$$

$$V_e = \frac{0.20}{0.075 - 0.035} = \$5.00$$

Financial problems

6.1 You have been offered an investment with the following cash flows:

End year	
1	50
2	80
3	300

If you have a discount rate of 7% pa, how much is this investment worth to you?

6.2 You expect Japonica Ltd to pay the following annual dividends for the next 3 years.

Year	Dividend
1	0.60
2	0.80
3	0.90

Dividends will be paid in two equal parts semi-annually. You also expect to be able to sell the share for \$9.75 right after you receive the final year 3 dividend. If your required return is 8% annually, how much would you be willing to pay for the share?

6.3 Hakka Ltd zero coupon bonds have a face value of \$100 000 and 5 years to maturity. Your nominal required return is 10% pa, compounded semi-annually. What is the intrinsic value of the bond?

6.4 Zed Ltd zero coupon bonds have a face value of \$500 000 and 2 years to maturity. Your nominal required return is 7% pa, compounded semi-annually. What is the intrinsic value of the bond?

6.5 A zero coupon bond has a face value of \$100 000 and 5 years to maturity. Interest accrues on the bond quarterly (4 times a year). If your required return is 8% pa, what is the value of the bond?

6.6 Crown Ltd bonds have 4 years to maturity, coupons of 9.5% and a face value of $100. Coupons are paid semi-annually. If your required return is 8% pa, what is the intrinsic value of a Crown bond?

6.7 Vision Systems bonds have a face value of $500 000, a coupon of 7.75% and 7 years to maturity. Coupons are paid semi-annually. If your required return is 11% pa, what is the intrinsic value of this bond?

6.8 Cowcall Ltd bonds have 3 years to maturity. They pay an 8% pa coupon and the payments are made semi-annually. The face value of the bond is $1000. If your required return is 10% pa, what is the intrinsic value of a Cowcall bond?

6.9 A bond with 5 years to maturity has a coupon of 6% pa paid quarterly. The face value is $100 000. If your required return is 8%, what is the value of the bond?

6.10 Amcor Ltd preference shares pay a dividend of $0.65 pa. If your required return is 8% pa, what is the intrinsic value of an Amcor preference share?

6.11 Croesus Mining NL preference shares pay an annual dividend of 8 cents. Two equal sized dividend payments are made each year. If your required return is 15% pa, what is the intrinsic value of a Croesus preference share?

6.12 Preference shares issued by Sydney Gas Ltd have a dividend of 11% pa based on a face value of 50 cents. Equal sized dividend payments are made twice a year. What is the intrinsic value of this share if your required return is 9% pa?

6.13 A preference share pays an annual dividend of $0.50. If your discount rate is 12% pa, what is the present value of the preference share's dividends?

6.14 XYZ pays semi-annual dividends. The last dividend was 50c and was paid yesterday. Your forecast growth rate is 3% pa. Forecast the dividends for the next 4 years.

6.15 You are considering the purchase of some shares. The shares pay semi-annual dividends and you have forecast the next four dividends to be 20c, 22c, 28c and 31c. You expect to sell the share for $6.75 right after you receive the fourth dividend. If your required return is 12% pa, what is the value of the share?

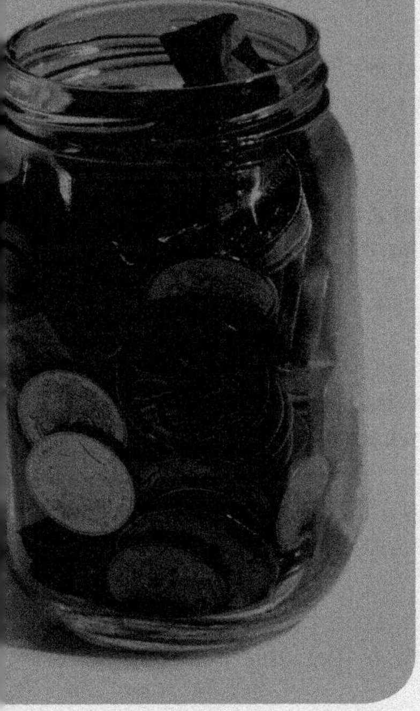

6.16 As part of your retirement funding strategy, you are considering the purchase of ordinary shares in Australian Ethical Investments Ltd. Dividends are paid semi-annually and you have forecast the next six. The first of these dividends will be received in 6 months' time.

	Dividend
1	0.20
2	0.20
3	0.27
4	0.30
5	0.32
6	0.35

You are planning to sell the shares when you have received the final dividend and you expect to get $14 for each share. If your required rate of return is 6% pa, what is the intrinsic value of a share?

6.17 Calliope Ltd has been listed for the last 20 years. Over this time, investors have enjoyed a steady stream of dividends. You expect the current annual growth rate of about 1% to be maintained into the foreseeable future. Dividends are paid semi-annually and the dividend paid last week was 13c per share. If your required return for Calliope is 5% pa, what is the intrinsic value of a share?

6.18 You have forecast an annual growth rate of 3% for MOP Ltd. Dividends are paid annually and the last dividend was 50c. If your required return is 12% pa, what is the value of an MOP share?

6.19 You have forecast the next annual dividend of Topboy Ltd at $1. You expect that the following dividends show a 5% increase for each of the next 2 years. After that, you forecast a growth rate of 1% pa and expect this growth to continue indefinitely. If your required return is 10% pa, what is the value of a Topboy share?

6.20 Shares in Cochlear Ltd have been trading on the ASX for about 12 years. Over that time, the company has experienced a phenomenal growth rate in dividends of about 25% pa. This growth has been achieved by expanding into overseas markets and, to a lesser extent, by new product development. You expect that growth in US sales will support the current growth in dividends for a further 5 years. After that time, you expect dividend growth to slow to about 10% pa and the new growth rate to be maintained for many years to come. Total dividends last year were 51 cents. The next dividend payment is due 6 months from now and dividends are paid semi-annually. What is the intrinsic value of a Cochlear share if your required rate of return is 16% pa?

6.21 Calliope Ltd (CLL) currently has a PE of 25 times. If CLL ordinary shares are selling at $6.82, what earnings per share does the market expect for the next period?

6.22 You are interested in the ordinary shares of Blackmores Ltd. Your forecast EPS for the coming financial year is 33c and your experience tells you that similar firms are trading at a PE of 19 times. What value would you give Blackmores shares?

6.23 You have forecast next year's earnings for Rontech Ltd at $2.5 million. The company has issued 1 million shares and the PE ratio for comparable firms in the industry is 12. Your required return is 15% pa. What is the value of Rontech?

6.24 A bond has 10 years to maturity, a face value of $1000 and a coupon rate of 7% pa paid semi-annually. What is the value of the bond if similar bonds are yielding:

(a) 6%?

(b) 11%?

6.25 Longhaul Ltd has issued bonds with 25 years to maturity and a face value of $100. The coupon rate will be 5% pa for the first 10 years. After that, the coupon will change to 8% pa. If the required rate of return is 7% pa, what is the value of the bond?

6.26 A preference share is selling for $6.36. Dividends are paid annually and the required rate of return is 5% pa. What is the dollar amount of each dividend payment?

6.27 (a) The last dividend on an ordinary share was $0.50. You expect the dividends to grow at 2% per annum for the foreseeable future. What is the value of the share if the required return is 10% pa?

(b) The next dividend on an ordinary share is expected to be \$0.50. You expect the dividends to grow at 2% per annum for the foreseeable future. What is the value of the share if the required return is 10% pa?

SOLUTIONS TO FINANCE WORKSHOPS

6.1 Using equation 6.3 $V_b = \dfrac{F}{(1 + r_b)^n}$

$$V_b = \frac{1000}{(1 + 0.05)^5} = \$783.52$$

6.2 Using equation 6.4 $V_b = \sum_{t=1}^{n} \dfrac{C_t}{(1 + r_b)^t} + \dfrac{F}{(1 + r_b)^n}$

$$\text{where} \quad C_t = \frac{0.03}{2} \times 100000 = 1500$$

$$r_b = \frac{0.04}{2} = 0.02$$

$$n = 2 \times 6 = 12$$

Use table 4 from the appendix to this book for the present value of an annuity factor for 2% and 12 periods (10.5753) and table 2 for the present value factor for 2% and 12 periods (0.7885)

$V_b = (1500 \times 10.5753) + (100000 \times 0.7885) = \$94\,712.95$

6.3 Using equation 6.5 $V_p = \dfrac{D}{r_p}$

$$V_p = \frac{5}{0.06} = \$83.33$$

6.4 Using equation 6.6 $V_e = \sum_{t=1}^{n} \dfrac{D_t}{(1 + r_s)^t} + \dfrac{P_n}{(1 + r_s)^n}$

$$V_e = \frac{0.50}{1.10} + \frac{0.75}{1.10^2} + \frac{0.80}{1.10^3} + \frac{0.85 + 6.50}{1.10^4}$$

$$= 0.4545 + 0.6198 + 0.6011 + 5.0201 = \$6.70$$

6.5 Using equation 6.7 $V_e = \dfrac{D_1}{r_e - g}$

$$V_e = \frac{0.15\left(1 + \frac{0.03}{2}\right)}{\frac{0.10}{2} - \frac{0.03}{2}}$$

$$= \$4.35$$

6.6 Using equation 6.8 $PE = \frac{P_0}{EPS}$

$$EPS = \frac{\text{net profit (loss)}}{\text{number of shares on issue}}$$
$$= \frac{2\,400\,000}{1\,000\,000}$$
$$= 2.40$$

$$PE = \frac{5}{2.40} = 2.083$$

End notes

1 Billabong — Aspect Huntley 2006, *Huntleys' Newsletters — ymw*, issue 33, 31 August, www.aspecthuntley.com.au; MYOB — Aspect Huntley 2006, *Huntleys' Newsletters — scg*, issue 33, 30 August, www.aspecthuntley.com.au.

2 If you would like to check the prices of some companies' shares, go to www.asx.com.au and access the 'Get price' link for shares. This allows you to search on the company's name, so you don't have to know the company code.

3 Table adapted from I/B/E/S forecasts from Datastream International.

4 *Investopedia*, www.investopedia.com.

5 Australian Ethical Investments 2001, 'Being an ethical investor', *Aim High*, February.

6 Beal, D & Goyen, M 1998, '"Putting your money where your mouth is." A profile of ethical investors', *Financial Services Review*, vol. 7, no. 2, pp. 129–43.

7 Call, S & Holahan, W 1983, *Microeconomics*, 2nd edn, Wadsworth Publishing Company, Belmont, California.

8 Emmerson, R 2006, 'Gold miner pays first dividend in 13 years', *Advertiser*, 7 September.

9 Webb, C 2005, 'Dental outfit fights decay in earnings', *Age*, 31 August 2006.

10 'Village Roadshow's win', *Hobart Mercury*, 3 June 2003, http://global.factiva.com.

11 Tippet, J 2000, 'Investors' perceptions of the relative importance of investment issues', *Accounting Forum*, vol. 24, no. 3, pp. 278–95.

12 Baker, H & Haslem, J 1974, 'Toward the development of client-specified valuation models', *Journal of Finance*, vol. 29, pp. 1255–63.

chapter 7

chapter

7

Cost of capital

Learning objectives

After studying this chapter, you should be able to:

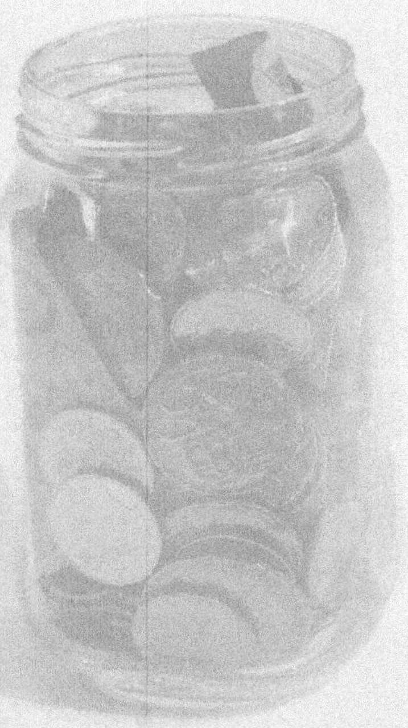

lo1 explain the concept of the firm's cost of capital

lo2 explain the impact of the taxation system on the cost of capital

lo3 calculate the before- and after-tax component costs for bonds, preference shares and ordinary equity

lo4 explain how the shareholders' capacity to utilise imputation credits affects the cost of capital

lo5 calculate the weighted-average cost of capital

lo6 explain the nature of capital structure and how taxation influences the capital structure choices of Australian companies

lo7 apply the EBIT–EPS technique to evaluate changes in capital structure and explain the limitations of this technique.

WHAT THE MARKET THINKS ABOUT A COMPANY'S COST OF CAPITAL

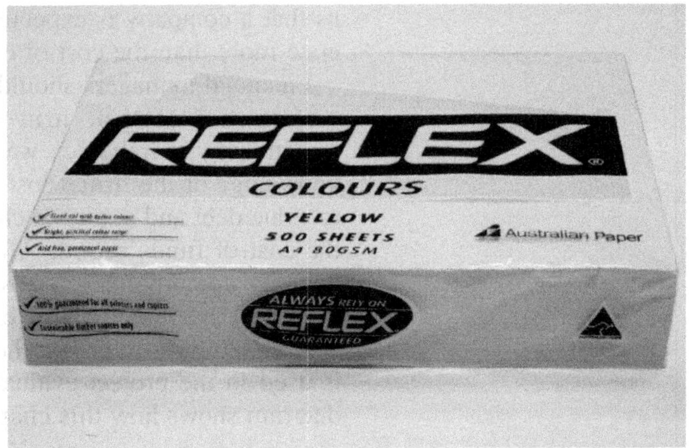

PaperlinX may be forced to write down the assets associated with its struggling Australian Paper business in a threat to the company's capacity to pay a dividend and that may wipe out all its second-half earnings.

Broker Goldman Sachs JBWere estimated Australian Paper is generating a return on assets of only about 2 per cent, far below the 9.5 per cent cost of capital...[1]

The wine division is years away from that, reporting earnings before interest and tax of $5.3 million in the six months to March 31. When Murray took the job almost two years ago, it is understood that he set an objective of $40 million by 2008, which he refers to as 'base camp'. Reaching its cost of capital or outdoing it to get to $40 million within two years would seem impossible, given its current structure, limited growth opportunities and market conditions.[2]

Telstra and Sensis also believe that Sensis has capabilities in directories and listings management and advertising pricing models that will add considerably to SouFun's value and potential, although the acquisition will not be earnings accretive until year three nor generate a return above Telstra's cost of capital under year four.[3]

Moreover, Virgin Blue's return on assets, at 16.3 per cent, is nearly double that of the Qantas group and, indeed, positions it at world-leading levels even among low-cost carriers — it is creating shareholder value by generating returns well above its cost of capital where Qantas is not covering its cost of capital.[4]

Telstra hasn't been investing in the network on the scale necessary to operate a world-class broadband network. The reason is that the interconnect price that allows Telstra's competitors to use the network isn't high enough to cover the cost of capital. Telstra takes the reasonable view that it should not be required to invest in infrastructure that can be accessed by its competitors at below cost to undercut Telstra in the retail market for fixed line and broadband services.[5]

Chapter preview

'Cost of capital' is a term you will often see discussed in the financial press. The quotes presented on the opening page of this chapter are taken from articles that appeared in the financial press. The quotes give us some examples of the cost of capital concept.

The first three quotes alert us to the use of the cost of capital as a yardstick for assessing the performance of the current and future investments of the firm. They compare the cost of capital to return on assets and earnings. Do you recall from our discussion of the objectives of the firm in chapter 1 that maximising wealth was a superior objective to maximising profit? Return on assets and earnings are accounting measures. Unless the profits and cash flows for PaperlinX and Lion Nathan (the second quote) are highly correlated, a return on assets higher than the cost of capital will not necessarily be associated with an increase in shareholder wealth (the primary objective of the firm that we identify in chapter 1). The fourth quote links Virgin Blue's cost of capital to shareholder value. As we see in chapter 8, returns above the cost of capital increase shareholder wealth. The final Telstra quote tells us that a company is expected to make investments in projects when the project can generate more than the cost of capital. We build on this idea in chapters 8 and 9.

Financial managers should be interested in the cost of capital as it is used to assess the performance of their firm and their own performance. A firm with the objective of maximising shareholder wealth can achieve this objective by assessing projects using knowledge of the firm's cost of capital. We apply models using investors' required returns to value debt and equity in chapter 6. In this chapter, we use those same models to estimate the cost of funds raised. After calculating the cost for each source of funds used by the firm, we combine these costs to develop an estimate of the cost of capital for the firm.

In this chapter, we will examine the impact of imputation tax credits and the shareholders' abilities to utilise them on the estimation of the cost of capital. The cost of capital is used in the project evaluation methods we explore in chapters 8 and 9. The following diagram shows how this chapter is structured.

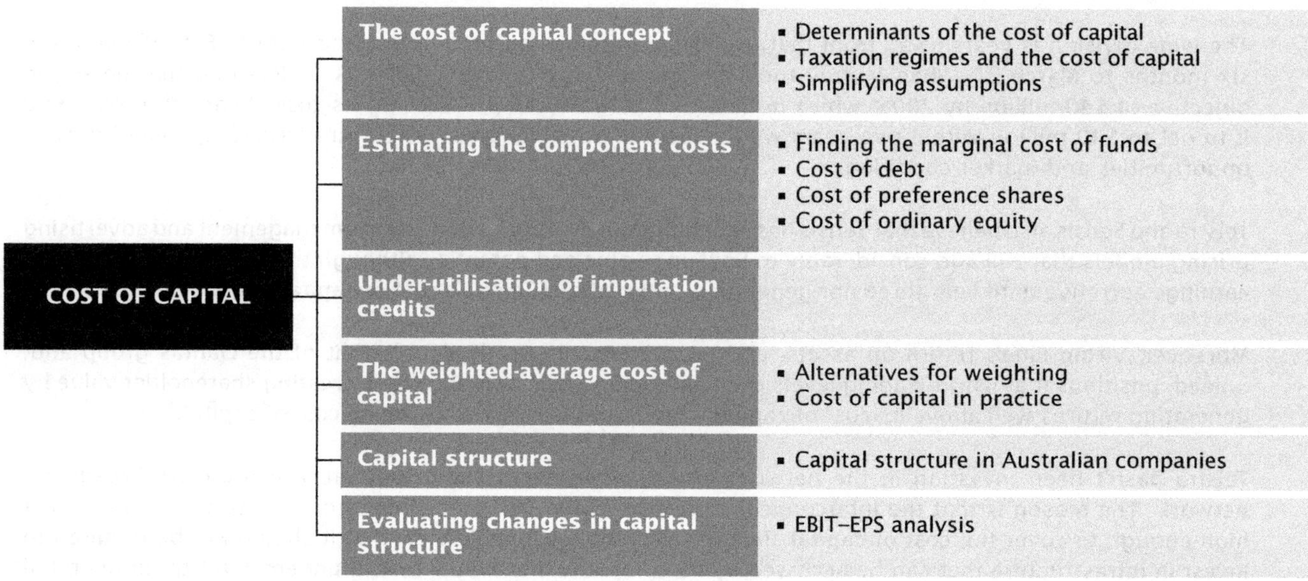

The cost of capital concept

lo1

Explain the concept of the firm's cost of capital.

Firms commonly raise capital from borrowings, preference shares and ordinary shares. As we see in chapter 5, investors expect a higher return for a higher level of risk. Therefore, investors will have lower required returns for the lower risk securities (secured debt, for example) issued by a firm, but higher required returns for the riskier securities like ordinary shares. Further, each source of finance will involve different costs. The cost of capital is therefore expressed as a weighted average that reflects the cost of permanent sources of financing. We will examine this in detail later in the chapter. As we see in chapters 8 and 9, a firm with the objective of maximising shareholder wealth must assess the return on any potential investment against the cost of capital. If the proposed investment has the same level of risk as the projects currently undertaken by the firm and the return is greater than the cost of capital, then the investment should be adopted. In this way the cost of capital forms the link between the firm's investment decisions and its value. The Virgin Blue example in the chapter opening quotes demonstrates this link where it states that 'it is creating shareholder value by generating returns well above its cost of capital'.[6]

We consider the role of the cost of capital when proposed projects do not have the same level of risk as the current projects of the firm in chapter 9. In this chapter we will assume that the operating risk of the firm is held constant for the calculation of the cost of capital. This means that the debt and equity holders of the firm have determined their required returns based on the current profile of the firm's investment projects and we will calculate the components of the cost of capital based on the required returns, given the firm's current level of risk.

As we have seen, the cost of capital represents all costs involved in raising funds. Therefore, the **cost of capital** is the minimum rate of return on the firm's investments that will compensate the suppliers of capital to the firm.

Cost of capital: the minimum rate of return on the firm's investments that will compensate the suppliers of capital to the firm

Some investment projects may be funded, for example, by a new issue of equity and at first glance we might think that the cost of capital for that investment is the investors' required return on the new share issue. However, a company usually consists of a collection of projects. Investors participating in a new issue made to finance a particular project participate in the profit generated by all the existing and future projects of the company, not just the project the new issue will be used to fund. This means that the cost of the particular source of finance for an investment made by the company does not tell the entire cost of capital story.

The company needs to be able to generate sufficient return to meet the claims of all providers of finance and still have enough to cover the required return of the ordinary shareholders. In addition to ordinary shareholders, most companies use debt as a source of finance and some use preference shares as well. Therefore, the company has to generate enough return from operations to make interest payments on its debt and pay dividends on its preference shares, then have enough left over to meet the ordinary shareholders' required return. If the company can earn more than the minimum rate of return on the firm's investments that will compensate the suppliers of capital to the firm, the share price should increase.

As we see in chapters 3 and 5, the cash flows to the debtholders of the firm are usually fixed coupon payments and the cash flows to garden-variety preference shares are fixed dividends. The coupon payments made to debtholders and the dividends paid to preference shareholders are paid before any dividend to the ordinary shareholders. Ordinary shareholders receive dividends and capital gains that depend on the level of profit the company generates. Any excess above the cost of capital that is generated by the firm belongs to the ordinary shareholders. The excess may be shared with the company's management if contracts specify that their bonuses use the cost of capital as a benchmark. A company generating less than the cost of capital still has to make fixed payments to debtholders and preference shareholders, so the shortfall means that a shareholder wealth decrease is reflected in a lower share price.

Determinants of the cost of capital

Each of the different sources of finance used by the company contributes to its total cost of funds. We discuss the risk–return relationship in chapter 5 and conclude that investors demand a higher expected return for taking on a higher level of risk. The relationship between risk and return leads us to expect that the more risky the company, the higher the return it will need to generate to keep the suppliers of capital from selling their investments.

The requirement for regular interest payments and the legal provisions that allow creditors to call for the winding up of a business mean that those supplying debt capital face the least risk. Therefore, we can expect creditors to have a relatively low required return. The reliability associated with the cash flows received by preference shareholders means that the suppliers of preference capital face lower risks than do ordinary shareholders. We would expect that the required return on this source of funds would be higher than debt, but lower than that for ordinary shareholders. As ordinary shareholders are the residual claimants, and therefore have the riskiest cash flows from their investments, we expect that their required return would be higher than that for preference shareholders and debtholders.

The level of risk for each source of capital drives the investors' required returns. The required returns for each category of capital suppliers contribute to the total cost of capital. We combine the component costs, and the cost of capital rate depends on how much reliance the company places on each source of capital. The cost of capital is a composite measure that includes the cost of each component (or source) of finance. As a very simple illustration of this concept, consider a firm that will be financed using half debt and half equity. Assuming the cost of debt is 8% and the cost of shares is 14%, the cost of capital would be 11% (that is, $0.5 \times 8 + 0.5 \times 14$). We will discuss the calculation of this composite measure later in the chapter.

Before a firm commits to a new investment project, management needs to assess the impact of the project on the firm's value. The cost of capital represents the minimum return that needs to be earned to compensate the suppliers of capital. As such, it provides an excellent place to begin the assessment of the adoption of a project on firm value. Simply speaking, if the proposed project returns the cost of capital, the firm's value will remain unchanged because all of the suppliers of capital to the firm are compensated for supplying that capital. If the proposed project returns more than the cost of capital, the value of the firm should increase. Alternatively, if the proposed project returns less than the cost of capital, we would expect firm value to decrease. We consider these issues further in chapters 8 and 9.

Our objective of calculating the cost of capital as a tool for project assessment directs our focus to the marginal cost of each source of funding. The **marginal cost** is the cost associated with raising the next dollar from a particular source. The firm needs new capital to expand its operations by investing in new projects. Therefore, the historic cost of funds raised is irrelevant when comparing how much a new project would have to earn to satisfy the suppliers of capital.

Marginal cost: for a particular source of capital, the cost associated with raising the next dollar from that source

lo2

Explain the impact of the taxation system on the cost of capital.

Taxation regimes and the cost of capital

We discuss in chapter 2 that dividends are taxed in the hands of the owners (shareholders) of companies in Australia, with shareholders receiving tax credits for the full amount of corporate tax paid. Germany, Italy and New Zealand have similar systems that pass on full imputation credits; while in Canada, Finland, France, Ireland, Mexico, Spain and Taiwan, shareholders receive imputation credits, but not for the full amount of corporate tax paid.[7] The value of imputation credits is higher for **resident shareholders** than for **foreign shareholders**. Resident shareholders can extract the full value of tax paid for them by the company. Foreign shareholders will not gain from receiving fully franked dividends unless the taxation office of the country in which they are resident allows Australian imputation credits to be counted as tax paid by the shareholder on dividend income.

Resident shareholders: those who live (and pay tax) in the same country as the company paying the dividends

Foreign shareholders: those who live (and pay tax) in a different country from that of the company paying the dividends

The common alternative to imputation is the classical taxation system, where tax is paid on dividends at the corporate level (that is, dividends are paid from after-corporate-tax profit) and tax is also paid by the shareholders when they receive the dividends. Rational investors assess their returns on an after-personal-tax basis. Therefore, we would expect to find that shareholders who can utilise all the benefits from receiving fully franked dividends will demand a lower before-tax required return than they would under a classical taxation system. Receiving imputation tax credits means that resident shareholders do not have to pay as much tax as they would under the classical system. If the risk of an investment before and after the introduction of imputation remains the same, the domestic investor's after-tax required return will not change. In this case, the value of imputation credits means that the resident shareholder's after-tax required return would be achieved by the receipt of a lower before-tax return from the company. The implication is that the cost of equity capital would decrease if companies paying fully franked dividends were owned by shareholders who could fully utilise the imputation credits. For resident shareholders of companies that do not frank dividends (that is, do not issue imputation credits for corporate tax paid), we would not expect to see a change in the before-tax required return of shareholders.

Black, Legoria and Sellers[8] studied the impact of the introduction of dividend imputation on corporate capital investment in Australia and New Zealand. They found evidence consistent with a lower cost of capital after the introduction of imputation for firms with high dividend payout ratios. The **dividend payout ratio** is the proportion of after-tax profit that is paid to shareholders as dividends. For firms with low payout ratios, the cost of capital increased because the benefits to shareholders of receiving franked dividends was more than offset by the introduction of the capital gains tax.

Dividend payout ratio: the proportion of after-tax profit that is paid to shareholders as dividends

Australian resident shareholders, complying superannuation and approved deposit funds, pooled superannuation trusts and endorsed tax-exempt charities receive a refund of excess imputation credits from the Australian Taxation Office. This means they can use all of the imputation credits they receive with their dividends. Therefore, a company with a shareholder register that consists only of these types of investors is considered to be fully integrated with the taxation system. Australian tax paid by a fully integrated company is passed on to shareholders and profit distributed as dividends is taxed only at the shareholders' personal tax rate. In this case, none of the imputation credits distributed by the company are lost and corporate taxes are not relevant in the determination of the cost of capital. For companies that are fully integrated with the dividend imputation tax system, the component costs should be calculated on a before-tax basis. Aspects of this issue are discussed in chapter 1.

At the opposite end of the scale are companies that don't pay any dividends. We discuss dividend policy in chapter 12. At this point it is sufficient to say that companies that do not pay dividends are not integrated into the dividend imputation tax system, as any available franking credits are not passed on to shareholders. For such companies, the level of corporate tax paid is relevant to the determination of the cost of capital.

Foreign shareholders, as we will see later, may gain no benefit from receiving fully franked dividends. A company that has a large proportion of foreign shareholders will not be fully integrated with the dividend imputation system. Again, the level of corporate tax paid should be considered when calculating the cost of capital.

The after-tax cost of capital is also appropriate for businesses structured as sole traders and partnerships as these do not distribute profits as dividends. Profits from sole traders and partnerships are taxed in the hands of the owners, rather than at the business level. As such, their profit distributions are excluded from the imputation system and it is the after-tax cost of capital that is relevant to decision making.

Between the two extremes of shareholders who can fully utilise imputation credits and those who gain no benefit from them lie cases where some of the company's shareholders cannot gain much from receiving fully franked dividends. The impact of these investors on a company's cost of capital depends on how much of the company they own. We explore this issue after learning how to calculate the elements of the cost of capital in the following sections.

Simplifying assumptions

Innovation in securities markets has resulted in an array of securities that can be used to raise funds. New types of securities are often based on the traditional debt and equity instruments, but offer investors new combinations of the features of debt and equity and new patterns of cash flows. To illustrate more clearly the concept of the cost of capital, we will use the 'garden varieties' of fixed interest debt, ordinary shares and preference shares. The exception is the inclusion of zero coupon bonds in our analysis. These securities do not represent an important component of the cost of capital for Australian companies. They have been included only to simplify demonstration of the trial and error method of calculating the cost of debt.

The cost of capital should include all permanent sources of funding used by the firm. The costs of term loans and leasing are sources of funding that should be included in the cost of capital. These costs are calculated in chapter 12. The cost of rollovers of discount securities (chapter 4) may also be included in the cost of capital.

We will also make a simplifying assumption with respect to the taxation of equities. While we will be including the impact of imputation credits on the cost of capital, we will not be including the impact of capital gains taxes. Capital gains tax is introduced in chapter 2 and is discussed further in chapter 9. As we see in chapter 2, capital gains are taxed differently for individuals and for companies. Further, the tax rate applied to the gain depends on the taxpayer's individual circumstances, making it difficult to make a realistic assumption about how capital gains and losses will change the after-tax wealth of all the investors in a company.

lo3

Calculate the before- and after-tax component costs for bonds, preference shares and ordinary equity.

Estimating the component costs

In this section, we will be estimating the costs of debt, preference shares and ordinary equity. Before we do this, we need to understand the importance of using marginal costs and how this factor makes the calculation of the components of the cost of capital slightly different to the calculation of the security holders' required returns. If a shareholder invests $100 and wants a 10% return, he or she will want that on the initial outlay. If issue costs are $5, the company gets only $95 of the shareholder's investment. The company needs to generate a $10 return on the $95 to get the shareholder's required return of 10%.

Finding the marginal cost of funds

Issue costs: the costs associated with bringing an issue of securities to the market

Net proceeds: the amount of cash received from investors minus any costs associated with the issue

With our focus on the marginal cost of each funding source, we need to include the costs of raising the funds. These are the costs associated with bringing an issue of securities to the market — called **issue costs** and also known as flotation costs for equity issues. They include any underwriting fees and costs of preparing a prospectus, in addition to costs associated with the advertising and promotion of the issue. It may be necessary for the firm to issue new equity securities at an offer price lower than the current market price to ensure sufficient funds are raised from the issue. This reduction in price can also be considered as a flotation cost. The **net proceeds** are the amount of cash received from investors minus any costs associated with the issue. Issue costs are often stated as a percentage of the issue price. As we will see in the following sections, net proceeds are used to calculate the component costs for new issues of debt, preference shares and ordinary shares. We use net proceeds because it is the cost of new funds from each source that is included in the cost of capital.

Equation 7.1 shows the relationship between net proceeds and issue costs, while example 7.1 demonstrates the calculation of net proceeds.

$$NP = P_i\,(1 - f) \qquad [7.1]$$

where NP = net proceeds per security from the issue

P_i = price per security at issue

f = issue costs as a percentage of price

EXAMPLE 7.1

Calculating net proceeds of an issue

Keating Ltd is planning the issue of 1 million ordinary shares. The shares will be offered to the market at $5 each. The investment bank handling the issue has agreed to bear all the costs of the issue for a fee of 4.6% of total funds raised. What net proceeds per share can Keating expect?

$NP = P_i (1 - f)$

$NP = 5 (1 - 0.046)$

$= \$4.77$

Total proceeds are therefore $4 770 000 (1 000 000 × $4.77)

We will be calculating the component costs of the cost of capital for the remainder of this section. The calculations show how to estimate the component costs on both a before- and after-tax basis. The tax rate used here will be the nominal corporate tax rate of 30%. The after-tax costs are for use by businesses that are not integrated with the dividend imputation systems and marginal tax rates should be used in these circumstances. The before-tax costs are for use by companies that are fully integrated with the dividend imputation system. We discuss the implications of partial integration at the end of the section.

Cost of debt

Cost of debt: the level of return that must be generated in order to meet the required return of debtholders

The cost of debt is the level of return that must be generated in order to meet the required return of debtholders. To estimate the cost of debt, we need to find the required return of debtholders. The analysis in this section applies equally to bonds, unsecured notes and debentures. For ease of discussion, the term 'bond' is used to represent all three types of security.

The face value, term to maturity and coupon rate are specified when fixed coupon bonds are offered to prospective purchasers. The issuer is locked into a series of payments that remain constant until the security matures. However, funds raised from previous issues of debt have already been used to finance assets held by the firm. The cost of previous issues is not relevant when we use the cost of capital as a yardstick for assessing new projects. Therefore, we measure the marginal cost of debt or the cost associated with a new issue.

Zero coupon bonds are not used as a major source of funds by Australian companies, but they are included here to help us understand how the cost of debt is calculated. The valuation equation for zero coupon bonds is given in chapter 6. Substituting the net proceeds for the intrinsic value in the zero coupon valuation equation gives:

$$NP_b = \frac{F}{(1+r_b)^n} \qquad [7.2]$$

where NP_b = net proceeds per bond from the issue

F = bond's face (or maturity) value

r_b = bondholder's required return

n = number of periods

The issuer will set the face value of the security and be able to estimate the net proceeds from the issue. This leaves us with the debtholders' required return, r_b, as the only unknown variable. As the before-tax cost of the zero coupon bond, $k_{z,\,bt}$, equals the required return of the debtholders, solving equation 7.2 will give us the before-tax cost of debt.

To find the required return or cost of debt, we need to find the discount rate that makes the present value of the future cash flows equal the net proceeds of the bond. This discount rate is also called the **internal rate of return** (IRR).

Internal rate of return: the discount rate that makes the present value of future cash flows equal to the net cash outlay

There are a couple of different methods for approximating the cost of debt. Each has its advantages and disadvantages and the one you choose in a given circumstance will depend on the cash flow pattern of the instrument and the facilities you have available at the time.

Interpolation: the process of approximating an unknown return using trial and error

One method is to use a trial and error approach called **interpolation**. The process begins with a guess at the discount rate that will make the present value of the future cash flows equal to the net proceeds of the bond. The guess can then be trialled in equation 7.2. If the answer from equation 7.2 does not equal the net proceeds of the bond, another guess is made and a new calculation using equation 7.2 is done. The same process continues until you get one discount rate that gives the nearest calculated price above the net proceeds and the next discount rate above that one gives a calculated price just below the net proceeds. The next step is to estimate where between our two discount rates the cost of debt lies. The ratio of the differences in the calculated prices is used to do this. The whole interpolation process is demonstrated to approximate the cost of a zero coupon bond in example 7.2.

EXAMPLE 7.2

Before-tax cost of zero coupon bonds

A zero coupon bond has a face value of \$100 000 and 3 years to maturity. Interest accrues on the bond annually. The net proceeds of the bond are \$90 000. What is the cost to the company of this source of finance?

$$NP_b = \frac{F}{(1+k_{z,bt})^n}$$

$$NP_b = \frac{100000}{(1+k_{z,bt})^3}$$

Try 5% as a first pass at the cost of debt:

$$= \frac{100000}{(1.05)^3}$$

$$= \frac{100000}{(1.1576)}$$

$$= \$86\,385.63$$

You can use table 2 of the financial tables in the appendix at the back of this book to look up the value of the denominator (in the same way as in chapter 4) if you would like to reduce the calculations involved. The calculation in this example (and all subsequent calculations in this chapter) has been rounded to four decimal places. If you do not round to four places, you will get a slightly different answer.

There is an inverse relationship between the discount rate and the value of a security. Keeping the cash flows constant (as we do in this example), the higher the discount rate the lower the calculated value. Conversely, the lower the discount rate the higher the calculated value (see figure 7.1).

Using the 5% discount rate, the calculated value of the bond is lower than the net proceeds. With our objective of getting the calculated value as close as possible to net proceeds, our next choice will be a lower discount rate to increase the calculated value. This means that the cost of debt must be lower than our first try of 5%. Let's try 4%.

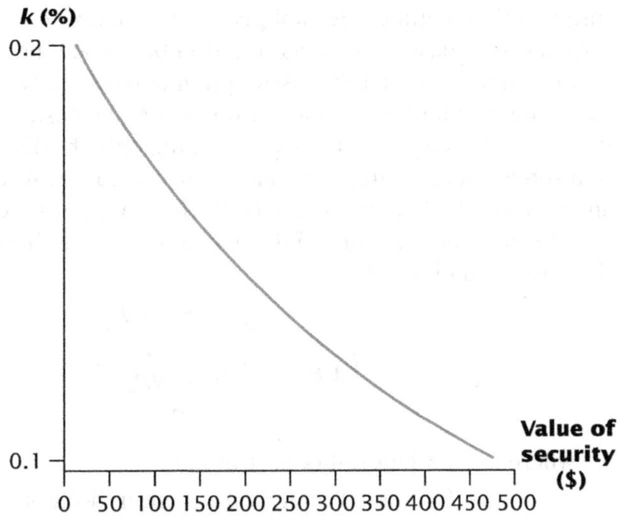

Figure 7.1 Inverse relationship of value and discount rate

Note: this figure is based on a series of cash flows of $50 per period for 10 periods.

$$NP_b = \frac{100\,000}{(1.04)^3}$$

$$= \frac{100\,000}{(1.1249)}$$

$$= \$88\,896.79$$

The calculated value has moved in the right direction by using the 4% discount rate, but is still lower than the net proceeds. This means that the cost of debt must be lower still, so we will try 3%.

$$NP_b = \frac{100\,000}{(1.03)^3}$$

$$= \frac{100\,000}{(1.0927)}$$

$$= \$91\,516.43$$

The calculated price using a 3% discount rate is now too high. As the next whole number percentage was too low, we can tell that the cost of debt is between 3% and 4%. To estimate where the cost of debt lies in that range we take the difference between the calculated value for the lower discount rate and the net proceeds (91 516.43 – 90 000 = 1516.43). We then divide that by the difference between the calculated value for the lower discount rate and that for the higher discount rate (91 516.43 – 88 896.79 = 2619.64). The ratio of these differences ($\frac{1516.43}{2619.64} = 0.5789$) approximates the distance from the lower discount rate. Therefore, using the trial and error method, the cost of debt for our zero coupon bond is 3.58% (or 3.0 + 0.5789). The interpolation between 3% and 4% is summarised as:

Difference of lower discount rate value and net proceeds 91 516.43 – 90 000 = 1516.43

Difference of lower and higher discount rate values 91 516.43 – 88 896.79 = 2619.64

Ratio of differences $\frac{1516.43}{2619.64} = 0.5789$

Lower rate plus ratio 3 + 0.5789 = 3.58%

The interpolation method does not give a precise cost of debt. The ratio approach we use with interpolation is based on the assumption that discount rates change in a linear fashion between whole numbers, and this assumption is not strictly correct. If you have access to a spreadsheet, the trial and error calculations are made easier if you set up the equations and data in cells so that each guess involves changing only the discount rate. However, if you have access to a spreadsheet or financial calculator you can simply use the internal rate of return (IRR) function to calculate the cost of debt. IRRs are discussed in detail in chapter 8.

Without a spreadsheet or financial calculator, a less tedious way to approximate the cost of debt is to use equation 7.3.

$$k_{d,\,bt} \cong \frac{I + \frac{(F - NP_b)}{n}}{\frac{(F + NP_b)}{2}} \qquad [7.3]$$

where $k_{d,\,bt}$ = before-tax cost of debt

I = annual interest payment in dollars

F = bond's face (or maturity) value

NP_b = net proceeds per bond from the issue

n = number of periods

The $\cong$ symbol indicates that the mathematical operation in equation 7.3 gives us an approximation of the cost of debt. If the equation were to give a strictly equivalent cost of debt, the 'equals' sign would be used. Example 7.3 uses the data for the zero coupon bond given in example 7.2.

EXAMPLE 7.3

Approximate before-tax cost of zero coupon bonds

$$k_{z,\,bt} \cong \frac{I + \frac{(F - NP)}{n}}{\frac{(F + NP)}{2}}$$

$$k_{z,\,bt} \cong \frac{0 + \frac{(100\,000 - 90\,000)}{3}}{\frac{(100\,000 + 90\,000)}{2}}$$

$$\cong \frac{3333.33}{95000}$$

$$\cong .0350\,88 \text{ or } 3.51\%$$

The approximate cost of the zero coupon bond is 3.51%. This is a little different from the 3.58% we estimated using the trial and error method. The difference is attributable to the methods we used to approximate. This method is less accurate than the previous method.

Coupon bonds have more cash flows than zero coupon bonds, further complicating the estimation of the cost of debt. The valuation equation for coupon bonds given in chapter 6 is adapted to reflect the net proceeds of the issue rather than the intrinsic value, as shown in equation 7.4.

$$NP_b = \sum_{t=1}^{n} \frac{C_t}{(1+r_b)^t} + \frac{F}{(1+r_b)^n} \qquad [7.4]$$

where NP_b = net proceeds per bond from the issue
F = bond's face (or maturity) value
C_t = coupon payment in period t
r_b = bondholder's required return
n = number of periods

Again, we need to find the debtholders' required rate of return by identifying the discount rate that makes the present value of the future cash flows equal the net proceeds of a coupon bond. The most efficient way to do this is by using the IRR function in a spreadsheet or financial calculator. Without access to a computer or financial calculator, the cost of debt on coupon bonds is approximated using trial and error or equation 7.3, as shown in example 7.4.

EXAMPLE 7.4

Before-tax cost of coupon bonds

A bond has a face value of \$100 000 and three years to maturity. The coupon rate is 5% and coupons are paid annually. The next coupon is due in 12 months' time and the issue will generate net proceeds of \$90 000. What is the cost to the company of this source of finance?

$$NP_b = \sum_{t=1}^{n} \frac{C_t}{(1+k_{b,bt})^t} + \frac{F}{(1+k_{b,bt})^n}$$

$$NP_b = \frac{5000}{(1+k_{b,bt})^1} + \frac{5000}{(1+k_{b,bt})^2} + \frac{5000+100\,000}{(1+k_{b,bt})^3}$$

Try 9% as a first pass at the cost of debt:

$$NP_b = \frac{5000}{(1+0.09)^1} + \frac{5000}{(1+0.09)^2} + \frac{5000+100\,000}{(1+0.09)^3}$$

$$= \frac{5000}{1.09} + \frac{5000}{1.1881} + \frac{5000+100\,000}{1.2950}$$

$$= 4587.16 + 4208.40 + 81\,081.08$$

$$= \$89\,876.64$$

If the before-tax cost of the bond ($k_{b,bt}$) was 9%, the net proceeds would be \$89 876.64. As the net proceeds are \$90 000, the cost must be a little lower. Let's try 8%.

$$NP_b = \frac{5000}{(1+0.08)^1} + \frac{5000}{(1+0.08)^2} + \frac{5000+100\,000}{(1+0.08)^3}$$

$$= \frac{5000}{1.08} + \frac{5000}{1.1664} + \frac{5000+100\,000}{1.2597}$$

$$= 4629.63 + 4286.69 + 83\,353.18$$

$$= \$92\,269.50$$

If $k_{b,bt}$ were 8%, the net proceeds would be \$92 269.50. We can tell from these calculations that a cost of 9% is too high and a cost of 8% is too low. We interpolate between these two rates to get a better estimate of the cost of debt as shown overleaf.

Difference of lower discount rate value and net proceeds 92 269.50 – 90 000 = 2269.50

Difference of lower and higher discount rate values 92 269.50 – 89 876.64 = 2392.86

Ratio of differences $\frac{2269.50}{2392.86} = 0.9484$

Lower rate plus ratio 8 + 0.9484 = 8.95%

The trial and error method gives $k_{b,\,bt}$ as 8.95%.

Example 7.4 was fairly simple because there were cash flows for only three periods. Discounting the cash flow for each period becomes cumbersome for bonds with longer terms. As the coupon payments for bonds represent a constant stream of cash flows, it is more efficient to use the present value interest factors for annuities that are included in the financial tables at the back of the book.

EXAMPLE 7.5

Approximate cost of debt

We can apply equation 7.3 to the data in example 7.4 as follows:

$$k_{b,\,bt} \cong \frac{I + \dfrac{(F - NP_b)}{n}}{\dfrac{(F + NP_b)}{2}}$$

$$k_{b,\,bt} \cong \frac{5000 + \dfrac{(100000 - 90000)}{3}}{\dfrac{(100000 + 90000)}{2}}$$

$$\cong \frac{8333.33}{95\,000}$$

$$\cong 0.087\,719 \text{ or } 8.77\%$$

The disparity between using trial and error and the approximate cost of debt equation grows with the introduction of the coupon cash flows. Equation 7.3 has greater accuracy for zero coupon bonds. It is necessary to use a financial calculator or spreadsheet to find accurately the before-tax cost of a coupon bond. Figure 7.2 shows a suggested format for calculating the cost of debt using the IRR function in Excel. The cash flows of the bond are entered in a column, with the net proceeds shown as a negative number in the first cell. In the cell where you want your answer to appear, enter '= IRR(values, [guess])' with the cell range containing your cash flows in the values section and any percentage as your guess at the cost of debt. Doing this for example 7.4 gives a cost of debt of 0.089 468, or 8.95%.

The cost of debt calculations we have done so far have been on a before-tax basis. The before-tax calculations are relevant when the company's shareholders can fully utilise imputation credits. When imputation credits are not available, maximising owners' wealth is achieved by maximising the after-tax return to owners. This means the appropriate measure of firm performance is after tax. We convert the before-tax cost of debt to an after-tax cost using equation 7.5.

$$k_{d,\,at} = k_{d,\,bt}\,(1 - t_r) \qquad [7.5]$$

where $k_{d,at}$ = after-tax cost of debt

$k_{d,bt}$ = before-tax cost of debt

t_r = nominal marginal tax rate

The before-tax cost of debt ($k_{d,bt}$) can be calculated by trial and error, approximation equation, spreadsheet or financial calculator.

For a company, the nominal marginal tax rate is the statutory tax rate for corporations.[9] As we see in chapter 2, partners and sole traders pay income tax individually rather than at the business level. Therefore the nominal marginal tax rate for partnerships and sole traders is the tax rate that applies to the next dollar of income in the hands of the individual owner.

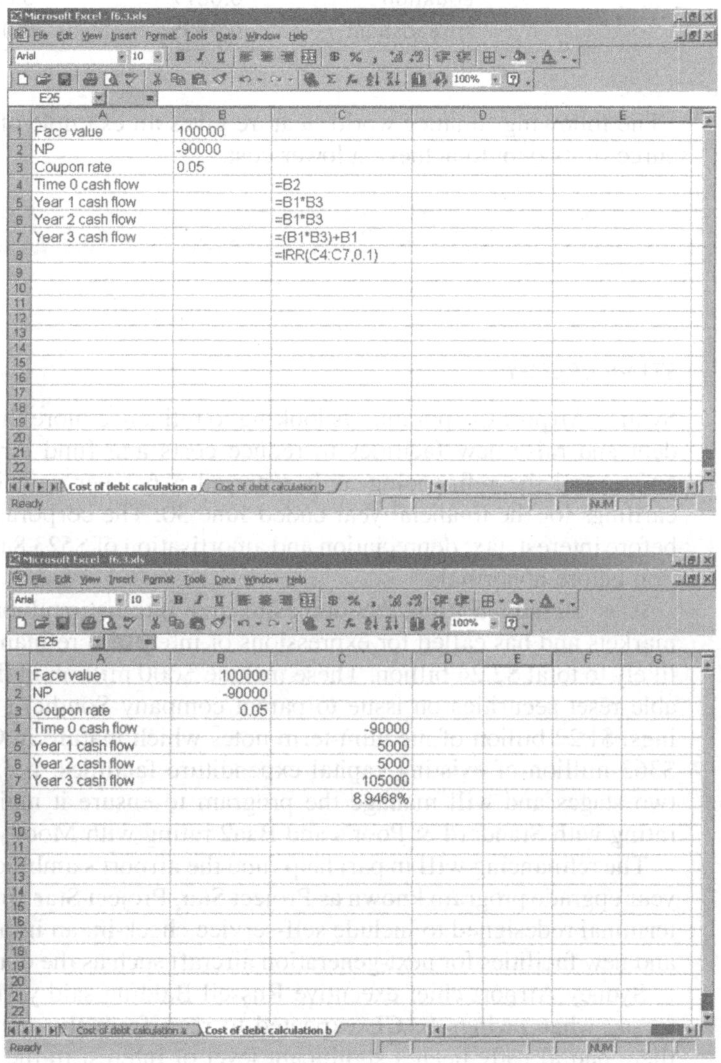

Figure 7.2 Cost of debt calculation spreadsheet

Given a non-zero marginal tax rate, the after-tax cost of debt is always lower than the before-tax cost of debt. This reflects the tax deduction allowed for interest payments made by a business. Example 7.6 converts the before-tax costs from examples 7.3 and 7.4 to after-tax costs.

EXAMPLE 7.6

After-tax cost of debt

The corporate issuer of the bonds in examples 7.3 and 7.4 faces a nominal tax rate of 30%. What is the after-tax cost of the coupon bond?

	Method	$k_{d,bt}$	$k_{d,at} = k_{d,bt}(1 - 0.3)$	$k_{d,at}$
Zero coupon	trial and error	0.0358	0.0358 × 0.7	2.51%
	equation	0.0351	0.0351 × 0.7	2.46%
Coupon	trial and error	0.0895	0.0895 × 0.7	6.27%
	equation	0.0877	0.0877 × 0.7	6.14%
	spreadsheet	0.0895	0.0895 × 0.7	6.27%

The following 'finance world' feature gives an example of a company changing the source of its debt to achieve a lower cost.

FINANCE WORLD

Sydney Airport rejigs debt in expansion plan

STEVE CREEDY

Sydney Airport Corporation is looking to refinance more than $2 billion worth of debt and raise new facilities to reduce costs and fund airport upgrades. SACL announced the refinancing as it reported a 6.2 per cent increase in unaudited earnings for the financial year ended June 30. The corporation reported earnings before interest, tax, depreciation and amortisation of $523.8 million, or $525.6 million before abnormals.

It is already testing the domestic and international bank debt and capital markets and has called for expressions of interest in refinancing facilities that are likely to total $2.24 billion. These include $600 million in floating IPO exchangeable reset securities on issue to parent company Southern Cross Airports Holdings, $1.22 billion of medium-term notes which mature in October next year and $363 million of existing capital expenditure facilities. It expects to refinance in two stages and will manage the program to ensure it maintains its BBB credit rating with Standard & Poor's and Baa2 rating with Moody's.

The refinancing wilI in part help fund the airport's ambitious $500 million, five-year upgrade program known as Project Star. Project Star will see the international terminal redesigned to include self-service check-in, an improved baggage system and new facilities for next-generation aircraft such as the double-decker A380.

Sydney Airport chief executive Russell Balding said yesterday it was too soon to say what savings SACL expected to reap from the refinancing exercise. But there had already been a significant level of interest in the transaction. 'We're in the process now of going to the market and we're looking forward to a highly competitive process of selecting our future financiers,' he said. Mr Balding described the airport's annual earnings as a solid result that underscored the resilience and strength of the business.

Growth in the commercial business continued to underpin earnings growth. SACL's figures show total revenues grew 6.5 per cent, with strong increases in the commercial trading and property portfolios, while total operating expenses rose 7.6 per cent. Aeronautical revenues grew 4.2 per cent to $269 million, retail revenues were up 4.4 per cent to $156 million, property revenues rose 8.2 per cent to $87 million and commercial trading increased 8.6 per cent to $85 million. Passenger traffic grew by 2.9 per cent and SACL said the fact revenues were ahead of passenger growth reflected improved yields from all commercial operations. The rise in expenses was principally due to increased spending on recoverable security requirements, it said.

Despite the sunny outlook, Sydney has yet to secure a long-term pricing agreement with airlines and some are pushing for aeronautical charges to be re-regulated. The airport also faces community and state government opposition to some of its property development plans, including a proposal to develop a shopping centre on airport land.[10]

FINANCE WORKSHOP 7.1

1. A zero coupon bond has a face value of $100 000 and 5 years to maturity. Interest accrues on the bond annually. The net proceeds of the bond are $60 000. Use interpolation to find the before-tax cost to the company of this source of finance.
2. Apply the approximate cost of debt equation to the data given in question 1 and determine the before-tax cost to the company of this source of finance.
3. You have calculated the before-tax cost of debt as 10.76%. What is the after-tax cost of the debt if the statutory tax rate is currently 30%?

Cost of preference shares

Cost of preference shares: the level of return that must be generated in order to meet the required return of preference shareholders

The **cost of preference shares** is the level of return that must be generated in order to meet the required return of preference shareholders. As was the case with debt, funds raised from past issues are not available for proposed investments. Substituting the net proceeds for the intrinsic value in the preference share valuation equation from chapter 6 gives:

$$NP_p = \frac{D}{r_p} \qquad [7.6]$$

where NP_p = net proceeds per preference share from the issue

D = dividend payment

r_p = preference shareholder's required return

The different types of preference shares are discussed in chapter 3. Difficulties in valuing preference shares with participating dividends and conversion features are mentioned in chapter 6. These same difficulties in forecasting cash flows that made valuation difficult also make finding the cost of preference shares difficult. In this section, we consider only 'standard issue' preference shares, where the dividend rate is fixed and is set prior to offer and the shares are irredeemable. As was the case for debt, the issuer should have a good idea of the price the shares will sell for at issue and the flotation costs involved in the issue. We estimate the cost of preference shares, k_p, by estimating the shareholders' required return, r_p. To make calculations easier, equation 7.6 can be restated as follows:

$$k_{p,at} = \frac{D}{NP_p} \qquad [7.7]$$

where $k_{p,at}$ = after-tax cost of preference shares
NP_p = net proceeds per preference share from the issue
D = dividend payment

There is no tax deduction associated with the payment of preference dividends, even though the regular stream of dividend payments is similar to coupons on debt. Dividends are paid from after-tax profits of a company. This means that the cost of preference shares estimated from equation 7.7 is the after-tax cost. The after-tax cost is relevant when the owners of the firm cannot use imputation credits. Example 7.7 shows the calculation of the after-tax cost of preference shares.

EXAMPLE 7.7

After-tax cost of preference shares

Legolas Ltd is planning the issue of preference shares at an offer price of $100 per share. Dividend payments of $5.35 will be made annually. Flotation costs are estimated at 3.5% of offer price. What is the after-tax cost of preference shares for Legolas?

$$k_{p,at} = \frac{D}{NP_p} \text{ and } NP = P_i\,(1 - f)$$

$$k_{p,at} = \frac{5.35}{96.50} \quad NP = 100(1 - 0.035) = 96.50$$

$$= 0.055\,44 \text{ or } 5.54\%$$

The after-tax cost of preference shares for Legolas is 5.54%.

The receipt of a fully franked dividend consists of the dividend cash flow and the credit for the corporate tax paid on profit. When investors can fully utilise imputation credits, the before-tax cost is relevant. In this case, it is necessary to adjust the dividends of preference shares to reflect the receipt of a fully franked dividend. We make the adjustment by grossing up the dividend to its before-tax value as follows:

$$k_{p,bt} = \frac{\dfrac{D}{(1 - t_c)}}{NP_p} \qquad [7.8]$$

where $k_{p,bt}$ = before-tax cost of preference shares
t_c = company tax rate
NP_p = net proceeds per preference share from the issue
D = dividend payment

EXAMPLE 7.8

Before-tax cost of preference shares

Given a corporate tax rate of 30% and the information about the Legolas Ltd preference shares issue in example 7.7, calculate the before-tax cost of preference shares.

$$k_{p,bt} = \frac{\frac{D}{(1-t_c)}}{NP_p}$$

$$k_{p,bt} = \frac{\frac{5.35}{(1-0.30)}}{96.50}$$

$$= \frac{7.64}{96.50}$$

$$= 0.0792 \text{ or } 7.92\%$$

The before-tax value of Legolas's dividend consists of the cash payment of $5.35 plus imputation credits of $2.29, giving a total before-tax value of $7.64. The before-tax cost of preference shares is 7.92%.

FINANCE WORKSHOP 7.2

Orange Ltd preference shares will be issued next week with an offer price of $50 per share. The issue costs for the preference shares will be 4.5% of the offer price. Dividend payments of $2 will be made annually and they will be franked to 100%. The corporate tax rate is currently 30%. Calculate the before- and after-tax cost of preference shares for the new issue.

Cost of ordinary equity

Cost of ordinary equity: the level of return that must be generated in order to meet the required return of the ordinary shareholders

The cost of ordinary equity is the level of return that must be generated in order to meet the required return of the ordinary shareholders. The costs of debt and preference shares were based on new issues of securities because funds from previous issues are not available for new projects. New issues of ordinary equity also generate funds for use in a company. However, in contrast to debt and preference securities, ordinary equity can also provide funds from existing shareholders without making a new share issue.

Retained earnings: represent the accumulated profit of the company that has not been paid out to shareholders as dividends

Ordinary shareholders are the owners of a company. Dividends are paid from profits and the ordinary shareholders' returns depend on how effectively the company operates. The ultimate purpose of company earnings is to be paid as dividends or to be reinvested in the company on the shareholders' behalf. Retained earnings represent the accumulated profit of the company that has not been paid out to shareholders as dividends. The level of retained earnings depends on the company's profitability and on the dividend payout policy. We examine dividend policy in detail in chapter 13. The important thing to note at this stage is that retained earnings are not a free source of funds for new projects. Retained earnings belong to the ordinary shareholders and the ordinary shareholders expect to get their required return on this source of funds. This feature of ordinary equity means we need to include both the cost of retained earnings (the ordinary shareholders' required return) and the cost of new issues as components in the cost of capital.

Cost of retained earnings

Cost of retained earnings: the required return of ordinary shareholders on shares that have already been issued

The **cost of retained earnings** is the required return of ordinary shareholders on shares that have already been issued. The following two sections are based on a mature company for which the constant growth model to value ordinary shares adequately reflects the future cash flows of ordinary equity. We are introduced to the constant growth model in chapter 6 and presented it in equation 6.7. The constant growth model is presented again in equation 7.9. If the company is expected to have a number of growth phases, equation 7.9 should be adapted to reflect these before the cost of equity is estimated.

$$V_e = \frac{D_1}{r_e - g} \qquad [7.9]$$

where V_e = intrinsic value of the ordinary share
D_1 = dividend to be paid in the next period
r_e = shareholder's required return
g = expected growth in dividends

By rearranging equation 7.9 to make the required return the focus of our calculations we get the equation shown below.

$$k_{re,at} = \frac{D_1}{P_O} + g \qquad [7.10]$$

where $k_{re,\,at}$ = after-tax cost of retained earnings
D_1 = dividend to be paid in the next period
P_O = current market price of one ordinary share
g = expected growth in dividends

We substitute the current price of an ordinary share (not net proceeds) for the intrinsic value when estimating the cost of retained earnings. This reflects the internal generation process of retained earnings, which come from profitable operations and a corporate policy of not paying out all profits as dividends. The following example demonstrates the calculation of after-tax cost of retained earnings.

EXAMPLE 7.9

After-tax cost of retained earnings

The ordinary shares of Legolas Ltd are currently trading at $4.72. A dividend of 50c was recently paid and the next dividend is due a year from now. The estimated growth rate is 4% per annum. What is the after-tax cost of retained earnings for Legolas?

The first step we need to take is to convert the last dividend paid to the forecast dividend, D_1, for next period. We achieve this by multiplying the last dividend by one plus the growth rate.

$$k_{re,\,at} = \frac{D_1}{P_O} + g$$

$$k_{re,\,at} = \frac{0.50(1 + 0.04)}{4.72} + 0.04$$

$$= \frac{0.52}{4.72} + 0.04$$

$$= 0.150\,169 \text{ or } 15.02\%$$

The before-tax cost of retained earnings (relevant when shareholders are integrated with the imputation tax system) for a company that pays a fully franked dividend uses the grossed up dividend amount. You will notice from the following equation and example that the grossing up process is identical to the one we followed for fully franked preference dividends.

$$k_{re,bt} = \frac{\frac{D_1}{(1-t_c)}}{P_O} + g \qquad [7.11]$$

where $k_{re,bt}$ = before-tax cost of retained earnings
D_1 = dividend to be paid in the next period
t_c = company tax rate
P_O = current market price of one ordinary share
g = expected growth in dividends

EXAMPLE 7.10

Before-tax cost of retained earnings

If the corporate tax rate is 30% and Legolas pays fully franked dividends, what is the before-tax cost of retained earnings?

$$k_{re,bt} = \frac{\frac{D_1}{(1-t_c)}}{P_O} + g$$

$$k_{re,bt} = \frac{\frac{0.50(1+0.04)}{(1-0.30)}}{4.72} + 0.04$$

$$= \frac{\frac{0.52}{0.7}}{4.72} + 0.04$$

$$= \frac{0.74}{4.72} + 0.04$$

$$= 0.1574 + 0.04$$

$$= 0.1974 \text{ or } 19.74\%$$

The entire balance of the retained earnings account in the company's balance sheet is rarely available as a source of funding for new projects. Some portion of the balance will represent funds that have already been used to finance existing projects. This portion of retained earnings corresponds to assets purchased for existing projects and these assets are shown in the balance sheet. Assets that are being used in the firm's current projects are not available for use in new projects unless the existing projects are terminated. Therefore, the proportion of retained earnings that can be used to finance existing projects is represented by cash not required for current operations, near cash assets and funds from the planned liquidation of existing assets. When these amounts have been used in the investment process, the company will have to raise equity funding by the issue of new shares.

BEHAVIOURAL PERSPECTIVE

Do investors sometimes make irrational decisions?

Most Australians like to pay less tax rather than more tax. If you are nodding as you read this, you might like to think of the relationship between taxable income and the amount of tax you pay! You pay more tax on higher levels of taxable income. If you don't want to pay tax, the sure way to achieve this is not to generate any income.

Some investors find the imputation credits attached to fully franked dividends to be the most attractive feature of purchasing shares. When investors place an undue importance on one particular aspect of a decision, we say they are 'fixated' on that particular variable (imputation credits in this case). For these investors, the future expectations of the company are not as important as the tax offset achieved by receiving fully franked dividends. Such investors have the objective of minimising their tax payable rather than maximising their total wealth position. They are likely to be mum and dad investors with relatively small holdings of shares rather than 'sophisticated' investors with large portfolios and relatively more investment experience. The irrational trades of tax minimising investors would not normally be expected to influence the price of a company's shares so the cost of retained earnings would not be affected. However, if a small listed company had a large proportion of this type of investor, the share price (and cost of retained earnings) would be expected to fall by more than the value of the franking credits if the company had to pay dividends without franking credits.

In addition to a fixation on imputation credits, recent research suggests that lunar phases contribute to determining share prices and returns. Yuan, Zheng and Zhu investigated returns on the market index for 48 countries (including Australia) and found that returns are significantly lower for days around the full moon compared to days around the new moon.[11] They suggest the association between lunar cycle and returns can be attributed to the psychological and biological effects of the cycle that have been documented in the scientific literature. The implication of this finding for managers who are determining the cost of capital is that the cost of retained earnings will be lower if the current share price is taken on a day around the full moon.

FINANCE WORKSHOP 7.3

Orange Ltd ordinary shares are currently trading at $12.70. A fully franked dividend of $1.25 was recently paid and the next one is due in 1 year's time. The annual growth rate for Orange is currently 1% and this rate is expected to continue for the foreseeable future. The corporate tax rate is currently 30%. Calculate the before- and after-tax cost of retained earnings.

Cost of new share issues

Cost of ordinary shares: the required return of shareholders on a new issue

The **cost of ordinary shares** is the required return of shareholders on a new issue. The cost of ordinary equity, as defined earlier, would include the cost of retained earnings and the cost of any new share issue. The term 'cost of ordinary shares' is used here to refer only to the cost of a new share issue. The main difference between estimating the cost of new ordinary shares and retained earnings is the use of net proceeds rather than current market price. We rearrange equation 7.10 and substitute net proceeds, NP_e, for price to estimate the after-tax cost of ordinary equity.

$$k_{e,\,at} = \frac{D_1}{NP_e} + g \qquad [7.12]$$

where $k_{e,at}$ = after-tax cost of ordinary shares
D_1 = dividend to be paid in the next period
NP_e = net proceeds per share from the issue
g = expected growth in dividends

Example 7.11 shows the calculation of the after-tax cost of an ordinary share issue for Legolas Ltd.

EXAMPLE 7.11

After-tax cost of new share issue

The ordinary shares of Legolas Ltd are currently trading at $4.72. A new share issue would be made at an offer price of $4.70. Issue costs are expected to be 3% of the proceeds of the issue. The last dividend was 50c and the next dividend is due a year from now. The estimated growth rate is 4% per annum. What is Legolas's after-tax cost of an ordinary share issue?

$$k_{e,\,at} = \frac{D_1}{NP_e} + g$$

$$k_{e,\,at} = \frac{0.50(1+0.04)}{4.70(1-0.03)} + 0.04$$

$$= \frac{0.52}{4.56} + 0.04$$

$$= 0.15404 \text{ or } 15.4\%$$

To obtain the before-tax cost of a new issue we gross up the dividend to reflect 100% franking credits. The equation for the before-tax cost of a new issue is:

$$k_{e,\,bt} = \frac{\dfrac{D_1}{(1-t_c)}}{NP_e} + g \qquad [7.13]$$

where $k_{e,bt}$ = before-tax cost of ordinary shares
D_1 = dividend to be paid in the next period
t_c = company tax rate
NP_e = net proceeds per share from the issue
g = expected growth in dividends

EXAMPLE 7.12

Before-tax cost of new share issue

If Legolas pays fully franked dividends and the corporate tax rate is 30%, what is the before-tax cost of a new issue of ordinary shares?

$$k_{e,\,bt} = \frac{\dfrac{D_1}{(1-t_c)}}{NP_e} + g$$

$$k_{e,\,bt} = \frac{\frac{0.50(1+0.04)}{(1-0.30)}}{4.56} + 0.04$$

$$= \frac{\frac{0.52}{0.7}}{4.56} + 0.04$$

$$= 0.1629 + 0.04$$

$$= 0.2029 \text{ or } 20.30\%$$

As we see in chapter 5, the CAPM provides a quantifiable relationship between expected return and systematic risk. We can use this relationship as an alternative to the dividend discount model we used to calculate the cost of ordinary shares. The after-tax cost of ordinary shares is given in equation 7.14 and demonstrated in example 7.13.

$$\boldsymbol{E(R) = R_f + \beta(E(R_m) - R_f)} \qquad [7.14]$$

where $E(R)$ = expected return on the investment

R_f = return on the risk-free asset

$E(R_m)$ = expected return on the market portfolio

β = systematic risk of the asset

EXAMPLE 7.13

CAPM and the after-tax cost of ordinary shares

Arwyn Ltd has a beta of 1.6. The current risk-free rate is 5.5% and the equity risk premium (ERP) is 5%. What is the after-tax cost for the ordinary shares of Arwyn?

$$E(R) = R_f + \beta(E(R_m) - R_f)$$

$$E(R) = 0.055 + 1.6 \times 0.05$$

$$= 13.5\%$$

The after-tax cost of ordinary shares is 13.5%.

While the CAPM does not require forecasts of dividends or assumptions about a dividend growth rate, it does need a forecast of the equity risk premium, $E(R_m) - R_f$, a measure of the risk-free rate, R_f, and a measure of the systematic risk, β, of the firm. As we discuss in chapter 4, an average of ex post risk premium is often used in place of the equity risk premium (ERP). This practice is based on the assumption that the ex post relationship between the realised market return and the risk-free rate for the corresponding time period is a good representation of what will happen in the future. The risk-free rate can be observed by calculating the returns on government-issued securities. You will, however, have to choose from a range of maturities on these securities.

You learn in chapter 5 that systematic risk is the risk that is common to all businesses and that beta is the relative measure of the systematic risk of the firm compared to that of the market. Beta is measured by regressing the realised returns on a share on the realised returns on the market. Different measures of beta can be obtained when daily, weekly and monthly data are used in the regression. The calculation of beta can also be dependent on the number of periods of data that are used in the regression (365 days versus 60 months versus 10 years, for example). Variable measures and the reliance on assumptions that the past is a good predictor of the future does cast doubt on the relevance of the expected returns calculated from the model.

Another complication with applying the CAPM to calculate the cost of ordinary shares is that the model does not incorporate flotation costs — net proceeds are not part of the calculation. The cost of capital should be based on the marginal cost of each source of finance. This complication can be overcome by adjusting project cash flows for issue costs rather than adjusting the component cost of capital.

A serious difficulty arises if we attempt to use the CAPM to calculate the before-tax cost of ordinary shares. The ERP should be higher under a dividend imputation tax system.[12] How much higher the ERP will be depends on the proportion of imputation credits that can be utilised by market participants. The proportion of imputation credits that can be utilised depends, in turn, on the proportions of investors who can fully utilise imputation credits, those who can partially utilise them and those that get no benefits from imputation credits. There is no readily available index that can be used to determine the ex post values of these proportions. Even if there were such an index, we would need to make the assumption that the level of franking credits on the market index would remain stable over time and that the proportions of investors with a certain ability to utilise credits would also remain constant. We discuss the issue of under-utilisation of imputation credits in the following section. We will not attempt to use the CAPM to calculate the before-tax costs of ordinary shares here.

FINANCE WORKSHOP 7.4

1. The ordinary shares of Orange Ltd are currently trading at \$12.70. A new share issue would be made at an issue price of \$12.50. Flotation costs are expected to be 3.5% of the proceeds of the issue. The last dividend was \$1.25 and the next dividend is due a year from now. Orange pays fully franked dividends. The estimated growth rate is 1% per annum and is expected to remain at this level. If the corporate tax rate is 30%, what is the after-tax cost of the new issue?
2. What is the before-tax cost of the new issue of Orange Ltd (see question 1 for data)?
3. Yellow Ltd has a beta of 0.9, the risk-free rate is currently 7% and the ERP is 4%. What is the after-tax cost of Yellow's ordinary shares?

lo4

Explain how the shareholders' capacity to utilise imputation credits affects the cost of capital.

Under-utilisation of imputation credits

Imputation credits can be lost when a company has shares held by foreign investors who are not Australian residents. As at June 2005, foreign investors held 28% of the total value of equities on issue in Australia.[13] With the exception of certain investors in the United States, UK and New Zealand, foreign investors have withholding tax deducted from any receipts of interest or dividends originating in Australia. The rate of withholding tax currently ranges from 15% to 30%, with tax at the lower end of the scale for those investors who live in the UK or the United States and hold at least 10% of the voting power in the company paying the dividend.[14] Foreign investors living in countries that have a double taxation agreement with

Australia usually pay 15% withholding tax on unfranked dividends.[15] If the investor is resident in a country that has a double taxation agreement with Australia, it is likely that the withholding tax will be the only tax that he will pay on the dividend income.

Foreign shareholders do not get a cash rebate for unused franking credits. Instead, the receipt of fully franked dividends means they are not liable for withholding tax. The tax paid by Australian companies is still passed on to investors but the exemption from withholding tax means that most of these investors cannot claim a rebate for the amount of withholding tax they would have paid on an unfranked dividend. In this situation, the franking credits cannot be used and have no value to the investor. Thus, foreign investors are likely to prefer unfranked dividends.

Consistent with our focus on marginal costs, Officer[16] developed a model for determining the cost of capital based on the consideration of the role a marginal investor plays in determining the price of a security. A marginal investor is the last one who is willing to purchase a security at the offer price at a given time. Officer argued that Australia is a small open economy so world market conditions contribute to the determination of the cost of capital for Australian companies. Thus, the marginal investor is a foreign one. In this case, imputation credits cannot be fully utilised by foreign shareholders and will not be reflected in the price of the share.[17] Following this reasoning, Wood[18] argues that strong linkages between the Australian and world capital markets reduce the value of imputation credits. Cannavan, Finn and Gray[19] found that imputation credits were not valued in the prices of 19 of Australia's largest companies. For these companies, the appropriate cost of capital would be after tax.

Foreign investors are much more likely to invest in large Australian companies. They are usually looking to make a large dollar value investment because they face higher transaction costs (especially the cost of searching for information) than do resident investors. While we expect relatively high levels of foreign investment in companies included in the market indices, we expect a much lower level of foreign investment in the remaining thousand or so listed companies. When the marginal investor in a company cannot use imputation credits, we would expect that the company would focus on generating capital gains, rather than maximising the size of a franked dividend. When the marginal investor is a resident shareholder, we would expect to see the company paying out the largest possible fully franked dividend. Evidence for a 'tax clientele effect' has been found in Australia[20] and New Zealand.[21]

At the time of writing, Australian companies can generate a credit in the franking account only when they pay Australian tax on income. Tax on foreign-sourced income is paid in the country of origin. If a company operates and generates a profit in Ireland, for example, a tax liability payable to the Irish government will arise. Because Australia has a double taxation agreement with Ireland, the Australian Taxation Office will not require the company to pay tax on the already-taxed Irish profits. Further, it will not allow an increase in the dividend franking account as no Australian tax has been paid on those profits. Australian companies that generate offshore income are only partially integrated with the dividend imputation taxation system because they are unable to pay out all of their profits as fully franked dividends. In this case, the amount of franking depends on how much tax the company has paid on Australian-sourced income. These dividends will be partially franked. Note that an Australian company exporting to Ireland will not pay tax in Ireland on the sales of exported products or services.[22]

The calculation of the component costs of capital in this chapter have been based on the implicit assumption that the company paying the dividend has Australian-sourced income, allowing the payment of fully franked dividends. The effective tax rate for companies with offshore income will be lower than the Australian statutory rate. In these cases, the effective rate should be used to adjust for partially franked dividends when calculating the component costs. However, the proportion of companies that pay partially franked dividends is very low,[23] suggesting companies with a significant amount of offshore income determine the size of the dividend payment in relation to the available franking credits. We further discuss dividends and franking credits in chapter 13.

The weighted-average cost of capital

lo5

Calculate the weighted-average cost of capital.

Weighted-average cost of capital: the sum of each component cost of capital weighted by each component cost's proportion of the firm's capital structure

The weighted-average cost of capital (WACC) is a compilation of the individual component costs of capital. When we assess a project to determine its impact on the value of the firm, we need to take a wider view than just determining if the project is expected to return more than the component cost of finance that would be used to fund the project. A company considering a relatively small project, such as purchasing delivery vehicles, for example, may intend to use a term loan or lease finance as the source of funds. If the project were evaluated by comparing its cash flows to the cost of debt, the financial manager would be ignoring the impact that a higher level of debt could have on the cost of equity and on the firm's ability to raise more debt in the future. On the other hand, the plan to fund a very large project might be to make a new issue of ordinary shares. If we were to assess the project making reference only to the cost of equity, we would be ignoring the impact of having greater equity in the firm on the cost of debt and the company's ability to raise more debt in the future. Relying on the component cost of capital in either of these examples could lead to the wrong decision about the impact of the project on the value of the firm.

Weighting each component cost by its relative importance in the firm's capital structure gives the financial manager a more reliable guide for assessing projects. Equation 7.15 shows how the weighted cost of capital is derived from the component costs. It tells us to take each component cost, k_x, and multiply it by the proportion, W_x, that k_x represents in the firm's capital structure.

$$WACC = \sum_{x=1}^{n} k_x W_x \qquad [7.15]$$

where $WACC$ = weighted-average cost of capital

k_x = component cost of capital from source x

W_x = proportion that x represents in the firm's capital structure

We need to have calculated the component costs and the proportion that each component represents in the firm's capital structure in order to determine the WACC. We have spent the entire chapter thus far on calculating the component costs. Example 7.14 shows how to calculate the proportions and how they are applied to the component costs to obtain the WACC.

EXAMPLE 7.14

Calculating WACC

The financial manager of Exa-Life Ltd has identified the amount of funds attributable to each component of the cost of capital. Therefore, we have the figures for k_x to use in equation 7.14, so the next step is to determine the weights, W_x. To do this, we total the amount derived from each source of funds to obtain the total funding used by the company, as shown in the second column of the table below. We then divide the amount attributable to each component by the total funding amount to identify the proportion of each source, as shown in the final column.

Source of funds	Amount of financing	Proportion of total financing (W_x)
Term loans	2000000	0.0244 $\left(\frac{2000000}{82000000}\right)$
Bonds	20000000	0.244 $\left(\frac{20000000}{82000000}\right)$
Preference shares	10000000	0.122 $\left(\frac{10000000}{82000000}\right)$
Ordinary shares	50000000	0.61 $\left(\frac{50000000}{82000000}\right)$
	82000000	1.00

We then apply the proportion that represents each component cost to weight each of the costs. Given the following component costs for Exa-Life Ltd, we calculate the WACC as follows.

Source of funds	Component cost (k_x)	Proportion (W_x)	Weighted cost
Term loans	0.067	0.0244	0.0016 (0.067 × 0.0244)
Bonds	0.081	0.244	0.0198 (0.081 × 0.244)
Preference shares	0.085	0.122	0.0104 (0.085 × 0.122)
Ordinary shares	0.125	0.61	0.0763 (0.125 × 0.61)
		WACC	0.108

The WACC for Exa-Life is 10.8%.

As an alternative to the table, the WACC can be calculated using equation 7.15 directly as follows:

$$WACC = \sum_{x=1}^{n} k_x W_x$$

$$\begin{aligned} WACC &= (0.067 \times 0.0244) + (0.081 \times 0.244) + (0.085 \times 0.122) + (0.125 \times 0.61) \\ &= 0.0016 + 0.0198 + 0.0104 + 0.0763 \\ &= 10.8\% \end{aligned}$$

We have not, thus far, discussed the alternative weighting schemes that could be used to determine the proportion of each component cost. This issue is considered in the following section.

Alternatives for weighting

There are two main alternatives for weighting the component costs of capital to obtain the WACC: 'book value' weights and 'target' weights. The first uses the weights based on the firm's current balance sheet. This results in a weighting scheme that reflects how the firm has been financed in the past. The balance sheet shows us the history of the firm's financing decisions. The **book values** shown in the balance sheet do not reflect the current value of the firm. We discuss book value and balance sheets in chapter 14. Making decisions that will impact on the firm's value in the future is not really related to the issue price of existing ordinary shares, for example. Current market values are more relevant to decisions that will impact on future market value.

Book value: the accounting measure of an asset's worth

We could improve a weighting system based on the balance sheet by using information that tells us how many securities in each category are currently on issue and multiplying this number by the current market price per security. There is no distinctly observable market value for retained earnings and they are not shown separate to the market value of ordinary shares when a market value weighting scheme is employed. Retained earnings belong to all of the ordinary shareholders and cannot be separated from the value of their ownership interest. The appropriate weight for retained earnings is calculated using the actual amount of financing available from this source.

We will not be able to get current market values for term loans or leases, for example, as these do not have secondary markets. For these sources of funds, we need to rely on the book values. While adjusting the book value proportions to reflect the market value of the company's securities is an improvement over simply using book value, this method implies that the firm will continue to fund its activities in the same proportions as it has done in the past. This may or may not be the case.

Target weights: weighting based on management's future plans for financing the company's operations

A better weighting alternative is to use **target weights** (based on market values) for each source of funding. The company may, for example, have used 50% ordinary equity and 50% debt to fund its activities. The directors may feel that a more appropriate funding structure is 70% equity and 30% debt. Further, a company that has used preference shares as a source of financing may have decided not to issue any more preference shares. In both these examples, the historic weights will not reflect the most appropriate WACC for decisions about the future. Therefore, a weighting system based on a target funding structure will provide a better yardstick for assessing projects.

Using a target structure weighting system accommodates situations where one project is funded only with debt and another uses only equity funding. If we consider the firm as a group of projects, it is not necessary for financial managers to apply the target proportions to each individual project. The target structure is applied to the set of projects undertaken. While each project may have a specific component cost of funds associated with it, when combined with other projects, the proportion of financing from each source should come close to the target structure. In the next section of this chapter we consider whether there are some ideal proportions of debt and equity sources of finance that may maximise firm value.

We have used the net proceeds from new issues to calculate the component costs for the cost of capital. The only exception has been when calculating the cost of retained earnings and this exception occurs because there are no issue costs associated with this source of funds. Implicit in our calculation of the cost of capital is the marginal cost approach — we have only included the costs of new funds raised to finance proposed projects.

Companies can not raise an infinite amount of new funds at any one component cost. As more debt is raised, for example, investors change their perceptions of the risk associated with the securities of the firm. This can result in a change in the component costs of capital, and therefore the weighted average cost of capital. To reflect the finite amount of funding investors are willing to supply at a given required return, we should recalculate the weighted average cost of capital for each band of dollar financing the firm can raise before one of the component costs changes.

The following 'finance world' feature includes some interesting observations on taxation and the cost of equity, debt and the WACC, and company size and WACC. The article also briefly discusses the concept of using WACC for evaluating projects (which we examine in chapters 8 and 9) and offshore investment (which we investigate in chapter 17).

FINANCE WORLD

The use and misuse of WACC

PAUL KERIN

It pays to be sceptical and focus on what creates value.

More executives are using the argument 'our cost of capital is different' to justify acquisitions, rationalise their losing out on deals or to advocate policy change. The arguments are usually fallacious. If acted upon, the result can be a substantial destruction of value. Companies estimate their weighted average cost of capital (WACC) to be the weighted average of the after-tax costs of each source of capital (such as debt, common equity and preferred stock). The calculation is simple. Unfortunately, simplistic thinking about WACC can lead to erroneous conclusions. Consider four common claims:

1. Australia's WACC is too high

This argument has often been used to advocate policy change, such as tax cuts. WACC may have differed between countries in decades past, when nations placed big barriers on capital inflows/outflows. But widespread liberalisation has largely eliminated these barriers. As liberalisation proceeded, differences in bond yields disappeared. Arbitrage generally eliminates them quickly.

True, bond yields can still vary substantially between countries, but this does not imply different WACCs. Five years ago, Japan's 10-year nominal government bond yield was about 1.3%, compared with Australia's 5.6% — a 4.3 percentage point difference. But this did not give Japanese companies a competitive advantage, nor did it cause Australian companies to raise more funds in Japan. For one thing, differences in bond yields reflect differences in expectations about inflation and, therefore, future exchange rates. Once these factors are taken into account, apparent WACC differences largely disappear.

In mid-2001, Japan experienced deflation of 1.3%, while Australia's inflation rate was 2.7%; a four percentage point difference, accounting for virtually all of the difference in nominal yields. That is, real (after inflation) government bond yields were virtually identical.

Differences in taxation and regulations affecting transaction costs can cause WACC differences. For example, when Australia introduced dividend imputation, the gross return that equity-holders required fell because their required net (after-tax) return could be met at a lower gross cost. Imputation reduced the cost of equity.

Although taxes and transaction costs can make a difference, the best independent studies over the past 15 years have found that Australian companies do not face

WACCs substantially different from overseas competitors; if anything, they may be lower.

2. We should use our lower WACC to make acquisitions overseas

Even if Australia's WACC was lower, this does not mean that Australian companies face lower WACCs on overseas acquisitions. A basic tenet of corporate finance (often ignored at acquirers' peril) is that the WACC that should be used in evaluating an acquisition is the target's WACC when fully geared, as this reflects the new risks taken on, not the acquirer's.

3. Companies cannot compete against the lower WACC of private-equity firms

Many executives think that debt is cheaper than equity and that private-equity firms leverage acquisitions to gain a WACC advantage. But debt is not cheaper than equity.

Although the direct cost of debt (the interest rate) is lower, taking on more debt raises the risks borne by providers of debt and equity — and therefore their costs. When a company's capital structure is optimised, the marginal costs of debt and equity are equal.

High leverage also places costs on private-equity firms. For example, the high risk causes debt providers to impose more restrictive covenants on private-equity firms; the cost is less flexibility. And with 90% debt financing, the cost of equity can be about triple that under 40% debt financing.

If private-equity firms really did have substantially lower WACCs than companies, they would win many more deals. In 2005, they accounted for 19% of merger and acquisitions volume in the United States and 15% in Britain. An important and growing share, but well short of 100%. And it is driven by private equity's operating advantages, not WACCs.

4. Companies should get bigger to reduce their WACC

Evidence confirms that smaller companies do have higher WACCs, but scale economies peter out before $500 million in market capitalisation is reached. The smallest market capitalisations of S&P/ASX 100 and S&P/ASX 150 companies are $2.3 billion and $1.3 billion, respectively. Scale-based WACC arguments for acquisitions are not credible for at least Australia's top 250 companies.

WACC is important. Financial engineering can sometimes create value in merger and acquisition deals. But it generally pays to be sceptical and focus on what creates value.[24]

FINANCE WORKSHOP 7.5

The target financing mix for Orange Ltd is $1 000 000 of preference shares, $5 000 000 of bonds and $20 000 000 of ordinary equity. The before-tax costs for bonds, preference shares and new ordinary share issues are 5.98, 7.9 and 15.95% respectively. What is the WACC for Orange Ltd?

Cost of capital in practice

As noted earlier in this chapter, we will use the cost of capital to determine the discount rate for the project evaluation techniques we discuss in chapter 8. Truong, Partington and Peat surveyed Australian companies to find out what financial managers do in practice. They reported that 88% of respondents use the cost of capital as the discount rate for project evaluation and that the majority of these estimated the cost of capital 'in house'.[25] Others use a combination of their own estimates and those obtained from financial institutions and analysts.

Truong, Partington and Peat found that the majority of Australian companies (72%) use the CAPM to determine the cost of equity and calculate the WACC. With respect to the weightings employed in calculating WACC, they reported that 60% use target weights while the rest use the current weights.[26] About half of the companies use weights based on market value while the other half use book value weights. As discussed in the previous section, target weights with market values are more relevant for making decisions about the future.

CAPM is used by 72% of Truong, Partington and Peat's survey respondents. The majority of companies reported that they use the return on Treasury bonds as the risk-free rate and an ERP between 5% and 8%. As we discussed earlier, there are difficulties in calculating the before-tax cost of equity from the CAPM. These difficulties are overcome in practice by ignoring any impact of imputation credits, even though the majority of respondents did think that imputation credits had some value to shareholders. Consistent with the use of the after-tax version of CAPM, the majority of companies (69%) use an after-tax cost of debt when calculating the WACC. However, in keeping with the value of imputation credits, the remaining 31% use the before-tax cost of debt.[27]

lo6

Explain the nature of capital structure and how taxation influences the capital structure choices of Australian companies.

Capital structure

Capital structure: the mix of contracted debt and equity used by a firm

So far in this chapter, we have calculated the before- and after-tax costs of the firm's long-term contracted sources of funds. We then combined these component costs in the WACC to get the complete picture of the cost of these contracted sources of funds for the firm. The weighting of each source of funds is determined by the firm's **capital structure**. Capital structure is the mix of contracted debt and equity used by a firm. Where financial structure (see page 68) includes long- and short-term funds, the capital structure excludes short-term funding.

The existing capital structure of a firm is a function of the past debt and equity raising activities. As retained earnings are included in the firm's capital structure, capital structure is also affected by profitability and dividend decisions. Recall that target weights were identified as the preferred weights for the WACC. This recommendation reflects the forward looking nature of decision making and fact that managers behave as if there is a target capital structure for the firm.

As discussed earlier, the cost of debt is usually lower than the cost of equity. If the objective of the firm is to maximise shareholder wealth by maximising the share price, could this not be achieved by a capital structure highly weighted with debt and relatively little equity? After all, the cost of debt is specified in the contracts for the debt securities issued by the firm while there is no upper limit on the returns that can be earned by the equity holders. If a firm is financed solely with equity, the returns generated by the firm are distributed proportionately to the owners. If a profitable firm is financed with debt and equity, we would expect that the equity holders would receive relatively higher returns than the debt holders. If they hold their securities to maturity, they only receive the return specified in their contracts, no matter how profitable the firm becomes. This implies that the

Financial leverage: the use of debt in a firm's capital structure to increase returns to equity holders

Debt-to-equity ratio: a measure of the proportion of debt relative to the amount of equity in the firm's capital structure

Financial risk: the risk involved in using debt as a source of finance

Financial distress: when a firm's financial obligations can not be met or can be met only with major difficulty

Optimal capital structure: the mix of contracted debt and equity that maximises the value of the firm

more debt used by a firm, the higher the returns to shareholders will be. Financial leverage is the use of debt in a firm's capital structure to increase returns to equity holders. Financial leverage is measured by the debt-to-equity ratio. As the name suggests, the debt-to-equity ratio measures the proportion of debt relative to the amount of equity in the firm's capital structure. A debt-to-equity ratio of 0.5 tells us that the firm uses twice as much equity as debt in its capital structure ($10 of debt for each $20 of equity, for example). A debt-to-equity ratio of 1 tells us that the firm uses equal amounts of debt and equity in the capital structure. We look at the debt-to-equity ratio in more detail in chapter 14.

If more debt in the capital structure means more returns to shareholders, why don't firms normally have more debt than equity in their capital structures? We define financial risk as the risk involved in using debt as a source of finance in chapter 3. More financial leverage creates higher financial risk. While the firm is not contractually bound to pay a dividend to ordinary shareholders in a period of lower than expected operating cash flows, the obligation to the holders of debt securities (including some preference shares) remains. As we see in chapter 3, a firm in this situation is facing financial distress.

Clearly, shareholders will not normally be attracted to a firm with a high probability of financial distress. While the shareholders' returns would be higher in good times, a slight downturn in operations could lead to the company being liquidated (or at least placed into receivership) and the shareholders could then lose their entire investment. To sum up the argument so far, no financial leverage would normally be associated with lower returns to shareholders and too much financial leverage would normally be associated with financial distress. This leads us to the idea that there may be some 'happy medium' where shareholders' returns are increased, but the financial risk is not too high. What amount of debt would get a company to this fortuitous position?

The optimal capital structure is the mix of contracted debt and equity that maximises the value of the firm. The optimal capital structure would include the 'right' proportion of debt to minimise WACC without decreasing the value of the firm. Maintaining the value of the firm with the lowest possible WACC is consistent with maximising shareholder value.

Unfortunately, there is no theory that adequately explains how to identify the optimal capital structure in practice. There isn't a model that can consistently identify the factors that affect capital structure choices. In addition to financial risk and the costs associated with financial distress, several other factors have been suggested as explanations for capital structure choice. These include agency costs, the firm's stage in the life cycle, the industry in which the firm operates and the relative level of profitability of the firm. An important influence of capital structure choice is the taxation environment. The impact of taxation on the capital structure of Australian firms is discussed in the next section.

Capital structure in Australian companies

Studies about the role of taxes on capital structure often use a change in the taxation system to determine how important corporate or personal tax rates are in the capital structure choices of firms. Twite examined the capital structure of Australian companies and found that the introduction of imputation resulted in:

- lower leverage
- lower retained earnings and
- relatively more new equity issues.[28]

The imputation system was designed to eliminate the double taxation of dividends. Debt enjoys a tax advantage over equity in a classical taxation system because interest payments are tax deductible, making the company's tax payments lower than they would be if equity was used instead of debt. Under the imputation system, interest payments are still tax deductible, but the less corporate tax a company pays, the lower the amount of franking credits there are to attach to dividends. If the company pays less tax by using debt, the resident shareholders have to make up the difference by paying tax on the unfranked portion of dividends. So, even though the interest tax shield remained at the corporate level, there was no benefit to resident shareholders after personal tax during the years included in Twite's study. As a result, the leverage of companies decreased. Lower debt-to-equity ratios were observed after the introduction of imputation in Canada and New Zealand.[29]

Ignoring capital gains tax for the moment, shareholders who are integrated with the dividend imputation system will prefer the company to pay as much in fully franked dividends as possible. The more a company pays in dividends, the less it can access as internally generated funds. Twite found that the level of retained earnings did decrease after the introduction of imputation. Companies that are using relatively less debt (lower leverage) and less internal funds (lower retained earnings) will need to raise capital by issuing new shares. Twite found that this was the case. He also reported that Australian companies generating income that is taxed overseas did not decrease their leverage as much as companies paying only Australian tax. Taken together, these results are consistent with personal taxes exerting a strong influence over the capital structure choices of Australian companies.

Resident shareholders will prefer the company to retain unfranked dividends when the tax rate on capital gains is lower than the tax rate on dividends. Capital gains tax is currently applied at the shareholder's marginal tax rate on half of the notional capital gain. If a shareholder had the choice of $100 paid as an unfranked dividend (and paying tax of $30 if the marginal tax rate is 30%) or taking a $100 capital gain (and paying tax of $15), he or she would be in a better after-tax position if the capital gain was chosen. This makes the retention of unfranked dividends attractive to resident shareholders and we would expect to see a relationship between the level of retained earnings and the proportion of income taxed overseas.

lo7

Apply the EBIT–EPS technique to evaluate changes in capital structure and explain the limitations of this technique.

Evaluating changes in capital structure

From our discussion so far, we can conclude that capital structure is relevant to the value of the firm (or at least management and investors behave as if it is). The relative attractiveness of debt and equity to the issuing firm is influenced by corporate and personal taxation regimes and the potential direct and indirect costs of bankruptcy. Agency theory suggests capital structures will be influenced by the desire to reduce costs arising from managers acting in their own (or the shareholders, in the case of debt) best interests. The pecking order hypothesis, based on information asymmetries, suggests that capital structure will be the result of managers' preferences for using firstly retained earnings, then debt, followed by new equity issues in a classical tax system. The life cycle approach modifies the pecking order hypothesis by suggesting that the firm's maturity will influence capital structure. Studies that investigate the observed capital structure of firms have been unable to clarify which of the theories of capital structure best explains how capital structure choices are made in firms. These studies have found that other factors, not included in the main theories, affect capital structure decisions. Thus, the question of which capital structure is optimal for a firm remains unanswered.

Graham and Harvey[30] surveyed CEOs in the United States and found that earnings per share (EPS) dilution was an important factor when assessing a new share issue as a source of funds. You learn in chapter 6 that EPS is the total earnings of the firm divided by the number of shares on issue. If earnings are expected to remain at a constant level, issuing new shares will reduce the amount of EPS. This reduction in EPS is called **dilution**. Example 7.15 shows how more shares on issue result in EPS dilution.

Dilution: the decrease in the proportion of income each share is entitled to

EXAMPLE 7.15

EPS dilution

Lummox Ltd has 2 million shares trading at $1 each on the ASX. The company has no debt. Earnings last year were $500 000. Lummox wants to purchase a property for an investment project that will begin generating cash inflows 1 year from now. The property costs $1 million and new shares can be sold at $1 each. (We will ignore transaction costs and, therefore, net proceeds in this example to keep it simple.) What is the impact of the new share issue on EPS?

$$\text{Current EPS} = \frac{\text{earnings}}{\text{number of ordinary shares}}$$

$$\text{EPS} = \frac{500\,000}{2\,000\,000}$$

$$= 0.25 \text{ or 25 cents per share}$$

$$\text{New EPS} = \frac{500\,000}{3\,000\,000}$$

$$= 0.1667 \text{ or 17 cents per share}$$

Thus, current investors in Lummox will find that EPS has fallen from 25 cents to 17 cents. This is really attributable to the ownership interest of the shareholder being diluted. If a shareholder does not participate in the new share issue, their proportional ownership of the firm will fall and they will be entitled to a smaller share of the earnings. If a shareholder currently owns 10% of the shares on issue and purchases 10% of the new shares that will be issued, they will still be entitled to the same proportion of earnings on their ownership stake. However, the EPS represents an earnings entitlement per share, not on the proportion of the company owned, so it will decrease when new shares are issued even if earnings remain the same.

EBIT–EPS analysis

Investors are interested in the firm's past and future EPS amounts. The historic or most recent EPS is often discussed in the financial press. Analysts forecast EPS to value companies and put their forecasts in the recommendations they make when giving investment advice. As we see in chapter 15, EPS is often reported in financial statements. It makes sense to evaluate the impact of a capital structure change on EPS, given that the market is so interested in this particular figure.

EBIT–EPS analysis: relates earnings before interest and tax to the after-tax income entitlement of each ordinary share

We use a technique called EBIT–EPS analysis to do this. **EBIT–EPS analysis** relates earnings before interest and tax to the after-tax income entitlement of each ordinary share. EBIT–EPS analysis relies on the existence of a tax advantage to debt, so is most appropriate in a classical taxation system or where shareholders are not integrated with the imputation system. Example 7.16 shows the impact on EPS of a change in capital structure.

EXAMPLE 7.16

EPS and capital structure change

The board of Multimax is considering issuing new equity to repay all of the firm's debt. The company currently has 5 million shares on issue trading at $2 and could issue new shares for this amount (ignore flotation costs). Debt is currently $600 000 and interest charges are 10% pa. The company is owned by investors who are unable to benefit from dividend franking and it generates an annual EBIT of $2 000 000. What would happen to Multimax's EPS if the new equity issue and debt repayment went ahead?

	Current capital structure	Proposed capital structure
Debt at 10% interest	600 000	0
Ordinary shares	10 000 000	10 600 000
Total debt and equity	10 600 000	10 600 000
Number of ordinary shares issued	5 000 000	5 300 000
EBIT	2 000 000	2 000 000
Less: interest expense	60 000	0
Earnings before tax (EBT)	1 940 000	2 000 000
Less: tax at 30%	582 000	600 000
Net income available to ordinary shareholders	1 358 000	1 400 000
EPS	0.2716	0.2642

The number of ordinary shares under the proposed capital structure is calculated as the amount of debt to be retired ($600 000) divided by the amount raised for each new share ($2) plus the existing number of shares on issue (5 000 000), so is 5 300 000. Notice that the total amount of funds used by the firm is unchanged because we are looking at a restructure rather than raising additional funds. Interest expense is calculated as the annual interest rate (10%) times the amount of debt outstanding ($600 000).

EPS is calculated as the net income available to ordinary shareholders divided by the number of shares issued. The EPS for the proposed capital structure is 26 cents, a decrease of 1 cent per share from current capital structure. Investors who have a negative reaction to this change have not considered the decreased risk of the firm with the new capital structure. By repaying the debt, Multimax has eliminated the financial risk of the firm and the shareholders will now be faced only with business risk.

Now you have an idea of how EBIT–EPS analysis works, we can use this technique to assess the impact of raising new funds to invest in positive NPV projects. The analysis is basically the same as the one we used in example 7.16, but we change the level of EBIT based on the expected impact of the adoption of new projects and compare the alternatives of debt and equity as the source of funds for the new project.

EXAMPLE 7.17

EBIT–EPS analysis and choice of capital structure

Lummox Ltd has 2 million shares trading at $1 each on the ASX. The company has no debt. Earnings last year were $500 000 and the current projects of the firm are expected to continue this level of earnings indefinitely. Lummox wants to raise $1 million for a new project that is expected to increase EBIT by $300 000 pa for the foreseeable future. The company can issue new ordinary shares and net $1 per share. Alternatively, the funds can be raised by issuing bonds with an annual coupon of 10%. Show the impact of the financing choice on Lummox's EPS.

	Capital structure		
	Current	New equity	New debt
Debt at 10% interest	0		1 000 000
Ordinary shares	2 000 000	3 000 000	2 000 000
Total debt and equity	2 000 000	3 000 000	3 000 000
Number of ordinary shares issued	2 000 000	3 000 000	2 000 000
EBIT	500 000	800 000	800 000
Less: interest expense	0	00	100 000
Earnings before tax (EBT)	500 000	800 000	700 000
Less: tax at 30%	150 000	240 000	210 000
Net income available to ordinary shareholders	350 000	560 000	490 000
EPS	0.1750	0.1867	0.2450

EPS rises from 18 cents to 19 cents if Lummox uses equity to finance the new project. Using equity means there is no interest tax shield from debt, so the increase is attributable to the relatively higher EBIT that is generated by the new project compared to the existing projects of the firm. The gain from leverage is a further 6 cents per share (that is, 25 – 19) if Lummox chooses debt finance. Remember, though, that this higher EPS is achieved by taking on financial risk.

Existing debt and preference shares should be taken into consideration when doing an EBIT–EPS analysis. Interest payments must be made on existing debt unless the debt is repaid and preference share dividends are a fixed cost that reduces the amount of income that is attributable to ordinary shareholders. In addition to a very simple capital structure, example 7.17 assumed that the new level of EBIT was certain. As we see in chapter 5, the future is uncertain. While the $300 000 increase in EBIT for Lummox might be the expected value of the new project, the actual level of EBIT could be higher or lower than this. Example 7.18 shows how existing debt and preference shares are incorporated into EBIT–EPS analysis and the following finance workshop shows the impact on EPS of EBIT that is higher or lower than expected.

EXAMPLE 7.18

EBIT–EPS analysis with existing debt and preference shares

Swimmingly Ltd operates aquatic fun centres in a number of cities. The company has decided to build another centre that is expected to generate a permanent increase in EBIT of $100 000 pa. Current EBIT is $350 000. Swimmingly currently has a capital structure that utilises bonds, ordinary equity and preference shares. The $200 000 of issued bonds pay 8% pa. Preference shares pay an annual fixed dividend of $150 000. 500 000 ordinary shares have been issued and are trading at $2 per share.

Swimmingly needs to raise $500 000 to construct the new aquatic centre. Assuming the company can issue new shares at the current market price, what is the impact on EPS if new shares are issued to fund the centre? If new debt can be raised at a 10% interest rate, what is the impact on EPS of using debt rather than a new equity issue?

	Capital structure		
	Current	New equity	New debt
Debt at 10% interest			500 000
Debt at 8% interest	200 000	200 000	200 000
Ordinary shares	500 000	1 000 000	500 000
Total debt and equity	700 000	1 200 000	1 200 000
Number of new shares issued		250 000	
Total number of ordinary shares issued	250 000	500 000	250 000
EBIT	350 000	450 000	450 000
Less: interest expense	16 000	16 000	66 000
Earnings before tax (EBT)	334 000	434 000	384 000
Less: tax at 30%	100 200	130 200	115 200
Net income (NI)	233 800	303 800	268 800
Less: preference dividend	150 000	150 000	150 000
NI available to ordinary shareholders	83 800	153 800	118 800
EPS	0.3352	0.3076	0.4752

Interest expense is the total of the interest charged on the existing debt plus the new debt raised under the debt financing plan. Preference share dividends are not tax deductible, so they reduce the amount of after-tax net income that is available for distribution to ordinary shareholders.

FINANCE WORKSHOP 7.6

Swimmingly Ltd depends on fine and hot summer weather to generate its expected EBIT. Use the information about Swimmingly Ltd in example 7.18 and the two possible outcomes outlined below to calculate the impact of the debt and equity financing alternatives if:

(a) future summers are especially hot with only a few rainy days and the new aquatic centre will increase EBIT by $150 000

(b) future summers are relatively short and cool and it rains for most of the time. In this case EBIT will fall to $320 000.

Your results from finance workshop 7.6 should show that poor weather will cause EPS to fall from the current level for both financing alternatives. However, the EPS under the equity financing plan in this case is higher than that for the debt plan. You will also notice that the EBIT for good summers results in the debt financing plan giving the highest EPS. Somewhere between these two EBIT extremes lies a point where EPS is equal for both financing alternatives. This is called the **indifference point** and it identifies the intersection of the linear representation of the debt and equity.

Indifference point: the level of EBIT that generates the same EPS for all financing alternatives under consideration

The indifference point for EBIT–EPS analysis is found using the following equation.

$$\overset{\textbf{EPS for plan 1}}{\frac{(EBIT - I)(1 - t_c) - DP}{\text{number of shares}_1}} = \overset{\textbf{EPS for plan 2}}{\frac{(EBIT - I)(1 - t_c) - DP}{\text{number of shares}_2}} \qquad [7.16]$$

where $EBIT$ = earnings before interest and tax

I = annual interest payment in dollars

t_c = company tax rate

DP = preference share dividend

Each side of equation 7.16 calculates the EPS for a proposed capital structure in the same way we calculated it in the previous examples. Example 7.19 shows the application of equation 7.16 to the capital structure choice faced by Swimmingly Ltd from example 7.18.

EXAMPLE 7.19

EPS indifference point

$$\begin{array}{ccc} \text{EPS — new equity} & & \text{EPS — new debt} \end{array}$$

$$\frac{(EBIT-16000)(1-0.3)-150000}{500000}=\frac{(EBIT-66000)(1-0.3)-150000}{250000}$$

$$\frac{0.7EBIT-11200-150000}{500000}=\frac{0.7EBIT-46200-150000}{250000}$$

$$0.7EBIT - 161\,200 = 2(0.7EBIT - 196\,200)$$

$$2(196\,200) - 161\,200 = 1.4EBIT - 0.7EBIT$$

$$231\,200 = 0.7EBIT$$

$$EBIT = 330\,286$$

The indifference point tells us that if EBIT is \$330 286, EPS will be equal under either financing plan. The EPS at the indifference point is 14c. You can calculate this for yourself by changing the EBIT in finance workshop 7.6 to \$330 286 in either the debt or equity fundraising proposals.

For EBIT lower than any given indifference point, the equity plan will generate higher EPS. For EBIT higher than the indifference point, the plan that uses debt will have the higher EPS. Look at your calculations for the Swimmingly Ltd finance workshop to satisfy yourself that this is correct. The relationship between the indifference point and the preference for either a debt or equity plan will always hold.

Limitations of EBIT–EPS analysis

EBIT–EPS analysis is not appropriate when shareholders are fully integrated with a dividend imputation tax system. Shareholders are interested in after-personal-tax returns and the corporate interest tax shield from debt does not provide benefits for shareholders who can fully utilise imputation credits. Even under a classical taxation system, EBIT–EPS analysis has the following disadvantages:

- higher EPS from increasing leverage does not take the increased financial risk into consideration
- higher leverage will lead to shareholders having higher required returns, so new shares need to be issued at a relatively lower price when more debt is used by the firm
- as we see in chapter 5, the variability of returns is an indication of risk. EBIT–EPS analysis ignores the variability of EBIT and focuses solely on the size of EBIT

- maximising EPS is not consistent with maximising shareholder wealth (as we see in chapter 1).

Taken together, these limitations mean that EBIT–EPS analysis should not be the only consideration in the choice of capital structure. If it were, capital structure changes that increased leverage would almost always be preferred to issuing new equity. We would expect sophisticated investors to be looking for increases in EPS that were attributable to growth in the firm and that these investors would not be impressed by EPS increases that came only from changes in capital structure. However, if financial managers think that shareholders are less rational and will be impressed by changes in EPS without considering the additional risk attached, EBIT–EPS analysis can have a role to play. We consider EPS further in chapter 15.

CORPORATE FINANCIAL GOVERNANCE

The cost of capital

We discuss the relative importance of corporate governance issues to share value in chapter 6 and conclude that the corporate governance issues rated by investors were unlikely to have a significant impact on the valuation of a company's shares. Linden and Matolcsy investigated the role of corporate governance ratings in determining share market returns and reported no association between the quality of corporate governance and return for Australian firms.[31] Using a different index for rating corporate governance. Matolcsy, Stokes and Wright found that a larger number of independent directors on the boards of Australian companies is not normally associated with higher values for equity (so it won't impact on the cost of capital).[32]

Another aspect of good corporate governance is the frequency and quality of information that is disclosed to the market. Beekes and Brown reported that better governed firms make more disclosures to shareholders via the ASX.[33] This aspect of corporate governance does have the capacity to influence share prices and the cost of equity capital because investors use information to value a company's shares. The first corporate governance disclosures required by the ASX were for listed companies to indicate the corporate governance principles they followed during the reporting period. Collett and Hrasky examined the corporate governance disclosure choices of Australian companies prior to the introduction of this requirement. They reported that only 10% of the top 300 Australian companies made any voluntary corporate governance disclosures.[34] They also found that voluntary disclosure is associated with the company's intention to raise equity capital during the period after this disclosure. This implies that company directors and managers think disclosure about corporate governance is important to investors considering the decision to participate in new equity issues.

executive summary

lo1 explain the concept of the firm's cost of capital

- The cost of capital is the link between the company's investment decisions and its value.
- It is the minimum rate of return on the firm's investments that will compensate the suppliers of capital to the firm.
- It is primarily used to assess project proposals and the performance of the firm.
- It is a composite measure that includes the cost of each component (that is, debt, preference shares and ordinary equity) of financing used by the firm.
- Acceptance of a proposed project that generates a higher return than the cost of capital will increase the value of the firm. If the project has a lower expected return than the cost of capital, it will reduce firm value if accepted.
- The marginal cost of a particular source of capital is the cost associated with raising the next dollar of funding from that source.
- The marginal cost of capital is the relevant cost for making decisions about future investments.

lo2 explain the impact of the taxation system on the cost of capital

- Under dividend imputation, dividends are taxed only once in the hands of the company's shareholders.
- Resident shareholders live (and pay tax) in the same country as the company paying the dividends. They gain the full value of imputation credits.
- Foreign shareholders live (and pay tax) in a different country from that of the company paying the dividends. They may not gain any value from receiving imputation credits.
- Rational investors assess their returns on an after-personal-tax basis.
- The cost of equity should decrease when companies owned by resident shareholders pay fully franked dividends.
- Australian resident shareholders, complying superannuation and approved deposit funds, pooled superannuation trusts and endorsed tax-exempt charities can fully utilise imputation credits because they receive a refund of excess credits from the ATO. The component costs of capital should be calculated on a before-corporate-tax basis when a company is owned by these investors.
- The component costs of capital should be calculated on an after-tax basis if the company does not pay dividends, or is owned by foreign investors, or the business is structured as a partnership or sole trader.
- The cost of capital should include all permanent sources of funding used by the firm.

lo3 calculate the before- and after-tax component costs for bonds, preference shares and ordinary equity

- The marginal cost of each source of funding includes the costs associated with raising the funds.
- Issue costs are the costs associated with bringing an issue of securities to the market.
- Net proceeds are the amount of cash received from investors minus any costs associated with the issue.

- The cost of debt is the level of return that must be generated in order to meet the required return of debtholders.
- The internal rate of return is the discount rate that makes the present value of future cash flows equal to the net cash outlay.
- Three methods of estimating the cost of debt are interpolation, using the approximate cost of debt equation, and using a spreadsheet or financial calculator to calculate the internal rate of return.
- Given a non-zero marginal tax rate, the after-corporate-tax cost of debt is always lower than the before-corporate-tax cost of debt.
- The cost of preference shares is the level of return that must be generated in order to meet the required return of preference shareholders.
- Dividends are grossed up to reflect the value of imputation credits when calculating the before-tax cost of preference and ordinary equity.
- The cost of ordinary equity is the level of return that must be generated in order to meet the required return of the ordinary shareholders.
- Retained earnings represent the accumulated profit of the company that has not been paid out to shareholders as dividends.
- The cost of retained earnings is the required return of ordinary shareholders on shares that have already been issued.
- The cost of ordinary shares is the required return of shareholders on a new issue.

lo4 explain how the shareholders' capacity to utilise imputation credits affects the cost of capital

- Foreign investors who receive imputation credits are not liable for withholding tax. Most do not receive a rebate from their local tax office in recognition of the receipt of franked dividends. Nor do they receive a cash rebate from the ATO.
- Foreign investors are more likely to invest in large Australian companies. For these companies, the cost of capital should be calculated on an after-tax basis.
- For smaller companies, the marginal investor is likely to be a resident shareholder. For these companies, the cost of capital should be calculated on a before-tax basis.

lo5 calculate the weighted-average cost of capital

- The weighted-average cost of capital (WACC) is the sum of each component cost of capital weighted by each component cost's proportion of the firm's capital structure.
- Projects should be assessed using WACC rather than the cost of the individual source of finance that was used to obtain funds.
- Book value is the historic dollar amount shown in the balance sheet.
- Weights based on current market values are superior to those based on historic values.
- Target weights are based on management's future plans for financing the company's operations. They provide the optimal weighting system.
- The weighted average cost of capital should be recalculated to reflect a change in one or more of the component costs.

lo6 explain the nature of capital structure and how taxation influences the capital structure choices of Australian companies

- Capital structure is the mix of contracted debt and equity used by a firm.
- The firm's current capital structure is determined by its past debt and equity raising.
- Financial leverage is the use of debt in a firm's capital structure to increase returns to equity holders.
- Debt-to-equity ratio measures the proportion of debt relative to the amount of equity in the firm's capital structure.
- Leverage increases returns to shareholders, but also increases financial risk.
- Financial risk is the risk involved in using debt as a source of finance.
- Financial distress occurs when a firm's financial obligations can not be met or can be met only with major difficulty.
- The optimal capital structure is the mix of contracted debt and equity that maximises the value of the firm.
- While it is not possible to empirically identify the optimal capital structure, the behaviour of managers suggests they aim for some 'target' capital structure.
- The introduction of the imputation system resulted in companies having lower leverage, lower retained earnings and relatively more new equity issues.
- The extent to which leverage decreased after the introduction of imputation was related to the amount of Australian tax paid by the company.

lo7 apply the EBIT–EPS technique to evaluate changes in capital structure and explain the limitations of this technique

- EPS dilution has been identified as a factor financial managers consider when making the choice to issue new equity. The market uses EPS in valuation decisions.
- EBIT–EPS analysis relates earnings before interest and tax to the after-tax income entitlement of each ordinary share.
- The indifference point is the level of EBIT that generates the same EPS for all financing alternatives under consideration.
- For EBIT lower than any given indifference point, the equity plan will generate higher EPS. For EBIT higher than the indifference point, the plan that uses debt will have the higher EPS.
- EBIT–EPS analysis is not appropriate when shareholders can fully utilise dividend imputation credits. Other limitations are that it ignores increases in financial risk, does not consider the change in shareholders' required return as leverage increases and it ignores the variability of EBIT.

Key terms

book value, p. 237
capital structure, p. 240
cost of capital, p. 213
cost of debt, p. 217
cost of ordinary equity, p. 227
cost of ordinary shares, p. 230
cost of preference shares, p. 225
cost of retained earnings, p. 228
debt-to-equity ratio, p. 241
dilution, p. 242
dividend payout ratio, p. 215
EBIT–EPS analysis, p. 243
financial distress, p. 241

financial leverage, p. 241
financial risk, p. 241
foreign shareholders, p. 214
indifference point, p. 246
internal rate of return, p. 218
interpolation, p. 218
issue costs, p. 216
marginal cost, p. 214
net proceeds, p. 216
optimal capital structure, p. 241
resident shareholders, p. 214
retained earnings, p. 227
target weights, p. 237
weighted-average cost of capital, p. 235

Learning chart

Learning objective	Questions	Self-test problems	Financial problems
lo1 explain the concept of the firm's cost of capital	7.1, 7.2, 7.3,		7.15
lo2 explain the impact of the taxation system on the cost of capital	7.4, 7.5, 7.6, 7.7, 7.8		
lo3 calculate the before- and after-tax component costs for bonds, preference shares and ordinary equity	7.9, 7.10, 7.11, 7.12, 7.13, 7.14, 7.15, 7.16	7.1, 7.2, 7.3, 7.4, 7.5	7.1, 7.2, 7.3, 7.4, 7.5, 7.6, 7.7, 7.8, 7.9, 7.10, 7.11, 7.12, 7.13, 7.14, 7.15, 7.16, 7.17
lo4 explain how the shareholders' capacity to utilise imputation credits affects the cost of capital	7.17		7.9, 7.12, 7.13, 7.15, 7.16, 7.17
lo5 calculate the weighted-average cost of capital	7.18, 7.19		7.12, 7.13, 7.14, 7.15, 7.16, 7.17
lo6 explain the nature of capital structure and how taxation influences the capital structure choices of Australian companies	7.20, 7.21, 7.22, 7.23		
lo7 apply the EBIT–EPS technique to evaluate changes in capital structure and explain the limitations of this technique	7.24	7.6	7.18

Questions

7.1 Explain the relationship between the cost of capital and the value of the firm.

7.2 What are marginal costs?

7.3 Why is the marginal cost of capital more relevant to making investment decisions than the historic cost of capital?

7.4 What basic distinction can be made between resident investors and foreign investors with respect to Australian taxation?

7.5 Do rational investors focus on before- or after-tax returns? Why?

7.6 What benefits do resident shareholders gain from receiving fully franked dividends?

7.7 Why don't most foreign investors benefit from receiving fully franked dividends?

7.8 Under which circumstances should a firm use the after-tax cost of capital?

7.9 What are issue costs? Give some examples of the sources of issue costs.

7.10 Explain the term 'net proceeds'. Explain how the use of net proceeds affects the calculation of a component cost.

7.11 Why would the debtholders of a company have a lower required rate of return than the shareholders of that same company?

7.12 Outline three methods that can be used to calculate the cost of debt. Which method would give you the most exact cost and which is the easiest to use?

7.13 What is the relationship between equation 7.6 (cost of a preference share) and the preference share valuation equation from chapter 6?

7.14 Can you use equations 7.6 and 7.7 to calculate the cost of all preference shares? Why or why not?

7.15 Define the cost of equity. Why do we separate the cost of equity into the cost of retained earnings and the cost of ordinary shares?

7.16 Explain how and why calculating the cost of retained earnings is different to calculating the cost of ordinary shares.

7.17 What is the implication for the calculation of the cost of capital if the marginal shareholder is:

(a) an Australian resident

(b) a foreign investor?

7.18 A proposed project will be financed by a new issue of ordinary shares. The marginal cost of ordinary equity is 15%. Is the marginal cost of ordinary equity the appropriate benchmark for assessing this project? What would you recommend?

7.19 Why are target financing structures considered more appropriate for weighting WACC than historic weights?

7.20 What is capital structure and how does it relate to the cost of capital?

7.21 Explain how increasing the proportion of debt in the firm's capital structure can increase returns to shareholders. Given this relationship, how can increasing the proportion of debt increase the required returns of shareholders?

7.22 What is meant by the term 'optimal capital structure'? How do you calculate the optimal capital structure for a firm?

7.23 What changes were observed in the capital structures of Australian companies after the introduction of dividend imputation?

7.24 What is EBIT–EPS analysis? When would it be appropriate to make capital structure decisions based on EBIT–EPS analysis?

Self-test problems

7.1 Tsunami Ltd is planning an issue of ordinary shares. Management have discussed the issue price per share with their sponsoring broker and underwriter and have decided to offer the shares at $0.80 each. They have also discussed the fees the company will be charged to get the offer to the market. The flotation costs will be 6.2% of the issue price. What will Tsunami's net proceeds per share be?

7.2 Typhoon Ltd is planning an issue of preference shares. The shares will be sold for $10 each and will pay an annual unfranked dividend of $1. Typhoon expects that most of the shareholders will be living in Asia. If flotation costs are $0.40 per share and the corporate tax rate is 30%, what is the cost of the new issue of preference shares?

7.3 Monsoon Ltd wants to raise $10 million in a bond issue. The face value of each bond will be $100 and it will be paying an annual coupon of 7% for 5 years. The offer price set in the prospectus is $90 per bond. Issue costs are estimated at 4.5%. The company is owned by Australian resident investors and the corporate rate of tax is 30%. Use the approximate cost of debt equation to determine the appropriate cost of debt for Monsoon.

7.4 Recalculate the cost of Monsoon's bond issue (described in problem 7.3) assuming that half of the shareholders are foreign investors.

7.5 Hurricane Ltd shares are currently trading at $7.70. Annual dividends are paid and these are expected to grow at 2% indefinitely. A fully franked dividend of $0.35 was paid yesterday and the corporate tax rate is 30%. What are the before- and after-tax costs of retained earnings for Hurricane?

7.6 Booyashaka Ltd has 3 million shares trading at $2.50 each on the ASX. The company has no debt at this point in time. Earnings last year were $1.5 million. Booyashaka wants to raise $1 million to invest in a project that will increase earnings to $1.6 million. Assuming that new shares can be issued at the current market price, what is the impact of the new issue on EPS?

Solutions to self-test problems

7.1 $NP = P_i(1 - f)$

$NP = 0.80\,(1 - 0.062)$

$= 0.80\,(0.938)$

$= \$0.75$

7.2 $NP = P\,(1 - f)$

$NP = 10 - 0.40$

$= \$9.60$

We use the after-tax calculation as the dividends will be unfranked and most of the shareholders are foreign investors.

$$k_{p,\,at} = \frac{D}{NP_P}$$

$$k_{p,\,at} = \frac{1}{9.60}$$

$$= 10.4167\%$$

7.3 $$k_{z,bt} \cong \frac{I + \dfrac{(F - NP_b)}{n}}{\dfrac{(F + NP_b)}{2}}$$

$$k_{z,bt} \cong \frac{(0.07 \times 100) + \dfrac{\{100 - [90 \times (1 - 0.045)]\}}{5}}{\dfrac{\{100 + [90 \times (1 - 0.045)]\}}{2}}$$

$$\cong \frac{9.81}{92.975}$$

$$\cong 0.1055 \text{ or } 10.55\%$$

7.4 As half of the shareholders are foreign investors, the marginal investor will be an overseas resident. Therefore, the after-tax cost is relevant.

$$k_{d,at} = k_{d,bt}\,(1 - \text{t})$$

$$k_{d,at} = 0.1055\,(1 - 0.30)$$

$$= 0.0739 \text{ or } 7.39\%$$

7.5 $$k_{re,\,at} = \frac{D_1}{P_0} + g$$

$$k_{re,\,at} = \frac{0.35 \times (1 + 0.02)}{7.70} + 0.02$$

$$= 6.6363\%$$

$$k_{re,\,bt} = \frac{\dfrac{D_1}{(1 - t_c)}}{P_0} + g$$

$$k_{re,\,bt} = \frac{\dfrac{0.35(1 + 0.02)}{(1 - 0.30)}}{7.70} + 0.02$$

$$= \frac{\dfrac{0.357}{0.7}}{7.70} + 0.02$$

$$= \frac{0.51}{7.70} + 0.02$$

$$= 8.6238\%$$

7.6 $$\text{Current EPS} = \frac{\text{earnings}}{\text{number of ordinary shares}}$$

$$= \frac{1\,500\,000}{3\,000\,000}$$

$$= 0.5 \text{ or 50 cents per share}$$

$$\text{New EPS} = \frac{1\,600\,000}{3\,400\,000}$$

$$= 0.47 \text{ or 47 cents per share}$$

Financial problems

7.1 A zero coupon bond has a face value of $100 and 10 years to maturity. Interest accrues on the bond annually. The net proceeds of the bond are $47.60. Use the trial and error method to determine the before- and after-tax costs of a zero coupon bond.

7.2 Use the approximate cost of debt equation to determine the before- and after-tax costs of the zero coupon bond described in problem 7.1.

7.3 Peenque Ltd is planning to issue bonds with 4 years to maturity and a face value of $100. The coupon rate of the bonds is 6.5% and coupons are paid annually. Peenque expects the net proceeds from each bond issued to be $95. Given the tax rate is 30%, determine the before- and after-tax cost of debt using either the trial and error method or by calculating the IRR.

7.4 Use the approximate cost of debt equation to determine the before- and after-tax costs of the bonds issued by Peenque Ltd in problem 7.3.

7.5 Currently, Agapanthus Industries Ltd can sell 10-year, $100 face value bonds with a 12% pa coupon, paid semi-annually. The bonds can be sold for $105 each. Flotation costs of $2.50 per bond will be charged by the underwriter handling the issue. The corporate tax rate is 30 per cent.

(a) Find the net proceeds from the sale of the bond.

(b) Use the approximation formula to estimate the before- and after-tax cost of debt.

7.6 Conrod Ltd is planning the issue of preference shares at an offer price of $80 per share. Dividend payments of $8 will be made annually and they will be fully franked. Flotation costs are estimated at 5.5% of offer price. What are the before- and after-tax costs of preference shares for Conrod?

7.7 Cashcow Co. has $3 million in retained earnings. Cashcow shares have a market value of $9.50 each. Fully franked dividends are paid annually. The next dividend of $1.50 is due in 12 months. New shares could be issued to raise net proceeds of $8.90 per share. Cashcow has a growth rate of 2.5% per annum and this rate is expected to continue for the foreseeable future. Given a tax rate of 30%, what are the before- and after-tax costs of retained earnings?

7.8 Use the information in problem 7.7 to complete the following.

(a) Assuming Cashcow is owned by Australian resident shareholders, what is the appropriate cost of a new share issue?

(b) Assuming Cashcow has a substantial proportion of foreign shareholders, what is the appropriate cost of a new share issue?

7.9 The ordinary shares of Firgold Ltd are currently trading at $2.60. A new share issue would be made at an offer price of $2.50. Issue costs are expected to be 5% of the proceeds of the issue. The last dividend was 27c and the next dividend is due a year from now. Dividends are fully franked. The estimated growth rate is 1.5% per annum and this rate is expected to continue. The corporate tax rate is 30%.

(a) Assuming Firgold is owned by Australian resident shareholders, calculate the appropriate costs of retained earnings and a new share issue.

(b) Now assume that the marginal investor in Firgold is a foreign shareholder. What impact does this have on the appropriate cost of retained earnings and a new share issue? Show calculations to support your answer.

7.10 The equity risk premium is expected to be 4.5%. Use the CAPM to estimate the cost of equity for Croesus Ltd with a beta of 1.79 if the risk free rate is:

(a) 4.3%

(b) 6.7%

(c) Are the costs you have calculated before- or after-tax costs? Explain.

7.11 Monty Ltd's ordinary shares are currently selling for $9.60. The firm pays annual dividends and expects the next one to be $0.97. After flotation costs, the firm expects to net $9.27 per share on a new issue. Dividends are expected to grow at 1.25% for the foreseeable future.

(a) Determine the before- and after-tax cost of retained earnings.

(b) Determine the before-and after-tax cost of a new issue.

7.12 The target financing mix for Grape Ltd is 8% preference shares, 32% debt (half bonds and half leases) and 60% ordinary equity. Grape Ltd does not have retained earnings available as a source of funds. The before- and after-tax component costs are as follows:

Source of funding	Before-tax cost %	After-tax cost %
Leases	9.5	6.65
Bonds	11.0	7.7
Preference shares	12.5	8.5
Ordinary shares	15.0	10.9

Calculate the WACC for Grape Ltd under the assumption that:

(a) Fully franked dividends are paid and the company is owned by Australian resident shareholders.

(b) Partially franked dividends are paid and the marginal investor in the company does not live in Australia.

7.13 Given a 30% corporate tax rate and the following information for Pitosporum Ltd:

- 10 000 bonds with a face value of $100, a coupon rate of 12%, an issue price of $92.30, and 5 years to maturity. Coupons are paid semi-annually. Use the approximate cost of debt method.
- 70 000 11% preference shares with a face value of $2 and net proceeds of $1.86.
- 500 000 ordinary shares with an issue price of $3.00, dividend growth rate 1% pa in perpetuity. The last dividend was $0.15 and the next dividend is due in about 1 year. Flotation costs will be 3.5% of the issue price.

(a) Calculate the cost of each source of finance if the marginal investor is an Australian resident who can fully utilise imputation credits. Using the weightings associated with issuing the proposed amount of each security, calculate the weighted average cost of capital.

(b) Calculate the cost of each source of finance if the marginal investor is an overseas resident. Using the weightings associated with issuing the proposed amount of each security, calculate the weighted average cost of capital.

7.14 Hydromat Ltd is interested in calculating its weighted average cost of capital and has presented you with the following data:

- $600 000 can be borrowed from the bank for a term of 10 years. The bank will charge Hydromat an annual effective rate of 13% pa.

- Preference shares have a market price of $8 and pay an annual dividend per share of $0.75. Flotation costs will be 3.9% of the issue price of $7.90.
- The firm has $500 000 of retained earnings available for investments.
- Hydromat's ordinary shares have a market value of $7.50 per share. The next dividend is expected to be $0.75. The current growth rate of 0.5% is expected to continue indefinitely. Flotation costs will be 2.8% for shares issued at $7.25 each.
- The corporate tax rate is 30%.
- The target capital structure is as follows:

Source	Weight
Long-term debt	40%
Preference shares	20%
Ordinary shares	40%

(a) Calculate the before- and after-tax WACC assuming no new ordinary shares will be issued.

(b) Calculate the before- and after-tax WACC assuming no retained earnings are available for investing in new projects.

7.15 Hotcakes Ltd is the Australian subsidiary of a large French company. Most of the shareholders are overseas residents who cannot utilise imputation credits. The company has identified the following projects as potential investments:

Project	Cost	IRR (at)
I	$3 000 000	10%
II	$4 000 000	13%
III	$4 750 000	11%
IV	$2 900 000	15%
V	$1 950 000	16%
VI	$3 500 000	9%

The firm's current capital structure (as well as its targeted future capital structure) consists of 40% long-term debt, 5% preference shares and 55% ordinary shares. The following data have been gathered in relation to each of these sources of finance:

- Hotcakes can raise $5 million in long-term debt at a before-tax cost of 15%.
- Preference shares can be sold at an after-tax cost of 10%.
- Hotcakes do not expect to have any retained earnings available for new investments in the coming year. The last annual dividend of $3.50 per share was paid recently. A new issue would be priced at $27, with flotation costs of $0.75 per share. The average dividend growth rate in recent years has been 1.5% pa and this growth rate is expected to continue for the foreseeable future.
- The corporate tax rate is 30%.

(a) Calculate the appropriate WACC for Hotcakes Ltd to use when evaluating new projects.

(b) Recommend which projects Hotcakes should accept.

7.16 In your position of CFO at Fantasy Fabrics Ltd, it is your job to recommend which investments the company should make. The investment alternatives are listed.

Investment	Initial outlay ($)	IRR before tax (%)	IRR after tax (%)
Cutting machine	120 000	9	8
Computer system	50 000	8.5	7
Premises upgrade	750 000	11	10
Automated loom	345 000	16.5	15
Bleaching vats	80 000	15	13

Fantasy Fabrics' current capital structure consists of the following:

Source of finance	Amount of finance ($)
Debt	900 000
Preference shares	525 000
Ordinary equity (including retained earnings)	900 000

The board have specified this pattern of funding as the target capital mix. To raise additional debt, Fantasy Fabrics would issue bonds with a face value of $1000. The coupon rate on the bonds would be 4% and interest would be paid annually. The bonds would mature in 10 years' time. Issue costs are 1.5% of the face value. Use the approximate cost of debt equation to calculate the cost of debt.

A new offering of preference shares would have issue costs of 3.5%. The preference shares are trading at $4.50 and new shares would be issued at this price. Fantasy Fabrics pays fully franked dividends of 42c per share.

The ordinary shares have a market price of $6. The next dividend ($0.45 per share, fully franked) will be paid at the end of the year. Dividends are expected to grow at an annual rate of 5% thereafter. Flotation costs for ordinary shares would be 5% of the issue proceeds of $5.80 per share. However, Fantasy Fabrics has sufficient cash to fund the equity portion for all of the proposed projects. Therefore, no new issue of ordinary shares is to occur. The corporate tax rate is 30%.

(a) Calculate the cost of capital if Fantasy's shareholders can fully utilise imputation credits. Recommend which projects should be accepted.

(b) Calculate the cost of capital if the marginal shareholders are foreign residents. Recommend which projects should be accepted.

(c) Would your recommendations change if Fantasy Fabrics did not have any cash that could be used to fund the equity portion of the proposed projects? Calculate the after-tax cost of capital to demonstrate.

7.17 The target financing mix for Taylor Ltd is 15% preference shares, 30% debt and the remainder as ordinary equity. The corporate tax rate is 30%.

- Preference shares can be issued at $3.20. The annual dividend will be $0.32 and will be fully franked. Flotation costs will be 4%.
- Bonds with a $100 face value can be issued at $98. The coupon rate is 10% and it will be paid annually. Flotation costs will be 3.5%. The bonds will mature in 7 years. Use the approximate cost of debt equation to determine the cost of bonds.
- Ordinary shares are currently trading at $7.70 and new shares would be issued at $7.50. The next annual dividend is expected to be $0.80 and will be fully franked. As Taylor's is a mature company, the current growth rate of 1.5% is expected to continue indefinitely. Flotation costs will be 4%. The company has

a retained earnings balance of $12 million and this is all being utilised in current operations.

- Taylor's shareholders are all resident Australian investors.

Calculate the appropriate WACC for Taylor Ltd.

7.18 Samurai Ltd manufactures garden tools and has decided to expand operations. The new operations are expected to increase EBIT from the current level of $750 000 to $1 million pa. Samurai has a capital structure that utilises bonds, ordinary equity and preference shares. The $500 000 of issued bonds pay 7% pa. Preference shares pay an annual fixed dividend of $75 000. The company has 1 000 000 ordinary shares that are trading at $5 per share. The Australian corporate tax rate is 30%. Most of the shareholders of Samurai live outside Australia and cannot fully utilise dividend imputation credits.

Samurai needs to raise $800 000 to fund the expansion. Assuming the company can issue new shares at the current market price, what is the impact on EPS if new shares are issued to fund the expansion? If new debt can be raised at a 9% interest rate, what is the impact on EPS of using debt rather than a new equity issue?

SOLUTIONS TO FINANCE WORKSHOPS

7.1 1. Using equation 7.2 $NP_b = \frac{F}{(1+r_b)^n}$

$$60\,000 = \frac{100\,000}{(1 + r_b)^5}$$

Try 11% as a first pass at the cost of debt:

$$NP_b = \frac{100\,000}{(1.11)^5} = \frac{100\,000}{1.6851}$$
$$= \$59\,343.66$$

The calculated value is a little below net proceeds, so our next choice will be a lower discount rate to increase the calculated value. Let's try 10%.

$$NP_b = \frac{100\,000}{(1.10)^5} = \frac{100\,000}{1.6105}$$
$$= \$62\,092.52$$

The calculated price is now too high, so the cost of debt must lie between 10% and 11%.

Difference of lower discount rate value and net proceeds	62 092.52 − 60 000 = 2 092.52
Difference of lower and higher discount rate values	62 092.52 − 59 343.66 = 2 748.86
Ratio of differences	2 092.52/2 748.86 = 0.7612
Lower rate plus ratio	10 + 0.7612 = 10.76%

2. Using equation 7.3 $k_{d,bt} \cong \dfrac{I + \left(\dfrac{F - NP_b}{n}\right)}{\left(\dfrac{F + NP_b}{2}\right)}$

$$k_{d,bt} \cong \frac{0 + \left(\dfrac{100\,000 - 60\,000}{5}\right)}{\left(\dfrac{100\,000 + 60\,000}{2}\right)}$$

$$= \frac{8\,000}{80\,000}$$

$k_{d,bt} = 0.10$ or 10%

3. Using equation 7.5 $k_{d,at} = k_{d,bt}(1 - t_r)$

$k_{z,bt} = 10.76\%$

$k_{z,at} = k_{z,bt}(1 - t_r)$

$= 0.1076\ (1 - 0.3)$

$= 0.0753$ or 7.53%

7.2 Using equation 7.1 $NP = P_i(1 - f)$, equation 7.7 $k_{p,at} = \dfrac{D}{NP_p}$

$NP = 50\ (1 - 0.045)$

$= 47.75$

$$k_{p,at} = \frac{2}{47.75}$$

$= 0.041\,88$ or 4.19%

and equation 7.8 $k_{p,bt} = \dfrac{\dfrac{D}{(1 - t_c)}}{NP_p}$

$$k_{p,bt} = \frac{\dfrac{2}{(1 - 0.3)}}{47.75}$$

$= 0.059\,84$ or 5.98%

7.3 Using equation 7.10 $k_{re,at} = \dfrac{D_1}{P_0} + g$ and equation 7.11 $k_{re,bt} = \dfrac{\dfrac{D_1}{(1 - t_c)}}{P_0} + g$

$D_1 = 1.25(1 + g)$

$= 1.2625$

$$k_{re,at} = \frac{1.2625}{12.70} + 0.01$$

$= 0.1094$ or 10.94%

$$k_{re,\,bt} = \frac{\dfrac{1.2625}{(1-0.3)}}{12.70} + 0.01$$

$$= 0.1520 \text{ or } 15.2\%$$

7.4 1. Using equation 7.12 $k_{re,\,at} = \dfrac{D_1}{NP_e} + g$ and equation 7.13 $k_{re,\,bt} = \dfrac{\dfrac{D_1}{(1-t_c)}}{NP_e} + g$

$$D_1 = 1.25(1+g)$$

$$= 1.2625$$

$$NP = 12.50\ (1 - 0.035)$$

$$= \$12.06$$

$$k_{re,\,at} = \frac{1.2625}{12.06} + 0.01$$

$$= 0.1147 \text{ or } 11.47\%$$

2. $NP = P_1(1 - f)$

$$= 12.50(1 - 0.035) = 12.06$$

$$k_{re,\,bt} = \frac{\dfrac{D_1}{(1-t_c)}}{NP_e} + g$$

$$k_{re,\,bt} = \frac{\dfrac{1.25(1+0.01)}{(1-0.3)}}{12.06} + 0.01$$

$$= 0.1595 \text{ or } 15.95\%$$

3. $E(R) = R_f + \beta(E(R_m) - R_f)$

$$= 0.07 + 0.9(0.04)$$

$$= 10.6\%$$

7.5 Using equation 7.15 $WACC = \sum_{x=1}^{n} k_x W_x$

Source of funding	Amount of funding	Before-tax cost	Weight	Weighted cost
Bonds	5 000 000	0.0598	0.1923	0.0115
Preference shares	1 000 000	0.079	0.0385	0.003
Ordinary shares	20 000 000	0.1595	0.7692	0.1227
	26 000 000		WACC	13.72%

7.6 Note there will be no changes to the interest expense or preference dividends as detailed in example 7.18, so the only change to net income available to ordinary shareholders will be the after-tax consequence of the change in EBIT.

(a) The new EBIT will increase by \$150 000 to \$600 000. If new equity is used the net income available to shareholders will be:
\$153 800 + (150 000 × 0.7) = \$258 800 and the EPS becomes 0.5176.
If new debt is used the net income available to shareholders will be:
\$118 800 + (150 000 × 0.7) = \$223 800 and the EPS becomes 0.8952.

(b) The new EBIT will fall to \$320 000, a decrease of \$130 000. If new equity is used the net income available to shareholders will be:
\$153 800 – (130 000 × 0.7) = \$62 800 and the EPS becomes 0.1256.
If new debt is used the net income available to shareholders will be:
\$118 800 – (130 000 × 0.7) = \$27 800 and the EPS becomes 0.1112.

End notes

1 Lee, T 2006, 'Axe poised over PaperlinX dividend', *Australian Financial Review*, 8 August, http://afr.com.

2 Ferguson, A 2006, 'Drink companies flirting', *Business Review Weekly*, 17 August, p. 13.

3 Batholomeusz, S 2006, 'Telstra deals are about radical changes to cost structures in traditional areas', *The Age*, 1 September, p. 10.

4 Batholomeusz, S 2006, 'Virgin Blue shows Qantas why it's the Red Baron of the air', *The Age*, 29 August, p. 10.

5 Davidson, K 2006, 'We shall all pay the price for the economic lunacy of T3', *The Age*, 31 August, p. 13.

6 Batholomeusz, S 2006, 'Virgin Blue shows Qantas why it's the Red Baron of the air'.

7 Fan, J, Titman, S & Twite, G 2005, *An international comparison of capital structure and debt maturity choices*, AFA 2005 Philadelphia Meetings, Social Science Research Network.

8 Black, E, Legoria, J & Sellers, K 2000, 'Capital investment effects of dividend imputation', *The Journal of the American Taxation Association*, vol. 22, no. 2, pp. 40–59.

9 Some authors recommend the use of effective tax rates, rather than the statutory tax rate. The effective tax rate can be defined as the ratio of tax paid to gross profits. Harris and Feeny show that the effective tax rate converges to the statutory tax rate for 'typical' Australian companies within two to three years. For this reason, and for the sake of simplicity, we have chosen to use only the statutory tax rate. If you are calculating the cost of debt for a company that benefits from industry specific tax shelters (write-off of exploration expenditure for mining, for example) the effective tax rate would be more appropriate. See Harris, M & Feeny, S 2003, 'Habit persistence in effective tax rates', *Applied Economics*, vol. 35, no. 8, pp. 951–9.

10 Creedy, S 2006, 'Sydney Airport rejigs debt in expansion plan', *The Australian*, 20 July, p. 23.

11 Yuan, K, Zheng, L & Zhu, Q 2006, 'Are investors moonstruck? Lunar phases and stock returns', *Journal of Empirical Finance*, vol. 13, issue 1, pp. 1–23.

12 Officer, B 1994, 'The cost of capital of a company under an imputation tax system', *Accounting and Finance*, vol. 34, no. 1, pp. 1–18.

13 Australian Bureau of Statistics 2006, *Year book Australia*, www.abs.gov.au.

14 Australian Taxation Office, 'PAYG withholding from interest, dividends and royalties to non-residents', www.ato.gov.au.

15 Australian Taxation Office, 'PAYG withholding from interest, dividends and royalties to non-residents', www.ato.gov.au. This website shows the countries with which Australia currently has a tax treaty and the rate of withholding tax that is to be paid on unfranked dividends and royalties.

16 Officer, B 1994, 'The cost of capital of a company under an imputation tax system', *Accounting and Finance*, vol. 4, no. 1, pp. 1–18.

17 Net proceeds from a new issue are highly correlated with the market price of a share, so the cost of equity capital relies on how investors value the security.

18 Wood, J 1997, 'A simple model for pricing imputation tax credits under Australias [sic] dividend imputation tax system', *Pacific-Basin Finance Journal*, vol. 5, pp. 465–80.

19 Cannavan, D, Finn, F & Gray, S, 'The value of dividend imputation tax credits in Australia', *Journal of Financial Economics*, vol. 73, no. 1, pp. 167–97.

20 Bellamy, D 1994, 'Evidence of imputation clienteles in the Australian equity market', *Asia Pacific Journal of Management*, vol. 11, no. 2, pp. 275–87.

21 Bartholdy, J & Brown, K 1999, 'Ex-dividend day pricing in New Zealand', *Accounting and Finance*, vol. 39, no. 2, pp. 111–29.

22 The effective tax rate (the Australian tax paid as a proportion of taxable income) is used to calculate before- and after-tax costs when a company is partially integrated with the imputation system. In the interest of simplicity, no examples or questions in this text deal with partially integrated companies.

23 Bellamy, D 1994, 'Evidence of imputation clienteles in the Australian equity market', *Asia Pacific Journal of Management*, vol. 11, no. 2, pp. 275–87.

24 Kerin, P 2006, 'The cost of capital furphies', *Business Review Weekly*, 20 July, p. 26.

25 Truong, G, Partington, G & Peat, M 2005, 'Cost of capital estimation and capital budgeting practice in Australia', AFAANZ Conference, Melbourne, 3–5 July, www.aemc.gov.au.

26 Truong, Partington & Peat 2005.

27 Truong, Partington & Peat 2005.

28 Twite, G 2001, 'Capital structure choices and taxes: evidence from the Australian dividend imputation tax system', *International Review of Finance*, vol. 2, no. 4, pp. 217–34.

29 Schulman, C, Thomas, D, Sellers, K & Kenedy, D 1996, 'Effects of tax integration and capital gains tax on corporate leverage', *National Tax Journal*, vol. 49, no. 1, pp. 31–54.

30 Graham, JR & Harvey, CR 2001, 'The theory and practice of corporate finance: evidence from the field', *Journal of Financial Economics*, vol. 60, pp. 187–243.

31 Linden, P & Matolcsy, Z 2004, 'Corporate governance scoring systems: what do they tell us?', *Australian Accounting Review*, vol. 14, no. 1, pp. 9–16.

32 Matolcsy, Z, Stokes, D & Wright, A 2004, 'Do independent directors add value?', *Australian Accounting Review*, vol. 14, no. 1, pp. 33–40.

33 Beekes, W & Brown, P 2006, 'Do better-governed Australian firms make more informative disclosures?', *Journal of Business Finance & Accounting*, vol. 33, nos 3 & 4, pp. 422–50.

34 Collett, P & Hrasky, S 2005, 'Voluntary disclosure of corporate governance practices by listed Australian companies', *Corporate Governance*, vol. 13, no. 2, pp. 188–96.

chapter

8

Planning investments — discounted cash flow techniques

Learning objectives

After studying this chapter, you should be able to:

lo1	define investment decisions and discuss their characteristics
lo2	explain how investment decisions relate to firm value and describe the characteristics of investment appraisal techniques that are consistent with increasing firm value
lo3	estimate the incremental cash flows of a project
lo4	describe and apply the net present value (NPV) technique
lo5	describe and apply the internal rate of return (IRR) technique.

WHAT HAPPENS WHEN INVESTMENT CHOICES DON'T GO TO PLAN?

It wasn't that long ago that Centennial Coal was the darling of the independent coal sector, feted for its reliable domestic coal contracts that compared favourably to its rivals' reliance on the volatile export makets.

Its purchase of miner Powercoal from the NSW government in 2002 for $331 million was feted as a company transforming transaction, vaulting Centennial from junior miner to major producer. Powercoal gave Centennial a large portfolio of mines in NSW and development opportunities including the Mandalong underground project, which began producing early last year, and the huge Anvil Hill deposit, which is due to be developed by 2008. But the purchase has been a mixed blessing.

The company shocked the market by announcing last week it was taking a $49 million charge against the Newstan mine, which will be the fifth powercoal pit shut by Centennial when production stops in 2008.

...

Newstan had been a reliable producer for 20 years. But Centennial inherited Powercoal's plan to move the mine's longwall underground mining machine to a different area of the deposit, and that new zone has been nothing but trouble, causing $47.8 million of write-downs in 2005–06, and further financial damage this year.

Centennial has concluded the investment required to get coal out of the new zone reliably isn't justified, and it will use the Newstan equipment and staff to boost production at two other mines, including Mandalong.

The company's profit tripled to $29 million in 2001–02, before the Powercoal deal. But since then, Centennial has become a serial source of disappointment, with its highest post-acquisition profit being $52 million in 2003–04, and last year's result being just $17 million, after losses from Newstan. Ironically, it was Centennial's big domestic sales contracts that exacerbated the damage from production shortfalls at Newstan. Centennial was forced to divert lucrative export tonnes from other mines to meet its less profitable commitments to supply NSW power stations.

Its shares rose 11¢ yesterday to $2.62, rebounding from three-year lows, less than half the price in mid-2005 before the Newstan problems emerged.

...

The Austral deal reflected a change in sentiment among investors, who saw rival miners profiting from export sales and exposure to coking coal, which has been selling for record prices.

Austral's Tahmoor mine gives Centennial export coking coal, but it has had a chequered history, with trouble installing a new longwall at the mine forcing the previous Austral mangement to put the company up for sale. And true to form, delays in the last move of Tahmoor's longwall to a new panel of coal in the mine contributed to last week's 40 per cent downgrade in Centennial's profit guidance for this year. The rest of the operating profit downgrade came from Newstan's operating problems, as the longwall struggled through the difficult ground which forced Centennial to give up on the mine.[1]

Chapter preview

As shown in the opening article for this chapter, the acquisition of the Powercoal business by Centennial Coal has not turned out as expected. Centennial purchased Powercoal to gain access to contracts and to expand its existing operations. We can draw some important conclusions about making major capital expenditures from the Centennial Coal situation. The first, and most obvious, is that the forecasts made when project proposals are being analysed don't always eventuate. This could be due to changing market conditions over the life of the project. Centennial Coal took over Powercoal's domestic contracts for delivering coal when it acquired the business. These domestic contracts guaranteed cash inflows. As the price for export coal increased, the domestic contracts meant that Centennial had to forego the higher cash inflows it could have obtained by exporting. Even without the market changes Centennial had to deal with, actual cash flows can be very different to those in initial analysis because the future is uncertain and very difficult to forecast reliably. It is unlikely that the additional time needed to get to the coal in the Tahmoor mine could have been forecast with much accuracy.

The second major conclusion we can draw is that capital projects are often difficult to reverse once the firm has made the investment. Centennial Coal's problems with the Newstan mine (and four others like it) were solved by closing the mines. These investment projects could not be 'reversed' by selling them — it would be very difficult to find buyers for coal mines that have costs of extraction higher than the cash inflows that could be generated from selling the coal. This second conclusion leads us to the fundamental issue of project appraisal. The forecast return for making the investment needs to be large enough to justify adopting the project. The cost of capital provides the decision maker with a good benchmark for making investment decisions when the risk of the proposed project is the same level as the risk of the projects that the firm currently has in place.

In chapter 4 we learn how to adjust dollar amounts from different periods so they are on a comparable footing. We discuss the nature of the risk–return relationship in chapter 5. In chapter 6 we learn how securities are valued and then extend these principles to determine the cost of capital in chapter 7. In this chapter, we use what we have learnt so far to help make some of the biggest decisions that managers face — decisions about the investments the firm will make.

The following diagram shows how this chapter is structured.

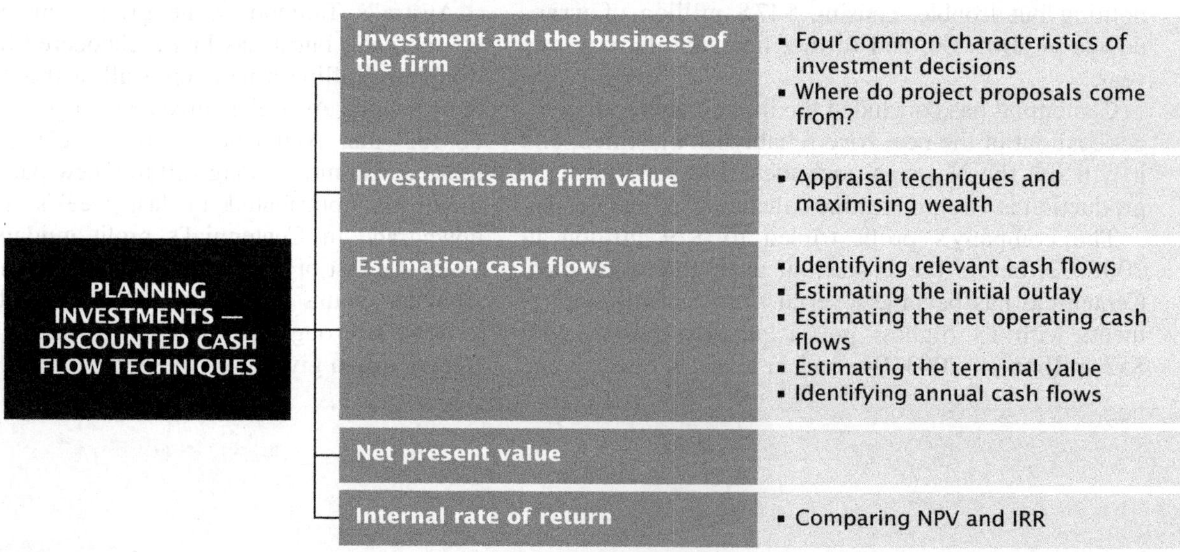

lo1

Define investment decisions and discuss their characteristics.

Investment: the outlay of capital made with a view to gaining future benefits

Investment and the business of the firm

An **investment** is the outlay of capital made with a view to gaining future benefits. Shareholders make an investment when they purchase the shares of a company and expect to gain future cash flows in the form of dividends and/or capital gains when they sell their investment. As we see in chapter 7, the cost of capital is the link between investment decisions and firm value. The management of the firm needs to make investments with the shareholders' capital to generate returns for them. Therefore, the appraisal of new projects is an important part of the role of managers. This applies equally to the management of listed firms and of small, privately held ones.

To remain viable in the longer term, firms need to respond to changes in their business environment and in available technology; exploit new opportunities; and replace existing projects and equipment. Managers in dynamic and stable firms need to make investment decisions.

Four common characteristics of investment decisions

Most investment decisions involve a relatively large initial outlay, have relatively long horizons, result in projects that are difficult to reverse, and involve risk. We will look at each of these characteristics in turn.

Relatively large initial outlay

Initial outlay: the capital expenditure made to implement an investment

Some investment decisions are relatively more important than others. The decision Centennial Coal made to expand its business by acquiring Powercoal is clearly an important investment decision (irrespective of how it turns out in the end!). The investment cost of replacing one damaged computer in a national bank would not justify using the techniques we will be discussing in this chapter. The cash benefits associated with one computer would be very difficult to estimate and the time taken on an appraisal would not be worth it for the size of the initial outlay. Conversely, replacing the entire computer system in a bank would involve a large **initial outlay**. Of course, the purchase of a computer in a small firm (rather than a large bank) could be a relatively large investment decision. Before management make the investment decision, they should be in a position to assure themselves that the expense is justified given the scale of the firm's operations. The owners of firms want the value of their investments to increase. Managers in turn should have the objective of making investments that will do that.

Relatively long horizons

In addition to having relatively large outlays, investment decisions often cover long periods of time. We would not expect managers to make a decision to replace the computer system each year. Even with rapid technological advances, we would expect a computer system to last at least five years. Because an investment decision covers a number of future years, it is important for managers to make the best decision they can at the time the investment is being considered. Coal miners like Centennial Coal would normally expect a mine to be productive for at least 10 years. Exactly how many years a mine operates depends on the price of coal relative to the costs of producing and delivering the coal to customers.

Projects can be difficult to reverse

As we saw at the start of the chapter, projects, once implemented, can be difficult and expensive to reverse. Assume our bank installed a new computer system that was expected to be in service for a minimum of five years. It could happen that, one year later, technological advances made the system obsolete and the new technology presented significant cost savings over the life of the system. Management then have two choices: they can keep the old system for the remaining four years and then upgrade to the new technology, or they upgrade now and try to recoup some of the cost of the 'old' system by selling it. The first option means the bank may lose some competitive edge if all the other banks adopt the new technology. The second could mean that the value of the firm decreases because the cost savings from operating the new technology might not offset the losses associated with abandoning the old system. What should management do? We can use the techniques of project appraisal in this chapter to compare the costs and benefits of each course of action and give management a decision tool to help make the choices that will have a positive impact on the value of the firm.

This brings us to the final characteristic of investment decisions — investment decisions involve risk.

Projects have risk

The longer the investment horizon, the more uncertain management will be about what will happen over the period. Products wax and wane in popularity, technological advances make equipment obsolete and legislative changes can have significant impacts on how a firm operates. The Centennial Coal situation is a good example of the risks encountered in the normal operations of a business. Implementing a project requires a capital outlay now, while the returns are received in the future. The future is always uncertain. We look at ways to incorporate risk into the project appraisal process in chapter 9.

Where do project proposals come from?

Investment decisions fall into two main categories:

1. new projects undertaken to increase cash flows
2. replacement of existing assets.

An example of a new project aimed at increasing revenue is opening a new coal mine. The bank's decision to install a new computer system is an example of a replacement decision, because it already has a computer system.

Many replacement projects or those suggested to save costs come from the non-management employees of the company. People on the factory floor are often in the best position to know when a machine is past its prime and are usually the ones to come up with more efficient ways of doing things. They pass their ideas on to their departmental managers who then pass them up the chain to the financial manager.

Cash-flow-increasing ideas, like new products or entering new markets, are usually more strategic in focus. We expect these to come from higher level management because it's their job to be looking at the 'big picture' of where the firm is heading. New product ideas might be generated in the research and development section or the marketing section of large firms.

CORPORATE FINANCIAL GOVERNANCE

Investment decisions

Corporate governance is about how the firm is managed. Managing a firm involves making decisions about allocating owners' resources to the various activities of the firm.

The current activities of the firm are determined by investment decisions that have been made in the past. The future activities of the firm are determined by the investment decisions managers make now. Therefore, the corporate governance system of a company is responsible for deciding what types of investments are made and who makes the decisions.[2] Corporate governance problems are often closely associated with the agency costs we discuss in chapter 1. Consider, for example, the company's decision to invest in a corporate jet. Will purchasing the jet increase shareholder wealth? It could if the CEO is very hands-on and regularly visits offices and production facilities that are geographically dispersed. Would it be more cost efficient to use commercial airline services in this case? Perhaps not if it results in longer travel time, given the hourly rate of the CEO! Is the decision to purchase a corporate jet unrelated to any personal benefits the CEO might gain? Yermack analysed the returns of US companies that disclosed personal managerial use of corporate jets.[3] He found that these firms did not perform as well as benchmark firms without jets for managerial use (that is, shareholder wealth was not maximised). Yermack also investigated the characteristics of CEOs to determine why they might need personal access to a corporate jet. He reported that the most important characteristic of the CEO for explaining personal use of jets is the CEO's membership of golf clubs that are distant from the CEO's normal place of work. It is hard to reconcile this rationale for purchasing a jet with maximising shareholder wealth.

Such an investment decision is consistent with a weak system of corporate governance. A strong system of corporate governance would ensure that investment decisions that generate large personal benefits are not made by the person who will receive those benefits.

FINANCE WORKSHOP 8.1

What four key features of investments make them so important and contribute to making them difficult to analyse?

lo2

Explain how investment decisions relate to firm value and describe the characteristics of investment appraisal techniques that are consistent with increasing firm value.

Investments and firm value

It is difficult to think of a business that does not require a start-up investment by its owners. Even in the least capital-intensive operations, like personal services, the business owner will need to advertise to make potential customers aware that the service is being offered. An important way to add value, or increase shareholder wealth, is by growth in operations and the firm needs to make investments to grow. Growth can be achieved by expanding the scale of current operations. For example, a bank could expand its customer base by opening mini-branches in supermarkets or operating in overseas markets. A second way to achieve growth is for the business to begin new activities. Our bank could establish stockbroking or financial planning services for its customers or offer insurance products in addition to its traditional banking business.

As we saw in the Centennial Coal case, growth in itself does not always add value to the firm. New projects should be adopted only after they have been analysed and have shown themselves capable of increasing shareholder wealth. We can do this only with analytical techniques that are consistent with the principles of wealth maximisation.

Appraisal techniques and maximising wealth

As we discuss in chapter 1, analysis of cash flows rather than profits is consistent with the objective of maximising owners' wealth. To be more confident that our decision outcomes achieve this objective, the techniques we use should be based on cash flows rather than profits. Cash flows represent real resources available to the firm. Profit figures are constructed by the application of accounting rules. A profit figure is determined by matching expenses and revenues in the period in which they are incurred to arrive at a periodic measure of performance. We discuss the accounting process further in chapter 14. The accounting matching process is not relevant when we are assessing the impact of a proposed project on shareholder wealth. With an objective of maximising wealth in mind, the timing of the cash flows is important (so, consistent with the principles we learn in chapter 4, they can be discounted appropriately) but we do not need a periodic measure of performance for each of the sub-periods of the project. We do not need to allocate a depreciation expense to our initial outlay because depreciation is not a cash flow. The only relevant decrease in the value of the assets of the project is the difference between the initial outlay and the **terminal value** of the assets at the end of the project. Shareholders sometimes do consider profits by using earnings per share (EPS) in their share purchase decisions, but profits are not a sound base on which to appraise projects.

Terminal value: the expected cash flow associated with disposal of the project assets at the end of the project's life

In addition to using cash flow rather than profits as the basis for project evaluation, the chosen technique should consider the time value of money. We mentioned earlier that many investment decisions result in projects that continue over a number of years. If managers ignore the time value of money, they may not choose the project that adds the most to firm value. For example, if we were evaluating a proposal to build a block of flats we could compare the initial outlay to the cash flows of selling each of the flats when the block was completed. Or we could compare the initial outlay to the net cash flows for renting the flats for the next 20 years then selling the building. The total cash flow from selling the flats is likely to be lower than the total from the rent then sell option. If we ignore the time value of money we would choose the rent and sell option. By doing this, we are ignoring the return that could be generated by investing the cash we would receive by selling the flats when the building was complete. If we sell the flats immediately we can use that cash to build another block of flats and sell them and repeat the project another 19 times over the life of the 'build and rent' project. Considering the time value of the cash flows is consistent with maximising shareholder wealth.

Finally, our analytical technique needs to have the capacity to include differences in risks between competing projects. We learn in chapter 5 that risk and expected return have a positive relationship. The debtholders and shareholders of the firm have determined their required returns based on the existing projects of the firm. If the firm adopts a project that is more risky than those it currently has in place, the contributors of capital will require a higher return. If the new project does not generate enough to cover this higher return, the share price will fall and the firm will decrease in value. We examine this issue further in chapter 9.

The project appraisal techniques that are consistent with shareholder wealth maximisation are the discounted cash flow techniques. We will look at the two discounted cash flow techniques — net present value (NPV) and internal rate of return (IRR) — in the following sections, but first we need to address the issue of estimating a project's cash flows.

lo3

Estimate the incremental cash flows of a project.

Estimating cash flows

The usefulness of any discounted cash flow technique is determined by the reliability of the data we use in it. The most difficult aspect of using the NPV and IRR techniques is the estimation of the future cash flows for a project. We generally don't expect our forecast cash flows to be 'accurate' unless we have the unusual case of having the cash inflows and outflows for a project specified in contracts. We plan investments by using the best available information at the time we are making the decision. As we see in chapter 5, this does not guarantee that our expected outcome will equal the actual outcome. Everyone has perfect hindsight, but perfect foresight is indeed a rare commodity! We can aim only to make the best decision at the time based on the best available information at that time.

Identifying relevant cash flows

The first step in conducting a discounted cash flow analysis is to identity the relevant cash flows. We will defer discussion of the impact of taxation to chapter 9; assume a tax-free environment and focus on the fundamental principles here. Before we start tossing numbers about, we need to know a little more about the cash flows that are relevant to an investment decision.

Marginal analysis: a method for making decisions to maximise our objective by comparing additional (marginal) benefits with additional relevant costs

Incremental cash flows: result from the acceptance of a project

One of the fundamental techniques of economic analysis is marginal analysis. **Marginal analysis** is a method for making decisions to maximise our objective by comparing additional (marginal) benefits with additional relevant costs. The relevant cash flows for investment evaluation are the marginal ones. We call these the **incremental cash flows** and they result from the acceptance of a project. Only incremental cash flows are relevant in discounted cash flow techniques; total cash flows are irrelevant. If a cash flow will occur with or without the new project, it is not incremental and it is irrelevant to the investment decision. If the cash flow exists only when the new project is adopted, it is an incremental cash flow.

Consider a firm that manufactures clothes washing products. Clean-O Ltd has a number of products that have been especially designed for normal washing, for washing wool and delicate fabrics, and one for those hard-to-shift stains. The managers have before them a proposal to develop a new product, called Greenwash, which contains lower levels of phosphates. The head of the marketing department is confident that Greenwash would appeal to the more environmentally conscious customer and that sales would increase. If the project was assessed by looking at the expected sales figures for Greenwash and comparing them to the costs of initiating the project, the managers of Clean-O could end up accepting a project that does not increase shareholder wealth. The reason is that some of the sales that are currently being made by Clean-O could be diverted to the new product. To determine the incremental cash flows for the Greenwash product, we need to subtract the cash inflows that would be lost by consumers switching from Clean-O's current products. This gives us the new cash inflows that are associated with the acceptance of the project.

What if the new Clean-O customers are so impressed with Greenwash that they decide to try some of Clean-O's other products? If this is the case, the introduction of the new product would increase the cash flows of the existing product range. To be consistent with the treatment of lost sales, these incidental cash flows from the existing range of products that can be attributed to the success of Greenwash should also be included in the relevant cash flows for analysis of the Greenwash project. They are incremental cash flows because they would not exist if the new project were rejected.

Clean-O's marketing department currently employs five full-time staff. If the Greenwash project were accepted, the number of marketing staff would not change. Therefore, the salaries of the marketing staff are irrelevant to the Greenwash investment decision. However, if a new marketing person were to be appointed to promote the Greenwash product, the salary and on-costs of that person would be a relevant cash flow for analysing the project. We need to include incremental cash outflows in the relevant cash flows.

Incremental outflows relevant to the initial outlay for the project include the cost of purchasing or modifying production equipment for the new product and increases in working capital. (We look at determining the initial outlay in the next section.) The next main group of incremental outflows include additional wages or salaries associated with producing and getting the product to market; increased electricity charges for running the machines; and the cost of the space that the machines occupy. Examples of how people depart from the principle of marginal analysis are included in the following 'behavioural perspective' feature.

BEHAVIOURAL PERSPECTIVE

Marginal analysis

Choices to acquire goods and services are made to equate marginal benefits (benefit from each additional unit gained) with marginal cost (cost of each additional unit gained). This rule seems to hold roughly true, even though people do not measure or value benefits and costs

accurately. Often, this rule means that people will go on acquiring units of some good or service until the marginal benefit, which has been steadily decreasing, comes down sufficiently to equal the marginal cost, which in many cases is constant.

To give you an example, consider a session in the pub with the boys. (Even if you are not a boy or are a boy not attracted to sessions in the pub with the boys, you will still be very aware of this scenario.) The marginal benefit rule applies reasonably well in this situation. A drinker will gain a good deal of benefit from his or her first drink, a little less from the second, less again from the third and so on. At some point, the marginal benefit has dropped to quite a low value and will approach marginal cost (measured in dollars and in potential pain from nausea, vomiting and tomorrow's hangover). At that point, most drinkers will stop drinking. For some people, this point comes quite quickly, even after one drink; for others it is delayed until after many drinks. Stopping drinking at the point where marginal benefit equals marginal cost will maximise the total pleasure from drinking. Continuing to drink past this point will reduce total pleasure as the cost of each additional drink in terms of pleasure will be greater than the benefits.

However, people do not keep to this rule in all decisions. Experimentation and anecdotal evidence have shown that people will drive across town and incur both the cash and time costs to save, for example, $9 on a discounted popular CD. But they will not make the same trip to save $9 on the price of a bigger item, such as a television set or a CD player. The anomaly here is relating the $9 saving to the total cost, respectively $30 and $400, not the marginal cost, which is the cost of the car trip. If the car trip costs less than $9, then it is worth going in both cases.

Operating costs: the cash outflows required in the daily activities of the project

Opportunity costs: the cash flows forgone when one path of action is chosen

The earlier example of employing new marketing staff indicates that incremental salaries are relevant cash flows. Salaries are calculated on an annual basis. Wages, on the other hand, are paid on an hourly basis and are the normal way production staff are paid. They rise and fall with changing levels of production, so they are called variable **operating costs**. Operating costs are the cash outflows required in the daily activities of the project. Increased utility costs, like water, power and heating, are also operating costs when they change with the level of production. Fixed utility costs, management salaries and rates are examples of overhead costs. The accountants among us will want to allocate a 'share' of these costs to each new project. However, if a new project has no impact on the total electricity bill, for example, this should not be included as a relevant cash flow because it is not incremental — it will not change if the project is accepted or rejected.

The cost of the space occupied by the project is an example of an **opportunity cost**. Opportunity costs are the cash flows forgone when one path of action (that is, accepting a new project) is chosen. If Clean-O had to rent new premises to manufacture Greenwash, we would include the rental cash outflow as an incremental cost of the project. If Clean-O can install a new machine to make Greenwash in an unused part of its existing factory, it is less clear if some of the costs of the existing factory should be allocated to the new product. This is where we apply our opportunity cost concept. If the firm adopting the new project has no alternative use for the space the project will occupy, then the opportunity cost of that space is zero — the firm is not giving up any return. If the firm is evaluating a number of projects that could occupy the same space, or the space could be rented out, there is an opportunity cost that should be included in the relevant cash flows of the new project. If the project were rejected, the firm could generate cash flows from the space needed for the project. Assuming the floor space could be rented out for $10 000 a year, the opportunity cost of accepting the new project is $10 000 each year. Operating cash inflows should be reduced by this $10 000 each year as this is the amount of cash flow the firm would have to forgo if the project is accepted. A real world example of the importance of opportunity costs is shown in the Centennial Coal article on the opening page of the chapter. Centennial's opportunity cost from being tied to domestic coal delivery contracts is the lost export sales at the higher price per tonne. The following 'behavioural perspective' feature contains some interesting observations on how people tend to consider opportunity costs.

BEHAVIOURAL PERSPECTIVE

Opportunity cost

The principle regarding opportunity cost is that opportunity cost and out-of-pocket costs should be considered as equivalent. Additionally, it is postulated that the willingness to pay (WTP) for a good should be equivalent to the willingness to accept (WTA). In other words, a good has a value at a particular time and an economic agent should be willing to buy the good if the price drops below the given level. It would then be a good deal. The same person should be a seller if the price rises above that level (it would also then be a good deal). Notwithstanding these two underlying postulates, most people do not view gains forgone in the same light as expenditures or losses of the same amount.

Consider the case of Will, a person who had inherited his mum's collection of mint condition punk records (vinyl, that is) from the mid- to late 1970s. New generation punk groups (as well as a couple of originals) enjoyed increased popularity in the mid 1990s. Will has Killing Joke's first single and found out that it is worth \$200. As an optimist, he thinks that the price could go up further over the next couple of years and decides not to sell. Irrespective of the price in a couple of years' time, the opportunity cost of the decision not to sell now is \$200. Will could have taken his \$200 and invested it to generate a return in the coming years. If Will sells the record for \$300 in two years' time he has made a realised gain of \$300. This does not alter his \$200 opportunity cost now. If Will cannot sell the record at all in two years' time he has not realised a loss at all because he paid nothing for the record and the opportunity cost is still \$200. Similarly, in the recent housing price boom in Australia, many people saw the prices of their houses double in four years. Did they view these rises, when they did not sell their houses, as losses? No, they viewed them as windfall gains even though prices may have fallen again by the time they do actually sell.

The WTA–WTP experiments have thrown light on some interesting facets of human nature. Theoretically, the amount an individual is 'willing to accept' to sell a good that is owned should be the same as the amount the same individual is 'willing to pay' to buy the same good. However, experimentation and observation of trading behaviour show this to be not so. Sellers, when assuming the reverse role of buyers, are often not willing to pay the prices they demanded when they were sellers. One experiment allowed respondents to either buy a lottery ticket for \$3 or to sell a ticket given to them for \$3. Only 18% of the potential sellers were willing to sell for \$3, whereas 38% of the potential buyers were willing to buy at that price. This effect is termed the 'endowment effect' and it has been observed in relation to both valued and valuable possessions as well as mundane and inexpensive goods. The endowment effect has been found to come into play almost instantaneously after a buyer has gained possession of a good.

Are the research and development costs of getting Greenwash to the project analysis stage relevant cash flows? New products often take a number of years to develop. The proportion of research projects that lead to a saleable product, especially in the area of scientific research, is low. Research and development can sometimes use years of human resources in addition to physical resources. However, they are not relevant cash flows because they are **sunk costs**. Sunk costs are cash outflows that occur prior to the evaluation of a project. Remember that only incremental cash flows are relevant to discounted cash flow methods. Will the research and development cash flow to date change depending on whether or not the project is accepted — it will not. Therefore, sunk costs are not incremental and are not relevant cash flows. Another example of a potential sunk cost is market testing and research. If this has happened before the proposal is analysed, it is a sunk cost. Market testing that occurs after the project is accepted is an incremental cost. See the following 'behavioural perspective' feature for some discussion on how people can misinterpret sunk costs.

Sunk costs: cash outflows that occur prior to the evaluation of a project

BEHAVIOURAL PERSPECTIVE

Sunk costs

Sunk costs are costs incurred in the past and they should not influence decisions, yet people making decisions often incorporate their sunk costs. Suppose you were a person very concerned about appearing in the latest fashion clothes. You bought a pair of expensive jeans and boots to match, put them on and found you looked terrible. Do you wear them even though you hate them or do you give them away? Some people will consider the sunk costs and continue to wear them (while gritting their teeth); others will ignore the sunk costs and give the clothes away. Would your decision be different if you had been given the clothes for nothing?

As a business decision example, suppose a firm has rented retail showroom space with a large amount of storage space behind. The rent is $1 per week per square metre and totals $4000 per week. The firm cannot negotiate a lower rent when it finds it has an excess of 1000 square metres of lockable space. It can, however, sub-lease the surplus space. Should it do so at any rent less than $1 per week? Answer: yes, it should rent the space out at the highest possible rent regardless of whether that rent is above or below $1 per square metre per week. Why? Because, the contracted rent is a sunk cost, and any revenue gained for the space is an additional benefit.

Airlines offering cheap stand-by fares use both these principles (sunk and marginal costs) all the time. If a 400-seat aircraft flies from Brisbane to Cairns with 40 empty seats, it does not matter that jet fuel and crew's wages cost $20 000 and $3000 respectively per trip. These are sunk costs. What matters is that the carrier is flying seats with no revenue-paying derrieres sitting in them. The additional expenses for each extra passenger may be no more than $1 for the cardboard box of juice and biscuits. Any fare greater than the marginal cost of $1 will enhance airline profits.

Finally, the cost of finance for the project should not be included in the project's cash flows. The cash flows of a proposed project with the same level of risk as the firm's existing projects are discounted using the firm's cost of capital. As you learn in chapter 7, the cost of capital represents the required returns of each group of capital contributors to the firm. Discounting at the cost of capital means we are already charging the project for its financing costs. Including dividends and interest payments as cash outflows of the project would mean double-counting the cost of finance.

To summarise, the relevant cash flows for a proposed project are incremental and occur only if a project is accepted. Changes of cash inflows and outflows from the firm's other activities that are attributable to the adoption of the new project should be included in the analysis of the new project. Any opportunity costs should be included as outflows in the analysis and sunk costs should be ignored. The cost of finance for a project is not included in the relevant cash flows because the discount rate implicitly charges the project for this cost.

Cash flows are grouped into three areas for analysis:

1. initial outlay
2. net operating cash flows
3. terminal value.

Each of these is discussed in the following sections.

Estimating the initial outlay

The initial outlay of the project is often the cash flow that can be identified with the highest degree of certainty. For our Greenwash example, we would start with the production equipment. If new equipment has to be purchased to manufacture Greenwash, the installed cost will be included in the initial outlay. The installed cost includes the purchase price of the equipment, delivery charges and any installation cost. Example 8.1 shows how to calculate the installed cost of a new machine used in an expansion project.

EXAMPLE 8.1

Calculating the installed cost of a new machine for an expansion project

Assume Clean-O will install a new production line for the specific purpose of manufacturing Greenwash. The purchase price of the machine is $1 million. Shipping and road transport costs are expected to be $150 000. There is enough space in Clean-O's existing factory and this space does not currently have any cash-generating potential. The company has obtained a quote of $10 000 from an electrician willing to do the installation when Clean-O wants it done. What is the installed cost for the Greenwash project?

Installed cost of new asset

Purchase price	1 000 000
Transport cost	150 000
Electrician	10 000
	1 160 000

Net working capital: the excess of current assets over current liabilities

Changes in net working capital are also included in the initial outlay. **Net working capital** is the excess of current assets over current liabilities. If the firm offers customers credit and a new project is expected to increase credit sales, net working capital will increase because the firm will have to fund the increase in the accounts receivable asset. Perhaps the firm will need to hold higher levels of raw materials inventory to support the manufacture of a new product. If so, the increase in the inventory asset will cause an increase in net working capital that should be reflected in the initial outlay of the project. The increase in the inventory may be fully or partially offset if the firm will receive credit from its inventory suppliers. The following example shows the incremental effect of adopting the project on net working capital.

EXAMPLE 8.2

Calculating the change to net working capital

The Greenwash project would require an additional $10 000 in raw materials. Finished goods inventories would increase by $30 000. The finished goods inventory would be established at the start of production as Clean-O is proud of its reputation for always being able to deliver stock. The accounting department has estimated an increase of $40 000 in accounts receivable from the sales of Greenwash made on credit. This increase would occur when the first orders of Greenwash are delivered, two weeks after the project commences. Suppliers of Clean-O's raw material offer the firm credit and accounts payable would increase by $10 000. What change in net working capital should be included in the initial outlay of the Greenwash project?

Change in net working capital

Add increase in raw materials	10 000
Add increase in finished goods	30 000
Add increase in accounts receivable	40 000
Subtract increase in accounts payable	(10 000)
	70 000

Outflows for any special training staff needed to operate the project should be included in the initial outlay of an expansion project. The costs of hiring new staff who will work on the project specifically should also be included. These employee-related cash outflows are included in the initial outlay because the payments need to be made at the start of the project. Wages are included in the period when they are paid. Finally, the cash outflows paid for advertising the launch of the product at commencement of the project are included in the initial outlay. Example 8.3 shows how these cash flows are included with the installed cost and the change in net working capital to determine the initial outlay.

EXAMPLE 8.3

Calculating initial outlay for an expansion project

The new production line for Greenwash is computerised and two current production employees will be trained by the manufacturer of the new equipment for a total cost of $2000. The marketing department want to spend $100 000 per annum on advertising, with a one-off campaign costing $50 000 at the start of the project. Using the installed cost calculated in example 8.1 and the change in net working capital from example 8.2, calculate the initial outlay for the Greenwash project.

Initial outlay	
Installed cost of new asset	1 160 000
Add increase in net working capital	70 000
Add training costs	2 000
Add initial advertising cost	50 000
	1 282 000

Determining the initial outlay for a replacement decision requires one additional element to be included. The cash flows from an asset that is being replaced will usually decrease, but can sometimes increase, the installed cost for a replacement decision. The asset being replaced may still have a value in either the second-hand or scrap markets. Here, the net cash flows from the sale of the existing asset are included as reductions in the initial outlay of the new machine. Sometimes there is a net cash outflow from the old asset. This can occur if the firm has to pay to have the asset dismantled and removed. Another potential cash outflow associated with existing assets is the cost of cleaning up any environmental damage that the asset has caused. Net cash outflows from existing assets increase the initial outlay of the replacement machine. We include the cash inflows and outflows from the disposal of the existing assets in the initial outlay of replacement decisions because they are incremental. They would not be generated unless the new project was accepted. That is, the replacement of the existing assets comes about because the new project involves the purchase of new assets that perform the same function.

Example 8.4 shows how the cash flows of an existing asset are included in the initial outlay. The net cash flow (that is, the amount received when the existing asset is sold minus any costs associated with getting the existing asset ready for sale) decreases the initial outlay for the replacement project.

EXAMPLE 8.4

Calculating the installed cost of a new machine for a replacement decision

After investigating new production facilities for the Greenwash project, Clean-O are considering replacing the existing production line they use for manufacturing their other products. The purchase price, transport costs and electrical are $1 million, $150 000 and $10 000 respectively. The new production line will occupy the space of the current machinery. Management have looked in trade magazines and estimated that the old machinery would sell for $50 000. It would cost around $1500 to dismantle the machine in preparation for sale. What is the installed cost for the replacement project?

Cash outflows for replacement machine	
Purchase price	1 000 000
Transport cost	150 000
Electrician	10 000
	1 160 000
Cash inflow from existing machine	
Sale of machine	50 000
Cash outflow from existing machine	
Dismantling cost	1 500
Total cash inflows from existing machine	48 500
Total installed cost of replacement project	1 111 500

A project to adopt new technologies to save costs should be classified as a replacement decision where existing technology is being exchanged for the new technology. This was the case in the replacement decision for Clean-O presented in example 8.4. At other times, new technology is adopted to run parallel to the existing assets of the firm. Department stores 'going online' is a good example. The stores may have no immediate plans to replace existing mail order services and accept sales only over the internet, but they can see that electronic order processing will save time and costs. In this case, the initial outlay for the project should be calculated as we did for the expansion project.

FINANCE WORKSHOP 8.2

1. Aster Ltd is considering a proposal to expand its operations by processing fresh flowers for sale as dried flowers. The drying equipment has a purchase price of $450 000. The company will house the equipment in a disused storage shed. The equipment can be installed and the shed refurbished at a cost of $50 000. Freight and insurance charges of $10 000 will be paid to have the equipment delivered. What is the installed cost of the project?

2. Aster currently has a very small amount of inventory. The raw materials inventory mainly consists of the cardboard boxes that the flowers are packed into for transport. The raw materials inventory would increase by about $2000 if the new project is adopted. The new drying project would need about $5000 of dried flowers to be held as the finished goods inventory. Aster's current suppliers of boxes, ribbon and wrapping paper for packaging the product are willing to offer the company credit for the additional packaging requirements associated with the project. Aster will not offer credit terms to its customers. What amount should be included in the initial outlay for the change in net working capital?
3. What is the initial outlay for Aster's flower drying project?

Estimating the net operating cash flows

After we have determined the initial outlay, the data we organise are the expected annual net cash flows from the proposed project. The sales department will supply their estimates of the inflows from sales over the life of the project. The production department might be the source of estimates for the project's operating costs. We investigate the issue of estimating cash flows further in chapter 14 when we prepare cash budgets.

The most important thing to remember when constructing a series of operating cash flows is to look at the incremental cash flows. If inflows will be diverted from other areas of the firm, these lost cash flows should be deducted from those of the new project. If there are synergistic (or incidental) increases in cash flows to other areas of the firm from the new project, then these should be added to the cash flows for the analysis of the new project. Similarly, costs should be incremental only to the new project. This is critical for the analysis of a cost saving project.

We will be using annual operating cash flows, even though the cash flows from the new project will occur throughout the course of the year. Given that we are using forecast inflows and outflows that are unlikely to exactly match the realised cash flows, the timing difference that will arise from discounting is insignificant. If you are analysing a project where cash flows are received fairly evenly and on a daily basis, you can use appendix table 5 at the end of this book to incorporate this feature into your analysis. Example 8.5 shows how to estimate the net operating cash flows for the Greenwash project.

EXAMPLE 8.5

Estimating operating cash flows for expansion and replacement decisions

The management of Clean-O have assembled the following annual forecasts of the operating cash flows for Greenwash:

- Sales of Greenwash for the first year: $1 000 000.
- Sales are expected to grow at a rate of 5% for years 2 and 3, then decline by 5% pa in years 4 and 5.
- Sales diverted from existing Clean-O products: $100 000.

- Raw materials will be 24% of sales.
- Labour: $90 000.
- Electricity: $7000.
- Advertising cost for years 1 to 4: $100 000.

These forecasts are the best available estimates for each year, ending in 5 years' time. What is the net annual operating cash flow for the Greenwash project?

	Year 1	Year 2	Year 3	Year 4	Year 5
Sales of Greenwash	1 000 000	1 050 000	1 102 500	1 047 375	995 006
Lost sales	−100 000	−100 000	−100 000	−100 000	−100 000
Raw materials	−240 000	−252 000	−264 600	−251 370	−238 801
Labour	−90 000	−90 000	−90 000	−90 000	−90 000
Electricity	−7 000	−7 000	−7 000	−7 000	−7 000
Advertising	−100 000	−100 000	−100 000	−100 000	
Net operating cash flow	463 000	501 000	540 900	499 005	559 205

The sales figure for year 2 is the year 1 sales figure, multiplied by 1.05 to reflect the 5% annual increase. Similarly, the sales figure for year 4 is the year 3 sales figure multiplied by 0.95 to reflect the 5% decrease.

The last set of cash flows we need to develop before applying the discounted cash flow techniques are terminal cash flows. These are discussed in the next section.

FINANCE WORKSHOP 8.3

The following annual operating cash flow estimates have been provided by Aster Ltd's management for the proposed flower drying project:

- Year 1 sales: $150 000.
- Sales are expected to increase by $15 000 for each of the following 6 years.
- Sales diverted from existing fresh flower sales: $1000 each year.
- Cost of growing additional flowers for drying: 30% of sales.
- Labour: $30 000 for the first 3 years and $50 000 for the following 3 years.
- Electricity: 15% of sales.
- Advertising cost for each of the first 2 years: $10 000; $5000 for years 3–6.

Determine the annual net operating cash flow for the flower drying project.

Estimating the terminal value

The terminal value of a project is the cash inflow or outflow that is expected at the end of the project's life. It is a relevant cash flow because it will not exist unless the project is accepted. The main sources of terminal cash flows are the salvage value of any assets used by the project and the return of net working capital. Net working capital is not used up in the production process because it is constantly replaced over the life of the project. An increase in the level of inventory, for example, is maintained while the project exists. During the last months of the project, this inventory can run down and not be replaced. This process returns the original increase in the value of inventory to the firm. Example 8.6 shows how the terminal value of the Greenwash project is calculated.

EXAMPLE 8.6

Estimating the terminal value

The Greenwash project is expected to continue for 5 years. At the end of that time, management expect to sell the production line that was purchased for the project for $400 000. The estimated cost of dismantling the production line is $4000. What is the terminal value of the project?

Cash flow at project termination

Sale of machine	400 000
Subtract dismantling cost	4 000
Cash inflow from machine	396 000
Add return of net working capital	70 000
Terminal value	466 000

FINANCE WORKSHOP 8.4

Aster Ltd's flower drying project is expected to continue for 6 years. The useful life of the flower drying machine is 6 years. At the end of this time the machine can be sold as scrap for $25 000. The net increase in working capital of $5000 at the project's inception will be returned upon completion of the project. What is the terminal value?

Identifying annual cash flows

The final step in preparing our cash flows for discounted cash flow analysis is to assemble the initial outlay, the net operating cash flows and the terminal value. We organise each of the cash flow components in sequence so we can properly adjust for the time value of the flows.

Example 8.7 shows the entire cash flow pattern for the Greenwash project. It uses the initial outlay we calculated in examples 8.1, 8.2 and 8.3, the operating cash flows from example 8.5 and the terminal value from example 8.6.

Time zero is when the initial outlay of the project is made. Operating cash flows commence in the period after the initial investment. The time line shows the first operating cash flows at the end of the first year (year 1) because we are measuring operating cash flows on an annual basis. Putting them at the end of year 1 is the same as assuming all of the operating cash flows are received on the last day of the year. Clearly, this will rarely be the case. However, as a simplifying assumption, this one makes much more sense than assuming that the cash flows are all received on the first day of the year when it's likely that no sales have been made! Alternatively, we could assume that flows occur daily, weekly or monthly but, for simplicity's sake, we will assume the last day of the year. The terminal value is included in the year 5 cash flows because this is when the project ends. It may not always be sensible to assume the terminal value occurs on the last day of the project. If the assets in the project are highly specialised, it may take some time to find a buyer for them. In this case, we would make our best estimate of how long it would take to dispose of the asset and extend the project time line if it were a significant length of time (say, over 6 months).

EXAMPLE 8.7

Annual cash flows for the Greenwash project

	Time zero	Year 1	Year 2	Year 3	Year 4	Year 5
Initial outlay	−1 282 000					
Net operating cash flow		463 000	501 000	540 900	499 005	559 205
Terminal value						466 000
Net cash flows	−1 282 000	463 000	501 000	540 900	499 005	1 025 205

Once we have assembled our cash flows, we are ready to apply our discounted cash flow techniques.

FINANCE WORKSHOP 8.5

Construct a table of the annual cash flows for Aster's flower drying project. Use the initial outlay, annual operating cash flows and the terminal value you have calculated in the last three finance workshops.

lo4

Describe and apply the net present value (NPV) technique.

Net present value: the sum of the discounted net cash flows over the life of a proposed project, minus the project's initial outlay

Net present value

The **net present value** (NPV) technique gives us a way of comparing the cash inflows and outflows of the project. The project's forecast cash flows are discounted (to allow for time value) at the firm's cost of capital (to allow for the debt and equity holders' required returns). The cost of capital can be thought of as the opportunity cost of the entire project. If the firm accepts a project, it is giving up the opportunity to earn a return on some other project. We do not show this opportunity cost in the project cash flows because, like financing costs, it is accounted for in the discount rate.

The discounted net cash inflows are the benefits of the project. These are compared to the initial outlay (or cost) of the project. We can calculate the NPV of a project by applying equation 8.1 to project cash flows.

$$NPV_i = \sum_{t=1}^{n} \frac{CF_t}{(1+k_a)^t} - IO \qquad [8.1]$$

where NPV_i = net present value of project i

CF_t = cash flow for period t

k_a = cost of capital for the firm

IO = initial outlay of the project

n = number of periods

A positive NPV tells us how much of the project's forecast net cash inflows are left after the debt and equity holders of the firm have been compensated and the initial outlay has been recovered. Positive NPV projects increase the value of the firm because they make more cash available for distribution to shareholders or for reinvestment in the firm.

If the project being evaluated has the same level of risk as the projects that the firm currently operates, the decision rules for use with the NPV technique are:

- accept a project if the NPV is greater than or equal to zero ($NPV \geq 0$)
- reject a project if the NPV is less than zero ($NPV < 0$).

A project with a zero NPV will leave the value of the firm unchanged because the suppliers of capital are receiving their required returns from the investment in the project. A project with a negative NPV will decrease the value of the firm. The cost of capital is not the appropriate benchmark when a project has more or less risk than the average of the projects currently being undertaken by the firm. We deal with this issue in chapter 9.

If management have adopted all the available positive NPV projects and have shareholder funds in excess of investment requirements, the excess funds should be returned to the owners. The following 'finance world' feature gives a real world example of a company returning excess cash to its shareholders. Brambles Ltd generated the excess cash from very strong operating performance and from the sale of assets. As we will see later in the book, cash can be returned to shareholders via a share buyback (as Brambles did) or by paying more dividends.

FINANCE WORLD

Returning excess cash to shareholders

17. Brambles Industries Ltd–BIL
Industry: Commercial Services & Supplies
1-year low/high: $8.69/$13.60
Share price: $12.65
CEO/MD: David Turner, appointed October 2003

BIL is a global commercial services group with operations in about 45 countries across six continents. The company's operations comprise two business units. CHEP is involved in pallets and containers and Recall is its information management business. BIL has been a great performer during the last 12 months, providing investors a return in excess of 50%. During FY06 BIL sold its Cleanaway businesses for $US3.6bn, a better than expected figure. BIL reported an annual net profit before tax and significant items of $887m, which was 89% above the FY05 figure. Both CHEP and Recall produced strong results.

The outlook for BIL is positive. In the three months to the end of September, sales and profits from the continuing businesses of CHEP and Recall were well ahead of the comparative period in the prior year. CHEP is expected to have another good year in FY07. So far, like for like sales have grown 6% in the three months to the end of September. Recall should build on the good performance of its second half of FY06, with sales 18% higher so far. This includes the return from its Ausdoc business acquired in December 2005. After recent asset sales, the company now has raised significant amounts of cash that will be used at least in part to finance a large share buyback.[4]

Example 8.8 applies the NPV technique to the cash flows for the Greenwash project we identified in example 8.7. Let's assume that the cost of capital for Clean-O is 10%.

EXAMPLE 8.8

Calculating the NPV of the Greenwash project

	Time zero	Year 1	Year 2	Year 3	Year 4	Year 5
Initial outlay	-1 282 000					
Net operating cash flow		463 000	501 000	540 900	499 005	559 205
Terminal value						466 000
Net cash flows	-1 282 000	463 000	501 000	540 900	499 005	1 025 205
		$(1 + 0.10)^{-1}$	$(1 + 0.10)^{-2}$	$(1 + 0.10)^{-3}$	$(1 + 0.10)^{-4}$	$(1 + 0.10)^{-5}$
Discount factor	1	0.9091	0.8264	0.7513	0.6830	0.6209
Present value	-1 282 000	420 913	414 026	406 378	340 820	636 550
NPV	936 687					

The NPV of the Greenwash project is positive. This tells the management of Clean-O that the project should be adopted. Accepting the project will increase the value of the firm by $936 687.

FINANCE WORKSHOP 8.6

Using a discount rate of 14% and the table of annual cash flows for Aster's flower drying project you constructed in finance workshop 8.5, calculate the project's NPV. Should the project be accepted? Why?

lo5

Describe and apply the internal rate of return (IRR) technique.

Internal rate of return: the discount rate that equates the present value of the project's cash flows to the initial outlay of the project

Internal rate of return

The second discounted cash flow technique we will learn is the **internal rate of return** (IRR). The concept of IRR is introduced in chapter 7, where it is defined as the discount rate that equates the present value of the project's cash flows to the initial outlay of the project. Where the NPV tells us the dollar amount of impact that a project has on firm value, the IRR tells us the rate of return that the project is earning. We apply equation 8.2 to the project's cash flows to determine the IRR.

$$IO = \sum_{t=1}^{n} \frac{CF_t}{(1 + IRR)^n} \qquad [8.2]$$

where IO = initial outlay of the project

IRR = discount rate that equates the present value of the cash flows to the IO

CF_t = cash flow for period t

n = number of periods

Where we solved equation 8.1 for the NPV, you will notice that the unknown factor (IRR in equation 8.2) is not isolated on one side of the 'equals' sign. We need to apply the techniques we use in chapter 7 to calculate the cost of debt. We can use the trial and error method or use a financial calculator or a spreadsheet to solve equation 8.2. Example 8.9 shows the IRR for the cash flows of the Greenwash project. It also demonstrates the relationship of the IRR to the NPV — the IRR is the discount rate that gives the project's net cash flows an NPV of zero.

EXAMPLE 8.9

Calculating the IRR of the Greenwash project

	Time zero	Year 1	Year 2	Year 3	Year 4	Year 5
Net cash flows	-1 282 000	463 000	501 000	549 000	499 005	1 025 205
IRR	32.4345%					

There are no calculations to show for the IRR as it was calculated using the IRR function in Excel. You would get the same result with a financial calculator. To demonstrate the relationship of the IRR to the NPV, the following table calculates the Greenwash NPV using the IRR as the discount rate.

	Time zero	Year 1	Year 2	Year 3	Year 4	Year 5
Net cash flows	-1 282 000	463 000	501 000	540 900	499 005	1 025 205
Discount factor	1	0.7551	0.5702	0.4306	0.3251	0.2455
(k = 0.3243)	-1 282 000	349 611	285 670	232 912	162 227	251 688
NPV	108					

The NPV of $108 is the result of rounding the discount rate to 4 decimal places and rounding the each cash flow to the nearest dollar. Calculate the IRR of the Greenwash project and use this to calculate the NPV to assure yourself that the IRR is the discount rate that gives a zero NPV.

FINANCE WORKSHOP 8.7

Using the table of annual cash flows for Aster's flower drying project that you constructed in finance workshop 8.5, calculate the project's IRR. Should the project be accepted if the hurdle rate is 14%? Why?

Hurdle rate: the minimum rate of return generated that will make a project acceptable

The decision rule to use with the IRR technique is to compare the project's IRR to the **hurdle rate**:

- accept a proposed project if IRR ≥ hurdle rate
- reject a proposed project if IRR < hurdle rate.

The hurdle rate for projects with the same level of risk as those already undertaken is the cost of capital. If the IRR is greater than the cost of capital, the project is earning greater returns than those required by the contributors of capital and firm value should increase by accepting the project. If the IRR is less than the cost of capital, the project is not generating sufficient returns to cover the cost of capital and firm value should decrease. An IRR equal to the cost of capital will leave the value of the firm unchanged. We will defer discussion of the appropriate hurdle rate for projects with different levels of risk to those currently operated by the firm until chapter 9.

We used the cost of capital as the discount rate for the Greenwash project in example 8.8 and to calculate NPV because we considered the risk of the Greenwash project to be the same as the other projects currently undertaken by Clean-O. The cost of capital is the appropriate hurdle rate for the IRR technique when the project risk is the same as that of current projects. The IRR for the Greenwash project is 32%, so by applying the decision rule:

- IRR ≥ hurdle rate accept proposed project
- 32% > 10% accept proposed project.

The following 'finance world' feature alludes to many of the issues we have discussed in the chapter so far.

FINANCE WORLD

IRR and firm value

LionOre gets go ahead for Activox project, Botswana

Sydney: Thursday, August 10 (RWE Australian Business News) — LionOre Mining (ASX: LIM) has received approvals for the Activox project, comprising the construction of a base metals refinery and associated projects at Tati Nickel in Botswana for US$620 million. It will include the US$482 million Activox Base Metal Refinery, US$114 million Dense Media Separation plant upgrade to the Tati concentrator and US$24 million power infrastructure installation.

Economics show an incremental IRR of 17 pc is achieved when compared against the current business plan, assuming a long-term nickel price of US$4.35 per pound.

Vertical integration increases the economic net back of payable nickel from 73 to 94 per cent.

Tati Nickel cash costs forecast to reduce significantly to US$1.69 per pound of nickel over the life of the project.

There is also the ability to lower cut-off grade to 0.10pc which doubles Phoenix mine reserves to 111.6 million tonnes containing 331 000 tonnes of nickel.

Project life of mine is 11 years with the potential to increase to more than 20 years when the Selkirk resource is factored in.

In addition to the Activox refining operation LionOre will continue to supply nickel concentrate to the BCL smelter.

LionOre shares were up 6c to 7.50.[5]

Comparing NPV and IRR

The NPV and IRR methods both share the disadvantage of requiring preparation of detailed estimates of cash flows. The use of these cash flows means that both methods share the benefit of being theoretically sound discounted-cash-flow methods that should result in decisions that increase the value of the firm.

Typical projects have a cash outflow at the start followed by net cash inflows over the life of the project. As we saw with the Greenwash example, the NPV and the IRR techniques will generate the same 'accept or reject' decision for typical projects. Because the IRR is the discount rate that equates the present value of the project's cash flows to the initial outlay, an IRR that is equal to the cost of capital will have a zero NPV for typical cash flow pattern projects. A negative NPV project would have an IRR that is less than the cost of capital, while a positive NPV project would have an IRR greater than the cost of capital.

Some projects have different patterns of cash flows and this can mean that the IRR and NPV relationship for typical cash flow patterns will not hold. A project might, for example, have a cash outflow at the start followed by several years of net cash inflows but then have a year where there is a net cash outflow. This could occur if the firm has to pay a large licence fee every few years for the right to manufacture a product. The following time line shows the cash flows for a project that has an initial outlay of \$100 000 (which includes a licence fee of \$80 000). The net operating cash inflows for the project are \$60 000 per year, but the licence fee of \$80 000 has to be paid at the start of each three-year period to obtain the right to continue manufacturing the product. This payment would occur at the start of the fourth year of operation, so we show it in the year 3 cash flows because these are assumed to occur at the end of year 3, The time value for one day (the difference between the start of year 4 and the end of year 3) is trivial. The net cash flow for year 3 is an outflow of \$20 000 (\$60 000 net operating inflow – \$80 000 licence fee).

t_0	t_1	t_2	t_3	t_4	t_5	t_6	t_n
−100 000	60 000	60 000	−20 000	60 000	60 000	−20 000	---

When a project's net cash flows have a reversal of sign (that is, net cash inflows followed by a net cash outflow, then return to net cash inflows) the IRR technique will fail to give a clear-cut decision that will maximise the value of the firm. In fact, the project will have as many IRRs as there are reversals in sign for the cash flows. The NPV technique is superior for projects with net cash outflows occurring during the life of the project.

While unusual, it is possible that some projects do not require an initial outlay. When this is the case, the IRR cannot be calculated because no investment is made on which to base the return. Again, the NPV technique is superior here. If the initial outlay of the project is zero, the NPV is simply the present value of the future cash flows and still represents the expected increase or decrease in value of the firm that would be attributable to accepting the project.

While the NPV and IRR techniques are both based on discounted cash flows, they make different assumptions about the cash flows that are received over the project's life. The NPV technique is based on the assumption that the net cash flows are invested at the discount rate we use to determine the present value of the future flows. For a project with the same risk as those currently operated by the firm, this will be the cost of capital. Basically, the NPV method works on the idea that cash flows from the project being assessed would be invested in new projects that will be adopted later and that these future projects will generate a return equal to the cost of capital for the firm. In our Greenwash example, the NPV of \$936 687 depends on the net cash flows of the project being used in future projects that will generate 10% per annum.

The IRR technique is based on the assumption that the cash flows are reinvested at the IRR of the project being analysed. In our Greenwash example, the IRR of 32% is dependent on the cash flows being used in future projects adopted by Clean-O that also have IRRs of 32%. An IRR that is more than three times the cost of capital makes the Greenwash project very attractive. However, the management of Clean-O may not be confident that they can find future projects that will generate such a high return. If they cannot, the IRR is misleading because it will not be achieved.

Further, it is illogical to assume different rates for reinvestment for projects with the same risk as the other projects in the firm. Say Clean-O was evaluating two projects and could adopt both of them. The first project has an IRR of 32% and the second has an IRR of 16%. Both projects are acceptable against a 10% hurdle rate, but we are assuming that the cash flows from the first are reinvested at 32% while the second are reinvested at 16%. Again, the NPV method is superior because it assumes that net cash flows over the life of the project are reinvested at the opportunity cost to the firm, not at some other rate that depends on the project that is currently being analysed.

Surveys about project appraisal techniques indicate that IRR is used as often as NPV. One survey of large enterprises (including private companies and government instrumentalities) found 75% used NPV and 72% used IRR.[6] Another survey of Australian listed companies found 96% of corporates used NPV and 96% used IRR.[7] Results for US and Canadian companies are similar, with 75% using NPV and 76% using IRR.[8] These results indicate that many financial managers use more than one discounted cash flow method of project evaluation for each project.

This brings us to the one advantage of IRR over NPV — it is easier for people without a formal finance background to interpret a rate of return than it is to understand what the dollar NPV amount means. The cost associated with conducting a discounted cash flow analysis comes in the collection of data for the best possible estimation of the size and timing of cash flows. Once you have the cash flow pattern, the incremental cost of running both analytical techniques is trivial. Managers have nothing to lose and perhaps more support to be gained by presenting both NPV and IRR measures.

In chapter 9, we continue our discussion of planning investments by investigating the issues that arise when projects compete for the same scarce resources, incorporating risk into project analysis, considering the impact of the taxation system and looking at the role of non-financial factors in the project analysis process.

executive summary

lo1 define investment decisions and discuss their characteristics

- An investment is the outlay of capital made with a view to gaining future benefits.
- The four common characteristics of investment decisions are that they have large initial outlays, they have relatively long project lives, they are difficult and expensive to reverse, and that they involve risk.
- Shareholders make investments to receive future returns from dividends and/or capital gains. They make their investments by purchasing shares.
- Companies make investments to generate the shareholders' required return.
- The two main categories of investment decisions are expansion and replacement projects.
- Projects with large outlays and relatively long lives should be evaluated as they represent a large commitment of the firm's resources.
- Projects that are difficult to reverse should be evaluated as it is usually expensive for the firm to divest itself of the project if it does not perform well.
- Not all investments made by a firm need to be rigorously evaluated. For example, if the purchased assets are inexpensive (purchasing paper for the printer), have a relatively short life (purchasing pens for the office) or are not too difficult to reverse (purchasing a new car for the CEO), the costs of the analysis are unlikely to be justified by the benefits.
- New projects are undertaken to increase net cash inflows.
- Replacement projects update the technology used in current projects, usually with the objective of saving costs (outflows).
- Often, ideas for projects are generated by management and employees.

lo2 explain how investment decisions relate to firm value and describe the characteristics of investment appraisal techniques that are consistent with increasing firm value

- Firms begin operations with an investment by the owners.
- Operations are maintained and expanded by making investment decisions.
- The objective of making investments is to maximise the wealth of the owners.
- To be consistent with this objective, project evaluation techniques should use cash flows rather than profits, consider the time value of money and be able to incorporate risk into the analysis.
- Cash flows are used in wealth maximising decisions because they are the real resources that are generated by the project. Profit, on the other hand, is the construct of accounting rules.
- The time value of money is considered in wealth maximising decisions because projects have relatively long lives. We cannot get a meaningful number if we add dollars from today to dollars received in five years' time.
- The ability of an evaluation technique to incorporate risk is important for wealth maximising decisions. The required rate of return for shareholders will change as the level of risk in the firm changes. We need to be able to include this factor in our decision making process.
- The discounted cash flow techniques of net present value (NPV) and internal rate of return (IRR) are consistent with the objective of wealth maximisation.

lo3 estimate the incremental cash flows of a project

- Marginal analysis is a method for making decisions to maximise our objective by comparing additional (marginal) benefits with additional costs.
- Marginal analysis helps the decision maker to focus on the important aspects of the project — how will the net cash flows of the firm change if the project is accepted?
- Incremental cash flows result from the acceptance of a project and it is incremental not total cash flows that are relevant to project evaluation.
- Incremental cash flows typically include the initial outlay of the project, the incremental cash inflows from sales, incremental outflows in the form of increased operating costs, opportunity costs of the project and the cash flow from the terminal value when the project is completed.
- The initial outlay is the capital expenditure made to implement an investment.
- Operating costs are the cash outflows required in the daily activities of the project.
- Opportunity costs are the cash flows forgone when one path of action is chosen.
- Terminal value is the expected cash flow associated with the disposal of the project's assets at the end of the project's life.
- Sunk costs are cash flows that occur prior to the evaluation of a project and are irrelevant to the analysis.
- Financing costs are not relevant cash flows because they are implicit in the discount rate used to evaluate the project.
- Relevant cash flows are estimated for the initial outlay, the operating cash flows and the terminal value of the project.
- The initial outlay includes the installed cost of any new equipment (less the terminal value of the old equipment in a replacement decision) plus any increase in net working capital.
- Net working capital is the excess of current assets over current liabilities.
- An increase in net working capital is included in the initial outlay because cash is required to fund the purchase of more inventory or higher levels of accounts receivable. This cash is then unavailable for other uses in the firm, so it is incremental to the project.
- A decrease in net working capital is included in the initial outlay because reduced levels of inventory or accounts receivable mean that there is more cash available for other uses in the firm.
- The initial outlay for an expansion project normally includes the cost of acquiring the assets for the project, the cost of getting the assets ready for use, the cost of training staff, and any change in net working capital.
- The initial outlay for a replacement project normally includes cash flow from disposing of the asset that is being replaced. It might be possible to sell the equipment that is being replaced. The cash from the sale of the old equipment will not occur unless the new project is accepted, so it is incremental. It reduces the cost of the replacement asset.
- Where the removal of the existing asset generates a net cash outflow, this outflow increases the initial outlay of the replacement project.
- Estimates of operating inflows and outflows are used to determine the annual net operating cash flow for the project.

- Terminal value is the cash inflow or outflow that is expected at the end of the project's life. The main sources of terminal value are the salvage value of any equipment and the return of net working capital.
- A time line of relevant cash flows normally shows the initial outlay at time zero (or today) then has the annual net cash flows for the project. The terminal value of the project is shown in the final year of the project's cash flows.
- The simplifying assumption used for annual net cash flows is that the cash flows are received at the end of each year.

lo4 describe and apply the net present value (NPV) technique

- The NPV of a project equals the discounted net cash flows received over the life of the project minus the project's initial outlay.
- The decision rules for use with the NPV technique for projects with the same level of risk as those currently undertaken are to accept a project if the NPV is greater than or equal to zero and to reject a project if the NPV is less than zero.
- Positive NPV projects increase the value of the firm.
- The appropriate discount rate for projects with the same risk as those currently undertaken by the firm is the cost of capital.
- The cost of capital incorporates the required returns of the shareholders and debtholders. It also represents the opportunity cost to the firm of not investing in other projects that would return the cost of capital.

lo5 describe and apply the internal rate of return (IRR) technique

- The IRR is the discount rate that equates the present value of the project's cash flows to the initial outlay of the project.
- The decision rules for use with the IRR technique for projects with the same level of risk as those currently undertaken are to accept a project if the IRR is greater than or equal to the hurdle rate and to reject a project if the IRR is less than the hurdle rate.
- The appropriate hurdle rate for projects with the same risk as those currently undertaken by the firm is the cost of capital.
- Projects with IRRs greater than the cost of capital should increase firm value.
- The internal rate of return is the discount rate that makes the net present value of a project equal to zero.
- Both the NPV and IRR are discounted cash flow techniques, so are consistent with wealth maximisation. They both require detailed cash flow forecasts and both give the same decision for projects with typical cash flow patterns.
- A disadvantage of the IRR technique is that there can be multiple IRRs for projects that do not have typical cash flow patterns.
- The IRR cannot be calculated for projects that have a zero initial outlay.
- The NPV assumes that the cash flows generated by the project are reinvested at the cost of capital (the discount rate).
- The IRR assumes that the cash flows generated by the project are reinvested at the IRR of the project. This assumption is less realistic than the assumption made in the NPV technique.

Key terms

hurdle rate, p. 287
incremental cash flows, p. 273
initial outlay, p. 269
internal rate of return, p. 285
investment, p. 269
marginal analysis, p. 273
net present value, p. 283
net working capital, p. 277
operating costs, p. 274
opportunity costs, p. 274
sunk costs, p. 275
terminal value, p. 272

Learning chart

Learning objective	Questions	Self-test problems	Financial problems
lo*1* define investment decisions and discuss their characteristics	8.1		
lo*2* explain how investment decisions relate to firm value and describe the characteristics of investment appraisal techniques that are consistent with increasing firm value	8.2, 8.3, 8.4, 8.5		
lo*3* estimate the incremental cash flows of a project	8.6, 8.7, 8.8, 8.9, 8.10, 8.11	8.1, 8.2, 8.3, 8.4	8.1, 8.2, 8.3, 8.4, 8.5, 8.6, 8.8, 8.9, 8.10, 8.11, 8.12, 8.13, 8.14, 8.15, 8.16, 8.17, 8.18, 8.19
lo*4* describe and apply the net present value (NPV) technique	8.12, 8.13, 8.16, 8.17, 8.18, 8.19, 8.20	8.4	8.4, 8.6, 8.7, 8.8, 8.9, 8.10, 8.11, 8.16, 8.17, 8.18, 8.19
lo*5* describe and apply the internal rate of return (IRR) technique	8.14, 8.15, 8.16, 8.17, 8.18, 8.19, 8.20	8.5	8.4, 8.7, 8.8, 8.9, 8.11, 8.16, 8.17, 8.18, 8.19

Questions

8.1 What is an 'investment'? Why do companies make investments?

8.2 Do you expect that every investment made by a firm would be rigorously evaluated? Why?

8.3 Identify two broad ways a business can grow. Is growth for its own sake a desirable objective? Why?

8.4 How do new projects generate wealth for the owners of the firm?

8.5 What are the criteria for investment evaluation techniques that are consistent with the firm objective of wealth maximisation? What two evaluation techniques meet these criteria?

8.6 What types of cash flows are relevant to the discounted cash flow techniques? Give some examples of cash flows that are irrelevant and explain why you would exclude these from an investment evaluation.

8.7 Why don't we include the cost of financing the project in the relevant cash flows?

8.8 Explain the concept of opportunity cost. What are the opportunity costs associated with your decision to study this course?

8.9 What are sunk costs? When are they relevant to investment decisions?

8.10 Define the term 'net working capital'. Why are increases or decreases in net working capital included in the initial outlay for a project?

8.11 Why are the terminal cash flows of an existing asset included in the calculation of the initial outlay for a replacement project, but not for an expansion project?

8.12 What are the decision rules for NPV? Explain what will happen to shareholder wealth if:

(a) NPV is positive

(b) NPV is zero

(c) NPV is negative.

8.13 What is the appropriate discount rate for evaluating a project with the same risk as the firm's existing projects? Why?

8.14 What are the decision rules for IRR? Explain what will happen to shareholder wealth if:

(a) IRR is greater than the hurdle rate

(b) IRR is equal to the hurdle rate

(c) IRR is less than the hurdle rate.

8.15 What is the appropriate hurdle rate for evaluating a project with the same risk as the firm's existing projects? Why?

8.16 What is the relationship between NPV and IRR? (*Hint:* what will the NPV of a project equal if the IRR equals the hurdle rate?)

8.17 What is the typical cash flow pattern for a project?

8.18 Is IRR or NPV more reliable when a project's cash flow pattern includes net outflows during the project's life? Why?

8.19 What assumptions do NPV and IRR make about the reinvestment of a project's cash flows over its life? Which assumption is more realistic? Why?

8.20 Do financial managers use IRR or NPV more? Why might managers use both techniques?

Self-test problems

8.1 Nesbitt Ltd is a biscuit manufacturer considering the addition of a new line of biscuits to its current range. The Hobgoblin project will require the purchase of a new mixing machine and a new oven. These will cost \$200 000 and \$500 000 respectively. The equipment will be installed in what is currently the factory storeroom. The cost to prepare the area and get the equipment ready for use is expected to be $20 000. What is the installed cost of the equipment for the new project?

8.2 Nesbitt Ltd estimates that an increase of $3000 in the level of raw materials and $5000 for finished goods inventories would be needed to support its new product. Accounts receivable are expected to increase by $10 000, and accounts payable by $2000. What is the net change in working capital for the Hobgoblin project?

8.3 Nesbitt's marketing department plans to spend $10 000 per annum advertising the product over its life. To really capture the market's attention, the marketing department will advertise to saturation level for the month around the product launch. This will involve an additional advertising cost of $60 000 to be spent in the month around the product launch date. What is the initial outlay for the Hobgoblin project?

8.4 Nesbitt expects to sell $100 000 of the Hobgoblin product next year. It expects sales will grow at a rate of 10% pa in years 2 to 6. The growth rate for sales in years 7 to 10 is expected to be a more modest 3%. Raw materials and labour are estimated at 20% and 15% of sales, respectively. Electricity and other variable costs will be 2% of sales. As mentioned in self-test problem 8.3, advertising the Hobgoblin product will cost $10 000 pa for each year of the project's operation. Nesbitt's annual insurance premiums of $5000 will not change with the introduction of the new project.

At the end of the tenth year, Nesbitt expects to use the equipment from the Hobgoblin project for some new biscuit product. At that time, they forecast the market value of the mixer to be $20 000 and the value of the oven to be $100 000. No net working capital will be lost over the life of the project. Nesbitt's cost of capital is 15%.

(a) Using this information and that included in self-test questions 8.1 to 8.3, calculate the NPV of the Hobgoblin project. Round all variables to whole dollar amounts.

(b) Should the project be accepted? Why or why not?

8.5 Using the information in self-test questions 8.1 to 8.4, calculate the IRR of the Hobgoblin project. Should the project be accepted? Why or why not?

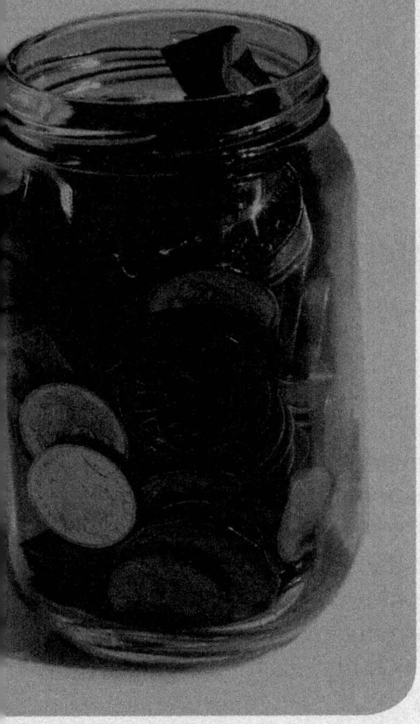

Solutions to self-test problems

8.1

Mixing machine	200 000
Oven	500 000
Set up costs	20 000
Installed cost	720 000

8.2

Raw materials	3 000
Finished goods	5 000
Accounts receivable (add)	10 000
Accounts payable (subtract)	(2 000)
Increase in net working capital	16 000

8.3

Installed cost of new machines	720 000
Increase in net working capital	16 000
Advertising for launch	60 000
	796 000

8.4 (a)

	0	1	2	3	4	5
Initial outlay	–796 000					
Sales		100 000	110 000	121 000	133 100	146 410
Raw materials		–20 000	–22 000	–24 200	–26 620	–29 282
Labour		–15 000	–16 500	–18 150	–19 965	–21 962
Electricity & other		–2 000	–2 200	–2 420	–2 662	–2 928
Advertising		–10 000	–10 000	–10 000	–10 000	–10 000
Terminal value						
Net cash flows	–796 000	53 000	59 300	66 230	73 853	82 238
PVF	1	0.8696	0.7561	0.6575	0.5718	0.4972
PV of cash flows	–796 000	46 089	44 837	43 546	42229	40 889
NPV	–387 329					

	6	7	8	9	10
Initial outlay					
Sales	161 051	165 883	170 859	175 985	181 265
Raw materials	–32 210	–33 177	–34 172	–35 197	–36 253
Labour	–24 158	–24 882	–25 629	–26 398	–27 190
Electricity & other	–3 221	–3 318	–3 417	–3 520	–3 625
Advertising	–10 000	–10 000	–10 000	–10 000	–10 000
Terminal value					120 000
Net cash flows	91 462	94 506	97 641	100 870	224 197
PVF	0.4323	0.3759	0.3269	0.2843	0.2472
PV of cash flows	39 539	35 525	31 919	28 677	55 421
NPV					

(b) The project has a negative NPV of $387 329. It would not increase the value of the firm so it should be rejected.

8.5 IRR = 2.6542%

The project has an IRR that is less than the hurdle rate (2.65%<15%). It should be rejected.

Financial problems

8.1 Cupsley Ltd is a manufacturer of cutlery. The firm's managers have asked you to evaluate a project proposal to diversify into manufacturing nailfiles. A new machine to mould the plastic on to the end of the nailfiles would need to be purchased at a cost of $150 000. Freight and insurance for the new machine will cost $3500 and installation will cost a further $1200. The files would be pressed on existing equipment. The files would be produced by introducing a night shift, so will not displace any current production capacity. The existing machine would be modified at a cost of $20 000.

If the new project goes ahead, Cupsley will need to increase the raw materials inventory by $2500. The finished goods inventory would need to be $4500 higher than its current level. Cupsley will supply 30-day terms to the distributors of the nailfiles and this is expected to result in an increase of $60 000 in accounts receivable. The increase in accounts receivable will occur during the first week of production for the project. Cupsley has arranged credit with suppliers of the plastic that will be used in the production process. This is expected to result in an increase of $15 000 to accounts payable.

(a) What is the installed cost of the project?

(b) What is the change in net working capital?

(c) What is the initial outlay for the nailfile project?

8.2 Cupsley Ltd has set a 5-year life for the proposed nailfile project. Cupsley's management have given you the following forecasts of operating cash flows:

- Sales of nailfiles for the first year are $120 000. The estimated growth rate for sales is 2% pa for the second and subsequent years of the project.
- Raw materials are estimated at 15% of sales.
- Labour costs for the project will be $30 000 per annum.
- Cupsley's annual electricity bill is $50 000. The electricity cost for the nailfile project is expected to be 12% of sales.

Determine the annual net operating cash flow for the nailfile project.

8.3 At the end of 5 years, Cupsley will terminate the nailfile project. It is expected that the plastic moulding machine that was purchased for the project will be sold for $30 000. Removal costs of $650 are expected for the moulding machine. The modifications to the machine used for pressing the metal part of the files will not affect the future use of that machine and will remain in place. The increase in net working capital (see problem 8.1) will be returned to the firm at the end of the project. What is the terminal value of the nailfile project?

8.4 Using your calculations in problems 8.1 to 8.3:

(a) Construct a table of the annual cash flows for Cupsley's nailfile project.

(b) Calculate the NPV of the project using a discount rate of 10%.

(c) On the basis of the NPV, is the project acceptable? Why?

(d) Calculate the IRR of the project and compare it to a hurdle rate of 10%.

(e) On the basis of the IRR, is the project acceptable? Why?

8.5 Four-poster Co. restores antique brass beds. As part of the restoration process, the beds are dipped into an acid bath to strip them of old paint. At present, the company uses an old hand winch to raise and lower the beds into the acid bath. A new computerised winch has been developed and is currently available for purchase. The new winch costs $27 000. Transport and insurance costs to get the new winch to the factory will be $790. An electrician has quoted $200 to install the machine. The old winch can be sold to the local museum for $500. Removal costs for the old winch are expected to be $150. What is the installed cost for the replacement winch?

8.6 Sales revenues at Four-poster Co. (see problem 8.5) will not increase if the new winch is purchased. However, the new winch will prevent employees from being splashed with acid. The safety improvements mean the company will save about $4000 each year on the cost of protective clothing. Currently, staff burnt by acid splashes do not come to work for an average of 3 days per incident. Elimination of acid splashes would save the company around $5000 per annum in sick leave payments. Payments for workers' compensation insurance would decrease by $1000 pa if the new machine was purchased. The annual electricity cost associated with operating the new machine is expected to be $2000.

The new winch would be operated for 12 years and could be sold for $5000 at the end of that time. Management tell you that the appropriate discount rate to use for analysis is 15%. Using these data and the information from problem 8.5, calculate the NPV of the new winch. Should the winch be purchased or not? Why?

8.7 Using 12% as the discount and hurdle rates, calculate the NPV and IRR for each of the following three projects:

	Project A	Project B	Project C
Time 0	–50 000	–75 000	–100 000
Year 1	15 000	10 000	25 000
Year 2	15 000	10 000	25 000
Year 3	15 000	15 000	35 000
Year 4	15 000	15 000	–10 000
Year 5	15 000	18 000	40 000
Year 6	15 000	18 000	45 000
Year 7	15 000	17 000	
Year 8	15 000	15 000	
Year 9	15 000		
Year 10	15 000		

Which projects should be accepted and which should be rejected? Why?

8.8 Babycare is considering a 4-year project to manufacture stain-resistant baby bibs. The firm has spent $10 000 researching the project and have estimated an annual demand of 20 000 units. The bibs will sell for $7.50 each and the cash costs per unit will be $3.25. An inventory of 25% of sales will be maintained over the life of the project. Additional equipment to manufacture the bibs will cost $70 000. Transport and insurance of the equipment will cost $2000 and a further $8000 will be needed to install the equipment and modify it to suit Babycare's needs. The project equipment will be sold for $10 000 at the end of the project and 80% of the working capital will be returned. The firm's cost of capital is 12% and the bib project has the same level of risk as current projects.

(a) Estimate the cash flows for the project.

(b) Calculate the NPV for the project. Should the project be accepted?

(c) Calculate the IRR for the project. Should the project be accepted?

8.9 Given your interest in sports and computers, you are considering establishing a computer games development business. You would like to run the business for the next 5 years and your required return is 18%. You would need hardware worth around $200 000 to start development and production of your first game 'Super Hoop Croquet'. The equipment would be scrapped at the end of the project.

You have decided to locate your business in a regional centre rather than the city in order to lower rental costs. Your annual rent will be $30 000. The going rate for programmers in the area is $70 000 pa and you would employ four programmers.

Sales for the first year are expected to be 3700 units and are expected to grow at 7% pa for the following 4 years of the project. The selling price will be around $130 per unit and the production costs will be $16 per unit. Marketing costs are expected to be 20% of annual sales and are paid at the start of each year, based on the sales estimate for the year. An inventory worth $52 000 will also be needed at the commencement of operations. The inventory cost will be recovered at the end of the project.

Showing all relevant cash flows, calculate the project's NPV and IRR. No incomplete units can be sold, so round the unit sales to the nearest whole number. Should you start this business?

8.10 Hard Rider designs, manufactures and sells motorcycle leathers. It currently has 15% of the market for these goods (the total market is worth $4 million pa). Hard Rider's fixed costs are $25 000 and variable costs are 45% of sales. The management of the firm believes that Hard Rider's market share would increase to 30% if it replaced the existing manufacturing equipment and spend an additional $150 000 pa on advertising. The current equipment has a market value of $25 000. New equipment would cost $800 000 and has an estimated resale value of $50 000 at the end of the 10-year project life. Hard Rider will continue to maintain working capital at 14% of sales.

Determine the relevant cash flows for the project and calculate the NPV using a required return of 15%.

8.11 Postal Chic is an upmarket mail-order fashion distributor. It is considering replacing its manual ordering system with a computerised system that allows customers to order online. The system will also be used to order stock from Postal Chic's suppliers and halve the current delivery time to the Postal Chic warehouses.

The computerised system will cost $3 million to purchase and install and will have annual running costs of $400 000. It will replace a manual system that costs $600 000 to operate. The new system is expected to last 6 years and will have no salvage value at the end of that time.

The attractiveness and accessibility of the new system is expected to increase sales from the current level of $2 million pa to $2.5 million for each of the next 6 years. Postal Chic will be able to cut its inventory from 60% of sale to 20%. The reduced inventory levels would apply at the commencement of the project. Postal Chic hopes this lower level of inventory would continue even when the proposed system is replaced in 6 years' time. The project has the same level of risk as those currently undertaken in the firm. Postal Chic has a cost of capital of 16%.

(a) Determine the relevant cash flows for the project.

(b) Calculate the NPV. Should the project be accepted?

(c) Calculate the IRR. Should the project be accepted?

8.12 The Entertainment Company operates 3 pay TV channels and a free-to-air radio station. It also manufactures CDs and DVDs. It is considering introducing an 'on-demand' movie channel that will allow customers to purchase latest release movies for viewing as many times as they wish within 24 hours of the purchase. It is currently estimating the cash flows for the on-demand movie project and is unsure how to deal with the following issues:

- *Copyright costs*: licence fees of $3.5 million are paid annually to movie studios so the Entertainment Company can reproduce movies on DVD and show the movies in any setting other than a cinema.

- *Server costs*: the firm currently has excess server capacity that could be used for the on-demand project. Before the project was proposed, management had planned to sell the excess server for $15 000.
- *Hardware costs*: the firm's current computer network would be used to meet the needs of the on-demand movie customers. The network was installed last year at a cost of $500 000.
- *Software costs*: ordering on-demand movies requires special software that was purchased last month. The software cost $5000 and the purchase was made to assess the technical feasibility of the project.
- *DVD sales and pay TV revenues*: the firm estimates that the demand for DVDs and pay TV subscriptions will decrease if an on-demand movie service is offered. Management expects that the firm's competitors will lose $3 million pa if the on-demand project goes ahead. They also expect that the Entertainment Company's sales of DVDs would fall by $50 000 pa and that $100 000 less would be received from pay TV subscriptions.

Which of these cash flows would be the relevant cash flows? Explain why you have included or excluded each of the 5 items.

8.13 The Entertainment Company is also considering replacing the broadcasting equipment for the pay TV channels. Management expects the following changes to be associated with replacing the equipment:

	$
Spare parts inventory decrease	−20 000
Accounts receivable increase	50 000
Accounts payable increase	−1 000
Cash increase	5 000

What is the change in net working capital associated with the replacement project?

8.14 Corrugated Metals wants to modernise the welding section of its production line. A new high-tech production system will cost $250 000 to purchase, $5000 to insure and transport to the plant and $3000 to install. The existing equipment cost $50 000 10 years ago and could be sold for $10 000 as is.

The new system would result in a significant annual sales increase and higher production levels. To support these, management have estimated that accounts receivable would increase by $30 000, accounts payable would increase by $20 000 and inventory would increase by $10 000. What is the initial outlay for the new welding system?

8.15 Sportique Ltd operates a chain of 114 sportswear and equipment stores nationwide. Sales last year were $700 million and cost of goods sold is 73% of sales. The selling and advertising expenses of the firm are fixed and will remain at $190 000 pa; 60 per cent of the advertising expense is charged to head office. The remainder of the cost is shared equally among the stores.

The company is considering opening a new store that will cost $500 000 to establish. Assume the new store will have the same costs as existing stores and that sales will be the same as those for the average existing store. Estimate the cash flows for the first 3 years of operation for the new store. Round your calculations for revenue and expenses to the nearest whole dollar.

8.16 You have decided to cash in on the dancing craze in your town, so you are thinking about setting up a dance studio. You can rent a warehouse close to the business district for $40000 pa paid in advance. In order to attract the 'right' sort of clientele, you will need to spend $120000 on redecorating and installing mirrors on all surfaces. You will also purchase some equipment at a cost of $70000. You expect that the equipment can be sold at the end of four years for $7000.

Your market research suggests you can attract and maintain 600 students. Each would pay an annual tuition fee of $900. Instructors are usually paid a salary of $43000 pa and you would employ 5 of these to keep the studio operating 7 days a week. You will operate the business for 4 years before retiring. If your cost of capital is 14%, should you set up the business? Calculate IRR and NPV to support your decision.

8.17 You have been asked to evaluate a proposal for the owner of Gloss Cosmetics. She has given you the following information about the project:

- it has a 7-year lifetime
- the installed cost of the project will be $430000
- the asset will be sold at the end of the project for an estimated $15000
- sales of $200000 are expected in the first year of the project
- sales will grow at a rate of 8% pa for each year of the project
- cost of goods sold (excluding depreciation) is expected to be 25% of sales
- the owner's required return is 18%.

Calculate both the IRR and NPV for the project, then advise the owner of Gloss Cosmetics on the acceptability of the project. Round each calculation to the nearest whole dollar.

8.18 Mick and Steve have a partnership that manufactures racing accessories that can be fitted to street cars. They would like you to evaluate a project for them and have provided the following details:

	Year 1	Year 2	Year 3	Year 4	Year 5	Year 6
Cash sales	300000	600000	700000	500000	500000	400000

- The initial investment in the project is $300000 for production equipment.
- The assets purchased at the commencement of the project will be sold at the end of year 6 for $90000.
- The assets require an overhaul that will cost $27000 at the end of year 4.
- Working capital will be 5% of revenues for each year. The working capital investment has to be made at the start of each period. All working capital will be recovered.
- Cost of goods sold is 50% of sales.
- Wages are $250000 pa.
- The required return of the partners is 17%.

(a) Calculate the relevant cash flows for the project.

(b) Calculate the NPV for the project. Make a recommendation about the acceptability of the project.

(c) Calculate the IRR for the project. Make a recommendation about the acceptability of the project

8.19 The managers of Patterns Ltd have asked you to evaluate a project for them. They have provided the following details:

	Year 1	Year 2	Year 3	Year 4
Revenue	220000	230000	240000	180000
Cost of goods sold	24200	25430	26400	19900

- The initial investment in the project is \$300000 and an additional investment of \$30000 is required at the end of year 2.
- The asset purchased at the commencement of the project will be sold at the end of the project for \$50000.
- Working capital will be 8% of revenues for each year. The working capital investment has to be made at the start of each period. All working capital will be recovered.
- The required return of the partners is 15%.

(a) Estimate the relevant cash flows for the project.

(b) Calculate the NPV for the project.

(c) Calculate the IRR for the project.

SOLUTIONS TO FINANCE WORKSHOPS

8.1 The four key features of investments that make them both important and difficult to analyse are that they:

1. have relatively large initial outlays
2. have relatively long horizons (lives)
3. can be difficult to reverse once they have been implemented
4. have risk.

8.2 1.

Purchase price	450000
Installation	50000
Transport cost	10000
	510000

2.

Add increase in raw materials	2000
Add increase in finished goods	5000
	7000

3.

Installed cost of equipment	510000
Increase in working capital	7000
	517000

8.3

	Year 1	Year 2	Year 3	Year 4	Year 5	Year 6
Sales	150 000	165 000	180 000	195 000	210 000	225 000
Lost sales	−1 000	−1 000	−1 000	−1 000	−1 000	−1 000
Raw material	−45 000	−49 500	−54 000	−58 500	−63 000	−67 500
Labour	−30 000	−30 000	−30 000	−50 000	−50 000	−50 000
Electricity	−22 500	−24 750	−27 000	−29 250	−31 500	−33 750
Advertising	−10 000	−10 000	−5 000	−5 000	−5 000	−5 000
	41 500	49 750	63 000	51 250	59 500	67 750

8.4

Sale	25 000
Returned working capital	5 000
Terminal value	30 000

8.5 and 8.6

	Time zero	Year 1	Year 2	Year 3	Year 4	Year 5	Year 6
Initial outlay	−517 000						
Net cash flows		41 500	49 750	63 000	51 250	59 500	67 750
Terminal value							30 000
Total cash flows	−517 000	41 500	49 750	63 000	51 250	59 500	97 750
	1	0.8772	0.7695	0.675	0.5921	0.5194	0.4556
	−517 000	36 403.8	38 282.63	42 525	30 345.13	30 904.3	44 534.9
NPV	−294 004						

The project should be rejected because the NPV is negative.

8.7 Reject Aster's project because IRR (−19.64%) < required (14%)

Greenwash IRR = 32.43%

End notes

1 Excerpts from Wisenthal, S 2006, 'Centennial falls out of favour', *Financial Review*, 23 November, p. 23.

2 Groenewegen, J 2004, 'Who should control the firm? Insights from new and original institutional economics', *Journal of Economic Issues*, vol. 32, no. 2, pp. 353–61.

3 Yermack, D 2006, 'Flights of fancy: corporate jets, CEO perquisites, and inferior shareholder returns', *Journal of Financial Economics*, vol. 80, pp. 211–42.

4 Deans, A 2006, 'Brambles Industries Ltd' (part of a report on listed companies), *The Bulletin*, 22 November, vol. 124, no. 48.

5 'LionOre gets the go ahead for Activox project, Botswana', *Ralph Wragg Australian Business News*, 10 August 2006.

6 Freeman, M & Hobbes, G 1991, 'Capital budgeting: theory versus practice', *Australian Accountant*, vol. 61, no. 8, pp. 36–41.

7 Kester, G, Chang, R, Erlinda, S, Haikal, S, Isa, M, Skully, M, Tsui, K & Wang, Chi 1999, 'Capital budgeting practices in the Asia-Pacific region: Australia, Hong Kong, Indonesia, Malaysia, Philippines and Singapore', *Financial Practice and Education*, spring/summer, pp. 25–33.

8 Graham, J & Harvey, C 2001, 'The theory and practice of corporate finance: evidence from the field', *Journal of Financial Economics*, vol. 60, pp. 187–243.

chapter 9

chapter

9

Planning investments — some real world complications

Learning objectives

After studying this chapter, you should be able to:

- lo1 explain the problems associated with evaluating mutually exclusive projects and apply techniques to overcome these problems
- lo2 incorporate risk in the project appraisal process
- lo3 explain and incorporate the impact of the taxation system on project appraisal
- lo4 describe and apply the payback method and the accounting rate of return (ARR) technique
- lo5 consider the implications of non-financial factors for the investment appraisal process.

RISKY BUSINESS

Mining is one of the riskiest businesses to be in, the main risks coming from uncertainty about the actual size and quality of mineral deposits and the variability of mineral prices. Establishing a mine requires large infrastructure investments to extract the minerals. As we see in the opening page for chapter 8, if it turns out that a particular mine cannot generate positive returns, much of the initial investment cannot be recovered. WMC Resources Ltd produces nickel, copper, uranium and fertilisers.

Analysts scrutinise Twiggy's scheme

MATTHEW STEVENS

Andrew Forrest's expanding crew have recently bemoaned the failure of Australia's serious investment houses to start coverage of the New Force in Australian iron ore. Well, JP Morgan has now become the first to formally review Fortescue Metals and Forrest's astoundingly ambitious Pilbara iron ore project. And the firm's opening report only goes to prove that getting what you wish for can sometimes be a bit uncomfortable.

Forrest's achievements cannot be underestimated. Over three years, he has defied sceptics (myself included) by finding $3.3 billion, largely from international investors, to set about building the biggest greenfields resource project under way in Australia. And there is nothing in the JP Morgan assessment to undermine the basic assumptions that drive Forrest's project. The analysts seem to accept the resource estimates that underpin the New Force and, while making a neutral recommendation, they put a 2007 target valuation of $10.55 on Fortescue.

Which is all well and good. But wait, there's more.

Boiled down to basics, the JB Morgan report suggests Forrest's project is going to be riskier, more costly and a longer slog than the ambitious bods at Fortescue want to admit. This is the first seriously independent, hard-headed public assessment of the challenge being embraced by Fortescue's shareholders and financiers. At the same time, though, the report offers the most certain view yet of Forrest's world-class ambitions for Fortescue.

The company has long-stated plans to produce 45 million tonnes per annum of Aussie iron ore for Chinese customers. But the way the Morgan team tells it, Forrest has plans to lift production from the Cloud Break and Christmas Creek mines to 60 million tonnes per annum [mtpa] by 2011, and then to something close to 90 mtpa.

At that level, to provide some sort of context, Fortescue would be matching BHP's current Pilbara output.

Fantastic stuff. Even more amazing, Fortescue seems to have foreshadowed that it will rewrite the bulk of the contracts (18 of 27) it has signed with its Chinese customer base between now and the start of production in 2008.

Interestingly, JP Morgan notes that, of the 39.8 mtpa that have been contracted, only 9.5 mtpa are for Fortescue's 'Super Value Product'. Fortescue has previously stated that the higher grade product will make up the majority of its start-up production. Which might, sort of, explain why Fortescue will work so hard at renegotiating its contracts.

Forrest has the customers. The question is, do they want to pay the price for the premium product he wants to sell?

The other big problem is going to be getting ore to customers on time and on budget. Fortescue has budgeted for a spend of $3.68 billion, but, by the time ore hits the ships, the costs will probably top $3.94 billion, according to Morgan. And within three years, Morgan believes the company will need to spend a further $1.1 billion on beneficiation technology.

The firm also reckons Fortescue will struggle to hit its 2008 production target. There has, apparently, been a delay in the issue of Fortescue's 'Special Railway Licence' and that might be exacerbated further by the next wet season.

Overall, JP Morgan expects a much slower ramp-up than foreshadowed by Fortescue. In particular, it is concerned by the unusual surface-mining equipment that Fortescue plans to deploy across its mines. The Wirtgen machines are more like road-scrapers than traditional iron ore mining equipment and they have never been used by iron ore producers. They remain a risk. And the prospect of delays only increases the sensitivity of Fortescue's project to iron ore prices. The risks there are stark, according to the JP Morgan analysis.

...

The other interesting revelation in the JP Morgan work is that Fortescue's debt covenants with its new senior note-holders would suggest it cannot spend more than $20 million on the contested Mindy Mindy iron ore project while it is developing its core operations.

Mindy Mindy, of course, is the deposit at the centre of Fortescue's dispute with BHP over railway access. It would cost something more than $100 million to mine that deposit. Which would suggest the debate with BHP is little but academic, until at least 2008.

The other core risk identified by JP Morgan is regulatory. Indeed, within the first three paragraphs of the 50-page report, the firm warns that Fortescue will not be 're-rated further' until the market sees 'tangible outcomes' from the Australian Securities and Investments Commission proceedings against both Andrew Forrest and Fortescue.[1]

Chapter preview

This chapter extends the basic knowledge of planning investments we gain in chapter 8. Here, we will focus on the real world complications to the simple investment analysis approach we take in the previous chapter. Firstly, we will consider how to evaluate a number of projects that are competing for the same corporate resources.

The article on the opening page of the chapter discusses some of the risks associated with the operations of Fortescue Metals. While analysts don't dispute the size of iron ore deposits that Fortescue have access to, they do question what the market will be willing to pay for Fortescue's iron ore and the company's ability to deliver the product 'on time and on budget'. The analysts at JP Morgan think the company has underestimated the cost of necessary technology and expect a large drain on cash flow in 2009. Fortescue needs a 'special railway licence' to transport the iron ore and this has not yet been granted. Further, Fortescue are using machines that may not work well in a mine environment. Finally, the company is involved in a dispute with BHP and both the CEO of Fortescue and the company itself are under investigation by ASIC. The situation at Fortescue demonstrates the types of operational risk that could be faced in almost any business. A firm is a set of risky projects and the risks of these projects need to be taken into consideration at the project evaluation stage. We will consider how to incorporate different levels of risk into project evaluation in this chapter.

The introductory project analysis techniques used in chapter 8 are based on the assumption that taxes are not paid by companies or investors — an assumption that is relaxed in this chapter. We then look at the payback period and the accounting rate of return. These are two main alternatives to discounted cash flow techniques of project evaluation. Finally, we consider if non-financial factors should ever be included in investment planning.

The following diagram shows how this chapter is structured.

PLANNING INVESTMENTS — SOME REAL WORLD COMPLICATIONS

- **Analysing a set of projects**
  - Capital constraints
  - Mutually exclusive projects
- **Incorporating risk into the analysis**
- **Taxation and investment planning**
  - Taxes and the initial outlay
  - Taxes and net operating cash flows
  - Taxes and terminal value
- **Non-discounted methods of project evaluation**
  - Payback period
  - Accounting rate of return
- **Non-financial factors in project choices**

lo1

Explain the problems associated with evaluating mutually exclusive projects and apply techniques to overcome these problems.

Analysing a set of projects

Our discussion so far has been about determining if a single project is acceptable or not using the NPV and IRR techniques. When we are evaluating more than one project at a time, additional complications may arise. What happens if managers cannot get access to all the funds they need to adopt value increasing projects? What happens if two or more proposed investments need to use the same resource? We will address these questions in the next two sections.

Capital constraints

Capital rationing: a self-imposed limit that is placed on the size of the capital budget

What happens if managers cannot get access to all the funds they need to adopt value increasing projects? This occurs when the firm is subject to a restriction on the amount of capital it has to invest. **Capital rationing** is a self-imposed limit that is placed on the size of the capital budget. When the amount of money available for investment in projects is unlimited, all positive NPV projects or all projects with IRRs greater than the hurdle rate should be accepted to maximise firm value. When the firm imposes a capital constraint, our decision rules have to be adapted to maximise firm value given the size of the capital budget.

Consider the case of a firm with five proposed projects to evaluate. The initial outlays, NPVs and IRRs are shown in table 9.1.

Table 9.1 Five projects and initial outlays

Project	Initial outlay $	NPV $	IRR %	Cumulative outlay $
A	50 000	2 273	15	50 000
B	45 000	1 819	14	95 000
C	55 000	1 364	13	150 000
D	25 000	455	12	175 000
E	80 000	−908	9	255 000

The NPV column of table 9.1 uses a discount rate of 10% and ranks the projects from the most acceptable (project A contributes most to firm value) to the unacceptable (project E should be rejected because it will decrease firm value). The rankings in the IRR column are based on a hurdle rate of 10% and give the same acceptances as the NPV technique. The final column shows a running total of investment given the most acceptable project is taken first, followed by the next most acceptable project and so on. To maximise the value of the firm, projects A through to and including D should be adopted. Figure 9.1 is a graphical display of the ranked project set contained in table 9.1.

We have chosen to use IRR on the vertical axis only because it is easier to make a visual comparison of returns than it is to digest the dollar amounts. The ranking for the project set is the same for the NPV and IRR techniques. The horizontal dashed line at 10% indicates the firm's unconstrained hurdle rate, or the return that would be required on all projects without capital rationing. The vertical dashed line represents the size of the capital budget ($120 000) under capital rationing. Figure 9.1 shows that using the standard NPV and IRR decision criteria with capital rationing would result in the acceptance of projects A and B. This selection would generate a total NPV of $4092 for an outlay of $95 000. Project C could not be accepted because the capital budget does not allow total investment of more than $120 000.

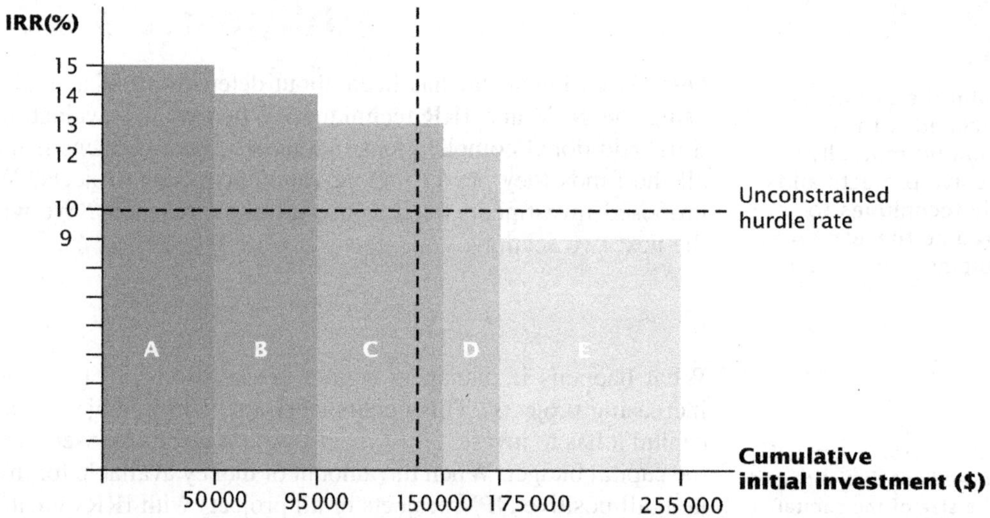

Figure 9.1 Project ranking under a capital constraint

The choice of A and B would leave $25 000 of the capital budget unused. We could feasibly undertake project D as it has an outlay of $25 000. This would give a total NPV of $4547, which is clearly preferable to the NPV when only projects A and B are adopted. By choosing project D over project C, we are departing from the standard NPV and IRR decision rules — we have chosen a project that has a lower NPV and IRR because it fits the capital budget constraint. The NPV rules are adapted under capital rationing so that the set of projects that gives the highest total NPV and remains within the capital budget constraint is chosen.

Independent project: a project that can be accepted or rejected without having to accept or reject some other project (that is, it is independent of other projects)

Mutually exclusive projects

What happens if two or more proposed investments need to use the same resource? The projects we consider in chapter 8 are independent of each other. The decision to accept or reject an **independent project** is unrelated to the acceptance or rejection of any other project. A firm with the objective of maximising shareholder wealth will accept all

Mutually exclusive projects: projects that either perform the same task or utilise the same scarce physical resources. Acceptance of one project means that the others must be rejected.

independent projects that have positive NPVs. **Mutually exclusive projects** either perform the same task or utilise the same scarce physical resources, so they are not independent. For example, a firm has the choice of two different machines to replace an existing metal press. The financial manager is looking at mutually exclusive projects because only one metal press is needed to replace the old one. Another example is the shop owner who has the choice of renting the premises to someone or setting up a hat shop. Setting up the hat shop means that the same shop premises can't be rented to someone else. As you will see later in this section, the opportunity cost concept we discuss in chapter 8 is incorporated into the way we analyse mutually exclusive projects. A capital constraint on the budget is a special case of mutual exclusivity where financial resources are limited.

Recall the Clean-O Company example introduced in chapter 8. If Clean-O is considering another product line (Bluewash, say) in addition to Greenwash, but has sufficient factory floor space to install only one new production line, Greenwash and Bluewash are mutually exclusive projects. When one is accepted, the other must be rejected because there is simply not enough room to adopt both projects. Mutual exclusivity does not present a problem for project selection if the initial outlays of the projects are the same size, the cash flow patterns are similar and the projects have the same life span. As an example, if the Greenwash and Bluewash projects both have an initial outlay of $100 000 (the projects are the same size), both have net cash inflows occurring evenly throughout their lives (similar timing), and both have the same life spans (that is, the time from initiation to completion of the project) we would accept the one that had the higher NPV or the higher IRR. The following sections examine the impact of a disparity in the size of initial outlay, a cash flow timing disparity, and unequal lives on the investment decision for mutually exclusive projects.

The size disparity

When mutually exclusive projects have different initial outlays we need to take this size disparity into consideration. In example 9.1 two mutually exclusive projects both have equal lives of one year and both have positive net inflows that occur at the end of the first year. The cost of capital is 10% and is used as the discount rate.

EXAMPLE 9.1

Mutually exclusive projects and the size disparity

	Project A		Project B	
	Time zero	Year 1	Time zero	Year 1
IO	−10 000		-50 000	
Cash flow		15 000		60 000
Discount factor	1	0.9091	1	0.9091
Present value	−10 000	13 636	-50 000	54 546
NPV	3637		4 546	
IRR	50%		20%	

If we use the NPV decision criteria, project B would be accepted because it has the higher NPV. If we used the IRR decision criteria, project A would be accepted because it has the higher IRR. This conflict in rankings between the two techniques is attributable to the difference in size of the initial outlay.

Given our previous discussion of the benefits of NPV over IRR, we would accept project B.

Choosing the NPV technique to rank projects is consistent with maximising the value of the firm even when the size disparity problem results in different rankings of mutually exclusive projects. However, if the firm is also subject to capital rationing, we would need to consider what could be gained by choosing project A, with its lower initial outlay, and freeing up $40 000 for investment in other projects. As we discussed earlier, a capital rationing constraint means we should consider the entire set of positive NPV projects that are feasible, given the size of the budget. If the total NPV of accepting project A plus some other positive NPV project that requires an investment of $40 000 or less is greater than the $4546 NPV of project B, then we should adopt this pair of projects.

Cash flow timing disparity

A second complication for mutually exclusive projects occurs when the projects have very different cash flow patterns over their lives, even when the initial outlay is identical. This disparity in the timing of cash flows causes different rankings under the NPV and IRR techniques and is attributable to the reinvestment assumptions we discuss in chapter 8 that are implicit in each of the techniques.

The two projects in example 9.2 have identical initial outlays and run for the same length of time. Again, a discount rate of 10% has been used to determine the project NPVs.

EXAMPLE 9.2

Mutually exclusive projects and the timing disparity

	Project C				Project D			
	Time zero	Year 1	Year 2	Year 3	Time zero	Year 1	Year 2	Year 3
IO	-50 000				-50 000			
Cash flow		25 000	25 000	25 000		5000	5000	75 000
Total cash flows	-50 000	25 000	25 000	25 000	-50 000	5000	5000	75 000
Discount factor	1	0.9091	0.8264	0.7513	1	0.9091	0.8264	0.7513
Present value	-50 000	22 728	20 660	18 783	-50 000	4546	4132	56 348
NPV	12 171				15 026			
IRR	23%				21%			

Project C's cash flows occur evenly over the life of the project, while the bulk of project D's cash flows come in the third and final year of the project. This cash flow pattern causes the NPV and IRR techniques to rank the projects differently. Using the NPV criteria, we would accept project D as it has the higher NPV. Using the IRR criteria, we would accept project C because it returns 2% more than project D. The NPV technique assumes that the cash flows received in years 1 and 2 are reinvested at the discount rate for the project (that is, 10%). The IRR method assumes that the cash flows from these years are reinvested at the IRR. This means that the $25 000 cash flow for years 1 and 2 in project C are reinvested at 23%, while the acceptance of project D would see the $5000 cash flow in years 1 and 2 generating only 21%.

Again, the NPV technique is recommended to overcome the timing disparity problem. Assuming differing reinvestment rates solely on the basis of which project is accepted is not logical.

Unequal lives

The final source of ranking differences for mutually exclusive projects results when projects have different lives. Consider the case where mutually exclusive projects occupy the same floor space and, further, that the cost of obtaining another factory is prohibitive or that management have strong reasons for keeping all the production facilities in the same location. Project E would run for two years while project F would run for four years. In example 9.3, we keep the initial outlays and the timing of cash flows consistent to isolate the impact of this effect. The discount rate for the NPV calculations is 10%, as is the IRR hurdle rate.

EXAMPLE 9.3

Mutually exclusive projects and unequal project life

	Project E			Project F				
	Time zero	Year 1	Year 2	Time zero	Year 1	Year 2	Year 3	Year 4
IO	-50 000			-50 000				
Cash flow		40 000	40 000		30 000	30 000	30 000	30 000
	-50 000	40 000	40 000	-50 000	30 000	30 000	30 000	30 000
Discount factor	1	0.9091	0.8264	1	0.9091	0.8264	0.7513	0.6830
Present value	-50 000	36 364	33 056	-50 000	27 273	24 792	22 539	20 490
NPV	19 420			45 094				
IRR	38%			47%				

If we accept project F on the grounds that it has the higher NPV, we are assuming that the floor space could be used in years 3 and 4 to generate the cost of capital. This assumption does not cause problems when we are evaluating projects that are not mutually exclusive. In that case, there is no constraint on the space available. However, if physical resources are limited, we need to consider other potential projects that could use the space in years 3 and 4 and have the potential to generate more than the cost of capital. By accepting the project with the longer life, we are rejecting future (but as yet unknown) projects that could occupy that space in the two years following the shorter project. Therefore, mutually exclusive projects with different lives are not directly comparable.

To make these projects comparable and include future investment opportunities, we need to make assumptions about future possible projects. This would be a difficult task indeed if we have no idea what projects may be possible at the end of the life of the shortest project. A compromise solution between trying to forecast a future that cannot be known and ignoring the problem altogether by simply selecting the project with the highest NPV is to assume that future projects will be similar to those that are currently available.

Replacement chain: a method that replicates the cash flows of the mutually exclusive projects until the two strings have equal lives

One way to incorporate this assumption is by repeating the short project as many times as is needed to match the length of the longer project. By doing this we create a **replacement chain** for the project. The replacement chain method replicates the cash flows of the mutually exclusive projects until the two strings have equal lives. If the life of the longer project cannot be divided equally by the shorter project, a chain also needs to be created for the longer project until we have two chains of identical length. We can then apply the discounted cash flow techniques to both the longer life project and the synthetic project that repeats the shorter project until the lives are equal.

Project F has a life of four years, so we would need to replicate project E twice (2 × two years) to make the lives of the projects comparable. The cash flows for the synthetic project E are shown in the replacement chain constructed in example 9.4.

EXAMPLE 9.4

Replacement chain for mutually exclusive projects with unequal lives

	Project E				
	Time zero	**Year 1**	**Year 2**	**Year 3**	**Year 4**
IO	-50000		-50000		
Cash flow		40000	40000	40000	40000
	-50000	40000	-10000	40000	40000
Discount factor	1	0.9091	0.8264	0.7513	0.6830
Present value	-50000	36364	-8264	30052	27320
NPV	35472				

The initial outlay for the second instalment of project E would need to occur on the first day of year 3, so it is included in the cash flows that are assumed to be received at the end of year 2. We then calculate the NPV for the synthetic project E as we would for any other project. The NPV for the replacement chain of project E is \$35472. We can compare this to the \$45094 NPV for project F. Thus, if we assume that the investment opportunities at the end of the 2 years of project F will be identical to those currently available, we would accept project F using the NPV criteria. We did not calculate the IRR for the synthetic project E because the cash flow of the chain has a negative cash outflow in year 2, making the cash flow pattern atypical and introducing the problem of multiple IRRs.

Equivalent annual annuity: the equal annual cash flows that would generate the project's NPV during the project's life

While the replacement chain method has been easy to construct for projects E and F, with their respective lives of two and four years, other mutually exclusive projects may involve greater differences in lives. If project E had a life of two years and project F had a life of 20 years, we would need to repeat project E 10 times to construct a chain that equalised the lives. A more efficient way to incorporate unequal lives is to use an **equivalent annual annuity** (EAA). An equivalent annual annuity is the equal annual cash flows that would generate the project's NPV during the project's life. Where the replacement chain method makes the lives of the projects equal, the EAA method annualises the cash flows over the life of each project to make them comparable.

We need to calculate the NPV for the life of each of the mutually exclusive projects before we can calculate the project's EAA. We did this for projects E and F in example 9.3. We then divide the NPV by the present value factor of an annuity, PVFA, that corresponds to the discount rate and the number of years that the project runs. Equation 9.1 shows how the EAA is calculated.

$$EAA_i = \frac{NPV_i}{PVFA_{k,n}} \qquad [9.1]$$

where EAA_i = equivalent annual annuity of project i

NPV_i = net present value of project i

$PVFA_{k,n}$ = present value factor for a rate of k and a time period of n

The decision rule for the EAA method is to select the project with the highest EAA. Example 9.5 shows how the EAA for projects E and F is calculated.

EXAMPLE 9.5

Calculating EAA

EAA for project E:

$$EAA_E = \frac{NPV_E}{PVFA_{0.10,\,2}}$$

$$EAA_E = \frac{19\,420}{1.7355}$$
$$= 11\,190$$

EAA for project F:

$$EAA_F = \frac{NPV_F}{PVFA_{0.10,\,4}}$$

$$EAA_F = \frac{45\,094}{3.1699}$$
$$= 14\,226$$

The PVFA can be calculated using equation 4.8 (see page 108) or you can use table 4 in the appendix at the back of this book. The EAA for project E is $11 190. This tells us that accepting project E is equivalent to receiving $11 190 per annum. Accepting project F would be equivalent to receiving $14 226 per annum. Project F has the higher EAA, so would be accepted and project E would then have to be rejected. This is the same 'accept' decision the replacement chain method gave us.

You may be faced with the choice between several sets of mutually exclusive projects but can ultimately only choose one project from all of the sets. In this situation, you should calculate the EAA for each project and choose the one with the highest EAA.

FINANCE WORKSHOP 9.1

Disco Kings is evaluating two mutually exclusive projects that have the following before-tax cash flow patterns:

	Mambo project	Samba project
Initial outlay	200 000	350 000
Annual net cash flow	80 000	90 000
Terminal value	60 000	80 000
Project life	3 years	6 years

The before-tax cost of capital is 15%. The company has asked you to advise on which project to accept, and want you to:

(a) use the replacement chain method to make a recommendation

(b) use the equivalent annual annuity method to make a recommendation.

lo2

Incorporate risk in the project appraisal process.

Incorporating risk into the analysis

The discussion so far has been based on decisions about proposed projects that have the same level of risk as the other projects that are currently being undertaken by the firm. In these cases, we have used the cost of capital as the discount rate for the NPV technique and as the hurdle rate for the IRR. However, many project proposals will be either more or less risky than those the firm is currently operating. The cost of capital is determined given the risk of the projects the firm is presently undertaking. When we consider projects with different levels of risk from current projects, we need to use a different discount rate. The cost of capital is too high to use as a discount rate for projects that are relatively less risky and it is too low for projects that are relatively more risky than those already in place.

Risk-adjusted discount rate: method incorporating differing levels of project risk by changing the required return or discount rate

The most common method used by Australian firms to incorporate risk is the **risk-adjusted discount rate** (RADR) method.[2] The RADR includes project risk in the discounted cash flow analysis by increasing the discount or hurdle rate for riskier projects and by decreasing the discount or hurdle rate for projects with less than the average risk experienced by the firm.

Table 9.2 Two alternative subjective risk classification schemes

Classification by risk		Classification by expenditure	
Risk category	**RADR %**	**Risk category**	**RADR %**
Low	8	Replacement	10
Average	10	Expansion	12
High	15	New products	15

Under the RADR method, projects are classified according to predetermined criteria. Table 9.2 shows the two main classification alternatives for using RADR. Classification by risk is the scheme most frequently used by Australian companies but classification by expenditure is not far behind.[3] The starting point for determining the RADR for each category is the firm's cost of capital and this provides an indicator for those projects that have 'average' risk. A subjective risk premium is then added to the cost of capital to set the RADR for the 'high' risk category. This risk premium could depend on how risk averse management are and/or their past experience with more risky projects. If the firm considers lower risk project proposals, the RADR is subjectively set to be lower than the cost of capital. A similar process is followed if the firm uses classification by expenditure (the second system in table 9.2).

Once the classification system and associated discount rates are established, proposed projects are put into groups so their RADR can be determined. The RADR is used to discount the project's cash flows or as the hurdle rate for the IRR technique. Example 9.6 shows how this is done.

EXAMPLE 9.6

Risk-adjusted discount rates

Hillsborough Ltd is a publisher of educational books for preschool children. It uses the RADR approach for incorporating risk into project evaluation. It has a cost of capital of 10% and assign proposed projects to the categories shown in the following table.

Risk category	RADR %
Low	8
Average	10
High	15

Hillsborough Ltd is considering two new independent projects. The first is to extend the current series of 'Learn about numbers' books by incorporating a new book called *Learning my tables*. The project has an initial outlay of $50 000 and cash flows are expected to be $20 000 per annum for the 5-year life of the project. It is classified as having average risk, so the RADR for the project is 10%.

	Project — Learning my tables					
	Time zero	Year 1	Year 2	Year 3	Year 4	Year 5
IO	-50 000					
Cash flow		20 000	20 000	20 000	20 000	20 000
Total CFs	-50 000	20 000	20 000	20 000	20 000	20 000
Discount factor	1	0.9091	0.8264	0.7513	0.6830	0.6209
Present value	-50 000	18 182	16 528	15 026	13 660	12 418
NPV	25 814					
IRR	29%					

The NPV for this project is $25 814 so the project should be accepted. Using the 10% RADR as the hurdle rate for the IRR, we would also accept the project if we chose to evaluate projects with this method.

The second project is to develop a new series of books for use in lower primary school. This new series would be called 'I can use numbers' and its success would depend on the series being adopted for use in the school curriculum. The initial outlay for this project is $200 000 and the project is expected to have a 5-year life. Net cash inflows for each year of operation are as follows:

Year 1	Year 2	Year 3	Year 4	Year 5
50 000	55 000	60 000	70 000	60 000

The 'I can use numbers' project is considered to have high risk because it is effectively a new line of business in which Hillsborough has no previous experience. The RADR for this risk category is 15%.

	Project — I can use numbers					
	Time zero	Year 1	Year 2	Year 3	Year 4	Year 5
IO	-200 000					
Cash flow		50 000	55 000	60 000	70 000	60 000
Total CFs	-200 000	50 000	55 000	60 000	70 000	60 000
Discount factor	1	0.8696	0.7561	0.6575	0.5718	0.4972
Present value	-200 000	43 480	41 586	39 450	40 026	29 832
NPV	-5 626					
IRR	14%					

Here, the NPV on a risk-adjusted basis is negative. If Hillsborough accepted this project, we would expect firm value to decrease by $5626. When we compare the IRR to the RADR hurdle rate (IRR 14%<RADR 15%) we also reject the project. If we had not allowed for the additional risk of this project, we would have accepted the project (IRR 14%>10%).

Three more theoretically correct ways to incorporate risk into project evaluation exist. The first is to estimate the divisional cost of capital and use this as a basis for adjusting for risk. For a firm that operates in the one line of business, the cost of capital would be a suitable discount rate for projects with similar risk to those already in place. However, the cost of capital for a large firm that has multiple and diverse business activities may not actually provide a suitable benchmark for projects proposed in any of the individual divisions. In this case, the cost of capital represents an overall assessment of firm risk, not for the risk of each group of activities. For diversified firms with multiple activities, a divisional cost of capital is a more suitable benchmark but is much more difficult to obtain. Wesfarmers Ltd, for example, have forestry and timber, retail hardware, livestock agency and rural supply divisions and we could not reasonably expect these divisions to all use the same benchmark.

The second way to incorporate risk into project evaluation is to use the CAPM model that is introduced in chapter 5 to estimate the project's level of systematic risk. To implement this procedure, we need to find a traded company that does the same thing as the proposed project. For Hillsborough to apply this method to the decision to diversify into school texts, a company that operates in that market (and no other) would need to be identified. We would then need to obtain the beta for that company and adjust it for any differences in the relative use of debt by Hillsborough and the proxy company. The difficulty of identifying a suitable proxy company makes this approach unfeasible in most situations.

Certainty equivalent: the amount of cash the decision maker would be willing to trade for the risky cash flow

The final method of adjusting for risk is by using certainty equivalents. This approach adjusts the project's cash flows so they can be viewed as 'riskless' and then uses the risk-free rate as the discount or hurdle rate. A **certainty equivalent** is the amount of cash the decision maker would be willing to trade for the risky cash flow. It indicates the certain amount that would make the decision maker indifferent between the sure cash flow and the uncertain one. While theoretically sound, determining certainty equivalent cash flows is time consuming and remains a subjective process.

The difficulties and costs associated with these more theoretically correct techniques deter management from using them. Less than a quarter of Australian companies use the CAPM for project evaluation and fewer than 5% use a divisional cost of capital.[4] Rational managers will use more complicated evaluation techniques only if the decisions resulting from the application of these are superior to the decisions that result from other available techniques.

lo3

Explain and incorporate the impact of the taxation system on project appraisal.

Taxation and investment planning

In chapter 8 we assume that projects are being evaluated in a world without tax. Yet, as we see in chapter 7, the way that cost of capital is calculated depends on the ability of the firm's owners to utilise dividend imputation credits. To achieve the objective of maximising shareholder wealth, a firm that is fully integrated with the taxation system should use the before-tax cost of capital as the discount rate for projects with similar risk to those already in place and as the hurdle rate for the IRR. If shareholders cannot utilise imputation credits, the after-tax cost of capital should be used to maximise shareholder wealth.

The shareholders' ability to utilise imputation credits determines whether the before-tax or after-tax discount rate is used. The integration of the firm with the dividend imputation system also determines on which basis the cash flows of projects should be evaluated. The treatment of cash flows and the discount rate needs to be consistent. The use of the before-tax cost of capital requires that before-tax cash flows are used in the discounted cash flow procedures. If shareholders can fully utilise imputation credits, the tax paid by the company is not relevant to the decision process. Any taxes paid by the firm are returned to the owners via imputation credits. Steps that the firm could take to minimise tax would only result in the shareholders having to pay the tax themselves when their franking credits were reduced. The process we have followed thus far in this chapter is consistent with what we would adopt for a firm that was fully integrated with the imputation system.

When the firm is not fully integrated with the imputation taxation system, the amount of tax paid does become relevant in the project-appraisal process. Tax paid is not available either for distribution to owners or for reinvestment in the firm, so it represents a decrease in firm value. When the firm is not integrated with the tax system, we should use the after-tax cost of capital and after-tax cash flows for evaluating project proposals. In the following sections we will investigate the impact of taxation on determining the initial outlay, the net operating cash flows and the terminal value of an asset.

The timing of taxation payments also becomes an issue when we are estimating net cash flows for project evaluation. As we discuss in chapter 2, companies generally pay tax in quarterly instalments, so the tax payment associated with an allowable deduction will frequently be received in the same year as the expenditure is made. Sole traders and partnerships are taxed as individuals, rather than businesses, but many of these individuals are taxed through the tax instalment system. For convenience we will assume that tax is paid when the revenues and expenditures are generated for these types of businesses. Net GST payments or receipts may also have an impact on a project's net operating cash flows. The net operating cash flow will be decreased by the net amount of GST payable on the sales of the project or increased if the net GST is a receivable. To keep our examples simple, GST cash flows have not been included.

Taxes and the initial outlay

The following sections use the Clean-O Greenwash project evaluation example we discussed earlier in the chapter. Here, however, we will assume that the owners of Clean-O cannot utilise dividend imputation credits because they are not Australian residents or because the firm is not structured as a company. This means that taxation is relevant in the project decision making process.

We calculate the installed cost of the new production facility in example 8.1 (see page 277) by including the purchase price of the machine, the shipping and road transport costs and the cost of the electrician. None of the components of the installed cost of a new asset in an expansion decision are affected by introducing tax to the evaluation. As we will see shortly, the installed cost becomes relevant at the end of the life of the project if the equipment is disposed of.

Taxation does not impact on the calculation of the change in working capital, so we can calculate this item as we do in example 8.2 (see page 277). Example 8.3 (see page 278) shows how the initial outlay for an expansion project is calculated. We include the installed cost of the new asset, the change in net working capital, and training and advertising costs. You learn in chapter 2 that section 8.1(1) of the *Income Tax Assessment Act 1997* allows a deduction from assessable income for expenses that are 'incurred in gaining or producing … assessable income'. Thus, taxation will have an impact on the training and advertising costs because they are business expenses. Example 9.7 shows how tax is incorporated into the calculation of the initial outlay for the Greenwash project.

EXAMPLE 9.7

Taxes and the initial outlay for an expansion project

Initial outlay		
Installed cost of new asset		1 160 000
Add increase in net working capital		70 000
Add training costs	2 000	
Add initial advertising cost	50 000	
	52 000	
Less tax at 30%	15 600	36 400
		1 266 400

The initial outlay for the Greenwash project is lower when taxation is relevant to the investment decision because the training and advertising costs are tax deductible.

The initial outlay for a replacement decision includes the terminal cash flows of the asset that is being replaced. This has taxation implications if the old asset is disposed of for a price that is different from its base value for taxation purposes. The base value each year is determined by subtracting the allowable **depreciation** deductions claimed in previous years from the installed cost of the asset. We will learn how to calculate the allowable depreciation deductions in the next section when we look at after-tax operating cash flows.

Depreciation: the amount allowed as a tax deduction by the ATO to recognise the decrease in the value of an asset that occurs as it is used and wears out over time

If the old asset in a replacement decision has been depreciated and is disposed of for an amount greater than the taxation book value, a taxable gain arises from the sale. A depreciable asset sold for less than its book value gives rise to an allowable deduction for taxation purposes. Example 9.8 shows how gains and losses on depreciable assets affect the net proceeds from the sale of the existing asset in a replacement decision.

EXAMPLE 9.8

Taxing gains and losses on the sale of depreciable assets

An asset was purchased 3 years ago for $100 000. It has been depreciated at $20 000 per annum for each of the last 3 years, so the book value for taxation purposes is $40 000.

Case 1: The asset can be sold for $50 000.

If the owner of the asset is a company, tax will be paid at the corporate tax rate of 30%.

Sale price	50 000
Taxation book value	40 000
Gain	10 000
Tax on gain at 30%	3 000
After-tax cash flow	47 000

Case 2: The asset can be sold for $30 000.

Sale price	30 000
Taxation book value	40 000
Loss	–10 000
Tax saving on loss at 30%	3 000
After-tax cash flow	33 000

Gains or losses on the disposal of non-depreciable assets (for example, land) are taxed differently to those on depreciable assets. The gain or loss on a non-depreciable business asset is subject to the rules for capital gains tax.

The rules for determining the tax payable on capital gains depend on how the business is structured. For companies, the capital gain is included in assessable income and taxed at the corporate tax rate. If the company has a capital loss, the loss does not represent an immediate tax deduction. Capital losses are carried forward until the company makes a capital gain. The past period loss is then deducted from the new capital gain. If the loss is larger than the gain, no gain is included in assessable income. If the loss does not fully offset the next gain, the remaining part of the gain is included in assessable income. Different capital gains rules apply to assets purchased prior to 21 September 1999.[5]

As we learn from our discussion of taxation in chapter 2, the income of sole traders and partnerships is taxed in the hands of the owners rather than at the business level. As for companies, the gain from the sale of an asset that is sold within 12 months of purchase is taxed at the marginal tax rate. However, because sole traders and partnerships are taxed as individuals, they are allowed a 50% discount on the amount of capital gain that they include in assessable income. The remaining 50% is taxed at the owner's marginal tax rate. Any losses that cannot be offset against current period gains are carried forward and offset against future gains as for companies. Example 9.9 shows how capital gains and losses are taxed for a company and for an individual carrying on a business.

EXAMPLE 9.9

Taxing capital gains and losses on the sale of assets

Two non-depreciable assets were sold in the same year. Asset A had an original purchase price of $60 000 and was sold for $50 000. Asset B was purchased for $20 000 and sold for $60 000. Calculate the after-tax cash flows from the sales of these assets.

Case 1: The business is structured as a company and the corporate tax rate is 30%. The first step is to calculate the capital gain or loss on each asset.

	Asset A	Asset B
Sale price	50 000	60 000
Purchase price	60 000	20 000
Capital gain (loss)	(10 000)	40 000

The capital loss on Asset A cannot be used to reduce assessable income, it can only be used to offset capital gains as follows.

Sale price of first asset	50 000
Sale price of second asset	60 000

Capital loss on sale of first asset	-10000
Capital gain on sale of second asset	40000
Taxable gain	30000
Tax on gain at 30%	9000
After-tax cash flow of first asset	50000
After-tax cash flow of second asset	51000

The capital loss on Asset A is used to reduce the size of the capital gain on Asset B. The remaining $30000 of capital gain is assessed at the marginal tax rate. The loss on the sale of the first asset has effectively increased the after-tax cash flow from the sale of the second asset. The cash flow from the sale of the first asset is not affected by tax — the associated loss can bring benefits only if there are other capital gains to offset.

Case 2: The business is structured as a sole trader or a partnership and the marginal tax rate of the owner is 48.5%.

The capital gain or loss on each asset is calculated as it was for the company in Case 1, but the calculation of the capital gains needs to incorporate the 50% discount.

Sale price of first asset	50000
Sale price of second asset	60000
Capital loss on sale of first asset	-10000
Capital gain on sale of second asset	40000
Net capital gain	30000
50% of capital gain	15000
Tax on gain at 48.5%	7275
After-tax cash flow of sale of assets	102725

The capital gain or loss for each asset is calculated the same as it was for the company in Case 1. For sole traders and partnerships, any capital loss is deducted from the gains before the 50% discount is applied. The owners then only have to pay tax on half of the net capital gain amount (that is, 0.5×30000). Tax is paid on the discounted amount at the marginal tax rate of the owner (that is, 0.485×15000).

Examples 9.8 and 9.9 had a gain and a loss occurring in the same year. What if the sale of both assets resulted in capital losses? The losses can be carried forward when there are no capital gains in the same tax year. At the project evaluation stage it would be difficult to estimate potential capital losses on assets that are unrelated to that project. However, if the business has capital losses carried forward from past years, these should be used to offset the impact of any capital gain arising from the replacement of an asset.

We calculated the before-tax installed cost of a new machine for a replacement decision in example 8.4 (see page 279). In example 9.10, we assume that Clean-O's shareholders cannot use the dividend imputation credits.

EXAMPLE 9.10

Taxes and the installed cost of a replacement machine

For the new machine, the purchase price, transport costs and electrical are $1 million, $150000 and $10000 respectively. The new production line will occupy the space of the current machinery. The expected sales price of the old machinery is $50000 and it has a book value of $40 000 for taxation purposes. The old machinery would have to be dismantled before it was sold and this would cost $1500. What is the installed cost for the replacement project?

Cash outflows for replacement machine	
Purchase price	1 000 000
Transport cost	150 000
Electrician	10 000
	1 160 000

Cash flow from sale of existing machine	
Sale of machine	50 000
Subtract dismantling cost	1 500
Subtract taxation book value	40 000
Gain	8 500
Tax on gain at 30%	2 550
AFter-tax cash flow from sale	45 950
Total installed cost of replacement project	1 114 050

The installed cost of the new machine does not change with the introduction of tax. Costs paid to get new equipment ready are capitalised into the cost of the asset, so are not allowed as deductions. The gain on the sale of the old machine is calculated as the sales price less the costs of getting the old machine to a saleable condition less the taxation book value of the old machine. Thus, the gain on the sale of an existing machine is lower when selling costs are involved. The after-tax cash inflow from the disposal of the existing machine is deducted from the installed cost of the new machine.

FINANCE WORKSHOP 9.2

The management of Markham Ltd is considering the replacement of their delivery trucks. The following figures are estimates for the acquisition of new trucks:

- purchase price $400 000
- delivery costs $2000
- registration $4000
- insurance $10 000.

Management has contacted some second-hand truck vendors and estimates that the old trucks would sell for $50 000. The current fleet of trucks has been fully depreciated for taxation purposes. Assume the registration and insurance costs are tax-deductible and any tax benefits will be obtained immediately. Given a corporate tax rate of 30%, what is the after-tax installed cost for the truck replacement project?

Taxes and net operating cash flows

We need to identify the taxable income to determine the size of the taxation cash outflow when taxation is relevant to project evaluation. For the most part, cash inflows are assessable income and attract a tax liability, while cash outflows are allowable deductions that reduce the amount of tax that needs to be paid. One major exception to this rule is the allowable deduction for depreciation.

How much depreciation expense the ATO will allow is normally determined by the Income Tax Assessment Act.[6] The ATO identifies assets and gives a standard effective life for each type of asset. The ATO allows a choice of two methods. The first is called the prime cost (or straight line) method because the cost of the asset is allowed as a deduction in equal instalments over the life of the asset. The installed cost of the asset is divided by the life of the asset to determine how much depreciation can be claimed as an expense for each year. This is shown in equation 9.2 and applied in example 9.11.

$$\textbf{Prime cost depreciation} = \frac{\textbf{installed cost of asset}}{\textbf{effective life}} \qquad [9.2]$$

EXAMPLE 9.11

Prime cost depreciation

The production line that Clean-O would install to operate the Greenwash project has an installed cost of $1 160 000. According to the ATO, the effective life of the asset is 10 years. Using the prime cost method, the depreciation expense that Clean-O could claim as an allowable deduction is:

$$\begin{aligned}\text{Prime cost depreciation} &= \frac{\text{asset cost}}{\text{effective life}}\\ &= \frac{1\,160\,000}{10}\\ &= 116\,000 \text{ per annum}\end{aligned}$$

Clean-O could reduce its taxable income by $116 000 per annum for each of the 5 years of the project if it chooses the prime cost method. As far as the ATO is concerned, the value of the production line at the end of the life of the project would be $580 000 [that is, 1 160 000 – (5 × 116 000)].

Diminishing value is the second method of determining depreciation that is allowed by the ATO. Equation 9.3 shows how the ATO specifies depreciation is to be calculated under the diminishing value method.

$$\textbf{Diminishing value depreciation} = \textbf{base value} \times \left(\frac{\textbf{150\%}}{\textbf{effective life}}\right) \qquad [9.3]$$

This method allows higher deductions in early years and relatively lower ones in the later years. In fact, a depreciation charge can be claimed for many more years than the asset's effective life if the asset continues to be used in the business. The depreciation charge in these later years is usually insignificant. Example 9.12 shows how the diminishing value method is applied in the case of Clean-O.

EXAMPLE 9.12

Diminishing value depreciation

Under the diminishing value method, the allowable deductions for the first year of the project would be as follows.

$$\text{Diminishing value depreciation} = \text{base value} \times \left(\frac{150\%}{\text{effective life}}\right)$$

$$= 1\,160\,000\left(\frac{1.5}{10}\right)$$

$$= 174\,000 \text{ in year 1}$$

Comparing this result with the prime cost one, we can see that the diminishing value method results in a higher allowable deduction in the first year. The base value that is used for the allowable deduction in year 2 is calculated as the asset cost minus the depreciation charge for year 1, so is \$986 000 (that is, 1 160 000 – 174 000). The allowable deduction for year 2 is calculated as:

$$\text{Diminishing value depreciation} = 986\,000 \times \left(\frac{1.5}{10}\right)$$

$$= 147\,900 \text{ in year 2}$$

The base value of the end of year 5 would be \$514 698.

FINANCE WORKSHOP 9.3

Calculate the diminishing value method depreciation charges for Clean-O's asset in years 3 to 5.

Given the choice between the prime cost and diminishing value methods, which would you choose? Keeping the time value of money in mind, you would choose the diminishing value method. It gives larger reductions in taxes in the early years of the project, so it generates a higher present value than the equal annual deductions provided by the prime cost method.

Those of you who have studied accounting will notice that the salvage value of the asset is not taken into account when determining the tax deduction for depreciation as it would be for calculating the depreciation expense in the Income Statement. The accounting depreciation expense is not relevant to determining a project's cash flows. It is important to remember that depreciation is not a cash flow. We consider depreciation only when determining the net cash flows of a project because it generates a tax deduction that will increase our net after-tax cash flows.

Example 9.13 (using the same data as example 8.5) shows how the net cash flows after tax are calculated for the Greenwash project.

EXAMPLE 9.13

Taxes and net operating cash flow

Sales of Greenwash for the first year: \$1 000 000.

Sales are expected to grow at a rate of 5% for years 2 and 3, then decline by 5% pa in years 4 and 5.

Sales diverted from existing Clean-O products: \$100 000.

Raw materials will be 24% of sales.
Labour: $90000.
Electricity: $7000.
Advertising cost for years 1 to 4: $100000.
Clean-O will use the prime cost method for calculating depreciation. The installed cost of the machine is $1 160000 and it has an effective life of 10 years.
Clean-O is structured as a company. The corporate tax rate is 30% and the shareholders cannot use imputation credits.
What is the after-tax operating cash flow for the Greenwash project?

Cash flows	Year 1	Year 2	Year 3	Year 4	Year 5
Sales of Greenwash	1 000 000	1 050 000	1 102 500	1 047 375	995 006
Lost sales	−100 000	−100 000	−100 000	−100 000	−100 000
Raw materials	−240 000	−252 000	−264 600	−251 370	−238 801
Labour	−90 000	−90 000	−90 000	−90 000	−90 000
Electricity	−7 000	−7 000	−7 000	−7 000	−7 000
Advertising	−100 000	−100 000	−100 000	−100 000	
Net cash inflow	463 000	501 000	540 900	499 005	559 205
Non-cash deductions					
Depreciation	116 000	116 000	116 000	116 000	116 000
Taxable income	347 000	385 000	424 900	383 005	443 205
Tax payable	104 100	115 500	127 470	114 902	132 962
After-tax cash flow	358 900	385 500	413 430	384 103	426 243

Revenues increase the amount of tax that the firm has to pay. Expenses related to the business reduce that amount of tax. We can net the inflows and outflows to determine how much tax has to be paid as we have done in example 9.13. At first glance, you might think it odd that lost sales are included in the calculation of after-tax income for the new project shown in example 9.13. However, we are looking at incremental cash flows, including incremental tax payable. This means that sales diverted from other products will not increase the tax payable by the firm. Clean-O already pays the tax corresponding to those sales, and so only the incremental sales level has an impact on the incremental amount of tax payable.

After calculating the annual net cash inflows, the next step is to consider any non-cash flow items that are allowed as expenses for taxation purposes. The most common of these is depreciation. The prime cost depreciation method for the new machine was calculated earlier as follows:

$$\text{Prime cost depreciation} = \frac{\text{asset cost}}{\text{effective life}} = \frac{1\,160\,000}{10} = 116\,000 \text{ per annum}$$

The depreciation expense for the new production line is not a cash flow, but is an allowable deduction for tax purposes, so reduces the taxation cash outflow. The after-tax net cash flows of the project are calculated as net cash inflows minus tax payable. The depreciation expense is used only to determine tax payable and is ignored for the rest of the calculations. The after-tax net cash flow for year 1, for example, is calculated as net cash inflow − tax payable ($463 000 − 104 100 = $358 900).

Taxes and terminal value

The issue of tax on asset sales was raised when we looked at the impact of taxation on determining the initial outlay for a replacement project. The same principles apply to assessing the after-tax terminal value of a new machine. Using the data from example 8.6 (see page 282), the terminal value of the Greenwash project is calculated in example 9.14.

EXAMPLE 9.14

Taxes and terminal value

At the end of the 5-year life of the Greenwash project, management expect to sell the production line for $400 000. It would cost $4 000 to dismantle the line to prepare it for sale. There was an increase of $70 000 in net working capital at the start of the project. The prime cost method of depreciation has been used with a 10-year effective life for the machine. What is the terminal value of the Greenwash project?

Cash flow at project termination	
Sale of machine	400 000
Subtract dismantling cost	4 000
Book value of machine	580 000
Loss on sale	−184 000
Tax saving on loss	55 200
After-tax cash inflow from machine	451 200
Add return of net working capital	70 000
Terminal value	521 200

Book value is needed to determine if there is a taxable gain or loss. This is calculated as the installed cost of the machine minus the total depreciation claimed during the time the machine was owned. Applying this in example 9.14, Clean-O has claimed $580 000 (that is, $116 000 × 5) as an allowable deduction, making the book value for taxation purposes $580 000 (that is, $1 160 000 – 580 000). With sales proceeds of $400 000 and costs associated with sales of $4000, Clean-O has made a loss on the sale of the production line of $184 000. Losses on disposal of depreciable assets are an allowable deduction against income in the year they are realised. If Clean-O is expecting sufficient taxable income in year 5 to absorb the loss from the Greenwash project, the loss would represent a tax saving of $55 200 (that is, $184 000 × 0.3) that increases the terminal value of the project.

The after-tax initial outlay (example 9.8), operating cash flows (example 9.13) and terminal value (example 9.14) are used in example 9.15 to calculate the after-tax NPV and IRR of the Greenwash project. For a project with the same risk as existing firm projects, the discount rate should be based on the after-tax cost of capital. We assume an after-tax cost of capital of 7% for Clean-O.

EXAMPLE 9.15

Calculating the after-tax NPV of the Greenwash project

	Time zero	Year 1	Year 2	Year 3	Year 4	Year 5
Initial outlay	−1 266 400					
Net operating cash flow		358 900	385 500	413 430	384 104	426 243
Terminal value						521 200

Net cash flows	−1 266 400	358 900	385 500	413 430	384 104	947 443
		$(1 + 0.07)^{-1}$	$(1 + 0.07)^{-2}$	$(1 + 0.07)^{-3}$	$(1 + 0.07)^{-4}$	$(1 + 0.07)^{-5}$
Discount factor	1	0.9346	0.8734	0.8163	0.7629	0.7130
Present value	−1 266 400	335 428	336 696	337 483	293 033	675 527
NPV	711 767					
IRR	22.58%					

lo4

Describe and apply the payback method and the accounting rate of return (ARR) technique.

Non-discounted methods of project evaluation

Discounted cash flow techniques require decision makers to generate extensive cash flow estimates and to determine an appropriate discount rate. As we saw earlier, the majority of companies use either NPV or IRR in their decisions. Some decision makers use other methods in addition to, or in place of, these for project evaluation. The two most popular non-discounted methods are the payback method and the accounting rate of return.[7] We will examine these methods in the next two sections.

Payback period

Payback period: measures the length of time it takes for the net cash inflows from a project to equal the initial outlay

The **payback period** (PP) measures the length of time it takes for net cash flows (annual cash inflow – annual cash outflow) to equal the initial outlay of the project. The payback method uses forecast cash flows, so if you have already estimated these for a discounted cash flow analysis (as in example 9.15) the incremental cost of using this method is low. Example 9.16 applies the technique to the cash flows of the Greenwash project.

EXAMPLE 9.16

Payback period for Greenwash

	Time zero	Year 1	Year 2	Year 3	Year 4	Year 5
Net cash flows	−1 266 400	358 900	385 500	431 430	384 104	947 443
Cumulative		358 900	744 400	1 175 830	1 559 934	

The net operating cash flows are added until the total inflows are greater than the initial outlay. This occurs in year 4 for the Greenwash project. As the year 4 cash flow more than covers the initial outlay we can say that it takes more than three years (but not as many as four) for recovery. How far into year 4 is it before the initial outlay is paid back?

$$\frac{1\,226\,400 - 1\,175\,830}{384\,104} = \frac{50\,570}{384\,104} = 0.1317$$

The cumulative cash flow for the last year where this amount does not exceed the initial outlay (that is, year 3 in our example) is subtracted from the initial outlay and divided by the cash inflow for the next year (year 4, in this case). If we assume that cash inflows occur evenly throughout the year, it will be about 7 weeks (that is, 0.1317 × 52) into year 4 when the cash inflows equal the initial outflow for the project. Thus the payback period for the Greenwash project is 3 years and 7 weeks.

Is this payback period of 3 years and 7 weeks for the Greenwash project an acceptable length of time? The decision rule for the payback period is to accept any project that has a payback shorter than the benchmark time. There is no generally accepted benchmark time. Managers may consider past experience or future cash flow needs to set the benchmark for the firm. The benchmark time is a type of decision making heuristic. The following 'behavioural perspective' feature explains more about heuristics and raises some personality issues that can reduce the effectiveness of using heuristics. If we assume the payback period for new projects at Clean-O is two years, we would reject the Greenwash project on the basis that it took longer than the benchmark payback time.

BEHAVIOURAL PERSPECTIVE

Rules of thumb

The processing of information is perhaps even more important than its collection. Human decision makers can make many mistakes in processing, such that the outcomes fall far short of the ideal. Some of the errors or biases include the use of approximate rules of thumb, inappropriate techniques and incorrect probabilities, inconsistent standards and inconsistent sources of information.[8] Additionally, decision makers may give way to personal stress, wishful thinking and delusions of control or grandeur.

A major processing problem is the use of rules of thumb or 'heuristics'. Heuristics are simplifying strategies that reduce the need to consider all information to reach a solution. We all use heuristics every day of our lives because re-analysing every problem is often not the most efficient thing to do. We work on our past experiences and learning. Rules of thumb certainly save time and therefore reduce the immediate costs of making a decision, but in the long term the costs of incorrect decisions may be very high indeed.

One heuristic is to select one variable alone and use that to decide between competing alternatives. Using the payback period benchmark time is an example of an heuristic. The benchmark is set for projects but does not make allowances for differences in the timing of the cash inflows and, depending on the firm's policy, may not even change for very different types of projects.

As another example, consider how financial institutions encourage potential borrowers to use a single-variable heuristic when they advertise 'honeymoon' discount interest rates for the first six-month period of loans to attract new borrowers. With full consideration of the whole interest rate and fees structure, it may be that such honeymoon loans are more expensive than other less publicised loans. Similarly, retailers advertise goods for 'no payment for 12 months'. A cheaper option may well be to pay cash obtained by personal loan from a financial institution. Hence, it is only full consideration of all the information that will produce an optimal outcome.

Some decision makers use 'representativeness' to excess. This is the heuristic of judging the likelihood of an event based on its similarity to a set of past events. Financial managers would be guilty of this processing fault if they allowed credit to all new customers bearing the title 'Doctor', without checking any further, merely because in the past they had not had any bad debts owed by medical practitioners. The new customers may well be medical practitioners, but also may be dentists, veterinarians, lowly paid PhD lecturers in universities or self-promoted frauds! Occupation by itself is not necessarily a reliable credit check.

When using either rules of thumb or more sophisticated analyses, decision makers are often inconsistent in applying decision standards. Even experts who are acknowledged as well versed and clever in their fields have been shown in experiments to vary in their judgements on a case-by-case basis. Variation occurs 'within' individuals and between individuals. Judgements can be influenced by personal factors such as stress, cultural and social norms, wishful thinking and essential outlook.

People's essential outlook is characterised in the literature by the phenomenon of locus of control. Under the locus of control dichotomy, individuals are classed as either internally controlled 'internals' or externally controlled 'externals'. Internally controlled individuals are self-motivated and driven, realise they are responsible for their own deeds and outcomes and understand that they can change things around them. 'Externals', on the other hand, see themselves essentially as flotsam. The world pushes them about, they can do nothing to change things, they are not responsible for their actions, and it is no use striving to achieve anything anyway, because it will not be successful. They are always victims. It is easy to see that people who are strongly at opposite ends of this spectrum will process information very differently. The business literature suggests strong internals, as exemplified by overconfident CEOs, tend to overestimate the quality of their investment proposals, while less strongly internally controlled CEOs tend to underestimate their project outcomes. Externally controlled managers are most likely doomed to eventual failure, as they do not react appropriately to challenges and changes in their business circumstances.

FINANCE WORKSHOP 9.4

Greengrow Ltd's management has provided the following net annual operating cash flow estimates for a proposed project.

Installed cost	Year 1	Year 2	Year 3	Year 4	Year 5
–100 000	30 000	36 000	38 000	40 000	45 000

(a) Calculate the payback period for the project.

(b) Does the payback period indicate that the project is acceptable? Why?

The payback period is often used in addition to the NPV or IRR techniques.[9] Accepting projects on the basis of their payback period will not be consistent with the objective of wealth maximisation. So while managers can use the payback period for a rough assessment of the short-run impact on the firm's liquidity of adopting the project, it should not be used as the primary method of evaluation for major investments. While it takes the timing of the cash flows (until the payback is completed) into consideration, this method ignores the time value of money. There is no way to incorporate risk into the analysis using the PP. It also ignores the cash flows that occur after the initial outlay has been recovered. Further, the cut-off time for comparison is set arbitrarily rather than being based on some objective criterion that is consistent with wealth maximisation.

Drawbacks aside, the payback period method is frequently used as the main appraisal technique for projects that are relatively small. For these projects, management might consider the use of IRR or NPV too costly given the size of the outlay.

Accounting rate of return

Accounting rate of return: measures a project's profitability using the ratio of average profits to average investment

The **accounting rate of return** (ARR) is different from the techniques we have discussed so far because it uses profits rather than cash flows in its calculation. A method that ignores cash flows and their time value, and risk — and has an accounting-based acceptance criterion — cannot be considered to be consistent with the objective of wealth maximisation.

What the accounting rate of return method does is give an indication of the impact of the project on the firm's profitability. Equation 9.4 shows how the ARR is calculated and example 9.17 applies the equation to some data.

$$ARR = \frac{\text{average net profit}}{\text{average investment}} \qquad [9.4]$$

EXAMPLE 9.17

Accounting rate of return

A company is evaluating a project and has forecast the following four annual profit figures over the project's life:

	Year 1	Year 2	Year 3	Year 4
Net profit	300000	350000	400000	375000

The project requires the purchase of a machine that costs $2500000 and that will be depreciated to zero (using straight line depreciation) by the end of year 4. What is the ARR of the project?

$$ARR = \frac{\text{average net profit}}{\text{average investment}}$$

$$ARR = \frac{\frac{(300000 + 350000 + 400000 + 375000)}{4}}{\frac{2500000}{2}}$$

$$= \frac{356250}{1250000}$$

$$= 28.5\%$$

Average net profit per annum is calculated by adding all profits for the project, then dividing total profits by the number of years the project will operate. The average investment can be calculated as the initial outlay divided by two when straight line depreciation is used and there is no salvage value. If there is a salvage value, it should be subtracted from the initial value when determining the average investment. The book value we calculate for average investment should be based on the accounting records rather than the allowable depreciation deduction for the ATO.

FINANCE WORKSHOP 9.5

Greengrow Ltd is evaluating a project and has forecast the following five annual profit figures over the project's life. The initial outlay for the project is $100000.

	Year 1	Year 2	Year 3	Year 4	Year 5
Net profit	25000	23000	15000	19000	18000

(a) Calculate the accounting rate of return for the project.

(b) Does the accounting rate of return indicate that the project is acceptable? Why?

The decision criterion for the ARR is that the return should exceed the hurdle of the minimum return considered acceptable by management. This minimum return is not objectively determined. As for the payback period, this method should not be used as the sole evaluation technique for large investments as it is not consistent with wealth maximisation.

Non-financial factors in project choices

lo5

Consider the implications of non-financial factors for the investment appraisal process.

The previous sections of this chapter have focused on the quantitative analysis of proposed projects. While this analysis is very important to the decision to accept or reject projects, it is not the whole story. Around three-quarters of decision makers from the largest Australian organisations reported that they had accepted projects that failed to pass the quantitative hurdles.[10] This means that decision makers are using qualitative criteria to override the outcome suggested by quantitative analysis. This may surprise you, given the efforts we have made to learn the discounted cash flow techniques and their consistency with the firm's objective of wealth maximisation. It does, however, bring us back to the point that forecast cash flows do not always eventuate. NPV and IRR help make the best decisions (on purely financial grounds) at the time but, with perfect hindsight, these sometimes turn out to be the wrong decisions. Managers learn this with experience and bring non-financial, or qualitative, factors into the decision process.

The main reason given for adopting quantitatively unacceptable projects is that they have strategic value for the firm.[11] While a particular project may not have a positive NPV, it may provide the firm with future opportunities in a particular market. A project that has a negative NPV may be a good fit with the long-term strategic goals of the firm, so accepting the project is expected to lead to a situation where shareholder wealth will increase when subsequent related projects come on line in the future.

Firms may also accept projects that have been rejected after quantitative analysis because the project might improve the reputation of the firm in the eyes of investors or regulators.

FINANCE WORLD

More than 'social welfare' in disguise

HUGH ALEXANDER GROSSMAN

Debate over the possible broadening of directors' duties exposes an inherent misunderstanding of corporate social responsibility (CSR) principles by business leaders and commentators.

The announcement that the Federal Government will explore the possibility of enacting legislation to extend directors' duties to include social and community obligations has sparked widespread discussion regarding the need for legislative reform. Meredith Hellicar, chairwoman of James Hardie, has suggested that directors' duties should be expanded to include responsibilities to all stakeholders. Such comments reinforce the erroneous perception that altruistic CSR is illegal and contribute to the incorrect view that CSR strategies are some sort of alternative to profitability.

Historic commentators such as Milton Friedman and more recently, since the Asian tsunami crisis, the Australian Shareholders Association, contend that CSR is merely profit sacrifice via the improvement of various social ills in the community.

These commentators fail to appreciate the inherent risk management attached to CSR; they erroneously view 'social welfare' as the only component of sincere engagement.

In practice, the adoption of CSR has a much wider application and may be more appropriately defined as a form of sound management to minimise conventional notions of non-financial risk in areas such as governance, environmental and social impact, and workplace practices. Sound management in such areas controls risk, increases productivity and enhances business opportunities.

Minimising risk in areas such as environmental impact, ethical compliance, community impact and workplace management ultimately places a company in a stronger, more sustainable market position. In the modern setting, a company must underpin its core profit maximisation objective through a proactive approach to CSR in order to manage and mitigate a broad array of risk factors. Companies that adopt a sincere CSR management approach gain advantages from an enhanced capacity to identify and control risk associated with new or altered demands from government regulators, employees, community stakeholders, shareholder activists and consumers. Effective risk management, therefore, reduces unexpected crises and strengthens the company's overall presence and stability.

Increasingly, global organisations, such as BHP Billiton for instance, are taking a leadership position on climate change in the knowledge that this will give the company an edge in the eyes of government officials with the power to deliver access to government-controlled oil deposits.

By contrast, companies adopting a non-integrated or insincere approach to CSR are more likely to be subject to constant stress resulting from the diverse range of issues relevent to external parties. Companies such as Gap and Nike, for example, failed to pay attention to social risks associated with poor management of supply chain issues in the 1990s. For these companies, poor risk management ultimately led to increased financial volatility; both are now leading proponents of sincere CSR.

Australian commentators have sidelined the issue of risk management, mistakenly defining CSR as only social welfare. Instead, CSR may be better defined as providing a sound approach to the management of non-financial risk. The positive link between effective risk management and a company's core objective of profit maximisation suggests that CSR activities may already be provided for under Australia's current Corporations Law and director's duties.[12]

As the 'finance world' article suggests, giving consideration to non-financial factors such as the environment, workplace practices and corporate governance is not only socially responsible — it also benefits the firm by reducing the level of non-financial risk. Of course, not everyone agrees, and some argue that the role of business is to generate wealth and create jobs without being overly concerned about factors outside the legal requirements that must be met by companies. Ethical or socially responsible investing has been an increasing phenomenon around the world. In Australia, ethics are a consideration for less than 1.5% of funds invested, compared to around 2% in the United States.[13] The size of ethical funds under management in Australia means that this group of investors is unlikely to be a force in determining the prices of most shares. However, it is evident that social issues play an increasing role in financial markets.

There is no standard way to incorporate qualitative factors into project evaluation — the weighting given to these factors will vary on a case-to-case basis. The important thing to remember is that analysis of projects goes beyond the purely quantitative. Non-financial factors may cause negative NPV projects to be accepted or positive NPV projects to be rejected.

Is the inclusion of qualitative factors in the decision making process consistent with wealth maximisation? Probably not in the short run. Consider a company that needs to reduce the level of pollution at its manufacturing plant by replacing its existing equipment. The NPV of the replacement is negative. The alternative to accepting the project and doing nothing now may mean the company has to pay to clean up the excessive pollution. As we consider the incremental cash flows in our analysis, the hard to quantify potential clean up costs should be included as savings to the firm from adopting the pollution reduction project and this may result in a positive NPV for the project. Even if the NPV remains negative, there are other potential threats to consider before the project is rejected.

If the company could prevent serious environmental damage, but chose not to, its reputation could be seriously damaged. Consumers might choose to boycott the firm's products. Shareholders might choose to raise the issue at the Annual General Meeting or to sell their shares. Management would need to consider the probability that the company may be forced to close the plant because of the level of pollution if the project is not adopted. In this case, failure to adopt the negative NPV pollution reduction project would result in a serious cash flow problem when the company could no longer make its products. This means considering qualitative factors (like the environment) can be consistent with maximising wealth in the longer term. A business needs to operate in a sustainable way if it wishes to continue operating in the future.

executive summary

lo1 explain the problems associated with evaluating mutually exclusive projects and apply techniques to overcome these problems

- Capital rationing is a self-imposed limit that is placed on the size of the capital budget. This means the firm can not undertake all identified positive NPV projects.
- The unconstrained hurdle rate is the return that would be required on projects in the absence of capital rationing.
- The NPV rule under capital rationing is to choose the set of projects that gives the highest total NPV while keeping the total initial outlays within the budget constraint.
- The imposition of a budget constraint is likely to result in a higher hurdle rate for projects than the unconstrained hurdle rate.
- This means that projects with positive NPVs are likely to be rejected when a capital budgeting constraint is implemented. Rejecting positive NPV projects is inconsistent with maximising shareholder wealth.
- Independent projects can be accepted or rejected without having to accept or reject some other project (that is, they are independent of other projects).
- Mutually exclusive projects either perform the same task or utilise the same scarce physical resources. Acceptance of one project means that the others must be rejected.
- Mutually exclusive projects can rank differently under the IRR and NPV techniques. The differences in ranking can be attributed to the size disparity, a cash flow timing disparity or unequal life projects.
- The size disparity arises when mutually exclusive projects have equal lives but have different sized initial outlays.
- The cash flow timing disparity arises when mutually exclusive projects have equal lives and the same size initial outlays but have different patterns of net cash inflows. One project, for example, may receive even cash flows over its life, while the other has relatively small net cash inflows at the start and relatively large inflows toward the end of the project.
- The use of NPV overcomes the size and timing disparities.
- Where mutually exclusive projects have unequal lives, we need to consider the return that could be generated on the resource that is required by both projects after the short-lived project is completed.
- It is not possible to reliably forecast the investment opportunities that will be available to the firm at the time of completion of the short-lived project. We use the simplifying assumption that the projects currently being evaluated can be repeated to overcome this forecasting difficulty.
- Note that unequal lives do not affect the analysis of independent projects — where projects are independent and in the absence of capital rationing all positive NPV projects should be adopted.
- Mutually exclusive projects with unequal lives should be evaluated using either a replacement chain or the equivalent annual annuity (EAA).
- The replacement chain method replicates the cash flows of the mutually exclusive projects until the two strings have equal lives.
- The inherent assumption in the replacement chain method is that the mutually exclusive projects will be repeated for as long as it takes to get the projects to a common lifespan.

- Where the initial outlay for a repeated project exceeds the expected net cash inflows for that year of operation, we should not use IRR. As we see in chapter 8, IRR is unreliable when the project cash flows have a reversal of sign subsequent to the first year.
- The replacement chain method becomes cumbersome when a large number of repeated projects is necessary to make the project lives comparable.
- The decision rule for the replacement chain method is to choose the project that has the highest NPV over the required number of project replacements.
- An EAA is the equal annual cash flow that would generate the project's NPV during the project's life.
- The inherent assumption in the EAA method is that each project is repeated an infinite number of times.
- The decision rule for the EAA method is to choose the project with the highest EAA.
- The EAA method gives the same accept/reject decision as the replacement chain while being less difficult to calculate.

lo2 incorporate risk in the project appraisal process

- The cost of capital is not the appropriate discount rate for projects with more or less risk than those currently undertaken by the firm.
- Using the cost of capital to evaluate projects with less risk than those that the firm currently undertakes will result in rejection of projects that would maximise shareholder wealth.
- Using the cost of capital to evaluate projects with more risk than those that the firm currently undertakes will result in acceptance of projects that would decrease shareholder wealth.
- Risk-adjusted discount rates (RADRs) incorporate differing levels of project risk by changing the required return or discount rate.
- A subjective risk premium is added to or subtracted from the cost of capital to obtain the RADR for each risk category.
- Projects are classified into risk categories and the subjectively determined discount rate for that category is used as the required return.
- Project cash flows are discounted at the RADR. The decision rule to apply with the RADR is to accept a project with a positive NPV and to reject a project with a negative NPV.
- Alternatives to the RADR are the use of a divisional cost of capital, estimating the project's beta using the CAPM and using certainty equivalents to adjust the cash flows for risk.

lo3 explain and incorporate the impact of the taxation system on project appraisal

- A firm that is fully integrated with the dividend imputation system will maximise shareholders' wealth by using before-tax cash flows and a before-tax discount rate to analyse projects.
- A firm that is not integrated with the dividend imputation system will maximise owners' wealth by using after-tax cash flows and an after-tax discount rate to analyse projects.

- Taxation does not normally have an impact on the installed cost of an asset or any change in net working capital for an expansion project.
- If the initial outlay included tax-deductible expenses such as training costs and some advertising expenses, there will be a tax impact on the initial outlay of an expansion project.
- There are tax implications for the initial outlays for most replacement projects because here the initial outlay included the terminal cash flow from the assets that are being replaced.
- Depreciable assets being replaced may attract a taxable gain or generate a deductible loss.
- Gains on disposal of depreciable assets are taxed at the marginal tax rate. Losses on these assets are allowed as tax deductions.
- The sale of non-depreciable assets in a replacement decision may generate a capital gain or loss.
- Depreciation is the amount allowed as a tax deduction by the ATO to recognise the decrease in the value of an asset as it is used and wears out over time.
- Capital gains are taxed differently for companies compared to sole traders and partnerships.
- Capital losses can be used only to offset current or future capital gains.
- The ATO currently allows the use of the prime cost and diminishing value methods of depreciation.
- The annual depreciation expense under the prime cost depreciation method is the cost of the asset divided by the asset's effective life.
- The annual depreciation expense under the diminishing value method is calculated as the base value (or asset cost) multiplied by the ratio of 150% to the effective life.
- The depreciation expense is not a cash flow and is calculated only to determine the amount of tax payable for the period.
- Taxes on the terminal value of the projects for depreciable assets depend on the taxation book value relative to the selling price of the asset. For non-depreciable assets, the tax on any capital gain depends on the sales price relative to the purchase price and the structure of the business.

lo4 describe and apply the payback method and the accounting rate of return (ARR) technique

- The payback period and accounting rate of return are non-discounted methods of evaluation.
- The payback period is the length of time it takes for the net cash inflows from a project to equal the initial outlay. A project is acceptable if it meets the subjectively determined payback time hurdle.
- The accounting rate of return measures a project's profitability using the ratio of average profits to average investment. A project is acceptable if it meets the subjectively determined minimum required ARR.
- Neither the payback nor ARR methods are consistent with maximising shareholder wealth, so should not be used as the sole method of evaluation for major investments.

- These methods are often used in conjunction with the discounted cash flow techniques or used as the sole method of evaluation for very small projects.

lo5 consider the implications of non-financial factors for the investment appraisal process

- Quantitative analysis is not the end of the story for project evaluation.
- Non-financial or qualitative factors are often considered in addition to the quantitative analysis.
- Qualitative factors include 'bigger picture' considerations such as the strategic fit of the project with the firm's long-run targets and ethical considerations.
- Qualitative analysis can mean that negative NPV projects are accepted, or positive NPV projects are rejected.
- Qualitative analysis may not be consistent with wealth maximisation in the short run, but may be in the long run.

Key terms

accounting rate of return, p. 330
capital rationing, p. 309
certainty equivalent, p. 318
depreciation, p. 320
equivalent annual annuity, p. 314
independent project, p. 310
mutually exclusive projects, p. 311
payback period, p. 328
replacement chain, p. 313
risk-adjusted discount rates, p. 316

Learning chart

Learning objective	Questions	Self-test problems	Financial problems
lo1 explain the problems associated with evaluating mutually exclusive projects and apply techniques to overcome these problems	9.1, 9.2, 9.3, 9.4, 9.5, 9.6, 9.7, 9.22	9.1	9.1, 9.2, 9.3, 9.4, 9.5, 9.6, 9.19
lo2 incorporate risk in the project appraisal process	9.8, 9.9	9.2, 9.3	9.7, 9.9, 9.10
lo3 explain and incorporate the impact of the taxation system on project appraisal	9.10, 9.11, 9.12, 9.13, 9.14, 9.15, 9.16, 9.17		9.8, 9.11, 9.12, 9.13, 9.14, 9.15, 9.16, 9.17, 9.18, 9.19
lo4 describe and apply the payback method and the accounting rate of return (ARR) technique	9.18, 9.19, 9.20	9.4, 9.5	9.15
lo5 consider the implications of non-financial factors for the investment appraisal process	9.21, 9.22		9.19, 9.20

Questions

9.1 What is capital rationing and how does it impact on the investment evaluation process?

9.2 Which projects should be accepted if there are no capital constraints on the firm?

9.3 What is an 'unconstrained hurdle rate'?

9.4 What are mutually exclusive projects? How are they different to independent projects?

9.5 Why is capital rationing a special case of mutual exclusivity?

9.6 How do you choose between mutually exclusive projects that have equal lives, the same initial outlay and similar cash flow patterns?

9.7 Which three factors can create ranking problems among mutually exclusive projects? Explain each factor and show how the associated ranking problem can be overcome.

9.8 Should riskier projects have a higher or lower required return than the current projects being undertaken in the firm? Why?

9.9 What is the most used method of incorporating risk into project appraisal? Why is it so often chosen over competing methods?

9.10 How do you determine if before- or after-tax cash flows are relevant to the investment evaluation process?

9.11 How are after-tax cash flows different to before-tax cash flows? To answer this question, discuss the impact of taxes on the initial outlay, the operating cash flows and the terminal value of a project.

9.12 What two methods of depreciation does the ATO allow for new assets? Describe how depreciation is calculated under each of these methods.

9.13 When is tax payable on the sale of the old depreciable asset? When is a tax benefit received from the sale of the old depreciable asset?

9.14 How are capital gains taxed if the business is structured as a company?

9.15 How are capital gains taxed if the business is structured as a sole trader or partnership?

9.16 What happens if the capital losses in a year are larger than the capital gains? What happens when capital gains are made in the years following capital losses?

9.17 Why are lost sales included in the calculation of after-tax cash flows?

9.18 Explain how the payback period is calculated and describe the decision rule for acceptance of projects.

9.19 Explain how the accounting rate of return is calculated and describe the decision rule for acceptance of projects.

9.20 What are the benefits of using non-discounted methods of project appraisal? Why are non-discounted methods of project appraisal considered inferior to the discounted cash flow methods?

9.21 Using an example, explain why using non-financial factors to override the decision from a quantitative analysis may be inconsistent with wealth maximisation in the short run, but consistent with it in the long run.

9.22 Daisy Co. has decided to take steps to reduce the impact of its operations on the environment. Two alternative projects are being considered. The first project involves the installation of equipment that reduces the company's greenhouse gas emissions. The equipment will cost $70000. The second project uses eucalyptus to absorb some of the company's emissions. The cost of purchasing the vacant land next to the factory and planting the trees would be around $90000. Neither of the projects will generate any cash inflows. What factors would you take into consideration if you had to decide which of the projects should be adopted?

Self-test problems

9.1 You are using a 15% discount rate to evaluate the following 5 projects.

Project	Initial outlay $	NPV $	IRR %
V	100000	4352	20
W	75000	1525	17
X	160000	13920	25
Y	225000	−7600	11
Z	65000	−4128	8

(a) Which projects would you accept? Why?

(b) Which projects would you accept if there is a capital constraint of $300000?

9.2 Disco King is evaluating two mutually exclusive projects that have the following before-tax cash flow patterns.

	Rumba project	Cha-cha project
Initial outlay	100000	200000
Annual net cash flow	50000	70000
Terminal value	30000	50000
Project life	2 years	4 years

The corporate tax rate is 30% and the shareholders of Disco King can fully utilise imputation credits. The before-tax cost of capital is 16%, and the after-tax cost is 12%. The company has asked you to advise on which project to accept, and want you to:

(a) use the replacement chain method to make a recommendation

(b) use the equivalent annual value method to make a recommendation.

9.3 The management of Radar Ltd is considering 2 new projects and has asked that you evaluate them. You have been supplied with the following cash forecasts:

	t = 0	Year 1	Year 2	Year 3	Year 4	Year 5
Project I	−250000	120000	100000	90000		
Project II	−300000	120000	100000	90000	80 0000	70000

Management estimates that Project I has a level of risk similar to that of most of the firm's current projects. Project II is a new line of business for Radar, so is considered to have higher than average risk. Radar's cost of capital is 12% and you have received the following risk-adjusted discount rates and categories:

Risk category	Discount rate (%)
Low	10
Medium	12
High	16

Use the NPV or IRR method to evaluate the projects and advise Radar of your recommendation.

9.4 TaxiCo Ltd will purchase 3 new computers to improve its scheduling system. The installed cost of the computers is $5000. The ATO specifies that the effective life for computers is 4 years. Calculate the depreciation charge for each year of the effective life using:

(a) the prime cost method

(b) the diminishing value method.

9.5 Muttaburra Ltd has forecast the profits for the proposed 'Saurus' project as follows:

	Year 1	Year 2	Year 3	Year 4
Profit	17 298	23 157	29 016	15 562

The project will require an investment of $209 900 and will have a zero terminal value. Calculate the accounting rate of return.

Solutions to self-test problems

9.1 (a) Projects V, W and X should be accepted as they have positive NPVs and IRRs that are greater than the hurdle rate.

(b) Project selection with capital constraint of $300 000:

The first step is to rank the projects by NPV or IRR. You then determine the cumulative outlay that is needed as projects are accepted in order of how much value they add to the firm.

Project	Initial outlay ($)	NPV ($)	IRR (%)	Total outlay ($)
X	160 000	13 920	25	–160 000
V	100 000	4 352	20	–260 000
W	75 000	1 525	17	–335 000
Y	225 000	–7 600	11	–560 000
Z	65 000	–4 128	8	–625 000

From the table, you can see that projects X and V can both be undertaken within the capital constraint. The next step is to identify any other feasible sets of projects that have total initial outlays under $300 000. These sets are projects X plus W, and projects V plus W. A set of projects V plus W plus Y is also feasible but there is no need to consider this set because the adoption of project Y decreases firm value (that is, firm value will be higher with the set of V plus W only).

Feasible set	Set outlay ($)	Set NPV ($)
X + V	−260000	18272
X + W	−235000	15445
V + W	−175000	5877

After consideration of the feasible sets of projects that will increase firm value, we would accept the set of projects X plus V.

9.2 (a) Replacement chain

	Rumba	Cha-cha	PVIF (table 2)	PV_{Rumba}	$PV_{Cha\text{-}cha}$
Initial outlay	−100000	−200000	1	−100000	−200000
Year 1	50000	70000	0.8621	43105	60347
Year 2	−20000	70000	0.7432	−14864	52024
Year 3	50000	70000	0.6407	32035	44849
Year 4	80000	120000	0.5523	44184	66276
			NPV	4460	23496

The Cha-cha project has the highest NPV so it should be accepted.

(b) EAA

	Rumba	Cha-cha
Initial outlay	−100000	−200000
Year 1	50000	70000
Year 2	80000	70000
Year 3		70000
Year 4		120000
NPV	2561	23496
PVFA (table 4)	1.6052	2.7982
EAA	1595	8397

The Cha-cha project has the highest EAA so it should be accepted.

9.3

Project I	Today	Year 1	Year 2	Year 3
Initial investment	−250000			
Net cash flow		120000	100000	90000
RADR = 12%				
NPV (tables)	$930	Accept		
IRR	12.23%	Accept		

Project II	Today	Year 1	Year 2	Year 3	Year 4	Year 5
Initial investment	−300000					
Net cash flow		120000	100000	90000	80000	70000
RADR = 16%						
NPV (tables)	$12934.96	Accept				
IRR	18.02%	Accept				

9.4 (a) Prime cost depreciation $= \dfrac{\text{asset cost}}{\text{effective life}}$

$$= \frac{5000}{4}$$

$$= 1250 \text{ pa for each of the 4 years}$$

(b) Diminishing value method = base value $\times \left(\dfrac{150\%}{\text{effective life}}\right)$

$$= 5000 \times \left(\frac{1.5}{4}\right)$$

$$= 1875 \text{ for year 1}$$

$$\text{Year 2} = 3125 \times \left(\frac{1.5}{4}\right)$$

$$= 1172$$

$$\text{Year 3} = 1953 \times \left(\frac{1.5}{4}\right)$$

$$= 732$$

$$\text{Year 4} = 1221 \times \left(\frac{1.5}{4}\right)$$

$$= 458$$

9.5 Average profit $= \dfrac{(17298 + 23157 + 29016 + 15562)}{4}$

$$= 21\,258.25$$

Average investment $= \dfrac{209900}{2}$

$$= 104\,950$$

$$\text{ARR} = \frac{2125.25}{104\,950}$$

$$= 20.26\%$$

Financial problems

9.1 The board of Redroll Ltd has stated that the capital expenditure budget for this year will not exceed $250 000. Management has given you 15 project proposals to analyse. The projects all have the same level of risk as those currently undertaken by the firm, so you used the company's WACC of 15% in your analysis. You have identified 7 projects that should be considered further:

Project	Initial outlay ($)	NPV ($)	IRR (%)
I	100 000	4352	17
II	150 000	0	15
III	45 000	7176	33

IV	25000	2827	28
V	75000	3264	20
VI	50000	437	16
VII	90000	1308	17

Identify the seven feasible project sets. Each set must contain more than one project. Calculate the NPV of each set then rank the sets in order of their ability to increase the wealth of the shareholders of Redroll Ltd.

9.2 Ratters Ltd is currently evaluating the following 5 projects. If Ratters has a capital budget constraint of $1 million, which of the 5 indivisible projects should the company accept?

Project	Initial outlay ($)	NPV ($)
A	290000	130000
B	250000	80000
C	690000	180000
D	460000	80000
E	600000	120000

9.3 Daisy Chain Shoes is a small company that has limited access to funds. They currently have a capital rationing constraint of $500000 and have asked you to recommend which investments they should make. Each project can be undertaken only once, and more than one project will be undertaken. The proposed investments are:

Project	Initial investment ($)	NPV ($)
Stilettos	125000	60000
Platforms	230000	61000
Sling backs	150000	15000
Creepers	95000	20000
Thongs	35000	15000

The management of Daisy Chain will only raise the amount of funds required to invest in the set of projects that will maximise the owners' wealth.

(a) Identify the wealth maximising set of projects from those available to Daisy Chain.

(b) How much money should Daisy Chain raise to fund these projects?

9.4 You have been asked to recommend the best of 3 mutually exclusive projects. The cost of capital is 10%. Each project has a 2-year life and the cash flows are as follows:

	$t = 0$	Year 1	Year 2
Red project	-150000	90000	90000
Blue project	60000	60000	-90000
Green project	-25000	15000	15000

(a) Recommend which project should be adopted.

(b) Explain how you chose between NPV and IRR as your tool of analysis.

9.5 As the financial manager of Nesbitt Ltd, you are currently evaluating 3 different mixing machines that could be used in the Hobgoblin expansion project. Each machine has an expected life of 5 years. However, the initial outlays for each machine and their potential cash flow patterns are quite different. The project has a 12% required return and you have made the following calculations:

	NPV	IRR
Mix-Right	$20 000	13%
Mix-O-Matic	$5 000	12.25%
Whizzer	$15 000	15%

(a) Identify any disparities in the ranking of the projects and explain why these disparities might occur.

(b) Which project would you choose? Why?

9.6 Jason's Publishing Co. wants to acquire a new printing machine so the firm can expand into the production of glossy magazines. Jason has identified two manufacturers that could supply the type of machine for the job. The manufacturers have provided the following details:

	Printley's machine	Page's machine
Purchase price	175 000	300 000
Transport	2 000	1 000
Installation	1 500	2 000
Annual maintenance charge	2 000	6 000
Estimated electricity usage pa	4 000	2 500
Estimated insurance pa	2 000	3 000
Scrap value at end of life	50 000	70 000
Useful life	3	9

Sales of $70 000 pa are expected from the magazine project. Jason's Printing has a WACC of 13% and the shareholders are fully integrated with the dividend imputation system. The project has about the same level of risk as those currently operating in the firm. Jason expects to be printing magazines for many years to come.

(a) Use the replacement chain method and advise which of the machines should be purchased.

(b) Use the EAA method to advise which of the machines should be purchased.

9.7 Learning Circle Ltd, the leading publisher of educational books for preschool children in Australia, is considering a project that would capitalise on the familiarity of their brand name. The company is owned by Australian-resident investors who can fully utilise dividend imputation credits.

The project proposal is for the establishment of 5 daycare centres. The set-up costs for the project would be: $1.5 million for the purchase of property and suitable buildings (no depreciation charge is allowed for these costs); a further $500 000 for equipment that can be depreciated over a 10-year useful life using the prime cost method. The corporate tax rate is 30%. The project is being evaluated over a 10-year useful life. At the end of the project, the land and buildings would be sold for $2.5 million and the equipment would be scrapped. Net operating cash flows of $350 000 are expected for each of the 10 years of operation.

Learning Circle has the following guidelines for evaluating projects:

Type of project	Before-tax required return	After-tax required return
Replacement decision	13%	10%
Expansion of current operations	14%	11%
Projects unrelated to current operations	15%	12%
Research and development	20%	18%

(a) Which discount rate should Learning Circle use to evaluate the new project? Why?

(b) Construct the relevant cash flow pattern for the 10 years of the childcare project.

(c) Calculate the NPV and the IRR of the childcare project.

(d) Should the project be accepted? Why?

9.8 Using the data in problem 9.7, assume now that Learning Circle is structured as a partnership and the business has no other capital gains or losses in year 10. The partners have a marginal tax rate of 45%.

(a) Which discount rate should Learning Circle use to evaluate the new project? Why?

(b) Construct the relevant cash flow pattern for the 10 years of the childcare project.

(c) Calculate the NPV and the IRR of the childcare project.

(d) Should the project be accepted? Why?

9.9 The management of Kaleidoscope Ltd is considering two new projects that you have been asked to evaluate. You have been supplied with the following cash forecasts:

	Today	Year 1	Year 2	Year 3	Year 4
Project Purple	−350 000	100 000	200 000	300 000	
Project Green	−300 000	150 000	110 000	100 000	90 000

Management estimates that Project Green has a level of risk similar to that of most of the firm's current projects. Project Purple is a new line of business for Kaleidoscope, so is considered to have higher than average risk. Kaleidoscope's cost of capital is 15% and you have received the following risk-adjusted discount rates and categories:

Risk category	Discount rate (%)
Low	11
Medium	15
High	20

Use the NPV method to evaluate the projects and advise Kaleidoscope of your recommendation.

9.10 Daft Girlie Ltd operates a chain of 179 fashion stores nation-wide. Sales last year were $400 million and cost of goods sold (not including depreciation) is 65% of sales. The selling and advertising expenses of the firm are $125 000 per annum. Three-quarters of this expense is fixed; the remainder of the cost is shared equally among the stores. The corporate tax rate is 30%.

The company is considering opening a new store that will cost $1.5 million to establish. The establishment costs would be depreciated straight line over an effective life of 8 years. Assume the new store will have the same costs as existing stores and that sales will be the same as those for the average existing store. Estimate the after-tax cash flows for the first 9 years of operation for the new store. Round your calculations for each cash inflow or outflow to the nearest whole dollar.

9.11 Minx Ltd is evaluating a project to manufacture faux fur. The equipment and set-up costs for the project will total $2.1 million. The equipment will be depreciated straight line over a 7-year effective life. Sales of $900 000 per annum are expected and cash operating costs will be 30% of sales. The project will run for 7 years and will have a zero salvage value. The corporate tax rate is 30%. The marginal shareholder of Minx is a foreign investor and the after-tax required return is 13%.

(a) Estimate the relevant cash flows. Round your calculations for each cash inflow or outflow to the nearest whole dollar. Calculate the NPV for the project.

(b) Assume that Minx is currently losing money on another major project. It does not expect to have a taxable income for the first 3 years of the faux fur project. Estimate the relevant cash flows and NPV of the project under these circumstances. Is your recommendation on the project different under this scenario?

9.12 You have decided to cash in on the fitness craze in your town, so you are thinking about setting up a gym. You can rent a warehouse close to the business district for $26 000 pa. In order to attract the 'right' sort of clientele, you will need to spend $70 000 on redecorating and installing mirrors on all surfaces. You will also purchase some equipment at a cost of $50 000. Both of these outlays can be depreciated straight line over a 4-year effective life. You expect that the equipment can be sold at the end of 4 years for $5000.

Your market research suggests you can attract and maintain 450 members. Each would pay an annual membership fee of $650. Instructors are usually paid a salary of $35 000 pa and you would employ 4 of these to keep the gym operating 7 days a week. Your marginal tax rate is 47% and you will operate the business for 4 years before retiring. If your cost of capital is 16%, should you set up the business? Calculate IRR and NPV to support your decision. Round your calculations for each cash inflow or outflow to the nearest whole dollar.

9.13 You have been asked to evaluate a proposal for the owner of Bamboo Traders. The owner's marginal tax rate is 47%. She has given you the following information about the project:

- it has a 5-year lifetime
- the installed cost of the project will be $250 000
- the ATO gives this type of asset an effective life of 4 years
- the asset will be sold at the end of the project for an estimated $20 000
- sales of $90 000 are expected in the first year of the project
- sales will grow at a rate of 5% pa for each year of the project
- cost of goods sold (excluding depreciation) is expected to be 30% of sales
- the owner's required return is 8%.

Using IRR and NPV, advise the owner of Bamboo Traders on the acceptability of the project. Round your calculations for each cash inflow or outflow to the nearest whole dollar.

9.14 How would your answer to problem 9.13 change if the owner of Bamboo Traders chose to use the declining balance method of depreciation? Assume that any tax losses from this project can be used to offset tax payable on other projects in the current year. Show calculations to support your answer, rounding each calculation to the nearest dollar.

9.15 Arkwright & Sons is a partnership where the partners all have a marginal tax rate of 38%. They would like you to evaluate a project for them and have provided the following information:

	Year 1	Year 2	Year 3	Year 4
Revenue	110 000	115 000	120 000	90 000
Cost of goods sold	12 100	12 650	13 200	9 900
Depreciation	50 000	45 000	40 000	35 000
Earnings before tax	27 900	37 350	46 800	25 100

- The initial investment in the project is $200 000 and an additional investment of $10 000 is required at the end of year 2.
- The asset purchased at the commencement of the project will be sold at the end of the project for its book value.
- Working capital will be 9% of revenues for each year. The working capital investment has to be made at the start of each period. All working capital will be recovered.
- The required return of the partners is 10%.

(a) Estimate the relevant cash flows for the project.
(b) Estimate the payback period.
(c) Calculate the accounting rate of return.
(d) Calculate the NPV for the project.

9.16 Recently, a meeting of the partners of your firm decided to investigate the viability of offering a babysitting service to the customers of the partnership's retail outlet. Consultants have been commissioned to conduct a survey of your current and target customers. The consultants' report was positive and they will be paid $15 000 next month for the work they have done.

You estimate that the licensing and set-up costs for the babysitting service will be $100 000. The service will cost about $5000 per month to operate and would open 1 month from today. The monthly sales of your retail outlet are $150 000 and you expect that offering the babysitting will increase these by 30%. The marginal cost of new sales will be 20% (excluding the costs of the new service). The partners' marginal tax rate is 40%. If the partnership's cost of capital is 12% and you expect the babysitting service to continue for 1 year, should the proposal be accepted? Show equations and calculations to support your answer.

9.17 Moddie and Millie have a partnership and both partners have a marginal tax rate of 42%. They would like you to evaluate a project for them and have provided the following information.

	Year 1	Year 2	Year 3	Year 4	Year 5
Cash sales	500000	600000	700000	500000	300000

- The initial investment in the project is $700 000 for production equipment. The ATO allows prime cost depreciation at the rate of 25% pa on these assets.
- The assets purchased at the commencement of the project will be sold at the end of the project for $50 000.
- The assets require a tax-deductible overhaul that will cost $15 000 before production can begin in year 4.
- Working capital will be 7% of revenues for each year. The working capital investment has to be made at the start of each period. All working capital will be recovered.
- Cost of goods sold is 30% of sales.
- Wages are $100 000 per annum.
- The required return of the partners is 15%.

(a) Calculate the relevant cash flows for the project.

(b) Calculate the NPV for the project. Make a recommendation about the acceptability of the project.

(c) Calculate the relevant cash flows for the project if the business is structured as a company rather than a partnership. The corporate rate of tax is 30%.

(d) Calculate the NPV for the cash flows in (c). Has your recommendation changed?

9.18 McAuber & Sons is a family owned partnership that sells books by mail order. Partnership income is shared among the three partners who all have a marginal tax rate of 47%. The corporate tax rate is 30%.

The youngest partner has suggested that posting catalogues and asking customers to return order forms by mail is a bit outdated. She has suggested that the firm set up an online catalogue that allows customers to order books and pay by credit card using their computer. The computerised system would replace the current mail system.

The current mail system used by McAuber costs $15 per 100 customer orders processed. Each customer spends an average of $30 per order and this is expected to continue under the new system.

Netlink Ltd has agreed to design and maintain the McAuber & Sons website for an upfront fee of $500 000. There will also be an ongoing service fee of $10 per 100 customers that order from the website. The contract with Netlink is for 4 years. At the end of 4 years, the entire ordering system will be reviewed. If McAuber decides to terminate the contract with Netlink prior to the contract date, it will have to pay Netlink a penalty of $100 000.

The new online advertising and ordering system is expected to increase sales from the current level of $750 000 pa to $1.2 million pa for the next 4 years.

Determine the relevant cash flows for the project and calculate the NPV using a required return of 10%. Show all relevant equations and calculations. Should the ordering system be changed?

9.19 Your brother owns a rental property and needs to replace the hot water system. He has provided you with the following 3 alternatives:

- A solar system which would cost $9000 to install and $200 pa operating costs. The system will last for 30 years and you can assume that the building will too.

- A gas system which would cost $3000 to install and $800 pa operating costs. This system would have a useful life of 15 years.
- An electric system with a cost of $2500 to install and $1200 pa operating costs. This system would have a useful life of 12 years.

(a) If your brother's cost of capital is 12% and the hot water systems do not generate any tax benefits, which system would you recommend to maximise your brother's wealth?

(b) Are there any non-financial factors your brother might consider in his investment decision?

9.20 Pillage Consolidated is an oil-producing company that has oil fields in a number of areas. The company is owned by investors who can fully utilise dividend imputation credits, and the before-tax cost of capital is 20%. Pillage has applied to the state government for a lease that would grant it the drilling rights over a field in the western district. The rights would cost $500 000, with the entire amount being paid to the state government on 1 January next year. Ongoing royalties would be paid to the government at the rate of 2% of the sales value of production for each year of the project. This project has a similar level of risk to those currently operated by Pillage and the company uses NPV to evaluate projects.

The company would begin production as soon as the payment has been made. No new equipment is required for the development of the field. The engineers at Pillage estimate that the field would produce oil for 10 years, with the following quantities for each year:

Year	Barrels of oil
1	10 000
2	9 000
3	8 000
4	7 000
5	6 000
6	5 000
7	4 000
8	3 000
9	2 000
10	1 000

Production costs and oil prices are expected to remain constant over the 10 years of operation. Pillage will be able to sell each barrel of oil for $50 with production costs of $10 per barrel.

A condition of the lease is that Pillage will have to close the wells and clean up the site when they have finished production. The engineers have estimated that the clean up would cost $500 000, and replacing the native vegetation that would be cleared for production would cost a further $500 000. Pillage's lawyers have examined the contract carefully and have found that there is no requirement to revegetate the site. They have recommended that the company not make this expenditure. While few contracts actually require the replacement of vegetation, this has become the normal practice of oil companies in the area.

(a) If management choose to follow the lawyer's advice, should they acquire the rights to drill in the area?

(b) What would the NPV of the project be if the management of Pillage chose to ignore the lawyer's advice and revegetate the site? Can such a decision be consistent with wealth maximisation? Why?

SOLUTIONS TO FINANCE WORKSHOPS

9.1 (a) The Mambo project needs to be repeated once to have the same project life as the Samba project.

Mambo	Time zero	Year 1	Year 2	Year 3	Year 4	Year 5	Year 6
Initial outlay	−200 000			−200 000			
Net cash flow		80 000	80 000	80 000	80 000	80 000	80 000
Terminal value				60 000			60 000
Total cash flow	−200 000	80 000	80 000	−60 000	80 000	80 000	140 000
	1	0.8696	0.7561	0.6575	0.5718	0.4972	0.4323
Present value	−200 000	69 568	60 488	−39 450	45 744	39 776	60 522
NPV (chain)	$36 648						

Samba	Time zero	Year 1	Year 2	Year 3	Year 4	Year 5	Year 6
Initial outlay	−350 000						
Net cash flow		90 000	90 000	90 000	90 000	90 000	90 000
Terminal value							80 000
Total cash flow	−350 000	90 000	90 000	90 000	90 000	90 000	170 000
	1	0.8696	0.7561	0.6575	0.5718	0.4972	0.4323
Present value	−350 000	78 264	68 049	59 175	51 462	44 748	73 491
NPV	$25 189						

Repeating the Mambo project gives a higher NPV than doing the Samba project for the same length of time. The Mambo project should be selected.

(b) Using equation 9.1, $EAA_i = \frac{NPV_i}{PVFA_{k,\,n}}$

$$EAA_{Mambo} = \frac{NPV_{Mambo}}{PVFA_{0.15,\,3}}$$

$$\begin{aligned} NPV_{Mambo} &= -200\,000 + 80\,000\,(0.8696) + 80\,000\,(0.7561) \\ &\quad + 140\,000\,(0.6575) \\ &= \$22\,106 \end{aligned}$$

$$EAA_{Mambo} = \frac{22\,106}{2.2832} = \$9682.02$$

$$EAA_{Samba} = \frac{NPV_{Samba}}{PVFA_{0.15,\,6}}$$

$$EAA_{Samba} = \frac{25\,189}{3.7845} = \$6655.83$$

The Mambo project has the higher EAA (9682.02 > 6655.83) so should be selected.

9.2 Cash outflows for replacement machine

Purchase price		400 000
Delivery costs		2 000
Registration	4 000	
Insurance	10 000	
	14 000	
Tax saving on expense at 30%	4 200	9 800
		411 800
Cash flow from sale of existing machine		
Sale of machine		50 000
Subtract taxation book value		0
Gain		50 000
Tax on gain at 30%		15 000
After-tax cash flow from sale		35 000
Total installed cost of replacement project		376 800

9.3 Depreciation charge = base value × $\frac{(150\%)}{\text{effective life}}$

Year 3 base value = 1 160 000 − (174 000 + 147 900)
Year 3 charge = 838 100 × 0.15
= 125 715
Year 4 base value = 1 160 000 − (174 000 + 147 900 + 125 715)
Year 4 charge = 712 385 × 0.15
= 106 857.75
Year 5 base value = 1 160 000 − (174 000 + 147 900 + 125 715 + 106 857.75)
Year 5 charge = 605 527.25 × 0.15
= 90 829.09

9.4

	Time zero	Year 1	Year 2	Year 3	Year 4	Year 5
Net cash flows	−100 000	30 000	36 000	38 000	40 000	45 000
Cumulative		30 000	66 000	104 000		

The payback period is more than 2 years ($66 000 cumulative cash flow at the end of year 2) but less than 3 years ($104 000 at the end of year 3).

$$\frac{100\,000 - 66\,000}{38\,000} = \frac{34\,000}{38\,000}$$

$$= 0.8947 \text{ or } 46.5 \text{ weeks}$$

The payback period is 2 years and 46.5 weeks. Without a benchmark payback period, we cannot say if this is acceptable or not.

9.5 (a) $ARR = \dfrac{\text{average net profit}}{\text{average investment}}$

$$ARR = \frac{\dfrac{25\,000 + 23\,000 + 15\,000 + 19\,000 + 18\,000}{5}}{\dfrac{100\,000}{2}}$$

$$= \frac{20\,000}{50\,000} = 0.40 \text{ or } 40\%$$

(b) The acceptability of this ARR depends on the minimum ARR hurdle that is considered acceptable by management.

End notes

1 Stevens, M 2006, 'Analysts scrutinise Twiggy's scheme', *The Australian*, 17 November, pp. 19, 22.

2 Kester, G, Chang, R, Erlinda, S, Haikal, S, Isa, M, Skully, M, Tsui, K & Wang, Chi 1999, 'Capital budgeting practices in the Asia-Pacific region: Australia, Hong Kong, Indonesia, Malaysia, Philippines and Singapore', *Financial Practice and Education*, spring/summer, pp. 25–33. Kester et al. found 61.9% of Australian respondents used subjectively defined risk categories.

3 Freeman, M & Hobbes, G 1991, 'Capital budgeting: theory versus practice', *Australian Accountant*, vol. 61, no. 8, pp. 36–41. Freeman and Hobbes reported that 27% of major Australian companies used classification by risk level and 23% used classification by expenditure type.

4 See Kester et al., p. 30.

5 Australian Taxation Office, 'Step by step guide to capital gains', www.ato.gov.au.

6 For some examples of the effective lives of assets see Australian Taxation Office, 'Taxation Ruling TR 2000/18W', http://law.ato.gov.au.

7 Kester et al. surveyed Australian listed companies and found 73% used the accounting rate of return, but did not rate it as important in their decision making process. They also found 93% used the payback period and these firms rated this method as more important than the accounting rate of return, but not as important as NPV or IRR. Freeman and Hobbes reported 33% and 43% of Australian organisations used the ARR and PP respectively.

8 Schwarz, H 1998, *Rationality gone awry: decision-making inconsistent with economic and financial theory*, Praeger, Westport, Connecticut, p. 64.

9 See Kester et al., p. 28 for use in Australia and for US results see Graham, J & Harvey, C 2001, 'The theory and practice of corporate finance: evidence from the field', *Journal of Financial Economics*, vol. 60, pp. 187–243.

10 See Freeman & Hobbes, p. 39.

11 See Freeman & Hobbes, p. 39.

12 Grossman, HA 2006, 'More than "social welfare" in disguise', *The Age*, 16 February, p. 8.

13 Ethical Investment Association 2006, 'Sustainable responsible investment in Australia', www.eia.org.au. These percentages are calculated on a narrow definition of what constitutes ethical investment. It excludes screened portfolios, shareholder advocacy and community investment.

Financing the firm

part 3

chapter

10

Short-term finance — working capital

Learning objectives

After studying this chapter, you should be able to:

- lo1 discuss the significance of having appropriate working capital in a business
- lo2 make a judgement about the level of net working capital within a firm
- lo3 describe the sources and costs of informal short-term finance
- lo4 discuss the sources and costs of formal short-term finance.

WORKING CAPITAL BOOST FOR SOUTH AUSTRALIAN EXPORTERS

South Australia's small-to-medium-sized exporters will be able to access more capital for export growth as a result of a new financial product launched in Adelaide today by the Minister for Finance and Administration, Senator Nick Minchin.

Announcing the SA launch of the Export Finance and Insurance Corporation's (EFIC) new product EFIC Headway, Senator Minchin said the product can boost access to working capital for small-to-medium-size enterprises (SMEs) involved in exporting by up to 20 per cent.

'Around 86 per cent of Australian exporters are SMEs, and this new product will provide a guarantee from EFIC to enable banks to lend additional funds to eligible SMEs with minimal documentation and without additional security,' he said.

'South Australian SMEs will now be able to take advantage of immediate export opportunities that would otherwise be lost due to working capital shortages. EFIC Headway is there to help South Australian SMEs to reach their full potential and grow—it is a breakthrough that will help local exporters build markets internationally.'

EFIC's research showed SMEs frequently missed out on export opportunities due to working capital constraints, and that 43 per cent of SMEs would borrow more if finance was available, according to EFIC Managing Director Angus Armour.

'EFIC Headway can help businesses turning over less than $50 million a year to export by providing a boost to working capital,' Mr Armour said. 'Export opportunities often grow faster than the assets SMEs can use as security, and EFIC Headway will open more doors for SME exporters looking to broaden their product range or expand their business into global markets.'

Distributed by six banks—Westpac, HSBC, ANZ, NAB, CBA and BankWest—EFIC Headway is available for a wide range of SME exporters at a competitive price.

EFIC Headway will encourage banks to lend more funds to SMEs, as EFIC provides a Triple-A rated guarantee for additional funding which would not otherwise be available.[1]

Chapter preview

As we see in previous chapters, businesses need funds in order to operate. Those funds are needed for both the short and the long term. This chapter deals with aspects of meeting the short-term financial needs of a business. As you can see from the press release that opens this chapter, having working capital is extremely important for businesses. The Export Finance and Insurance Corporation (EFIC) had identified that many firms, especially SMEs, could not take advantage of export opportunities because they had insufficient working capital.

Why 'working capital'? What is working capital? Doesn't all capital work? Working capital comprises cash, debtors and stock. We will be dealing with these items in this chapter and chapter 11. As chapter 11 deals with the management of current assets, we will discuss receivables and cash management there. Thus, this chapter will deal with working capital in general, and payables in particular, by examining both the sources and the cost of short-term finance.

The following diagram shows how this chapter is structured.

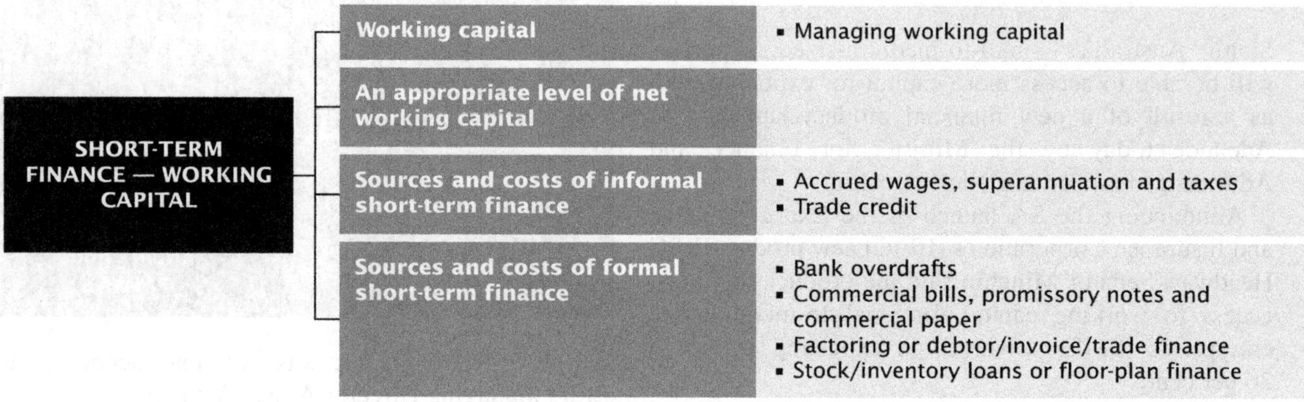

lo1

Discuss the significance of having appropriate working capital in a business.

Working capital

Working capital: the funds invested in current assets

Current assets: the assets the firm expects to be able to convert to cash in the normal course of business within the next 12 months

Net working capital: the excess of current assets over current liabilities

Current liabilities: debts that will be paid within the next 12 months

Working capital is usually defined as the funds invested in current assets. **Current assets** are the assets the firm expects to be able to convert to cash in the normal course of business within the next 12 months. Thus, current assets comprise cash, debtors or accounts receivable and stock or inventory. While a bakery may plan to sell a delivery truck within the next 12 months, the truck is not classed as a current asset because the firm is not in the business of selling trucks (that is, the truck is not stock or inventory). Conversely, a second-hand truck dealer would class a similar truck as 'stock' and therefore a current asset.

The **net working capital** concept introduced in chapter 8 is a more sophisticated one than simple working capital. Net working capital is the excess of current assets over current liabilities (that is, current assets net of current liabilities). **Current liabilities** are debts that will be paid within the next 12 months or accruals for which the accounting entries will be shortly reversed or written out of the books. Current liabilities normally include trade creditors, accrued expenses (accrued at balance day and normally acquitted shortly into the new accounting period), taxation liabilities, short-term debt such as commercial bills, and provisions for current liabilities such as dividends declared but not yet paid. We will examine trade creditors and short-term debt in this chapter.

Managing working capital

In managing the level of working capital, and indeed net working capital, the firm is concerned with three things:

- the need to maintain liquidity
- the need to earn the required rate of return on the assets
- the cost and risk of short-term funding.

Liquidity: a measure of the ease of conversion of an asset into cash

Liquidity is a simple concept that has been applied to a multitude of situations. Liquidity is simply a measure of the ease of conversion of an asset into cash. Thus, cash is 100% or totally liquid. Bank current (cheque) account balances normally have high liquidity in that the depositor can write a cheque and have what is really an instruction to the bank accepted as cash. Equities have high liquidity in Australia as the standard settlement time after sale is three days.

As an extension of the concept, firms are said to have liquidity when they have sufficient cash to pay their bills on time. As you can readily appreciate, businesses really run on trust and short-term credit, and businesses want to be paid by their debtors or they themselves may be in danger of failure. Therefore, being able to maintain that trust within the immediate business environment by paying bills on time is vitally important.

To maintain liquidity, firms may pursue one of three policies:

- keep a tight rein on cash and use cash budgeting extensively and accurately to ensure enough cash is available at all times
- maintain a 'better safe than sorry' policy of keeping an overestimate of the cash needed on hand at all times
- use a bank overdraft as a 'cushion' to provide the cash needed at times when cash is short — a 'she'll be right' policy. An overdraft is a loan facility attached to a current (cheque) account.

The first policy requires most time and effort. The second and third policies normally cost more, the second in terms of opportunity costs and the third in real cash costs. You will recall from chapter 8 that opportunity costs are the cash flows forgone when one path of action is chosen (that is, they are the cost of benefits forgone). Thus, for example, if a firm habitually overestimated its cash needs and kept $100 000 too much in its current account which earned 0.25% pa when it could earn 4.25% in a term deposit or commercial bill investment, then the cost of this policy is $4000 pa pre-tax. The third policy is used by most firms, as either a stand-alone option or in conjunction with one of the other policies. The cost of this policy is the account establishment and maintenance fees, plus interest on the amount borrowed in any period.

In chapter 1 we discuss the goal of business and settle on the financial goal, for the purposes of financial analysis, of maximising investors' wealth. An extension of this concept is that investors will have a rate of return that they require in order to invest or to maintain their investment in a firm. This requirement applies not only to long-term capital investment such as land, factory buildings and production machinery, but also to working capital. Thus, working capital must 'pull its weight'. Investors do not differentiate. (As investors have a required return, it is easier to achieve that return if all assets are earning acceptable returns.)

If working capital is not managed competently, then it can easily fail to 'pull its weight'. How does this happen? Working capital, as you know, comprises cash, debtors and stocks. All of these assets effectively earn little or no return and thus can easily reduce the average rate of return on investors' funds. Yet, at the same time, most firms have to keep some of all these assets. Remember, current assets generally earn low returns but they also decrease the risk of a lack of liquidity (illiquidity).

Can a firm work without having some cash? Probably not. Can a firm work without having some debtors? Yes, it can, but it is almost surely limiting its growth and potential for growth. Can a firm work without having some stock? Yes, it can. It depends on the type of business. Real estate agencies and sharebrokers, for example, normally do not keep stock as their businesses involve acting as agents for the people who own the goods that they sell. So, most firms have to have some cash, but not all firms keep debtors and stock.

The third aspect that firms must manage — apart from the trade-off between illiquidity and the need to minimise the holdings of low-yielding assets — is the cost and risk of current liabilities. Current liabilities, as already noted, comprise mainly for our purposes trade creditors and short-term finance. A firm can increase its holdings of cash, debtors and stock at any time so long as it is able to contract for adequate funds to finance the expansion. The finance has a cost, normally comprising both fees and interest, and the financial manager must be convinced that the benefits to the firm exceed the cost.

Funds may be raised through either short- or long-term debt. Here the financial manager faces something of a paradox, because the more the firm relies on short-term debt, the more likely its liquidity will be decreased. How is this so? Firstly, short-term debt must be repaid more often. Thus, the firm may face a cash squeeze in the normal course of its business just when it needs to repay debt. The only way out of this position is to raise more debt quickly. Strict cash budgeting can help to minimise these occasions. Secondly, the cost of funds may be more volatile when funds must be raised continually by means of short-term instruments. This may impact on the firm's liquidity.

On the other hand, short-term debt normally costs less in interest charges than long-term debt. For every borrowing firm with its unique credit history, perceived credit risk, liquidity and expectations of the future, there is a term structure of interest rates. Under normal circumstances in the debt markets, interest yields show a rising trend over the short to medium term with a flattening as the time to maturity approaches and exceeds, say, 10 years. This is known as the **normal yield curve**. Thus, 90-day funds from the market might cost 5%, 180-day funds 5.2%, one-year funds 6%, three-year funds 7% and 10-year funds 9.5%. The reason for the increase in yields is the expectation by investors that short-term funds in the future will attract higher interest rates. Of course, other expectations are possible. If investors expect interest rates to fall in the future, the yield curve may be downward sloping and this is known as an **inverse yield curve**.

Normal yield curve: shows investors expect future short-term interest rates to be higher than current rates over the medium term

Inverse yield curve: shows short-term interest rates are expected to fall over the medium term

Thus, in normal circumstances, a firm raising short-term funds can expect to pay less for the money than it would if it raised long-term funds. This is obviously attractive, but this source of funding carries additional risks. On the other hand, the funding is flexible in that financial managers can match the timing of raising the funds with the timing of the need for funds. Additionally, the financial manager has no need to try to find a place to park surplus funding and earn the required return, if short-term funds are needed and raised. This contrasts with the position of using long-term funds for short-term finance needs. In summary then, current liabilities tend to be less expensive than long-term liabilities but increase the risk of illiquidity.

An appropriate level of net working capital

lo2

Make a judgement about the level of net working capital within a firm.

How does a financial manager judge what is an appropriate level of net working capital? The hedging principle, often more appropriately called the principle of **self-liquidating debt**, provides loose guidance to the maintenance of an appropriate level of net working capital. The concept of self-liquidation in regard to debt incorporates the notion that the cash inflows that result from the investments made with the debt funding will be received at times when repayments of principal are necessary. A level where the firm maintains the ability to meet its financial obligations on time is considered appropriate. However, this principle does not give any guidance on the level that provides the optimal return.

Self-liquidating debt: occurs when debt-funded investments generate cash inflows that are received when the debt payments are due

The **hedging principle** is based on the idea of matching the maturity of the source of funding with its use. The financial manager has control over the maturity of funding for which contracts are entered into. Thus, a retail toy store preparing for the Christmas trading period will order extra stock in October for delivery in early November.

Hedging principle: based on matching the maturity of the source of funding with its use

The invoices will be payable by 7 December. By this time, the store will already have sold some of the stock for cash, but it will not have recouped all of the funds. To be on the safe side, it could arrange for 30-day funding repayable on 6 January on the basis that it will have recouped all of the outlays plus earned a profit margin by that date. The funding will cost, say, 5% pa or 0.41% for the 30 days. This is an additional cost of doing business, but it ensures the firm is able to pay its bills on time and maintain a good reputation.

Let's look at another scenario. The toy shop could stretch the payment until 24 December. With the disruption to the postal service and banking over the Christmas period, the chances are the cheque would not be banked and cleared until 2 January. By this time, the toy store may have sold all the extra stock and thus effectively financed the purchases at no cost. This action, however, is likely to annoy the supplier and gain the toy store a reputation as a 'slow payer'. Supplying firms may continue to supply for a while, but then they will either refuse to supply or supply for cash only. Such restrictions interrupt the smooth running of business and ultimately cost the transgressing firm. It is far better for the successful long-term continuation of business for firms to strive for and maintain their reputations as ethical businesses and 'good payers'.

Permanent funding: comprises funding with maturities greater than one year and includes long-term debt, leases and ordinary shares

Temporary funding: comprises the short-term formal sources of finance, such as commercial bills and bank loans

Spontaneous sources of funding: those that arise in an unplanned way in the ordinary course of business

In order to make the hedging principle more useful, it is constructive to think in terms of permanent, temporary and spontaneous sources of funding. **Permanent funding** comprises funding with maturities greater than one year and includes long-term debt, leases and ordinary shares. **Temporary funding** comprises essentially the short-term formal sources of finance, such as commercial bills and bank loans. 'Formal' is used here to indicate that some sources of short-term finance are not classed as temporary, but instead are classed as 'spontaneous'. The **spontaneous sources of funding** are those that arise in a substantially unplanned and unstructured way in the ordinary course of business. Examples are trade creditors and the various forms of accrued expenses. Accrued expenses include wages, superannuation contributions, interest and taxes.

Even though employees come to work on a daily basis, they are not paid daily. Most firms in Australia today pay either weekly or fortnightly. A fortnightly pay cycle may end on a Friday, but the pays may be disbursed on the Thursday before. Effectively, the employees are providing finance to the firm until the ninth day of the cycle and, on the tenth day, the firm is financing the employees until the payment is acquitted at closing time, when neither party owes the other either wages or work. Thus, accrued wages are a significant source of spontaneous finance. Similarly, with the withholding of pay-as-you-go (PAYG) tax instalments from employees' pay, as Australian taxation law requires, firms enjoy a significant source of funding. Many firms pay the total of these instalments to the ATO quarterly with their GST returns. A firm with a $1 million per quarter payroll will normally have about $250 000 in accrued tax instalments to pay each period. This is an important free source of funding.

FINANCE WORLD

Initial working capital

ITSA, the Insolvency and Trustee Service Australia, manages the *Bankruptcy Act 1966* throughout all states and territories in Australia. People who get into financial difficulties, for whatever reasons, may apply to ITSA to lodge a debtor's petition or to propose that they go bankrupt or enter a Part IX debtor's agreement. They must lodge a Statement of Affairs. As you can see from the excerpt in figure 10.1, one of the reasons businesses commonly fail is insufficient working capital.

Part A – Personal Details **CONFIDENTIAL**

18 About your Insolvency

What do you believe is the main cause of your insolvency?

Tick one cause only in ***either*** *18A* ***or*** *18B that best describes the main cause of your financial difficulties.*

18A Non Business Related

- [ ] Unemployment or loss of income
- [ ] Adverse legal action
- [ ] Liabilities due to guarantees
- [ ] Gambling, speculation & extravagance in living
- [ ] Ill health or absence of health insurance
- [ ] Domestic discord or relationship breakdowns
- [ ] Excessive use of credit facilities including losses on repossessions, high interest payments and pressure selling

18B Business Related *(only applies if you have personally operated a business)*

- [ ] Economic conditions affecting industry, including competition, credit restrictions, fall in prices or increases in costs
- [x] Lack of business ability including underquoting or failure to assess potential of business
- [ ] Excessive interest payments on loan monies and capital losses on repayments
- [ ] Excessive drawings including failure to provide for taxation
- [x] Inability to collect debts due to disputes, faulty work or bad debts
- [ ] Failure to keep proper books of account and costing records
- [x] Lack of sufficient initial working capital
- [ ] Gambling or speculation
- [ ] Seasonal conditions including floods and drought

If other reason not listed please specify.

[ ]

18C When did you first have difficulty paying your debts? Month [ ] Year [ ]

18D Where did you obtain information about bankruptcy and the alternatives? *(tick one only)*

ITSA	[ ]	Financial Counsellor	[ ]	Accountant	[ ]
ITSA pamphlets	[ ]	Registered Trustee	[ ]	Solicitor	[ ]
ITSA website	[ ]	Debt agreement consultant/administrator	[ ]	Other	[ ]

18E Have you previously been bankrupt or entered into a formal arrangement with creditors? No [ ] Yes [ ] *please give details*

What type of administration was it?

1.		2	
Bankruptcy	[ ]	Bankruptcy	[ ]
Part X Arrangement	[ ]	Part X Arrangement	[ ]
Part IX Debt agreement	[ ]	Part IX Debt agreement	[ ]
Part X Personal Insolvency Agreement	[ ]	Part X Personal Insolvency Agreement	[ ]
Year	[ ]	Year	[ ]

There are penalties under the Bankruptcy Act for providing false or misleading information Page 8

Figure 10.1 Page 8 of ITSA's Statement of Affairs form

Source: Insolvency and Trustee Service Australia.[2]

In addition, since the 1993 introduction of compulsory employer superannuation contributions made on behalf of employees, employers have been able to use these as yet another source of free funding. Some employers pay their superannuation contributions to their employees' superannuation funds fortnightly; others pay monthly or at longer intervals. Because some employers were very slow in paying superannuation contributions, the government changed the legislation so that contributions must be paid at least quarterly from 1 July 2003.

The principles for using the permanent, temporary and spontaneous classifications to advantage are:

- permanent assets should be financed with permanent and spontaneous sources of funding
- temporary assets should be financed with temporary sources of funding.

Why, you might ask, would it be a good idea to finance permanent assets with spontaneous sources of funding? The answer lies in the fact that there remains a core level of funding that is virtually fixed, even though the balances of the various types of spontaneous funding are continually changing. Thus, if the totals of spontaneous funding from all sources over several periods were \$50 000, \$90 000, \$80 000, \$100 000 and \$60 000, the core level is \$50 000 which may be treated as virtually permanent funding. The \$50 000 comprises the minimum level that is always available.

What are the costs of getting this matching principle wrong? If long-term funding is used to finance temporary assets, cost is normally increased and risk is decreased. In contrast, if short-term funding is used to finance fixed assets, cost is normally decreased and risk is increased. Either way, getting the funding recipe wrong can lead to ultimate business failure. Have a look at figure 10.1 in the 'finance world' feature opposite where lack of sufficient initial working capital is so common a cause of bankruptcy that the Insolvency and Trustee Service (ITSA) Form 3 lists this as a possible bankruptcy determinant.

Finally, as noted briefly in the introduction to this section, the hedging principle does not give any guidance as to the level of net working capital that provides the optimal return. Such an assessment involves several cost–benefit analyses. The cost of holding additional cash is the opportunity cost of forgoing higher returns available elsewhere and the benefit is the reduced expectation of illiquidity or, finally, bankruptcy. The cost of carrying higher debtors is again an opportunity cost if internally financed or a true cash cost of the additional external funding necessary, while the benefits stem from increasing sales, both currently and in the future (goodwill). The cost and benefits of holding additional stock are similar to those of holding higher debtors. These analyses are difficult to carry out as many of the valuations rest on heroic assumptions. Hence, finding the appropriate level of debtors and stock especially is more a matter of trial and error and 'gut feeling'.

FINANCE WORKSHOP 10.1

Think of a retail business that handles a large amount of cash. Perhaps you have thought of a fast-food business such as a local McDonald's store.

1. Is the store likely to have all three components of working capital?
2. Are all three likely to be in roughly equal proportions?
3. If one or more is likely to be larger than the others, which do you think would be the largest component?
4. If you were the manager of such a store, how many days of stock would you keep on hand? (Give your answer in terms of the inventory needed for the expected sales each day.)

lo3

Describe the sources and costs of informal short-term finance.

Sources and costs of informal short-term finance

The most common sources of informal short-term finance for businesses are:

- accrued wages, superannuation and taxes
- trade credit.

Accrued wages, superannuation and taxes

Accrued wages, superannuation and PAYG withholding instalments have already been discussed as examples of spontaneous sources of funding. A business such as an educational institution pays a high proportion of its cash expenses as wages and salaries. Consider such an institution with a $4 million fortnightly wage bill. On average, this institution effectively owes its employees $2 million all the time. This $2 million of funding is provided free of charge. In addition, the majority of the academic staff will be labouring under a 43.5% or 48.5% marginal tax rate, so that the average tax paid by staff may be in the order of 30%. Many staff members will also pay up to 20% in superannuation contributions. Hence, the institution may be able to retain up to $2 million every payday and pay the aggregate of $4 million to the ATO and the superannuation funds only monthly. This source of funding is also free.

With the advent of the GST in Australia, most firms making taxable supplies — most goods except food, exports, health care, education and child care — collect the tax of 10% on the sales price. Collected tax is remitted to the ATO either quarterly or monthly (if annual turnover is greater than $20 million). Thus a firm with $4.4 million of sales per quarter will collect $400 000 of tax by the end of each quarterly period. The firm has the use of this daily-increasing source of free funding from day 1 in the cycle to about week 16 when the total, less allowance for tax paid, must be paid to the ATO.

Trade credit

Trade credit is possibly the most important source of short-term credit for business. This is because such credit arises during the normal course of business and it usually is extended without formal agreements. Moreover, it is normally unsecured (although some suppliers will impose Romalpa clauses, which are discussed in the next chapter) and requires nothing additional to normal accounting practices for its successful management. In contrast, the imposition and the availability of the GST as a source of finance for business (not that it was imposed for this purpose) required major redevelopment of accounting systems for almost all businesses.

Trade credit these days is most likely to be offered on a 'net 30 days' or even 'net 7 days' basis. This means that the full amount of the invoice must be paid within 30 days or seven days, respectively. Often, where a customer makes many purchases within the monthly accounting period, a statement of account is sent out to the customer at the end of the month and then the customer has 30 days in which to pay the whole amount.

Sometimes, firms offer discounts for early payment. Thus, an invoice may be marked '2/10, net 30', which means a 2% discount will be granted if the bill is paid within 10 days, but no discount will be available if the bill is paid within 30 days. Even though a 2% discount is attractive for the period for which it is granted, many firms do not try to gear up their accounts-payable departments to take advantage of these offers. They prefer to keep to the standard billing cycle, as it is easier to manage.

However, neglecting to earn the discount can be costly in terms of the effective annual rate forgone. Given that this is a simple interest problem and that interest equals *Pin*, then:

$$\textbf{Cost of forgoing cash discount} = \frac{\textbf{interest}}{Pn} \quad [10.1]$$

where P = principal (or net price after discount)

n = length of period (in annual terms)

EXAMPLE 10.1

Cost of forgoing a discount

Suppose Countrywide Ltd receives an account for $100, marked '2/10, net 30'. A 2% or $2 discount will be granted if the bill is paid within 10 days. The principal is thus $98. The discount is lost if Countrywide uses the supplier's money for another 20 days (the 30 days less the 10-day discount period) and pays the full $100 on day 30. The effective annual cost Countrywide is imposing on itself by not paying the bill within 10 days is:

$$\text{Cost of forgoing cash discount} = \frac{2}{\left(98\frac{20}{365}\right)}$$

$$= 37.24\%$$

Thus, the supplier has indicated that the goods could have been 2% cheaper, but by not taking that discount and using the supplier's funds for another 20 days, the customer has made use of funds with an annual charge of 37.24%.

Some suppliers add a threat to their invoices that interest will be charged at a given rate if the invoice is not paid within 30 days. Even though these interest charges appear to be quite small — for example, 1–2% per month — only a little thought will convince the purchaser that they are in fact quite punitive. Of course, whether a firm actually tries to collect the interest is another matter that relates to the competitive situation within the particular industry. A firm is not likely to try to collect the extra charge in a highly competitive industry or where the customer has been previously highly valued.

A glance at some Telstra phone bills will reveal another method of encouraging customers to pay on time. 'Should payment of this bill not be received by the due date, a late payment fee of $5.50 (incl. GST) may apply.' Phone, electricity, reticulated gas and water companies have additional means of successfully persuading customers to pay — the threat of cutting off supplies! Another means of giving an incentive to pay on time is to impose an 'account keeping' fee of $20 or more per month while the account is outstanding.

lo4

Discuss the sources and costs of formal short-term finance.

Sources and costs of formal short-term finance

The most common sources of formal short-term finance for businesses are:

- bank overdrafts
- commercial bills, promissory notes and commercial paper
- factoring or debtor/invoice/trade finance
- stock/inventory loans or floor-plan finance.

Each of these products is priced according to the level of the cash rate, the base rate in the markets at the time and the perceived degree of risk undertaken by the provider. The effect for individual firms being assisted by the EFIC initiative described in the opening pages of this chapter is the reduction in the cost of borrowed funds, as EFIC essentially agrees to share risk with the loans providers.

Bank overdrafts

Overdraft: a permitted over-drawing of funds beyond the credit balance in the account

As we see in chapter 2, an **overdraft** is a permitted over-drawing of funds beyond the credit balance in the account. Essentially, it is a loan facility attached to a current (cheque) account. The loan is drawn down only as required, when cheques written on the account exceed positive balances. The intention of overdraft finance is that the balance in the account will fluctuate from day to day between positive and negative as cash flows into and out of each business.

Overdrafts are useful for businesses, because firms are able to carry on their normal activities without being forced to track their cash with 100% accuracy every day, so long as they are not operating near their overdraft limits. A firm may be solvent and nowhere near financial distress, but news that a financial institution had 'bounced' (rejected and returned) the firm's cheques due to a shortage of cash in the firm's current account could do untold damage to its reputation and ability to operate successfully in the future. Having an overdraft reduces the possibility of such an event happening.

Overdrafts thus provide a cushion of liquidity beyond that provided by the firm's own balance of cash. Firms arrange overdrafts with their bankers and contract for funding limits beyond which cheques will normally not be honoured. The fees attached to overdrafts comprise establishment and account-keeping fees. Establishment fees are in the order of 0.75–1% with a minimum fee of about $500–600. Account-keeping fees (loan administration charges or line service fees) are about 0.4–0.5% pa.

Banks used to impose 'unused limit' fees to compensate them for providing for the possibility that overdrafts will not be used in full. When banks agree to overdraft limits, they are aware that many customers will not be operating near those loan limits. (Indeed, banks discourage customers from financing semi-permanent needs by overdrafts.) However, banks must still be prepared to honour the cheques of all customers up to their overdraft limits. Thus, based on their previous experience, the banks will make estimates of the expected use of the limits and plan their cash needs accordingly. A check of banks' websites has shown that unused limit fees are unusual in the current competitive banking environment.

The interest rate charged on overdrafts normally lies towards the middle of the range of common interest rates at any time. Starting with the overnight interbank rate — the cash rate set by the board of the Reserve Bank of Australia (RBA) — a margin of 2–3% pa is added to compensate lenders for the increased risk associated with even the best and most creditworthy customers. This is known as the 'prime', 'indicator' or 'index' rate. Other less creditworthy customers suffer an additional penalty rate of perhaps another 2–4.75% pa. At least one bank will honour some cheques that over-draw the overdraft limit but charge another 4% penalty on the excess drawings. This means a customer getting into this position could pay up to about 17% for the funds (assuming an overnight interbank rate of about 5%). These fees are normally charged on daily balances and debited to accounts monthly. The various margins that banks charge vary over time, but enhanced competition in the last few years has seen interest margins pared down considerably.

In the days before the substantial deregulation of the banking sector, it was common for banks to provide overdraft finance to businesses where the overdrafts were in effect permanent loans. Firms with persistent cash shortages tended to operate with ever-increasing overdraft balances. As regulation was lifted, the banks converted many of these loans to long-term finance products such as fully drawn advances, and started the firms off again with overdrafts that, under the agreed conditions, had to be operated as intended with widely fluctuating balances.

EXAMPLE 10.2

Cost of using an overdraft

Cheeta Trading Co. has an overdraft with its bank for $100000. Because Cheeta has not had a good credit history, the bank has added extra risk margins to its prime rate and Cheeta is paying 15% pa on daily balance for the overdraft funds. Funds in credit earn 0.25% pa on daily balance. The account-keeping fees are 0.5% pa charged on minimum monthly balance and debited monthly. On 1 July, Cheeta's balance is $10009.90 O/D. The following transactions are processed and shown on the bank statement during July.

Date	Details	Debit	Credit	Balance
1 July	Chq 00987	5000.10		15010.00 O/D
	Chq 00978	1897.50		16907.50 O/D
3 July	Deposit		20076.00	3168.50 cr
	Chq 00986	3854.35		685.85 O/D
10 July	Chq 00985	1000.00		1685.85 O/D
	Deposit		5098.90	3413.05 cr
16 July	Chq 00988	2541.86		871.19 cr
	Chq 00989	4567.45		3696.26 O/D
	Chq 00990	3267.65		6963.91 O/D
	Chq 00991	23432.89		30396.80 O/D
23 July	Deposit		2874.40	27522.40 O/D
30 July	Chq 00992	21674.00		49196.40 O/D
	Interest cr		0.14	49196.26 O/D
	Interest dr	202.70		49398.96 O/D
	Fee	20.30		49419.34 O/D

Interest of 0.25% pa is earned only on the $3413.05 credit balance for the 6-day period 10–15 July, making a gain of 14c (that is, $3413.05 \times 0.0025 \times \frac{6}{365}$). Interest of 15% pa is charged on the outstanding overdraft balances: $16907.50 for 2 days, $685.85 for 7 days, $30396.80 for 7 days, $27522.40 for 7 days and $49196.40 for 1 day. The total of these five amounts of interest is $202.70. (To help check that you have at least computed the correct number of days, add the days for interest charged to days for interest earned and see if you get the correct number of days for the given month.) The fee of 0.5% pa is charged on the minimum monthly balance of $49399.04, making a charge of $20.30 (that is, $49\,398.96 \times 0.005 \times \frac{30}{365}$).

We consider the role of overdraft financing further in chapter 14 when we look at cash budgeting.

Commercial bills, promissory notes and commercial paper

These three terms — commercial bills, promissory notes and commercial paper — essentially describe the same instrument. The differences between them normally stem from the markets in which they are traded rather than substantive elements. During the 1980s in Australia, commercial bill finance became very popular. From a low base the commercial bill market grew to \$5 billion in 1980, and to more than \$68 billion in 1990. Since that time, the total has varied between \$50 billion and \$69 billion, which was achieved in July 2001.[3] Basically, this situation arose because banks promoted this form of finance to their customers and these funds normally were cheaper than overdraft or other short-term funding. Why did banks do this, rather than sell customers a loan? To understand this issue, you have to understand how bill finance works.

There are normally three parties to the issue of a bank-accepted commercial bill (BAB). A firm (borrower) wanting to access the bill market would normally approach its financier and make its request known. Normally, the financier would draw up a bill because it has the software and staff with the expertise to do the job properly and efficiently, but it is possible for borrowers to produce the bill. We now have introduced one party to the BAB process, and this is the drawer (borrower). The bank then finds an investor (the 'discounter', party two) who has funds to invest and is happy with the yield that is possible from this product. However, the investor may be relatively small and may be worried about the risk involved in lending to this borrower. The bank then facilitates the deal even further by 'accepting' the bill. In this context, this means the bank has guaranteed that the bill will be honoured at maturity. The bank, in other words, has assumed the credit risk on the bill in return for a fee and becomes the 'acceptor' — party three.

Why did banks promote commercial bills so strongly? The answer stems from the facts that the banks earned fees rather than interest from loans; they did not provide the loan funds; and they did not have to have either deposits or capital to support the loans. While ultimately loans are limited by the regulatory need to back them with capital, fee income is unlimited and banks could sell commercial bill finance so long as they could find investors willing to invest. Consistent with our discussion of the risk–return relationship in chapter 5, investors earn low-risk interest and borrowers gain a relatively cheaper source of finance.

BABs are often standardised in maturity to 90 and 180 days to facilitate marketability although other periods, normally about 30, 60 or 120 days, are available. A range of fees, such as a drawdown, handling and the bank's acceptance fees, may be charged. There is also the interest payable to the discounter on the loan. Often, financial institutions add all their fees into the interest rate charged and thus express all charges in a single interest rate. This is a reasonable approach given that the banks are normally merely 'retailing' a product where external investors are providing the funds.

You will remember from chapters 3 and 4 that commercial bills are discount instruments. This means that the borrower effectively pays the interest up front and receives the face value less the prepaid interest. The interest may be expressed as a rate — either as a yield or as a discount.

Promissory notes (PNs) are similar to BABs, but they are not endorsed by an acceptor. They are often called 'one name paper' in recognition that the borrower is the only party that is responsible for the repayment of the debt. As there is no other party involved in guaranteeing the repayment, the raising of finance by means of PNs tends to be restricted to larger firms that have good reputations and excellent credit ratings. While financial institutions may still act as intermediaries to bring borrowers and lenders together, the fact that there is no financial guarantee offered by the bank means that, once sold, each

PN represents a completed transaction and irrevocably 'off the books'. There is no contingent liability. That makes this form of finance attractive to intermediaries. PNs for large amounts transacted by major borrowers and lenders are often called 'commercial paper'.

EXAMPLE 10.3

Calculating funds raised from a promissory note

The Bank of the Nation is approached by a customer looking for about \$500 000 for 120 days. The bank can find an investor who will supply the funds for 5% pa. The bank quotes the customer 5.78% pa as the full price of the funds, including the bank's fees. How much will the customer receive?

The interest rate for the period of 120 days is 0.0190 (that is, $0.0578 \times \frac{120}{365}$). The customer will therefore receive \$490 677.13 (that is, $\frac{\$500\,000}{1 + 0.0190}$).

FINANCE WORLD

CBA variable rate bill facility

The Commonwealth Bank of Australia (CBA), in common with many other financial institutions, provides commercial bill finance. Here is a brief description of a bill facility offered by the CBA.

Bill facility

Need a loan that can offer a range of repayment options, and take care of your short- and long-term financial needs?

The BetterBusiness Bill Facility may be a solution for your business. A bill is your promise to pay to the bank a specified amount (face value) on a specified future date (maturity date).

A bill is issued at a discount to the face value. This means that the bank takes the bill and pays you an amount less than the face value (settlement price). At maturity you pay to the bank the face value, and so you repay the settlement price plus interest.

Features

Features of a BetterBusiness Bill Facility include:

- a minimum borrowing amount of \$500 000 or more
- a variable facility which offers you the ability to have a fixed rate on a short-term basis. This provides you with the flexibility to reset your interest rate every 30, 60, 90, 120, 150 or 180 days.
- fixed rates available up to seven years
- principal reductions at each rollover can be established
- bill rates priced off market related rates.

Structure is up to you

Your BetterBusiness Bill Facility can be used as a revolving line of credit (where you draw funds down as you need), or a term loan (if you want to pay it back over time).

Flexible interest rates

Interest rates can be fixed for up to seven years. Alternatively, you can choose to reset your fixed rate every 30, 60, 90, 120, 150 or 180 days on a variable facility. Interest rates are priced off market related benchmarks, which fluctuate according to money market movements.

Interest rate management options

The BetterBusiness Bill Facility also provides a range of strategies to help protect your business from movements in interest rates. These products come under the Flexi Bill Solutions which can be attached to your bill facility. They can be individually tailored to protect businesses from adverse movements with interest rates or potentially take advantage of fluctuations in interest rates over an agreed period.

You may elect to include one of the following Flexi Bill Solutions to your BetterBusiness Bill Facility.

- Cap Advantage
- Range Advantage
- Rate Reset Advantage
- Forward Start Advantage
- Principal Range Advantage
- Participator

How can your business benefit?

The BetterBusiness Bill Facility can help you to:

- manage cash flow more effectively, by making payments only on the maturity of the bill
- provide interest rate protection and flexibility.

Source: Commonwealth Bank of Australia.[4]

St George Bank also offers bill discounting facilities. If you are interested in the mechanics of the 'Cap Advantage' and the 'Range Advantage' type facilities offered by the Commonwealth Bank, look at the 'Capped Bills' and 'Collared Bills' descriptions on the St George Bank website at www.stgeorge.com.au.

FINANCE WORKSHOP 10.2

Note that the 'finance world' example says that 'a bill is issued at a discount to the face value'. This is true as bills are a discount product.

Assume that a borrower requires about \$590 000 for 3 months. The bank agrees to purchase a bill with a face value of \$600 000 maturing in 91 days. The rate is 5.57%. Is the bill priced at a discount of 5.57% to the face value or to yield 5.57%? Why would the bill mature in 91 days and not 90 days? Calculate how much the borrower will receive and how much interest they will pay.

Factoring or debtor/invoice/trade finance

So far, we have examined sources of short-term finance that are normally unsecured. We turn now to secured or quasi-secured sources of finance. Consider the nature of accounts receivable or debtors for any business. The total is made up of the many smaller amounts that are owed by the customers of the business to the firm. What could be a better and less risky asset than many entities' undertakings to pay rather than the undertaking of a single entity? Sure, there could eventually be some bad debts where debtors do not pay, but in the main the debtors will pay and the risk is spread over many entities.

Financial institutions have been inventive in finding ways to use the security of debtors to back business loans. The variety includes:

- pledging a general line of receivables
- invoice discounting or pledging specific invoices
- factoring.

With pledging a general line of receivables, the borrower offers its debtors in total as security for a loan. This method is simple and inexpensive to implement. However, as the lender has no control over the quality of the debts and there may be some potentially bad debts included, normally the loan does not exceed a loan-to-value ratio (LVR) of 70–75%. Thus, a firm with $200 000 in receivables may be able to access a loan of $150 000.

Invoice discounting involves the pledging of specific invoices. Because the quality of the invoices based on the perceived creditworthiness of each customer can be ascertained, the LVR is often as high as 85%. Thus, a firm writing a new invoice for $20 000 may go to an invoice discounting finance company and receive $17 000 with the invoice pledged as security. Why do you think a *new* invoice is specified? This is because new invoices have a higher probability of being paid in full than old invoices. Why? New invoices cover the whole spectrum of clients, the good, the bad and the maybes. Old invoices typically relate to the bad and the maybes. Thus, the risk for the lender increases if it lends on invoices that are in the process of getting 'stale' or old.

With the pledging of a general line of receivables and invoice discounting, customers know nothing of the financial arrangements that are being made on the basis that they will pay their bills on time. The borrowing firm collects its debts in the normal way and repays the financier according to the conditions underlying each cash advance.

Factoring: involves businesses selling their invoices at a discount for cash to another party that takes over the right to collect the amounts owing

The third method of using accounts receivable as security is quite different. **Factoring** is a method of obtaining short-term finance, but the borrower gives the lender the right to collect the cash owing on its invoices. Essentially the factor (lender) discounts the invoices and hands over the cash. It then collects the amounts owing by the borrowing firm's customers through its specialised debt collection processes. In some cases, once the discounting process is complete and the cash paid, that is the end of the transaction between the borrower and the factor. In other cases, the factor gives the loan, collects the outstanding amounts, subtracts its fees and the loan amount and then returns the balance to the borrower. Factoring fees may be quite high. A fee of 5%, for example, when converted to a nominal annual basis, becomes 61%, if the 5% was for the use of the funds for 30 days.

Factoring has been growing strongly in the last decade, both in Australia and worldwide. In 2005–06, factoring and discounting amounted to $39.4 billion in Australia, representing an average annual compound growth rate of 27.6% pa over the last eight years.[5] One reason for this growth is that businesses subject to heightened forces of competition are less liable to demand payment at or within a short time of delivery. Instead, firms are offering their customers increasingly attractive trade credit conditions and, as a result, they have a greater volume of account receivables to finance and to use for financing.

Apart from the benefit of quickly converting sales invoices to cash, many businesses find factoring facilitates their entry to overseas markets, where collection of trade debts may be more difficult than collection domestically. Firms thus may exploit the international expertise of global factoring firms to offset some of the costs associated with international sales. Additionally, factoring firms may reduce the foreign exchange risk by contracting to pay for invoices in the home currency.

Factoring and discounting businesses normally require client firms using their services to:

- sell goods on normal. credit terms
- have efficient debtors' ledgers and credit assessment systems
- have a spread of debtors so that no one debtor is responsible for a large part of the total outstanding debt
- have a projected minimum annual turnover of $200 000.

Factoring and discounting are normally highly suitable for businesses that have rapid sales growth, are unable to meet large orders or seasonal peaks and that regularly exceed their current overdraft limits and are fully borrowed against fixed assets. Factoring and discounting are not suitable for businesses with disproportionate levels of trade disputes or retailers with their myriad small sales. Besides, retailing finance normally is closely aligned with the credit card networks.

BEHAVIOURAL PERSPECTIVE

Debt financing grows strongly?

Debt financing has grown rapidly during the last decade, with nearly 30% pa growth on average. However, although there are nearly three million businesses in Australia, fewer than 5000 used this form of finance in 2006. Consider the following news report and suggest why this is so.

SMEs turn to debt financing for growth

The number of businesses using debt financing has risen 12 per cent in the year to March as small and medium enterprises (SMEs) look to expand.

According to the Institute of Factors and Discounters (IFD), 4665 businesses used debt financing in the 12 months to March 31, compared to 4160 in the previous corresponding period.

This comes on the back of three years continuous growth in the industry.

Through discounting and factoring businesses sell invoices to a third party who then takes a portion of the money owed—usually 9.6 per cent to 9.8 per cent—although the size of the charge can vary depending on the size of the payment and the risk profile of the client.

IFD chairman Peter Langman said SMEs were waking up to the fact that debt financing allowed them to fill gaps in their cash flow, allowing them to finance rapid growth or survive in tough times.

'Improved cash flow means better buying power. Usually businesses want money to solve a problem and hopefully it's a growth problem,' he said.

Most debt financing, around 90 per cent, is supplied by the banks, who Mr Langham said have also fuelled growth in the market because they see it as a safe form of credit and a good way to expand their footprint in the SME market. Mr Langham expects the industry will continue to grow as SMEs seek alternative forms of cash flows, particularly as the housing market starts to moderate.

'The growth isn't going to slow down,' he said. 'You have got an economy that is still strong ... you have got a flattening of the housing market in places like New South Wales. Historically in NSW when house prices were going through the roof and you wanted to increase funding for your small business you could just go to the bank every six months and say "my house has gone up in value, can you lend me some more money?". But you can't do that anymore.'

Australia's factoring and discounting industry generated annual turnover of $39.4 billion in the year to the end of March, up 21 per cent on the corresponding period last year.[6]

Stock/inventory loans or floor-plan finance

The final asset which can be used to secure short-term finance is stock. The quality of stock as a security depends on its nature. Essentially, quality, age, perishability and marketability all impact on the usefulness of stock as security for a loan. Think of some examples where you would not like to lend funds with that sort of stock as the security.

How about a $100 000 load of 'high-quality' extra-thick bicycle tubes all packed tightly in their little boxes? The only thing wrong with them is that each fold in each tube perishes the rubber after only a few months when the storage temperature is too high. What is the security worth when each tube falls apart when unpacked from its little box? How about a load of high-protein flour? Only six months old. What's it worth? The weevils are included, no charge. Many seemingly valuable stocks can be perishable and thus lose their usefulness as loan security. Additionally, some stocks are difficult to sell even though they have cost the owners a good deal of money. Examples are 'works in progress', whether they be metal fabrications at an engineering shop, false teeth at a dental technician's laboratory or partly completed books at a printery and bindery.

We introduce the concept of floor-plan finance in chapter 3. Floor-plan finance is the most important example of stock or inventory finance and it is very commonly found in the motor vehicle (cars, trucks and motorbikes) retail sector. There are two types of floor-plan lenders — captives and independents. Captive floor-plan lenders are often affiliates or subsidiaries of manufacturers that were established to offer financing to their retail dealer networks and thus facilitate sales for the manufacturers. Examples here in Australia are DaimlerChrysler Financial Services, Ford Credit Australia Wholesale, General Motors Acceptance Corp., Trident Jet (Australia) and Volvo Group Treasury Australia. The independent financiers lend to dealers in many different industries. Examples are Primus Automotive Financial Services, St George Motor Wholesale and Suncorp Finance. Global firms such as GE Finance provide inventory finance worldwide (see the 'finance world' feature on the next page for an example of the types of finance offered).

Floor-plan lenders generally write, service and monitor loans to dealers. To write loans, lenders examine bank references and other credit reports, past sales volumes and inventory turnover. Inventory turnover is especially important. Analyses of inventory can tell much about the competence of management — whether ordering of stock is appropriate for the sales area (is stock ordered in the colours, models and configurations which are appropriate for the client base?) and whether sales staff are doing an efficient job.

Servicing and monitoring functions are normally fairly labour-intensive as lenders are concerned with the ageing of both the receivable and the collateral stock. If dealers are not regularly paying down their loans, lenders will be interested to know the reasons. Should stock have to be sold by lenders, it may be sold back to the manufacturers at a contracted price, sold to another dealer or sold by public auction.

The lending arrangements with floor-plan finance involve three parties — the lender, the manufacturer and the borrower (the retail dealer). After the initial contracts outlining each party's responsibilities are in place, the dealer places an order with the manufacturer who then contacts the lender to see if the dealer's credit for that amount is good. If so, the order is filled, the dealer gets the stock and the lender receives the invoice to pay. Until the stock is sold, the dealer pays interest monthly to the lender and has an obligation to repay the principal as soon as the stock is sold.

Have you ever bought a new car or gone with a family member to a car dealer's showroom to buy a vehicle? If you have, you will have noticed that the dealer and the staff are desperate to sell you a vehicle that is standing on the showroom floor or in storage next door. Why is that? The answer stems from inventory ageing. The dealer does not want to be left with colours or models that the public does not seem to want. (Additionally, dealers are worried that buyers might repudiate contracts to buy if they don't get delivery immediately.) So, dealers have found that selling current stock as fast as possible is the best business plan.

Sometimes the system as described is varied and the lender in fact becomes the purchaser of the stock. This system is known as 'bailment', where the lender is the 'bailor'. Possession is granted to the dealer, the 'bailee', for display purposes alone. The dealer then sells the vehicles in the normal way. However, the bailor gives final approval of each sale. Where the ownership is passed from financier to dealer and then on to buyers, the retail customers have no inkling that all these financial transactions have taken place when they place orders.

FINANCE WORLD

GE Commercial Finance: inventory

Our range of customised floorplan inventory finance products enables distributors and dealers in a broad range of industries to hold more stock without cash flow strain and to generate more sales.

We can provide customised floorplan (inventory) financing to distributors and dealers in a broad range of sectors such as industrial, construction, computer, office, telecommunications, agricultural/viticultural, motorcycle, road transport, airline and marine industries. And managing your inventory finance with GE Commercial Finance is now easier than ever with our new customised eP@L — your electronic Priority Account Link eP@L allows customers to manage their inventory finance facility and make payments online.

Distributor supported programs

Provide your dealers with an initial interest-free period on their stock purchases and have a refinancing option available for any unsold stock.

Direct line programs

Dealers can access a direct line of credit where they can fund stock purchases for both new and approved used stock. Refinance options are also available for unsold stock.

Scheduled payment programs

We can arrange finance with payments made on specific dates rather than sales — and make cash flow management easy for dealers with high turnover and high stock volumes. This program particularly suits non-serialised products.

Trade bills/business loans

Extend credit beyond normal trading terms with a source of funds to complement the floorplan customer's normal line of credit.

International trade finance

Help dealers to stay financially competitive when dealing with overseas suppliers.

Accounts receivable funding

We can provide back-to-back inventory and accounts receivable facilities to alleviate extended accountancy terms for business-to-business operators.

Source: GE Commercial.[7]

CORPORATE FINANCIAL GOVERNANCE

The need for management of floor-plan finance has encouraged the development of a specialised branch of the accounting and business advice industry. For example, the following excerpt from a brochure issued by PPB, an Australia-wide accounting firm, illustrates some of the firm's work in corporate governance.

Significant motor group

Background

- Financier alarmed by significant variations with stock audit versus floor plan
- PPB retained informally to monitor the motor group while an alternative financier was sought and ensure security position of original financier not further eroded

Actions

- Stocktake to ascertain eroded security position under the floor plan
- Full investigation and strategy report to financier
- Suggested alternative ways financier could recover security

Results

- Original financier paid out in full by an alternative financier
- Motor group still trading

Source: PPB.[8]

executive summary

lo1 discuss the significance of having appropriate working capital in a business

- Working capital is defined as the funds invested in current assets.
- Current assets are the assets the firm expects to be able to convert to cash in the normal course of business within the next 12 months.
- Net working capital is current assets net of current liabilities.
- Current liabilities are debts that will be repaid within the next 12 months.
- In managing the level of working capital and indeed net working capital, the firm is concerned with three things:
  - the need to maintain liquidity
  - the need to earn the required rate of return on the assets
  - the cost and risk of short-term funding.
- Liquidity is a measure of the ease of conversion of an asset into cash.
- Current assets generally earn low returns but decrease the risk of illiquidity.
- Managing working capital involves a trade-off between risk and costs.

lo2 make a judgement about the level of net working capital within a firm

- The hedging principle, often more appropriately called the principle of self-liquidating debt, provides loose guidance to the maintenance of an appropriate level of net working capital.
- A level of net working capital where the firm maintains the ability to meet its financial obligations on time is appropriate.
- The hedging principle is based on the idea of matching the maturity of the source of funding with its use.
- The financial manager has control over the maturity of contracted funding.
- In order to make the hedging principle more useful, it is constructive to think in terms of permanent, temporary and spontaneous sources of funding.
- Permanent funding comprises funding with maturities greater than one year and includes long-term debt, leases and ordinary shares.
- Temporary funding comprises essentially the short-term formal sources of finance, such as commercial bills and bank loans. 'Formal' is used here to indicate that some sources of short-term finance are not classed as temporary, but instead are classed as 'spontaneous'.
- The spontaneous sources of funding are those that arise in a substantially unplanned and unstructured way in the ordinary course of business.
- Permanent assets should be financed with permanent and spontaneous sources of funding.
- Temporary assets should be financed with temporary sources of funding.

lo3 describe the sources and costs of informal short-term finance

- The most common sources of informal short-term finance for businesses are:
  - accrued wages, superannuation and taxes
  - trade credit.

- Accrued wages have been earned by employees but not yet paid.
- Accrued wages, superannuation and taxes are free forms of finance for businesses.
- Trade credit is a cheap and significant form of business finance.
- Trade credit arises during the normal course of business and is normally extended without formal agreements.
- It is normally unsecured and requires nothing additional to normal accounting practices for its successful management.
- Trade credit is most likely to be offered on a net 30 days or even net 7 days basis.
- Sometimes, firms offer discounts for early payment.
- Not taking discounts is a costly expense.

lo4 discuss the sources and costs of formal short-term finance

- The most common sources of formal short-term finance for businesses are:
  - bank overdrafts
  - commercial bills, promissory notes and commercial paper
  - factoring or debtor/invoice/trade finance
  - stock/inventory loans or floor-plan finance.
- Bank overdrafts are drawn down only as required when cheques written on the account exceed positive balances.
- The intention of overdraft finance is thus that the balance in the account will fluctuate between being positive and negative from day to day as cash flows into and out of each business.
- Bank overdrafts are normally more expensive than commercial bills.
- There are normally three parties to the issue of a bank-accepted commercial bill (BAB):
  - A firm (the borrower — party one) wanting to access the bill market would normally approach its financier and make its request known.
  - Normally, the financier draws up a bill because it has the software and staff with the expertise to do the job properly and efficiently, but it is possible for borrowers to produce the bill.
  - The bank then finds an investor (the 'discounter' — party two) who has funds to invest and is happy with the yield that is possible from this product.
  - The bank then facilitates the deal even further by 'accepting' the bill. In this context, it means the bank has guaranteed that the bill will be honoured at maturity.
  - The bank has assumed the credit risk on the bill in return for a fee and becomes the 'acceptor' — party three.
- Factoring and debt finance are based on the security of debts or accounts receivable.
- Factoring and debt finance have costs which vary widely according to the conditions attached to the finance.
- Stock, inventory or floor-plan finance is based on the security of stock or inventory.
- The cost of floor-plan finance is normally quite similar to the cost of overdraft finance.

Key terms

current assets, p. 358
current liabilities, p. 358
factoring, p. 371
hedging principle, p. 361
inverse yield curve, p. 360
liquidity, p. 359
net working capital, p. 358
normal yield curve, p. 360
overdraft, p. 366
permanent funding, p. 361
self-liquidating debt, p. 360
spontaneous sources of funding, p. 361
temporary funding, p. 361
working capital, p. 358

Learning chart

Learning objective	Questions	Self-test problems	Financial problems
lo1 discuss the significance of having appropriate working capital in a business	10.1, 10.2, 10.3, 10.4, 10.5		
lo2 make a judgement about the level of net working capital within a firm	10.6, 10.7, 10.8, 10.9, 10.10, 10.11, 10.12		10.2
lo3 describe the sources and costs of informal short-term finance	10.13, 10.14, 10.15	10.1, 10.2,	10.3, 10.4, 10.5, 10.6
lo4 discuss the sources and costs of formal short-term finance	10.16, 10.17, 10.18, 10.19, 10.20, 10.21	10.3, 10.4, 10.5	10.1, 10.2, 10.7, 10.8, 10.9, 10.10, 10.11, 10.12, 10.13, 10.14, 10.15, 10.16, 10.17, 10.18

Questions

10.1 How are working capital and net working capital different?
10.2 What is the trade-off that a financial manager must juggle in deciding on the most appropriate level of working capital?
10.3 How can having excessive working capital reduce the profitability of the firm?
10.4 Explain the apparent paradox that the excessive use of short-term funds could increase the risk of illiquidity for a firm.
10.5 What does a normal yield curve show?
10.6 Explain in your own words and with examples the operation of the hedging principle.
10.7 What is self-liquidating debt?
10.8 What is temporary funding?
10.9 'Spontaneous sources of funding have something to do with fire' wrote Billy in his exam. Is he correct? Give your definition.
10.10 Are spontaneous sources of funding important to a small business such as a local newsagent? Give examples to back your view.
10.11 Temporary assets should be funded with temporary sources of funding. Why?
10.12 Permanent assets should be financed with which sources of funding?
10.13 Explain why accrued expenses are sources of short-term funding?
10.14 What is the cost of accrued-expense funding?

10.15 Why is trade credit so useful as a funding source for business? What other advantages does it confer?

10.16 What is the cost of trade credit to the buyer, given today's interest rate structure?

10.17 Why are the terms of BABs often standardised?

10.18 Explain the difference between a BAB and a promissory note (PN).

10.19 If a commercial bill was priced to yield 6%, would the same price give a higher or lower discount percentage?

10.20 Explain the differences between factoring and discounting invoices.

10.21 Auditing by lenders is essential for successful floor-plan financing. Why?

Self-test problems

10.1 A swimming pool construction firm has had trouble getting clients to pay for their pools after construction has been completed. The firm charges a well-padded price and allows a 10% discount for payment received within 10 days of issue of the bill, net 40 days. What is the effective annual interest rate on funds used if a customer does not take advantage of the discount? The bill for the most popular pool is $10 000.

10.2 Franks Fish issues a $5000 prawn invoice marked '3/10, net 30'. How much will Frank be owed if the client pays in 7 days? What is the effective annual interest rate on funds used if the client pays in 25 days?

10.3 Sentrale Trading Co approaches its financier for about $100 000 and is offered a commercial bill at 6.35% for 180 days. How much will Sentrale receive?

10.4 George Smythe Floors Ltd (GSF) occasionally buys promissory notes in the short-term money market. A note for $500 000 is discounted at 8% and has 45 days to maturity. How much does GSF pay for the note? How much will GSF receive when the note matures?

10.5 A2Z Bank accepts a bill on behalf of a client. The face value of the bill is $100 000. The term is 3 months — from 1 December to 1 March in a leap year. The yield is 5.8%. How much will the investor have to provide to the borrower?

Solutions to self-test problems

10.1 To solve this problem, you can use the $10 000 as the base for your calculation or you can do the calculation in thousands (which is a bit easier). The discount is 10% or $1 for every $10, so the net price is $9. The discount is forgone for 30 days.

$$\text{Cost} = \frac{\text{interest}}{Pn}$$

$$\text{Cost} = \frac{1}{\left(9 \times \frac{30}{365}\right)}$$

$$= \frac{1}{0.7397} \text{ or } 135\%$$

10.2 At 7 days, Frank will be owed 97% of \$5000 (that is, \$4850).

$$\text{Cost} = \frac{\text{interest}}{Pn}$$

$$\text{Cost} = \frac{3}{\left(97 \times \dfrac{15}{365}\right)}$$

$$= \frac{3}{0.9863} \text{ or } 75.26\%$$

10.3 $i = 0.0635 \times \dfrac{180}{365}$

$$= 0.031\,315$$

$$\text{Amount} = \frac{100\,000}{1.031\,315}$$

$$= \$96\,963.58$$

10.4 $i = 0.08 \times \dfrac{45}{365}$

$$= 0.098\,63$$

$$\text{Price} = 500\,000\,(1 - 0.009\,863)$$

$$= 500\,000\,(0.990\,137)$$

$$= \$495\,068.50$$

$$\text{Repayment} = \text{face value}$$

$$= \$500\,000$$

10.5 $i = 0.058 \times \dfrac{91}{365}$

$$= 0.014\,460$$

$$\text{Amount} = \frac{100\,000}{1.014\,460}$$

$$= \$98\,574.61$$

Financial problems

10.1. David Pride Fashions has an overdraft account at its bank with a limit of \$100 000. Interest is charged at the rate of 11.25% pa on daily balance, debited monthly. The balance remains at \$26 833.25 O/D for 7 days and then falls to \$55 800.02 O/D for the remaining 23 days in the month. What is the monthly interest expense?

10.2 Georg Zeller is a conservative chief financial officer. He often over-estimates the need for cash in his firm. The internal auditor has just reported to the board that Georg kept \$250 000 more in the current account than was necessary for a particular 6-month period. Funds in the current account earned 0.25% while funds in the almost risk-free short-term money market earned 5.25%. The internal audit reported a cost to the firm post-tax through this action. What amount would you report to the board as the cost? Would it be pre- or post-tax?

10.3 Eastern Slopes Advisory Group (ESAG) receives a government grant for $220000 (GST inclusive) on 1 April. ESAG reports to the ATO quarterly. ESAG uses contractors predominantly to carry out its work. No payments were made to contractors in that quarter. How much extra finance did ESAG gain through the GST system? If funds in the short-term money market earned 6% pa, what benefit did ESAG derive from this extra funding?

10.4 Arco Ltd submits its BAS and pays its dues to the ATO monthly. In a particular February, the reported figure for wages paid was $600000. The value of the payroll each payday was stable in the period and the paydays were the 14th and the 28th of the month. Average tax withheld with the PAYG system was 25%. Arco paid the required amount of PAYG at the post office on 13 March and the cheque was cleared through its account on the night of 14 March. How much funding for how long did Arco gain through this situation?

10.5 David Lawrence receives a $10000 invoice marked '4/10, net 42'. How much can he save by paying within 10 days? Is there any advantage in paying in 5 days? What is the effective cost of funds if he pays on the 42nd day?

10.6 What is the effective cost of funds for a firm that pays an invoice marked '2/20, net 30' on the 35th day?

10.7 Marti Motors has an overdraft at the local bank. The account for a given month had a positive balance for the first 5 days only and was in overdraft for the remaining 25 days. The average positive balance was $3500 and the average daily overdrawn balance (excluding interest charges) was $25600. The account pays 0.25% pa interest computed monthly on lowest daily positive balance. Interest is charged monthly on each day's overdrawn balances at 15% pa. What is the net interest charge for the month?

10.8 Jani Soki approaches her bank for commercial bill finance. She wants about $100000 for 90 days. The bank indicates she can have the funds at 6.1% pa and the 90-day period ends on a Sunday. How much will Jani receive?

10.9 Bill Smith Sportstore has funds to invest for a short period. Bill, the owner, approaches his bank and finds he can lend funds to other businesses for short periods via the bank-accepted bill medium. Bill is happy that there is little risk with the bank acceptance of the security. Bill pays over the funds to finance a $100000 commercial bill for 180 days at 6.3% yield. How much does Bill pay to the bank? How much will Bill be repaid at the end of the period?

10.10 James Soo decides to buy an already issued promissory note in the market. He buys a $200000 note to yield 5.95%. The note has 67 days to maturity. How much does James pay?

10.11 Fleur's Fashions (FF) wants some extra funding for the Christmas rush period. Fleur arranges a BAB with her bank — $100000 face value, 90 days to yield the investor 5.7%. How much will FF have credited to her account?

10.12 Two $100000 commercial bills are discounted at 7.3%. They have 45 days to maturity. How much is paid for the bills?

10.13 A $100000 BAB is discounted at 8.1% with 152 days to maturity. How much is paid for the bill?

10.14 Acme Trading Co. factors its whole accounts receivable file. The factoring charge is 6.3% and the total value of the debtors is $430000. How much does Acme receive for the invoices?

10.15 Ace Discounters buys $600 000 of invoices for a 4.3% fee. Ace collects 90% of the debts in 30 days and 10% in 61 days. If funds cost Ace 6.0% pa, and assuming the costs of collecting the debts amounts to 2% of face value per month for debts collected within 30 days and 3% of face value per month for debts collected within 2 months, was this deal worth doing for Ace? Why? How could Ace manage a better outcome?

10.16 MyStore Retail has about $200 000 in credit sales each month. Payment terms are net 30 days after the end of the purchase month. MyStore factors all these invoices at a 5% fee. What is the effective annual percentage cost of this action?

10.17 Adam's Barbeques uses stock finance to fund the business. The firm builds up stock during the winter in preparation for the summer barbequeing season. The financier charges 12% interest on a loan of 60% of stock value. The stock value is $100 000 and the loan is for 3 months. There are also other fees of $500, including a valuation fee. What is the effective annual percentage cost of this finance?

10.18 A floor-plan financier agrees to lend a car dealer funds to buy stock up to a limit of $1 million. The first order under this scheme is for 25 sedans which average $23 000 each with all ordered optional extras included. The cars are delivered and the invoice paid by the financier on Monday, 1 October. The interest is 6.5% pa, charged monthly on the balance at 5.00 pm each Friday. Five vehicles are sold in the first week, and six in the second week, at an average price of $30 000 each. The dealer pays the financier at cost price electronically on Saturday each week for the vehicles sold during that week. The dealer re-orders vehicles at the end of the second week, and 10 new vehicles are delivered and paid for by the financier on the Monday of the fourth week at the same average price as the original lot. Sales comprise five vehicles in each of weeks 3 and 4, and two in the last few days in the month. How much does the dealer owe the financier on the first day of the new month?

SOLUTIONS TO FINANCE WORKSHOPS

10.1
1. A retail store like a fast-food outlet could have all three forms of current assets.
2. No, cash and stock would be greater than debtors.
3. Cash at most times may be greater than stock as stock is continually turned over.
4. Most items of stock would be delivered fresh daily; only long shelf-life items such as frozen meats and oils would be kept in sufficient quantities to last for several days.

10.2 The bill is priced to yield 5.57%

$$i = 0.0557 \times \frac{91}{365}$$
$$= 0.013\,886\,849$$

$$\text{Sum} = \frac{\$600\,000}{1.013\,886\,849}$$
$$= \$591\,786$$

If the bill were priced at a discount of 5.57%, the sum received would be:

$$\text{Sum} = \$600\,000\ (1 - 0.013886849)$$

$$= 250\,000 \times 0.986113151 = \$591\,672$$

The bill would mature in 91 days if the 90-day period ended on a Sunday.

End notes

1 Export Finance and Insurance Corporation 2006, 'Working capital boost for South Australian exporters', media release, 26 October.

2 Insolvency and Trustee Service Australia 2006, 'Statement of Affairs' form, p. 8, www.itsa.gov.au.

3 *Reserve Bank of Australia Bulletin*, various dates, RBA, Sydney.

4 Commonwealth Bank of Australia Business Centre 2006, 'Bill facility', http://business.commbank.com.au.

5 'SMEs turn to debt financing for growth', *Sydney Morning Herald*, 16 May 2006.

6 'SMEs turn to debt financing for growth', *Sydney Morning Herald*, 16 May 2006.

7 GE Commercial Australia and New Zealand 2006, 'GE Commercial Finance: inventory', www.gecommercial.com.au.

8 PPB 2007, 'Industry experience: significant motor group', www.ppb.com.au.

chapter

11

Managing current assets

Learning objectives

After studying this chapter, you should be able to:

- **lo1** describe the dual meaning of 'cash'
- **lo2** discuss the motives for holding cash
- **lo3** discuss the issues related to the management of cash
- **lo4** describe some electronic methods of transferring funds
- **lo5** discuss some aspects of the management of accounts receivable
- **lo6** discuss the issues pertaining to the management of inventories.

THE IMPORTANCE OF CASH

The following extract comes from a report on the effects of the closure of the last bank branch in small to medium sized country towns. The research was undertaken by the Centre for Australian Financial Institutions (CAFI) at the University of Southern Queensland in Toowoomba. It highlights the importance of cash to business and some of the effects of having impediments to the smooth management of cash.

Where there is no local bank, businesses can expect high denomination notes will accumulate over time at the expense of 'change' — lower denomination notes and coinage. To try to overcome change shortages, many businesses have increased their change floats. However, there is an upper limit to this practice, because change in hand poses security problems and costs either opportunity interest or the relevant portion of the interest charge on an overdraft.

Change shortages affect turnover. Because other arrangements can be made to overcome the problem, there may be little effect on sales where the customer is a local person. However, the situation is quite different where the customer is just passing through town. Mungindi, for example, has a large itinerant population at times, because of the casual labour requirements of the cotton crop. Where a shopkeeper cannot cash cheques because of change shortages, those sales are lost. Customers usually will not go to another store, make some purchases in order to cash a cheque, and then return to the first store. Respondents to the survey reported an average of $4475 per month of lost sales by HCH [high cash-handling] businesses and an average of $675 per month in lost sales by LCH [low cash-handling] businesses.

Requests to cash cheques have increased for many respondent businesses since the bank branch closures. All types of businesses except primary producers have been affected. 'To get money you have got to go where your bank is. If cashing a cheque in town, it is only for a small amount or you have to wait two or three days to get a large one cashed. Also if I go to the bank, it costs for petrol and wear on the car. I also shop there.' (survey response) The HCH businesses reported an average monthly increase in cheque cashings of $12 100; the LCH businesses, $4750 per month; the community and professional services businesses, $500 per month; and the government and semi-government businesses reported an average monthly increase of $2000.

The accumulation of high denomination notes similarly has implications for security and has an effect on interest charges or interest earned. The significance of this problem depends on the type of business. Respondents in HCH businesses reported excess cash accumulated to the extent of an average of $4100 per month, while LCH businesses reported an average of $1000 'unwanted' cash per month, with primary producers accumulating an average of $850 per month in unwanted cash.[1]

Chapter preview

This chapter discusses the management of current assets. All the current assets — cash, debtors and inventory — are extremely important to the health of most types of businesses. As you will see from reading the opening to this chapter, most businesses rely on having adequate supplies of cash in the form of change to facilitate the making of sales. Additionally, businesses need cash in the form of readily available funds with which to pay financial commitments on time. Allowing customers credit also plays a vital role in facilitating sales, but how much credit is too much? Finally, the chapter considers the holding of stock or inventories and stock management techniques. Just as there is skill in managing an appropriate level of debtors or accounts receivable, so too there is skill in keeping an appropriate level of stock. Studying this chapter should give you tools with which to develop these skills.

The following diagram shows how this chapter is structured.

MANAGING CURRENT ASSETS

- **The dual meaning of 'cash'**
- **The motives for holding cash**
  - The transactions motive
  - The precautionary motive
  - The speculative motive
- **Managing cash**
  - The timing of cash flows
  - The financial imperative of having sufficient cash
  - The cost of holding cash
  - The cost of not having enough cash
- **Using electronic funds transfer (EFT)**
  - Benefits and costs of EFTPOS
  - Using direct entry (DE)
- **Debtors or accounts receivable**
  - Benefits and costs of granting credit
  - Determinants of the level of debtors
  - Romalpa clauses
- **Managing inventories**
  - Types of inventories
  - Benefits and costs of holding inventories
  - Management techniques
  - Just-in-time

lo*1*

Describe the dual meaning of 'cash'.

Cash: all the currency that the firm has on hand. Cash is also all the liquid or near liquid assets that a firm holds or has ready access to.

The dual meaning of 'cash'

'Cash' to the proverbial people in the streets is the coins and notes in their pockets, purses, wallets or handbags, plus any money kept at home in biscuit tins, bottles and wall safes. In other words, cash is often regarded by people as restricted to currency alone. 'Cash' to a business manager is currency plus the funds kept in cheque accounts and term deposits at banks, cash management trusts, commercial bills and other short-term loans. The business equivalent of cash in the pocket is cash in tills, cash registers, on-site safes and petty cash tins.

Thus, cash is all the currency that the firm has on hand. Cash is also all the liquid or near liquid assets that a firm holds or has ready access to. Some authors classify liquid assets as currency plus marketable securities, but this classification is not strictly complete. Cash includes cheque account (demand) deposits, but does not include term deposits. Term deposits are not marketable securities but, on the other hand, are available on demand after the payment of a high 'break' fee.

lo2

Discuss the motives for holding cash.

The motives for holding cash

In 1936 John Maynard Keynes, the famous economist, gave the reasons that any entity (including individuals) holds cash. No work since has been generally accepted to have improved on Keynes's view in this area. Keynes suggested that there are three reasons that cash is held:

1. the transactions motive
2. the precautionary motive
3. the speculative motive.

The transactions motive

Cash is held so transactions — sales and purchases — may be completed successfully. This motive has implications for both meanings of cash. In regard to the holdings of currency, a shortage of change can impact on a business, as can be seen from the part of the report in the opening to this chapter. This effect on sales can be especially important in rural and remote areas and areas of high passing trade. The minimum amount of currency, or change, that should be held by a business depends on the type of business being run. A bookmaker, for example, with the same annual turnover as a local bread shop would hold significantly more currency than the shop. With modern payment mechanisms such as credit and debit cards, holding currency to pay for purchases is normally not so important as it was previously.

With regard to the larger meaning of cash, it is important that firms have enough liquid assets to pay for their purchases in a timely manner. The absolute and relative (to total current assets) amounts of cash held by various firms depend on the types of business and the patterns of their cash flows. A farm machinery dealership specialising in grain harvesters selling for about $500 000 each, for example, would minimise its year-round holdings of cash but would provide for the pre- and during-harvest burst of sales activity and stock re-ordering. A department store or supermarket, on the other hand, is likely to keep a reasonably high proportion of current assets as cash, even though daily cash flow both in and out is high. Table 11.1 gives the absolute and relative (to total current assets) amounts of cash held by three firms at 30 June 2006. Note how different the proportions are, but remember these values are only a single snapshot. There may be specific reasons for balances to be smaller or larger than usual.

Table 11.1 Cash held by three Australian firms at 30 June 2006

Firm	Industry	Cash held ($m)	
ABC Learning Centres	Child care	132*	47
CSL Ltd	Vaccines and blood products	754	32
Woolworths	Retail supermarket	526	13

* This high value of cash is likely to relate to the recent capital raising.

Sources: Data from the 2006 annual reports for the respective firms.

The precautionary motive

Precaution: involves prudent actions taken early to ensure a good outcome or to forestall an adverse effect

At the same time as firms provide for the transactions that they know they must have sufficient cash to service, well-managed firms also keep a buffer of cash that is available should it be needed. This need for a buffer arises from the precautionary motive. Firms careful of, and determined to keep, their good reputations maintain a buffer of cash so that they are not embarrassed by unexpected events. A manager exercising **precaution** has a cash buffer planned and maintained. Well-managed travel agencies, for example, may factor into their planning the risk of industrial unrest and strike actions by airline employees.

Holding cash reserves normally has an opportunity cost (see chapters 8 and 10) through the loss of interest or alternative investment earnings (and this will be discussed in more detail later). However, to a large extent businesses can 'have their cake and eat it too' by holding some funds in short-term marketable securities. A purchased commercial bill, for example, which may be used to hold excess cash at the current market rates may be sold to another investor without penalty to achieve liquidity if required, even at short notice.

The speculative motive

Speculation: involves the purchase of an asset for eventual resale with a view to profit, but where there is a strong element of risk

The speculative motive involves holding cash to make speculative purchases when the opportunity arises. **Speculation** involves the purchase of an asset for eventual resale with a view to profit, but where there is an element of risk. Of the three motives, this is the least likely motive for most businesses. However, there are some firms which openly speculate by buying significant parcels of shares in other companies, then wait for prices to rise to sell later at a profit. At an individual level, 'day traders' — people who buy and sell shares on the same day or in the next few days — are speculators not investors.

Often there are media reports that large firms such as News Ltd and National Australia Bank are holding large volumes of cash in order to make big purchases of assets, or takeovers, in the near future. Would these takeovers be speculation? The answer to this is 'no'. The takeovers would be of firms in allied industries; that is, news and entertainment media and banking and financial services, respectively. The objective of such takeovers is not speculation, but an increase in critical mass and market share.

Another common situation occurs when firms purchase raw materials early because they believe there will be price rises or scarcity in the future. If a sawmill buys a tract of undeveloped land with good timber stands, is this speculation? Strictly speaking, it is not. The sawmill is in the business of buying logs or rights to fell timber and selling sawn timber. Thus, buying timber stands even several years before they are needed can be viewed as hedging, not speculation.

lo3

Discuss the issues related to the management of cash.

Managing cash

The issues that are related to the management of cash include:

- the timing of cash flows
- the financial imperative of having sufficient cash
- the cost of holding cash
- the cost of not having enough cash.

The timing of cash flows

Cash moves into the firm from possibly six major sources. These are:

- cash sales
- credit sales, when the debtors eventually pay their accounts
- sales of used or unwanted assets
- capital injections
- short-term loans
- long-term loan funding.

Cash flows out from the firm to service a further four needs:

- purchase of inventories
- purchase of labour, materials and other services

- purchase of assets (fixed or intangible)
- payment of taxes.

The cash flows associated with loans are two-way in nature for many firms, with cash initially inflowing and then being paid back and, in the case of short-term funding, sometimes outflowing first as excess cash is 'parked' for a period then repaid by the borrower. Figure 11.1 shows these flows in diagrammatic form.

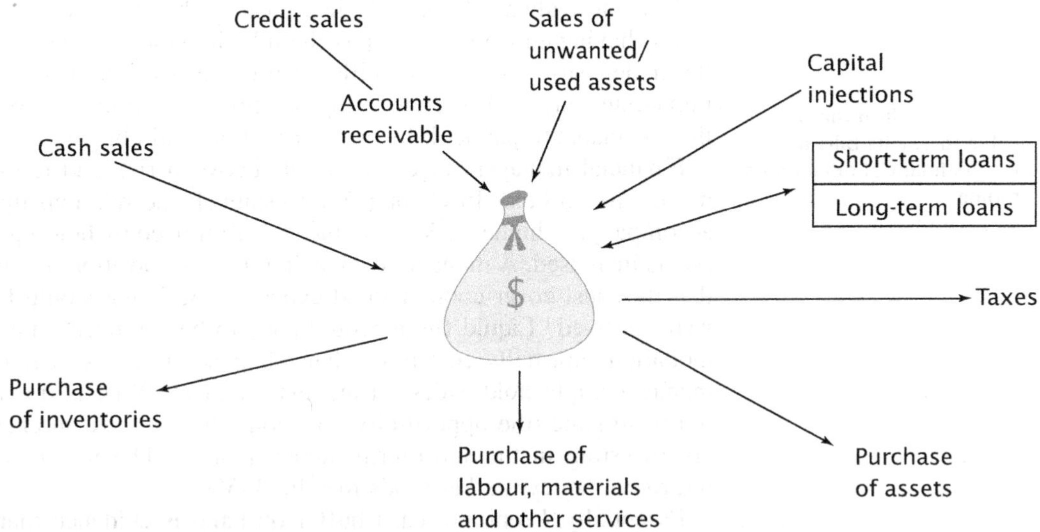

Figure 11.1 The cash flow within a firm

The timing of most of these flows is variable, the only exceptions being the cash sales and payments by debtors (both inflows), the payment of wages, mostly fortnightly these days, and the payment of taxes. Even though cash sales are normally made by most firms every trading day, cash sales will bring in more funds some days than others. For example, many different types of businesses have busier trading days on Fridays than they have on Mondays.

Similarly, debtors may pay on any day of the week, but there will normally be a larger inflow of funds in the first few days of the month as debtors pay their bills in the first few days after the end of the previous month. Moreover, the firm itself will normally pay its trade creditors in the first few days after the end of the previous month and there will be a major cash drain during this period.

The taxes a firm pays comprise mainly income tax, fringe benefits tax and possibly capital gains tax. In addition, the firm must handle the cash flows for the PAYG for its employees and for the GST. Thus, even though the firm does not actually bear the liability for these latter taxes, it still must have the cash available to make the payments when they fall due. For most firms, these taxes are paid either quarterly or monthly, depending on the size of the firm and its turnover.

Budget: a plan that includes forecasts of future transactions

Cash budget: a detailed plan of expected cash receipts and cash payments that highlights any probable cash surpluses or deficits

The firm can plan the timing of the purchase and sale of assets, and the requirements for capital injections, to suit its needs. Similarly, in contracting for loans or placing funds in the short-term money market, it can negotiate timing that best suits its needs. How does the firm know what timing is most appropriate? A little thought will convince you that the firm must have some tools to hand to allow it to analyse and plan these needs. An important element of cash management is the preparation of a cash budget. We look at techniques to develop cash forecasts and budgets in chapter 14. Suffice to say here, a **budget** is a plan that includes forecasts of future transactions. A **cash budget** is a detailed plan of expected cash receipts and cash payments in terms of the most appropriate time period for the business. That time period may be daily, weekly, monthly or annually, depending on the type of business. The cash budget highlights any probable cash surpluses or deficits and allows the manager to plan for investing surpluses or providing for deficits in plenty of time so that the most advantageous arrangements may be made.

The financial imperative of having sufficient cash

A firm must always have sufficient cash on hand to meet its financial obligations. This means having enough cash to pay the bills in hand, and having sufficient cash or near-cash (term deposits, commercial bills or pre-approved credit) to meet expected bills in the immediate future. The contrasting position is described as being **insolvent**. An insolvent firm is unable to pay its bills or meet its financial obligations on time.

Insolvent: a firm that is unable to pay its bills or meet its financial obligations on time

Financial managers face a trade-off between risk and return when contemplating how much cash to hold. In chapter 5 we establish the relationship of higher expected returns accompanying higher risk. Cost may be minimised by holding as little cash as possible, but risk is increased. A manager overseeing the cash position of a firm can cut cash holdings so that they just cover contemplated expenses, but what would happen if an unexpected bill were received? Liquid funds would have to be arranged quickly and such speedy accommodations normally cost more than planned increases in liquidity. On the other hand, a manager might hold excess cash, 'just in case'. What is the cost of this? The cost is the return forgone (the opportunity cost concept discussed in chapter 8) by holding cash and not investing in the short-term money market. The return on cash in hand is zero; the return on money-market funds may be 4–5%.

Essentially, keeping a cash buffer on hand is evidence that the firm's business is such that it cannot synchronise its cash receipts and cash payments. This is the norm for most businesses. Additionally, the cash buffer is recognition that most firms find it virtually impossible to budget with total accuracy for whatever planning period is used. Even if a firm could forecast its own expenses, it is in the hands of its customers as to when its accounts are paid by them.

The cost of holding cash

The cost of holding cash may be thought of in terms of two issues:

- the opportunity cost of holding currency, rather than short-term securities, or the cost of holding very short-term securities instead of longer short-term securities
- the cost of ensuring physical security of currency.

Cash held in the form of currency earns no return. No one will pay a firm for the use of its cash if it does not lend it out for someone to use. In contrast, cash lent overnight, or for a week, or a month, does have a positive return and the cost of keeping funds as cash or in current accounts is the return forgone from not investing in the short-term market. Similarly, funds kept in seven-day deposits or one-month securities normally would involve a sacrifice in returns possible from a longer short-term period.

In addition to these opportunity costs, there is also the cost of ensuring funds kept as currency are secure. Most firms have some sort of security system on site to keep cash reasonably secure — a safe, burglar alarm systems and physical barriers to entry. These systems can be quite expensive and, normally, the more money that is handled, the more sophisticated and expensive the security systems.

There are other issues relating to the management of cash (not just currency) as a firm's asset. One such issue is the installation of secure systems to prevent or enable detection of **embezzlement** by the firm's employees. Embezzlement is the illegal diversion of funds from the firm by employees for their own benefit. Embezzlement may take the form of stealing

Embezzlement: the illegal diversion of funds from the firm by employees for their own benefit

currency from cash registers or diverting funds from bank accounts. Some employees in larger companies are given access to bank accounts. This expands the scope for embezzlement far beyond pilfering the till. For example, a finance director of the APP newsagency managed to write himself cheques totalling $300 000 before he was detected.[2] An employee of Bank Leumi Le-Israel embezzled around $400 million and the situation caused an international scandal.[3] Systems to overcome embezzlement are expensive to put in place, but may be cheaper in the long run than not having them. Such systems include secure till systems, where cash sales are recorded and tills are balanced at the end of each trading day. In addition, 'the banking' (counting notes and coin, and listing cheques) should be made up by two people so that successful embezzlement will normally involve conspiracy as well as stealing. (It is harder to steal successfully over a long period as the number of people involved increases.)

Moreover, one of the weakest links in a secure system of managing cash is the actual trip to the bank. Many firms send the same person to the bank at the same time of day by the same route. This is a very dangerous practice. With relatively small bankings, an alert employee should use different routes and go at different times of the day. The reason for this is to undermine any robbery plans that rely on known time and place. In addition, the banking 'parcel' should be made substantially unidentifiable to reduce the chance of spontaneous mugging. Next time you are near a bank branch, look out for the people you can positively identify as carrying business banking. You will find many! The cost of getting this area of business management wrong includes the loss of the funds, the cost of trying to reconstruct the banking records and perhaps employee compensation. Firms may take out insurance to cover this risk, but that too has a cost.

The cost of not having enough cash

The cost of not having enough cash at the required time may be the loss of the business. HIH failed because it ran out of cash. One.Tel failed because it ran out of cash. Both these firms ran out of cash because their businesses were inherently unprofitable and were badly managed. However, it was the deficit in cash — insolvency — which finally killed them. The penalty for insolvency is normally the winding up of the business.

It is possible to put the lack of cash into a continuum and trace the effects. Figure 11.2 shows such a continuum. As we saw on the chapter opening page, temporary change shortages affect turnover, especially in isolated businesses and businesses that attract a high proportion of 'passing trade'. Lost turnover is profit forgone and represents an opportunity cost.

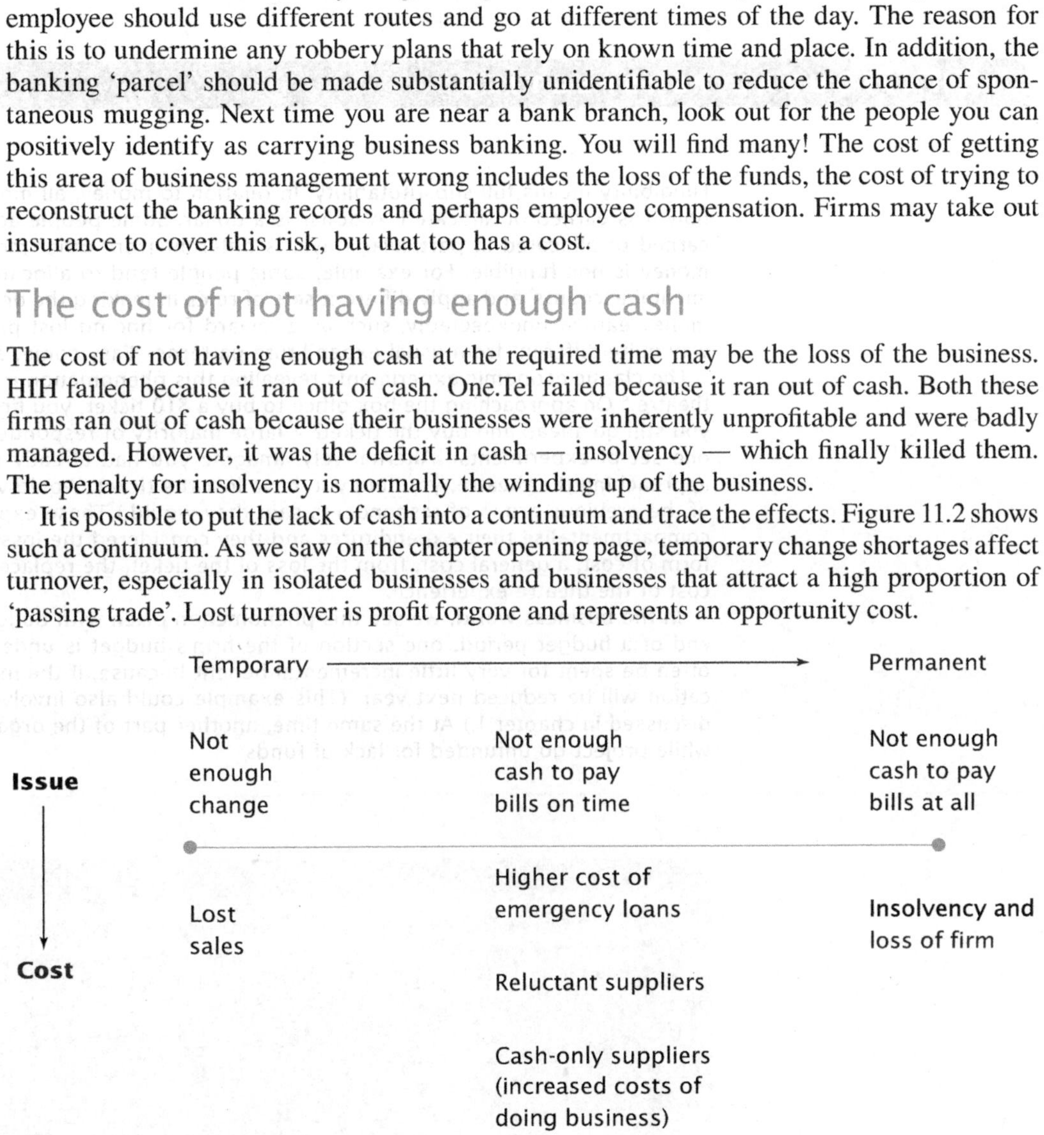

Figure 11.2 The cost of a lack of cash

Temporary cash shortages may be overcome by arranging emergency loans. However, as a general rule, the more desperate the need, the higher the cost of emergency funds. If a firm gains a reputation as a 'late payer', its suppliers become progressively more reluctant to supply. Eventually, some suppliers will supply only for cash. This decree introduces a whole new suite of problems. If suppliers will supply only for cash, the purchasing firm must find out the value of each invoice and have the correct amount of cash or a made-out cheque available when the goods are collected. This involves extra time on the part of office personnel and more security problems. In effect, the cost of doing business has increased. The final stage on the continuum occurs when firms become insolvent. Trading while insolvent is illegal and the insolvent firm is normally wound up.

Throughout this section of the chapter we have followed the normal idea that any one dollar has the same value as any other dollar at that point in time. Another way to say this is that money is 'fungible'. The following 'behavioural perspective' feature provides some discussion about how people do not always view money as a fungible asset.

BEHAVIOURAL PERSPECTIVE

Fungibility

Fungibility means full substitutability. In relation to money, all money is the same, no matter how it is earned or allocated. A dollar is a dollar. Some people act as if some money, either earned or allocated in particular ways, is different from other money; that is, they act as if money is non-fungible. For example, some people tend to allocate their regular income into 'mental accounts' and apply different sets of rules in making the decisions to spend it. Further, money earned unexpectedly, such as a reward for finding lost property, is often spent in a way quite different from usual expenditure patterns. 'Easy come, easy go.'

The classic economic experiments revealing this phenomenon involved people going to the theatre.[4] On approaching the box office to buy a $10 ticket, you find you have lost $10. Would you still go ahead and buy the ticket? A large majority of respondents say they would (88% in one set of experiments). Alternatively, imagine you had already bought a ticket and, when approaching the theatre, you find you have lost the ticket. Would you buy another? (Only 46% of the previous group of respondents said they would.) These experiments show that people compartmentalise their expenditures and they considered the loss of money to be a different form of cost, a general cost, from the loss of the ticket, the replacement of which doubled the cost of the theatre experience.

In the business world, we see this phenomenon often with budgeted funds. If, towards the end of a budget period, one section of the firm's budget is underspent, then the funds will often be spent for very little incremental benefit because, if the money is not spent, the allocation will be reduced next year. (This example could also involve the agency problem first discussed in chapter 1.) At the same time, another part of the organisation can have a worthwhile project go unfunded for lack of funds.

FINANCE WORKSHOP 11.1

'Most firms must have a stock of cash on hand at all times.'

1. Is this statement as true for a real estate sales partnership with no employees (only partners) as for a retail bakery?
2. What are the costs of holding cash?
3. What are the costs of not having enough cash?

lo4

Describe some electronic methods of transferring funds.

Using electronic funds transfer (EFT)

Those of you who have lived all of your lives in cities will probably find the opening extract — the disruption to business that the closure of the last bank in a town caused during the 1990s — slightly unbelievable. 'Why didn't they just use plastic?' you ask. Well, many people did and many others were forced into the EFT world more quickly than they would have preferred.

The Bankcard was introduced to the Australian public by a consortium of nine Australian banks in 1974. By using a range of means including general advertising, direct mailing of cards, predetermined credit limits and so on, the banks encouraged their customers and others to take and use this new method of making payments. People who are inherently 'early adopters', people who could see an easy means of getting some 'no questions asked' credit funding and people who could see how they could change and improve their payment method quickly adopted Bankcard. In the early 1980s, MasterCard and Visa entered the Australian market and a new wave of advertising encouraged more people to take up at least one credit card. The additional advantage of having a credit card branded by either of these global organisations is that the card is recognised and usable worldwide, and thus Australians can easily gain access to local currency while in other countries and repay the debt in Australian dollars in the normal way.

By November 2006, there were more than 13 million bank-linked credit cards on issue in Australia and the outstanding debt on them was $38 billion.[5] People holding these cards used them for more than 110 million transactions each month and these transactions amounted to more than $16 billion in most months.[6] Debit cards were introduced in the late 1980s. By November 2006, there were more than 26 million accounts linked to debit cards[7] but their pattern of activity is different from that of credit cards. During early 2006–07, there were on average about 200 million transactions each month valued at about $22 billion.[8] From these statistics, it is apparent that more people have more debit cards than credit cards and that each credit card is used on average slightly more often than each debit card.

Unlike credit cards, where less than 3% of total transactions are cash advances, about 34% of debit card transactions are cash advances from automatic teller machines (ATMs). The remaining 130 million transactions (in December 2006) worth $9.4 billion are thus of interest to us here, as these transactions (with an average value of about $70) are made through electronic funds transfer point of sale (EFTPOS) devices.[9] EFTPOS terminals were introduced in the late 1980s and 15 000 terminals had been installed throughout the country by 1990.[10] This number doubled in three years, doubled again in the next two years and nearly doubled again the following year, 1997. By 1999, there were 278 000 terminals installed and by 2006 more than 540 000.[11] These terminals are installed in non-financial institution businesses, and they all accept both credit cards and debit cards.

Benefits and costs of EFTPOS

Why have businesses taken up this technological advance with such alacrity? Your study of this chapter so far will help you answer this question. By offering EFTPOS to their customers, businesses can:

- attract more sales and increase turnover
- decrease the need for change and the opportunity costs of keeping it
- reduce currency inflow and thus reduce security and banking risks and costs
- be paid faster.

On the negative side, there are additional costs attached to offering EFTPOS to customers.

The first three of the four benefits listed need no further elaboration. They follow from the previous discussion on the costs of cash and the costs of not keeping enough cash. Being paid faster is a significant benefit. Ideally, financial managers would like their firms to be paid immediately by their customers but to pay their own suppliers as slowly as possible. In this way, cash would remain as long as possible within the firm and could earn an optimal return through judicious investment. Unfortunately, most financial managers have the same idea, and thus delaying payments too long is not a good idea. However, the introduction of EFTPOS has allowed the immediate collection of sales revenue without the attendant costs of collecting cash.

But what of the costs of EFTPOS to merchants? To understand these costs, we have to know a little more about how credit and debit cards operate. Figure 11.3 shows how credit cards, the so-called four party schemes, work.[12] Two of the parties are the holder of the credit card — the customer who buys the goods — and the merchant who sells the goods and wants to be paid. Interspersed between these two parties are two financial institutions, the merchant's bank and the customer's credit card provider. In some cases, this will be the same institution.

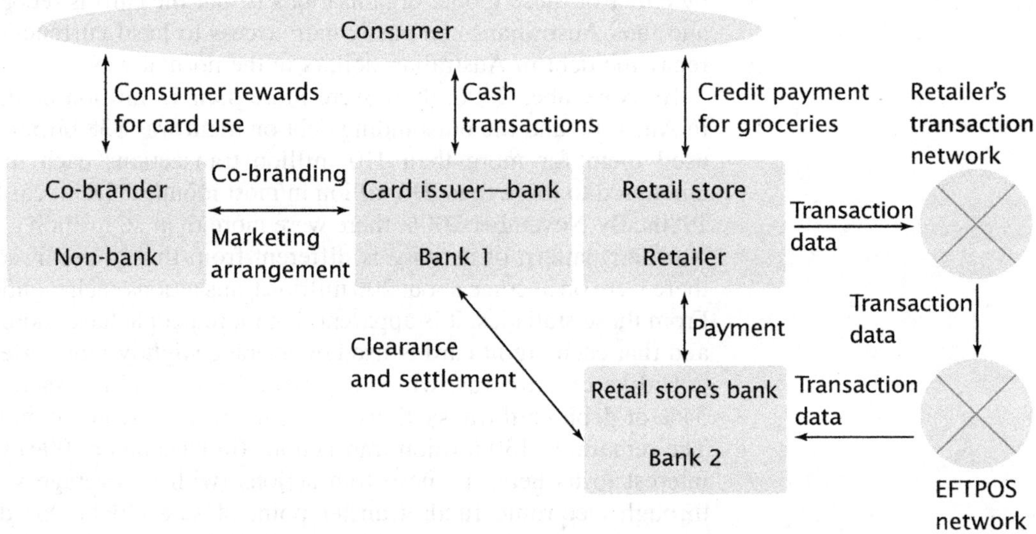

Figure 11.3 Credit card transactions

Source: Australian Bankers' Association.[14]

The merchant's bank charges a merchant service fee. This fee varies according to the merchant's annual turnover and provider. The reforms implemented by the RBA in the early 2000s have caused a decrease in these fees. In June 2005, the average credit card (Bankcard, Visa and Mastercard) fee was 0.92%, while for charge cards (Amex and Diners Club) the fee was about 2.3%.[13] Many merchants would prefer not to accept the cards more costly to them and, indeed, it is now commonplace for firms not to accept some cards. Alternatively, they may charge customers a fee to use such cards. For example, Telstra charges an extra 1% fee on payments made with Diners Club cards. Debit card fees are considerably less.

Now you might be tempted to think that, for a merchant, EFTPOS is not worth it. After all, most merchants do not charge their customers an extra fee for using plastic. You may think this is a legal restriction. In fact, it is not. As far back as 1980, the Trade Practices Commission, the predecessor of the Australian Competition and Consumer Commission (ACCC), authorised the Bankcard system on the condition that merchants were free to determine, according to market conditions, the prices they charged with payment by either cash or Bankcard. During the early 1990s, this view was ratified by two government inquiries and the passage of the Uniform Credit Code. However, Visa and MasterCard originally made it a condition of their contracts with merchants that they were not free to pass on the merchant service fees to customers as passing on the fee would have introduced differential pricing for goods and services. Even though this restriction has now been removed, this is the reason that, in the vast majority of cases, the same price is still charged for goods regardless of the method of payment.

What are the costs of different forms of payment? In 2001 the Australian Retailers Association gave evidence to the RBA of these costs in terms of the percentage of average transaction values and they can be seen in table 11.2. These costs are unlikely to have changed much in the last few years. However, the cost of handling credit card transactions has fallen from around 2% in 2001 to less than 1% in 2007. The cost of charge card transactions has decreased, but not to the same extent.

Table 11.2 Approximate costs of various retail payment methods, 2001

Payment method	Cost as percentage of average transaction value
Debit card	0.3
Cash	0.7
Cheque	1.4

Source: Reserve Bank of Australia.[15]

We are now in a better position to make a judgement about the worth of EFTPOS to any merchant. EFTPOS attracts more sales and increases turnover, decreases the need for and costs of keeping change, reduces currency inflow and banking risks and costs, and effects faster payment (direct to bank) than any other payment method. The cost of all these benefits is about a net 0.2–0.3% for credit card payments compared with cash and a net 0.5% for credit card payments compared with cheque payments. With debit card payments, there is no net cost. (Indeed there is a net 0.4% gain over receiving cash and a 1.1% gain over receiving cheques.) The rapid increase in the number of businesses offering EFTPOS facilities to their customers would suggest that, overall, the benefits exceed the costs.

Using direct entry (DE)

A final non-cash method of payment to be considered is direct entry (DE). DE transactions are effected by direct computer-to-computer links. While some countries use a central clearing house, in Australia the systems process the transactions bilaterally; that is, direct from payer's terminal to receiver's terminal. The great attraction of DE is its low cost in relation to either cash or non-cash methods such as cheques and, in the case of receipts by firms, the significantly reduced incidence of late payments and bad debts.

Both direct credit and direct debit are possible (indeed each transaction comprises a credit and a debit), but each transaction is classified according to its nature. Direct credit is currently used more widely than direct debit. The most common examples of direct credit are the payment of wages and salaries by large and medium-sized firms to their employees; the payment of dividends and interest to investors; and the payment of suppliers by large firms with thousands of suppliers such as Woolworths. In 2002–03, about 900 million direct credit transactions worth $3400 billion were made in Australia. By early 2007, the number had grown to more than 110 million transactions worth about $470 billion each month.[16] At an average of about $6000 per transaction, these transactions are considerably larger than the average debit or credit card transaction.

Direct debits are currently being used by many different types of firms, especially for (customers') regular payments such as telephone, water, electricity and gas bills, local government rates, insurance premiums, loan repayments including automatic payments of credit card monthly balances, newspaper and magazine subscriptions, and so on. In 2006–07, about 40 million direct debits worth $370 billion were effected monthly.[17] These transactions averaged $8500. Just think of the advantages this payment method — the right to extract the amount owed directly from the customers' bank accounts — gives to business enterprises. No more late receipts, no cash to count, no banking to be done and a reduced chance of never being paid. No wonder more and more firms are arranging this facility with their banks and offering the service to their customers.

FINANCE WORKSHOP 11.2

All payments, be they in the form of cash, cheque, credit card or debit card, require management, recording and control by those who receive them.

1. Trace the processes needed in a business receiving payments by cash to manage and control this facet of the business.
2. Why do cheques as a form of receiving payments cost more than cash?

lo5

Discuss some aspects of the management of accounts receivable.

Debtors or accounts receivable

Debtors or accounts receivable are a normal, and usually significant, component of most businesses. The most common exceptions to this statement are to be found in retail industries, such as fast-food outlets like KFC and McDonald's, and large supermarkets, such as Woolworths and Coles, where credit sales are a comparatively small component of total sales. Even retail stores that you might think would not have receivables, such as service stations, newsagents and pharmacies, do in fact extend credit to their better customers. Table 11.3 gives some selected data of receivables owed to some Australian firms. Note that receivables are a small proportion of current assets for Woolworths, but a large proportion for both ABC and CSL.

Table 11.3 Debtors of three Australian firms at 30 June 2006

Firm	Industry	Debtors ($m)	Proportion of current assets (%)
ABC Learning Centres	Child care	77	27
CSL	Vaccines and blood products	594	25
Woolworths	Retail supermarket, electronics	221	5

Sources: Data from the 2006 annual reports for the respective firms.

Benefits and costs of granting credit

Why do firms sell goods or provide services to their customers on the promise that they will be paid, when they are well aware that there is a chance that they won't be paid? As with most financial decisions, there are benefits and costs, and financial managers face a trade-off between those advantages and disadvantages. With careful management, it is hoped that benefits can be maximised and costs minimised.

The benefits of granting credit include:

- increased sales, because of:
  - attracting new customers from other cash-only suppliers
  - encouraging customers to bring planned purchases forward
  - attracting impulsive purchases
  - attracting customers who would not otherwise have purchased at all
- reduced cost of making sales, such as in the case where counter staff merely fill out delivery dockets and specialist pricing people calculate actual charges.

The costs of granting credit include:

- the opportunity cost of the funds tied up; there is no direct return to funds as there would be if the funds were invested on the money market
- the cost of the (hopefully small) proportion of slow payers and bad debts; even with the best of credit rating and collection systems there will normally be a small percentage of debtors who will be slow to pay or will not pay at all
- the cost of administering the system, including cost of office staff, stationery, postage, telephone and possibly specialist collection services.

Determinants of the level of debtors

The value of debtors carried by any firm depends on a number of policies and processes that the firm determines and manages. Figure 11.4 gives an overview of these determinants and we will discuss each of the determinants in turn.

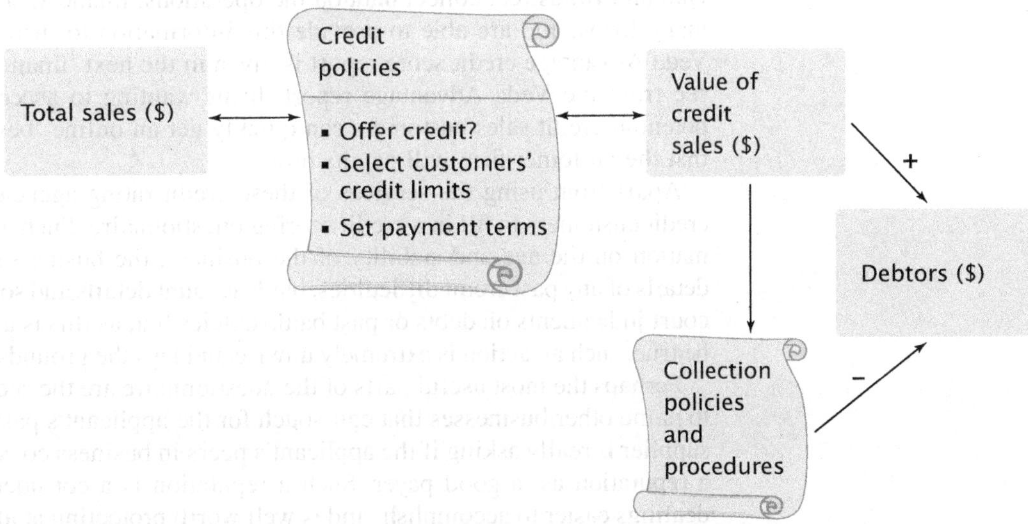

Figure 11.4 Determinants of the level of debtors

Total sales

The value of total sales has an impact on the value of credit sales, so long as the firm exercises a policy of offering sales on credit. Thus, it follows that the greater the total sales, the greater the credit sales and the greater the value of debtors. Once credit policies have been formulated, the financial manager is likely to have little impact on the value of total sales. Rather, this is the preserve of the marketing manager and other sub-administrators such as the pricing, advertising and quality control managers. Total sales and credit policies have an impact on the level of credit sales. Moreover, credit policies also have an impact on total sales, as we saw in the previous section.

Credit policies

Credit policies determine the value of credit sales. Credit policies may be conveniently broken up into four parts, all of which are managed by financial managers. These parts are all decision variables, in that financial managers are free to make whatever decisions they think best to achieve the firms' objectives. The four parts are:

- deciding to offer credit, or not
- selecting suitable creditworthy customers
- setting credit limits
- deciding payment terms.

Of the four parts, the first is where financial managers have the least control. Competition in markets normally forces suppliers to offer similar services and trading terms. The stronger the competitive pressures, the more likely no firm can stand out from the pack and offer significantly less advantageous selling terms. If a firm's competitors offer credit, it too will be forced to offer credit sales. Additionally, in terms of pure economics and the 'economic line of thought', it is highly likely that the marginal revenue from credit-induced sales at normal profitable prices, initially at least, will exceed the marginal cost of these sales. In other words, a firm not offering credit sales at all is very likely reducing its potential profitability.

Businesses seeking to determine the creditworthiness of potential customers face different tasks, depending on the size and status of the applicant customer. Very large firms may be rated by the global ratings agencies, such as Moody's and Standard & Poor's, and these ratings are publicly available. Other mercantile agents such as Veda Advantage and Dun and Bradstreet collect data on the operations, financial standing and credit history for many firms, and are able to provide this information to firms which require it. A sample Veda Advantage credit score report is given in the next 'finance world' feature. As you can see from the Veda Advantage report, firms wanting to ascertain the creditworthiness of potential credit sales customers can quickly get an online 'best estimate' of the likelihood that the customer firm will pay its bills.

Apart from using the services of these credit rating agencies, many firms ask potential credit customers to fill in a credit scoring questionnaire. Such a questionnaire asks for information on the age and stability of the business, the business's accountants and solicitors, details of any past credit difficulties, bank account details and so on. A firm may lie about past court judgements on debts or past bankruptcies but, as this is a signed statement certified to be true, such an action is extremely unwise and lays the grounds for further legal difficulties.

Perhaps the most useful parts of the questionnaire are the sections requiring the applicant to name other businesses that can vouch for the applicant's past creditworthiness. Thus, the supplier is really asking if the applicant's peers in business consider that firm to be, and have a reputation as, a good payer. Such a reputation is a considerable benefit as it makes all dealings easier to accomplish, and is well worth protecting at almost all costs.

More sophisticated businesses may use more complex credit scoring models. These models rely on quantifying the answers to questions about issues considered to be determinants of creditworthiness and combining the quantitative data into a model. The data are compared with past experience in that particular industry. The result is a numerical estimate of creditworthiness. This type of modelling has several advantages:

- consistency
- quantification of risk
- consistent refinement of knowledge of predictor variables
- efficiency in decision making
- delegation of decision making to lower-level staff.

Firms granting credit normally set an upper credit limit, either explicitly or implicitly. The credit limit is set with regard to the level of knowledge of the customer and the expected size of the sales during any period. Thus, a new customer about which little is known may have a relatively low credit limit imposed. On the other hand, a potato grower contemplating a new contract with Woolworths to supply potatoes all year round is not at all likely to impose a low credit limit. Similarly, when a firm expects the monthly sales to a customer to be $20 000, it will not set a $5000 credit limit. Normally, credit limits are increased as time passes and the business relationship has been successful.

The final of the four decisions that a financial manager must make relates to the terms of credit to be offered. Credit terms involve the possibility of a discount for early payment, (if so) what discount for what period, and the total allowed credit period. The use of trade credit was discussed in the last chapter, as were discount terms and the cost of not taking advantage of such allowances when offered. To reiterate, discount terms are often stated in the form '1/10, net 30', meaning 1% discount if paid in 10 days and net if paid within 30 days. The standard net period is 30 days in most industries, although many firms that do not want to finance large amounts of debtors often state their term as 'net 7 days'.

The aim of granting a discount is to provide a monetary incentive for debtors to pay quickly. A 2% discount naturally reduces a $100 invoice to $98, which is not a large difference, but it also reduces a $100 000 invoice to $98 000, which is probably a savings worth having in most businesses. Also, as we discussed in the previous chapter, by not taking discounts, firms are using the suppliers' funds but the annualised interest cost of those funds is very high.

Some firms set penalty interest rates, or accounting charges, if accounts are not paid during the credit period. Still others, and we saw an example in the case of inventory financing, in effect charge their customers interest for the use of trade credit immediately from the day of supply. This practice is standard in the motor vehicle and farm machinery industries. Suppliers such as Ford, Volvo, General Motors and John Deere have set up finance subsidiaries to formalise the supply of credit, but essentially the manufacturer is supplying stock on credit and charging customers interest immediately.

Collection policies and procedures

Customer Jane wants a washing machine, goes to Harvey Norman and buys an electronic whiz-bang machine for $1000 on credit. She is extremely grateful, as the old machine was not worth repairing, and the baby's nappies are piling up. She agrees to pay the full amount in 60 days. The account arrives and she pays up, just as every other customer does. Right? No, not all customers pay on time. They were grateful for the credit and they've made use of the goods, but things happen. They're having difficulty finding the money. There are just so many bills!

What does a supplier do to ensure it collects the highest possible proportion of its accounts receivable? The answer is to have set policies and procedures in place, monitor the ageing of accounts and apply the procedures rigorously. These days, when almost all firms have computerised accounting packages (post the introduction of the GST which forced many smaller firms to install electronic systems), accessing a debtors' ageing schedule is easy as such schedules are standard in accounting packages. Ageing schedules identify which accounts are unpaid and overdue. Additionally, these overdue accounts are classified by the period overdue, such as 30 days, 60 days, 90 days and so on. The following 'corporate financial governance' feature gives you an extract from the CSL Ltd 2006 annual report showing an example of an ageing schedule.

The collection process often follows a pattern like this:

- send an 'account rendered' statement which reiterates the amount owing
- post an 'account overdue' letter which reminds the debtor of the account

- telephone to speak to the responsible person, who normally finds it difficult to deny that the account *should* be paid and may make some structured payment arrangement
- put the unpaid account into the hands of a solicitor or collection agency
- in some cases with goods that have not been substantially transformed by the buyer, the goods may be reclaimed by the seller. (See the next section for a discussion of Romalpa clauses.)

The timing of these steps should be established and set down in the firm's collection policy documentation. Otherwise, things tend to drift on, steps are not taken, the accounts are inexorably getting older, and experience has shown all businesspeople that the older an account the less likely it will ever be collected. An account not collected is a loss to the firm — a loss of profit and a loss of all the other expenses which have been put into the making and selling of the good or service.

CORPORATE FINANCIAL GOVERNANCE

Here is an example of an ageing schedule for trade receivables. It is an extract from the 2006 annual report for CSL Ltd. Note the process the company uses to identify impaired assets. Only 16% of the aged (> 90 days) receivables are considered impaired, and this amount is only 2.6% of total trade receivables.

CSL Limited and its controlled entities

Notes to the Financial Statements continued for the year ended 30 June 2006

36 Financial Instruments (continued)

Credit Risk (continued)

An analysis of trade receivables that are past due and the allowance for doubtful debts is as follows: All other financial assests are less than 30 days overdue.

Financial assets are considered impaired where there is objective evidence that the consolidated entity will not be able to collect all amounts due according to the original trade and other receivable terms. An allowance for doubtful debts is created for the difference between the assets carrying amount and the present value of estimated future cashflows. The consolidated entity's trading terms do not generally include the requirement for customers to provide collateral as security for financial assets.

For the period ended 30 June 2006	Not impaired	Impaired	Allowance for doubtful debts
Trade and other receivables:			
less than 30 days overdue	357451	–	–
more than 30 but less than 90 days overdue	84605	–	–
more than 90 days overdue	82926	13744	13744
	524842	13744	13744

Source: CSL Limited.[18]

Getting the timing right is an art and depends to some extent on the type of industry and the norms within each industry. Sending out an account rendered is usually not a problem. Customers are normally happy to admit to themselves that they have not paid and that the suppliers have a right to ask again for their money. However, account overdue letters, which often contain carefully worded threats, can be the end of a business relationship if the customers feel they have been sent out prematurely. Telephoning customers to ask for payment, while not a pleasant task, can be successful when carefully done. Rational people are usually happy to admit they are having financial difficulty and are often quite pleased to be offered a way to pay either at some future date or by a structured series of payments over time.

The final step in the process is to put the matter into the hands of a collection agency, although many collection agencies prefer to be involved quite early in the process. Collection agencies issue final letters of demand or notices of intention to take legal action, make telephone calls and personal visits, and finally take action in the courts.

Collecting debts costs money, due both to the staff time and cash costs associated with the processes. The more time and money allocated to the activity, the greater will be the collection success and the shorter will be the collection period. However, there is not likely to be a fixed relationship between collection costs and collection success. In other words, the forgetful and timid debtors will pay early in the process at little cost, while the ruthless, manipulative and deceitful will be costly to overcome and eventually collect the debts. Indeed, many debts are not collected at all. On the other hand, looking at the problem from an economics viewpoint again, the firm that has never had a bad debt has almost certainly denied itself business based on credit and that would have increased its profits.

Firms may judge the effectiveness of their collection policies and processes by making use of ratio analysis. The most useful ratio is average collection period (ACP), which is average debtors divided by average daily credit sales. In other words, the ratio gives the number of days of the credit sales value which remain outstanding. This number may then be compared with:

- previous periods for the same firm
- industry benchmarks.

A decreasing ACP may indicate more effective collection processes, which is good, but may also indicate that too much time and effort is being put into collections or that credit policy has become so restrictive that the firm is missing out on sales. Conversely, an increasing ACP may indicate less effectiveness in collections, too little expenditure or too lenient a credit policy.

Another measure of the success of collection policies is the percentage of bad debt — bad debts divided by credit sales for the same period. As before, a firm may compare this value with the values computed for previous periods or against industry benchmarks. The same comments relate to either decreasing or increasing values as were noted for decreasing or increasing ACPs.

Credit sales to debtors

Now that we have examined total sales, credit policies, and collection policies and procedures we can review the whole of the determinants of the level of debtors. Credit policies to some extent impact on total sales, and total sales when considered in conjunction with credit policies determine the value of credit sales. Credit sales increase the value of debtors at any point of time, but collection policies also impact on the value of debtors. Efficient collection decreases the value of debtors.

In summary, this discussion has shown you that managing debtors in any firm is not a straightforward scientific process. There are many policies and procedures to establish and manage and many value judgements to be made. The financial manager draws on past

FINANCE WORLD

Online business score

Veda Advantage is the largest single source of data-based business information in Australia and New Zealand. It offers a wide range of credit scoring and credit risk modelling products as well as being active in debt collection. This is their sample credit score report.

veda ADVANTAGE

www.vedaadvantage.com
Veda Advantage Information Services and Solutions Ltd.
ACN: 000 602 862

Business Express

Current Date: 13/02/2007 15:19

Business Name:	MALVERN BATHROOM SHOP *
Business Number:	0314558W
Business Status:	Registered
Nature of Business:	BATHROOM SHOP
Date Commenced:	23/03/1973

Principal Place of Business
19 CLAREMONT AVE , MALVERN , VIC 3144

Bureau Score Details
Bureau Scorecards utilise all available data to calculate a risk estimate. This is based on analysis of the association of all the data with future adverse outcomes.

Bureau Score Result
Relative Risk: -3.37 times worse than Veda Advantage average.

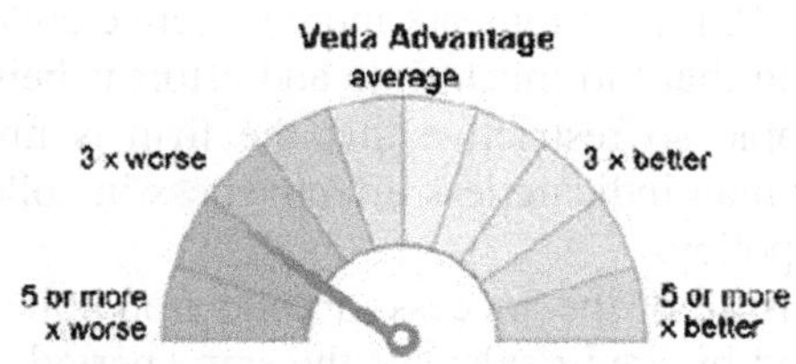

About The Credit Score
The credit score for this business has been calculated using Veda Advantage's Company/Business scorecard. The relative Risk position indicated is based on a comparison with the Veda Advantage population. The odds of recording adverse credit information within 24 months of an enquiry are 16:1

Key Contributing Factors impacting this assessment are:	Impact on Risk
Defaults recorded	Greatly Increases Risk
History of type of Credit sought	Marginally Increases Risk
Time Since Incorporation	Marginally Decreases Risk
Shopping Pattern	Marginally Increases Risk

Figure 11.5: Veda Advantage business score report

Source: Veda Advantage.[19]

experience, current knowledge and a 'delicate touch' to be successful. In conjunction with these, financial managers have access to financial tools, one of which is the Business Express report referred to in the 'finance world' feature opposite.

Romalpa clauses

One of the most vexing of many legal issues pertaining to the sale of goods is how sellers may reserve their rights to the goods if buyers who are extended credit fail to pay. Normally when goods are sold, title passes at the time the parties intend. Under the Sale of Goods Acts of each state and territory, the property in the deliverable goods passes to the buyer when the contract is made, regardless of when payment is made. 'Deliverable' in relation to goods merely indicates that the goods are in a condition or have been transformed to a state that is acceptable to the buyer.

When a credit buyer contracts for goods, title normally passes then to the buyer. If the buyer does not pay the account, the seller may pursue the buyer for the debt. If the buyer goes bankrupt, the seller joins all the other creditors who come forward with unpaid accounts and may eventually be paid a few cents in the dollar as the final outcome. In order to try to achieve a better outcome for themselves, sellers have tried to isolate their goods from the other remaining assets of the failed buyer. They have done this by inserting retention of title clauses in contracts of sale or on the invoices that give the details of each sale.

Romalpa clauses: legal conditions included on credit sales documentation to ensure title to the goods described does not pass to the buyer until the goods are fully paid for

Retention of title clauses are generally called **Romalpa clauses** after the case in the UK Court of Appeal, *Aluminium Industrie Vaassen BV v. Romalpa Aluminium Ltd* [1976] 1 WLR 676. (This decision and others following have been upheld in Australian courts.) The purpose of Romalpa clauses is to allow sellers to recover the goods (or the proceeds of the sale of the goods if they have already been sold), if the buyer becomes insolvent. Essentially, the sellers are trying to ensure that the value of their goods does not become part of the general pool of funds that will eventually be divided among all creditors.

Romalpa clauses are worded along the following lines:

> Ownership in these goods is retained by the supplier until payment is made for the goods and all other goods supplied by the supplier. If such goods are sold by the customer before payment to the supplier and if they become constituents of other goods then the proceeds of the sale thereof shall be the property of the supplier.

Managing inventories

lo6

Discuss the issues pertaining to the management of inventories.

Inventories or stock normally form part of the stock of current assets for most firms involved in manufacturing or the sale of goods. Firms selling services, on the other hand, normally have insignificant values of stock, as stocks are limited to office supplies, vehicle maintenance supplies, and so on. The purpose of holding stock for retail firms is to ensure that sales can be effected immediately. Manufacturers hold stock so that production can be carried on without undue hold-ups due to lack of raw materials, should there be any disruption in the normal course of supply.

Table 11.4 gives the value of inventories at 30 June 2006 for the three Australian firms we have been tracking in this chapter. The information in this table provides evidence for the statements in the previous paragraph. The first firm — a service organisation — has virtually no stock. ABC Learning Centres only has stocks because its has expanded into the importing of educational toys. CSL is a manufacturer and wholesaler, so carries large stocks, while Woolworths is a large retailer carrying nearly 60% of its current assets as inventories.

Table 11.4 Value of inventories of several Australian firms at 30 June 2006

Firm	Industry	Inventories ($m)	Proportion of current assets (%)	Proportion of total assets (%)
ABC Learning Centres	Child care	5	2	0.2
CSL	Vaccines and blood products	973	42	23
Woolworths	Retail supermarket, electronics	2316	56	17

Sources: Data from the 2006 annual reports for the respective firms.

Types of inventories

There are three types of inventories:

1. raw materials
2. work in progress
3. finished goods.

Raw materials are held by all types of manufacturers to ensure that production may be carried on without delay, should there be interruption in normal receivals. Thus, beef producers keep stocks of fencing materials; sawmills keep stocks of logs; brickmakers keep stocks of clay; bakers keep stocks of flour, sugar and yeast; candlemakers keep stocks of wax and wicks. Goodman Fielder, an integrated grain processor and baker, carries stocks that include unmilled grains at its flour mills and milled flour at its bakeries, oilseeds at its vegetable oil plants and vegetable oils at its margarine factories.

Work in progress or work in process (WIP) consists of goods (or services) where some of the required work operations have been completed and some have not. Normally, the more complex the transformation process, the more likely a firm will have WIP stocks. These come about for two reasons:

- The firm is unable to adjust all sectors of the process so that the 'steadily being transformed' material flows forward at a constant rate.
- The firm desires to hold some stocks at each point so that interruptions at any one point do not stop the whole factory. The stocks are then available at each point to take up the slack.

Thus a foundry where aluminium gearbox casings are cast may have three processes — casting, rough grinding and precision finishing. Stocks of rough casts are held as feedstock for the grinding section and stocks of ground units as feedstock for the precision finishers. In this way, the work of the factory can seldom be held up due to an internal breakdown or disruption.

In addition to manufacturing firms managing their WIP stocks, some service firms also account for and manage such stock where the values are significant. Thus in large advertising agencies, where advertising campaigns have significant staff time expended before the final 'product' is completed, accounting firms, audit firms, software developers and architects are all likely to have to manage WIP.

Benefits and costs of holding inventories

Managing inventories is an art, although there are many techniques managers can use to transform much of the role into a science. We discuss many of these techniques later in this chapter. First, we must consider the benefits and costs of holding inventories. Suppose you manage a truck stop on a major highway and you sell a wide variety of products including fuel, oil, spare parts such as radiator hoses and spark plugs, fast food, ice-cream, sweets, drinks and newspapers. How much of each type of goods should you stock? What are the benefits and what are the costs of holding the stocks?

The benefits of holding stocks are:

- sales are made and profits gained
- cross-sales are made and profits increased (trucks drivers stop for fuel, but also buy meals, drinks, ice-cream and newspapers)
- goodwill is built up ('that place always has what you want') and 'no stock' costs are avoided ('that place never has what you want, let's go elsewhere').

However, there are costs that must be balanced against the benefits. The costs of holding stocks include:

- ordering costs
- holding costs.

Ordering costs include the time and cash costs involved in placing orders, freight and handling costs imposed by suppliers, and quantity discounts forgone if only small orders are made. In general, the larger the order, the smaller and less significant will be the sum of these costs. However, making only large orders may not be possible because of the nature of the goods. Large orders also increase the holding costs.

Holding costs include:

- storage and display costs
- insurance costs
- deterioration and obsolescence
- wholesale price changes
- theft
- financing costs.

Storage costs can be quite high for some types of goods. The grains, oilseeds and flours held by Goodman Fielder, for example, must all be held in specially built silos which must be weatherproof and vermin-proof. In addition, some may be climate controlled to manage the changes that inevitably happen with 'living' or organic materials. Coming back to your truck stop, fuel is stored underground in large tanks and the storage must be managed to minimise the build-up of water through condensation or leakage into the fuel. Similarly, ice-cream and milk drinks must be stored at the correct temperatures to ensure public health but also to minimise storage damage and product deterioration.

Another holding cost involves display costs. Think about some of the modern bright and airy truck stops you've patronised, with whole banks of tall fridges of cold water, colas, other soft drinks, fruit juices and milk drinks. Compare those with some of the older places with a few battered old drink coolers that you have to rummage through to find your desired drink. The display costs of the first places are high, but the throughput is large; the costs of the second type are low but throughput and profitability are very low.

Stock should be insured unless the manager believes the firm can afford to lose the lot or that the risk is so small that losing the lot is hardly possible. Stock can be insured for storm and water damage, fire, theft and fusion (loss of refrigeration due to malfunction of electric motors). Normally, the higher the value of inventory, the higher the premium. There may be some economies of scale for very large inventories because the rate per $1000 of cover may decrease as the sum insured increases.

Deterioration and obsolescence are always risks with the holding of stock for resale. Back to the truck stop. Fuel deteriorates over a long period, milk deteriorates over a few days and bread deteriorates over a matter of hours. Stocks have to be managed to ensure that losses are minimised. Diesel fuel comes in either winter or summer blends. Summer blends have more impurities in the form of wax left in the fuel, because it costs more to remove them and they do not constitute a problem in warm periods. However, a diesel engine fuelled with summer fuel and run during a cold snap can have wax solidify in its injectors and refuse to run. Our truck stop would soon get a very nasty reputation if it sold summer fuel in wintertime. Similarly, a radiator hose for a 1975 FE Holden left in stock in 2008 has a poor chance of selling.

When wholesale prices change, the value of inventory changes. What is the correct valuation method for inventory? The correct answer to this question probably depends on the purpose of the valuation. The easiest method to use is historical cost, the most usual accounting method, because normally these values are easy to find and are built into an appropriate management accounting system. However, if the firm were to be sold as a going concern, then the most appropriate method is market value. Market value may be the same as historical cost if none of the stock is very old and prices have not changed. If prices have gone up, for example, then market value of the stock will be higher than historical cost. If prices have gone down significantly, market value will be less than historical cost. If prices are regularly rising, a manager might make a conscious decision to hold larger stocks to take advantage of this situation. In this case, if the rises are large enough, holding costs may be cut to the point where there are no net costs. Indeed there may be gains made by holding stocks through negative net holding costs.

Theft or shoplifting occurs in practically all retail situations and indeed in almost all businesses. Theft can be insured for but, in many smaller instances, managers do not make claims. This is because it may not be economic to spend the time making the claim. Additionally, many insurance policies include minimum claim clauses to reduce the number of small claims that might otherwise be made. The more open and self-service display shelving is, the higher the rate of shoplifting is likely to be. On the other hand, the more open and self-service the display shelving is, the higher sales are likely to be as people give in to spur-of the-moment decisions to buy those goods.

Finally, there are the financing costs. Funds tied up in inventory could be invested elsewhere, so have an opportunity cost. If the best alternative investment yields 5%, then the cost of holding inventory, from only the financing viewpoint, is 5% or $50 per $1000 of stock. In practice, the best alternative investment is probably an investment elsewhere in the firm, but it may be an investment externally on the short-term money market.

In making the decision about the level of stocks to be held, the manager must trade off all these costs against the benefits. Normally, holding stocks is an incremental thing. As businesses become established, turnover improves, cash flow improves and stocks tend to build up as managers see the need to hold more of this, hold more of that and to try this and try that.

Management techniques

Three management techniques are discussed in this section to show how financial managers may be assisted in their management of inventories. The techniques are:

- anticipatory buying
- maintaining minimum safety level of stock
- economic order quantity (EOQ) theory.

The first two techniques are used very frequently by managers working in all sizes of firms, from small sole traders and partnerships to large companies. The third technique is likely to be found in use only in larger, more sophisticated operations.

Anticipatory buying is undertaken to buy in stock before an anticipated or known shortage or price rise occurs. For example, in February 2007, it was reported in Adelaide that grape growers who had previously lacked buyers for their wine grapes had now found markets. Late in 2006 the large wine companies had decided to buy in more fruit because of an anticipated short harvest in 2007 due to frost and drought.

Many managers maintain either an explicit or implicit minimum safety level of stock. The level is explicit when documented in stock management records, or implicit when the requisite level is an idea or 'feeling' on the part of the manager. For example, stock would be replenished at our truck stop either by telephone or email, with the order initiated by the manager, or by means of travelling salesmen who travel with stocks on board large vans. This latter means is normally the way confectionery and drinks are replenished at many such outlets. Do we need some more Jumbo-Jubes? How many are there on the shelf? Only one packet. OK, give me another dozen packets. How many packets of Wrigley's peppermint? Only one outer and three loose packets. Better have another five outers. And so the process goes on, looking at every relevant stock item and ordering if the level of stock is down below some re-order point.

While many such re-order points are in the heads of managers, it would be better if they were documented. Why? Managers gain a good deal of experience in knowing their usual customers, knowing usual demand patterns and knowing how long it takes to get supplies from ordering point to display. A new manager can also learn these patterns in time. However, the learning period is reduced when a manager retires or leaves suddenly or a business is sold if this knowledge that has been gained from past experience is written down.

The third technique involves the economic order quantity (EOQ) theory. The EOQ tool is based on the knowledge that the cost of stock consists of the holding costs and the ordering costs. EOQ calculates the optimal size of each new order by combining the increasing holding costs with the fixed order cost which, of course, declines per unit as the order size increases (see figure 11.6). EOQ theory combines inventory carrying costs, ordering costs and total demand over a planning period to estimate the optimal size of each order. The EOQ theory assumes Q is the inventory order size. If no stock were re-ordered until inventory had fallen to zero, the average inventory level over a planning period would be $\frac{Q}{2}$. Total inventory costs equal holding costs plus ordering costs. If holding costs per unit equal H, then total holding costs equal $\frac{Q}{2} \times H$ or $\frac{QH}{2}$. Similarly, if total demand over the planning period is D, orders are made in lot sizes of Q and the ordering cost is O per order, then total ordering cost is $\frac{D}{Q} \times O$ or $\frac{DO}{Q}$. The total cost is calculated using equation 11.1.

$$\boldsymbol{TC = \frac{QH}{2} + \frac{DO}{Q}} \qquad [11.1]$$

where TC = total cost
D = demand per period
O = order cost per order
Q = the economic order quantity
H = holding cost per unit

We can graph these curves as shown in figure 11.6. The holding costs curve must be a rising line through the origin. Substitute a few values for Q into the equation to prove this to yourself. Ordering costs must be a negatively (downward) sloped line, as the fixed amount (fixed for each scenario), DO, is spread over ever-increasing order sizes, Q. These two curves may be summed vertically to give a total cost curve, $\frac{QH}{2} + \frac{DO}{Q}$. The total cost curve will be U-shaped or concave to the horizontal axis, and the minimum cost point will be where the two curves intersect at Q_1.

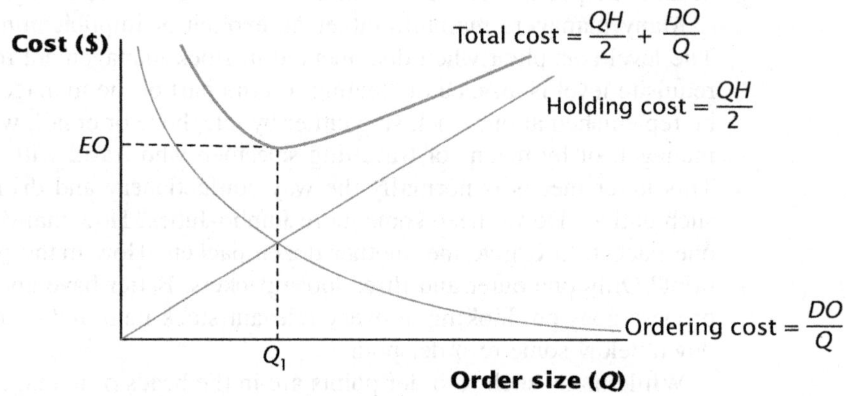

Figure 11.6 Total cost of order

For those of you learned in calculus (and this bit of knowledge is unimportant for those of you who are not), you will know that the minimum point of the total cost curve can be found by taking the first derivative with respect to Q, setting that equation equal to 0 and solving for Q.

$$\text{If } TC = \frac{QH}{2} + \frac{DO}{Q}$$

$$TC = 0.5HQ + DOQ^{-1}$$

$$\text{Let } \frac{dTC}{dQ} = 0.5H - DOQ^{-2} = 0$$

$$0.5H = \frac{DO}{Q^2}$$

$$Q^2 = \frac{2DO}{H} \quad \text{and so} \quad Q = \sqrt{\frac{2DO}{H}}$$

$$Q = \sqrt{\frac{2DO}{H}} \qquad [11.2]$$

Equation 11.2 calculates the economic order quantity.

EXAMPLE 11.1

Calculating EOQ

Suppose Bennie's Truck Stop sells 1000 cases containing 24 cans of Coke each year. Ordering costs are $1 per order and holding costs are $1 per case. What is the EOQ?

$$Q = \sqrt{\frac{2DO}{H}}$$

$$Q = \sqrt{\frac{2 \times 1000 \times 1}{1}}$$

$$= \sqrt{2000}$$

$$= 45 \text{ cases}$$

This order would last about 16 days (that is, $\frac{45 \times 365}{1000}$) at a constant rate of demand.

The EOQ model, like all theories in economics, rests on several assumptions. If these assumptions are violated, the model usually will not suggest an appropriate solution and must be amended to take account of the new circumstances. These are the assumptions.

- Demand is known and constant from day to day. If this assumption is violated and managers are not able to forecast demand accurately from day to day, then a minimum safety level of stock must be kept to ensure stock is available at all times.
- Ordering and holding costs are known and constant. Businesses use best estimates all the time to ascertain costs. If costs change, the calculation may be repeated with the new data. One calculation does not last a lifetime.
- Delivery is instantaneous. While no delivery is likely to be instantaneous, many delivery times are known and these times can be factored into the model by bringing order times forward or increasing safety stocks to cope with delivery delays.

Just-in-time

Inspection of the EOQ equation will show you that the estimated EOQ in any set of circumstances will drop as holding costs rise, as H is the denominator in the equation (and the larger the denominator, the smaller the quotient). Price inflation in Australia was severe in the 1970s and 1980s, with the index of prices of traded goods rising from 20.7 in 1971–72 to 63.0 in 1980–81 and 100 in 1989–90. In the two decades prior to 1971–72, the index had moved very little each year, from 21.4 in 1951–52 to 20.7 in 1971–72.[20] As a result of the sharp rises in prices throughout the 1970s and 1980s, businesses tended to cut their holdings of inventory to save costs. The need to cut costs also drew managers' attention to the 'just-in-time' (JIT) philosophy.

The JIT manufacturing philosophy was originally developed by the Toyota Motor Company of Japan in the 1960s. JIT spread rapidly through Japanese manufacturing and helped manufacturers to offer high-quality, cheap consumer goods, delivered on short lead times. The apparent benefits of JIT attracted other firms to adopt JIT and it spread throughout the world. An additional driving force behind the adoption of JIT in Australia was a program sponsored by the Technology Transfer Council and the Department of Industry, Technology and Commerce in 1985. The program involved groups of manufacturers in both Victoria and New South Wales being provided with funding to aid the implementation of JIT.

The JIT philosophy encompasses more than merely limited inventories. It emphasises demand-driven production (a pull rather than a push system), reduction in setup times, high quality (zero defects), continuous improvement and multiskilled workers as well as smaller inventories. Essentially, JIT production is concerned with the elimination of activities that do not add value to the product being manufactured.

The reduction of inventories provides the benefits of savings in carrying costs through reduced storage and handling costs, lower insurance costs, smaller losses due to spoilage, obsolescence and theft, and decreased opportunity costs associated with having money tied up in inventory. However, the reduction of inventories also exposes inefficiencies in the manufacturing system, as the unplanned increase or decrease in inventories no longer masks manufacturing problems.

To achieve reduced raw material inventory, long-term relationships with reliable suppliers are important. Additionally, it is claimed the JIT system allows businesses to become more responsive to customer requirements and to be more able to compete in an increasingly competitive business environment.

Although JIT has many benefits, adopting JIT production does not automatically increase profit because the benefits from JIT adoption may be offset by its many direct and indirect costs. Significant training and implementation costs are associated with the adoption of JIT. Reducing raw materials inventory levels increases a firm's dependence on the stability of its supply chain and may result in increased shipping and receiving costs due to small, frequent trips. Small inventories can increase the risk of shut-down when there are truckers' strikes, suppliers are unreliable or there are excessive machinery breakdowns.

FINANCE WORKSHOP 11.3

Mack's Market and General Store is the only store within 200 km on a highway running across a desert area. Mack's stocks 'everything', ranging from fuel and some emergency parts for vehicles, food, drinks, clothing and agricultural requirements to tissues, pharmaceuticals and toothpaste. What are the benefits and costs of holding stock for the owners of Mack's?

executive summary

lo1 describe the dual meaning of 'cash'

- Cash is all the currency that the firm has on hand.
- Cash is also all the liquid or near liquid assets that a firm holds or has ready access to.

lo2 discuss the motives for holding cash

- There are three reasons that cash is held:
  - the transactions motive
  - the precautionary motive
  - the speculative motive.
- The transactions motive is that cash is held so that sales and purchases may be completed easily.
- Well-managed firms, as a precaution, keep a buffer of cash that is available should the need for it arise.
- The speculative motive involves holding cash to make speculative purchases when the opportunity arises.
- Forward purchases of materials likely to be in short supply in a later period is not speculation.

lo3 discuss the issues related to the management of cash

- The issues which are related to the management of cash include:
  - the timing of cash flows
  - the financial imperative of having sufficient cash
  - the cost of cash
  - the cost of not having enough cash.
- The timing of cash flows depends on their sources, which include:
  - cash sales
  - credit sales, when the debtors eventually pay their accounts
  - sales of used or unwanted assets
  - capital injections
  - short-term loans
  - long-term loan funding.
- Cash flows out from the firm to service a further four needs:
  - purchase of inventories
  - purchase of labour, materials and other services
  - purchase of assets (fixed or intangible)
  - payment of taxes.
- A firm must always have sufficient cash on hand to meet its financial obligations.
- The cost of holding cash may be thought of in terms of two issues:
  - the opportunity cost of holding currency, rather than short-term securities, or the cost of holding very short-term securities instead of longer short-term securities
  - the cost of ensuring physical security of currency.
- The cost of not having enough cash may be the loss or failure of the business.

lo4 describe some electronic methods of transferring funds

- The use of EFTPOS helps in the continuing problem of managing cash.
- By offering EFTPOS to their customers, businesses can:
  - attract more sales and increase turnover
  - decrease the need for change and the opportunity costs of keeping it
  - reduce currency inflow and thus reduce security and banking risks and costs
  - be paid faster.
- On the negative side, there are additional costs attached to offering EFTPOS to customers.
- Direct electronic entry transactions are widely used and growing strongly for regular payments such as wages, superannuation payments and dividends, and for regular supplies such as gas, electricity, rates, loan repayments and subscriptions.

lo5 discuss some aspects of the management of accounts receivable

- The benefits of granting credit include:
  - increased sales, through attracting new customers from other cash-only suppliers, encouraging customers to bring planned purchases forward, attracting impulsive purchases and attracting customers who would not otherwise have purchased at all
  - reduced cost of making sales such as in the case where counter staff merely fill out delivery dockets and specialist pricing people calculate actual charges.
- The costs of granting credit include:
  - the opportunity cost of the funds tied up as there is no direct return to funds as there would be if the funds were invested on the money market
  - the cost of the (hopefully small) proportion of slow payers and bad debts, as even with the best of credit ranking and collection systems there will normally be a small percentage of debtors who will be slow to pay or will not pay at all
  - the cost of administering the system including office staff, stationery, postage, telephone and possibly specialist collection services.
- The level of debtors carried by a firm depends on policies and processes the firm decides on and manages.
- Credit policies are a vital determinant of credit sales.
- Collection policies and procedures affect the value of debtors.
- Firms use Romalpa clauses to try to protect their revenue should some of their debtors go bankrupt.

lo6 discuss the issues pertaining to the management of inventories

- Inventories comprise raw materials, work in progress and finished goods.
- The benefits of holding stocks are:
  - sales are made and profits gained
  - cross-sales are made and profits increased (truck drivers stop for fuel, but also buy meals, drinks, ice-cream and newspapers)
  - goodwill is built up ('that place always has what you want') and 'no stock' costs are avoided ('that place never has what you want, let's go elsewhere').

- Costs must be balanced against the benefits.
- The costs of holding stocks comprise ordering costs and holding costs.
- EOQ theory may guide ordering by suggesting the optimal order size.
- The EOQ tool allows the cost of ordering to be allocated over possible order size and combined with the increasing cost of holding stock.

Key terms

budget, p. 389
cash, p. 386
cash budget, p. 389
embezzlement, p. 390
insolvent, p. 390
precaution, p. 387
Romalpa clauses, p. 403
speculation, p. 388

Learning chart

Learning objective	Questions	Self-test problems	Financial problems
lo1 describe the dual meaning of 'cash'	11.1		
lo2 discuss the motives for holding cash	11.2, 11.3, 11.4		
lo3 discuss the issues related to the management of cash	11.5, 11.6, 11.7, 11.8, 11.9, 11.10, 11.11	11.1,	11.1, 11.2
lo4 describe some electronic methods of transferring funds	11.12, 11.13, 11.14, 11.15, 11.16, 11.17	11.2	11.3, 11.4,
lo5 discuss some aspects of the management of accounts receivable	11.18, 11.19	11.3	11.5, 11.6, 11.7
lo6 discuss the issues pertaining to the management of inventories	11.20	11.4, 11.5	11.8, 11.9, 11.10, 11.11, 11.12, 11.13, 11.14, 11.15, 11.16, 11.17, 11.18, 11.19, 11.20

Questions

11.1 A firm has some petty cash, a cheque account with a positive balance, another cheque account with a $100 000 overdraft limit that is $25 000 'in the red' and a long-term term deposit at a very favourable interest rate that it would prefer not to break in the event of a liquidity squeeze. Which of these items constitute 'cash'? Why?

11.2 Explain to a friend what the 'transactions motive' is in relation to the holding of cash.

11.3 What is the basis for firms to hold cash reserves over and above the likely everyday need?

11.4 Acme Rubber Imports consignments of rubber from Malaysia. Apart from its normal contractual purchases, it also buys cargoes that sometimes become available when other firms' deals fall apart. Acme keeps extra cash available because it has found from past experience that it can get better prices if it offers cash deals, payable immediately. What motive would you attribute to the holding of these extra cash balances? Why?

11.5 Acme Rubber sells mostly on credit, but sometimes for cash. Assuming Acme has no financing (capital injections, loan repayments or establishment) transactions on a particular day, from what sources might the $258 067 banked that day stem?

11.6 Acme also wrote a few cheques that day. For what expenses might these cheques pay?

11.7 Acme has 20 employees and about $50 million in turnover each year. There are 12 days each year when the sum of the cheques written is quite large. From what obligations might the extra payments arise?

11.8 As financial manager for a firm like Acme, what technique would you use to plan your cash needs for the next 12 months?

11.9 Explain the trade-off between risk and return in relation to holding enough cash.

11.10 What are the costs of holding cash reserves?

11.11 Trace all the effects on a retailer of not having enough cash on hand at a particular time or day.

11.12 Why is EFTPOS attractive to retailers?

11.13 What approximately is the current average merchant service fee for MasterCard and Visa transactions?

11.14 Charge cards (such as Amex, Diners Club) charge higher merchant service fees than the principal credit card providers. How is that possible?

11.15 Why don't most retailers refuse to take the cards with higher merchant service fees?

11.16 Define 'direct debit'.

11.17 How is 'direct debit' different from 'direct credit'?

11.18 Why do trading firms that are not financial service firms offer credit?

11.19 Explain the purpose of a Romalpa clause.

11.20 From what needs or bases do holding costs arise in relation to inventories?

Self-test problems

11.1 March Materials (MM) is a wholesaler of perishable goods. The firm sells to all its customers on credit with payment nominally within 30 days of the issue of each invoice. Evidence from past performance has show the financial manager that she can rely on 80% of sales being settled during the next calendar month and 20% in the month thereafter. Purchases are settled by the firm always within the next calendar month. Inventory remains fairly stable. Employment and other operating costs amount to about $20 000 per month. Here are the sales, purchases and other costs for MM for the first three months of a particular year.

	January ($'000)	February ($'000)	March ($'000)
Sales	300	200	250
Purchases	150	110	160
Operating costs	20	20	20
Depreciation	10	10	10
Wastage	30	10	20

Construct a cash budget for February and March.

11.2 Custom Irrigation Co. (CIC) determines that credit card and charge card sales will cost 1.9% and debit card sales 0.4% of transaction value, which must be paid to its bank for servicing the facility. It estimates that an average \$5000 and \$10 000 per week of credit sales will be paid for immediately by credit card and by debit card, respectively, if it installs EFTPOS equipment. The average collection time of credit sales is 8 weeks. Funds invested on the short-term money market currently earn 6%. Using these data and taking into account no other benefits or costs, is it worth it for CIC to offer an EFTPOS facility?

11.3 Harrigan Hay Supplies is a wholesaler of hay. The firm sells mainly for cash but sometimes extends credit to selected customers. To speed payment, Harrigan offers '2/10, net 30' terms. About 10% of its \$1 million turnover is sold on credit, and 80% of those credit sales are settled within 10 days. 5% of the remainder of the credit sales normally turn into bad debts, which are written off. What is the cost of the credit policy?

11.4 Joe's Cafe sells 365 cases of Popola each year. Ordering costs are \$0.50 per order and holding costs are \$1.50 per case. What is the EOQ?

11.5 Becky's Place has a different clientele from Joe's. They love Popola and Becky sells 1000 cases each year. Becky calculates her ordering costs at \$1 per order and reckons on \$1.20 as holding costs. What is her EOQ?

Solutions to self-test problems

11.1 Cash budget

	February (\$'000)	March (\$'000)
Sales	240	60 + 160
Purchases	(150)	(110)
Operating expenses	(20)	(20)
Cash surplus	70	90 + 70*

*\$70 from the previous month

Depreciation is a non-cash expense; wastage has no cash flow.

11.2 Credit card:debit card sales = 1:2, so cost of credit sales is

$0.019 \times 0.333 + 0.004 \times 0.667 = 0.09$

Funds earn 6% pa, so in 8 weeks earn

$0.06 \times \frac{8}{52} = 0.0923$

Thus, the cash benefit marginally outweighs the cost.

11.3 \$100 000 credit sales — \$80 000 take discount of 2% = \$1600

Bad debts — 5% of \$20 000 = \$1000

Total cost = \$2600.

11.4
$$Q = \sqrt{\left(\frac{2DO}{H}\right)}$$
$$= \sqrt{\left(2 \times 365 \times \frac{0.5}{1.5}\right)}$$
$$= \sqrt{243.33} \text{ or 16 cases}$$

11.5 $Q = \sqrt{\left(\frac{2DO}{H}\right)}$

$= \sqrt{\left(2 \times 1000 \times \frac{1}{1.2}\right)}$

$= \sqrt{1666.67}$ or 41 cases

Financial problems

11.1 Shower Sales Ltd sells plumbing fittings in a rapidly developing area. Its sales in June are \$500 000. From recent experience, the manager can confidently predict that sales will increase 10% each month cumulatively. 10% of sales are for cash, 80% are paid for in the next calendar month and 10% in the following calendar month. Purchases are \$380 000 in June. The manager decides to keep stock levels high and makes purchases in any month to the value of 80% of the previous month's sales. These purchases are paid for in the next calendar month. Cash operating expenses are \$50 000 per month. Calculate a monthly cash budget for July to December.

11.2 SuperTyre Retail sells tyres, makes tyre repairs and does wheel balancing for passenger vehicles. Sales average about \$300 000 each month. About 10% of these sales are for cash and the rest are paid for by 'plastic'. Of these sales, 80% are paid for by Visa or MasterCard and the rest by charge card. The credit card companies charge 1% merchant service fees and the charge card companies charge 2.5%. Purchases amount to 50% of sales and these are paid for in the next calendar month. There are three permanent employees who average \$4000 each per month in wages. Employment on-costs are 25% of wages. Other operating expenses average 25% of sales. Depreciation on the equipment is \$35 000 pa. Calculate a monthly cash budget for January to June.

11.3 Burton Resteel (BR) is offered an EFTPOS facility by its bank at a set fee of 1.0% of each transaction for credit card sales and 0.3% of each transaction for debit card sales. BR declines to accept Amex and Diners Club. BR calculates that customers will use credit cards and debit cards in a 2:3 ratio for the \$100 000 of EFTPOS transactions each month. Funds may be invested on the short-term money market at 5% pa on average. Average credit sales collection time has been running at 6 weeks. BR also estimates that there are additional benefits to the firm equal to \$1000 monthly from these EFTPOS transactions. Advise BR whether it should go ahead and install the facility, based on these figures.

11.4 Foye's Plastics Ltd makes and sells plastic catering goods. Many of its customers are small retailers; others are large wholesale catering houses. Foye's bank offers EFTPOS at a set fee of 1.0% of each transaction for credit card sales, 2.5% for charge card sales and 0.3% of each transaction for debit card sales. After checking with other managers, Foye's manager estimates its sales would probably fall into the ratio 2:5:1:2 for cash, credit card, charge card and debit card sales respectively. Funds may be invested on the short-term money market at 5% pa on average. Average credit sales collection time has been running in the past at 5 weeks. Bad debts have been recently equal to 0.5% of credit sales. Advise Foye's whether it should go ahead and install the facility, based on these figures.

11.5 Sunny Pools Ltd has always had a very tight credit policy because the pool industry is noted for its bad debts. The new manager of Sunny thinks the firm has been missing out on business because of this policy. He decides to take a calculated risk by increasing the firm's planned debtor level. Make a sketch of figure 11.4 (see page 397); show the determinants you think will change and indicate how they will change (positively or negatively).

11.6 How might Sunny Pools try to protect itself against bad debts after it has decided to increase the carrying value of its debtors?

11.7 Jedda's Paints and Tees sells artifacts to tourists. The firm sells mainly for cash but sometimes extends credit to selected wholesale customers. To speed payment, Jedda's offers '2/10, net 30 terms'. About 30% of its $2 million turnover is sold on credit, and 80% of those credit sales are settled within 10 days. 5% of the remainder of the credit sales normally become bad debts, which are written off. What is the cost of the credit policy?

11.8 ABC News has just announced that a motor parts manufacturer has suffered industrial trouble and its employees are on strike. As a consequence, the Ford Motor Company has had to cease assembly and send its employees on their annual leave. If the lack of parts continues beyond a few days, the Ford employees will be deemed to be on leave without pay. Which issues regarding current assets does this news highlight?

11.9 Why, in your view, would Ford jeopardise production (as in the circumstances in problem 11.8) by having its current policy?

11.10 Billabong Bagel Bakery specialises in making bagels to an original Jewish recipe, but adds distinctively Australian flavours such as wattle seed and lemon myrtle. Wattle seed is harvested seasonally from a number of species that produce edible seed. Billabong uses about 52 kg of seed a year and does not like to run out of supplies. Seed is packed in 100 g packets; there are no bulk packs. Additionally, seed must be kept refrigerated to retain the best flavour. Billabong estimates that order costs average $30 because often it takes an hour of an employee's time and several phone calls to different sellers to find supplies. Holding costs are also relatively high at $5 per 100 g due to the need for refrigeration. What would you advise Billabong to do about the supply problem?

11.11 Given the circumstances in problem 11.10, what is the EOQ?

11.12 Given the circumstances in problem 11.10, how long will each order last, if stocks run down to zero each time and use is constant?

11.13 Bob's Corner Store gets his soft drink supplies from the sales delivery truck which visits his store every week in summer and every fortnight in winter. Bob sells about 10 cases of drinks a week in the warmer 6 months and 3 cases of drinks a week in the cooler half of the year. Order costs, he says, are zero, even though he does spend time talking to the salesman. Holding costs are about 10 cents per case.

(a) What is the effect on EOQ of the so-called zero order costs?

(b) What solution do you suggest?

(c) How sensitive is the EOQ to the value of this variable?

11.14 Refer to problem 11.13 (Bob's Corner Store). What is the EOQ in summer?

11.15 Refer to problem 11.13 (Bob's Corner Store). What is the cooler-period EOQ?

11.16 Toowoomba Seed and Herbicide (ToSH) buys 20-litre drums of Rounddown herbicide by the pallet of 50 drums. Each drum sells for $200 and costs $150 landed in the store. About 3000 drums of this size are sold each year. Occasionally (averaging one drum in every 8 pallets) a drum is holed in the store and is unsaleable. It costs $10 additionally to dispose of the holed drum and contents and clean up the mess. Other holding costs average $10 per pallet. Order costs are estimated to be $1. What is the EOQ?

11.17 Given the circumstances in problem 11.16, how long will each order last?

11.18 A change in environmental protection guidelines requires ToSH (see problem 11.16) to install secure lockups for its herbicides and to use more expensive chemicals in the cleanup of spills. These changes add $20 per pallet to its holding costs. What effect will this increase in costs have on the EOQ?

11.19 A Woolies Petroleum outlet has a throughput of 140 000 litres of ULP fuel each week. Purchases are always made in multiples of 1000 litres. Holding costs including evaporation and variation in volumes due to temperature changes are estimated to be $10 per 1000 litres. Ordering costs are $1 per order. What is the EOQ, calculated on weekly data?

11.20 Given the circumstances in problem 11.19, do you believe the company would keep strictly to the EOQ with each order it submits to its suppliers? Why or why not? If you calculated the EOQ on daily turnover data, what values must change to achieve the same EOQ as calculated on a weekly basis?

SOLUTIONS TO FINANCE WORKSHOPS

11.1 1. The bakery would need a greater volume of cash as change and also cash as liquid funds to pay employees, to buy flour and other ingredients, and for fixed costs such as rent and rates. The real estate partnership would need possibly petty cash and liquid funds to pay overheads and drawings for the partners.

2. The opportunity costs and the security costs.

3. Lost sales, higher cost of emergency loans, interrupted supplies and cash-only supplies, insolvency and loss of firm (as a continuum from minor to major costs).

11.2 1. For cash sales — receipt/cash sale docket for receiving the cheque, reconciliation of cheques received by recording office with cheques received by sales departments, bank deposit records.

For credit sales — cheque receival lists, recording of payments against customers' accounts, bank deposit records and reconciliation with receival lists.

2. Depending on processes, there may be greater office-staff time involved in handling them; banks charge clearance fees and the small percentage of dishonoured cheques increase costs through the process of getting payment.

11.3 Benefits are sales, cross-sales and future sales. Costs are ordering costs and holding costs including storage and display costs, insurance, deterioration, theft and financing. The possible reduction in wholesale prices is not likely to be relevant at an isolated store as customers who need a good will pay any reasonable price.

End notes

1 Beal, D & Ralston, D 1997, 'Economic and social impacts of the closure of the only bank branch in rural communities', Centre for Australian Financial Institutions, University of Southern Queensland, Toowoomba, pp. 18–19.

2 Milligan, L 2003, 'Director stole to please his wife', *The Australian*, 5 December, p. 15.

3 Carson, V & Leys, N 2004, 'More Aussies in Swiss fraud net', *The Australian*, 19 April, p. 1.

4 Kahneman, D & Tversky, A 1982, 'The psychology of preferences', *Scientific American*, January, pp. 136–42.

5 *Reserve Bank of Australia Bulletin*, February 2007, table C.1.

6 *Reserve Bank of Australia Bulletin*, February 2007, table C.1.

7 *Reserve Bank of Australia Bulletin*, February 2007, table C.4.

8 *Reserve Bank of Australia Bulletin*, February 2007, table C.4.

9 *Reserve Bank of Australia Bulletin*, February 2007, table C.4.

10 *Reserve Bank of Australia Bulletin*, February 2007, table C.7.

11 *Reserve Bank of Australia Bulletin*, February 2007, table C.7.

12 Australian Bankers' Association (ABA) 1996, Submission to the Financial Systems Inquiry, viewed 12 November 2002, <http://fsi.treasury.gov.au/content/downloads/PubSubs/000126.doc p. 61>.

13 RBA 2005, 'Merchant service fees and market shares for credit and charge cards', *Reserve Bank of Australia Bulletin*, August, p. 68.

14 Australian Bankers' Association 1996, 'A credit card transaction', Submission to the Financial System Inquiry, September, fig. 4.4, p. 61.

15 Data derived from the Reserve Bank of Australia 2002, 'Reform of credit card schemes in Australia IV', p. 7, www.rba.gov.au.

16 *Reserve Bank of Australia Bulletin*, February 2007, Table C5.

17 *Reserve Bank of Australia Bulletin*, February 2007, Table C5.

18 CSL Limited 2006, *Annual report 2005–2006*, p. 119.

19 Veda Advantage 2007, 'Business Express', p. 1 of the business score report, http://services.au.vedaadvantage.com.

20 Foster, RA 1996, *Australian economic statistics 1949–50 to 1994–95*, RBA, Sydney, table 1.14a.

chapter 12

Long-term external finance

Learning objectives

After studying this chapter, you should be able to:

lo1	discuss the range of loans offered by financial institutions together with their normal terms and conditions
lo2	discuss the issues relating to the lease or buy decision
lo3	describe market sources of debt
lo4	discuss hybrid finance in the Australian markets
lo5	describe international sources of funding
lo6	discuss sources and the raising of equity finance.

SOURCES OF FUNDING

The firms we have been tracking through this textbook are both large and small and they are in very different industries. They have used various sources of funding and table 12.1 gives you the long-term debt and the contributed equity for each firm, together with the debt-to-equity and the debt to total assets ratios. Note that the debt figure used here is long-term debt excluding deferred tax liabilities and provisions. Also note that the equity figure is 'contributed equity'; that is, equity contributed by the public. This equity figure does not include internally generated reserves or retained profits. For firms that have been profitable it is normal for total equity or total shareholders' funds to be more than contributed equity as total equity includes reserves which have been built up over time. See how high Woolworths' debt-to-equity ratio is, but even then debt is still only a minor proportion of total assets.

Table 12.1 Long-term debt and contributed equity funding for several Australian firms at 30 June 2006

Firm	Long-term debt ($m)	Contributed equity ($m)	Debt: equity (%)	Debt: total assets (%)	Source of debt funds
ABC Learning Centres	235	1635	14.4	10.1	FI[a]
CSL	595	994	59.9	14.2	FI; M; P[b]
Woolworths	3704	2948	125	27.7	FI; M[c]

FI = financial institutions; M = markets; P = private.

a. ABC Learning Centres had $58 million of debt sourced from converting preference shares.

b. CSL had $179 million in FI loans; $317 million in notes funded by the financial markets; and $99 million funded privately by vendors of property purchased.

c. Woolworths had $505 million drawn down in bank loans; $800 million sourced from the domestic financial markets; US$1808 million sourced from US financial markets; and $591 million outstanding in Woolworths Notes.

Sources: Data from the 2006 annual reports for the respective firms.

Chapter preview

This chapter deals with the sources of funding for the long-term needs of businesses. Both small and large businesses use financial institutions as sources of intermediated finance. Intermediated finance is that gained through the services of a financial intermediary or financial services provider such as a bank, merchant bank or finance company. Generally, only businesses towards the larger end of the spectrum use the markets to raise debt finance. As you can see from table 12.1, even though ABC Learning Centres is a company worth more than a billion dollars, it still has not raised much finance from the debt markets. It prefers to use equity financing from the markets and debt financing from the financial institutions. Additionally, both relatively small and large businesses raise funds through equity funding, but mostly only the relatively larger firms are publicly listed and raise equity funds from the public through the market. Table 12.1 at the start of the chapter shows you how larger firms use more sophisticated sources of debt finance.

The following diagram shows how this chapter is structured.

LONG-TERM EXTERNAL FINANCE

Intermediated finance	▪ Fixed rate business loans ▪ Variable rate business loans ▪ Instalment loans ▪ Interest-only loans ▪ Commercial bills ▪ Fully drawn advances (FDAs) ▪ Leases
The lease or buy decision	▪ Leasing and debt in a firm's capital structure ▪ Taxation treatment of lease payments ▪ Potential benefits of leasing ▪ Lease or buy decision analyses
Debt finance from the Australian market	▪ Corporate bonds ▪ Floating rate notes (FRNs) ▪ Debentures
Hybrid finance from the Australian market	▪ Convertible notes ▪ Convertible preference shares
International sources of funding	
Equity finance securities	▪ Ordinary shares ▪ Preference shares
Raising equity finance	▪ Initial public offers ▪ Raising more equity finance

Intermediated finance

lo1

Discuss the range of loans offered by financial institutions together with their normal terms and conditions.

Intermediated finance: uses the services of a financial intermediary or financial services provider such as a bank, merchant bank or finance company

Australian business tends to look to the financial institutions as suppliers of **intermediated finance** in the first instance. While larger business firms with standing in the community (or internationally) are able to access the financial markets as well as financial institutions for funds, smaller firms typically approach one or several financial institutions for long-term funding. At September 2006, total bank lending to business was over $460 billion.[1] In contrast, long-term direct (non-intermediated) debt securities issued by non-financial corporations at the same date totalled about 10% of this value, $48 billion, after subtracting asset-backed securitisation securities, and a further $90 billion was raised by business directly from overseas markets.[2]

Banks offer a range of long-term finance options to business. Each bank gives its products different names for marketing purposes, but essentially all the products fit into several generic categories. These are:

- fixed rate business loans
- variable rate business loans
- instalment loans
- interest-only loans
- commercial bills
- fully drawn advances
- lease finance.

See the following 'finance world' feature for ANZ's suite of products. The terms and conditions of similar products may vary slightly among the various financial institutions, and in these days of intense competition financial institutions are often willing to amend conditions to suit the requirements of customers.

FINANCE WORLD

Business finance: options to suit whatever financial need arises

Your Business Need ...	ANZ Solution ...
Business Loans	
A low cost, flexible business loan for customers with residential security — for amounts above $25 000.	ANZ Business Mortgage Loan
A no-frills, low cost business loan for amounts above $50 000.	ANZ Business Saver
A capital boost with flexible repayment and interest rate options — for amounts above $10 000.	ANZ Business Loan
Finance vehicles or equipment using the asset as security.	Esanda Vehicle and Equipment Finance
Managing Your Cash Flow	
Cover seasonal and working capital requirements for amounts above $2 000.	ANZ Business Overdraft
Funding for important investment opportunities such as equipment, shares or property — for amounts above $25 000.	ANZ Business Credit Facility
Use an ANZ Commercial Card to help improve your cash flow with all of the convenience of a Visa credit card.	ANZ Business Credit Cards
Other Finance Needs	
Finance to cover major cash needs from $100 000.	ANZ Commercial Bill
Protect your business against adverse variations in interest rates.	ANZ Structured Business Finance
A formal guarantee from ANZ to pay a financial obligation to a third party.	ANZ Indemnity and Guarantees
Provide salary packaged vehicles options to your employees using a novated lease facility.	Esanda FleetPartners Packaged Vehicle Program

Source: ANZ.[3]

Fixed rate business loans

Fixed rate business loans are available from most of the major financial institutions for the purchase of many types of business assets. Many institutions impose a minimum loan condition that it must be greater than $100 000. Many financial institutions offer loans of up to $2 million. Terms are usually given for up to 25 years, with the interest rate being fixed for only the first three, five or 10 years. After the expiry of the initial period, the rate may be fixed for a further period or converted to a variable rate. Some financial institutions impose application fees; others levy no application fee, as part of their marketing packages. These loans may be unsecured, secured with business assets or secured with residential property. The availability of acceptable security naturally affects the interest rates charged. Financial institutions generally charge a 3–6% pa margin above the cash rate for these loans. Repayment conditions are negotiated to suit the business conditions of customers.

Variable rate business loans

Variable rate business loans are also available from most of the major financial institutions. Amounts available vary up to about $2 million. Terms are available up to 25 years. Interest rates vary in line with changes in the markets and, in March 2007, were about 2.5–4% above the cash rate, depending on security and loan terms and conditions. Many financial institutions offer flexible drawdown of the contracted loan amounts. In other words, not all of the loan must be taken up at the outset. Similarly, many financial institutions offer flexible repayment schedules — weekly, fortnightly or monthly. Additionally, these loans may be taken on an interest-only repayment basis during the terms of the loans.

Instalment loans

Instalment loans: have fixed repayment schedules negotiated at the outset

Instalment loans differ from business loans in that fixed repayment schedules are negotiated at the outset. Minimum loan amounts vary between financial institutions and may be as low as $10 000 from some suppliers and $50 000 from others. The loan periods also vary between suppliers but are often in the range 1–15 years. Both fixed rate and variable rate loans are available. Normally, the interest rates increase with the term of the loan. In March 2007, in a climate of relative uncertainty in the interest-rate markets, the 10-year rate quoted by banks was generally five basis points below the one-year rate. Remember that we define a basis point in chapter 3 as a one-hundredth part of 1%, so there are 100 basis points in a full 1%. Fixed rate loans can be extended with variable rate periods added after the fixed rate terms expire.

The amount of each instalment to repay such a loan is, as you will no doubt realise from your study of chapter 4, the instalment amount calculated by means of the present value of an annuity equation where the PV is the initial amount of the loan. Thus, a $100 000 loan taken out for 15 years at 7.2%, compounded monthly, would be repayable by 180 monthly instalments of $910.05, disregarding any fees.

Interest-only loans

Interest-only loans are taken out to finance special situations. During the term of the loan only interest is paid, while the repayment of the principal amount is made in full at the expiry of the term. These types of loans are suitable for situations where, say, an asset is bought (and used) for a specific period with the expectation that it will be sold at the end of the period. The sale of the asset then provides funds to repay the loan. Thus, the payment of interest in the intervening period may be considered a holding cost for owning the asset.

Interest-only loans are used by speculators who buy assets (such as real property or equities) with the expectation of resale at an enhanced price to achieve a capital gain. Additionally, such loans are used by hedgers or businesspeople for ordinary operations where the one lump sum repayment suits the cash flows associated with the investment. Loans are normally secured. The terms of interest-only loans vary normally from six months to 10 years. The amounts available are often greater than $50 000 and the interest rates are normally fixed.

Commercial bills

Commercial bills are introduced in chapter 3 and discussed as a form of short-term funding in chapter 10. Bills may also be used as a form of long-term funding by rolling over one bill to another. In other words, the first bill is repaid with the proceeds of taking out another bill. With this means of financing, effectively interest is paid each time a bill is rolled over. Given that each bill has the same face value, each new bill will yield less than the face value of the maturing bill. For example, assume a firm has arranged for one \$100 000 bill with 180-day maturity. The firm receives \$98 000 in return for the first bill. At the expiry of 180 days, it arranges for another 180-day bill and uses the \$98 000 receipt to repay the first bill. The firm must also find another \$2000 to repay the first bill in full. Thus, the firm can use commercial bills to provide long-term finance. However, as discussed previously, this practice involves extra managerial time and may expose the firm to additional financing risk.

Fully drawn advances (FDAs)

Fully drawn advances: loans that are initially drawn down to the full amount and repaid over the term of the loan by means of a fixed repayment schedule

Fully drawn advances (FDAs) are loans that are initially drawn down to the full amount and repaid over the term of the loan by means of a fixed repayment schedule. FDAs are a major form of business financing. Amounts available may vary from as little as \$5000 to any amount at all with some financial institutions. Terms are normally for up to 10 years. Rates are normally variable. Some financial institutions offer capped rates, where the variable rate charged cannot exceed a negotiated maximum rate for a specific term. Often financial institutions will set a system where interest is charged to a separate account, while the FDA account merely keeps track of the balance of the principal. Normally a regular repayment schedule is set up initially, so that the balance in the FDA account decreases continually over the term of the loan. FDA loans are usually secured. Interest rates charged are similar to those for instalment loans.

Leases

Leasing is a significant form of debt finance for business, with new leasing approvals by the major financial institutions averaging more than \$500 million per month in 2006–07.[4] The major financial institutions provide a full range of leasing options and products to complement their other loans and to assist business with financing specific assets such as motor vehicles, construction and manufacturing plant, and IT and office equipment. Some financial institutions, normally through their finance company subsidiaries, offer complete management of vehicle fleets. These specialist services involve fixed cost servicing, more efficient administration, reduced used vehicle price risk and cost benchmarking to best practice standards. Some of the characteristics of leasing options offered by financial institutions are given in table 12.2.

Table 12.2 Characteristics of leasing products offered by financial institutions

Product	Deposit	Tax deduction for: rental	Tax deduction for: interest and depreciation	Guaranteed ownership by customer at end
Lease	No	Yes	No	No
Novated lease	No	Yes	No	No*
Hire-purchase	Yes	No	Yes	Yes

*Employee is registered owner.

Source: National Australia Bank Limited.[5]

Lease: a contract by which an owner of property (the lessor) allows another person or entity (the lessee) the use of the asset

Lessor: the owner of property that is being leased

Lessee: the person or entity that gains the use of the leased asset by entering the lease contract

Novated lease: involves a three-party agreement between an employee, an employer and a financial institution to provide a motor vehicle to the employee as part of a salary package

Hire-purchase agreement: involves a financial institution buying the equipment required by the customer then hiring it to the customer. The customer purchases the asset outright at the end of the lease period.

As can be seen from table 12.2, there are many permutations of the leasing option. The chief issues of concern with leasing are the ownership of the subject assets, the availability of tax deductions and the extent of financing available (that is, can 100% of the value of the assets be financed or is a deposit necessary?).

First, we should consider exactly what is meant by each leasing term. A **lease** is a contract by which an owner of property (the **lessor**) allows another person or entity (the **lessee**) the use of the asset for a specific period in return for rent or lease payments. When leasing is arranged with financial institutions, the lessors are both owners and financiers. (This contrasts with the case of an equipment loan where the customer owns the asset and the financier may or may not have a right over the asset as security.)

A **novated lease** is a relatively new form of finance. It involves a three-party agreement between an employee, an employer and a financial institution. Novated leases are normally used to provide motor vehicles to employees as part of salary packages. The cost of providing the vehicle is part of the employee's salary, but is paid directly to the financial institution. The employee is able to select the vehicle of choice and to reduce annual taxable income. The financial institution is able to claim from the ATO the GST component of the new price of the vehicle, and this credit effectively reduces the lease payments. Novated leases are normally fully portable between employers, at least from the point of view of the financial institutions.

Under a **hire-purchase agreement**, a financial institution buys equipment required by the customer then hires it to the customer for use during the agreed period. At the end of the period, the deal is settled by the payment of any outstanding balances and ownership passes to the customer. This is a very common form of lease that is arranged every business day for the purchase of machinery, vehicles and other types of fixed assets. Hire purchase finance was once very common among consumers, but is now less so due to the attraction of credit-card finance and personal loans.

As can be seen from table 12.2, the first two products are relatively straightforward. The underlying assets are used by the customer in return for a rental payment. The rental or lease payments are tax deductions for the customer firms in each case. There are no tax deductions for interest or depreciation and there is no guarantee of ownership of the assets at the end of the period by the customer. The fact that there is no such guarantee, however, does not mean that the customer firms cannot purchase the assets. Often they do, by paying a final lump sum, which is called a 'balloon' or residual payment.

In contrast with hire-purchase, the payments made by the lessees are treated as ownership costs, and deductions are allowable for interest and depreciation. Consistent with this view, ownership at the expiry of the terms of the agreements resides not with the financial institutions but with the lessees. The following 'finance world' feature gives more detailed information on National Australia Bank's lease and equipment-loan products.

Finance leases: non-cancellable contractual obligations to make payments in return for the use of an asset for the majority of its useful life

Operating leases: contractual agreements, but they are cancellable upon given notice and tend to be of much shorter term than the useful life of the asset

All of these forms of leasing may be classified as **finance leases**. Finance leases are non-cancellable contractual obligations to make payments in return for the use of an asset for the majority of its useful life, and are essentially just one of many forms of financing the use of assets. Lessees that are party to finance leases enjoy most of the benefits of ownership and are normally responsible for maintenance and upkeep. Conversely, some leases may be classed as **operating leases**. These include the sorts of agreements that you might enter for the hire of a car for a two-week holiday in a foreign land, the hire of a floor sander or, indeed, the rental of a house. Operating leases are contractual agreements, but they are cancellable upon given notice and tend to be of much shorter term than the useful life of the asset. Owners, not lessees, tend to be responsible for repairs and continued 'fitness for purpose'.

FINANCE WORKSHOP 12.1

1. The range of loans available to business may be classified according to various characteristics. What do you consider to be the two most important characteristics?
2. Loans may be repaid by three different methods of which one is the fixed-value instalment. What are the other two methods?
3. Each repayment method is particularly suitable for some business circumstances. Give an example of three separate business circumstances that in turn would make a particular repayment method more attractive to a financial manager.

FINANCE WORLD

NAB: Your options at a glance

Attribute	Finance Lease	Hire Purchase	Equipment Loan
Finance amount	100% finance is mandatory	Any amount up to 100% can be financed	Any amount up to 100% can be financed
Accounting treatment	Liability on customer's balance sheet	Liability on customer's balance sheet	Liability on customer's balance sheet
Depreciation	Tax deduction for Lessor (Bank)	Tax deduction for Hirer (Customer)	Tax deduction for Borrower (Customer)
Tax effect for user	Rentals may be deductible for Lessee (Customer) to the extent the asset is used in producing assessable income	Hirer claims tax deduction for interest on contract plus depreciation of asset to the extent the asset is used in producing assessable income	Borrower claims deduction for interest on the loan plus depreciation of the asset to the extent the asset is used in producing assessable income
Residual/balloon payment	Residual is mandatory and is an estimate of value at end of term. Lessee indemnifies the Lessor for residual	Balloon payment is optional	Balloon payment is optional
Interest rate for transactions < $500 000	Rate fixed for the term of the contract	Rate fixed for the term of the contract	Rate fixed for the term of the contract
Interest rate for transactions equal to or greater than $500 000	Fixed, floating, capped, range or any combination (must be a minimum of two)	Fixed, floating, capped, range or any combination (must be a minimum of two)	Fixed, floating, capped, range or any combination (must be a minimum of two)
Deposit/trade ins	No deposit allowable	Deposit is optional	Deposit is optional
Structures for seasonal income	Yes	Yes	Yes

Equipment ownership	Equipment owned by NAB.	Ownership passes to Hirer once all rent instalments are made.	Borrower provides, as security, a mortgage to NAB over the goods.
Treatment of GST and input tax credit (ITC) on acquisition	NAB purchases equipment and claims an ITC. The GST exclusive amount is financed under the agreement.	Liability to GST arises at the time of supply of equipment. The GST amount can be paid up front, funded or paid as well as the repayment that coincides with the Hirer's ITC claim.	Agreement has no GST consequence as Borrower acquires goods directly from the supplier and claims ITC as per a normal purchase.
Treatment of GST on rentals/ repayments, residuals/ balloons and payouts	GST is included in the amount paid by the Lessee for the rentals, residual and any purchase of the asset. Lessee can generally claim and GST paid as an ITC.	As GST is assessed on the equipment when it is supplied, the Customer is subsequently liable for GST on the stamp duty component of any repayment. No GST liability for the balance of repayment, balloon or final transfer of the asset to the Customer.	There are no GST consequences on repayments, balloons or pay out.

Source: National Australia Bank Limited.[6]

FINANCE WORKSHOP 12.2

1. Define three different types of leasing arrangements.
2. Give examples of circumstances where each of the different forms of lease is most appropriate.

lo2

Discuss the issues relating to the lease or buy decision.

The lease or buy decision

Deciding whether to lease or buy equipment is a major area of decision making for financial managers. The term 'lease' here is used as a generic category for all the permutations of finance leasing. Similarly, while 'buy' is a specific term, effectively a company buying an asset must finance that purchase through internally generated funds, for which there is an opportunity cost, or through borrowed funds, for which there is a realised cash cost.

Before looking at the potential benefits of leasing, it is worthwhile to spend a little time considering two issues:

- leasing and debt in a firm's capital structure
- the taxation treatment of payments associated with leases.

Both these issues have had a significant impact on the growth of lease finance, and taxation treatment still drives the selection of some lease products over others, depending on individual firms' circumstances.

Leasing and debt in a firm's capital structure

Leasing has become firmly established in business's toolbox of debt financing options only in the last 40–50 years. Early in this period, one of the promoted advantages was that leasing could provide firms with assets but that there were no consequences for the firms' capital structures and balance sheets. In other words, leasing was said to be an off-balance sheet form of finance. This made it attractive to some firms in that they could obtain extra finance but appear, from the financial records, not to have done so. This argument of no structural consequences is not true, in fact, and omitting leases from accounting records is no longer possible.

Lenders consider firms' capital structures when making funding decisions. Suppose a firm had decided on a 3:7 debt-to-equity ratio. The debt might be made up of an overdraft and an FDA. If the firm then decides to lease \$100 000 of equipment, some of the earlier debt would have to be repaid to maintain the 3:7 ratio. In other words, a 'place' has to be made in the debt structure for the lease finance, if the target ratio is to be maintained.

While lease finance is usually secured by the assets purchased, potential financiers are very interested in obtaining full details of the debt structures and the quality of the equity before advancing lease funding. Lease funding may be relatively easy to obtain, but financiers are still very interested in the ability of firms to repay what they see as debt.

With respect to accounting records and the off-balance sheet argument, it was recognised more than 20 years ago that finance leases usually confer valuable rights and some obligations on firms. Consequently, these rights and obligations should be recognised and reported in the accounting records. Accountants are guided in their decisions regarding the appropriate treatment of various transactions by accounting standards. AAS 17 was issued in 1987 to guide accountants in their treatment of leases. Subsequently AASB 117 was issued and this standard came into operation from 1 January 2007.

AASB 117 classifies leases based on the extent to which the risks and rewards attached to the ownership of the subject assets lie with the lessor or the lessee. Risks stem from technological obsolescence and variations in expected returns. Rewards are the expected profits from operations and gains in value. Leases are classified as finance leases if substantially all the risks and rewards are transferred from lessor to lessee. Conversely, a lease is considered to be an operating lease if it does not transfer substantially all the risks and rewards of ownership.

Thus it is apparent that, contrary to the view of some lay persons, leasing is not 'Clayton's finance', but finance that does appear in the financial reports. Similarly, leasing is not finance to be accessed when all else fails. It has a place in certain circumstances, which will be apparent later.

Taxation treatment of lease payments

The treatment of the payments associated with leasing and leased assets for taxation purposes can be quite complex, with both legislation and taxation rulings applicable. However, the general principle is that the lease payments made periodically are tax-deductible provided that (a) the leased asset is used to produce assessable income and (b) the lease is a genuine lease rather than an instalment purchase arrangement. If the arrangement were really an instalment purchase agreement, the lessee firm would be requesting an unfair advantage in that the firm would effectively be claiming accelerated depreciation or deductions for capital payments. One test the ATO uses is that, if a lessee has the guaranteed right to purchase the asset at the expiry of the lease period, it is more inclined to believe the arrangement is an instalment purchase agreement. Look back to table 12.2 to see this ruling reflected in the attributes of the lease products on the market. The first two products are forms of leases where the lease rental payments are tax-deductible. Hence, there is no guaranteed right of purchase at the expiry of the term.

No guaranteed right of purchase at the expiry of the lease term does not mean that lessees do not purchase the leased assets. Indeed, in the majority of cases, the lessees (and in the case of novated leases, the employee user of the asset) buy the assets and ownership transfers at that point. Normally, the purchase involves the payment of one final lump sum, the residual or balloon payment. The size of the final payment is set at the start of the contract and is an approximation of the market value of the used asset at that time.

A moment's quiet thought will suggest to you another issue that could provoke contention between the ATO and the tax-paying public. If lessees can purchase the leased assets for one final payment, then they would want that payment to be as small as possible. Hence, they would want the lease payments to be maximised so that the residual was minimised. The ATO has issued rulings to guide the calculation of acceptable values for both the residual and the lease payments.

Hire-purchase agreements are different in character from other leases. Ownership passes to the lessee on receipt by the lessor of the final payment. Thus, there is guaranteed right of purchase at the expiry of the lease term. The lessee is not technically the owner of the asset until all payments are made, but the lessee may be treated as the owner of a depreciating asset during the term of the lease. Thus, the lessee may claim as tax deductions the interest paid on the finance and depreciation of the asset. Such lessees may not claim lease payments as tax deductions as well.

GST also impacts on lease products. Lease payments are construed as payments for a supply and thus are taxed under the GST legislation. If a lease payment were calculated as \$500, then the actual payment in each period would increase 10% to \$550. However, GST-registered entities are able to claim back their net GST payments (GST payments less GST receipts), so effectively such firms have not paid any GST. Only some very small firms and community groups are likely not to be registered for GST, and these entities are also unlikely to lease assets, so overall the GST has little impact on the leasing industry.

Lease products which have the nature of hire purchase, and repayments of loans used to purchase assets, are classified as financial services and are GST-free. Additionally, financial institutions providing hire-purchase products also normally offer innovative options regarding the GST components of the sale part of each deal.

Potential benefits of leasing

There are advantages and disadvantages associated with leasing in comparison with buying. As with many other financial decisions, the lease–buy decision is complicated and each case should be analysed individually. Managers should not rely on 'usual practice' or rules of thumb. In addition, some of the benefits that are claimed by finance providers may not eventuate or in fact be likely in any circumstances.

In evaluating any argument in favour of leasing, one very basic principle must be remembered. A potential lessor takes over some of the ownership duties of the potential lessee. Thus, leasing inserts a third entity into the demand–supply transaction for the acquisition of an asset. That third party needs to be compensated for the services rendered. Thus, for the deal to be advantageous for the demander of the asset (the potential lessee), the third party (the potential lessor) must be able to provide some part of the transaction better or more cheaply than the demander could do itself. Doing something better may come from specialist skills; doing something more cheaply may stem from specialist skills but may also emerge from differences in the legal environment (such as the taxation system) for lessors and lessees.

Potential benefits associated with leasing may include:

- taxation benefits
- efficiency of asset management and disposal
- speed in acquisition of assets
- avoidance of obsolescence
- improved cash flows and conservation of capital.

Taxation benefits

One of the arguments in favour of leasing most commonly aired is that leasing is cheaper because the taxation system rewards firms that lease over firms that borrow. Is this really so? Individual circumstances dictate the taxation effects. (In the examples that are provided later in this chapter, consideration will be given to the effect of dividend imputation for corporate lessees, as well as to situations where after-tax values are important.)

Lease payments comprise an interest component and a component to compensate the lessor for the using up of value of the underlying asset. At the end of the lease period, the used asset is theoretically worth exactly its residual value, which should be the market value of that used asset. Lease payments are 100% tax-deductible. Compare this with the case of an asset purchased on borrowed funds. The asset is used and depreciated annually. At the end of the relevant period, it has a (market) sale price or residual value. The interest charges are 100% tax-deductible, as are the depreciation charges. How are the two situations different? The answer is that they generally are not. However, there are several matters that could introduce differences. These include:

- timing
- interest rates and perceived risk
- different tax rates.

Lease payments can be negotiated and structured so that equal payments are made at regular intervals or unequal payments are made at intervals to suit the cash flows of the lessee business. Sole traders and partnerships could structure lease payments so that they were paid during a period of high income, when marginal rates of tax of 48.5% were payable. However, this is also true with many types of loans.

Depreciation is another area where timing is involved. For taxation purposes, a deduction is available for the decline in value of a depreciating asset during each taxation period. The decline in value is calculated on the basis of the effective life of each asset and taxpayers are free to determine what those effective lives will be. The ATO publishes recommended periods as effective lives, which taxpayers may choose as 'safe' periods for which there will be no ATO objections. These periods are, in the main, quite liberal. For example, motorbikes are accorded effective lives of three years. Now, while it is possible to wreck a motorbike in much less than three years, careful maintenance and reasonable riding will see most bikes last considerably longer than that. Similarly, drums (musical, not oil) are accorded lives of five years, but they too normally last much longer. Once the effective life of any asset is settled upon, taxpayers must choose to use either the prime cost or the diminishing value method of allocating the cost of using the asset (see chapter 9). Thus, claims for deductions for depreciation are relatively inflexible. On the other hand, as already noted, lease payments can be negotiated to be relatively flexible so that resultant claims for tax deductions are similarly flexible.

The interest rates charged for a lease to a client firm may be different from the rate charged on a loan to the same firm. Why is this so? Before examining this issue, it is fair to say that the two rates cannot be very different. Why not? Because, if they were strikingly different (say, leases were always charged out at a higher rate), there would be no demand for lease finance except in unusual cases. However, there may be small differences and these may stem from lenders' perceptions of differences in risk. For example, a finance provider may view a lease as imposing less risk to its business as the provider still owns the asset as security. On the other hand, where the asset in question is highly specialised, such as a purpose built saffron-harvesting machine, another financial institution might view a loan as having less risk because the specialist machine would be hard to sell for reasonable value. It is better from the financial institution's point of view for the customer to own the machine. Additionally, the financial institution could take security in the form of other, more easily realised assets.

Finally, there may be different tax rates payable by potential lessors and potential lessees. Where this is so, it may be possible for the parties to share the difference so that both parties enjoy a net gain through going ahead with the deal.

Efficiency of asset management and disposal

One of the most valid arguments in favour of leasing is concerned with efficiency of asset management and disposal. Lessor companies often develop specialist units that develop high expertise in managing selected groups of assets such as computers and fleets of motor vehicles, long-distance haulage trucks, construction equipment, forklifts and tractors. Some large firms find it more efficient to have a lessor track the physical locations, service and upgrade status as well as maintain the IT equipment in all their branches.

The ANZ Bank, through its finance company subsidiary, Esanda, runs Esanda Fleetpartners which offers complete vehicle fleet management — fixed cost servicing, efficient administration, reduced used vehicle price risk and cost benchmarking to best practice standards. Efficiencies are gained in servicing and administration through specialisation and high throughput. Thus, the costs of use and maintenance of the assets are less. Additionally, it is widely accepted that vehicle management firms can purchase standard Australian sedans and wagons for about 10%, or $3000, less than private purchasers. Another example of a specialist lessor is Alltech Finance. This business specialises in technology leasing and provides computer equipment to organisations such as the University of Sydney, QBE Insurance and Ernst & Young.[7]

Apart from more efficient purchasing, specialist lessors are often able to dispose of used assets at higher prices than other people. This is because they have the right contacts in the industry (they know who normally deals in that type of asset), they are able to put together large packages of assets of similar specifications or they are able to draw large crowds of potential buyers to asset auctions. Overall, according to this argument, the net cost of using these sorts of assets under lease is less.

Avoidance of obsolescence

Avoidance of obsolescence is to some extent a corollary of the argument given in the previous section. Potential lessors argue that firms are able to turn over leased equipment faster so that they may keep up with improved technology more easily. For one thing, payments are normally relatively small (but frequent) and new equipment can be obtained by increasing the payments marginally. On the other hand, the scrapping of owned equipment, especially in fast developing areas such as IT, may involve relatively large write-offs which impact negatively on net profits. As noted previously, whether this argument has merit depends on many individual factors.

Improved cash flows and conservation of capital

Leasing, according to this argument, involves regular small cash outflows over the relevant period. Purchasing, on the other hand, involves a large initial outflow which must be planned and financed one way or another. However, planning is never a bad thing and debt finance, too, normally involves regular smaller outflows than the initial purchase price.

The conservation of capital argument runs in parallel to the cash flow issue. It is true that capital not spent on new assets could be used elsewhere, but this argument is also true where conventional debt finance is being considered. Another variation of this argument is that leasing is 100% financed, but financial institutions require a deposit and a loan to value ratio (LVR) of perhaps no more than 80%. This may be true, but it is really a 'smoke and mirrors' argument. If a lessor requires a first lease payment equivalent to, say, 30% on signing a three year lease agreement, then the lease has effectively required an LVR of less than 80%.

Lease or buy decision analyses

The lease–buy decision only needs to be made after analysis of the project that requires the assets (see chapter 8 and 9). If the project has a positive NPV, the manager can then consider whether or not the assets should be leased. If the project has a small negative NPV, the benefits of leasing may make the project acceptable by shifting the NPV to positive. The manager should, however, exercise extreme caution in the analysis in the latter case.

When analysing lease or buy decisions, firms may find themselves in one of three different positions with regard to their owners' taxation situations, as discussed in chapter 2:

- Their owners are unable to take advantage of dividend imputation, as with sole traders, partnerships and companies with major proportions of shareholders who cannot make use of the system, and therefore they should use post-tax values.
- Their owners can use dividend imputation to advantage, so that pre-tax values are relevant.
- Their owners can only partially take advantage of dividend imputation, so that post-effective-tax values should be used.

Let us now look at the analysis of some lease–buy problems.

Suppose Bob Matuzzi, a farmer with his business structured as a sole trader, decides to spend more time out contracting as a haymaker for other farmers in his district. He needs a new mower-conditioner, rake and baler. The new equipment will cost \$70 000. With the cash earnings from the haymaking, Bob reckons he will be paying the 40% marginal rate of income tax plus Medicare Levy — making 41.5%. (This income is classified as non-primary production income and therefore is not eligible to be included in his income subject to averaging.) The depreciation allowance for the machinery is 10% straight line, based on a 10-year life. Bob can borrow the \$70 000 from the finance company arm of his bank at 12% interest over five years or he can take out a lease for five years with lease payments of \$15 000 due at the start of each new year. He can purchase the machinery at the end of five years by paying a residual of \$35 000. If he borrows the funds, he similarly will own the machinery outright at the end of five years.

There are two ways we can analyse this problem. We can look at the cash flows that would eventuate from taking the loan and using it to buy the machinery, disregarding the income the machinery will earn and the cash costs of servicing and maintenance. Then we can examine the cash flows that would occur if the machinery were leased. In this case, again we are interested only in the ownership cash flows, not the cash operating costs nor the revenue that will be earned by the machinery (as it is the same for both financing options). A final step in this process is to compare the two outcomes and decide which source of funding is the better.

An alternative way of examining the problem is to do the analysis in one step by building the comparison into the figures as we consider each cash flow. We will use this shorter and more efficient method in example 12.1.

EXAMPLE 12.1

Lease–buy analysis when owners are not integrated with the imputation system

In the analysis for Bob Matuzzi, we deal with six time periods:

$t = 0$ (now, or the start of $t = 1$)
$t = 1$ (end of year 1 or beginning of year 2)
$t = 2$ (end of year 2 or beginning of year 3) and so on.

Lease payments are normally required to be paid at the start of each period. We assume other cash flows occur on the last day of each period, for easc of calculation. Mathematically, there is very little difference when present values are being computed between a cash flow being received or expended on 31 December one year or on the next day, 1 January in the new year. Hence, there is a need for $t = 0$, as the payments which occur on day 1 of $t = 1$ can be assumed to have occurred on the last day of $t = 0$. Thus, all cash flows will occur at the end of equal length periods — periods of exactly one year.

Table 12.3 Analysis of cash flows ($000)

Item	$t = 0$	$t = 1$	$t = 2$	$t = 3$	$t = 4$	$t = 5$
Lease proceeds[a]	+70					
Lease payments	-15	-15	-15	-15	-15	-35
Tax benefit from lease payments		+6.225	+6.225	+6.225	+6.225	+6.225
Tax benefit forgone (depreciation)		-2.905	-2.905	-2.905	-2.905	-2.905
Net benefits	+55	-11.68	-11.68	-11.68	-11.68	-31.68

a. Gaining possession of the machinery is equivalent to receipt of $70 000.

The lease payments of $15 000 pa are tax deductible, thereby reducing tax payable each year by 0.415 × $15 000, which is $6225. In this example it is assumed this tax benefit is received in the year following each lease payment, but we could assume that tax is paid in the period of income, as we do in chapter 9. No tax deduction is available for the residual payment. A tax benefit from a deduction for depreciation would be available for purchased machinery. However, this benefit is not available with a lease, so this benefit is forgone. The value of the benefit forgone through leasing is $2905, made up of 0.415 × $7000, when $7000 is the annual depreciation at 10% for $70 000 of machinery.

The final step in the analysis is to find the present value, PV, of the outflows so that the aggregated PV of the outflows may be compared with the net benefit of $55 000 at the outset. To find the PV, we must use a discount rate. What is the most appropriate discount rate? The answer to this question is the loan interest rate. The net lease cash flows are discounted by the *loan after-tax interest rate.* This means that like will be compared with like. Why use after-tax rates? The interest payable on the loan, if it were the chosen method of finance, is tax deductible. Hence, by using the after-tax interest rate as the discount rate, the benefits of the tax deductions for the interest that might have been paid are automatically built into the model.

The interest rate that would have been charged on the loan was 12%. After tax of 41.5%, the interest rate is 7.02%, that is, 0.12 (1 – 0.45). This rate is used to discount the cash flows, as in table 12.4. The annuity equation may be used to find the PV of $11 680 cash flow in years 1–4, which is $39 548. The equation for the PV of a single sum is used to calculate the value of $22 566 as the PV of $31 680. The negative values on the second line of the table add to $62 114, and the net value of the third line is –$7114.

Table 12.4 PV of cash flows ($000)

Item	$t = 0$	$t = 1$	$t = 2$	$t = 3$	$t = 4$	$t = 5$
Net benefits	+55	-11.68	-11.68	-11.68	-11.68	-31.68
PV	+55		39.548			22.566
	+55			-62.114		
Net PV			-7.114			

A net PV of –$7114 means that the lease is not as good an option as the loan. The lease has given a net inflow at the outset of $55 000 for the PV 'cost' of $62 114. Had the analysis given the alternative answer — that the outflow in PV terms was lower with the lease than the initial net proceeds — then the lease would have been the better financing option.

EXAMPLE 12.2

Lease–buy analysis when owners are fully integrated with the imputation system

Now suppose a firm structured as a company wants to buy or lease plant worth $70 000 and wants to do a similar analysis. The lease payment schedule and residual value are the same as before, as is the loan interest rate of 12%. All of the shareholders of the firm are Australian residents for tax purposes and all thus claim dividend imputation credits. Cash flows at pre-tax values are thus appropriate for the analysis. The PVs of the lease payments are found by using the loan interest rate of 12%.

Table 12.5 Analysis of pre-tax cash flows ($000)

Item	$t = 0$	$t = 1$	$t = 2$	$t = 3$	$t = 4$	$t = 5$
Lease proceeds	+70					
Lease payments	-15	-15	-15	-15	-15	-35
Net benefits	+55	-15	-15	-15	-15	-35
PV	+55		-45.560			19.860
	+55			-65.42		
Net PV			-10.42			

The net PV of the $t_1 - t_4$ lease payments is $65 420 while the lease proceeds are $55 000. Thus, the lease is 'costing' in PV terms $10 420 more than the loan, and the loan is the preferable finance option.

The third possibility in analysing lease–buy problems occurs where not all the owners of a company are able to take advantage of the dividend imputation system. In that case, an effective rate of taxation based on the percentage of its shareholders eligible to benefit from the dividend imputation system may be calculated and the after-tax values used in these analyses.

FINANCE WORKSHOP 12.3

An Australian company with a share register comprising only resident Australians wants to finance new equipment costing $110 000. The financial manager must choose between borrowing and lease finance. A lease is available over 3 years and the loan will cost 7.6%. The lease payments comprise three payments of $30 000 payable at the start of each period and one final payment of $40 000 payable at the end of the third year. Which funding should the firm take?

lo3

Describe market sources of debt.

Debt finance from the Australian market

Firms wanting to raise debt finance from the Australian market have corporate bonds, notes and debentures to choose from as the financing media. To a great extent, these securities are similar methods of financing; their differences mainly lie in their historical roles. Essentially, borrowing firms issue bonds, notes or debentures as proof that debts exist. After that, if the securities are traded, the security itself (the physical piece of paper) or the proof of registration with issues that are electronically recorded merely acts as proof of current ownership. Naturally, the owner of a bond at maturity is the entity that receives the repayment of face value from the issuer.

Bonds have been traditionally associated in Australia with the Commonwealth Government, the state governments or state-owned instrumentalities. Corporate bonds were seldom issued until the 1990s. In 1990, for example, only about $4 billion of corporate bonds were on issue.[8] Debentures and unsecured notes were traditionally issued by finance companies directly to the public. They were a popular finance product which gave unsophisticated 'mums and dads' a higher risk — higher return option than bank term deposits at a time when there was little choice for savers with funds to invest. In 1990, finance companies raised $19 billion by this method.[9] Since then, the value of funds raised has dropped gradually so that, in September 2002, the value of finance company debentures and unsecured notes on issue was only $13 billion, and has since dropped every further to be less than $7 billion in December 2006.[10]

Corporate bonds

Corporate bonds: debt instruments where the issuer receives the face value of the bonds at the outset and pays a coupon, usually six-monthly. The face value is repaid when the bonds mature.

As noted here and in chapter 3, **corporate bonds** have grown in popularity in Australia during the 1990s. In chapter 3, we define corporate bonds as debt instruments where the issuer receives the face value of the bonds at the outset and pays a coupon, usually six-monthly. The face value is repaid when the bonds mature. Corporate bonds are unsecured, so good credit rankings by the ranking agencies, Moody's and Standard & Poor's, are extremely important to potential issuers of bonds. At June 2001, there were about 50 corporate bond issues in Australia valued at about $21 billion.[11] (These figures exclude securitisation issues, financial corporation issues and funds supplied by non-residents.) Credit ratings or rankings of specific bond issues determine the interest rates that must be offered at any given time to make the bonds attractive to the market. For example, on 31 May 2006, corporate bonds of 1–5 years maturity with AAA ratings were priced to yield 6.13%. At the time, AA bonds yielded 6.20% and A bonds 6.32%. These yields represented margins of 44–64 basis points above the yields of similar Commonwealth Government bonds.[12] Bonds ranked 'BBB' and below are considered 'junk bonds' and not suitable for the conventional investment market.

Over-the-counter (OTC) market: that part of a market where deals are arranged privately between two parties

Traditionally, corporate bonds have been lightly traded among institutions. This trade is an example of the so-called **over-the-counter (OTC) market**. The OTC market is that part of a market where deals are arranged privately between two parties. OTC deals start with an asking price, just as you would start with an asking price when making a private sale of your car. The eventual sales prices may be the same as the initial asking prices or may be different, depending on the relative power and strength of desire to buy (or sell) among the parties.

Currently, about 25% of corporate bonds issued are traded on the ASX. The ASX website at www.asx.com.au has full details of corporate bond product specifications, prospectus summaries and prices. Table 12.6 gives a selection of corporate bonds on issue and traded on the ASX. The issue price for all these bonds was $100 and their coupon payments are made semi-annually or quarterly as indicated.

Table 12.6 Selected corporate bonds traded on the ASX

Security	ASX code	Coupon (% pa)	Maturity date
Australian Food and Fibre Ltd debentures	AFFHA	7.0[b]	16/07/10
Australian Central Credit Union unsecured notes	ACDHC	9.0[a]	31/07/15
Ale Property Group unsecured cumulative redeemable notes	LEPHB	7.265[b]	30/09/11
Timbercorp Orchard Trust debenture	TODHA	9.0[c]	15/12/10

a. Paid quarterly.
b. Paid semi-annually.
c. 9.0% pa paid until December 2008. Then BBSW plus 3.5% pa.

Source: Australian Securities Exchange.[13]

Corporate bonds are typically issued for periods of 5–10 years, although they have been issued for up to 15 years. For example, table 12.6 shows ACDHC notes that were issued on 7 July 2000 with a 15-year term. In the interest rate and investment climate at the time of writing, when interest rates are relatively low (the cash rate is 6.25%), corporate bonds with coupons in this relatively high range typically trade at a higher price, a premium, to face value. A premium of about 1–3% takes account of the higher yield of these bonds while still giving due emphasis to their higher risk status (higher than, for example, bank term deposits).

Subordinated debt: debt ranked below other similar classes of debt in the event that a firm is liquidated

Unsubordinated debt: does not take a lower ranking than other debt of similar characteristics

In the event of the issuing entity's becoming insolvent, unsecured notes rank for repayment of both principal and any unpaid interest behind secured creditors, equally with any other unsecured creditors and ahead of owners of ordinary shares. Some notes are issued as **subordinated debt**. This means that the issue is ranked below other similar classes of debt. Investors would normally demand a higher return from this debt to compensate them for the higher risk involved. In contrast, some issues are **unsubordinated debt**, which means that the issue does not take a lower ranking than other debt of similar characteristics.

Floating rate notes (FRNs)

Floating rate notes: loans that pay a variable coupon amount that is based on a short-term benchmark rate such as the bank bill swap rate (BBSW)

Floating rate notes (FRNs), as their name implies, pay a variable coupon amount that is based on a short-term benchmark rate such as the bank bill swap rate (BBSW). Normally, a fixed margin of perhaps 1–4% is paid above the BBSW and this varies according to market conditions. FRNs can be secured or unsecured. Many FRNs are perpetual, although some have fixed, normally long-term maturities such as 30 years. Additionally, many issues carry a right of redemption for the issuing firm at the face value after the expiry of an initial period. The issue price of notes is normally $100.

Some FRNs are traded on the ASX and table 12.7 gives details of some selected issues.

Table 12.7 Selected FRNs traded on the ASX

Security	ASX code	Coupon (% pa)
Adelaide Bank FR capital note	ADBHB	BBSW + 0.73%[a]
HY-FI Securities Ltd	HYFHA	BBSW + 1.35%[a]
Mahogany Capital Ltd	MHYHA	BBSW + 4.0%[b]
Macquarie income security	MBLHB	BBSW + 1.70%[a]
National income security	NABHA	BBSW + 1.25%[a]
Suncorp Metway FR capital note	SUNHB	BBSW + 0.75%[a]
Woolworths income security	WOWHA	BBSW + 2.00%[a]

a. Paid quarterly.
b. Paid semi-annually.

Source: Australian Securities Exchange.[14]

In the event that the issuing entity becomes insolvent, FRNs (if unsecured) rank for repayment of both principal and any unpaid interest behind secured creditors, equally with any other unsecured creditors and ahead of owners of ordinary shares. Noteholders are not entitled to share in the distribution of any surplus assets.

Debentures

Debentures: fixed-term debt securities issued under a prospectus. Debentures are secured by assets

Debentures (which are often untraded) are issued by firms to raise debt funds in a similar fashion to the issuing of unsecured notes. We define debentures in chapter 3 as fixed-term debt securities issued under a prospectus. They may be offered by finance companies and general financiers to the large institutional investors by way of a private issue, or they may be issued to the public after the full details of the issue and the firm are given in the publication of a prospectus. Information of interest in regard to the issue includes the minimum investment amount, the total amount of the issue, the maturity dates (normally 1–10 years), redemption details, interest rate offered (normally fixed), interest payment dates and the security that is being offered to investors should the firm become insolvent. Financial information includes the previous year's balance sheet and income statement (profit and loss account).

Debentures are secured by assets and may be offered with either a fixed or floating charge over the assets. A fixed charge means that specific assets are listed as security. A floating charge is held over a group of like assets that have not been offered as security to another lender and thus are free to be offered in this particular case. The advantage of offering a floating charge is that borrowers are free to manage their assets. In contrast, a fixed charge restricts the free sale of an asset if that were necessary in the normal course of business.

Unsecured notes are also issued by finance companies and general financiers. These are similar in characteristics to debentures except that they are unsecured. Normally they have maturities of 3–10 years and carry a fixed coupon. Because they are unsecured, they carry a higher coupon to compensate investors for the higher risk. These unsecured notes normally take the form of a certificate issued by the borrower and made out to the lender for the amount invested. Borrowers stipulate in the prospectus that amounts will be received in multiples of $100 or $1000. Where issues are not traded, investors must wait until maturity of each issue to be repaid their funds.

lo4

Discuss hybrid finance in the Australian markets.

Hybrid securities: securities that have characteristics of both debt and equity

Convertible preference shares: shares that pay dividends and convert on or before a specific date to the issuer's ordinary shares

Hybrid finance from the Australian market

Hybrid securities are securities that have characteristics of both debt and equity. The principal hybrid debt securities are convertible notes and convertible preference shares. **Convertible notes** pay interest and ultimately convert to the issuer's ordinary shares. **Convertible preference shares** convert to the issuer's ordinary shares but pay dividends in the interim. The principal difference between the two is that convertible notes pay interest and convertible preference shares pay dividends that are usually fully franked. With both types of securities, however, the issuer receives cash only on issue. Eventual conversion to ordinary shares is a cashless transaction.

Convertible notes

Convertible notes, while all converting ultimately to the issuer's ordinary shares, nevertheless are issued with varying conditions. However, firms issuing convertible notes are generally interested in claiming tax deductions for the interest payable on them, so the notes are normally issued with conditions that are acceptable to the ATO under the legislation. Chief among these conditions are:

- the interest rate is fixed
- note holders, not issuers, decide when to convert notes to ordinary shares
- conversion must take place between two and 10 years from date of issue so long as the note maturity is not less than two years.

The notes are normally unsecured and often subordinated, but some notes may not be issued with these conditions. Subordinated notes are issued when a firm has several issues of similar notes and wishes to indicate precedence in redemption should the firm fail. Most notes have a stated maturity date, but some may be issued as perpetual. Interest is paid either semi-annually or quarterly, with semi-annually being more common. Interest rates vary according to the perceived risk profile of the issuer. Each note normally converts to one ordinary share, although it is not uncommon for notes to convert to two or more ordinary shares.

Table 12.8 gives details of some selected notes traded on the ASX. Note that the fourth letter in the ASX code is 'G', which is the indicator letter for convertible notes. To illustrate some of the conditions of issue, APNG is cumulative and subordinated and GTPGA is a perpetual subordinated reset convertible note. Many issues with complex names are given attractive acronyms to help improve the security's marketability. For example, KZLG is designated as 'convertible unsecured redeemable listed early repayable securities' to give the acronym CURLERS and GTPGA is marketed as 'TREES2'. When examining the information in the table, note the difference in the interest rates payable. The rates directly reflect the perceived 'riskiness' of the issuing firm.

Table 12.8 Selected convertible notes traded on the ASX

Security	ASX code	Coupon (% pa)	Issue price ($)	Maturity date
APN News and Media unsecured cn	APNG	7.25[b]	3.95	31/10/08
Babcock & Brown Ltd	BNBG	8.182[b]	100.00	15/11/15
Dragon Mining NL	DRAG	10.00[a]	1.00	10/02/11
Great Southern Plantations Ltd	GTPGA	6.4[b]	100.00	31/12/36
Kargara Zinc Ltd unsecured cn	KZLG	9.75[b]	0.85	09/05/07

a. Paid quarterly.
b. Paid semi-annually.

Source: Australian Securities Exchange.[15]

The APN notes are redeemable by the issuer, at their issue price, on 31 October 2008 unless converted or redeemed earlier. Holders of the notes (investors) may convert some or all of their notes on fixed dates twice a year into one ordinary share per note. Alternatively, the issuer may redeem the notes prior to the maturity date under given circumstances. KZLG notes (CURLERS) introduce a further option to the normal set of conditions. The issuer may repay 50% of the value of CURLERS early and thus before the normal at-maturity condition. In this case, investors are compensated with an additional return. CURLERS also convert to two ordinary shares per note.

Convertible preference shares

Convertible preference shares (CPS), sometimes called hybrid securities, are perhaps the most popular interest rate security (IRS) traded on the ASX. Even so, the number of companies issuing and listing for trading CPS is small compared with the total number of firms which have their ordinary shares traded on the ASX. Possibly firms prefer the certainty of issuing either debt (which is likely to be cheaper) or ordinary shares. Table 12.9 gives details of some selected issues. The fourth letter in the ASX code, 'P', is the indicator code for convertible preference shares.

Table 12.9 Selected convertible preference shares (CPS) traded on the ASX

Security	ASX code	Dividend (% pa)	Issue price ($)	Maturity conversion date
ABC Learning Centres Ltd	ABSPA	6.75[b]	5.00	30/11/08
Adelaide Bank Ltd	ADBPB	floating[a]	100.00	10/10/14
ANZ Banking Group Ltd	ANZPA	BBSW + 1.00[a]	100.00	15/09/08
David Jones Ltd	DJSPA	at least 8%[b]	100.00	01/08/07
St George Bank SAINTS	SGBPA	floating[a]	100.00	perpetual
Timbercorp cps	TIMPA	9.00[b]	1.00	01/12/06

a. Paid quarterly.
b. Paid semi-annually.

Source: Australian Securities Exchange.[16]

CPS generally do not convert to ordinary shares in a fixed ratio, such as one for one or one for two, as was the case with convertible notes. Normally, the conversion ratio is calculated by taking into account volume-weighted average sale price on the ordinary shares on the market in the past 5–20 days before the conversion date. Additionally, a discount rate of 2.5–10% is applied to the average market price to enhance the conversion ratio and increase the benefits to the investor. For example, if the average price of ABC Learning Centres (ABS) shares during the 20 business days prior to the conversion date were $7.00, then the conversion ratio for each $5 ABSPA is 5:7 or $\frac{5}{7}$ ordinary shares for each ABSPA. [ABS has another proviso that the minimum number of shares to be issued on conversion is one (1:1) and the maximum number is five (5:1).] (In each case, the prospectus stipulates the number of decimal places the conversion rate is calculated to and also whether allocations, including part of a share, will be rounded up.)

Dividends payable on CPS are normally paid semi-annually until maturity in 5–7 years and are franked if the issuer has sufficient franking credits available. Dividends are normally fixed, as is the case with preference shares.

lo5

Describe international sources of funding.

International sources of funding

Australia as a nation has traditionally relied heavily on overseas capital as a source of funds to assist in our development. The need for international capital stems directly from our inability, for one reason or another, to save enough ourselves and therefore to provide sufficient 'home grown' capital. Foreign investment in Australian industry occurs when overseas investors make direct equity investments and lend directly, or make portfolio investments in equities or debt. **Direct investment** is defined by the Reserve Bank (RBA) as capital invested in an enterprise by an investor that has significant influence over the key policies of the enterprise. A proxy for that definition is that the investor owns at least 10% of the voting stock in the business. In contrast, **portfolio investment** is assumed to mean that the investor has no control over the key policies of the enterprise and that the investor owns less than 10% of the voting stock.[17] Australian companies can attract international funding by offering securities for sale in overseas markets or by attract foreign investors to purchase securities in Australian markets.

Direct investment: capital invested in an enterprise by an investor that has significant influence over the key policies of the enterprise

Portfolio investment: the investor has no control over the key policies of the enterprise

An example of a direct equity investment is the establishment of Virgin Blue in Australia. This airline was established through the direct investment of Sir Richard Branson's UK group into the Australian economy. (Virgin Blue has since listed on the ASX, so that Australian investors now own some of the airline.) An example of direct debt investment was included in the opening page of this chapter. Woolworths has raised debt in foreign capital markets and denominated in foreign currencies. In its 2006 annual report, Woolworths notes that, at 30 June, it had USD1326 million raised by debt securities in the US markets.[18]

While finance raised in global financial markets may often bear lower interest rates than those available in Australia for the same terms and maturities, borrowers have to be mindful of exchange rate risk. If the exchange rate moves against the borrower during the term of the loan, then the periodic interest payments will effectively rise, and the funds will no longer be cheap. The Australian dollar (AUD) value of the loan will also rise. For example, the value of the Australian dollar dropped from about USD1.15 in 1981 to about 77 cents in 1991, then to about 74 cents in 1997 and to 55 cents in late 2002. For practically any medium- to long-term borrowing period during this time, borrowers would have the exchange rate going against them. (Remember, when USD1.15 is worth AUD1, USD1 is worth about AUD0.87, and when AUD1 is worth USD0.55, USD1 is worth AUD1.82. So for every USD1 million that a firm borrows and receives AUD870000 at the former exchange rate, it must pay back AUD1820000 at the latter exchange rate.) Risk-averse borrowers hedge against exchange rate risk by using derivatives (see the Woolworths example in the following 'corporate financial governance' feature). Hedging costs a relatively small, known amount to guard against the risk of losing what could possibly be a very large amount.

CORPORATE FINANCIAL GOVERNANCE

Woolworths, as we have seen, has raised large sums in the US markets. The firm then uses sophisticated derivatives to manage the additional risks associated with these borrowings. This extract from their 2006 annual report highlights the company's policies regarding these risks.

(ii) Fair value hedge

A fair value hedge is a hedge of a fair value (i.e. 'mark-to-market') exposure arising on a recognised balance sheet asset or liability. A fair value hedge results in the fair value exposure being offset. Woolworths' fair value hedges include:

- Cross-currency interest rate swaps (CCIRS) that convert fixed interest rate foreign currency borrowings into floating rate Australian dollar borrowings. The CCIRS offsets the foreign currency and fixed interest rate fair value exposures arising on those borrowings.

Changes in the fair value of derivatives that are designated and qualify as fair value hedges are recorded as profit or loss immediately, together with any changes in the fair value of the hedged asset or liability that is attributable to the hedged risk.

Hedge accounting is discontinued when the hedge instrument expires or is sold, terminated, exercised, or no longer qualifies for hedge accounting. The adjustment to the carrying amount of the hedged item arising from the hedged risk is amortised to profit or loss from that date.

(iii) Hedge of monetary assets and liabilities

When a derivative financial instrument is used to hedge economically the foreign exchange exposure of a recognised monetary asset or liability, hedge accounting is not applied and any gain or loss on the hedging instrument is recognised in the income statement.

Source: Woolworths.[19]

Investors who do not have large amounts of funds to invest are normally portfolio investors. They will still want to diversify their holdings to decrease their risk and one way to diversify is to do so by geographical area. Thus, the proverbial 'French dentist' (newspapers often quote the views of this investor) who wants to gain exposure to international assets may invest in the Australian share market through purchases of shares, equity unit trusts, fixed interest trusts or cash trusts. Whatever their preferred investments, investors such as these are investing in Australian businesses.

Table 12.10 gives details of international investment in the Australian private sector for selected years since 1980. Note how international investment has grown. These data are given in current prices, and thus do not allow for inflation. However, even adjusting for the effects of inflation, the increase in foreign investment has been significant. To complement the data in table 12.10, table 12.11 gives the net foreign debt position of the Australian private sector at 30 June in recent years. These data allow for Australian investments overseas.

Table 12.10 International investment in the Australian private sector (A$ billion)

Year (at 30 June)	Direct investment			Portfolio investment		
	Equity	Debt	Total	Equity	Debt	Total
1980	16.8	2.3	19.1	6.3	4.0	10.3
1990	70.7	19.1	89.8	23.6	71.8	95.4
1997	130.1	28.9	159.0	86.9	160.0	246.9
1998	138.9	32.7	171.6	110.6	183.4	293.9
1999	152.7	33.5	186.2	134.2	182.1	316.3
2000	171.5	40.2	211.7	166.7	230.4	397.1
2001	184.2	52.4	236.6	173.2	275.6	448.8
2002	187.9	60.0	247.9	162.3	287.5	449.8
2003	209.8	72.0	281.9	155.2	301.8	457.0
2004	230.7	72.4	303.2	203.1	377.0	580.0
2005	231.8	74.6	306.4	199.8	416.2	616.0
2006	240.0	77.6	317.6	262.1	578.2	780.3

Source: Reserve Bank of Australia.[20]

Table 12.11 Australia's net foreign private sector debt and equity investment (billion)

Year (at 30 June)	Net debt (A$)	Net equities (A$)	Total (A$)
1995	182.5	64.7	247.2
1997	191.0	81.5	272.5
1999	230.5	91.0	321.5
2001	325.5	63.0	388.5
2002	345.0	41.0	386.0
2003	382.1	58.9	452.3
2004	423.4	61.3	499.2
2005	465.6	71.8	557.0
2006	542.9	50.5	593.4

Source: Reserve Bank of Australia.[21]

Eurobonds: debt securities issued outside the domestic capital market of the issuer in a currency that is neither the domestic currency of the issuer nor the domestic currency of the place of issue

The Woolworths example discussed previously illustrates the types of securities used by Australian firms to raise funds in the global financial markets. Woolworths used 6, 10, 12 and 15 year notes. Other firms such as Telstra have used **eurobonds** and bonds denominated in US and Singapore dollars, French francs and Japanese yen. Eurobonds are securities issued outside the domestic capital market of the issuer in a currency that is neither the domestic currency of the issuer nor the domestic currency of the place of issue. The name 'eurobond' has nothing to do with the currency of the European Union. While that currency is called the euro, the term 'eurobond' was being used long before the European Union came into existence. Telstra's issue of Deutschmark eurobonds, for example, was issued by an Australian company so the domestic currency of the issuer is Australian dollars. The issue was denominated in Deutschmarks, so coupon and maturity payments would have been made in Deutschmarks.[22] The place of issue was not ascertainable from Telstra's annual report, but it must have been in a market other than Germany or Australia (possibly London) for it to be a eurobond. Telstra's euro eurobonds have coupons and maturity payments made in the euro, but were issued outside Europe (possibly in the United States).

Foreign bonds: debt securities issued overseas in the currency of the country of issue

Foreign bonds are securities issued overseas in the currency of the country of issue. Telstra's US dollar loans include bonds issued by Telstra in the US market and the issue is denominated in US dollars, so is classified as foreign bonds.

Commercial paper: a generic term for unsecured loans which are normally issued only by borrowers of high repute with excellent credit ratings

Eurobonds, euroloans and euro-commercial paper (ECP) are all forms of borrowing in the Euromarkets. **Commercial paper** is a generic term for unsecured loans that are normally issued only by borrowers of high repute with excellent credit ratings. ECP is normally arranged through either an Australian bank or merchant bank. That bank acts as a lead agency which issues the securities through smaller groups of dealers who act as market makers in the secondary markets. The fact that there is an active secondary market gives investors confidence to invest in these issues. The chief investors are funds managers, financial institutions, businesses with surpluses, money and capital market dealers and affluent individuals ('French dentists'?). The lead agency normally arranges underwriting which, while costing the borrower extra, ensures that the issue raises the required amount of funding and is a success.

lo6

Discuss sources and the raising of equity finance.

Equity finance securities

Owners may at times wish to expand their businesses or liquidate some or all of their ownership rights. They achieve this by selling ownership rights to other investors. The means by which ownership rights are packaged, sold (and bought) and transferred are ordinary shares and preference shares. Ordinary shares are by far the more common of the two. All companies issue ordinary shares; some, but not all, companies issue preference shares.

Ordinary shares

Ordinary shares: evidence of part-ownership of a company

We defined **ordinary shares** as evidence of part-ownership of a company. They are the standard security by which companies divide and sell ownership rights to investors who wish to buy part-ownership of the firms. Ordinary shares have an initial issue price but, after they are issued, their price is set by the secondary market. If the company is listed with a stock exchange such as the ASX, price discovery is simple as the stock is quoted and in most cases sold every day. If the stock is not listed (and it is quite possible for a public company not to be listed), then price discovery is more difficult. In some cases of public but non-listed firms, brokers make OTC markets in the shares, and thus investors owning the stocks are able to find buyers relatively easily.

In the case of private companies, ownership is normally still divided up into shares, but often there may be as few as five or 10 shares only in each firm. The value of each share is usually very difficult to ascertain. Additionally, as these are often family-owned companies, there may be a family tradition or unwritten principle that the shares are not sold outside the family.

Ordinary shares have no fixed maturity date, unlike most forms of debt. The shares continue to exist so long as the firm exists. However, individual shares may undergo transformations such as share consolidations or share splits. These actions are discussed later in this section. The payments attaching to shares are dividends, the amounts of which are not guaranteed. Directors decide upon and declare dividends, normally twice a year, after the profitability of the firm for the relevant period has been calculated. Determinants of dividend policies are discussed in chapter 13. However, if there are no or insufficient profits after interest and taxes have been paid, dividends may not be paid and ordinary shareholders do not have any cumulative rights.

Ordinary shares conventionally rank last in the event of the winding up of the firm. However, the certainty of this ranking is now somewhat clouded following the successful *Sons of Gwalia vs Margaretic* case. The decision in this case has since been upheld by the High Court; thus, shareholders may in some circumstances rank equally with unsecured creditors. The claims of people holding debt (the senior ranked debt being paid first) are settled first, followed by the claims of preference shareholders. In most insolvencies, ordinary shareholders receive no repayment of their invested funds at all, because the pool of cash accumulated through the liquidation of assets is insufficient to pay out in full all those who rank above them. This chance increases the risk associated with ordinary shares. The collapses of HIH and One.Tel are good examples. Ordinary shareholders are unlikely to receive any repayments.

One of the major attractions of ordinary shares is their limited liability. Just imagine the behavioural differences that would exist in the investor community if shareholders were held responsible and liable for all the actions of the employees of the firms in which they had invested funds. Most reasonably risk-averse people would not invest in shares, but would merely invest in debt securities. The stock exchanges as we know them today would not exist! Thus, limited liability for shareholders enables firms to raise equity capital where otherwise they would be unable to do so. Shareholders are liable only to the extent of their subscribed capital in the case of initial shareholders and to the extent of the price paid for shares in the case of later shareholders.

Ordinary shareholders exercise their rights of ownership through their voting powers. An annual general meeting (AGM) must be held under the *Corporations Act 2001*. At this meeting, directors report to the owners, and owners vote new directors onto the board and approve changes to the constitution and possibly major changes in direction by the company. In practice, institutional shareholders and shareholdings associated with the directors normally hold a majority of the votes and seldom do the 'mums and dads' shareholders have enough voting power to effect major changes.

Share consolidations: reduce the number of shares on issue in direct proportion to the consolidation ratio

Share consolidations are not a source of equity finance — they are undertaken to:

- reduce the number of shares on issue
- increase the share price so that trading takes place within a popular price range
- 'hide' past losses (or at least draw attention away from the past losses or current lack of profitability that an extremely low share price indicates)
- improve public perception of the worth of the firm.

As an example, Centaur Mining and Exploration, now liquated, consolidated its shares on a 1:10 basis in the early 2000s and reduced its issued shares to 10% of the former number. Additionally, share consolidations may take place after companies demerge and adjust their capital structures. This occurred when Boral Ltd divided its energy and building products interests.

Share splits: reduce the share price and increase the number of issued shares

Share splits are not a source of equity finance — they are used to reduce the share price and increase the number of issued shares. They are normally undertaken for a number of reasons which are essentially the reverse of those for consolidation. Possibly the most important reason is that companies want their shares to be liquid and well traded. It is thought that high priced shares suffer reduced trading, even though an investment of a given amount buys the same proportion of the firm at any particular time, no matter whether that amount buys 5000 shares initially worth $1 or 25 000 shares initially issued at 20 cents. Westfield Holdings split their shares on a 5:1 basis in November 1997 when their share price climbed into the $30–40 range to reduce the market price at that time to less than $10. Additionally, when shares are closely held, there are fewer available for trading. Share splits can thus increase the number of shares available for trading. This was the principal reason given for the 5:1 split of ABC Learning Centres Ltd shares in November 2002. 'This [capital reconstruction]... is expected to significantly enhance the liquidity of ABC shares in the market.'[23]

Preference shares

Preference shares: hybrid equity instruments that have some characteristics of equity and some of debt which normally have a fixed dividend that has preference over the payment of ordinary dividends

As we see in chapter 3, **preference shares** are hybrid equity instruments with some characteristics of equity and some of debt that normally have a fixed dividend which has preference over the payment of ordinary dividends. In contrast to the convertible notes already discussed, preference shares tend to lean more towards equity than debt. Issuers are able to attach different sets of rights to their issues of preference shares, so the debt and equity characteristics vary between securities. Preference shares are regarded legally to be equity and preference dividends are regarded as a distribution of profits, not a tax-deductible expense.

Preference shares cater for investors who do not wish to be confronted with as much risk as is attached to investment in ordinary shares. So preference shares rank ahead of ordinary shares for repayment in the event of winding up the company and payment of preference share dividends ranks ahead of the payment of ordinary dividends. In addition, preference shares usually have a fixed dividend, such as 10% of issue price, rather than a dividend that fluctuates according to the profitability of the firm.

Among the different rights that may be attached to preference shares are:

- *franking* — companies can choose whether to attach franking credits.
- *cumulativeness* — preference shares are cumulative when past unpaid dividends accumulate until paid. In other words, a debt attaches to the shares until the firm is able to pay the dividends and ordinary dividends cannot be paid until the outstanding preference dividends are paid.
- *non-participation* — preference shares tend to be non-participating, which means they do not participate in additional profits or dividends to the stated dividend.
- *non-redemption* — while redeemable (by the issuer) preference shares have been issued in Australia, nowadays preference shares are normally not redeemable by the issuer.
- *voting* — preference shares generally do not have voting rights attached, but may gain such rights if the payment of dividends is in arrears or the value of the security is at risk.

As discussed, some preference shares are issued as converting preference shares so that eventually the shares convert to ordinary capital. A further point to note about preference shares is that they are usually not issued as partly paid. In this, they mimic debt. A firm issuing preference shares does so to collect the full amount of funds that they represent at the time of issue.

Firms issue preference shares to gain the following advantages:

- ownership rights are not diluted by the issue of preference shares, while the preference shares have no voting rights
- non-participation, being the norm, gives firms certainty in the cost of this form of funding
- cumulation or non-cumulation, non-payment of preference dividends cannot pose the solvency risk of debt
- the fixed cost of preference share capital allows firms to enhance earnings per ordinary share.

Raising equity finance

Raising equity finance generally takes place in two general circumstances:

- initial floats or initial public offers (IPO) to sell a part or the whole of previously private firms to the public or to start new companies
- the raising of further finance through private placements or rights issues.

Initial public offers

Initial public offer or **float:** the first issue of capital made to the public

As noted, firms decide to offer shares to the public when the current owners wish to diversify their own investment portfolios. (Typically owners of private businesses have put substantial proportions of their own investible funds into the businesses.) An **initial public offer** (IPO) is the first issue of capital made to the public. IPOs are also called '**floats**'. They are made when the current owners either no longer wish to be in that sort of business (as in the case of government privatisations), or when the current owners perceive that sharing ownership of their businesses with the public will be an easier and less risky option than continuing to try to raise funds for expansion through debt. See the following 'finance world' feature for a report on the IPOs of 2005.

The *Corporations Act 2001* and the listing rules of the ASX for public offers of firms that will be listed govern the conduct of floats. Shares are offered to the public by means of the publication of a prospectus, which includes all the information that a potential investor is thought to want and need to know in order to make an informed decision about the investment. The prospectus includes, among other information, the final financial reports of the previous period for established businesses and may also include a directors' forecast of future income which must be ratified by an independent accountant. Prospectuses must be approved by the Australian Securities and Investments Commission (ASIC) before being released to the public.

FINANCE WORLD

Perfect year to offer public a piece of the action

MICHAEL EVANS

The top five 2005 IPOs	Issue price	Close	Change %
Iron Ore Holdings	20c	$2.66	1230
PIPE Networks	40c	$2.34	485
Monaro Mining	20c	80c	300
Echelon Holdings	20c	71c	255
Energy Metals	25c	82.5c	230
The bottom five 2005 IPOs			
Narhex Life Sciences	20c	8.3c	–59
ZBB Energy	50c	21c	–58
Real Brand Holdings	20c	8.5c	–58
Buka Gold	50c	23c	–54
Westralian Gas & Power	25c	13c	–48

There were big ones, small ones, wildly successful ones and the occasional dog. But with confidence high and the market gaining another 17 per cent to record levels in 2005, there was no better time to tap investors for cash and go public.

Nearly 250 companies launched initial public offerings in 2005 which, while not a record, still raised more than $16 billion by the end of November.

There were floats that shone a light on the Melbourne establishment when the once-secret benefactors of gaming house Tattersall's were revealed. There were floats repackaging old favourites like Goodman Fielder — the year's biggest at $2.6 billion. And the big names were in there making a motza. Having paid $33 million for a 25 per cent stake in online job site Seek before it went public, the Packer-controlled Publishing & Broadcasting Ltd watched a scramble for stock that pushed its stake to around $210 million by Friday. There were also more Macquarie spin-offs than you could poke a stick at, including cash boxes, property trusts and media funds.

With China's appetite for raw materials roaring along, nearly one-third of 2005's floats were from mining companies while 20 per cent were financials. There was also plenty of infrastructure.

Given the extent of the resources boom, it shouldn't be a surprise that a company named Iron Ore Holdings was the IPO of the year. Its share price had risen 1230 per cent by year's end. After raising $6 million at 20c per share in May, its stock soared with the assistance of a 70 per cent price rise producers secured from steel makers. That made one man in particular, the little know Iron Ore Holdings founder and technical director Derek Ammon, a very wealthy person.

Mr Ammon has 20 year of experience in mineral exploration and mining, and a track record of identifying iron ore deposits. He has also seen his 50 per cent stake in the company jump from $3 million to around $36 million.

The worst float of the year was biotech Narhex Life Sciences, which raised $8 million in January at 20c only to see its shares lose nearly 60 per cent by Friday's close of 8.3c.

Successful floats included telecom tiddlers like PIPE Networks, which raised $3.5 million in May at 40c before closing at $2.30.

The best of the larger listings was Transpacific Industries, which raised nearly $500 million in May at an offer price of $2.40. It closed the year at $5.65. Transpacific chairman Terry Peabody appears to be a man in a hurry, telling shareholders at the annual meeting he would go all out for a big acquisition if it presented itself in the next 12 months. Just weeks later, Transpacific threw its lot in with cashed-up private equity investor CHAMP to examine a multimillion-dollar bid for Brambles's waste management operations in Australia.

Among big name players, the Packer-backed online job classifieds site Seek raised more than $160 million in April at $2.10 and with sentiment in the media sector leaning towards the internet, finished the year at $3.02.

Robert Whyte's Trafalgar Corporate Group raised $113 million in July and was up around 10 per cent by year's end.

Frank Cicutto didn't get much early joy from RUN Corp, which raised $25 million in December at $1 and had eased 1c by Friday.

Celebrity-backed stocks this year included Reverse Corp, promoted by former tennis player Pat Rafter, who reportedly took stock in the company as payment for his endorsement. The company raised $75.5 million at $1.65 this month before closing at $1.72.

Visible brand names like Domino's Pizza did well, raising $75 million at $2.20c in May and closing at $3.25.

Mining stocks weren't just at the top of the pile this year but also at the bottom. It's hard to imagine that a uranium miner ended up near the bottom but Uranium Exploration Australia managed to do so, turning its 20c listing price from November into 12.5c.

And big didn't always mean best. Macquarie Bank's listed cash box, Macquarie Capital Alliance Group, raised $1 billion with a first instalment of $2 and made plenty of acquisitions. But its share price closed the year at $1.665.

And the one that got away for the year? Affinity Health's hospital portfolio never made it to market. Ramsay Health Care saw to that, snaffling the one-time Mayne Group hospitals for nearly twice the amounts ($1.4 billion) Mayne had sold them for 18 months earlier.[24]

In order to ensure that IPOs are successful, issues are often underwritten by brokers or investment bankers. This means that the sponsoring brokers or bankers agree to guarantee that the whole of the required funds will be raised. These guarantees are given in return for underwriting fees. The underwriters use their contacts with both institutional and private investors to bring the floats to their attention to ensure there is strong demand for the issues. IPOs are not always underwritten. The decision depends on the issuer's assessment of the risk of undersubscription and the size of the underwriting fees. Underwriting fees normally are in the order of 2–5%, but the actual fees vary with the size of the float and the relative power of all parties. Apart from earning underwriting revenues, brokers are keen to become managing agents for large IPOs because of the transaction fees attached. This is especially true in times where enhanced competition has pared normal brokerage fees down to just above the cost of production.

Firms thinking about raising funds from the public through a float obviously have to consider the costs as well as the benefits, already discussed. There are cash costs in the additional accounting services required to prepare and submit the prospectus. There are printing and distribution costs, commissions paid to brokers, transaction fees paid to share registries (unless the firm decides to manage its own share register, which would necessitate the employment of extra staff and resources) and listing fees paid to the ASX. About 75% of industrial firms elect to underwrite IPOs. Why do they do it, at a cost of, say, 4% of the raised funds? There are many reasons.

- Firms can never be totally sure how popular an issue will be.
- Conditions in the stock market may deteriorate dramatically between the time of deciding to go public and the time investors have to commit funds.
- Firms want to be sure of raising the required amount of funds.
- Directors do not want to be seen to preside over a failed float.

Another issue to be considered very carefully is the matter of price. What price should a firm set as the value of each of its shares when there is no historical record to refer to? Directors of issuing firms solve the problem of the offer price in two ways:

Book-build: uses a bidding system to combine the expertise of large investors to determine the price of an issue

- set a fixed price
- hold a **book-build**.

When a fixed price issue is made, the offer price for the shares is specified in the prospectus. If the issuers choose to use a book-build to set the offer price, they will solicit bids from large investors to determine the price of an issue. Even though book-builds have been used for such high-profile issues as Telstra and Sanity, they are used relatively rarely in Australia. Over the last few years, book-builds have comprised fewer than approximately 5% of issues.

You may remember several book-build floats and so may be surprised to learn that the majority of issues are not book-builds. The following 'behavioural perspective' feature will shed some light on how you may have drawn the wrong conclusion.

BEHAVIOURAL PERSPECTIVE

Inappropriate weights

The ready availability of information leads many decision makers to overestimate the probability of occurrence. Experiments have shown that people also overvalue certainty and the appearance of certainty and undervalue low probabilities.[25] For evidence of these propositions, can you remember reading about a flood through a housing area in your state? After a flood has drained away, the value of affected housing normally falls dramatically, as if a flood were due again next week. On the other hand, after several years without flooding, people act as if a flood had never occurred in the area and even complain that local government rules to prevent building in the potentially worst-affected areas are unfair, unnecessary and a ridiculous over-reaction when worthy citizens need the space.

Book-build issues tend to be used for privatisations of government enterprises and the larger private sector floats. As such, they attract a lot of media attention. Because they are familiar to many people, they can pose a problem of 'representation bias'. If you have heard more about this type of float and have seen more examples of it, you might assume that it is the most popular means of setting the offer price for floats. When this happens, you are extrapolating the probability from a small and unrepresentative sample of floats to the entire population and coming up with an erroneous conclusion.

Setting a fixed offer price

A firm that is considering going public will find an advisor to the float. The advisor may be a broker, an investment bank or the underwriter if the firm plans to use one. Advisors tend to use a 'comparable firms' approach to setting the offer price. Comparable firms are listed firms of about the same size and in the same industry. Advisors take the comparable firms' P/E ratios (see chapter 6) and derive an appropriate multiple. This P/E is applied to the IPO firm's forecast earnings to estimate a base value for each share. A further step is then to adjust the base price for perceived differences in risk, level of retained ownership, size and growth prospects. Advisors then often estimate a range within which the final price should lie and negotiate with the issuing firm to set the final price. Mining companies frequently use fixed price offers, but the prices are calculated on the basis of the present value of the expected cash flows from mineral reserves. For miners, geologists' reports are used to assess the production capacity of the reserves.

A risk for the owners of the firm with a fixed price issue is that the general direction of the stock market will move dramatically during the time the issue is open. In Australia, the typical period from issuing the prospectus to the close of a fixed price offer is about two months. If investors hold off subscribing until the final few days of an offer period of, say, eight weeks, the market may have lost 5% of its value, the issue will be seen as expensive and may close undersubscribed. Contrarily, if the market has gained 5% during the offer period, the issue will probably be oversubscribed and directors will believe they have set the price too low and have short-changed the current owners.

Book-building an offer price

An alternative to setting the offer price in the prospectus is to conduct an issue that takes a book-building approach. A book-build uses a bidding system to combine the expertise of large investors to determine the price of an issue. A benefit of book-builds is that they have a much lower time from setting the offer price to the time of issuing the shares. However, setting an issue price even a day or so before listing by using a book-build cannot exactly mirror rapid changes in the general level of the market. Large investors, particularly institutional investors, are invited to bid for blocks of shares, and in this way the final price of the issue is set. Book-builds for the sale of equities exactly replicate the process whereby the RBA sells Treasury notes in the money market.

Two systems are available in setting up a book-build. One system uses open pricing, where investors submit bids for stock with no constraints on either the prices or desired volumes. To use a simplified example, suppose Tara Products (TP) offers 10 million shares to the public through a book-build. Table 12.12 gives the assumed bids, listed in descending order of price.

Table 12.12 Bids received for TP shares

Price ($)	No. of shares required (m)
5.05	1
5.00	3
4.90	3
4.85	4
4.80	4
4.70	2
4.60	2

TP's directors, who want to maximise the funds raised from the float, will accept the individual offers down to $4.85. Whether they allocate the whole four million shares at $4.85 or allocate only three million depends on the conditions set out in the prospectus. Some firms are prepared to accept oversubscriptions and allocate more shares. Others will keep to the limit initially proposed and will allocate shares according to a method indicated in the prospectus. By taking this approach, the directors have extracted as much as possible for the shares and have made use of the combined wisdom of the market.

The alternative system with a book-build is to offer shares within a given range of prices and then set the final price as a weighted average of the bids received. Thus, in the TP example, the directors might stipulate that the final price will be in the range of $5.05 and $4.70. Investors are then invited to make bids. Suppose bids were made as in table 12.12, ignoring the $4.60 bid. The weighted average of the six bids is $4.87 and this is set as the final price for all bidders. Again, the method of allocation among bidders is described in the prospectus. Sometimes, there are two rounds of bidding among institutional investors, so that those who bid too low initially have another chance to receive an allocation of shares at the final price.

Australian book-builds are normally accompanied by a retail offer that smaller shareholders can participate in. The retail offer usually gives an indicative range for the final offer price and the final price to retail investors is based on the final book-build price. The price for retail investors may be at a discount to the price established for the institutional investors.

Book-builds have been used in Australia since the early 1990s. The process of collecting bids to establish offer price is relatively more expensive than the price setting process for fixed price offers, so it is not surprising that book-builds are used fairly infrequently and for only very large issues. Book-builds were used by the Commonwealth Government in selling the final part of Qantas in 1995–96 and half of Telstra in 1997 and 1998. Book-building is the predominant method used for setting offer prices in the United States. Their use in Australia has possibly been influenced by the growth in importance of institutional investors, with the rapid increase in funds under management stemming from the new superannuation arrangements and the large number of government privatisations in the last decade of the twentieth century.

Many investors perceive that IPOs are underpriced and that there will be good profits to be made by applying for shares and selling on the first day of trade.[26] This practice is known as **stagging** and such an investor is a 'stag'. This perception exists in the market because there have been many cases where supplies of shares are short of demand and the price does rise significantly on the first day of trade. However, this is not invariably the case and sometimes stags get 'burnt' and make substantial losses.

Stagging: the practice of applying for and buying shares issued under a prospectus and selling them on the first day of trade on the market for a profit

Raising more equity finance

Firms pursuing growth need more capital from time to time. Companies, after flotation, may source the needed funds through more debt or through the issue of rights or through private placements or offers to the public under a prospectus. A company putting in place a plan for the future raising of funds may also issue options. This section discusses the issue of rights and options.

Rights

A **rights issue** is the issue of new shares to existing shareholders in proportion to the number of shares they already hold. The 'rights' terminology refers to the entitlement of existing shareholders to subscribe. Normally there is a benefit attached to the right in that the new issue of shares is made available at a price that is below the current market price.

Rights issue: the issue of new shares to existing shareholders in proportion to the number of shares they already hold

The number of rights a shareholder receives depends on how many shares are already owned by the shareholder. For example, ABC Learning Centres at 30 June 2002 showed equity of $27.5 million in its balance sheet, made up of $20.3 million of contributed capital from the issue of 14.8 million shares and $7.2 million in reserves. ABC wanted to double its capital approximately. Shares in ABC were selling at that time at about $14 on the market. Directors had two decisions to make:

- What subscription price should be set for shares?
- What ratio should the issue represent to current shareholdings?

With 14.8 million shares on issue, a 1-for-1 issue (one right issued for each share held) at $2 subscription a share would raise nearly $30 million less costs. On the other hand, a 1-for-6 issue (one right for every six shares held) at $13 a share would also raise a similar amount, and there are many other combinations that would achieve the desired result. How do directors make this decision? They want the issue to be attractive to investors and they want to optimise costs. ABC settled on a 2-for-11 issue at $10.80 per share. Thus, an investor with 5500 shares received rights to subscribe to 1000 more shares at $10.80 per share, with none of the normal transaction costs that accrue with purchases through a broker on market.

What if an investor does not want to invest more funds in this company or does not have any free cash available to invest at the time? Most rights issues are **renounceable**. That is, shareholders are free to sell their rights to subscribe on the market. (Some issues are **non-renounceable**, which means that investors are not able to sell the rights even though they may decline to subscribe more funds.) The value of each right to subscribe to one share naturally depends on the discount implied with the rights subscription price.

Renounceable: rights that can be sold on the market if the shareholder does not wish to subscribe to the issue

Non-renounceable: rights that cannot be sold on the market. The shareholder has to subscribe to the issue or let the offer lapse.

In the case of ABC, with a subscription price of $10.80 and a market price of $14, the discount was $3.20. The theoretical value of each right thus is about $2.71. We will examine the calculation of this value shortly. Shareholders who did not wish to subscribe further funds could sell their rights for about this price, the actual price depending on supply and demand conditions on the day. It is interesting to learn in an ABC information release to the ASX on 30 October 2002 that 98.09% of the rights were taken up. This means that the owners of about 280 000 shares and about 52 000 rights did not take up rights and nor did they sell the rights, each worth about \$2.71. These investors must not have understood that the company was handing them a free bonus of about \$140 000 in total.

The theoretical price of a right, R, is calculated with the aid of the following equation:

$$RP = \frac{N(P_m - S)}{N + 1} \qquad [12.1]$$

where RP = theoretical price of a right
N = number of shares that must be held to receive one right
P_m = price of a share with the rights entitlement attached
S = rights issue subscription price

$P_m - S$ is the discount implied by the difference between the market price of a share and the subscription price. $\frac{N}{(N+1)}$ reduces the difference to account for the increase in the number of shares once the rights issue is made. In the ABC case:

$$\begin{aligned} RP &= \frac{N(P_m - S)}{N+1} \\ &= \frac{5.5(14 - 10.80)}{6.5} \\ &= \$2.71 \end{aligned}$$

Another way of coming to the same conclusion is that a shareholder must own 11 shares worth \$154 (11 × \$14) and pay another \$21.60 (2 × \$10.80) when taking up the two rights, making an investment of \$175.60. The shareholder then owns 13 shares. This makes each share worth approximately \$13.51. As the subscription price for the rights share is \$10.80, the right must be worth \$2.71 (\$13.51 – \$10.80).

This latter way of thinking about the value of a right also allows the valuation of the shares after the rights issue or the valuation of the shares **ex-rights** using the following equation:

Ex-rights: the share price quoted without the right to purchase further shares attached

$$P_x = \frac{(NP_m + S)}{N + 1} \qquad [12.2]$$

where P_x = ex-rights price
N = number of shares that must be held to receive one right
P_m = price of a share with the rights entitlement attached
S = rights issue subscription price

To confirm the reasoning above:

$$\begin{aligned} P_x &= \frac{(5.5 \times 14 + 10.80)}{6.5} \\ &= \$13.51 \end{aligned}$$

Because a company issuing capital through rights is asking the public for funds just the same as a company making an initial issue, a rights issue must have a prospectus approved by ASIC. Normally, with renounceable issues, a rights trading period of 25 to 60 days is set to allow shareholders who do not wish to subscribe more capital the opportunity to sell their rights. When companies announce a rights issue, they normally also announce the record date on which the names registered on the share register and their holdings will be taken as the correct record of current shareholders. To cope with the need to allow time for recent sales to be recorded, the shares trade ex-rights four trading days previously. In other words, if you buy shares fewer than five trading days before the record date for a rights issue, you will not receive the entitlement to rights.

A rights issue will normally be underwritten by the company where the issue is large in terms of the absolute amount of capital or large in relation to the current contributed capital, the subscription price does not give a substantial discount to market price or the issue is non-renounceable. As already discussed, the underwriting is an expense, but the alternatives of perhaps not raising the required capital or having to give a larger discount are also expensive. As a matter of interest, the ABC rights issue was underwritten for a fee of 3%. The lead manager of the issue also received another $100 000 fee for its services.

Options

Option: grants the right but not the obligation to undertake a trade by a given date at a given price

The other method which companies use to raise further capital is by means of options. An **option** to purchase shares is the right to subscribe to shares at a price and time that are pre-determined. The difference between this company option and the so-called exchange-traded options (ETOs) such as puts and calls is that the relevant company issues these options itself. ETOs, on the other hand, are created as contracts between buyers and sellers separate from the companies whose shares are the underlying assets involved in each contract. (Just to confuse the issue, these company options are also traded on stock exchanges.)

Normally the exercise price of options is set at a value which may be near the current market price but which is thought to be at a substantial discount to the expected market price at the time the options may last be exercised. Thus, a company might give options exercisable until a final date in five years' time at $2, when the current share price is $1.80. An option exercisable by, say, 1 August 2012 may be exercised at any time until expiry at that date. In the meantime, the option has value and may be traded, the price being dependent on the difference between the exercise price and the current market price of the underlying shares. If the option is not exercised by the expiry date, the option expires and is worthless. Options with exercise prices that are above the market price of the shares are worth very little while this situation exists. The value of an 'out-of-the-money' option, if it has any at all, lies in the chance that the relevant market price might change to such a degree that it becomes 'in the money' before it expires.

Companies issue options for four main purposes:

- to set in place a programmed raising of funds in the future
- to reward and motivate employees, usually senior in rank, and directors so that their financial health is aligned with that of the company
- as an additional benefit attached to an equity issue to make the current issue more attractive, but also to put in place the opportunity to raise more capital
- as an additional benefit attached to a debt contract to secure the funds or to benefit from a lower interest rate.

We discuss options further in chapter 15.

executive summary

lo1 discuss the range of loans offered by financial institutions together with their normal terms and conditions

- Firms may gain funding through the financial institutions or from the markets. Financial institutions offer a wide range of loans with varying terms and conditions.
- Terms are usually given for up to 25 years, with the interest rate being fixed only for the first three, five or 10 years.
- Variable rate business loans are also available from most of the major financial institutions with similar conditions to fixed rate loans with the exception that interest rates vary from the outset in line with changes in the markets.
- Instalment loans differ from other business loans in that fixed repayment schedules are negotiated at the outset.
- Interest-only loans are taken out to finance special situations and only interest is paid during the term of the loan, while the repayment of the principal amount is made in full at the expiry of the term.
- FDAs are a major form of secured business financing, normally with variable interest rates and regular repayment schedules.
- Leasing is a significant form of finance for business with new leasing approvals by financial institutions annually aggregating to several billion dollars.

lo2 discuss the issues relating to the lease or buy decision

- The classification of leases depends on the extent to which the risks and rewards of ownership are transferred.
- Leases are classed as finance leases when substantially all the risks and rewards of ownership are transferred.
- Leases are operating leases when substantially all the risks and rewards of ownership remain with the lessor.
- Lease payments are tax-deductible if the asset is used to produce assessable income and the lease is not a purchase by instalment arrangement.
- The potential benefits of leasing include:
  - taxation benefits
  - efficiency of asset management and disposal
  - speed in acquisition of assets
  - avoidance of obsolescence
  - improved cash flows and conservation of capital.
- Lease or buy analyses may or may not include taxation effects.

lo3 describe market sources of debt

- Firms wanting to raise debt finance from the Australian market have corporate bonds, notes and debentures to choose from as the financing media.
- Corporate bonds are unsecured, so good credit rankings by the ranking agencies, Moody's and Standard & Poor's, are extremely important to potential issuers of bonds.

- Corporate bonds are typically issued for periods of 3–6 years, although they have been issued for up to 15 years.
- FRNs pay a variable coupon amount that is based on a short-term benchmark rate such as the bank bill swap rate (BBSW).
- FRNs can be secured or unsecured.
- Debentures may be offered to the large institutional investors by way of a private issue or may be issued to the public after the full details of the firm and the issue are given in the publication of a prospectus.
- Debentures may be offered with either fixed or floating charge over assets.
- A fixed charge means that specific assets are listed as security.
- A floating charge is held over a group of like assets that have not been offered as security to another lender and thus are free to be offered in this particular case.

lo4 discuss hybrid finance in the Australian markets

- Hybrid securities have characteristics of both debt and equity.
- Hybrid securities comprise convertible notes and convertible preference shares.
- Convertible notes, while all converting ultimately to the issuer's ordinary shares, are issued with varying conditions, including:
  - the interest rate is fixed
  - note holders, not issuers, decide when to convert notes to ordinary shares
  - conversion must take place between two and 10 years from date of issue so long as the note maturity is not less than two years.
- Convertible preference shares convert eventually to ordinary shares generally on a current value basis less a discount to enhance attraction to investors.
- Dividends paid on convertible preference shares are generally fixed as with preference shares.

lo5 describe international sources of funding

- Foreign investment in Australian industry occurs when overseas investors make direct equity investments and lend directly, or make portfolio investments in equities or debt.
- Portfolio investment is normally undertaken by investors who do not have very large amounts of funds to invest but still want to diversify their holdings geographically to decrease their risk.
- Portfolio investment is assumed to mean that the investor has no control over the key policies of the enterprise and that the investor owns less than 10% of the voting stock.
- Australian companies can attract international funding by offering securities for sale in overseas markets or by attracting foreign investors to purchase securities in Australian markets.
- Eurobonds are debt securities issued outside the domestic capital market of the issuer in a currency that is neither the domestic currency of the issuer nor the domestic currency of the place of issue.
- Foreign bonds are debt securities issued overseas in the currency of the country of issue.

- Eurobonds, euroloans and euro-commercial paper (ECP) are all forms of borrowing in the Euromarkets.
- Commercial paper is a generic term for unsecured loans which are normally issued only by borrowers of high repute with excellent credit ratings.
- ECP is normally arranged through either an Australian bank or a merchant bank.
- That bank acts as a lead agency which issues the securities through smaller groups of dealers who act as market-makers in the secondary markets.
- An active secondary market gives investors confidence to invest in these issues.
- The chief investors are funds managers, financial institutions, businesses with surpluses, money and capital market dealers and affluent individuals.

lo6 discuss sources and the raising of equity finance

- Ordinary shares are the standard security by which companies divide and sell ownership rights to investors who wish to buy part-ownership of the firms.
- Ordinary shares have an initial issue price but, after that time their price is set by the secondary market.
- The payments attaching to shares are dividends, the amounts of which are not guaranteed.
- Ordinary shares rank last in the event of the winding up of the firm.
- One of the major attractions of ordinary shares is their limited liability.
- Preference shares are a hybrid form of capital, which lean more towards equity than debt.
- Firms issue preference shares to gain the following advantages:
  - ownership rights are not diluted by the issue of preference shares, while the preference shares have no voting rights
  - non-participation, being the norm, gives firms certainty in the cost of this form of funding
  - cumulation or non-cumulation, non-payment of preference dividends cannot pose the solvency risk of debt
  - the fixed cost of preference share capital allows firms to enhance earnings per ordinary share.
- Firms need more capital from time to time, and may source needed funds through the issue of rights, private placements or the issue of options.

Key terms

book-build, p. 449
commercial paper, p. 444
convertible notes, p. 439
convertible preference shares, p. 439
corporate bonds, p. 436
debentures, p. 438
direct investment, p. 441
eurobonds, p. 443
ex-rights, p. 453
finance leases, p. 426
float, p. 447
floating rate notes, p. 438
foreign bonds, p. 444
fully drawn advances, p. 425
hire-purchase agreement p. 426
hybrid securities, p. 439
initial public offer, p. 447
instalment loans, p. 424
intermediated finance, p. 422
lease, p. 426
lessee, p. 426
lessor, p. 426
non-renounceable, p. 452

novated lease, p. 426
operating leases p. 426
option, p. 454
ordinary shares, p. 444
over-the-counter (OTC) market, p. 437
portfolio investment, p. 441
preference shares, p. 446
renounceable, p. 452
rights issue, p. 452
share consolidations, p. 445
share splits, p. 445
stagging, p. 452
subordinated debt, p. 437
unsubordinated debt, p. 437

Learning chart

Learning objective	Questions	Self-test problems	Financial problems
lo1 discuss the range of loans offered by financial institutions together with their normal terms and conditions	12.1, 12.2, 12.3, 12.4, 12.5, 12.6	12.1, 12.2, 12.3	12.1, 12.2, 12.3, 12.4, 12.5
lo2 discuss the issues relating to the lease or buy decision	12.7, 12.8, 12.9	12.4	12.6, 12.7, 12.8, 12.9, 12.10
lo3 describe market sources of debt	12.10, 12.11		12.11, 12.12, 12.13
lo4 discuss hybrid finance in the Australian markets	12.12, 12.13, 12.14, 12.15, 12.16		
lo5 describe international sources of funding	12.17, 12.18		
lo6 discuss sources and the raising of equity finance	12.19, 12.20	12.5	12.14, 12.15, 12.16, 12.17

Questions

12.1 Explain to a friend the difference between intermediated finance and direct finance. Give an example.

12.2 Under what conditions do you think a financial manager would want to lock in a fixed rate for a 5-year loan?

12.3 Would you expect a fixed rate for a 3-year loan to be higher or lower that a quoted fixed rate for a 5-year loan?

12.4 Why might the owners of a small business structured as a partnership prefer an instalment loan rather than a business loan?

12.5 Explain to a friend the principle of an interest-only loan and give two examples of appropriate uses.

12.6 How can commercial bills which are inherently short-term in nature be used as long-term finance?

12.7 Explain what a novated lease is and how they are commonly used. What are the advantages to an employee entering such an arrangement?

12.8 Explain how it is possible that a bank could manage a suburban courier firm's vehicle fleet more efficiently than the operating firm.

12.9 Critically evaluate the avoidance of obsolescence argument with regard to leasing of IT equipment.

12.10 What is the chief difference between a corporate bond and an FRN?

12.11 What is the chief difference between a corporate bond and a debenture?

12.12 Explain to your long-suffering friend the meaning of hybrid finance.

12.13 How do convertible notes convert?

12.14 Do convertible preference shares convert in the same manner as convertible notes? Explain.

12.15 Define subordinated debt.

12.16 What does 'OTC' imply in relation to a finance deal?

12.17 What is the difference between direct and portfolio investment in the international arena, according to the RBA?

12.18 How might companies raising finance internationally protect themselves against the additional risk incurred when compared with domestic finance?

12.19 If you were the owner of a company which had decided to become public and listed, what factors would govern the timing of the IPO? Would you use an underwriter? Explain the issues.

12.20 Explain how a constrained book-build for pricing equities works.

Self-test problems

12.1 James Strand is a sole trader who runs a machinery and road-vehicle tyre business in a major country town. James needs funds to increase his stock. He decides to take out a $500 000 instalment loan, repayable on a fixed monthly schedule, at 6% fixed for 3 years.

(a) How much must James repay at the end of each month?

(b) What is the total amount repaid?

12.2 Instead of taking out the loan in problem 12.1, how much would James owe at the end of 3 years if he had taken out a $500 000 interest-only loan for that period at 6% pa, compounded monthly.

12.3 AGH Ltd arranges for an instalment loan with its bank. The loan is for $1 million, the rate is fixed at 8.8% pa and the period is 15 years. Repayments are due quarterly starting in 3 months and the interest is compounded quarterly. How much is each instalment?

12.4 Campco is the trading name for a camping-gear store structured as a partnership. Campco runs a fleet of three delivery vehicles which need replacing. Campco can borrow funds to buy the vehicles costing $100 000 in total for 7.2% pa after tax, compounded semi-annually. Alternatively, their financier will arrange lease finance over 3 years with 6 semi-annual payments of $13 000; the first payment to be made when the lease is signed. A residual payment of $40 000 will secure ownership of the three vehicles if Campco decides to buy them at the end of the lease period. This value is considered to be fair market value for the vehicles. Campco intends to buy the vehicles at that time and keep them for another year. These vehicles are normally depreciated at a prime rate of 20% pa. Campco's owners pay tax on average at the rate of 30% and pay an instalment of tax every quarter. Assume for simplicity's sake that the tax benefits from each lease payment and the tax benefits forgone for depreciation are received without time lag in each half-year period. Should the vehicles be leased or purchased?

12.5 Energiservices (EGS) wants to raise more funds and decides on a rights issue. The issue will be on the basis of 1 for 3 and the subscription for each share in the rights issue will be \$3. EGS are currently selling for \$5.10. What are the theoretical ex-rights share and rights prices?

Solutions to self-test problems

12.1 This is a PV problem. The PV is \$500 000, k is 0.005 and n is 36.

$$PV = C\left\{\frac{1-(1+k)^{-n}}{k}\right\}$$

$$500\,000 = C\left\{\frac{1-1.005^{-36}}{0.005}\right\}$$

$$= C \times 32.87102$$

$$C = \$15\,210.97$$

$$\text{Total amount} = \$15\,210.97 \times 36$$

$$= \$547\,594.92$$

12.2 $FV = P(1+i)^n$

$$= 500\,000\ (1.005)^{36}$$

$$= \$598\,340.26$$

12.3 This is a PV problem. PV is \$1 000 000, k is 0.022 and n is 60.

$$PV = C\left\{\frac{1-(1+k)^{-n}}{k}\right\}$$

$$1\,000\,000 = C\left\{\frac{1-1.022^{-60}}{0.022}\right\}$$

$$1\,000\,000 = C \times 33.137$$

$$C = \$30\,177.73$$

12.4 Analysis of cash flows (\$'000)

Item	$t = 0$	$t = 1$	$t = 2$	$t = 3$	$t = 4$	$t = 5$	$t = 6$
Lease proceeds	+100						
Lease payments	−13	−13	−13	−13	−13	−13	−40
Tax benefit from lease payments		+3.9	+3.9	+3.9	+3.9	+3.9	+3.9
Tax benefit forgone (depreciation)		−3	−3	−3	−3	−3	−3
Net benefits	+87	−12.1	−12.1	−12.1	−12.1	−12.1	−39.1

The PV of −\$12 100 for 5 periods at a discount of 3.6% per period, using the annuity formula, is −\$54 478. The present value of the single sum of −\$39 100 is −\$31 624. Together with the \$87 000 initial net benefits, the NPV of the cash flows is \$898. The result of \$898 indicates that the lease finance is a better option than the loan of funds to purchase the vehicles.

12.5 $P_x = \dfrac{(NP_m + S)}{N + 1}$

$= \dfrac{(3 \times 5.10 + 3)}{4}$

$= \$4.57$

$R = \dfrac{N(P_m - S)}{N + 1}$

$= \dfrac{3(5.10 - 3)}{4}$

$= \$1.57$

Financial problems

12.1 Penline Partnership wants to but some new production equipment — sorters and graders. The equipment will cost $450 000. Penline's bank manager advises the manager to take out a fixed interest loan for 5 years at 7.8%. Payments are due monthly and the interest is compounded monthly.

(a) What is the monthly repayment?

(b) How much interest will Penline pay in total over the 5 years?

12.2 Dog-eared Books buys and sells second-hand paperback books. The manager needs to reorganise the business's finances from short-term to long-term debt. She decides to take out an FDA for $50 000 at 7.5% pa, compounded monthly over 4 years. She also agrees to repay the loan on a fixed monthly schedule. What is the monthly payment?

12.3 The manager of Dog-eared Books is offered a one-off opportunity to distribute the 4000 copies of a remaindered Accounting textbook. The cost is $80 000. She has sufficient contacts and she is fairly sure she can sell the whole lot within 6 months. She is offered an interest-only loan at 6.4% pa, compounded monthly, for 6 months or a 180-day commercial bill at 6.4% pa discount to fund the purchase. Note that the commercial bill will have a higher face value than $80 000 in order to give her a full $80 000 in funding. Which source of finance costs less in dollar terms?

12.4 Joseph Beete Enterprises (JBE) needs two new computers plus a rather expensive plan printer. Joe, the owner/manager, goes to one dealer who offers a deal involving a repayment-free period of 25 months, then 24 payments of $800 per month. Another dealer offers similar equipment financed by a finance company loan requiring 20 payments of $750 per month starting in one month. Which is the better deal for JBE?

12.5 Glass Blowers Inc. is a group of keen craftspeople who blow glass and produce high-quality ornamental glassware. They have a regular cash flow and are considered reliable customers by their bank. They need $95 000 – $100 000 funding for about 1 year and their bank manager suggests two commercial bills for 180 days maturity. They take out the first bill ($100 000 at 5.8% yield) and the second bill for $100 000 at 6.0% yield. Advise Glass Blowers of the exact cash flows they will receive or need to pay out during the 360-day period (ignoring any extra fees).

12.6 Brown's Foundry, structured as a partnership with all partners on the maximum individual marginal tax rate of 48.5%, needs a new casting line which will cost $250 000. Brown's can borrow the funds at 6% pa after tax compounded semi-annually over 3 years. Alternatively, it can arrange lease finance comprising 6 payments of \$52 000, one every 6 months starting immediately. Because the casting line at the end of the lease period cannot be sold as a whole and can only be broken up and sold as scrap, there is no residual value built into the contract. The leasing company, however, has agreed to transfer the ownership of the line to Brown's for the payment of \$1. Casting lines are normally depreciated at the rate of 33% pa. Which method of financing would you recommend? Assume for simplicity's sake that the tax benefits from each lease payment and the tax benefits forgone for depreciation are received without time lag in each half-year period. Show your calculations as evidence to support your conclusions.

12.7 The financial controller of Brown's Foundry likes to understand all the implications of each financial deal the firm is offered. Calculate the implied interest rate for the lease finance in problem 12.6 so that you can advise him. (Note that this is a trial and error problem. Try 10% as your first semi-annual discount rate and then 9%. Once you have discovered how the values are 'running', you can estimate the nominal annual implied interest rate. Alternatively, you can use Excel or a financial calculator.)

12.8 If Brown's lease (described in problem 12.6) were restructured so that there was a residual payment of \$100 000 due exactly 3 years after the deal is made, what would each of the 6 lease payments be, given an implied interest rate of 19.6%?

12.9 Greenridge Nursery has just contracted to supply eucalypt seedlings in tubes to five mining companies for their landscape rehabilitation work after open-cut mining. The contracts are for the supply of 20 000 tubes monthly for the next 3 years. Greenridge needs to upgrade its propagation house including the hotbeds and watering system and to increase the size of the growing-out area with its automatic watering system. The expansion works will cost \$100 000. Greenridge is offered lease finance for \$100 000 over 2 years or 3 years, with lease payments due semi-annually, starting immediately. The lease finance is available at 9.00% pa.

(a) What is the amount of each lease payment with the 3-year option with no residual?

(b) What is the amount of each lease payment with the 2-year option with no residual?

(c) What is the amount of each lease payment with the 3-year option with a \$20 000 residual payable 3 years from now?

(d) What is the amount of each lease payment with the 2-year option with a \$20 000 residual payable 2 years from now?

12.10 Greenridge is also offered loan funds of \$100 000 at 8.2% pa after tax, compounded semi-annually for 2 years. Greenridge is structured as a partnership and the partners pay income tax at an average rate of 30%. The ATO allows depreciation at the rate of 50% pa on this equipment. Advise Greenridge which is the better deal — the loan or a 2-year lease with 4 equal payments of \$26 674 starting with the first payment at the signing of the contract. Assume for simplicity's sake that the tax benefits from each lease payment and the tax benefits forgone for depreciation are received without time lag in each half-year period.

12.11 E2Z Bank has issued \$20 million in corporate bonds. The bonds are rated as A. The coupon is 6.8%, paid half-yearly. The bonds have a 5-year maturity and a face value of \$1000. What is the price of a bond that yields 7.2% and has exactly 3.5 years to maturity, the day after the regular coupon payment has been made?

12.12 Jeanette's Fashions Ltd needs funds and the company's financial adviser suggests going to the market directly. The company issues $1 million in 5-year 8% bonds, interest payable 6-monthly. The company has a better year than expected in the second year the bonds are on issue, so decides to try to buy back the bonds $100 000 or so at a time. What will be the cost of the first bond buy-back of $100 000 face value when there are 3 years exactly to maturity and price implies a yield of 8.2%?

12.13 Jeanette's Fashions (see problem 12.12) continues the buy-back program the next year and plans to buy back another $100 000 of bonds. This time, when there are exactly 2 years to maturity, corporate bonds are shorter in supply in the market and the price is such that the yield is 7.8%. What is the price of $100 000 face value of bonds?

12.14 AON is a South Australian biotechnology company that develops vaccines. It needs to raise $20 million to fund new research. It has 10 million ordinary shares on issue, and these are currently selling on the ASX for $13.20. The directors decide to make a 1 for 5 rights issue at $10 subscription. What are the theoretical ex-rights and rights prices?

12.15 Mary White Botany Ltd does environmental surveys and consulting. The company has 2 million shares on issue, currently selling for $5.60. The company decides to make a rights issue to raise $6 million and the directors think the subscription price should be about $4.

(a) How many new shares must be sold?

(b) How many shares must each shareholder own to be granted one right?

(c) What are the theoretical ex-rights and rights prices?

12.16 Jupiter Gold Explorers Ltd is a geological exploration business in Western Australia. Jupiter has just made a rights issue at the rate of 1:5 and there were 10 million shares outstanding before the rights issue. The subscription price for the rights shares was $2.50 and the theoretical ex-rights price was $3.25. What was the market price before the rights issue?

12.17 Planet Breeding Supplies Ltd is a small listed company which keeps stud beef bulls which are performance tested for beef production through the growth rates of their progeny. Planet sells tested semen across the nation and internationally. Planet wants to raise more funding through an equity issue. Currently it has 20 million shares on issue with a market price of $1.55. The company wants to raise about $5 million; costs of the issue are expected to be $500 000. The directors are attracted by the idea of making the issue price $1.20.

(a) How many new shares must be sold?

(b) How many shares must each shareholder own to be granted one right?

(c) What are the theoretical ex-rights and rights prices?

SOLUTIONS TO FINANCE WORKSHOPS

12.1 1. Interest rate specification (such as fixed vs variable, compounding period), repayment schedule (fixed amount, fixed timing, variable amounts and timing, no repayments until maturity).

2. Instalments variable in amounts and timing, lump sum at maturity.

3. Fixed repayments — loan to fund the purchasing of manufacturing equipment for a product which enjoys a steady demand such as flour.

   Variable repayments — loan to fund the purchase of more land by a banana grower whose returns are highly variable and strongly influenced by the weather.

   Interest-only loan — loan to fund the building of accommodation where the principal will be repaid when the building is sold.

12.2 1. Finance lease; novated lease (where employees benefit); hire-purchase agreement.

2. Finance lease — lease of vehicles from car hire and leasing firm.

   Novated lease — lease of car by employee as part of salary package with payments made by employer.

   Hire-purchase — FI buys specialised car transporter equipment needed by a transport company and leases/hires it to the transport company.

12.3 1. As this company has resident Australian shareholders only, they will be able to take advantage of dividend imputation. Decision should be based on pre-tax values.

Item	Y_0 (\$'000)	Y_1 (\$'000)	Y_2 (\$'000)	Y_3 (\$'000)
Flows	+110 – 30	−30	−30	−40
PVs at 7.6%	+80	−27.88	−25.91	−32.11
Sum PVs	+80	−85.90		
Net PV	−5.90			

The value is negative. Therefore the loan is preferable to the lease.

End notes

1 *Reserve Bank of Australia Bulletin*, February 2007, table D.7.

2 *Reserve Bank of Australia Bulletin*, February 2007, table D.4.

3 ANZ 2006, 'ANZ Business: business finance', www.anz.com.au. The information is current as at the date of publication and is subject to change. Esanda products are provided by Esanda Finance Corporation Limited (a wholly owned subsidiary of ANZ).

4 *Reserve Bank of Australia Bulletin*, February 2007, table D.6.

5 Data from National Australia Bank Limited 2006, 'Leasing options at a glance', www.nab.com.au.

6 Extracted from National Australia Bank Limited 2006, 'Your options at a glance', www.nab.com.au. Use of the extracted information is governed by Australian law and is subject to the disclaimers set out on the www.nab.com.au website

7 Crowe, D 2004, 'Lease deal lightens uni burden', *Australian Financial Review*, 10 May, p. 52.

8 *Reserve Bank of Australia Bulletin*, June 2001, p. 6.
9 *Reserve Bank of Australia Bulletin*, January 1994, table C.6.
10 *Reserve Bank of Australia Bulletin*, November 2002 and February 2007, table B.10.
11 *Reserve Bank of Australia Bulletin*, June 2001, p. 6.
12 *Reserve Bank of Australia Bulletin*, June 2006, Table F3.
13 Data from ASX 2006, 'Interest rate security prices', www.asx.com.au.
14 Data from ASX 2006, 'Interest rate security prices', www.asx.com.au.
15 Data from ASX 2006, 'Interest rate security prices', www.asx.com.au.
16 Data from ASX 2006, 'Interest rate security prices', www.asx.com.au.
17 *Reserve Bank of Australia Bulletin*, November 2002, p. S99.
18 Woolworths Ltd., 2006 Annual Report p. 106.
19 Woolworths Ltd., 2006 Annual Report, p. 83.
20 Data derived from *Reserve Bank of Australia Bulletin*, December 1994, table H.5 and *Reserve Bank of Australia Bulletin*, February 2007, table H.4.
21 Data derived from *Reserve Bank of Australia Bulletin*, February 2007, table H.5.
22 As Germany is a participant in the European Monetary Union, the Deutschmark has been replaced by the Euro as the currency of Germany.
23 ABC Learning Centres Limited, media statement, 26 August 2002.
24 Evans, M 2005, 'Perfect year to offer public a piece of the action', *Sydney Morning Herald*, 31 December, p. 28.
25 Schwarz, H 1998, *Rationality gone awry: decision-making inconsistent with economic and financial theory*, Praeger, Westport, Connecticut, p. 65.
26 Australian academic research supports this widely held belief.

chapter

13

Dividend policy and internal financing

Learning objectives

After studying this chapter, you should be able to:

lo1	discuss fundamental dividend concepts and dividend policy in corporate Australia
lo2	explain the dividend irrelevance theory
lo3	explain how dividend policy may affect shareholders' wealth with particular attention to the tax treatment of dividends and capital gains
lo4	describe the use of bonus shares, share repurchase and dividend reinvestment as alternatives to cash dividends
lo5	discuss rationales for dividend policies generally adopted by Australian companies.

AN OPTIMAL DIVIDEND POLICY?

Table 13.1 shows variations in the indicators of dividend policy of selected Australian firms of various sizes, with market capitalisation ranging from $7 million to $90 billion. Most of these firms pay a significant portion of earnings as cash dividends as reflected in the high dividend payout ratios. Macquarie Goodman Group has a high payout ratio of about 80.17%. However, it pays an unfranked dividend; that is, a dividend paid from profits on which no Australian corporate taxes were paid. Recipients of unfranked dividends are not eligible for an imputation tax credit, which can be used to reduce their personal tax liabilities. Wesfarmers Limited provides a high dividend of 6.09 cents pa per dollar of share price, and its dividend is fully franked. BHP, on the other hand, has a lower dividend yield and payout ratio than all companies mentioned, but its dividends are fully franked. Thus, we find a wide variation in indicators of dividend policy in a small sample of Australian firms. In this chapter, we examine the fundamental and institutional factors guiding a firm's dividend decision and search for an optimal dividend policy.

Table 13.1 Dividend policy indicators of selected Australian companies at October 2006

ASX Code	Company name	Payout ratio (%)	Dividend yield (%)	Total franking (%)	Market capitalisation ($m)
BHP	BHP Billiton Limited	21.63	1.68	100.00	90364.6
QBE	QBE Insurance Group Limited	52.83	3.62	50.00	19605.0
MBL	Macquarie Bank Limited	56.24	3.32	95.80	17333.0
SGB	St. George Bank Limited	85.67	4.91	100.00	15976.4
WES	Wesfarmers Limited	92.27	6.09	100.00	13265.5
LEI	Leighton Holdings Limited	66.00	3.80	50.00	5538.2
MGQ	Macquarie Goodman Group	80.17	4.58	0.00	10875.7
SNL	Supply Network Limited	81.78	4.67	100.00	7.7

Source: Aspect Financial Pty Limited.[1]

Chapter preview

The fundamental question we address in this chapter is: 'Can a firm's dividend policy affect shareholders' wealth?' The answer is unambiguously 'no' in a perfect capital market — one with no taxes, no transaction costs, no agency costs or information asymmetry. If this is the case, why do we observe share price fluctuations in response to dividend announcements, alternative dividend policies accommodating needs of heterogeneous shareholders, and a stable dividend payout despite volatility in company earnings? Why do Australian and New Zealand firms provide higher dividend payouts from earnings than US firms? Why don't Australian companies return cash to shareholders primarily through share repurchases, like their US counterparts? This chapter explores the answers to these questions. We demonstrate that with corporate and personal taxes, transaction costs, and asymmetric information about firms, dividend policy does matter to shareholders. As suggested by table 13.1, there is no one policy that suits all firms.

This chapter begins with a discussion of fundamental dividend concepts — the dividend payment process for publicly listed companies in Australia; commonly used indicators of dividend policy; and the cross-sectional and historical patterns of dividend payout underlying the dividend policies of Australian firms. We then examine the major schools of thought on dividend policy. The most remarkable of the theories put forward is Miller and Modigliani's dividend irrelevance theory, which argues that dividends do not matter due to their irrelevance to the riskiness and cash flows of a firm.[2] This theory is considered to be a significant contribution to corporate finance.

Next we focus on theories that argue that dividend policy influences share value. One school of thought within the family of dividend relevance theories relies on the tax treatment of dividends and capital gains. Others argue that investors perceive dividends as less risky than capital gains, and they would prefer to invest in companies with a high dividend policy. Finally, we consider other arguments for the relevance of dividend policy, which are based on asymmetric information, agency costs, transaction costs and clientele effects.

There are alternative ways to return funds to shareholders. In recent years, some large Australian companies returned cash to shareholders through share repurchases. Bonus shares and dividend reinvestment are other forms of dividend plans. Potential benefits of these alternatives to cash dividends are examined.

In the last section of the chapter, we discuss alternative dividend policies in practice and highlight the important factors firms take into account in developing an optimal dividend policy.

The following diagram shows how this chapter is structured.

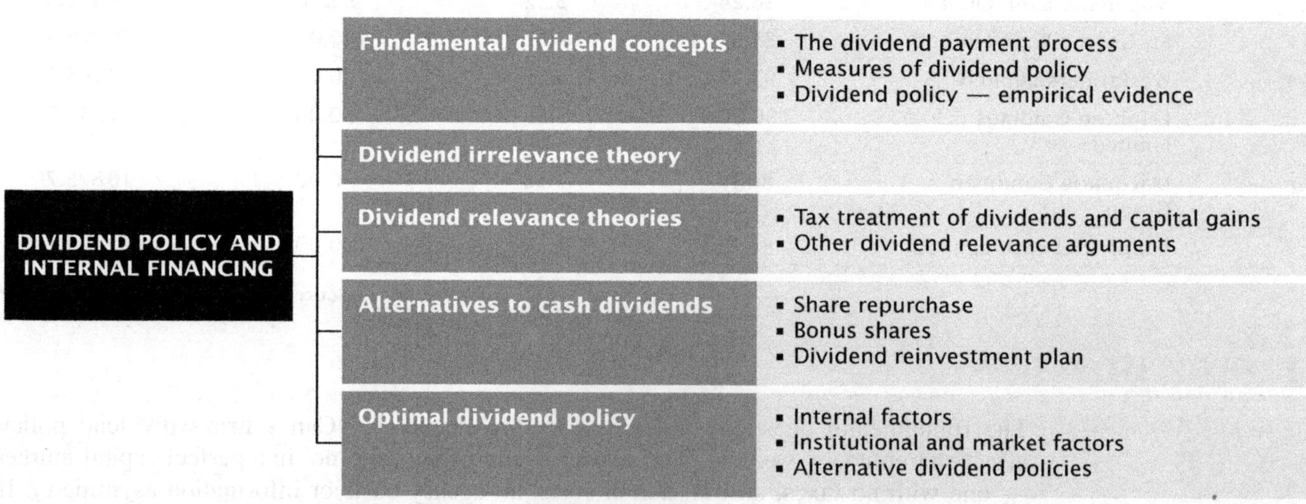

lo1

Fundamental dividend concepts

Discuss fundamental dividend concepts and dividend policy in corporate Australia.

Dividend policy: involves the allocation of profits between dividend payments to shareholders and retention for reinvestment in the company

Companies make decisions about whether they will return profits to shareholders as dividends or retain profits for reinvestment. This is called the **dividend policy**.

In this section we will discuss cash dividend payment procedures in Australia, various commonly used measures of dividend policy (such as dividend payout ratio, dividend yield and dividend stability) and present some facts about dividend policies in Australia.

The dividend payment process

Australian and New Zealand companies generally pay cash dividends twice a year (interim dividend and final dividend), whereas US companies usually make dividend payments every quarter. In Australia, a final dividend is normally paid following the annual general meeting and an interim dividend is paid typically six months prior to the final dividend. Whether to pay dividends in a publicly listed company, and how much to pay, are recommendations made by the board of directors. The directors take into account the last period's financial performance and dividend payment and future growth opportunities in recommending the amount of dividend to pay. The date of the directors' meeting at which a recommendation for dividend payment is made is known as the **announcement date**. The announcement date is important for investors because, if dividends do matter, a firm's share price is likely to respond on this date.

Announcement date: date of the directors' meeting when the dividend is recommended

Record date: date used to identify all shareholders on the register of members so they can receive a dividend

Ex-dividend date: four working days prior to the record date

Cum-dividend: shares that have a current entitlement to receive a dividend

In announcing a dividend, the board of directors also sets a **record date**. All shareholders whose names are listed on the company's register of members on the record date may receive a dividend. The Australian Securities Exchange (ASX) has determined the **ex-dividend date** to be four business days prior to the record date, to allow time for registering changes in share ownership in the Register of Members by the record date. Investors who purchase shares before the ex-dividend date are entitled to a dividend payment and they are said to own shares **cum-dividend**. On the ex-dividend date, the share price normally drops because investors who purchase shares on or after the ex-dividend date do not receive a dividend. An example of a dividend announcement is presented in figure 13.1. The top part of the figure shows Supply Network Ltd's announcement of a fully franked dividend of 1 cent per share. The bottom part shows the corresponding dividend payment time line and other details.

Directors have declared a fully franked final dividend of 1.0 cent per share, payable on 22 September 2006 to shareholders registered on 1 September 2006.

Code	Company name	Div amount	Ex Div Date	Record date	Date payable	% Franked	Type	Further information
SNL	SUPPLY NETWORK	1c	28/08/2006	01/09/2006	22/09/2006	100%	Final	1C FRANKED @ 30%

Figure 13.1 Announcement of final dividend payment, Supply Network Ltd and the corresponding dividend payment time line

Source: Australian Securities Exchange.[3]

Measures of dividend policy

A firm's dividend policy is primarily reflected in the dividend payout ratio, dividend yield and stability of dividends over time. Each of these indicators of dividend policy will now be explained using real world examples.

Dividend payout ratio

Dividend payout ratio: the ratio of dividends to earnings

The **dividend payout ratio** measures the amount of dividend paid per dollar of earnings.

$$\textbf{Dividend payout ratio} = \frac{DPS}{EPS} \qquad [13.1]$$

where DPS = dividend payment per share
EPS = earnings per share

EXAMPLE 13.1

Calculating the payout ratio

If the National Australia Bank's dividend per share and earnings per share were \$1.66 and \$2.52, respectively, this indicates a dividend payout ratio of 66% $\left(\frac{1.66}{2.52}\right)$.

Retention ratio: the proportion of earnings retained in the company, not returned to shareholders as dividends

The dividend payout ratio can be used to estimate the firm's future earnings growth rates. The proportion of earnings reinvested in the company is called the **retention ratio**, which is one minus the payout ratio. A firm with a high retention ratio is normally expected to have higher future growth in earnings and share prices. The expected growth rate of a firm depends on the retention ratio as well as the rate of return on retained profits — the return on equity.

$$\textbf{Growth rate} = (1 - \textbf{payout ratio}) \times \textbf{return on equity} \qquad [13.2]$$

The return on equity (ROE) is the ratio of net profit to equity, measuring the rate of return on investment of ordinary shareholders. We discuss the ROE further in chapter 14.

EXAMPLE 13.2

Calculating the growth rate

The Commonwealth Bank of Australia (CBA) increased its dividend payout ratio from 65% in 2005 to 75.5% in 2006. Over the same period the return on equity increased from 16.45% to 18.18%. The estimated growth rate under the new high payout ratio is calculated as follows:

$$\text{Estimated growth rate}_{\text{High payout ratio}} = (1 - 0.755) \times 0.1818 = 4.45\%$$

As you can see, this is relatively low (despite a slightly higher return on equity) compared to the estimated growth rate that would be calculated under the previous moderate payout ratio:

$$\text{Estimated growth rate}_{\text{Moderate payout ratio}} = (1 - 0.65) \times 0.1645 = 5.76\%$$

Dividend yield

Dividend yield: the ratio of dividend per share to the share price

The second measure of dividend policy is **dividend yield** — a component of total return on a share. Total return on a share typically consists of dividend yield and capital gain.

$$\textbf{Dividend yield} = \frac{\textbf{dividends per share}}{\textbf{price per share}} \qquad [13.3]$$

EXAMPLE 13.3

Calculating dividend yield

If Telstra paid a dividend of 40c per share and its share price was around $4.94 at the end of the year, Telstra's dividend yield was 8.1%.

The dividend yield is often viewed as an important indicator of future performance of a share. It is believed that shares with high dividend yields outperform those with low dividend yields. However, this assertion does not fit well with the recent share price performance of Telstra. In 2005, Telstra's dividend yield was 8.1 — significantly higher than the median dividend yield of approximately 4.2 for the top 300 companies listed on the ASX — but its share price declined by over 25% over the first nine months of 2006.

FINANCE WORKSHOP 13.1

1. In the 2005 financial year, Cochlear Ltd's dividend per share totalled 80c. If earnings per share for the period were $1, what was Cochlear's payout ratio?
2. Cochlear Ltd decreased its dividend payout ratio from 86.4% in 2004 to 74.4% in 2005. Over the same period the return on equity remained more or less constant at 36%. What was the estimated growth rate for 2004 and 2005?
3. Cochlear's dividend per share for the year ended 30 June 2005 was 80c. The share price at the end of June 2005 was around $40. What was Cochlear's dividend yield?

Dividend stability

Dividend stability: shows the volatility of dividend yields or dividend per share over time

The third indicator of dividend policy is **dividend stability**. Companies generally attempt to pay a stable stream of dividends to shareholders despite fluctuations in earnings. In particular, companies are reluctant to reduce dividend payout when earnings decline and they increase dividends when a persistent increase in earnings is anticipated. There is no standard measure of dividend stability. We focus on two alternative measures of dividend stability proposed in the literature.[4]

Standard deviation of dividend yields

We introduce the concept of the standard deviation in chapter 5. Here, the standard deviation of dividend yields gives an indicator of volatility of dividend yields around the mean dividend yield.

$$SDY = \sqrt{\frac{\sum_{t=1}^{n}(DY_i - \overline{DY})^2}{n-1}} \qquad [13.4]$$

where SDY = standard deviation of dividend yields

DY_i = dividend yield in period i

$\overline{DY}$ = mean dividend yield

n = number of observations in the sample

For cross-sectional comparison of dividend instability we should use the coefficient of variation, the standard deviation divided by the mean dividend yield, or $\frac{SDY}{\overline{DY}}$. The coefficient of variation is free of the unit of measurement.

Dividend instability indicator

This measure is based on the incidence of cuts to dividend payout.

$$ST = \frac{\sum_{t=1}^{n} (D_i - D_{i-1})^2}{\bar{D}} \quad \text{for all } D_i < D_{i-1} \qquad [13.5]$$

where ST = indicator of dividend instability

D_i = dividend payment in period i

n = number of times the condition $D_i < D_{i-1}$ is satisfied

$\bar{D}$ = mean dividend payment for the whole sample

Unlike the standard deviation, this measure considers only downward movements in dividends. The following 'finance world' feature demonstrates an application of both measures of dividend instability for Coles and the National Australia Bank.

FINANCE WORLD

Dividend stability

Table 13.2 illustrates calculations of instability of dividends for Coles and the National Australia Bank. Over the period 1996–2005, Coles had an average dividend yield of 3.74% and a standard deviation of 1.09%, providing a coefficient of variation of 0.29. The instability indicator, *ST*, for Coles was 0.09, as shown in panel B of table 13.2. The last panel of this table presents annual dividends per share and dividend yields for the same period for National Australia Bank. You may verify that NAB had a coefficient of variation of 0.13 for dividend yields, significantly lower than that of Coles. As NAB did not cut dividends during 1996–2005, the instability indicator, *ST*, was zero. Thus, we may conclude that NAB has followed a more stable dividend policy than Coles in recent years.

Table 13.2 Dividend instability, Coles and National Australia Bank

Panel A Standard deviation of dividend yields, Coles			
Year (ending 30 June)	Dividend yield (DY_i)	$(DY_i - \overline{DY})$	$(DY_i - \overline{DY})^2$
1996	5	1.26	1.59
1997	3.3	-0.44	0.19
1998	1.9	-1.84	3.39
1999	2.9	-0.84	0.71
2000	4.1	0.36	0.13
2001	5.8	2.06	4.24
2002	4.1	0.36	0.13
2003	3.5	-0.24	0.06

2004	3.3	−0.44	0.19
2005	3.5	−0.24	0.06
Total			10.68
Mean	3.74		

Variance = 1.19

Standard deviation = 1.09

Coefficient of variation = 0.29

Panel B Instability of dividend per share, Coles

Year (ending 30 June)	Dividend per share (DPS)	$(D_i - D_{i-1})$ for all $D_i < D_{i-1}$	$(D_i - D_{i-1})^2$
1996	0.2200		0
1997	0.2300		0
1998	0.1150	−0.115	0.0132
1999	0.2550		0
2000	0.2700		0
2001	0.3550		0
2002	0.2550	−0.1	0.0100
2003	0.2600		0
2004	0.2900		0
2005	0.3325		0
Total			0.0232
Mean	0.2583		

$$\text{Instability index} = \frac{0.032}{0.2583} = 0.0898$$

Panel C Dividend instability, National Australia Bank

Year (ending 30 September)	Dividend per share	Dividend yield
1996	0.87	6.6
1997	0.94	4.4
1998	1.02	5
1999	1.12	5
2000	1.23	4.8
2001	1.35	5.3
2002	1.47	4.4
2003	1.63	5.3
2004	1.66	6.2
2005	1.66	5
Mean	1.30	5.2

Standard deviation of dividend yields = 0.6738

Coefficient of variation = 0.1296

Instability index = 0 because $D_i \geq D_{i-1}$ For all i.

Source: Aspect Financial Pty Limited.[5]

Dividend policy — empirical evidence

Having developed an understanding of the key indicators of dividend policy, we now present the salient facts about dividends in corporate Australia. First, the dividend payout ratio is very high in Australia compared to the United States. The percentage of US companies paying dividends declined from 85% to around 20% over the period 1950–99 because of tax disadvantages of dividends over capital gains. In contrast, most Australian companies with profits pay dividends, producing an average payout ratio of 69%. The payout ratio for US companies is only 28%. Figure 13.2 shows the variation in dividend payout ratios across countries. Some analysts interpret a low payout ratio as a reflection of the company's commitment towards investing in future growth. As shown in equation 13.2, the lower the payout ratio, the higher the expected growth rate.

Second, since the mid-1980s, dividend yields in Australia have been similar to those of the UK but higher than dividend yields in the United States. New Zealand has outperformed all other markets in terms of dividend yields since 1991, which is consistent with its high payout ratio of 82%, as shown in figure 13.2. Figure 13.3 shows dividend yields over the period 1976–2005 for Australia, New Zealand, UK and the United States.

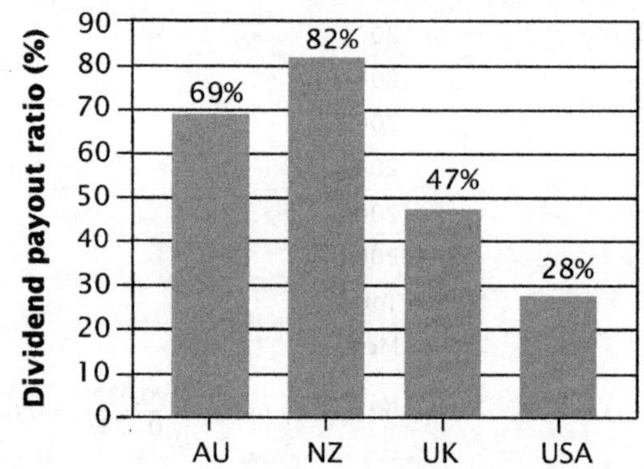

Figure 13.2 Dividend payout ratios across countries

Source: Australia and New Zealand Banking Group Limited.[6]

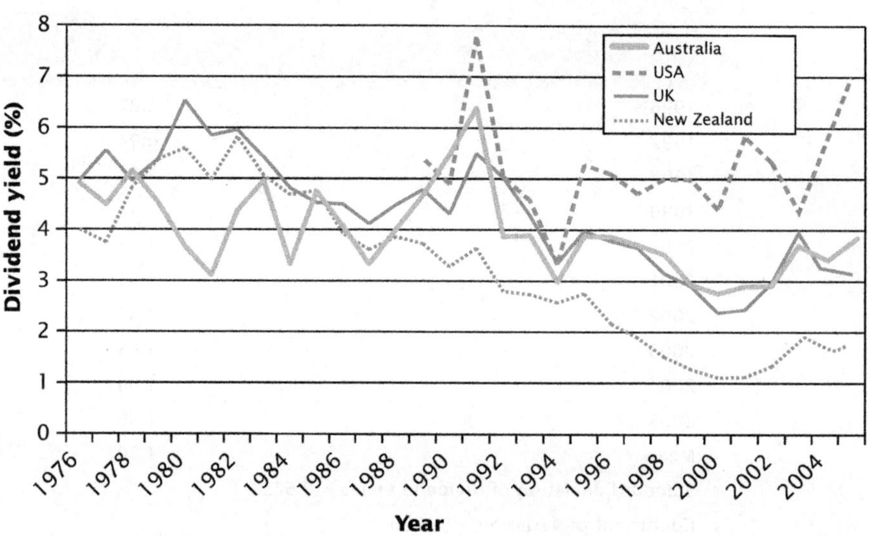

Figure 13.3 Dividend yields in Australia, New Zealand, UK and the USA, 1976–2005

Sources: Datastream, World Federation of Exchanges and Stern School of Business, New York University.[7]

Third, the volatility in dividend yields may be attributed to either fluctuations in share prices or fluctuations in dividends per share. The latter possibility can be ruled out because dividends typically tend to follow a more stable path. As indicated earlier, companies are generally reluctant to reduce their dollar dividends despite any transitory decline in earnings. The movements in earnings, dividends per share and dividend yields from 1973 through 2005 for the National Australia Bank are demonstrated in figure 13.4. Both earnings and dividends series exhibit a significant upward trend but dividends follow a smoother path than earnings, and earnings changes lead dividend changes. Thus, the National Australia Bank's dividends and earnings history fits well with the typical patterns hypothesised in the literature.[8]

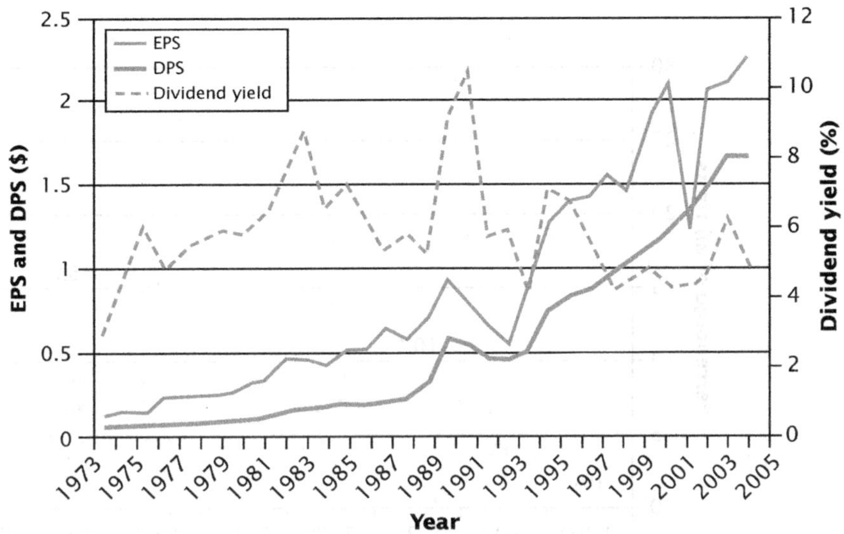

Figure 13.4 Earnings, dividends and dividend yields for the National Australia Bank

Sources: Datastream and Aspect Financial Pty Limited.[9]

Fourth, we observe some variations in indicators of dividend policy across Australian firms. Figure 13.5 plots dividend yields on shares listed on the Australian Securities Exchange in October 2006. Most Australian firms provide a reasonable dividend yield, unlike firms in the United States. A vast majority of Australian firms generate dividend yields over 4% and about 24% of firms pay a dividend yield of more than 7%. The distribution of the dividend payout ratio is graphed in figure 13.6. Around 16% of firms have payout ratios greater than 100%, signifying that these firms' dividend payments are more than their current earnings.

lo2

Explain the dividend irrelevance theory.

Dividend irrelevance theory

Theories of dividend policy are concerned with the potential impact of a dividend decision on share value of a company. Broadly speaking, these theories can be categorised into two groups: those proposing that dividends are irrelevant to share value, and those proposing that dividends are relevant to share value. This section focuses on the 'dividend irrelevance' theory.

Dividend irrelevance theory argues that what a company pays in dividends has no influence on its share value. This theory was put forward by Miller and Modigliani (M&M),[12] and is based on the notion that, if there are no taxes, investors will care only about total return, not the components of total return — dividend and capital gain Companies that pay lower dividends and retain more earnings for reinvestment are likely to provide higher future earnings growth and capital gains than companies paying higher dividends. The M&M theory relies on this fundamental trade-off between dividends and capital gain and is based on the following assumptions:

1. The investment decisions of the company (the decisions discussed in chapters 8 and 9) are independent of its dividend policy. This assumption is useful in isolating the impact of dividend policy from the influence of investment decisions.
2. Capital markets are perfect. This assumption implies that there are no business or personal taxes, investors can buy or sell shares with no transaction costs, companies can issue new shares without flotation costs, and complete information about companies is available to investors with no costs.

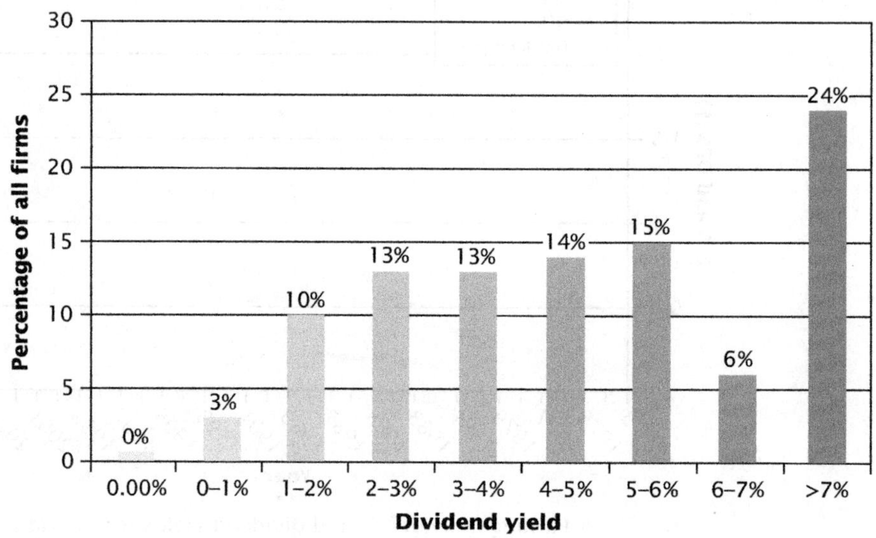

Figure 13.5 Dividend yields of 628 ASX-listed firms, October 2006

Source: Aspect Financial Pty Limited.[10]

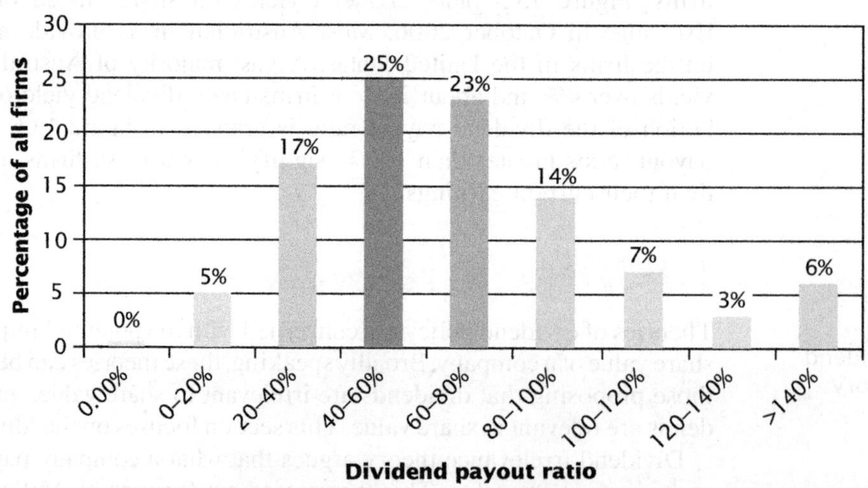

Figure 13.6 Dividend payout ratios of 654 ASX-listed firms, October 2006

Source: Aspect Financial Pty Limited.[11]

Under these assumptions, it can be shown that there is no relationship between a company's dividend policy and its market value. As noted earlier, shareholders are concerned about total return. In a perfect capital market, they are indifferent to receiving dividends or share price appreciation. To understand this assertion, let us consider the valuation of a hypothetical tourism firm, Hunter Valley Corporation, which is financed solely by equity. Assume that the firm has an after-tax operating income of $250 million and a cost of capital of 15%. The firm has 110 million outstanding shares and it requires $100 million per year for reinvestment. The firm's after-tax operating income is expected to grow at 10% annually. In table 13.3 we demonstrate total value accruing to existing shareholders under three alternative policies. We examine each policy in examples 13.4, 13.5 and 13.6.

EXAMPLE 13.4

Hunter Valley Corporation, moderate dividend payout

We examine the dividend discount model in chapter 6. An alternative approach to firm valuation is to discount the firm's free cash flows. Free cash flows constitute cash flows from operations left over after undertaking desired investment projects. Suppose the company pays free cash flow of $150 million as dividend. The value of the firm is the present value of the future stream of free cash flows:

$$\begin{aligned}\text{Value of the firm} &= \frac{\text{free cash flow }(1+g)}{k-g}\\ &= \frac{\$150(1.10)}{0.15-0.10}\\ &= \$3300 \text{ million}\end{aligned}$$

The price per share is $30 (that is, $\frac{\$3300}{110}$) and dividend per share is $1.36 (that is, $\frac{\$150}{110}$), yielding total value accruing to shareholders of $31.36.

EXAMPLE 13.5

Hunter Valley Corporation, high dividend payout

Now, consider an increase in dividend payment from $150 million to $200 million. Hunter Valley Corporation decides to replace this additional dividend payment by issuing $50 million worth of new shares to ensure that its original reinvestment target is exactly met. The value of the firm will not be affected by this strategy because cash flows from the project, the growth rate and cost of capital are unaffected by an increase in dividend payment. Although the value of the firm remains at $3300 million, ownership of existing shareholders in the value of the firm declines to $3250 after issuing $50 million worth of new shares. Thus, price per share decreases to $29.55 (that is, $\frac{\$3250}{110}$) and dividend per share increases to $1.82 (that is, $\frac{\$200}{110}$). Now we can verify that total value accruing to existing shareholders is $31.37 (that is, $29.545 + $1.818). Therefore, in spite of an increase in dividend payment, total value accruing to shareholders is the same as before (a slight discrepancy arises from rounding errors).

EXAMPLE 13.6

Hunter Valley Corporation, zero dividend payout

Next we consider a scenario where Hunter Valley Corporation decides to pay no dividend and holds $150 million as a cash balance. The value of the company can now be found as the sum of present value of free cash flows and excess cash balance of $150 million.

$$\text{Value of the firm} = \frac{\$150(1.10)}{0.15 - 0.10} + \$150$$
$$= \$3450 \text{ million}$$

Price per share increases to $31.364 (that is, $\frac{\$3450}{110}$). The loss of cash dividend is compensated by an increase in the share price, leaving the total value derived from each share unchanged.

Thus, total value accruing to existing Hunter Valley Corporation shareholders remains unchanged under alternative dividend policies, as summarised in table 13.3.

Table 13.3 Irrelevance of dividend policy, Hunter Valley Corporation

	Moderate dividend	High dividend	Zero dividend
After-tax operating income	$250m	$250m	$250m
Reinvestment requirement	$100m	$100m	$100m
Free cash flow[a]	$150m	$150m	$150m
Dividend	$150m	$200m	0
Value of the firm[b]	$3300m	$3250m	$3450m
Price per share[c]	$30	$29.55	$31.36
Dividend per share[d]	$1.36	$1.82	0
Total value accruing to existing shareholders per share[e]	$31.36	$31.37	$31.36
Number of shares owned by existing shareholders	110m	110m	110m

a. Free cash flow = after-tax operating income − reinvestment requirements

b. $\text{Value of the firm} = \frac{\text{free cash flow}(1+g)}{k-g} + \text{cash balance}$

c. $\text{Price per share} = \frac{\text{value of the firm}}{\text{number of shares}}$

d. $\text{Dividend per share} = \frac{\text{dividends}}{\text{number of shares}}$

e. Total value accruing to existing shareholders = price per share + dividend per share

Regardless of the firm's dividend policy, shareholders can create a dividend stream of their choice. If the firm pays no dividend, the shareholder can sell shares to generate cash flow. On the other hand, if the firm pays a large dividend, the shareholder can use it to purchase additional shares. In a perfect capital market, the shareholder can create a 'homemade dividend stream' without any transaction costs. Thus, from a shareholder's perspective, dividend policy may not provide any net benefit.

The dividend irrelevance argument relies on the fundamental premise that the value of a company depends on its cash flows, which in turn depend on investment decisions — not dividend decisions. In a perfect capital market, a company can always change its dividend policy by changing the number of shares on issue, and individuals can create a desired dividend stream by adjusting their shareholdings. These are costless strategies with no relevance for the value of the company.

lo3

Explain how dividend policy may affect shareholders' wealth with particular attention to the tax treatment of dividends and capital gains.

Dividend relevance theories

Dividend policy may affect the market value of a firm under various circumstances. In this section, we discuss theories that highlight benefits and costs of dividend payout for shareholders. Arguments for dividend relevance are based on the tax treatment of dividends as compared to capital gains, riskiness of capital gains, 'informativeness' of dividends payout, agency costs, transaction costs and the clientele effect.

Tax treatment of dividends and capital gains

In examining the relationship between dividend policy and share value, so far it has been assumed that there are no personal or corporate taxes. Relaxing this assumption, the proponents of low dividend policy argue that dividends are taxed more heavily than capital gains. Since investors are concerned about after-tax return, they would be willing to pay less for shares of firms distributing a high dividend at the expense of a capital gain. This assertion is made under the classical tax system (as discussed in chapter 6), where dividends are taxed at both corporate and individual levels. Companies pay tax on earnings at the company tax rate. Any dividends received from after-tax company earnings are then taxed at the personal income tax rates. This tax system induces firms to retain more earnings or repurchase shares rather than pay a high cash dividend.

Taxation of dividends

Until 30 June 1987, Australia had a classical tax system, featuring double taxation of dividends. Countries like the United States and Japan still have a classical tax system. In Australia, this tax system was replaced by the dividend imputation system on 1 July 1987 with the aim of eliminating double taxation of dividends. Figure 13.7 presents data for dividend taxation in 10 OECD countries, including Australia. The figure illustrates data for the top dividend tax rates, combining both individual and corporate taxes imposed by all levels of governments. The top dividend tax rate for Australia is shown as 48.5%, which includes 1.5% of Medicare levy. Australia's major trading partner, Japan, has a very high dividend tax rate of about 65%. Norway has the lowest dividend tax rate in the 30-nation OECD.

As we see in chapters 2 and 7, dividends are taxed at the shareholder's personal tax rate and taxes paid by a company on its taxable earnings are deducted from the shareholder's personal tax bill under the Australian dividend imputation system. The amount of corporate tax passed on to shareholders with the dividend is called the **imputation tax credit**. As discussed in chapter 2, a dividend containing an imputation credit is known as a franked dividend. Franked dividends can be paid out of company earnings taxed in Australia. From July 2000, shareholders with a tax liability less than the imputation credit are eligible for a refund of surplus imputation credits, making the imputation system more attractive to investors with low personal tax rates. Dividend franking is a common practice at Australian firms. As shown in figure 13.8, 63% of Australian firms pay 100% franked dividend.

Imputation tax credit: represents the amount of tax on a dividend that has been paid by the company on behalf of a shareholder

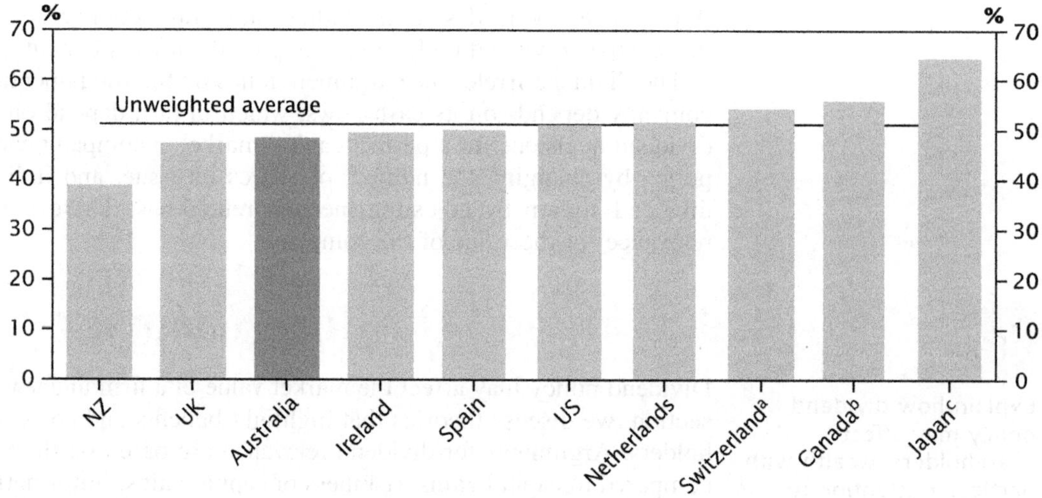

Notes: Overall statutory tax rates on distributions of domestic source income to a resident individual shareholder, incorporating corporate income tax, personal income tax and any type of shareholder relief.

a. The corporate income tax rate includes the church tax, while the personal income tax rate excludes it.
b. Canada recently announced a reduction in personal income taxes on eligible dividends.
c. The 2005 rate for Japan was not available, the 2004 rate is presented.

Figure 13.7 Top overall statutory tax rates on domestic source dividend income

Source: Warburton & Hendy.[13]

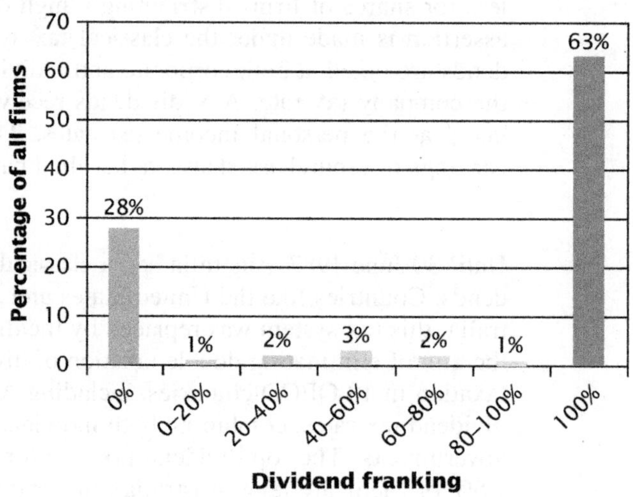

Figure 13.8 Dividend franking at Australian firms, October 2006

Source: Aspect Financial Pty Limited.[14]

Imputation credit for a fully franked dividend is calculated as:

$$\textbf{Imputation credit} = \left[\frac{D_f}{1 - t_c}\right] t_c \qquad [13.6]$$

where D_f = fully franked dividend

t_c = company tax rate

$$\frac{D_f}{1 - t_c} = \text{grossed up dividend}$$

We examine how companies record changes in the dividend franking account in chapter 2. Here, we will further examine imputation from the shareholders' perspective. To demonstrate benefits of dividend imputation, we assume that a fully franked dividend of \$100 is received by each shareholder in the following three examples. The company tax rate is 30% and shareholders have different tax rates on dividend income. The Medicare levy of 1.5% is ignored in calculating the after-tax dividend in these examples.

EXAMPLE 13.7

Marginal personal tax rate higher than the corporate tax rate

Tran received a fully franked dividend of \$100. He is in the 45% marginal tax bracket. His after-tax dividend income is calculated as follows:

Fully franked dividend = \$100.00

$$\text{Grossed up dividend} = \frac{\$100}{1 - 0.30} = \$142.86$$

Tax at 45% = \$142.86 × 0.45 = \$64.29

$$\text{Imputation credit} = \left[\frac{\$100}{1 - 0.30}\right] \times 0.30 = \$42.86$$

Net tax liability = \$64.29 – \$42.86 = \$21.43

After-tax dividend = \$100 – \$21.43 = \$78.57

EXAMPLE 13.8

Marginal personal tax rate lower than the corporate tax rate

Anita is currently in the 15% personal income tax bracket. She received a fully franked dividend of \$100.

Fully franked dividend = \$100.00

$$\text{Grossed up dividend} = \frac{\$100}{1 - 0.30} = \$142.86$$

Tax at 15% = \$142.86 × 0.15 = \$21.43

$$\text{Less imputation credit} = \left[\frac{\$100}{1.0 - 0.30}\right] \times 0.30 = \$42.86$$

Net tax liability = \$21.43 – \$42.86 = –\$21.43

After-tax dividend = \$100 + \$21.43 = \$121.43

Anita's tax on her grossed up dividend is less than her imputation credit. She is entitled to a refund of \$21.43, the surplus imputation credit. Therefore, her after-tax dividend income is more than the fully franked dividend.

EXAMPLE 13.9

Imputation credits and superannuation funds

Suppose the HESTA super fund received $100 of franked dividend. A superannuation fund is subject to a 15% flat tax rate.

Therefore, a surplus imputation credit of $21.43 arises from a franked dividend of $100 as in example 13.8. Like low income shareholders, superannuation funds are also entitled to a refund of surplus imputation credits.

We can further simplify calculations of after-tax dividends. Denoting t_p as the shareholder's personal marginal tax rate, after-tax dividend can be expressed as:

$$\text{After-tax dividend} = \underbrace{D_f}_{\substack{\text{Fully}\\\text{franked}\\\text{dividend}}} - \underbrace{\left[\frac{D_f}{1-t_c}\right]t_p}_{\substack{\text{Tax on}\\\text{grossed-up}\\\text{dividend}}} + \underbrace{\left[\frac{D_f}{1-t_c}\right]t_c}_{\substack{\text{Imputation}\\\text{credit}}}$$

This expression can be further simplified as:

$$\textbf{After-tax dividend} = D_f\left[\frac{1-t_p}{1-t_c}\right] \qquad [13.7]$$

where D_f = fully franked dividend

t_p = investor's marginal tax rate

t_c = company tax rate

You may verify that your calculations of after-tax dividend based on equation 13.7 are the same as those obtained in examples 13.7, 13.8 and 13.9.

FINANCE WORKSHOP 13.2

1. Rosie received a fully franked dividend of $250. Her marginal tax rate (excluding the Medicare levy) is 40%. If the corporate tax rate is 30%, what is Rosie's after-tax dividend?
2. Julio's marginal tax rate is 15% (excluding the Medicare levy). If Julio receives a fully franked dividend of $250 and the corporate tax rate is 30%, what is his after-tax dividend?

Taxation of capital gains

We introduce the concept of capital gains in chapter 2 and see how they are calculated in chapter 9. Capital gains on shares are not taxable in many countries, including Hong Kong, Switzerland, New Zealand and Taiwan. In Australia, a capital gains tax is applicable to assets purchased after 19 September 1985. Historically, this tax has been applicable to real capital gain, which is the difference between an inflation indexed cost base and the selling value. A capital gain discount is available for assets purchased after 11.45 am on 21 September 1999 and held for at least 12 months. For individuals and trusts, 50% of nominal capital gain (that is, not adjusted for inflation) is taxable. Superannuation funds are entitled to a 33.33% discount but companies are not eligible for any discount. For assets purchased before 11.45 am on 21 September 1999 but sold after that date, investors may choose either indexation of cost base or the discount method. Figure 13.9 shows that, in a group of 10 OECD countries considered by Warburton and Hendy, Australia has the third highest top marginal tax rate on capital gains on shares.

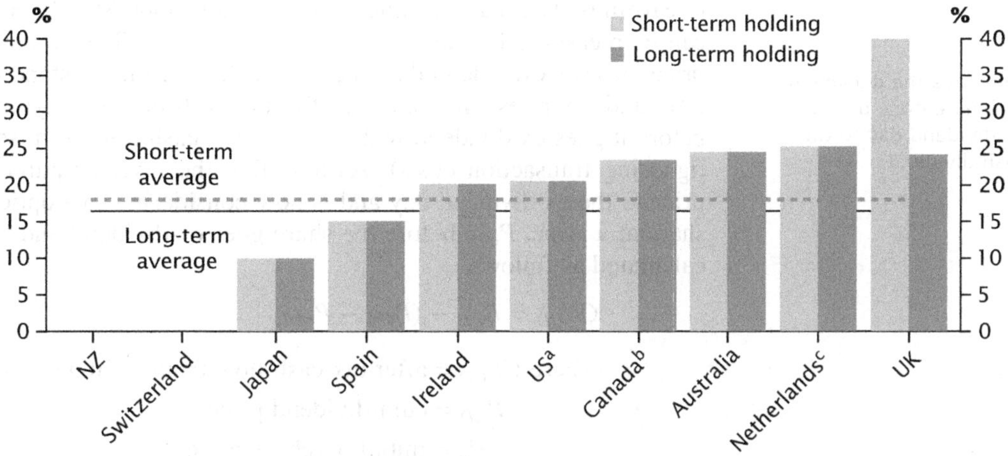

Notes: Where relevant based on top marginal income tax rates, short-term holdings are greater than one year but less than two years, long-term holdings are where the shares have been held for 10 years.

a. The rate includes federal, state and city taxes with the last two being based on Michigan and Detroit.
b. Cumulative lifetime capital gains exemption (C$500 000) under certain conditions. Rate includes national and sub-national taxes, the latter being based on the representative Province of Ontario.
c. For substantial shareholders (direct or indirect ownership more than 5%): otherwise exempt.

Figure 13.9 Top marginal tax rate on capital gains on shares

Source: Warburton & Hendy.[15]

The timing of tax payments is also an important consideration for taxpayers. Although the introduction of the imputation system eliminated double taxation, dividends still have a tax disadvantage. Taxes on dividends are payable when investors receive dividend income, but capital gain taxes are payable when gains are realised. Investors have some control over the timing of receiving a capital gain but they don't have a choice about when they receive a dividend. By realising capital gain in periods of low income or realising capital losses to offset against gains, shareholders can minimise tax liability. In addition, the 1999 capital gain tax reform has made dividend income a less attractive option for shareholders.

The argument for a low dividend policy was advanced in the context of a classical tax system. The introduction of the dividend imputation system in July 1987 has made dividend income relatively attractive but this has been partly offset by the provision of capital gains tax discount. Thus, it may no longer be possible to argue for either a high or a low dividend policy based solely on tax considerations because shareholders differ with respect to their tax status.

Market value of franked dividends

In this section, we focus on market valuation of franked dividends. The extent of tax advantages of dividends over capital gains depends on dividend franking and the shareholder's tax status and investment horizon.

As indicated earlier, an investor who holds shares for less than 12 months will not be entitled to a tax discount on capital gains. Thus, a short-term investor might be indifferent between unfranked dividends and capital gains because both are taxed at the investor's marginal tax rate with no tax discount for capital gains and no imputation credits for dividends. On the other hand, an investor who holds shares for at least 12 months is entitled to a tax discount on capital gains and would prefer capital gains over unfranked dividends. Thus, unfranked dividends have no tax advantage over capital gains in Australia.

Franked dividends may have a tax advantage over capital gains resulting from retention of earnings. The market value of this tax advantage should be reflected in share prices and can be measured by the **dividend drop-off ratio**. This is the ratio of the decline in share price on the ex-dividend day to cash dividend. To understand the relationship between this ratio and tax rates, we compare after-tax cash flow to a typical investor if a share is sold before it goes ex-dividend with the after-tax cash flow from selling on the ex-dividend day (ignoring transaction costs). Assume that the investor purchased a share at a price, P_p, prior to the ex-dividend day and is now considering two options. The investor can sell the share at a price, P_{CD}, before the share goes ex-dividend and receive an after-tax cash flow calculated as follows:

Dividend drop-off ratio: compares the decline in the share price on the ex-dividend day to the cash dividend

$$CF_{CD} = P_{CD} - (P_{CD} - P_p)\, t_g$$

where CF_{CD} = after-tax cash flow from selling cum-dividend shares
P_{CD} = cum-dividend price
P_p = initial purchase price
t_g = tax rate on capital gain

Alternatively, the investor can sell the share after the ex-dividend day at a price, P_{XD}, and receive a fully franked dividend payout, D_f, but suffer a capital loss. The after-tax cash flow to the investor from this action is calculated as follows:

$$CF_{XD} = P_{XD} - (P_{XD} - P_p)t_g + D_f\left[\frac{1-t_p}{1-t_c}\right]$$

where CF_{XD} = after-tax cash flow from selling ex-dividend shares
P_{XD} = ex-dividend price
P_p = initial purchase price
D_f = fully franked dividend
t_g = tax rate on capital gain
t_p = investor's marginal tax rate
t_c = company tax rate

The investor would not be able to make arbitrage (that is, riskless) profits if the after-tax cash flow is the same from selling shares before and after the ex-dividend day. That is:

$$P_{CD} - (P_{CD} - P_p)t_g = P_{XD} - (P_{XD} - P_p)t_g + D_f\left[\frac{1-t_p}{1-t_c}\right]$$

This equation can be solved for the price decline on the ex-dividend day as follows:

$$\mathbf{P_{CD} - P_{XD} = D_f\left[\frac{1-t_p}{(1-t_c)(1-t_g)}\right]} \qquad [13.8]$$

where P_{CD} = cum-dividend price
P_{XD} = ex-dividend price
D_f = fully franked dividend
t_p = investor's marginal tax rate
t_g = tax rate on capital gain
t_c = company tax rate

Let us now consider three possible scenarios to interpret equation 13.8:

- If dividends and capital gains are taxed at the same rate ($t_P = t_g$), the price drop-off should be equal to the grossed up value of the dividend, $\frac{D_f}{(1-t_c)}$.
- If dividends are taxed more heavily than capital gains, the price drop-off will be less than the grossed up value of the dividend.
- If capital gains are taxed more heavily than dividends, the price drop-off will be more than the grossed up value of the dividend.

The drop-off ratio can be found by dividing both sides of equation 13.8 by the cash dividend, D_f.

$$\frac{P_{CD} - P_{XD}}{D_f} = \frac{1 - t_p}{(1 - t_c)(1 - t_g)} \qquad [13.9]$$

where P_{CD} = cum-dividend price
P_{XD} = ex-dividend price
D_f = fully franked dividend
t_p = investor's marginal tax rate
t_g = tax rate on capital gain
t_c = company tax rate

EXAMPLE 13.10

Calculating dividend drop-off ratio

Suppose the typical investor in New England Biotech holds shares for less than 12 months and faces a personal tax rate of 45%. The company is expected to pay a fully franked dividend this year. Given the company tax rate of 30%, estimate the expected price decline as a percentage of dividend payout on the ex-dividend day.

In this example, $t_p = t_g$ because the typical investor in New England Biotech is not eligible for a capital gains tax discount. Thus, the drop-off ratio can be found as:

$$\frac{P_{CD} - P_{XD}}{D_f} = \frac{1 - 0.45}{(1 - 0.30)(1 - 0.45)}$$

$$= \frac{1}{1 - 0.30}$$

$$= 1.43 \text{ or } 143\%$$

That is, for each dollar of fully franked dividend, the price decline would be \$1.43 on the ex-dividend day.

EXAMPLE 13.11

Deriving the personal tax rate from the drop-off ratio

Assume that a typical investor in KLM Ltd holds shares for more than 12 months. On the recent ex-dividend day, the price decline was 117.65% of the company's fully franked dividend. Estimate the marginal personal tax rate for the typical investor in KLM Ltd.

The typical KLM shareholder is entitled to a 50% capital gains tax discount because shares are held for more than 12 months. Thus, equation 13.9 can be modified as:

$$\frac{P_{CD} - P_{XD}}{D_f} = \frac{1 - t_p}{(1 - t_c)\left(1 - \frac{t_p}{2}\right)}$$

Substituting $\frac{P_{CD} - P_{XD}}{D_f} = 117.65\%$ and $t_c = 30\%$ into this equation,

$$t_p = 30\%$$

Therefore, a typical KLM shareholder is in the 30% personal tax bracket.

Early Australian studies generally report a drop-off ratio of less than 1, signifying that the market value of $1 of cash dividend is less than $1. For example, Brown and Walter[16] found an average drop-off ratio of 0.72 for daily data over the period 1973–74 to 1984–85 when Australia had a classical tax system. Once daily share price data were adjusted for overall market movements, the average drop-off ratio became 0.68. Analysing data after the introduction of the dividend imputation system, over the period 1987–92, Bellamy[17] found that the average drop-off ratio was 0.66 for unfranked dividends and 0.89 for franked dividends. This finding indicates that franked dividends create an incremental value for investors. Brown and Clarke's study, however, showed no significant increase in the drop-off ratio following the introduction of dividend imputation in July 1987.[18]

A typical limitation of this line of study is that cum-dividend and ex-dividend prices are non-contemporaneous. Researchers generally estimate the price drop-off from the closing cum-dividend price to either opening or closing ex-dividend price. This measure of the drop-off ratio is subject to a bias resulting from arrival of new market or company specific information over this time interval. Following the introduction of trading of cum-dividend shares during the ex-dividend period by the ASX, we can now observe cum-dividend and ex-dividend prices contemporaneously. Taking advantage of this new information base, Walker and Partington[19] estimated an average drop-off ratio of 1.23 for fully franked dividends. Their sample included 1015 ex-dividend trades arising from 93 ex-dividend events over the period 1 January 1995 to 1 March 1997. Unlike previous Australian studies, they demonstrated that the market value of $1 of fully franked dividend is significantly more than $1.

FINANCE WORKSHOP 13.3

1. Rahnee is representative of the average investor in Meringandan Mercantile Ltd. Like the majority of shareholders in the company, she has held her shares for less than 12 months and her marginal tax rate is 40%. The company

will pay a fully franked dividend in the coming year and the corporate tax rate is 30%. What is the expected price decline as a percentage of the dividend payout on the ex-dividend day?

2. A typical investor in Rosalie Ltd holds shares for more than 12 months. The price decline on a recent ex-dividend day was 112.56% of the company's fully franked dividend. What is the marginal personal tax rate for the typical investor in Rosalie Ltd?

Other dividend relevance arguments

This section presents non-tax arguments for the relevance of dividend policy to the market value of a firm. We begin with a discussion of riskiness of capital gains as compared to current dividends. We will then turn our attention to various sources of market imperfections to understand the potential role of dividend policy in providing positive signals to financial markets, reducing agency costs, and meeting investor preferences for dividend payouts.

Riskiness of capital gains

Although dividend policy cannot change the present value of cash flows of a company, it can influence the temporal pattern of cash payment to shareholders. It has been argued that shareholders consider dividends to be paid in the distant future more unpredictable and riskier than dividends to be paid in the near future.[20] Thus, dividends anticipated in the distant future will be discounted at a higher rate to reflect this differential risk. Put differently, investors prefer 'a bird in the hand' over 'two in the bush'. Thus, share value might be increased by increasing current dividends at the cost of future growth in earnings and capital gains. Investors prefer a dollar of current dividends over capital gains anticipated from a dollar of retained earnings because future cash flows are riskier. If this is the case, investors would be willing to pay a higher price for shares paying higher current dividends. That is, dividend policy does matter. Note that this argument does not depend on the tax treatment of dividends and capital gains.

However, the fallacy of the 'bird in hand' reasoning can be recognised by focusing on the basic valuation principle. The risk of a company depends on the riskiness of the cash flows from its assets, not on the temporal pattern of dividend payout. A change in dividend policy has no impact on the expected cash flows or its volatility. Thus, where shareholders are rational wealth maximisers, high dividends are not expected to increase the value of a company.

Signalling and asymmetric information

Corporate insiders know more about the firm's capacity to generate cash flows and earnings than outsiders. This asymmetric information is an important source of market imperfection. Insiders can convey their private information to markets through announcing a change in dividend payout. Unlike other methods of conveying information, such as earnings forecasts and annual reports, a dividend announcement generally gives a credible signal to markets about future cash flows of the firm. A firm with good future prospects can adopt a signalling device, which cannot be imitated by firms with bad future prospects. One such signalling device is increasing dividend. An increase in dividend is costly to a firm and generally viewed as a positive signal because it reflects the firm's ability to generate adequate cash flow to meet its dividend payments and debt obligation in the future. A firm without good future growth prospects would have to rely on external financing to increase dividend payout and so incur additional costs. Thus, signalling theories suggest that an increase in dividend gives a signal for a permanent increase in earnings and elicits share value.[21]

Agency costs

As we discuss in chapter 1, agency costs arise from the separation of ownership and day-to-day management of companies. Managers may make decisions to maximise their own benefits rather than shareholders' wealth. If this is the case, the market value of the company with the separation of ownership and managerial control may be less than the market value of a comparable owner-managed company. This gap in market value is interpreted as agency costs because it results from the conflict between a principal's interest and an agent's interest. It has been argued that dividend payments may reduce agency costs in two ways.

First, dividend payments may facilitate external monitoring of a manager's performance. Higher dividend payments may induce a company to raise external capital by issuing either new shares or debt instruments. The process of capital raising typically involves publicising information about the company's recent performance and future growth prospects in a prospectus. This information is scrutinised by investors, the stock exchange, regulators and other market participants. Thus, the capital raising process exposes a manager's performance to external monitoring and encourages managers to act in the interest of the shareholders.

Second, dividend payments may restrain managers from spending free cash flows on unprofitable activities. Managers may prefer to retain free cash flows (rather than pay dividends) and use the funds to provide themselves with attractive salary packages or to spend on projects to enhance their corporate powers rather than shareholders' wealth. Therefore, a high dividend policy can be effective in reducing agency costs and increasing share value of the firm.

Transaction costs and clientele effect

The dividend irrelevance theory assumes that companies can issue new shares without incurring flotation costs and investors can buy and sell shares without any transaction costs. In practice, these assumptions do not hold. If a company adopts a high dividend policy, it may have to raise capital by issuing new shares, which involves flotation costs. Thus, flotation costs may induce a company to adopt a low dividend policy and rely more on retained earnings to meet investment needs.

Transaction costs also constrain shareholders from creating a 'homemade dividend stream'. If there is a mismatching between a shareholder's consumption needs and dividend payments, the shareholder may buy or sell shares to create a desired stream of cash flows. However, transaction costs of buying and selling shares limit the shareholder's ability to achieve this goal.

Therefore, companies paying a regular stream of dividends may attract investors, such as pensioners, who need additional income to meet their consumption needs. On the other hand, companies paying low or no dividends typically attract investors at the middle stage of their life cycle who usually have adequate income to meet their consumption needs. Recognising this 'dividend clientele effect', companies generally try to avoid any significant changes to their dividend payout ratios. The clientele effect was first identified by Miller and Modigliani.[22] However, they argued that the clientele effect did not change the fundamental conclusion of the dividend irrelevance theory.

> If, for example, the frequency distribution of corporate payout ratios happened to correspond exactly with the distribution of investor preferences for payout ratios, then the existence of these preferences would clearly lead ultimately to a situation whose implications were different in no fundamental respect from the

perfect market case. Each corporation would tend to attract itself a 'clientele' consisting of those preferring its particular payout ratio, but one clientele would be as good as another in terms of the valuation it would imply for the firm.

lo4

Describe the use of bonus shares, share repurchase and dividend reinvestment as alternatives to cash dividends.

Alternatives to cash dividends

Cash dividends are still the primary means of returning cash to shareholders in Australia. Over the last decade, many Australian companies have introduced alternative dividend plans to accommodate the differing needs of shareholders. These plans include share repurchase, bonus shares and dividend reinvestment.

Share repurchase

Share repurchase: the company purchases its own shares

A **share repurchase** refers to the company buying back its own shares and is a substitute for a cash dividend. Both forms of dividend involve a reduction in the company's cash balance. A cash dividend payment leads to a drop in the share price on the ex-dividend day, with the number of outstanding shares unchanged. A share repurchase, on the other hand, reduces the number of outstanding shares and usually increases the share price. Example 13.12 demonstrates that a share repurchase can be a perfect substitute for a cash dividend under certain conditions.

EXAMPLE 13.12

The substitutability between cash dividend and share repurchase

Suppose XYZ Corporation is considering two alternative dividend plans — paying cash dividends of $2 million or spending $2 million on a share repurchase. The company's relevant financial data are:

Earnings = $4 000 000
Number of ordinary shares = 2 000 000
Earnings per share = $2
Expected ex-dividend price = $50
P/E ratio = 25 (see chapter 6)

If the company spends $2 million on cash dividends, the cum-dividend share price will reflect a dividend per share of $1. That is, total value accruing to a shareholder would be $51 under the cash dividend plan.

Alternatively, the company may announce a repurchase price of $51, constituting the $50 anticipated ex-dividend price and $1 of cash dividend per share. At the $51 repurchase price the company can buy back about 39 215 shares ($2 million/$51). Following the share buyback, earnings per share are expected to increase to $2.04, which can be found as:

$$\text{EPS after buyback} = \frac{\text{earnings}}{\text{number of outstanding shares after buyback}}$$

$$= \frac{\$4\,000\,000}{2\,000\,000 - 39\,215}$$

$$= \$2.04$$

If the P/E ratio remains stable at 25, share price is expected to increase after the buyback.

New share price = P/E ratio × EPS after buyback
= 25 × \$2.04
= \$51

Therefore, a buyback plan provides the same total value per share to a shareholder through share price appreciation rather than the cash dividend.

Share repurchase process

In Australia, under the *Corporations Act 2001*, a company can generally repurchase up to 10% of its own shares in a 12-month period. This provision is known as the 10/12 limit. The legislation permits five different kinds of buybacks:

1. *Equal access purchase.* Under this plan, all ordinary shareholders can sell the same percentage of their shareholdings to the company.
2. *On-market purchase.* The company can repurchase its shares on the stock exchange at prevailing market prices.
3. *Selective purchase.* A share repurchase offer can be made to a specific group of shareholders.
4. *Employee share purchase.* Buyback offers can be made to employees who obtained the company's shares under an employee share scheme.
5. *Odd lot purchase.* This refers to buying back small parcels of shares that are not considered as a marketable parcel by the stock exchange.

Rationales for share repurchase

As we previously discussed, for countries that have a classical tax system, dividends are taxed more heavily than capital gains. Share repurchases have gained popularity in such countries, including the United States. Buybacks lead to an increase in earnings per share (EPS) and are often accompanied by a share price appreciation or capital gain. Investors have discretion over the timing of receiving a capital gain, which can be useful in manipulating temporal patterns of personal income and reducing tax liability.

Share buybacks can also perform a signalling function. Managers are equipped with better information than outsiders and they can use share buybacks to provide positive signals to investors about the company's future earnings prospects. Put differently, share buybacks allow managers to convey their assessment of share price to investors.

Another advantage of the share buybacks arises from their financial flexibility. Cash dividend payments usually involve a long-term commitment and the company may not meet this commitment if there are unanticipated changes in earnings. On the other hand, investors do not expect a company to repurchase its own shares regularly. Thus, share buybacks are a more flexible way to return cash to shareholders.

CORPORATE FINANCIAL GOVERNANCE

Share repurchase and capital discipline

We have presented share repurchase as an alternative to a cash dividend. Like a cash dividend, share repurchase also reduces cash balance and encourages capital discipline within the company. It encourages the board of directors to invest in growth businesses instead of channelling funds in activities conducive to improving their corporate power and personal wealth. Thus, returning cash to shareholders through either a cash dividend or a share repurchase may promote the quality of corporate governance. The following article shows that the recent share buyback program of BHP has been welcomed by shareholders.

Investors overwhelm BHP $3.5b buyback

JAMIE FREED

BHP Billiton's $3.5 billion off-market buyback of its Australian-listed shares received a very warm reception from shareholders.

The miner bought back $250 million more than expected at $24.81 a share, which was a 14 per cent discount to the average price its shares traded at last week.

The company received so many oversubscriptions that investors who signed up for the buyback were only able to sell 37.57 per cent of the shares they had offered for tender.

'We are pleased with the strong support we have received from shareholders in this transaction,' BHP chief financial officer Alex Vanselow said. 'Our progressive dividend policy, together with sizeable capital initiatives, demonstrate our continued commitment to capital discipline as well as our confidence in our outlook and strong cash generative capabilities.'

The off-market buyback in Australia is only the first phase of a US$10 billion ($12.4 billion) global buyback program. The company was set to resume an on-market buyback of its UK-listed stock in London last night.

Shareholders who successfully tendered to the local off-market buyback will have $22.31 of the purchase price treated as a fully-franked dividend. The deemed proceeds, as agreed by the tax office, for capital gains purposes are $7.39 a share.

Last month, BHP said its off-market buyback would have a targeted maximum size of $3.25 billion to ensure it retained enough franking credits for its dividends.

'We had really strong demand at the maximum discount and decided to take advantage of that to satisfy some of the oversubscriptions,' said BHP spokeswoman Emma Meade.

ABN Amro analyst Rob Clifford said he was not surprised the miner purchased an extra $250 million of shares. 'I thought they had some franking credits up their sleeve,' he said. 'It's such an attractive deal for them. They'll buy back as much as they can.'

BHP shares closed 84c higher at $30.04 yesterday.[23]

FINANCE WORKSHOP 13.4

Quoll Ltd is considering a $1.5 million share repurchase. Quoll's relevant financial data are as follows:

Current earnings: $7 000 000

Number of ordinary shares: 10 000 000

Price–earnings ratio: 18

1. What is Quoll's current EPS?
2. What is the current market price of Quoll's shares?
3. How many shares will Quoll repurchase?
4. If the dollar amount of current earnings is maintained after the repurchase, what is the new EPS?
5. What is the post share repurchase price if the P/E ratio remains unchanged?

Bonus shares

Bonus shares: dividends paid in the form of additional shares

Companies may issue **bonus shares** to provide dividends to existing shareholders. For example, a 5% bonus share issue means that every shareholder in the company is given one new share for every 20 currently owned shares. There are four main motivations for providing bonus shares (share dividends).

First, a share dividend can be given without using cash, which is an attractive way of paying dividends for cash-strapped companies. Second, a company in a high-growth phase of its life cycle may reinvest most of its earnings on profitable investment projects and offer a share dividend scheme to supplement its low cash dividend policy. Third, a bonus issue increases the number of shares outstanding and may reflect the company's confidence in future earnings growth and ability to pay dividends on an augmented share base. Thus, a bonus share plan may yield positive signalling benefits to the company. Fourth, some managers believe that market liquidity of the company's shares can be improved by making more shares available to potential investors, at a lower price per share, through a bonus issue.

Bonus share issues are not a common practice in corporate Australia. Companies issuing bonus shares often justify the issue in terms of improvement in liquidity, but there is some evidence that market price does not drop to the expected theoretical price following a bonus issue.

EXAMPLE 13.13

Effects of a bonus share issue

Aloca Ltd shares are selling at about $66 per share with a P/E multiple (ratio) of 49.4 and they have an EPS of approximately $1.34. Now suppose a senior financial analyst considers that the current share price of $66 is too expensive and advises Aloca Ltd to issue a 50% share dividend; that is, a 1-for-2 bonus issue. This dividend plan will lead to a 50% increase in the number of issued shares and a decline in share price to $44 (that is, $\frac{66}{1.5}$). An investor holding 100 Aloca Ltd shares would receive 50 bonus shares, but the market value of 150 shares theoretically will be $6600 (that is, 150 × $44), which is the same as the market value of 100 shares prior to a bonus issue. Thus, a bonus share issue theoretically would not create any value for shareholders of Aloca Ltd.

FINANCE WORKSHOP 13.5

A share in Selina Ltd currently sells at $34.04 and the company has a P/E ratio of 37. Management are considering a 1-for-3 bonus issue.

1. What would the share price be if management went ahead with the bonus issue?
2. Consider an investor who owns 900 shares in Selina prior to the bonus issue. How many shares would the investor own after the bonus issue?
3. What is the value of our investor's shares before and after the bonus issue?

Dividend reinvestment plan

Dividend reinvestment plan: provides shareholders with an option to invest their cash dividends in the company's shares

A **dividend reinvestment plan** (DRP) provides shareholders with an option to invest their cash dividends in the company's shares. This type of plan emerged in Australia in the early 1980s and has gained popularity since the introduction of the dividend imputation system in 1987. A DRP has some attractive properties.

- A DRP allows existing shareholders to acquire more shares in the company without incurring transactions costs.
- Many companies offer a discount of about 5% of the prevailing market price, making the DRP more rewarding to existing shareholders.
- Participation in a DRP is voluntary. Shareholders have a right, not an obligation, to participate in this plan. Thus, a DRP offers flexibility to shareholders in making an investment decision.
- A DRP may be useful in conserving the company's cash balance. It generally allows a company to get back part of a cash dividend by issuing additional shares.

However, there are some disadvantages to a DRP. In particular, shares issued at a discount from market price may increase the cost of capital for the company. Furthermore, new shares may dilute earnings per share of the company.

FINANCE WORLD

Dividend plans of National Australia Bank

Cash dividend

If you are not presently in a plan you will automatically receive $A cash dividends.

As an alternative to cash dividends, shareholders may elect to participate in one or more of the following dividend alternatives.

Dividend Reinvestment Plan

The Dividend Reinvestment Plan (DRP) enables shareholders to use cash dividends for the purchase of additional fully paid ordinary shares. Shares are issued under the DRP at the Current Market Price. (The 'Current Market Price' means, for any dividend the arithmetic average of the Volume Weighted Average Price (VWAP) during the seven trading days commencing on the trading day after the record date for that dividend (or such other date as specified by the directors), or any other period specified by the directors and as announced to the market through the Australian Securities Exchange Limited's company announcements platform, calculated to two decimal places.

No brokerage or commission is payable on shares issued under the Dividend Reinvestment Plan.

Participation in our Dividend Reinvestment Plan is restricted to a minimum of 35 National shares and a maximum of 15 000 National shares, unless you are maintaining a broker's clearing account or acting as a trustee or nominee.

If you maintain a broker's clearing account or act as trustee or nominee you may participate in the Dividend Reinvestment Plan up to a maximum of 15 000 National shares for each person for whom you hold shares.

If you maintain a broker's clearing account or act as trustee or nominee for other persons and wish to participate in the Dividend Reinvestment Plan in excess of 15 000 National shares in aggregate you must complete the statutory declaration, and forward this together with Dividend Nomination Advice to the National's share registry. Unless a correctly completed statutory declaration is received, your holding participation in the Dividend Reinvestment Plan will be limited to 15 000 National shares.

Bonus Share Plan

The Bonus Share Plan (BSP) enables shareholders to receive bonus shares in lieu of cash dividends. These shares are issued at the Current Market Price. (For BSP purposes, 'Current Market Price' is defined in the same manner as for the DRP above.)

Participation in the Bonus Share Plan is restricted to a minimum of 35 National shares. If you elect partial participation in the Bonus Share Plan, you must specify the exact number of shares you wish to participate in that plan.

You will be deemed to have instructed us that you wish to participate in the plans in the following order:

- the Bonus Share Plan; and then
- the Dividend Reinvestment Plan,

subject to the maximum participation in the respective plans set out in your Dividend Nomination Advice and the limits that apply to participation in the Dividend Reinvestment Plan. You will also be deemed to have instructed that any balance of your holding will receive cash dividends. It is important that you update your Dividend Nomination Advice before the relevant record date if your shareholding has changed and you wish to change your instructions.

No brokerage or commission is payable on shares issued under the Bonus Share Plan.

United Kingdom Dividend Plan

The United Kingdom Dividend Plan (UKDP) allows dividends to be received from a United Kingdom subsidiary and paid in pounds sterling rather than in Australian dollars. Participation in the Dividend Reinvestment Plan is also possible.

New Zealand currency payments

Shareholders who wish to receive their dividends in New Zealand currency may do so, provided it is deposited directly into an account at a bank in New Zealand.

Please be aware that the variable exchange rates which apply between Australia and New Zealand, will require the relevant rate to be set in advance of the payment date. The conversion rate will be at a rate as determined on the record date for determination of dividend entitlements.

Source: National Australia Bank Limited.[24]

lo5

Discuss rationales for dividend policies generally adopted by Australian companies.

Optimal dividend policy

An optimal dividend policy refers to the policy that maximises the market value of the firm. Firms generally take into account internal, institutional and market factors when determining how large a dividend they will pay to shareholders.

Internal factors

Dividends are paid from cash available after meeting the financial needs of the firm. High profits may not induce the firm to pay a high cash dividend because profits are not necessarily in the form of cash. They may be tied up in other forms of assets and financing dividend payouts by debt is not perceived as a value-generating action in the capital market. In addition, lenders generally prefer to make loans for activities that generate cash flows. If a significant part of profits is returned to shareholders as dividends, the firm may have to attract external funding to support its investment needs. Thus, the firm's profitability as well as its borrowing capacity influence its dividend decision.

Although dividends are normally paid from the firm's current or recent-past profits, the firm takes into account its future growth prospects and investment needs in determining current dividends. A firm's investment needs, earnings and dividends generally follow a predictable pattern over its life cycle. Five stages in the life cycle of the firm are recognised in the literature: start-up, rapid expansion, high growth, mature growth and decline. Figure 13.10 illustrates a typical firm's life cycle path of dividend payout.

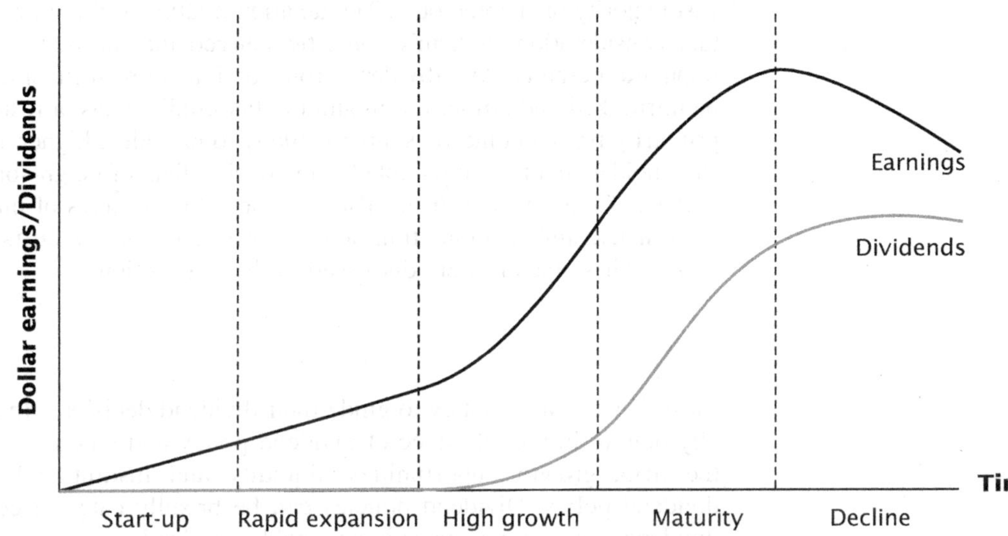

Figure 13.10 Life cycle profile of dividend policy

At the start-up stage the primary source of financing for a typical firm is owners' equity. If the firm succeeds in establishing a business, it attempts to expand business operations by relying on private equity as well as venture capital. At the start-up and rapid expansion stages, the firm may not have adequate free cash flow to pay dividends. Many firms make the transition to a publicly listed firm at the rapid expansion stage and move to the high growth phase. Now the firm has more choices with regard to sources of financing, but its investment needs are also high. Thus, firms generally adopt a low dividend policy at the high growth stage. As the firm moves to the mature growth stage of its life cycle, earnings continue to increase rapidly but reinvestment needs decline. Mature firms with stable and large cash flows return more of their earnings to shareholders as dividends. At the final stage of the firm's life cycle its market share may decline as new competitors enter the market. Although the firm's revenues and earnings may decline, it can afford to pay a high dividend because of its declining need for investments. Thus, dividend policy may be related to the firm's life cycle. For example, analysing data from 1990 to 1998 for 810 firms listed on the (then) Australian Stock Exchange, Jones and Sharma[25] found that high growth firms are associated with lower dividend yields.

Institutional and market factors

An Australian firm is prohibited from paying dividends out of its legal capital (paid-in ordinary share capital). Under Section 201(1) of the *Corporations Act 2001*, dividends can be given only from the distributable earnings of the firm. This legal restriction on dividend payment shields the equity capital of the firm and protects creditors from potential losses. Creditors can also protect their claims by a restrictive clause in a loan covenant. This clause might include a prohibition on dividend payout or linking dividend payout with the firm's performance indicators.

Another institutional constraint in determining a dividend policy is the taxation system. The evolution of the taxation treatment of dividends and capital gains in Australia has already been discussed. The firm must devise a dividend policy that maximises shareholders' wealth within their tax environment. However, shareholders differ in term of tax status and it might not be possible to develop a dividend policy that suits every shareholder. The firm may adopt a dividend policy that maximises after-tax total return for the vast majority of shareholders. The taxation treatment of the firm's income is also an important consideration. A firm's domestic-sourced income that is taxed in Australia attracts imputation credits. Any dividend from foreign-sourced income that is taxed offshore will be unfranked and attract no imputation tax credit. Thus, a resident firm deriving earnings primarily from a domestic source is likely to provide a higher after-tax dividend income to shareholders than a comparable firm with significant foreign-sourced income.

Apart from taxation, firms also consider other sources of market imperfections such as asymmetric information, transaction costs and agency costs in developing a dividend policy. These factors were discussed in the last section.

Alternative dividend policies

Most firms adopt a policy to guide their dividend decisions. In the real world, firms generally believe in the relevance of dividend policy and take into account the performance of the firm, growth opportunities, liquidity and institutional constraints in adopting a dividend policy. Dividend policies can be broadly categorised into three types: residual dividend, constant payout ratio and stable dividend.

Residual dividend policy

Under this policy, dividends are paid from residual earnings — the part of earnings left over after financing a firm's investment needs. Under this policy, dividend payout varies inversely with investment opportunities. In a perfect capital market with no flotation costs of issuing new shares, the firm would be indifferent between capital raised through the sale of new shares and retention of earnings. As we discuss in chapter 7, the firm incurs flotation costs and the cost of new shares is more than the cost of retained earnings. Therefore, the firm will first try to meet its investment needs using internal equity, and then pay a dividend if any earnings are left over after financing all desired projects. As we see in chapters 8 and 9, positive NPV projects will be accepted to increase firm value, while some negative NPV projects might be accepted for strategic reasons.

This argument relies on the presence of transaction costs in issuing new shares and gives priority to meeting investment needs over shareholders' dividend needs, in the anticipation of having a favourable impact on share value through minimising the cost of capital.

Constant payout ratio policy

Under this policy, dividend payment as a percentage of earnings is constant. The dollar amount of dividend can vary with earnings fluctuations but the payout ratio is fixed. Thus, dividends will reduce to zero when the firm's earnings are non-positive. As the firm's earnings increase, the dollar amount of dividends will increase. A majority of Australian firms have explicit target payout ratios, with the aim of returning a fixed proportion of earnings as dividends, and the payout ratios are positively associated with the size of the firm.[26] Generally, a firm can't maintain a constant payout ratio over its entire life cycle, as explained in example 13.14.

EXAMPLE 13.14

Constant payout ratio and a firm's life cycle

Suppose XYZ Corporation is operating at the high growth stage of its life cycle and is considering adopting the policy of a constant payout ratio. It is considering two alternative payout ratios, 80% and 35%, but before making a decision on a target payout ratio the corporation wants to examine the impact on the firm's growth rate. XYZ Corporation's current EPS is $2.00 and return on equity is 15%. Under the lower payout ratio it can expect a growth rate of 9.75% (that is, 0.65×0.15) but the higher payout ratio will yield a growth rate of only 3% (that is, 0.20×0.15).

The firm is likely to adopt the low payout ratio, but in the future, at the mature stage of its life cycle, it may adopt the higher payout ratio. Thus, the payout ratio is likely to vary over a firm's life cycle.

Stable dividend policy

This policy is in favour of paying a fixed dollar dividend per share. Investors (such as pensioners) requiring a regular stream of income might prefer this policy. Mature firms with a good earnings history are likely to commit themselves to a stable dividend policy. In practice, firms may increase their dollar dividend if there is a permanent increase in earnings but typically refrain from reducing dividends in the event of a decrease in earnings.

A minor variation of the stable dividend policy can be a low regular dividend and an occasional 'extra' dividend linked to the company's performance. The regular component of the dividend is determined based on the firm's normal earnings, while the extra dividend is given when earnings exceed the normal level. This policy provides shareholders with a low but steady stream of cash, keeping open the option of an upward revision of dividends.

In general, managers have significant discretion over dividend payouts and they typically follow a more or less stable dividend policy. On the other hand, earnings reporting is subject to stringent conditions specified in both corporation law and accounting standards, giving managers limited control over reporting of earnings figures. The greater stability of dividends relative to earnings provides financial analysts with an edge in forecasting dividends more accurately than earnings. An investigation of the consensus dividend forecasts of Australian financial analysts over the period 1991–98[27] supports this assertion. Financial analysts provide regular forecasts of dividends, indicating that dividends perhaps provide useful signals about future cash flows of the firm. If this were not so, resources would not be channelled to forecast them.

executive summary

lo1 discuss fundamental dividend concepts and dividend policy in corporate Australia

- Cash dividends are usually paid twice a year in Australia — an interim dividend and a final dividend.
- Investors who own shares before the ex-dividend day are entitled to a dividend.
- Dividend payout ratio, dividend yield and dividend stability over time are the key indicators of a firm's dividend policy.
- Australian firms generally follow a high dividend policy relative to US firms and usually pay a stable stream of dividends.

lo2 explain the dividend irrelevance theory

- The dividend irrelevance theory was developed by Miller and Modigliani to demonstrate that changes in dividend policy have no impact on the market value of a company.
- The dividend irrelevance arguments are based on the assumptions that a dividend decision is separable from an investment decision and capital markets are perfect.
- The market value of a firm depends on the present value of cash flows from its assets, which in turn depend on investment decisions not on dividend decisions.

lo3 explain how dividend policy may affect shareholders' wealth with particular attention to the tax treatment of dividends and capital gains

- Dividend relevance arguments are primarily based on the tax treatment of dividends as compared to capital gains, asymmetric information, agency costs, transaction costs and the clientele effect.
- A vast majority of Australian firms pay a 90–100% franked dividend, providing shareholders imputation tax credit for offsetting their personal tax liabilities.
- A capital gains tax is applicable to assets acquired after 19 September 1985. A capital gains tax discount of up to 50% was introduced in 1999.
- The market value of a franked dividend can be measured by the dividend drop-off ratio, which depends on the company tax rate and a typical shareholder's marginal tax rates on dividend income and capital gains.
- Signalling theories suggest that an increase in dividend provides a signal for persistent increase in earnings, leading to a rise in share value. Higher dividend payments may also reduce agency costs.

lo4 describe the use of bonus shares, share repurchase and dividend reinvestment as alternatives to cash dividends

- Although the cash dividend is still the primary means of returning cash to shareholders in Australia, many firms ha.ve provided alternatives to cash dividends over the last decade.
- Like a cash dividend, a share buyback also reduces the firm's cash balance. A share buyback may provide a positive signal about the firm's future cash flows and is often accompanied by a rise in share price.

- Bonus shares (share dividends) can be given to shareholders without using cash. It is not a common practice in Australia.
- A dividend reinvestment plan allows existing shareholders to acquire more shares in the company, usually at a discount price, without incurring transaction costs.

lo5 discuss rationales for dividend policies generally adopted by Australian companies

- Firms take into account internal, institutional and market factors in determining the size of the dividend they will pay to shareholders and in what form.
- Internal factors include the firm's profitability, liquidity and capacity to attract external financing. Generally, these factors vary with the stage of a firm's life cycle. A mature firm pays a higher dividend than a firm at the rapid expansion or high growth stage.
- Under the Corporations Act, an Australian firm can pay a dividend from its distributable earnings, but not from its legal capital. Firms also take into account various sources of capital market imperfections in developing a dividend policy.
- Dividend policies can be categorised into three types — the residual dividend policy, constant payout ratio policy and stable dividend policy. Managers typically follow a more or less stable dividend policy.

Key terms

Learning chart

Learning objective	Questions	Self-test problems	Financial problems
lo1 discuss fundamental dividend concepts and dividend policy in corporate Australia	13.1, 13.2, 13.3	13.2, 13.3	13.1, 13.2, 13.7
lo2 explain the dividend irrelevance theory	13.4, 13.5		
lo3 explain how dividend policy may affect shareholders' wealth with particular attention to the tax treatment of dividends and capital gains	13.6, 13.7, 13.8, 13.9	13.1, 13.2, 13.3	13.3, 13.4, 13.5, 13.7, 13.10

continued

lo4 describe the use of bonus shares, share repurchase and dividend reinvestment as alternatives to cash dividends	13.10	13.3	13.6, 13.8, 13.9
lo5 discuss rationales for dividend policies generally adopted by Australian companies	13.11		

Questions

13.1 What are the indicators of dividend policy? Define each indicator.

13.2 Explain the dividend payment process in Australia.

13.3 Why do Australian companies pay a higher cash dividend than their US counterparts?

13.4 Explain the dividend irrelevance arguments advanced by Miller and Modigliani.

13.5 'The investment decision is separable from the dividend decision.' Do you agree with this statement? Explain your answer.

13.6 Should all investors prefer franked dividends over capital gains?

13.7 Explain the possible impacts of each of the following tax rate changes on the dividend drop-off ratio for shares paying a franked dividend:

(a) an increase in the company tax rate

(b) an increase in the personal tax rate

(c) abolition of capital gains tax.

13.8 How can a firm's dividend policy give a positive signal to financial markets?

13.9 'An increase in dividends reduces agency cost.' Briefly explain this proposition.

13.10 Discuss the potential advantages of each of the following over a cash dividend:

(a) a share repurchase

(b) a share dividend.

13.11 Why do firms adopt a stable dividend policy in the presence of earnings volatility?

Self-test problems

13.1 Suppose ANT Super Fund owns 5000 Gotel shares. Gotel has just paid a fully franked dividend of \$1.25 per share. Find the after-tax dividend income of ANT Super Fund.

13.2 On 22 September, Aberdeen Leaders Ltd, an ASX-listed company, announced a fully franked dividend of 1c per share to be paid on 22 October. The record date for determining dividend entitlement was 8 October.

(a) What was the ex-dividend date for Aberdeen shares?

(b) Suppose the typical investor in the company faced a personal marginal tax rate of 47% and was not entitled to a capital gains tax discount. The company tax rate is 30%. Given this information, estimate the impact of a fully franked dividend of 1c per share on the share price on the ex-dividend date.

13.3 Melbourne Health Care Ltd has 1 million outstanding ordinary shares with $1.5 million of earnings available for ordinary shareholders. The company's shares are expected to be sold at $50 per share on the forthcoming ex-dividend day.

(a) If the firm pays a cash dividend of $2.50 per share, what would be the cum-dividend share price? Ignore dividend franking and taxation.

(b) Suppose the company decides to buy back shares at the cum-dividend price instead of paying a cash dividend of $2.50 per share. Find the number of outstanding shares after buyback.

(c) Calculate the impact of the buyback on the company's EPS.

(d) Estimate the share price after buyback.

(e) Evaluate the impact of the cash dividend and buyback options on a shareholder's wealth. Which option would you recommend to the company?

Solutions to self-test problems

13.1 A superannuation fund is subject to a 15% tax on dividend income. As shown in equation 13.7:

$$\text{After-tax dividend} = D_f\left[\frac{1-t_p}{1-t_c}\right]$$

$$= \$1.25\left[\frac{1-0.15}{1-0.30}\right]$$

$$= \$1.25 \times 1.2143$$

$$= \$1.52$$

13.2 (a) The ex-dividend data for Aberdeen shares was 1 October, four business days prior to the record date.

(b) The price drop-off on the ex-dividend day can be estimated using equation 13.8.

In this case, the price drop-off is equal to the grossed up value of dividend because dividends and capital gains are taxed at the same rate.

13.3 (a) Ignoring dividend franking and taxes, equation 13.8 can be rewritten as:

$$P_{CD} - P_{XD} = D$$

Thus, the cum-dividend share price is:

$$P_{CD} = P_{XD} + D$$

$$P_{CD} = \$50 + \$2.50 = \$52.50$$

(b) The company can spend $2.5 million (1 million shares × $2.50) on share repurchase. At the cum-dividend price of $52.50, the company can buy 47 619 shares (that is, $\frac{\$2.5 \text{ million}}{\$52.50}$).

(c) $$\text{EPS after buyback} = \frac{\text{earnings}}{\text{number of outstanding shares after buyback}}$$

$$= \frac{\$2\,500\,000}{1\,000\,000 - 47\,619}$$

$$= \$2.63$$

$$\text{EPS before buyback} = \frac{\text{earnings}}{\text{number of outstanding shares before buyback}}$$
$$= \frac{\$2\,500\,000}{1\,000\,000}$$
$$= \$2.50$$

Thus, the share buyback has led to an increase of EPS by 13 cents.

(d) $$\text{New share price} = \text{P/E ratio} \times \text{EPS after buyback}$$
$$= \left[\frac{\$50}{\$2.50}\right]\$2.625$$
$$= 20 \times \$2.625$$
$$= \$52.50$$

(e) Under a cash dividend option the cum-dividend share price would reflect a dividend per share of $2.50. Thus, the total value accruing to a shareholder would be $52.50, as shown in part (a).

The buyback option provides the same value to the shareholder through a capital gain.

If there are no taxes, a cash dividend is a perfect substitute for share repurchase. However, if dividends are taxed more heavily than capital gains for the majority of the company's shareholders, the share buyback would be preferable over a cash dividend.

Financial problems

13.1 Gotel Inc. has a dividend payout ratio of 60% and a return on equity of 15%. The firm wants to increase its payout ratio to 80%. What will be the impact of this change in the payout ratio on the growth rate of Gotel Inc?

13.2 KLM Corporation's dividends per share and dividend yields over the last 10 years are given below.

(a) Calculate the standard deviation of dividend yields.

(b) Find the dividend instability index.

Year	Dividend yield (%)	Dividend per share (cents)
1998	3.04	112
1999	2.98	94
2000	3.12	120
2001	4.25	122
2002	5.65	125
2003	4.30	90
2004	6.00	105
2005	5.10	95
2006	3.98	102
2007	4.75	105

13.3 John has just received a fully franked dividend of $200 and he is currently at the 15% personal income tax bracket. The current company tax rate is 30%. Find his after-tax dividend income.

13.4 Suppose a typical shareholder of Central Coast Bank (CCB) holds shares for more than 12 months and pays 45c of personal tax on each dollar of additional ordinary income. The company has just announced a fully franked dividend of \$1.50 per share. The company tax rate is 30%. CCB shares are currently selling at a cum-dividend price of \$20 per share. Estimate the ex-dividend price of CCB shares.

13.5 In question 13.4, if the typical investor of CCB shares holds shares for less than 12 months, what would be your estimate of the ex-dividend price?

13.6 Bell Corporation has 1 million ordinary shares outstanding and a P/E multiple of 25. The firm's annual earnings are \$500 000. It is considering a 20% bonus share issue to supplement its current low cash dividend policy.

(a) What is the firm's current share price? How will this be affected by the proposed bonus share issue?

(b) Suppose you hold 100 Bell shares. What will be the impact of a bonus issue on the total value of your shares?

13.7 On 4 September 2006, Commonwealth Bank of Australia (CBA) made the following announcement:

> On 5 October 2006, Commonwealth Bank of Australia will be paying its final dividend for the year ended 30 June 2006 of 130 cents per share, amounting to \$1 688.2 million.
> This dividend will be a 100% franked dividend with the imputed credit being at the rate of 30%.
> The dividend will be paid to all Commonwealth Bank shareholders who were recorded on the register as at the record date of 18 August 2006.[28]

(a) What was the ex-dividend date for CBA shares?

(b) Suppose a typical investor in CBA shares faced a personal marginal tax rate of 40% and was entitled to a capital gains tax discount on CBA shares. The company tax rate is 30%. Using this information, approximate the impact of a fully franked dividend of 130 cents per share on the share price on the ex-dividend date.

13.8 Suppose New England Bank is an all-equity firm with an after-tax operating income of \$350 million pa; it has 200 million outstanding shares. The firm needs \$180 million to meet its annual reinvestment target. The firm expects after-tax operating income to grow at the rate of 5% pa indefinitely and the cost of capital to remain at its current rate of 12% in the foreseeable future.

Estimate the market value of the firm and total value per share accruing to existing shareholders, assuming that the company pays all of its free cash flows as dividend.

13.9 How would your answer to problem 13.8 change under the following alternative dividend policies?

(a) The firm pays no dividend and holds all of its free cash flows in the form of cash balance.

(b) The firm pays dividend of \$200 million, financed by all of its free cash flows and new ordinary shares.

13.10 Queensland Ecolights pays a 60% franked dividend. It has just announced a dividend of \$2.00 per share. If the cum-dividend share price is \$30.00, the company tax rate is 30% and the marginal tax rate of a typical shareholder in the company is 42%, what would be the ex-dividend share price?

SOLUTIONS TO FINANCE WORKSHOPS

13.1 1. Payout ratio $= \dfrac{D}{E}$

$$= \frac{0.80}{1.00} = 0.80$$

Thus, Cochlear Ltd paid 80% of its earnings as dividend in 2005.

2. As shown in equation 13.2:

$$\text{Growth rate} = (1 - \text{payout ratio}) \times \text{return on equity}$$

$$\text{Growth rate in 2004} = (1 - 0.864) \times 0.36 = 0.049$$

$$\text{Growth rate in 2005} = (1 - 0.744) \times 0.36 = 0.092$$

The estimated growth rate increased from 4.9% in 2004 to 9.2% in 2005.

3. Using equation 13.3, we obtain:

$$\text{Dividend yield} = \frac{D}{P} = \frac{0.80}{40} = 0.02$$

Investors earned 2 cents per dollar of investment in Cochlear's shares.

13.2 1.

$$\text{After-tax dividend} = D - \left[\frac{D}{1-t_c}\right]t_p + \left[\frac{D}{1-t_c}\right]t_c$$

$$= D\left[\frac{1-t_p}{1-t_c}\right]$$

$$= \$250\left[\frac{1-0.40}{1-0.30}\right] = \$214.29$$

2.

$$\text{After-tax dividend} = D\left[\frac{1-t_p}{1-t_c}\right]$$

$$= \$250\left[\frac{1-0.15}{1-0.30}\right] = \$303.57$$

13.3 1. The drop-off ratio can be found as:

$$\frac{P_{CD} - P_{XD}}{D} = \frac{(1-t_p)}{(1-t_c)(1-t_g)}$$

Since shares are held less than 12 months, the investors are not entitled to a capital gains tax discount.

$$\text{Thus, } \frac{P_{CD} - P_{XD}}{D} = \frac{(1-0.40)}{(1-0.30)(1-0.40)}$$
$$= 1.4286 \text{ or } 142.86\%$$

The market value of $1 of franked dividend is $1.43.

2. The investor is entitled to a capital gain tax discount because shares are held more than 12 months.

$$\frac{P_{CD} - P_{XD}}{D} = \frac{(1-t_p)}{(1-t_c)\left(1-\frac{t_p}{2}\right)}$$

$$1.1256 = \frac{(1-t_p)}{(1-0.30)\left(1-\frac{t_p}{2}\right)}$$

$$1.1256(1-0.30)\left(1-\frac{t_p}{2}\right) = 1-t_p$$

$$t_p = 0.35$$

13.4 1. $\text{Current EPS} = \frac{\text{Current earnings}}{\text{Number of shares}}$

$$= \frac{\$7\,000\,000}{10\,000\,000} = \$0.70$$

2. $\text{Current market price} = \left(\frac{P}{E}\right) \times EPS$

$$= 18 \times \$0.70 = \$12.60$$

3. Quoll will be able to re-purchase about 119 047 shares $\left(= \frac{\$1.5\text{ million}}{\$12.60}\right)$

4. $\text{New EPS} = \left(\frac{\$7\,000\,000}{10\,119\,047}\right)$

$$= \$0.69$$

5. $\text{Share price after re-purchase} = \left(\frac{P}{E}\right) \times EPS$

$$= 18 \times \$0.69 = \$12.42$$

13.5 1. This plan is expected to decrease share price from $34.04 to $25.53.

That is, $\frac{\$34.04}{\left[1+\frac{1}{3}\right]} = \$25.53$

2. Number of shares = 900 x $\left[1+\frac{1}{3}\right]$ = 1200

3. Pre-bonus issue value = $34.04 x 900

= $30 636

Post-bonus issue value = \$25.53 x 1200
= \$30 636

This example shows that a bonus issue does not change the market value of the investor's share portfolio.

End notes

1 Data from Aspect Financial Pty Limited, *Aspect Fin Analysis*, www.aspectfinancial.com.au.

2 Miller, M & Modigliani, F 1961, 'Dividend policy, growth and the valuation of shares', *Journal of Business*, vol. 34, no. 4, pp. 411–33.

3 Dividend payment timeline available from the ASX, www.asx.com.au.

4 For further details see Gwilym, O, Morgan, G & Thomas, S 2000, 'Dividend stability, dividend yield and stock returns: UK evidence', *Journal of Business Finance and Accounting*, vol. 27, nos 3 & 4, pp. 261–81; Gombola, M & Liu, F 1993, 'Considering dividend stability in the relation between dividend yields and stock returns', *Journal of Financial Research*, vol. 16, no. 2, pp. 139–50.

5 Data on dividend yields and dividend per share from *Aspect Fin Analysis*.

6 Reproduced from figure 'Dividend policy', p. 3 of 'Is your dividend policy liquidating your business? Dividend policy and shareholder value', © 2002 Australia and New Zealand Banking Group Limited.

7 Data for 1976–2003 are from Datastream; data for 2004–05 for Australia, New Zealand and the UK are from World Federation of Exchanges, www.world-exchanges.org; data for 2004–05 for the US are from Stern School of Business, New York University.

8 These general patterns were first hypothesised by John Lintner in Lintner, J 1956, 'Distribution of incomes of corporations among dividends, retained earnings and taxes', *American Economic Review*, vol. 46, no. 2, pp. 97–113, based on interviews with the management of 28 firms.

9 Data for 1973–2003 are from Datastream; data for 2004–2005 are from *Aspect Fin Analysis*.

10 Data from *Aspect Fin Analysis*.

11 Data from *Aspect Fin Analysis*.

12 Miller & Modigliani 1961.

13 Reproduced from Warburton, R & Hendy, P 2006, *International comparison of Australia's taxes* (a report submitted to the Treasurer, Commonwealth of Australia), p. 205.

14 Data from *Aspect Fin Analysis*.

15 Reproduced from Warburton & Hendy, p. 207.

16 Brown, P & Walter, T 1986, 'Ex-dividend day behaviour of Australian share prices', *Australian Journal of Management*, vol. 11, no. 2, pp. 139–52.

17 Bellamy, D 1994, 'Evidence of imputation clienteles in the Australian equity market', *Asia–Pacific Journal of Management*, vol. 11, no. 2, pp. 275–87.

18 Brown, P & Clarke, A 1993, 'The ex-dividend day behaviour of Australian share prices before and after dividend imputation', *Australian Journal of Management*, vol. 18, no. 1, pp. 1–40.

19 Walker, S & Partington, G 1999, 'The value of dividends: evidence from cum-dividend trading in the ex-dividend period', *Accounting and Finance*, vol. 39, no. 3, pp. 275–96.

20 Gordon, M 1962, ch. 5 in *The investment, financing and valuation of the corporation*, Irwin, Homewood, Ill.

21 Dividend signalling theories were developed by John and Williams, Bhattacharya and Miller and Rock. See John, K & Williams, J 1985, 'Dividends, dilution and taxes: a signalling equilibrium', *Journal of Finance*, vol. 40, no. 4, pp. 1053–70; Bhattacharya, S 1979, 'Imperfect information, dividend policy and "The bird in the hand" fallacy', *Bell Journal of Economics*, vol. 10, no. 1, pp. 259–70; Miller, M & Rock, K 1985, 'Dividend policy under asymmetric information', *Journal of Finance*, vol. 40, no. 4, pp. 1031–51.

22 Miller & Modigliani 1961, p. 431.

23 Freed, J 2007, 'Investors overwhelm BHP $3.5b buyback', *Sydney Morning Herald*, 27 March.

24 Extracted from National Australia Bank Limited 2007, 'Dividend information', www.nabgroup.com. Use of the extracted information is governed by Australia law and is subject to the disclaimers set out on the www.nabgroup.com website.

25 Jones, S & Sharma, R 2001, 'The association between the investment opportunity set and corporate financing and dividend decisions: some Australian evidence', *Managerial Finance*, vol. 27, no. 3, pp. 48–64.

26 Ho, H 2003, 'Dividend policies in Australia and Japan', *International Advances in Economic Research*, vol. 9, no. 2, pp. 91–100.

27 Brown, P, Clarke, A, How, JCY & Lim, KJP 2002, 'Analysts' dividend forecasts', *Pacific-Basin Finance Journal*, vol. 10, pp. 371–91.

28 Announcement available on the ASX company announcements database, www.asx.com.au.

chapter

14

Forecasting to evaluate financial decisions

Learning objectives

After studying this chapter, you should be able to:

lo1	describe the structure of financial statements
lo2	explain the rationale for and importance of financial forecasting
lo3	construct a cash budget
lo4	explain the use of pro-forma financial statements
lo5	construct the pro-forma income statement and balance sheet
lo6	explain the role of financial ratio analysis
lo7	identify and calculate key ratios and interpret your results.

FORECASTING YOUR ABILITY TO STAY AFLOAT

The bank reserves the right to withdraw [certain] facilities if, in the opinion of the bank, there have been material adverse changes in the financial condition or operation of the business. In addition certain ratios are to be maintained to the satisfaction of the bank.

Source: Harvey Norman Holdings Limited.[1]

Moody's gave it a Ba2 rating, noting its financial metrics would weaken as it invested in finding alternative outlets for its coal when its existing long-term contract with Verve Energy expires in 2010.

Standard & Poor's gave it a BB– long-term rating with a stable outlook.

It said the stable outlook anticipated Griffin would complete its growth plans over the next three years while maintaining appropriate financial ratios.

Source: *The West Australian.*[2]

Multiplex says its foreshadowed asset sales are unrelated to any breaches of loan covenants.

It said: 'Wembley has caused breaches of various financial ratios and covenants. We are in ongoing dialogue with bankers and insurance bond providers, and based on discussions to date, we expect they will continue to support the company.'

Source: *The Age.*[3]

Chapter preview

This chapter introduces you to techniques for forecasting the cash flows and financing requirements of the firm. We begin by looking at the content and format of financial statements. We then learn to develop cash budgets. Control over cash is a critical aspect of maintaining a firm's liquidity. Identifying future cash needs and forecasting periodic balances helps managers to anticipate cash shortfalls and allows them to plan how to best finance any shortfall. Taking information from the cash budget and using our knowledge of the financial statements, we then move on to forecasting the next period's financial statements. We use our forecast financial statements to assess the likely impact of management decisions on the perceptions investors and creditors have about the firm. To do this, we use ratio analysis.

The quotes on the chapter's opening page demonstrate the importance of maintaining specific levels for financial ratios to ensure the firm does not breach its debt covenants. Debt covenants are contracts with lenders and they are used to minimise the probability that the borrower will default on the loan. Debt covenants are normally written in terms of minimum performance for certain financial ratios. Breaching debt covenants causes difficulty for the firm with lenders (who can terminate the borrowing agreement and insist on immediate repayment) and generates 'bad press' for the firm. Forewarned is forearmed — by developing the cash budget and pro-forma financial statements we will learn to construct in this chapter, managers can take steps to minimise potential future problems.

Company insiders have access to much more useful information than the published financial statements to predict events like insolvency. But because managers know creditors and investors use the published financial statements to form an opinion about the company, they are interested in how their decisions will be viewed by the users of financial statements.

The following diagram shows how this chapter is structured.

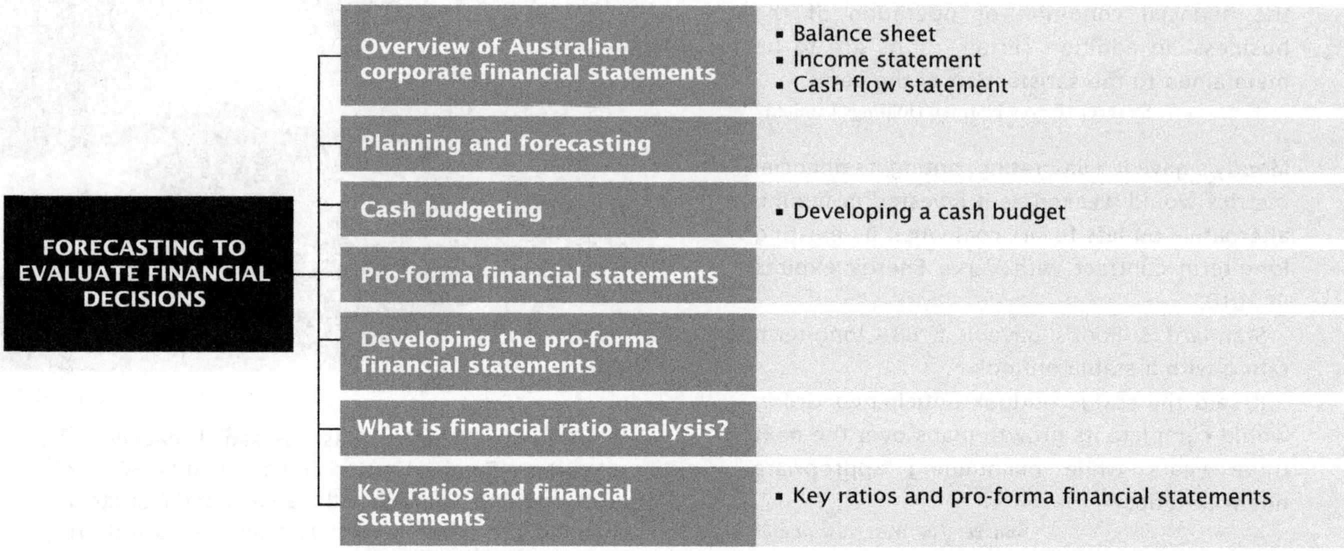

Overview of Australian corporate financial statements

lo1

Describe the structure of financial statements.

Accounting system: the collection of records of financial transactions

Financial statements: the balance sheet, the income statement and the cash flow statement

Firms keep records of all financial transactions for legal reasons (taxation and reporting requirements, for example) and to help managers monitor and control operations. These financial records are stored in the **accounting system**. The accountant produces the financial statements from these records. Managers use data from the accounting system to prepare budgets, forecast performance and assess past performance. Our focus in this chapter is on management's use of the accounting system. Before we investigate this further, we need to have some understanding of the content and structure of financial statements.

The term **'financial statements'** collectively refers to the balance sheet, the income statement and the cash flow statement. Each of these statements tells us something different about the company. The financial statements relate to a particular period of time. A company's annual report will have a reporting period that is one year long. Companies listed on the stock exchange are also required to produce half-yearly reports. The financial statements for these reports are based on a six-month reporting period.

Balance sheet

Balance sheet: shows the assets, liabilities and equity of the company at the end of the reporting period

The **balance sheet** shows the assets, liabilities and equity of the company at the end of the reporting period. It gives us a 'stock' measure of the company by telling us the book value of the assets controlled by the company and the liabilities owed by it. Figure 14.1 provides an example of a company balance sheet.

Maximus Printing Limited Balance sheet as at 30 June	2008 $'000	2007 $'000
Current assets		
Cash	670	960
Receivables	3 375	4 725
Inventories	750	625
Other financial assets	9 700	6 320
Total current assets	14 495	12 630
Non-current assets		
Land	26 800	16 975
Buildings	23 959	26 458
Plant and equipment	6 987	8 734
Total non-current assets	57 746	52 167
Total assets	72 241	64 797
Current liabilities		
Payables	1 050	1 490
Interest-bearing liabilities	14 200	5 412
Current tax liability	6 000	1 125
Total current liabilities	21 250	8 027
Non-current liabilities		
Interest-bearing liabilities	14 000	33 000
Total non-current liabilities	14 000	33 000
Total liabilities	35 250	41 027
Equity		
Contributed equity	11 335	11 335
Reserves	2 047	7 548
Retained profits	23 609	4 887
Total equity	36 991	23 770

Figure 14.1 Balance sheet

Assets: probable future economic benefits that the firm is able to utilise

Liabilities: future sacrifices of economic benefits that the firm is obliged to make

Equity: the book value of the ownership interest in the firm

Net assets: total assets minus total liabilities

This financial statement contains the three broad categories: 'assets', 'liabilities' and 'equity'. **Assets** are defined as probable future economic benefits that the firm is able to utilise. **Liabilities** represent future sacrifices of economic benefits that the firm is obliged to make. Assets and liabilities are each divided into 'current' and 'non-current', based on how long the company expects to be holding the asset or liability. Current assets are those that management expects to liquidate within the next 12 months. Current liabilities are those that have to be paid within the next 12 months. **Equity** represents the book value of the ownership interest in the firm. The book value of equity equals the **net assets**, or assets minus liabilities.

Income statement: shows the revenues and expenses that were generated over the reporting period

Revenues: inflows of future economic benefits that come from the operations of the firm

Expenses: consumption or losses of future economic benefits

Income statement

The **income statement** shows the revenues and expenses that were generated over the reporting period. **Revenues** are inflows of future economic benefits that come from the operations of the firm. Sales and interest income are examples of revenues. The funds raised from a new issue of shares, however, are not revenues — they are increases in equity. **Expenses** are the consumption or losses of future economic benefits. Cost of goods sold and interest payments are examples of expenses. The payment of dividends is not considered an expense because dividends belong to the owners of the firm. That is why they are shown below

Retained earnings: the accumulated profits (net of dividend payments) that are shown in the equity section of the balance sheet

Profit: the excess of revenues over expenses

the net profit figure and why they reduce the amount of profit that is transferred to retained earnings. Profit (revenues minus expenses) is often used as a measure of performance.

The income statement for Maximus Printing Ltd is shown in figure 14.2. This statement distinguishes between revenues and expenses from ordinary operating activities and those from any other areas.

Maximus Printing Limited Income statement for the financial year ended 30 June	2008 $'000	2007 $'000
Revenues from sales	81 435	46 497
Cost of goods sold	28 502	16 274
Gross profit	52 933	30 223
Interest revenue	20	15
	52 953	30 238
Administration and marketing	10 080	7 374
Depreciation	3 070	3 346
Electricity and other operating expenses	407	232
Employee benefits		2 000
Borrowing costs expense	1 222	975
Profit (loss) from ordinary activities	38 174	16 311
Income tax expense relating to ordinary activities	11 452	4 893
Net profit (loss)	26 722	11 418
Dividends paid	8 000	8 000
Transfer to retained earnings	18 722	3 418
Basic earnings per share	2.67	1.14
Dividends per share	0.80	0.80

Figure 14.2 Income statement

Why don't we have a current/non-current classification in the income statement? It is because this statement represents 'flows' through the firm rather than the 'stock' picture presented in the balance sheet. The profit that a company generates is used to make distributions to owners (dividends are paid from profit), to reduce liabilities and to increase assets. What happens to any profit that is left over after these three types of applications are completed? The remaining profit is transferred to the retained earnings account in the equity section of the balance sheet. The balance sheet and income statement are linked because the change in net assets (that is, assets minus liabilities) over the reporting period is matched by the change in retained earnings.

Accrual accounting: the process of matching revenues to the period in which they are earned and liabilities to the period in which they are incurred

The balance sheet and income statement are based on an accrual accounting system. This means that revenues are matched to the period in which they are earned and liabilities for the period when they are incurred. Think about a company purchasing inventory on 60-day terms a month before the end of the reporting period. The company will have received the inventory and may even have sold all of it well before the cash payment to the supplier is made in the following reporting period. Under accrual accounting, this transaction is recorded as an inventory asset and a creditor liability in the reporting period the inventory benefit was obtained. Without the accruals, the profit in this case is higher than it should be in the first period, but lower than it should be in the second period when the goods are paid for.

Accountants use accrual accounting because the objective of preparing financial reports is to report on *past performance*. Finance, on the other hand, has a forward-looking focus that involves making decisions about the future. While we only include cash flows in the period they are received, the allocation of revenues and expenses used in accrual accounting helps to meet the objective of reporting on the past decisions of the firm's management.

Cash flow statement

Cash flow statement: shows the amount of cash that came into and went out of the company over the reporting period

The **cash flow statement** shows the amount of cash that came into and went out of the company over the reporting period. Like the income statement, the cash flow statement represents a 'flow' rather than a 'stock' picture of the company's activities. It is not based on accrual accounting. You will recall from chapter 1 that profit and cash flows are two very different concepts. This difference is illustrated when we compare the income statement and the cash flow statement. The profit and loss statement applies accounting rules to arrive at a profit figure, while the cash flow statement does not use accrual accounting principles and presents a picture of the business's cash flows. Transactions in the cash flow statement represent cash payments and receipts that occurred during the reporting period. It relates to the balance sheet in that the cash at the end of the financial year is shown as a current asset. Reductions in liabilities in the income statement appear as cash outflows from financing activities. The purchase or sale of additional assets is represented as a cash outflow or inflow from investing. If the company borrowed money to purchase the asset, the borrowed amount is shown as an inflow from financing activities. Changes in asset values that are due to depreciation or revaluations do not appear in the cash flow statement because there are no cash transactions involved. Figure 14.3 shows the cash flow statement for Maximus Printing Ltd.

Maximus Printing Limited Cash flow statement for the financial year ended 30 June	2008 $'000	2007 $'000
Cash flows from operating activities		
Receipts from customers	78 356	45 567
Payments to suppliers and employees	(39 467)	(27 767)
Dividends received	0	0
Interest and bill discounts paid	(22)	(13)
Borrowing cotss	(1 250)	(947)
Income taxes paid	(9 870)	(4 650)
Net cash provided by operating activities	27 747	12 190
Cash flows from investing activities		
Payments for property, plant and equipment	(9 825)	(795)
Proceeds from sale of property, plant and equipment	0	250
Net cash used in investing activities	(9 825)	(545)
Cash flows from financing activities		
Proceeds from issue of shares	0	0
Proceeds from borrowings	14 200	4 550
Repayment of borrowings	(24 412)	(7 970)
Distributions paid	(8 000)	(8 000)
Net cash used in financing activities	(18 212)	(11 420)
Net increase (decrease) in cash held	(290)	225
Cash at the beginning of the financial year	960	735
Cash at the end of the financial year	670	960

Figure 14.3 Cash flow statement

Cash inflows and outflows are classified as 'operating', 'investing' or 'financing'. These categories tell the net cash story for each activity in the reporting period. Our focus throughout this text has been on cash flows rather than profits. The reporting requirement for cash flow statements was introduced to provide investors with more information on which to base their decisions. The cash flow statement does not have as much potential for being used to misrepresent the company's performance as do the accrual statements.

FINANCE WORLD

Cochlear financial statements

The financial statements presented in figures 14.1 to 14.3 have been adapted from the usual format of those in annual reports. Go to the Cochlear Limited website[4] and download the most recent financial statements. Financial statements for 2006 and onwards are based on the International Accounting and Financial Reporting Standards (IFRS). Form an opinion about the trend in operating cash flow for Cochlear Ltd.

lo2

Explain the rationale for and importance of financial forecasting.

Planning and forecasting

Financially viable businesses don't just happen — they require efficient management and planning. If the production manager doesn't make sure there are enough staff rostered on to operate the line, that urgent order might not be filled (or might be filled only by having to pay staff hefty overtime rates). If the sales manager doesn't allocate the sales reps to specific regions, sales will be lost when areas are not serviced and competitors may take market share. What if the financial manager doesn't make sure there is enough cash to pay suppliers? The company's reputation might be damaged or a more expensive source of short-term finance might have to be called on.

The main tools available to help the financial manager in planning are the cash budget and the pro-forma financial statements. Cash budgets focus on maintaining the solvency of the firm. Pro-forma financial statements are concerned with forecasting profit for the coming period and the position of the firm at the end of the period.

lo3

Construct a cash budget.

Budget: a plan that includes forecasts of future transactions

Cash budgeting

Control over cash is a critical aspect of maintaining a firm's liquidity. The cash flow statement tells us about the past cash flows of the firm but identifying future cash needs and forecasting periodic balances helps managers to anticipate cash shortfalls and allows them to plan how to best finance any shortfall. A **budget** is a plan that includes forecasts of future transactions. A cash budget involves detailed forecasts of cash inflows and outflows for the firm over the budget period and is a planning tool for the financial manager, rather than a historical document for the benefit of investors. Another difference between the cash budget and the cash flow statement is that the level of detail required for a cash budget is much higher than that which is presented in the cash flow statement.

How long is a budget period? This depends on the specific use of the budget. Large companies that have many daily cash transactions use daily cash budgets.[5] Firms that do not have such high volumes of transactions need weekly or monthly cash budgets. Budgets to suit different purposes have different budget periods. Weekly or monthly cash budgets are useful for planning how much cash to hold in the company's bank account. Annual cash budgets are useful for identifying the financing needs of the company. Forecasting cash transactions gives the firm a blueprint to determine in advance if it will have to borrow money to meet working capital needs or to make an equipment purchase at a particular time. Knowing in advance when additional financing will be needed allows the financial manager to optimise the choice of funding source.

One aspect common to forecasts of any kind is that the closer you get to the end of the forecast period, the more reliable your forecasts become. Can you reliably forecast how much you will earn this week? Can you reliably forecast how much you will earn this year? You probably answered yes to both these questions, but could you reliably forecast your earnings in 10 years' time? The longer the budget period, the lower the expected accuracy of the forecasts. Even though they are less accurate, preparing longer term budgets is a useful exercise. The most effective budgeting systems have nests of budgets that fit together rather than one single annual cash budget.

Cash cycle: the progression of cash into and out of the business

The quality of a forecast also depends on how well the manager understands the firm's cash cycle. The **cash cycle** refers to the progression of cash into and out of the business. As we see in chapter 10, managing liquidity is a critical component of keeping the business running. The capacity to identify and forecast the cash inflows and outflows of the firm is a very important aspect to maintaining liquidity. The flows for a typical manufacturing firm are shown in figure 14.4.

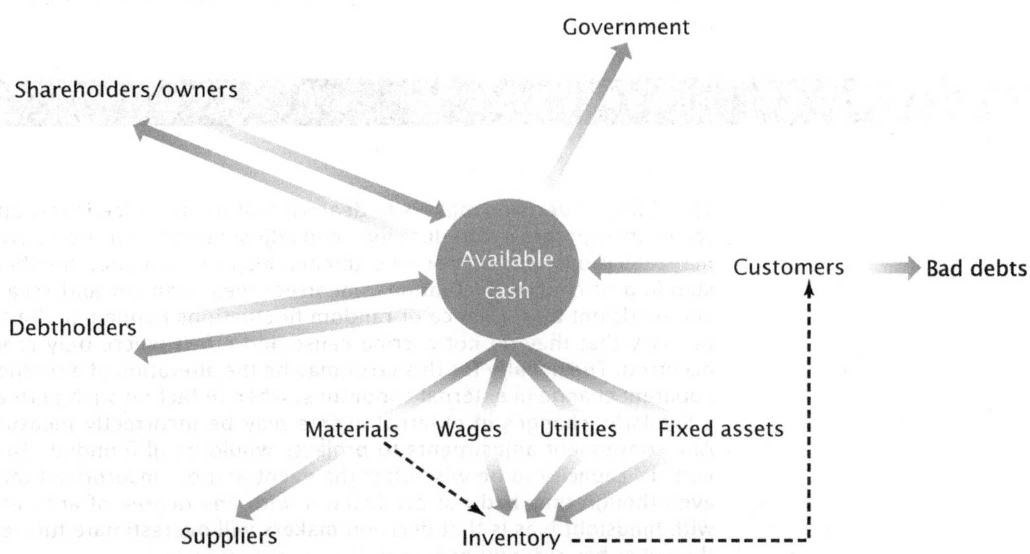

Figure 14.4 The cash cycle of a firm

A firm begins life with an inflow of assets from owners. The owners expect that this equity they contribute will result in future cash outflows (such as dividends) from the firm. Debtholders contribute cash inflows and they require future cash outflows in the form of interest and principal repayments. Cash outflows are made to acquire the fixed assets needed to carry on operations. In a manufacturing firm, for example, these fixed assets could include the purchase of a factory, necessary machinery, delivery vans and office equipment.

Once the production process begins, materials are obtained from suppliers in return for a cash outflow. Payment to suppliers may be on account, in which case the cash outflow is not immediate. Other cash outflows required for production include wages, power and other services. The manufacturing process results in an inventory that is offered for sale to customers. Customers provide cash inflows in return for the supply of goods from the inventory. These inflows may be immediate (cash sales) or deferred (on account). Bad debts from unpaid customer accounts represent a loss of cash to the firm.

Cash generated from sales is used to make payments for the inputs required to maintain or increase inventory levels. It is used to make payments to owners and debtholders. As the business expands, further inflows might be sought from owners and debtholders. The government becomes a recipient of cash outflows when taxes and rates are paid.

Developing a cash budget

The key ingredient when preparing a cash budget is the sales forecast figures. If the company has fairly stable monthly sales, this will not be too difficult. For most firms, however, sales figures will require a significant amount of judgement in their estimation.

It is a good idea to develop sales forecasts after consultation with the people in the firm that are most knowledgeable about sales trends (both for the firm and for the firm's main competitors) and also about any advertising campaigns or other events that are likely to impact on sales. When you have developed a couple of cash budgets, you can go back and see how good your forecasts turned out to be. You can then adjust your current forecasts based on the accuracy of your past forecasts. Read the following 'behavioural perspective' feature to learn about a serious pitfall that can occur in the process of evaluating your past forecasts.

BEHAVIOURAL PERSPECTIVE

Dealing with information feedback

The ability of decision makers to deal with information feedback, appraise the information correctly, incorporate it into decisions and adjust actions appropriately is critical to the success of many decisions, projects or investments. Major information feedback issues are the misunderstanding of chance fluctuations, incorrect measurement and recall of environmental events, and hindsight bias. Chance or random fluctuations happen all the time. Decision makers must be wary that they do not ascribe cause and effect where only random variation has actually occurred. The penalty for this error may be the alteration of a budget or project to adjust to the apparent change in external conditions, when in fact no such permanent change has occurred.

Similarly, changes in external events may be incorrectly measured or incorrectly recalled. Any consequent adjustments to projects would be ill founded. 'Hindsight bias' refers to individuals' capacity to be wise after the event and be unsurprised that an event has occurred — even though they had not predicted it with any degree of accuracy or certainty. The danger with hindsight bias is that decision makers will overestimate future probabilities, just because the event has recently occurred.

After forecasting the sales figures, the next step is to estimate the timing of the cash inflows associated with the level of sales. A good understanding of the cash cycle of the firm is critical to forecast the timing of cash flows. Cash sales will result in cash being received when the sale is made, so we need to estimate the proportion of sales that will be made for cash. The cash from credit sales will come later. Past data are useful because they can help to identify the firm's cash flow cycle. If, on average, half of the sales are made for cash and half are made on credit, we can reflect this in the cash budget. We then need to look at the collection rate for credit sales. If credit is offered on 30-day terms and the firm does not usually have problems receiving payments on time, we show the credit sales from this month as collections in the next month. As discussed in chapter 11 terms of, say, 1/30 net 60 mean the customer will receive a 1% discount if the account is paid in

30 days and that the account should be paid within 60 days if the discount is forgone. If terms are 1/30 net 60 we will need to estimate the proportion of customers who will take the discount and show the discounted amount in the month following the sale, with the remainder of collections two months after the time of the sale. Example 14.1 shows how this is done.

EXAMPLE 14.1

Cash inflows

Maximus Printing is developing a cash budget for July, August and September. Sales in June were $6 750 000. Forecast sales are $7 000 000 for July, $7 250 000 for August and $7 750 000 for September. Half of all sales are usually made for cash. Credit terms are net 30 days. Maximus has an excellent collection record and bad debts are most unusual. Maximus also has money in term deposits that generate a cash receipt of $6000 each quarter. The next interest will be received in August.

Table 14.1 Developing the cash budget — cash inflows

	July $	August $	September $	Quarterly $
Sales	7 000 000	7 250 000	7 750 000	22 000 000
Cash sales	3 500 000	3 625 000	3 875 000	11 000 000
Accounts collected	3 375 000	3 500 000	3 625 000	10 500 000
Total sales inflows	6 875 000	7 125 000	7 500 000	21 500 000
Interest received		6 000		6 000
Total cash inflows	6 875 000	7 131 000	7 500 000	21 506 000

Table 14.1 shows the sales inflows for each month. Total sales are broken down into their cash and credit components. The cash inflows are then put in the column that corresponds to the time of receipt. Total cash inflows from sales for each month are shown on the fourth line of the budget.

After determining forecast sales inflows, the next step is to estimate any other cash inflows the firm expects. There are many possible sources of non-sales cash inflows. They may be payments received from licensing or rental agreements, dividends or interest from investments the firm has made or receipts from the sale of assets.

Once we have identified and forecast all of the cash inflows for the budget period, we follow the same process for the cash outflows. These typically include raw materials costs, wages, operating costs, rent for premises, interest payments and dividends. The expected cash outflows for Maximus are outlined in example 14.2.

EXAMPLE 14.2

Cash outflows

- Raw materials cost 15% of sales. The time taken from ordering the raw materials to making the sale of the product is, on average, two months. Raw materials are ordered based on the monthly forecast sales. Maximus Printing's suppliers give the company credit terms of 30 days. This means raw materials are paid for in the month before the goods are sold. The forecast sales figure for October is $8 million.

- Wages are paid in the month they are earned. Administration and marketing staff salaries and expenses will be $800 000 per month. Monthly production staff wages are forecast to be 20% of sales for the month.
- Electricity and other operating expenses are forecast at 0.05% of sales for the month.
- $6 000 000 in tax is payable quarterly, with the next instalment due in September.
- Dividends of $3 500 000 will be paid in July.
- A company director has decided to take early retirement in September. He will receive $1 000 000 when he goes.
- Maximus have ordered a highly specialised and state-of-the art printer from Germany. The cost of the printer is estimated at $7 million and payment will be made in August.
- The company has an overdraft facility of $10 000 000. The overdraft has not been used for the last year. Interest of 12% pa is charged on the month-end debt balance on the first day of the following month. No interest is paid when the account is in credit.
- Maximus has $670 000 cash in the bank account on 30 June.

Table 14.2 Developing the cash budget — cash outflows

	July $	August $	September $	Quarterly $
Trade accounts payable[a]	1 087 500	1 162 500	1 200 000	3 450 000
Production wages[b]	1 400 000	1 450 000	1 550 000	4 400 000
Admin. & marketing expenses	800 000	800 000	800 000	2 400 000
Other expenses[c]	35 000	36 250	38 750	110 000
Tax paid			6 000 000	6 000 000
Dividends	3 500 000			3 500 000
Director's payment			1 000 000	1 000 000
New printer		7 000 000		7 000 000
Total cash outflows	6 822 500	10 448 750	10 588 750	27 860 000

a. July forecast: 15% of the following month sales forecast 1 087 500 = 7 250 000 × 15%

b. July forecast: variable wages at 20% of monthly sales 1 400 000 = 0.2 × 7 000 000

c. July forecast: sales times 0.05% 35 000 = 7 000 000 × 0.005

After we have collected the best estimates for all cash flows and identified the time period in which they are most likely to occur, the final step is to put the inflows and outflows together to determine the net impact on the firm's cash position. Look at table 14.3 to see how to do this.

The cash inflow section in table 14.3 comes directly from table 14.1. The cash outflows mostly come from table 14.2. We subtract the total cash outflows from the total cash inflows numbers to arrive at our net change in cash figure. This amount will indicate an increase or decrease to opening cash balance. We adjust the opening cash balance by the net change to get to the closing cash balance for the month. This closing cash balance becomes the opening cash balance for the following month.

Maximus will need to consider additional finance when the closing cash balance is negative. The cash budget in table 14.3 assumes that the financing needs in August are met by using the overdraft facility. The interest cost for the use of overdraft finance is then included as a cash outflow for September. This interest charge was not included in table 14.2 as we need to determine the final cash position before calculating it. Given the cash balance remains negative in August, using the overdraft is not likely to be the most cost effective method of raising the additional cash needed to purchase the new printer. The point of doing the cash budget is to highlight time periods where additional financing is needed, so management can plan ahead. The financial manager may decide to use a long-term source of finance for the entire cost of the printer and thus match the cash flows of the asset to the loan repayments. Alternatively, the manager may decide that the company generates sufficient cash flow to repay a loan over a shorter time frame. Cash budgeting is the tool that provides the necessary information to make this decision.

Table 14.3 Developing the cash budget — identifying financing requirements

	July $	August $	September $	Quarterly $
Sales	7 000 000	7 250 000	7 750 000	22 000 000
Cash sales	3 500 000	3 625 000	3 875 000	11 000 000
Accounts collected	3 375 000	3 500 000	3 625 000	10 500 000
Total sales inflows	6 875 000	7 125 000	7 500 000	21 500 000
Interest received		6 000		
Total cash inflows	6 875 000	7 131 000	7 500 000	21 506 000
Trade accounts payable	1 087 500	1 162 500	1 200 000	3 450 000
Production wages	1 400 000	1 450 000	1 550 000	4 400 000
Admin. & marketing expenses	800 000	800 000	800 000	2 400 000
Other expenses	35 000	36 250	38 750	110 000
Tax paid			6 000 000	6 000 000
Dividends	3 500 000			3 500 000
Director's payment			1 000 000	1 000 000
New printer		7 000 000		7 000 000
Interest payment[a]			25 953	25 953
Total cash outflows	6 822 500	10 448 750	10 614 703	27 885 953
Net change in cash	52 500	−3 317 750	−3 114 703	−6 379 953
Opening cash balance	670 000	722 500	−2 595 250	670 000
Closing cash balance	722 500	−2 595 250	−5 709 953	−5 709 953
Financing needed		2 595 250	5 709 953	5 709 953

a. closing overdraft balance times $\frac{0.12}{12}$ (25 953 = 2 595 250 × 0.01). This assumes the overdraft is used to finance the printer purchase.

The budgets in table 14.3 are monthly budgets. If we wanted a quarterly budget, we could sum the totals for each of the three months. The monthly budgets 'nest' in the quarterly budget and the quarterly budgets 'nest' in the annual budget. Which one we use depends on the level of detail that is required. If the daily or weekly cash flows of the firm are highly variable, the financial manager would also need to produce shorter horizon budgets that nest in the monthly budget. Weekly cash budgets, for example, would be constructed using the same method we used for the monthly budgets. A firm with volatile daily or weekly cash flows could easily run out of cash a number of times during the month, even though the monthly budget shows a positive cash balance at the end of the month.

Our application of cash budgeting so far has relied on the assumption that the input forecasts are pretty reliable. What happens if the financial manager is not so confident in the forecasts? The sales forecasts may have been developed last month and current economic data show that the economy looks like it may be going into recession. In this case, it is useful to develop a second budget that incorporates estimates under these less favourable conditions. Alternatively, the financial manager might have reason to be more optimistic than the sales forecasts would suggest. Again, a budget that reflected these more favourable conditions can be prepared and used in conjunction with the original budget. As more information becomes available, the budgets can be adjusted so they reflect the most likely outcomes.

FINANCE WORLD

Uncertainty of cash flows

Airlines the world over ran into financial difficulties after two passenger jets were flown into the Twin Towers in New York on 11 September 2001. Cash budgets (for those airlines that survived the post-9/11 drop in passenger demand for flights) must have been thrown into turmoil in early 2003. Firstly, the continuing threat of terrorism resulted in dramatic decreases in the number of people willing to take flights, reducing the cash inflows from sales. Next, the SARS epidemic in parts of South-East Asia meant health concerns (and quarantine restrictions) made fewer people willing to fly and resulted in a further reduction in airline cash inflows. Finally, oil prices rose in the lead-up to war in Iraq as it was predicted that production would be disrupted. Fuel prices remained high until late 2006. Fuel is the major cost component for operating an airline and rising oil prices increased the cash outflows of the airlines. Budgeting is a particularly difficult process when cash inflows are decreasing and outflows are increasing over an unpredictable horizon.

It's not always bad news, though. Future cash flows are risky and, as we see in chapter 5, risk includes the chance of losses and gains. Oil prices have been volatile since the US-led war with Iraq. The unseasonably mild start to the northern hemisphere winter of 2007 resulted in lower than normal demand for oil and a corresponding price fall. Australian airlines were charging a 'fuel tariff' to recover the cost of higher oil prices. The fuel tariff remained in place even when oil prices were lower than had been expected.

FINANCE WORKSHOP 14.1

What budget period would you recommend the financial manager of Maximus use to help decide the term of financing for the printer purchase decision?

lo4

Explain the use of pro-forma financial statements.

Pro-forma financial statements: projections of a future position and of future period performance

Pro-forma financial statements

We looked at the financial statements of Maximus Printing Ltd at the start of the chapter. The financial statements report on a position at a given point in time and on performance for a past period. **Pro-forma financial statements** contain projections of a future position and of future period performance. Management use the pro-forma financial statements to map the impact of their decisions on the financial statements.

In chapter 1, we identify maximising shareholder wealth as the primary objective for a company and in chapter 8 we see that discounted cash flow methods of project evaluation were consistent with this objective. We use the discounted cash flow valuation models in chapter 6 that rely on dividend cash flows, so why would management bother assessing the impact of their decisions on the financial statements?

A company's published financial statements are an important means of communicating information about the firm to those outside the firm. The larger listed companies usually have a following of analysts who are searching for new information about the company. Even though the analysts are often better informed than ordinary investors, they still use the financial statements when they are forming an assessment of a company. Analysts tend to forecast earnings more frequently than they do dividends. Consider the three alternative dividend policies discussed in chapter 13. To forecast the dividends of a company using a residual dividend policy, the analyst needs to forecast earnings and the dollar amount of future investments for the firm. It is the difference between these two variables that determines the dividend amount. A constant payout ratio policy for dividends requires the identification of the proportion of earnings that will be paid as dividends and, again, the future level of earnings. Dividends are more predictable for a firm with a stable dollar dividend policy, but even under this regime, the analyst should seek assurance that future earnings will be sufficient to maintain the policy as dividends can be paid only from current or past earnings. The popular alternative share valuation method to the dividend discount model is the application of the price–earnings ratio. As we see in chapter 6 this method relies on forecast earnings to determine the value of a company. The market pays attention to earnings figures for companies and a prudent financial manager should do the same.

Smaller companies tend not to receive such close attention from investment analysts. Thus, the published accounts are an even more important source of information when they are produced by smaller companies. Although the published accounts can be misleading at times, the auditing process means the accounts are usually considered to be reliable.

Companies occasionally specify target levels of performance (as measured by the financial statements) in their corporate objectives. Before these targets can be announced, management needs to assess if the company is likely to reach the target. Pro-forma financial statements can help them do this. As we have already discussed, the financial statements are an important source of information for analysts and investors making decisions about the purchase or sale of a company's shares. They use the past and current financial statements as a starting point for their assessments of future performance. The financial manager will be in a much better position to forecast next year's performance and some companies make their forecast earnings available to the public. However, firms that provide earnings forecasts find their actual performance is measured against the forecast. The financial manager would need to provide the best possible forecast in this case and can use pro-forma financial statements to achieve this.

As we will see later in the chapter, many companies include key financial statement ratios in their annual reports, especially when there is a positive trend over time. Pro-forma statements provide advance warnings when management plans are going to have a negative impact on the key ratios. If forecast deterioration in the ratios is associated with the adoption of a positive NPV project, management could forestall a negative share price reaction by disclosing more information about the new project. After all, analysts and investors use financial statements because they do not get access to detailed information about the company's future plans. By disclosing additional information about the new project, management help the market to reassess future performance. Of course, the market will respond to this additional information only if analysts and investors think that the company's management is credible. We will be looking at the use of financial ratios in the last section of this chapter.

Contracts with the firm are often specified in terms of financial statement data. Lenders may require that the proportion of liabilities to assets does not exceed a certain amount. If such a covenant is breached, the lender has the right to call in the loan. Using 'pro-formas' can indicate if a course of action will result in a breach of the company's debt contracts. Remuneration contracts for top management are often specified in terms of the accounting numbers in the financial statements.

Pro-forma financial statements are a tool that allows management to evaluate different alternatives in terms of the impact on profits and other key figures and ratios that are employed by the users of financial statements.

Developing the pro-forma financial statements

lo5

Construct the pro-forma income statement and balance sheet.

The first step in developing our pro-forma financial statements is to get the previous year's financial statements. We use last period's financial statements as the base for our pro-forma statements. They show us the types and levels of assets and liabilities held by the firm, the opening balances for these accounts and the types and levels of revenues and expenses generated.

While we will use as many 'concrete' predictions as we can (the purchase of the new printing machine, for example), there will still be some accounts in the financial statements that we will have to estimate without any additional information. This is usually done by assuming that past financial statement relationships are a good indicator of future relationships.

Percent of sales method: expresses items in the income statement as a percentage of sales. The calculated percentage is applied to the forecast sales figure.

The sales level is a critical factor in the company's ability to generate profits and some items in the income statement vary with the level of sales. We saw this when we constructed our cash budget. The cost of raw materials and production workers' wages were forecast as a percentage of the monthly sales. This method of forecasting is called the **percent of sales method**. Unless you are expecting the cost of a major input into the production process to change, it is reasonable to assume that the inputs will continue to be the same proportion of sales as they were in the previous period. It would, however, be naïve to make a blanket application of the percent of sales method to all items in the income statement. Dividend payments and interest revenues, for example, are unlikely to vary with the sales level. The percent of sales method is best kept for those items that have a direct and predictable relationship to sales and those you have no better forecast for.

EXAMPLE 14.3

Using the percent of sales method

The income statement for Maximus Printing is included in figure 14.2. Use the percent of sales method to establish the relationship between cost of goods sold and sales for 2008.

$$\frac{\text{Cost of goods sold}}{\text{sales}} = \frac{28\,502\,000}{81\,435\,000}$$

$$= 0.35$$

This calculation tells us that cost of goods sold was 35% of sales revenue in 2008.

FINANCE WORKSHOP 14.2

Using the percent of sales method, calculate for Maximus Printing the relationship of the following accounts to sales for 2007:

(a) cost of goods sold

(b) electricity and other expenses.

The next thing we need is the sales forecast for the coming period. As we discussed earlier in the chapter, these should be developed using information known by the people most conversant with the firm's sales levels. Forecasts should also take economic conditions into consideration. We then need to collect information from within the firm that will help to produce the most accurate pro-forma statements possible. This information is identified as 'management information' in figures 14.5 and 14.6. Management information includes any planned expenditures (such as the new printing machine in our example), the company policy on inventory levels, the accounting depreciation rates for assets, the expected dividend payment, the planned amount of finance that will be raised and any associated borrowing costs.

The pro-forma financial statements in figures 14.5 and 14.6 also show the cash budget as a forecasting source for quite a few accounts. If you have made your best estimates for developing the cash budget, why would you neglect these forecasts when you are assessing the impact of management decisions on the financial statements? The planning process is an iterative one. The forecast level of interest expense in the projected income statement depends on the amount and source of finance chosen by management. This means we need to develop the cash budget first, then the income statement and balance sheet in conjunction with each other. Example 14.4 shows how the pro-forma income statement and balance sheet are developed.

EXAMPLE 14.4

Pro-forma income statement and balance sheet

From the financial statements for the year ended 30 June 2008, we have the following:

- The opening balance for accounts receivable for July 2008 is $3 375 000.
- The opening balance for accounts payable for July 2008 is $1 050 000.
- The 30 June 2008 cash balance is $670 000.

Management have collected the following additional information:

- Sales for the 2009 financial year are forecast at $108 400 000.
- An investment in current financial assets of $800 000 will be made during the year and this will generate $24 000 interest income.
- It is expected that inventory levels of $1 084 000 are needed to maintain the forecast sales level.
- Administrative and marketing wages and expenses are expected to be $9 600 000.
- Interest expense and borrowing costs during the period are $639 000.
- Depreciation is charged at 5% of closing book value per annum on buildings and 20% of closing book value on plant and equipment.
- The current portion of interest-bearing liabilities in the 2008 balance sheet will be repaid in October.

- The planned purchase of the new printer in August ($7 000 000) will be financed with a long-term loan.
- Cost of goods sold is forecast to be 35% of sales.
- A vacant lot next door to the land purchased last year will be acquired for $10 000 000. This land will be used in the development of a retail outlet during 2009.
- Employee entitlements of $1 671 000 will be paid during the year.
- The income tax rate is 30%. The current portion of the tax liability at 30 June is estimated at $4 160 000.
- Dividends of $10 000 000 will be declared during the year.
- Repayments of long-term debt during the year will be $14 000 000.
- There will not be any transfers to or from reserves during the year.
- The number of shares on issue is 10 million.
- There are no plans to issue new shares during the coming year.

Maximus Printing Limited Projected income statement for the financial year ended 30 June		
	2009	Forecast source
Revenue from sales	108 400 000	Management information
Cost of goods sold	37 940 000	Percent of sales
Gross profit	70 460 000	Forecast position statement
Interest revenue	24 000	plus management information
	70 484 000	
Administration and marketing	9 600 000	Management information
Depreciation	3 995 350	Management information
Electricity and other expenses	542 000	Percent of sales
Employee benefits	1 671 000	Management information
Borrowing costs expense	639 000	Cash budget
Profit (loss) from ordinary activities	54 036 650	
Income tax expense	16 210 995	
Net profit (loss)	37 825 655	
Dividends paid	10 000 000	Management information
Transfer to retained earnings	27 825 655	
Basic earnings per share	3.78	
Dividends per share	1.00	

Figure 14.5 Pro-forma income statement

Maximus Printing Limited Projected balance sheet as at 30 June		
	2009	Forecast source
Current assets		
Cash	9 526 000	Cash budget
Receivables	5 250 000	Cash budget
Inventories	1 084 000	Management information
Other financial assets	800 000	Management information
Total current assets	16 660 000	

Non-current assets		
Land	36 800 000	Opening balance plus management information
Buildings	22 761 050	Opening balance less depreciation
Plant and equipment	11 189 600	Opening balance less depreciation plus cash budget
Total non-current assets	70 750 650	
Total assets	87 410 650	
Current liabilities		
Payables	1 650 000	Cash budget
Interest-bearing liabilities	0	Cash budget
Current tax liability	4 160 000	Management information
Total current liabilities	5 810 000	
Non-current liabilities		
Interest-bearing liabilities	7 000 000	Opening balance plus cash budget
Total non-current liabilities	7 000 000	
Total liabilities	12 810 000	
Equity		
Contributed equity	11 335 000	Opening balance
Reserves	2 047 000	Opening balance plus amount from income statement
Retained profits	51 434 655	Opening balance plus amount from income statement
Total equity	64 816 655	
Financing required	9 783 995	

Figure 14.6 Pro-forma balance sheet

We developed the cash budget for the first quarter of the year in examples 14.1 and 14.2. The first lot of data in example 14.4 comes from extending this budget for the full financial year (not shown in the chapter). We start our 'pro-formas' with outlines of the financial statements that contain the accounts, but no numbers. We can then put the data we have from our cash budget into the pro-forma statements.

The balances for accounts receivable and accounts payable go into the balance sheet. We can read the accounts receivable figure from the cash budget by calculating the expected collections for the month of July. If 50% of sales are on credit and credit customers pay within one month, the expected collections are the credit sales for June ($0.5 \times 10\,500\,000 =$ \$5 250 000). Given the ordering and payment schedule for accounts payable, the closing balance for one month is the next month's cost of goods sold figure. Therefore, we can use an estimate of July's sales and the cost of goods sold as a proportion of sales to get the closing accounts payable figure for June. We do not include the opening balance from the 2008 statement because these accounts should be received early in the forecast period.

The closing cash balance from the cash budget is shown in the current assets section of the income statement. We can also deduce the changes to the interest-bearing liabilities accounts from the cash budget as this should include debt repayments made during the period. Our cash budget would show a cash outflow of \$14 200 000 in October. As this amount is the opening balance of current interest-bearing liabilities, we know that this debt has been paid, reducing the balance to zero. If the cash budget does not show any cash inflows associated with raising short-term interest-bearing debt, then we know the closing balance is zero (that is, \$14 200 000 − \$14 200 000 = 0). If the cash budget showed that there were inflows from short-term debt, we would add the inflows (and subtract any further repayments made in the period) to get the final balance for the pro-forma balance sheet. We would take the same approach for long-term interest-bearing liabilities. As long-term debt is usually serviced by regular repayments, we total the principal components of these outflows and deduct them from the long-term interest-bearing liabilities account to get our pro-forma balance ($14 000 000 in our example). Any new debt raised (such as the loan associated with the new printer) is added to the account.

The cash budget should also allow us to approximate the interest expense for the reporting period. We can add the cash outflows to get a total for interest paid. Interest expense in the balance sheet should include any interest accrued for the reporting period. This means that the interest-paid amount from the cash budget will not be exactly the same amount as it will be in the financial statements that are prepared by the accountant when the forecast period is over. The difference should not be too significant and, if management are aware that there usually is a large difference, they can use this knowledge to adjust the amount that goes into the pro-forma statements.

Once we have taken all the information we can from the cash budget, we can continue with the additional information that is based on management expectations of how the firm will operate through the forecast period. Current financial assets are those that are expected to be sold during the 12 months after the financial report date. This means our cash budget should include inflows totalling $9 700 000 from the liquidation of current assets held at the last reporting date. These cash flows would reduce the balance to zero. We then add any expected investment in current financial assets ($8 000 000 in our example) to get the forecast balance for the pro-forma balance sheet. These financial assets generate interest revenue of $24 000 and this amount needs to be shown in the pro-forma income statement.

The forecasts for closing level of inventory, the current portion of the tax liability and any other assets and liabilities are included in the balance sheet. We discussed the inclusion of a $7 000 000 loan to finance the new printer. Acquiring the printer gives rise to an increase to debt, but also an increase of $7 000 000 to the plant and equipment asset account. Similarly, the forecast purchase of land will increase the asset account 'land' by the $10 000 000 paid for the land. Management have not indicated how this purchase will be financed — we will discuss this further in the next section.

The forecast levels of administrative and marketing wages and expenses, employee entitlements and any other revenues or expenses are shown in the income statement. The forecast corporate tax rate is used to calculate the tax expense for the period. We also have information on how depreciation is calculated for the Maximus financial statements. Once all of the planned asset acquisitions have been added to the balances in the income statement, we can multiply the balance by the depreciation rate to calculate the depreciation expense for the income statement. We also reduce the balance of the depreciable asset accounts by this expense to calculate the closing book values for the assets. This will not result in the exact depreciation charge in the actual financial statements prepared at the end of the forecast period because accountants charge depreciation based on the proportion of the year that the asset was held and use a range of different depreciation methods for reporting purposes.

Management's forecast dividend payment is included at the bottom of the income statement. We use the percent of sales method for the remaining accounts (cost of goods sold and electricity and other expenses) because we have no better information available.

The final stage of constructing our pro-forma income statement is to fill in the calculations for gross profit, profit from ordinary activities, income tax expense, transfer to retained earnings, EPS and DPS. We then take the amount 'transferred to retained earnings' from the income statement and add it to the retained earnings balance from last period's balance sheet. To complete our pro-forma balance sheet, we calculate the totals for current assets, non-current assets, total assets, current liabilities, non-current liabilities and equity.

The pro-forma balance sheet gives us an estimate of the amount of long-term funding that will be required during the forecast period. No new long-term funds will be needed if net assets are equal to or less than total equity. New funding will be needed if net assets exceed equity. In our example a total of $9 783 995 in new debt and equity is needed to support the forecast level of operations.

We now have two methods for determining how much additional financing the company will need to support the forecast level of operations and asset acquisitions. The cash budget helps us identify the timing of the financing required. The pro-forma balance sheet helps us identify the amount of financing required. We could estimate the total amount of financing required from the cash budget for the forecast period, so why bother with the pro-forma financial statements? We use the pro-forma statements to show how the impact of proposed management decisions might be interpreted by the owners, creditors and potential investors of the company.

If we automate the process of constructing the cash budget and pro-forma statements by developing a spreadsheet, we can utilise 'what if' scenarios. For example, management would be interested in the impact of choosing to finance the required amount with long-term debt. Will this cause the company to be in technical breach of any debt covenants? They would also be interested in the impact of substituting the issue of shares for debt when raising new finance. Will the higher number of shares on issue mean that EPS looks unfavourable compared to those of competitors? This shouldn't matter if the market for the company's shares is efficient, but EPS is a number often cited by analysts and is reported in the press! A new set of 'pro-formas' can easily be generated for each of the different scenarios. How do investors and creditors manage to digest the large amount of information in the financial statements? We investigate the use of key ratios in the next section.

lo6

Explain the role of financial ratio analysis.

Financial ratios: data reduction techniques that express one account as a proportion of another

What is financial ratio analysis?

Financial ratios are data reduction techniques that express one account as a proportion of another. They allow us to compare different aspects of a company's performance and position to those of other companies or to the same company over time. Financial ratio analysis employs relative rather than absolute concepts. Rather than simply comparing the outstanding debt figures for two different companies, we standardise the debts by relating them, for example, to the amount of equity invested in the firm. By considering debt relative to equity, we have a more informative means of making the comparison.

Investment advisors' reports always comment on the strength of the financial ratios of the companies they recommend to their clients. Credit rating services like Standard & Poor's often discuss the financial ratios when a change in credit rating is announced. When debt covenants are used in loan contracts, the restrictions placed by the lenders are often specified in terms of target profit figures and leverage ratios. Suppliers of capital use the financial statements to analyse the results of management's previous decisions. This helps them to assess the likely quality of management's future decisions.

Even though theory tells us that investors focus on the present value of future cash flows when making their decisions, they rarely have access to sufficient information to allow them to do so. They make use of the published financial statements instead. Given that people make decisions about the firm based on the financial statements, it makes sense for managers to assess the impact of their decisions for the coming period on the financial statements that will be produced at the end of the period.

lo7

Identify and calculate key ratios and interpret your results.

Key ratios and financial statements

There are literally dozens of financial ratios that are employed by the users of financial statements. The ones that are the most important depend on the objectives of the analysis. Creditors place greater emphasis on solvency and capacity to make interest and principal repayment. Investors have their main focus on the returns the company will generate for their investments. A brief survey of the 2006 annual reports for 10 companies (chosen in a random fashion) shows that eight of the 10[6] companies report what they consider to be key financial ratios. The results of this survey are presented in table 14.4 and the most commonly reported ratios are discussed in the following section.

Table 14.4 Commonly reported financial ratios

Company	Earnings per share	Dividends per share	Return on equity	Debt to equity	Net debt to capital employed	Times interest	Net tangible assets per share	Other[a]
Adsteam Marine Ltd[7]	1							
Amcor Ltd[8]	2	1	1		1	1	1	
Blackmores Ltd[9]	1	1	1		1	2	1	4
Cochlear Ltd[10]	2	1			2			
Harvey Norman Holdings Ltd[11]	1	1					1	
Sigma Pharmaceuticals Ltd[12]	2	1	1		1	1		2
Southern Cross Broadcasting (Australia) Ltd[13]	1	1		1		1	1	1
Wesfarmers Ltd[14]	1	1	1	1		1	1	1
Total reported	11	7	4	2	5	6	5	8

a. Other reported ratios (and the number of companies reporting them) included the 'dividend payout ratio' as discussed in chapter 13 (3), 'current ratio' (2), 'return on assets' (1), 'EBIT to sales' (1), 'return on adjusted capital employed' (1), 'net debt to EBITA' (1), 'net cash to debt' (1) and 'operating cash flow per share' (1).

Sources: Data from the annual reports of the various organisations, available on the corporate websites (see end notes for details).

These ratios were reported in a prominent position on the first couple of pages in the annual report, most often in a section called '5 year summary'. Users of financial statements could easily calculate these ratios for themselves from the financial statements. Why then would management waste space in the financial report by showing these ratios? It could be that they consider the ratios so important that they present them prominently to show how well the firm is performing. It could also be that management report the ratios selectively, ignoring those that do not present such a good picture of the company. To investigate this issue, we examined four years of past annual reports available on the internet for the eight firms sampled in table 14.4. The trend for ratios reported by six of these companies was to maintain or increase the number of ratios included in the annual report. The other two companies selectively reduced the ratios they reported. One company stopped reporting the ratio of sales to earnings before interest and tax (EBIT) when sales decreased by 8% and EBIT decreased by 43%, showing a very poor performance for this ratio. Both companies dropped the net tangible asset backing per share ratios. The

Intangible assets: non-physical assets that will give the company future benefits, but that are difficult to separate from the business

acquisition of intangibles resulting from a merger resulted in a fall of this ratio from $1.82 to $0.27 for one company. Recognised intangibles rose from 2% of total assets to 38% of total assets for the other company, resulting in more intangibles than net assets. **Intangible assets** are non-physical assets that will give the company future benefits, but that are difficult to separate from the business.

The most frequently reported ratio identified in table 14.4 is earnings per share (EPS). This ratio compares the total earnings figure to the number of shares issued. As we saw earlier, EPS is the figure most frequently forecast by analysts for use with a P/E multiple for valuation and can be crucial to forecasting dividend when a specific dividend policy is adopted by the company.

$$\textbf{EPS} = \frac{\textbf{net profit (loss)}}{\textbf{number of shares on issue}} \qquad [14.1]$$

We get the net profit figure from the income statement. Using the data from the 2008 financial statements for Maximus Printing Limited we can calculate the EPS as follows:

$$\text{EPS} = \frac{26\,722\,000}{10\,000\,000}$$
$$= \$2.67$$

This tells us that $2.67 of profit was generated for each share issued by Maximus. This calculation is for 'basic' EPS. It does not make any adjustment for the timing of any new issue of shares over the previous financial year. If, for example, 5 000 000 shares were issued in May 2007 the basic EPS calculation ignores the fact that half of the company's closing capital was not available to generate the profit figure for 11 months of the financial year. Complications also arise when share buybacks occur and splits or bonus issues are made. 'Diluted EPS' calculations are included in the income statement to overcome this problem. We can't use the EPS ratios of two companies to make a comparison, but analysts use the ratio to assess the earnings trend over time for a company.

The next most frequently reported ratio is dividend per share (DPS). This ratio relates the total dividend payment to the number of shares on issue. Use of the dividend discount model requires us to come up with some forecast about future dividends. When combined with EPS figures, the historic series of DPS can contain important clues about the dividend policy of the firm that can help establish a growth rate or other forecasts of future dividends.

$$\textbf{DPS} = \frac{\textbf{dividends paid}}{\textbf{number of shares on issue}} \qquad [14.2]$$

Taking the dividend amount from the 2008 income statement for Maximus:

$$\text{DPS} = \frac{8\,000\,000}{10\,000\,000}$$
$$= 0.80$$

We find that each share received total annual dividend payments of 80 cents. The EPS and DPS ratios are popular with investors as they provide indicators of the profitability of the company and how much of that profit is paid to investors.

Return on equity (ROE) is also a key ratio for investors. It is used to assess how well management has employed the funds invested in the firm to generate profits. It measures profitability by calculating the accounting return on the ordinary shareholders' investment. In the absence of any better information, ROE can be used by analysts to derive estimates of future growth in dividends based on past data.

$$\text{Return on equity (ROE)} = \frac{\textbf{net profit}}{\textbf{ordinary shareholders' equity}} \qquad [14.3]$$

The net profit figure is obtained from the income statement. Make sure the net profit figure is after any preference dividends have been paid because ordinary shareholders do not receive preference dividends.

The figure for ordinary shareholders' equity in the ROE ratio is most often calculated as total equity minus goodwill (and other intangibles) minus preference equity. Each of these accounts can be found in the balance sheet. Earlier in the chapter we defined intangible assets as non-physical assets that will give the company future benefits, but that are difficult to separate from the business. Goodwill is an example of an intangible asset. Goodwill is valued in the company accounts as the excess of purchase price over net tangible assets when a business is first acquired. Accounting standards require the book value of goodwill to be written down when an impairment test suggests it has decreased. However, the book value of goodwill does not increase as the company's reputation strengthens.

If the company has issued preference shares, we need to consider the characteristics of these shares before including them in ordinary equity. If the preference shareholders enjoy the ability to sell their shares back to the company whenever they wish, the shares really have more in common with debt than equity. If the preference shares have more of the characteristics usually associated with debt, they should not be included in the calculation of equity for this ratio. If, on the other hand, the preference shares are convertible to equity and have an element of profit participation in their dividend payments, they should be treated as equity here.

We can use the book value of equity from the balance sheet in our example because Maximus does not have any intangible assets or preference shares. The return on equity is calculated as follows:

$$\text{Return on equity} = \frac{26\,722\,000}{36\,991\,000}$$
$$= 0.72$$

Maximus's ordinary shareholders get a 72% return on the equity invested in the firm. The higher the return on equity, the more profitable the firm is considered to be. There is no general standard for this ratio, but 72% would more than delight most investors.

Intangible assets are excluded from the net tangible asset backing per share (NTA) ratio because of the difficulty of selling them without liquidating the company. Net tangible assets are calculated as the book value of tangible assets less the book value of liabilities.

$$\text{NTA} = \frac{\textbf{assets} - \textbf{intangibles} - \textbf{liabilities}}{\textbf{number of ordinary shares}} \qquad [14.4]$$

The net tangible asset backing gives an indication of what the asset value per share would be after all the company debt is repaid. This rests on the assumption that all of the company's tangible assets are sold for their book values and the debt is repaid so there are no further claims on the company. Analysts and investors use it as a gauge of how much would be returned to the shareholders if the company ceased operations now. The NTA backing for Maximus Printing is:

$$\text{NTA} = \frac{72\,241\,000 - 0 - 35\,250\,000}{10\,000\,000}$$
$$= \$3.70$$

The market can be interpreted as placing value on the company's intangible assets or as having confidence in the way the company is being managed if Maximus Printing's shares are selling for above $3.70 each. A company with an NTA backing higher than the current market share price is at risk of being taken over. If Maximus shares could be purchased for $2 each, it would be worth someone's effort to purchase the shares and then sell the assets to liquidate the company. Such a strategy would net a gain of about $1.70 per share, assoming assets can be sold for at least their book value and that transaction costs are low.

What would investors think about Maximus Printing's profitability? We can't say much about the EPS or DPS results unless we compare them to past results for Maximus to find any trends. ROE is very high and we could compare this to other firms in the printing industry to see if this is a 'normal' result. It is unusual for an industry average ROE to be half that of Maximus Printing's ROE. The most likely explanation is that Maximus is experiencing a growth phase in its revenues and is managing to keep costs well under control. To make meaningful comment on the NTA backing per share, we need to compare the result to the market price of the shares.

The gearing ratios (debt-to-equity and net debt to capital employed) and times-interest ratio are used to assess the degree of indebtedness of the company and its ability to meet its fixed financial obligations in the longer term. Financial leverage is a result of the commitment to pay fixed financial costs. Higher financial leverage means higher risk for the company because fixed payments have to be made even when the business is in difficult times. The financial leverage of a company provides an indication of how much a company has borrowed as well as how much more it can afford to borrow.

Gearing ratios address the question of how much the company has borrowed. The debt-to-equity ratio provides an indication of how much of the firm is owned by lenders and creditors by comparing total liabilities to owners' equity.

$$\textbf{Debt to equity} = \frac{\textbf{total liabilities}}{\textbf{ordinary shareholders' equity}} \qquad [14.5]$$

We use the total liabilities and shareholders' equity figures from the balance sheet. As we discussed earlier, the amount of shareholders' equity should be determined after the nature of any preference shares has been identified. If preference shares are not included as equity, they should be included in the total debt amount. The debt-to-equity ratio for Maximus Printing is:

$$\text{Debt to equity} = \frac{35\,250\,000}{36\,991\,000}$$

$$= 0.95$$

A debt-to-equity ratio of 1:1 indicates that a firm is taking a balanced approach to financing (that is, half of the firm is financed by debt and half by equity). However, the appropriate level of gearing can be very sensitive to the nature of the industry. Maximus's ratio of 0.95:1 indicates that not quite half of the total financing is provided by debt. You may come across other ways of calculating this gearing ratio. One is the 'net debt to equity', where the approach is to reduce the level of liabilities by the amount of any financial assets the company holds. Another variation, 'net interest-bearing debt to equity', excludes from liabilities the amounts included in 'provisions' and 'accounts payable' where interest is not charged.

According to our small survey of contemporary Australian annual reports, the net debt to capital employed ratio is now reported more frequently than the debt-to-equity ratio.

$$\textbf{Net debt to capital employed} = \frac{\textbf{net debt}}{\textbf{net debt + ordinary shareholders' equity}} \qquad [14.6]$$

Net debt is measured as financial liabilities (the interest-bearing borrowings of the firm) minus financial assets (cash, debt securities held by the firm and money the firm has lent to parties outside the firm). Net debt plus ordinary shareholders' equity measures capital employed. The net debt to capital employed ratio for Maximus Printing is:

$$\text{Net debt to capital employed} = \frac{(14\,200 + 14\,000) - (9\,700 + 670)}{(14\,200 + 14\,000) - (9\,700 + 670) + 36\,991}$$
$$= 0.33$$

The net debt to capital employed ratio for Maximus tells us that 33% of the total funds employed by the firm are from interest-bearing debt. The debt-to-equity ratio shows us that about half of the firm is financed by debt, so why is the net debt to capital employed ratio different? First, the debt-to-equity ratio includes total liabilities, not net financial liabilities. The debt-to-equity ratio includes non-interest-bearing liabilities that are part of working capital (accounts payable, for example) and it makes no allowance for any financial assets (cash, for example) that could be used to reduce the liabilities. Second, the denominator in the net debt to capital employed ratio includes net debt in addition to equity to provide the full financing picture of the firm. The net debt to capital employed ratio therefore gives a more refined measure of the debt position of the firm relative to all the firm's funding sources.

To get some indication of a company's ability to sustain its level of debt, we can use the interest cover or times-interest-earned ratio. This ratio indicates the firm's ability to meet its interest payments from earnings generated by operations. The lower the times-interest-earned result, the more likely it is that the company will not be able to meet its interest payments.

$$\textbf{Times interest earned} = \frac{\textbf{profit before interest and tax}}{\textbf{annual interest expense}} \qquad [14.7]$$

The profit before interest and tax figure (or profit from ordinary activities) is derived from the income statement. Profit before interest and tax is not usually shown as a separate item in the income statement. We add the interest expense back on to the profit from ordinary activities figure to get the number we need for analysis. The annual interest expense is shown in the Maximus income statement, but it is normally disclosed in the notes to the accounts rather than as an item in the statement. As an insider of the company, a manager doing a financial analysis should be able to access the figure from the accounting system.

$$\text{Times interest earned} = \frac{38\,174\,000 + 1\,222\,000}{1\,222\,000}$$
$$= 32.23 \text{ times}$$

This calculation tells us that Maximus Printing generated profit before interest and tax of about 31 times the amount of interest it paid. As a general benchmark, profit before interest and tax should be at least 3 times the interest expense. Creditors would be very happy with Maximus Printing's result for this ratio.

Two other approaches are sometimes used to calculate this ratio. The first uses cash flow from operations (rather than profit) to interest. This approach gives an indication of the actual amount of cash that is available to make interest payments. The second variation is the use of net interest paid (that is, interest paid – interest received) rather than simply using the interest expense. This approach will provide a higher times interest for companies that receive interest income.

What would creditors think about Maximus Printing's leverage? The debt-to-equity and net debt to capital employed ratios show us that the company has not taken an aggressive approach to the use of debt. They can easily meet their interest payments from profit before interest and tax as shown by the times-interest-earned ratio. These ratios support the capacity of the company to have higher debt levels and its ability to service the debt.

Key ratios and pro-forma financial statements

If our forecasts turn out to be pretty accurate, how will the users of Maximus Printing's financial statements view the company at the end of the forecast period? We can calculate the key ratios on the pro-forma statements to get an idea. To do this, we need to identify how we will finance the \$9 783 995 shortfall identified in figure 14.6. Firstly, let's assume it is financed by issuing 500 000 ordinary shares and that the funding amount raised after all costs associated with the issue will be \$9 783 995. The only impact this financing transaction will have on the pro-forma financial statements is to increase the contributed equity account to \$21 118 995 (that is, 11 335 000 + 9 783 995) and total equity then becomes \$74 600 650.

$$\text{EPS} = \frac{\text{net profit (loss)}}{\text{number of shares on issue}}$$

$$\text{EPS} = \frac{37\,825\,655}{10\,500\,000}$$

$$= \$3.60$$

The projected EPS is \$3.60, which shows a hefty increase over the \$2.67 achieved for 2008. This will be viewed as a positive change by investors.

$$\text{DPS} = \frac{\text{dividends paid}}{\text{number of shares on issue}}$$

$$\text{DPS} = \frac{10\,000\,000}{10\,500\,000}$$

$$= \$0.95$$

The DPS decreased because the rise in number of shares on issue was not offset by the rise in the total forecast dividend payment. How this is viewed by investors depends on the factors we discuss in chapter 13.

$$\text{ROE} = \frac{\text{net profit}}{\text{ordinary shareholders' equity}}$$

$$\text{ROE} = \frac{37\,825\,655}{74\,600\,650}$$

$$= 0.51$$

The return on equity is forecast to fall substantially. The ROE for the company in 2008 is unusually high compared to average ROEs across different industries. Given that the ROE will remain very high in comparison to other investments, investors would expect the ROE to fall over time so that it is more in line with other listed companies.

$$\text{NTA} = \frac{\text{assets} - \text{intangibles} - \text{liabilities}}{\text{number of ordinary shares}}$$

$$\text{NTA} = \frac{87\,410\,650 - 0 - 12\,810\,000}{10\,500\,000}$$

$$= \$7.10$$

The forecast net tangible asset backing per share is $7.10. This is a significant increase over the $3.70 for 2008 and reflects the increased asset base acquired, coupled with a proportionally lower increase in liabilities.

$$\text{Debt to equity} = \frac{\text{total liabilities}}{\text{ordinary shareholders' equity}}$$

$$= \frac{12\,810\,000}{74\,600\,650}$$

$$= 0.17$$

The forecast debt-to-equity ratio is 0.17:1. This tells us that Maximus will rely much more heavily on equity than debt compared to the 2007 relationship.

$$\text{Net debt to capital employed} = \frac{\text{net debt}}{\text{net debt + ordinary shareholders' equity}}$$

$$= \frac{(0 + 7\,000\,000) - (9\,526\,000 + 800\,000)}{(0 + 7\,000\,000) - (9\,526\,000 + 800\,000) + 74\,600\,650}$$

$$= -0.05$$

The net debt to capital employed ratio has fallen from 33% to about –5%. The negative ratio shows that Maximus has net financial assets, not net debt. The result supports that of the debt-to-equity ratio.

These ratios will be considered very favourably by creditors as they show that the company will have a greater capacity to use more debt in the future. This greater capacity will make existing creditors feel more secure and potential creditors more disposed to lending to the company.

$$\text{Times interest earned} = \frac{\text{profit before interest and tax}}{\text{annual interest expense}}$$

$$= \frac{54\,036\,650 + 639\,000}{639\,000}$$

$$= 85.56 \text{ times}$$

The pro-forma statements show that Maximus is expected to generate profit before interest and tax about 86 times greater than its forecast interest expense. This result is attributable to the forecast reduction in debt (and corresponding reduction of interest expense) from the 2008 levels. The other main factor is the large forecast increase in profit. Creditors will view this as another positive signal.

Overall, the pro-forma financial statements show that if management can meet the forecast results, the users of the financial statements will be likely to view the results in a very favourable light.

This analysis assumed that the requirement for financing was met by an equity issue. What would happen if management chose to use long-term debt instead? The first thing to note is that raising debt of $9 783 995 as identified in figure 14.6 (p. 525) will not balance the balance sheet. Consider an interest expense of $900 000 for the forecast period associated with this debt. The interest expense in the pro-forma income statement increases to $1 539 000 (639 000 + 900 000). A higher interest expense means a lower tax expense ($15 940 995 compared to $16 210 995) and a lower net profit figure of $37 195 655. Our financing requirement figure was based on a transfer of $27 825 655 profit to retained earnings. Given the new interest expense and lower tax, debt financing will result in a transfer of $27 195 655 to retained earnings. The $630 000 reduction in profit will not be available for the company to use in its activities. Therefore, the amount of debt that has to be raised is $10 413 995 (the original financing requirement of $9 783 995 plus the after-tax interest paid of $630 000).

One way to overcome this problem is to prepare a different cash budget for each of the methods proposed for financing. That way, you can build the different cash at bank balances and any differences in interest expense and tax into a unique set of pro-forma statements that forecast the financing alternatives. You then do your key ratio analysis on the sets of pro-forma statements and use the results to assess the impact of management's choices.

EXAMPLE 14.5

Comparing key ratios

Assume Maximus will borrow $10 413 995 for five years. The interest expense for the coming year will be $900 000. What is the impact on the key financial ratios for the company?

Non-current interest-bearing liabilities will increase to $17 413 995 (that is, 10 413 995 + 7 000 000). The interest expense for the forecast period increases to $1 539 000 (that is, 639 000 + 900 000). The tax expense decreases to $15 940 995 and the net profit figure is forecast as $37 195 655. The impact on the key ratios is shown in table 14.5.

Table 14.5 Comparison of key ratios under debt and financing

	Equity financing	Debt financing
EPS	$3.60	$3.72
DPS	$0.95	$1.00
ROE	51%	58%
NTA	$7.10	$6.42
Debt to equity	0.17:1	0.36:1
Net debt to capital employed	–5%	10%
Times interest	86 times	36 times

FINANCE WORKSHOP 14.3

1. Prepare the pro-forma balance sheet and income statement under the debt financing scenario described in example 14.5 to see how interest and tax expenses impact on retained earnings.
2. Use the information from these pro-forma statements to calculate the ratios under the debt financing option.

Earnings per share increases if management chooses debt financing rather than equity. This reflects the leverage effect of using more debt. The tax deduction associated with the higher interest payment and the relatively lower number of shares issued result in higher earnings per share. We need to be careful when assessing how investors will interpret a change in the EPS. Investors will be pleased with an increase in EPS stemming from an increase in debt finance only if they cannot utilise the dividend imputation credits. If investors can use the imputation credits, paying less corporate tax means that shareholders will receive a lower franking percentage on their dividends. Keeping the total dividends paid constant, debt financing also results in higher DPS than would be the case with increased equity finance. This happens because there are fewer shares on issue.

Return on equity is higher under the debt financing option largely because of the relatively lower equity base. Although there are more shares issued under the equity financing option, net tangible asset backing per share is higher here because net assets are higher and the amount of financing needed when equity was chosen is lower.

The largest impact of the choice of financing is reflected in the debt-related ratios. Under either financing option, the debt-to-equity ratio has decreased in comparison to 2008. At 0.36:1 under the debt financing option, Maximus would not be considered as overgeared (remember that 1:1 shows the firm has equal proportions of debt and equity). A ratio of 0.36:1 tells us that Maximus uses about three times as much equity as debt in the company's financing structure. The main reason this ratio has fallen significantly under both financing options is that relatively large increases in retained earnings are forecast. The increase in retained earnings is due to operations. The times interest earned is dramatically different under the two options. Under either financing option, the forecast profit before interest and tax is much higher than it was in 2008. If Maximus chooses equity financing, the interest expense is relatively low. Combining these factors gives a times interest of 86. For the debt option, times interest increases to only 36 times compared to the 31 times for 2008.

Does this comparison tell management which financing option it should choose? Unfortunately the answer is no. What we can tell from analysis of the pro-forma financial statements is how the users of the financial statements are likely to react under the different scenarios. For example, if management were planning to use more debt and the pro-forma statements showed that the higher debt levels would put the company in breach of its borrowing agreements, it would be reasonable to predict that the forecast breach of contract would result in the loans being recalled.

FINANCE WORLD

Setting performance targets

The annual reports of Sigma Pharmaceuticals Ltd for 2004 and 2005 disclose the company aim to hold gearing at between 25% and 40% for the medium term. The 2004 report also discloses an EBIT margin target of 2.4% for the next financial year, but does not include such performance targets in 2005 and 2006.

You don't often see boards of directors that are brave enough to publish financial targets. Good forecasting skills combined with the tools of cash budgeting and pro-forma financial statement analysis are essential if the company wants to show stakeholders that it is serious about financial targets and that it is willing to be assessed on the basis of performance relative to the targets set.

executive summary

lo1 describe the structure of financial statements

- Financial statements are prepared from the transactions stored in the firm's accounting system.
- The accounting system is the collection of records of financial transactions.
- Financial statements are the balance sheet, the income statement and the cash flow statement.
- The balance sheet shows the assets, liabilities and equity of the firm. Assets and liabilities are classified as current and non-current.
- Assets are probable future economic benefits that the firm is able to utilise.
- Liabilities represent future sacrifices of economic benefits that the firm is obliged to make.
- Equity (in the balance sheet) is the book value of the ownership interest in the firm.
- Net assets equal the total assets minus the total liabilities.
- Retained earnings are the accumulated profits (net of dividend payments) that are shown in the equity section of the balance sheet.
- The income statement shows the revenues, expenses and profit for the reporting period.
- Revenues are inflows of future economic benefits that come from the operations of the firm.
- Expenses are the consumption or losses of future economic benefits.
- Profit is the excess of revenues over expenses.
- Accrual accounting is the process of matching revenues to the period in which they are earned and liabilities to the period in which they are incurred.
- After dividends are paid, the remaining profit is transferred to retained earnings in the balance sheet.
- The cash flow statement shows the amount of cash that came into and went out of the company over the reporting period.
- The cash flow statement classifies inflows and outflows as cash from:
  - operating activities
  - investing activities
  - financing activities.

lo2 explain the rationale for and importance of financial forecasting

- Financially viable businesses require efficient management and planning.
- Financial managers use cash budgets and pro-forma financial statements for planning purposes.
- A budget is a plan that includes forecasts of future transactions.
- Cash budgets focus on maintaining the solvency of the firm.
- Pro-forma financial statements are used to forecast profit for the future period and forecasting the financial position of the firm at the end of the future period.
- Preparing cash budgets helps the firm to maintain liquidity by identifying when and how much financing will be required.
- The budget period is determined by the volume of cash transactions and management's purpose in preparing the budget.

- The most effective budgeting systems have nests of budgets that fit together. For example, weekly, monthly, quarterly and annual cash flow budgets could be prepared to help the firm keep control of its cash position.
- The progression of cash inflows and outflows to the business is called the cash cycle.
- The person preparing the cash budget needs to have a detailed understanding of the firm's cash cycle to make realistic forecasts of the cash inflows and outflows.

lo3 construct a cash budget

- Good sales forecasts are the key ingredient to preparing cash budgets.
- Inflows including cash sales, credit sales and interest receipts are forecast.
- The sales forecast needs to separate cash sales from sales on account because the cash from account sales will not be received at the time the sale is made.
- Further, the timing of the cash receipts from account sales need to be forecast. Reference to customers' past payment patterns will aid this process.
- Outflows including payments to suppliers, wages and dividends are forecast.
- Cash outflows are deducted from the cash inflows to determine the firm's net cash flow for the period.
- A negative ending cash balance indicates that financing is required.

lo4 explain the use of pro-forma financial statements

- Pro-forma financial statements are projections of a future position and of future period performance.
- They are used to map the impact of management decisions on the financial statements.

lo5 construct the pro-forma income statement and balance sheet

- Using the financial statements for the previous period as a base, forecasts from the cash budget are included in the forecast pro-forma accounts.
- Information about management's plans (asset sales and purchases, for example) is collected and reflected in the pro-forma statements.
- Shareholders use the company's published financial statements as an important source of information about the firm's performance.
- Analysts tend to forecast earnings figures rather than dividend cash flows.
- Some companies set target levels of performance for the coming period in their annual reports. Management needs to be confident that these levels can be achieved and they set the target performance levels after they have constructed the pro-forma financial statements.
- Pro-forma financial statements allow managers to assess the impact of a proposed course of action on the key financial ratios that are used by the market to evaluate the firm's performance.
- They are also used to ensure the firm does not breach any of its debt covenants.
- Pro-forma financial statements can be used to forecast financing requirements.
- The pro-forma balance sheets and income statements should be developed simultaneously.

- For items that relate directly to sales (and there is no change expected in the historic relationship), the percent of sales method can be used for the forecasts.
- The percent of sales method expresses items in the income statement as a percentage of sales. The calculated percentage is applied to the forecast sales figure.
- The balance for accounts receivable can be calculated from the cash budget.
- The balance for accounts payable is calculated from the forecast of sales and the proportion of cost of goods sold that will be represented by purchases on account.
- The cash balance is obtained from the cash budget.
- The interest-bearing liabilities can be calculated from the opening balance and the changes in this item shown in the cash budget.
- Interest expense is calculated as a combination of interest paid in the cash budget and the accrued interest for the period.
- Other asset accounts are based on opening balances, depreciation for the period and management's plans for sale and acquisition of assets.
- Dividends are based on management's forecast dividend payments.
- 'What if' scenarios are facilitated by the use of a spreadsheet to construct the pro-formas.

lo6 explain the role of financial ratio analysis

- Financial ratios are data reduction techniques that express one account as a proportion of another.
- Financial ratios facilitate the comparison of a firm's performance across time and against that of other firms for the same period.
- Analysts, credit rating agencies and the suppliers of capital use financial ratios when they are assessing a firm.

lo7 identify and calculate key ratios and interpret your results

- The key ratios are: earnings per share (EPS), dividends per share (DPS), return on equity (ROE), debt to equity (D/E), times interest earned and net tangible asset backing per share (NTA).
- EPS equals net profit (or loss) divided by the number of shares on issue.
- DPS equals dividends paid divided by the number of shares on issue.
- ROE equals net profit divided by ordinary shareholders' equity.
- Ordinary shareholders' equity (in the ROE ratio) is usually calculated as total equity minus goodwill (and other intangibles) minus preference equity.
- Intangible assets are non-physical assets that will give the company future benefits, but that are difficult to separate from the business.
- NTA equals assets minus intangibles minus liabilities all divided by the number of ordinary shares.
- D/E equals total liabilities divided by ordinary shareholders' equity.
- Times interest earned equals profit before interest and tax divided by the annual interest expense.
- Ratio analysis can be applied to published financial statements and to pro-forma financial statements.
- Managers can assess the impact of their plans on the financial statements by preparing pro-forma statements and doing ratio analysis on these statements.

Key terms

accounting system, p. 510
accrual accounting, p. 512
assets, p. 511
balance sheet, p. 510
budget, p. 514
cash cycle, p. 515
cash flow statement, p. 513
equity, p. 511
expenses, p. 511
financial ratios, p. 527
financial statements, p. 510
income statement, p. 511
intangible assets, p. 529
liabilities, p. 511
net assets, p. 511
percent of sales method, p. 522
profit, p. 512
pro-forma financial statements, p. 520
retained earnings, p. 512
revenues, p. 511

Learning chart

Learning objective	Questions	Self-test problems	Financial problems
lo1 describe the structure of financial statements	14.1, 14.2, 14.3, 14.4, 14.5		
lo2 explain the rationale for and importance of financial forecasting	14.6		
lo3 construct a cash budget	14.7, 14.8, 14.9, 14.10, 14.11, 14.12, 14.13	14.1, 14.2	14.1, 14.2, 14.3, 14.4, 14.5, 14.6, 14.7
lo4 explain the use of pro-forma financial statements	14.14, 14.15		
lo5 construct the pro-forma income statement and balance sheet		14.3, 14.4, 14.5	14.8, 14.9, 14.10, 14.11, 14.12, 14.13
lo6 explain the role of financial ratio analysis	14.16		
lo7 identify and calculate key ratios and interpret your results	14.17, 14.18, 14.19, 14.20		14.14, 14.15, 14.16

Questions

14.1 What are financial statements and what are they used for?
14.2 Describe the structure of the balance sheet. What is measured in this statement?
14.3 Describe the structure of the income statement. What is measured in this statement?
14.4 Describe the structure of the cash flow statement. What is measured in this statement?
14.5 What is accrual accounting and how is it different from cash flow?
14.6 Why is control over a firm's cash so important?

14.7 What is a budget? What length period should a budget cover?

14.8 What is a cash cycle?

14.9 What similarities and differences would you expect to find when comparing the cash cycle of a supermarket chain to that of an investment advisor?

14.10 Why is a good understanding of the firm's cash cycle necessary when developing the cash budget? Use examples to illustrate your answer.

14.11 Would you use information from previous periods when you are preparing the cash budget? Why?

14.12 Explain why information feedback is important in the cash budgeting process.

14.13 Should the 'total sales' forecast be included in the cash budget? Why?

14.14 What is the percent of sales method for forecasting? When is it appropriate to use this method?

14.15 What are pro-forma financial statements and what are they used for?

14.16 What is financial ratio analysis and what is it used for?

14.17 How is EPS calculated? Why is this ratio important?

14.18 What are intangible assets? Why are they usually excluded from the calculation of ordinary shareholders' equity when the ROE is calculated?

14.19 What does the NTA ratio tell us?

14.20 Which group of financial statement users do you think would be most interested in the debt-to-equity ratio, the net debt to capital employed ratio and the times-interest-earned ratio? Explain your answer.

Self-test problems

14.1 Canning Limited makes all of its sales on account. The sales manager has provided you with the following sales forecasts.

	$
July	600 000
August	490 000
September	450 000
October	495 000
November	525 000

The actual sales for June were $500 000. You make an assessment of the past payment histories of creditors and find that 70% of accounts are paid in the month following the month the sale was made. Of the remaining accounts, the 1% of sales revenue that is not collected in the second month after the sale is usually bad debts. What are the total sales inflow figures for each month from August to November?

14.2 You have forecast the following monthly sales for Franklin Fittings Ltd.

	$
January	825 000
February	900 000
March	950 000
April	875 000
May	850 000
June	815 000
July	790 000

After analysis of past records, you find that all of Franklin's production costs vary with the level of sales. Raw materials are 17% of sales. They are purchased on account and are paid for in the month following the sale of the inventory. Production wages are 34% of sales and are paid in the month of the sale. Water expenses average 3% of sales and are paid quarterly. The next water bill will be paid in April and will charge for usage from January to March. The electricity bill is paid monthly and is usually about 4% of the previous month's sales. What are the production cost outflow figures for each month from February to July?

14.3 Use the percent of sales method and the following information to construct the pro-forma income statement for Thibault Ltd.

Cost of goods sold	0.15
Administration	0.09
Marketing	0.08
Electricity	0.03
Wages	0.25
Freight charges	0.07

- Sales for the next period are forecast as $2 000 000.
- The corporate tax rate is 30%.

14.4 This is the income statement for Pascale Ltd:

Pascale Limited Income statement for the financial year ended 30 June	
Sales revenue	5 000 000
Cost of goods sold	1 350 000
Gross profit	3 650 000
Administration	550 000
Marketing	650 000
Electricity	350 000
Wages	750 000
Freight charges	650 000
Interest expense	100 000
Profit before tax	600 000
Income tax expense	180 000
Profit for the period	420 000

Management have also supplied you with the following information:

- The corporate tax rate is 30%.
- $7 000 000 sales are forecast for the coming year.
- The ratio of expenses to sales is expected to continue into the future.

Calculate the after-tax profit of Pascale Ltd for the coming year.

14.5 As financial manager of Fox-Vixen Ltd, it's your job to analyse the financial ratios on the pro-forma financial statements. Fox-Vixen has 500 000 ordinary shares on issue. Use the following information to calculate:

(a) earnings per share (EPS)
(b) dividends per share (DPS)
(c) return on equity (ROE)
(d) debt to equity (D/E)
(e) times interest
(f) net tangible asset backing per share (NTA).

	$
Net profit	214 424
Dividends paid	7 500
Total assets	1 993 620
Intangible assets	3 791
Total liabilities	736 320
Ordinary shareholders' equity	1 257 300
Profit before interest and tax	275 000
Interest	57 600
Transfer to retained earnings	190 197

Solutions to self-test problems

14.1

	June	July	August	September	October	November
Sales	500	600	490	450	495	525
Month 1 collections[a]			420	343	315	346.5
Month 2 collections[b]			145	174	142.1	130.5
Total sales inflows			565	517	457.1	477

a. Month 1 collections = 0.7 × sales for previous month

b. Month 2 collections = 0.29 × sales for 2 months ago

14.2

	Jan.	Feb.	March	April	May	June	July
Sales	825	900	950	875	850	815	790
Accounts pay[a]		140.25	153	161.5	148.75	144.5	138.55
Wages[b]		306	323	297.5	289	277.1	268.6
Water[c]				80.25			76.2
Electricity[d]		33	36	38	35	34	32.6
Total outflows		479.25	512	577.25	472.75	455.6	515.95

a. 140 250 = 0.17 × 825 000

b. 306 000 = 0.34 × 900 000

c. 80 250 = 0.03 × (825 000 + 900 000 + 950 000)

d. 33 000 = 0.04 × 825 000

14.3

Sales	2 000 000
Cost of goods sold	300 000
Gross profit	1 700 000
Administration	180 000
Marketing	160 000
Electricity	60 000
Wages	500 000
Freight charges	140 000
Profit before tax	660 000
Tax	198 000
Profit for the period	462 000

14.4

	This year	Percent of sales	Next year
Sales revenue	5 000 000		7 000 000
Cost of goods sold	1 350 000	0.27	1 890 000
Gross profit	3 650 000		5 110 000
Administration	550 000	0.11	770 000
Marketing	650 000	0.13	910 000
Electricity	350 000	0.07	490 000
Wages	750 000	0.15	1 050 000
Freight charges	650 000	0.13	910 000
Interest expense	100 000	0.02	140 000
Profit before tax	600 000		840 000
Income tax expense	180 000		252 000
Profit for the period	420 000		588 000

14.5 (a) $$\text{EPS} = \frac{\text{net profit (loss)}}{\text{number of shares on issue}} = \frac{\$214\,424}{500\,000} = \$0.43$$

(b) $$\text{DPS} = \frac{\text{dividends paid}}{\text{number of shares on issue}} = \frac{\$7500}{500\,000} = \$0.015$$

(c) $$\text{ROE} = \frac{\text{net profit}}{\text{ordinary shareholders' equity}} = \frac{\$214\,424}{\$1\,257\,300} = 0.17$$

(d) $\text{Debt to equity} = \dfrac{\text{total liabilities}}{\text{ordinary shareholders' equity}}$

$$= \frac{\$736\,320}{\$1\,257\,300}$$

$$= 0.59$$

(e) $\text{Times interest earned} = \dfrac{\text{profit before interest and tax}}{\text{annual interest expense}}$

$$= \frac{\$275\,000 + \$57\,600}{\$57\,600}$$

$$= 5.77 \text{ times}$$

(f) $\text{NTA} = \dfrac{\text{assets} - \text{intangibles} - \text{liabilities}}{\text{number of ordinary shares}}$

$$= \frac{\$1\,993\,620 - \$3\,791 - \$736\,320}{500\,000}$$

$$= \$2.51$$

Financial problems

14.1 The Tapestry Place makes 7% of sales each month from its small shop in Canberra. Most of the firm's sales come from orders from other craft shops. The wholesale customers are given accounts and have 40 days to pay. Normally, 33% of customers pay by the end of the month and 65% pay by the end of the month following the sale. The firm writes off any accounts unpaid by the second month as bad debts. The firm has an excellent reputation for shipping orders on the day the order is received.

	Nov.	Dec.	Jan.	Feb.	Mar.	Apr.	May	June
Monthly sales	87 000	95 000	42 000	49 000	57 000	55 000	61 000	63 000

Use the information above to calculate the total sales inflow figures for each of the months from January to June.

14.2 Construct a monthly cash budget for The Tapestry Place using the sales figures in problem 14.1 and the following information:

- The cost of importing tapestries from overseas suppliers is 45% of sales.
- The tapestries are purchased on account and are paid for the month the sale of the inventory is made.
- Three part-time employees staff the shop and pack the customers' orders for shipping. Monthly wages total $2200.
- Rent for the business premises is $2700 per month. Rent payments are made quarterly, in advance. The next rent payment is due in February.
- Postage is 25% of credit sales and is paid at the time the order is shipped.

Your cash budget should identify the net change in cash for each of the months from January to June.

14.3 The Grammar School mails out accounts for school fees at the start of each school term (that is, quarterly, commencing in January). The total amount of fees charged each term is \$3 000 000 and 80% of accounts are paid within a week of the accounts being mailed. A further 10% are paid within the month; 8% of parents pay in two months after the mailing of the accounts; and the remaining accounts are paid a week or two before next term's accounts are mailed. The school has no problem with bad debts as students with accounts unpaid at the beginning of the new term are expelled. Calculate the total fee revenue for each month of the year.

14.4 Use the monthly cash inflows from problem 14.3 and the following information for The Grammar School:

- The school employs 32 full-time staff at an average annual salary of \$90 000 per staff member.
- Casual staff are also employed by the school. They are needed for the second and third months of each term. The monthly bill for casual wages is \$28 800.
- Rates of \$14 000 per quarter. The next payment is due in February.
- Water rates of \$3000 per quarter. The next payment is due in March.
- The Grammar School is located in a warm climate, so all buildings are air-conditioned. The electricity bill for each of the summer months (November to January inclusive) is \$2000 and the remaining months cost \$1000 per month.
- Other expenses include stationery, printing and craft supplies. These expenses total \$9500 per month.
- The balance of the School's bank account is \$100 000 at the start of the year.

(a) Prepare a cash budget to identify the net change in cash and the closing balance for the bank account for each of the months from January to December.

(b) The Grammar School is planning an upgrade to the sporting facilities in July. This upgrade will cost \$20 000 000. Will the school have sufficient cash to pay for the sporting facilities by the end of July?

14.5 You are hired by Sid and Nancy's Bookstore on 1 January to prepare a cash budget for the next three months. The bookstore provides you with the following data.

	Cash sales	Credit sales	Total sales
October 2007 (actual)	9 900	13 975	23 875
November 2007 (actual)	10 000	15 500	25 500
December 2007 (actual)	12 400	14 600	27 000
January 2008 (forecast)	8 500	12 250	20 750
February 2008 (forecast)	8 750	13 125	21 875
March 2008 (forecast)	9 250	13 875	23 125
April 2008 (forecast)	9 750	14 625	24 375
May 2008 (forecast)	7 600	11 400	19 000

Sid and Nancy have based their sales forecast on past experience. They also tell you that approximately 85% of credit sales are collected in the month following the month of the sale, 8% in the second month and 4% are collected in the third month after the sale.

Books are sold in the second month after they are ordered from Sid and Nancy's suppliers. Sid and Nancy have to pay for the books at the time of order and base their orders on the forecast sales level for 2 months ahead. Cost of goods sold is 27% of sales. Rent on the bookshop costs \$1000 per month and is paid in advance.

Sid and Nancy work in the shop themselves and need to employ casual staff only at peak periods. They expect that wages will be around 8% of sales and wages will be paid in the same month as the staff are employed. They also expect the monthly electricity cost to be 2% of sales. The electricity bill is paid in the month following the sales.

Sid and Nancy tell you that they had $750 in the business bank account on 1 January.

(a) Prepare a cash budget for the months of January, February and April.

(b) Credit sales collections total 97%. What has happened to the other 3% of credit sales?

14.6 Easter Island Ltd is a travel company that specialises in island cruises in the Pacific. The peak travel times are November to December and April to August.

	Forecast sales
April 2008	950 000
May 2008	1 250 000
June 2008	1 123 000
July 2008	1 005 000
August 2008	1 897 000
September 2008	500 000
October 2008	500 000
November 2008	1 564 000
December 2008	1 756 000
January 2009	550 000
February 2009	545 000
March 2009	560 000

- Sales of $500 000 per month were made in January and February 2008. Sales for March 2008 were $550 000.
- Customers must book 2 months in advance of travel and pay 20% of the cost of travel at the time of booking. Sales are recorded in the month the booking is made. The remaining amount must be paid the month prior to travel. The company does not have any bad debts as customers who do not pay prior to travel have their bookings cancelled.
- Easter Island pays 35% of sales to the cruise ship operators who carry their passengers. The payments are remitted 3 months after the sale is made.
- Customers receive accommodation and meals on their island stopovers. The company pays 12% of sales for this service. The payment is remitted 2 months after the sale is made.
- Salaries and wages are paid to employees monthly. The forecast amount for each month is $52 000.
- Premises rental is $3000 per month and is paid monthly. This amount is fixed for the budget period.
- Other overheads run at 2% of total sales and are paid in the month following the sales.
- Equal-sized tax payments are made quarterly. The next payment of $94 000 is due in April.

- The company borrowed $6 000 000 in 2007. Monthly repayments associated with this loan are $500 000. The final payment will be made in September 2008.
- A new computer system designed especially for taking bookings and tracking payments is due to be installed in June 2008. Easter Island will make two $360 000 payments for the system. The first payment is due in May and the second is to be paid in June when the system is installed.
- The opening cash balance for April is $2000.

(a) Given this information, prepare a cash budget for each month from April 2008 to March 2009.

(b) Will Easter Island need to raise any additional financing? If yes, when would the financing be required?

14.7 Williams Ltd subcontracts to the government to construct highways. The board has been advised that the current fleet of graders will need to be replaced at the end of March. The estimated cost of a new fleet of graders is $5.6 million. You have collected the following information.

	Estimated contract receipts
October	2 365 000
November	1 986 000
December	2 500 000
January	1 976 000
February	1 579 000
March	2 357 000
April	2 250 000

- The company bills the government at the end of each month for that month's work. The government pays the account in the following month.
- Contract receipts for September were $2 674 000.
- Wages are 41% of contract receipts for the following month. They are paid to employees in the month they do the work.
- Materials are forecast as 21% of contract receipts and, like wages, are paid the month the work is done.
- Fuel and transportation are estimated at 18% of contract receipts and are paid in the same month as the contract payment is received.
- Monthly maintenance costs are expected to be $200 000.
- Insurance of $1.2 million per annum is paid in equal quarterly instalments. The next payment is due in November.
- Monthly debt repayments are $100 000 and will continue at this level for the next 12 months.
- The opening cash balance for October is $10 000.

(a) Prepare a cash budget to determine the cash balance at the end of March.

(b) Is sufficient cash being generated from operations to allow Williams to purchase the new fleet of graders without raising additional finance?

14.8 You have been asked to calculate the profit after tax for next period for Jennox Limited. The following is last period's financial statement:

	% of sales
Cost of goods sold	37
Administration	6
Marketing	12
Electricity	2
Rent	2
Freight charges	12

You have also been informed that:

- The ratio of expenses to sales is expected to continue into the future.
- Forecast sales for the next period are $3 500 000.
- The corporate tax rate is 30%.

What after-tax profit will Jennox Ltd expect in the next period?

14.9 The following income statement is for Maurice Ltd:

Maurice Limited Income statement for the financial year ended 30 June	
Sales revenue	1 000 000
Cost of goods sold	410 000
Gross profit	590 000
Administration and other	50 000
Advertising	30 000
Wages	150 000
Rent	130 000
Freight charges	120 000
Interest expense	30 000
Profit before tax	80 000
Income tax expense	24 000
Profit for the period	56 000

Management have also supplied you with the following information:

- The corporate tax rate is 30%.
- $1 500 000 sales are forecast for the coming year.
- Except for the freight expense, the ratio of expenses to sales is expected to continue into the future for all expense items. A contract with a new freight provider will result in a ratio of freight to sales that is half that of its current level.

Calculate the after-tax profit of Pascale Ltd for the coming year.

14.10 The following financial statements are for Trefoil Ltd.

Trefoil Limited Income statement for the year ended 30 June 2008	
Revenues from sales	7 500 000
Cost of goods sold	2 775 000
Gross profit	4 725 000
Dividend revenue	550 000
	5 275 000
Electricity and other operating expenses	525 000
Administration and marketing	540 000
Depreciation	146 500
Borrowing costs expense	726 000
Profit (loss)	3 337 500
Income tax expense	1 001 250
Net profit (loss)	2 336 250
Dividends paid	2 000 000
Transfer to retained earnings	336 250

Trefoil Limited Balance sheet as at 30 June 2008	
Current assets	
Cash	250 000
Receivables	600 000
Inventories	1 275 000
Other financial assets	100 000
Total current assets	2 225 000
Non-current assets	
Land	12 400 000
Buildings	2 630 000
Plant and equipment	500 000
Total non-current assets	15 530 000
Total assets	17 755 000
Current liabilities	
Payables	300 000
Interest-bearing liabilities	250 000
Current tax liability	272 800
Total current liabilities	822 800
Non-current liabilities	
Interest-bearing liabilities	2 500 000
Total non-current liabilities	2 500 000
Total liabilities	3 322 800
Equity	
Contributed equity	13 188 550
Reserves	470 000
Retained profits	773 650
Total equity	14 432 200

You have also collected the following information.

- Sales are forecast at $8.7 million for 2009.
- Dividend revenue is expected to be the same as in 2008.
- The corporate tax rate is 30%.
- There are 7 million Trefoil ordinary shares on issue.
- The depreciation expense of $98 750 is estimated for builidings and $30 850 for plant.
- The estimated administration and marketing expense is 15% higher than it was in 2008.
- The current tax liability for the 2008 pro-forma balance sheet will be 25% of the tax expense in the pro-forma income statement.
- Dividends of $2 million are expected to be paid in 2009.
- The closing balance for cash at bank is expected to be 20% higher than the amount for 2008.
- No major capital outlays are expected for the coming financial year.
- No transfers to reserves are expected to occur.
- Trefoil do not expect to be holding any current assets in the 'other financial assets' account.
- Short-term interest-bearing liabilities are expected to remain at the 2008 amount.
- Long-term interest-bearing liabilities are expected to decrease to $1 500 000.
- The annual interest expense is expected to be 13% of the closing balances for interest-bearing liabilities.
- You decide to use the percent of sales method for the cost of goods sold, electricity, receivables, inventories and payables accounts. You will assume that the relationship between these accounts and sales remains the same as it was in 2008.

(a) Prepare the pro-forma income statements for 2009.

(b) Would any new financing be required for 2009? If so, how much new equity would be required?

14.11 Using the information for Trefoil Ltd from problem 14.10, construct the pro-forma financial statements to identify how much debt would need to be raised. The interest expense for the additional debt would be $75 000 in the forecast year.

14.12 The following financial statements are for Williams Ltd.

Williams Limited Income statement for the year ended 31 October 2008	
Contract revenues	19 876 000
Cost of goods sold	15 900 800
Gross profit	3 975 200
Maintenance	1 800 000
Insurance	1 100 000
Depreciation and amortisation	750 000
Borrowing costs expense	157 500
Profit (loss)	167 700
Income tax expense	50 310
Net profit (loss)	117 390
Dividends paid	50 000
Transfer to retained earnings	67 390

Williams Limited Balance sheet as at 31 October 2008	
Current assets	
Cash	10000
Receivables	2674000
Inventories	1000
Total current assets	2685000
Non-current assets	
Land and buildings	570000
Plant and equipment	7600000
Goodwill	500000
Total non-current assets	8670000
Total assets	11355000
Current liabilities	
Payables	481320
Interest-bearing liabilities	50000
Current tax liability	12578
Total current liabilities	543898
Non-current liabilities	
Interest-bearing liabilities	7000000
Total non-current liabilities	7000000
Total liabilities	7543898
Equity	
Contributed equity	3000000
Retained profits	811102
Total equity	3811102

You have also collected the following information.

- Contract revenue of $2 million is forecast for October 2009. You will use this amount to estimate the balances for 'receivables' and 'payables'.
- Contract revenues for the year ending October 2009 are forecast to be $29530500.
- Williams keeps only a minimal amount of inventory and you do not expect this amount to change.
- The closing cash balance is expected to be $30000.
- Total depreciation and amortisation charges of $700000 are expected. Depreciation of $50000 will be charged on buildings and $640000 will be charged on plant and equipment. The same amount of dividends is expected to be paid in 2009.
- Amortisation of goodwill is expected to be $10000. Therefore, the balance of the goodwill account is expected to be $490000.
- Of the $1.2 million repayments made on long-term interest-bearing liabilities during the year, $1042000 will be principal payments.
- Short-term interest-bearing liabilities are forecast as $40000.
- The interest expense for the year is forecast to be $161200.
- The current portion of the tax liability is 25% of the income tax expense from the pro-forma income statement.

- There are 1 million ordinary shares currently issued.
  - (a) Using this information and that given in problem 14.7, construct the pro-forma financial statements for the year, November 2008 to October 2009.
  - (b) Does Williams Ltd need to raise additional financing? If yes, how much equity would need to be raised?

14.13 Using the information for Williams Ltd from problem 14.12, construct the pro-forma financial statements assuming debt would be used to fund the shortfall. The interest expense for the additional debt would be $55 000 in the forecast year.

14.14 (a) Using the 2008 financial statements of Trefoil Ltd presented in problem 14.10 calculate the key ratios.

(b) If investors were expecting Trefoil to generate a return on equity of 18% would they be happy with the results for 2008?

14.15 (a) Include the new equity funding in the pro-formas you constructed for Trefoil Ltd in problem 14.10. Issue one new share for each dollar of financing required. Dividends paid will be the same as the previous year. Calculate the key ratios.

(b) Include the new debt funding in the pro-formas you constructed for Trefoil Ltd in problem 14.11. Calculate the key ratios.

(c) Compare your results for the alternate funding strategies.

14.16 (a) Using the 2008 financial statements of Williams Ltd presented in problem 14.12, calculate the key ratios.

(b) Assume 500 000 ordinary shares are issued to raise the amount of financing you identified in the pro-forma statements for 2009. Reflect this change in the balance sheet and calculate the key ratios.

(c) How do you think lenders would view the forecast performance compared to the current performance of Williams Ltd?

SOLUTIONS TO FINANCE WORKSHOPS

14.1 If the firm can make fairly reliable monthly cash forecasts over a period of a couple of years, Maximus might consider using these to determine how much cash it will have available from operations to repay a loan and the timing of the loan repayments (for example, monthly or quarterly). If Maximus has problems forecasting monthly cash flows a few years ahead, the firm should consider using annual cash budgets to identify the appropriate term for the loan.

14.2 (a) $$\frac{\text{cost of goods sold}}{\text{sales}} = \frac{16\,274\,000}{46\,497\,000} = 0.35$$

(b) $$\frac{\text{electricity and other expenses}}{\text{sales}} = \frac{232\,000}{46\,497\,000} = 0.00499$$

14.3 1. The solution is based on an interest expense of $900 000 for the additional borrowing. This increases total forecast interest to $1 539 000 for the planning year.

Maximus Printing Limited
Projected income statement under debt financing alternative
for the year ended 30 June 2009

	2009	Forecast source
Revenues from sales	108 400 000	See figure 14.5
Cost of goods sold	37 940 000	See figure 14.5
Gross profit	70 460 000	
Interest revenue	24 000	See figure 14.5
	70 484 000	
Administration and marketing	9 600 000	See figure 14.5
Depreciation	3 995 350	See figure 14.5
Electricity and other expenses	542 000	See figure 14.5
Employee benefits	1 671 000	See figure 14.5
Borrowing costs expense	1 539 000	Figure 14.5 forecast plus $900 000 from the new debt
Profit (loss)	53 136 650	
Income tax expense	15 940 995	30% of forecast profit
Net profit (loss)	37 195 655	
Dividends paid	10 000 000	See figure 14.5
Transfer to retained earnings	27 195 655	
Basic earnings per share	3.72	
Dividends per share	1.00	

Maximus Printing Limited
Projected balance sheet under debt financing alternative
as at 30 June 2009

	2009	Forecast source
Current assets		
Cash	9 526 000	See figure 14.6
Receivables	5 250 000	See figure 14.6
Inventories	1 084 000	See figure 14.6
Other financial assets	800 000	See figure 14.6
Total current assets	16 660 000	
Non-current assets		
Land	36 800 000	See figure 14.6
Buildings	22 761 050	See figure 14.6
Plant and equipment	11 189 650	See figure 14.6
Total non-current assets	70 750 650	
Total assets	87 410 650	

Current liabilities		
Payables	1 650 000	See figure 14.6
Interest-bearing liabilities	0	See figure 14.6
Current tax liability	4 160 000	See figure 14.6
Total current liabilities	5 810 000	
Non-current liabilities		
Interest-bearing liabilities	17 413 995	Figure 14.6 forecast plus $10 413 995 from new debt
Total non-current liabilities	17 413 995	
Total liabilities	23 223 995	
Equity		
Contributed equity	11 335 000	See figure 14.6
Reserves	2 047 000	See figure 14.6
Retained profits	50 804 655	Opening balance plus pro-forma income statement
Total equity	64 186 655	

2. $\text{EPS} = \dfrac{\text{net profit (loss)}}{\text{number of shares on issue}}$

$= \dfrac{37\ 195\ 655}{10\ 000\ 000}$

= $3.72 — higher than the equity alternative because lower total profit is more than offset by the lower number of shares on issue

$\text{DPS} = \dfrac{\text{dividends paid}}{\text{number of shares on issue}}$

$= \dfrac{10\ 000\ 000}{10\ 000\ 000}$

= $1— higher than the equity alternative because the total dividends are spread over fewer shares on issue

$\text{Return on equity (ROE)} = \dfrac{\text{net profit}}{\text{ordinary shareholders' equity}}$

$= \dfrac{37\ 195\ 655}{64\ 186\ 655}$

= 0.58 or 58% — higher than the equity plan because relatively less equity has been contributed by shareholders

$$\text{NTA} = \frac{\text{assets} - \text{intangibles} - \text{liabilities}}{\text{number of ordinary shares}}$$

$$= \frac{(87\,410\,650 - 0 - 23\,223\,995)}{10\,000\,000}$$

= \$6.41 — less than under equity financing as total liabilities have been increased by the new loan

$$\text{Debt to equity} = \frac{\text{total liabilities}}{\text{ordinary shareholders' equity}}$$

$$= \frac{23\,223\,995}{64\,186\,655}$$

= 0.36:1 — shows the higher gearing under the debt plan

$$\text{Times interest earned} = \frac{\text{profit before interest and tax}}{\text{annual interest expense}}$$

$$= \frac{53\,136\,650 + 1\,539\,000}{1\,539\,000}$$

= 36 times — much lower than under equity financing, but still more than adequate from a creditor's perspective

End notes

1 Harvey Norman Holdings Limited, *Annual report 2006*, p. 81.

2 Bolt, C 2006, 'Raising gives hint of Griffin', *The West Australian*, 28 October, p. 81.

3 Cummins, C 2006, 'Multiplex on back foot over sell-off', *The Age*, 28 February, p. 2.

4 Cochlear Limited, www.cochlear.com.au.

5 Khoury, T, Smith, K & MacKay, P 1999, 'Comparing working capital practices in Canada, the United States, and Australia: a note', *Canadian Journal of Administrative Sciences*, vol. 16, p. 1.

6 The two companies that did not provide ratios were Amcom Ltd and Envestra Ltd. At the time of writing (February 2007) the most recently available annual report for Amcom was for the year ended 31 December 2005. The annual reports for these companies are available at the company websites.

7 Adsteam Marine Ltd, *Annual report 2006*, www.adsteam.com.au.

8 Amcor Ltd, *Annual report 2006*, www.amcor.com.

9 Blackmores Ltd, *Annual report 2006*, www.blackmores.com.au.

10 Cochlear Ltd, *Annual report 2006*, www.cochlear.com.

11 Harvey Norman Holdings Ltd, *Annual report 2006*, www.harveynorman.com.au.

12 Sigma Pharmaceuticals Ltd, *Annual report 2006*, www.sigmaco.com.au.

13 Southern Cross Broadcasting (Australia) Ltd, *Annual report 2006*, www.southerncrossbroadcasting.com.au.

14 Wesfarmers Ltd, *Annual report 2006*, www.wesfarmers.com.au.

part 4

Special topics in corporate finance

chapter

15

Risk management

Learning objectives

After studying this chapter, you should be able to:

lo1	discuss risk management in non-financial services firms
lo2	identify the various types of traders in the markets
lo3	describe the role and operations of the futures markets
lo4	describe the roles and operations of FRAs
lo5	discuss the roles and operations of swaps markets
lo6	describe how companies manage risk with options
lo7	discuss the principles that should govern hedging operations.

MANAGING RISK

What women want

KEN BOAG

The insurance industry must devise the next generation of insurance products to meet the increasing needs of women as they outlive men.

Women live longer on average than men and have different patterns of morbidity. These differences result in differentiation in premium rates for death, disability and critical illness (trauma) products.

The premium rates for female death-cover products are less expensive than those of men, reflecting the increased life expectancy. The tables show the extent of these differences, which can be quite significant. The companies chosen are simply a sample from the available universe of products offered.

Premium tables

Death cover: $200 000 benefit, yearly stepped premiums

	Non-smokers						Smokers					
Age next birthday	**25**		**35**		**45**		**25**		**35**		**45**	
	Male	**Female**	**Male**	**Female**	**Male**	**Female**	**Male**	**Female**	**Male**	**Female**	**Male**	**Female**
Asteron—Term Life Insurance	$307	$295	$295	$273	$405	$347	$417	$351	$427	$385	$711	$533
Aviva—Life Cover	$219	$176	$217	$178	$327	$262	$330	$255	$368	$279	$680	$466
COMM—Total Care Plan	$258	$250	$250	$250	$353	$276	$337	$274	$383	$285	$774	$508
ING—One Care	$242	$200	$218	$200	$318	$272	$308	$258	$346	$272	$642	$446
Tower—Life Protection Plan	$233	$220	$220	$220	$312	$250	$350	$262	$356	$260	$662	$458
Zurich—Term Life Plus	$261	$201	$221	$201	$349	$293	$361	$260	$375	$281	$767	$470

Critical illness cover: $200 000 benefit, yearly stepped premiums

	Non-smokers						Smokers					
Age next birthday	**25**		**35**		**45**		**25**		**35**		**45**	
	Male	**Female**	**Male**	**Female**	**Male**	**Female**	**Male**	**Female**	**Male**	**Female**	**Male**	**Female**
Asteron—Standalone Recovery Insurance	$371	$340	$424	$466	$863	$825	$558	$470	$762	$705	$1 915	$1 539
Aviva—Standalone Recovery Money	$409	$409	$447	$454	$1 122	$1 125	$671	$643	$853	$805	$2 687	$2 334
COMM—Total Care Plan	$290	$299	$416	$460	$1 069	$998	$471	$451	$793	$865	$2 504	$2 156

Age next birthday	25		35		45		25		35		45	
	Male	Female	Male	Female	Male	Female	Male	Female	Male	Female	Male	Female
ING—One Care Premier Trauma	$426	$523	$460	$544	$1100	$985	$697	$704	$909	$974	$2394	$1980
Tower—Crisis Protection Plan	$384	$379	$499	$490	$1180	$1077	$642	$578	$973	$936	$2523	$2201
Zurich—Standalone Trauma Insurance Plus Extended	$312	$319	$436	$458	$1054	$962	$559	$452	$911	$881	$2465	$2074

The extent of the differences does vary from one product to another as a result of a number of factors. For married couples, it is often the case that the woman is younger than her partner and the amount of insurance required is also smaller for a number of reasons, usually reflecting differences in typical family structures.

All of these influences act in a similar direction to produce smaller costs associated with the provision of death-cover insurance protection for females.

For critical-illness protection, this pattern is not as clear cut in that many conditions are covered and what is covered varies from product to product. The more common cancers that affect women result in costs in products covering such risks being relatively more expensive. Certainly, it pays to do careful comparisons of critical-illness products to attempt to ascertain value.

Expert advice that takes into account the many factors involved can be rewarding and also can help to mitigate against an unfortunate situation that could arise where a claim may not be paid due to the condition not being covered or in some way being restricted. Another factor in any comparison of critical illness products is that many include a death benefit as part of the standard cover.

Income-protection cover reflects relatively higher female morbidity rates, particularly during child-bearing years. Again, these effects can be seen in the sample of rates shown in the tables. Broadly, it can be said that income-protection premiums are higher for females. This is the opposite of death cover.

Arguably the most problematic area is the difficulty that women face in obtaining disability cover during periods out of the paid workforce raising children. While there are a few companies that offer some cover, it is nevertheless an area where the need for protection is not matched by available products.

It should not be beyond the ingenuity of the insurance industry to devise a form of disability cover that is not dependent on the receipt of an income.

Clearly, the inability to perform the not insignificant duties involved in maintaining a home and looking after a family involves a burden, including a financial one. There is a real need but as yet there is no really satisfactory, commonly available product.[1]

Chapter preview

This chapter deals with risk management from the point of view of businesses not involved as heavily in the financial markets as are financial services firms such as banks, finance companies and funds managers. Thus, it deals with the practices and tools available to, and likely to be used by, such firms. It does not deal with the many other derivatives available to, and used by, sophisticated investors and speculators.

The opening page of the chapter introduces two different types of insurance policy that are available to individuals and firms. Insurance is the most common risk-management tool used in society today. This article points out that even such a standard option as insurance must change to remain relevant and useful in our fast-changing society. Firms use such insurance products to protect themselves and their employees from some of the many risks they confront.

The following diagram shows how this chapter is structured.

RISK MANAGEMENT

- **Managing risk**
- **Types of traders in the markets**
- **Futures markets**
  - The terminology of futures
  - The anatomy of a futures trade
  - Options on futures
  - Reading the media reports
- **The FRA market**
- **The swaps markets**
  - Interest rate swaps
  - Currency swaps
- **Company-issued options**
- **Rules for hedgers using derivatives**
  - Recent disasters among those who ignored the rules

lo1

Discuss risk management in non-financial services firms.

Risk: (in finance) the chance that the actual outcome from an investment will be different from the expected outcome

Managing risk

As we see in chapter 5, **risk** in finance is defined as the chance that the actual outcome will be different from the expected outcome. It is quantified by the standard deviation. You also learn from chapter 5 that standard deviation for a series of outcomes or values measures the dispersion of observed outcomes about the mean or average. For example, if you decided to sell 20 of your old textbooks and achieved sales of six at $15 each, one at $14, three at $12 and ten at $8, your average price is $11 and the standard deviation is $3.15. The $3.15 includes in one figure all the observed variation in your individual textbooks' sale prices.

Firms face risky outcomes with respect to many business variables. These include:

- prices for own products (unless the firm has market power)
- sales of products (depending on competitors' actions and consumers' preferences)
- costs of business inputs including interest rates and exchange rates.

Other factors such as national and international economic policies, government regulation and the weather also impact on individual businesses.

Firms are able to manage risk. Managing or reducing risk is a benefit and, like most benefits, reducing risk comes at a cost. Firms manage risk commonly by one or more of the following methods:

- insurance
- fixed rate finance
- forward contracting.

The most common way of reducing risk is to buy insurance. Firms buy insurance to cover all sorts of perils or unwanted events — damage to property through fire, storm and tempest, flood and theft, loss of key employees, claims of unsafe products, claims of damage to the public through actions of the firms' employees, professional negligence and so on. In these cases, the insured firms are paying a relatively small amount each year, by means of the insurance premiums, to insurance companies to take over their individual risks. (This raises the issue of the various parties in risk markets and we will discuss them in the next section.)

The insurance companies take on risk and charge premiums that they hope will be high enough to cover all the claims in each period and leave some over to compensate them for the business risks that they are taking. When you insure your car comprehensively, for example, you are handing over to the insurance company:

- the risk of loss, theft or damage to your vehicle
- your legal liability to pay for any damage that you cause to other vehicles
- your legal liability to pay for any compensation for death or injuries arising from your use of your vehicle.

Your insurance premium may be, say, $400 per year, but a compensation payment could be several million dollars. Have a good look at the premiums quoted on the opening page of this chapter and compare them with the sums insured.

A further common method that firms use to manage a business risk is to enter contracts to fix the interest rates on loans. In Australia, the interest rates charged for loans closely follow the movements of the cash rate, which is set by the Board of the Reserve Bank for monetary policy purposes. Many types of loans are available in the markets at variable rates, and thus firms contracting for debt under these conditions face interest rate variability. One way to overcome this risk is to arrange for fixed rate loans. When interest rates are stable but expected to rise, fixed rate loans will always be higher priced (have a higher interest rate) than variable rate loans. Borrowers are willing to pay higher rates in order to enjoy the certainty that rates for their loans will not rise even further. Financial institutions supplying the loans, on the other hand, require compensation for the risk that market rates will rise and they will have to pay more in the finance markets to replenish their stocks of funds. When interest rates are expected to fall in the market, fixed rate loans may be cheaper than variable rate loans, as the suppliers are anticipating that market rates will fall even further.

Another method of reducing risk is forward contracting. Suppliers of goods and users of the same goods may meet and negotiate prices for the goods for future delivery. In this way, the suppliers lock in certainty of revenue flows and the purchasers stabilise their costs. These contracts are normally not organised in any structured way, but happen on a case-by-case basis. However, it is not unusual for third parties to perceive that there are profits to be made by finding buyers for sellers and sellers for buyers. These information services cut the transaction costs that the parties would otherwise bear, and hence there are benefits to be gained by all three parties.

Forward contracting applies to commodities, debt through (interest) forward rate agreements, foreign exchange (forex) and equity though company-issued options. A special type of forward contract that covers the exchange-based trading of standardised quantities of commodities or financial products is known as a **futures contract**. In Australia, the Sydney Futures Exchange (SFE), part of the Australian Securities Exchange, manages trade in futures contracts for commodities (cattle, wool and electricity) and financial products. Other futures exchanges around the world deal in a much greater number of commodities which businesses use as inputs, such as oil, grains, orange juice and minerals. Although delivery of the underlying product is possible with some contracts, the normal expectation is that settlement will be effected by undertaking a further, but opposing, contract for the same product. The general principles of futures trading will be dealt with in more detail later in the chapter, and emphasis will be placed on the financial products rather than the commodities, as the financial products have greater general applicability.

Futures contract: a type of forward contract that is traded in a futures market and covers the purchase or sale of a set quantity of an asset to fix forward prices

Derivatives: synthetic financial products whose value is derived from an underlying product

Apart from these three most common methods of managing risk, there are many new and not-so-new financial products which are available to manage business risks. These are the products known collectively as 'derivatives'. **Derivatives** are so named because they are financial products whose value is derived from an underlying product. The underlying product could be a real asset (like cattle, wool, gold or silver) or financial assets (debt and equity instruments). In this chapter, we are not concerned with all the sophisticated products available, but rather we are interested in those products that businesses looking to hedge risk are likely to use. Table 15.1 gives a schematic representation of the tools available for various financial needs. This chapter will cover futures, swaps and company-issued options in greater detail.

Table 15.1 Tools for managing price risk for various business needs

Tools	Commodities	Debt	Forex	Equity
Forward contracting	✓	✓	✓	✓
Futures	✓	✓	✓	✓
Swaps		✓	✓	
Company-issued options				✓
Exchange-traded options[a]				✓

a. May be used by strongly growing firms to manage price risk of equity in the case of future mergers and takeovers.

One study undertaken in Australia provided the following indication of the use of derivatives among large listed firms. Table 15.2 shows the risks and the tools used by the firms in the sample (100 Australian respondents from the top 500 listed companies in Australia). From the data in this table, you can see that swaps in particular have become very popular to manage interest rate and forex risks, as has forward contracting for fixing currency prices.

Table 15.2 Tools used by 100 listed firms in Australia (%)*

Tools	Commodity price risk	Interest rate risk	Forex risk
Forwards	21	27	52
Futures	9	11	9
Swaps	12	57	38
Options	19	32	39

*Equity risks were not specifically reported.

Source: Benson and Oliver.[2]

FINANCE WORLD

Management motivation for using financial derivatives in Australia

Following are extracts and a table from Benson and Oliver's paper.[3] As you will see, firms use derivatives to change the volatility of their cash flows and to improve the value of the firms. Potential motivations such as increasing the use of debt finance, reducing taxation and improving personal compensation were little supported.

In this study a direct approach is taken to the determination of why firms use derivatives. A sample of managers of Australian publicly listed firms is surveyed to determine incentives for the use of derivatives. Theoretical incentives are incorporated and managements' views requested on the importance of these variables. The types of financial risks that are managed are also assessed. Data are collected on the types of derivative contracts used and the extent to which managements use derivatives to cover their financial exposure. Consideration is given as to how managements assess their risk exposure and how much of the exposure is covered. The results are considered in the context of the empirical evidence on financial risk exposure.

Guay and Kothari (2003), in a study of large US corporations, examine the amount of financial exposure managed with derivatives. They find that the cash flow generated from a derivative portfolio is relatively small in comparison to economic exposure and operating cash flows. They argue an increase in firm value is not driven by derivative investment and derivatives are a noisy proxy for risk management.

The majority of the empirical studies that attempt to identify the determinants of derivative use obtain data from annual financial statements. Disclosure in financial statements regarding derivative use can be limited. Firms disclose the value of derivatives at year-end. It is feasible that a long and short position at this time results in a net value of zero. Similarly, the year-end position is not necessarily representative of the firm's derivative and risk management policy throughout the year.

The top 500 listed companies in Australia were sampled through a mailed questionnaire.

One hundred useable responses were received representing a response rate of approximately 23%.

Table 2 Summary of responses in relation to derivative use from both non-derivative users and derivative users (ranked on mean response)

Issues	Mean	Standard deviation	Rank	Number of responses: Most important 1	2	< > 3	4	Least important 5
Change volatility of cash flows	2.17	1.32	1	39	20	14	8	8
Change the volatility of accounting earnings	2.20	1.26	2	29	35	11	3	10
Improve value of firm	2.40	1.22	3	21	35	19	4	10
Reduce risks faced by management	2.41	1.34	4	27	27	16	7	11
Reduce the cost of capital	3.08	1.26	5	6	28	23	11	18
Budgeting purposes	3.11	1.17	6	4	29	22	19	14
The firm has alternative means to manage financial risks	3.47	1.29	7	6	14	26	12	27
Change balance sheet accounts or ratios	3.57	1.15	8	2	15	26	18	25
Reduce bankruptcy and financial distress	3.73	1.37	9	8	11	13	17	36
The perceptions of derivative use by investors, regulators and the public	3.83	1.16	10	2	11	21	18	34

Types of traders in the markets

lo2

Identify the various types of traders in the markets.

The futures, swaps, forwards and company-issued options markets are fast growing markets. This is because they have filled a need and have thus been successful. There are normally three types of traders who operate in these markets. They are:

- hedgers
- speculators
- arbitrageurs.

Hedgers and speculators operate almost all of the time; arbitrageurs operate only when they are assured of profits.

Hedgers: traders who enter a market to try to reduce the price risk in their normal business operations

Hedgers are traders who enter a market to try to reduce the price risk in their normal business operations. Thus, the cattle producer enters a futures contract to sell cattle at a fixed price, or an Australian cotton exporter sells US dollars forward to fix the return in Australian dollars of US-dollar sales of cotton. Further, a lender can lock in the price of a loan or a borrower the price of funding.

EXAMPLE 15.1

Fixing a future exchange rate

James Stevensen is an Australian cotton exporter who holds contracts to export US\$1 million of cotton in June, 10 months away. In order to carry on his business he needs to convert the US dollars (USD) he will receive into Australian dollars (AUD). What will that US\$1 million be worth in AUD at that time? No one knows for sure, so James faces the risk that the amount of AUD into which he will be able to convert the USD will not be as much as it is now. James is able to lock in an exchange rate by trading now the USD he expects to receive for delivery of cotton to the USD buyer next June. He contracts to buy AUD, using several of the A\$100 000 contracts traded on the SFE. The conversion price is set in the contract and he settles his purchase next June by paying USD and receiving AUD. Thus, James has fixed the future exchange rate for the USD he expects to receive.

Speculators: take on risk in order to make profits

Speculators take on risk in order to make profits. We introduce the concept of speculation in chapter 11. The whole insurance industry is, by definition, speculation. Insurers assume other entities' risks in return for payments that they plan will more than cover the cost of restitution after damage or loss has occurred. You, too, would be a speculator if you bought one futures contract for the purchase of cattle (so long as you are not an abattoir, beef retailer or exporter) with the intention of later selling the cattle at a higher price. If you don't need 5000 kg dressed weight equivalent of beef for your normal business operations, by definition your purchase of the contract is a speculation. You assume risk by buying the cattle in order to make a profit when you sell later.

EXAMPLE 15.2

Speculating in the share market

Dolores Rodrigues is an analyst who day-trades in equities. She has noticed that the market often rises in the first hour after opening, then falls in the second hour. It often rises again about lunchtime and falls again in the afternoon. Dolores often buys shares late in the morning or afternoon with the intention to sell each parcel of shares within a few trading hours (either just after lunch or early the next morning). Dolores is a speculator. She buys shares, not to hold as investments, but in order to make profits on short-term price rises. She assumes the risk that the price of the shares, once purchased, will fall rather than rise. She does not have to assume this risk, but she does so for profit.

Arbitrageurs: enter markets and trade to make profits without risk by making complementary trades in two or more markets virtually instantaneously to exploit price differences

Arbitrageurs enter markets and trade to make profits without risk. How do they achieve this? They make complementary trades in two or more markets virtually instantaneously to exploit price differences. Arbitrage trades may be simple and involve only two markets, such as the physical and the financial. An example of this is selling a $1 million 90-day Australian bank-accepted bill futures contract and at the same time buying a bank bill for $1 million in the market at a price that is less than the futures contract price less the transaction and opportunity costs. The effect of these sorts of transactions is to ensure that the physical and financial markets keep in line with each other.

Much more complicated arbitrage transactions take place. Three-way, four-way or *n*-way transactions may be undertaken. The number of 'legs' in a transaction is limited only by the trader's ability to cope with information and track the deals made. An arbitrageur may put together, for example, complicated foreign exchange deals that combine several currencies and several interest rate futures. Arbitrage deals add volume and liquidity to markets and, as noted, serve to keep prices in separate but related markets in line. Any aberrant pricing in a market is quickly noticed by traders, and is traded away through these sorts of transactions. Thus, the only differences in prices between markets is likely, ultimately, to be the transaction costs necessary to complete deals.

EXAMPLE 15.3

Arbitraging in the forex market

George Li is an Australian foreign exchange arbitrageur. He mostly trades at night when overseas forex markets are open and busy. He specialises in three-way currency deals. Here is a typical deal. George sees the following quotes on his computer screen:

AUD1 = USD 0.73
AUD1 = ¥78
USD1 = ¥106.6 and rising

The first two quotes have been relatively stable in the time George has been watching the market in this trading session. There is then a flurry of activity as several dealers sell Japanese yen (¥) and buy USD. The USD/YEN quote goes to 109.1, so George immediately sells AUD, buys USD, uses the USD to buy YEN, then sells the YEN and buys AUD. All these trades happen within a few seconds, before the markets have time to move very much. George uses about A$500 000 to fund each of his plays, so that the small profit made on each single dollar is multiplied many times. That way he covers his transaction costs and makes a reasonable profit.

Let's look at the maths of his trade in terms of a single AUD. George sells AUD1 to buy USD 0.73; he then sells the USD 0.73 to buy ¥79.6 (that is, 109.1 × 0.73). Lastly, he sells the ¥79.6 to buy AUD1.0205. He is thus 2.05 Australian cents better off after the trades. After allowing for the trading costs, he has made about A$10 000 on the play.

lo3

Describe the role and operations of the futures markets.

Futures markets

A futures contract is a derivative security where the contract stipulates the transfer of a specified quantity of the underlying asset. Thus, the futures contract for cattle specifies a sale of 5000 kg of beef carcases of young cattle, the 90-day bank-accepted bill contract is for $1 million and the AUD contract is for AUD100 000. A firm wanting to buy (lock in the supply of) a product for which there are futures contracts traded would buy one (or several) futures contract(s) just as you would enter a contract to buy a house if you wanted (and could afford) it. In contrast, a firm wanting to lock in a price at which it could supply the product would sell futures contracts, just as the house owner would sign a contract to sell the house. The futures contract sets the price so that both buyer and seller know exactly the price they will pay and receive, respectively.

The SFE deals in three contracts for wool (of three different thicknesses), three contracts for electricity and one cattle contract. For interest rates, there are six Australian contracts: 30-day interbank cash rate, three- and 10-year bonds, three- and 10-year interest rate swaps and 90-day bank-accepted bills (BABs); and three NZ contracts. The 90-day BAB contract is an extremely successful and liquid contract with 60 000–80 000 contracts traded daily. See the ASX website at www.asx.com.au for further information on these contracts. In addition, the SFE trades put and call options on futures contracts. An **option** grants the right, but not the obligation, to undertake a trade by a given date at a given price. A **call option** gives the buyer the right, but not the obligation, to buy an asset by a given date at a given price. A **put option** gives the buyer the right, but not the obligation, to sell an asset by a given date at a given price. These are discussed in greater detail later in the chapter.

Option: grants the right but not the obligation to undertake a trade by a given date at a given price

Call option: gives the buyer the right but not the obligation to buy an asset by a given date at a given price

Put option: gives the buyer the right but not the obligation to sell an asset by a given date at a given price

There are futures exchanges in all the major countries in the world. The largest futures exchanges, however, are in the United States and Europe. The Chicago Board of Trade (www.cbot.com), the Chicago Mercantile Exchange (www.cme.com) and the New York Board of Trade (www.nybot.com) are large US exchanges. These exchanges trade an interesting range of commodities such as corn, oats, soybeans, soybean meal, soybean oil, wheat, canola, barley, cattle, pigs, pork bellies, cocoa, coffee, sugar, cotton and orange juice, as well as financial futures. The largest exchanges in Europe are the London International Financial Futures and Options Exchange (www.liffe.com) and Eurex (www.eurexchange.com). Other exchanges around the world trade metals, copper, gold, platinum and silver, as well as petroleum products such as crude oil, heating oil, natural gas and unleaded petrol. National exchanges also trade in commodities in which their countries have a particular interest; for example, Tokyo and Osaka Commodity Exchanges both trade rubber futures.

Forward contracting and futures market contracts achieve the same outcomes. The differences between the two lie in the specification of the contracts. While forward contracts between two parties are customised to each particular situation, futures contracts are standardised — standard quantities of the product, standard delivery dates, standard trading conditions and so on. Firms wanting to trade more than the standard amount in one contract are able to trade as many contracts as necessary to make up the desired amount.

The terminology of futures

Let's look now at some of the terminology of futures that you must understand before coming to grips with how the market works. The key terms in futures markets are:

- spot market
- contract unit or contract size
- contract or delivery months

- last trading day
- clearing house
- delivery
- cash settlement price
- minimum price movements
- margin
- mark-to-market
- position limits.

Spot market: a futures trading term to indicate the market where trading for immediate delivery occurs

The **spot market** is a futures trading term to indicate the market where trading for immediate delivery occurs. Many markets are effectively spot markets. If you go into your local town on a Sunday morning and buy something at your farmers' market, craft market or swap market, then you are buying for immediate delivery and are in effect trading on a spot market. Cattle sold at the local saleyards, cars sold by the local dealers and second-hand houses sold by real estate agents are all examples of trading in spot markets. (The fact that you might not get delivery of your car for seven days or your house for a month confuses the issue a bit. However, it still does not make these markets into futures markets, because delivery is arranged for as soon as practically possible and not at some set time in the future.) In contrast, the trading in futures markets is arranged for delivery or deal-completion at set times in the future.

Contract unit: the standard quantity of the product that is the subject of each contract; also called contract size

The **contract unit** or contract size is the standard quantity of the product that is the subject of each contract. We have already noted that, for cattle, the standard unit is 5000 kg dressed weight in carcase and for AUD the standard contract size is AUD100 000. Futures contracts are subject to immutable rules of 'survival of the fittest'. In other words, only the 'fit' or most suitable contracts are popular in the marketplace, develop the necessary trading volume and liquidity and therefore survive into the long term. Unsuitable contracts do not attract sufficient trade and are quickly killed off by the offering of futures exchange. Contracts may be unsuitable because the product specification is not what the market wants or because the unit is too high. (The contract unit may also be too small, but this is a nuisance rather than a lethal impediment.) Contracts for agricultural commodities tend to be formulated so that one contract sells for about $10 000 to $15 000. The SFE cattle contract, for example, has a total value of about $13 000 to $15 000. The cocoa contract on NYBOT is for 10 tonnes and settles for about US$10 000. Financial product contracts, on the other hand, tend to be formulated for much larger amounts $ $100 000 up to $1 million. The LIFFE long gilt (UK government bonds) contract is for £100 000. These are the sizes that suit these particular markets.

In addition to the contract unit, the contract must specify exactly what is being traded. This is necessary so that all parties are getting or supplying what they want or, with contracts where the product is not actually delivered, the settlement price can be accurately found. With financial products, there is no problem because there is no ambiguity. An AUD is an AUD, a yen is a yen, a $100 000 bank-accepted bill is a $100 000 bank bill. But what about cattle? We have all eaten a steak that we would rather not have started. Cattle are marketed at different ages and weights, and their meat will have different levels of tenderness, fat content and flavour. The cattle contract specifies young cattle as represented by the Eastern Young Cattle Indicator (EYCI). The EYCI is a seven-day weighted rolling average of prices for 24 local trade classes of vealers and yearlings from 25 saleyards in eastern Australia.[4] The Chicago Mercantile Exchange has a timber futures contract which specifies that the timber must be 8–20 feet (2.4–6 metres) long, 4 inch × 2 inch (100 mm × 50 mm) sawn lengths of a specified grade range of Englemann spruce, hem fir, lodgepole pine or spruce pine fir grown in specified areas of western United States or Canada.[5] Thus, the asset being traded is specified as closely as necessary to define it accurately.

Contract months or **delivery months:** months in which deliveries are made or contracts are settled

Each contract specifies the **contract months** or **delivery months** — the months in which deliveries are made or contracts are settled. A futures exchange could allow contracts to be traded with deliveries every month but, to make operations more efficient and to improve liquidity in each contract class, many exchanges restrict deliveries to four to six months each year. For example, AUD futures deliver in the months ending each quarter (March, June, and so on).

Last trading day: the last day on which trading occurs in a particular contract

The **last trading day** is just that, the last day on which trading occurs in a particular contract. Last trading days are normally specified as the business day 'following the third Wednesday' of the month or 'prior to the third Wednesday'. The purpose of this specification rather than 'the third Wednesday' is to cope with public holidays or any other unexpected interruption to trading. The actual time when trading in a contract is to cease is also stipulated.

Clearing house: facilitates settlement of contracts and transfer of ownership between the parties to transactions

A **clearing house** attached to a market or exchange facilitates settlement of contracts and transfer of ownership between the parties to transactions. In the case of futures exchanges, clearing houses provide guarantees of contract performance and collect margins to ensure performance is effected.

Deliverable contracts: contracts that may be settled by physical delivery

Some futures contracts are settled by physical delivery, if required, but most are not. Contracts that may be settled by physical delivery are called **deliverable contracts**. For example, the contracts on individual shares, such as those of the National Australia Bank, are settled by the physical delivery of the shares. Holders of buy contracts or 'bought positions' receive shares and holders of sell contracts or 'sold positions' transfer their shares. The 90-day BAB contract is deliverable, but only about 2% of all open positions are delivered.

Mandatory-settled contracts: settled by the clearing house at a cash settlement price which is calculated according to principles laid down for each contract

Cash settlement price: (for a futures contract) the current market value for the assets that are the subject of the contract

Non-deliverable or **mandatory-settled contracts**, such as the cattle, electricity and Treasury bonds are settled by means of a **cash settlement price**. The cash settlement price for the cattle contract is determined by the EYCI, as already discussed. This measure is an approximation of the price being received for young cattle of the required weight range at the time of settlement and thus is a proxy for actual sale and delivery of the cattle. The electricity and bonds contracts are settled by cash. See the ASX website at www.asx.com.au for further contract specifications.

In order to keep some control of market movements, trading exchanges stipulate how the prices of their contracts will be quoted and the minimum price changes that are acceptable. Thus, the cattle contract on the SFE is quoted with price movements of 0.25 cents per kilogram. This means that each 0.25 cents change in price equates to a $12.50 change per contract. The AUD contract is quoted in USD. (It could not be quoted in AUD, because prices of any 'item' cannot be quoted in the same 'currency'. In other words, you can't quote the price of one dozen oranges in oranges of the same quality and still be accepted as a rational being.) The minimum price fluctuation for the AUD contract is US$0.0001 or US$10 per contract. In the USA, oil futures price changes are quoted in cents per barrel or US$10 per contract.

It will be apparent to you by now that futures contracts may involve reasonably large amounts of money. What happens if a firm, which wants USD in two months' time (in June), sells an AUD contract for US$70 000 and then finds the value of AUD has risen and it could get US$74 000 for A$100 000 on the spot market? This firm would be better off by forgetting the futures contract and spending A$94 595 to buy US$70 000, instead of honouring its contract and spending A$100 000 to buy US$70 000. Why don't firms do this?

Margin: a deposit or bond that ensures completion of the futures contract

Initial margin: the first payment required for a futures contract

The answer lies in the margin requirements system. A **margin** is a deposit or bond that ensures completion of the futures contract. When two parties enter a futures contract, one buys (termed to be 'going long' on the asset) and the other sells or 'goes short' on the asset. Both buyers and sellers must lodge deposits with their brokers to pass on to the clearing house attached to each market. These initial deposits or **initial margins** are set by the clearing house according to the value of the contract, its liquidity and the likely volatility of its price based on previous experience. The margin for the SFE 10-year bond contract, in March 2007, was $2800, while the margin for the 90-day bank bill contract was $750.[6] Margins are also varied by the SFE clearing house from time to time to reflect changes in price volatility and liquidity experienced by each contract.

The purpose of the margin requirements is to ensure that holders of contracts have no incentive to renege or repudiate a contract. A margin is thus essentially a bond which ensures performance, just as a rental bond is supposed to ensure tenants pay their rents on time and don't indulge in property wrecking as a hobby. In addition to the initial margin requirements, there are also daily settlement margins that must be paid.

Marking-to-market: involves valuing each open futures contract daily according to the closing price in the futures market and adjusting margin accounts at the clearing house to show the consequent gains or losses

Clearing houses manage margin requirements and ensure contracts are successfully settled by a process known as **marking-to-market**. Marking-to-market involves valuing, daily, each open futures contract according to the end-of-day settlement price for the contract. If the futures market has risen during the day, holders of bought positions will have made gains on the day and their accounts at the clearing house will be adjusted to show those gains. If the market has fallen, holders of bought positions will have made losses on the day and their accounts at the clearing house will be adjusted to reflect those losses. Conversely, where the market has risen, holders of sold positions will have made losses on the day and, where the futures market has fallen, holders of sold positions will have made gains on the day. Trades are marked to market on every day each contract remains open, including on the day of purchase. The clearing house goes through this process to reduce its business risk by preventing traders from accumulating losses over a period greater than one business day. **Daily-settlement margin calls** are demands for extra funds to be placed in traders' margin accounts to cover any shortfalls in the value of open positions in comparison with current market prices at the end of any trading day. They are based on each day's trading results and are issued by 7.00 am the following morning, with payments expected by 10.30 am. Clearing houses also make **intra-day margin calls** during periods of extreme price volatility to further protect themselves from business risk. An intra-day margin call is a demand for extra funds to be placed in traders' margin accounts to cover any shortfalls in the value of open positions in comparison with current market prices during a trading day. An intra-day call at 12.30 pm, for example, is likely to be payable by 3.00 pm.

Daily-settlement margin calls: demands for extra funds to be placed in traders' margin accounts to cover any shortfalls in the value of open positions in comparison with current market prices at the end of any trading day

Intra-day margin calls: demands for extra funds to be placed in traders' margin accounts to cover any shortfalls in the value of open positions in comparison with current market prices during a trading day

In effect, margin calls mean that both parties to the futures contract realise gains and losses on the day they occur, rather than at the end of the contract. If this did not occur, a trader with a large loss position on the contract at settlement would have greater incentive to default. Thus, the margin system provides more than a convenient way of settling the contract payments.

Closed out: when the clearing house takes out an opposite contract to the open contract for the same goods for the same delivery terms so that the two contracts cancel each other in all details except price

If payments are not received on time, open positions are **closed out** or compulsorily cancelled by the clearing house before the balances in margin accounts can be reduced to zero or less, should the market continue to move against the traders' positions. Closing out an open buy contract by the clearing house, for example, involves taking out a sell contract for the same goods for the same delivery terms so that the two contracts cancel each other in all details except price. The margin account of the defaulting trader is decreased by the loss represented by the difference between the value of the open position and the value of the closing-out contract. As we will see later, a trader can close out an open position by taking an opposite contract. A company holding a futures contract to buy the underlying asset can, for example, avoid the obligation to settle at maturity by taking a contract to sell the same underlying asset with the same contract date as the original contract.

Position limits: maximum numbers of contracts that speculators may hold for any individual type of commodity or asset

Some futures exchanges impose **position limits** on speculators. Position limits are maximum numbers of contracts that speculators may hold for any individual type of commodity or asset. The reason for this limit is to prevent speculators from 'cornering the market' (tying up the majority of trade) in order to squeeze out excessive profits. Bona fide hedgers are usually not affected by such rules, as it is quite possible for a larger user or supplier to want to effect a large number of contracts. The CME, for example, limits speculators in timber to 1000 open contracts in any one contract month, with a further constraint of no more than 435 contracts in any expiring month.[7]

The anatomy of a futures trade

Now we understand the terminology of the market, let's look at a futures trade. Suppose Cashmere Coats (CC) needs nearly \$1 million for the purchase of extra fibre and material stock over the summer period to prepare for the following winter's sales. CC is worried that interest rates will rise significantly before it is able to arrange the physical loans in December. The firm decides it might use the futures market to lock in the price of about \$1 million by selling a 90-day bank bill (BAB) contract on the SFE, if the price is right. (CC sells the contract [not buys] to fix the supply of cash.) The contract month is December and settlement day is the second Friday in December. Suppose December BABs are trading at 95.05. What does this mean? Look at the contract specifications in the 'finance world' feature on page 575. BAB futures are quoted in terms of 100 minus the nominal annual yield. Thus, 95.05 means a nominal annual yield of 0.0495 or 4.95%. If CC believes a cost of 4.95% is cheaper funding than it will be able to access funds in the physical market, even after allowing for the transactions costs of the futures trade, it will go ahead with selling a futures contract. For example, if the best (lowest) price for which CC believes it could obtain funds from alternative sources were 6.5% and transaction costs of the futures trade were equal to 0.15%, then there is still a 1.4% cost reduction to be had in entering the futures contract.

EXAMPLE 15.4

Pricing an interest rate futures contract

The quoted price of the contract CC is interested in is 95.05. Translated, the price of the futures contract is \$987 942. How is this derived? The answer is 'the same way as the price of any discount security', as you found using equation 4.3 (see page 98).

$$P = \frac{FS}{(1+in)}$$

$$P = \frac{1000\,000}{\left(1+0.0495\times\dfrac{90}{365}\right)}$$

$$= \frac{1000\,000}{1.012\,205}$$

$$= \$987\,942$$

CC has two options to consider to complete its funding strategy. It can:

- reverse its futures position by entering a buy contract which will cancel its obligation and make a profit or loss in the futures market and then raise funds from the physical money markets at the current price ('spot' price), or
- issue a bill, have it accepted by a bank and deliver the resultant BAB to the buyer of the futures contract who will hand over cash in return.

Let's look at each of these situations in turn. CC has locked in a futures price of 95.05, which equates to receivable funding of \$987 942, a yield of 4.95%. During the time between selling the futures contract ('going short on BABs') and the December settlement date, the yields will vary on both the futures and physical money markets. However, as settlement day approaches, the yields in both markets will tend to converge. Let's assume interest rates have risen, and the yield in both markets on settlement day is 5.5%. The futures quote will thus be 94.50.

CC can reverse its position by buying one December futures contract prior to settlement day. The value of the contract will be $986 620. CC now no longer has a futures market obligation but it also has not raised any funds yet. The futures trading has yielded a profit of $1322. CC can then go back to the money market (physical market) and issue a bill or bills and receive funding of $986 620. Remember we established the yields on the day in both the futures and physical markets were the same — 5.5%. CC can then add its profit of $1322 from the futures market to its received funding to get a total of $987 942, which represents the yield of 4.95% which it originally locked in some months previously.

If interest rates had declined on the money market, the futures trading would have resulted in a loss. Then, when CC raised funds from the money market, those funds less the trading loss would equal the locked-in yield of 4.95%. Additionally, in reality there may be a slight difference in yields between the futures and physical markets. This slight difference will either increase or decrease the gain or marginally change the value of the trading loss. Eventually, the effect of this minor variation is that the locked-in rate will vary slightly.

The alternative option for CC is to deliver against the futures contract. (On average, delivery is effected on only 2% of the SFE BABs contracts, as was noted previously.) CC wants the funds so, at settlement day, CC will receive approximately $987 942 (less transaction costs which are minor) and hand over bank-accepted bills or, more likely in these days of more efficient electronic instruments, electronic bank-accepted bills (EBAs) or electronic certificates of deposit (ECDs) with the face value of $1 million. **EBAs** and **ECDs** are electronically recorded debt obligations that obviate the need for paper securities. In Australia, Austraclear Ltd runs an electronic debt security clearing system and members of that network are responsible for giving and taking delivery of the bills required in this transaction. Before settlement day, CC is obliged to arrange for the issue of appropriate securities with a face value of $1 million. The securities must have been either issued or accepted by banks approved by the SFE. Only the four major banks in Australia are approved banks.

Electronic bank-accepted bills (EBAs) and **electronic certificates of deposit (ECDs):** electronically recorded debt obligations that obviate the need for paper securities

In this second situation, CC has delivered the asset that was the subject of the futures contract. With some contracts, as we noted previously, physical delivery is not taken as it is too difficult to arrange. In these cases, open contracts may be settled through the payment of a cash settlement price that stems from prices currently being quoted in the physical market. Cash settlements will normally be more or less than the contract prices, and the parties thereby make the expected gains or suffer losses.

The futures trading just discussed referred to locking in the price of money in the short term. Firms wanting to lock in the price of longer term funds can do so by using a run of sequential 90-day BAB futures. The simultaneous sale of a run of futures contracts with sequential contract dates is called a **strip hedge**. BAB contracts are available for five years or 20 quarters ahead, so theoretically BABs could be used to fix interest rates for five years. However, it is unlikely that firms would extend a strip hedge to that extent when other means of hedging interest rates are available.

Strip hedge: the simultaneous sale of a run of given futures contracts with sequential contract dates that is undertaken to fix prices over a longer term than the term of each contract

Alternatively, firms wanting longer term funds could use three-year and 10-year bond futures. While non-financial institution firms are unlikely to have Commonwealth bonds on hand to supply when they enter a sold futures position, they can still use the futures market to fix their cost of funds. They do this by entering contracts as already discussed and then fulfilling their obligations — not by delivery, but by cash settlement which is the approved method of settling bond futures contracts.

The commodities catered for by SFE contracts cover beef, wool and electricity. Firms that supply these goods are able to fix their supply prices per unit if they so desire. Firms that use these goods (practically all firms, in the case of electricity) are similarly able to fix their input costs by use of the futures markets. With regard to small users of electricity, however, many — perhaps even most — regard the learning curve as too steep and too costly of time to use the markets in this way. Finally there is the special case of foreign exchange, forex. Many export contracts are written in terms of USD. The SFE trades a A$100 000 futures contract that is nominally settled in USD. However, the contract is actually settled on a cash settlement basis, and holders of trading positions settle by paying or receiving in AUD the losses or gains on each contract.

To summarise, futures trading allows firms that produce relevant goods to lock in sales prices through taking sold positions. Conversely, firms that buy relevant inputs are able to fix purchase costs by taking bought positions. If prices in the physical market move against these firms (that is, move down for sellers and move up for purchasers), their futures trading will bring gains. This is because they will be able to make or take delivery of the goods at advantageous prices when compared with the current physical market prices. Alternatively, they will be able to close their futures positions by taking out reverse trades. If hedgers reverse their futures trades rather than take or make delivery, they are able to use the futures gains to supplement the actual prices received or to reduce the prices paid in the physical market for the goods they supply or need in the normal course of their operations. The opposite occurs if prices in the physical market move up for sellers and down for buyers of the goods. In these cases, futures positions will show losses, but the hedgers will gain through higher sales prices or lower input costs, so the futures losses are compensated for by the better outcomes in the physical market.

In all these cases, hedgers have fixed their sales or input prices, sometimes with a futures market gain and sometimes with a futures market loss. (Remember, it is implicit that a futures market loss comes with a physical market gain.) Hedgers showing losses on their futures trades no doubt wish they could walk away from these contracts, and just take the gains they have made on the physical market. In this way, they could make additional gains, because they would have no futures losses to fund. However, they cannot repudiate their futures contracts because the margin requirements imposed by their brokers and the clearing house systems do not allow them to do so.

Where there is a need, someone will come up with the goods! And this is true in the case of futures trading losses. The product to deal with these situations is options on futures and these are discussed in the next section.

Options on futures

An option to do anything confers the right, but not the obligation, to do that thing. A financial option grants the right, but not the obligation, to undertake a trade by a given date at a given price. A call option gives the buyer the right, but not the obligation, to buy an asset by a given date at a given price. A put option gives the buyer the right, but not the obligation, to sell an asset by a given date at a given price. Options on futures contracts therefore give the buyers of those options the rights, but not the obligations, to buy or sell futures contracts.

How do these work? We saw in the previous section that sometimes futures contracts make losses. A trader who buys an option to buy or sell a contract has the right to take up that contract at any time and will do so if the physical market moves in the desired direction and gains are to be made on the futures contract. If, on the other hand, the physical market moves against the trader's position, then the option will not be exercised. The trader will not crystallise the futures market loss. Instead, the only loss will be the costs involved in purchasing the option.

EXAMPLE 15.5

Using options on futures

Eureka Gold Mines NL wants to manage some of the price risk associated with its gold sales. It decides to enter options on futures contracts which will give it the right (but not the obligation) to sell gold futures contracts. As Eureka is worried about a decline in the future gold price and is a producer of gold, it pays a premium of $1000 each to purchase June 350 gold put options. These options each give Eureka the right to sell one 100-ounce gold futures contract at $350 per ounce.

The price of gold does decline so that the June futures price is only $300 per ounce. Eureka may sell the option or exercise its right and gain $5000 (50 × 100) per contract less the $1000 premium, making a $4000 gain on each contract. If the market price had increased, contrary to Eureka's expectations, the firm would have allowed its options to lapse and thus would have incurred only the cost of the premium of $1000 per contract.

Option trades have two sides, just as any other commercial transaction, as we have seen. Hedgers may buy options that confer the right to buy or the right to sell. The party on the other side of an option trade is called the writer. The **writer of an option**, therefore, is the party that grants the right to the option buyer and the writer therefore must sell or buy the asset, if the option is exercised. Writers are not hedgers. Writers are taking on risk and are therefore, by definition, speculators. They make these deals to profit from the sale prices of the options, which are non-refundable when options are not exercised. Conversely, writers make losses when options are exercised. Generally, settlement takes place by means of payment of cash for the gains made rather than delivery of the underlying assets.

Writer of an option: the party that grants the right to the option buyer

EXAMPLE 15.6

Gains and losses on options on futures

In the previous example of Eureka Gold Mines, when Eureka exercised its option to sell, the writer of each contract was forced to buy the contract for the supply of gold at $350 an ounce when the current futures price was $300. Thus the writers all made $5000 losses per contract, less the $1000 premiums which they had received, making a $4000 loss per contract. If the market price had increased, in accordance with their expectations, the writers would have made gains of the $1000 premiums on each contract as Eureka would have allowed the options to lapse.

The SFE has traded options on futures contracts since 1985. Options are currently offered on the 90-day BAB, three-year Treasury bond and 10-year Treasury bond contracts. Additionally, there are intra-day or overnight options traded on Treasury bonds.

Reading the media reports

Financial managers thinking about using the futures market to hedge business risk are able to look in the financial print media or on the ASX website to gain a 'feel' for current market prices and movements. Table 15.3 shows the sort of information available.

Table 15.3 Futures market data — SFE 90-day bank bills

Expiry	Bid	Ask	Open	High	Low	Last trade	Time last trade	Volume
Dec 07	93.280	93.290	93.280	93.290	93.280	93.290	14:42	3699
Mar 08	93.160	93.170	93.160	93.180	93.160	93.170	12:37	2791
Jun 08	93.080	93.090	93.080	93.100	93.080	93.090	14:35	1500
Sep 08	93.040	93.060	93.050	93.050	93.040	93.050	14:36	713

Source: Sydney Futures Exchange.[8]

The 'expiry' column gives the month of expiry of each contract; there are thus five different contracts listed in this table. The 'bid' prices are the prices traders are bidding to buy contracts. Remember '95.26' means that the contract is priced to yield 4.74% on a nominal annual basis. Sellers are asking the prices in the 'ask' column. The market opened that morning with the price in the 'open' column and, since trading began at 8.30 am, trades with prices as high as that in the 'high' and as low as that in the 'low' columns have been made. The 'time last trade' column gives the time of the last trade before the time the report was printed. The 'volume' column gives the number of trades in each contract from 8.28 am to the time of the report. Note that this report was printed relatively early in the trading day and relatively few trades had been made. The BAB contract normally trades about 30 000 times each day. Note also that the 'sooner to expiry' contracts trade more heavily than later contracts.

FINANCE WORLD

90-day BAB futures

This is the specification for the SFE's 90-day BAB futures contract. This contract is one of the top 10 traded futures contracts in the world, and currently trades about $80 billion daily.

90 Day Bank-Accepted Bills Futures

Contract unit:	A$1 000 000 face value 90-Day Bank Accepted Bills of Exchange or EBAs.[1]
Contract months:	March/June/September/December up to 20 quarter months or five years ahead.
Commodity code:	IR
Listing date:	17/10/1979
Minimum price movement:	One hundred minus annual percentage yield quoted to two decimal places. (The minimum fluctuation of 0.01% equals approximately $24 per contract, varying with the level of interest rates.)
Last trading day:	12.00 noon on the business day immediately prior to settlement day.[2]
Settlement day:	The second Friday of the delivery month.
Trading hours:	5.08 pm – 7.00 am and 8.28 am – 4.30 pm[2] (during US daylight saving time)[3]
	5.08 pm – 7.30 am and 8.28 am – 4.30 pm[2] (during US non daylight saving time)[3]

Settlement method:	Ten bank accepted bills or EBAs or ten bank negotiable certificates of deposit (NCDs) or ECDs each of face value A$100 000, or two bank accepted bills or EBAs or bank negotiable certificates of deposit or ECDs each of face value A$500 000 or one bank accepted bill or EBA or bank negotiable certificate of deposit or ECD of face value A$1 000 000 maturing 85–95 days from settlement day.

1 EBAs and ECDs are electronically recorded debt obligations as defined within the definition of 'Dematerialised Security' in the Operating Manual of Austraclear Limited.

2 Unless otherwise indicated, all times are Sydney times.

3 US daylight saving begins first Sunday in April and ends last Sunday in October.

Source: Sydney Futures Exchange.[9]

FINANCE WORKSHOP 15.1

Fifi Fashions (FF) imports high-quality women's clothing from Italy into Australia. FF needs about $1 000 000 in 2 months' time (in December) to pay for winter stock. The manager of FF is sure that interest rates will start to rise soon and wants to lock in the price of 90-day funds. She sells a December 90-day BAB futures contract quoted at 93.90. Instead of taking delivery, she reverses her position at 94.50. She then issues BABs for $1 000 000 and raises funds in the money market at a yield of 5.6%.

(a) What is her gain or loss on the futures trading?

(b) What is her eventual cost of funding?

lo4

Describe the roles and operations of FRAs.

Forward rate agreement (FRA): a deal between two parties that fixes an interest rate (or foreign exchange rate) for a period which begins some time in the future

Trade date: the date on which the FRA contract is signed

Settlement date: the date FRA settlement takes place at the start of the contract period

Maturity date: the date at the end of the FRA contract period

The FRA market

A **forward rate agreement** or **FRA** is a deal between two parties that fixes an interest rate for a period which begins some time in the future. Thus, firms can reduce their borrowing cost risk by coming to an agreement about the rate that will prevail at some future date. FRAs have been around for about 20 years, and have grown strongly in importance over the last few years. In 2005–06, the annual turnover in FRAs was reported by the Australian Financial Markets Association (AFMA) as more than $3100 billion, an increase of 20% over the trading the year before.[10] Clearing houses are not involved with FRAs because the contracts are not traded on an open market. They are party-to-party agreements.

With FRAs, there is no commitment to lend or borrow the principal amount. They are therefore effectively a non-deliverable discount security. Thus, they are like many futures contracts where delivery does not take place, but settlement is made in cash. FRAs are, however, unlike futures contracts in that the contract specifications are not standardised. They are customised according to the needs of both parties. Additionally, there are no margin requirements so there is a risk of non-execution. Financial institutions act as facilitators in most cases.

FRAs are signed on the **trade date** and settled on the **settlement date**, which is the start of the contract period. The date at the end of the contract period is the **maturity date**. FRAs are normally signed for three-month or six-month contract periods, but may be executed for periods up to two years ahead. FRAs are often described in terms of the time from trade to settlement and the contract period. Thus, an agreement reached four months before a three-month contract period is described as a 4:7 FRA.

FRAs are settled by the payment of the difference in interest payable on a notional principal at the agreed rate and at the current market rate. Suppose a 3:6 FRA was signed at 5.2% and at settlement the market in three-month BABs had risen to 5.4%. The notional principal is $10 million. The settlement amount is the difference between the price of a discount security for $10 million at 5.2% yield and a similar security at 5.4% yield. Assuming there are 90 days in the relevant quarter, the price of the 5.2% bill is $9 873 404.02 and the price of the 5.4% bill is $9 868 598.92. The difference between these two amounts is $4805.10.

If the market has risen (as in this case), the seller must pay the buyer of the FRA who is the potential borrower. Effectively, the potential borrower has been shielded from the rise in interest rates on the market. The borrower may now go to the market and borrow at the current rates, but the borrower has the $4805 compensation to cover the extra interest payable now rates have risen. The borrower is thus accessing funds at the rate agreed to in the FRA and has reduced interest rate risk. The converse occurs when interest rates fall on the market. The borrower will be able to access cheaper funds in the market than previously but, because the FRA has been entered into, the borrower will have to compensate the other party to the FRA, which will effectively increase the price of the funds.

Forward rate agreements are also contracted for foreign exchange. Exporters and importers often need to manage foreign exchange price risk. They can deal with financial institutions that offer forward foreign exchange contracts. Buying or selling forex forward manages the risk associated with trading in goods and services in foreign currencies.

FINANCE WORKSHOP 15.2

Barnacle Boats needs about $1 million in 60 days' time to pay a contracted deposit on a new catamaran that is being built for them. Barnacle needs the funds for 90 days, until the revenue from the sale of other boats is received. Barnacle's bank quotes 6.25% for a 2:5 FRA and agrees also to provide the funds at market price when supplied. At settlement, the interest rate in the market has fallen to 6%. What is the settlement figure for Barnacle?

lo5

Describe the roles and operations of swaps markets.

The swaps markets

In the last section, we dealt with forward contracting by means of the formal mechanism of the futures market. **Swaps** are just an extension of the idea of a forward contract. The chief difference is that several payments in the future are involved rather than just one transaction.

Swap: the exchange of two sets of cash flows that, although different in character, have the same expected present value

The swaps market has grown dramatically over the last few years. In 1993–94, for example, the swaps market aggregated to about $270 billion in annual turnover. In the five years to 1998–99, that turnover had doubled to $577 billion. Turnover then almost doubled annually and reached more than $2600 billion in 2001–02 and $3768 billion in 2002–03. In 2005–06, turnover was $4633 billion.[11]

The swaps markets are normally concerned with two sources of business risk — interest rates and foreign currencies. Just as in the case with forward contracts, firms enter swaps agreements in order to manage the risk they face. We will deal firstly with interest rate swaps and then with currency swaps.

Interest rate swaps

Interest rate swaps are used by borrowers to convert obligations to pay interest on a fixed rate basis to obligations to pay on a floating rate basis, or conversely to convert floating rate obligations to fixed rate commitments. Australian firms generally source their debt funding from the domestic financial markets, where the debt instruments predominantly carry variable or floating rate interest obligations. However, fixed rate loans are available from overseas capital markets and, to a lesser extent, from domestic sources. Firms use the swaps markets to vary their current obligations or to vary the mix of their current obligations.

Woolworths' *2005 financial report to shareholders* gives a fine example of this mechanism in operation.[12]

> Woolworths Ltd is party to financial instruments with off-balance sheet risk in order to hedge exposure to fluctuations in interest and foreign exchange rates. The interest rate instruments that may be used include swaps and forward rate agreements... Under the swap agreements the consolidated entity will receive interest at variable rates and pay interest at fixed rates. The contracts are used to protect against rising interest rates on the variable interest component of the underlying debt. The contracts are settled on a net basis...

The most common form of interest rate swap is just like that undertaken by Woolworths — fixed for floating or floating for fixed. This is also known as a 'plain vanilla' swap or, in other words, an ordinary kind with no great sophistication. Of all swaps transactions, fixed rate to floating rate interest swaps have the highest turnover, and generally account for 70–80% of all swap transactions. Other types of swaps are possible, but an essential feature is that the interest rates must be set on different bases. The floating rate used in Australian swaps is the bank bill swap rate (BBSW). This rate is widely reported, and can be found in the financial press and on financial institutions' websites. The BBSW is an average of the bid and offer BAB rates provided by eight of Australia's largest banks; the BBSW is reset daily.

Swaps are undertaken because the two principals who are party to each agreement can do so to their mutual advantage, as a result of lenders having differing perceptions of the risk they are facing in lending to that of the principals. Swaps exploit differences in interest rates in different markets and also allow firms to take advantage of differences in risk margins that financial institutions impose on them.

The terminology of swaps

As with FRAs, swaps do not have an organised trading market. There are no set swaps contracts. The parties to swaps contracts negotiate the conditions that each requires. Trades are made over the counter (OTC) and the large financial institutions are major participants in the market. There are, however, a number of conventions or characteristics that most swaps deals include.

1. There is no exchange of principal amount. The parties have contracted for loans with lenders outside the swaps agreement and the obligations to these lenders remain unchanged. Because the principal is not part of the deal, it is called a **notional amount of a swap**.
2. Swaps normally deal with very large notional amounts — a minimum of $10 million and frequently as much as $50 million or $100 million.
3. Swaps are normally concerned with the relatively short or medium term. The most frequent term for swaps is less than one year and more than half are for less than two years.
4. Swap obligations are settled when one party pays to the other the net monetary effect of the swap. This settlement process happens relatively frequently and, in Australia, this is

Notional amount of a swap: the hypothetical principal amount on which the payment of the swap obligations is based

Swaps reset period: the period for which each determination of the value of BBSW is valid

mostly quarterly for shorter term swaps and half-yearly for longer term swaps. This period is called the **swaps reset period**.

5. At the start of each reset period, the parties agree to the value of BBSW that will apply for the next period. The payment, however, is made at the end of the period, even though the amount is known at the start of the period. Swaps can be thought of as a series of discrete periodical payments that are made between two parties. The size of each payment depends on how market interest rates change.

The mechanics of an interest rate swap

In a swap transaction, the two principals agree to swap their interest rate obligations. Suppose there are two companies, Alfio Algoods (AA) and Beta Bathtubs (BB). AA has the better credit rating and has contracted for a $1 million loan at 7% fixed for one year. We discuss credit ratings in chapters 11 and 12. AA is also aware it could have contracted for the loan at BBSW + 0.2%. BB has also investigated the debt markets and has contracted for a $1 million loan at BBSW + 1.4%. BB is aware it could have arranged for a fixed rate loan at 9%. AA has subsequently decided it would rather have floating rate obligations and BB has decided it would rather have fixed. Can these two companies each improve their positions? Yes, they can, but they have to find each other and the circumstances have to be favourable.

First, the firms want to change their interest rate obligations. Second, the rates arranged and quoted by the market are different. AA has an absolute advantage over BB as it has the better credit rating. AA can get fixed rate funds at 2% cheaper than BB and it could have arranged for floating rate funds at 1.2% cheaper than BB. There is no rational reason for this difference in the risk premium charged between the two markets, and it is this difference in risk perception by the market that is the basis for the gains that each firm can make.

The difference between the fixed rate differential (2%) and the floating rate differential (1.2%) is 0.8%. This margin may be shared between AA and BB in any ratio they like, but let's suppose they share it equally. In such a case, AA and BB will have the use of the funds 0.4% more cheaply than otherwise. How does this occur?

AA has arranged for its loan and is paying 7% to its lender. BB similarly is paying BBSW + 1.4% to its lender. If AA pays BB exactly the floating rate, BBSW, it will be exposed to floating rates, just as it desires. It will thus be paying out BBSW + 7% in total, but it must receive a payment from BB.

BB pays BBSW + 1.4% to its lender and receives BBSW from AA. BB's net payment so far is 1.4%. BB wants to pay fixed, but it can save only 0.4% off the fixed rate it has been quoted. This is 9%, so with the saving the fixed payment will be 8.6%. BB must thus pay another 7.2% (that is, 8.6 – 1.4) to AA. Does this work out for AA? Remember, we left AA above paying out BBSW + 7%. AA will receive 7.2% from BB, so the net interest payment is BBSW – 0.2%, which is a 0.4% saving over BBSW + 0.2%, the best it could find in the market.

Table 15.4 shows how both parties are better off by 0.4% than they were before the swap.

Table 15.4 An interest rate swap

	Firm AA	Firm BB
Fixed	7%	9%
Floating	BBSW + 0.2%	BBSW + 1.4%
Pays to lender	(–) 7%	(–) BBSW + 1.4%
Pays to other	(–) BBSW	(–) 7.2%
Receives from other	(+) 7.2%	BBSW
Net interest paid	BBSW – 0.2%	8.6%

The example continues in table 15.5, which shows the payments AA and BB make to their lenders and between themselves for four reset periods. BBSW is assumed for illustrative purposes to vary much more rapidly than it normally does. The notional amount is \$40 million and the cash flows in the table are in thousands of dollars. The first line data are derived as follows. AA pays 7% to its lender, and this amount is \$700 000 per quarter for a notional amount of \$40 million. AA receives 7.2% from BB and pays 5% (BBSW) to BB, making a net receipt of 2.2% from BB ($0.022 \times 40\,000\,000 \times 0.25 = 220\ 000$). The net cost to AA of funding is thus \$480 000 or 4.8%. Similarly, BB pays BBSW + 1.4% (6.4%) to its lender (\$640 000), pays \$220 000 to AA and thus pays \$860 000 in total for \$40 million for this quarter.

Table 15.5 Loan and swap net cash flows, quarterly (\$'000)

		Firm AA			Firm BB		
Period	**BBSW (%)**	**Pays to lender**	**Swap**	**Net cost**	**Pays to lender**	**Swap**	**Net cost**
1	5	−700	+220	480	−640	−220	860
2	6	−700	+120	580	−740	−120	860
3	7	−700	+20	680	−840	−20	860
4	8	−700	−80	780	−940	+80	860

Is this table correct? How can we check? The net cost of funds for AA we calculated as BBSW − 0.2%. Is that so in the table? Yes, it is, so the calculations must be correct. The net cost of funds for BB we calculated as 8.6% pa. Is that also so? Yes, \$860 000 per quarter equals \$3.44 million pa and equates to 8.6% of \$40 million.

To summarise, there are six steps in working out an interest rate swap:

1. Calculate the difference in fixed rates.
2. Calculate the difference in floating rates.
3. Calculate the net difference between the two rates. (If there is a net difference, a swap will advantage both parties.)
4. Ascertain how the net benefit will be split between the two parties.
5. Calculate the final outcome or net cost of borrowing for both parties.
6. Calculate the swaps necessary between the two parties. This is normally the subject of negotiation between the swap parties. (If you are constructing the swap, it is useful to start with BBSW as one side of the swap and then calculate the necessary fixed rate payment to make the deal work.)

Once the mechanics of the swap are worked out the actual cash flows, as in table 15.6, may be calculated.

Currency swaps

Currency swaps involve the exchange of loan obligations in one currency for the payments on loans made in another currency. The simplest version of a currency swap involves the exchange of both principal and fixed interest payments. However, more complicated swaps might involve fixed and floating interest rate swapping as well, in order to change the exposure to interest rate movements. One Australian company, for example, may have borrowed in USD or euro, then decided to hedge the foreign currency exposure risk by swapping obligations with another company that had borrowed in AUD but wanted USD or euro obligations. Woolworths again provides us with a real example.[13]

> To hedge the US dollar denominated Senior Notes ... the consolidated entity entered into cross currency swap agreements to fully hedge the US dollar value of the notes issued. The effect of the cross currency swaps is to offset all of the US dollar exposure on both interest and principal payments associated with the notes... The exposure to the consolidated entity subsequent to the cross-currency swap agreements is in Australian dollars...

Currency swaps are undertaken for two principal reasons: to lower the final cost of funds and to hedge foreign exchange risk. Borrowing funds from international sources has long been an Australian business practice, because of the ready availability of funds from overseas capital markets. In the early years of this decade, interest rates in the United States were 3–4% lower than in Australia and interest rates in Japan were practically zero. Borrowing cheap funds is attractive, but involves high risk when the funds are sourced overseas. The danger for Australian firms borrowing overseas is that the value of AUD will fall and thus disadvantage the borrowers at the times when interest payments are due, and especially when the principal must be repaid. A cheap source of funding becomes rather more expensive if the AUD falls in value by 25%; immediately $1.33 million must be repaid for every $1 million borrowed. Currency swaps provide certainty about the size of the cash flows that are exchanged under the swap agreement.

Currency swaps are used in at least three situations:

- by firms that operate predominantly in their domestic markets and can borrow in their home countries more cheaply than elsewhere but need foreign currency funds; for example, Australian firms will swap their AUD loan payments for foreign currency cash flows
- by firms which can borrow more cheaply internationally (or do not wish to issue more securities onto local markets); for example, Australian firms will swap their foreign loan payments for AUD cash flows
- by firms which operate in both domestic and overseas markets and have foreign cash flows that may be used to service debt internationally, but which may borrow more cheaply in their home countries. In these situations, there is no need to hedge exchange rate risk, because the operating cash flows of the firms are used to repay the debt, so they are not exposed to foreign exchange risk in servicing the loans.

Financial institutions often act as facilitators of currency swaps. Their services cut the search costs of firms looking for currency exchange partners. Indeed many financial institutions nowadays offer swaps with themselves as principals, initially through taking all offered business and then laying off the risk through subsequent deals which operate in the opposite direction. In other words, they warehouse deals until they can be sold to a complementary party. In return for their services, the financial institutions charge fees that reduce slightly the magnitude of the savings available to the parties to the deals.

The mechanics of a currency swap

Suppose STV, a large Australian multinational company with operations in the United States, found it could borrow the funds it needed in Australia at 8.0% and it could also borrow the equivalent funds in the United States for 6.0%. Another firm, NYK, also needs funds and it can borrow in the United States for 4.0% and in Australia for 7.5%. NYK obviously has a better credit rating than STV, because it can borrow at better rates in both markets. STV, on the other hand, has a comparative advantage in AUD, as its funding cost is only 50 basis points higher than NYK's whereas, in USD, STV's funding cost is a full 2.0% (200 basis points) higher (see table 15.6). STV would like to borrow in USD and use its USD cash flow to fund the regular interest payments, but the comparative advantage in interest rates makes it worthwhile for STV to borrow in AUD and enter a swap. NYK, on the other hand, can borrow more cheaply in USD but wants an AUD loan.

Table 15.6 Data for a currency swap

Debt market	Firm STV	Firm NYK	Differences
Fixed-rate AUD	8.0%	7.5%	0.5%
Fixed-rate USD	6.0%	4.0%	2.0%
		Difference	1.5%

Just as with interest rate swaps, the first steps are to calculate the differences in cost in each market and the net difference in interest cost. These values are 0.5%, 2% and 1.5%, respectively. Each party borrows the funds in the currency where it has comparative advantage, and delivers the funds to the other party. The principal borrowed in each currency will not be the same 'number', unless the exchange rate is at parity, but will be equivalent in value. Thus, the current exchange rate determines the sums in each currency that are equivalent in value. The exchange rate used is normally the market rate on the day. That exchange rate is normally fixed by the parties by means of currency derivatives, so that the same rate applies to all further transactions associated with the swap. Let's assume the rate is AUD: USD 0.6000. Thus, A$50 million equals US$30 million, and STV borrows A$50 million that it transmits to NYK. NYK in turn borrows US$30 million and transmits that to STV.

At this time, the two parties agree how the interest rate differential is to be split between them. Suppose NYK is the stronger firm and won't enter the deal unless it gets a 1% (100 basis points) reduction on its AUD loan. STV is then left to benefit from the remaining 0.5% reduction. STV agrees to pay NYK 4.0% on the USD loan and NYK agrees to pay 6.5% on the AUD loan. Through the deal, each party eventually pays the best rate it could get from the market in the other currency less the savings that have been agreed between them. Table 15.7 shows the payments.

Table 15.7 Payments between parties to the swap

Payments	Firm STV	Firm NYK
To home lender	−8%AUD	−4.0%USD
To other party	−4%USD	−6.5%AUD
From other party	+6.5%AUD	+4%USD
Net interest paid	4%USD + 1.5%AUD	6.5%AUD

From the table, it is clear that the US firm (NYK) has benefited in that its USD interest commitments are covered and its AUD interest commitment is limited to 6.5%, a full 100 basis points below the best it could arrange in the market. For STV, the situation is a little more complex. It is left with its AUD interest payments not fully covered to the extent of 1.5% by the payment by the US firm but, by paying 4% on its US notional loan, it is 1.5% better off. The question now is whether the 1.5% owing on the AUD loan has the same value as the 1.5% gained on the USD loan. The answer is — yes, it has. Check the calculations yourself. The AUD loan is $50 million and 1.5% of that amount is A$750 000. Convert that amount to USD at the assumed 0.6000 exchange rate to get US$450 000. The USD loan is $30 million and 1.5% of that amount is $450 000. So 1.5% on the AUD loan has the same value as 1.5% on the USD loan, and firm STV pays effectively 5.5% of its USD loan, 50 basis points less than the best it can get on the market.

This solution is just one of the possible outcomes where the two parties share the benefits. Under this solution, STV still carries some foreign exchange risk. In practice, financial institutions arrange currency swaps for client firms and cover the exchange-rate risk in return for the payment of fees. The fees paid use up some of the benefits of the swap, but still leave net benefits for the principal parties to the deal. For example, in the above swap, the deal facilitator might charge 0.5% and leave the parties the 1% benefit to share among themselves.

At the time of each interest payment, STV pays interest to NYK in USD, and NYK pays STV in AUD. If interest were paid quarterly, STV would pay US$300 000, and NYK would pay A$812 500. Additionally, at the conclusion of the swap and maturity of the original loans, the parties re-exchange principals and repay their lenders. STV repays the USD to NYK and NYK repays the AUD to STV. The firms face no exchange rate risk, because all the transactions are conducted at the exchange rate which prevailed at the commencement of the swap and which has been fixed by entering appropriate risk management deals.

FINANCE WORKSHOP 15.3

1. Calculate the payments made and received for the interest rate swap illustrated in table 15.5 for periods 2–4.
2. Two companies, Columbine Traders (CT) and Porphyry and Granite (PG) need to borrow $1 million each. CT has the better credit rating and has contracted for a $1 million loan at 7% fixed for one year. It also is aware it could have contracted for the loan at BBSW + 0.2%. PG has also investigated the debt markets and has contracted for a $1 million loan at BBSW + 0.6%. PG is aware it could have arranged for a fixed rate loan at 8%. CT has subsequently decided it would rather have floating rate obligations and PG has decided it would rather have fixed. Can these two companies each improve their positions? Show how, numerically, if they share the gain equally.

lo6

Describe how companies manage risk with options.

Company-issued options

Company-issued options are options to buy shares in the company at a future date at a stipulated price. As noted in chapter 12, companies issue options to reward and motivate employees, as additional benefits to sweeten debt and equity issues and to put in place a program of future funds raising.

How does issuing options assist with company risk management? Regarding the issue of options to employees, options may be used as 'golden handcuffs' which help to keep valuable senior employees. Additionally, many companies run employee share plans that allow employees to take up shares in the company at a discount to market price. The aim of employee shares and options plans is to try to ensure that good employees do not leave and that employees' personal interests and the interest of the company are aligned. Normally, the option conditions are structured so that benefits do not flow to the employees if they leave the employ of the firm. Thus, firms try to facilitate stability in their workforces, retain the benefits of costly training and capitalise on developed knowledge of corporate culture among their employees. Employee satisfaction and stability reduces business risk for firms.

Options may be used as sweeteners to make it easier for firms to raise funds. Strictly speaking, one would expect that options attached to either equity or debt issues would have an effect on the original issues prices. In practice, however, the price effect may be negligible. Further, it is only when the price effect is negligible that the attachment of an option could be regarded as a sweetener. For example, suppose the 'correct' price of an equity issue is $2. The issuing firm decides to add an options sweetener, but increases the price of one share to $2.30. Effectively, the firm is forcing investors to pay $0.30 for an option that they may not want. This behaviour is likely to decrease the popularity of the issue, not increase it. However, if investors perceive the correct price of one share to be $2 and they are issued with one share plus one option, then the options may be realistically regarded as a sweetener. The same argument can be run with debt issues and the 'correct' interest rate.

Finally, a firm might use options to put in place a program of future funds raising. This is not likely to be of major significance, but there may well be a reduction in compliance and transactions costs with this method. Suppose a firm raises new capital by means of shares issued under a prospectus with all the attendant compliance and transactions costs. It might attach options that are exercisable by a given future date at a given price. If the market price of the company's shares does not reach the exercise price, the options will lapse, as it would cost investors more for each share issued under the options plan than it would to buy shares directly on the market. If, however, the market price exceeds the options exercise price, most of the options will be exercised and the company will raise additional revenue without being forced to go back to the market formally to do so. (Normally, not all the options will be exercised in this situation, because some investors do not keep abreast with market movements and may not realise the options are worth exercising. Others may miss the closing date for investment or may find they have better investment alternatives for their funds.)

From the point of view of the firm, the issue of options in this situation puts in place the ability to raise future funds as part of the initial capital raising. Does it reduce risk? Yes, it does in the sense that the firm does not have to set a price for the new shares. We discuss the complexities of pricing IPOs in chapter 12. Even though the option issuing company's share price is observable on the market, a new share issue requires an offer price. Setting the offer price could involve forecasting the market price a month or so ahead. Further, issuing options means that the firm does not run the risk of poor publicity in the event of an undersubscribed issue (if the issue is undersubscribed through the lapse of some options, the firm can merely report the fact in the next annual report in a small note to the accounts).

The cost of an options plan is another consideration that we will not pursue in full. Suffice to say, if the market price of the firm's shares is $5 and it has issued a large quantity of options exercisable at $2, there is a large opportunity cost attached to the exercise. The firm may have reduced capital raising risk, but it has done so at a high cost to the existing shareholders who may not have received the options.

Rules for hedgers using derivatives

lo7

Discuss the principles that should govern hedging operations.

The most important rule for firms using the derivatives markets to manage risk is to ensure that their trading is always carried out in a kind and magnitude consistent with hedging, not speculating. Remember, hedgers use the underlying assets in the course of their normal businesses and they use derivatives to reduce the risk of pricing falling for produced output, or of prices increasing for inputs including funding (and exchange rates moving adversely if forex transactions are part of normal business operations). Speculation, on the other hand, is involved if a firm takes on risk in the quest of profits or makes bigger deals than are necessary to hedge normal business operations.

This general principle implies that:

- trading or risk limits should be set by each company's board
- individual traders should have personal risk limits set and rigorously monitored
- sensitivity analyses should be carried out to identify the worst-case situations
- duties must be separated so there are different people performing the various duties associated with trading
- relevant senior managers must fully understand the trading systems
- the trading section must not be made a profit centre
- accounting for trades must be conservative.

The boards of firms which decide to use derivatives to hedge risk must make it very clear to employees that company policy is only to reduce the risk the firm already faces and that any excursions to the realm of speculation will be punishable by dismissal. Thus, firms using futures at any time take sold or bought positions only for amounts that are commensurate with the output or input requirements of the firm. For example, a beef producer such as AA Company would take sold positions for the number of contracts necessary to cover their planned turnoff of fat stock in the relevant period. Additionally, individual employees who manage these trades must be given trading limits that they must not exceed.

Because many derivative products are relatively new, it is possible that not all the senior management understand derivative products and how they operate to reduce risk. The board must appoint at least one senior manager who fully understands the trading systems and is responsible for oversight of the firm's activities. This person or a nominee should conduct sensitivity analyses to ensure the firm's activities are correctly focused on the areas of greatest risk. Moreover, the senior manager must ensure that the tasks associated with trading are split so that different people undertake various parts of each trade. This means that trading operations, risk assessment and recording of trades are carried out by different people. The danger in having one person attend to all these tasks is that there are no checks for suitability attendant with each trade.

Finally, accounting for trades must be conservative, so that profits and losses are properly recognised, and on no account should the trading section be made a profit centre. By making hedge trading a profit centre, the firm is immediately sending out an inappropriate and inconsistent message. The rules say, on one hand, that the firm is merely reducing risk through its trading, but the profit centre message is that the firm is out to make profits through speculation. See the following 'corporate financial governance' feature for a discussion of governance, risk management and compliance.

CORPORATE FINANCIAL GOVERNANCE

Managing derivatives trading

The following extracts are from an article reporting a roundtable discussion involving several business leaders. The speaker is Gautam Banerjee, executive chairman, Pricewaterhouse-Coopers.

> Derivatives trading is becoming an essential tool for companies to manage their risks and to turn volatile markets to their advantage. But, if not properly managed, using derivatives can sometimes bring down an entire company,
>
> How can businesses reap the most benefits from derivatives trading — and is corporate governance the foundation of it all?

...

Derivatives are not dangerous; the misuse of derivatives is. A two-way relationship exists in derivatives trading: you can be a buyer or a seller of risk — a salient factor that many overlook. Be it an individual or an organisation that is involved in derivatives trading, it is critical that the incumbent assess his own risk appetite, and carefully. The incumbent needs to first decide the amount of risk to take on. Next, distinguish the risks that present opportunities from those that present undesirable threats. And finally, decide if more of the profitable risks should be taken on, while eliminating those risks which pose a threat.

The understanding of the transfer of risk from the original owner to the new owner is critical. Typically, problems emerge when there is inappropriate taking-on of risks, where risks are not properly controlled, or where risks are not reported to management in a timely fashion — or at all. To tackle volatility effectively, trading companies should simply get their corporate governance right. And that essentially is all about understanding the different types of risks they are exposed to, and formulating a plan to continually manage, measure and report the risks to management.

...

Good risk management starts with governance. If you get governance right, everything else should fall nicely into place. The root cause of most — if not all — catastrophic losses in derivatives trading is poor governance. Many examples of the breakdown of governance in the past can attest to this. For instance, we have witnessed the same derivative disasters in National Australia Bank, Allied Irish Banks, Sumitomo Corp and Barings Bank. The PricewaterhouseCoopers' eighth annual global CEO survey 2005 attests that many CEOs recognise the growing importance of governance, risk management and compliance (GRC), particularly of the value and competitive advantage GRC provides for their organisations.

From the survey, despite acknowledging that implementing GRC is a significant investment, and not an easy task, the CEOs recognise the tangible benefits of GRC. CEOs in GRC-effective organisations confirm that GRC reduces legal liabilities, enhances reputation and brand, and significantly improves financial performance, operational excellence, and product/service excellence.

GRC-effective organisations possess the following eight elements: corporate/organisational codes of conduct; policies and procedures; compliance and ethics training; demonstrating expected behaviour; ongoing process improvement; real-time reporting; monitoring/measuring GRC performance; as well as accurate, timely, complete, and consistent information.[14]

Recent disasters among those who ignored the rules

In the last decade or so, there have been some spectacular financial disasters among firms that ignored some or many of the rules. Often the crashes have been among firms that entered the derivatives markets merely to hedge but ended up, through failure of their systems, taking on more risk. In other cases, especially among financial institutions, the failures were due to speculation based on views of 'superior' knowledge.

Futures trading

Metallgesellschaft AG (MG) is a German conglomerate that deals largely in metal and energy products. MG ventured into the derivatives markets in 1991 and, by December 1993, was forced to admit it had lost about US$1.5 billion. MG built up over time an enormous trading position, reported to be about equal to three days' normal trading in the whole market. Eventually the firm was not able to support the funding necessary to maintain its positions and the losses were realised. The board pleaded ignorance of their position.

In 1995, Sumitomo Bank in Japan lost US$1.8 billion when a single unauthorised trader decided to corner the copper market with futures and immediate trades coupled with options deals. China Aviation Oil lost US$550 million in 2004 after speculative trading in the oil futures market. These losses were completely overshadowed in 2006 when a US-based hedge fund, Amaranth Advisors, lost $6 billion in trading natural-gas futures.

Forex trading

The Queensland Graingrowers Association in the early 1980s was a thriving organisation representing the interests of grain growers in the state. It sold grains on behalf of growers and had significant financial reserves in the form of property. As part of its grain trading activities, it began to hedge forex. The currency trader was substantially unsupervised, began to trade well beyond the needs to hedge currencies derived from grain sales and eventually bankrupted the organisation. The business and property were lost; only the lobby group activities survived.

AWA, an Australian communications and electrical goods company, made annual profits after tax of about $20–30 million in the late 1980s. The company began hedging its foreign exchange exposure (resulting from its imports of components from Japan) through currency futures. At first, results were favourable and the company moved from hedging to speculating. Its principal trader, aged 24 years, was hailed as a whiz kid in early 1987. However, on 8 July 1987, the company was forced to disclose to the ASX that it may have sustained forex trading losses of up to $30 million and that its earlier reported gains may have been overstated. The whiz-kid trader, formerly extremely confident of his ability to make money easily in the forex market, was bitter in his comments when he was sacked one week later.

In 1991, the UK brewer, food and hotel group, Allied Lyons, lost £150 million (A$370 million at early 2000s exchange rates) by selling call options on the USD–GBP (British pound) exchange rate.

In 1993, a single unsupervised employee at Showa Shell Shekiyu, the Japanese subsidiary of Shell Petroleum, lost ¥165 billion (about A$2 billion at early 2000s exchange rates) in trading forex forward contracts. The next year, Kashima Oil, a Japanese oil refiner and transporter, lost US$1.5 billion in forex trading. In most cases, the trading moved from hedging deals to pure speculation where risk was assumed rather than minimised.

National Australia Bank was severely embarrassed in early 2004 when it was revealed that a group of forex traders in the bank had consistently exceeded their stipulated trading limits and had taken positions which assumed the value of the AUD would fall. Over about three months of unsanctioned trading, the traders lost about $360 million of the bank's funds as the AUD continued to gain value. The episode cast significant doubt over the bank's risk management procedures, the efficiency of its record keeping and its trading authorisation processes. The market saw this loss as one more black mark against the management of the bank. Ultimately, the bank's CEO resigned and the board suffered significant instability. APRA subsequently required the bank to increase its capital adequacy ratio to 10% — a very public statement of the regulator's view of the bank's prudential management.

Interest rate derivatives

One of the most notable early disasters was that of a British local authority, Hammersmith and Fulham, which in 1988 lost about £500 million (A$1.2 billion at early 2000s exchange rates) on sterling interest rate swaps and options. Much to the chagrin of the financial institutions that were counter-party to its deals, the courts later declared all contracts null and void. US local authorities were also shown not to be immune to the attractions of gambling with the ratepayers' funds. In the mid-1990s, Robert Citron, the treasurer of Orange County, a local authority in California, speculated in interest rate derivatives and lost close to US$2 billion. Similarly, Glaxo, a drugs company, lost in the order of £150 million (A$375 million at early 2000s exchange rates) with interest rate derivatives.

No account of the great derivative losses of our times would be complete without mention of the case of Barings Bank. Barings was an old (more than 200 years old) well-established and well-respected British bank. It was bankrupted in 1995 by the trading activities of a junior employee in Singapore, Nick Leeson. Nick was supposed to arbitrage Nikkei 225 equity futures between Singapore and Osaka, Japan, with all deals bringing no increase in risk. Instead, Nick used futures and options trades to try to make a killing by outguessing the market on the future direction of the Japanese stock market. Nick failed to predict the Kobi earthquake that shook the confidence of the market and sent prices rapidly down. The bank lost close to £1 billion and went bust. The subsequent inquiry showed that Barings broke almost all the rules discussed earlier for managing derivatives trading. Enron was the seventh largest company in the United States in 2000, and the world's largest trader in the energy markets. The next year it went bankrupt. Although there were several contributing factors, energy and interest rate derivatives were involved.

That these losses and many others occurred in the 1980s and 1990s and few significant losses were reported after 1997 is not accidental. The losses showed the senior management of firms the power of derivatives to destroy their best efforts in other parts of their business operations, if traders were not strictly controlled and if systems were not in place to monitor activities accurately and in a timely manner. Additionally, the boards and senior management had to understand derivatives themselves rather than leave their supervision to trust and luck.

What compels some derivatives traders to have positions that are far too large for their organisations to cover? A highly plausible explanation is that traders are overconfident in their abilities to predict the future (or to have reliable gut instincts!).

executive summary

lo1 discuss risk management in non-financial services firms

- Risk in finance is defined as the chance that the actual outcome will be different from the expected outcome and is quantified by the standard deviation.
- Common methods to manage risk are through the purchase of insurance, fixing interest rates and forward contracting.
- Insurance companies are willing to take on risk in return for the payment to them of premiums. They pool risk, pay out for claims and plan to make a profit in the process.
- Interest rates are fixed through fixed price loans, futures contracts, forward rate agreements and swaps.
- Forward contracting applies to commodities, debt through (interest) forward rate agreements, foreign exchange (forex) and equity though company-issued options.

lo2 identify the various types of traders in the markets

- Hedgers are traders who enter a market to try to reduce the price risk in their normal business operations.
- Speculators take on risk in order to make profits.
- Arbitrageurs enter markets and trade to make profits without risk by making complementary trades in two or more markets virtually instantaneously to exploit price differences.

lo3 describe the role and operations of the futures markets

- A futures contract is a derivative security where the contract stipulates the transfer of a specified quantity of the underlying physical product at a future time at an agreed price.
- The principal futures market in Australia is run by the Sydney Futures Exchange (SFE), which is part of the Australian Securities Exchange.
- The SFE deals in three contracts for wool (of three different thicknesses), three contracts for electricity and one cattle contract. For interest rates, there are six Australian contracts: 30-day interbank cash rate, three- and 10-year bonds, three- and 10-year interest rate swaps and 90-day bank-accepted bills (BABs); and three NZ contracts.
- The key terms in futures markets are:
  - spot market
  - contract unit or contract size
  - contract or delivery months
  - last trading day
  - clearing house
  - delivery
  - cash settlement price
  - minimum price movements
  - margin
  - mark-to-market
  - position limits.

- Futures exchanges ensure performance of contracts by means of margin requirements.
- Clearing houses manage margin requirements and ensure contracts are successfully settled by a process known as marking-to-market.
- Futures trading allows firms to lock in future prices.
- Another growing risk management tool is options on futures.
- Options give the holder the right but not the obligation to exercise a contract.

lo4 describe the roles and operations of FRAs

- A forward rate agreement or FRA is a deal between two parties which fixes an interest rate for a period which begins some time in the future.
- FRAs are signed on the trade date and settled on the settlement date, which is the start of the contract period. The date at the end of the contract period is the maturity date.
- There is no commitment to lend or borrow the principal amount with FRAs.
- FRAs normally have maturities of 3–6 months, but may be executed for periods up to two years ahead.
- FRAs are settled by the payment of the difference in interest payable on a notional principal at the agreed rate and at the current market rate.
- If the market rate has risen, the seller must pay the buyer of the FRA who is the potential borrower. The borrower may now go to the market and borrow at the current rates, but the borrower has compensation in hand which will cover the extra interest payable now that rates have risen. The borrower is thus accessing funds at the rate agreed to in the FRA and has reduced interest rate risk.
- The converse occurs when interest rates fall on the market. The borrower will be able to access cheaper funds in the market than previously but, because the FRA has been entered into, the borrower will have to compensate the other party to the FRA which will effectively increase the price of the funds to the agreed rate.

lo5 discuss the roles and operations of swaps markets

- Interest rate swaps are used by borrowers to convert obligations to pay interest on a fixed rate basis to a floating rate basis, or conversely to convert floating rate obligations to fixed rate commitments.
- Swaps are undertaken because the two principals who are party to each agreement can do so to their mutual advantage, as a result of lenders having differing perceptions of the risk they are facing in lending to the principals.
- Swaps exploit differences in interest rates in different markets and allow firms to take advantage of differences in risk margins that financial institutions impose on them.
- Swaps do not have an organised trading market. Trades are made over the counter (OTC) and the large financial institutions are major participants in the market.
- There are no set swaps contracts. The parties to swaps contracts negotiate the conditions that each requires.
- There is no exchange of principal amount with interest rate swaps. Because the principal is not part of the deal, it is called a 'notional' amount.
- The parties have contracted for loans with lenders outside the swaps agreement and the obligations to these lenders remain unchanged.

- Interest rate swaps normally deal with very large notional amounts — a minimum of $10 million and frequently as much as $50 million or $100 million.
- Interest rate swaps are normally concerned with the relatively short or medium term. The most frequent term for swaps is less than one year and more than half are for less than two years.
- Currency swaps involve the exchange of loan obligations in one currency for the payments on loans made in another currency.
- The simplest version of a currency swap involves the exchange of both principal and fixed interest payments.
- Currency swaps are undertaken for two reasons: to lower the final cost of funds and to hedge foreign exchange risk.
- Currency swaps are used in at least three situations:
  - by firms which operate predominantly in their domestic markets and can borrow in their home countries cheaper than elsewhere but need foreign currency funds
  - by firms which can borrow more cheaply internationally (or do not wish to issue more securities onto local markets)
  - by firms which operate in both domestic and overseas markets and have foreign cash flows which may be used to service debt internationally, but which may borrow more cheaply in their home countries. In these situations, there is no need to hedge exchange rate risk, because the operating cash flows of the firms are used to repay the debt, so they are not exposed to foreign exchange risk in servicing the loans.
- Financial institutions often act as facilitators of currency swaps. Their services cut the search costs of firms looking for currency exchange partners.
- Many financial institutions nowadays offer swaps with themselves as principals initially through taking all offered business and then laying off the risk through subsequent deals which operate in the opposite direction.
- The financial institutions involved charge fees which reduce slightly the magnitude of the savings available to the parties to the deals.

lo6 describe how companies manage risk with options

- Company-issued options are options to buy shares in the company at a future date at a stipulated price.
- Options may be used as 'golden handcuffs' which help to keep valuable employees.
- Options may be used as sweeteners as additional benefits given for 'free' to make it easier for firms to raise funds.
- The issue of options puts in place the ability to raise future funds as an extension of a prior capital raising.

lo7 discuss the principles that should govern hedging operations

- Hedgers must ensure that their trading is always carried out in kind and magnitude consistent with hedging not speculating.
- This general overarching principle implies that:
  - trading or risk limits should be set by each company's board
  - individual traders should have personal risk limits set and rigorously monitored

- sensitivity analyses should be carried out to identify the worst-case situations
- duties must be separated so there are different people doing the various duties associated with trading
- relevant senior managers must fully understand the trading systems
- the trading section must not be made a profit centre
- accounting for trades must be conservative.

Key terms

arbitrageurs, p. 566
call option, p. 567
cash settlement price, p. 569
clearing house, p. 569
closed out, p. 570
contract months, p. 569
contract unit, p. 568
daily-settlement margin calls, p. 570
deliverable contracts, p. 569
delivery months, p. 569
derivatives, p. 563
electronic bank-accepted bills (EBAs), p. 572
electronic certificates of deposit (ECDs), p. 572
forward rate agreement (FRA), p. 576
futures contract, p. 562
hedgers, p. 565
initial margin, p. 569
intra-day margin calls, p. 570
last trading day, p. 569
mandatory-settled contracts, p. 569
margin, p. 569
marking-to-market, p. 570
maturity date, p. 576
notional amount of a swap, p. 578
option, p. 567
position limits, p. 570
put option, p. 567
risk, p. 561
settlement date, p. 576
speculators, p. 565
spot market, p. 568
strip hedge, p. 572
swap, p. 577
swaps reset period, p. 579
trade date, p. 576
writer of an option, p. 574

Learning chart

Learning objective	Questions	Self-test problems	Financial problems
lo1 discuss risk management in non-financial services firms	15.1, 15.2, 15.3		
lo2 identify the various types of traders in the markets	15.4, 15.5, 15.6, 15.7	15.2	15.1
lo3 describe the roles and operations of the futures markets	15.8, 15.9, 15.10, 15.11, 15.12	15.1, 15.3	15.2, 15.3, 15.4, 15.5, 15.6
lo4 describe the roles and operations of FRAs	15.13, 15.14	15.4	15.7, 15.8, 15.9, 15.10, 15.11
lo5 discuss the roles and operations of swaps markets	15.15, 15.16	15.5	15.12, 15.13, 15.14, 15.15, 15.16, 15.17
lo6 describe how companies manage risk with options	15.17, 15.18		15.18, 15.19
lo7 discuss the principles that should govern hedging operations	15.19, 15.20		

Questions

15.1 Think of a business with no market power such as a pumpkin grower. In what areas does such a business face risk?

15.2 Compare the business in 15.1 with Woolworths Ltd. How is the risk structure facing the two businesses different?

15.3 What is the most common method for business to manage risk?

15.4 Discuss the role of speculators in a futures market. Give a numerical example of a successful speculation.

15.5 Speculators generally have a bad name. Is this justified?

15.6 Explain how an arbitrageur would profit from a deal in the forex markets.

15.7 Joseph Cotter and Co. hedges in the cotton futures market. In what business does the firm trade?

15.8 What is meant by the term 'contract unit' in relation to a futures contract? Give three examples.

15.9 Explain how margin requirements work in the futures markets.

15.10 What are mandatory-settled futures contracts? Are they not all mandatorily settled? Why do you think they are called mandatory-settled contracts?

15.11 Why would a hedger take an option on a futures contract?

15.12 A 90-day BAB is traded at 93.3. What does this mean?

15.13 Explain with a worked example how an FRA is settled.

15.14 At settlement, the buyer of an FRA pays the seller. Explain what has happened and how the buyer has fixed her interest rate.

15.15 How are interest rate swaps possible and able to benefit the parties?

15.16 Explain why Cubbyhouse Partnership, a large Australian cotton-growing firm, would enter a currency swap.

15.17 Why would a company issue options instead of fully paid shares?

15.18 Explain one of the downside risks in a company issuing a large number of options.

15.19 Why should firms dealing in the derivatives markets split the duties associated with trading? What are the three tasks associated with each day's trading?

15.20 Grain Handlers Ltd regularly used the derivative markets to hedge grain prices for its growers. If its derivatives traders exceeded their limits while on a profit-making quest, is the firm still hedging?

Self-test problems

15.1 A cattle fattener decides in February to lock in the sale price of his 2-year-old cattle which will average 250 kg dressed weight (DW) at turn-off. (Dressed weight is carcase weight with bone in, but hide, head, tail, hooves and organs off.) These cattle suit the specifications of the Eastern Young Cattle Indicator (EYCI). The producer has 60 steers and heifers which will be ready for sale in July.

(a) How many contracts will the producer need to buy or sell?

(b) The contract price is 330 c/kg. On settlement day, the EYCI is 360 c/kg. What price has the producer fixed for his cattle?

(c) How will the futures trade be settled?

15.2 Mick Mikimoto is an Australian of Japanese extraction who trades on his own behalf in shares and currencies. Mick has been watching the quotes for AUD, USD and JPY (Japanese yen). Here are the current quotes:

AUD1 = USD 0.7543

AUD1 = JPY 86.10

USD1 = JPY 115.25

If transaction costs are about $600 for a three-trade deal, can Mick make a profit by starting the trading round with AUD100 000? Is he likely to do this deal?

15.3 Learmonth Leather Co Pty Ltd wants to raise $1 million for 3 months in 6 months' time, in December. Learmonth is persuaded by its financial adviser to sell a 90-day BAB December futures contract. The price is 93.65. Learmonth later reverses its futures position at 93.15. How much better or worse off is Learmonth after the second trade?

15.4 ACE, a computer services company, asks its financial institution for a quote for an FRA for 91 days with the start date in 45 days' time. The quote is 5.65%. ACE needs to borrow $5 million. ACE contracts for the FRA with the bank. At settlement, the interest rate in the market for 91-day money has risen to 5.85%.

(a) What is the settlement amount and who pays whom?

(b) How does this FRA assist ACE?

15.5 Andy's, an Australian retailer, borrows $10 million from the market at 7.0% to fund the purchase of stock and some specialised bar-coding and stock-control equipment. The firm decides to enter an interest rate swap as it believes interest rates may fall. Another firm, Barnacle Boats, which has borrowed from its bank at BBSW + 4.6%, decides it would rather have fixed rate funds, as it believes the cost of its funds will fall. Andy's gets a quote for floating rate funds of BBSW + 3% and Barnacle's best alternative quote is 9%. Andy's and Barnacle get together and arrange a swap where they share the gain equally. What will the cost of funds be for each party and what would be the swap if Andy's pays BBSW without a margin to Barnacle?

Solutions to self-test problems

15.1 (a) The cattle contract is for 5000 kg DW, so three contracts are needed.

(b) Regardless of the current market price, the producer has fixed 330 c/kg for his cattle.

(c) The trade will be settled by the producer paying the buyer (the holder of the bought contract) the difference between the contract price (330 c/kg) and the EYCI (360 c/kg). The difference is $\$0.30 \times 5000 \times 3$, which is $4500. Even though the producer has lost money on his futures trade, he can sell his stock in his usual saleyards or direct to works and receive the current market price, which should be about 360 c/kg. In practice, it may be a bit more or a bit less, depending on the quality of his stock, trading conditions on the day, etc. The EYCI is an average of prices for different classes of stock at many different centres.

15.2 AUD100 000 = USD75 430, which buys JPY8 693 307.5 ($75\,430 \times 115.25$), which in turn will buy AUD100 967.56 $\left(\dfrac{8\,693\,307.5}{86.1}\right)$.

The round robin yields $967.56, but $600 must be paid in costs so the net profit is $367.56. Is it worth doing? Probably not worth the bother.

15.3 Learmonth sells the contract at 93.65 or 6.35% yield. For 90 days, this is 0.015657.

$$\text{Price} = \frac{1\,000\,000}{1.015657} = \$984\,584.44.$$

The company buys back at 93.15 or 6.85%. For 90 days, this is 0.016890.

$$\text{Price} = \frac{1\,000\,000}{1.016890} = \$983\,390.53.$$

The difference of $1193.91 is a gain.

15.4 The interest rates for 91 days for the FRA and market rates are 0.01409 and 0.01458, respectively $\left(0.0565 \times \frac{91}{365} \text{ and } 0.0585 \times \frac{91}{365}\right)$.

$$P_1 = \frac{1\,000\,000}{1.015657} = \$4\,930\,528.85$$

$$P_2 = \frac{5\,000\,000}{1.01458} = \$4\,928\,147.61$$

$$\text{Settlement price} = \$4\,930\,528.85 - \$4\,928\,147.61 = \$2\,381.24$$

The market rate has risen, so the financial institution pays ACE the settlement price. ACE can go to the market and borrow the funds. The payment by the financial institution will compensate ACE for the increase in the cost of funds on the market.

15.5

	Andy's	Barnacle Boats	Difference
Fixed	7.0%	9.0%	2.0%
Floating	BBSW + 3.0%	BBSW + 4.6%	1.6%
Net difference			0.4%
Pay to market	−7.0%	−(BBSW + 4.6%)	
Pay to other	−BBSW	−4.2%	
Receive from other	+4.2%	+BBSW	
Net cost of funds	BBSW + 2.8%	8.8%	

Financial problems

15.1 Hank Harnencort is a Brisbane forex dealer, recently arrived from Boston. Hank sees these quotes on his screen and decides to use US$400 000 to make an arbitrage deal. The quotes are:

AUD1 = USD0.7484
AUD1 = JPY85.22
USD1 = JPY110.59

How much gain would Hank make at these rates, disregarding transaction costs?

15.2 A firm buys two SFE September 90-day BAB futures contracts at 93.15. At settlement, the firm receives what and pays what?

15.3 A small credit union sells an SFE June 90-day BAB futures contract at 92.85. At settlement, what does it receive? When the bill matures, what happens?

15.4 An Australian exporter decides to hedge receivables in USD. Accordingly, it buys 10 SFE June AUD futures contracts at 0.6410. In early June, it decides to reverse its position in the futures market by selling 10 contracts at 0.6620. How much has the exporter gained or lost on the futures trade? Explain what these prices indicate about the movement of the physical exchange rate.

15.5 A New Zealand exporter, Kiwanis, does business with the United States and is to receive about US$700 000 next September. Kiwanis decides to hedge the USD and does so at the SFE at 0.6990. Kiwanis is happy to receive AUD as it buys a large amount of goods from Australia.

(a) How many AUD contracts will Kiwanis buy or sell?

(b) Kiwanis reverses its position at 0.6300. Has the futures trading brought a loss or gain? Of how much?

15.6 Comet Mines NL wants to lock in the price of some of its future gold production. Rather than enter the futures market directly, it decides to purchase some December 850 gold put options. Each option gives Comet the right to sell one 100-ounce gold futures contract for $850 per ounce; each option costs $1200. The price of gold in the physical market increases to $925. What will Comet do? What are its gains and losses?

15.7 CGT Ltd wants to fix the interest rate of some future borrowings. Accordingly it makes a deal with its financier to buy a 5:8 FRA for a notional principal of $10 million at 5.9%. At settlement, the market rate for 90-day funds has risen to 6.4%. Who pays what to whom?

15.8 Given the circumstances in problem 15.7, what payments would be made if the market price of 90-day funds at settlement had fallen to 5.65%?

15.9 GS Trading Co Ltd's financial manager thinks interest rates will rise. Hence, he wants to lock in the cost of future borrowings. He arranges to buy a 6:9 FRA for a notional $10 million at 6.2%. At settlement the market has risen to 6.45%. How much does the firm pay or receive?

15.10 Given the circumstances in problem 15.9, what payments would be made if the market had fallen to 6.05%?

15.11 GS Trading is so pleased with its FRA deal that it decides to extend the fixing of its interest rate. If settlement in problem 15.9 took place in September, how would you describe another FRA deal which locked in the notional $10 million for another three months after the maturity of the current deal?

15.12 Australian Avocados (AA) can borrow at 8.2% and BBSW + 3.5%; Ptero Traders (PT) can borrow at 9.8% and BBSW + 4.1%. The managers of the two firms know each other and decide to arrange an interest rate swap. AA borrows fixed and really wants floating, and PT is happy to borrow floating and swap to fixed. Arrange a swap with any benefit shared equally and AA paying PT no more than BBSW.

15.13 Allen's Autos (AA) can borrow at 7.2% and BBSW + 2.8%; Davidson Fruits (DF) can borrow at 8.8% and BBSW + 3.2%. The managers of the two firms decide to arrange an interest rate swap. AA borrows fixed and really wants floating, and DF is happy to borrow floating and swap to fixed. Arrange a swap with any benefit shared equally and AA paying DF no more than BBSW.

15.14 Build a table such as table 15.4 (see page 579) showing the actual payments for your swap solution in problem 15.12 during one year with four reset periods, a nominal loan amount of $40 million, and BBSW increasing by 100 basis points each reset period from a start of 5%.

15.15 Build a table such as table 15.4 (see page 579) showing the actual payments for your swap solution in problem 15.13 during one year with four reset periods, a nominal loan amount of $40 million, and BBSW increasing by 100 basis points each reset period from a start of 5%.

15.16 Austra Global can borrow at fixed rates in Australia at 8.2% and in the United States at 6.2%. New Texas, a US firm, has a better credit rating and can borrow at 7.2% in Australia and 4.8% in the United States. Austra borrows in Australia and New Texas in the United States; they want loans denominated in the other currency so arrange a currency swap for principal and interest. They decide to share the benefits equally. Structure a swap and calculate the quarterly payments on a A$10 million and equivalent USD loan with the AUD:USD exchange rate at 0.6000.

15.17 Design a currency swap for the following situation with a financial institution earning 50 basis points and assuming all foreign exchange risk.

	AA	BB
AUD loan	9.6%	10.0%
USD loan	5.0%	6.5%

15.18 Directors in ABG Ltd granted themselves two million options exercisable at $2 each as part of their remuneration packages. The options will lapse in December 2012, if not exercised before this time. When the market price of the fully paid ordinary shares is $6.30 and the company has recently issued rights at $5, how much do you believe the company has forgone in granting the options?

15.19 Fanta Ltd is a software company looking to increase its capital. Its adviser reports that it can raise the $100 million in funds needed by issuing shares at $2.50 each. This issue, according to the adviser, should be underwritten at a fee cost of 4%. Alternatively, the adviser suggests directors should consider attaching a free option to the issue. The option should be exercisable by investors at $2 any time before 30 September 2011. The adviser notes that the issue will now be more attractive and the underwriting fee will drop to 3%. Advise the directors of the issues and costs involved here.

SOLUTIONS TO FINANCE WORKSHOPS

15.1 Sell for $985 181.79

Buy for $986 619.81

Loss $1 438.02

Funds from market $986 379.85

less loss 1 438.02 $984 941.83

$$\text{Cost of funds} = \frac{(1\,000\,000 - 984\,941.83)}{984\,941.83} = 0.015\,288\,385$$

$$\text{Nominal annual rate} = 0.015288385 \times \frac{365}{90} = 0.062 \text{ or } 6.2\%$$

15.2 At 6.25%, price = $984 822.93

At 6%, price = $985 421.17

Difference = $598.24

Market rate has fallen so borrower pays lender.

15.3

	Firm CT	Firm PG
Fixed	7%	8%
Floating	BBSW + 0.2%	BBSW + 0.6%
Pays to lender	(–) 7%	(–) BBSW + 0.6%
Pays to other	(–) BBSW	(–) 7.1%
Receives from other	(+) 7.1%	(+) BBSW
Net result	(–) BBSW – 0.1%	(–) 7.7%

Both parties are better off by 0.3% than they were before the swap.

End notes

1 Boag, K 2006, 'What women want', *Asset*, July, p. 58.

2 Benson, K & Oliver, B 2004, 'Management motivation for using financial derivatives in Australia', *Australian Journal of Management*, vol. 29, no. 2, pp. 225–42. Data derived from figure 2, p. 237.

3 Extracts from Benson & Oliver, pp. 226, 228, 231.

4 Sydney Futures Exchange (SFE) 2007, 'Contract specifications', www.asx.com.au; Meat & Livestock Australia (MLA) 2007, 'Eastern young cattle indicator', www.mla.com.au.

5 Chicago Mercantile Exchange (CME) 2006, 'Contract specifications', www.cme.com.

6 SFE 2006, 'Margins', www.asx.com.au.

7 CME 2006, 'Contract specifications'.

8 Data from Sydney Futures Exchange 2007, '90-day bank bills', www.asx.com.au.

9 SFE 2007, 'Contract specifications'.

10 Australian Financial Markets Association (AFMA) 2007, 'Summary of market turnover', www.afma.com.au.

11 AFMA 2003, 'Summary of market turnover', www.afma.com.au.

12 Woolworths 2005, *2005 financial report to shareholders*, Woolworths Ltd, Sydney, p. 92.

13 Woolworths 2005, p. 93.

14 Extracts from 'Managing derivatives trading', *Business Times* (Singapore), 26 May 2005.

chapter 16

chapter

16

Capital restructuring — takeovers and divestments

Learning objectives

After studying this chapter, you should be able to:

lo*1*	define the key terminology of takeovers
lo*2*	explain the procedures for takeovers
lo*3*	outline the rationales for takeovers and critically analyse these
lo*4*	calculate the NPV of a proposed takeover
lo*5*	describe how and why companies change from public to private ownership and from private to public ownership using takeovers
lo*6*	explain how and why companies use sell-offs and spin-offs to divest their assets.

LION NATHAN LTD'S RESTRUCTURING ACTIVITIES

Acquiring new assets to expand a firm's line of business and divesting parts of the business are regular occurrences for some firms. The following article gives some real life examples of these activities in Lion Nathan Ltd.

Market wonders when Lion will roar

SIMON EVANS

Lion Nathan's reputation as being a bit of a miser when it comes to acquisitions is earning some plaudits in the market, but questions remain about what is required to ignite some serious profit growth.

The share price climbed almost 8 per cent in the two months to February 9 as the company kept its hands in its pockets in the battle for Australasian ready-to-drink spirits firm Independent Liquor. While RTDs is the one area in which Lion is weakest in its portfolio of beer, wine and spirits, it refused to go all out in the bidding process for Independent.

The latter is viewed by some as a maverick company not afraid to take risks. It may have found the transition into a more sober and disciplined management style under Lion more difficult.

Private equity firms CCMP Capital Asia and Pacific Equity Partners bought Independent for $1.1 billion, representing an earnings multiple of about 11 times. But the uncertainties around what Lion might buy have not disappeared.

Lion chief executive Rob Murray signalled last week that the company was looking at several opportunities, but he cautioned they would be nowhere near the size of Independent.

A planned share buyback of up to 5 per cent of the company's capital, which would soak up more than $200 million, is on ice in the short term pending the resolution of some corporate action. Credit Suisse speculated on Tuesday it might involve a potential divestment of Lion's wine division. A decision on whether Lion intends selling its Auckland brewery, which could fetch up to $150 million, is also due in the next few months and might provide more clarity on the company's direction.

Some analysts suspect the purchase of a spirits brand is possible to complement the fledgling McKenna Kentucky Straight Bourbon portfolio that Lion is introducing around Australia after the brand hit its sales targets in a trial period in Queensland. This might go some way towards addressing the concerns among fund managers that while Lion is a safe and conservative company, it is battling to find much growth.

Alleron Investment Management's chief investment officer, Albert Hung, said the decision in May last year to increase the dividend payout ratio to 80 per cent of net profit attracted the attention of some investors, but over the past two years Lion had become a 'dull company'. 'They have been very conservative and obviously doing things like tidying up the portfolio and focusing on cost containment,' he said.

Credit Suisse cut its rating on Lion last week after the share price gains of the past two months.[1]

Chapter preview

The article about Lion Nathan raises a number of issues we will be examining in this chapter. Firstly, the article discusses a takeover attempt by Lion Nathan for Independent Liquor. This takeover did not eventuate because another bidder (the private equity consortium of CCMP Capital Asia and Pacific Equity Partners) offered more for Independent than Lion Nathan was willing to pay. The article also raises the question of some takeover plans Lion Nathan might bring into play in the future. In this chapter, we build on our previous knowledge of investment decisions (chapters 8 and 9) by investigating the rationale for takeovers. Secondly, the article links the timing of a proposed share buyback to the 'resolution of some corporate action'. This action turned out to be a takeover of the Beenleigh Distillery and its brand 'Inner Circle Rum' three weeks after this article was published. Finally, the article refers to the possible sale of Lion Nathan's wine division. The divestment of lines of business will also be discussed in this chapter.

The following diagram show how this chapter is structured.

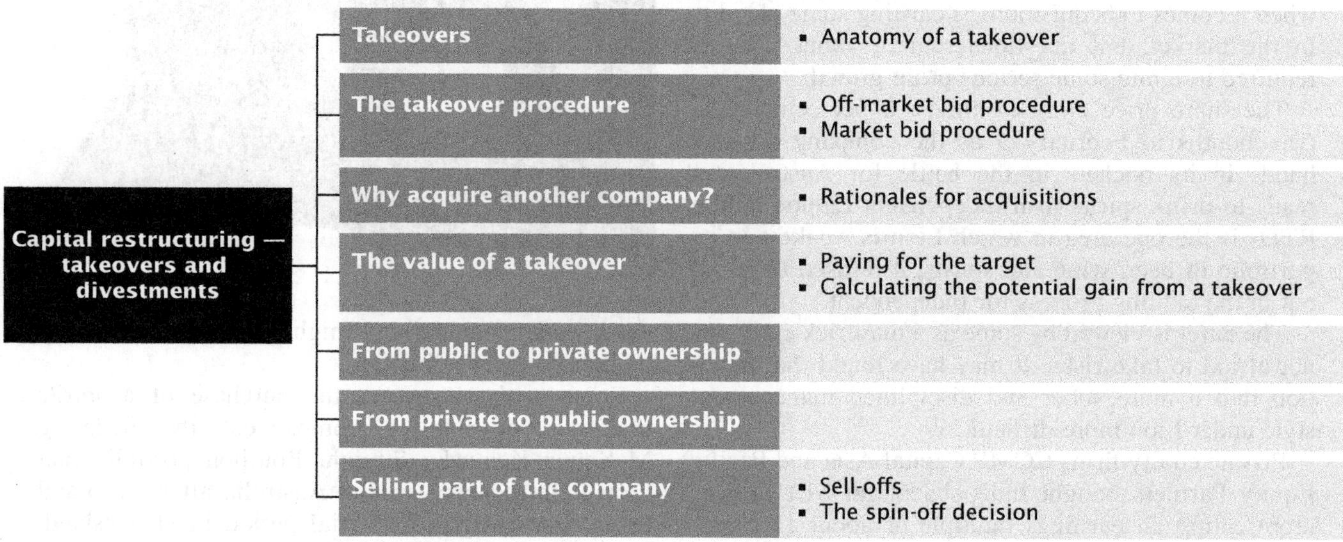

lo1

Define the key terminology of takeovers.

Takeover: a company (or group of companies and/or individuals) gains control of an existing company

Bidder: the party that makes an offer for shares in the company it wishes to acquire

Takeovers

As noted in the chapter preview, the analysis of the decision to take over another firm is an extension of the investment evaluation techniques we learn in chapters 8 and 9. A **takeover** allows a company (or group of companies and/or individuals) to gain control of an existing company

Takeovers are a special case of the investment decision because they have unique features that make the estimation of net present value difficult. We will explore these issues for determining the value of a takeover later in the chapter. Before we do, we will identify the key terms associated with takeovers and examine the takeover process. To help understand some of these definitions and processes, we will use the events associated with a proposed takeover of Qantas to put our knowledge into context.

Before we begin our anatomy of a proposed takeover of Qantas, we need a couple of fundamental definitions. We have already defined a takeover as gaining control of an existing company. The **bidder** is the party making an offer for the shares of the

Target: the company that the bidder wants to acquire

Merger: the combination of two (or more) businesses into a single entity

target company. A merger, on the other hand, is the combination of two (or more) businesses into a single entity. When two companies merge, their shareholders normally swap their existing shares for shares in the new combined business. When a company is the target of a successful takeover, the target's shareholders might sell their shares for cash to the bidder or they might swap their shares for shares in the bidding company. We will return to the issue of how payment for shares is made later in the chapter.

Anatomy of a takeover

The APA consortium's proposed takeover of Qantas involved delisting the public company and changing to a private ownership structure. The business would be managed by the current management team, who would also invest in the consortium. The share price for Qantas on 3 November 2006 was $4.23. Following is an outline of the events associated with the proposed takeover of Qantas up to the time of writing this book.[2] As you read through the sequence of events, you can trace the related price changes on figure 16.1 (page 608).

6 November 2006
UBS Nominees Pty Ltd is identified as becoming a substantial shareholder in Qantas. UBS Nominees does not purchase shares for itself, but holds the shares on behalf of 'various custodians', 'unknown custodians' and some specific firms that purchase shares on behalf of undisclosed clients. Qantas shares close at $4.20.

7 November 2006
The Australian Financial Review reports takeover rumours based on the presence in Australia of senior figures from global private equity firms. Qantas shares close at $4.31.

22 November 2006
Qantas notifies the ASX that 'an approach has been made by Macquarie Bank and Texas Pacific Group on behalf of a consortium they represent'. Qantas shares close at $5.00.

24 November 2006
CEO and managing director of Qantas advises the ASX that he has not discussed with the bidders his 'future role, remuneration or equity in any new company'. Qantas shares close at $4.94.

13 December 2006
Qantas advises the ASX that 'a non-binding conditional proposal to acquire 100% of the Company from a Consortium including Allco Equity Partners, Allco Finance Group, Macquarie Bank, Onex and Texas Pacific Group' had been received. The first three consortium members are Australian companies listed on the ASX while the other two are based overseas. The off-market takeover bid is $5.50 cash and a minimum acceptance of 90% is required for the takeover to proceed. Qantas shares close at $5.09.

14 December 2006
Qantas requests that the ASX halts trading for its shares. Trading halts until an announcement is made by the board giving a recommendation about the offer.

The chairman advises the ASX that:

- The consortium offer has been increased to $5.60 after the initial offer was rejected by the board of Qantas. She states that the new offer price is '33% higher than the closing share price of $4.20 on 6 November 2006, the day before the first speculation about the offer'. She also notes that the average share price for the previous six months is $3.48 and that the consortium bid price is 61% higher than this average.
- The interim dividend due in April will not be paid, but a fully franked special dividend may be paid during the bid period. If a special dividend is paid, the offer price per share will decrease by the dividend amount.
- Most consortium members are Australian and the inclusion of foreign consortium members is justified by their international experience of airline operations. An assurance is given that 'Qantas will remain a majority Australian-owned, Australia-based airline'.
- The non-executive directors will be selling their shares to the consortium.
- The executive directors (who will be involved in the consortium) did not participate in the board's decision to accept the takeover offer.

Qantas shares close at $5.28.

15 December 2006

ACCC notifies ASX that it is reviewing the proposed acquisition of Qantas. Qantas shares close at $5.29.

27 December 2006

The board sends a letter to shareholders outlining the conditions of the takeover offer and recommending that the offer be accepted. Qantas shares close at $5.21.

28 December 2006

The bidding consortium sends a letter to shareholders, outlining how the takeover is in the best interests of the company. Some information about the consortium members is provided. The letter also includes a statement that the takeover will have no impact on the Frequent Flyer Program. Qantas shares close at $5.22.

2 February 2007

Bidder's statement released to the ASX and ASIC. Offer is to open on 5 February 2007 and close on 9 March 2007.

- Shareholders are supplied with forms to complete to enable the sale of their shares to the bidder.
- The document contains large print statements about the proportion of the business that will remain Australian owned, increasing future investments to expand capacity, the industry-specific experience of the consortium and a lot of pictures of aeroplanes.
- Seven reasons for accepting the offer are given: the directors recommend acceptance, the offer price is at a premium to the market price, the business will continue to have majority ownership by Australians, the business will continue to exist, significant risks to the value of Qantas shares are removed, the share price will fall if the offer does not proceed, and shareholders will receive a 'certain' value for their shares by accepting the offer.

A media release is made that alerts the public to the fact that 46% of Qantas is currently owned by foreign investors (mostly foreign institutions). The consortium highlights that its foreign ownership component has experience in the airline industry. Qantas shares close at $5.39.

5 February 2007
The consortium owns 0.27% of Qantas shares. Qantas shares close at $5.37.

7 February 2007
Consortium announces to the ASX that it made a voluntary notification of the takeover bid to the Foreign Investment Review Board on 5 February. The first supplementary bidder's statement is issued to convey this information to shareholders. Qantas shares close at $5.36.

8 February 2007
Qantas announces a special fully franked dividend of $0.15 per share. Qantas shares close at $5.35.

12 February 2007
Target's statement released.

- The recommendation to accept the offer is in large print on the first page of the document. This is followed by the chair of the board of directors' letter that states that the directors' recommendation is unanimous and that the advice of the independent expert concluded that the APA consortium offer was fair and reasonable.
- Six reasons for accepting the offer are given: the offer price is more than the market price of Qantas has ever been, the offer price includes a significant premium over the current market price, the independent expert considers the offer to be fair and reasonable, the independent expert thinks any price above $5.18 is worth taking, the bidder negotiated with the board prior to releasing the bidder's statement, and the expectation that the share price will fall if the takeover does not go through.
- A statement that there are no other serious bidders for Qantas.
- A list of 21 'frequently asked questions' about the takeover proposal and answers.
- A profile of the Qantas business including a summary of financial performance for the most recent six months.
- An outline of five important matters for Qantas shareholders to consider, including: how the board has managed potential conflict of interest issues, a direction to read the attached independent expert's report, the consequences of a minority ownership position if the takeover is unsuccessful and the consortium does not sell the shares it has acquired, the impact on the Qantas share price if the takeover does not proceed, and a direction to some advice on the possible tax implications of selling shares to the consortium.
- A statement about the directors' interests and what they would receive under the offer.
- A summary of the key feature of the consortium's offer and a profile of the members of the consortium.
- Other material information — what happens to shares under the employee share plan, the likely impact of the takeover on contracts with Qantas, the

implementation deed with the consortium with respect to the bid period, litigation that Qantas is currently involved in, the consents of the experts whose views are expressed in the target statement and a statement that Qantas is subject to the continuous disclosure requirements of the ASX.

- A glossary and interpretation of terms.
- The independent expert's report on the bidder's offer.
- The audited interim financial statements for the six months to 31 December.

Independent expert's valuation statement released to the market. The independent expert states that any 'price above $5.18 would be fair value' and that Qantas shares would be unlikely to reach $5.60 if it continued as a listed company. Qantas shares close at $5.36.

13 February 2007
Second supplementary bidder's statement is released. This statement announces a special facility for institutional investors to accept the consortium's offer and that the cash consideration for each share would fall from $5.60 to $5.45 to reflect the payment of the special dividend announced by Qantas on 8 February 2007. Qantas shares close at $5.22.

15 February 2007
Expert's report on management rollover offer confirms that management will receive no more than the price offered to other shareholders. Qantas shares close at $5.21.

20 February 2007
Consortium announces to the ASX that the offer price of $5.60 is final and will not be increased. Qantas shares close at $5.19.

28 February 2007
Offer period extended from original close date of 9 March to new close date of 3 April. The consortium has acquired 6.09% of Qantas shares at this date. Qantas shares close at $5.15.

2 March 2007
ACCC announces it will not oppose the takeover of Qantas.

Third supplement to bidder's statement is released. It tells Qantas shareholders that the ACCC does not view the takeover as anti-competitive and that one member of the consortium (Texas Pacific Group), which had been involved with Continental Airlines, America West Airlines and Ryanair, does not have any current investment interests in those companies. Qantas shares close at $5.23.

5 March 2007
Takeovers Panel advises the ASX that it has received an application from the Pilot's Association complaining that the bidder's statement and the third supplement to the bidder's statement contain deficiencies in disclosure with respect to Texas Pacific Group's experience in the airline industry. Qantas shares close at $5.20.

7 March 2007
The Australian government announces that it will not oppose the takeover of Qantas. The consortium now owns 12% of the total shares on issue. 37% of

shareholders have accepted the consortium's offer. Taken together, these two percentages indicate that large individual investors and institutional investors have not been prompt in taking up the offer.

Fourth supplement to the bidder's statement is released. It contains details of the consortium's commitment made to the Australian government to expand the airline's services internationally and domestically, maintain the Frequent Flyer Program and maintain majority Australian ownership of Qantas after the takeover. Qantas shares close at $5.32.

8 March 2007
Fifth supplement to the bidder's statement announces that the consortium will pay the handling fees charged by brokers for the sale of Qantas shares by retail investors to the consortium. Qantas shares close at $5.31.

20 March 2007
Sixth supplement to the bidder's statement details the airline experience of consortium member (Texas Pacific Group) in response to the application made by the Pilot's Association to the Takeovers Panel. Qantas shares close at $5.14.

23 March 2007
Bid period extended to 20 April. Over 50% of Qantas shareholders have accepted the offer at this point and the consortium holds 29% of Qantas shares.

Balanced Equity Management, holder of about 4% of Qantas shares, announces that it will not be accepting the consortium's offer. Qantas shares close at $5.06.

6 April 2007
Media reports that the consortium's bankers have agreed to accept a controlling interest in Qantas as security for their loan instead of taking Qantas's assets as security. This frees the consortium from the requirement to acquire 90% of Qantas shares to proceed with the takeover.

12 April 2007
Seventh supplementary bidder's statement — APA consortium announces that it will accept 70% of Qantas shares as the minimum required acceptance condition. The share price rises to $5.39.

18 April 2007
First supplementary target's statement reiterates the board's support for acceptance of the takeover offer. It also outlines the implications for shareholders who do not accept the offer when they become minority shareholders Qantas share close at $5.37.

23 April 2007
Eighth supplementary bidder's statement outlines acceleration of cash payments to selling shareholders and the conditions that allow shareholders to withdraw their acceptances of the consortium's offer for shares. Qantas shares remain at $5.37.

30 April 2007
APA consortium announces that the takeover offer will lapse if they do not own 50% of Qantas shares by 4 May. Qantas share price remain unchanged at $5.32.

7 May 2007
Qantas requests a trading halt on its shares when the Takeovers Panel questions whether the consortium held 50% of Qantas shares when the offer closed. Shares prices falls to $5.22 at close on 8 May.

17 May 2007
The APA consortium announces to the market that it will not be renewing its takeover offer for Qantas. Qantas shares close at $5.25.

18 May 2007
Qantas chairman announces her retirement plans to the market.

31 May 2007
Qantas shares close at $5.70. This price is higher than during or just prior to the takeover bid.

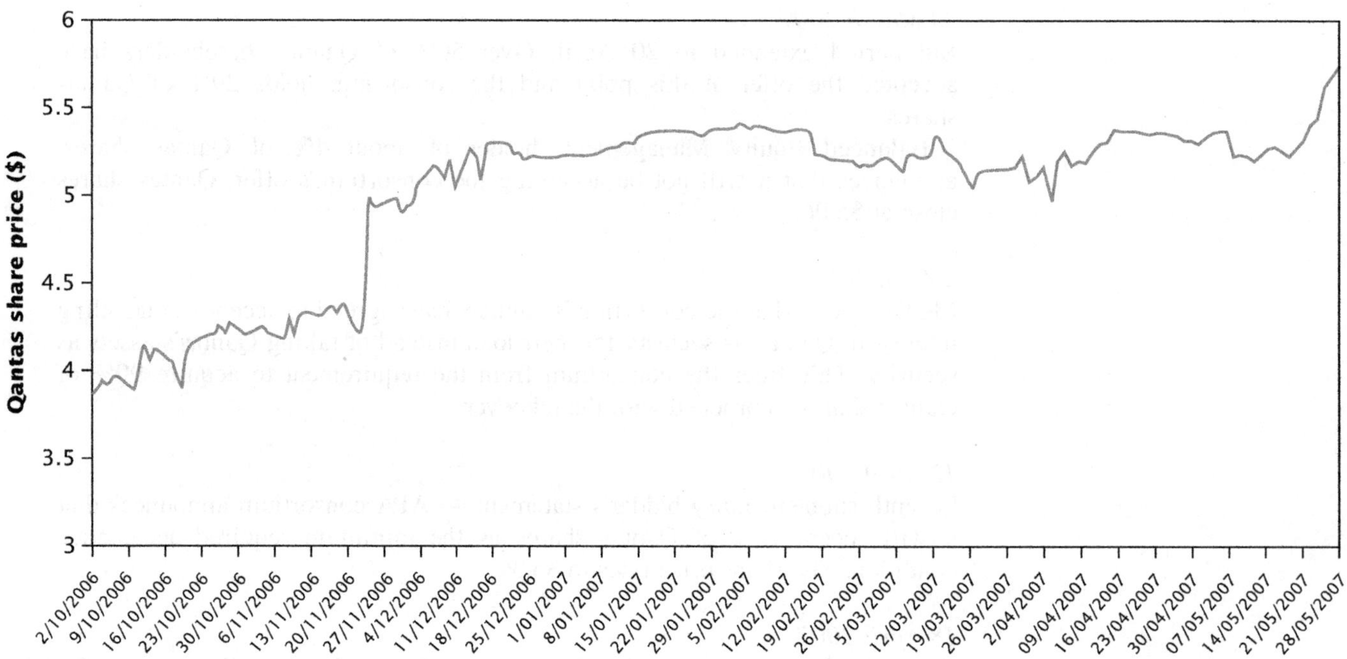

Figure 16.1 Qantas share prices, October 2006 to May 2007

Source: Yahoo Finance.[3]

Substantial shareholding: the ownership of 5% or more of the voting shares of a listed company

Section 671B of the *Corporations Act 2001* specifies that the market must be notified within two days if a shareholder obtains a substantial shareholding in a listed company. Section 9 of the *Corporations Act 2001* defines a **substantial shareholding** as the ownership of 5% or more of the voting shares of the company. A substantial shareholder must notify the market if there is a change of at least 1% of their holding. The information release about the substantial shareholding acquired by UBS Nominees may have encouraged rumours about Qantas becoming a takeover target.

The price of Qantas shares increased 2.6% based on rumours that international private equity firms were looking for Australian investments. **Private equity firms** acquire listed companies and operate them as private businesses. They normally use a relatively large proportion of debt to fund their acquisitions. We will discuss the rationales for taking a public company private later in the chapter.

Private equity firms: firms that acquire listed companies and operate them as private businesses

Two weeks after the takeover rumours began, Qantas announced that the board of directors had been approached by a consortium of investors to purchase the company. This consortium consisted of a group of companies that wanted to make a private equity investment in Qantas to gain control of the company. The price of Qantas shares increased 15% that day with confirmation of the takeover rumour. This price increase tells us that the market expected the consortium to offer more than $4.35 (the previous day's closing price) for each share. The consortium had not made a firm offer to purchase shares at this point and had not indicated a price that it would be prepared to pay for the shares. Why would Qantas announce that there was an interested bidder for the company without having firm details? One possible reason would be that the Qantas board wanted to attract more bidders to increase the eventual price paid for Qantas shares, but this could only be a secondary reason. Regulation 3.1 of the ASX Listing Rules requires listed companies to make immediate disclosure of information that would 'have a material effect on the price or value of the entity's securities'. This listing rule is given the force of law by section 674(1) of the *Corporations Act 2001*. We can tell by the share price increase that the news of a potential takeover offer did have a very material effect.

Can you think of a reason the CEO would announce that he had not been involved in discussion with the consortium about what might be in it for him if the takeover offer was accepted? As we have seen, the board of directors made a recommendation to the shareholders about accepting the takeover offer. The CEO is also the managing director of the company and has a seat on the board. This raises some interesting corporate governance issues that will be discussed in the 'corporate financial governance' feature at the end of the chapter.

Qantas then released some preliminary details of the offer, including the percentage of shares that the bidder wished to acquire (100% in this case). A **proportional takeover bid** specifies a proportion of shares (less than 100%) that the bidder wants to purchase. The APA consortium wanted to end up with all Qantas shares because they planned to delist the company and operate the business assets with private ownership. Therefore, the consortium's bid is not a proportional takeover bid.

Proportional takeover bid: a bid that specifies a proportion of shares (less than 100%) that the bidder wants to purchase

Market takeover: a takeover in which the bidder purchases the shares of the target by normal trading on the stock exchange

Section 9 of the *Corporations Act 2001* defines a **market takeover** transaction as one that occurs in the ordinary course of trading on the market. The APA consortium bid for Qantas was an off-market takeover. In an **off-market takeover**, the bidder gives the target's shareholders an application form to complete the sale of their shares. The consortium also indicated that they would pay $5.50 cash per share. We will discuss other methods of compensation later in the chapter.

Off-market takeover: a takeover in which the bidder gives the target's shareholders an application form to complete the sale of their shares at a specified offer price

The consortium's takeover bid was **conditional** on it acquiring 90% of Qantas shares. Section 625(2) of the *Corporations Act 2001* allows off-market bids to have some attached conditions. Bidders who want control of a company to gain access to particular assets make the takeover offer conditional on those assets not being sold prior to the completion of the takeover. If a 'defeating condition' is not met, the bidder can cancel any acceptances of the offer and the takeover offer is void (section 650G). The bidder is not allowed to set conditions that limit the maximum number of shares they will purchase (section 626(1)) or conditions that result in some people's shares being purchased under the offer but other

Conditional bid: a takeover offer in which certain requirements have to be met for the offer to proceed

people's not being purchased (section 627). The effect of the consortium's condition was that the takeover would be withdrawn if the consortium did not obtain 90% of the shares by the end of the bid period. The **bid period** is the time from when the bidder makes the takeover offer to when that offer closes. The bid period must be not less than one month and not more than one year (section 624(1)).

Bid period: the time from when the bidder makes the takeover offer to when that offer closes

Why did the consortium choose 90% as the condition rather than the 100% ownership they would need to transfer to private ownership? Section 661A of the *Corporations Act 2001* requires a bidder who holds 90% or more of the voting shares of a target to make a **compulsory acquisition** of the remaining shares. This means any shares that have not already been sold to the bidder must now be sold. Compulsory acquisition can occur during or at the end of the bid period. If the bidder does not reach the 90% threshold, an application for compulsory acquisition can be made to the court (section 661A(3)). The price paid for these shares must be the same as the price paid to shareholders who accepted the bidder's offer (section 661C(1)). It might seem harsh at first glance that a shareholder who did not want to sell to the bidder is forced to sell under a compulsory acquisition, but what is the shareholder going to do with the shares when the company is no longer listed on the exchange? The bidder must also make a compulsory acquisition of any convertible securities that have been issued by the target (section 663A) as these securities cannot convert to shares in a company that is no longer listed.

Compulsory acquisition: occurs when the bidder is allowed to purchase any shares in the target company it does not already own

The board of Qantas said what they thought of the takeover proposal the day after it was announced to the market. The chair indicated that negotiations with the bidder had resulted in an increase in the offer from $5.50 to $5.60. It is important for a bidder to get support from the board of the target for the takeover to be successful. It is easier for the bidder to increase the offer price prior to releasing their formal bidder's statement and negotiating prior to this means the bidder is more likely to get the support of the target's board.

Why does the payment of a dividend during the bid period reduce the offer amount from the bidder? Paying a dividend reduces the amount of cash or near liquid assets in the target firm, so the bidder will not be receiving as many assets as it would have if there were no dividend payment. This is similar to a takeover offer being conditional on the retention of assets in the target prior to the takeover.

The content of the **bidder's statement** is specified in section 636(1) of the *Corporations Act 2001*. The bidder's statement must be in writing and specify the length of the bid period. It must state who the bidder is, what the intentions for the future of the target company are (including the use of the target's assets and current employees), details of how the offer can be accepted and what the selling shareholders will receive in return for their shares, the details of any on-market purchases of shares in the target in the previous four months, the bidder's current shareholdings and voting rights in the target and any other information that would be considered material. The bidder's statement must be sent to the target company, ASIC and the ASX. If you would like to look at the bidder's statement for Qantas, go to the ASX website and check the 'announcements' section under 'company research' for 2 February 2007 (but don't try this unless you have a fast internet connection!).

Bidder's statement: sets out the terms and conditions of the takeover offer

When the bidder for an Australian company is not an Australian resident, the takeover has to be approved by the Foreign Investment Review Board. The APA consortium was obviously concerned about the negative media reports that the 'Australian icon' of Qantas was going to be owned by foreigners and this concern explains the media release that accompanied the bidder's statement on 2 February. To really emphasise the point that foreign ownership of Qantas would not be higher after the takeover, the consortium made a voluntary notification of the takeover to the Foreign Investment Review Board. The consortium was not obliged to make this notification as its ownership is predominantly Australian. The first **supplementary bidder's statement** was used to tell the Qantas

Supplementary bidder's statement: a statement distributed to advise shareholders of new circumstances that could affect their decision on the bid or to correct any misstatement or omission in the original bidder's statement

shareholders about this notification. A supplementary bidder's statement is required to correct a misleading statement, or to rectify an omission in the original bidder's statement, or to advise of some new and relevant circumstance. The bidder's statements are cumulative — when a supplementary statement is issued, it is to be added to information in the original bidder's statement and any previous supplementary statements (section 646). The supplementary bidder's statement is sent to the target company, ASIC and the ASX. The APA consortium made six supplementary bidder's statements to provide shareholders with clarification on a number of issues.

Target's statement: a statement that contains the target's directors' recommendations on the acceptability of the takeover offer and the reasons for their recommendations

The directors of the target company respond to a bidder's statement by releasing their own **target's statement.** The content of the target's statement is specified by section 638 of the *Corporation Act 2001.* It should include all information (within reason) that would help shareholders decide on the acceptability of the takeover offer (section 638(1)). The target's statement should contain a recommendation from each of the target's directors about accepting the offer and the reasons for that recommendation (section 638(3)). Where the target's statement includes an expert's opinion about accepting the offer, as the Qantas statement does, it should also contain the formal consent of any person whose opinion has been included in the statement. If you would like to look at the target's statement for Qantas, go to the ASX website and check the 'announcements' section under 'company research' for 12 February 2007 (this file is even larger than the bidder's statement). Section 644 of the *Corporations Act 2001* requires a **supplementary target's statement** to be produced and distributed under the same circumstances as those for a supplementary bidder's statement.

Supplementary target's statement: a statement distributed to advise shareholders of new circumstances that could affect their decision on the bid or to correct any misstatement or omission in the original target's statement

There are no legal requirements to present experts' reports in either the bidder's statement or the target's statement, but they can be included to support the positions in either document. Section 648A(2) requires that the expert must be independent of the bidder and the target. Disclosure of any relationship is required by section 648A(3). The expert is also required to disclose any interest that might affect his or her capacity to give an unbiased opinion and the fees or other benefits that will be received. The expert report provided in the Qantas target's statement includes a valuation statement that the consortium's bid is 'fair and reasonable', based on an independent valuation of a fair value price range of $5.18 to $5.98. The expert's report states that it used discounted cash flow and earnings multiples as the basis for its conclusion.

Section 50 of the *Trade Practices Act 1974* prohibits anti-competitive behaviour by businesses. In 2005, companies were given the option to gain clearance from the ACCC prior to acquiring shares or other assets to avoid uncertainty about how the ACCC would view the acquisition. The potential for anti-competitive behaviour in the Qantas case was not from competition for flight routes, but from the participation of the owner of Sydney Airport in the consortium.[4] The share price increase of about 2% that accompanied the ACCC clearance shows that the announcement increased investor confidence that the takeover would proceed.

The Takeovers Panel is the forum for disputes between parties to takeover offers during the bid period. After the bid period is completed, any disputes need to be settled in court. Court proceedings generally take a long time to complete so the Takeovers Panel was established to provide guidance swiftly enough to allow the target or the bidder to fix any problems. To avoid delaying tactics that could be used by parties opposing the bid, the panel has the power to determine if some circumstances associated with the takeover are unacceptable. In the Qantas case, the Takeovers Panel agreed with the claims made by the Pilot's Association. While the consortium disagreed with the panel's decision, it released the third supplementary bidder's statement to clarify the issues raised. There has been media speculation that the Pilot's Association's approach to the Takeovers Panel was an attempt by the Qantas pilots, who did not support it, to delay the takeover.[5]

At the time of writing, the APA bid for Qantas had failed. Did any new bidders for Qantas emerge? Complete finance workshop 16.1 by doing some research on this issue.

FINANCE WORKSHOP 16.1

Was the APA consortium's takeover bid for Qantas the only recent takeover attempt? If you haven't heard about the outcome from the press, use the company announcements facility on the ASX website to find out what happened.

lo2

Explain the procedures for takeovers.

The takeover procedure

As we saw in the previous section, the APA consortium made an off-market bid for Qantas. In this section, we will look at the general procedures for off-market and market bids.

Off-market bid procedure

We defined an off-market bid as a takeover proposal where the bidder purchases the shares of the target through shareholders completing the form attached to the bidder's statement. The rules for off-market bids are covered by section 632 of the *Corporations Act 2001*. Figure 16.2 summarises the steps that must be followed when making an off-market bid.

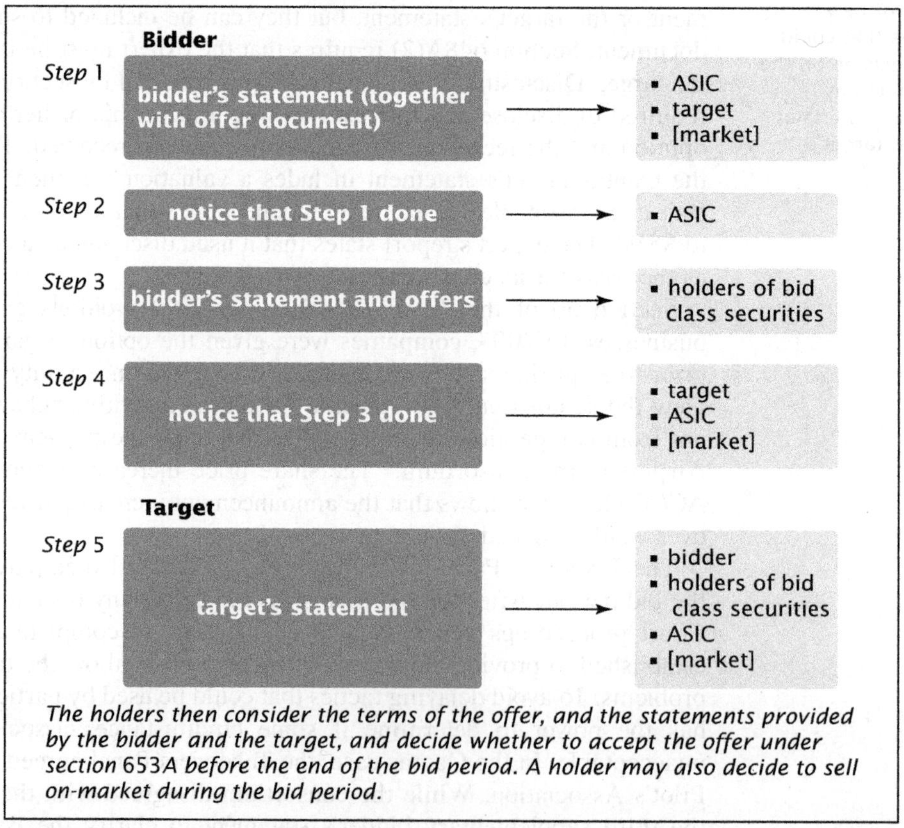

Figure 16.2 Overview of steps for an off-market bid

Source: *Corporations Act 2001,* section 632.

The first step in the off-market process is the preparation of the bidder's statement. As we saw in the Qantas case, the bidder's statement outlines the terms and any conditions of the offer. To maximise the likelihood of the target's board of directors supporting the takeover offer, the bidder might approach the board before releasing the bidder's statement. The consortium took this approach in its bid for Qantas, with the result that some conditions were removed and the offer price was increased. The bidder's statement is then sent to the target's board so it can prepare the target's statement. The bidder's statement is also released to the ASX to meet continuous disclosure requirements and it is lodged with ASIC so they can perform their oversight functions. The second step in the process is for the bidder to formally notify ASIC when Step 1 has been completed.

The third step is for the bidder to send its statement to the target's shareholders. This will help the shareholders to decide if they should accept or reject the bidder's offer. The bidder is then required to notify ASIC, the target's board and the market that this step has been completed.

As we saw in the proposed takeover of Qantas, the target's board of directors responds to the bidder's statement with their target's statement (see page 605 for the contents of the target's statement). The target's statement is sent to the bidder, the target's shareholders and ASIC. Shareholders who want to sell their shares to the bidder follow the procedure outlined in the bidder's statement to transfer ownership.

The note at the bottom of figure 16.2 draws our attention to the option shareholders have to sell their shares on the market during the bid period. Hedge funds had purchased about 40% of Qantas shares during the bid period, indicating that many Qantas shareholders must have chosen to sell their shares on the market rather than sell them to the bidder. Why would shareholders do this instead of selling to the bidder and receiving a higher price? The ones who sold on the market might have been worried that the bid would be withdrawn and their shares returned to them if they accepted the bidder's offer. By selling on the exchange, these shareholders gain from the rise in market price and do not take the risk that the bid is withdrawn. The hedge funds take this risk in the expectation that the offer will proceed and they will gain the difference between the price they paid for the shares and the price offered by the bidder. As we saw in the Qantas case, the failure of a proposed takeover bid is expected to cause the market price of shares to fall. One reason for the price fall would be the sale of shares by the hedge funds. Hedge funds do not want to be long-term investors in Qantas. They want to buy shares at lower than the offer price and sell a short time later for the offer price. When the consortium's bid for Qantas did fail, those shareholders who sold shares on the market during the bid period would have expected the post-bid share price to fall. Unusually, in the Qantas case it did not. If the share price fell to below the price paid by the hedge funds, these investors would have made a loss.

An off-market bid must be an offer to buy all the ordinary shares that have been issued by the target or, for a proportional bid, the same proportion of shares from each shareholder (section 618(1)). For example, if the bidder makes a proportional bid for 50% of the target's shares, it must purchase 50% of each shareholder's ownership interest in the target. The bidder cannot purchase all of the shares of some shareholders and refuse to purchase any more from the remaining shareholders.

The same offer price must be received by all shareholders who sell their shares to the bidder in an off-market bid (section 619(1)). If the bidder has purchased shares in the target company before the bid was announced, the minimum amount that can be paid for the purchase of shares under the offer is the highest price it paid for a share in the four months prior to making the offer (section 621(3)). If the APA consortium had purchased some shares at $4.25 in the four months prior to announcing their takeover proposal, they would have to offer at least $4.25 for their bid. The consideration given for shares in the target company can be cash, securities (normally those issued by the bidder) or a combination of cash and securities (section 621(1)).

The offer price and the bid period can be varied during the bid period for off-market bids. The amount of consideration offered can be increased during an off-market bid (section 650B(1)). This means that the bidder can offer more cash, more shares, switch from share only consideration to the same number of shares plus some cash or some other additional alternative type of consideration. The new higher amount of consideration must be paid to all shareholders — any that have not yet accepted the offer get the higher price and so do those shareholders who accepted earlier for the lower offer price (section 650B(2)). The bid period can be extended any time before the end of the period (section 650C(1)).

The bidder can withdraw a takeover offer with written consent from ASIC (section 652A) or if the conditions of the bid are not met.

Market bid procedure

Market takeovers occur where the bidder purchases the shares of the target by normal trading on the stock exchange. The main differences between this and an off-market bid are that market bids must be for the acquisition of all the issued ordinary shares, be unconditional, only offer cash as consideration and the bidder can vary the offer price during the bid period without paying all shareholders the same price. Figure 16.3 summarises the steps that must be followed when making a market bid.

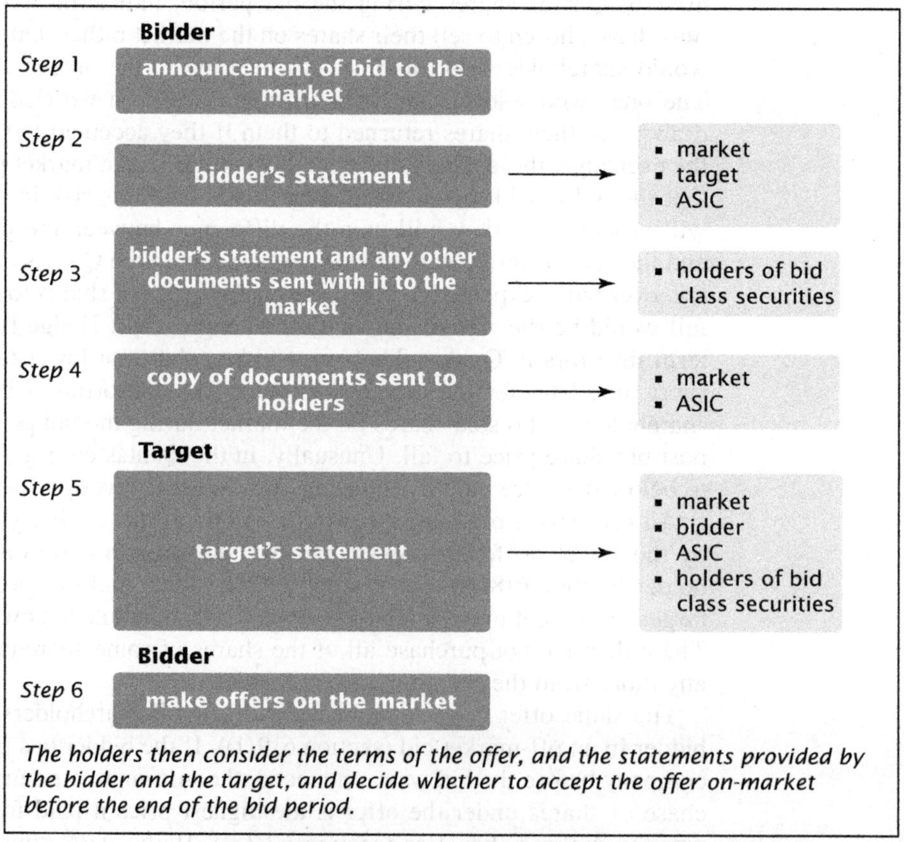

Figure 16.3 Overview of steps in a market bid

Source: *Corporations Act 2001*, section 634.

The first step in a market bid is to announce the offer to the market. The *Corporations Act 2001* does not require this step in an off-market bid but, as we saw with the Qantas case, the target announced that it was discussing a potential takeover offer to comply with the continuous disclosure requirements of the ASX Listing Rules. The next step for a market bid is the release of the bidder's statement to the market, the target's board and ASIC. The bidder's statement must be released the same day that the proposed takeover is announced to the market. The third step is to provide the shareholders with the bidder's statement and any other relevant documents (an independent valuation report, for example). These other documents must then be released to the market and supplied to ASIC. As for the off-market offer, the target prepares its statement and supplies this to the market, the bidder, ASIC and its shareholders. The final step is for the bidder to make offers on the market to purchase shares in the target during the bid period.

Market bids must be for all of the shares of the target company (section 618(3)). This means that proportional bids can only be conducted using an off-market bid. Further, the only type of payment for purchasing shares in the target is cash (section 621(2)). The same minimum consideration rule is applied to market bids as we discussed in the off-market bid section.

The bidder in a market bid can vary the price offered and the bid period. The offer price can be increased as long as this occurs more than five trading days before the end of the bid period (section 649B). The bid period can normally be extended any time prior to the last five trading days of the bid period (section 649C(1)). Extensions can also occur in the last five trading days when there are rival bidders for the target. The only procedure for obtaining an extension is to make the announcement to the market. While off-market bids can contain conditions (such as acquiring 90% of the shares in the Qantas case), market bids must be unconditional.

If the bidder holds less than 50% of the target's voting power, the takeover offer to shareholders who have not yet accepted can be withdrawn under section 652(1) of the *Corporations Act 2001*. This section allows the bidder to withdraw if the target makes certain changes to the number of shares it has on issue including: consolidating or splitting shares, buybacks, issues of convertible securities or grants of options over the shares. The offer can also be withdrawn if the target sells substantial assets, makes a resolution to wind up the company, goes into liquidation or enters a deed of arrangement. In the next section we will examine some rationales for proposing a takeover.

FINANCE WORKSHOP 16.2

1. Outline the procedure for an off-market bid.
2. Lookin the financial press to see if you can find a recent example of an off-market takeover.

lo3

Outline the rationales for takeovers and critically analyse these.

Why acquire another company?

In this section, we will look at some of the reasons given for making a takeover offer. However, before we do that, we will look at the level of takeover activity in Australia.

The RBA estimated takeover and merger activity for the 2006 calendar year as around 10% of the total capitalisation of Australian listed companies.[6] This means that about 10% of the total value of shares listed was sold to bidders in a takeover or merger. However, not all of the companies acquired by bidders were listed on the ASX when the offer was made. The number of private companies taken over by listed companies in the period 1997–2006 is not readily available, but there were 155 takeover bids for private companies during the seven years up to and including 1998.[7] Figure 16.4 shows both the total numbers and aggregate values for takeover and merger activity for the 10 years up to and including 2006.

The columns in figure 16.4 show the dollar value of completed takeover and merger deals for each year (read the value from the left-hand side) and for 2006, the value of those deals not yet completed. The line that travels across the graph shows the number of deals for each year (read the number from the right-hand side). You can see that there were more than 900 takeover and merger proposals during 2006. About half (by value) had been completed by January 2007 and the remainder were still in process. Not all takeover bids are successful. Finn and Hodgson[8] find about 62% of Australian takeovers were successfully completed during the period from 1972 to 1996 and Maheswaran and Pinder[9] report a successful completion rate of about 90% during the period from 1992 to 2001. Compare the number of completed and proposed takeovers to the number completed in 1997 (the first bar on the graph). Even after allowing for about 40% of the uncompleted takeovers for 2006 to be unsuccessful, the number of takeovers and mergers for 2006 would be roughly four times as many as reported for 1997. If you look at the trend line in figure 16.4, you might conclude that takeovers and mergers are occurring more frequently in Australia and that this pattern will continue — don't make this conclusion. Ten years of data in financial markets is not enough to conclude that takeovers will continue to increase.

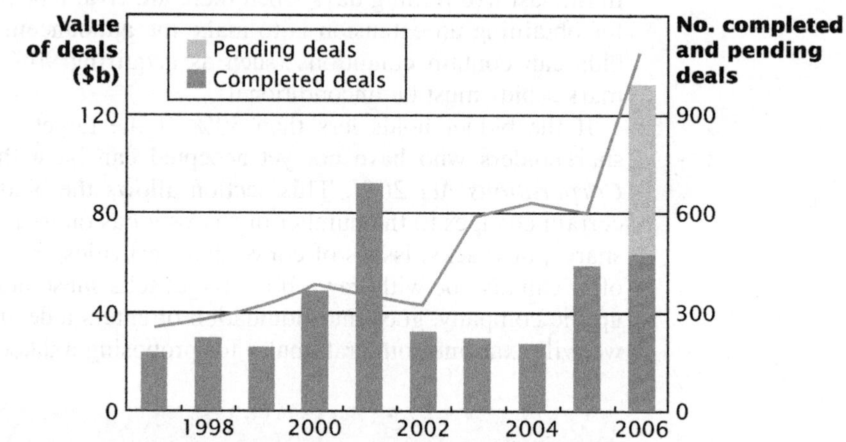

Figure 16.4 Takeover and merger activity, 1997–2006

Notes: This excludes real estate transactions. 'Pending' indicates transactions announced in 2006 but not completed.

Source: Reserve Bank of Australia.[10]

Peaks and troughs in takeover activity (or 'takeover waves') have occurred over the history of the share market. High levels of takeover activity in Australia have occurred in the early and late 1970s, the latter half of the 1980s and the middle of the 1990s[11] — and a wave that commenced at the turn of this century was still rising at the start of 2007. Are these takeover waves driven by the reasons bidders have for making offers?

Rationales for acquisitions

Theory suggests three main types of motives for making a takeover bid.[12] Synergistic gains, target undervaluation and managerial desires are each discussed in the next sections.

Synergistic gains

Synergy: when the value of two assets combined is greater than the sum of the individual values

Horizontal takeover: when two companies in the same business are combined

Vertical takeover: the acquisition of a related business that either supplies the buyer or is closer to the consumer of the buyer's goods or services

Economies of scale: efficiency gains from producing more of a good or service

Synergy occurs when the value of two assets combined is greater than the sum of the individual values. Synergistic benefits occur when one plus one equals three (and not in an accounting sense). At first, it seems difficult to imagine how the combined value of two fleets of trucks, for example, can be higher than the sum of the individual values of the two separate fleets. What if you owned a well-established transport company on the west coast of Australia? You find that you do not have sufficient access to customers on the east coast because your firm has limited exposure in that market. What if you combine your business with a transport company on the east coast? The new combined business could be worth more than the two existing businesses because it has access to a national customer base and the two separate infrastructures can be combined to give you a national network of trucking routes.

Our trucking firm example demonstrates a **horizontal takeover**. A horizontal takeover occurs when two companies in the same business are combined. Here, the size of the business changes, not the nature of the business. A vertical takeover, on the other hand, changes the nature of the acquirer's business. **Vertical takeovers** are the acquisition of a related business that either supplies the buyer or is closer to the consumer of the buyer's goods or services. Our transport company would be making a vertical takeover if it acquired a tyre manufacturer because the tyre manufacturer would give the company control over its supply of the tyres that are necessary to keep the fleet moving. The synergy in this acquisition would come from the tyre manufacturer gaining access to a permanent market for its products and from the transport company having control over a large cost component of its operations.

The synergistic gains in our transport company example come from operations — the transport company could potentially gain from economies of scale and from increased market power. **Economies of scale** are efficiency gains from producing more of a good or service. The transport company may enjoy economies of scale by paying lower prices on its inputs because it orders in larger amounts. If there was spare capacity in the company's booking system it may be fully utilised when the firm has a national client base. In addition to the benefits of economies of scale, our transport company could enjoy increased market power by becoming a national operator. Further, it may have the capacity to offer an expanded range of services that would improve the net cash flow of the company.

Financial synergies might also arise in takeovers. These could include tax effects and higher debt capacity. The impact of dividend imputation and the legislation about trading 'tax loss' companies should be carefully evaluated before you accept tax benefits as a reasonable rationale for a takeover. Throughout this book we have discussed how dividends are effectively taxed in the hands of the shareholder and how steps taken by managers to reduce the amount of corporate tax payable do not benefit Australian resident shareholders. Tax losses that a target company might have can only be used by the buyer if there is continuity in the target's line of business. Even if this condition can be met, a takeover is a very expensive way of obtaining a tax deduction.

Larger companies may gain access to debt more cheaply than smaller ones. Interest rates can be relatively lower when a takeover makes the bidder large enough to access the public debt markets in Australia (or the Euromarkets if the company becomes really large) rather than relying on bank finance. This lower cost of debt will be a real gain if it is achieved by economies of scale in making the debt issues. If the interest rate is lower because the new company has more assets and cash flows to meet the repayment of debt obligations, then the reduction in the interest rate carries an implicit cost. This cost comes from each part of the combined company effectively insuring the debt of the other part of the company.

Operating synergies provide real economic gains for the bidder's shareholders. We can't make the same unequivocal conclusion about claims of financial synergies.

Target undervaluation

Gains from takeovers can occur when the bidding company can correctly identify target companies with share prices lower than the intrinsic value of the company. We see how CAPM could be used to help investors identify overpriced and underpriced shares in chapter 5. In this case, the bidding company is just another investor, but one that has significantly more capacity to make changes to the target firm than the standard investor.

A bidder might be able to identify targets selling for less than their value if the bidder has access to superior skills of analysis. This rationale is plausible for smaller listed companies given the relatively low (or no) analyst following for most Australian companies. While most of the top 200 (by market capitalisation) listed Australian companies are followed by analysts, only half of the next 400 had any following in November 2006.[13] As we can safely assume that the majority of smaller companies are not monitored by professionals there should be opportunities for bidders to identify underpriced companies and to gain from their acquisition.

The market may be undervaluing companies because they do not believe the current management is efficient. A buyer can improve the performance of a target by replacing an inefficient management team if the buyer has a current excess of management talent available. A note of caution is justified when evaluating undervaluation as a takeover rationale — you would have to be sceptical if the bidder offered this as a reason for acquiring a company like Qantas that has a large national and international analyst following.

Managerial desires

We explore the possibility that managers might act in their own interests rather than in the interests of shareholders when we discuss agency costs in chapter 1. Managers following such a path will be interested in acquiring companies so they can diversify the risk they personally bear from placing all of their human capital in one company, to increase the size of the company or to increase the amount of their own compensation.

Conglomerate takeover: the acquisition of a business that is unrelated to the current operations of the buyer

The acquisition of a business that is unrelated to the current operations of the buyer is called a **conglomerate takeover**. Managers have claimed that synergies can be achieved in conglomerate takeovers from the centralisation of administrative services such as accounting. Conglomerate takeovers were popular in the 1970s and 1980s. If you look in the recent annual reports of many of the conglomerates, you will see that most are accounting for significant 'restructuring costs' that are associated with getting rid of lines of business that are not important for the company's core business.

We learn about diversification in chapter 5. Recall the example of the wheat producer who diversified risk by planting crops on both sides of the Pacific (page 151). We said that the risk reduction by diversification was good for the owners of a private business but that it was not expected to bring benefits to the shareholders in a company. Managers acting in their own interests will gain from diversifying the operations of the company because such diversification means that the manager's stream of income becomes less risky. Shareholders won't benefit from the diversification activities of a company because they can diversify more effectively and efficiently by purchasing shares in two separate companies. A company engaging in diversification via conglomerate takeovers might lose some of its shareholders because corporate diversification will alter the risk profile of the shareholders' portfolios.

The costs of integrating another business can be very high. Management needs to deal with cultural differences between the firms and they need to devote a large amount of time to the integration of corporate systems. Shareholders, on the other hand, only have search costs and brokers' fees when they want to diversify their portfolios. Shareholders can't create synergies by combining their shares. Managers can increase shareholder wealth by recognising synergies and taking steps to capture them, but if a proposed takeover doesn't have synergies it is unlikely that shareholders will be pleased with the proposal.

In addition to diversifying their personal level of risk, managers might look for potential takeover targets to build their empires. Managers often gauge their success by the size of the company they manage. They have personal incentives to increase the size of the company rather than return any free cash flows to shareholders. This behaviour increases agency costs and agency costs are ultimately borne by the shareholders. A related incentive for managers to initiate a program of takeovers occurs when managers are rewarded for achieving higher earnings per share. Example 16.1 shows how higher earnings per share can be achieved without any real gains resulting from the takeover.

EXAMPLE 16.1

Increasing EPS without real gains

Bidder has proposed a takeover of Target. There will not be any synergies or other economic benefits from the takeover. The number of shares issued, total earnings, EPS, share price, total market value and price per share for Bidder and Target immediately prior to the takeover are as follows.

	Pre-takeover		Post-takeover
	Bidder company	Target company	
Issued shares	1 000 000	500 000	1 375 000
Earnings	3 000 000	1 500 000	4 500 000
EPS	3	3	3.27
Share price	24	18	24
PE ratio	8	6	7.34
Total market value	24 000 000	9 000 000	33 000 000

Bidder will pay three of its shares in exchange for every four Target shares. As four Target shares have the same market value as three Bidder shares, the exchange is at fair value. Bidder will issue 375 000 new shares to pay the Target shareholders, so the post-takeover company will have 1 375 000 issued shares (Bidder's original 1 000 000 plus the new shares issued as consideration). The total market value (or market capitalisation) of the combined company will be the sum of the pre-takeover market capitalisations of the separate companies as no economic benefits will come from the takeover.

The total earnings of the combined firm will be the sum of the earnings from both firms. You will notice that EPS for the combined firm has increased from the EPS of the separate firms pre-takeover. This occurs because Bidder will acquire $1 500 000 of earnings by issuing 375 000 new shares. If Bidder had grown its own business rather than conduct the takeover, it would have to issue 500 000 shares (given that it could maintain its current EPS of $3) to achieve the same increase in earnings. By acquiring a target with a lower price–earnings ratio, a bidder can immediately increase earnings per share, even when the takeover does not generate any real gains.

Because there are no real economic gains in this example, the new share price is calculated by dividing total market value for the combined entity by the total number of shares post-takeover. After establishing EPS and share price, we have enough information to

Bootstrapping: the capacity to increase EPS in a takeover in the absence of any economic gains for shareholders coming from the takeover

calculate the new PE ratio. The new PE will fall between the two PEs of the pre-takeover entities. When evaluating takeovers, it is important to be aware of this **bootstrapping** effect that increases EPS. Takeovers should be conducted to maximise shareholder wealth, not management compensation tied to increases in earnings per share.

Now we have established the rationales for takeovers, we will see how takeover decisions are evaluated.

FINANCE WORKSHOP 16.3

1. The acquisition of the tyre manufacturer by a transport company is an example of the buyer moving back along its supply chain to acquire a supplier. Can you think of an example where the tyre manufacturer might acquire a firm to move closer to its end customers?
2. Is the Lion Nathan takeover of Inner Circle Rum (see the opening page of this chapter) a horizontal, vertical or conglomerate takeover? Can you think of any possible sources of synergy in this takeover?

lo4

Calculate the NPV of a proposed takeover.

The value of a takeover

We will be using an extension of the investment evaluation techniques we learned in earlier chapters to evaluate takeovers. To be consistent with the objective of maximising shareholder wealth, the value of a business that combines both the bidder and the target should be greater than the sum of the values of the bidder and the target when they are operating separately. Equation 16.1 shows this necessary relationship for shareholder wealth maximisation.

$$\textbf{Takeover gain} = PV_C - (PV_B + PV_T) \qquad [16.1]$$

where PV_C = present value of the combined entity post-takeover
PV_B = present value of the bidder pre-takeover
PV_T = present value of the target pre-takeover

Takeover premium: the amount paid for the target's shares less the present value of the target's operations

A negative PV_C would reduce the wealth of the bidder's shareholders so should not proceed. An acquisition with positive PV_C would be expected to increase shareholder wealth if the premium paid by the bidder is less than the size of the gain. The **takeover premium** is the difference between the amount paid for the target's shares and the present value of the target's operations. Premiums offered to target shareholders are normally around 33% higher than the share price four weeks before the date of the takeover announcement.[14] Equation 16.2 shows the relationship between the takeover premium, the consideration paid by the bidder and the pre-takeover value of the target.

$$\textbf{Takeover premium} = \textbf{payment} - PV_T \qquad [16.2]$$

where PV_T = present value of the target pre-takeover

Once we have established the takeover gain and premium, we can estimate the takeover's NPV with equation 16.3. Equations 16.1 and 16.2 are used to estimate the gain and premium shown in equation 16.3.

$$\textbf{NPV} = \textbf{gain} - \textbf{premium} \qquad [16.3]$$

EXAMPLE 16.2

Calculating a takeover's NPV

The management of Seek Ltd are considering making a takeover offer for the shares of Found Ltd. The present value of Seek is \$5 000 000 and Found has a present value of \$2 000 000. Synergies with a present value of \$1 000 000 are expected from the merger. Seek will have to pay \$2 200 000 to purchase the shares of Found. The takeover gain is calculated as:

$$\begin{aligned}\text{Takeover gain} &= PV_C - (PV_B + PV_T)\\ &= (5\,000\,000 + 2\,000\,000 + 1\,000\,000) - (5\,000\,000 + 2\,000\,000)\\ &= 1\,000\,000\end{aligned}$$

You should not be surprised that the takeover gain in this example is exactly equal to the present value of the synergies expected from combining the operations of Seek and Found. The takeover premium is calculated as:

$$\begin{aligned}\text{Takeover premium} &= \text{payment} - PV_T\\ &= 2\,200\,000 - 2\,000\,000\\ &= 200\,000\end{aligned}$$

The NPV of Seek's takeover of Found will be:

$$\begin{aligned}\text{NPV} &= \text{gain} - \text{premium}\\ &= 1\,000\,000 - 200\,000\\ &= 800\,000\end{aligned}$$

If the market makes the same assessment of the gain on the takeover, the price of Seek's shares should increase by about \$800 000 when the takeover bid is announced. The price of Found's shares should increase so the market capitalisation equals the \$2 200 000 that Seek will pay.

We don't always see the bidder's share price increase by the takeover gain and the target's share prices increase to the offer price when takeovers are announced. The first reason is that the market might not agree with management on the size of the gain. The second reason is that the market might have some concerns about the likelihood of success for the takeover offer. We can see this in the Qantas case shown earlier in the chapter. The market was first concerned that the government would not allow the takeover of the national carrier. It was then concerned that institutional shareholders would refuse to sell so the 90% of shares condition on the bid would not be met. The third reason we may not observe much change in the target's price upon the announcement of a takeover is that the market might have predicted a takeover offer, so part of the takeover premium is already impounded into the target's share price. As we will see in the next section, the ability of the market to include takeover expectations in the target's share price complicates the calculation of the premium and the amount that the bidder should pay for the target.

Paying for the target

As we saw earlier, a bidder can offer the target's shareholders cash, shares in the bidder or a combination of cash and bidder shares in return for the sale of the target's shares. We can estimate the maximum amount that the bidder should pay for the target using equation 16.3 to get the cost that will give the takeover a zero NPV. Recall from chapter 8 that a zero NPV project will not change the value of a firm if the new project has the same level of risk as the firm's current operations. Assuming the target has the same level of risk as the bidder, a bidder paying less than the takeover gain to acquire the target will increase value for its shareholders.

EXAMPLE 16.3

Calculating the maximum bid

The management of Seek Ltd are considering making a takeover offer for the shares of Found Ltd. The present value of Seek is $5 000 000 and Found has a present value of $2 000 000. Synergies with a present value of $1 000 000 are expected from the merger. There are 1 000 000 shares in Found Ltd. We calculated the takeover gain of $1 000 000 in example 16.2.

$$\begin{aligned} NPV &= \text{gain} - \text{premium} \\ &= 1\,000\,000 - (\text{payment} - PV_T) \end{aligned}$$

Setting the NPV equal to zero, we have

$$0 = 1\,000\,000 - (\text{payment} - PV_T)$$

$$\begin{aligned} \text{payment} &= 1\,000\,000 + PV_T \\ &= 1\,000\,000 + 2\,000\,000 \\ &= 3\,000\,000 \end{aligned}$$

The NPV of the acquisition of Found will not decrease Seek's shareholders' wealth as long as the total amount paid to Found's shareholders is less than $3 000 000. The maximum amount that Seek would pay for each Found share is:

$$\frac{3\,000\,000}{100\,000} = \$3 \text{ per share}$$

We assumed that PV_T was equal to $2 000 000 in examples 16.2 and 16.3, but how would we determine the present value of a listed company without the detailed information that a manager normally has about a proposed project? Recall from chapter 6 that market price approximates the aggregate values of individual traders. This means that market price (in the absence of any behavioural biases) should reflect the present value of the firm's future cash flows. The problem with using the target's market price is that investors price the probability of a takeover offer being made (that is, they can pick which companies are likely to become targets). Go back to figure 16.1 (page 608) and have a look at the share prices for Qantas in the six weeks prior to the consortium's takeover bid. The large jump in the share price on the day news of the takeover is officially released is obvious, but look at the prices prior to the announcement date. Although the Qantas price fluctuates, there is an obvious upward trend in prices which is most likely due to speculation about a takeover offer before the market could have known the identity of the potential bidders. A market price that includes a speculative component can't be expected to reflect the present value of the future cash flows of the company. If we are using the share price of the target to estimate its present value, we need to find a share price prior to the advent of any takeover speculation.

Think about the maximum of $3 per share we calculated as the bid price that Seek Ltd could offer the shareholders of Found Ltd. Say the directors of Seek have decided to offer $2.50 per share to give Found's shareholders a premium of 25% and to give the acquisition an NPV of $500 000 ($3 000 000 – $2 500 000). If Seek is making a cash bid and Found's price is $2.20 per share at the time of the offer, the NPV of the takeover is not affected by any speculative component ($0.20 in this situation) in Found's share price. Found's price increase means that shareholders who sold at $2 have lost their part of the takeover premium. When the takeover offer is made, shareholders might reject the offer because they think the premium is too low at 23% (0.50/2.20). Have a look at example 16.4 to see what happens when Seek makes a share bid to Found's shareholders.

EXAMPLE 16.4

Calculating the cost of a share bid

The present value of Seek is $5 000 000 and Found has a present value of $2 000 000. Synergies with a present value of $1 000 000 are expected from the merger. There are 1 000 000 shares in Found Ltd and 2 000 000 in Seek.

If the market price of Seek reflects the company's present value, the price will be:

$$\frac{5000\,000}{200\,000} = \$2.50 \text{ per share}$$

If the market price of Found reflects its present value of $2 per share when Seek are working out the share exchange ratio, they could offer 1 Seek share for each 1.25 Found shares. This is a fair value exchange as one Seek share is worth $2.50 and 1.25 Found shares are worth $2.50 (1.25 × $2). However, Found's shareholders would be likely to reject this offer as they won't make a gain and they would be expecting to get something extra for selling to the bidder. Let's say that Seek offers a one-for-one share exchange so that Found gets the equivalent of $2.50 per share. Seek would then have a total of 3 000 000 issued shares after the takeover. We would expect the share price of the post-takeover company to be higher than the current price of the bidder — if it isn't the expectation, then the takeover bid should not proceed. We would expect the post-takeover share price of Seek to be:

$$\frac{5000\,000 + 2000\,000 + 1000\,000}{300\,000} = \$2.67$$

This means Found's shareholders effectively get $2.67 in exchange for each share.

Every extra dollar of gain for the target's shareholders is a dollar lost to the bidder's original shareholders when the bidder is using either cash or shares. The bidder wants to acquire the target for the lowest possible amount that will still result in a successful takeover. As we can see from example 16.4, the bidder's shareholders can potentially pay much more for the target if the acquisition's impact on the post-takeover share price is not considered when determining the number of shares to offer in exchange for the target's shares. The gain to the target's shareholders can be measured as the difference between the cash offered for the purchase of shares in a cash bid, but their gain in a share offer depends on the accuracy of the bidder's estimate of the present value of the synergies from the takeover.

What happens to the bidder's share price when takeover offers are made? This depends on the type of consideration offered. The bidder's original shareholders, on average, see the price of their shares fall when announcements of share exchange takeovers are made. The announcement of a cash offer normally generates positive returns for the bidder's shareholders.[15] Now we have had a closer look at determining the present value of the target, we will discuss how to determine the gains from a takeover.

Calculating the potential gain from a takeover

The economic gain from a takeover is the present value of the incremental cash flows that will accrue to the post-takeover combined company. Sources of incremental cash flows include higher net operating cash flows, inflows from selling surplus assets and outflows associated with planned upgrades of the post-takeover company's assets.

The incremental cash inflows in our transport company takeover would include higher sales and operating costs, but there should be savings in operating costs from the capacity to make bulk purchases of inputs and negotiate a lower price per unit. It might be possible to generate cost savings by centralising administrative functions or reducing the size of the management team. It might be possible to sell one of the pre-takeover head offices, or at least save the rental on one of these spaces. If it turned out that the combined entity had too many trucks, the excess could be sold to generate a cash inflow. Basically, we use forecast incremental cash flows and discount them as we did for the cash flows in chapter 8.

The choice of discount rate will be important in determining the present value of the gain. If the capital structures of the two pre-takeover firms are similar with respect to their proportions of debt and equity and the risks of the two companies are similar, the bidder's weighted average cost of capital would be an appropriate discount rate. The WACC would probably be suitable for the acquisition of Inner Circle Rum by Lion Nathan (see the opening page of this chapter) as the lines of business are similar and the target company was much smaller than the bidder, so it is unlikely that there would be much impact on Lion Nathan's capital structure after the acquisition. If the risks of the target's operations are different to those of the bidder, a higher or lower discount rate than the bidder's WACC should be used. If the capital structure of the post-takeover company is different, then a new WACC will have to be estimated to discount the incremental cash flows. This will be the most likely scenario in the private equity takeovers discussed in the next section.

FINANCE WORKSHOP 16.4

The board of Carpet Ltd are evaluating the takeover of Rug Ltd. The present value of Carpet is currently \$10 million and Rug has a present value of \$2.5 million. Synergies with a present value of \$750 000 are expected for the post-takeover company. Carpet would pay \$3 375 000 to acquire Rug.

1. What is the NPV of the takeover?
2. Should Carpet proceed with a takeover bid?

lo5

Describe how and why companies change from public to private ownership and from private to public ownership using takeovers.

Leveraged buyout: when the purchase of a listed company is financed predominantly with debt

From public to private ownership

Historically, the bidders for Australian listed companies have been other companies. The **leveraged buyout** (LBO) is a more recent trend in the Australian takeover market. A leveraged buyout involves highly-geared bidders taking over listed companies. Rather than look for synergies in the takeover, the bidders in the LBO aim to change the ownership structure of the firm so they can better control costs and make improvements to management. The bidders in Australian LBOs are typically private equity funds. These funds often have the intention of acquiring a listed company, delisting it when they acquire control, improving the operating performance of the firm then selling it to some other private buyers or re-floating the company on the exchange to make their profits. The Qantas case we have discussed throughout this chapter is an example of an LBO.

While leveraged buyouts were not unknown during the 1980s and 1990s, they became more common in 2001 and their number increased dramatically in 2006. The average annual total value of successful LBOs for the period 2000 to 2005 was $1.5 billion. The value of successful LBOs in 2006 was $27 billion.[16] Figure 16.5 highlights the increase in the total dollar value of LBOs in Australia from 1999 to 2006.

Although the value of LBOs has increased rapidly, they only represented about 15% of Australian takeovers in 2006.[17] Further, during the peak year of 2006 LBOs were only worth about 1% of the entire value of the Australian corporate sector.[18]

The RBA attributes the meteoric growth in value of LBOs to the relatively low cost of debt recently experienced in the Australian market, a favourable economic outlook and the superannuation funds' investments into private equity funds.[19] The cost of debt is a very important factor in the LBO decision because the bidders finance most of the acquisition with borrowed funds. This is why it was essential for the APA consortium to get the approval of their bankers before they lowered the proportion of Qantas shares necessary for the takeover to proceed.

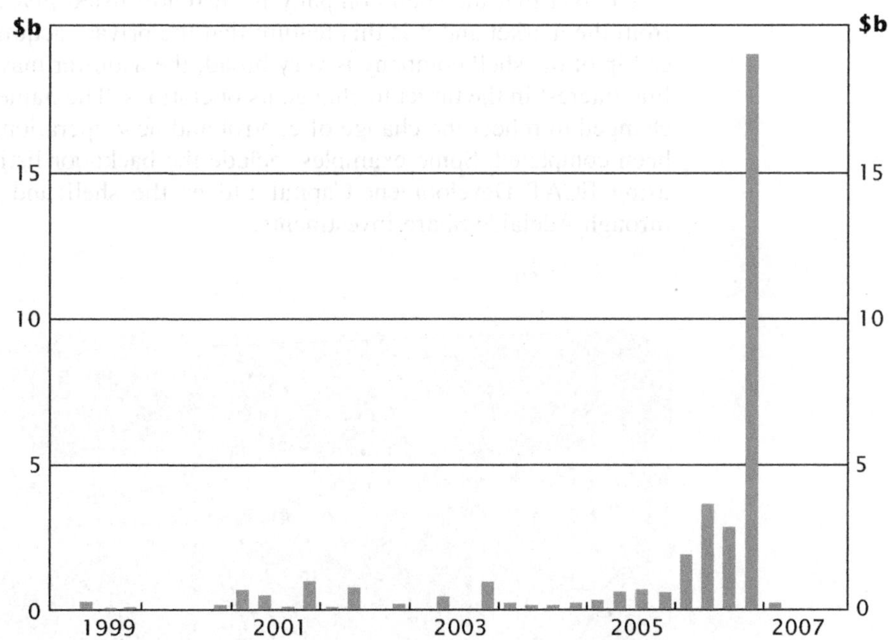

Figure 16.5 LBO activity in Australia, 1999–2006

Source: Reserve Bank of Australia.[20]

Strong economic performance is necessary for the private equity fund to generate sufficient cash to repay the money they borrowed to pay the target's shareholders. The high gearing of the post-LBO firm means the target companies need to have strong and smooth operating cash flows and low levels of debt to make positive returns for their post-takeover owners.

Management buyout: an LBO where the managers of the target firm lead the private equity bid

A **management buyout** (MBO) is an LBO where the managers of the target firm lead the private equity bid. Although the CEO of Qantas became involved with the bidder by agreeing to participate in the post-takeover firm and contributing some equity, the Qantas bid is an LBO rather than an MBO as the bid was not obviously initiated by the existing management of Qantas.

From private to public ownership

Backdoor listing: a takeover of a listed company by a private company, where the listed company continues trading on the exchange and the shares represent an ownership interest in the previously private company's assets

We discuss the IPO process in chapter 12. **Backdoor listing** is an alternative way to take a private company public. Backdoor listing is a takeover of a listed company by a private company, where the listed company continues trading on the exchange and the shares represent an ownership interest in the previously private company's assets. Backdoor listing allows a private company to avoid some of the costs of listing and shortens the amount of time it takes for the 'new' company's shares to trade on the exchange.

The 'target' in a backdoor listing is most likely to be a distressed company that has few or no assets on its balance sheet. Therefore, the operations of the listed company have effectively ceased. These companies are often called 'shell' companies because the inner working bits are missing. Backdoor listing was a popular method of listing for dot.coms during their boom. Backdoor dot.coms often used shells that had been mining companies. Interestingly, many failed dot.coms were used as shells by mining companies after the dot.com bubble collapsed.

The fact that the shell company is currently listed gives it the potential to raise capital from the market and it is this feature that the private acquirer is willing to pay for. If ownership of the shell company is very broad, the acquirer may only need to acquire a controlling interest in the target to change its operations. The name of the shell company is usually changed to reflect the change of control and new operations when the backdoor listing has been completed. Some examples include the backdoor listing of Clinical Cell Culture Ltd using ECAT Development Capital Ltd as the shell and Cockatoo Ridge Wines listing through Adelaide Share Investments.

FINANCE WORKSHOP 16.5

1. Go to www.delisted.com.au and see if you can identify any likely backdoor listings by looking at company name changes. Small name changes like 'H Pettiford Holdings Ltd' to 'Pettiford Holdings Ltd' are unlikely to be backdoor listings. Very different names (like those in the previous paragraph) are worth investigating.
2. Click the links for some companies without a ticker code (the ASX trading code shown in brackets next to the company names). Have a look to see if they have been takeover targets or have delisted for some other reason.

lo6

Explain how and why companies use sell-offs and spin-offs to divest their assets.

Sell-off or divestiture: the sale of a major asset by the company

Spin-off: the creation of a new company from an existing line of business

Conglomerate: a company with several subsidiaries that operate in unrelated lines of business

Selling part of the company

In this section we examine two main ways a company can restructure by selling some of its assets. A sell-off or divestiture is the sale of a major asset by the company. Often, the major asset forms the basis of a line of business. A spin-off is a special case of a sell-off, where the sale of a line of business results in the creation of a new company.

Sell-offs

Major assets should be sold by a company if the sales price is larger than the NPV of operating the asset. Shareholder wealth will be increased if the assets are more valuable to the purchaser (as reflected in the sale price) than they are in their current use. Cooney, Finn and Karl[21] find that shareholder wealth increases with the announcement of a sell-off of assets that are unrelated to the company's core business. Often, a sell-off is the consequence of a previous takeover. Earlier, we identified the potential for the sale of excess or unwanted assets that were acquired with the target to generate cash inflows from a takeover. Another reason for divesting assets after a takeover is that the ACCC might require the sale of some assets post-takeover to prevent the new company having too much market power. Toll Holdings, for example, was required to sell its interests in Pacific National after its takeover of Patrick Corporation.[22]

After a history of acquisitions, the boards and shareholders of some conglomerates decide to refocus their companies back to one core business. Dunlop Pacific Ltd provides a good example of this phenomenon. Originally listed in 1899, Dunlop commenced its operations with the manufacture of bicycle tyres. The company then expanded operations by manufacturing other rubber products like footwear. Dunlop then commenced a program of acquisitions that took the company into the production of sporting goods, bedding and several ranges of clothing. In response to poor performance, the decision to divest all but the core business of rubber glove and condom manufacture was made and the company sold the non-core assets to a private equity consortium in 2001.[23] Dunlop changed its name to Ansell in 2002. The private equity owners who purchased Dunlop's non-core assets floated a new company, Pacific Brands, in 2004.[24] We will discuss a special case of selling an existing line of business as a separate company in the next section.

The spin-off decision

A company can effect a spin-off in two main ways. The first is to make a pro-rata distribution of shares to existing shareholders and list the new company on the exchange so these shares can be traded. Shareholders do not pay anything for the shares in this case. The second method is to sell the line of business in an IPO. Current shareholders may receive preference in the allocation of shares and/or pay a lower price for the shares. This differs from the first type of spin-off because new capital is raised for the spin-off company. Some Australian spin-offs have combined a free distribution of shares with a new capital raising in the IPO.[25]

The new owners of a spin-off might be old owners of the assets, so do spin-offs increase shareholder wealth? Durand, Woodliff and Richards studied Australian spin-offs and found that that shareholder wealth does increase when a spin-off is announced.[26] They concluded that the wealth gains are attributable to information asymmetries — the market finds it easier to value two separate entities with fewer lines of business than it does to value one company with several lines of business. They also found that moving back to a core business is viewed positively by the market. This means that even though the spin-off doesn't involve a cash inflow to the company, the shareholders gain.

Another potential reason for a spin-off is to avoid legislative restrictions that currently affect the firm as a whole. The following 'finance world' feature discusses how a spin-off of non-bank assets would improve the operation of Macquarie's banking business by allowing the non-bank assets to be freed of the capital adequacy requirements placed on the bank.

FINANCE WORLD

Macquarie's proposed spin-off

Application to APRA for a non-bank spin-off

SCOTT MURDOCH

Macquarie has stepped up its campaign to spin off its non-bank assets into a separate entity that will allow it to operate outside the restrictions of its banking licence.

Macquarie has applied to APRA to establish the non-operational holding company, and is awaiting a decision.

Macquarie is believed to be part of a group of banks that has discussed the issue with Treasury officials in Canberra.

For the move to proceed, Treasury will have to alter legislation to allow the proposed bank restructure.

National Australia Bank is another player believed to be involved, as it thinks it could put its agribusiness assets in the holding company.

Macquarie announced plans to create the company last year.

The idea is to give it flexibility and a business model more similar to its rival, Babcock and Brown, the pure investment bank.

At its annual meeting last year, Macquarie told shareholders that having a banking licence was onerous. It said placing the businesses not covered by the licence in another entity would be beneficial.

Analysts said APRA had made Macquarie hold more regulatory capital than commercial banks because of its investment banking businesses.

At the time, the bank said its international operations were growing at a faster rate than its domestic banking.

The proposed regulatory changes come as the Macquarie old guard changes again, with the resignation of deputy chairman Mark Johnson.

A Macquarie spokesman said the application had been lodged with APRA.

Bank staff are understood to have met with Treasury experts but the Government has given no indication on whether it will give the official go-ahead.

APRA refused to comment, but it is believed Macquarie is sticking to its original time frame, putting the deal to shareholders later this year.

It says it could be 18 months from the time of the announcement in July last year, before the separate company is operating.[27]

FINANCE WORKSHOP 16.6

Look in the financial press to see if you can find an example of a recent sell-off or spin-off. Are any reasons given for the sales of the assets?

CORPORATE FINANCIAL GOVERNANCE

Restructuring decisions

We have discussed the role of corporate governance in the decision making processes a number of times throughout this book. So far, we haven't been able to establish a clear link between changes in corporate governance and increases in shareholder wealth. Corporate restructuring is one area where strong corporate governance is crucial. Think back to the Qantas case. The chair of the board went to great lengths to assure shareholders that those members of the management team who would be involved in the post-takeover company were not involved in the board's decision to recommend the offer. This did not stop media speculation that management had been involved in attracting a bidder and formulating the first offer.[28]

Some potential corporate governance issues that could arise with restructures include:

- the purchase of potential target company shares by insiders before a takeover announcement is announced
- the possibility that management have been involved in discussions with the bidder and have made 'sweetheart' deals in return for supporting the bidder when the offer goes to the target's board
- a corporate advisor obtaining inside information when providing services to the target then using the inside information to formulate either a leveraged buyout or participating in a management buyout.

On a more positive note, Ahn and Walker[29] find that spin-offs in the US are more likely to be undertaken by companies that have characteristics associated with good corporate governance. These characteristics include boards with diverse membership, higher levels of share ownership by independent directors and generally smaller boards.

executive summary

lo1 define the key terminology of takeovers

- Takeovers allow a company (or group of companies and/or individuals) to gain control of an existing company.
- The bidder makes an offer for shares in the company it wishes to acquire.
- The takeover target is the company that the bidder wants to acquire.
- A merger is the combination of two (or more) businesses into a single entity.
- A substantial shareholding is the ownership of 5% or more of the voting shares of a listed company.
- Private equity firms acquire listed companies and operate them as private businesses.
- A proportional takeover bid specifies a proportion of shares (less than 100%) that the bidder wants to purchase.
- Market takeovers occur where the bidder purchases the shares of the target by normal trading on the stock exchange.
- Off-market takeovers occur when the bidder gives the target's shareholders an application form to complete the sale of their shares at a specified offer price.
- A conditional takeover offer is one where certain requirements have to be met for the takeover offer to proceed. Only off-market takeovers can be conditional bids.
- The bid period is the time from when the bidder makes the takeover offer to the time that the offer closes.
- The bidder's statement sets out the terms and conditions of the takeover offer.
- A supplementary bidder's statement is distributed to advise shareholders of new circumstances that could affect their decision on the bid or to correct any misstatement or omission in the original bidder's statement.
- The target's statement contains the target's directors' recommendations on the acceptability of the takeover offer and the reasons for their recommendations.
- A supplementary target's statement is distributed to advise shareholders of new circumstances that could affect their decision on the bid or to correct any misstatement or omission in the original target's statement.
- A compulsory acquisition occurs when the bidder is allowed to purchase any shares in the target company it does not already own.
- The ACCC reviews takeovers to make sure the post-takeover company would not breach the anti-competitive behaviour provisions of the *Trade Practices Act 1974*.
- The Takeovers Panel is the forum for disputes between parties to takeover offers during the bid period.

lo2 explain the procedures for takeovers

- To increase the probability that shareholders will accept their bid, bidders in an off-market bid might approach the board of the target company prior to issuing a bidder's statement. The formal bidder's statement is then prepared.
- The first official step in an off-market bid is for the bidder to give the bidder's statement and the offer document to ASIC and the target's board of directors, and to release the statement to the market (that is, notify the ASX).
- The second step is to notify ASIC that the target's board and the ASX have received the bidder's statement and offer document.

- The third step is to supply the bidder's statement to all shareholders for their consideration.
- The fourth step is to notify the target's board, ASIC and the ASX that the bidder's statement has been made available to all shareholders.
- The final step in an off-market offer is for the board of the target to release its statement. The target's statement recommends the acceptance or rejection of the offer. This document must be sent to the bidder, the shareholders, ASIC and the ASX.
- The first step in a market bid is to announce the bid to the ASX.
- The second step is to release the bidder's statement to the ASX, the target's board of directors and ASIC.
- Next, the bidder's statement for a market bid is made available to all shareholders. The bidder might also supply other documentation to the shareholders with the bidder's statement, such as independent valuations of the target's shares.
- The four step is to supply any documentation that was sent to shareholders in addition to the bidder's statement to the ASX and ASIC.
- Release of the target's statement to the ASX, the bidder, ASIC and the target's shareholders is the fifth step in the market bid procedure.
- The final step is for the bidder to make offers on the market to purchase the target's shares.

---

lo3 outline the rationales for takeovers and critically analyse these

- Australian listed companies make bids for other listed companies and for unlisted companies.
- Not all takeover bids are successful.
- The three broad groups of rationales for takeovers are synergistic gains, target undervaluation and managerial desires.
- Synergy occurs when the value of two assets combined is greater than the sum of the individual values.
- Synergies can come from combining the operations of two companies or they may arise from financial characteristics (increased company size gives access to Euromarkets, for example).
- A horizontal takeover occurs when two companies in the same business are combined.
- Vertical takeovers are the acquisition of a related business that either supplies the buyer or is closer to the consumer of the buyer's goods or services.
- Economies of scale are efficiency gains from producing more of a good or service.
- The majority of Australian listed companies do not have an analyst following. This means there may be potential for a bidder to spot an undervalued company that will generate a takeover gain.
- A conglomerate takeover is the acquisition of a business that is unrelated to the current operations of the buyer. Managers may propose conglomerate takeovers to build their empires or to diversify their personal levels of risk.
- Compensating managers for increasing EPS may result in takeovers without any real gains to the shareholders of the bidder.
- Bootstrapping is the capacity to increase EPS in a takeover in the absence of any economic gains for shareholders coming from the takeover.

lo4 calculate the NPV of a proposed takeover

- To be consistent with the objective of maximising shareholder wealth, the value of a business that combines both the bidder and the target should be greater than the sum of the values of the bidder and the target when they are operating separately.
- Takeover premium is the amount paid for the target's shares less the present value of the target's operations.
- The market value of the target firm is unlikely to be a good indicator of the target's present value because the market prices the probability of a takeover offer prior to the offer being made.
- The gain to target shareholders in a cash bid is the difference between the cash they receive and the market price of their shares.
- The gain to target shareholders in a share bid depends on the value of the bidder's shares at the completion of the takeover.
- Net cash inflows from the takeover should be discounted using an appropriate discount rate.

lo5 describe how and why companies change from public to private ownership and from private to public ownership using takeovers

- A leveraged buyout (LBO) occurs when the purchase of a listed company is financed predominantly with debt.
- After cutting costs and improving management, private equity companies sell the companies they have acquired to make their return.
- A management buyout (MBO) is an LBO where the managers of a target firm lead the private equity bid.
- Backdoor listing is a takeover of a listed company by a private company, where the listed company continues trading on the exchange and the shares represent an ownership interest in the previously private company's assets.
- Backdoor listing is a faster way of achieving listing than conducting an IPO and making an application to the exchange.

lo6 explain how and why companies use sell-offs and spin-offs to divest their assets

- A sell-off (or divestiture) is the sale of a major asset by the company.
- Major assets should be sold by a company if the sales price is larger than the NPV of operating the asset.
- A conglomerate is a company with several subsidiaries that operate in unrelated lines of business.
- A spin-off creates a new company from an existing line of business.
- The shares of a spin-off can be given to the existing shareholders of the company.
- An IPO can be conducted to achieve the spin-off. In this case, existing shareholders may be given shares in the new company. They may also be given preferential treatment when it comes to acquiring shares in the new company.

Key terms

backdoor listing, p. 626
bid period, p. 610
bidder, p. 602
bidder's statement, p. 610
bootstrapping, p. 620
compulsory acquisition, p. 610
conditional bid, p. 609
conglomerate, p. 627
conglomerate takeover, p. 618
divestiture, p. 627
economies of scale, p. 617
horizontal takeover, p. 617
leveraged buyout, p. 625
management buyout, p. 626
market takeover, p. 609
merger, p. 603
off-market takeover, p. 609
private equity firms, p. 609
proportional takeover bid, p. 609
sell-off, p. 627
spin-off, p. 627
substantial shareholding, p. 608
supplementary bidder's statement, p. 610
supplementary target's statement, p. 611
synergy, p. 617
takeover, p. 602
takeover premium, p. 620
target, p. 603
target's statement, p. 611
vertical takeover, p. 617

Learning chart

Learning objective	Questions	Self-test problems	Financial problems
lo1 define the key terminology of takeovers	16.1, 16.2, 16.3		
lo2 explain the procedures for takeovers	16.4		
lo3 outline the rationales for takeovers and critically analyse these	16.5, 16.6, 16.7, 16.8		16.1, 16.2, 16.11, 16.12
lo4 calculate the NPV of a proposed takeover	16.9, 16.10, 16.11, 16.12	16.1, 16.2, 16.3, 16.4, 16.5	16.2, 16.3, 16.4, 16.5, 16.6, 16.7, 16.8, 16.9, 16.10, 16.12, 16.13, 16.14, 16.15, 16.16, 16.17, 16.18, 16.19, 16.20
lo5 describe how and why companies change from public to private ownership and from private to public ownership using takeovers	16.13, 16.14, 16.15		
lo6 explain how and why companies use sell-offs and spin-offs to divest their assets	16.16, 16.17, 16.18, 16.19, 16.20		

Questions

16.1 What is a proportional takeover bid?

16.2 What is a conditional takeover offer?

16.3 Explain how a bidder can end up with 100% of the target's shares when it has only purchased 90% of the shares at the end of the bid period.

16.4 Outline four main differences between market and off-market bids.

16.5 What does synergy mean? What are the general sources of synergies?

16.6 Explain the difference between vertical and horizontal takeovers. Give an example of each type.

16.7 Assume you are a manager looking for an undervalued takeover target. What type of firm would you look for?

16.8 Apart from maximising shareholder wealth, what reasons might managers have for proposing takeovers?

16.9 Is the market price of the target a good indication of the target's present value at the time the bid is made? Why?

16.10 Is the takeover premium known with certainty at the time of a bid that has shares as consideration? Why?

16.11 What types of cash flows should be included in the NPV analysis of a takeover? Give some examples.

16.12 What discount rate should a bidder use when evaluating a takeover proposition?

16.13 How do the acquirers in a leveraged buyout make their returns?

16.14 What is a management buyout? How is it different to a leveraged buyout?

16.15 What is a backdoor listing? Why do backdoor listings occur?

16.16 What are sell-offs and spin-offs? How are they different?

16.17 Why would a company sell its major assets?

16.18 When will a sell-off increase shareholder wealth?

16.19 What are two ways a company can issue shares in a spin-off? How are the two methods different?

16.20 Do spin-offs create wealth for shareholders? Why?

Self-test problems

The management of Chocolate Ltd is considering making a takeover offer for the shares of Biscuit Ltd. The present value of Chocolate is \$3 000 000 and Biscuit has a present value of \$1 500 000. Synergies with a present value of \$500 000 are expected from the takeover. There are 500 000 shares in Biscuit Ltd and 500 000 in Chocolate. Use this information to answer the following questions.

16.1. What is the expected gain from the takeover?

16.2. What is the maximum price per share Chocolate would offer for Biscuit?

16.3. If Chocolate decides to offer a premium of 30%, how much will it offer for each share in Biscuit? Assume that Biscuit's share price reflects the present value of the company.

16.4. Calculate the NPV of the takeover. Chocolate will make cash payments per share of the amount you calculated in problem 16.3.

16.5. Should Chocolate proceed with the takeover? Why?

Solutions to self-test problems

16.1. The gain on takeover is the \$500 000 synergy.

16.2. NPV = gain – premium

Setting the NPV to zero, we have

$$0 = 500000 - (\text{payment} - PV_T)$$

$$\text{Payment} = 500000 + PV_T$$
$$= 500000 + 1500000$$
$$= 2000000$$

$$\text{Payment per share} = \frac{2000000}{500000} = \$4$$

16.3. Current price of Biscuit shares $= \dfrac{1500000}{500000} = \$3$ per share

Bid price $= 3 \times 1.3 = \$3.90$

16.4. NPV = gain − premium

$$= 500000 - [(3.9 \times 500000) - 1500000)]$$
$$= 50000$$

16.5. The takeover should proceed as the NPV is positive. Chocolate's shareholders will increase their wealth.

Financial problems

16.1 Each member of the management team of Bird Ltd receives a bonus if they achieve an annual increase of 5% in EPS in any year. They have identified Feather Ltd as a potential takeover target. They do not expect any synergies to arise from the takeover and Feather is not currently undervalued by the market. Complete the table and answer the following questions.

	Pre-takeover		Post-takeover
	Bird Ltd	Feather Ltd	
Issued shares	3 000 000	1 000 000	3 600 000
Earnings	3 500 000	1 500 000	
EPS			
Share price	20	12	
PE ratio			
Total market value			

(a) What will the EPS and PE ratio for the post-takeover company be?

(b) What is the exchange ratio of shares in the takeover?

(c) Will the management of Bird receive their bonuses in the year of the takeover?

(d) Will Bird's shareholders gain or lose from the takeover?

16.2 As noted in the previous question, the management team of Bird Ltd each receives a bonus if they achieve an annual increase of 5% in EPS in any year. In addition to Feather Ltd, they are also considering Cage Ltd as a potential takeover target. There will be synergies from the acquisition of Cage as this would be a horizontal takeover. The present value of these synergies would be $1 000 000. Complete the table and answer the following questions.

	Pre-takeover		Post-takeover
	Bird Ltd	Cage Ltd	
Issued shares	3 000 000	1 000 000	3 800 000
Earnings	3 500 000	2 000 000	
EPS			
Share price	20	12	
PE ratio			
Total market value	60 000 000	12 000 000	73 000 000

(a) What will the EPS and PE ratio for the post-takeover firm be?

(b) What is the exchange ratio of shares in the Cage takeover?

(c) Will the management of Bird receive their bonuses in the year of the takeover?

(d) Will Cage's shareholders gain or lose from the takeover?

(e) Will Bird's shareholders gain or lose from the takeover?

16.3 The management of Apex Ltd is considering a takeover of Nadir Ltd. The present value of Apex is $10 000 000 and Nadir has a present value of $2 500 000. Synergies with a present value of $1 500 000 are expected from the takeover. There are 1 250 000 shares in Nadir Ltd and 2 500 000 in Apex. What is the maximum price per share Apex would offer for Nadir?

16.4 If Apex (see problem 16.3) decides to offer a premium of 30%, how much will it offer for each share in Nadir? Assume that Nadir's share price reflects the present value of the company.

16.5 Calculate the NPV of the Apex takeover (see problem 16.3). Assume Apex will make cash payments per share of the amount you calculated in problem 16.4. Should Apex proceed with the takeover? Why?

16.6 (a) Calculate the NPV of the Apex takeover (see problem 16.3). Assume Apex will give one of its shares for each 1.5 Nadir shares. Should Apex proceed with the takeover?

(b) What percentage gain would the shareholders of Nadir receive? Round to the nearest share in your calculations.

16.7 Bank Ltd is considering the takeover of Branch Ltd. You have received the following information about the cash flows for the two companies.

	Bank Ltd	Branch Ltd
Revenues	50 000 000	15 000 000
Operating costs	20 000 000	6 000 000
Administrative costs	5 000 000	2 000 000

Bank's management believes it can halve the operating costs of Branch. As Bank has a highly efficient computerised administration system with excess capacity, the administrative costs for Branch are expected to fall to zero after the acquisition. Both banks have a cost of capital of 12%. The cost savings would continue indefinitely and revenues are expected to remain unchanged.

(a) Calculate the present value of Bank Ltd.

(b) Calculate the present value of Branch Ltd.

(c) Calculate the gain on takeover.

16.8 Bank (see problem 16.7) wants to acquire Branch for $80 000 000.

(a) Calculate the size of the takeover premium. Would you expect the shareholders of Branch to accept this offer? Why?

(b) Should Bank go ahead with the takeover?

16.9 Films Ltd is considering the acquisition of Sport View Ltd. These companies both operate pay TV channels and significant benefits are expected from the takeover. You have received the following information about the companies' cash flows.

	Films Ltd	Sport View Ltd
Revenues	5 000 000	3 000 000
Operating costs	800 000	500 000
Administrative costs	700 000	500 000

Films Ltd's management plans to use excess capacity at its transmitting stations to broadcast the channels currently offered by Sports View. The facilities that Sports View currently use could be sold for $1 000 000. Sports View's advertising department would be closed down, generating cost savings of $400 000 pa. Films expects that the centralisation of the advertising function would result in an annual increase of $200 000 in the post-takeover company's revenue. Both companies have a cost of capital of 15%.

(a) Calculate the present value of Films Ltd.

(b) Calculate the present value of Sports View Ltd.

(c) Calculate the gain on takeover.

16.10 Films Ltd (see problem 16.9) wants to acquire Sports View for $15 000 000.

(a) Calculate the size of the takeover premium. Would you expect the shareholders of Sports View to accept this offer? Why?

(b) Should Films Ltd go ahead with the takeover?

16.11 Members of the management team of Sweep Ltd each receive a bonus if they achieve an annual increase of 20% in EPS in any year. They have identified Broom Ltd as a potential takeover target. They do not expect any synergies to arise from the takeover and Broom is not currently undervalued by the market. Complete the table and answer the following questions.

	Pre-takeover		Post-takeover
	Sweep Ltd	Broom Ltd	
Issued shares	4 500 000	3 200 000	6 633 333
Earnings	4 200 000	3 500 000	
EPS			
Share price	12	8	
PE ratio			
Total market value			

(a) What will the EPS and PE ratio for the post-takeover company be?

(b) What is the exchange ratio of shares in the takeover?

(c) Will the management of Broom receive their bonuses in the year of the takeover?

(d) Will Sweep's shareholders gain or lose from the takeover?

16.12 As noted in problem 16.11, the members of the management team of Sweep Ltd each receive a bonus if they achieve an annual increase of 20% in EPS in any year. In addition to Broom Ltd, they are also considering Mop Ltd as a potential takeover target. The synergies that are expected to arise from the acquisition of Mop are $750 000. Complete the table and answer the following questions.

	Pre-takeover		Post-takeover
	Sweep Ltd	Mop Ltd	
Issued shares	4 500 000	1 000 000	5 500 000
Earnings	4 200 000	1 000 000	
EPS			
Share price	12	12	
PE ratio			
Total market value	54 000 000	12 000 000	66 750 000

(a) What will the EPS and PE ratio for the post-takeover firm be?
(b) What is the exchange ratio of shares in the Mop takeover?
(c) Will the management of Sweep receive their bonuses in the year of the takeover?
(d) Will Mop's shareholder gain or lose from the takeover?
(e) Will Sweep's shareholders gain or lose from the takeover?

16.13 The management of Wide Ltd is considering a takeover of Narrow Ltd. The present value of Wide is $4 000 000 and Narrow has a present value of $1 750 000. Synergies with a present value of $400 000 are expected from the takeover. There are 1 000 000 shares in Narrow Ltd. What is the maximum price per share Wide would offer for Narrow?

16.14 If Wide (see problem 16.13) decides to offer a premium of 40%, how much will it offer for each share in Narrow? Assume that Narrow's share price reflects the present value of the company.

16.15 Calculate the NPV of the Wide takeover (see problem 16.13). Assume Wide will make cash payments per share of the amount you calculated in problem 16.14. Should Wide proceed with the takeover? Why?

16.16 (a) Calculate the NPV of the Wide takeover (see problem 16.13). Wide currently has 500 000 shares on issue and will give one of its shares for each 4 Narrow shares. Should Wide proceed with the takeover?
(b) What percentage gain would the shareholders of Narrow receive? Round to the nearest share in your calculations.

16.17 Flower Ltd is considering the takeover of Tree Ltd. You have received the following information about the cash flows for the two companies.

	Flower Ltd	Tree Ltd
Revenues	12 000 000	9 000 000
Operating costs	6 000 000	5 000 000
Administrative costs	1 000 000	900 000

Flower's management believe they can use economies of scale to reduce the operating costs of Tree by $2 000 000. The administrative costs for Tree are expected to halve after the acquisition. Both companies have a cost of capital of 17%. The cost savings would continue indefinitely and revenues are expected to remain unchanged.

(a) Calculate the present value of Flower Ltd.

(b) Calculate the present value of Tree Ltd.

(c) Calculate the gain on takeover.

16.18 Flower (see problem 16.17) wants to acquire Tree for $30 000 000.

(a) Calculate the size of the takeover premium. Would you expect the shareholders of Tree to accept this offer? Why?

(b) Should Flower go ahead with the takeover?

16.19 Woollen Ltd spins and dyes wool for the retail market. The managers are considering the acquisition of Kwik Knit Ltd. Kwik Knit manufactures and distributes knitting patterns to retail outlets. Woollen plans to use Kwik Knit's current customers to market packages of wool, patterns and needles. You have received the following information about the companies' cash flows.

	Woollen Ltd	Kwik Knit Ltd
Revenues	15 000 000	7 000 000
Operating costs	8 000 000	1 500 000
Administrative costs	500 000	300 000

As the lines of business are different, no changes to operating costs are expected. The administrative costs of each operation are expected to fall by 10% after the takeover. The big gain is expected from sales of Woollen's products. Management estimate that Woollen's revenue would increase 20% on the current level and that the higher level of sales can be maintained indefinitely. Both companies have a cost of capital of 14%.

(a) Calculate the present value of Woollen Ltd.

(b) Calculate the present value of Kwik Knit Ltd.

(c) Calculate the gain on takeover.

16.20 Woollen Ltd (see problem 16.19) wants to acquire Kwik Knit for $48 000 000.

(a) Calculate the size of the takeover premium. Would you expect the shareholders of Kwik Knit to accept this offer? Why?

(b) Should Woollen Ltd go ahead with the takeover?

SOLUTIONS TO FINANCE WORKSHOPS

16.1 No solution is available for this question. Your answer depends on the research you have done.

16.2 1. Step 1: the bidder gives the bidder's statement and the offer document to ASIC and the target's board of directors, and releases the statement to the market (that is, notifies the ASX).

Step 2: ASIC is notified that the target's board and the ASX have received the bidder's statement and offer document.

Step 3: the bidder's statement is supplied to all shareholders.

Step 4: the target's board, ASIC and the ASX are notified that the bidder's statement has been made available to all shareholders.

Step 5: the board of the target releases its statement. This document must be sent to the bidder, the shareholders, ASIC and the ASX.

2. No solution is available for this question. Your answer depends on the research you have done.

16.3 1. A tyre manufacturer might make a takeover of a chain of retail tyre outlets. This would be a vertical takeover because it brings the manufacturer one step closer to its consumers.

2. Lion Nathan's takeover of Inner Circle Rum is a horizontal takeover. Lion Nathan already owns a line of business that manufactures spirits, so the acquisition of the rum brand is similar to its current operations.

16.4 1. Takeover gain = PVC − (PVB + PVT)

= (10 000 000 + 2 500 000 + 750 000) − (10 000 000 + 2 500 000)

= 13 250 000 − 12 500 000

= 750 000

Takeover premium = payment − PV_T

= 3 375 000 − 2 500 000

= 875 000

NPV = gain − premium

= 750 000 − 875 000

= −125 000

2. The NPV of the takeover is negative, so Carpet should not proceed with a takeover offer.

16.5 No solution is available for this question. Your answer depends on the research you have done.

16.6 No solution is available for this question. Your answer depends on the research you have done.

End notes

1 Evans, S 2007, 'Market wonders when Lion will roar', *Australian Financial Review*, 14 February, p. 28.

2 Sequence of events compiled from Qantas company announcements to the ASX, www.asx.com.au; Qantas share prices from Yahoo Finance, htttp://au.finance.yahoo.com.

3 Qantas share prices from Yahoo Finance, http://au.finance.yahoo.com.

4 ACCC 2007, *ACCC not to oppose proposed acquisition of Qantas Airways Limited by Airline Partners Australia Limited*, media release MR 050/07, 1 March, www.accc.gov.au.

5 Firth, B 2007, ‘Qantas union’s appeal to the Takeovers Panel a tactical strike’, *The Australian*, 23 March, p. 22.

6 Reserve Bank of Australia (RBA) 2007, ‘Domestic financial markets and conditions’, *Statement on monetary policy — February 2007*, www.rba.gov.au.

7 da Silva Rosa, R, Limmack, R, Supriadi, S & Woodliff, D 2004, ‘The equity wealth effects of method of payment in takeover bids for privately held firms’, *Australian Journal of Management*, vol. 29, special issue, pp. 93–110.

8 Finn, F & Hodgson, A 2005, ‘Takeover activity in Australia: endogenous and exogenous influences’, *Accounting and Finance*, vol. 45, pp. 375–94.

9 Maheswaran, K & Pinder, S 2005, ‘Australian evidence on the impact and determinants of takeover resistance’, *Accounting and Finance*, vol. 45, pp. 613–33.

10 RBA 2007, graph 61.

11 Finn & Hodgson 2005 and Reserve Bank of Australia 2007.

12 Lev, B 1992, ‘Observations on the merger phenomenon: a review of the evidence’, in J Stern and D Chew (eds), *The revolution in corporate finance*, 2nd edn, Blackwell Publishing, Oxford.

13 FINSIA 2006, *ASX and FINSIA combine to provide equity research coverage for ASX-listed companies*, media release, 14 November, www.finsia.edu.au.

14 Maheswaran & Pinder 2005.

15 Maheswaran & Pinder 2005.

16 RBA 2007.

17 Reserve Bank of Australia 2006, ‘Domestic financial markets and conditions’, *Statement on monetary policy — November 2006*, www.rba.gov.au.

18 RBA 2006.

19 RBA 2007.

20 RBA 2007.

21 Cooney, M, Finn, F & Karl, A 2004, ‘Australian divestiture activity: an examination of gains to sell-off announcements’, *Australian Journal of Management*, vol. 29, special issue, pp. 135–51.

22 Knight, E 2006, ‘Toll got jigsaw puzzle but not the picture’, *Sydney Morning Herald*, 2 August, p. 20.

23 Maiden, M, 2003, ‘Freed from the dead hand of conglomerate’, *Sydney Morning Herald*, 14 July, p.28.

24 Williams, J 2004, ‘Aussie icon soars on debut — investors rush offer’, *The Courier-Mail*, 3 April, p. 75.

25 Durand, R, Woodliff, D & Richards, O 2003, ‘Spin-offs in Australia’, *Accounting Research Journal*, vol. 16, no. 2, pp. 90–101.

26 Durand, Woodliff & Richards 2003.

27 Murdoch, S 2007, ‘Application to APRA for a non-bank spin-off’, *The Australian*, 13 March, p. 23.

28 Evans, M 2007, ‘Qantas deal was out of the blue’, *Sydney Morning Herald*, 7 March, p. 23.

29 Ahn, S & Walker, M 2007, ‘Corporate governance and the spinoff decision’, *Journal of Corporate Finance*, pp. 76–93.

chapter

17

International corporate finance

Learning objectives

After studying this chapter, you should be able to:

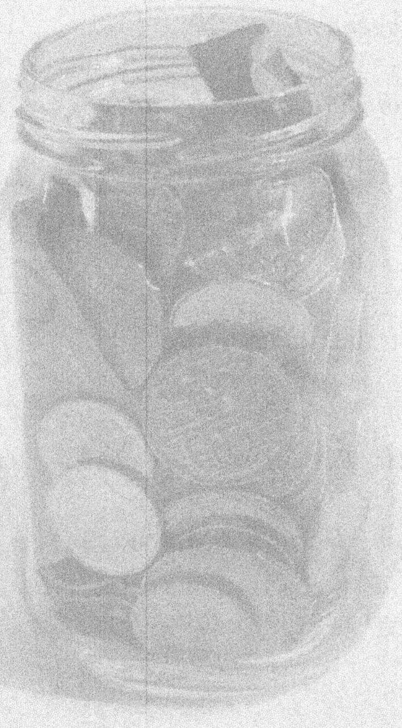

lo1	describe the roles of market participants
lo2	understand foreign exchange rate quotations
lo3	calculate return on foreign currency denominated securities and cross exchange rates
lo4	explain the purchasing power parity, the covered interest rate parity and the unbiased forward rate conditions
lo5	discuss the implications of the uncovered interest parity and the international Fisher effect
lo6	discuss the foreign exchange exposure of firms
lo7	undertake international capital budgeting using the home currency and foreign currency methods.

WESTPAC'S FOREIGN EXCHANGE EXPOSURE

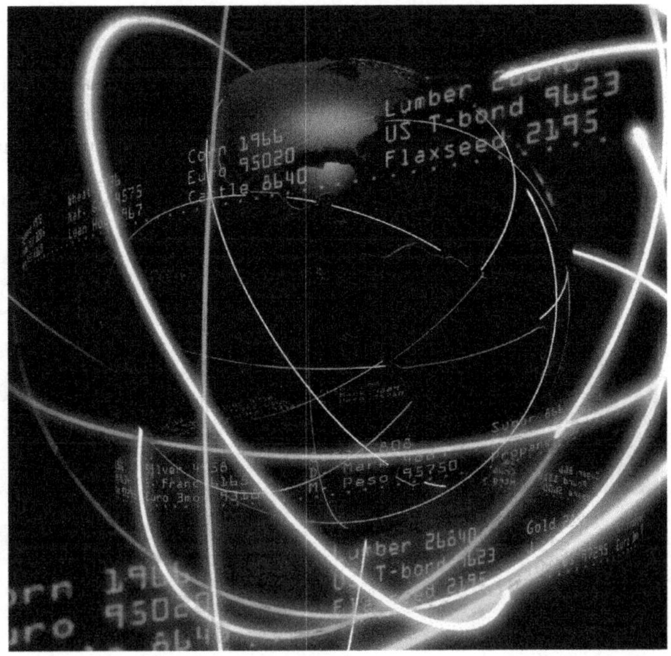

Table 17.1 shows the foreign exchange exposure of Westpac Banking Corporation, a major commercial bank in Australia with significant operations in New Zealand and other overseas locations. The distribution of assets, liabilities and net profits by geographic markets is summarised in this table.

Westpac's foreign currency denominated assets exceeded its foreign currency denominated liabilities, which implies that any depreciation of a foreign currency (for example, the New Zealand dollar) against the Australian dollar would lead to erosion in the market value of its foreign currency denominated net assets. The distribution of net profits by geographic markets also suggests that a significant part of Westpac's net profits is generated from overseas operations, which are exposed to foreign exchange as well as country risks.

Table 17.1 Foreign exchange exposure of Westpac Banking Corporation

	Australia		New Zealand		Other overseas		Australia	New Zealand	Other overseas
Year*	Total assets (A$m)	Total liabilities (A$m)	Total assets (A$m)	Total liabilities (A$m)	Total assets (A$m)	Total liabilities (A$m)	Net profit (A$m)	Net profit (A$m)	Net profit (A$m)
2005	210 682	196 512	40 054	38 521	35 436	33 927	1 841	592	385
2004	197 901	186 706	38 062	36 165	32 368	29 143	1 584	638	317
2003	179 908	170 778	32 945	31 263	26 454	23 270	1 604	386	193
2002	151 918	145 230	30 972	28 693	22 807	21 306	1 866	466	–140
2001	151 421	146 014	28 977	26 913	26 209	23 975	1 301	336	266
2000	133 578	128 126	24 973	23 479	25 853	23 447	1 161	329	225

*Assets and liabilities figures are for 30 September and net profits figures are for years ended 30 September.

Source: Data derived from Westpac Banking Corporation annual reports.

Chapter preview

So far in this book, we have studied corporate finance decisions primarily in the context of firms operating domestically. In practice, many firms buy raw materials and equipment abroad, sell products in foreign markets, raise funds from foreign capital markets, invest in foreign countries and pay dividends to their overseas shareholders. This process has created new investment and financing opportunities for the firms, but at the same time exposed them to foreign exchange and political risk. Although the previously discussed decision rules for investment, capital structure and dividend policy are relevant for a firm with foreign currency denominated assets and liabilities, some unique aspects of financial decisions of a firm with international risk exposure will be examined in this chapter.

First, we will examine the operations of the foreign exchange market. Second, the fundamental determinates of the foreign exchange rate are examined. Third, foreign exchange risk faced by a firm with international operations is discussed. Fourth, capital budgeting decisions of this type of firm are analysed.

The following diagram shows how this chapter is structured.

INTERNATIONAL CORPORATE FINANCE		
	The foreign exchange market	• Market participants • Foreign exchange rate quotation • Return on foreign currency denominated securities • Cross exchange rates
	Determinants of the foreign exchange rate	• Absolute purchasing power parity • Relative purchasing power parity • Covered interest rate parity • Unbiased forward rate • Uncovered interest parity • The international Fisher effect
	Exchange rate risk	
	International capital budgeting	• The home currency method • The foreign currency method

lo*1*

Describe the roles of market participants.

The foreign exchange market

The foreign exchange market is undoubtedly the largest market in the world in terms of volume of trading. Foreign currencies are traded in the over-the-counter (OTC) markets, not in a single unified foreign exchange market. The major trading centres for international currencies are London, New York, Tokyo and Singapore.

The Australian foreign exchange market is the sixth largest in the world. In April 2006, the daily average turnover in the Australian spot foreign exchange market was over $70 billion. Although Australia is only the fifteenth largest economy in the world, the Australian/US currency pair (AUD/USD) is the fourth most traded pair in the world, reflecting the high liquidity of the market.

Market participants

Arbitrageur: a market participant who buys and sells identical assets in different markets to make riskless profit from small differences in prices between the different markets

Hedger: a market participant who engages in financial market transactions to reduce risk

Speculator: a market participant who assumes risk in the expectation of earning a high return

Major participants in the foreign exchange market can be classified into three groups based on their motives for foreign exchange trading: arbitrageurs, hedgers and speculators.

Arbitrageurs participate in the market with the aim of making risk-free profits by exploiting price anomalies. For example, if the AUD/USD exchange rate in one market differs from that in another market, an arbitrageur can make a riskless profit by buying at a low price from one market and then selling at a high price in another market at the same time.

Hedgers participate in the foreign exchange market to reduce or even eliminate risk resulting from an open position in a foreign currency. For example, importers with foreign currency payables or exporters with foreign currency receivables in the future might shield their open position by taking an opposite position in the forward market.

Speculators assume risk by intentionally taking an open position in the currency in the anticipation of favourable exchange rate movements in that currency. For example, a speculator would take a long position in the US dollar (that is, a contract to purchase USD with AUD) if he/she expects USD to appreciate against AUD in the future.

Major market participants can also be categorised based on the characteristics of the participating entity: commercial firms, commercial banks, non-bank financial institutions, brokers and central banks.

Commercial firms can be viewed as price takers (that is, they do not have the power to negotiate better deals than the prices offered in the market) in the foreign exchange market. They buy or sell foreign currencies to support their foreign trade and investment operations. Exporters, importers, multinational corporations and international investors are the primary customers in the foreign exchange market. They buy (demand) foreign currency to purchase foreign goods, services and assets, and sell (supply) foreign currency received from selling goods, services, assets or financial securities to foreign countries.

Large *commercial banks* are the price makers, willing to buy or sell currencies at their quoted exchange rates. Foreign exchange trades are executed through their dealers at the dealing desk. Commercial banks participate in both the wholesale and the retail foreign exchange markets. In the wholesale market, transactions take place between banks, while in the retail market transactions take place with the customers, such as commercial firms and individuals.

Non-bank financial institutions — such as merchant banks, insurance companies and investment management firms — undertake foreign currency transactions, either directly with the counter parties or indirectly through brokers. The broker ensures anonymity of the institutions.

Unlike foreign exchange dealers, *brokers* take neither a short nor a long portion in any foreign currencies. They act as a 'middle man' to facilitate trades by matching buy and sell orders placed by customers and financial institutions. In return, brokers receive commission fees for their service.

Central banks are major players in the foreign exchange market. They participate in the foreign exchange market as bankers for the government. In developed countries, central banks are given autonomy to implement monetary policy and control excess volatility in the foreign exchange rates.

Banks and non-bank financial institutions are the major traders in the foreign exchange market. Table 17.2 shows that the top three institutions — Deutsche Bank, UBS AG and Citigroup — between them account for 37% of the volume of world trade in foreign currencies. A significant part of the transactions in the foreign exchange market is essentially undertaken by a few large financial institutions. In spite of this high degree of market concentration, the foreign exchange market is highly competitive and efficient.

Table 17.2 Top ten currency traders in the world

Rank	Name	Percentage of total volume of currency trade
1	Deutsche Bank	17.0
2	UBS AG	12.5
3	Citigroup	7.5
4	HSBC	6.4
5	Barclays	5.9
6	Merrill Lynch	5.7
7	J.P. Morgan Chase	5.3
8	Goldman Sachs	4.4
9	ABN AMRO	4.2
10	Morgan Stanley	3.9

Source: *The Wall Street Journal* (Europe).[1]

lo2

Understand foreign exchange rate quotations.

Foreign exchange rate quotation

There are two ways of quoting the price of a foreign currency: the direct method and the indirect method. Under the *direct quotation method* the price of one unit of a foreign currency is expressed in terms of the domestic currency. In Australia, the *indirect quotation method* is used. The indirect method expresses the price of one unit of the domestic currency in terms of a foreign currency.

There are two types of foreign exchange transactions: spot transactions and forward transactions. In the case of a spot transaction, the exchange of currencies takes place immediately. The exchange rate at which this transaction takes place is known as the spot exchange rate. For a wholesale or interbank transaction, the delivery of foreign currencies occurs within two business days, so a liberal interpretation of the word 'immediate' is needed when we think about spot transactions. The spot exchange rate between two currencies, x and y, can be denoted as $S(x/y)$, indicating the number of units of x required to purchase 1 unit of y. The reciprocal of this exchange rate provides the number of units of y required to purchase 1 unit of x.

Table 17.3 shows international three-letter currency codes and buy/sell quotes for different foreign currencies in the retail foreign exchange market. The indirect buy/sell quotes are obtained from Westpac. Looking at these quotes you might get the wrong impression that Westpac is ready to 'buy high and sell low'. Once the corresponding direct buy/sell quotes are derived by inverting the indirect buy/sell quotes, this confusion disappears. As the last two columns of table 17.3 suggest, Westpac is willing to 'buy low and sell high'. For example, for the day shown in the table, Westpac wanted to buy one British pound (pound sterling) for 2.3923 Australian dollars and sell one British pound for 2.5853 Australian dollars, yielding a spread of AUD0.193. The spread (difference between the buy and sell quotes) is the profit for the dealers. The spread is usually greater in the retail foreign exchange market than in the wholesale market. However, the spread in the foreign exchange market is significantly lower than that of the markets for other financial securities.

Table 17.3 International currency codes and foreign currency quotations, 2 March 2007

			Indirect quotations*		Direct quotations*	
	Currency	International currency codes	Spot buy	Spot sell	Spot buy	Spot sell
United States	Dollars	USD	0.8088	0.7659	1.2364	1.3057
United Kingdom	Pounds	GBP	0.418	0.3868	2.3923	2.5853
Brunei Darussalem	Dollars	BND	1.3211	1.1275	0.7569	0.8869
Canada	Dollars	CAD	0.9672	0.8835	1.0339	1.1319
Denmark	Kroner	DKK	5.0639	4.2364	0.1975	0.2360
Europe	Euro	EUR	0.6309	0.5717	1.5850	1.7492
Fiji	Dollars	FJD	1.5093	1.2445	0.6626	0.8035
French Pacific	Francs	XPF	78.22	66.59	0.0128	0.0150
Hong Kong	Dollars	HKD	6.5716	5.8667	0.1522	0.1705
Japan	Yen	JPY	100.03	88.85	0.0100	0.0113
Malta	Lire	MTL	0.2818	0.2371	3.5486	4.2176
New Zealand	Dollars	NZD	1.1958	1.0954	0.8363	0.9129
Norway	Kroner	NOK	5.3055	4.4892	0.1885	0.2228

Saudi Arabia	Riyals	SAR	3.2422	2.739	0.3084	0.3651
Singapore	Dollars	SGD	1.2852	1.1483	0.7781	0.8709
South Africa	Rand	ZAR	6.3008	5.2999	0.1587	0.1887
Sweden	Kronor	SEK	6.0767	5.1811	0.1646	0.1930
Switzerland	Francs	CHF	1.0368	0.9161	0.9645	1.0916
Thailand	Baht	THB	29.17	24.14	0.0343	0.0414
Tonga	Pa anga	TOP	1.7659	1.3632	0.5663	0.7336
Vanuatu	Vatu	VUV	96.03	74.24	0.0104	0.0135
Samoa	Tala	WST	2.4266	1.8409	0.4121	0.5432

Notes: These rates are applicable to transactions up to and including AUD10 000 for bank note currency and travellers cheque transactions and for up to AUD25 000 for telegraphic transfers and bank draft transactions.

Currencies without both the buy and the sell quotes were excluded from the table.

*Indirect foreign exchanges rates are quoted by WBC. Direct quotations are obtained by inverting indirect quotations.

Source: Westpac Banking Corporation.[2]

EXAMPLE 17.1

Buying British Pounds

Suppose you wish to invest 1000 Australian dollars in British pound denominated financial securities. To this end you want to purchase British pounds. Given the spot exchange rates in table 17.3, how many British pounds would you receive for 1000 Australian dollars?

WBC is willing to sell one British pound for 2.5853 Australian dollars. Thus, the investor would receive GBP368.80 for AUD1000. More formally:

$$\text{AUD}1000 \times \frac{1}{2.5853} = \text{GBP}368.80$$

lo3

Calculate return on foreign currency denominated securities and cross exchange rates.

Return on foreign currency denominated securities

The total return on investment in a foreign currency denominated security depends on the rate of return on the security as well as the rate of appreciation of the foreign currency. We learn how to calculate the rate of return on a security in chapter 5. Suppose a market participant invests in securities denominated in foreign currency, *y*. For a security without interim cash flows, like dividends or interest payments, the rate of return in terms of currency *y* over the time interval $[t-1, t]$ would be:

$$\boldsymbol{R_t = \frac{c_t}{c_{t-1}} - 1} \qquad [17.1]$$

where R_t = rate of return on the security

c_{t-1} = outlay at period $t-1$

c_t = value of investment at period t

Note that R_t represents the rate of return on the security, disregarding any change in the value of the currency. Now denoting *x* as the domestic currency, the rate of appreciation of the foreign currency, *y*, can be expressed as shown overleaf.

$$\hat{S}_t(x/y) = \frac{S_t(x/y)}{S_{t-1}(x/y)} - 1 \qquad [17.2]$$

where $\hat{S}_t(x/y)$ = the rate of change in the value of currency y (in terms of currency x) over the time interval $[t-1, t]$.[3]

The total return on the foreign currency denominated security can now be determined.

$$TR_t = (1 + R_t)(1 + \hat{S}_t(x/y)) - 1 \qquad [17.3]$$

EXAMPLE 17.2

Determining return on a US dollar denominated security

Suppose you invest 1000 Australian dollars for 12 months in a US dollar denominated stock. Stock prices and exchange rates over your investment horizon are given in the following table. The US investment does not pay dividends. Find the annual rate of return and how many Australian dollars your investment will represent at the end of the year.

Year	Stock price	S(AUD/USD)
0	USD50	1.2878
1	USD53	1.3305

$$R_t = \frac{53}{50} - 1 = 0.06 \text{ and } \hat{S}_t(\text{AUD/USD}) = \frac{1.3305}{1.2878} - 1 = 0.033$$

Then, the annual rate of return is:

$$TR_t = (1 + R_t)(1 + \hat{S}_t(\text{AUD / USD})) - 1$$
$$= (1 + 0.06)(1 + 0.033) - 1 = 0.0950$$

You could sell your investment and convert the proceeds to AUD1095 (= 1000 × 1.0950) at the end of the year.

Cross exchange rates

The exchange rate for any pair of currencies can be derived from the exchange rate of each currency in the pair against a third currency. In general, one can calculate the cross exchange rate between any two currencies, $S(x/y)$, as follows:

$$S(x/y) = \frac{S(x/z)}{S(y/z)} \qquad [17.4]$$

where $S(x/y)$ = the amount of currency x required to purchase 1 unit of y
$S(x/z)$ = the amount of currency x required to purchase 1 unit of z
$S(y/z)$ = the amount of currency y required to purchase 1 unit of z

EXAMPLE 17.3

Calculating the cross rate

Ignoring the distinction between the buy and sell quote for the time being, calculate the exchange rate between Samoan tala (WST) and Fijian dollars (FJD) implied by the exchange rates for the WST/AUD and FJD/AUD currency pairs. Suppose the value of one Australian dollar is equal to 2.1338 in terms of the Samoan tala and 1.3769 in terms of the Fijian dollar. Then the value of one unit of Samoan tala in terms of Fijian dollars can be calculated as follows:

$$S(\text{FJD/WST}) = \frac{S(\text{FJD/AUD})}{S(\text{WST/AUD})}$$

$$= \frac{1.3769}{2.1338} = 0.6453$$

If a market quote for the FJD/WST currency pair deviates from that implied by the cross rate, one might be able make an arbitrage profit. For example, if $S(\text{FJD/WST})$ is 0.6812, an arbitrageur with, say, AUD1000 can undertake the following transactions to exploit price anomalies:

1. Buy 2133.8 Samoan tala for 1000 Australian dollars (AUD1000 × 2.1338 = WST2133.8).
2. Use the 2133.8 Samoan tala to buy 978.98 Fijian dollars (WST2133.8 × 0.6812 = FJD1453.5).
3. Convert 1453.5 Fijian dollars into 1055.66 Australian dollars $(\text{FJD}\frac{1453.5}{1.3769} = \text{AUD } 1055.66)$

This process of round-trip trading would yield an instantaneous risk-free profit of AUD55.66 or 5.57% (ignoring transaction costs).

In an efficient foreign exchange market, the profit opportunity illustrated in example 17.3 cannot persist. Traders will quickly spot the pricing misalignment. Their trades will result in the prices of the currencies moving until the profit opportunity is gone. Even in an efficient market, any deviation of the market quote for a currency pair from the corresponding cross rate can be justified in terms of transactions costs of round-trip trading, possible illiquidity of the market for the currency pairs and capital gains tax.

lo4

Explain the purchasing power parity, the covered interest rate parity and the unbiased forward rate conditions.

Determinants of the foreign exchange rate

In this section we examine the possible determinants of the foreign exchange rate. The purchasing power parity, the covered interest rate parity and the unbiased forward rate conditions are discussed. These theorems highlight the key role of the inflation rate differential or the interest rate differential between two countries in explaining changes in exchange rates.

The absolute purchasing power parity

Purchasing power parity: the idea that the exchange rate changes to keep purchasing power of currencies constant across countries

The **purchasing power parity** (PPP) theorem suggests that the exchange rate changes to keep the purchasing power of currencies constant across countries. The absolute form of the purchasing power parity is based on the 'Law of One Price'. That is, a commodity should be traded at the same price regardless of the currency of denomination or the market where it is traded. For example, if a commodity costs £1.42 in the United Kingdom and the AUD/GBP exchange rate is \$2.5641 per British pound, then the same commodity should cost \$3.64 in Australia. To generalise this simple relationship, P and P^* are the domestic and foreign prices of a commodity, respectively, in local currency. The absolute purchasing power parity suggests that:

$$P = S \times P^* \quad [17.5]$$

where S is the value of one unit of foreign currency expressed in terms of units of domestic currency. This equation states that the price of a commodity at home should be the exchange rate times the price of the same commodity in the foreign country. If the price of a calculator is \$20 in Sydney and £8.15 in London, the exchange rate implied by the absolute PPP is:

$$S(\text{AUD/GBP}) = \frac{P}{P^*}$$

$$= \frac{\text{AUD20}}{\text{GBP8.15}} = \text{AUD2.4540}$$

If the actual exchange rate deviates from the exchange rate implied by the absolute PPP, arbitrageurs will exploit this pricing anomaly to earn riskless profit. Suppose the actual exchange rate is \$3.0303 for British pounds and that there are no taxes, transportation costs or other transaction costs. The arbitrageur can buy the commodity for \$20 from Australia, sell it in the United Kingdom for £8.15 and then convert the proceeds into Australian dollars. At the exchange rate of \$3.0303, the arbitrageur will receive \$24.6969, yielding a profit of \$4.6969. This risk-free profit opportunity cannot persist because other traders will try to replicate this activity, which will lead to changes in commodity prices. More specifically, the price of the calculator will increase in Australia and decrease in the United Kingdom as calculators move from Australia to the United Kingdom. This profit-seeking activity will increase supply of British pounds and demand for Australian dollars in the market, leading to an appreciation of Australian dollars against pounds. Ultimately, the exchange rate must be restored to \$2.4540 per British pound to reduce arbitrage profit to zero.

FINANCE WORLD

Burgernomics

One of the most prominent theories of how exchange rates are determined is the theory of purchasing power parity. It states that, in the long run, the exchange rate between countries that produce identical products wiil adjust over time to a level at which the costs of similar goods in any country are the same. Simply put, a dollar should buy the same things anywhere in the world. As a light-hearted test of whether exchange rates for currencies are at their 'correct' level, in 1986 *The Economist* began publishing the Big Mac Index. Big Macs are a relatively homogeneous product in that the recipe is roughly the same in the 118 countries in which McDonald's operates. Comparing a country's PPP rate with the market-determined exchange rate is a test of whether a country's currency is overvalued or undervalued.

The table shows the price of Big Macs in dollars for select countries from *The Economist.* If purchasing power parity holds, the burgernomics test should show that the cost of a Big Mac is the same worldwide. Column 3 converts the local prices into US dollars at the prevailing market foreign exchange rate. The average price of a Big Mac in Australian outlets during May 2006 was about A\$3.25 or US\$2.44. To determine how much a currency is over- or undervalued, column 4 calculates a country's purchasing power parity exchange rate. For example, dividing the local Australian Big Mac price by the US price gives a dollar purchasing power parity of 1.05. Column 6 shows the implied under- or overvaluation of each currency [(exchange rate – implied rate)/exchange rate)]. Therefore, for Australia: (1.33 – 1.05)/1.33 = 21% undervaluation of the Australian dollar. Note from this table the places that Australians find very expensive to visit.

Why does burgernomics not validate the theory of purchasing power? First, regardless of the Big Mac Index outcome, economists are comfortable with the theory of purchasing power parity as the major behavioural force that drives the exchange rate to purchasing power parity equilibrium in the long run. Second, it is no surprise that the Big Mac prices are not in purchasing power parity equilibrium. The theory assumes that products can be easily traded across borders: in the case of perishable Big Macs, this does not seem likely. Further more prices between countries in the real world are distorted by taxes, tariffs differences in profit margins and differences in the cost of nontradable items such as rent, Finally, in the long run there are other factors that influence exchange rates, such as relative price levels, preferences for foreign versus domestic goods and a country's productivity.

The hamburger standard

1	2	3	4	5	6
	Big Mac prices In local currency	in US dollars	Implied PPP* of the dollar	Actual dollar exchange rate 22 May	Under (–)/ over (+) valuation against the dollar, %
United States†	$3.10	3.10	–	–	–
Argentina	Peso 7.00	2.29	2.26	3.06	–26
Australia	A$3.25	2.44	1.05	1.33	–21
Brazil	Real 6.40	2.78	2.06	2.30	–10
Britain	£1.94	3.65	1.60‡	1.88‡	+18
Canada	C$3.52	3.14	1.14	1.12	+1
Chile	Peso 1 560	2.94	503	530	–5
China	Yuan 10.5	1.31	3.39	8.03	–58
Czech Republic	Koruna 59.05	2.67	19.0	22.1	–14
Denmark	DKr 27.75	4.77	8.95	5.82	+54
Egypt	Pound 9.50	1.65	3.06	5.77	–47
Euro area§	2.94	3.77	1.05**	1.28	+22
Hong Kong	HK$12	1.55	3.87	7.75	–50
Hungary	Forint 560	2.71	181	206	–12
Indonesia	Rupiah 14 600	1.57	4 710	9 325	–49
Japan	¥250	2.23	80.6	112	–28
Malaysia	Ringgit 5.50	1.52	1.77	3.63	–51
Mexico	Peso 29.00	2.57	9.35	11.3	–17
New Zealand	NZ$4.45	2.75	1.44	1.62	–11
Peru	New Sol 9.50	2.91	3.06	3.26	–6
Philippines	Peso 85.00	1.62	27.40	52.6	–48
Poland	Zloty 6.50	2.10	2.10	3.10	–32
Russia	Rouble 48.00	1.77	15.5	27.1	–43
Singapore	S$3.60	2.27	1.16	1.59	–27
South Africa	Rand 13.95	2.11	4.50	6.60	–32
South Korea	Won 2 500	2.62	806	952	–15
Sweden	SKr 33.00	4.53	10.6	7.28	+46
Switzerland	SFr 6.30	5.21	2.03	1. 21	+68
Taiwan	NTS 75.00	2.33	24.2	32.1	–25
Thailand	Baht 60.00	1.56	19.4	38.4	–50
Turkey	Lire 4.20	2.72	1.35	1.54	–12
Venezuela	Bolivar 5 701	2.17	1 839	2 630	–30

* Purchasing power parity
† Average price
‡ Dollars per pound
** Dollars per euro
§ Weighted average price

Source: *The Economist.*

The absolute PPP may not hold literally in the real world. The exchange rate implied by the absolute PPP will hold under the following conditions:

1. There are no transportation, insurance, storage or other forms of transaction costs.
2. There are no taxes, tariffs or any other forms of foreign trade barriers or capital control.
3. Identical commodities are available in both countries.

These conditions seldom hold in reality. Hence, the PPP condition is often presented in terms of relative prices, as discussed in the next section.

FINANCE WORKSHOP 17.1

Does the absolute PPP hold for internationally non-traded goods and services? Do you expect to pay the same price for a haircut in both Australia and India? Explain your answer.

Relative purchasing power parity

Relative purchasing power parity attempts to explain movements in exchange rates over time rather than determining the absolute value of the exchange rate. More specifically, the relative PPP suggests that the rate of change in the exchange rate depends on the difference between the foreign and domestic expected inflation rates. For example, suppose the current value of 1 British pound is 2.4540 Australian dollars and the general price level in the United Kingdom is expected to rise by 8% over the next 12 months. If the general price level in Australia remains unchanged over the same period, the value of British pounds in terms of dollars would increase by 8%. That is S(AUD/GBP) should decrease to $2.2577 (= 2.4540 × 0.92) per pound. However, the depreciation of the British pound (or appreciation of Australian dollar) would be lower if the general price level in Australia also increases by 5%. Thus, the difference between the British and the Australian inflation rates is 3% and the value of a British pound would decrease to $2.3804 (= $2.4540 × 0.97). The relative PPP suggests that the expected rate of change in the exchange rate is determined by the inflation differential. As shown in the previous section, according to the absolute PPP, the domestic price level at two points in time, 0 and 1, can be expressed as:

$$P_1 = S_1 P_1^* \qquad [17.6]$$

$$P_0 = S_0 P_0^* \qquad [17.7]$$

where P = the domestic price level

P^* = the foreign price level

S = the foreign exchange rate represented as units of domestic currency per unit of foreign currency

Dividing equation 17.6 by equation 17.7, we can derive the relative PPP as follows:

$$\frac{P_1}{P_0} = \frac{S_1}{S_0} \times \frac{P_1^*}{P_0^*} \text{ or}$$

$$(1+\hat{S}) = \frac{(1+\hat{P})}{(1+\hat{P}^*)} \qquad [17.8]$$

where $\hat{S}$ = the rate of change in the exchange rate

$\hat{P}$ = domestic inflation rate

$\hat{P}^*$ = foreign inflation rate

To predict the exchange rate, we can rearrange equation 17.8 as follows:

$$S_1 = S_0\left(\frac{1+\hat{P}}{1+\hat{P}^*}\right) \quad [17.9]$$

The relative PPP implies that the higher the foreign inflation rate (or the lower the domestic inflation rate), the lower the value of foreign currency. This prediction simply echoes the general notion that higher inflation leads to the erosion of the purchasing power of a currency. Equation 17.8 can also be rewritten as equation 17.10. Here, we ignore the term $S\hat{P}^*$ because of its small absolute magnitude:

$$\hat{S} = \hat{P} - \hat{P}^* \quad [17.10]$$

This is the approximate version of relative PPP, stating that the rate of change in the exchange rate is the difference between the inflation rates. If the inflation rate is the same in both countries, the exchange rate should remain unchanged.

EXAMPLE 17.4

Predicting the spot exchange rate

The following table provides the current (Year 0) and anticipated (Year 1) consumer price indices (CPI) in Australia and the United States and the current exchange rate.

Year	Australian CPI	US CPI	Foreign exchange rate, S(AUD/USD)
0	100	140	1.25
1	102	148	

$$\hat{P} = \frac{P_1}{P_{01}} - 1 = \frac{102}{100} - 1 = 2\%,\quad \hat{P}^* = \frac{P_1^*}{P_0^*} - 1 = \frac{148}{140} - 1 = 5.7\% \text{ and}$$

$$S_1 = S_0\left(\frac{1+\hat{P}}{1+\hat{P}^*}\right)$$

$$= 1.25\left(\frac{1+0.02}{1+0.057}\right) = 1.2062$$

The value of one US dollar decreased from AUD1.25 to AUD1.2062, a 3.5% depreciation of the US dollar against the Australian dollar, which is slightly less than the anticipated inflation gap of 3.7% between the two countries. Thus, the approximate version of the relative PPP would overestimate the rate of depreciation by 0.2%.

FINANCE WORKSHOP 17.2

Suppose you expect the annual inflation rates to remain at 2% and 5% in Australia and Singapore, respectively, over the next five years. If the current spot exchange rate is S(SGD/AUD) = 1.21, what will be the exchange rate in five years?

Covered interest rate parity

In this section we introduce the equilibrium relationship between spot exchange rates, forward exchange rates and interest rates. The term 'equilibrium' is used to refer to a situation where one cannot make an instantaneous profit by simply 'buying at a low price' and 'selling at a high price' without bearing any risk. To derive the equilibrium relationship, let F_1 be the forward exchange rate for the settlement at time 1, i is the domestic risk-free interest rate and i^* is the foreign risk-free interest rate. Suppose an Australian investor can invest in either a domestic risk-free asset or a US risk-free asset for one year. Investing AUD1 in a domestic risk-free asset, the investor will receive $(1 + i)$ Australian dollars at the end of the year. Alternatively, the investor can convert AUD1 into US dollars at the current spot exchange rate to obtain $(1/S_0)$ US dollars and sell a US dollar forward contract. Next, $1/S_0$ is invested in a US risk-free asset, which yields $\frac{1}{S_0}(1 + i^*)$ US dollars at the end of the year. At the end of the investment horizon, the investor can convert $\frac{1}{S_0}(1 + i^*)$ US dollars back to Australian dollars to meet the forward contract obligation. Thus, the future value of the US investment in terms of domestic currency will be $\frac{F_1}{S_0}(1 + i^*)$ with certainty. In order to preclude the possibility of an arbitrage profit, both domestic and foreign investments must generate the same future value at the end of the year. That is:

$$(1 + i) = \frac{F_1}{S_0}(1 + i^*) \text{ or}$$

$$\frac{F_1}{S_0} = \frac{(1 + i)}{(1 + i^*)} \qquad [17.11]$$

Equation 17.11 represents the interest rate parity (IRP) condition.

EXAMPLE 17.5

Determining the forward exchange rate

Suppose the current spot price of one British pound is 2.5641 Australian dollars. The interest rate in Australia is $i = 6\%$ and the interest rate in the United Kingdom is $i^* = 3.5\%$. The forward exchange rate implied by the IRP condition (equation 17.11) is:

$$F_1 = S_0\left(\frac{1 + i}{1 + i^*}\right)$$

$$= 2.5641 \times \frac{1.06}{1.035} = 2.6260$$

Thus, the British pound is selling at a forward premium and the Australian dollar is selling at a discount.

The IRP condition represented by equation 17.11 is often expressed in terms of the forward spread, $f = (F_1 - S_0)/S_0$ as follows:

$$(1 + f)(1 + i^*) = (1 + i) \qquad [17.12]$$

Ignoring the term i^*f, the approximate version of the IRP can be derived, which suggests that the forward spread is equal to the interest differential.

$$f = i - i^* \quad [17.13]$$

or

$$F_1 = S_0[1 + (i - i^*)] \quad [17.14]$$

Thus, the IRP suggests that the currency with a higher interest rate is traded at a forward discount. The currency with a lower interest rate is traded at a forward premium, to compensating investors for the adverse investment outcome resulting from a lower interest rate.

Unbiased forward rate

The unbiased forward rate (UFR) condition states that on average the forward rate should be equal to the expected future spot rate. That is:

$$F_t = E(S_t) \quad [17.15]$$

The forward rate for settlement at the time t is equal to the expected future spot rate at the time t. The UFR condition is based on the principle that market participants can't consistently make profits by simply taking either a long or a short position in a forward contract. If $F_t > E(S_t)$, everyone interested in purchasing foreign currency in the future would avoid a forward contract and enter into a spot contract at time t. This process will lead to a fall in the forward exchange rate relative to the future spot exchange rate. Ultimately, the profit opportunity will simply disappear. The UFR condition does not imply the forward rate will always be equal to the future spot rate. It simply argues that, on average, the forward rate is equal to the future spot rate so that the one can't consistently make profits by entering into forward contracts for any currency pair.

lo5

Discuss the implications of the uncovered interest parity and the international Fisher effect.

Uncovered interest parity

The uncovered interest parity (UIP) condition states that the expected change in the spot rate depends on the interest rate differential. This relationship can be derived from the IRP and the UFR conditions.

IRP $\dfrac{F_1}{S_0} = \dfrac{(1+i)}{(1+i^*)}$

UFR $F_1 = E(S_1)$

Substituting UFR into IRP, we obtain the uncovered interest parity condition:

$$\frac{E(S_1)}{S_0} = \frac{(1+i)}{(1+i^*)} \quad \text{or} \quad E(S_1) = S_0\frac{(1+i)}{(1+i^*)} \quad [17.16]$$

The international Fisher effect

Now we want to focus on real interest rates across countries. Recall the PPP and UIP conditions from the previous sections:

PPP $E(S_1) = S_0\left(\dfrac{1+\hat{P}}{1+\hat{P}^*}\right)$

UIP $E(S_1) = S_0\left(\dfrac{1+i}{1+i^*}\right)$

These two conditions together imply the equality of real interest rate across countries.[4]

$$\left(\frac{1+i}{1+\hat{P}}\right)=\left(\frac{1+i^{*}}{1+\hat{P}^{*}}\right) \qquad [17.17]$$

International Fisher effect: the idea that the difference in the nominal interest rates between two countries determines the movement of the exchange rate between their currencies

This is a strong result, indicating that an asset must yield the same real returns in all countries. Otherwise, capital will move from a country with lower real returns to a country with higher real returns. This process, known as the **international Fisher effect**, will eventually lead to equalisation of real returns through changes in asset prices. In practice, real returns may vary across countries due to government restrictions on international capital mobility, the difference in the risk characteristics of assets and differential risk profiles of investors and countries.

lo6

Discuss the foreign exchange exposure of firms.

Exchange rate risk

Firms with international operations are exposed to exchange rate risk. As exchange rates cannot be predicted accurately, any firms with receivables and payables and assets and liabilities denominated in foreign currencies are exposed to foreign exchange risk. Even firms without any operations in foreign countries are not fully immune to foreign exchange risk because changes in exchange rates affect prices of internationally traded goods and services as well as cost of capital, which in turn may indirectly affect cash flows of these firms. The exchange rate risk can be broadly classified into translation exposure, transaction exposure and economic exposure.

Translation exposure: any changes in exchange rates affect domestic currency denominated value of items on the income statement and balance sheet

Translation exposure arises from the translation of foreign currency denominated financial statement items into domestic currency. Any changes in exchange rates affect domestic currency denominated value of items on the income statement and balance sheet. For example, Westpac Banking Corporation had more New Zealand dollar denominated assets than liabilities in every year over the period 2000–05 (see table 17.1, page 643). Hence, any depreciation of the New Zealand dollar against the Australian dollar would have reduced the book value of the bank's equity.

Transaction exposure: the domestic currency value of foreign currency denominated receivables and payables is affected by changes in exchange rates

Transaction exposure arises from the difference between foreign currency denominated receivables and payables, which give rise to cash inflows and outflows, respectively. The domestic currency value of these contractual cash flows is affected by changes in exchange rates.

Economic exposure: the sensitivity of the market value of the firm with respect to the exchange rate

Economic exposure measures the sensitivity of the market value of the firm with respect to the exchange rate. The market value of the firm can be viewed as the present value of the firm's future net cash inflows. Changes in exchange rates may affect sales revenues, operating expenses and the cost of capital of a firm, which in turn influence the present value of future net cash flows.

lo7

Undertake international capital budgeting using the home currency and foreign currency methods.

International capital budgeting

As indicated in the first section of this chapter, the fundamental methods of project evaluation are valid for both domestic and foreign projects. In the context of a foreign investment project there are additional sources of risk, such as foreign exchange and political risk, which need to be taken into account in estimating cash flows and the required rate of return. There are two alternative methods of calculating discounted cash flows of a foreign project.

The home currency method

Under this method, cash flows from a foreign project are estimated in terms of domestic currency and then the net present value of the project is calculated using the required rate of return for a comparable domestic project. To implement this method, the firm must forecast future exchange rates and use them to express cash flows from the foreign project in terms of the domestic currency. Exchange rates can be predicted using the uncovered interest parity condition (equation 17.16), which suggests that the expected spot exchange rate in t years will be:

$$E(S_t) = S_0 \frac{(1+i)^t}{(1+i^*)^t} \quad [17.18]$$

Now suppose Hunter Resources, an Australian company, is considering a new project in South Africa with a life of five years. The current spot exchange rate for South African rand (ZAR) is 0.17 Australian dollars. The current Australian interest rate is 6% pa, while the South African interest rate is 8% pa. The company's required rate of return for this type of project is 12%. Initial investment outlay and cash flows denominated in ZAR are given in the second column of table 17.4. The third column presents the current spot exchange rate as well as the expected exchange rates for the years 1 to 5. The expected exchange rates are calculated using equation 17.18 as follows:

$$E(S_t) = 0.17 \times \frac{(1+0.06)^t}{(1+0.08)^t}, \text{ where } t = 1, 2, \ldots, 5$$

For example, $E(S_3) = 0.17 \times \dfrac{(1+0.06)^3}{(1+0.08)^3} = 0.1607.$

Cash flows in Australian dollars are reported in the fourth column. The final column provides discounted cash flows using the discount rate of 12%. The net present value denominated in the Australian dollar is \$3.10 million. Hence, the project should be accepted.

Table 17.4 Foreign project evaluation using the home currency method

Year	Cash flows (in million ZAR)	Expected exchange rate	Cash flows (in million AUD)	Discounted cash flows (in million AUD)
0	−185	0.17	−31.45	−31.45
1	30	0.1669	5.01	4.47
2	70	0.1638	11.46	9.14
3	80	0.1607	12.86	9.15
4	65	0.1578	10.25	6.52
5	60	0.1548	9.29	5.27
NPV (using a discount rate of 12%)				3.10

The foreign currency method

This method first determines the foreign currency cash flows and then translates these into domestic currency to calculate the NPV. To calculate NPV in the foreign currency, we need a required rate of return in the foreign currency:

Required rate of return in rand

= [(1+ Required rate of return in AUD) × Expected change in the exchange rate] − 1

$$= (1.12) \times \left(\frac{1.08}{1.06}\right) - 1 = 14.1132\%$$

This required rate of return is used to discount cash flows in rand. Table 17.5 provides a net present value of 18.22 million in the foreign currency. Multiplying this amount by the exchange rate of $0.17 (per unit of the foreign currency), we find a net present value of $3.10 million, which is the same as that found using the home currency method.

Table 17.5 Foreign project evaluation using the foreign currency method

Year	Cash flows (in million ZAR)	Discounted cash flows (in million AUD)
0	−185	−185
1	30	26.29
2	70	53.76
3	80	53.84
4	65	38.33
5	60	31.01
NPV in rand (using a discount rate of 14.1132%)		18.22
NPV in Australian dollars (= NPV in rand × $0.17)		3.10

It is worth noting that further modification of the capital budgeting techniques may be required to take into account political risk or restrictions on repatriation of cash flows to the parent firm. One can either adjust the cash flows or the discount rate to incorporate potential impacts of these factors. Information on country risk ranking can be used to determine the appropriate discount rate. For example, a risk premium can be added to the discount rate for a country in the high political risk category, similar to the way we use risk category discount rates in chapter 9. Cash flows can be adjusted downward if remittance constraints are expected.

executive summary

lo1 describe the roles of market participants

- Based on their motives for foreign exchange trading, market participants can be classified as arbitrageurs, hedgers and speculators.
  - Arbitrageurs participate in the market with the aim of making risk-free profits by exploiting exchange rate anomalies.
  - Hedgers participate in the foreign exchange market to reduce or eliminate risk resulting from an open position in a foreign currency.
  - Speculators assume risk by intentionally taking an open position in the currency in the anticipation of favourable exchange rate movements in that currency.
- Based on the characteristics of the participating entity, market participants can be classified as commercial firms, commercial banks, non-bank financial institutions, brokers and central banks.
  - Commercial firms are price takers in the foreign exchange market, buying and selling foreign currencies to support their foreign trade and investment operations.
  - Commercial banks are price makers in the foreign exchange market, buying and selling currencies at their quoted exchange rates.
  - Non-bank financial institutions, such as merchant banks, insurance companies and investment management firms, undertake foreign currency transactions.
  - Brokers act as the 'middle man' to facilitate trades by matching buy and sell orders placed by customers and financial institutions.
  - Central banks participate in the foreign exchange market as bankers for the government.
- Banks and non-bank financial institutions are the major traders in the foreign exchange market.

lo2 understand foreign exchange rate quotations

- The price of a foreign currency can be quoted in two ways: direct quotation and indirect quotation.
- A direct quotation expresses the price of one unit of a foreign currency in terms of the domestic currency.
- An indirect quotation expresses the price of one unit of the domestic currency in terms of a foreign currency.

lo3 calculate return on foreign currency denominated securities and cross exchange rates

- Return on a foreign currency denominated security includes return on the security and return on the associated foreign currency.
- The cross exchange rate for any pair of currencies is derived from the exchange rate of each currency in the pair against a third currency.

lo4 explain the purchasing power parity, the covered interest rate parity and the unbiased forward rate conditions

- The purchasing power parity theorem proposes that the exchange rate changes to keep purchasing power of currencies constant across countries.
- The covered interest rate parity outlines the equilibrium relationship between spot exchange rates, forward exchange rates and interest rates.
- The unbiased forward rate condition suggests that generally the forward rate should be equal to the expected future spot rate.

lo5 discuss the implications of the uncovered interest parity and the international Fisher effect

- The uncovered interest parity condition shows that the expected change in the spot exchange rate depends on the interest rate differential.
- The international Fisher effect suggests that in equilibrium real interest rate across countries should be same.

lo6 discuss the foreign exchange exposure of firms

- Firms with international operations are exposed to foreign exchange risk, which can be classified into translation exposure, transaction exposure and economic exposure.
  - Translation exposure arises from the translation of foreign currency denominated financial statement items into domestic currency. Any changes in exchange rates affect the domestic currency denominated value of items on the income statement and balance sheet.
  - Transaction exposure arises from the difference between foreign currency denominated receivables and payables, which give rise to cash inflows and outflows, respectively. The domestic currency value of foreign currency denominated receivables and payables is affected by changes in exchange rates.
  - Economic exposure measures the sensitivity of the market value of the firm with respect to the exchange rate.

lo7 undertake international capital budgeting using the home currency and foreign currency methods

- Under the home currency method, cash flows from a foreign project are expressed in terms of domestic currency and then the net present value of the project is calculated using the required rate of return for a domestic project with comparable risk characteristics.
- The foreign currency method estimates the NPV of the project in terms of the foreign currency and then expresses the NPV in terms of domestic currency.

Key terms

arbitrageurs, p. 644
economic exposure, p. 656
hedgers, p. 644
international Fisher effect, p. 656
purchasing power parity, p. 649
speculator, p. 644
transaction exposure, p. 656
translation exposure, p. 656

Learning chart

Learning objective	Questions	Self-test Problems	Financial problems
lo1 describe the roles of market participants	17.1		
lo2 understand foreign exchange rate quotations	17.2	17.1	17.1, 17.4, 17.5
lo3 calculate return on foreign currency denominated securities and cross exchange rates		17.1	17.2
lo4 explain the purchasing power parity, the covered interest rate parity and the unbiased forward rate condition	17.3, 17.4, 17.5	17.2	17.3, 17.6, 17.7
lo5 discuss the implications of the uncovered interest parity and the international Fisher effect	17.6, 17.7	17.3	17.8, 17.9, 17.10
lo6 discuss the foreign exchange exposure of firms	17.8		
lo7 undertake international capital budgeting using the home currency and foreign currency methods	17.9		

Questions

17.1 Briefly describe the role of arbitrageurs, hedgers and speculators in the foreign exchange market.

17.2 Distinguish between direct and indirect foreign exchange quotations.

17.3 Explain the relative purchasing power parity theorem. How does relative PPP differ from the absolute purchasing power parity condition?

17.4 Suppose the exchange rate implied by the absolute purchasing power parity for the US dollar is AUD1.23 but the current spot exchange rate for the US dollar is AUD1.19. How would you exploit the deviation of the spot exchange rate from its theoretical value? Ignore transaction costs.

17.5 Provide some examples of goods and services for which the absolute PPP may not hold. Explain your answers.

17.6 If the general price level in Thailand is expected to increase at a faster rate than that in Australia, what is likely to happen to the dollar/bhat exchange rate?

17.7 Suppose euros are trading at AUD1.60 per euro at the spot market and AUD1.76 in the 180-day forward market. Is the euro selling at a discount or premium against the Australian dollar? Do you expect the Australian dollar to appreciate relative to the euro? Explain your answer.

17.8 Is the depreciation of Australian dollar bad for all Australian companies? Explain your answer with particular reference to transaction exposure, translation exposure and economic exposure.

17.9 Discuss the alternative methods of estimating the net present value of a foreign project?

Self-test problems

17.1 On 31 December 2005, a US resident invested USD10 000 in an Australian managed fund that closely tracks the ASX/S&P 200 Index.

End-of-month	ASX/S&P 200 Index	Units of US dollars per Australian dollar
December 2005	4763	0.7337
January 2006	4930	0.7510
February 2006	4921	0.7382
March 2006	5130	0.7159
April 2006	5259	0.7542
May 2006	5002	0.7636
June 2006	5074	0.7433
July 2006	4986	0.7658
August 2006	5115	0.7627
September 2006	5154	0.7480
October 2006	5384	0.7692
November 2006	5482	0.7850
December 2006	5670	0.7913

(a) Calculate the monthly rate of return denominated in the US dollar.

(b) Calculate the cumulative value of investment denominated in US dollars at the end of each month.

17.2 The British pound is currently trading for AUD2.55. If the interest rate in Australia is 5.5% and the interest rate in the United Kingdom is 6.5%, what would be the one-year forward exchange rate?

17.3 Suppose GoTech International is considering a new project in Thailand with a life span of 3 years. The current spot exchange rate for the Thai bhat (THB) is 0.0339 Australian dollars. The interest rate in Australia is 6% pa, while the Thai interest rate is 7.5% pa. The required rate of return for a comparable domestic project is 10% pa. Given the following cash flows from the project, estimate the net present value using the foreign currency method.

Year	Cash flows (in million THB)
0	–200
1	50
2	85
3	110

Solutions to self-test problems

17.1 (a) Monthly rates of return denominated in USD are calculated using equation 17.3 and shown in the seventh column of the following table. For example, the rate of return for January 2006 can be calculated as follows:

$$R_t = \frac{4930}{4763} - 1 = 0.0351 \text{ and } \hat{S}_t(\text{USD/AUD}) = \frac{0.751}{0.7337} - 1 = 0.0236$$

Then, the annual rate of return is:

$$TR_t = (1 + R_t)(1 + \hat{S}_t(\text{USD / AUD})) - 1$$
$$= (1 + 0.0351)(1 + 0.0236) - 1 = 0.0595 \text{ or } 5.95\%$$

(b) The cumulative value at the end of March 2006, for example, can be found as follows:

USD10 000(1 + 0.0595)(1 – 0.0188)(1 + 0.0110) = USD10 509

End-of-month	ASX/ S&P 200 Index	Units of US dollars per Australian dollar	Return on ASX/ S&P Index in AUD (R_t)	Return on foreign currency – AUD $\hat{S}_t$(USD/AUD)	Return on ASX/ S&P Index in USD (TR_t)	Cumulative value of investment in US dollars
1	2	3	4	5	6	7
Dec 05	4763	0.7337				10 000
Jan 06	4930	0.751	0.0351	0.0236	0.0595	10 595
Feb 06	4921	0.7382	–0.0018	–0.0170	–0.0188	10 395
Mar 06	5130	0.7159	0.0425	–0.0302	0.0110	10 509
Apr 06	5259	0.7542	0.0251	0.0535	0.0800	11 350
May 06	5002	0.7636	–0.0489	0.0125	–0.0370	10 930
June 06	5074	0.7433	0.0144	–0.0266	–0.0126	10 792
July 06	4986	0.7658	–0.0173	0.0303	0.0124	10 926
Aug 06	5115	0.7627	0.0259	–0.0040	0.0217	11 163
Sep 06	5154	0.748	0.0076	–0.0193	–0.0118	11 032
Oct 06	5384	0.7692	0.0446	0.0283	0.0742	11 851
Nov 06	5482	0.785	0.0182	0.0205	0.0391	12 314
Dec 06	5670	0.7913	0.0343	0.0080	0.0426	12 839

17.2 The forward exchange rate implied by the IRP condition (equation 17.11) is:

$$F_1 = S_0\left(\frac{1+i}{1+i^*}\right) = 2.55 \times \frac{1.045}{1.065} = 2.5021$$

Thus, the British pound is selling at a forward discount and the Australian dollar is selling at a premium.

17.3 Required rate of return in rand = [(1 + Required rate of return in AUD) × Expected change in the exchange rate] − 1

$$= \left[[(1 + \text{Required rate of return in AUD}) \times \frac{(1+i)}{(1+i^*)} \right] - 1$$

$$= (1.10) \times \left(\frac{1.075}{1.06} \right) - 1 = 11.56\%$$

The expected change in the exchange rate is estimated using the uncovered interest parity condition (equation 17.16).

Year	Cash flows (in million THB)	Discount factor	Discounted cash flows (in million THB)
0	−200	1	−200
1	50	0.8964	44.82
2	85	0.8035	68.30
3	110	0.7202	79.23
NPV in THB			−7.66
NPV in AUD (= NPV in THB × 0.0339)			−0.2597

The project should be rejected since the net present value is negative.

Financial problems

17.1 The following retail foreign exchange buy/sell quotations are from the Westpac Banking Corporation.

International currency codes and foreign currency per Australian dollar (AUD)

			Indirect quotations	
	Currency	International currency codes	Spot buy	Spot sell
Canada	Dollars	CAD	0.9672	0.8835
Denmark	Kroner	DKK	5.0639	4.2364
Europe	Euro	EUR	0.6309	0.5717

Suppose a Canadian investor wants to convert CAD1000 into Australian dollars. Given the spot exchange rates in this table, how many Australian dollars would the investor receive?

17.2 Suppose you invest A$1000 in a British pound denominated stock for 1 year. Given the following stock prices and the spot exchange rates, determine the annual rate of return denominated in Australian dollars. Ignore the buy/sell spread.

Year	Stock price	Exchange rate S(AUD/GBP)
0	GBP50	2.4078
1	GBP48	2.5305

17.3 The price of a Big Mac is AUD3.25 in Australia and USD3.10 in the US. The spot exchange rate for the US dollar is AUD1.2106. Determine the absolute PPP exchange rate. Is the Australian dollar overvalued or undervalued against the US dollar? Explain.

17.4 Suppose you can buy or sell selected foreign currencies at the following spot exchange rates:

	Currency	International currency codes	Australian dollar per unit of foreign currency
United States	Dollars	USD	1.2711
Canada	Dollars	CAD	1.0829
Denmark	Kroner	DKK	0.2168

Given these foreign exchange quotes, find the following cross exchange rates:

(a) *S*(USD/DKK)

(b) *S*(CAD/DKK)

(c) *S*(USD/CAD).

17.5 Suppose you can buy or sell Saudi Arabian riyals (SAR), Singapore dollars (SGD) and Australian dollars at the following spot exchange rates:

SGD1 = SAR2.6510

AUD1 = SGD1.2129

AUD1 = SAR2.9691

(a) If transaction costs are zero, how could you make an arbitrage profit given these spot rates?

(b) What exchange rate between SGD and SAR would eliminate arbitrage profits?

17.6 Suppose the current exchange rate for the Singapore dollar is AUD0.8245. The expected inflation rate over the next 12 months is 3% in Australia and 2% in Singapore. What will be the spot exchange rate in 12 months' time?

17.7 The Swiss franc is currently trading at AUD0.9731 per franc. If the interest rate in Australia is 6% and the interest rate in Switzerland is 3.5%, what would be the 1-year forward exchange rate?

17.8 Suppose the inflation rate in Australia is 3% pa and Treasury notes are traded at an annual yield of 5.5%. New Zealand short-term government securities yield 6.6% pa. Estimate the inflation rate in New Zealand.

17.9 Telcom Australia is considering a new project in Malaysia with a life span of 6 years. The current spot exchange rate for the Malaysian ringgit (MYR) is 0.3540 Australian dollars. Currently, the interest rate in Australia is 6% pa, while the Malaysian interest rate is 8% pa. The required rate of return for this type of project is 12%. Initial investment outlay and expected cash flows denominated in MYR are given in the following table. Use the home currency method to determine whether or not the company should accept this project.

Year	Cash flows (in million MYR)	Year	Cash flows (in million MYR)
0	–285	4	90
1	60	5	60
2	85	6	30
3	110		

17.10 Repeat your calculations in problem 17.9 using the foreign currency method.

SOLUTIONS TO FINANCE WORKSHOPS

17.1 The absolute purchasing power parity does not hold for internationally non-traded goods and services. Internationally non-traded goods and services are usually traded at different prices across countries and arbitrageurs can't take advantage of this price differential to make profits. A good example of internationally non-traded services is a haircut. The price of a haircut in a less developed country like India would be significantly less than in Australia.

17.2 Using the relative purchasing power parity (equation 17.9), we can predict the exchange rate in 5 years.

$$E(S_t) = S_0\left(\frac{1+\hat{P}}{1+\hat{P}^*}\right)^t$$

or

$$E(S_5) = \left(\frac{1}{1.21}\right)\left(\frac{1+0.02}{1+0.05}\right)^5 = 0.7149$$

Thus, the price of one Australian dollar in terms of Singapore dollars in 5 years will be:

$$S_5(\text{SGD/AUD}) = \frac{1}{S_5(\text{AUD/SGD})} = \frac{1}{0.7149} = 1.3988$$

End notes

1 Information from *The Wall Street Journal* (Europe), 2 September 2006, p. 20.

2 Westpac Banking Corporation 2007, 'Today's rates', 2 March, www.westpac.com.au.

3 From this expression, the rate of appreciation of currency x, $\hat{S}_t(y/x)$ can also be found as:

$$\hat{S}_t(y/x) = \frac{1}{1+\hat{S}_t(x/y)} - 1$$

4 The approximate version of the international Fisher effect is $(i - \hat{P}) = (i^* - \hat{P}^*)$, which can be found from equation 17.17 by setting $\hat{P}i^* = \hat{P}^* i = 0$.

The following 'behavioural perspective' feature wraps up our discussion of the behavioural influences on financial decision making.

BEHAVIOURAL PERSPECTIVE

The problem of economic man — *Homo economicus*

Economic man, sometimes light-heartedly called *Homo economicus*, depicts a simple model of human behaviour. This character is driven by one pure motive — self interest; one cognitive process — perfect rationality; and happily, one level of resources — perfect information. We are all well aware that economic man as a model is oversimplified, but the simplification is used to assist in the analysis of human actions and decision making. Critics of *Homo economicus* have pointed out that, for most people, emotions drive their behaviour and their intellect takes a subservient role. Strong emotions can very quickly destroy rational thinking and decision making processes. Think of anger, hate, greed, anxiety, love — these emotions can quickly turn reasoned judgements into irrational thoughts and actions.

The 'behavioural perspective' features in this book have dealt with the nature of rationality and how research has shown that people contravene some of the tenets of rationality every day in their decision making. We have also looked at the problems arising with collecting and processing information. We will now explore one further issue — economic *man*. Traditional thinking deals with economic man as a generic term including both man and woman, but women and men think, process information and tolerate risk sufficiently differently that studies have found sex to be a statistically significant variable impacting on financial decision making.

The result of the differences in tolerance for risk and perhaps in wealth-maximising behaviour is that women make different investment decisions. Studies in the USA* using large data sets have questioned women about their risk tolerance and measured their risk aversion by statistical methods. Women were found to perceive themselves as more risk averse than men. When asked about their willingness to accept risk for the potential benefit of higher returns, 63% of single women (compared with 43% of single men) reported they were unwilling to accept any financial risk. Additionally, estimated measures of risk aversion showed single women to be more risk averse than either single men or couples.

The implications of these findings may be transposed to business financial decisions. Women in managerial roles will make different decisions from their male counterparts. Women are less likely to take on projects with higher measured risk, less comprehensive information, high and uncertain development costs, or marginal projected outcomes. Moreover, women are also less likely to be overconfident in their forecasting ability and consequently less likely to risk their firms' funds in 'barge on and win through' strategies.

Even though people, both women and men, do not always make the best or most appropriate decisions, or even reasonable decisions, understanding the methods and tools that have been discussed in this textbook will help you make *good* decisions. That is, decisions made when they are needed and by incorporating necessary information and using appropriate tools and methodology.

The majority of this textbook has been devoted to providing you with these tools. The 'behavioural perspective' features have been included to alert you to the fact that decision makers are first and foremost people who are driven by forces, impulses, pressures and urges that sometime impact on the appropriateness of their decisions and ultimately on the outcomes of business enterprises.

* Bajtelsmit, VL & Bernasek, A 1996, 'Why do women invest differently than men?', *Financial Counseling and Planning*, vol. 7, pp. 1–10.

Case studies

Case study contents

This case matrix shows you, at a glance, the appropriate case study to use during your course of study based upon the preferred concepts and topics to be covered.

	Chapter 1 Introducing the firm and its goals	**Chapter 2** Business structures and taxation	**Chapter 3** Business and the financial markets	**Chapter 4** Financial mathematics	**Chapter 5** Understanding risk and return	**Chapter 6** Valuation of bonds and shares	**Chapter 7** Cost of capital
Case 1 ▪ Financial advisory service				✓	✓		
Case 2 ▪ Next Net		✓					✓
Case 3 ▪ Solar Sail Ltd		✓					
Case 4 ▪ Hygienic Solutions and the EnviroMist		✓					✓
Case 5 ▪ Spring Chickens	✓			✓			
Case 6 ▪ Financial advisory service II				✓			
Case 7 ▪ Greenfish Ltd							
Case 8 ▪ Rebellion Flour Ltd					✓		✓
Case 9 ▪ Financial advisory service III			✓	✓	✓		
Case 10 ▪ Financial advisory service IV				✓			
Case 11 ▪ Romantic Roses		✓					
Case 12 ▪ Speedy Concrete							
Case 13 ▪ Financial advisory service V				✓			
Case 14 ▪ Palmer Hardware Ltd							✓
Case 15 ▪ First Blush Ltd							

Chapter 8 Planning investments — discounted cash flow techniques	Chapter 9 Planning investments — some real world complications	Chapter 10 Short-term finance — working capital	Chapter 11 Managing current assets	Chapter 12 Long-term external finance	Chapter 13 Dividend policy and internal financing	Chapter 14 Forecasting to evaluate financial decisions	Chapter 15 Risk management	Chapter 16 Capital restructuring — takeovers and divestments	Chapter 17 International corporate finance
✓	✓								
✓	✓	✓							
✓	✓			✓					
		✓	✓						
✓				✓	✓				
		✓		✓		✓			
✓	✓					✓			
✓	✓								
✓	✓								
✓									
						✓			

case 1

Financial advisory service

As a finance student, you are naturally inclined to want to share your skills for the benefit of others. You and a couple of friends have decided to open a free financial counselling service for students from other disciplines. The level of demand for your services has been most pleasing and you have interviewed a number of clients. Your assessments of each person's requirements are outlined below.

Client one — Roberto (Bob) Minicelli

Bob needs a car for travelling from campus to his part-time job. He has done some research, chosen to purchase a new Hynight and checked out what is on offer from three dealers in town. The list price for the Hynight is $15 000. Bob found that the market for new small cars in his town is highly competitive.

- Baker Autos is offering interest-free terms on the retail price. Bob would be required to pay $1500 deposit and monthly instalments of $450 for the next 30 months. The first loan instalment is due one month after the car is purchased.
- Bridge Cars does not offer interest-free terms, but has offered Bob a discount of $2000 from the retail price.
- Brown Motors will provide a no-deposit finance deal. Under the terms of the contract, Bob would borrow the retail price of the Hynight and make monthly payments of $100 for 23 months with the first payment due one month after purchase. Bob will pay the balance of the loan at the end of the 2-year term. Interest will be compounded monthly at the market rate. If Bob signs up for financing from Brown Motors, they will give him free floor mats and a sound system with a combined value of $500. (If Bob takes the Baker Autos or Bridge Cars deal, he would purchase the floor mats and sound system separately.)

Bob wants to know which company is offering the best deal. The market rate of interest is 6% per annum.

Client two — Athena Stratopoulos

Athena has just enrolled in a combined degree in Accounting and Astrology. Over the 5 years it will take her to complete her degree, Athena wants to save enough money for a quick trip round Europe. Given the current exchange rate, she estimates that she will need $30 000. She plans to leave for Europe the day after her graduation (5 years from now). Athena has an investment account that pays 12% per annum and has interest compounded monthly. She wants to make equal monthly deposits into her account. She has no money now, so her first deposit would be in one month's time. Athena wants to know what the size of her deposits should be.

Although she is not very good at forecasting yet, Athena is an optimist. She thinks it is possible that the exchange rate will improve. If this happens, she will need to have only $20 000 to fund her trip. What size monthly deposits would she have to make to achieve this amount?

Athena has also told you that her granny has had a look at the tea leaves and thinks that her time is almost up. Granny told Athena that she would bequeath her either a chestnut Arabian horse or enough to fund the trip to Europe. Athena has asked you to tell her how much money she would need today to pay for a trip that costs $30 000 the day she leaves. Interest will be compounded monthly.

Client three — Ivy Chan

Ivy, a final year engineering student, has been awarded a prize for academic excellence. The publishers who fund the prize have given Ivy a choice of five ways to receive her payments. She needs to choose one of the following:

1. \$900 now
2. \$1500 at the end of 7 years
3. \$35 at the end of each year forever
4. \$75 at the end of each year for the next 20 years
5. \$50 at the end of one year, with the amount increasing 10% each year until 10 payments have been made.

Ivy wants you to recommend the choice that is the most valuable. Interest rates are 4% per annum.

Client four — Boris Ropolov

One of the teaching staff from Nursing has heard that you are giving excellent advice. Boris is willing to contribute \$50 to the faculty students club in return for your advice. Boris is considering these two alternative investments that cost the same amount:

(a) an investment that offers \$1200 per annum in perpetuity. The \$1200 is paid at the end of each year

(b) an investment that offers \$1200 per annum in perpetuity with the payment received at the beginning of each year.

If Boris has an opportunity cost of 6%, which investment should he make?

Client five — Chris Van Noorden and Glen Livvet

Chris and Glen have no children of their own, so they decide to keep their memories alive by making a perpetual endowment to the local home for wayward cats. They will make provision to support 100 cats each year. The home estimates that this level of support would require \$4700 per annum. The endowment will be handed over to the cats' home in 8 years' time, and \$4700 will be withdrawn on that first day. To fund the endowment, Chris and Glen will make deposits every 6 months into an account, the first deposit to be made today. The rate of interest is 4% per annum, compounded semi-annually. They want you to advise them on the following:

(a) What will be the amount of the endowment to be handed over to the cats' home in 8 years' time?

(b) How much must they deposit every 6 months to accumulate the required amount?

(c) Chris and Glen are also considering the purchase of a house. They will be borrowing \$363 700 for a term of 18 years, payable by equal monthly repayments in arrears. The current interest rate is 6% per annum, compounded monthly. They have asked you to tell them what dollar amount the monthly repayments on the mortgage will be.

Client six — Professor Cash

Hearing of the good work you are doing with your student service, Professor Cash decides to support your initiative by paying for advice. She has a sum of money that she has accumulated over the last 15 years and has decided it is time to invest in the share market. Professor Cash's daughter is a first-year Finance undergraduate and Professor Cash has asked her to do some research and then advise on which shares to purchase. Professor Cash has given you the data her daughter has collected:

Share	Beta	Expected return
ABC Ltd	0.5	7%
DEF Ltd	1.9	19%
GHI Ltd	−0.9	−3%
JKL Ltd	0.8	10%
MNO Ltd	−0.2	1%
PQR Ltd	1.2	12%
STU Ltd	0.7	8%
XYZ Ltd	2.1	23%

Professor Cash is not sure if she wants to purchase some shares in each company, or if she would be better off putting all of her money into XYZ Ltd. From your knowledge of the current state of the market, you assess the risk-free rate as 2% and the return on the market at 9%.

She would like you to give her a measure of risk for XYZ Ltd. She wants you to explain how risky a portfolio of shares is both compared to leaving the money in the bank and to purchasing only XYZ shares.

REQUIRED

1.1 Answer each of your client's questions. Show all calculations and equations you use to prepare your answer for each client.

1.2 Write a paragraph for each client explaining the approach and concepts you have used in developing your answer.

case 2

Next Net

Next Net is a provider of internet services. It has been listed on the ASX for 6 months. The shares of Next Net are held by resident Australian investors who all have marginal tax rates of 42%. Next Net's marginal tax rate is 30%. The company will maintain its current capital structure as shown.

Ordinary shares	60
Preference shares	10
Debt	30
	100%

Section one

Next Net has a young and innovative team in its project division. The team is constantly generating so many new projects that the managing director has decided that it is time for the company to adopt a systematic approach to the analysis of the projects. The manager of the project division has identified the best 6 projects and proposed that these be adopted. Some details of the 6 projects are as follows:

Investment	Initial outlay	IRR (before tax)	IRR (after tax)
1	175 000	24	16
2	100 000	21	15
3	125 000	18	13
4	200 000	15	12
5	250 000	13	9
6	150 000	12	8

The managing director of Next Net would like your advice on which projects to accept. You collect the following details in your interview.

- *Ordinary shares.* Retained earnings are currently $150 000 but Next Net has little cash in the bank and a very low level of current assets. Ordinary shares can be issued at the current market price of $7.20 and have issue costs of 15%. The last annual dividend paid was 27.5c per share and the long-term growth rate for dividends is 9%.
- *Preference shares.* New issues would have a face value of $10 and pay annual dividends of 85c per share. The company would receive a net price of $8. The current market price of Next Net's preference shares is $10.
- *Debt.* The before-tax cost of raising debt is 8%.

REQUIRED

You must take the following steps to prepare for your meeting with the Next Net directors:

2.1 Calculate the weighted marginal cost of capital for Next Net if the marginal investor is a foreign resident.

2.2 Identify the appropriate size of the capital budget and indicate which projects should be accepted.

2.3 Show how your results would be different if Next Net's marginal shareholder is an Australian resident (you will need to repeat parts 1 and 2 to do this).

2.4 Show how your results would be different if Next Net's marginal shareholder is an Australian resident and the company has $150 000 cash available for new investments. In this situation, no new shares would be issued.

2.5 Prepare a two-page report that explains your methodology and results.

Section two

The project division of Next Net is constantly coming up with more ideas than the company can handle. Next Net's share price has been rising rapidly and the managing director wants to see this continue. The company wants you to advise on the dilemma caused by the large choice of projects they could undertake. In all, 23 projects have been suggested for implementation in the coming quarter. Fifteen of these have been accepted after NPV analysis conducted within the company. Management were less confident about evaluating the remaining 8 projects. One team member suggested that the nature of the projects meant that a straight comparison of the project NPVs could be misleading. Most of the team agreed with this, but disagreed about how the projects should be evaluated. One suggested IRR, another suggested the payback period, while another was sure the NPV method could be used with some adaptations.

To resolve the matter, the management suggested you be consulted. They asked that you use all three approaches and explain to them which approach is the most suitable for these projects. You have collected the following information about the projects:

Project one

Developing an internet site dedicated to gardening information. This site would provide gardeners with answers to any gardening questions they may have. There would be an online gardening encyclopaedia, a gardening newsgroup, chat rooms for each of the more popular species of plants, a directory of suppliers for the whole of Australia, downloadable video clips of the best segments of the 'Grubby Gardener' television program and an advice service provided by Australia's most respected gardening experts.

Revenues would be generated according to the amount of time clients spent at the site. Revenues are expected to rise over the life of the project (3 years) as more gardeners get used to the internet. The popularity of the site would mean that one of Next Net's seven servers would have to be used exclusively for this purpose. Next Net currently has one server in excess of its needs. The cash flows for this project are presented in table 1.

Project two

Developing an internet site dedicated to motor racing information. This site would provide race fans with answers to any motor sport questions they may have. There would be an online motor racing magazine, newsgroups and chat rooms for each of the different types of motor racing, race guides to each of the coming major racing events worldwide and for all Australian motor sports, downloadable video clips of the most memorable moments in motor sports and an advice service on vehicle maintenance. Revenues would be generated according to the amount of time clients spent at the site. Because motor racing fans tend to be technologically sophisticated, revenues are expected to remain constant over the 3-year life of the project. This site is expected to be every bit as popular as the gardening site and would also require one of Next Net's seven servers. The cash flows for this project are presented in table 1.

Project three

Projects three and four are both based on the development of a new search engine. The project team really outdid themselves on this one. They have developed an entirely new system of searching the internet and have patented the process. Next Net could sell the patent rights to Microsplat (a major vendor of software). To prepare the patented system to a saleable stage, Next Net would have to do minor testing and development over the coming year. The patent would be sold at the end of that year. The cash flows for this project are presented in table 1.

Project four

As an alternative to project three, Next Net could retain the patent, develop the product and market the search engine itself. To get the product to a saleable stage would require considerable development and testing. Special care would have to be taken to make the search engine 'user friendly' if it is going to be competitive. This phase can be completed in one year if the team starts work immediately. The cash flows for this project are presented in table 1.

Project five

Next Net is convinced that producing CDs will be a major generator of income for the company for the foreseeable future. They currently have one small CD burner that has met their production needs so far, but will not be able to meet their future needs. They have identified the best two machines for the production of CDs. Project five is the evaluation of one of these machines. This 'project five' machine is moderately priced and extremely efficient with an expected productive life of 5 years. The cash flows for this project are presented in table 1.

Project six

Project six is the evaluation of the other CD burner. The 'project six' machine is about the same price as the one evaluated in project five. It has a longer estimated productive life (10 years) but it is not as efficient as the project five machine. This lower efficiency would mean that Next Net would not be able to fully satisfy the demand for its product. The cash flows for this project are presented in table 1.

Project seven

The clerical duties at Next Net are currently undertaken by the managing director's secretary (Nick) and one part-time staff member. Nick is the only secretary employed at the company and has great difficulty maintaining the accounts receivable records in addition to his other duties. Inventory control is the job of the part-time staff member, whose primary responsibility is to ensure that the project division has a plentiful supply of coffee and chocolates. Although the project division is very happy with this arrangement, the managing director thinks that the company may not be giving its accounts receivable and inventory sufficient attention. Two alternatives have been identified to improve this situation. The first of these is project seven.

Project seven is the outsourcing of customer billing control. The Family & Co. would do all the billing and bookkeeping currently done by the secretary. This would save Next Net considerable overtime costs as well as providing a more efficient billing and bookkeeping system. The Family & Co. would also do credit analysis to identify delinquent customers and they claim to be expert in the collection of overdue accounts. The cash flows for this project are presented in table 1.

Project eight

Project eight would keep the billing, bookkeeping and account collection functions within the company. However, the current system would be completely overhauled — a new computer system would be leased for one year and a new staff member would be employed to run this system. The computer would be fitted with proper accounting software that would generate invoices, record accounts receivable and allow for analysis of credit accounts. Although it could not offer the effective collection services of The Family & Co., it would facilitate better inventory management. Software is available for inventory control — this would allow Next Net to keep track of all raw materials and parts in stock, reorder when necessary and reduce the number of times production is held up by lack of inventory. The cash flows for this project are presented in table 1.

Table 1 Project cash flows

Year	Project one	Project two	Project three	Project four	Project five	Project six	Project seven	Project eight
0	-75 000	-75 000	-30 000	-271 500	-500 000	-500 000	-8 000	-20 000
1	10 000	43 000	210 000	100 000	225 000	150 000	11 000	25 000
2	30 000	43 000		100 000	225 000	150 000		
3	100 000	43 000		100 000	225 000	150 000		
4				100 000	225 000	150 000		
5				100 000	225 000	150 000		
6				100 000		150 000		
7				100 000		150 000		
8				100 000		150 000		
9				100 000		150 000		
10				100 000		150 000		

REQUIRED

2.1 Analyse each of these eight projects for Next Net using the methods suggested by the directors. Assume all projects have the same level of risk and use an opportunity cost of 10% where appropriate. Show all equations and calculations you use in your analysis (you will need to identify the 'adapted NPV method' that would be appropriate for these projects). Recommend which projects would be accepted under each method. The benchmark payback period for Next Net is two years.

2.2 Prepare a report explaining the methodologies you have used and summarising the result of the analysis for each methodology. Make a recommendation on which methodology is most appropriate for Next Net and explain why you have made that recommendation.

case 3

Solar Sail Ltd

Solar Sail is an Australian listed company whose shareholders can fully utilise taxation imputation credits. The company manufactures small solar panels for use on boats and caravans. Their operations have been highly successful and the directors are considering expanding company sales by exporting.

All of Solar Sail's sales are currently made in Australia. The sales department has informed the board that there has been an increasing number of requests from overseas retailers. Solar Sail has never advertised overseas and the marketing manager thinks that the South-East Asian market would be a good place for Solar Sail to start.

Section one

The directors have requested information from the division heads, and their replies are included in the following memoranda.

MEMO ONE

SOLAR SAIL LTD

To: CFO, Solar Sail

From: Marketing department

Date: 31 March 2008

Subject: Advertising budget and projected sales for South-East Asia

We have conducted our own rigorous market research into demand for our product in South-East Asia. Our results are as follows:

- The demand for solar panels for use on boats and caravans is currently small. Boating and caravanning are not popular leisure activities in the region. We estimate that sales of solar panels for this use would not increase significantly above the amount we already supply to the region.
- There are no local producers of solar panels of any sort.
- We have identified a small but unmet demand for solar panels for use in regional areas. There are significant population levels in rural villages relying on diesel generators to supply electricity.
- We propose to market a system that uses our currently produced solar panels combined with storage batteries. These systems would meet the needs of the small- to medium-sized regional households.
- Batteries would be supplied by Energon (see memo two).
- We have estimated the number of units that would be sold, the price we could get per unit and the marketing costs for the next 8 years. We are not confident of forecasting beyond 8 years as it is likely that market conditions would be significantly different after that time.
- Initially, marketing expenses would be high and sales would be relatively low. However, as our figures show, this situation is reversed in year 4.
- Freight costs of $300 per unit are expected over the life of the project.

The following table shows the forecast number of unit sales, the forecast price per unit and the annual marketing expense forecast for years 1 to 8 for the project.

Year	Units	Sales price per unit ($AUD)	Marketing ($AUD)
1	2000	2500	5000000
2	3000	2500	3000000
3	4000	2500	3000000
4	6000	2300	1000000
5	9000	2300	750000
6	12000	2200	500000
7	16000	2200	500000
8	20000	2000	500000

MEMO TWO

SOLAR SAIL LTD

To: Terri Wilson, Marketing Manager, Solar Sail Ltd

From: Mark Brown, Sales Manager, Energon Ltd

Date: 7 April 2008

Subject: Supply of storage batteries for solar systems

We have received your request for technical information and quotes for storage batteries that would suit solar systems. Energon currently manufactures a product that would meet your needs. The wholesale price per unit is $750. We expect to be able to supply the number of units you would need at this price over the next 8 years. We look forward to a happy business relationship with Solar Sail.

MEMO THREE

SOLAR SAIL LTD

To: CFO, Solar Sail Ltd

From: Production department

Date: 4 April 2008

Subject: Production costs — South-East Asia project

- Due to the recent upgrade, our production facility has enough excess capacity to be able to meet both domestic needs and the forecast demand for the South-East Asia project for the next 3 years. To meet demand after that (that is, from the start of year 4 of the project) we would need to install additional production facilities.
- The expansion of facilities would require additional equipment. We estimate that this would cost $1 200000 at the time of installation. The equipment can be depreciated at $300000 pa over its 4-year life. This equipment would be scrapped at the end of 4 years.
- Adoption of the new project would require an increase of working capital of $40000. This amount would be recovered at the end of the project.
- Raw materials, labour and other variable costs per unit are forecast at $800 for the first 2 years, $750 for years 3–5 and $725 per unit for the final 3 years.

MEMO FOUR

SOLAR SAIL LTD

To: CFO, Solar Sail Ltd

From: Georgie Greengrass, Finance department

Date: 5 April 2008

Subject: Financial considerations — South-East Asia project

The following information has been collated by the finance department:

- The before-tax cost of capital is 9%.
- The after-tax cost of capital is 7%.
- The rate of return on Treasury bills is 5%.
- The company's after-tax cost of debt is 5.5%.
- The corporate tax rate is 30%.

New projects with similar risks as existing projects are evaluated at the cost of capital. Any new projects that have different characteristics to our current range of projects are evaluated using a risk-adjusted discount rate. A further 5% is added to the cost of capital for projects that are not similar to our current operations.

REQUIRED

3.1 The directors have asked you to advise them on the acceptability of the project. They have requested that you use the NPV approach. Show all equations and calculations used.

3.2 As some of the directors have no formal qualifications in finance, you are also asked to include an explanation of your approach. To do this you will need to write a report that explains the NPV method and a justification of the cash flows you have included or excluded from your analysis.

3.3 Currently, all of Solar Sail's shareholders are Australian residents who can fully utilise taxation imputation credits. The directors think there may be interest from offshore investors if this project is successful. They have asked you to explain the impact (if any) that a large number of new offshore investors would have on the capital budgeting process. Write the directors a report on this matter.

3.4 Analyse the project (that is, repeat the first requirement in this section) assuming the majority of Solar Sail's shareholders are overseas residents. Ignore any withholding tax transactions.

Section two

Six months after implementing the project, the company has plenty of product but has not been able sell any of it in South-East Asia. The company had not anticipated that it would take so long to gain the necessary import permits from governments. Nor did it anticipate the waterside workers' strike that lasted for a further 2 months. Management estimate that sales revenues will not be received for another month. This has caused a short-term liquidity problem for the company. The directors are seeking your advice on potential sources of short-term finance and for identification of the source that might best suit their needs.

REQUIRED

Prepare a report and make a recommendation to Solar Sail.

case 4

Hygienic Solutions and the EnviroMist

Hygienic Solutions is an Australian business that has specialised in producing environmentally friendly cleaning products. The business is structured as a partnership and is owned by Bill and Ben Weed. It has been a highly successful operation and is large enough to have several divisions. Hygienic Solutions' 'Earth Safe' range currently includes low-phosphate detergents, washing liquids, bathroom and oven-cleaning products.

Section one

Bill and Ben want you to advise on the feasibility of a proposal to introduce a steam cleaning machine (the 'EnviroMist') for the domestic market. The EnviroMist would be very different from the current range of products — Hygienic Solutions has not been involved in producing appliances before. Bill and Ben have provided you with the following information.

MEMO ONE

HYGIENIC SOLUTIONS

To: Bill and Ben

From: New projects division

Date: 20 December 2008

Subject: Equipment requirements

Our engineers have estimated the following costs of equipment needed to produce 15 000 units of the EnviroMist a year:

- The installed cost of the main machine is $500 000. The machine would have a useful life of 10 years. The machine could be sold at the end of 5 years for an estimated $100 000, or at the end of 10 years for an estimated $20 000. The Australian Taxation Office (ATO) allows prime cost depreciation at the rate of 20% pa.
- $36 000 of specialised small tools are also required. The ATO allows prime cost depreciation at 33.33% pa. The tools will have a useful life of 15 years, after which time they would be scrapped.
- You can assume that any benefits from tax deductions are received in the year in which the deduction is incurred.

MEMO TWO

HYGIENIC SOLUTIONS

To: Bill and Ben

From: Production manager

Date: 20 December 2008

Subject: Production costs

Our department has estimated the following costs for production of the EnviroMist:

- Staff training would need to be conducted at the start of the project. The estimated cost of training is $7500. Training costs are tax deductible.
- Each unit of EnviroMist would require 3 hours of labour. Hygienic currently has an enterprise bargaining agreement with our production workers. Wages are fixed at $15 per hour for the next 5 years. After year 5, wages are expected to increase to $20 per hour and remain at that rate for at least the following 5 years.
- Material cost per unit would be $85 for the first 3 years of the project. The EnviroMist is made from recycled materials. As advances in recycling technology are forecast, the material cost is expected to fall to $60 per unit after year 3.
- Raw materials and parts inventories costing $10 000 would be needed to facilitate production of the EnviroMist.
- Electricity, machine maintenance and other variable expenses are $3 per unit of production.
- Insurance and other tax-deductible fixed overhead expenses associated with the project will be $8000 per annum.

MEMO THREE

HYGIENIC SOLUTIONS

To: Bill and Ben

From: Marketing

Date: 20 December 2008

Subject: Product sales forecasts

Only one other competitor (K-Star) currently sells a steam cleaner in the Australian market. From what we can gather, K-Star has been increasing sales at a rate of 5% for each of the 3 years their product has been on the market. K-Star sold 7000 units in the year just ended. We think that K-Star's growth in sales is more closely linked to the environmental benefits of steam cleaning than to the quality of their product.

K-Star's product is manufactured overseas. We believe we can capitalise on our use of recycled products and the use of domestic labour to gain market share from K-Star. If our estimates of the market size and the effectiveness of our marketing strategy are correct, we expect to sell 6000 units in the first year. We estimate that sales growth will be at 10% per annum for the following 6 years. After that time, we expect a stable level of sales. Round forecast sales to the nearest whole unit. We also expect to maintain a constant $175 per unit price.

An advertising campaign costing $30 000 per annum would be needed to gain market share and meet our growth forecasts. The advertising expense is tax deductible. A one-off increase of $15 000 in accounts receivable would be necessary to support the expected level of sales (not tax deductible).

A small downside of introduction of the EnviroMist is that current customers purchasing the appliance will be able to substitute it for our Earth Safe range. This will result in a before-tax annual loss of $75 000 net cash flows.

MEMO FOUR

HYGIENIC SOLUTIONS

To: Bill and Ben

From: CFO

Date: 20 December 2008

Subject: Financial considerations

The following information has been collated by the finance department:

- The before-tax cost of capital is 15%.
- Bill and Ben's marginal tax rate is 47%.
- The after-tax cost of capital is 11%.
- The rate of return on Treasury bills is 3%.
- The company's after-tax cost of debt is 4.5%.
- New projects with similar risks as existing projects are to be evaluated at the cost of capital. Any new products that have different characteristics to our current product line are evaluated at the cost of capital plus 3%.
- The current financing structure of Hygienic is 30% debt and 70% equity.
- All working capital will be recovered at the end of the project.

The owners of Hygienic Solutions have asked you to help them with their investment decision. Specifically, they want you to produce a report that develops a recommendation on the acceptance or rejection of the EnviroMist project. You have decided to use the net present value approach.

REQUIRED

4.1 Analyse the project using NPV.

4.2 Write a report that includes an essay outlining the benefits of the NPV approach. Your essay will also discuss how you determined your discount rate. Make a recommendation about the project.

4.3 Explain the processes you have used to determine your cash flows to Bill and Ben. As they do not have any formal qualifications in Finance, you will need to give your explanation in a manner that is clearly understandable to them.

Section two

Given the success of their business, Bill and Ben have been considering listing on the ASX. They have asked you to advise them on how to go about becoming a listed company. They would also like to know if listing would have an impact on your analysis of the EnviroMist project.

REQUIRED

4.1 Explain the process of listing on the ASX.

4.2 Explain how the change of ownership would require modifications to the project appraisal. Assume that the shareholders in the listed company can fully utilise imputation credits and re-evaluate the project under this assumption.

Section three

Bill and Ben have had a quick look at the memos and have noticed the large fall in salvage value on the machine after year 5. They think they might be better off if they produce the EnviroMist for only 5 years, rather than 10. Should Bill and Ben terminate the project at the end of year 5? The partnership will not change to a company.

REQUIRED

Advise Bill and Ben. You will need to show calculations and include an explanation that justifies your conclusion.

case 5

Spring Chickens

A local company, Spring Chickens, has been selling a rejuvenating face cream for the last 12 months. Although the face cream performed well in the laboratory tests conducted on rabbits, there has been an unfortunate side effect when the cream is used on people over 40. The company had received a few positive comments from satisfied male customers, but the number of complaints from women has been increasing. The pharmacist responsible for developing the product conducted further tests (this time on frogs) and found that the cream greatly increased facial hair.

Section one

The local law firm has always handled legal matters for Spring Chickens. They have advised the company that a class action taken to court by Spring Chickens' customers would be guaranteed to succeed. The lawyers estimate the court case would take one year to complete and that the judge would award $5000 per plaintiff. The managing director of Spring Chickens tells you that 10 000 customers have been unhappy with the side effects produced by the cream.

The management team at Spring Chickens has identified several different ways of dealing with this situation:

1. Purchase bonds that return 4% pa to create a 'damages reserve'. The managing director wants you to tell her the dollar amount of a bond purchase made today that would provide sufficient funds to pay damages when the court case is settled. Coupons and face value would be used to settle the claims.
2. Settle out of court. The managing director wants you to tell her how much the company could offer the plaintiffs today and be indifferent to waiting for the court case to be settled.
3. Get a big city lawyer. The managing director has a cousin with a legal contact who estimates that the case could be delayed for a further year. This approach is unlikely to change the outcome, but will mean that Spring Chickens Ltd does not have to pay damages until 2 years from now. Spring Chickens' cost of capital is 10%. The managing director wants to know the maximum amount of money she should pay for the lawyer to use delaying tactics.

REQUIRED

5.1 Which of the alternatives would you recommend if you were told the objective of the firm was to minimise the costs to shareholders?

5.2 Are there any ethical issues that might cause you to modify your conclusion? Why might ignoring such an issue have a negative effect on shareholder wealth?

Section two

Due to the large amount of damages and legal expenses faced by the company, Spring Chickens have asked you how they can manage their cash flows more efficiently. After discussing the matter with the managing director, you think there could be significant savings if the raw materials inventory and accounts payable were better managed.

Raw materials

The main component of the raw materials inventory of Spring Chickens is lanolin. Being a natural product, lanolin has a shelf life of only 18 months before it has to be discarded. The company made a large purchase of heavily discounted lanolin from a competitor's liquidator 2 years ago. About one-third of this purchase was discarded in the last 6 months and the company has had trouble getting the inventory level right ever since then. A new and regular source of lanolin has been found, but the supplier is located interstate so shipments take 2 weeks to arrive after an order has been placed. This has meant that Spring Chickens often runs out of lanolin, which is critical to almost all of their products. Management are reluctant to authorise large orders as they know that ordering too much will have adverse financial consequences.

The line manager has estimated the usage of lanolin for the coming year as 1500 kilograms. The supplier will accept orders only in 50 kilogram lots at a price of $30/kg. The cost of placing an order is $75. Lanolin is quite bulky, so the carrying cost per kilogram is $2.50. To avoid running out of lanolin and holding up production, a safety stock of 100 kg is to be maintained, even during the 2-week period it takes for a new order to be delivered.

Accounts payable

A second supplier of lanolin has been identified and has agreed to supply Spring Chickens for the same costs. The only difference between the two suppliers is the credit terms they offer. The first offers terms of 1/45 net 90, while the second gives 2/15 net 60.

REQUIRED

5.1 Calculate the optimal order quantity of lanolin.

5.2 Identify the number of orders that will be placed each year.

5.3 Determine when new inventory should be ordered.

5.4 Calculate the average inventory level under the new policy.

5.5 Prepare a report that explains the methodology you have used and discusses your results.

5.6 Recommend which supplier should be used.

Show the equations and calculations you have used.

case 6

Financial advisory service II

Given the experience and excellent reputation you developed while providing financial advice to your fellow students, you have been offered a part-time position advising corporate clients. Your new boss has passed the following clients over to you and wants to be impressed by the quality and thoroughness of your analysis of each client's situation.

Client one — University Staff Union

Part one

The University Staff Union (USU) is currently negotiating with university employers for improved conditions for staff. As part of the package, the university employers have developed the following proposals to help staff finance further studies:

- *Proposal one.* Reimbursement of eligible education expenses of $2300 each year for 3 years.
- *Proposal two.* A $19 200 loan at 2%, principal and interest to be repaid at the end of 5 years.

The USU members want you to assist them to decide which proposal to accept. They tell you that a 'typical' university staff member's opportunity cost is 6% per year. Specifically, the USU would like to know:

(a) the present value of proposal one to the typical employee

(b) how much a typical employee will have to pay at the end of 5 years under proposal two and the present value of this amount to an employee

(c) if the typical employee would prefer proposal one or proposal two. (To address this issue, assume the present value calculated in the previous question is the amount a typical employee could normally borrow from a bank. You can then subtract this from the $19 200 to determine the present value of the university subsidy.)

(d) if employees with higher opportunity costs than the typical employee make the same choice. No calculations are required here, but be sure to explain your answer.

REQUIRED

Answer the four questions posed by USU. Show all equations and calculations.

Part two

USU, like many other unions in Australia, is finding it increasingly difficult to attract new members. They are currently looking for ways to increase the success of the next membership drive. One member suggested that they offer discounted domestic travel to members. Domestic airlines offer discounted fares (5% off the regular price) for travel booked 6 months in advance. They require payment for the discounted fare within 2 weeks of booking. The scheme would involve members booking their travel through USU to get the 5% discount and paying for the travel 60 days after booking. USU would book and pay for the member's travel the same day the member booked with USU. USU has an opportunity cost of 10%.

REQUIRED

Calculate the cost of the scheme and identify any ways the cost could be reduced.

Client two — Deterrent Dogs Ltd

Deterrent Dogs is a company that provides security services to residential and commercial properties in all the major cities of Australia. The company has been operating for 20 years and has achieved impressive market penetration and a stable growth rate of 1% per annum. Reported earnings for the financial year just ended were $495 000.

Deterrent Dogs Ltd issued 1 000 000 shares when the company first floated and has not made any further issues. Deterrent shares are currently trading at $5.00 and the last annual dividend paid was $0.05. In fact, the company has always paid an annual dividend of $0.05. Earnings of $500 000 and capital expenditure of $50 000 are forecast for next year.

The board of Deterrent is considering the adoption of a new dividend policy in the coming year. They have asked you to analyse the situation for them.

REQUIRED

6.1 Explain the three main dividend policy alternatives to the board.

6.2 Calculate the dividend per share under each of these three policies.

6.3 Identify the factors that the board should consider when trying to determine the optimal dividend policy for Deterrent Dogs.

Client three — Nix Noodles

Nikki is the manager of a division of a large manufacturing firm, Nix Noodles. She is currently faced with the decision of leasing or buying a specialised noodle-making machine. If the machine were to be purchased on 1 January the cash price of $92 000 would be financed by a loan on which interest would be payable at 16% per annum. The loan would be repaid in four equal annual instalments at the end of each year. The machine would be used for 4 years and then it would be transferred to the shoelace division of the company at its written-down value.

If a lease were to be taken out, four annual rentals of $20 000 would be paid starting on 30 June. There is an option to purchase the machine for $25 000 at the end of the 4-year lease. Nikki expects to exercise this option.

The company has a 31 December balance date and tax is payable in the year of income. Nikki expects that the tax rate of 35% will continue. She has calculated that the after-tax cost of the loan is 12%. The firm is structured as a partnership. All partners currently have a marginal tax rate of 35%. The prime cost depreciation rate allowed by the ATO is 25% per annum.

REQUIRED

6.1 Should Nikki lease the machine or purchase it using the cash raised from the loan? Show all calculations and explain your conclusion.

6.2 Would your analysis have been different if Nix Noodles were a listed company (with investors who could fully utilise imputation credits) rather than a partnership? Show calculations and explain your answer.

6.3 Prepare a report that outlines the advantages and disadvantages of leasing for Nikki.

Case 7

Greenfish Ltd

As one of the first companies to mass-produce DVDs, Greenfish Ltd is well positioned in this market. As demand for Greenfish products has steadily increased over the last few years, the board thinks it appropriate to put more effort into managing the financial aspects of the business. You have been asked to prepare a cash budget and pro-forma financial statements. The directors are particularly interested in finding out how much (if any) finance will need to be raised for next year's operations. You have collated the following information:

Income statement Greenfish Ltd for the year ended 30 April 20X8	
Sales revenue	500000
Less: Cost of goods sold	150000
Gross profit	350000
Less: Operating expenses	100000
Depreciation	75000
Interest expense	16000
Net profit before tax	159000
Less: Tax (30%)	47700
Net profit after tax	111 300
Dividends paid	20000
	91 300

Balance Sheet Greenfish Ltd as at 30 April 20X8			
Assets		**Liabilities and equities**	
Cash	32000	Trade accounts payable	23400
Property, plant & equipment	3000	Other current liabilities	5000
Accounts receivable	32592		
Inventories	25000		
Total current assets	92592	*Total current liabilities*	28400
Net fixed assets	350000	Long term debt	200000
		Ordinary shares	100000
		Retained earnings	114192
Total assets	442592	*Total liabilities and equity*	442592

Additionally:

- Estimated sales for the 20X8–X9 financial year are $960000. Sales occur evenly throughout the year. Sales for March and April 20X8 were $76000 and $78000 respectively.
- The dividend for 20X8–X9 is expected to be $100000 and will be paid in December.
- Accounts receivable are expected to be 42% of sales each month. Greenfish offers a credit period of one month and 80% of customers adhere to the credit period. The remaining customers pay in the second month after purchase. Fortunately, Greenfish has no bad debts.

- Inventory changes directly with the level of sales. Greenfish orders goods from suppliers in the same month as the inventory is sold. Trade accounts are paid one month after the goods are sold. Other current liabilities remain at the same level.
- Other expenses (excluding interest) vary directly with sales and are paid in cash in the month they are incurred.
- The depreciation charge for existing fixed assets will be the same as the most recent financial year. A new DVD machine costing $150 000 will be purchased in August. The annual depreciation charge for this asset for 20X8–X9 will be $50 000. No other fixed assets will be purchased. If there is not enough cash in the bank, any gap needed to purchase the machine will be raised using long-term debt.
- Taxes are payable quarterly, with the first payment due at the end of July. Tax payable will be one quarter of the tax expense in the pro-forma income statement.
- Of the current portion of property, plant and equipment, machinery with a book value of $2000 will be sold for that amount in May. Plant with a book value of $1000 will be sold for that amount in June. No further sales of PP&E are planned for the coming year.
- The interest rate on long-term debt is 8% pa. The debt is long-term bonds issued by Greenfish. Interest is paid quarterly, with the next payment due in May. $50 000 of the bonds matures in May. No ordinary shares will be issued during the coming year.
- The tax rate of 30% will be maintained for the coming financial year.
- The firm will maintain a minimum cash balance of $30 000.
- Long-term debt will be used to finance any forecast shortfall. Bonds with a total face value of $70 000 will be issued for a net price of $70 000. The new debt will be issued on the first day of the first month where the forecast cash balance is below $30 000. The bonds will pay a coupon of 10% per annum, with semi-annual payments commencing one day before the 6-month anniversary of the issue.

REQUIRED

Will Greenfish have sufficient cash for operations to purchase the new DVD equipment?

7.1 Present a monthly cash budget so you can make a recommendation to the board on when the funding will be needed. Round all cash flows to the nearest dollar.

7.2 Prepare a report that contains a pro-forma income statement for the year ended 30 April 20X9, using the percent of sales method for those items you have not been given any specific information about. Also include the pro-forma balance sheet dated 30 April 20X9. Round your percentages to two decimal places.

7.3 Calculate the EPS, DPS, ROE, debt-to-equity and times-interest-earned ratios for the year ended April 20X8, and on the pro-forma financial statements for the year ended April 20X9. Greenfish issued 2 million shares when the company floated and has not made any further issues. Give your opinion on how investors will view any changes in the ratios calculated on the pro-forma financial statements.

7.4 None of the directors of Greenfish has any formal training in finance. To help them make an informed choice on meeting any funding shortfalls, write an essay that outlines some alternative sources of long-term and short-term finance.

case 8

Rebellion Flour Ltd

A local company, Rebellion Flour Ltd, has grown quite a lot over the last few years. The board of directors has decided that it is time to employ a full-time CFO. You find the package offered by Rebellion is very attractive and decide to apply for the position. Your written application has impressed the directors and they have asked you to make a presentation to them. This is your big chance to display your impressive skills — the board have asked that you deal with some specific problems that the company currently faces.

Section 1

The management at Rebellion Flour are considering the purchase of the patent for a new flour bleaching system. The technology is highly innovative, but has not been adequately tested yet. Given the large risk associated with the patent, the directors of Rebellion have decided against borrowing the necessary $500 000 to acquire the patent. They have asked you to advise them on whether or not the company will be able to generate sufficient cash flow from operations to purchase the patent at the end of January next year. You decide to prepare a cash budget for Rebellion to answer the directors' question and to be able to show them why they can or can't generate sufficient cash for the purchase.

Working closely with Rebellion's accountant, you have collected the following information.

- Sales forecasts for June to February are as follows:

June	75 000
July	95 000
Aug.	105 000
Sept.	155 000
Oct.	230 000
Nov.	320 000
Dec.	175 000
Jan.	135 000
Feb.	125 000

Actual sales for April and May were $125 000 and $190 000 respectively.

- 25% of Rebellion's sales are made for cash. Trade credit is extended to the company's larger customers. This results in 50% of credit sales being collected in the month following the sale. Apart from bad debts of 1% of credit sales, the remainder of the sales amount is collected during the second month following the sale.
- Rebellion's production department keeps one month ahead by using estimates of company sales for the following month to set the level of production. The purchasing department orders and pays for the wheat and other necessary raw materials in the month the flour will be produced. The total cost of raw materials is 75% of the following month's sales forecast.
- Rebellion's land and factory are mortgaged. The payments on this loan are $4000 per month.
- Wages, electricity and other cash overheads total $15 000 per month.

- Corporate tax is paid quarterly, with the next payment due in August. The next four payments have been estimated at $17 250.
- The rolling machine used in the factory is financed by a hire purchase contract. The equal payments for this contract are made quarterly. The next payment of $5000 is due in June.
- Rebellion issued 100 bonds 18 months ago. The bonds mature in December and will not be rolled over. The bonds have a face value of $1000 and a coupon rate of 10%. The coupon is paid semi-annually.
- The company's cash balance is $12 000 at 31 May this year. The directors have told you that it is company policy to maintain a minimum cash balance of $7500 at all times.
- If it is forecast that insufficient cash will be generated in any month, Rebellion uses short-term financing to fund the gap. The amount of funds raised is based on the estimated shortfall for each month. The amount borrowed must be a multiple of $10 000. If the funding shortfall was $15 000, for example, Rebellion would need to borrow $20 000. The funds are borrowed at the start of the month in which there is an estimated shortfall. Interest is payable for the whole month and is paid on the first day of the month following the borrowing. If sufficient funds are generated in the month following a short-term borrowing, the loan is repaid then (that is, in the month after it was borrowed). When there are insufficient funds to repay one of the loans, the balance is rolled over. Interest on short-term borrowings is 6% per annum.
- Round all cash flows for each line item to whole dollars.

REQUIRED

8.1 Prepare a cash budget for the months from June up to and including January. Show all calculations and present your work in a manner that will impress the board.

8.2 Advise the board on whether or not the company will be able to generate sufficient cash flow from operations to purchase the patent at the end of January next year.

Section two

Management at Rebellion are currently considering a strategy for the vertical integration of the business. The first phase of the strategy involves expanding into the production of pasta products. The board likes the idea, but has insisted that marketing research be conducted before any capital commitment is made. A consulting firm has been hired to facilitate the product and packaging designs, then to test these using market surveys. The fee charged by the consultants is $500 000. The market testing phase of the project would take one year. The board is willing to commit funds to the project if the market testing shows sufficient demand for the new product.

As there is insufficient room at their existing factory, Rebellion would have to extend their premises. They have paid $100 000 for a purchase option over one acre of land close to their existing factory. The purchase option allows them to buy the land for $750 000 when the market testing phase has been completed. Rebellion will take this option if the results of the market testing are positive and the project receives the final approval of the board. If Rebellion does not go ahead with the project, the $100 000 paid for the option will not be refunded. Construction of the new factory would take one year to complete at an estimated cost of $1 500 000. Payment for the building would be made upon completion.

Plant and equipment for the production process is highly specialised and would cost $950 000. The equipment has an expected useful life of 10 years. The equipment will be ready for installation when the building is completed. The contract with the supplier specifies that payment for the equipment be made on delivery. Installation of the equipment would be done on the day the equipment is delivered and would cost $15 000. Pasta production will commence the day following the installation.

Staffing levels will need to be increased. New staff members receive one week's specialist training and will be ready to start work when the equipment has been installed. Staff on-costs and training will total $7000 after tax. Holdings of raw materials and finished goods inventories associated with the project will be $35 000.

Although the report on market testing has not yet been completed, management have already made a best estimate of annual sales figures. Year 1 applies to the first year of production.

Year 1	900 000
Year 2	1 000 000
Year 3	1 500 000
Year 4	1 750 000
Year 5	1 750 000
Year 6	1 750 000
Year 7	1 500 000
Year 8	1 500 000
Year 9	1 250 000
Year 10	900 000

Raw materials will cost 40% of sales revenue. Wages are forecast to be $300 000 per annum. Other cash expenses associated with production are 10% of sales.

Management doubt that revenues and expenses can be accurately forecast out beyond 11 years. They want you to assess the project on the assumption that it will be terminated 10 years from the beginning of production. The estimated sales proceeds for the land and buildings at termination is $3 000 000 (this amount is deemed as $2 000 000 for the land and $1 000 000 for the buildings for tax purposes). The plant and equipment would be scrapped at a cost of $5000.

Rebellion is integrated with the taxation system. The relevant tax rate is 30%. The Australian Taxation Office allows 20% per annum depreciation on the installed cost of plant and equipment. The depreciation rate for buildings is 5% of cost per annum. The market testing expense would not be tax deductible. Tax deductions can be claimed in the same year as the expenditure is incurred and tax is paid in the same year that the associated revenue is generated. Tax losses are carried forward and offset against the tax payable amounts in future years.

Rebellion's board members have asked you to evaluate the pasta project for them. To do this, you will need to calculate the net present value (NPV) of the project. You have calculated that Rebellion's before-tax cost of capital is 10% and the after-tax cost is 8%. Your presentation to the board will be made at the same time that the contract with the marketing consultants is signed.

REQUIRED

8.1 Evaluate the project for the board. Show all calculations. Explain your rationale for the items you have included in your analysis. To assist the board members to understand your presentation, prepare an explanation of the concept of NPV and explain to them why they should accept or reject the project based on your calculations.

8.2 Even though you have been asked to prepare your analysis using NPV, you are concerned that some of the directors might ask you what the internal rate of return is for the project. You really want to impress the board, so prepare a response to this question.

Section three

The board of Rebellion have approved a new project that requires an outlay of $2 000 000. They are unsure as to which source of funds they should use. They have given you the following information:

- Bonds can be issued with a face value of $1000 and annual coupon payments of 6% pa. The bonds would have a 10-year term. Rebellion would receive 95% of the $1200 issue price. You have decided to calculate the cost of the bonds using the approximate cost of debt equation.
- Preference shares can be issued with a face value of $5. They would pay an annual dividend of $0.50. The issue price of the shares would be $6. Rebellion would net 92% of the proceeds.
- The company's ordinary shares (500 000 have been issued) are currently selling for $7.50. A new issue would be made at this price. Issue costs would be 10% of the proceeds. The expected annual dividend for the first year is expected to be $0.30. Dividends are expected to grow at the constant rate of 2% pa. Investors have a 12% required rate of return for this type of investment.
- Information about Rebellion's taxation status was presented in section two.
- The new project will generate earnings before interest and tax of $1 000 000.
- Some members of the board feel that the project should be financed with the cheapest source of funds; others think the source that gives the highest earnings per share should be chosen. You have been asked to give your opinion on the matter.

REQUIRED

8.1 Calculate the cost of each source of funds, showing all equations and calculations.

8.2 Prepare a short essay that identifies the appropriate cost of finance for the new project and clearly states the reasons for your selection.

8.3 Use EBIT–EPS analysis to calculate the impact each source of finance (if it were the only one chosen) would have on Rebellion's EPS. Round to the nearest whole security when calculating the number of securities to be issued. Do you think EBIT–EPS analysis is appropriate for Rebellion Flour? Why?

Section four

In your discussion with Rebellion, you have ascertained that the majority of the board have not had any formal training in the field of finance. You know that your presentation will be much more impressive if the audience understands the relationship between risk and return and the implications of this relationship to the activities of Rebellion.

REQUIRED

Prepare an essay that explains the relationship between risk and return and how the relationship impacts on Rebellion's activities and on the analyses you have presented.

case 9

Financial advisory service III

As a finance student, you are naturally inclined to want to share your skills for the benefit of others. You and a couple of friends have decided to open a free financial counselling service for retirees. The level of demand for your services has been most pleasing and you have interviewed a number of clients. Your assessments of each person's requirements are outlined below.

Client one — Vida's shares

Vida lives in the local retirement village. She owns shares in a number of companies and wants to sell some so she can take a trip to Bhutan. Vida's required return is 15%. She has owned the shares for many years and will not have to pay capital gains tax on any sales.

- ABC Ltd pays semi-annual unfranked dividends. The last dividend was $0.30. The company is well established and you have forecast the dividend growth rate to be 2% pa. The current market price of ABC shares is $7.70.
- KLM Ltd pays semi-annual unfranked dividends. The last dividend was $0.50. The company is well established and you have forecast the dividend growth rate to be 2.5% pa. The current market price of KLM shares is $8.05.
- HIJ Ltd pays annual unfranked dividends. The last dividend was $0.90. The company is well established and you have forecast the dividend growth rate to be 1.5% pa. The current market price of HIJ shares is $13.00.
- DEF Ltd pays constant annual dividends of $0.75 that are unfranked. The current market price of DEF is $4.90.

Vida has asked you for a recommendation about which shares to sell. She wants you to provide a rationale and calculations to support your decision.

Client two — Paddy's bonds

Paddy has quite a lot of money from the sale of his house and he wants to invest this in bonds. He is not sure which bond to purchase. He has given you the following information about each of the bonds. All bonds have 20 more coupon payments to maturity. The final coupon is paid with the face value.

- Bond A has a face value of $100 000 and a coupon rate of 5%. Coupons are paid semi-annually with the first coupon received the day after purchase. Paddy's required return is 7% and Bond A is selling at $88 300.
- Bond B has a face value of $100 000 and a coupon rate of 5%. Coupons are paid semi-annually with the first coupon received 6 months after purchase. At maturity date, Bond B will pay face value and one more coupon. Paddy's required return is 7% and Bond B is selling at $85 700.
- Bond C has a face value of $50 000 and a coupon rate of 6%. Coupons are paid semi-annually with the first coupon received 6 months after purchase. Paddy's required return is 8.5% and Bond C is selling at $41 600.

Paddy wants you to recommend which bonds to purchase. He also wants you to show calculations to support your recommendation and to provide him with a rationale that supports your recommendation.

Client three — Mavis's bills

Mavis has $1 million she wants to leave to her grandchildren when she dies. She accumulated the money from property and share investments over her lifetime, but has sold these assets and has the money in a bank account that generates 2% pa compounded monthly. Her friend at the retirement village told her she could invest the money for short periods in the bill market. Mavis doesn't expect to live much longer, so she wants her million to be highly liquid for division among her grandchildren when she is gone. She has given you the following information and wants you to tell her if she should purchase any of the bills or if she should simply leave the money in the bank.

To give your advice, you have decided to compare the returns on each of the bills to the annual return of keeping the money in the bank. To do this, you will need to calculate the return on the bank account.

- Bill X has a purchase price of $98 400 and a face value of $100 000. It has 180 days to maturity.
- Bill Y has a purchase price of $98 900 and a face value of $100 000. It has 120 days to maturity.
- Bill Z has a purchase price of $99 560 and a face value of $100 000. It has 60 days to maturity.

Should Mavis leave her money in the bank or purchase bills if she wants to maximise her wealth? If she should purchase bills, should she purchase X, Y or Z? Assume the bills have the same level of risk as the bank account. Mavis has instructed you that she does not have to place every last dollar of the million in bills, and has advised you not to worry about the return on any money left in the bank after she has purchased the bills.

REQUIRED

9.1 Answer each of your clients' questions. Show all calculations and equations.

9.2 Write a paragraph for each client that explains why you have made your recommendation. To do this, you will need to provide a rationale to support your choice.

9.3 Prepare a short essay that explains the nature of the risk–return relationships for your clients. Be sure to define all key terms.

case 10

Financial advisory service IV

As a finance student, you are naturally inclined to want to share your skills for the benefit of others. You and a couple of friends have decided to open a free financial counselling service for students from other disciplines. The level of demand for your services has been most pleasing and you have interviewed a number of clients. Your assessments of each person's requirements are outlined below.

Client one — Yani's gift

Yani's grandparents want to help him with his studies. They will give him $4000 pa for 4 years. They made a similar offer to Yani's cousin and so Yani won't receive the first payment until 3 years from today.

(a) If Yani can earn 7.5% on his investments, what is the present value of the gift?

(b) If Yani can earn 5% on his investments, what is the present value of the gift?

(c) What is the present value of the gift if Yani only has to wait one year for his first payment and he can earn 7.5% on his investments?

(d) What is the present value of the gift if Yani receives his first payment today and he can earn 7.5% on his investments?

Client two — Jin's investment

Jin has been offered a special set of annuities by his insurance company. He would receive $45 000 a year for the next 8 years and $52 000 for the following 8 years.

(a) How much should Jin pay for this set of annuities if his discount rate is 9% pa? The payments are received annually and are made at the beginning of each year.

(b) How much should Jin pay for this set of annuities if his discount rate is 9% pa and the annuity payments are made semi-annually? Jin would still receive a total of $45 000 each year for the next 8 years and $52 000 for the following 8 years. The first payment is made on the day of the purchase.

(c) How much should Jin pay for this set of annuities if his discount rate is 9% pa and the annuity payments are made semi-annually? The first payment is made 6 months after the day of the purchase.

Client three — BankSouth superannuation

BankSouth has unfunded superannuation (pension) liabilities of $1 million due in 15 years. BankSouth can earn 8% pa, compounded semi-annually on its investments.

(a) What size payments have to be invested every 6 months to meet the superannuation liability in 15 years? The first payment would be made in 6 months' time.

(b) What size payments have to be invested each year to meet the superannuation liability in 15 years if the first payment would be made in one year's time.

(c) How much would BankSouth have to invest today to have enough to meet the liability in 15 years' time?

Client four — Peter's trip

Peter is planning to travel around Europe in 5 years' time. He expects that his trip will cost $20 000. Peter estimates that he can deposit the following amounts at the end of each year:

Year 1	Year 2	Year 3	Year 4	Year 5
$2000	$3000	$4000	$5000	$5000

(a) If he can earn 7% pa on his investments, will he have enough saved at the end of 5 years to take the trip?

(b) Will he have enough if he can earn 5% pa on his investments?

(c) Will Peter have enough for his trip if he expects it will cost $28 000 in 5 years and he can earn 20% compounded monthly on his investments?

REQUIRED

10.1 Answer each of your clients' questions. Show all calculations and equations.

10.2 Prepare a short essay for your clients explaining the nature of present and future values. Be sure to define all key terms.

case 11

Romantic Roses

Dianna and Peter established their business partnership 'Romantic Roses' 5 years ago. Peter has a degree in horticulture and leaves the marketing and financing of the firm to Dianna as she has a Commerce degree.

The business has experienced a solid level of success growing roses for the cut-flower market. It is located on a 6-hectare property north of Hobart. Five hectares are currently under cultivation and Dianna and Peter have been discussing expanding the business by utilising the spare hectare. They have asked you to analyse the following data and provide them with a recommendation as to the acceptability of the project. Peter and Dianna tell you that they will retire 10 years from today. The business will not be sold as Dianna and Peter live on the property.

Peter has been developing three new varieties of roses over the last 2 years. Development costs of the roses so far has been $70 000. Details of the new roses are as follows:

- 'Byron' has a large flamboyant pink flower. The rose bush is sturdy and well suited to commercial growing conditions. The Byron is well suited to the temperate climate where Romantic Roses operates, but it is not expected to do well in warmer climates.
- 'Shelley' has been developed for its delightful fragrance. The rose bush is not as robust as the Byron, but is expected to perform reasonably well under commercial growing conditions. It will require a lot of pruning to prevent it turning into a monster.
- 'Keats' has a less exciting flower than the Byron and a milder perfume than the Shelley, but it does have the advantage of longevity as a cut flower. It is a relatively low-maintenance rose bush to cultivate.

Peter estimates that it will take 6 months for further development and testing of the new roses if the decision is made to expand the operation of Romantic Roses with cultivation of these three roses. It would then take another 6 months to generate sufficient stock to plant a hectare of land. The operating cash outflow associated with the further development and stock production is $140 000 and is tax deductible. The hectare of land that would be planted would need to be cleared, graded and cultivated. Dianna estimates that this would cost $20 000. The soil would need to be enriched with 10 tonnes of manure at a cost of $100 per tonne. The clearing and fertilising costs are tax deductible. The clearing and fertilising of the land would occur the day before the new roses are taken from the greenhouse for planting out.

The time from planting to a commercial quantity of flower buds is 3 years after the roses are transferred from the greenhouse to the soil. After the roses are transplanted from the greenhouse to the soil, the labour cost per hectare of roses under cultivation is $10 000 pa, pest control will cost a further $5000 pa and the annual fertiliser cost is $500 per hectare. Additional labour costs of $3000 pa are required when the roses are cut and packed in boxes for sale. The new project will utilise the existing cultivation equipment. This equipment was purchased 5 years ago for a total cost of $90 000 and is being depreciated using the prime cost method over 10 years. It is used for all current projects.

A marketing consultant was contracted 6 months ago to provide market research on the new rose varieties. Romantic Roses received an invoice for $5000 and the following advice this week.

MEMO ONE

To: Romantic Roses

From: Brilliant Marketing

Date: 31 December 2007

Subject: Market response to the Byron, Shelley and Keats roses

At your request, we have conducted rigorous market research into the demand for your three new varieties of roses. Our results are as follows:

- The large flowers and fashionable colours of the Byron rose were well received by florists. Many commented that they had never seen a rose more suited to bridal bouquets, where the size and colour of the flowers are the critical features.
- The fragrance of the Shelley makes this rose ideal for supermarket sales of cut flowers. Buyers for supermarkets commented Shelley bunches in stores would generate large sales as customers would be drawn to the stunning fragrance.
- The Keats rose was especially attractive to florists who specialise in funeral wreaths. The long-lasting flowers and sedate perfume of the Keats are ideal characteristics for this market.
- We conclude that each of the three new varieties of roses would fill market niches very successfully.
- We have estimated how many boxes of 100 roses would be sold and the price per box for 10 years.
- We also estimate that the new range of roses would reduce sales of your current product by $30 000 per annum.
- Initially, marketing expenses would be relatively high as we work to familiarise the market with the new roses. The charge for marketing your new products would be $20 000 pa for the first 3 years of sales. The charge for subsequent years would be $4500 pa.

Year	Boxes	Price per box ($)
1	500	200
2	700	225
3	1 200	250
4	1 500	275
5	1 400	300
6	1 200	300
7	1 000	300
8	700	275
9	500	250
10	500	250

Romantic Roses currently uses Brilliant Marketing to advertise the firm's existing range of roses. Dianna and Peter would contract Brilliant Marketing for the new project if they decide to adopt it. Peter is confident that the firm can supply as many boxes of roses as the market demands.

Peter would need more greenhouse capacity to develop the new roses and grow them to the required size for planting. He has received the following quote for extending the current facilities to the size he needs.

MEMO TWO

To: Peter, Romantic Roses

From: Glassy Greenhouses

Date: 2 January 2008

Subject: Extension of greenhouse at Romantic Roses

- Thank you for asking us to provide the following quote to extend the facilities we built for you 5 years ago.
- The expansion of the greenhouse would require a cement slab equipped with appropriate drainage. We estimate that this would cost $35 000.
- Materials for the structure would cost $60 000
- Labour and associated insurance will cost $12 000.

The greenhouse can not be depreciated for taxation purposes.

In addition to the extension to the greenhouse, Peter would need racks for storing the roses while they grow. This equipment would cost $7000 and can be depreciated using the prime cost method over 3 years. A new drip watering system would also need to be installed at a cost of $6000. The watering system can be depreciated using prime cost over 4 years.

Peter recently attended a conference about future trends in the rose growing business. At one of the sessions Peter heard a leading rose market researcher discussing a change in the home gardening market for rose bushes. While 90% of current rose bush sales in the home gardening market are for bare-rooted plants about 12 months old, the researcher expects a very strong growth in the market for more mature roses in pots. Peter thinks that the Byron, Shelley and Keats varieties would do well in this new market. Given the different qualities of each rose, Romantic Roses would be able to capture a large share of the potted rose market. He expects that each of the 1000 roses that would be planted on the spare hectare of land could be sold for $50 in 7 years from the commencement of the project. The costs of growing the roses up to this point would be the same as they are for the cut-flower market and the flowers could be sold until the rose bushes are transferred to pots for sale. The rose bushes would be harvested after flowering has finished for the year. The bushes would be presented in pots that would appeal to the upper end of the market and each pot would cost $10.

Romantic Roses currently uses Quickest Couriers to deliver their flowers. Dianna requested a quote for freight rates and received the following from the couriers.

MEMO THREE

To: Dianna and Peter, Romantic Roses

From: Quickest Couriers

Date: 2 January 2008

Subject: Quote for delivery of boxes of roses

We have received your request for a quote to expand your current delivery contract. We are pleased to be able to continue to offer you the fixed rate of $25 per box. The delivery price for potted roses will be $4 per pot. We look forward expanding our happy business relationship with Romantic Roses.

Dianna has provided the following information about the firm's cost of capital:

- The before-tax cost of capital is 15.25%.
- The after-tax cost of capital is 10.75%.
- The rate of return on Treasury Bills is 6.5%.
- The company's after-tax cost of debt is 8%.

New projects with similar risks as existing projects are evaluated at the cost of capital. Any new projects that have different characteristics to the current Romantic Roses projects (that is, those that do not involve growing roses) would be evaluated using a risk-adjusted discount rate. A further 7% would be added to the cost of capital for projects that do not involve growing roses.

Peter and Dianna both have a marginal tax rate of 42%. The corporate tax rate is 30%. Assume that any tax losses from this project can be used to offset tax payable on other operations conducted by Romantic Roses.

Dianna and Peter have asked to you advise them on the acceptability of the project. They have requested that you use the NPV and IRR approaches.

REQUIRED

11.1 Advise Dianna and Peter on their decision about accepting or rejecting the project. Show all equations and calculations.

11.2 To support your calculations in 11.1, prepare a justification of the cash flows you have used in your analysis. That is, you should identify why you have included each cash inflow and outflow to arrive at your net cash flows. If you have omitted cash flows discussed in the information provided, you should also explain why these have not been used in the analysis.

11.3 Justify your choice of discount rate for the analysis.

11.4 Currently, Romantic Roses is structured as a partnership. Peter and Dianna are thinking about listing the firm on the ASX if this project is successful. They have asked you to explain the impact (if any) that listing would have on the capital budgeting process. Write a short essay to advise them on this matter.

11.5 Include a reworked analysis of the project (that is, repeat requirement 11.1) assuming Romantic Roses is structured as a company that is fully integrated with the dividend imputation system. Show all calculations.

case 12

Speedy Concrete

Your aunt and uncle own Speedy Concrete, a firm that mixes and delivers concrete in the local area and is structured as a partnership. Your aunt and uncle want you to tell them if they should purchase new delivery trucks or keep the old ones. They have sent you the following information:

MEMO

To: Financial Advice Service

From: Speedy Concrete

Re: Truck fleet decision

- Speedy Concrete expects to generate $75 000 of sales over the next year. Sales are expected to grow at 4.5% pa for the foreseeable future.
- The corporate tax rate is 30% and your aunt and uncle both have a marginal tax rate of 47%.
- The current delivery fleet is 4 trucks purchase 4 years ago. Each truck cost $20 000. The total monthly fuel cost for these trucks is $2000. The service and maintenance cost for each truck is $2500 pa. These trucks could be used for another 3 years. The scrap value of the trucks is $3000 per truck at the end of 3 years, or they could be sold today for $6000 per truck. The current fleet will be sold if you recommend the purchase of new trucks.
- New Mini-Max trucks: 6 trucks would be required to meet demand. The purchase price per truck is $21 000. The total monthly fuel cost for these trucks is $1000. The service and maintenance cost for each truck is $1100 pa. These trucks have a useful life of 3 years. The scrap value of the trucks would then be $5000 per truck.
- New Maxi-Boy trucks: 3 trucks would be required to meet demand. The purchase price per truck is $27 000. The total monthly fuel cost for these trucks is $1900. The service and maintenance cost for each truck is $1600 pa. These trucks have a useful life of 6 years. The scrap value of the trucks would then be $5000 per truck.
- The Australian Taxation Office allows depreciation of 20% pa on concrete trucks.
- Annual registration cost per truck is $800.
- Fuel prices are expected to increase by 5% pa over the planning horizon. The increase will occur on the first day of each year.

REQUIRED

12.1 Show the relevant cash flows for the Mini-Max and Maxi-Boy projects.

12.2 Identify and describe three discounted cash flow evaluation methods that could be used to make a decision in this case. Is one particular method of evaluation superior to the others, given the decision to be made in this case? Give reasons for your answer. Be sure to define all key concepts.

12.3 If the cost of capital is 13%, evaluate the alternatives using the appropriate discounted cash flow method you chose in requirement 12.2.

12.4 If the cost of capital is 19%, evaluate the alternatives using the appropriate discounted cash flow method you chose in requirement 12.2.

12.5 Evaluate the alternatives using the appropriate discounted cash flow method you chose in requirement 12.2 using a corporate tax rate of 35% or a partner tax rate of 25% (not the 30% and 47% rates in the memo). The cost of capital is 19%.

12.6 Evaluate the alternatives using the appropriate discounted cash flow method you chose in requirement 12.2 with sales increasing at 1% pa (not the 4.5% rate from the memo). The tax rates identified in the memo should be used in this analysis. The cost of capital is 19%.

12.7 Evaluate the alternatives again with fuel price increases of 10% pa (not the 5% in the memo), annual truck registration of $1000 per truck and an allowable deduction for depreciation of 25% pa. The sales increase proportion and tax rates should be those specified in the memo. The cost of capital is 19%.

case 13

Financial advisory service V

As a finance student, you are naturally inclined to want to share your skills for the benefit of others. You and a couple of friends have decided to open a free financial counselling service for students from other disciplines. The level of demand for your services has been most pleasing and you have interviewed a number of clients. Your assessments of each person's requirements are outlined below.

Client one — Lei's gift

Lei's uncle wants to help her with her studies. He will give her $6000 pa for 3 years. He will put half of the annual amount in Lei's account every 6 months, with the first deposit made today.

(a) If Lei can earn 5.25% on her investments, what is the present value of the gift?

(b) If Lei can earn 6.5% on her investments, what is the present value of the gift?

(c) What is the present value of the gift if Lei has to wait one year for her first payment and she can earn 6.5% on her investments? Lei will still receive the same number of payments and the payments are for the same amount.

(d) What is the present value of the gift if Lei receives her first payment 2 years from today and she can earn 5.25% on her investments? Lei will still receive the same number of payments and the payments are for the same amount.

Client two — Sally's investment

Sally is about to retire and is considering her options for the way she receives her superannuation payments. She can receive $30 000 a year for the next 12 years and $40 000 for the following 12 years.

(a) What amount of money would Sally be willing to trade today for the cash flows identified above? Sally's discount rate is 11.5% pa and the payments are received annually.

(b) Would your answer to (a) change if the payments are made quarterly? Sally would receive the same total annual amount nominated initially. The first payment would be made 3 months after her retirement.

(c) What amount of money would Sally be willing to trade today if the payments are made semi-annually? Sally would receive the same total annual amount nominated initially and the first payment would be made today.

Client three — The Cladding Company

The Cladding Company has been involved in a legal case. As a result, the company has been ordered to provide sufficient funds to compensate workers for exposing them to dangerous substances. The substances cause a lung disease that can take up to 20 years to develop. The company ceased its dangerous operations 7 years ago, so there is still a lot of uncertainty about the amount that will have to be paid. The company has enough cash to pay the current claims against it, but must provide $400 000 per worker for all new claims as they arrive over the next 13 years.

(a) Assuming 2000 new claims are made at the end of 13 years, how much would have to be invested every quarter to meet the liability? The first investment amount would be made in 3 months' time. The Cladding Company can earn 10% pa, compounded quarterly, on investments.

(b) Assuming 5000 new claims are made at the end of 13 years, how much would have to be invested semi-annually to meet the liability? The first investment amount would be made today. The company can earn 9.75%, compounded semi-annually, on investments.

(c) How much would The Cladding Company have to invest today if 1000 claims are received at the end of each year for the next 13 years? The Cladding Company can earn 9.5% pa.

Client four — William's postgraduate study

William is planning to study in Europe in 4 years' time and expects that his study will cost \$100 000. He estimates that his mother can deposit the following amounts at the end of each year:

Today	Year 1	Year 2	Year 3	Year 4
\$15 000	\$20 000	\$20 000	\$20 000	\$15 000

(a) If William's mother can earn 5.25% on her investments, will she have enough saved at the end of 4 years to pay for William's study?

(b) Will she have enough if she can earn 5.75% on her investments?

(c) Will she have enough for William's study if they expect it will cost \$105 000 in 4 years and she can earn 4% compounded quarterly on her investments?

REQUIRED

13.1 Answer each of your clients' questions. Show all calculations and equations.

13.2 Prepare a short essay for your clients explaining the concepts of present and future values. Also explain why you have chosen to use either present or future value to answer the questions for each client. Be sure to define all key terms.

case 14

Palmer Hardware Ltd

Palmer Hardware Ltd is a listed company with plans for expansion into different markets and products. The Board of Directors has determined that it is time to improve the processes for deciding on which new projects should be undertaken and have advertised a senior financial officer position. You find the package offered by Palmer is very attractive and decide to apply for the position. Your written application has impressed the directors and they have asked you to make a presentation to them. This is your big chance to display your impressive skills — the Board have asked that you deal with some specific problems that the company currently faces.

The Board of Palmer Hardware has been presented with the following projects by the departmental managers of the business. All of the identified projects have a similar level of risk to those currently undertaken by the company.

Project	IRR%	Initial investment
Greenfingers kids gardening club	5	50000
Australian natives seed raising kits	7	500000
Landscape gardening service	10	900000
Garden consulting service	14	750000
Turf laying service	15	600000
Introduction of lawnmowers to product range	13	375000
Introduction of water features to product range	14	450000
Production of garden tools	16	1500000
Production of potting mixes	22	1200000

The Board are unsure about which should be accepted and which should be rejected. They have given you the following information:

- Palmer issued 1000 bonds 18 months ago. The bonds mature in December 2008. They have a face value of $100, a coupon of 8% pa and are currently trading at $115. The most recent coupon was paid at the start of January.
- Up to 1000 bonds can be issued with a face value of $100 and annual coupon payments of 5%. The bonds would have a 10-year term. Palmer would receive 95% of the $105 issue price. If Palmer decides to issue more than 100 bonds with the same face value and coupon rate, the issue price would fall to $100.
- Palmer issued 50 000 preference shares 5 years ago with a face value of $7. They pay an annual dividend of $0.30 and are currently trading at $5.70. It is expected that Palmer could issue a further 50 000 — paying the same dividend — at an issue price of $5.70. Palmer would net 93.7% of the proceeds. Any further preference shares would have to be issued at $5.50 to ensure full subscription of the issue. Such shares would still have a dividend of $0.30, but the net proceeds would only be 90% of the issue price.
- The company's ordinary shares (500000 have been issued) are currently selling for $4.50. A new issue would be made at this price. Issue costs would be 10% of the proceeds. The dividend for the first year is expected to be $0.30 and would be paid in one year's time. Dividends are expected to grow at the constant rate of 2% pa. Palmer's current and future shareholders are all Australian residents for taxation purposes.

- The financial statements show that Palmer has a retained earnings balance of \$250 000. The directors estimate that \$100 000 of this would be available for investment in new projects.
- The corporate tax rate is 30%.

Palmer's current and target capital structures are as follows:

Source of capital	Current structure	Target structure
Long-term debt	100 000	500 000
Preference shares	350 000	500 000
Ordinary equity	2 350 000	2 500 000

REQUIRED

14.1 What is the marginal cost of each source of funds? Show all calculations and equations.

14.2 Recommend which of the projects should be adopted by Palmer, giving reasons for your recommendations.

14.3 Tell the Board how much new financing is required.

14.4 Some members of the Board feel that the project should be financed with the cheapest source of funds; others think the source that gives the highest earnings per share should be chosen. Prepare a short essay that advises the Board on the matter.

case 15

First Blush Ltd

First Blush is an Australian company listed on the ASX. The company has been manufacturing natural health and beauty products for over 30 years. First Blush supplies retailers in Australia, New Zealand, South-East Asia and the UK.

Income statement for year ended 30 June				
		20X7	20X6	20X5
	Note	($'000)	($'000)	($'000)
Revenue from ordinary activities	1	82 933	76 557	79 806
Promotional and other rebates		-3 386	-3 257	-1 775
Changes in inventories		-221	-567	-1 850
Raw materials and consumables used		-24 430	-25 672	-28 975
Employee benefits expense		-20 291	-18 517	-13 094
Depreciation and amortisation expense		-1 549	-1 257	-1 168
Interest paid		-1 222	-998	-371
Selling and marketing expenses		-9 566	-8 853	-23 997
Operating lease rental expenses		-1 555	-1 278	
Professional and consulting expenses		-1 563	-1 462	
Repairs and maintenance expenses		-1 001	-817	
Book value of assets disposed		-1 143	-160	
Freight expenses		-1 370	-1 248	
Other expenses		-8 163	-4 099	
Profit before income tax expense		7 473	8 372	8 576
Income tax expense		-2 371	-2 883	-3 193
Profit after income tax expense		5 102	5 489	5 383

Balance sheet as at 30 June				
		20X7	20X6	20X5
	Note	($'000)	($'000)	($'000)
Current assets				
Cash assets		3 670	2 049	3 534
Receivables		15 856	14 296	13 680
Inventories	2	7 281	7 510	8 711
Other financial assets	3	0	70	61
Other	9	1 388	1 309	1 038
Total current assets		28 195	25 234	27 024
Non-current assets				
Land	4	2 700	3 051	3 033
Buildings and leasehold improvements	4	5 198	5 922	5 626
Plant and equipment	4	7 278	5 434	2 805
Other	10	2 451	2 729	2 687
Total non-current assets		17 627	17 136	14 151
Total assets		45 822	42 370	41 175

Current liabilities				
Payables		6 565	6 158	10 289
Interest bearing liabilities	5	14 200	13 700	6 400
Current tax liabilities		38	386	2 118
Provisions	6	4 680	2 387	4 311
Total current liabilities		25 483	22 631	23 118
Non-current liabilities				
Deferred tax liabilities		1 141	710	249
Provisions	7	443	383	392
Total non-current liabilities		1 584	1 093	641
Total liabilities		27 067	23 724	23 759
Net assets		18 755	18 646	17 416
Equity				
Contributed equity	8	11 335	11 335	10 524
Reserves		2 533	2 773	2 893
Retained profits		4 887	4 538	3 999
Total equity		18 755	18 646	17 416

Statement of cash flows for year ended 30 June	20X7	20X6	20X5
	($'000)	($'000)	($'000)
Cash flows from operating activities			
Receipts from customers	76 566	76 509	77 462
Payments to suppliers and employees	-67 006	-69 381	-67 698
Interest received	112	63	61
Interest and other costs of finance paid	-1 222	-938	-142
Income tax paid	-2 532	-4 094	-2 614
Net cash provided by operating activities	5 918	2 159	7 069
Cash flows from investing activities			
Payments for property, plant and equipment	-3 435	-4 573	-1 361
Proceeds from sale of property, plant and equipment	1 314	0	147
Proceeds from sale of equity investments	72	0	5
Net cash provided by/(used in) investing activities	-2 049	-4 573	-1 209
Cash flows from financing activities			
Proceeds from issues of equity securities	0	811	-4 461
Payment for employee share plan loans	0	-698	0
Proceeds from borrowings	500	7 300	5 890
Dividends paid	-2 852	-7 030	-6 391
Other	172	413	-467
Net cash provided by/(used in) financing activities	-2 180	796	-5 429

(continued)

Net increase in cash held	1 689	−1 618	431
Cash at the beginning of the financial year	2 049	3 534	3 099
Effects of exchange rate changes on the balance of cash held in foreign currencies	−68	133	4
Cash at the end of the financial year	3 670	2 049	3 534

Notes to the accounts:

		20X7($'000)	20X6 ($'000)	20X5 ($'000)
1	Sales revenue (all credit)	81 435	76 497	79 598
	Interest revenue	112	60	61
	Total operating revenue	81 547	76 557	76 659
	Sale of investment shares	72		
	Sale of property, plant and equipment	1 314		147
	Total non-operating revenue	1 386	0	147
2	Cost of goods sold	32 234	30 203	34 088
	Raw materials and work in progress	2 453	2 458	3 467
	Finished goods	4 828	5 052	4 497
	Ending inventory	7 281	7 510	8 711

3 Shares in listed corporations.

4 Land, buildings, leasehold improvements, plant and equipment and motor vehicles at net book value.

5 Secured bank bills.

6 Employee entitlements $4 373 000
Directors retirement $307 000

7 Employee entitlements.

8 15 011 585 fully paid shares, (20X6: 15 011 585), (20X5:14 871 585)

9 Other current assets: the total amount of this account is due from employee loan schemes. All the loans are due 10 March 20X8.

10 Loans to directors.

Additional information:

1 First Blush offers credit terms of 65 days. 70% of accounts are collected in the month following the sale. The remaining 30% of accounts are collected in the second month following the sale.

2 Monthly sales for April, May and June 20X7 were 6 000 000, 6 500 000 and 6 750 000, respectively. These sales figures matched the forecast sales. See memo one for the sales forecasts for July 20X7 to September 20X8.

3 Dividends of 20 702 000 will be paid on 15 July 20X7.
Employee entitlements — 1 000 000 will be paid in September 20X7 and the remaining payment will be made in April 20X8.
The retiring director will receive his payout on 21 January 20X8.

4 The time taken from ordering the raw materials to making the sale of the product is, on average, 2 months. Raw materials are ordered based on the forecast sales for the month the goods are expected to be sold. First Blush's suppliers give the company credit terms of 30 days. Raw materials costs are 15% of sales.

5 Total interest revenue of $120 000 is forecast for the 20X7–X8 financial year. The two equal interest payments will be received in August and February.

6 Wages are paid in the month they are earned. Administration and marketing staff wages will be $1 400 000 per month. Production staff wages are forecast to be 20% of sales. Other expenses are forecast at 0.05% of sales.

7 The payables amount in current liabilities includes the amount due to suppliers for raw materials purchased in May 20X7. The remaining payables are to be paid in August 20X7.

8 Tax is payable quarterly, with the current tax liability due in September. The forecast for remaining tax instalments is $411 000 per quarter.

9 An interim dividend of $90 000 will be paid in January 20X8.

10 The secured bank bills mature in October 20X7. First Blush will have to pay the amount shown in the balance sheet when the bills mature.

11 First Blush has an overdraft facility of $5 000 000. It has not been used for the last year. The overdraft interest is 12% pa and interest on the end of month balance is charged to the account in the following month. No interest is paid when the account is in credit.

12 The company will have to pay $128 000 for a research and development contract in May 20X8.

Hints:

1. Gross profit = sales – cost of goods sold.
2. Net income = profit after income tax expense.

MEMO ONE

To: CFO, First Blush

From: Arthur Daley, Marketing Manager

Date: 30 June 20X7

Subject: Requested sales forecasts

Monthly sales forecasts for the 15 months beginning July 20X7

July	7 000 000
August	7 250 000
September	7 750 000
October	8 000 000
November	8 500 000
December	9 500 000
January	9 700 000
February	9 900 000
March	9 900 000
April	9 900 000
May	10 500 000
June	10 500 000
July	11 000 000
August	11 000 000
September	11 500 000

REQUIRED

15.1 The directors have asked you to report on the key ratios of First Blush. To do this, you will need to compare the firm's performance for 20X7 with that of 20X6. Your analysis should include an explanation of each of the ratios and a commentary on the company's performance.

(a) The directors have asked you to advise if size of the overdraft is sufficient to meet the financing needs of the company for the coming financial year.

(b) The company is considering a marketing program to boost sales in the UK. The program would commence in July 20X8. The directors want to know how much cash will be available at the end of June 20X8.

15.2 Construct a cash budget for First Blush for the 20X7–X8 financial year to provide answers to the directors' questions in 15.2 and 15.3.

Glossary of equations

Equation 1.1	$PV = \frac{CF_1}{(1+k)} + \frac{CF_2}{(1+k)^2} + \frac{CF_3}{(1+k)^3} + \ldots + \frac{CF_n}{(1+k)^n}$	*p. 7*
Equation 4.1	$\text{Interest} = Pin$	*p. 96*
Equation 4.2	$FS = P(1 + in)$	*p. 97*
Equation 4.3	$P = \frac{FS}{(1+in)}$	*p. 98*
Equation 4.4	$SP = FS(1 - in)$	*p. 101*
Equation 4.5	$FV_n = PV(1 + k)^n$	*p. 103*
Equation 4.6	$PV = \frac{FV_n}{(1+k)^n}$	*p. 104*
Equation 4.7	$k_{eff} = \left(1 + \frac{j}{m}\right)^m - 1$	*p. 106*
Equation 4.8	$PVA = C\left\{\frac{1-(1+k)^{-n}}{k}\right\}$	*p. 108*
Equation 4.9	$FVA_n = C\left\{\frac{(1+k)^{-n} - 1}{k}\right\}$	*p. 108*
Equation 4.10	$FVA_D = C\left\{\frac{[(1+k)^{n+1} - 1]}{k} - 1\right\}$	*p. 113*
Equation 4.11	$PVA_D = C\left\{\frac{[1-(1+k)^{-(n-1)}]}{k} + 1\right\}$	*p. 114*
Equation 4.12	$PVA_B = C\left\{\frac{[1-(1+k)^{-n}]}{k}\right\}(1+k)^{-b}$	*p. 115*
Equation 4.13	$PVP = \frac{C}{k}$	*p. 116*
Equation 5.1	$R = \frac{P_t - P_{t-1} + D}{P_{t-1}} \times 100$	*p. 132*
Equation 5.2	$E(R) = \sum_{i=1}^{n} O_i p_i$	*p. 135*

Equation 5.3	$\sigma^2 = \sum_{i=1}^{n} (O_i - E(R))^2 p_i$	*p. 141*
Equation 5.4	$\sigma = \sqrt{\sum_{i=1}^{n} (O_i - E(R))^2 p_i}$	*p. 141*
Equation 5.5	$\sigma^2 = \frac{\sum_{t=1}^{T} (R_t - \bar{R})^2}{T - 1}$	*p. 142*
Equation 5.6	$\bar{R} = \frac{\sum_{t=1}^{T} R_t}{T}$	*p. 143*
Equation 5.7	$\sigma = \sqrt{\frac{\sum_{t=1}^{T} (R_t - \bar{R})^2}{T - 1}}$	*p. 143*
Equation 5.8	$E(R) = R_f + \beta\,(E(R_m) - R_f)$	*p. 152*
Equation 6.1	$\text{Book value of a share} = \frac{\text{total assets} - \text{total liabilities}}{\text{number of ordinary shares issued}}$	*p. 181*
Equation 6.2	$V = \sum_{t=1}^{n} \frac{CF_t}{(1+r)^t}$	*p. 182*
Equation 6.3	$V_b = \frac{F}{(1 + r_b)^n}$	*p. 184*
Equation 6.4	$V_b = \sum_{t=1}^{n} \frac{C_t}{(1+r_b)^t} + \frac{F}{(1+r_b)^n}$	*p. 185*
Equation 6.5	$V_p = \frac{D}{r_p}$	*p. 187*
Equation 6.6	$V_e = \sum_{t=1}^{n} \frac{D_t}{(1+r_e)^t} + \frac{P_n}{(1+r_e)^n}$	*p. 188*
Equation 6.7	$V_e = \frac{D_1}{r_e - g}$	*p. 191*
Equation 6.8	$PE = \frac{P_0}{EPS}$	*p. 195*
Equation 7.1	$NP = P_i\,(1 - f)$	*p. 216*
Equation 7.2	$NP_b = \frac{F}{(1 + r_b)^n}$	*p. 217*

Equation 7.3	$k_{d,bt} \cong \dfrac{I + \dfrac{(F - NP_b)}{n}}{\dfrac{(F + NP_b)}{2}}$	p. 220
Equation 7.4	$NP_b = \sum_{t=1}^{n} \dfrac{C_t}{(1 + r_b)^t} + \dfrac{F}{(1 + r_b)^n}$	p. 221
Equation 7.5	$k_{d,\,at} = k_{d,\,bt}\,(1 - t_r)$	p. 222
Equation 7.6	$NP_p = \dfrac{D}{r_p}$	p. 225
Equation 7.7	$k_{p,\,at} = \dfrac{D}{NP_p}$	p. 226
Equation 7.8	$k_{p,\,bt} = \dfrac{\dfrac{D}{(1 - t_c)}}{NP_p}$	p. 226
Equation 7.9	$V_e = \dfrac{D_1}{r_e - g}$	p. 228
Equation 7.10	$k_{re,\,at} = \dfrac{D_1}{P_O} + g$	p. 228
Equation 7.11	$k_{re,\,bt} = \dfrac{\dfrac{D_1}{(1 - t_c)}}{P_O} + g$	p. 229
Equation 7.12	$k_{e,\,at} = \dfrac{D_1}{NP_e} + g$	p. 231
Equation 7.13	$k_{e,\,bt} = \dfrac{\dfrac{D_1}{(1 - t_c)}}{NP_e} + g$	p. 231
Equation 7.14	$E(R) = R_f + -(E(R_m) - R_f)$	p. 232
Equation 7.15	$WACC = \sum_{x=1}^{n} k_x W_x$	p. 235
Equation 7.16	$\dfrac{(EBIT - I)(1 - t_c) - DP}{\text{number of shares}_1} = \dfrac{(EBIT - I)(1 - t_c) - DP}{\text{number of shares}_2}$	p. 246
Equation 8.1	$NPV_i = \sum_{t=1}^{n} \dfrac{CF_t}{(1 + k_a)^t} - IO$	p. 283
Equation 8.2	$IO = \sum_{t=1}^{n} \dfrac{CF_t}{(1 + IRR)^n}$	p. 286

Equation 9.1	$EAA_i = \frac{NPV}{PVFA_{k,n}}$	p. 314
Equation 9.2	$\text{Prime cost depreciation} = \frac{\text{installed cost of asset}}{\text{effective life}}$	p. 324
Equation 9.3	$\text{Diminishing value depreciation} = \text{base value} \times \left(\frac{150\%}{\text{effective life}}\right)$	p. 324
Equation 9.4	$ARR = \frac{\text{average net profit}}{\text{average investment}}$	p. 330
Equation 10.1	$\text{Cost of forgoing cash discount} = \frac{\text{interest}}{Pn}$	p. 365
Equation 11.1	$TC = \frac{QH}{2} + \frac{DO}{Q}$	p. 407
Equation 11.2	$Q = \sqrt{\frac{2\,DO}{H}}$	p. 408
Equation 12.1	$RP = \frac{N(P_m - S)}{N+1}$	p. 453
Equation 12.2	$P_x = \frac{(NP_m + S)}{N+1}$	p. 453
Equation 13.1	$\text{Dividend payout ratio} = \frac{DPS}{EPS}$	p. 470
Equation 13.2	Growth rate = (1 − payout ratio) × return on equity	p. 470
Equation 13.3	$\text{Dividend yield} = \frac{\text{dividends per share}}{\text{price per share}}$	p. 470
Equation 13.4	$SDY = \sqrt{\frac{\sum_{t=1}^{n}(DY_i - \overline{DY})^2}{n-1}}$	p. 471
Equation 13.5	$ST = \frac{\sum_{t=1}^{n}(D_i - D_{i-1})^2}{\bar{D}}$ for all $D_i < D_{i-1}$	p. 472
Equation 13.6	$\text{Imputation credit} = \left[\frac{D_f}{1 - t_c}\right] t_c$	p. 480
Equation 13.7	$\text{After-tax dividend} = D_f \left[\frac{1 - t_p}{1 - t_c}\right]$	p. 482

Equation 13.8	$P_{CD} - P_{XD} = D_f\left[\dfrac{1-t_p}{(1-t_c)(1-t_g)}\right]$	p. 484
Equation 13.9	$\dfrac{P_{CD} - P_{XD}}{D_f} = \dfrac{1-t_p}{(1-t_c)(1-t_g)}$	p. 485
Equation 14.1	$\text{EPS} = \dfrac{\text{net profit (loss)}}{\text{number of shares on issue}}$	p. 529
Equation 14.2	$\text{DPS} = \dfrac{\text{dividends paid}}{\text{number of shares on issue}}$	p. 529
Equation 14.3	$\text{Return on equity (ROE)} = \dfrac{\text{net profit}}{\text{ordinary shareholders' equity}}$	p. 530
Equation 14.4	$\text{NTA} = \dfrac{\text{assets} - \text{intangibles} - \text{liabilities}}{\text{number of ordinary shares}}$	p. 530
Equation 14.5	$\text{Debt to equity} = \dfrac{\text{total liabilities}}{\text{ordinary shareholders' equity}}$	p. 531
Equation 14.6	$\text{Net debt to capital employed} = \dfrac{\text{net debt}}{\text{net debt} + \text{ordinary shareholders' equity}}$	p. 532
Equation 14.7	$\text{Times interest earned} = \dfrac{\text{profit before interest and tax}}{\text{annual interest expense}}$	p. 532
Equation 16.1	$\text{Takeover gain} = PV_C - (PV_B + PV_T)$	p. 620
Equation 16.2	$\text{Takeover premium} = \text{payment} - PV_T$	p. 620
Equation 16.3	$\text{NPV} = \text{gain} - \text{premium}$	p. 620
Equation 17.1	$R_t = \dfrac{c_t}{c_{t-1}} - 1$	p. 647
Equation 17.2	$\hat{S}_t(x/y) = \dfrac{S_t(x/y)}{S_{t-1}(x/y)} - 1$	p. 648
Equation 17.3	$TR_t = (1+R_t)(1+\hat{S}_t(x/y)) - 1$	p. 648
Equation 17.4	$S(x/y) = \dfrac{S(x/z)}{S(y/z)}$	p. 648
Equation 17.5	$P = S \times P^*$	p. 649
Equation 17.6	$P_1 = S_1 P_1^*$	p. 652

Equation 17.7	$P_0 = S_0 P_0^*$	p. 652
Equation 17.8	$(1+\hat{S}) = \dfrac{(1+\hat{P})}{(1+\hat{P}^*)}$	p. 652
Equation 17.9	$S_1 = S_0\left(\dfrac{1+\hat{P}}{1+\hat{P}^*}\right)$	p. 653
Equation 17.10	$\hat{S} = \hat{P} - \hat{P}^*$	p. 653
Equation 17.11	$\dfrac{F_1}{S_0} = \dfrac{(1+i)}{(1+i^*)}$	p. 654
Equation 17.12	$(1+f)(1+i^*) = (1+i)$	p. 654
Equation 17.13	$f = i - i^*$	p. 655
Equation 17.14	$F_1 = S_0[1 + (i - i^*)]$	p. 655
Equation 17.15	$F_t = E(S_t)$	p. 655
Equation 17.16	$\dfrac{E(S_1)}{S_0} = \dfrac{(1+i)}{(1+i^*)}$ or $E(S_1) = S_0\dfrac{(1+i)}{(1+i^*)}$	p. 655
Equation 17.17	$\left(\dfrac{1+i}{1+\hat{P}}\right) = \left(\dfrac{1+i^*}{1+\hat{P}^*}\right)$	p. 656
Equation 17.18	$E(S_t) = S_0\dfrac{(1+i)^t}{(1+i^*)^t}$	p. 657

Key to symbols

b	number of periods before the annuity begins
C	periodic cash flow
C_t	coupon payment in period t
CF	cash flow for the period
CF_t	cash flow for period t
c_t	value of investment at period t
c_{t-1}	outlay at period t–1
D	dividend payment
$\frac{D_f}{1-t_e}$	grossed-up dividend
$\bar{D}$	mean dividend payment for the whole sample
D_1	dividend to be paid in the next period
D_f	fully franked dividend
D_i	dividend payment in period i
D_t	dividend payment in period t
D_v	value of debt
DP	preference share dividend
$\overline{DY}$	mean dividend yield
DY_i	dividend yield in period i
E	earnings
E_v	value of equity
$E(R)$	expected return on the investment
$E(R_m)$	expected return on the market portfolio
$E(S_t)$	expected spot rate at time t
EAA_i	equivalent annual annuity of project i
$EBIT$	earnings before interest and tax
EPS	forecast earnings per share
F	bond's face (or maturity) value
f	issue costs as a percentage of price; forward spread
FS	sum that must be repaid
F_t	the forward exchange rate for the settlement at time t
FVA_D	future value of an annuity due
FVA_n	future value of an ordinary annuity at the end of the nth period
FV_n	future value at the end of the nth period
g	expected growth in dividends
i	the domestic risk-free interest rate
I	annual interest payment in dollars
i^*	the foreign risk-free interest rate
IO	initial outlay of the project
IRR	discount rate that equates the present value of the cash flows to the IO
j	nominal annual rate
k	compounding or discount rate
k_a	cost of capital for the firm
k_d	cost of debt
$k_{d,\ at}$	after-tax cost of debt
$k_{d,\ bt}$	before-tax cost of debt
k_e	cost of equity
$k_{e,\ at}$	after-tax cost of ordinary shares
$k_{e,\ bt}$	before-tax cost of ordinary shares
k_{eff}	annual effective rate
$k_{p,\ at}$	after-tax cost of preference shares
$k_{p,\ bt}$	before-tax cost of preference shares
$k_{re,\ at}$	after-tax cost of retained earnings
$k_{re,\ bt}$	before-tax cost of retained earnings
k_x	component cost of capital from source x
m	number of compounding periods each year
$\bar{R}$	mean return of the observed outcomes
n	number of periods, observations, possible outcomes, or times a condition is satisfied; length of period
N	number of shares that must be held to receive one right
NP	net proceeds per security from the issue
NP_b	net proceeds per bond from the issue
NP_e	net proceeds per share from the issue
NP_p	net proceeds per preference share from the issue
NPV_i	net present value of project i
O_i	i^{th} possible outcome
$\hat{P}$	domestic inflation rate
P	the domestic price of a commodity in local currency; principal sum borrowed
P^*	foreign price of a commodity in local currency

$\hat{P}^*$	foreign inflation rate
P_{CD}	cum-dividend price
PE	price–earnings ratio
P_i	price per security at issue
p_i	probability of the ith possible outcome occurring
P_m	price of a share with the rights entitlement attached
P_n	market price of the share at time n
P_O	current market price of one ordinary share
P_t	price of the share at the end of the period
P_{t-1}	price of the share at the start of the period
PV	present value
PVA	present value of an annuity
PVA_B	present value of a deferred annuity
PVA_D	present value of an annuity due
PV_B	present value of the bidder pre-takeover
PV_C	present value of the combined entity post-takeover
PV_{DAC}	present value of debt-related agency costs
PV_{FDC}	present value of the financial distress costs
$PVFA_{k,\,n}$	present value factor for a rate of k and a time period of n
PV_{ITS}	present value of *ITS*
PVP	present value of the perpetuity
PV_T	present value of the target pre-takeover
P_x	ex-rights price
P_{XD}	ex-dividend price
r	investor's required rate of return
R	percentage return on share
r_b	bondholder's required return
r_e	shareholder's required return
R_f	return on the risk-free asset
r_p	preference shareholder's required return
RP	theoretical price of a right
R_t	rate of return on the security
R_t	observed outcome for time period t
S	the foreign exchange rate represented as units of domestic currency per unit of foreign currency
S	rights issue subscription price
$\hat{S}$	the rate of change in the exchange rate
$S(x/y)$	the amount of unit currency x required to purchase 1 unit of y
$\hat{S}_t(x/y)$	rate of change in the value of currency y (in terms of currency x)
SDY	standard deviation of dividend yields
SP	selling price (or present value)
ST	indicator of dividend instability
t	nominal marginal tax rate
T	number of observations
t_c	company tax rate
t_g	tax rate on capital gain
t_p	investor's marginal tax rate
TR	total return on foreign currency denominated security
V	intrinsic (or present) value of a security producing expected future cash flows, CF_t in periods 1 to n
V_b	intrinsic value of the bond
V_e	intrinsic value of the ordinary share
V_L	after-tax value of a levered firm
V_p	intrinsic value of the preference share
V_U	after-tax value of an unlevered firm
$WACC$	weighted average cost of capital
W_x	proportion that x represents in the firm's capital structure
β	systematic risk of the asset
σ	standard deviation
σ^2	variance

Glossary

Accounting rate of return Measures a project's profitability using the ratio of average profits to average investment. *p. 330*

Accounting system The collection of records of financial transactions. *p. 510*

Accrual accounting The process of matching revenues to the period in which they are earned and liabilities to the period in which they are incurred. *p. 512*

Agency costs The losses borne by the owners of the firm that can be attributed to the agent having different objectives from the owners (or principals). *p. 11*

All Ordinaries Accumulation index Constructed by taking the share prices of a group of companies listed on the ASX and weighting them according to their relative size in the market. It is assumed that dividends paid by the companies are reinvested, so they increase the index. *p. 133*

Allowable deductions Generally, for the computation of income tax liability, expenses incurred to earn assessable income. *p. 42*

Announcement date Date of the directors' meeting when the dividend is recommended. *p. 469*

Annuity A series of equal cash flows that are evenly spaced over time. *p. 107*

Annuity due The first payment is made at the inception of the annuity. *p. 107*

Arbitrage Pricing Theory Systematic risk comes from a number of factors. *p. 158*

Arbitrageurs Enter markets and trade to make profits without risk by making complementary trades in two or more markets virtually instantaneously to exploit price differences. *pp. 566, 644*

Assessable income Includes most forms of income earned by resident taxpayers, both in Australia and overseas. *p. 42*

Assets Probable future economic benefits that the firm is able to utilise. *p. 511*

Australian business number (ABN) A discrete number that identifies each business registered with the ATO so that the regulation of taxation is facilitated. *p. 34*

Backdoor listing A takeover of a listed company by a private company, where the listed company continues trading on the exchange and the shares represent an ownership interest in the previously private company's assets. *p. 626*

Balance sheet Shows the assets, liabilities and equity of the company at the end of the reporting period. *p. 510*

Benchmark Sets the standard for assessing the level of risk and the expected return. *p. 152*

Beta A relative measure that describes how the return on the asset is related to the return on the market portfolio. *p. 154*

Bid The price a trader is willing to pay for a security. *p. 180*

Bid period The time from when the bidder makes the takeover offer to when that offer closes. *p. 610*

Bidder The party that makes an offer for shares in the company it wishes to acquire. *p. 602*

Bidder's statement Sets out the terms and conditions of the takeover offer. *p. 610*

Blue chip Companies that are well established and have a good track record for financial stability. *p. 193*

Bonus shares Dividends paid in the form of additional shares. *p. 491*

Book-build Uses a bidding system to combine the expertise of large investors to determine the price of an issue. *p. 449*

Book value The accounting measure of an asset's worth. *pp. 181, 237*

Bootstrapping The capacity to increase EPS in a takeover in the absence of any economic gains for shareholders coming from the takeover. *p. 620*

Budget A plan that includes forecasts of future transactions. *pp. 389, 514*

Call option Gives the buyer the right but not the obligation to buy an asset by a given date at a given price. *p. 567*

Capital Asset Pricing Model (CAPM) Generates an expected return for a risky asset based on the asset's level of systematic risk, the expected return on the market portfolio and a risk-free asset. *p. 152*

Capital gain Arises when the price of an asset increases. *p. 132*

Capital loss Arises when the price of an asset decreases. *p. 132*

Capital markets Deal in long-term instruments; that is, instruments with maturities greater than one year. *p. 68*

Capital rationing A self-imposed limit that is placed on the size of the capital budget. *p. 309*

Capital structure The mix of contracted debt and equity used by a firm. *p. 240*

Cash All the currency that the firm has on hand. Cash is also all the liquid or near liquid assets that a firm holds or has ready access to. *p. 386*

Cash budget A detailed plan of expected cash receipts and cash payments that highlights any probable cash surpluses or deficits. *p. 389*

Cash cycle The progression of cash into and out of the business. *p. 515*

Cash flow Funds flowing either into or out of a business; that is, cash receipts or cash expenses. *p. 94*

Cash flow statement Shows the amount of cash that came into and went out of the company over the reporting period. *p. 513*

Cash settlement price (for a futures contract) The current market value for the assets that are the subject of the contract. *p. 569*

Certainty equivalent The amount of cash the decision maker would be willing to trade for the risky cash flow. *p. 318*

Clearing house Facilitates settlement of contracts and transfer of ownership between the parties to transactions. *p. 569*

Closed out When the clearing house takes out an opposite contract to the open contract for the same goods for the same delivery terms so that the two contracts cancel each other in all details except price. *p. 570*

Commercial bills Promises by the borrowers to repay at a stated future date the face value of the instrument, which is normally guaranteed by a third party such as a bank. *p. 71*

Commercial paper A generic term for unsecured loans that are normally issued only by borrowers of high repute with excellent credit ratings. *p. 444*

Company An association of entities with a common objective formed under the *Corporations Act 2001* that is legally separate from its owners. *p. 37*

Compound interest Interest calculated on the actual amount outstanding each period. *p. 102*

Compulsory acquisition Occurs when the bidder is allowed to purchase any shares in the target company it does not already own. *p. 610*

Conditional bid A takeover offer in which certain requirements have to be met for the offer to proceed. *p. 609*

Conglomerate A company with several subsidiaries that operate in unrelated lines of business. *p. 627*

Conglomerate takeover The acquisition of a business that is unrelated to the current operations of the buyer. *p. 618*

Contract months or **delivery months** The months in which deliveries are made or contracts are settled. *p. 569*

Contract unit The standard quantity of the product that is the subject of each contract; also called contract size. *p. 568*

Contributing shares or **partly paid shares** Ordinary shares where the full subscription amount has not yet been paid to the issuing company. *p. 74*

Convertible notes Notes that pay interest and convert before maturity to the issuer's ordinary shares. *p. 439*

Convertible preference shares Shares that pay dividends and convert at maturity to the issuer's ordinary shares. *p. 439*

Corporate bonds Debt instruments where the issuer receives the issue price (net of costs) at the outset and pays a coupon, usually six-monthly. The face value is repaid when the bonds mature. *pp. 72, 436*

Corporate governance The management of the firm so that the actions of managers are in accord with the stated objectives. *pp. 10, 38*

Corporate social responsibility The firm has wider responsibilities in relation to objectives and people apart from the owners or shareholders. *p. 17*

Correlation A measure of the way two variables move relative to each other. *p. 150*

Cost of capital The minimum rate of return on the firm's investments that will compensate the suppliers of capital to the firm. *p. 213*

Cost of debt The level of return that must be generated in order to meet the required return of debtholders. *p. 217*

Cost of ordinary equity The level of return that must be generated in order to meet the required return of the ordinary shareholders. *p. 227*

Cost of ordinary shares The required return of shareholders on a new issue. *p. 230*

Cost of preference shares The level of return that must be generated in order to meet the required return of preference shareholders. *p. 225*

Cost of retained earnings The required return of ordinary shareholders on shares that have already been issued. *p. 228*

Coupon The stated rate of interest paid on a bond. *pp. 72, 183*

Coupon payments The regular interest payments received by the holder of a bond. *p. 181*

Cum-dividend Shares that have a current entitlement to receive a dividend. *p. 469*

Current assets The assets the firm expects to be able to convert to cash in the normal course of business within the next 12 months. *p. 358*

Current liabilities Debts that will be paid within the next 12 months. *p. 358*

Daily-settlement margin calls Demands for extra funds to be placed in traders' margin accounts to cover any shortfalls in the value of open positions in comparison with current market prices at the end of any trading day. *p. 570*

Debentures Fixed-term debt securities issued under a prospectus. Debentures are secured by assets. *pp. 72, 438*

Debt-to-equity ratio A measure of the proportion of debt relative to the amount of equity in the firm's capital structure. *p. 241*

Deep discount A purchase price (at the time of issue) for a security that is well below its face value. *p. 184*

Deferred annuity The first payment is made after several periods have elapsed. *p. 107*

Deliverable contracts Contracts that may be settled by physical delivery. *p. 569*

Delivery months or **contract months** The months in which deliveries are made or contracts are settled. *p. 569*

Depreciation The amount allowed as a tax deduction by the ATO to recognise the decrease in the value of an asset that occurs as it is used and wears out over time. *p. 320*

Derivatives Synthetic financial products whose value is derived from an underlying product. *p. 563*

Dilution The decrease in the proportion of income each share is entitled to. *p. 242*

Direct investment Capital invested in an enterprise by an investor that has significant influence over the key policies of the enterprise. *p. 441*

Discount rate (in relation to pricing a security) The percentage difference between the face value and the purchase price of the security. *p. 101*

Discount rate The interest factor that is used to calculate a present value (PV) from a future value (FV). *p. 104*

Discounting The process of calculating the present value (PV) of a future amount. The discount factor incorporates the possible or required return for the funds. *p. 7*

Diversification The spread of different assets held in a portfolio. *p. 150*

Divestiture or **sell-off** The sale of a major asset by the company. *p. 627*

Dividend drop-off ratio Compares the decline in the share price on the ex-dividend day to the cash dividend. *p. 484*

Dividend imputation The system where dividends carry an additional benefit in the form of an attached tax credit for the relevant amount of tax paid by the company on its profits. *p. 45*

Dividend payout ratio The proportion of after-tax profit that is paid to shareholders as dividends. *pp. 215, 470*

Dividend policy Involves the allocation of profits between dividend payments to shareholders and retention for reinvestment in the company. *p. 469*

Dividend reinvestment plan Provides shareholders with an option to invest their cash dividends in the company's shares. *p. 492*

Dividend stability Shows the volatility of dividend yields or dividend per share over time. *p. 471*

Dividend yield The ratio of dividend per share to the share price. *p. 470*

Earnings per share The total earnings of the firm divided by the number of ordinary shares on issue. *p. 195*

EBIT–EPS analysis Relates earnings before interest and tax to the after-tax income entitlement of each ordinary share. *p. 243*

Economic exposure The sensitivity of the market value of the firm with respect to the exchange rate. *p. 656*

Economies of scale Efficiency gains from producing more of a good or service. *p. 617*

Effective rate Reflects the impact of multiple compounding during the year. *p. 106*

Electronic bank-accepted bills (EBAs) Electronically recorded debt obligations that obviate the need for paper securities. *p. 572*

Electronic certificates of deposit (ECDs) Electronically recorded debt obligations that obviate the need for paper securities. *p. 572*

Embezzlement The illegal diversion of funds from the firm by employees for their own benefit. *p. 390*

Equity The book value of the ownership interest in the firm. *p. 511*

Equity risk premium Indicates how much additional return can be expected by moving from the risk-free asset to the market portfolio of risky assets. *p. 153*

Equivalent annual annuity The equal annual cash flows that would generate the project's NPV during the project's life. *p. 314*

Ethics Moral principles or rules of conduct that indicate the acceptability of behaviour within a community. *p. 13*

Eurobonds Debt securities issued outside the domestic capital markets of the issuer in a currency that is neither the domestic currency of the issuer nor the domestic currency of the place of issue. *p. 443*

Ex ante returns Those that investors expect to receive in the future. *p. 134*

Ex ante standard deviation The square root of the ex ante variance. *p. 140*

Ex ante variance The probability-weighted average of squared deviation of possible returns from the expected return. *p. 140*

Ex-dividend date Four working days prior to the record date. *p. 469*

Ex post or **realised returns** Those returns that relate to past periods. *p. 132*

Ex post standard deviation The square root of the ex post variance. *p. 142*

Ex post variance The weighted average of the squared deviations of observed returns from the mean return. *p. 142*

Ex-rights The share price quoted without the right to purchase further shares attached. *p. 453*

Expected return The probability-weighted average of possible outcomes associated with the investments. *p. 135*

Expenses Consumption or losses of future economic benefits. *p. 511*

Face value The amount that will be repaid upon maturity of the bond. It is specified at the time the bond is issued. *p. 71*

Factoring Involves businesses selling their invoices at a discount for cash to another party that takes over the right to collect the amounts owing. *p. 371*

Fair game One where the expected value of participating is zero. *p. 146*

Finance leases Non-cancellable contractual obligations to make payments in return for the use of an asset for the majority of its useful life. *p. 426*

Financial derivatives Contracts that are derived from the value of some underlying assets and are used to manage risk. *p. 9*

Financial distress When a firm's financial obligations can not be met or can be met only with major difficulty. *pp. 69, 241*

Financial governance The financial and management accounting systems and other financial processes that are put in place to achieve the objectives of the firm. *p. 10*

Financial leverage The use of debt in a firm's capital structure to increase returns to equity holders. *p. 241*

Financial ratios Data reduction techniques that express one account as a proportion of another. *p. 527*

Financial risk The risk involved in using debt as a source of finance. *pp. 69, 241*

Financial statements The balance sheet, the income statement and the cash flow statement. *p. 510*

Financial structure The mix of all sources of debt and equity that funds the assests owned by the business. *p. 68*

Fixed interest The coupon received on the bond stays the same over the bond's life. *p. 185*

Float or **initial public offer** The first issue of capital made to the public. *p. 447*

Floating rate notes Loans that pay a variable coupon amount that is based on a short-term benchmark rate such as the bank bill swap rate (BBSW). *p. 438*

Floor-plan finance or **inventory finance** Provided to car and whitegoods dealers to buy stock to place on showroom floors; secured by the stock itself. *p. 71*

Foreign bonds Debt securities issued overseas in the currency of the country of issue. *p. 444*

Foreign shareholders Those who live (and pay tax) in a different country from that of the company paying the dividends. *p. 214*

Forward rate agreement (FRA) A deal between two parties that fixes an interest rate (or foreign exchange rate) for a period that begins some time in the future. *p. 576*

Franked dividend A dividend carrying an attached franking or tax credit. *p. 45*

Fully drawn advances Loans that are initially drawn down to the full amount and repaid over the term of the loan by means of a fixed repayment schedule. *p. 425*

Fully franked dividend A dividend that carries a tax credit equal to the full 30% company tax paid on the underlying profit. *p. 45*

Future value The value of an amount of today's dollars at a specific time in the future; future value is calculated by compounding at a given rate. *p. 102*

Futures contract A type of forward contract that is traded in a futures market and covers the purchase or sale of a set quantity of an asset to fix forward prices. *p. 562*

Hedger A market participant who engages in financial market transactions to reduce risk. *pp. 565, 644*

Hedging principle Based on matching the maturity of the source of funding with its use. *p. 361*

Hire-purchase agreement Involves a financial institution buying the equipment required by the customer then hiring it to the customer. The customer purchases the asset outright at the end of the lease period. *p. 426*

Hoarding Savings held outside the financial system and thus not available for financial investment. *p. 63*

Holding period return The return an investor would earn if the share was purchased at the start of the period and sold at the end of the period. *p. 132*

Horizontal takeover When two companies in the same business are combined. *p. 617*

Hurdle rate The minimum rate of return generated that will make a project acceptable. *p. 287*

Hybrid securities Securities that have characteristics of both debt and equity. *p. 439*

Imputation tax credit Represents the amount of tax on a dividend that has been paid by the company on behalf of a shareholder. *p. 479*

Income statement Shows the revenues and expenses that were generated over the reporting period. *p. 511*

Incremental cash flows Result from the acceptance of a project. *p. 273*

Independent project A project that can be accepted or rejected without having to accept or reject some other project (that is, it is independent of other projects). *p. 310*

Indifference point The level of EBIT that generates the same EPS for all financing alternatives under consideration. *p. 246*

Initial margin The first payment required for a futures contract. *p. 569*

Initial outlay The capital expenditure made to implement an investment. *p. 269*

Initial public offer or **float** The first issue of capital made to the public. *p. 447*

Insolvent A firm that is unable to pay its bills or meet its financial obligations on time. *p. 390*

Instalment loans Have fixed repayment schedules negotiated at the outset. *p. 424*

Intangible assets Non-physical assets that will give the company future benefits, but that are difficult to separate from the business. *p. 529*

Interest The price charged for the temporary use of money. *p. 95*

Intermediated finance Uses the services of a financial intermediary or financial services provider such as a bank, merchant bank or finance company. *p. 422*

Internal rate of return The discount rate that makes the present value of future cash flows equal to the net cash outlay. *pp. 218, 285*

International Fisher effect The idea that the difference in the nominal interest rates between two countries determines the movement of the exchange rate between their currencies. *p. 656*

Interpolation The process of approximating an unknown return using trial and error. *p. 218*

Intra-day margin calls Demands for extra funds to be placed in traders' margin accounts to cover any shortfalls in the value of open positions in comparison with current market prices during a trading day. *p. 570*

Intrinsic value (of a security) The present value of expected future cash flows discounted at the investor's required rate of return. *p. 181*

Inventory finance or **floor-plan finance** Provided to car and whitegoods dealers to buy stock to place on showroom floors; secured by the stock itself. *p. 71*

Inverse yield curve Shows short-term interest rates are expected to fall over the medium term. *p. 360*

Investment The outlay of capital made with a view to gaining future benefits. *p. 269*

Issue costs The costs associated with bringing an issue of securities to the market. *p. 216*

Joint venture An association of individuals or corporations who agree under a contract to pursue a common goal or engage in a common undertaking with the aim of making a profit by combining their resources without forming a legal partnership. *p. 37*

Last trading day The last day on which trading occurs in a particular contract. *p. 569*

Lease A contract by which an owner of property (the lessor) allows another person or entity (the lessee) the use of the asset. *p. 426*

Lessee The person or entity that gains the use of the leased asset by entering the lease contract. *p. 426*

Lessor The owner of property that is being leased. *p. 426*

Leveraged buyout When the purchase of a listed company is financed predominantly with debt. *p. 625*

Liabilities Future sacrifices of economic benefits that the firm is obliged to make. *p. 511*

Liquidity A measure of the ease of conversion of an asset into cash. *p. 359*

Management buyout An LBO where the managers of the target firm lead the private equity bid. *p. 626*

Mandatory-settled contracts Settled by the clearing house at a cash settlement price that is calculated according to principles laid down for each contract. *p. 569*

Margin A deposit or bond that ensures completion of the futures contract. *p. 569*

Marginal analysis A method for making decisions to maximise our objective by comparing additional (marginal) benefits with additional relevant costs. *p. 273*

Marginal cost For a particular source of capital, the cost associated with raising the next dollar from that source. *p. 214*

Marginal tax rate The tax rate applied to the next dollar of taxable income. *p. 40*

Market capitalisation The total dollar value of all issued shares. Market value is used to determine the dollar value per share. *pp. 7, 195*

Market takeover A takeover in which the bidder purchases the shares of the target by normal trading on the stock exchange. *p. 609*

Market value The price willing buyers are prepared to pay and willing sellers are prepared to accept. *p. 7*

Marking-to-market Involves valuing each open futures contract daily according to the closing price in the futures market and adjusting margin accounts at the clearing house to show the consequent gains or losses. *p. 570*

Maturity or **term to maturity** The contracted time that may elapse before the borrowed funds are to be repaid. *p. 68*

Maturity date The date at the end of the FRA contract period. *p. 576*

Merchant bank A financial institution that is not registered or regulated under the *Banking Act 1959* but which carries out many of the functions of a bank, especially in the wholesale or commercial banking areas. *p. 67*

Merger The combination of two (or more) businesses into a single entity. *p. 603*

Money markets Deal in short-term debt; that is, debt that has less than one year to maturity. *p. 67*

Mutually exclusive projects Projects that either perform the same task or utilise the same scarce physical resources. Acceptance of one project means that the others must be rejected. *p. 311*

Net assets Total assets minus total liabilities. *p. 511*

Net present value The sum of the discounted net cash flows over the life of a proposed project, minus the project's initial outlay. *p. 283*

Net proceeds The amount of cash received from investors minus any costs associated with the issue. *p. 216*

Net working capital The excess of current assets over current liabilities. *pp. 277, 358*

Nominal rate The advertised or quoted annual rate that does not reflect the impact of multiple compounding periods during the year. *p. 105*

Non-renounceable Rights that cannot be sold on the market. The shareholder has to subscribe to the issue or let the offer lapse. *p. 452*

Normal distribution A symmetric and bell-shaped curve centred on the expected value of a variable. *p. 138*

Normal yield curve Shows investors expect future short-term interest rates to be higher than current rates over the medium term. *p. 360*

Notional amount of a swap The hypothetical principal amount on which the payment of the swap obligations is based. *p. 578*

Novated lease Involves a three-party agreement between an employee, an employer and a financial institution to provide a motor vehicle to the employee as part of a salary package. *p. 426*

Off-market takeover A takeover in which the bidder gives the target's shareholders an application form to complete the sale of their shares at a specified offer price. *p. 609*

Offer The price a trader is willing to accept to sell a security. *p. 180*

Operating costs The cash outflows required in the daily activities of the project. *p. 274*

Operating leases Contractual agreements, but they are cancellable upon given notice and tend to be of much shorter term than the useful life of the asset. *p. 426*

Opportunity costs The cash flows forgone when one path of action is chosen. *p. 274*

Optimal capital structure The mix of contracted debt and equity that maximises the value of the firm. *p. 241*

Option Grants the right but not the obligation to undertake a trade by a given date at a given price. *pp. 454, 567*

Ordinary annuity A series of equal cash flows that are evenly spaced over time and are received at the end of each period. *p. 107*

Ordinary shares Evidence of part-ownership of a company. *pp. 74, 444*

Over-the-counter (OTC) market That part of a market where deals are arranged privately between two parties. *p. 437*

Overdraft A permitted over-drawing of funds beyond the credit balance in the account. *pp. 71, 366*

Partly franked dividend A dividend that carries a tax credit less than the full 30% company tax paid on the underlying profit. *p. 45*

Partly paid shares or **contributing shares** Ordinary shares where the full subscription amount has not yet been paid to the issuing company. *p. 74*

Partnership An association of two or more people carrying on a business in common with a view to profit. *p. 35*

Payback period Measures the length of time it takes for the net cash inflows from a project to equal the initial outlay. *p. 328*

Percent of sales method Expresses items in the income statement as a percentage of sales. The calculated percentage is applied to the forecast sales figure. *p. 522*

Permanent funding Comprises funding with maturities greater than one year and includes long-term debt, leases and ordinary shares. *p. 361*

Perpetuity An ordinary annuity that has cash flows that continue forever. *p. 107*

Portfolio A collection of different assets. *p. 150*

Portfolio investment The investor has no control over the key policies of the enterprise. *p. 441*

Position limits Maximum numbers of contracts that speculators may hold for any individual type of commodity or asset. *p. 570*

Precaution Involves prudent actions taken early to ensure a good outcome or to forestall an adverse effect. *p. 387*

Preference shares Hybrid equity instruments that have some characteristics of equity and some of debt which normally have a fixed dividend that has preference over the payment of ordinary dividends. *pp. 75, 446*

Present value The value (in today's dollars) of a future amount calculated for a given discount rate. *p. 102*

Price The amount of money needed to acquire an asset. *p. 179*

Price discovery The process of finding and settling on a price that is acceptable to both parties to a transaction. *p. 66*

Price–earnings ratio Compares the price per share to the forecast EPS. *p. 195*

Primary market The market in which securities are offered for the first time. *p. 66*

Principal–agent problem The scope for conflict or division between principals (owners) and agents (managers) over the goals of the firm that are being pursued by its policy and management decisions. *p. 11*

Private equity firms Firms that acquire listed companies and operate them as private businesses. *p. 609*

Private placements Issues of securities made by negotiation directly with purchasers. *p. 67*

Profit The excess of revenues over expenses. *p. 512*

Profit maximisation Implies a business is managed to maximise the difference between revenues and expenses in any period. *p. 6*

Pro-forma financial statements Projections of a future position and of future period performance. *p. 520*

Promissory notes 'P-notes' are promises by the borrowers to repay the face value of the instrument at a stated future date. *p. 71*

Proportional takeover bid A bid that specifies a proportion of shares (less than 100%) that the bidder wants to purchase. *p. 609*

Prospectus A document that provides details of a new issue of securities to the public. *p. 66*

Public issues Issues of securities to the public; they require the release of a prospectus. *p. 66*

Purchasing power parity The idea that the exchange rate changes to keep purchasing power of currencies constant across countries. *p. 649*

Put option Gives the buyer the right but not the obligation to sell an asset by a given date at a given price. *p. 567*

Rational behaviour Implies decisions are made after an amount of reasoning so that ultimate decisions are not foolish or absurd, and are based on the desire to satisfy objectives and maximise or at least optimise outcomes. *p. 21*

Realised returns or **ex post** Those returns that relate to past periods. *p. 132*

Record date Date used to identify all shareholders on the register of members so they can receive a dividend. *p. 469*

Renounceable Rights that can be sold on the market if the shareholder does not wish to subscribe to the issue. *p. 452*

Replacement chain A method that replicates the cash flows of the mutually exclusive projects until the two strings have equal lives. *p. 313*

Re-purchase agreements or **repos** Securities that are bought or sold with an agreement to reverse the original transaction at a later date. *p. 67*

Repos or **re-purchase agreements** Securities that are bought or sold with an agreement to reverse the original transaction at a later date. *p. 67*

Required rate of return (on an investment) The minimum level of return that is acceptable to an investor, given the level of risk associated with that investment. *p. 150*

Resident shareholders Those who live (and pay tax) in the same country as the company paying the dividends. *p. 214*

Retained earnings Represent the accumulated profit of the company that has not been paid out to shareholders as dividends. *pp. 227, 512*

Retention ratio The proportion of earnings retained in the company, not returned to shareholders as dividends. *p. 470*

Return The gain or loss achieved by making an investment. *p. 131*

Revenues Inflows of future economic benefits that come from the operations of the firm. *p. 511*

Rights issue The issue of new shares to existing shareholders in proportion to the number of shares they already hold. *p. 452*

Risk (in finance) The chance that the actual outcome from an investment will be different from the expected outcome. *pp. 69, 137, 561*

Risk-adjusted discount rate Method incorporating differing levels of project risk by changing the required return or discount rate. *p. 316*

Risk-averse A person who will not participate in a fair game. *p. 145*

Risk-neutral Person who is indifferent to participating in a fair game. *p. 146*

Risk preference Represents a person's attitude to risk. *p. 145*

Risk-seeking A person who will reject a certain outcome in favour of a riskier game that has an equal or lower expected return. *p. 146*

Romalpa clauses Legal conditions included on credit sales documentation to ensure title to the goods described does not pass to the buyer until the goods are fully paid for. *p. 403*

Secondary markets Deal with sales of securities that have been issued by their respective firms in the past and do not increase the stock of securities. *p. 66*

Securities Tradable instruments that represent an ownership interest or the right to receive payment on a debt. *pp. 66, 180*

Self-liquidating debt Occurs when debt-funded investments generate cash inflows that are received when the debt payments are due. *p. 360*

Sell-off or **divestiture** The sale of a major asset by the company. *p. 627*

Settlement date The date FRA settlement takes place at the start of the contract period. *p. 576*

Share consolidations Reduce the number of shares on issue in direct proportion to the consolidation ratio. *p. 445*

Share repurchase The company purchases its own shares. *p. 489*

Share splits Reduce the share price and increase the number of issued shares. *p. 445*

Simple interest Interest calculated on the original sum borrowed. *p. 96*

Sole proprietorship A business owned by an individual, who owns assets used in the business, incurs liabilities and reaps the annual profits or losses. *p. 34*

Speculation Involves the purchase of an asset for eventual resale with a view to profit, but where there is a strong element of risk. *p. 388*

Speculator A market participant who assumes risk in the expectation of earning a high return. *pp. 565, 644*

Spin-off The creation of a new company from an existing line of business. *p. 627*

Spontaneous sources of funding Those that arise in an unplanned way in the ordinary course of business. *p. 361*

Spot market A futures trading term to indicate the market where trading for immediate delivery occurs. *p. 568*

Stagging The practice of applying for and buying shares issued under a prospectus and selling them on the first day of trade on the market for a profit. *p. 452*

Standard deviation The square root of the variance. *p. 139*

Strip hedge The simultaneous sale of a run of given futures contracts with sequential contract dates that is undertaken to fix prices over a longer term than the term of each contract. *p. 572*

Subordinated debt Debt ranked below other similar classes of debt in the event that a firm is liquidated. *p. 437*

Substantial shareholding The ownership of 5% or more of the voting shares of a listed company. *p. 608*

Sunk costs Cash outflows that occur prior to the evaluation of a project. *p. 275*

Supplementary bidder's statement A statement distributed to advise shareholders of new circumstances that could affect their decision on the bid or to correct any misstatement or omission in the original bidder's statement. *p. 610*

Supplementary target's statement A statement distributed to advise shareholders of new circumstances that could affect their decision on the bid or to correct any misstatement or omission in the original target's statement. *p. 611*

Swap The exchange of two sets of cash flows that, although different in character, have the same expected present value. *p. 577*

Swaps reset period The period for which each determination of the value of BBSW is valid. *p. 579*

Synergy When the value of two assets combined is greater than the sum of the individual values. *p. 617*

Systematic risk The risk that is common to all business. *p. 151*

Takeover A company (or group of companies and/or individuals) gains control of an existing company. *p. 602*

Takeover premium The amount paid for the target's shares less the present value of the target's operations. *p. 620*

Target The company that the bidder wants to acquire. *p. 603*

Target weights Weighting based on management's future plans for financing the company's operations. *p. 237*

Target's statement A statement that contains the target's directors' recommendations on the acceptability of the takeover offer and the reasons for their recommendations. *p. 611*

Taxable income Assessable income less legitimate deductions. *p. 42*

Temporary funding Comprises the short-term formal sources of finance, such as commercial bills and bank loans. *p. 361*

Term to maturity or **maturity** The contracted time that may elapse before the borrowed funds are to be repaid. *p. 68*

Terminal value The expected cash flow associated with disposal of the project assets at the end of the project's life. *p. 272*

Time line A diagrammatic representation of cash flows, either received or paid or both. *p. 102*

Time value of money The concept that a dollar is worth more the sooner it is received. *pp. 6, 95*

Total risk Includes both systematic and unsystematic risk. *p. 151*

Trade credit Allows a purchase to be made without the immediate payment of cash. *p. 71*

Trade date The date on which the FRA contract is signed. *p. 576*

Transaction costs The costs, in terms of both time and explicit cash costs, of effecting a transaction or deal. *p. 63*

Transaction exposure The domestic currency value of foreign currency denominated receivables and payables is affected by changes in exchange rates. *p. 656*

Translation exposure Any changes in exchange rates affect domestic currency denominated value of items on the income statement and balance sheet. *p. 656*

Trust A legal structure where property is nominally owned by one party, the trustee, on behalf of others who are the beneficiaries. *p. 40*

Unfranked dividend A dividend that carries no tax credit. *p. 45*

Unsecured notes Fixed-term debt securities issued under a prospectus. Unlike debentures, they are not secured by assets. *p. 72*

Unsubordinated debt Does not take a lower ranking than other debt of similar characteristics. *p. 437*

Unsystematic risk Comes from the way a particular business conducts its activities. *p. 151*

Value The worth of an asset to an individual. *p. 179*

Variance The squared deviation of the variable from its expected value. *p. 139*

Vertical takeover The acquisition of a related business that either supplies the buyer or is closer to the consumer of the buyer's goods or services. *p. 617*

Wealth maximisation Implies that the business is managed so that the present and future cash flows discounted at an appropriate rate will give a present value (PV) that is maximised. *p. 6*

Weighted-average cost of capital The sum of each component cost of capital weighted by each component cost's proportion of the firm's capital structure. *p. 235*

Whistleblowing Informing (usually by employees of the perpetrators) the relevant authorities of malpractice or dangers to the public or the environment. *p. 16*

Working capital The funds invested in current assets. *p. 358*

Writer of an option The party that grants the right to the option buyer. *p. 574*

Yield The amount produced or the return based on the initial investment. *p. 100*

appendix

The time value of money

Table 1

Future value of $1 at the end of *n* periods = $(1 + k)^n$										
n	Compounding rate									
	1%	2%	3%	4%	5%	6%	7%	8%	9%	10%
1	1.0100	1.0200	1.0300	1.0400	1.0500	1.0600	1.0700	1.0800	1.0900	1.1000
2	1.0201	1.0404	1.0609	1.0816	1.1025	1.1236	1.1449	1.1664	1.1881	1.2100
3	1.0303	1.0612	1.0927	1.1249	1.1576	1.1910	1.2250	1.2597	1.2950	1.3310
4	1.0406	1.0824	1.1255	1.1699	1.2155	1.2625	1.3108	1.3605	1.4116	1.4641
5	1.0510	1.1041	1.1593	1.2167	1.2763	1.3382	1.4026	1.4693	1.5386	1.6105
6	1.0615	1.1262	1.1941	1.2653	1.3401	1.4185	1.5007	1.5869	1.6771	1.7716
7	1.0721	1.1487	1.2299	1.3159	1.4071	1.5036	1.6058	1.7138	1.8280	1.9487
8	1.0829	1.1717	1.2668	1.3686	1.4775	1.5938	1.7182	1.8509	1.9926	2.1436
9	1.0937	1.1951	1.3048	1.4233	1.5513	1.6895	1.8385	1.9990	2.1719	2.3579
10	1.1046	1.2190	1.3439	1.4802	1.6289	1.7908	1.9672	2.1589	2.3674	2.5937
11	1.1157	1.2434	1.3842	1.5395	1.7103	1.8983	2.1049	2.3316	2.5804	2.8531
12	1.1268	1.2682	1.4258	1.6010	1.7959	2.0122	2.2522	2.5182	2.8127	3.1384
13	1.1381	1.2936	1.4685	1.6651	1.8856	2.1329	2.4098	2.7196	3.0658	3.4523
14	1.1495	1.3195	1.5126	1.7317	1.9799	2.2609	2.5785	2.9372	3.3417	3.7975
15	1.1610	1.3459	1.5580	1.8009	2.0789	2.3966	2.7590	3.1722	3.6425	4.1772
16	1.1726	1.3728	1.6047	1.8730	2.1829	2.5404	2.9522	3.4259	3.9703	4.5950
17	1.1843	1.4002	1.6528	1.9479	2.2920	2.6928	3.1588	3.7000	4.3276	5.0545
18	1.1961	1.4282	1.7024	2.0258	2.4066	2.8543	3.3799	3.9960	4.7171	5.5599
19	1.2081	1.4568	1.7535	2.1068	2.5270	3.0256	3.6165	4.3157	5.1417	6.1159
20	1.2202	1.4859	1.8061	2.1911	2.6533	3.2071	3.8697	4.6610	5.6044	6.7275
25	1.2824	1.6406	2.0938	2.6658	3.3864	4.2919	5.4274	6.8485	8.6231	10.8347
30	1.3478	1.8114	2.4273	3.2434	4.3219	5.7435	7.6123	10.0627	13.2677	17.4494
35	1.4166	1.9999	2.8139	3.9461	5.5160	7.6861	10.6766	14.7853	20.4140	28.1024
40	1.4889	2.2080	3.2620	4.8010	7.0400	10.2857	14.9745	21.7245	31.4094	45.2593
45	1.5648	2.4379	3.7816	5.8412	8.9850	13.7646	21.0025	31.9204	48.3273	72.8905
50	1.6446	2.6916	4.3839	7.1067	11.4674	18.4202	29.4570	46.9016	74.3575	117.3909

Future value of $1 at the end of n periods = (1 + k)^n										
Compounding rate										n
11%	12%	13%	14%	15%	16%	17%	18%	19%	20%	
1.1100	1.1200	1.1300	1.1400	1.1500	1.1600	1.1700	1.1800	1.1900	1.2000	1
1.2321	1.2544	1.2769	1.2996	1.3225	1.3456	1.3689	1.3924	1.4161	1.4400	2
1.3676	1.4049	1.4429	1.4815	1.5209	1.5609	1.6016	1.6430	1.6852	1.7280	3
1.5181	1.5735	1.6305	1.6890	1.7490	1.8106	1.8739	1.9388	2.0053	2.0736	4
1.6851	1.7623	1.8424	1.9254	2.0114	2.1003	2.1924	2.2878	2.3864	2.4883	5
1.8704	1.9738	2.0820	2.1950	2.3131	2.4364	2.5652	2.6996	2.8398	2.9860	6
2.0762	2.2107	2.3526	2.5023	2.6600	2.8262	3.0012	3.1855	3.3793	3.5832	7
2.3045	2.4760	2.6584	2.8526	3.0590	3.2784	3.5115	3.7589	4.0214	4.2998	8
2.5580	2.7731	3.0040	3.2519	3.5179	3.8030	4.1084	4.4355	4.7854	5.1598	9
2.8394	3.1058	3.3946	3.7072	4.0456	4.4114	4.8068	5.2338	5.6947	6.1917	10
3.1518	3.4785	3.8359	4.2262	4.6524	5.1173	5.6240	6.1759	6.7767	7.4301	11
3.4985	3.8960	4.3345	4.8179	5.3503	5.9360	6.5801	7.2876	8.0642	8.9161	12
3.8833	4.3635	4.8980	5.4924	6.1528	6.8858	7.6987	8.5994	9.5964	10.6993	13
4.3104	4.8871	5.5348	6.2613	7.0757	7.9875	9.0075	10.1472	11.4198	12.8392	14
4.7846	5.4736	6.2543	7.1379	8.1371	9.2655	10.5387	11.9737	13.5895	15.4070	15
5.3109	6.1304	7.0673	8.1372	9.3576	10.7480	12.3303	14.1290	16.1715	18.4884	16
5.8951	6.8660	7.9861	9.2765	10.7613	12.4677	14.4265	16.6722	19.2441	22.1861	17
6.5436	7.6900	9.0243	10.5752	12.3755	14.4625	16.8790	19.6733	22.9005	26.6233	18
7.2633	8.6128	10.1974	12.0557	14.2318	16.7765	19.7484	23.2144	27.2516	31.9480	19
8.0623	9.6463	11.5231	13.7435	16.3665	19.4608	23.1056	27.3930	32.4294	38.3376	20
13.5855	17.0001	21.2305	26.4619	32.9190	40.8742	50.6578	62.6686	77.3881	95.3962	25
22.8923	29.9599	39.1159	50.9502	66.2118	85.8499	111.0647	143.3706	184.6753	237.3763	30
38.5749	52.7996	72.0685	98.1002	133.1755	180.3141	243.5035	327.9973	440.7006	590.6682	35
65.0009	93.0510	132.7816	188.8835	267.8635	378.7212	533.8687	750.3783	1051.6675	1469.7716	40
109.5302	163.9876	244.6414	363.6791	538.7693	795.4438	1170.4794	1716.6839	2509.6506	3657.2620	45
184.5648	289.0022	450.7359	700.2330	1083.6574	1670.7038	2566.2153	3927.3569	5988.9139	9100.4382	50

Table 2

				Present value of $1 received at the end of *n* periods = $\frac{1}{(1+k)^n}$						
n	Discount rate									
	1%	2%	3%	4%	5%	6%	7%	8%	9%	10%
1	0.9901	0.9804	0.9709	0.9615	0.9524	0.9434	0.9346	0.9259	0.9174	0.9091
2	0.9803	0.9612	0.9426	0.9246	0.9070	0.8900	0.8734	0.8573	0.8417	0.8264
3	0.9706	0.9423	0.9151	0.8890	0.8638	0.8396	0.8163	0.7938	0.7722	0.7513
4	0.9610	0.9238	0.8885	0.8548	0.8227	0.7921	0.7629	0.7350	0.7084	0.6830
5	0.9515	0.9057	0.8626	0.8219	0.7835	0.7473	0.7130	0.6806	0.6499	0.6209
6	0.9420	0.8880	0.8375	0.7903	0.7462	0.7050	0.6663	0.6302	0.5963	0.5645
7	0.9327	0.8706	0.8131	0.7599	0.7107	0.6651	0.6227	0.5835	0.5470	0.5132
8	0.9235	0.8535	0.7894	0.7307	0.6768	0.6274	0.5820	0.5403	0.5019	0.4665
9	0.9143	0.8368	0.7664	0.7026	0.6446	0.5919	0.5439	0.5002	0.4604	0.4241
10	0.9053	0.8203	0.7441	0.6756	0.6139	0.5584	0.5083	0.4632	0.4224	0.3855
11	0.8963	0.8043	0.7224	0.6496	0.5847	0.5268	0.4751	0.4289	0.3875	0.3505
12	0.8874	0.7885	0.7014	0.6246	0.5568	0.4970	0.4440	0.3971	0.3555	0.3186
13	0.8787	0.7730	0.6810	0.6006	0.5303	0.4688	0.4150	0.3677	0.3262	0.2897
14	0.8700	0.7579	0.6611	0.5775	0.5051	0.4423	0.3878	0.3405	0.2992	0.2633
15	0.8613	0.7430	0.6419	0.5553	0.4810	0.4173	0.3624	0.3152	0.2745	0.2394
16	0.8528	0.7284	0.6232	0.5339	0.4581	0.3936	0.3387	0.2919	0.2519	0.2176
17	0.8444	0.7142	0.6050	0.5134	0.4363	0.3714	0.3166	0.2703	0.2311	0.1978
18	0.8360	0.7002	0.5874	0.4936	0.4155	0.3503	0.2959	0.2502	0.2120	0.1799
19	0.8277	0.6864	0.5703	0.4746	0.3957	0.3305	0.2765	0.2317	0.1945	0.1635
20	0.8195	0.6730	0.5537	0.4564	0.3769	0.3118	0.2584	0.2145	0.1784	0.1486
25	0.7798	0.6095	0.4776	0.3751	0.2953	0.2330	0.1842	0.1460	0.1160	0.0923
30	0.7419	0.5521	0.4120	0.3083	0.2314	0.1741	0.1314	0.0994	0.0754	0.0573
35	0.7059	0.5000	0.3554	0.2534	0.1813	0.1301	0.0937	0.0676	0.0490	0.0356
40	0.6717	0.4529	0.3066	0.2083	0.1420	0.0972	0.0668	0.0460	0.0318	0.0221
45	0.6391	0.4102	0.2644	0.1712	0.1113	0.0727	0.0476	0.0313	0.0207	0.0137
50	0.6080	0.3715	0.2281	0.1407	0.0872	0.0543	0.0339	0.0213	0.0134	0.0085

Present value of $1 received at the end of n periods = $\frac{1}{(1+k)^n}$										
Discount rate										n
11%	12%	13%	14%	15%	16%	17%	18%	19%	20%	
0.9009	0.8929	0.8850	0.8772	0.8696	0.8621	0.8547	0.8475	0.8403	0.8333	1
0.8116	0.7972	0.7831	0.7695	0.7561	0.7432	0.7305	0.7182	0.7062	0.6944	2
0.7312	0.7118	0.6931	0.6750	0.6575	0.6407	0.6244	0.6086	0.5934	0.5787	3
0.6587	0.6355	0.6133	0.5921	0.5718	0.5523	0.5337	0.5158	0.4987	0.4823	4
0.5935	0.5674	0.5428	0.5194	0.4972	0.4761	0.4561	0.4371	0.4190	0.4019	5
0.5346	0.5066	0.4803	0.4556	0.4323	0.4104	0.3898	0.3704	0.3521	0.3349	6
0.4817	0.4523	0.4251	0.3996	0.3759	0.3538	0.3332	0.3139	0.2959	0.2791	7
0.4339	0.4039	0.3762	0.3506	0.3269	0.3050	0.2848	0.2660	0.2487	0.2326	8
0.3909	0.3606	0.3329	0.3075	0.2843	0.2630	0.2434	0.2255	0.2090	0.1938	9
0.3522	0.3220	0.2946	0.2697	0.2472	0.2267	0.2080	0.1911	0.1756	0.1615	10
0.3173	0.2875	0.2607	0.2366	0.2149	0.1954	0.1778	0.1619	0.1476	0.1346	11
0.2858	0.2567	0.2307	0.2076	0.1869	0.1685	0.1520	0.1372	0.1240	0.1122	12
0.2575	0.2292	0.2042	0.1821	0.1625	0.1452	0.1299	0.1163	0.1042	0.0935	13
0.2320	0.2046	0.1807	0.1597	0.1413	0.1252	0.1110	0.0985	0.0876	0.0779	14
0.2090	0.1827	0.1599	0.1401	0.1229	0.1079	0.0949	0.0835	0.0736	0.0649	15
0.1883	0.1631	0.1415	0.1229	0.1069	0.0930	0.0811	0.0708	0.0618	0.0541	16
0.1696	0.1456	0.1252	0.1078	0.0929	0.0802	0.0693	0.0600	0.0520	0.0451	17
0.1528	0.1300	0.1108	0.0946	0.0808	0.0691	0.0592	0.0508	0.0437	0.0376	18
0.1377	0.1161	0.0981	0.0829	0.0703	0.0596	0.0506	0.0431	0.0367	0.0313	19
0.1240	0.1037	0.0868	0.0728	0.0611	0.0514	0.0433	0.0365	0.0308	0.0261	20
0.0736	0.0588	0.0471	0.0378	0.0304	0.0245	0.0197	0.0160	0.0129	0.0105	25
0.0437	0.0334	0.0256	0.0196	0.0151	0.0116	0.0090	0.0070	0.0054	0.0042	30
0.0259	0.0189	0.0139	0.0102	0.0075	0.0055	0.0041	0.0030	0.0023	0.0017	35
0.0154	0.0107	0.0075	0.0053	0.0037	0.0026	0.0019	0.0013	0.0010	0.0007	40
0.0091	0.0061	0.0041	0.0027	0.0019	0.0013	0.0009	0.0006	0.0004	0.0003	45
0.0054	0.0035	0.0022	0.0014	0.0009	0.0006	0.0004	0.0003	0.0002	0.0001	50

Table 3
In this table it is assumed that the payments are received at the end of each period.

Future value of \$1 received per period for n periods = $\frac{[(1+k)^n - 1]}{k}$

n	Compounding rate									
	1%	2%	3%	4%	5%	6%	7%	8%	9%	10%
1	1.0000	1.0000	1.0000	1.0000	1.0000	1.0000	1.0000	1.0000	1.0000	1.0000
2	2.0100	2.0200	2.0300	2.0400	2.0500	2.0600	2.0700	2.0800	2.0900	2.1000
3	3.0301	3.0604	3.0909	3.1216	3.1525	3.1836	3.2149	3.2464	3.2781	3.3100
4	4.0604	4.1216	4.1836	4.2465	4.3101	4.3746	4.4399	4.5061	4.5731	4.6410
5	5.1010	5.2040	5.3091	5.4163	5.5256	5.6371	5.7507	5.8666	5.9847	6.1051
6	6.1520	6.3081	6.4684	6.6330	6.8019	6.9753	7.1533	7.3359	7.5233	7.7156
7	7.2135	7.4343	7.6625	7.8983	8.1420	8.3938	8.6540	8.9228	9.2004	9.4872
8	8.2857	8.5830	8.8923	9.2142	9.5491	9.8975	10.2598	10.6366	11.0285	11.4359
9	9.3685	9.7546	10.1591	10.5828	11.0266	11.4913	11.9780	12.4876	13.0210	13.5795
10	10.4622	10.9497	11.4639	12.0061	12.5779	13.1808	13.8164	14.4866	15.1929	15.9374
11	11.5668	12.1687	12.8078	13.4864	14.2068	14.9716	15.7836	16.6455	17.5603	18.5312
12	12.6825	13.4121	14.1920	15.0258	15.9171	16.8699	17.8885	18.9771	20.1407	21.3843
13	13.8093	14.6803	15.6178	16.6268	17.7130	18.8821	20.1406	21.4953	22.9534	24.5227
14	14.9474	15.9739	17.0863	18.2919	19.5986	21.0151	22.5505	24.2149	26.0192	27.9750
15	16.0969	17.2934	18.5989	20.0236	21.5786	23.2760	25.1290	27.1521	29.3609	31.7725
16	17.2579	18.6393	20.1569	21.8245	23.6575	25.6725	27.8881	30.3243	33.0034	35.9497
17	18.4304	20.0121	21.7616	23.6975	25.8404	28.2129	30.8402	33.7502	36.9737	40.5447
18	19.6147	21.4123	23.4144	25.6454	28.1324	30.9057	33.9990	37.4502	41.3013	45.5992
19	20.8109	22.8406	25.1169	27.6712	30.5390	33.7600	37.3790	41.4463	46.0185	51.1591
20	22.0190	24.2974	26.8704	29.7781	33.0660	36.7856	40.9955	45.7620	51.1601	57.2750
25	28.2432	32.0303	36.4593	41.6459	47.7271	54.8645	63.2490	73.1059	84.7009	98.3471
30	34.7849	40.5681	47.5754	56.0849	66.4388	79.0582	94.4608	113.2832	136.3075	164.4940
35	41.6603	49.9945	60.4621	73.6522	90.3203	111.4348	138.2369	172.3168	215.7108	271.0244
40	48.8864	60.4020	75.4013	95.0255	120.7998	154.7620	199.6351	259.0565	337.8824	442.5926
45	56.4811	71.8927	92.7199	121.0294	159.7002	212.7435	285.7493	386.5056	525.8587	718.9048
50	64.4632	84.5794	112.7969	152.6671	209.3480	290.3359	406.5289	573.7702	815.0836	1163.9085

Future value of $1 received per period for *n* periods = $\frac{[(1+k)^n - 1]}{k}$

Compounding rate										*n*
11%	12%	13%	14%	15%	16%	17%	18%	19%	20%	
1.0000	1.0000	1.0000	1.0000	1.0000	1.0000	1.0000	1.0000	1.0000	1.0000	1
2.1100	2.1200	2.1300	2.1400	2.1500	2.1600	2.1700	2.1800	2.1900	2.2000	2
3.3421	3.3744	3.4069	3.4396	3.4725	3.5056	3.5389	3.5724	3.6061	3.6400	3
4.7097	4.7793	4.8498	4.9211	4.9934	5.0665	5.1405	5.2154	5.2913	5.3680	4
6.2278	6.3528	6.4803	6.6101	6.7424	6.8771	7.0144	7.1542	7.2966	7.4416	5
7.9129	8.1152	8.3227	8.5355	8.7537	8.9775	9.2068	9.4420	9.6830	9.9299	6
9.7833	10.0890	10.4047	10.7305	11.0668	11.4139	11.7720	12.1415	12.5227	12.9159	7
11.8594	12.2997	12.7573	13.2328	13.7268	14.2401	14.7733	15.3270	15.9020	16.4991	8
14.1640	14.7757	15.4157	16.0853	16.7858	17.5185	18.2847	19.0859	19.9234	20.7989	9
16.7220	17.5487	18.4197	19.3373	20.3037	21.3215	22.3931	23.5213	24.7089	25.9587	10
19.5614	20.6546	21.8143	23.0445	24.3493	25.7329	27.1999	28.7551	30.4035	32.1504	11
22.7132	24.1331	25.6502	27.2707	29.0017	30.8502	32.8239	34.9311	37.1802	39.5805	12
26.2116	28.0291	29.9847	32.0887	34.3519	36.7862	39.4040	42.2187	45.2445	48.4966	13
30.0949	32.3926	34.8827	37.5811	40.5047	43.6720	47.1027	50.8180	54.8409	59.1959	14
34.4054	37.2797	40.4175	43.8424	47.5804	51.6595	56.1101	60.9653	66.2607	72.0351	15
39.1899	42.7533	46.6717	50.9804	55.7175	60.9250	66.6488	72.9390	79.8502	87.4421	16
44.5008	48.8837	53.7391	59.1176	65.0751	71.6730	78.9792	87.0680	96.0218	105.9306	17
50.3959	55.7497	61.7251	68.3941	75.8364	84.1407	93.4056	103.7403	115.2659	128.1167	18
56.9395	63.4397	70.7494	78.9692	88.2118	98.6032	110.2846	123.4135	138.1664	154.7400	19
64.2028	72.0524	80.9468	91.0249	102.4436	115.3797	130.0329	146.6280	165.4180	186.6880	20
114.4133	133.3339	155.6196	181.8708	212.7930	249.2140	292.1049	342.6035	402.0425	471.9811	25
199.0209	241.3327	293.1992	356.7868	434.7451	530.3117	647.4391	790.9480	966.7122	1181.8816	30
341.5896	431.6635	546.6808	693.5727	881.1702	1120.7130	1426.4910	1816.6516	2314.2137	2948.3411	35
581.8261	767.0914	1013.7042	1342.0251	1779.0903	2360.7572	3134.5218	4163.2130	5529.8290	7343.8578	40
986.6386	1358.2300	1874.1646	2590.5648	3585.1285	4965.2739	6879.2907	9531.5771	13203.4242	18281.3099	45
1668.7712	2400.0182	3459.5071	4994.5213	7217.7163	10435.6488	15089.5017	21813.0937	31515.3363	45497.1908	50

Table 4
In this table it is assumed that the payments are received at the end of each period.

Present value of $1 received per period for n periods = $\frac{[1-(1+k)^{-n}]}{k}$										
n	Discount rate									
	1%	2%	3%	4%	5%	6%	7%	8%	9%	10%
1	0.9901	0.9804	0.9709	0.9615	0.9524	0.9434	0.9346	0.9259	0.9174	0.9091
2	1.9704	1.9416	1.9135	1.8861	1.8594	1.8334	1.8080	1.7833	1.7591	1.7355
3	2.9410	2.8839	2.8286	2.7751	2.7232	2.6730	2.6243	2.5771	2.5313	2.4869
4	3.9020	3.8077	3.7171	3.6299	3.5460	3.4651	3.3872	3.3121	3.2397	3.1699
5	4.8534	4.7135	4.5797	4.4518	4.3295	4.2124	4.1002	3.9927	3.8897	3.7908
6	5.7955	5.6014	5.4172	5.2421	5.0757	4.9173	4.7665	4.6229	4.4859	4.3553
7	6.7282	6.4720	6.2303	6.0021	5.7864	5.5824	5.3893	5.2064	5.0330	4.8684
8	7.6517	7.3255	7.0197	6.7327	6.4632	6.2098	5.9713	5.7466	5.5348	5.3349
9	8.5660	8.1622	7.7861	7.4353	7.1078	6.8017	6.5152	6.2469	5.9952	5.7590
10	9.4713	8.9826	8.5302	8.1109	7.7217	7.3601	7.0236	6.7101	6.4177	6.1446
11	10.3676	9.7868	9.2526	8.7605	8.3064	7.8869	7.4987	7.1390	6.8052	6.4951
12	11.2551	10.5753	9.9540	9.3851	8.8633	8.3838	7.9427	7.5361	7.1607	6.8137
13	12.1337	11.3484	10.6350	9.9856	9.3936	8.8527	8.3577	7.9038	7.4869	7.1034
14	13.0037	12.1062	11.2961	10.5631	9.8986	9.2950	8.7455	8.2442	7.7862	7.3667
15	13.8651	12.8493	11.9379	11.1184	10.3797	9.7122	9.1079	8.5595	8.0607	7.6061
16	14.7179	13.5777	12.5611	11.6523	10.8378	10.1059	9.4466	8.8514	8.3126	7.8237
17	15.5623	14.2919	13.1661	12.1657	11.2741	10.4773	9.7632	9.1216	8.5436	8.0216
18	16.3983	14.9920	13.7535	12.6593	11.6896	10.8276	10.0591	9.3719	8.7556	8.2014
19	17.2260	15.6785	14.3238	13.1339	12.0853	11.1581	10.3356	9.6036	8.9501	8.3649
20	18.0456	16.3514	14.8775	13.5903	12.4622	11.4699	10.5940	9.8181	9.1285	8.5136
25	22.0232	19.5235	17.4131	15.6221	14.0939	12.7834	11.6536	10.6748	9.8226	9.0770
30	25.8077	22.3965	19.6004	17.2920	15.3725	13.7648	12.4090	11.2578	10.2737	9.4269
35	29.4086	24.9986	21.4872	18.6646	16.3742	14.4982	12.9477	11.6546	10.5668	9.6442
40	32.8347	27.3555	23.1148	19.7928	17.1591	15.0463	13.3317	11.9246	10.7574	9.7791
45	36.0945	29.4902	24.5187	20.7200	17.7741	15.4558	13.6055	12.1084	10.8812	9.8628
50	39.1961	31.4236	25.7298	21.4822	18.2559	15.7619	13.8007	12.2335	10.9617	9.9148

Present value of $1 received per period for *n* periods = $\frac{[1-(1+k)^{-n}]}{k}$

Discount rate										n
11%	12%	13%	14%	15%	16%	17%	18%	19%	20%	
0.9009	0.8929	0.8850	0.8772	0.8696	0.8621	0.8547	0.8475	0.8403	0.8333	1
1.7125	1.6901	1.6681	1.6467	1.6257	1.6052	1.5852	1.5656	1.5465	1.5278	2
2.4437	2.4018	2.3612	2.3216	2.2832	2.2459	2.2096	2.1743	2.1399	2.1065	3
3.1024	3.0373	2.9745	2.9137	2.8550	2.7982	2.7432	2.6901	2.6386	2.5887	4
3.6959	3.6048	3.5172	3.4331	3.3522	3.2743	3.1993	3.1272	3.0576	2.9906	5
4.2305	4.1114	3.9975	3.8887	3.7845	3.6847	3.5892	3.4976	3.4098	3.3255	6
4.7122	4.5638	4.4226	4.2883	4.1604	4.0386	3.9224	3.8115	3.7057	3.6046	7
5.1461	4.9676	4.7988	4.6389	4.4873	4.3436	4.2072	4.0776	3.9544	3.8372	8
5.5370	5.3282	5.1317	4.9464	4.7716	4.6065	4.4506	4.3030	4.1633	4.0310	9
5.8892	5.6502	5.4262	5.2161	5.0188	4.8332	4.6586	4.4941	4.3389	4.1925	10
6.2065	5.9377	5.6869	5.4527	5.2337	5.0286	4.8364	4.6560	4.4865	4.3271	11
6.4924	6.1944	5.9176	5.6603	5.4206	5.1971	4.9884	4.7932	4.6105	4.4392	12
6.7499	6.4235	6.1218	5.8424	5.5831	5.3423	5.1183	4.9095	4.7147	4.5327	13
6.9819	6.6282	6.3025	6.0021	5.7245	5.4675	5.2293	5.0081	4.8023	4.6106	14
7.1909	6.8109	6.4624	6.1422	5.8474	5.5755	5.3242	5.0916	4.8759	4.6755	15
7.3792	6.9740	6.6039	6.2651	5.9542	5.6685	5.4053	5.1624	4.9377	4.7296	16
7.5488	7.1196	6.7291	6.3729	6.0472	5.7487	5.4746	5.2223	4.9897	4.7746	17
7.7016	7.2497	6.8399	6.4674	6.1280	5.8178	5.5339	5.2732	5.0333	4.8122	18
7.8393	7.3658	6.9380	6.5504	6.1982	5.8775	5.5845	5.3162	5.0700	4.8435	19
7.9633	7.4694	7.0248	6.6231	6.2593	5.9288	5.6278	5.3527	5.1009	4.8696	20
8.4217	7.8431	7.3300	6.8729	6.4641	6.0971	5.7662	5.4669	5.1951	4.9476	25
8.6938	8.0552	7.4957	7.0027	6.5660	6.1772	5.8294	5.5168	5.2347	4.9789	30
8.8552	8.1755	7.5856	7.0700	6.6166	6.2153	5.8582	5.5386	5.2512	4.9915	35
8.9511	8.2438	7.6344	7.1050	6.6418	6.2335	5.8713	5.5482	5.2582	4.9966	40
9.0079	8.2825	7.6609	7.1232	6.6543	6.2421	5.8773	5.5523	5.2611	4.9986	45
9.0417	8.3045	7.6752	7.1327	6.6605	6.2463	5.8801	5.5541	5.2623	4.9995	50

Table 5

Present value of $1 received throughout the year on a daily basis										
n	Discount rate									
	1%	2%	3%	4%	5%	6%	7%	8%	9%	10%
1	0.9950	0.9900	0.9851	0.9802	0.9753	0.9705	0.9657	0.9609	0.9562	0.9515
2	0.9851	0.9704	0.9560	0.9418	0.9278	0.9140	0.9004	0.8871	0.8739	0.8610
3	0.9753	0.9512	0.9277	0.9049	0.8825	0.8608	0.8396	0.8189	0.7987	0.7790
4	0.9656	0.9324	0.9003	0.8694	0.8395	0.8107	0.7828	0.7559	0.7300	0.7049
5	0.9560	0.9139	0.8737	0.8353	0.7986	0.7634	0.7299	0.6978	0.6672	0.6378
6	0.9465	0.8958	0.8479	0.8025	0.7596	0.7190	0.6805	0.6442	0.6097	0.5772
7	0.9371	0.8781	0.8228	0.7711	0.7226	0.6771	0.6345	0.5946	0.5573	0.5222
8	0.9277	0.8607	0.7985	0.7408	0.6873	0.6377	0.5916	0.5489	0.5093	0.4725
9	0.9185	0.8437	0.7749	0.7118	0.6538	0.6006	0.5517	0.5067	0.4655	0.4276
10	0.9094	0.8270	0.7520	0.6839	0.6219	0.5656	0.5144	0.4678	0.4254	0.3869
11	0.9003	0.8106	0.7298	0.6571	0.5916	0.5327	0.4796	0.4318	0.3888	0.3501
12	0.8914	0.7945	0.7082	0.6313	0.5627	0.5016	0.4472	0.3986	0.3553	0.3168
13	0.8825	0.7788	0.6873	0.6066	0.5353	0.4724	0.4169	0.3680	0.3248	0.2866
14	0.8737	0.7634	0.6670	0.5828	0.5092	0.4449	0.3888	0.3397	0.2968	0.2594
15	0.8650	0.7483	0.6473	0.5599	0.4844	0.4190	0.3625	0.3136	0.2713	0.2347
16	0.8564	0.7334	0.6281	0.5380	0.4607	0.3946	0.3380	0.2895	0.2479	0.2124
17	0.8479	0.7189	0.6096	0.5169	0.4383	0.3716	0.3151	0.2672	0.2266	0.1921
18	0.8395	0.7047	0.5916	0.4966	0.4169	0.3500	0.2938	0.2467	0.2071	0.1739
19	0.8311	0.6907	0.5741	0.4771	0.3966	0.3296	0.2740	0.2277	0.1893	0.1573
20	0.8228	0.6771	0.5571	0.4584	0.3772	0.3104	0.2554	0.2102	0.1730	0.1424
25	0.7827	0.6126	0.4795	0.3753	0.2938	0.2300	0.1800	0.1409	0.1103	0.0863
30	0.7445	0.5543	0.4127	0.3073	0.2288	0.1704	0.1269	0.0945	0.0703	0.0524
35	0.7082	0.5016	0.3552	0.2516	0.1782	0.1262	0.0894	0.0633	0.0449	0.0318
40	0.6737	0.4538	0.3058	0.2060	0.1388	0.0935	0.0630	0.0424	0.0286	0.0193
45	0.6408	0.4107	0.2632	0.1687	0.1081	0.0693	0.0444	0.0285	0.0182	0.0117
50	0.6096	0.3716	0.2265	0.1381	0.0842	0.0513	0.0313	0.0191	0.0116	0.0071

Present value of $1 received throughout the year on a daily basis										
Discount rate										n
11%	12%	13%	14%	15%	16%	17%	18%	19%	20%	
0.9468	0.9422	0.9376	0.9330	0.9284	0.9239	0.9194	0.9150	0.9105	0.9061	1
0.8482	0.8357	0.8233	0.8111	0.7991	0.7873	0.7757	0.7643	0.7530	0.7419	2
0.7599	0.7412	0.7229	0.7052	0.6878	0.6709	0.6545	0.6384	0.6227	0.6075	3
0.6807	0.6574	0.6348	0.6131	0.5921	0.5718	0.5522	0.5333	0.5150	0.4974	4
0.6098	0.5831	0.5575	0.5330	0.5096	0.4872	0.4659	0.4454	0.4259	0.4072	5
0.5463	0.5171	0.4895	0.4634	0.4386	0.4152	0.3931	0.3721	0.3522	0.3334	6
0.4894	0.4587	0.4298	0.4028	0.3775	0.3538	0.3316	0.3108	0.2913	0.2730	7
0.4384	0.4068	0.3775	0.3502	0.3250	0.3015	0.2798	0.2596	0.2409	0.2235	8
0.3928	0.3608	0.3315	0.3045	0.2797	0.2570	0.2361	0.2169	0.1992	0.1830	9
0.3519	0.3200	0.2911	0.2647	0.2408	0.2190	0.1992	0.1811	0.1648	0.1499	10
0.3152	0.2838	0.2556	0.2301	0.2072	0.1866	0.1680	0.1513	0.1363	0.1227	11
0.2824	0.2517	0.2244	0.2001	0.1784	0.1590	0.1418	0.1264	0.1127	0.1005	12
0.2530	0.2233	0.1971	0.1739	0.1535	0.1355	0.1196	0.1056	0.0932	0.0823	13
0.2266	0.1980	0.1731	0.1512	0.1321	0.1155	0.1009	0.0882	0.0771	0.0673	14
0.2030	0.1756	0.1520	0.1315	0.1137	0.0984	0.0851	0.0737	0.0637	0.0551	15
0.1819	0.1558	0.1334	0.1143	0.0979	0.0839	0.0718	0.0615	0.0527	0.0452	16
0.1629	0.1382	0.1172	0.0994	0.0843	0.0715	0.0606	0.0514	0.0436	0.0370	17
0.1460	0.1226	0.1029	0.0864	0.0725	0.0609	0.0511	0.0429	0.0360	0.0303	18
0.1308	0.1087	0.0904	0.0751	0.0624	0.0519	0.0431	0.0359	0.0298	0.0248	19
0.1171	0.0964	0.0793	0.0653	0.0537	0.0442	0.0364	0.0300	0.0247	0.0203	20
0.0676	0.0529	0.0414	0.0324	0.0254	0.0199	0.0156	0.0122	0.0095	0.0075	25
0.0390	0.0290	0.0216	0.0161	0.0120	0.0089	0.0067	0.0050	0.0037	0.0027	30
0.0225	0.0159	0.0113	0.0080	0.0057	0.0040	0.0028	0.0020	0.0014	0.0010	35
0.0130	0.0087	0.0059	0.0040	0.0027	0.0018	0.0012	0.0008	0.0006	0.0004	40
0.0075	0.0048	0.0031	0.0020	0.0013	0.0008	0.0005	0.0003	0.0002	0.0001	45
0.0043	0.0026	0.0016	0.0010	0.0006	0.0004	0.0002	0.0001	0.0001	0.0001	50

Index

Printed in Australia
04 Jan 2024
LP025823